The Oxford Handbook of Feminist Multicultural Counseling Psychology

OXFORD LIBRARY OF PSYCHOLOGY

OXFORD LIBRARY OF PSYCHOLOGY

Editor in Chief PETER E. NATHAN

The Oxford Handbook of Feminist Multicultural Counseling Psychology

Edited by

Carolyn Zerbe Enns

Elizabeth Nutt Williams

OXFORD
UNIVERSITY PRESS

OXFORD
UNIVERSITY PRESS

Oxford University Press is a department of the University of Oxford. It furthers the University's objective of excellence in research, scholarship, and education by publishing worldwide.

Oxford New York
Auckland Cape Town Dar es Salaam Hong Kong Karachi
Kuala Lumpur Madrid Melbourne Mexico City Nairobi
New Delhi Shanghai Taipei Toronto

With offices in
Argentina Austria Brazil Chile Czech Republic France Greece
Guatemala Hungary Italy Japan Poland Portugal Singapore
South Korea Switzerland Thailand Turkey Ukraine Vietnam

Published in the United States of America by
Oxford University Press
198 Madison Avenue, New York, NY 10016

Library of Congress Cataloging-in-Publication Data

The Oxford handbook of feminist multicultural counseling psychology / edited by Carolyn Zerbe Enns, Elizabeth Nutt Williams.
p. cm. — (Oxford library of psychology)
ISBN-13: 978–0–19–974422–0
ISBN-10: 0–19–974422–X
1. Cross-cultural counseling. 2. Feminist therapy. I. Enns, Carolyn Zerbe. II. Williams, Elizabeth Nutt.
BF636.7.C76O94 2012
158.3082—dc23
2012015009

9 8 7 6 5 4 3 2
Printed in the United States of America
on acid-free paper

SHORT CONTENTS

OXFORD LIBRARY OF PSYCHOLOGY

The *Oxford Library of Psychology*, a landmark series of handbooks, is published by Oxford University Press, one of the world's oldest and most highly respected publishers, with a tradition of publishing significant books in psychology. The ambitious goal of the *Oxford Library of Psychology* is nothing less than to span a vibrant, wide-ranging field and, in so doing, to fill a clear market need.

Encompassing a comprehensive set of handbooks, organized hierarchically, the *Library* incorporates volumes at different levels, each designed to meet a distinct need. At one level are a set of handbooks designed broadly to survey the major subfields of psychology; at another are numerous handbooks that cover important current focal research and scholarly areas of psychology in depth and detail. Planned as a reflection of the dynamism of psychology, the *Library* will grow and expand as psychology itself develops, thereby highlighting significant new research that will impact on the field. Adding to its accessibility and ease of use, the *Library* will be published in print and, later on, electronically.

The *Library* surveys psychology's principal subfields with a set of handbooks that capture the current status and future prospects of those major subdisciplines. This initial set includes handbooks of social and personality psychology, clinical psychology, counseling psychology, school psychology, educational psychology, industrial and organizational psychology, cognitive psychology, cognitive neuroscience, methods and measurements, history, neuropsychology, personality assessment, developmental psychology, and more. Each handbook undertakes to review one of psychology's major subdisciplines with breadth, comprehensiveness, and exemplary scholarship. In addition to these broadly-conceived volumes, the *Library* also includes a large number of handbooks designed to explore in depth more specialized areas of scholarship and research, such as stress, health and coping, anxiety and related disorders, cognitive development, or child and adolescent assessment. In contrast to the broad coverage of the subfield handbooks, each of these latter volumes focuses on an especially productive, more highly focused line of scholarship and research. Whether at the broadest or most specific level, however, all of the *Library* handbooks offer synthetic coverage that reviews and evaluates the relevant past and present research and anticipates research in the future. Each handbook in the *Library* includes introductory and concluding chapters written by its editor to provide a roadmap to the handbook's table of contents and to offer informed anticipations of significant future developments in that field.

An undertaking of this scope calls for handbook editors and chapter authors who are established scholars in the areas about which they write. Many of the nation's and world's most productive and best-respected psychologists have agreed to edit *Library* handbooks or write authoritative chapters in their areas of expertise.

For whom has the *Oxford Library of Psychology* been written? Because of its breadth, depth, and accessibility, the *Library* serves a diverse audience, including graduate students in psychology and their faculty mentors, scholars, researchers, and practitioners in psychology and related fields. Each will find in the *Library* the information they seek on the subfield or focal area of psychology in which they work or are interested.

Befitting its commitment to accessibility, each handbook includes a comprehensive index, as well as extensive references to help guide research. And because the *Library* was designed from its inception as an online as well as a print resource, its structure and contents will be readily and rationally searchable online. Further, once the *Library* is released online, the handbooks will be regularly and thoroughly updated.

In summary, the *Oxford Library of Psychology* will grow organically to provide a thoroughly informed perspective on the field of psychology, one that reflects both psychology's dynamism and its increasing interdisciplinarity. Once published electronically, the *Library* is also destined to become a uniquely valuable interactive tool, with extended search and browsing capabilities. As you begin to consult this handbook, we sincerely hope you will share our enthusiasm for the more than 500-year tradition of Oxford University Press for excellence, innovation, and quality, as exemplified by the *Oxford Library of Psychology.*

Peter E. Nathan
Editor-in-Chief
Oxford Library of Psychology

ABOUT THE EDITORS

Carolyn Zerbe Enns

Carolyn Zerbe Enns is Professor of psychology and a contributor to the ethnic studies and women's studies programs at Cornell College. Her scholarly interests include multicultural, feminist, and transnational perspectives on psychotherapy and pedagogy. She has published approximately 60 articles and chapters on topics that focus primarily on gender, pedagogy, and feminist theory and psychotherapy. She is the author of *Feminist Theories and Feminist Psychotherapies: Origins, Themes, and Diversity* (2004), and the co-editor (with Ada L. Sinacore) of *Teaching and Social Justice: Integrating Multicultural and Feminist Theories in the Classroom* (2005). Carolyn spent a substantial portion of her childhood in Japan and has served as Resident Director for the Japan Study Program in Tokyo.

Elizabeth Nutt Williams

Elizabeth Nutt Williams has been a Professor of psychology at St. Mary's College of Maryland, The Public Honors College, since 1997, where she has served as Coordinator for the Women, Gender and Sexuality Cross-Disciplinary Studies Program, Department Chair in Psychology, and Dean of the Core Curriculum and First Year Experience. Dr. Williams has been awarded honors for her teaching as well as for her scholarship, receiving two Early Career Awards in 2006 from the Division of Psychotherapy of the American Psychological Association (APA) and from the Society for Psychotherapy Research. She served as President of the Division of Psychotherapy of the APA in 2011, Chair of the Section for the Advancement of Women for the Division of Counseling Psychology at the APA from 2008–2010, and Newsletter Editor for the Society of Counseling Psychology of the APA from 2005–2007. She has served on the editorial boards for the journals *Psychotherapy, Psychotherapy Research*, and the *Psychology of Women Quarterly*. Her scholarly interests focus primarily on psychotherapy process, qualitative research methods, and feminist/multicultural approaches to counseling.

CONTRIBUTORS

Elizabeth M. Abrams
Department of Educational Psychology
University of Utah
Salt Lake City, UT

Muninder K. Ahluwalia
Department of Counseling and Educational Services
Montclair State University
Montclair, NJ

Anjali Alimchandani
Department of Applied Psychology
New York University
New York, NY

Julie R. Ancis
Department of Counseling and Psychological Services
Georgia State University
Atlanta, GA

Lauren Appio
Teachers College
Columbia University
New York, NY

Kiran S. K. Arora
Department of Counseling and School Psychology
University of Massachusetts Boston
Boston, MA

Stephanie San Miguel Bauman
Department of Psychology
Washington State University
Tri-Cities, WA

Kalina M. Brabeck
Feinstein School of Education and Human Development
Rhode Island College
Providence, RI

Mary M. Brabeck
Steinhardt School of Culture, Education, and Human Development
New York University
New York, NY

Jeanett Castellanos
School of Social Sciences
University of California – Irvine
Irvine, CA

Jennifer Chang
Teachers College
Columbia University
New York, NY

Christine A. Courtois
Psychologist, Private Practice
Courtois & Associates, PC
Washington, DC

M. Meghan Davidson
Department of Educational Psychology
University of Nebraska – Lincoln
Lincoln, NE

Kurt A. DeBord
Department of Social and Behavioral Sciences
Lincoln University
Jefferson City, MO

Carolyn Zerbe Enns
Department of Psychology
Cornell College
Mount Vernon, IA

Ruth E. Fassinger
College of Graduate and Professional Studies
John F. Kennedy University
Pleasant Hill, CA

Ann R. Fischer
Department of Psychology
Southern Illinois University Carbondale
Carbondale, IL

Freda Ginsberg
Department of Counselor Education
SUNY Plattsburgh
Plattsburgh, NY

Alberta M. Gloria
Department of Counseling Psychology
University of Wisconsin-Madison
Madison, WI

Barbara Gormley
College of Education
Governors State University
Chicago, IL

Gail Hackett
Office of the Provost
University of Missouri, Kansas City
Kansas City, MO

Katharine Hahn Oh
Oberlin College Counseling Center
Oberlin College
Oberlin, OH

Donna Hawxhurst
Women's Resource Center
University of Utah
Salt Lake City, UT

Angela N. Hilton
Department of Psychology
University of Tennessee
Knoxville, TN

Sharon G. Horne
Department of Counseling and School Psychology
University of Massachusetts Boston
Boston, MA

Denise A. Isom
Ethnic Studies Department
Cal Poly San Luis Obispo
San Luis Obispo, CA

Dana L. Joseph
Department of Psychology
University of Central Florida
Orlando, FL

Cindy L. Juntunen
Department of Counseling Psychology & Community Services
University of North Dakota
Grand Forks, ND

Susan Kashubeck-West
Division of Counseling and Family Therapy
University of Missouri – St. Louis
St. Louis, MO

Anusha Kassan
Department of Counselling Psychology
University of British Columbia
Vancouver, British Columbia, Canada

Julie D. Kohlhart
School of Education
University of Missouri, Kansas City
Kansas City, MO

Stefanie Lindlau
Graduate Studies in Counseling
Rollins College
Winter Park, FL

Amina Mahmood
College of Education
The University of Iowa
Iowa City, IA

Laurie B. Mintz
Department of Psychology
University of Florida
Gainesville, FL

Marie L. Miville
Teachers College
Columbia University
New York, NY

Susan L. Morrow
Department of Educational Psychology
University of Utah
Salt Lake City, UT

Kathryn L. Norsworthy
Graduate Studies in Counseling
Rollins College
Winter Park, FL

Roberta L. Nutt
Department of Educational Psychology
University of Houston
Houston, TX

Alayne J. Ormerod
School of Psychology
Fielding Graduate University
Champaign, IL

Barbara J. Palombi
Mental Health Consultant
Allendale, MI

Pam A. Remer
Department of Educational, School, and Counseling Psychology
University of Kentucky
Lexington, KY

Ada L. Sinacore
Department of Educational and Counselling Psychology
McGill University
Montreal, Quebec, Canada

Laura Smith
Teachers College
Columbia University
New York, NY

Suzette L. Speight
Department of Psychology
The University of Akron
Akron, OH

Lisa A. Suzuki
Department of Applied Psychology
New York University
New York, NY

Dawn M. Szymanski
Department of Psychology
University of Tennessee
Knoxville, TN

David Tager
Student Health Center
University of Missouri
Columbia, MO

Lori Tagger
Psychological Services
St. Anthony's Medical Center
St. Louis, MO

Anita J. Thomas
School of Education
Loyola University Chicago
Chicago, IL

Lauren M. Weitzman
University Counseling Center
University of Utah
Salt Lake City, UT

Elizabeth Nutt Williams
Department of Psychology
St. Mary's College of Maryland
St. Mary's City, MD

Erin Winterrowd
Department of Psychology
University of Wisconsin Oshkosh
Oshkosh, WI

CONTENTS

Part Three • Feminist Multicultural Counseling Psychology Applications: Theory, Research, and Practice

Part Four • Education, Advocacy, and Social Justice

Part Five • Afterword

PART 1

Foundations of Feminist Multicultural Counseling Psychology

CHAPTER

1 Feminist Multicultural Psychology: Evolution, Change, and Challenge

Carolyn Zerbe Enns, Elizabeth Nutt Williams, *and* Ruth E. Fassinger

Abstract

This chapter traces the "herstory" of feminist multicultural perspectives in counseling psychology from 1970 to the present. It highlights the activities, events, products, groups, and organizations that have contributed to feminist multicultural and social justice perspectives. The chapter chronicles the challenges of integrating multicultural and feminist perspectives and notes developments and changes with regard to (a) defining sex and gender; (b) conceptualizing the intersections of oppression, power, and privilege; (c) understanding complex and subtle forms of bias in the twenty-first century; (d) exploring research methods for studying complex intersections of multiple identities; and (e) clarifying concepts and structures that support feminist multicultural theory, ethics, and practice. Chapter themes provide a foundation for the contents of this handbook, which focus on contemporary frameworks for feminist multicultural counseling psychology; the contributions and experiences of diverse groups of women and persons with multiple social identities; major theory and practice areas in feminist multicultural counseling psychology; and advocacy, training, and social justice applications.

Key Words: Herstory (history), feminism, multiculturalism, social justice, counseling psychology

Feminist Multicultural Counseling Psychology: Evolution, Change, and Challenge

The title of this handbook underlines its major goal: the integration of multicultural and feminist perspectives in counseling psychology. Although this goal has been important for many decades (see, for example, Griscom, 1979; Thompson, 2002), the effective implementation of this holistic approach to diversity often has been challenging and elusive (Williams & Barber, 2004). Louise Silverstein (2006) stated, for example, that multicultural theorists typically have paid limited attention to gender and feminism, and feminist theorists have tended to pay limited attention to class and race/ethnicity themes, focusing primarily on the realities of White, middle class women. Silverstein's statements echoed Pamela Trotman Reid's (2002) earlier observation that in the feminist literature, "the dominant ethnicity is assumed unless otherwise specified" (p. 104), while "researchers who examine ethnicity or race often define their interests narrowly to ignore issues of gender and the impact of sexism" (p. 104).

Multicultural and feminist perspectives are characterized by a variety of similarities, including: an emphasis on the ways in which sociocultural environments affect life trajectories, goals, and challenges; attentiveness to social, institutional, and individual power structures and their relationships to privilege, oppression, and "isms;" a recognition of the roles of consciousness-raising and critical consciousness for gaining insights and facilitating equality and empowerment; and the valuing of social as well as individual change as major methods for meeting goals (Enns & Forrest, 2005; Williams & Barber, 2004; Reynolds & Constantine, 2004). The reasons for the slow (or lack of) integration of these approaches are multiple, and include, among other factors, myopic or narrow conceptualizations of feminism and multiculturalism, difficulties defining the complexity of feminist and multicultural factors in inclusive and meaningful ways, the limited willingness of White individuals to acknowledge and give up privileged status, and the outsider status of both feminist and multicultural perspectives within psychology (Enns, 2004; Williams & Barber, 2004).

Although integrative work remains challenging, both Reid and Silverstein emphasize the value of and hope for a complexity paradigm that involves "a commitment to examining all of the salient features of personal identity and social locations" (Silverstein, p. 26). This volume represents one effort to explore the complex biopsychosocial intersections of multiple identities, multiple privileges, and multiple oppressions as they emerge during multiple time periods, multiple developmental phases, and multiple life tasks. Reid and Silverstein also proposed that a commitment to social justice offers a unifying approach for implementing a complexity paradigm, and the theme of social justice is explored throughout this handbook. As the concept implies, a "complexity paradigm" is not easily defined, and, as this volume reflects, there are many content areas and methods of working toward implementing an inclusive complexity approach.

The title of this handbook uses the following sequence of words: "feminist multicultural counseling psychology." The title could have reversed this order as "multicultural feminist." The ordering of these two words is not intended to prioritize one approach over the other, but rather to move toward the integration of multicultural feminist approaches in an inclusive, holistic perspective. Some readers may prefer multicultural feminist, others feminist multicultural, and still others, an alternative phrase that emphasizes a social justice orientation. It is also possible that different situations may call for "differential consciousness" (Moya, 2001), which results in heightened awareness of multicultural issues in some contexts, and heightened awareness of feminist concerns in other situations. It is important to value the efforts of psychologists and activists who have worked toward the integration of multicultural and feminist goals in a variety of organizations and initiatives, some of which use multicultural approaches as an umbrella framework and others which use feminism as an overall scaffold or framework.

The final component of this book's title refers to counseling psychology, which also provides an orienting foundation for this book's approach to multiculturalism and feminism. Counseling psychology values lend themselves to forms of integration that emphasize (a) human dignity, strengths, resilience, and optimal functioning; (b) a life span approach that is attentive to the varying educational, career, and personal needs of individuals across the life span; (c) person-environment interactions and a holistic ecological perspective that is attentive to microsystems as well as macrosystems; (d) educational and prevention interventions that focus on health enhancement; (e) the creative synthesis and integration of theory, science, and practice; (f) collaborative, egalitarian, and multidisciplinary networks and knowledge foundations; and (e) advocacy and social justice (Packard, 2009; Whalen et al., 2004). The multiple topics included in this volume are intended to reflect these priorities.

This initial chapter is intended to introduce a variety of issues and themes that are developed in greater detail throughout this volume. To provide a context for feminist multicultural (or multicultural feminist) perspectives, we begin with a herstory/history of important developments that have moved counseling psychologists toward adopting a complexity paradigm and more integrative, intersectional approaches. This summary speaks to both the positive outcomes and the tensions that have characterized the past 50 years. Space does not permit a comprehensive history/herstory of all important approaches to enhancing integrative work. Given the fact that the editors and many of the authors of this volume began their exploration of diversity issues within feminist contexts, the herstory that follows places particular emphasis on changes within feminism that have contributed to multicultural understandings. The second part of this chapter highlights domains in which our understanding of multiculturalism and feminism have evolved, with the goal of providing a road map for reading other chapters in this volume.

Feminist Multicultural Counseling Psychology: A Herstorical Perspective

During the 1960s, as the civil rights and second wave women's movements gained strength, feminist psychologists in both the United States and Canada began to focus on women's issues within psychology. One of the most frequently cited critiques of that time came from Naomi Weisstein

([1968] 1993), who stated that "psychology has nothing to say about what women are really like" (p. 197). Weisstein described three major flaws with psychology. First, she identified the problem of theory without evidence, especially in the subfields of personality and psychotherapy, and was especially critical of classical psychoanalysts who proposed that women were essentially passive, masochistic, and dependent. The second problem was psychology's tendency to decontextualize human experience, to explain behavior in terms of inner traits rather than on the basis of the social context that modifies and shapes behavior. Third, Weisstein was critical of reductionist biologically based theories of sex and gender differences that permeated the field. In other work, Weisstein (1977) also documented the type of biased, sexist treatment experienced by women in graduate psychology programs. Each of the problems that she discussed is relevant to the corrective measures that both multicultural and feminist psychologists have addressed.

In both the United States and Canada, psychologists such as Weisstein encountered professional organizations and institutions that were unresponsive to their concerns and proposals (Pyke, 2001; Tiefer, 1991). Thus, they stepped outside the formal structures of the American Psychological Association (APA) and the Canadian Psychological Association (CPA) to initiate change. In the United States, after coping with various forms of resistance, denial, disinterest, and marginalization within the APA (Tiefer, 1991), feminist psychologists established an independent organization in 1969, the Association for Women in Psychology (AWP). In response to their frustration (Pyke, 2001), Canadian feminist psychologists also ventured outside psychology's formal structure, sponsoring an "underground symposium" at a hotel adjacent to the CPA convention in 1972.

The early to mid-1970s were years marked by high levels of energy for women in both the CPA and the APA. Following the "walk-out" of feminist psychologists in both the United States and Canada, both the CPA and the APA acknowledged the disadvantaged status of women psychologists and provided structures for fostering research and knowledge relevant to the psychology of women (Hogan & Sexton, 1991; Mednick & Urbanski, 1991; Pyke, 2001). For example, the APA created a Task Force on the Status of Women in Psychology, which led to the establishment of APA's Society for the Psychology of Women (Division 35) (Mednick & Urbanski, 1991). APA's Division 35 and the AWP have enjoyed a close and mutually enriching relationship since that time. Division 35 organized a Task Force on Black Women's Priorities in 1976, and a Task Force on the Concerns of Hispanic Women in 1977, emphasizing the important role that women of color have played within the psychology of women (Mednick&Urbanski). Today, the Society for the Psychology of Women includes sections on lesbian, bisexual, and transgender concerns; Black women; Hispanic women and Latinas; Asian Pacific American women; and Alaska native, American Indian, and indigenous women. Both APA's Society for the Psychology of Women and AWP have assumed leadership roles in considering the intersections of multiple forms of diversity.

Within counseling psychology, the Ad Hoc Committee on Women was established in 1970 (Farmer, 2002), and its members historically have been active members of the Society for the Psychology of Women (Division 35) and multiple other APA structures that emphasize diversity and social justice concerns. Much of the content that appears in subsequent chapters of this handbook is the outgrowth of the priorities, scholarship, and initiatives that emerged from the ad hoc committee and evolving structures that eventually were formalized as the Section for the Advancement of Women (SAW) in 1996. Helen Farmer (2002) identified five major goals of SAW: (a) providing professional support for members, including supporting women's advancement as leaders and journal editors, and nominating women for awards; (b) advancing education and training, such as through crafting principles and guidelines for psychological practice, sponsoring workshops and conferences, and ensuring that training programs and accreditation guidelines emphasized social change as well as gender and multicultural concerns; (c) contributing to the advancement of science, especially through the publication of major journal contributions; (d) highlighting professional practice issues relevant to the changing needs of women, as well as ethics (e.g., boundary crossings in therapy, competent practice with sexual abuse memories); and (e) addressing diversity, public interest and social change, and the intersections of gender, race, sexual orientation, and other social locations. Across these five areas, SAW has maintained an activist focus and has supported a variety of task forces designed to effect change within psychology and beyond (see Farmer, 2002, for a detailed summary).

Efforts to create a more inclusive climate consistent with feminist multicultural priorities have been enriched by a variety of ethnic minority organizations within psychology, which also originated during the late 1960s and early 1970s (Franklin, 2009; Holliday, 2009; Leong & Okazaki, 2009; Sue, 2009; Trimble & Clearing-Sky, 2009). Ethnic minority psychological associations (e.g., Association of Black Psychologists, Asian American Psychological Association, Society of Indian Psychologists) emerged out of a need to "transform the status quo in the profession" (Franklin, 2009, p. 416), and to protest the lack of or limited responsiveness to ethnic minority issues and realities in the APA and within psychology more broadly (Holliday, 2009; Pickren, 2009). Ethnic minority associations (a) gave voice to the "deeply scarring indignities" (Franklin, 2009, p. 352) of people of color, as well as their pride and resilience; (b) challenged the marginalization and underrepresentation of psychologists and people of color within psychology, as well as biases and racism embedded in theory and research; (c) provided a foundation for personal and professional support, the development of new knowledge, and activism; and (d) paved the way for "unity in through diversity" (Comas-Diaz, 2009, p. 402) within the Society for the Psychological Study of Ethnic Minority Issues (Division 45). Although the APA first established the Committee on Equality of Opportunity in Psychology in 1963, the structure of APA Division 45 was not formalized until 1986. The inclusive model on which it was founded focused on "representing all major ethnic minority groups balanced with gender" (Comas-Diaz, 2009, p. 402).

Within counseling psychology, the Section on Ethnic and Racial Diversity (SERD) and the Section on Lesbian, Gay, Bisexual, and Transgender Issues (SLGBTI) also have been instrumental in supporting consciousness-raising, scholarship, and practice relevant to ethnic/racial groups and sexual minorities. A variety of contributors to feminist multicultural psychology have provided significant leadership and knowledge through these structures, and overlap of Division 17 membership with APA's Divisions 45 (Society for the Psychological Study of Ethnic Minority Issues) and 44 (Society for the Psychological Study of Lesbian, Gay, Bisexual and Transgender Issues) has been considerable. In addition, the Association for Multicultural Counseling and Development (originally named the Association for Non-White Concerns), a Division of the American Counseling Association, also played an important role in the advancement of multicultural issues. Its journal, the *Journal of Multicultural Counseling and Development* (JMCD), included a series of articles based on the outcomes of the Centralizing Multiculturalism and Feminism in Counseling Psychology conference (see Fassinger, 2004; JMCD 32 (Extra) 2004; JMCD 34(2), 2006).

Nonsexist Psychological Practice with Women: The 1970s and 1980s

This section provides background about a variety of important initiatives within psychology during the 1970s and 1980s that emphasized features of non-sexist practice. We place emphasis on the Principles Concerning the Counseling and Psychotherapy of Women (1979), which were an outgrowth of work within counseling psychology. This narrative also makes reference to parallel developments that occurred within Canada and discusses how these projects provided a foundation for later work.

From the 1970s to the mid-1980s, a variety of task forces within both the APA and the CPA challenged sexism and developed guidelines for non-sexist language (APA, 1975a, 1977), non-sexist research (Denmark, Russo, Frieze, & Sechzer, 1988), and non-sexist psychotherapy (APA 1975b, 1978; see also Hogan & Sexton, 1991; Pyke, 2001). A survey of women psychologists, conducted by the Task Force on Sex Bias and Sex Role Stereotyping in Psychotherapeutic Practice (1975b), revealed problems encountered by women in therapy, including (a) the fostering of traditional women's roles; (b) the devaluation and biased expectations of women; (c) the sexist application of psychoanalytic concepts; and (d) the treatment of women as sex objects. The Task Force (APA, 1978) proposed 13 guidelines to counteract and rectify these biases.

In addition to association-wide efforts, psychologists representing counseling psychology participated in a multi-year project that led to the crafting and adoption of the Principles Concerning the Counseling and Psychotherapy of Women (APA, 1979; Fitzgerald & Nutt, 1986). A 1977 planning meeting focused on identifying basic philosophical values; clarified the need for specific knowledge, skills, and attitudes in counseling women; and noted areas in which specific competencies and expertise were necessary. One year later, a group of approximately 30 women met to develop specific recommendations that could be endorsed by "broad-based groups of professionals" (Hill et al., 1979, p. 2). As a part of proceedings that were characterized by "lively debate," and "reasoned zeal" (Blimline & Birk, 1979, p. 49), participants worked as a group to craft and approve 13 guidelines, seeking compromise when consensus did not emerge immediately. Some participants criticized the resulting principles for endorsing non-sexist rather than feminist perspectives, and as offering an insufficient analysis of power dynamics within society that impede women's development and mental health (e.g., Lerman, 1979). Hannah Lerman noted that some participants believed that the principles went too far, and acknowledged that "despite the carefully chosen neutral (as opposed to political) words, we may have committed ourselves to political dynamite" (p. 51). Despite some tension, the Principles Concerning the Counseling and Psychotherapy of Women (APA, 1979) were endorsed by the Division of Counseling Psychology (17) in 1978, adopted by a variety of other divisions within the APA, including Divisions 12 (Clinical Psychology), 16 (School Psychology), 29 (Psychotherapy), and 35 (Psychology of Women) (Farmer, 2002), and were endorsed by the APA Education and Training Board (Mintz, Rideout, & Bartels, 1994).

A special issue of *The Counseling Psychologist* published a series of short supporting articles that described sexist psychotherapy practices, documented women's "footnote" status in psychology, provided background regarding general knowledge and skills for counseling women, and identified skills for working with subgroups of women (e.g., lesbians, school-age girls, Black women). Two of the authors of these short articles are contributors to this volume (Courtois, 1979; Nutt, 1979). In addition, Joan Griscom (1979) articulated the need to attend to the diverse race, class, and sex differences between women, noting that, whereas early feminist visions had emphasized sisterhood and similarities among women, contemporary challenges require "recognizing and facing crucial differences among women" (p. 11). She added: "Both class and race analyses become crucial for an integrated perspective, and for building real bridges between women from different groups" (p. 11).

Within Canada, the CPA Status of Women Committee was largely responsible for the writing of the 10 Guidelines for Therapy and Counselling with Women, which were approved and adopted by the CPA Board of Directors in 1980 (CPA, 1980). Although the APA and CPA groups worked independently of each other, there are remarkable similarities within the two documents, and these overlapping themes can be grouped within eight broad categories. The following list labels these categories and associated behaviors for enhancing non-sexist practice.

1. Awareness of values: Monitoring values and attitudes, including understanding one's own values and socialization, developing awareness of the potential impact of one's personal functioning, and avoiding double standards when considering the choices of clients. (APA principles 11 and 12; CPA principle 9)
2. Knowledge: Gaining knowledge of unique concerns and issues faced by women. (APA principle 1 and 3, CPA principle 5)
3. Theory: Avoiding the use of biased theories, and adopting theoretical frameworks that support women's potential. (APA principle 2; CPA principles 3 and 4)
4. Women's life choices: Expanding women's options by helping them explore a variety of options that transcend gender role socialization and restrictions. (APA principle 7; CPA principles 1 and 2)
5. Oppression and power: Recognizing and working toward eliminating oppressions and power abuses, including physical violence and sexual abuse, sex biases in institutions, and forms of oppression that interact with sexism. (APA principles 4 and 13; CPA principle 7)
6. Therapeutic relationships: Developing optimal therapist-client relationships and process/intervention skills that facilitate sharing responsibility with clients, treating clients as full adults, using skills that support growth, and recognizing occasions when the gender of the therapist might be important to achieving therapeutic goals. (APA principles 5, 6, and 8; CPA principle 8)
7. Communication: Using non-sexist language, being aware of the impact of non-verbal and verbal variables as they reinforce the sharing of responsibility and power, and avoiding language that demeans women or conveys bias. (APA principles 5 and 9; CPA principle 6)
8. Sexualization and objectification: Avoiding the sexualization of clients, including avoiding the treatment women as sex objects or engaging in sexual activity with clients. (APA principle 10; CPA principle 10)

Both the APA and CPA principles/guidelines reflected salient concerns and goals of the late 1970s and emphasized (a) eliminating the gender-biased attitudes of practitioners; (b) understanding the socialization processes that limit the self-definitions of women and men; and (c) moving research, knowledge, and practice regarding the psychology of women and gender from marginalized status to a central, legitimate area of study. The guidelines and principles, along with an expanded rationale and implementation statement (Fitzgerald & Nutt, 1986), called on practitioners to work with women from an informed, sensitive, non-sexist perspective; provided useful guidance for work and research with women through the 1980s and much of the 1990s; and established a framework for organizing and discussing gender issues in counseling (see Enns, 2000; Yoder, 1999).

As understandings of feminism matured and expanded during the 1990s and beyond, the limitations of non-sexist approaches for guiding contemporary practice became apparent. Growing knowledge of diversity among women and the limitations of "one size fits all" approaches were among the catalysts for efforts to transform initial frameworks. More specifically, the 1979 principles spoke to the confining socialization influences that women and men face, but placed less emphasis on power differences and structures that influence women's lives and mental health experiences. They called for the elimination of sex bias in institutions and individuals, but provided limited guidance for initiating systemic change. Second, although the 1979 principles referred to the importance of being knowledgeable about "special problems of subgroups of women" (principle 3) and recognizing "all forms of oppression and how they interact with sexism" (principle 4), themes of diversity were not central to the document. In their commentary about the guidelines, Fitzgerald and Nutt (1986) noted that:

> The theories that are only now being constructed about female psychology are often, ironically, as irrelevant to the description and explanation of the experience and behavior of black, Chicano, poor, elderly, and gay women as were the androcentric formulations of mainstream psychology to the behavior of white, middle-class women a decade ago. (p. 189)

Thus, it was becoming apparent that an approach that was simply non-sexist was inadequate for meeting the needs of diverse women in multiple contexts. This growing awareness led to important events in subsequent decades that shaped a feminist multicultural agenda.

Feminist and Multicultural Developments during the 1990s and the Twenty-first Century

This section includes commentary about a variety of developments and conferences that were held during the 1990s and beyond, highlighting the sequence of events and the emerging awareness of the importance of and methods for feminist multicultural practice. In keeping with the focus of this volume on counseling psychology, most of the events and developments described below were centered within Division 17, the Society of Counseling Psychology.

Centralizing Multiculturalism and Feminism in Psychology

The need for greater attentiveness to intersections of multiculturalism and feminism became a major focus for working conferences in the 1990s. Catalysts for these conferences included growing knowledge of feminist frameworks and diversity among women, and the need to assess and organize the rapid expansion of knowledge, research, and practice within the psychology of women and gender. Janet Hyde (2007), for example, author of seven editions of a psychology of women text, noted that, whereas in 1974 "the problem was that the field was too new and the research therefore too thin" (p. xi), by 2005 "there was almost too much research" (p. xi), and she faced the challenge of making decisions about topics and research that were most important for an introductory text. Major changes that she brought to later editions focused on diversity and multiculturalism.

In 1993, Division 35 (then Psychology of Women) hosted a conference that focused on "shaping the future of feminist psychology" (Worell & Johnson, 1997). One of the conference working groups focused on diversity (Greene & Sanchez-Hucles, 1997). This working group called for an analysis of privilege and power among women, reminded psychologists that emphasizing gender as a primary source of oppression posed an obstacle to inclusive definitions of diversity, and spoke of the importance of developing alliances across specific social identities.

In 1998, the Section for the Advancement of Women (SAW) in counseling psychology hosted a national working meeting titled Advancing Together: Centralizing Multiculturalism and Feminism in Counseling Psychology (Fassinger, 2004). The goal of the conference chairs (Ruth Fassinger, Linda Forrest, and Freda Ginsberg) was to bring together women who represented diverse social identities (e.g., race, sexual orientation, age, disability) and different experiences within counseling psychology for the purpose of defining a multicultural feminist knowledge base relevant to ten major topics (most of which also are addressed in this handbook). Working groups focused on the topics of counseling and psychotherapy, ethics, supervision, mentoring and professional development, education, pedagogy, career development, research and science, assessment, consultation and advocacy, and diversity and multiculturalism. Other goals included fostering large-scale mentoring and fostering the production and dissemination of scholarly outcomes relevant to the working group topics (Farmer, 2002). Many of these products appeared in two issues of the *Journal of Multicultural Counseling and Development* (Volume 32, Extra 2004; Volume 34, Issue 2, 2006) and a special issue of the *Career Development Quarterly* (see Cook, Heppner, & O'Brien, 2002).

One of the most profound outcomes of this conference was the recognition that bringing together multicultural and feminist themes within counseling psychology is not an uncomplicated task, and that difficult dialogues across identities would be necessary for moving forward (Fassinger, 2004). Women of color assumed leadership in identifying a number of issues that limited full inclusion of all women (e.g., Bowman, Rasheed, Ferris, Thompson, McRae, & Weitzman, 2001; Steward & Phelps, 2004). Some women of color experienced subtle pressure to prioritize a feminist identity over other identities, and viewed the feminism of their White co-participants as ethnocentrically glossing over multiple oppressions and identities, especially race, class, and cultural dimensions. As one woman of color noted: "I refuse to take the label feminist" (Bowman et al., p. 788), noting that for her, that term is associated with a movement by and for White middle-class women. Another woman of color commented that, although gender had been an "element in discrimination against me" (Bowman et al., p. 789), "race is more significant in U.S. society than being a woman" (Bowman et al., p. 789). She stated that, while women and men of color share discrimination and work toward liberation on a daily basis, white men and women share power and privilege, and "women of color understand that feminism was and is not necessary to liberate us" (Bowman et al., p. 791).

Women of color emphasized the importance of honest, open discussion of imbalances of power, and expressed anger not only about their experiences of racism, but about the responses of their White colleagues, noting that, when faced with the direct expression of anger, White women often deny their associations with privilege and power, adopting "internalized perceptions of themselves as weak, passive, and powerless" (p. 792); in addition, "they cry; they whine; they shut down" (p. 792), a behavioral pattern that limits direct management of conflict. They observed that this response pattern on the part of White women also implies that women of color need to take care of White women and to raise issues "in a way that allows White women to hear it on an intellectual level" (p. 793). They challenged their White sisters to be honest, noting that, for genuine progress to be made, "holding back or being polite" (p. 796) will not lead to substantial change; rather, real progress requires the willingness to share and experience intense emotion, to listen to pain, and to tolerate discomfort and feelings associated with distrust. As noted by Ruth Fassinger (2004) in her summary of the meeting:

> We learned that trust takes time to build and that we do not always listen as well as we think we do. We learned that hierarchy is extraordinarily difficult to dismantle even under the best efforts. We learned how hard it is to keep perspective and momentum after highly charged interpersonal interactions.... We glimpsed how far we have to go. (p. 345)

In short, the concerns of women of color underlined the in-depth level of dialogue that was and continues to be necessary in formulating inclusive models of integrating multiculturalism and feminism. For White women, in particular, recognizing and sharing power and privilege and centralizing the perspectives of those who often have been marginalized or underrepresented are crucial areas of learning.

Multicultural Summits and Diversity in Psychology

One year after the Centralizing Multiculturalism and Feminism working conference, the first National Multicultural Conference and Summit (NMCS) was sponsored by a group of four APA divisions committed to social justice issues. In a fortuitous circumstance in which the presidents of Divisions 17, 35, 44, and 45 all were people of color that year, these individuals collaborated to create a space in which multicultural issues were central. Major themes at the first summit focused on (a) raising consciousness about the impact of monoculturalism and

"Whiteness" in psychology and society; (b) creating space for difficult dialogues about race, gender, and sexual orientation; (c) building a psychology that is responsive to the changing and ever more diverse landscape of North American society; (d) supporting the teaching of multiculturalism and diversity; and (e) acknowledging and integrating dimensions associated with spirituality within the psychology knowledge base (Sue, Bingham, Porché-Burke, & Vasquez, 1999). Another major goal of the conference was to build multicultural alliances to support advocacy and political action. As noted by organizers, multiculturalism was defined broadly to include a wide range of social identities such as sexual orientation, gender, race/ethnicity, disability, religion, class, age, and other identities and differences. An integrative approach was adopted to facilitate challenging dialogues between underrepresented and/or marginalized groups and to transcend "who is more oppressed" arguments. Although there are potential tensions associated with defining multiculturalism broadly (e.g., perceptions of a dilution of issues or diversion away from key issues faced by people of color), a more inclusive definition has the potential to support productive activist alliances and approaches that are attentive to the intersectional, multiple identities held by individuals.

Like its predecessor meetings and conferences, the Multicultural Summit revealed the presence of deep and difficult tensions and misunderstandings among the diverse groups represented at the Summit; the chasm between conservative religious beliefs and the affirmative inclusion of sexual minorities has been particularly difficult to bridge, for example, as has been the ongoing invisibility of disability in the multicultural discourse. However, the NMCS continues to be held on a biennial schedule, and it continues to grow and evolve, contributing importantly to enriched understandings of what it means to think inclusively about multicultural psychology and its relation to other foci in our field. The NMCS held in 2011, for example, highlighted themes of unification through diversity and the integration of science and practice in psychology, both important issues for feminist multicultural psychology.

Social Justice, Advocacy, and Multiculturalism in Counseling Psychology

In 2001, a national counseling psychology conference held in Houston was organized around the following theme: Psychologists are Everywhere and Making a Difference (Fouad et al., 2004). The conference explored the many new and different roles that counseling psychologists play in a changing society, and the roles of social advocacy and social justice in counseling psychology. In addition to keynote addresses that explored topics such as counseling psychology's emphasis on health and diversity, counseling psychology's growth toward greater inclusiveness, and the role of political advocacy, the conference structure included social action groups (SAGs). Nine groups organized their efforts around topics such as domestic violence, community violence, child abuse and neglect, homelessness and welfare, care for the chronically mentally ill, issues of poor and working class persons, racism, and social justice and ethics. In addition, members of sections within the Society of Counseling Psychology that emphasize social justice concerns met to explore potential alliances (e.g., Section for the Advancement of Women [SAW], Section on Race and Ethnic Diversity [SERD], and the Section on Lesbian, Gay, Bisexual, and Transgender Issues [SLGBTI]). They chose the label "More Pie." Rather than competing for the limited resources (or, a slice of the pie) that are typically designated for social justice groups, the name "More Pie" underlined efforts to collaborate to maximize and increase resources (Fouad, Gerstein, & Toporek, 2006).

Subsequent to initiatives explored in Houston, a variety of important articles on social justice in counseling psychology were published (e.g., Goodman et al., 2004; Speight & Vera, 2004; Toporek, Gerstein, Fouad, Roysircar, & Israel, 2006; Vera & Speight, 2003). Elizabeth Vera and Suzette Speight's (2003) contribution linked social justice to the APA's (2003) endorsement of the Guidelines on Multicultural Education, Training, Research, Practice, and Organizational Change for Psychologists. The six guidelines are highly relevant to multicultural feminist perspectives in counseling psychology. The first two guidelines emphasize the importance of self-examination of values and attitudes and the development of multicultural sensitivity, knowledge, and understanding of ethnically, racially, and culturally diverse persons. The third guideline calls on psychologists to embed multicultural and diversity constructs in education, and the fourth guideline elaborates on qualities of research that informs culture-centered and ethical research with persons from ethnic, linguistic, and racial minority backgrounds. The fifth guideline explores skills necessary for applied psychological practice, and the sixth guideline outlines the importance of organizational change processes (see Appendix A for a complete list of the six major guidelines).

Shortly thereafter, Lisa Goodman and colleagues (2004) called attention to both feminist and multicultural building blocks for social justice (for more information, see Miville, chapter 23 of this volume; Norsworthy et al., chapter 25 of this volume). In addition, the *Handbook for Social Justice in Counseling Psychology* (Toporek et al., 2006) expanded on various aspects of social justice, including ethical dimensions, education and training implications, themes relevant to marginalized communities, career dimensions, advocacy, and international aspects. Several contributions in this volume specifically focused on the nexus of feminism and multiculturalism, for example, chapters on advocacy in education and work (Fassinger & Gallor, 2006), intimate partner violence (Bell and Goodman, 2006), and women with disabilities (Palombi & Mundt, 2006). Thus, recent developments relevant to social justice in psychology have contributed to substantial movement toward integrative frameworks of multiculturalism and feminism.

Guidelines for Psychological Practice With Girls and Women

In 2000, the presidents of the Society of Counseling Psychology (Nadya Fouad) and the Society for the Psychology of Women (Jan Yoder) appointed three co-chairs (Roberta Nutt, Joy Rice, and Carolyn Zerbe Enns) to an interdivisional task force charged with revising the Principles Concerning the Counseling and Psychotherapy of Women and crafting a new set of guidelines that reflected twenty-first-century realities. The resulting guidelines, eventually adopted in 2007 by the APA Council of Representatives, are referred to frequently in later chapters of this Handbook. The 11 guidelines are included in Appendix B of this chapter, along with brief commentary about each guideline.

Consistent with the group process that provided a framework for the 1979 Principles, organizers of the 26-member task force that crafted the initial statements and literature review for the guidelines were committed to feminist process—a belief that how colleagues work together is central to achieving goals that ensure inclusivity and widespread involvement and endorsement. Knowing that integrating multicultural and feminist perspectives was central to the work ahead, task force members spent substantial time discussing the relationships between multiculturalism and feminism and discovered (to no one's surprise) that group members' thinking about entry points and methods for integration varied. For some, feminism was a point of entry and a vehicle for enriching our understanding of the complexities of girls' and women's rich multicultural experiences. For others, especially for women of color, multiculturalism was seen as encompassing a commitment to understanding diverse cultures, including gender cultures. From the latter perspective, the multiplicity of cultures in which we live provides the umbrella; feminism is more specific and provides a vehicle or methodology for generating change within cultures.

Discussions among task force members led to greater appreciation of the ways in which multiculturalism and feminism intersect, and the ways in which the positionalities and social identities of individuals are related to diverse forms of integration. Task force members concluded that understanding the diversity of women's lives requires being attentive to oppression, privilege, and the celebration of differences; and that although one social identity or aspect of diversity may be experienced as preeminent in a given person's life, other aspects of diversity and other identities are not erased but may be prioritized or relevant in different ways. A shared goal of this group was to be attentive to the multiple diversities, identities, and realities of women's and girls' lives (Enns & Rice, 2008).

The feminist process underlying the 2007 guidelines included (a) brainstorming via Internet and preliminary planning meetings; (b) small task group work products; (c) plenary sessions designed to identify overlap, similarities, and differences among small working groups; and (d) opportunities for members to "check in" to ensure that feelings and thoughts about the process itself were articulated. During the initial work phase (April 2002), small working groups met and were charged with developing guideline statements in four categories: (a) gender socialization, (b) power, (c) diversity, and (d) practice applications. After posting the 22 initial guideline statements that emerged in these groups, statements were placed into eight major clusters. After many hours of lively discussion, finessing of language, and restatement and clarification, a group of statements that correspond closely to the 11 statements that appear in the current guidelines emerged. Over time, multiple readers and groups within the APA (2002–2007) contributed to the further honing of the guidelines and the completion of literature reviews that supported each component (Enns & Rice, 2008; Nutt, 2008). Seven years after the appointment of task force chairs, the Guidelines for Psychological Practice With Girls and Women

(APA, 2007a) were approved by the APA Council of Representatives. The 11 guidelines are organized into three broad categories: (a) diversity, social context, and power; (b) professional responsibility; and (c) practice applications (see Appendix B).

The guidelines reflect contemporary realities and perspectives, and represent an expansion of the original Principles in a variety of ways. First, they emphasize diversity among girls and women as well as intersectionality, or the interactions of specific social identities such as gender, race, sexual orientation, and class. The salience, impact, and importance of any specific social identity (such as gender, race, or class) vary substantially among girls and women. Furthermore, some girls and women experience the benefits of White, upper middle class, and heterosexual privilege; differences based on both privilege and oppression are acknowledged within these guidelines. In addition, the supporting literature review focuses on the impact of contemporary and more subtle forms of bias and oppression (e.g., racism, classism, sexism, heterosexism).

Second, these guidelines attend more explicitly than previous documents to the impact of power differences within society and address the importance of social change and social activism. In other words, gender neutral or non-biased treatment of individuals alone is not adequate for erasing social barriers and enduring problems such as violence against women, racism, classism, heterosexism, ableism, and other oppressions. The guidelines are consistent with the notion that social locations such as gender, race, and ethnicity are socially constructed and are intimately connected to power structures and to the "doing," or enactment, of gender, culture, and other social identities.

Third, the guidelines emphasize a life span perspective and are based on the accumulated knowledge of more than 40 years of psychological research and theory about women's and girls' lives. They emphasize the complex knowledge relevant to working with girls and women at different life stages, and with different life experiences, ethnicities, abilities, and socioeconomic and class backgrounds. Integrated with this life span perspective is a biopsychosocial perspective on girls' and women's lives; biological, psychological, and cultural analyses are applied to female life span issues and events such as menstruation, reproduction, reproductive choice, childbirth, and menopause.

Fourth, contemporary issues relevant to assessment and diagnosis receive more explicit attention within the current guidelines than in previous guidelines. For example, the current guidelines address more explicitly the strengths, resources, creativity, and forms of resilience of girls and women. As such, they represent a "positive" feminist psychology, which is in line with counseling psychology's historical focus on strengths and resilience (Gelso & Fretz, 2001). In addition, a more comprehensive and ecological systems perspective is prioritized. Since the initial publication of guidelines during the 1970s, the American Psychiatric Association's (2000) *Diagnostic and Statistical Manual* has gained a more powerful and pervasive hold on perceptions of distress and systems of treatment, and the guidelines refocus attention to ways in which social systems inform life tasks and challenges, and thus attempt to counteract the heavy emphasis in the field of psychology on deficits and remediation.

Finally, unlike the original guidelines, which focused primarily on counseling and psychotherapy applications, these guidelines are based on an expansive definition that encompasses practice in its broadest sense. Psychological practice includes education, research, advocacy, psychotherapy, prevention, supervision, and consultation.

It is important to note that while task force members were crafting a new set of guidelines in the United States, a parallel process was again occurring in Canada. The Canadian process emerged from internal efforts to reexamine all policy statements (Church, Pettifor, & Malone, 2006). The committee charged with reviewing the Canadian guidelines in 2002 noted that much had changed since the first set of guidelines had been adopted in 1980. Although there was less need to document the existence of sexism (it had already been done) and women had made substantive gains in Canada, the momentum of feminist change had slowed during the 1990s, and many issues remained. A revision of the guidelines sought to take contemporary issues into account, including the need to (a) challenge systemic inequities that perpetuate women's lower status; (b) address the well-documented physical and sexual victimization of girls and women; (c) emphasize the complexity of women's lives based on their multiple contexts and diverse oppressions related to social identities such as nationality, race, religion, relationship status, sexual orientation, physical and mental abilities, age, and so on; and (d) highlight issues related to power differentials and overlapping relationships in psychotherapy relationships (Church, Pettifor, & Malone, 2006).

A new set of guidelines, named the Guidelines for Ethical Psychological Practice with Women, was approved by the CPA Board in 2007 (CPA). Each of the 21 guidelines is linked directly to one of the four major moral values that support the Canadian Code of Ethics for Psychologists. The CPA document also includes both positive and negative examples of the application of the guidelines. That the Canadian guidelines bear similarity to the guidelines developed within the APA in the United States is perhaps not surprising, and, in concluding this subsection, we note that our summary highlights North American practice themes. The development of guidelines that support inclusive and competent transnational practice represents an important future direction (Enns & Machizawa, 2008). The APA's (2004a) Resolution on Culture and Gender Awareness in International Psychology represents one step toward this goal.

On Integrating Practice Guidelines

During the past decade, a variety of practice guidelines have been approved by the APA, including the Guidelines for Multicultural Education, Training, Research, Practice, and Organizational Change for Psychologists (APA, 2003); Guidelines for Psychological Practice with Lesbian, Gay, and Bisexual Clients (APA, 2012a); Guidelines for Psychological Practice with Girls and Women (APA, 2007a); Guidelines for Psychological Practice with Older Adults (APA, 2004b); and Guidelines for Assessment of and Intervention with Persons with Disabilities (2012b). A variety of reports have been tasked by the APA, and resolutions relevant to diverse social identities have been passed, such as the Resolution on Poverty and Socioeconomic Status (APA, 2000); the Report of the APA Task Force on Gender Identity and Gender Variance (APA, 2008); the Report of the APA Task Force on Appropriate Therapeutic Responses to Sexual Orientation (APA, 2009); the Report of the APA Task Force on the Sexualization of Girls (APA, 2007b); and the Resolution on Gender and Culture Awareness in International Psychology (APA, 2004a). These kinds of documents and governance actions within the APA make clear the professional expectation that psychologists attend to human diversity in all of their work.

Each of the guidelines, reports, and resolutions also speaks to the importance of identifying biases and providing competent practice based on knowledge and sensitivity to the social identity addressed by the specific set of guidelines. In light of the growing complexity of being familiar with and applying these guidelines, a special task group was charged by the APA Society of Counseling Psychology and the Council of Counseling Psychology Training Programs (CCPTP) to explore and develop a framework for integrating the information contained within the various guidelines and promoting competence in multiple aspects of diversity (Miville et al., 2009; see also Miville, chapter 23 of this volume).

Marie Miville and co-authors (2009) proposed an integrative model that emphasized four cyclical stages: (a) understanding the multicultural self; (b) understanding others based on common themes across guidelines that are attentive to general social justice goals; (c) developing understanding and knowledge (e.g., specific cultural sensitivity and empathy) specific to each set of guidelines; and (d) building skills and strategies for competence. First, understanding oneself in the context of person-environment interactions, including one's privileges and oppressions, "is a prerequisite for understanding the social and cultural experiences of others" (p. 540). Second, at the level of broad understanding, each set of guidelines shares the theme that "social oppression is a core experience of people with one or more minority statuses" (p. 540), and the development of critical consciousness of social, political, and economic oppressions is a crucial step for adopting a social justice approach to counseling psychology. Developing specific understanding and intervention skills requires the integrated application of all relevant guidelines to the specific client (e.g., related to the confluence of multiple identities), the application of specific guidelines as they are relevant to the specific concerns of a client (e.g., aging), and the application of multiple levels of intervention that are appropriate to the circumstances (e.g., social change/activism and/or individual counseling).

The task force (Miville et al., 2009) also identified a variety of challenges to applying this model. For example, although being attentive to multiple parallels between different identities and forms of privilege or oppression is important, it is crucial to validate the realities, struggles, and strengths associated with the individual's unique identity. In addition, shared issues (e.g., interpersonal violence) may hold different meanings based on one's multiple intersecting identities. Finding optimal approaches to pedagogy and the assessment of competence also pose challenges and will need further testing and refinement over time.

Counseling Psychology in Global Perspective

During the past decade, multiple Society of Counseling Psychology (Division 17) presidents have prioritized transnational efforts in counseling psychology (e.g., Louise Douce, Puncky Heppner, Roberta Nutt, Linda Forrest). A section within the division devoted to international counseling psychology also has been formed and is thriving. In her presidential address, Louise Douce (2004) spoke of the value of linking scholarship and practice relevant to domestic and international/transnational aspects of multiculturalism in order to support counseling psychology in a global context. In keeping with a global theme, the most recent national counseling psychology conference was titled the International Counseling Psychology Conference: Counseling Psychologists in a Changing World (see Forrest, 2010). In addition to featuring keynote addresses that were delivered by international scholars and a wide range of concurrent sessions relevant to the expanding roles of counseling psychologists, the conference incorporated a variety of working groups on topics such as transgender concerns, immigration, internationalizing counseling psychology, international collaborations and alliances, advocacy, practicing feminist/multicultural therapy in a conservative environment, and global psychological practice with girls and women. As psychologists move further into the twenty-first century, implications relevant to the integration of multiculturalism and feminism continue to expand.

Feminist Multicultural Counseling Psychology: Evolving Perspectives

Across the time periods and events relevant to feminist and multicultural psychology, growth and positive change have been evident, despite the enormous complexity of the integrative task. With growing knowledge of this complexity, early understandings and definitions have been reworked and continue to evolve. In this section, we briefly outline some of these major areas of evolution, growth, and change, noting their relevance to the contents of this handbook.

Evolving Concepts of Sex, Gender, Sexuality, and Intersecting Social Identities

Researchers and theorists have focused on defining and differentiating between the terms "sex" and "gender" since the 1950s (Muehlenhard & Peterson, 2011). Rhoda Unger and Mary Crawford (1992) defined gender as "what culture makes out [of] the 'raw material' of biological sex" (p. 18). Consistent with this idea, feminist psychologists consistently have endorsed the notion that gender is about "doing" or activity, and often involves self-presentation efforts that can be referred to as "gender display" or "gender accomplishment" (West & Zimmerman, 1987; Golden, 2008). Differentiating between sex as biology and gender as the enactment of social meanings associated with cultural views of maleness and femaleness has offered good utility during the past 40 years, in part because it allowed feminist psychologists to challenge myths about biological sex/gender differences and to emphasize the social creation and social construction of sex and gender-related behaviors. It also has provided a framework for understanding multicultural variations in gender, as well as how ecological contexts modify gender.

However, boundaries between sex and gender, or nature and nurture, increasingly are seen as less distinct. As noted by Jan Yoder (2003), "sex isn't as immutable as we might have thought at first" (p. 17), leading her to suggest that we regard "*sex and gender as inseparable and intertwined*" (p. 17). Marecek, Crawford, and Popp (2004) noted that "sex, like gender, draws meaning from shifting cultural understanding and ever-changing social practices" (p. 207). Similarly, feminist theorist Judith Butler (1990) argued that physical bodies are gendered from birth, and sex does not exist without gender. Growing awareness of queer, intersexual, transsexual, transgendered, and other non-dichotomous identities also is consistent with the view that differentiating strictly between sex and gender can lead to placing individuals in arbitrary, dichotomous categories.

Recent research on sexuality, sexual orientation, and sexual minority women's experiences also reveals that change, fluidity, multidimensional identities, and boundary crossing often are more normative than stability and consistency (Diamond & Butterworth, 2008; Fassinger & Israel, 2010). A "gender transgressive" (Fassinger & Arseneau, 2007) approach to understanding the identity development of sexual minorities allows for a more flexible approach that takes into account intersections among sexual orientation, gender orientation, and cultural orientation (including ethnicity/race, social class, disability, and religion), as well as individual differences and developmental experiences.

Whereas gender and sex once were defined as distinctive (biological and social aspects), there is now greater awareness in psychology of the "messiness," fluidity, and complexities of these boundaries.

Changing views of gender and sex also are reflected in more complex understandings of factors that interact with sex and gender, such as culture, ethnicity/race, age, ability/disability, and sexual orientation (Bieschke, Hardy, Fassinger, & Croteau, 2008; Greene, 2003; Moradi, Mohr, Worthington, & Fassinger, 2009; Shields, 2008). Multiple social identities characterize individuals' lives, and these identities (e.g., ethnicity/race, class, sexual orientation), vary in salience and significance for the individuals across contexts and a life span, and "*mutually constitute*" (Shields, 2008, p. 302) each other such that gender and sex take on meaning only in relationship to other identities. In other words, our greater difficulty differentiating precisely between sex and gender also is reflected in our growing understanding that we cannot neatly carve out "effects" related to multicultural and feminist definitions and understandings. Both feminism and multiculturalism need to be flexible enough to reflect ways in which culture, gender, and many other social identities mutually constitute each other. This sense of reciprocal influence is reflected across most of the chapters in this volume, such as life span development (Juntunen & Bauman, chapter 3), concepts of mental health (Ancis & Davidson, chapter 4), feminist identity development (Fischer & DeBord, chapter 5), and career development (Hackett & Kohlhart, chapter 14).

Evolving Concepts of Power, Oppression, and Privilege

Oppression historically has been considered a central concept within feminist theory, and as stated by Marilyn Frye (1983), "it is a fundamental claim of feminism that women are oppressed" (p. 1). Although recognizing the reality of diverse "isms" that affect individuals, second wave radical feminists tended to define gender and sexism as the original, fundamental, and most pervasive form of oppression experienced by women. Lesbian Black feminist members of the Combahee River Collective (1982) were among the first to challenge this view, and made important contributions that are a cornerstone of contemporary feminist multicultural thought. Central to the Collective's thinking was the "simultaneity of oppression" (Smith, 1983, p. xxxii) and a refusal to rank oppressions related to class, race, or gender. Collective members also recommended that specific groups of women (e.g., Black women, Latinas) should identify the ways in which multiple identities and oppressions inform their experiences. This encouragement to explore specific realities of diverse groups of women (e.g., women of color, lesbians) has supported the development of knowledge and feminisms by, about, and for specific groups of women (e.g., Collins, 2000; Hurtado, 2003; Nam, 2001). Becky Thompson (2002) also provided evidence that although second wave feminism has been stereotyped as a White women's movement, multicultural and multiracial feminisms have challenged feminists to provide inclusive and intersectional visions of feminism since the early 1970s.

Black feminist theorist Patricia Hill Collins (1991) built on themes in the Combahee River Collective by speaking of race, class, and gender as interlocking systems of oppression; and used the phrase "matrix of domination" (p. 225) to signify the complex, exponential ways in which "isms" interact. She noted: "Depending on the context, an individual may be an oppressor, a member of an oppressed group, or simultaneously oppressor and oppressed" (p. 225). Collins also used the term "intersectionality" to refer to an "analysis claiming that systems of race, social class, gender, sexuality, ethnicity, nation, and age form mutually constructing features of social organization" (2000, p. 299). This emphasis on context, which was also elaborated by other multiracial (e.g., Zinn & Dill, 1996), anti-racist (Calliste, Dei, & Aguiar, 2000), and women of color feminists (e.g., Hurtado, 2003, 2010), contributed to the growing awareness of ways in which power, privilege, and oppression interact. Peggy McIntosh's (1989) discussion of White privilege also led to enhanced recognition of ways in which social power contributes to invisible and unearned privilege, and her analysis has been expanded to encompass male privilege, heterosexual privilege, class privilege, Western privilege, Christian privilege, and other forms of privilege (Israel, 2012).

Power is also central to oppression, privilege, and the enactment of various "isms." Consistent with this theme, Abigail Stewart and Christa McDermott (2004) indicated that "gender is increasingly understood as defining a system of power relations embedded in other power relations" (p. 519). The multiple social identities held by individuals are realized in power structures and social locations, and an individual may experience power and empowerment in some contexts and not others. During the past 40 years, feminists have moved from relatively simplistic and singular assumptions about oppression to recognizing the complexity and the interwoven, seemingly infinite number of combinations of interacting effects of power, privilege, and oppression. This complexity informs a feminist multicultural perspective and defies "one size fits all" types of analyses and solutions. Within the third section of this volume, authors focus on specific identity categories in order to inform readers of central, shared, and unique issues that characterize their life experiences. They also use an intersectional perspective to reflect the ways in which women with any shared identity also represent multiple forms and levels of diversity.

This volume features chapters relevant to a wide range of women's social identities and diversities, but given the diversity of women's identities, our coverage is not comprehensive (e.g., the volume does not include a separate chapter on indigenous or American Indian women). Specific chapters focus on African American women (Speight, Isom, & Thomas, chapter 6); lesbians, bisexual women, and transgender individuals (Szymanski & Hilton, chapter 7); women in poverty (Smith, Appio, & Chang, chapter 8); Latinas (Gloria & Castellanos, chapter 9); women with disabilities (Palombi, chapter 11); American Muslim women (Mahmood, chapter 12); and transnational contexts (Horne & Arora, chapter 13).Finally, social identity models (e.g., feminist or identity), which conceptualize individual development in response to marginalized, low-power status, provide lenses for thinking about how individuals negotiate personal identities in response to oppression. Although past models have tended to focus on single identities (e.g., gay identity, feminist identity, racial/ethnic identity), recent emphasis on intersectionality and the borders and boundaries between identities indicate that it is important to rethink theory and research on this topic, a direction that is explored by Ann Fischer and Kurt DeBord (chapter 5).

Evolving Concepts of Bias and "Isms"

At the dawn of the civil rights and feminist movements of the 1960s, much research focused on studying relatively blatant or obvious forms of bias and prejudice and the ways in which they were manifested. By the mid-1990s, researchers concluded that blatant racism and sexism had decreased substantially, and that assessing these "isms" had become increasingly difficult in a social climate in which appearing unprejudiced was expected and expressing racist or sexist attitudes was becoming increasingly unpopular (Campbell, Schellenberg, & Senn, 1997). Psychologists also became more aware that acts of bias, racism, sexism, heterosexism, or classism cannot be conceptualized as individual acts alone, but often are embedded in institutional structures and social norms that perpetuate the status quo but are difficult to change (Herek & Garnets, 2007; Margolis & Romero, 1998; Ridley, 2005). However, one's ability to recognize and acknowledge the power of institutionalized "isms" may be compromised by the individualistic values that permeate much of Western society, supporting the notion that individuals can overcome negative circumstances through their personal efforts alone.

Modern racist and modern sexist attitudes (Swim, Aikin, Hall, & Hunter, 1995; Swim, Becker, Lee, & Pruitt, 2010) are characterized by denial that racism and sexism exist within contemporary society and the assumption that people of various marginalized groups expect special favors. Resentment about perceived unearned advances of those from low-power groups and the presence of "reverse racism" also is a common feature. Even more subtle than these modern "isms" are the behaviors of well-intentioned individuals who, though desiring to be unprejudiced, often are influenced by internal conflicts as well as non-conscious attitudes and behaviors that limit their ability to relate to others in genuinely egalitarian ways. For example, ambivalent racism and ambivalent sexism (Glick & Fiske, 2001) are characterized in part by benevolent forms of bias. Benevolent biases are characterized by apparently positive acts and attitudes that also serve (often unconsciously) to reinforce existing power differences and justify existing systemic biases. Furthermore, research on aversive racism (Dovidio, Gaertner, Kawakami, & Hodson, 2002) reveals that subtle racist acts or attitudes only are manifested when they can be "explained away" by other variables. Implicit, non-conscious biases can have a negative impact on productivity and task quality. For example, research reveals that stereotypes about one's group can be internalized as "stereotype threat" at a non-conscious level, and depress the performance of otherwise high-achieving individuals (Steele, 2010). The impacts of both benevolent "isms" and stereotype threat are that they are difficult for the target to detect and also are challenging to identify or legitimize as forms of bias. As a result, the performance or self-concept of victims of these subtle interpersonal dynamics may suffer due to the internalization and self-questioning that these behaviors often induce (Dardenne, Dumont, & Bollier, 2007).

Although blatant forms of racism and sexism are less obvious within contemporary society, opposition to the civil and legal rights of gender-transgressive sexual minorities still is considered acceptable in many contexts (Fassinger & Arseneau, 2007). Gregory Herek has been documenting the effects of individual and institutional stigma on the mental health of sexual minority populations for at least two decades (e.g., Herek, 1991, 1995, 2007, 2010), and Ilan Meyer (e.g., 1995) has applied the minority stress model to LGBT populations to account for the well-documented negative mental health outcomes associated with prejudice and discrimination. Moreover, despite some recent gains in securing legal rights relevant to marriage, parenting, and health care for sexual minority people, it bears pointing out that even these legislative gains are hard-won in public battles that exhibit almost unthinkable hatred and anti-gay rhetoric. Research demonstrates the negative effects of these anti-gay political and legislative events on sexual minority populations, even when outcomes are generally positive (Rostosky, Riggle, Horne, & Miller, 2009). Thus, it is quite clear that equality is still elusive for many LGBT people, and continues to be an important civil rights issue that ultimately translates into mental health issues that need to be addressed by psychologists.

In general, contemporary and subtle forms of bias and intricate interactions of sexism, racism, heterosexism, ageism, ableism, and classism inform the intersectional analyses of authors within this handbook. The actions emanating from subtle forms of bias also are addressed, such as Barbara Palombi's analysis (chapter 11) of microaggressions experienced by women with disabilities. The concept of "gendered racism" (Thomas, Witherspoon, & Speight, 2008) is based on the assumption that racism and sexism are inseparable as experienced by many women of color. Suzette Speight, Denise Isom, and Anita Thomas (chapter 6) provide analysis of gendered racism by examining stereotyped images of African American women. Assessment of the interacting aspects of various "isms" experienced by women also is a feature of feminist multicultural therapy (see Remer & Hahn, chapter 16).

Evolving Approaches to Research and Evidence

As noted in the first section of this chapter, some of the first efforts to reduce bias in research focused on expanding the purview and scope of research by implementing non-sexist practices, asking unbiased questions, using representative samples (e.g., women, people of color), interpreting data objectively, and attending to interactions influenced by cultural values (Denmark, Russo, Frieze, & Sechzer, 1988). However, Sandra Harding (1986) argued that the attempted non-sexist use of quantitative methods did not provide tools for challenging flawed assumptions about the structure of knowledge. Janice Yoder and Arnold Kahn (1993) also noted that, even when researchers expanded their participant pools to include persons who were marginalized, these groups often were compared to samples of White women, which reinforced the implicit assumption that White heterosexual women's experiences were normative, and imposed a yardstick for assessing how other groups "measured up" to dominant White women's cultural standards. In contrast, "standpoint theories" and qualitative research methods were seen as emphasizing the in-depth exploration of the experiences of diverse groups of individuals. These methods purportedly allowed marginalized persons to explore their deep and personal knowledge as persons with outsider status who had gained insider perspectives. This knowledge had been acquired by living according to the rules of dominant society and by developing fine-tuned lenses for detecting nuances, hypocrisies, contradictions, and inconsistencies that powerful individuals had difficulty seeing in themselves (Collins, 1991; Harding, 1986).

By the late 1980s and early 1990s, psychologists (e.g., Hare-Mustin & Marecek, 1990; Peplau & Conrad, 1989; Riger, 1992) made a case for approaching research through multiple lenses and approaches. More specifically, the claim began to be made that all research methods, including "objective" methods, are embedded within a value system, that all epistemologies and related research practices have both strengths and limitations, and that all findings represent "snapshots" at a particular point in time and are subject to political, social, and historical forces and interpretations. During the past two decades, multicultural and feminist psychology have been enriched by a rich array of research approaches and findings, typically based on a combination of qualitative and quantitative findings. Social justice emphases in counseling psychology also have led to increased interest in participatory action research (PAR). PAR centralizes the needs of specific, typically underserved communities; entails collaboration with community members in the designing, implementation, and interpretation of research; and results in an action phase designed to address problems that are clarified by the research findings (see Smith, Appio, & Chang, chapter 8).

Unlike many handbooks within psychology, this volume does not include a separate chapter on research approaches. As can be seen from the contents of the chapters, authors value many different forms of theoretical and research evidence, and emphasize the importance of raising questions about the function and implications of all forms of research. In their chapter on social identity development, for example, Ann Fischer and Kurt DeBord (chapter 5) use critical power analysis to evaluate existing models of feminist social identity. Tools for engaging in this analysis include asking who benefits from specific research framing or findings, how power and privilege shape perspectives, who is or is not represented in findings, and how contexts or power dynamics may be obscured by the research approach. Critical power analysis also involves raising critical thinking questions about research questions, methods, interpretations, and the motivations of researchers. We invite readers who wish to gain more specific information about the uses of qualitative and quantitative methods in counseling psychology to refer to the excellent and multiple sources that provide more specific description; Betz and Fassinger (2011) provide a thorough overview of both quantitative and qualitative approaches, and other resources focus on either qualitative or qualitative methods more specifically (e.g., Carter, 2006a, 2006b; Carter & Morrow, 2007; Haverkamp, Morrow, & Ponterotto, 2005; Hill, 2012).

Evolving Concepts of Feminist Multicultural Theory, Ethics, Practice, and Social Justice

As noted earlier in this chapter, the ethnocentrism of White feminists often has been identified as a barrier to inclusive feminisms and social justice (see Enns, 2004, for a history). The "grand theories" (Jaggar, 2008) that emerged from the second wave women's movement often sought to provide comprehensive, unified explanations of gender oppression, and provided limited information about borders and intersections among oppressions, power, and privilege. In general, these theories quickly outlived their utility and gave way to social constructionist, multicultural, and diversity feminisms that critiqued hidden assumptions underlying grand theories, such as the assumption that women across cultures, time periods, and circumstances share similar needs and oppressions. Multicultural and locational feminisms (Enns, 2010) increasingly underlined the geography and time specificity of privilege, power, and oppression and provided a foundation for flexible feminisms and practice. Women of color feminists provided insightful analyses from their specific standpoints as African American women (e.g., Collins, 1991, 2000), Chicana feminists (e.g., Hurtado, 2003; Moya, 2001), Asian American women (e.g., Chin, 2000), and Native American women (Smith, 2005). In addition, lesbian feminists and queer theorists identified heterosexism within feminist theory and published correctives that focus on the diversity of lesbian/queer experience (Bieschke et al., 2008; Brown, 1994; Garber, 2001; Rudy, 2001).

Locational, multicultural feminisms and feminist multicultural ethics (see Brabeck & Brabeck, chapter 2) highlight the (a) socially constructed, variable, and changing nature of all social identities; (b) decenter and restructure dominant and Eurocentric forms of knowledge; (c) explain oppressions based on multiple social identities, while highlighting strengths and survival skills based on such identities that support empowerment and decolonization; and (d) emphasize the importance of embedding all theoretical understanding in the concrete realities of individuals' lives. A variety of feminist multicultural practices are built on these themes across psychotherapy practice (see Remer & Hahn, chapter 16; Morrow & Hawxhurst, chapter 18; Nutt, chapter 19), teaching/pedagogy (Sinacore, Ginsberg, & Kassan, chapter 22), supervision (Miville, chapter 23), mentoring (Gormley, chapter 24), and social justice (Norsworthy, Abrams, & Lindlau, chapter 25). Given the fact that counseling and psychotherapy are major activities and priorities of counseling psychologists, this volume also features feminist multicultural counseling practices with specific groups such as men (Mintz & Tager, chapter 17), traumatized individuals (Courtois, chapter 20), individuals with eating and body image problems (Kashubeck-West & Tagger, chapter 21), and couples/families (Nutt, chapter 19). These latter chapters represent a sample of the areas in which feminist multicultural counseling psychologists have developed expertise.

Organization of This Handbook

The chapters following this introductory overview survey theory, research, and practice with the intent of presenting a snapshot of the current status of feminist multicultural counseling psychology. Part I introduces foundational topics that have been central to counseling psychology over time: ethical foundations (Brabeck & Brabeck, chapter 2), life span development (Juntunen & Bauman, chapter 3), mental health in ecological context (Ancis & Davidson, chapter 4), and social identity development (Fischer & DeBord, chapter 5). Part II explores perspectives relevant to specific social locations or identities: African American women (Speight, Isom, & Thomas, chapter 6); lesbians, bisexual women, and transgendered persons (Szymanski & Hilton, chapter 7); women in poverty (Smith, Appio, & Chang, chapter 8), Latinas (Gloria & Castellanos, chapter 9), Asian American women (Suzuki, Ahluwalia, & Alimchandani, chapter 10), women with disabilities (Palombi, chapter 11), American Muslim women (Mahmood, chapter 12), and women in transnational contexts (Horne & Arora, chapter 13). Authors have brought a variety of approaches to these chapters, sometimes providing a broad overview, sometimes emphasizing a subset of issues and concerns facing women with specific social identities, and sometimes integrating personal stories within the chapter. In all cases, authors speak to the complexity and diversity of women in a given category and bring an intersectional focus to their writing. Although the topics in this section discuss many social identity categories of interest to feminist multicultural counseling psychologists, we also are aware that this section easily could have been doubled in length and still would have been less than comprehensive! When identities of interest to the reader are missing, we hope that the approaches taken by authors in this section will provide direction for those seeking information about additional groups of women.

Part III explores a variety of theory and practice areas to which counseling psychologists have contributed. Career theory and practice (Hackett &Kohlart, chapter 14), and work challenges related to sexual harassment and career-life balance (Ormerod, Joseph, Weitzman, & Winterrowd, chapter 15) highlight distinctive and unique contributions of counseling psychologists to psychological theory and practice. As the title of the specialty implies, counseling psychologists also contributed to the early literature on feminist therapy (e.g., Gilbert, 1980) and multicultural counseling (Sue, Arredondo, & McDavis, 1992) as well as to multicultural guidelines (APA, 2003) and guidelines for practice with women and girls (APA, 2007). It should come as no surprise that explorations of the intersections of feminism and multiculturalism within counseling and therapy have been a priority. In light of this reality, Part III features the empowerment model of feminist therapy (Remer & Hahn, chapter 16), feminist therapy with men (Mintz & Tager, chapter 17), multicultural feminist therapy (Morrow & Hawxhurst, chapter 18), couples and family counseling/therapy (Nutt, chapter 19), feminist multicultural therapy with traumatized individuals (Courtois, chapter 20), and feminist multicultural perspectives on body image and eating disorders (Kashubeck-West & Tagger, chapter 21). As with the major section on specific social identities (Part II), this section could also have been expanded substantially to focus on many other applications of feminist multicultural themes to counseling and psychotherapy.

The final section of this handbook, Part IV, explores the major practice areas of training, advocacy, and social justice. Chapter 22 (Sinacore, Ginsberg, & Kassan) on multicultural feminist and social justice pedagogies outlines principles that are relevant to teaching at all levels of education, and chapter 23 (Miville) on multicultural feminist training, supervision, and continuing education explores themes relevant to graduate and lifelong learning. Chapter 24 (Gormley) on feminist multicultural mentoring discusses themes for supporting women's growth and development across life domains, and the final chapter (Norsworthy, Abrams, & Lindlau) speaks about the extension of feminist multicultural perspectives in the service of social change.

Concluding Thoughts

The topics addressed in this chapter represent a brief introduction to the rich content that follows in the next 24 chapters. The contents of these chapters represent the culmination of more than 40 years of theory, research, and practice relevant to the lives of diverse groups of women. We hope that readers find the information in this handbook to be useful for research, training, practice, and advocacy. Likewise, we hope that readers are challenged to re-analyze their own perspectives on the issues in this handbook, and that they use a feminist multicultural counseling psychology framework to guide future work that propels counseling psychology into new, courageous, and pioneering directions.

References

American Psychiatric Association. (2000). *Diagnostic and statistical manual of mental disorders: Fourth edition text revision.* Washington, DC: American Psychiatric Association Press.

American Psychological Association, Task Force on Issues of Sexual Bias in Graduate Education. (1975a). Guidelines for nonsexist use of language. *American Psychologist, 30,* 682–684. doi: 10.1037/h0076869

American Psychological Association. (1975b). Report of the task force on sex bias and sex-role stereotyping in psychotherapeutic practice. *American Psychologist, 30,* 1169–1175. doi: 10.1037/0003-066X.30.12.1169

American Psychological Association, Publication Manual Task Force. (1977). Guidelines for nonsexist language in APA journals. *American Psychologist, 32,* 487–494. doi: 10.1037/0003-066X.32.6.48

American Psychological Association, Task Force on Sex Bias and Sex Role Stereotyping in Psychotherapeutic Practice. (1978). Guidelines for therapy with women. *American Psychologist, 33,* 1122–1133. doi: 10.1037/0003-066X.30.12.1169

American Psychological Association. (1979). Principles concerning the counseling and psychotherapy of women. *Counseling Psychologist, 8,* 21.

American Psychological Association. (2000). Resolution on poverty and socioeconomic status. *Roeper Review,* 02783193, 20030301, *25*(3). Also available at www.apa.org/about/governance/council/policy/poverty-resolution.aspx.

American Psychological Association. (2003). Guidelines on multicultural education, training, research, practice, and organizational change for psychologists. *American Psychologist, 58,* 377–402. doi: 10.1037/0003-066X.58.5.377

American Psychological Association. (2004a). *Resolution on culture and gender awareness in international psychology.* Washington, DC: Author.

American Psychological Association. (2004b).Guidelines for psychological practice with older adults. *American Psychologist, 59,* 236–260. doi: 10.1037/0003-066X.59.4.236

American Psychological Association. (2007a). Guidelines for psychological practice with girls and women. *American Psychologist, 62,* 949–979. doi: 10.1037/0003–066X.62.9.949

American Psychological Association. (2007b). *Report of the APA task force on the sexualization of girls.* Available at: www.apa.org/pi/wpo/sexualization.html.

American Psychological Association. (2008). *Report of the APA task force on gender identity and gender variance.* Available at: www.apa.org/pi/lgbt/resources/policy/gender-identity-report-pdf.

American Psychological Association. (2009). *Report of the APA task force on appropriate therapeutic responses to sexual orientation.* Available at: www.apa.org/pi/lgbt/resources/therapeutic-response.pdf.

American Psychological Association. (2012a). Guidelines for psychological practice with lesbian, gay, and bisexual clients. *American Psychologist, 67,* 10–42. doi: 10.1037/a0024659

American Psychological Association. (2012b). Guidelines for assessment of and intervention with persons with disabilities. *American Psychologist, 67,* 43–62. doi: 10.1037/a0025892

Bell, M. E., & Goodman, L. A. (2006). Seeking social justice for victims of intimate partner violence: Real-world struggles in pursuit of systemic change. In R. Toporek, L. Gerstein, N. Fouad, G. Roysircar, and T. Israel (Eds.), *Handbook for social justice in counseling psychology: Leadership, vision, and action* (pp. 155–169). Thousand Oaks, CA: Sage.

Betz, N. E., & Fassinger, R. E. (2011). Methodologies in counseling psychology. In E. M. Altmaier & J. Hansen (Eds.), *The Oxford handbook of counseling psychology* (pp. 237–269). New York: Oxford.

Bieschke, K. J., Hardy, J. A., Fassinger, R. E., & Croteau, J. M. (2008) Intersecting identities of gender-transgressive sexual minorities: Toward a new paradigm of affirmative psychology. In W. B. Walsh (Ed.), *Biennial review of counseling psychology* (pp. 177–207). New York: Routledge/Taylor & Francis Group.

Blimline, C. A., & Birk, J. M. (1979). A note of impatience. *The Counseling Psychologist, 8*(1), 48–49.

Bowman, S. L., Rasheed, S., Ferris, J., Thompson, D. A., McRae, M., & Weitzman, L. (2001). Interface of feminism and multiculturalism: Where are the women of color? In J. G. Ponterotto, J. M. Casas, L. A. Suzuki, & C. M. Alexander (Eds.), *Handbook of multicultural counseling* (2nd ed.) (pp. 779–798). Thousand Oaks, CA: Sage.

Brown, L. S. (1994). *Subversive dialogues: Theory in feminist therapy.* New York: Basic Books.

Butler, J. (1990). *Gender trouble.* New York: Routledge.

Calliste, A. M., Dei, G. J. S., & Aguiar, M. (Eds.). (2000). *Anti-racism feministm: Critical race and gender studies.* Halifax, NS, Canada: Fernwood Publishing.

Campbell, B., Schellenberg, E. G., & Senn, C. Y. (1997). Evaluating measures of contemporary sexism. *Psychology of Women Quarterly, 21,* 89–102. doi: 10.1111/j.1471-6402.1997.tb00102.x

Canadian Psychological Association. (1980). Guidelines for therapy and counseling with women. *Canadian Psychology, 21,* 185–186.

Canadian Psychological Association, CPA Section on Women in Psychology (SWAP). (2007). *Guidelines for ethical psychological practice with girls and women.* Ottawa, ON: Author.

Carter, R. T. (2006a). Special issue: Quantitative issues and analyses in counseling psychology: Part I [Special issue]. *The Counseling Psychologist, 34* (5).

Carter, R. T. (2006b) Special issue: Quantitative issues and analyses in counseling psychology: Part II [Special issue]. *The Counseling Psychologist, 34* (6).

Carter, R. T., & Morrow, S. L. (2007). Special issue: Qualitative issues and analysis in counseling psychology: Part III [Special issue]. *The Counseling Psychologist, 35*(2).

Chin, J. L. (Ed.). (2000). *Relationships among Asian American women.* Washington, DC: American Psychological Association.

Church, E., Pettifor, J. L., & Malone, J. (2006). Evolving Canadian guidelines for therapy and counseling with women. *Feminism and Psychology, 16,* 259–271. doi: 10.1177/0959353506067846

Collins, P. H. (1991). *Black feminist thought.* New York: Routledge.

Collins, P. H. (2000). *Black feminist thought* (2nd ed.). New York: Routledge.

Comas-Diaz, L. (2009). Changing psychology: History and legacy of the Society for the Psychological Study of Ethnic Minority Issues. *Cultural Diversity and Ethnic Minority Psychology, 15,* 400–408. doi: 10.1037/a0016592

Combahee River Collective. (1982). A Black feminist statement. In G. T. Hull, P. B. Scott, & B. Smith (Eds.), *All the women are white, all the Blacks are men, but some of us are brave* (pp. 13–22). Old Westbury, NY: The Feminist Press.

Cook, E. P., Heppner, M. J., & O'Brien, K. M. (2002). Career development of women of color and white women: Assumptions, conceptualization, and interventions from an ecological perspective. *The Career Development Quarterly, 50,* 291–305. doi: 10.1002/j.2161-0045.2002.tb00574.x

Courtois, C. A. (1979). Victims of rape and incest. *The Counseling Psychologist, 8*(1), 38–40.

Dardenne, B., Dumont, M., & Bollier, T. (2007). Insidious dangers of benevolent sexism: Consequences for women's performance. *Journal of Personality and Social Psychology, 93,* 764–779. doi: 10.1037/0022-3514.93.5.764

Denmark, F., Russo, N. F., Frieze, I. H., & Sechzer, J. A. (1988). Guidelines for avoiding sexism in psychological research: A report of the ad hoc committee on nonsexist research. *American Psychologist, 43,* 582–585. doi: 10.1037/0003-066X.43.7.582

Diamond, L. M., & Butterworth, M. (2008).Questioning gender and sexual identity: Dynamic links over time. *Sex Roles, 59,* 365–376. doi: 10.1007/s11199-008-9425-3

Douce, L. A. (2004). Globalization of counseling psychology. *The Counseling Psychologist, 32,* 142–152. doi: 10.1177/0011000003260009

Dovidio, J. F., Gaertner, S. L., Kawakami, K., & Hodson, G. (2002). Why can't we just get along? Interpersonal biases and interracial distrust. *Cultural Diversity and Ethnic Minority Psychology, 8,* 88–102. doi: 10.1037/1099-9809.8.2.88

Enns, C. Z. (2000). Gender issues in counseling. In S. Brown & R. Lent (Eds.), *Handbook of counseling psychology* (3rd ed., pp. 601–638). New York: Wiley.

Enns, C. Z. (2004). *Feminist theories and feminist psychotherapies: Origins, themes, and diversity* (2nd ed.). New York: Haworth.

Enns, C. Z., & Forrest, L. M. (2005). Toward defining and integrating multicultural and feminist pedagogies. In C. Z. Enns & A. L. Sinacore (Eds.), *Teaching and social justice: Integrating multicultural and feminist theories in the classroom* (pp. 3–23). Washington, DC: American Psychological Association.

Enns, C. Z., & Machizawa, S. (March 2008). *Psychological practice with women and girls: Global perspectives.* Working group conducted at the 2008 International Counseling Psychology Conference, Chicago, Illinois.

Enns, C. Z., & Rice, J. K. (August 2008). History and evolution of the guidelines for psychological practice with girls and women. In P. Remer (Chair), *Guidelines for psychological practice with girls and women—Inspirations and challenges.* Symposium conducted at the 116th meeting of the American Psychological Association, Boston, MA.

Enns, C. Z. (2010). Locational feminisms and social identity analysis. *Professional Psychology: Research and Practice, 41,* 333–339. doi: 10.1037/a0020260

Farmer, H. S. (2002). Focus on Division 17's Committee on Women/Section for the Advancement of Women (SAW) 1970–2030: Achievements and challenges. *The Counseling Psychologist, 30,* 417–440. doi: 10.1177/0011000002303004

Fassinger, R. E. (2004). Centralizing feminism and multiculturalism in counseling: Introduction to the special section. *Journal of Counseling and Development, 34,* 344–345.

Fassinger, R. E. & Gallor, S. M. (2006). Tools for remodeling the master's house: Advocacy and social justice in education and work. In R. Toporek, L. Gerstein, N. Fouad, G. Roysircar, and T. Israel (Eds.), *Handbook for social justice in counseling psychology: Leadership, vision, and action* (pp. 256–275). Thousand Oaks, CA: Sage.

Fassinger, R. E., & Arseneau, J. R. (2007). "I'd rather get wet than be under that umbrella": Differentiating the experiences and identities of lesbian, gay, bisexual, and transgender people. In K. J. Bieschke, R. M. Perez, & K. A. DeBord (Eds.), *Handbook of counseling and psychotherapy with lesbian, gay, bisexual, and transgender clients* (pp. 19–49). Washington, DC: American Psychological Association.

Fassinger, R. E., & Israel, T. (2010). Sanctioning sexuality within cultural contexts: Same-sex relationships for women of color. In H. Landrine & N. F. Russo (Eds.), *Handbook of diversity in feminist psychology* (pp. 211–232). New York: Springer.

Fitzgerald, L. F., & Nutt, R. (1986). The Division 17 principles concerning the counseling/psychotherapy of women: Rationale and implementation. *The Counseling Psychologist, 14,* 180–216. doi: 10.1177/0011000086141019

Forrest, L. (2010). Linking international psychology, professional competence, and leadership: Counseling psychologists as learning partners. *The Counseling Psychologist, 38,* 96–120. doi: 10.1177/0011000009350585

Fouad, N. A., McPherson, R. H., Gerstein, L., Blustein, D. L., Elman, N., Helledy, K. I., & Metz, A. J. (2004). Houston, 2001: Context and legacy. *The Counseling Psychologist, 32,* 15–77. doi: 10.1177/0011000003259943

Fouad, N. A., Gerstein, L. H., & Toporek, R.L. (2006). Social justice and counseling psychology in context. In R. L. Roporek, L. H. Gerstein, N. A. Fouad, G. Roysircar, & T. Israel (Eds.), *Handbook for social justice in counseling psychology* (pp. 1–16). Thousand Oaks, CA: Sage.

Franklin, A. J. (2009). Reflections on ethnic minority psychology: Learning from our past so the present informs our future. *Cultural Diversity and Ethnic Minority Psychology, 15,* 416–424. doi: 10.1037/a0017560

Frye, M. (1983). *The politics of reality: Essays in feminist theory.* Trumansburg, NY: Crossing Press.

Garber, L. (2001). *Identity poetics: Race, class, and the lesbian-feminist roots of queer theory.* New York: Columbia University Press.

Gelso, C. J., & Fretz, B. R. (2001). *Counseling psychology.* Fort Worth, TX: Harcourt College Publishers.

Gilbert, L. A. (1980). Feminist therapy. In A. Brodsky & R. T. Hare-Mustin (Eds.), *Women and psychotherapy* (pp. 245–265). New York: Guilford Press.

Glick, P., & Fiske, S. T. (2001). An ambivalent alliance: Hostile and benevolent sexism as complementary justifications for gender inequality. *American Psychologist, 56,* 109–118. Doi: 10.1037/0003-066X.56.2.109

Golden, C. (2008). The intersexed and the transgendered. In J. C. Chrisler, C. Golden, & P. D. Rozee (Eds.), *Lectures on the psychology of women* (4th ed., pp. 137–152). New York: McGraw Hill.

Goodman, L. A., Liang, B., Helms, J. E., Latta, R. E., Sparks, E., & Weintraub, S. R. (2004). Training counseling psychologists as social justice agents: Feminist and multicultural principles in action. *The Counseling Psychologist, 32,* 793–837. doi: 10.1177/0011000004268802

Greene, B., & Sanchez-Hucles, J. (1997). Diversity: Advancing an inclusive feminist psychology. In J. Worell & N. G. Johnson (Eds.), *Shaping the future of feminist psychology: Education, research, and practice* (pp. 173–202). Washington DC: American Psychological Association.

Greene, B. (2003). Beyond heterosexism and across the cultural divide: Developing an inclusive lesbian, gay, and bisexual psychology: A look to the future. In L. D. Garnets & D. C. Kimmel (Eds.), *Psychological perspectives on lesbian and gay male experience* (2nd ed.) (pp. 357–400). New York: Columbia University Press.

Griscom, J. L. (1979). Sex, race, and class: Three dimensions of women's experience. *The Counseling Psychologist, 8*(1), 10–11.

Harding, S. (1986). *The science question in feminism.* Ithaca, NY: Cornell University Press.

Hare-Mustin, R., & Marecek, J. (Eds.). (1990). *Making a difference: Psychology and the construction of gender.* New Haven, CT: Yale University Press.

Haverkamp, B. E., Morrow, S. L., & Ponterotto, J. G. (2005). Special issue: Knowledge in context: Qualitative methods in counseling psychology research. [Special issue]. *Journal of Counseling Psychology, 52*(2).

Herek, G. M. (1991). Stigma, prejudice, and violence against lesbians and gay me. In J. Gonsiorek & J. Weinrich (Eds.), *Homosexuality: Research implications for public policy* (pp. 60–80). Newbury Park, CA: Sage.

Herek, G. M. (1995). Psychological heterosexism in the United States: In A. D. Augelli & C. Patterson (Eds.), *Lesbian, gay, and bisexual identities over the lifespan: Psychological perspectives* (pp. 321–346). New York: Oxford University Press.

Herek, G. M. (2007). Confronting sexual stigma and prejudice: Theory and practice. *Journal of Social Issues, 63,* 905–925.

Herek, G. M. & Garnets, L. D. (2007). Sexual orientation and mental health. *Annual Review of Clinical Psychology, 3,* 353–375. doi: 10.1146/annurev.clinpsy.3.022806.091510

Herek, G. M. (2010). Sexual orientation as deficits: Science and stigma in the history of American psychology. *Perspectives on Psychological Science, 56,* 693–699. doi: 10.1177/1745691610388770

Hill, C. E., Birk, J. M., Blimline, C. A., Leonard, M. M., Hoffman, M. A., & Tanney, M. F. (1979). Guest editors' introduction. *The Counseling Psychologist, 8*(1), 2–3.

Hill, C. E. (Ed.). (2012). *Consensual qualitative research: A practical resource for investigating social science phenomena.* Washington, DC: American Psychological Association.

Hogan, J. D., & Sexton, V. S. (1991).Women and the American Psychological Association.*Psychology of Women Quarterly, 15,* 623–634. doi: 10.1111/j.1471-6402.1991.tb00435.x

Holliday, B. G. (2009). The history and visions of African American Psychology: Multiple pathways to place, space, and authority. *Cultural Diversity and Ethnic Minority Psychology, 15,* 317–337. doi: 10.1037/a0016971

Hurtado, A. (2003). *Voicing Chicana feminisms: Young women speak out on sexuality and identity.* New York: New York University Press.

Hurtado, A. (2010). Multiple lenses: Multicultural feminist theory. In H. Landrine & N. F. Russo (Eds.), *Handbook of diversity in feminist psychology* (pp. 29–54). New York: Springer.

Hyde, J. S. (2007). *Half the human experience: The psychology of women* (7th ed.). Boston: Houghton Mifflin.

Israel, T. (2012). Exploring privilege in counseling psychology: Shifting the lens. *The Counseling Psychologist, 40,* 158–180. doi: 10.1177/0011000011426297

Jaggar, A. M. (Ed.). (2008). *Just methods: An interdisciplinary feminist reader.* Boulder, CO: Paradigm.

Leong, F. T. L., & Okazaki, S. (2009). History of Asian American psychology. *Cultural Diversity and Ethnic Minority Psychology, 15,* 352–362. doi: 10.1037/a0016443

Lerman, H. (1979). The professional-political influence of principles for practice with women. *The Counseling Psychologist, 8*(1), 51.

Marecek, J., Crawford, M., & Popp, D. (2004). On the construction of gender, sex, and sexualities. In A. H. Eagly, A. E. Beall, & R. J. Sternberg (Eds.), *The psychology of gender* (2nd ed.) (pp. 192–216). New York: Guilford Press.

Margolis, E., & Romero, M. (1998). "The department is very male, very white, very old, and very conservative": The functioning of the hidden curriculum in graduate sociology departments. *Harvard Educational Review, 68,* 1–32.

McIntosh, P. (1989). White privilege: Unpacking the invisible knapsack. *Peace and Freedom,* July/August, 10–12.

Mednick, M. T., & Urbanski, L. L. (1991). The origins and activities of APA's Division of the Psychology of Women. *Psychology of Women Quarterly, 15,* 651–663. doi: 10.1111/j.1471-6402.1991.tb00437.x

Meyer, I. H. (1995). Minority stress and mental health in gay men. *Journal of Health and Social Behavior, 36,* 38–56. doi: 10.2307/2137286

Mintz, L. B., Rideout, C. A., & Bartels, K. M. (1994). A national survey of interns' perceptions of their preparation for counseling women and of the atmosphere of their graduate education. *Professional Psychology, 25,* 221–227. doi: 10.1037/0735-7028.25.3.221

Miville, M. L., Duen, C., Nutt, R. L., Waehler, C. A., Suzuki, L., Pistole, M. C., Arredondo, P., Duffy, M., Mejia, B. X., & Corpus, M. (2009). Integrating practice guidelines into professional training: Implications for diversity competence. *The Counseling Psychologist, 37,* 519–563. doi: 10.1177/0011000008323651

Moradi, B., Mohr, J. J., Worthington, R. W., & Fassinger, R. E. (2009). Advances in research with sexual minority people. *Journal of Counseling Psychology, 56(1)(special issue).*

Moya, P.M.L. (2001). Chicana feminism and postmodernist theory. *Signs: Journal of Women in Culture and Society, 26,* 441–483.

Muehlenhard, C. L., & Peterson, Z. D. (2011).Distinguishing between *sex* and *gender*: History, current conceptualizations, and implications. *Sex Roles, 64,* 791–803. doi: 10.1007/s11199-011-9932-5

Nam, V. (2001). *Yell-oh girls: Emerging voices explore culture, identity, and growing up Asian American.* New York: HarperCollins.

Nutt, R. L. (1979). Review and preview of attitudes and values of counselors of women. *The Counseling Psychologist, 8*(1), 18–20.

Nutt, R. L. (August, 2008). Implications of the guidelines for training. In P. Remer (Chair), *Guidelines for psychological practice with girls and women—Inspirations and challenges.* Symposium conducted at the 116th meeting of the American Psychological Association, Boston, MA.

Williams, E. N., & Barber, J. S. (2004). Power and responsibility in therapy: Integrating feminism and multiculturalism. *Journal of Multicultural Counseling and Development, 32*(Extra), 390–401.

Packard, T. (2009). Core values that distinguish counseling psychology: Personal and professional perspectives. *The Counseling Psychologist, 37,* 610–624. doi: 10.1177/0011000009333986

Palombi, B. J. & Mundt, A. M. (2006). Achieving social justice for college women with disabilities: A model for inclusion. In R. Toporek, L. Gerstein, N. Fouad, G. Roysircar, and T. Israel (Eds.), *Handbook for social justice in counseling psychology: Leadership, vision, and action* (pp. 170–184). Thousand Oaks, CA: Sage.

Peplau, L. A., & Conrad, E. (1989). Beyond nonsexist research: The perils of feminist methods in psychology. *Psychology of Women Quarterly, 13,* 379–400. doi: 10.1111/j.1471-6402.1989.tb01009.x

Pickren, W. E. (2009). Liberating history: The context of the challenge of psychologists of color to American psychology. *Cultural Diversity and Ethnic Minority Psychology, 15,* 425–433. doi: 10.1037/a0017561

Pyke, S. W. (2001). Feminist psychology in Canada: Early days. *Canadian Psychology, 42,* 268–275. doi: 10.1037/h0086895

Reid, P. T. (2002). Multicultural psychology: Bringing together gender and ethnicity. *Cultural Diversity and Ethnic Minority Psychology, 8,* 103–114. doi: 10.1037/1099-9809.8.2.103

Reynolds, A. L., & Constantine, M. G. (2004). Feminism and multiculturalism: Parallels and intersections. *Journal of Multicultural Counseling and Development, 32,* 346–357.

Ridley, C. R. (2005). *Overcoming unintentional racism in counseling and therapy: A practical guide to intentional intervention* (2nd ed.). Newbury Park, CA: Sage.

Riger, S. (1992). Epistemological debates, feminist voices: Science, social values, and the study of women. *American Psychologist, 47,* 730–740. doi: 10.1037/0003-066X.47.6.730

Rostosky, S. S., Riggle, E. D., Horne, S. G., & Miller, A. D. (2009). Marriage amendments and psychological distress in lesbian, gay, and bisexual (LGB) adults. *Journal of Counseling Psychology, 56,* 56–66. doi: 10.1037/a0013609

Rudy, K. (2001). Radical feminism, lesbian separatism, and queer theory. *Feminist Studies, 27*(1), 191–222.

Shields, S. A. (2008). Gender: An intersectionality perspective. *Sex Roles, 59,* 301–311. doi: 10.1007/s11199-008-9501-8

Silverstein, L. B. (2006). Integrating feminism and multiculturalism: Scientific fact or science fiction? *Professional Psychology: Research and Practice, 37,* 21–28. doi: 10.1037/0735-7028.37.1.21

Smith, A. (2005). Native American feminism, sovereignty, and social change. *Feminist Studies, 31,* 116–132.

Smith, B. (Ed.). (1983). *Home girls: A Black feminist anthology.* New York: Kitchen Table, Women of Color Press.

Speight, S. L., & Vera, E. M. (2004). A social justice agenda: Ready, or not? *The Counseling Psychologist, 32,* 109–118. doi: 10.1177/0011000003260005

Steele, C. M. (2010). *Whistling Vivaldi and other clues to how stenotypes affect us.* New York: Norton.

Steward, R. J., & Phelps, R. E. (2004). Feminist and multicultural collaboration in counseling supervision: Voices from two African American women. *Journal of Multicultural Counseling and Development, 32,* 358–365.

Stewart, A., & McDermott, C. (2004). Gender in psychology. *Annual Review of Psychology, 55,* 519–544. doi: 10.1146/annurev.psych.55.090902.141537

Sue, D. W., Arredondo, P., & McDavis, R. J. (1992). Multicultural counseling competencies and standards: A call to the profession. *Journal of Counseling and Development, 70,* 477–486. doi: 10.1002/j.2161-1912.1992.tb00563.x

Sue, D. W., Bingham, R. P., Porché-Burke, L., & Vasquez, M. (1999). The diversification of psychology: A multicultural revolution. *American Psychologist, 54,* 1061–1069. doi: 10.1037/0003-066X.54.12.1061

Sue, S. (2009). Ethnic minority psychology: Struggles and triumphs. *Cultural Diversity and Ethnic Minority Psychology, 15,* 409–415. Doi: 10.1037/a0017559

Swim, J. K., Aikin, K. J., Hall, W. S., & Hunter, B. A. (1995). Sexism and racism: Old fashioned and modern prejudices. *Journal of Personality and Social Psychology, 68,* 199–214. doi: 10.1037/0022-3514.68.2.199

Swim, J. K., Becker, J. C., Lee, E., & Pruitt, E. (2010). Sexism reloaded: Worldwide evidence for its endorsement, expression, and emergence in multiple contexts. In H. Landrine & N. F. Russo (Eds.), *Handbook of diversity in feminist psychology* (pp. 137–171). New York: Springer.

Thomas, A. J., Witherspoon, K. M., & Speight, S. L. (2008). Gendered racism, psychological distress, and coping styles of African American women. *Cultural Diversity and Ethnic Minority Psychology, 14,* 307–314. doi: 10.1037/1099-9809.14.4.307

Thompson, B. (2002). Multiracial feminism: Recasting the chronology of second wave feminism. *Feminist Studies, 28,* 337–360.

Tiefer, L. (1991). A brief history of the Association for Women in Psychology: 1969–1991. *Psychology of Women Quarterly, 15,* 635–649. doi: 10.1111/j.1471-6402.1991.tb00436.x

Toporek, R. L., Gerstein, L. H., Fouad, N. A., Roysircar, G., & Israel, T. (Eds.). (2006). *Handbook for social justice in counseling psychology.* Thousand Oaks, CA: Sage.

Trimble, J. E., & Clearing-Sky, M. (2009). An historical profile of American Indians and Alaska natives in psychology. *Cultural Diversity and Ethnic Minority Psychology, 15,* 338–351. doi: 10.1037/a0015112

Unger, R. K., & Crawford, M. E. (1992). *Women and gender: A feminist psychology.* New York: McGraw-Hill.

Vera, E. M., & Speight, S. L. (2003). Multicultural competence, social justice, and counseling psychology. *The Counseling Psychologist, 31,* 253–272. doi: 10.1177/0011000003031003001

Weisstein, N. (1977). "How can a little girl like you teach a great big class of men?" the chairman said, and the other adventures of a woman in science. In S. Ruddick & P. Daniels (Eds.), *Working it out: 23 writers, artists, scientists, and scholars talk about their lives and work* (pp. 241–250). New York: Pantheon Books.

Weisstein, N. (1993). Psychology constructs the female: or the fantasy life of the male psychologist. *Feminism and Psychology, 3,* 195–210. (Original work published 1968).

West, C., & Zimmerman, D. G. (1987). Doing gender. *Gender and Society, 1,* 125–151.

Whalen, M., Fowler-Lese, K. P., Barber, J. S., Williams, E. N., Judge, A. B., Nilsson, J. E., & Shibazaki, K. (2004, Extra). *Journal of Multicultural Counseling and Development, 32,* 379–389.

Worell, J., & Johnson, N. G. (Eds.). (1997). *Shaping the future of feminist psychology: Education, research, and practice.* Washington, DC: American Psychological Association.Yoder, J. D., & Kahn, A. S. (1993). Working toward an inclusive psychology of women. *American Psychologist, 48,* 846–850.

Yoder, J. D. (1999). *Women and gender: Transforming psychology.* Upper Saddle River, NJ: Pearson/Prentice Hall.

Yoder, J. D. (2003). *Women and gender: Transforming psychology* (2nd ed.). Upper Saddle River, NJ: Pearson/Prentice Hall.

Zinn, M. B., & Dill, B. T. (1996). Theorizing difference from multiracial feminism. *Feminist Studies, 22,* 321–331.

Appendix A: Guidelines on Multicultural Education, Training, Research, Practice, and Organizational Change for Psychologists (APA, 2003)

Commitment to Cultural Awareness and Knowledge of Self and Others
Guideline 1: *Psychologists are encouraged to recognize that, as cultural beings, they may hold attitudes and beliefs that can detrimentally influence their perceptions of and interactions with individuals who are ethnically and racially different from them.*
Guideline 2: *Psychologists are encouraged to recognize the important of multicultural sensitivity/responsiveness to, knowledge of, and understanding about ethnically and racially different adults.*

Education
Guideline 3: *As educators, psychologists are encouraged to employ the constructs of multiculturalism and diversity in psychological education.*

Research
Guideline 4: *Culturally sensitive psychological researchers are encouraged to recognize the importance of conducting culture-centered and ethical psychological research among people from ethnic, linguistic, and racial minority backgrounds.*

Practice
Guideline 5: *Psychologists are encouraged to apply culturally appropriate skills in clinical and other applied psychological practices.*

Organizational Change and Policy Development
Guideline 6: *Psychologists are encouraged to use organizational change processes to support culturally informed organizational (policy) development practices.*

Appendix B: Guidelines for Psychological Practice with Girls and Women (APA, 2007)

***Section One:* Diversity, Social Context, and Power**
Guideline 1: *Psychologists strive to be aware of the effects of socialization, stereotyping, and unique life events on the development of girls and women across diverse cultural groups.*

From the text: "Each girl and woman is socialized within a unique cultural milieu and set of visible and invisible social group memberships that may include, but are not limited to, gender, race/ethnicity, class, age, sexual orientation, SES, spiritual orientation, nationality, physical or cognitive ability, and body size. The multiple group memberships of girls and women intersect and influence each other and are enacted within the family and cultural institutions (schools, religion), through peer influences, and within media" (p. 960).

Guideline 2: *Psychologists are encouraged to recognize and utilize information about oppression, privilege, and identity development as they may affect girls and women.*

From the text: "Because girls and women have multiple personal and social group memberships, they may simultaneously belong to both socially privileged and disempowered groups (e.g., White, heterosexual, lower SES, and female) or to multiple socially oppressed groups (e.g., African American, female, lesbian, disabled).... Saliency of a particular identity is determined by several factors, including socialization experiences and the amount of social support received in a particular situation.... Psychologists are encouraged to identify the social group memberships of girls and women, the extent to which they accept or deny these memberships, their experiences of oppression and/or privilege within the context of these memberships, and their abilities to resist confining or oppressive messages" (p. 961).

Guideline 3: *Psychologists strive to understand the impact of bias and discrimination on the physical and mental health of those with whom they work.*

From the text: "Bias and discrimination are embedded in and driven by organizational, institutional, and social structures. These dynamics legitimize and foster inequities, influence personal relationships, and affect the perception and treatment of a person's metal and behavioral problems" (p. 961). The narrative elaborates further on the impact of the following systems: health, education, the workplace, religious institutions, legal systems, family and couple systems, and research methods and language.

Section Two: Professional Responsibility

Guideline 4: *Psychologists strive to use gender sensitive and culturally sensitive, affirming practices in providing services to girls and women.*

From the text: "Psychologists strive to be knowledgeable about the theoretical and empirical support for the assessment, treatment, research, consultation, teaching, and supervision practices they use with girls and women. Psychologists are encouraged to be aware of assumptions in theory, research, and practice that are noninclusive and to use theories and practices that pay equal attention to relational and autonomous qualities.... They are urged to show caution when using methods that have not been developed with the specific needs of diverse groups of girls and women in mind" (p. 964).

Guideline 5: *Psychologists are encouraged to recognize how their socialization, attitudes, and knowledge about gender may affect their practice with girls and women.*

From the text: "The practice of psychologists is likely to be influenced by their culture, values, biases, socialization, and experiences of privilege and oppression or disempowerment. Limited self-knowledge may contribute to subtle belief systems that can be potentially harmful to girls and women with diverse social identities.... Psychologists are encouraged to gain specialized education, training, and experience with issues particularly relevant to the experiences and problems of women and girls" (p. 965).

Section Three: Practice Applications

Guideline 6: *Psychologists are encouraged to use interventions and approaches that have been found to be effective in the treatment of issues of concern to girls and women.*

From the text: "Psychologists are therefore encouraged to (a) implement interventions that encourage the development of protective factors, such as healthy relationships and body image, (b) reframe girls' and women's concerns from a coping and ecological perspective, and (c) emphasize a strength and empowerment perspective in psychotherapy treatment, research, advocacy, teaching, consultation, and supervision" (p. 966).

Guideline 7: *Psychologists strive to foster therapeutic relationships and practices that promote initiative, empowerment, and expanded alternatives and choices for girls and women.*

From the text: "Cooperative mutuality and connection facilitate psychotherapy, supervision, teaching, and consultation (p. 966). Empowerment flourishes in an environment of safety, and this condition is protected by appropriate boundaries.... Psychologists are encouraged to make efforts to help women develop an improved sense of initiative, resilience, and personal power and to help them expand their nonstereotyped alternatives and choices" (p. 967).

Guideline 8: *Psychologists strive to provide appropriate, unbiased assessments and diagnoses in their work with girls and women.*

From the text: "Psychologists, therefore, strive to make unbiased, appropriate assessments and diagnoses by considering ... the following: development experiences, physical and psychological health, violence and other traumatic events, life history (including experiences of privilege and discrimination), social and kinship support systems, educational and work experiences, geographical and national affiliation influences, various multiple group memberships, and other relevant aspects related to the cultural context as it uniquely interacts with gender. Assessment tools, such a social, cultural, and gender-role identity analyses, may be especially useful.... Psychologists are also urged to show caution when using assessment procedures and tests developed in the United States in countries in which cultural differences and norms have not been considered" (p. 968).

Guideline 9: *Psychologists strive to consider the problems of girls and women in their sociopolitical context.*

From the text: "To support the personal growth, independence, and empowerment of girls and women, psychologists strive to integrate cultural and contextual information into their conceptualizations and interventions. Such contextual factors include immigration, race, ethnicity, geography (e.g., rural or urban residence), sexual orientation, disability, SES, age, and other sociocultural influences" (p. 968).

Guideline 10: *Psychologists strive to acquaint themselves with and utilize relevant mental health, education, and community resources for girls and women.*

From the text: "Psychologists strive to become knowledgeable about community resources and to consult others with expertise about community resources" (p. 969).

Guideline 11: *Psychologists are encouraged to understand and work to change institutional and systemic bias that may impact girls and women.*

From the text: "Psychologists are encouraged to participate in prevention, education, and social policy as forms of psychological practice that improve the mental health and lives of women and girls ... [and] to support their clients' contributions to positive microlevel and/or macrolevel actions that increase a sense of empowerment and influence" (p. 969).

CHAPTER

2 Feminist and Multicultural Ethics in Counseling Psychology

Mary M. Brabeck *and* Kalina M. Brabeck

Abstract

This chapter examines the origins and major themes of feminist and multicultural ethics, as well as the contributions of counseling psychology to feminist and multicultural ethics. Finally, these ethical frameworks are applied to the American Psychological Association's (APA) Ethical Principles of Psychologists and Code of Conduct (2003) to demonstrate the benefit of incorporating feminist and multicultural ethics in professional psychology.

Key Words: Feminist, multicultural, ethics, counseling psychology

Counseling psychology has embraced the lenses of multicultural ethics and feminist ethics in its ongoing mission to serve individuals as well as society through psychological practice. This chapter explores the contributions of multicultural and feminist ethics to psychological practice. We first discuss the origins of feminist and multicultural ethics. We next compare multicultural ethics with five common themes (Brabeck, 2000) of feminist ethics, thereby illustrating how these lenses intersect. Finally, we apply feminist and multicultural ethical frameworks to the principles of ethical psychological practice articulated in the current American Psychological Association's Ethical Principles of Psychologists and Code of Conduct (2003a) (hereafter, APA Ethics Code). This examination will reveal both the limits of the current understanding of the ethical principles in the APA Code (2003a) and the unique contributions that feminist and multicultural ethics make to ethical psychological practice.

During the late 1800s, when William James held chairs at Harvard in both psychology and philosophy, the two disciplines were closely allied. As psychology has become more concerned with evidence-based practice and the empirical claims that support interventions, and as important gains have been made in the learning sciences, neuropsychology, and cognitive psychology, philosophical theory has received less emphasis. However, a discussion of ethics, and, for the purposes of this chapter, feminist and multicultural ethics, puts us squarely in the domains of philosophy, theology, political theory, and psychological theory. The great value of theory is its ability to organize information in ways that provide useful lenses for organizing, understanding, and explaining phenomena. Both multicultural ethics and feminist ethics aim to identify ethical principles or aspirational goals of ethical behavior, as well as standards for acting in specific situations. The multicultural and feminist lenses, which are distinct and yet overlap substantially, provide important perspectives for assessing the adequacy of the APA Ethics Code's (2003a) principles.

Ethics is the branch of philosophy concerned with how people ought to act, what principles should guide behavior, and how people should live together. Professional ethics is the application of ethics to professional practice. Since 1952, the American Psychological Association has adopted a code of ethics that enjoins psychologists to act ethically in all psychological practice, including psychotherapy, research, teaching, assessment, advocacy, and supervision. The 2003 APA Ethics Code (amended in February 2010) represents professional psychology's best attempt to identify both general principles that are aspirational in nature and the standards for judging the ethical action of professional psychologists.

History of Feminist and Multicultural Ethics

History of Feminist Ethics

As early as 1792, Mary Wollstonecraft asserted in *A Vindication of the Rights of Women* (1792) that women, like men, have the potential to be equally moral and that education is instrumental in the development of the moral person. However, Wollstonecraft claimed that society too often teaches boys morals and girls manners, and then negates those qualities, like gentleness and kindness, associated with women: "When it is the submissive demeanor of dependence, the support of weakness that loves, because it wants protection; and is forbearing because it must silently endure injuries; smiling under the lash at which it dare not snarl" (Wollstonecraft, 1792, p. 117).

John Stuart Mill (1869) discussed women's morality in the nineteenth century and Catherine Beecher, Charlotte Perkins Gilman, Elizabeth Cady Stanton, and Simone de Beauvoir developed theories of women's morality in the twentieth century (Eisenstein, 1981; Tong, 1993). However, since the second wave of feminism in the 1970s, there has been an explosion of feminist theory and feminist philosophy. This work lays the groundwork for feminist ethics.

The phrase "feminist ethics" first was used in the late 1970s in the context of Carol Gilligan's (1982) assertion that women's moral voice reflects the ethic of care. Broadly speaking, feminist ethics represent an effort to revise or correct the dominant views of Western ethics that devalue women, ignore women's moral experiences, and denigrate the characteristics associated with women (Jaggar, 1991). In psychology, male experience historically has been privileged over female experience, leading to distorted empirical findings. For example, achievement motivation research generally did not include women as research subjects until Matina Horner (1972) called attention to these lacunae.

Women's moral issues, like rape, violent pornography, or intimate partner abuse, have been ignored or have been associated with the "private sphere" of home and family. In addition, Western philosophers and theologians (Plato, Aristotle, Augustine, through Descartes and Kant), psychologists (Freud), and sociologists (Talcott Parsons) have deemed women morally inferior to men. The Western philosophical tradition of moral theory is predominantly written by males and emphasizes rules, universality, and impartiality, traits that are assumed to be masculine (Jaggar, 1991). Historically, traits culturally associated with men (e.g., independence, autonomy, individuality, objective rationality) and male experiences (e.g., war and work) have been privileged over traits associated with women (e.g., empathy, sympathy, connection, emotion) and female experiences (e.g., mothering and peace work).

Feminist ethics include moral critiques of acts and policies that keep women subordinate and envision emancipatory moral alternatives that enhance the lives of women and all marginalized people. Philosopher Patricia Ward Scaltsas (1992) writes, "The project of criticizing, analyzing, and when necessary, replacing the traditional categories of moral philosophy in order to eradicate the misrepresentation, distortion, and oppression resulting from the historically male perspective is, broadly speaking, the project of feminist ethics" (p. 16). For example, a feminist ethical lens is used to examine the problems of violence against children and women (Herman, 1997), rape as a weapon of war (Brownmiller, 1993), stigma and prejudice associated with people with disabilities (Banks, 2008), sexuality (Fine, 2006), and workplace discrimination (Gilbert & Brownson, 1998).

Feminist ethics are not based on one agreed-upon feminist perspective, just as there is no singular psychodynamic or multicultural perspective (Enns, 1997). Rather, feminist ethics draw from multiple feminist theories. For example, liberal feminists advocate the use of legal and political systems to achieve gender justice. Marxist/socialist feminists note that class intersects with gender and that power and money are equated. Relational feminists call attention to the importance of women's moral experience, especially concerning mothering and caregiving. Radical separatist feminists caution that women's ethical and moral selves are at risk in the patriarchal society that threatens that special self. Neo-psychoanalytic feminists find the origin of gender identity in the experience of the mother-child relationship. French feminists see woman's nature as deeply embodied and believe that psychological development results from her natural experiences in menstruation, gestation, and female sexuality.

There are heated and ongoing debates among and within these traditions. Many of these debates and the ways in which they impact feminist ethics are discussed in this chapter. The theorists cited here, however, differ from those who espouse a "feminine ethics" (Grimshaw, 1993; Houser, 2006). Feminine ethics, like feminist ethics, valorize the culturally constructed qualities associated with women, for example, care, obedience, subordination, humility, generosity, helpfulness, emotionality, and sympathy, but they do so uncritically. Socially sanctioned roles such as caring for children or the elderly are assumed as "natural" roles for women. Without a critique of who benefits when women care, or the costs of care (e.g., job opportunities, physical and mental health), feminine ethics may harm women. In contrast, feminist ethicists reclaim the value of moral attributes associated with women *and* critically analyze how they enhance or limit the lives of women. Feminist ethics do not limit moral concern to the liberation of only girls and women, but, in contrast to feminine ethics, feminist ethics explicitly seek to eliminate the subordination of women. In this way, feminist ethics are compatible with ethical efforts to enhance the human condition for all individuals and are consistent with other social justice initiatives, including multiculturalism.

Despite the many different feminist perspectives, Brabeck (2000) identified five broad themes common to feminist ethics:

1. The assumption that women and their experiences are of moral significance;
2. The assertion that attentiveness and non-rational subjective knowledge can illuminate moral issues;
3. The claim that a feminist critique of male oppression must be accompanied by a critique of racist, classist, and homophobic distortions;
4. The admonition that feminist ethics engage in analysis of the context and of the power dynamics inherent in that context; and
5. The injunction that feminist ethics require action directed at achieving systemic social justice.

Following a discussion of the history of multicultural ethics, these five tenets will be examined to illustrate and elucidate the contributions of feminist and multicultural ethics to psychological work in general and to the APA Ethics Code (2003a) in particular.

History of Multicultural Ethics

Both feminist ethics and multicultural ethics arose out of a need to correct biases in traditional, Western ethics. Multicultural ethical theorists (e.g., Appiah, 2006; Hinman, 1998, 2007; West, 1994) identified bias in attempts to rationalize the subordination of people of color. Like feminist ethicists, multicultural ethicists examined the experiences of marginalized people, identified the ethical values associated with those experiences, and claimed moral significance for these experiences.

While many philosophers who concentrate on ethics have emphasized the universality of ethical principles (e.g., Beauchamp & Childress, 1994), contemporary multicultural philosophers have examined issues of diversity, multiple and intersecting cultural identities, and pluralistic ethics. Such work within philosophy has examined issues of minority rights, ethical pluralism, ethnic and cultural diversity in ethical thought, and the influence of race and ethnicity on identity. For example, Hinman (1998, 2007) argued that an ethical theory must include an understanding of the moral agent or one's identity as a moral person. Identity, Hinman argued, is profoundly influenced by one's culture and experiences within that culture. Furthermore, there are different interpretations of the same behavior within different cultures, and different cultures have different norms for behaving. The question, then, is how can morality be determined in the face of such diversity of moral views?

Hinman (1998, 2007) identified a number of responses to this question. The first response, which he called a separatist model, stresses the importance of cultural identity and involves a voluntary isolation from groups that would threaten, demean, or damage the cultural group. This response can be seen among radical feminists, ultra-orthodox Jews, and Mennonites, but also those who espouse separate experiences for African American boys and youth (Noguera, 2008). This stance assumes a "live and let live" relativistic attitude toward differences in moral norms and behaviors and does not claim superiority for any one cultural group. However, separations are difficult to maintain without comparisons, and comparisons lead to rankings. When separatists claim a superior culture, they are in danger of becoming supremacists, a morally suspect position; supremacists demean others in order to support their own superiority. Thus, they are neither just nor caring, neither respectful nor beneficent in their attitude and conduct. The conduct of supremacists has led to some of the most heinous crimes toward groups of people such as African Americans, Native Americans, and Jews. Therefore, Hinman rejects the separatist model.

Hinman's (1998, 2007) second model, the Assimilationist model, de-emphasizes the importance of race and assumes a "melting pot" metaphor. The goal for assimilationists is the elimination of cultural identities in favor of a common humanity. The problem is that assimilation is almost always in the direction of joining the dominant (White, male, Western) culture. The moral danger for assimilationists is the opposite of that for separatists: In attempting to be part of the dominant group, they may lose what is particular and valuable to the cultural identity of the minority group.

Hinman (1998, 2007) argues that a third model, the Pluralist model, offers a morally supportable position. Pluralists assume that while there are many unique cultural groups, every person shares membership in several such groups. Individuals belong to groups identified by gender, linguistic background, religious affiliation, ethnicity, and so on. Pluralists accept that different standpoints, histories, and experiences shape individuals and hence different claims of "truth" and "reality" can be defended from a number of perspectives. From this perspective, diversity is an asset to be preserved and is compatible with harmonious living: "A *cultural pluralism* that sees diversity as a source of strength, emphasizes the value of *dialogue*, and approaches such dialogues with a *fallible* attitude... also recognizes that we need to learn to live together while honoring our differences (emphases in original)" (Hinman, 1998, p. 413). Hinman stresses the importance of virtues like understanding, tolerance, standing up for what is right, and fallibility as requisite for a multicultural ethical stance.

The pluralist position has, however, the problem of relativism. If all cultures are equally important, how does one argue for access, benefits, and special treatment for any single group? What does one do when there are conflicting values among different groups? The philosopher Kwame Anthony Appiah (1990, 2006) argues that while there are many differences that mark each individual and each group, there is also a common trait, which he labels "cosmopolitanism," which we all share. "Cosmopolitanism" is a term that goes back to the fourth century b.c.e. Greek philosopher Diogenes of Sinope, who famously claimed, "I am a citizen of the world"—a *kosmopolitis*. Diogenes meant that neither geography nor culture limited him. Appiah (2006) argues that while one belongs to one's own ethnic group, culture, or race, to be a cosmopolitan is to see oneself as a citizen of the world. A cosmopolitan maintains her sense of place, country, ethnicity, religion, and culture, even as she embraces, learns from, adapts to, and respects global diversity. Appiah presents his theory of cosmpolitanism as a set of moral standards for living in a global society.

For Appiah, leaders in this global society are "cosmopolitan patriots":

> In a world of cosmopolitan patriots, people would accept the citizen's responsibility to nurture the culture and the politics of their homes. Many would, no doubt, spend their lives in the places that shaped them, and that is one of the reasons local cultural practices would be sustained and transmitted. But many would move, and that would mean that cultural practices would travel also (as they have always travelled). The result would be a world in which each local form of human life was the result of long-term and persistent processes of cultural hybridization: a world, in that respect, much like the world we live in now. (Appiah, 2006, p. 22)

Psychologists Fowers and Davidov (2006) argue that there is an ethical intent inherent in multicultural approach: do no harm (in particular to marginalized groups) and promote social understanding, inclusion, and harmony in a pluralistic world. Fowers and Davidov (2006) suggest Aristotelian virtue ethics as a systematic ethical theory for enhancing multicultural competence in psychology. Drawing on Aristotle's virtue ethics that center on cultivation of character strengths as the pathway for ethical action, and the idea that acting right grows out of good character, the authors suggest that multiculturalism can be seen as the pursuit of worthwhile goals; this requires virtues, knowledge, consistent actions, proper motivation, and practical wisdom. They argue that the central virtue of "openness to the other" is at the core of multiculturalism, and that attaining this virtue extends far beyond simply acquiring skills. Rather, it requires a transformation of character and one's sense of who one is (Fowers & Davidov, 2006).

All people are defined by their social identities, which are multiple and intersecting. We claim our race, gender, sexual orientation, and ethnicity, and these multiple social categories intersect: "Intersectionality is the mutually constitutive relations among social identities. By *identity* I mean social categories in which an individual claims membership as well as the personal meaning associated with those categories (emphasis in original) " (Ashmore, Deaux & McLaughlin-Volpe, 2004). Intersectionality implies that identity is multiply determined, and that the multiple aspects of identity cannot be disaggregated. Black feminists like Patricia Collins (1990, 2000) noted that being African American cannot be separated from being a woman. Being gay, lesbian, bisexual, or transgender is inseparable from being Latino/a or Asian, Catholic, or Jewish. One's privileged status because of education and income profoundly impacts one's experience of being African American, Latino/a, or White. Any adequate ethical theory, multiculturalists argue (Hinman, 1998, 2007), must include attention to the multiple aspects of identity that influence our development as moral agents.

Since Aristotle, we have known that it is unjust to treat equals unequally, and it is also unjust to treat unequals equally. For example, children who have not reached the age of reason and those who have severe and persistent mental illnesses are not treated as mature and able-minded adults in our court systems or our schools. The critical issue is whether differences are relevant to the policy or treatment. For example, a nursing mother might be offered a longer parental leave than a male partner because her ability to nurse is a benefit to her baby, and this in turn benefits society by making the baby healthy and productive. On the other hand, treating non-significant aspects of identity as important may be racist or sexist, that is, the fact that the nursing mother is a woman and a mother does not affect her ability to do her job; persons of different genders (or races, ethnicities, etc.) should therefore not be afforded differential access to work. Multicultural ethicists both call attention to the ways in which differences distinguish us, and also caution against ways in which differences are used as the basis for discrimination.

Counseling Psychology's Contributions to Multicultural Ethics

With its emphasis on wellness rather than disease, resilience rather than deficits, and celebration of diverse strengths rather than weaknesses, it is not surprising that counseling psychology has taken the lead in defining and applying a multicultural ethical framework to psychological work. Multicultural ethics in psychology developed primarily from counseling psychology's commitment to prepare competent professional practitioners to work with an increasingly diverse society (Miville et al., 2009). For example, Ted Packard, in his 2008 Leona Tyler Award address (2009), claimed that "cultural and individual diversity, inclusion, equity, and social justice" are central values for counseling psychology (p. 615).

Ethical strands of both feminist and multicultural ethics have been embraced within Counseling Psychology and have been incorporated into counseling psychology training programs (Miller, Forrest, & Elman, 2009). Competence to address the needs of diverse people is a necessary requisite of ethical practice within professional psychology (Oyserman, Coon, & Kemmeleier, 2002; Watson, Herlihy, & Pierce, 2006). Sue et al. (1982) developed a set of multicultural competencies that involve developing awareness, knowledge, and skill sets to work with diverse populations; Sue and Sue (2008) define cultural competency as: "... the ability to engage in actions or create conditions that maximize the optimal development of client and client systems ... The acquisition of awareness, knowledge, and skills needed to function effectively in a pluralistic democratic society (ability to communicate, interact, negotiate, and intervene on behalf of clients from diverse backgrounds), and on an organizational/ societal level, advocating effectively to develop new theories, practices, policies and organizational structures that are more responsive to all groups" (p. 46). Additionally, counseling psychologists were instrumental in developing the APA Guidelines for Psychological Practice with Girls and Women (2007). The Guidelines build on the work of the Feminist Therapy Institute's guidelines (Feminist Therapy Institute, 2000) and the work in feminist psychology.

Pedersen (1989) traced the evolution of the integration of multiculturalism into the APA Ethics Code until the late 1980s and suggested a number of revisions to the 1986 APA Ethics Code. Pedersen (1989) argued that psychologists need to recognize culturally determined differences in moral and legal standards and should make public their degree of competence and training in working with persons from a specific culture. Issues such as language barriers, non-verbal communication, and cultural variations in communication styles need to be considered in order to responsibly conduct research with cultural groups for whom informed consent may carry different meanings and to avoid misinterpretations and inappropriate pathologizing in therapy.

Pedersen (1989) suggested that psychologists are ethically required to prevent disparagement of a group's cultural values and that they must consider cultural information and values when interpreting assessment data and conducting research with diverse populations. He invoked the metaphor of cultural encapsulation (Wrenn, 1962) to suggest that counseling professionals too often revert to stereotypes because of inadequate information and ignore important differences between counselors and clients that affect the counseling process. Finally, he warned against relying on "technique-oriented" interventions that lack sensitivity to cultural variability (Pedersen, 1989). The remedy for cultural encapsulation is a multicultural or cosmopolitan ethical response.

Counseling psychology was instrumental in the 2003 APA task force charged with providing a rationale for multiculturalism in education, research, practice, and organizational change; amassing relevant information, empirical research, and terminology; compiling appropriate references; and suggesting paradigms that broaden the scope of psychology as a profession. This task force developed a list of guidelines of multicultural competence and based their work on premises of the APA Ethics Code (2003a), namely, that psychologists must be competent to work with diverse populations (Principle A), respect others' rights (Principle D), not harm others (Principle E), and contribute to social justice (Principle F). Core assumptions underlying the guidelines include the assumptions that all encounters are cross-cultural; that race and ethnicity impact psychological practice and interventions; that psychologists advocate respect and inclusiveness for all; that psychologists recognize cultural contexts as defining forces for individuals and groups; and that external forces (historical, economic, sociopolitical) deeply influence people's lives. Ethical conduct of psychologists can be enhanced by knowledge of differences in beliefs and practices that emerge through socialization in particular groups; understanding how race and ethnicity intersect with other social identities (class, race, religion, gender, etc.) enhances treatment.

From these principles, the APA task force authors (2003b) identified six guidelines, including a call for an awareness of psychologists as cultural beings who hold attitudes and beliefs that can detrimentally influence their perceptions and interactions with those who are different from themselves (Guideline 1). Psychologists ought to increase their knowledge of and sensitivity to ethnically and racially different individuals, which includes knowledge both of worldview and also of oppressed groups' experiences with marginalization (Guideline 2). In recognition of the fact that, historically, culture was omitted from education in psychology, psychologist educators are encouraged to employ the constructs of multiculturalism and diversity in psychological education (Guideline 3). Since traditional research often relied on all-White samples, used culturally inappropriate measures, and treated culture as a "nuisance variable," psychologists must recognize the importance of conducting culture-centered research with diverse individuals as a prerequisite of ethical research (Guideline 4). Psychologists are encouraged to apply culturally appropriate skills in clinical and other applied psychological practices, including viewing the client in the context of her or his social group identities, worldview, sociopolitical factors, historical factors (e.g., slavery), and experiences with discrimination and oppression (Guideline 5). Finally, psychologists are encouraged to use organizational change processes to support culturally informed organizational development and practices, including pursuing the multicultural legislative agenda (Guideline 6). These guidelines were set to expire in 2009, but were extended to 2011.

As a result of these efforts, some within the fields of counseling and counseling psychology have delineated ethical decision-making models that specifically integrate multicultural ethical considerations. For example, Garcia, Cartwright, Winston, and Borzuchowska (2003) proposed a transcultural integrative model of ethical decision making. Reflecting Rest's (1983) influential four-component model of morality, each of Garcia et al.'s, four steps includes culturally responsive components. In Step One (Interpreting the Situation through Awareness and Fact Finding), practitioners are enjoined to be aware of the influences of their own worldviews, cultural identities, and theoretical orientation; to be attuned to intra-group differences; and to gather culture-specific information. Step Two (Formulating an Ethical Decision) involves reviewing cultural information and potential discriminatory regulations; ensuring that courses of action reflect the different worldviews of those involved; consulting with cultural experts; and selecting a course of action that best represents the agreement of those involved. In Step Three (Weighing Competing, Non-moral Values and Affirming the Course of Action), practitioners identify how their non-moral values might reflect a culture different from that of the client. Finally, Step Four (Planning and Executing the Selected Course of Action) includes identifying culturally relevant resources and strategies for implementation of the plan; anticipating cultural barriers to executing the plan; and using culturally appropriate measures to evaluate the effectiveness of the plan (Garcia et al., 2003).

Themes of Feminist and Multicultural Ethics

In this section, we use the five themes of feminist ethics identified and discussed in Brabeck (2000) and explore how multicultural ethics coincide with and inform each of them.

Theme 1: Women and Their Experience Are of Moral Significance

All feminist ethicists assume that women and their experiences are of moral significance. Valuing women's experience is the bedrock of feminist ethics; as Jaggar notes (1991), feminist ethics are distinguished from humanist ethics, Kantian ethics, or virtue ethics by their explicit commitment to respect women's moral experiences and to avoid rationalizing women's subordination. In a similar vein, Hinman proposes that "what is morally right depends (at least in part) on one's identity as a moral agent" (1998, p. 403), and one's identity is shaped by one's culture, ethnicity, and race. For that reason, understanding the moral agent must include attention to a person's race, ethnicity, and culture. It seems obvious that all persons' experiences should have moral significance, since all persons share a common human nature. But this has not always been a valid assumption. The personhood of women (as compared to men) has been debated since Aristotle (Shields, 1975), and the dehumanization of enslaved people has always been a reality of human evil and atrocities.

Virtues associated with women and people of color have continually been devalued (Miller, 1976; Moraga & Anzaldua, 1981). For example, caring has been viewed as a "natural" attribute of women, and therefore not a rational aptitude that is acquired with experience and perseverance. Roles associated with women have been both elevated beyond what is humanly possible and degraded to what is subhuman (the virgin/whore dichotomy). Rigid, narrow roles that women are assigned are often transformed into pervasive caricatures of women (the "good mother," the "temptress," etc.), and women have been legally deemed as property.

Similarly, people of color (and other groups, e.g., Jews, marginalized ethnic groups such as Armenians, Bosnians, the Maya, and the Tutu) throughout history have been called subhuman, denied claims of personhood, sold as property, and treated worse than animals. They have also been the victims of rigid and often pernicious stereotypes. Such stereotypes are unethical because they fail the moral tests of justice and beneficence. They are inadequate from a psychological perspective because they fail to capture the complexity of what it means to be a person. To counteract all persons' tendency to engage in stereotyping, the APA (2003b) encourages psychologists to recognize that, as cultural beings, they may hold attitudes and beliefs that can detrimentally influence their perceptions of and interactions with individuals who are ethnically and racially different from themselves.

To restore a more adequate understanding of the complexities and diversities of human experience, feminists and multiculturalists bring the experiences of women and other marginalized groups to any ethical process. An examination of the experiences of women and other groups challenges dominant Western philosophy. For example, women's experiences with children, students, research participants, and the particularities of their own lives have led some feminists to question the ethical limitations of abstract ethical principles. Sarah Ruddick (1980) identified "maternal thinking" as involving a particular attentiveness to the needs of children. She argued that maternal thinking is expressed in an ethical stance characterized by "attentive love." Janice Raymond (1986) explored a philosophy of friendship that was both ethical and feminist and rooted in women's connections to each other. Nel Noddings's (1984) ethic of care theory, grounded in the examination of women's relationships, particularly the mother-child relationship, is an ethical theory of responsibility to and for others.

The most well-known effort to articulate the moral dimension of women's experiences was Carol Gilligan's (1982) assertion of the ethic of care. Gilligan (1982) described a "different" (woman's) moral voice: "This voice emerges with great clarity, defining the self and proclaiming its worth on the basis of the ability to care for and protect others" (p. 79). Gilligan argued that this moral voice develops because women are encouraged to define their identity through relationships of intimacy and care (Gilligan, 1982, p. 164). In contrast, Gilligan argued, the masculine voice is socialized to be concerned with abstract rules of justice. She claimed that the male identity is defined in separation and "instead of attachment, individual achievement rivals the male imagination and great ideas or distinctive activity defines the standard of self-assessment and success" (Gilligan, 1982, p. 161). Female identity, on the other hand, develops in a context of belonging and connection to others.

Beginning with an examination of women's experience with mothering and peace-making, relational feminists, like Gilligan, Noddings, and Miller, have generally advanced three assertions that are relevant to ethical deliberations. First, they have offered a critique of Kantian moral theory, which holds abstract reasoning as the pinnacle of human thought. Relational theorists (Belenky, Clinchy, Goldberger, & Tarule, 1987; Gilligan, 1982) claim that women's subjective knowing, revealed in discussions about moral issues, is equally valid. Second, relational feminists emphasize the value of empathy, nurturance, and caring over—or in addition to—justice, rights, and abstract moral rules. They insist that the qualities associated with women must be valued equally with those associated with men. For example, what has been dismissed as women's passivity may be reconceptualized as peacefulness; maternal work may be associated with the ethic of care or beneficence. Third, relational feminists challenge notions of individualistic moral choice derived from universal moral imperatives. Instead, they emphasize human connections over autonomy as the moral ideal. Some (e.g., Flax, 1990; Noddings, 1984) propose that the mother-child relationship is the paradigmatic caring relationship. As an alternative to rights-based morality, which ensures that one's individual rights are guaranteed, relational feminists offer a relationship-based morality, grounded in our connections to each other (Held, 1987; Whitbeck, 1989).

Claims by Gilligan and others that women have a different moral voice have not been substantiated by empirical research (Brabeck, 2000). Rather, research indicates that the care perspective can be reliably and validly assessed, and that men and women, boys and girls, are equally likely to use care when the moral situation involves people, relationships, and interpersonal issues. Likewise, males and females are equally likely to invoke an ethic of justice when reasoning about issues of conflicting rights and claims. The value of the feminist lens is in bringing a care perspective to moral issues and reasserting the importance of "feminine" attributes as important for all persons.

Multicultural theorists have challenged feminist theory for being too Eurocentric and failing to include the multiple ways in which people's characteristics intersect (Collins, 1990, 2000). We are not only gendered, but we are born with skin color, into a language group, within a culture, and with special abilities and disabilities, all of which shape our identity, and that identity has moral aspects (Appiah, 1990). Moreover, while all women might be subjected to oppression in patriarchal societies, they are not all equally oppressed on the basis of other aspects of identity, for example, immigrant status, socioeconomic status, and so forth. Multicultural ethicists focus on the ways that culture, race, and other social group identities uniquely inform our moral identities and selves.

Edward Sampson (1989) argued that the American notion of the individualistic, self-contained person stifles our ability to solve pressing social problems. Sampson identified two conceptions of self. The first, which he labeled "ensembled individualism," is characteristic of pre-modern understandings of self and develops in societies with strong communal ties. Ensembled individualism is defined by fluid self-other boundaries; a sense of control that includes, but goes beyond the individual; and a conception of other persons as included within one's notion of self.

In contrast, "self-contained individualism" is characterized by firm self-other boundaries, a sense of personal control, and a conception of self that excludes other people (Kim, Triandis, Kagitcibasi, Choi, & Yoon, 1994). Similar ideas have been expressed by Wheeler, Reis, and Bond (1989), who labeled their notions of self as "collectivism" (akin to ensembled individualism) versus "individualism" (akin to self contained individualism).

Sampson (1989) dates the beginning of our contemporary self-contained individualism to the fifteenth century. Prior to that time, he argued, persons were understood as intrinsically and unalterably embedded in culture, and meanings of self, relationships, and values were derived within this context. However, over the past three centuries, we have shifted from a notion of persons as molded within the particular experience of their culture, to a notion of individuals who possess, as MacIntyre (1988) describes, "their identity and their essential human capacities apart from and prior to their membership in any particular social and political order" (p. 210).

As individuals became detached from their communities and more affluent and mobile (Triandis, 1989), they were free to establish their own identities, thus rendering communities as derivative of the individual. Rather than the person being created through her or his attachments within community, in modern times, community has come to be defined by the needs and the desires of the individual. Like Gilligan, cross-cultural theorists and researchers have associated different values with these different conceptions of self (Schwartz & Bilsky, 1990). For example, Triandis (1989) associates a collective self with the values of conservatism, hierarchy, harmony and cooperation. In contrast, he claims that individualistic selves are associated with autonomy, mastery, equality, and competition.

While the neat dichotomy associating selves, cultures, and values has not been uniformly supported by empirical evidence (Brabeck, 1983, 1996), the experiences of marginalized groups provide a different lens for understanding personhood and the ethical values associated with a worldview. For both multiculturalists and feminists, the experiences of diverse groups must be a starting place for identifying ethical responses. Feminist and multicultural ethicists value grounded knowledge, that is, knowledge that is derived from lived experience. They examine the cognitive, affective, and subjective realities of people's experience to define a way of seeing and sensing the world and making moral decisions. In so doing, they reinstitute the primacy of women's and cultural groups' experiences and offer an alternative lens to that developed within a European-dominant, patriarchal society.

Theme 2: Attentiveness and Subjective Knowledge Can Illuminate Moral Issues

The ethical stance is that feminist consciousness should become as familiar as the dominant patriarchal lens, serving as "another mother tongue" (Brabeck & Brown, 1997) for understanding and responding. This "other tongue" is informed by subjective knowledge, in contrast to the impartial rational knowledge privileged by patriarchy.

In part, feminist subjective knowledge claims the body as a source of information and insight and reverses the Platonic/Cartesian/Kantian duality that separates mind and body and reifies mind. The idea that feelings rather than rationality alone can lead to moral impulses was proposed by David Hume in the eighteenth century. Hume held that ethics are based on moral sentiment rather than abstract moral principles.

For many feminist theorists (e.g., Baier, 1994) and some multicultural theorists (e.g., Fowers & Davidov, 2006), ethical responses are guided by subjectivity, rather than reason alone. Reflection on personal experience is not objectively verifiable, and is informed by both cognition and affect. This is similar to Fowers and Davidov's (2006) suggestion that, over and beyond abstract knowledge or skills, personal transformation and character virtues, in particular openness to the other, are necessary for true multicultural competence.

Ethical theories that acknowledge that we are sensing, feeling, and emotionally complex persons emphasize what is situated within contexts, immediate, unverifiable, and particular. The emphasis on physicality reveals our existence as interdependent and embedded in particular relationships, cultures, and communities, in contrast to the Cartesian notion of universal and impartial rationality. Recognizing that this embodied state is a permanent aspect of all human experience leads to different ethical issues and responses. It requires attentiveness to the particular, concrete, and unique experiences of persons, a loving attentiveness (Frye, 1983; Noddings, 1984), rather than universal ideal principles that are uniformly applied. Recognizing that each person's subjectivity is unique requires empathy, along with reason and caring relationships, as well as acknowledgment of universal rights and justice.

In 1951, Simone Weil laid the philosophical foundation for a subjectivist moral view that was later developed by feminist philosophers. Weil believed that pure attentiveness, or attentive seeking, was a form of prayer that ultimately could reveal God. Later, Iris Murdoch (1970) developed Weil's ideas and argued that loving regard, patience, and just discernment are the "characteristic and proper mark of the moral agent" (p. 34). Marilyn Frye (1983), concerned that women not be limited or suppressed in the role of caring for the other, described attention as an active act. For Frye, attention involves not only perceiving reality, but also constructing it. Since we can construct other people through our perceptions of them, proper attentiveness may be understood as a moral and an instrumental/agentic act. Consequently, according to Frye, we must be careful about how we are attentive to others as well as how we attend to ourselves.

Standpoint theory (Wood, 1992) is invoked by both feminist and multicultural ethicists as a way to understand the unique and objectively unknowable experiences of diverse persons and to reinstate the primacy of subjective lived experience as the basis for knowing. Standpoint theory can be traced back to Hegel's reflection on the slave-master relationship (Bell, 1993). Hegel realized that the distinct standpoints occupied by slave and master produce radically different understandings of both their relationship and the world. Hegel and other standpoint theorists contend that the viewpoints of oppressed and dominant groups are not merely distinct, but qualitatively unequal. Those in positions of power have substantial interest in preserving their hierarchical place, and they invest considerable effort in making their standpoint the dominant reality. Thus, to know the totality of human potential, one must actively engage in attentive knowing to discern the experiences of marginalized people, from their unique standpoints.

Feminist standpoint theory, as described by feminist philosophers Jane Flax (1990), Nancy Hartsock (1983), Alison Jaggar (1991), and others, extends this notion to ask how various standpoints arise out of conditions surrounding them and how these are construed within subjective consciousness and are expressed in an individual's narrative or story. An individual's reality is located at the intersection of time and place and forms an ongoing narrative. Feminist ethics recognize that any moral obligation to act arises out of a person's or a community's story and will continue into that person's or community's future. For this reason, attending to group membership is essential; moral adequacy depends on paying loving attention to the particularities of an individual's and community's narratives while examining these particularities in light of their unique sociocultural contexts. Such attentiveness reveals the ways in which people's lives are affected by bigotry, prejudice, and other distortions. Multicultural and feminist ethical psychologists seek to understand the distinctive features of individuals' experiences as they take place in a gender-stratified and racist culture. They assume that the subjective, interpretive capacities of individuals are the best sources of information about the cultural contexts that shape people. People who are oppressed are in the best position for engaging in the analysis of how power is used to oppress individuals and groups.

However, emphasizing the unique experiences of individuals or groups, rather than universal human qualities, can, as discussed earlier, result in separatist views. For example radical feminists (Daly, 1978, 1984; Marks & de Courtivron, 1981; Raymond, 1986) view women's attributes, moral sensibilities, and affective relational skills as innately different or arising from biologically based experiences, such as women's ability to give birth and nurse (Marks & de Courtivron, 1981). This view of women's superior morality that is threatened by patriarchal society has its roots in Charlotte Perkins Gilman's utopian novel about an all-female society, *Herland*, published in 1915. Radical feminists argue that women's values and virtues are unique to women and are not available to men. For example, Audre Lorde (1984) asserted, "The master's tools will never dismantle the master's house" (p. 110).

Radical feminists, like some multicultural separatists, exhort women and people of color to free themselves from oppressive socioeconomic, political, and linguistic patriarchy. They denounce patriarchal and hegemonic attempts to name (and thereby assert power over) and to determine the limits and boundaries of women's and other marginalized groups' experiences and knowledge. Some (e.g., French feminists, see Marks & de Courtivron, 1981) argue that subjective, unverifiable knowing is special to women, and they urge women to build on their own understanding of the moral domain by paying attention to the subjectivities of women that arise out of their experiences. If patriarchy is at the root of all oppressions, radical feminists try to save themselves by separating from flawed patriarchal social systems. Similarly, multiculturalists who see racism as endemic to U.S. society urge separation and isolation from that society.

However, other feminists and multiculturalists (Appiah, 1990; Weisstein, 1997) criticize those who completely reject objective knowledge and focus on the subjective. For example, Weisstein (1997) claims that such arguments are "leading us back into the cave, away from reality, and away from an understanding of our world and how to change it" (p. 146). She urges engagement in order to change the world to become more just. Multicultural and feminist ethicists who have adopted Hinman's (1998, 2007) notion of pluralism embrace the ethical perspectives that arise from different cultural contexts, even as they would warn against the dangers of separatism and isolationism.

Many feminists and multiculturalists (Greene & Sanchez-Hucles, 1997; hooks, 1993; Spelman, 1988) have warned about the danger of essentialism and false universalism, that is, arguing that a trait is essential to all members of a group (e.g., "all women are nurturing"). For example, if care is assumed to be an essential virtue for all women, it may lead some women to believe that they must provide care to others, even if they are damaged in the process (Puka, 1989). Such an assertion might lead some women to falsely believe that even if they are battered, they are morally obligated to continue to care about the batterer and to maintain the relationship (Applebaum, 1997). Furthermore, there is a moral danger in claiming an essential nature for women or any cultural group; as Calhoun (1988) writes, "Unless moral theory shifts its priority to knowledgeable discussions of human differences—particularly differences tied to gender, race, class, and power—these lists are likely to be sexist, racist, and classist" (p. 456). This observation leads feminist and multiculturalists to assess the ways that claims about women or about cultural groups may lead to distortions, which will be discussed next.

Theme 3: Feminist Critiques of Male Distortions Must Be Accompanied by a Critique of Racist, Classist, and Homophobic Distortions

Multicultural and feminist ethicists agree that oppression is a unit of analysis that must include gender, class, race, ethnicity, disability, and sexual orientation. The feminist goal is not to show that women are oppressed, but to remove the oppression and replace it with empowerment of marginalized groups. It is further recognized that at different times, in different contexts, and for different individuals, one social identity may be more salient than another. Feminist and multicultural ethics complement each other by drawing attention to our intersecting identities: "Multiculturalism advocates respect for patterns of behavior and consciousness within cultural diversity.... Feminism advocates respect for patterns of behavior and consciousness within cultural diversity" (Cervantes & Cervantes, 1993, pp. 164, 168).

Sexism and racism refer to attitudes, actions, laws, policies, and practices that treat anyone differently based solely on gender or ethnicity. Both racism and sexism might involve either intentions (attitudes that disparage people on the basis of ethnicity or gender) or consequences (actions that impact persons, e.g., denying housing to an ethnic group). Moreover, they include personal (e.g., individuals' attitudes) as well as systemic (e.g., policies and institutions that systematically privilege one group and marginalize another) aspects. David Wellman's (1993) definition of racism as a "system of advantage based on race" (p. 360) reflects the idea that racism and sexism and other "isms" go beyond the individual and imply a systematic advantage. One personally may not consider herself a racist, but as a White person, she would have to acknowledge that she benefits from a system that privileges her.

A further distinction can be made between overt and covert institutional racism and sexism. Overt racism includes visible acts of discrimination such as hate crimes, ethnic and gender slurs, and so on. Institutional racism and sexism exist in social and institutional structures that disadvantage individuals based on their sex or race (or other social group memberships). Racism and sexism can be sanctioned by the United States government (e.g., historically, Jim Crow laws, denial of voting privileges to women). Alternatively, racism might not be sanctioned by law, but may still be perpetrated by individuals (e.g., discrimination in housing; hate crimes; low expectations of poor, homeless, or undocumented children). Finally, racism may be active, for example, actively using homophobic language, or it may be passive, for example, failing to challenge another individual who is using homophobic language in one's presence (Tatum, 1997). Feminist and multicultural ethics attempt to identify the ethical problems in all sexist and racist structures, acts, and attitudes, and to work toward removing them.

Both feminist and multicultural ethics subscribe to a liberational ethic, that is, ethical concern for liberating oppressed persons. Both embrace human diversity as a requirement and foundation for practice, and advocate that psychologists examine the limitations of their own knowing, shaped by experience and positions of privilege (APA, 2003b; Frame & Williams, 2005; Sue & Sue, 2008). They espouse self-interrogation about the ways in which our own context leads us to oppress others (Applebaum, 1997; Sue & Sue, 2008).

Theme 4: Feminist Ethics Engage in Analysis of the Context and of the Power Dynamics in That Context

Feminism and multiculturalism, like most philosophical thought in the twentieth nd twenty-first centuries, have been informed by postmodernism. Postmodernism is the epistemological stance that maintains that all knowledge is constructed and deeply influenced by political and historical forces. Postmodernism challenges the assertion of absolute objective reality and uncovers power inequities embedded in all constructions of knowledge.

All feminist and multicultural ethics recognize that power and domination may be overt or covert, may be structural or interpersonal, and may be subtle or blatantly expressed acts of coercion, control or aggression (Jaggar, 1991; Wellman, 1993). Multicultural and feminist ethics recognize such acts as diminishing or distorting persons and therefore as ethically wrong, and both value efforts to resist such forces.

Postmodernism offers powerful tools for analyzing power and a method for deconstructing how labels such as "woman," "Latino," and "African American" have been defined (or constructed) within patriarchal and European-White-dominated society. Multiculturalists and feminists share a concern about how, by whom, and for whose benefit knowledge is constructed. Like postmodernists, they question claims of certainty about truth and assume that alternative ways of knowing and constructing reality (including subjectively) always exist. Like postmodernists, they interrogate ways of knowing and the inherent power hierarchies that affect what we accept as "knowledge," especially gendered knowledge. For feminists and multiculturalists, this interrogation of how power affects claims of ethics or truth also includes interrogation of how one's own situation of power and privilege affect one's own knowledge and ethical stance. Feminist and multicultural ethics require such self-reflection.

However, postmodernism poses some dilemmas for feminist and multicultural ethics. If we believe our realities to be only constructions arising out of specific contexts, it follows that no universal experience may be claimed. Within this epistemological stance, neither universal truth nor moral absolutes exist. The radical relativism of postmodernism is a dangerous framework for the multiculturalist and feminist enterprises, not because it legitimizes oppression, but because it helps maintain it. Postmodernism rejects the grand narrative, which provides a theoretical explanation for forces such as patriarchy, racism, and sexism. As Hawkesworth (1989) writes, "In a world of radical inequality, relativistic resignation supports the status quo" (p. 351).

As importantly, postmodernism leaves one with a philosophy of negation (Alcoff, 1989). One can say what is *not* (woman, truth, Latina, virtue) but not what *is* (women, truths, Latino/as, virtues). For feminists and multiculturalists committed to making the world more just, and for those working to identify ethical responses to complex situations, a philosophy of negation is not an option. Feminist and multicultural ethics seek a moral basis for improving the condition of all of humanity. That requires ethical aspirations and ethical action. Without an affirmative agenda, how then are we to develop a moral argument against heinous acts such as torture, hate crimes, and battering? How are we to decide on the ethical action that is required of an ethical practitioner? Under the radical relativism of postmodernism, how do we even justify the question of what ought the feminist/multiculturalist researcher (or multiculturalist/feminist therapist, teacher, activist, administrator) do? Feminists and multiculturalists seek to discover instances of racism, sexism, classism, or any other system of exploitation, and then work to eradicate them.

Theme 5: Feminist Ethics Require Action Directed at Achieving Social Justice

As previously discussed, though they developed as parallel lines of work, feminist and multicultural ethics share a number of commonalities and commitments. Most noteworthy, both ethical frameworks make the pursuit of social justice an aspirational goal, a motive for ethical action, and a principle of judging moral worth. Both approaches attempt to rectify the wrong that is done by discrimination on the basis of social group membership, including gender and ethnicity. Both approaches see moving groups of people from positions of marginalization to the center as ethical goals. Both attempt to try to make visible groups who have been ignored.

Feminist and multicultural ethics are concerned not only with what ought to be, but also with how to bring *what is* to be more in line with *what ought to be* (Bell, 1993). As Prilleltensky (1997) states, "Discourse without action is dangerous because it creates the impression that progress is taking place when in fact only the words have been changed" (p. 530). This work is overtly political:

> All feminisms share an explicit political urge—to reform or to remake the world in line with a deeply held conviction that women have been the victims of faulty and exploitative social institutions. One cannot separate feminist politics from ethics; they are entangled at each and every point, from the assumptions that undergrid alternative feminist theories to the explicit projects that feminists endorse. This holds whether one is addressing radical, liberal, Marxist or socialist, or what is now called ecofeminism. (Elshtain, 1991, p. 128)

Tong (1993) notes that in classical times, politics and ethics were joined. For Plato, the virtues of the individual and those of the city were isomorphic; for Aristotle, ethics and politics together led to the human good. Practical wisdom led to doing good. "To say that feminist approaches to ethics are 'political' in the classical sense of the term is to say... that feminists pay attention to issues of power because in so doing they liberate themselves and others. Politics is indispensable to ethics in the sense that only an empowered person has the capacity to self-reflectively make this a better world" (Tong, 1993, p. 183).

As discussed above, the etiology of all behavior is complex and multidetermined. Caring discernment attends to the particular circumstances of individuals and groups. Simultaneously rational and affective, it both perceives and constructs realities, and pays attention to the ways that sexism and racism, homophobia, and other distortions of human experience and worth affect people. Loving attention reveals the power hierarchies inherent in each particular situation, and feminist ethics require us to critique the ways in which our own positions in the hierarchy of power within any context affect our perceptions and moral sensitivities. In these ways, feminist and multicultural ethics inform and enhance moral actions that make the world more just and communities more caring.

Similarly, counseling psychologists (e.g., Goodman, et al., 2004; Toporek, Gerstein, Fouad, Roysicar, & Israel, 2006) have drawn from feminist and multicultural principles and recommended that social justice ethics be incorporated into the work of counseling psychologists. Counseling psychologists convened a Social Justice and Ethics Social Action Group at the National Counseling Psychology Conference in Houston in 2001 and developed a definition of social justice as "a concept that advocates engaging individuals as coparticpants in decisions which directly affect their lives; it involves taking some action, and educating individuals and their group identities, considering power differentials in all areas of counseling practice and research" (Blustein, Elman & Gerstein, 2001, p. 9).

One research model that reflects both feminist and multicultural ethics, and that challenges traditional models of knowledge production, explicitly links research with the goal of social action and change, and reinstates the primacy of marginalized groups' voices is participatory action research (PAR). Building on the work of social psychologist Kurt Lewin (1946), Brazilian educator Paulo Freire (1970), and Colombian sociologist Orlando Fals Borda (2001), PAR involves university- and community-based co-researchers collaboratively engaging in research, reflection, and knowledge generation, and together taking collective actions that strive to bring about more just and equitable life conditions in communities (Park, 1993; Reason & Bradbury, 2008). In PAR, researchers and community members collectively identify and investigate an issue or problem and determine how to investigate the problem and analyze the results. Throughout the iterative process, they continuously engage in dialogue and self- and collective refection, and jointly decide how to disseminate research findings (McIntyre, 2008). The ultimate goals of PAR are to collaboratively create action as a catalyst for social change and to build leadership and capacity in the community, as community members move from being passive "objects" of academic inquiry to active participants in their own research process (Grant, Nelson, & Mitchell, 2008; Park, 1993).

Of course, changing the system will change us. Thus, according to Bell (1993), it is not surprising that this is the juncture where many of us walk away from the challenge of change, and avoid confronting institutional and structural moral considerations. Yet, she urges that without such an analysis and accompanying agendas for change, the larger systems of repression will remain intact.

Recommendations from Feminist and Multicultural Ethics to the APA Ethical Principles (2003)

Feminist and multicultural ethics share many similarities, including the critique of traditional psychological theories as embedded within a worldview of the privileged; the understanding of the significance of race, gender, and culture; the belief that psychologists must be self-aware and educated about their own culture and that of the client/student/participant; the awareness of multiple and intersecting identities; the credence afforded to subjective lived experience; the respect paid to the cultural values and norms of clients, students, and participants; and the recognition of the influence that power dimensions and dynamics have on inter-group and within-group relations.

One way to examine how feminist and multicultural ethics inform professional practice is to look at how they might act as a corrective to, or expansion of, the American Psychological Association's (APA's) Ethical Principles of Psychologists and Code of Conduct (2003a). The general ethical principles included in the APA Code are those that are central to ethical conduct in psychology (Department of Health and Human Services, 2001; National Commission for the Protection of Human Subjects of Biomedical and Behavioral Research, 1978).

Principle A: Beneficence and Nonmaleficence

An overall criticism that feminist and multicultural ethics might make of the APA Code is that it is highly individualistic and less concerned about the wellbeing and ethical treatment of groups. Moreover, scant attention is paid to the ways in which social embeddedness affects individual persons. For example, the first principle, Beneficence and Nonmaleficence, mandates that psychologists "do no harm" and enjoins psychologists to ensure that people with whom they work are helped by the intervention or interaction, to avoid misusing the influence that they hold over another, and to strive to be aware of how their own state of well-being impacts those they seek to help. Thus, the emphasis is on the well-being of the individual, be it client, student, or psychologist.

Feminist and multicultural ethics would expand the understanding of beneficence to include awareness of the impact of contexts on the well-being of persons. In addition to helping individuals, feminist and multicultural ethics would question whether the community at large is being left a more just and equitable place. In examining one's own influence on others, feminist and multicultural ethics would explicitly mandate an examination of one's cultural lens and worldview, as well as one's positions of privilege and power.

Feminist and multicultural ethics would further encourage psychologists to avoid psychologizing individuals' responses to a harmful context; as we learn more about the biological and neurological bases of behavior, we risk ignoring the contexts that impact well-being. A feminist and multicultural psychologist, for example, would not stop at diagnosing and treating a single working mother's physical, emotional, and cognitive symptoms of depression. Rather, he or she would also help the client understand the sources of emotional distress located outside the individual, that is, within the contexts of racism, sexism, classicism, and other discriminatory systems that affect the well-being of individuals, and would strive to reduce their impact. The ethical feminist and multicultural psychologist would further help the client to consider how her or his multiple and intersecting social group identities impact psychological well-being; for example, how inevitably failing to live up to the standards for one's gender (e.g., perfect mother) impacts one's emotional state, and how this is complicated when gender intersects with, for example, a religion that reinforces unattainable ideals for women.

Principle B: Fidelity and Responsibility

The second APA Ethics Code (2003a) principle, Fidelity and Responsibility, requires psychologists to become aware of their responsibility to "society and the specific communities in which they work" (APA Code, 2003a, p. 3). This principle requires psychologists to give some portion of their time and talent "for little or no compensation or personal advantage" (APA Code, 2003a, p. 3). A feminist and multicultural psychologist would expand this to include examination of who benefits from a psychologists' work. For example, how does research benefit the participants and the communities in which they live? An ethical feminist/multicultural researcher might look to PAR as a model of how research might benefit both the participants, who develop organizing potential and consciousness, and the community through collective actions toward social change. The feminist and multicultural ethical psychologist would further recognize that the individual is embedded within the collective; hence to advance one is to promote the other. For example, if a suicidal Latina client fails to attend a therapy appointment, and the psychologist is aware that she lives in a home with several undocumented immigrants, the psychologist would consider the impact on the client's immediate community before sending emergency responders to her home to ensure her safety. The psychologist would recognize that the individual clients' well-being is necessarily connected to the well-being of her community.

A feminist and multicultural psychologist would see psychological research as itself embedded in a context that has values, assumptions, and limitations. He or she would notice how academic institutions may impede psychologists from engaging in action that is responsible to the community and involves the community in empowering ways. Truly participatory work requires time and patience to develop meaningful and trusting relationships, particularly with marginalized communities who are accustomed to outside researchers dropping in, collecting data, and leaving. The tenure clock, "publish or perish" academic environment, as well as distrust of alternative ways of constructing knowledge, pose obstacles to ethical feminist and multicultural psychologists. Including relevant persons in the research project and using research as a catalyst for creating sustainable and meaningful change in communities calls for a very different approach from that of laboratory studies. Ironically, failing to include marginalized groups may also impede the development of knowledge. Yet, ethical psychologists recognize the potential risks of participating in research posed to marginalized participants (e.g., undocumented immigrants, battered women) and honor their decisions to decline; as Fantuzzo, McWayne, and Childs (2006) point out, "The concerns of the *no's* [those who decline participation] genuinely embody the spirit of the guiding ethical principles: beneficence, autonomy and justice. The fundamental reality is that the participant is the primary source of confirmation of the beneficence, autonomy, and justice of their involvement in the research" (p. 32).

Principle C: Integrity

According to Principle C of the APA Ethics Code (2003a), psychologists are required to be honest and truthful in all encounters and actions. A feminist and multicultural ethicist would expand this to include self-knowledge of how one's own situated condition affects perceptions, views of others, and emotional responses. A feminist and multicultural psychologist would engage in self-interrogation regarding how one's own positions of power, privilege, and advantage affect one's self and prevent one from being maximally able to be attentive and open to understanding the subjective realities of clients, research participants, students, or community activists. For example, a White female therapist working with an African American female client may understand the client's distress in terms of gender and sexism, but may fail to see how her own positions of racial privilege vis-à-vis the client impact the client-counselor relationship and limit her full understanding of the client's experiences and concerns. An ethical psychologist recognizes the limits of her or his "openness to the other" (Fowers & Davidov, 2006) and continuously works to expand this virtue. Additionally, the ethical psychologist would be truthful about the limitations of historical psychological research, theory, and practice with regard to underrepresented groups, and would acknowledge other valid and powerful indigenous paths toward healing (Sue & Sue, 2008).

Principle D: Justice

The principle of Justice requires that there be equity and fairness in all that psychologists undertake. But justice need not be equated solely with individual rights. An ethic of justice informed by an ethic of care would encourage psychologists to resolve conflicts, including conflicts over how one spends one's time, in ways that strengthen relationships, enhance trust, and reflect attentiveness and love at least as much as regard for impartial fairness, autonomy, and individual rights. When working, for example, with a client who is considering whether to pursue her own dreams of attending a distant university, or to stay home and take care of a sick parent, the feminist/multicultural psychologist would invoke both the ethic of justice and of care to recognize her right to follow her individual path, along with her commitment to her relationships and loving attentiveness for others. Additionally, the feminist/multicultural psychologist would argue that principles of justice and fairness should extend beyond individual interactions. As discussed earlier, working toward social justice, equity, and equality for all is a mandate of the ethical psychologist.

Principle E: Respect for People's Rights and Dignity

Principle E is based on the principle of autonomy of persons and their right to privacy, confidentiality, and self-determination. A feminist and multicultural ethics would encourage psychologists to expand the understanding of respect and autonomy to include an understanding of how different contexts limit the choices of some more fully than others. A feminist and multicultural ethics would attend to the subjective experience of people and understand how oppression shapes that subjectivity. He or she would further recognize that for many, "autonomous" decisions are inextricably linked to the social context. For example, in working with a client who migrated to the United States and left three children in her native country, the feminist/multicultural psychologist would recognize that what might appear as an "autonomous" decision to migrate in fact reflected the client's responsiveness to her social context, that is, her best option to support her family. Moreover, the psychologist would recognize that this decision results from structural conditions (in particular between the first and developing world) that preclude her from being able to support her family in her country of origin. Additionally, a feminist and multicultural ethics would question traditional assumptions about the importance of confidentiality. For example, in PAR work, some participants may want to be named as co-researchers and take credit for their work. In giving testimonials as part of qualitative research, interviewees (including, for example, rape survivors, torture survivors) may wish to own their stories as part of the process of breaking silence.

In summary, adding the lenses of multicultural and feminist ethics to the obligations of all psychologists under the APA Ethics Code (2003a) raises new issues that may lead to more competent and ethical action.

Future Directions and Questions

In conclusion, we pose the following questions regarding the intersections of feminist and multicultural ethics with psychological practice:

In what ways might feminist and multicultural ethics conflict with state and federal legislative mandates for psychologists? How might these conflicts be resolved?

In what ways might feminist and multicultural attentiveness to social and community well-being conflict with psychology's traditional emphasis on the well-being of the individual?

Is it important for practicing psychologists to be familiar with the philosophical roots of their ethical principles? How well do training programs teach the philosophical bases of ethical principles and codes? What impact does such education have on ethical practice?

How well do current counseling psychology training programs incorporate feminist and multicultural ethics into their training? How might we challenge them to include such ethical lenses?

If all cultures are equally important, how does one argue for access, benefits, and special treatment for any single group? How might an ethical psychologist respond when ethical claims from different groups are in conflict?

References

Alcoff, L. (1989). Cultural feminism versus post-structuralism: The identity crisis in feminist theory. In M. R. Malson, J. F. O'Barr, S. Westphal-Wihl, & M. Wyer (Eds.), *Feminist theory in practice and process* (pp. 405–436). Chicago: University of Chicago Press.

American Psychological Association. (2003a). Ethical principles of psychologists and code of conduct. Retrieved October 10, 2010, from http://www.apa.org/ethics/code/index.aspx

American Psychological Association. (2003b). Guidelines on multicultural education, training, research, practice and organizational change for psychologists. *American Psychologist, 58,* 377–402.

American Psychological Association. (2007). Guidelines for psychological practice with girls and women. Retrieved October 10, 2010, from http://www.apa.org/practice/guidelines/girls-and-women.pdf

Appiah, K. A. (1990). "But would that still be me?" Notes on gender, "race," ethnicity, as sources of "identity." *The Journal of Philosophy, 87,* 493–499.

Appiah, K. A. (2006). *Cosmopolitanism: Ethics in a world of strangers.* New York: W. W. Norton.

Applebaum, B. (1997). Good liberal intentions are not enough! Racism, intentions and moral responsibility. *Journal of Moral Education, 26,* 409–421.

Ashmore, R. D., Deaux, K., & McLaughlin-Volpe, T. (2004). An organizing framework for collective identity: Articulation and significance of multidimensionality. *Psychological Bulletin, 130,* 80–114.

Baier, A. (1994). *Moral prejudices: Essays on ethics.* Cambridge, MA: Harvard University Press.

Banks, M. (2008). Women with disabilities: Cultural competence in rehabilitation psychology. *Disability and Rehabilitation, 30,* 184–190.

Beauchamp, T. L., & Childress, J. F. (1994). *Principles of biomedical ethics* (4th ed.). Oxford: Oxford University Press.

Belenky, M. F., Clinchy, B. M., Goldberger, N. R., & Tarule, J. M. (1987). *Women's ways of knowing: The development of self, voice, and mind.* New York: Basic Books.

Bell, L. (1993). *Rethinking ethics in the midst of violence: A feminist approach to freedom.* Lanham, MD: Rowman & Littlefield.

Blustein, D. Elman, N., & Gerstein, L. (August, 2001). *Executive report: Social Action Groups National Counseling Psychology Conference.* Houston, TX: Authors.

Brabeck, M. (1983). Moral judgment: Theory and research on differences between males and females. *Developmental Review, 3,* 274–291.

Brabeck, M. (1996). The moral self, values and circles of belonging. In K. F. Wyche & F. J. Crosby (Eds.), *Women's ethnicities: Journeys through psychology* (pp.145–165). Boulder, CO: Westview Press.

Brabeck, M. & Brown, L., et al. (1997). Feminist theory and psychological practice. In N. Johnson & J. Worell (Eds.), *Shaping the future of feminist psychology: Education, research, and practice* (pp. 15–35). Washington, DC: American Psychological Association Press.

Brabeck, M. (Ed.). (2000). *Practicing feminist ethics in psychology.* Washington, DC: Division 35 (Psychology of Women) Book Series, American Psychological Association Press.

Brownmiller, S. (1993). *Against our will: Men, women, and rape.* Minneapolis, MN: Milkweed Editions.

Calhoun, C. (1988). Justice, care, gender bias. *Journal of Philosophy, 85,* 451–463.

Cervantes, N., & Cervantes, J. M. (1993). A multicultural perspective in the treatment of domestic violence. In M. Hansen & M. Harway (Eds.), *Battering and family therapy: A feminist perspective* (pp. 156–174). Newbury Park, CA: Sage Publications.

Collins, P. (1990/2000). *Black feminist thought: Knowledge, consciousness, and the politics of empowerment.* Boston: Unwin Hyman.

Daly, M. (1978). *Gyn/ecology: The metaethics of radical feminism.* Boston: Beacon Press.

Daly, M. (1984). *Pure lust: Elemental feminist philosophy.* Boston: Beacon Press.

Department of Health and Human Services. (2001). *Title 45 Public Welfare, Part 46, Code of Federal Regulations, Protection of Human Subjects.* Washington, DC: Government Printing Office.

Eisenstein, H. (1981). *Contemporary feminist thought.* Boston: G. K. Hall.

Elshtain, J. B. (1991). Ethics in the women's movement. *The Annals of the American Academy, 515,* 126–139.

Enns, C. Z. (1997). *Feminist theories and feminist psychotherapies: Origins, themes and variations.* Binghamton, NY: The Haworth Press.

Fals Borda, O. (2001). Participatory (action) research in social theory: Origins and challenges. In P. Reason & H. Bradbury (Eds.), *Handbook of action research: Participative inquiry and practice* (pp. 27–37). Thousand Oaks, CA: Sage Publications.

Fantuzzo, J., McWayne, C., & Childs, S. (2006). Scientist-community collaborations: A dynamic tension between rights and responsibilities. In J. E. Trimble & C. B. Fisher (Eds.), *Handbook of ethical research involving ethnocultural populations and communities* (pp. 27–49). Thousand Oaks, CA: Sage Publications.

Feminist Therapy Institute. (2000). *Feminist therapy code of ethics.* Retrieved October 10, 2010, from http://www.chrysalis counseling.org/Feminist_Therapy.html

Fine, M., &McClelland, S. (2006) Sexuality education and desire: Still missing after all these years. *Harvard Educational Review, 76,* 297–338.

Flax, J. (1990). *Thinking fragments: Psychoanalysis, feminism and postmodernism in the contemporary West.* Berkeley: University of California Press.

Fowers, B. J., & Davidov, B. J. (2006). The virtue of multiculturalism: Personal transformation, character, and openness to the other. *American Psychologist, 61,* 581–594.

Frame, M. W., & Williams, C. B. (2005). A model of ethical decision-making from a multicultural perspective. *Counseling and Values, 49,* 265–179.

Freire, P. (1970). *Pedagogy of the oppressed.* New York: Continuum.

Frye, M. (1983). *The politics of reality: Essays in feminist theory.* Trumansburg, NY: The Crossing Press.

Garcia, J., Cartwright, B., Winston, S. & Borzuchowska, B. (2003). A transcultural integrative model for ethical decision-making in counseling. *Journal of Counseling and Development, 81,* 268–277.

Gilbert, L. A. & Brownson, C. (1998). Current perspectives on women's multiple roles. *Journal of Career Assessment, 6,* 433–448.

Gilligan, C. (1982). *In a different voice: Psychological theory and women's development.* Cambridge, MA: Harvard University Press.

Goodman, L. A., Liang, B., Helms, J. E., Latta, R. E., Sparks, E., & Weintraub, S. R. (2004). Training counseling psychologists as social justice agents: Feminist and multicultural principles in action. *The Counseling Psychologist, 32,* 793–837.

Grant, J., Nelson, G. & Mitchell, T. (2008). Negotiating the challenges of participatory action research: Relationships, power, participation, change and credibility. In P. Reason & H. Bradbury (Eds.), *The SAGE handbook of action research* (2nd ed.) (pp. 581–601). Thousand Oaks, CA: Sage Publications.

Greene, B., & Sanchez-Hucles, J. B. (1997). Diversity: Advancing an inclusive feministpsychology. In J. Worell & N. G. Johnson (Eds.), *Shaping the future of feminist psychology: Education, research, and practice* (pp. 173–202). Washington, DC: American Psychological Association Press.

Grimshaw, J. (1993). The idea of a female ethic. In P. Singer (Ed.), *A companion to ethics* (pp. 491–499). Malden, MA: Blackwell.

Hartsock, N. (1983). The feminist standpoint: Developing the ground for a specifically feminist historical materialism. In S. Harding & M. B. Hintikka (Eds.), *Discovering reality: Feminist perspectives on epistemology, metaphysics, methodology and philosophy of science* (pp. 283–310). Dordrecht, Netherlands: D. Reidel.

Hawkesworth, M. (1989). Knowers, knowing, known: Feminist theory and the claims of truth. In M. Malson, J. F. O'Barr, S. Westphal-Wihl, & M. Wyer (Eds.), *Feminist theory in practice and process* (pp. 327–352). Chicago: University of Chicago Press.

Held, V. (1987). Feminism and moral theory. In E. F. Kittay & D. T. Meyers (Eds.), *Women and moral theory* (pp. 111–128). Totowa, NY: Rowman and Littlefield.

Herman, J. (1997). *Trauma and recovery.* New York: Basic Books.

Hinman, L. M. (1998). *Ethics: A pluralistic approach to moral theory* (2nd ed.). Toronto: Harcourt Brace.

Hinman, L. M. (2007). *Ethics: A pluralistic approach to moral theory* (4th ed.). Belmont, CA: Thomson Higher Education.

hooks, b. (1993). *Sisters of the yam: Black women and self-recovery.* Cambridge, MA: South End Press.

Horner, M. S. (1972). Toward an understanding of achievement-related conflicts in women. *The Journal of Social Issues 28*(9), 157–174.

Houser, R. (2006) Feminine and feminist ethics and counselor decision-making. In R. Houser, F. L. Wilczenski, & M. Ham (Eds.), *Culturally relevant ethical decision-making in counseling* (pp. 39–46). Thousand Oaks, CA: Sage Publications.

Jaggar, A. M. (1991). Feminist ethics: Projects, problems, prospects. In C. Card (Ed.), *Feminist ethics* (pp. 78–106). Lawrence: University Press of Kansas.

Kim, U., Triandis, H. C., Kagitcibasi, C., Choi, S. C., & Yoon, G. (Eds.). (1994). *Individualism and collectivism: Theory, method and applications: Cross-cultural research and methodology.* Thousand Oaks, CA: Sage Publications.

Lewin, K. (1946). Action research and minority problems. *Journal of Social Issues, 2,*34–46.

Lorde, A. (1984). *Sister outsider: Essays and speeches.* Berkeley, CA: Crossing Press.

MacIntyre, A. (1988). *Whose justice? Which morality?* South Bend, IN: Notre Dame Press.

Marks, I., & de Courtivron, E. (Eds.). (1981). *New French feminisms.* New York: Schocken.

McIntyre, A. (2008). *Participatory action research.* Thousand Oaks, CA: Sage Publications.

Mill, J. S. ([1869] 1997). *The subjection of women.* London: Dover Thrift Editions.

Miller, D. S., Forrest, L., Elman, N. S. (2009). Training directors' conceptualizations of the intersections of diversity and trainee competence problems: A preliminary analysis. *The Counseling Psychologist, 37,* 519–563.

Miller, J. B. (1976). *Toward a new psychology of women.* Boston: Beacon Press.

Miville, M. L., Duan, C., Nutt, R. L., Wachler, C. A., Suzuki, L., Pistole, M., Arredondo, P., Duffy, M., Mejia, B. X., & Corpus, M. (2009). Integrating practice guidelines into professional training. *The Counseling Psychologist, 37,* 519–563.

Moraga, C., & Anzaldua, G. (1981). *This bridge called my back: Writings of radical women of color.* Watertown, MA. Persephone Press.

Murdoch, I. (1970). *The sovereignty of good.* Routledge: London.

National Commission for the Protection of Human Subjects of Biomedical and Behavior Research. (1978). *The Belmont report: Ethical principles and guidelines for the protection of human subjects research* (DHEW Publication No. (OS) 78–0012). Washington, DC: Government Printing Office.

Noddings, N. (1984). *Caring: A feminine approach to ethics and moral education.* Berkeley: University of California Press.

Noguera, P. A. (2008).*The trouble with Black boys and other reflections on race, equity and the future of public education.* Hoboken, NJ: John Wiley and Sons, Inc.

Oyserman, D., Coon, H. M., & Kemmeleier, M. (2002). Rethinking individualism and collectivism: Evaluation and theoretical assumptions and meta-analyses. *Psychological Bulletin, 128,* 3–72.

Packard, T. (2009). Core values that distinguish counseling psychology: Personal and professional perspectives. *The Counseling Psychologist, 37,* 610–624.

Park, P. (1993). What is participatory research? A theoretical and methodological perspective. In P. Park, M. Brydon-Miller, B. Hall, & T. Jackson (Eds.), *Voices of change: Participatory research in the United States and Canada* (pp. 1–20). Westport, CT: Bergin & Garvey.

Pedersen, P. (1989). Developing multicultural ethical guidelines for psychology. *International Journal of Psychology, 24*, 643–652.

Perkins Gilman, C. (1915). *Herland.* London: Dover Thrift Editions.

Prilleltensky, I. (1997). Values, assumptions, and practices: Assessing the moral implications of psychological discourse and action. *American Psychologist, 47,* 517–535.

Puka, B. (1989). The liberation of caring: A different voice for Gilligan's "different voice." In M. M. Brabeck (Ed.), *Who cares? Theory, research and educational implications of the ethic of care* (pp. 19–44). New York: Praeger.

Raymond, J. (1986). *A passion for friends: Toward a philosophy of female affection.* Boston: Beacon Press.

Reason, P., & Bradbury, H. (Eds.). (2008). *The SAGE handbook of action research II.* London: Sage Publications.

Rest, J. (1983). Morality. In *Carmichael's manual of child psychology,* vol 3: *Cognitive development,* P. Mussen (Ed.) (pp. 556–629). New York: John Wiley.

Ruddick, S. (1980). Maternal thinking, *Feminist Studies, 1,* 342–367.

Sampson, E. (1989). The challenge of social change for psychology: Globalization and psychology's theory of the person. *American Psychologist, 44,* 914–921

Scaltsas, P. W. (1992). Do feminist ethics counter feminist aims? In E. B. Cole & S. Coultrap-McQuin (Eds.), *Explorations in feminist ethics: Theory and practice* (pp. 15–26). Bloomington: Indiana University Press.

Schwartz, S. H., & Bilsky, W. (1990). Toward a theory of the universal content and structure of values: Extensions and cross cultural replications. *Journal of Personality and Social Psychology, 58,* 878–891.

Shields, S. A. (1975). Functionalism, Darwinism and the psychology of women: A study in social myth. *American Psychologist, 30,* 739–754

Spelman, E. (1988). *Inessential woman: Problems of exclusion of feminist thought.* Boston: Beacon Press.

Sue, D. W., Bernier, Y., Durran, A., Feinberg, L., Pedersen, P. B., Smith, E. J., & Vasquez-Nuttal, E. (1982). Position paper: Cross-cultural counseling competencies. *The Counseling Psychologist, 10,* 45–52.

Sue, D. W., & Sue, D. (2008). *Counseling the culturally diverse: Theory and practice* (5th ed.). Hoboken, NJ: John Wiley and Sons.

Tatum, B. (1997). *Why are all the Black kids sitting together in the cafeteria? And other conversations about race.* New York: Basic Books.

Tong, R. (1993). *Feminine and feminist ethics.* Belmont, CA: Wadsworth.

Toporek, R. L., Gerstein, L. H., Fouad, N. A., Roysircar, G., & Israel, T. (2006). *Handbook for social justice in counseling psychology: Leadership, vision, and action.* Thousand Oaks, CA: Sage Pub.

Triandis, H. C. (1989). The self and social behavior in differing cultural contexts. *Psychological Review, 96,* 506–520.

Watson, Z. E., Herlihy, B. R., & Pierce, L. A. (2006). Forging the link between multicultural competence and ethical counseling practice: A historical perspective. *Counseling and Values, 50,* 99–107.

Weil, S. (1951). *Waiting for God.* (E. Craufurd, Trans.). New York: G. P. Putnam's Sons.

Weisstein, N. (1997). Power, resistance and science. *New Politics, 6,* 145–151.

Wellman, D. T. (1993). *Portraits of White racism.* New York: Cambridge University Press.

West, C. (1994). *Race Matters.* New York: Vintage Books.

Wheeler, L., Reis, H. T. & Bond, M. H. (1989). Collectivism-individualism in everyday social life: The middle kingdom and the melting pot. *Journal of Personality and Social Psychology, 57,* 79–86.

Whitbeck, C. (1989). A different reality: Feminist ontology. In A. Garry & M. Pearsall (Eds.), *Women, knowledge and reality: Explorations in feminist philosophy* (pp. 64–88). Boston: Unwin Hyman.

Wollstonecraft, M. (1792). *A vindication of the rights of women.* Boston: Peter Edes for Thomas and Andrews.

Wood, J. T. (1992). Gender and moral voice: Moving from woman's nature to standpoint epistemology. *Women's studies in communication, 15,*1–24.

Wrenn, G. (1962). The culturally encapsulated counselor. *Harvard Educational Review, 32,* 444–449.

CHAPTER

3 Life Span Development: Childhood, Adolescence, and Adulthood

Cindy L. Juntunen *and* Stephanie San Miguel Bauman

Abstract

This chapter examines human development in the context of multiple identities. It begins with an exploration of the complexity of human development through the lens of ecological systems theory (Bronfenbrenner, 1977; Bronfenbrenner & Morris, 2006), as augmented by multicultural and feminist psychology (Gilligan, 1982, 1996; Hurtado, 2010; Neville & Mobley, 2001; Yakushko, Davidson, & Williams, 2009). The roles of resilience and empowerment in development are then presented in the context of social identities. The remainder of the chapter explores important developmental concerns across the life span, including physical, emotional, social, and cognitive and academic/vocational development. Across each of these life domains, the specific contributions of feminist multicultural counseling psychology perspectives are identified, with an emphasis on fostering positive development throughout the life span.

Key Words: Life span development, ecological systems theory, multicultural feminist theory, resilience, empowerment, multiple social identities

Human development is often conceptualized as a relatively orderly and predictable progression through stages of growth and change. Major developmental theorists, including Piaget (1926), Erikson (1964), and Kohlberg (1963), have addressed the ways in which people develop cognitively, socially, and morally. These "classic" theories do not explicitly address the role of culture or gender, but instead were generalized to women and other cultures from the experience of primarily White and male humans. Feminist psychologists, including Carol Gilligan (1982) and the scholars at the Stone Center (Jordan, Kaplan, Miller, Stiver, & Surrey, 1991), challenged these generalizations and noted the qualitatively different importance of relationship and interpersonal connection in the development of women and girls. In turn, early feminist psychology has been criticized as being primarily Eurocentric and was subsequently challenged by scholars focusing on the implications of multiple identities and the unique experiences of girls and women of color (Landrine, 1995; Russo & Landrine, 2010).

Both feminist and multicultural psychology scholars have pointed out significant limitations in the classic developmental theories. Despite their origin in the experience of White males, developmental theories do provide an important basis for understanding human development from a feminist multicultural perspective. For example, although it is criticized for being both andro- and ethnocentric, the biopsychosocial framework proposed by Erikson (1964) provides a significant foundation for most postmodern and feminist perspectives on development because it envisions development as a process that is lifelong and shaped by an individual's participation in multiple social relationships (Sorell & Montgomery, 2001). However, early theories did little to integrate or address the development of social identity, which refers to the sense of being emotionally connected to a socially and politically identified group (Hurtado, 2010). Such social identities evolve in a meaningful sociopolitical context, or environment, in which the individual develops.

Many recent developmental theories attend more closely to sociocontextual factors, emphasizing the relational nature of the interaction between individual and environment (Lerner, 2002, 2006); the importance of understanding development in the context of environmental factors (Bronfenbrenner & Morris, 2006); and the interaction of culture, individual perceptions, and social policy on development (Spencer, 2006). In fact, the emphasis on the interaction of the individual and his or her social context has become a hallmark of developmental research over the last 25 years (Lerner & Steinberg, 2009a). This increasing emphasis on social context has contributed to "understanding how development, at any point across the life span, involves the relations of diverse and active individuals and diverse, active, and multitiered ecologies" (Lerner & Steinberg, 2009b, p. 9).

When human development is conceptualized as a function of person-context interaction, the groundwork is laid to examine the influence of social systems on individual development, as well as the impact of the individual on social systems. The feminist multicultural perspective, which utilizes the analysis and critique of social hierarchies and norms, allows a deeper understanding of the impact of social identity and social context. Specifically, feminist multicultural theory directly and fundamentally considers the intersectionality (Hurtado, 2010) of multiple identities in the development of a given individual.

In this chapter, we examine human development in the context of multiple identities. We begin with an exploration of the complexity of human development through the lens of ecological systems theory (Bronfenbrenner, 1977; Bronfenbrenner & Morris, 2006), building on expansions by multicultural counseling psychology (Neville & Mobley, 2001) and feminist psychology (Yakushko, Davidson, & Williams, 2009). (See Ancis and Davidson, chapter 4 of this volume, for additional discussion of the ecological model.) We then discuss the role of resilience and empowerment in development in the context of social identities. In the remainder of the chapter, we explore important developmental concerns across the life span, including physical, emotional, social, and cognitive and academic/vocational development. Across each of these life domains, we identify the specific contributions of feminist multicultural counseling psychology perspectives, with an emphasis on fostering positive development throughout the life span.

Development in the Context of Multiple Identities

Richard Lerner (2006) has argued that early developmental psychology theories, which assumed uniform and permanent change, viewed diversity factors as sources of deviation or deficit from optimal development. In contrast, contemporary developmental science is a multidisciplinary area of study that significantly extends early theories of developmental psychology. Importantly, contemporary theories embrace a systems framework with an appreciation for diversity, both intra-individual change and inter-individual differences, in the development process. Diversity is also recognized as a key part of the systems in which change occurs (Lerner, 2006).

Models within counseling psychology, specifically feminist and multicultural models, expand on this appreciation of diversity by articulating the ways in which individuals develop social identities. Discussed more thoroughly in a later chapter (Fischer and DeBord, chapter 5 of this volume), social identity development models provide important insights into the process by which people come to understand themselves in the context of their ethnic, gender, sexual, religious, social class, and other identities. Human development is made more complex by the recognition that social identities are fluid and evolve at least partially independently of each other, at different times, as individuals encounter new situations across different environments. This is recognized in several locational feminisms (Enns, 2010) as "acknowledge[ing] the messy and complex nature of constructing healthy identities (p. 336)." In the framework of ecological systems theory, "development is a function of forces emanating from multiple settings and from the relations among these settings" (Bronfenbrenner & Morris, 2006, p. 817).

Bronfenbrenner (1977, 1993) conceptualized an ecological system consisting of four major subsystems, which interact to influence human development. These subsystems include (a) the microsystem, which consists of the interpersonal interactions that occur in a given setting such as home, school, work, or social group; (b) the mesosystem, in which two or more microsystem environments interact, such as the relationship between work and home; (c) the exosystem, which consists of social structures and linkages that indirectly impact individuals, such as community resources or neighborhood characteristics; and (d) the macrosystem, which is most distal from the individual and includes norms and values of the larger society.

Bronfenbrenner's model has been adapted to specifically address multicultural counseling psychology processes (Neville & Mobley, 2001). Although the authors were focusing on counseling and training in their proposal of the Ecological Model of Multicultural Counseling Psychology Processes (EMMCPP), the constructs they used are readily adaptable to examining human development from a perspective in which culture is an integral influence on human behavior. Neville and Mobley also incorporated the individual as a system within the ecological framework, resulting in five interacting systems that influence human development.

The complexity of human identity has been explored in the Identity Salience Model (ISM; Yakushko, Davidson, & Williams, 2009), which is also anchored in Bronfenbrenner's model of development. Responding to the criticism that both multiculturalism and feminism have been marginalized in psychology because of their lack of intersectionality (Silverstein, 2006), Yakushko and colleagues applied ecological theory to the psychotherapy process, explicitly identifiying the ways in which multiple identities might have greater or less salience in the psychotherapy relationship. The ISM also provides promising application for research and theory development beyond psychotherapy (Allen, 2010). Both the ISM and EMMCPP provide a clear link between ecological development theory, counseling psychology tenets, feminism, and multiculturalism. Together, these ideas support a comprehensive framework for understanding the complexity of human development across multiple domains and identities.

Illustrative Case Example: Mikayla

Within the core system of the individual exist multiple social identities, each of which develop and change at different points in time. Imagine the case of Mikayla, a biracial female of divorced parents, currently living with her father and his male partner. Mikayla's mother is Latina and her father and stepfather are both White, of European descent. Mikayla has no known physical or mental disabilities. She and all of her parents identify as Catholic, and they live in a predominantly Jewish neighborhood. Mikayla's family is considered "well-to-do" by community standards, although her parents do not flaunt their wealth. As she grows into adolescence and young adulthood, Mikayla dates both males and females, and eventually identifies as bisexual.

Mikayla's earliest identity may be defined primarily by genetic and heritability factors, such as sex, race, and temperament. However, as she grows and has more social interactions, Mikayla's understanding of her own identity will likely change numerous times. Given the diversity of her family, she may have some understanding of her social identities from a fairly young age, but that cannot be assumed. Nor will these identities stay constant, as she will continuously be influencing and influenced by her social environment. Her identity may change as she encounters a sexist event in middle school (microsystem-individual interaction); might evolve again as she becomes aware of the impact of her family's social class on the way in which teachers respond to her in high school (mesosystem-microsystem-individual interaction); may again change as a young adult when she begins to question the role of sexual orientation and laws about same-sex marriage in her selection of a life partner (exosystem-individual interaction); and may be altered when a woman is elected president of the United States or when the Catholic Church votes to ordain gay priests (macrosystem). Each of these potential system interactions may be enacted in different ways at different points of the life span, as Mikayla becomes a member of the workforce, becomes a parent or chooses not to do so, accesses the health care system, moves out of the workforce, and potentially enters a community living environment as an older adult.

In each of these, and myriad other instances, Mikayla's development is significantly influenced by the ecological systems in which she lives. However, these environments also influence and are influenced by her social identities, which are numerous and vary in salience depending on the situation at hand (Yakushko et al., 2009). The reality of these multiple identities can serve as an exemplar of three core concepts of multicultural feminist theory—intersectionality, self-reflexivity, and accountability (Hurtado, 2010).

The *intersection* of Mikayla's multiple identities strongly influences her process of development, even though a specific aspect of her identity may be more salient at a given moment, such as gender identity in the face of a sexist event. Her understanding of herself in new situations is constantly informed by her recognition (or lack of recognition) of other social identities. Given that these intersecting identities may be at various levels of awareness for Mikayla, this process can produce stress as well as renewed understanding, and the internal conflicts that emerge can either inhibit or promote development. For example, Mikayla's resiliency, or the ability to foster resiliency through empowerment, can provide her with the opportunity to thrive or flourish, following such challenges (O'Leary & Bhaju, 2006).

In general, *self-reflexivity* refers to having an image or representation of one's self. Through a feminist multicultural lens, this includes understanding one's self in the context of a social structure that includes oppression and privilege (Hurtado, 2010). It is important to attend to the reality that individuals are likely to experience social locations in which they both experience oppression and contribute to oppression. Mikayla may experience gender oppression in the context of a sexist or null (Betz, 1989) environment, and may simultaneously be a member of the dominant group if she "passes" as White, is assumed to be heterosexual, or is able to afford a higher education. As Mikayla develops, self-reflexivity will help her become increasingly aware of the system of privilege and oppression, as well as her own position as privileged or oppressed, or both.

Further, Mikayla is impacted by and is impacting the social environment in which she lives, learns, works, and relates to others. As a member of social groups, she becomes *accountable* to the well-being of others, as well as herself. "Accountability assumes that the self is not constituted in the individual; rather it is encased in a body that is socially connected" (Hurtado, 2010, p. 36). As she recognizes her own place in the social environment, and the relationship between community well-being and her own well-being, Mikayla may become empowered to contribute to social change. For example, Mikayla may become more aware and intolerant of homophobia on a national level (exosystem and macrosystem), and more specifically to the lack of response by high school administration and teachers when homophobic slurs are made (microsystem). This awareness could then lead to Mikayla and her father's efforts to establish a gay student association in her high school (individual-microsystem-exosystem interaction).

In this thumbnail sketch of a case example, only a small number of Mikayla's possible identities are acknowledged, and the complexity of her environment is only briefly realized. Yet even within this simplistic scenario, the factors that can either inhibit or promote Mikayla's development are numerous. As pointed out by Lerner (2006), traditional theories of development may have pointed to several sources of risk in Mikayla's development related to factors of social identity: her biracial identity, her father's sexual orientation, her gender, and her religious identity may all have been viewed as potential contributors to Mikayla deviating from successful human development. In contrast, a multicultural feminist perspective on Mikayla's developmental context highlights the potential for strengths to emerge from these same factors, and particularly highlights the value of empowerment and resilience as Mikayla encounters challenges in her ecological system.

Resilience and Empowerment

The variability of social contexts and the complexity inherent in intersectional identities present numerous sources of both strain and strength across the life span. Inevitably, individuals encounter stressors and sources of adversity that have the potential to enhance or impair human development. Whether or not an individual is able to respond effectively to such stressors is often attributed to resiliency, as a personality trait, or resilience, the process of adapting to adverse situations (Luthar, Cicchetti, & Becker, 2000). Enhancing the individual's ability to respond to adversity can be achieved through feminist empowerment-focused interventions (O'Leary & Bhaju, 2006). Both resilience and empowerment are consistent with the strengths-based, contextually informed, life span development approach of counseling psychology, as exemplified by the work of the Society of Counseling Psychology Section for the Advancement of Women (Whalen, Fowler-Lese, Barber, Williams, Judge, Nilsson, & Shibazaki, 2004).

Resilience

The construct of resilience began to receive serious attention in the psychological literature several decades ago, primarily in its application to understanding positive and negative outcomes among groups of at-risk children (Garmezy, 1993; Masten, Best, & Garmezy, 1990; Rutter, 1987). Several models of resilience have been proposed, varying in terms of the relationship between stressors and adaptation. The compensatory model (Garmezy, Masten, & Tellegen, 1984) proposes that compensatory factors (which can take many forms, such as positive attitude, spiritual beliefs, or problem-solving approach to barriers) neutralize the potential negative impact of stressors. In contrast, the challenge model views moderate stressors as potentially enhancing adaptation (Garmezy et al., 1984) as the individual learns from successfully meeting the challenge. The protective factor model (Garmezy et al., 1984) proposes that protective factors can moderate the influence of risk factors to reduce the likelihood of a negative outcome. The reserve capacity model (Gallo & Matthews, 2003) proposes that sociocultural and contextual factors will influence the availability or amount of resources (be they tangible, interpersonal, intrapersonal, or culture-specific) available to either promote or protect health in the face of adversity.

Similarities across these models are apparent when one considers the functions of resilience, which cut across models. These functions, as identified by Rutter (1987), include reducing the impact of risk factors; reducing negative chain reactions; helping to establish and maintain self-identity and self-efficacy; and enhancing opportunities. Through these functions, resilience has significant influence on the interaction of subsystems within the ecological system of human development.

The existence of several models of resilience does highlight an ongoing challenge in clearly defining the term. Resilience as a psychological construct is perhaps most widely understood as a "dynamic process encompassing positive adaptation within the context of significant adversity" (Luthar et al., 2000, p. 543). The explicit inclusion of contextual factors in this definition provides several opportunities for intersection with feminist multicultural perspectives, as does the implicit rejection of pathological and deficit models (O'Leary & Bhaju, 2006). Clauss-Ehlers (2008) noted that "significant differences in the experience of childhood stressors when socioeconomic variables are considered further suggests that overcoming adversity (i.e., resilience) needs to move beyond a mere focus on individual traits to incorporate the ecological context" (p. 209). Drawing from sociology and ecology, as well as cross-cultural psychology, Ungar (2010) recently defined resilience as "the capacity of individuals to access resources that enhance their well-being and the capacity of their physical and social ecologies to make those resources available in meaningful ways" (p. 6). With this expansion, Ungar clearly locates resilience in the interaction of the individual, the exosystem of community, and potentially the macrosystem of the larger society.

RESILIENCE IN A FEMINIST MULTICULTURAL FRAMEWORK

Until quite recently, studies of the development of children in racial/ethnic minority groups tended to focus on negative outcomes and deficiency models (Coll et al., 1996). Consistent with the increasing attention to diversity among developmental theories in general (Lerner & Sternberg, 2009b), current research in resiliency also attends more closely to specific diversity factors as they relate to positive outcomes. The specific contributions of culture to the development of resilience and coping have been explored in a model of cultural resilience developed through the work of Clauss-Ehlers (2003, 2004, 2008) and her colleagues (Clauss-Ehlers, Yang, & Chen, 2006). Cultural resilience includes "a developmental trajectory within a cultural matrix composed of norms, family structure, and peer relationships" (Clauss-Ehlers, 2008, p. 198).

Cultural resilience is supported by empirical evidence that cultural resources, including cultural beliefs, family ties, and social support, are related to resilience among Latino youth (Clauss-Ehlers & Levi, 2002) and adults (Gallo, Penedo, de los Monteros, & Arguelles, 2009), African American girls (Belgrave, Chase-Vaughn, Gray, Addison, & Cherry, 2000), and culturally diverse college women (Clauss-Ehlers et al., 2006). Among diverse college women, Clauss-Ehlers and colleagues (2006) found that a strong engagement with ethnic and gender identity predicted greater resilience in response to stressors, including those related to racial or gender discrimination. In another diverse sample of college women, Clauss-Ehlers (2008) found that sociocultural support, including specific cultural traditions and attributes, was predictive of adaptive coping (or resilience).

The cultural resilience model articulated in developmental psychology is congruent with a counseling psychology emphasis on strengths-based counseling, which assumes, among several other key propositions, that (a) strength is the outcome of a process that includes struggle with adversity; (b) all strengths are based in culture; and (c) that race, class, and gender are integral parts of all experience, including counseling interactions (Smith, 2006). Specifically, Smith has posited that "cross-cultural counseling should focus on clients' cultural and individual strengths rather than on the victimizing effects of racial or ethnic discrimination" (p. 17). In order to meet this goal, Smith proposes ten steps to strengths-based counseling, which include instilling hope, using a solution-oriented framework, empowering clients, and building resilience.

This emphasis on strengths is not intended to overlook the realities of social disparity in the larger cultural context. As Vera and Shin (2006) noted in their response to Smith, health disparities and differences in academic and vocational achievement that disadvantage lower-income people of color may well be due to social context. The authors go on to note that several social toxins, including poverty, limited adult supervision, excessive exposure to television, and limited connection to community, need to be addressed at the environmental, rather than individual, level. They suggest that counseling psychologists can take a more active stand in influencing public policy and advocating for families. Engaging in community outreach and prevention strategies, as well as educating families so that they can advocate for themselves, are all ways of influencing the exo-, meso- and metasystems in which children and families develop. This call to action echoes Bauman (2002), who pointed out the need to intervene at the levels of the environment, the community, the school, and the family in order to foster resilience in children.

While Smith (2006), Vera and Shin (2006), and Bauman (2002) focus their interventions on different levels of the ecological system, their strategies share a common focus on the interaction of the individual with his or her sociopolitical experience. All of them point to the need for counseling psychologists to engage with the larger political and ecological experience of clients, and all describe strategies that empower the client, be that an individual, a family, or a community, to make positive changes.

Empowerment

Empowerment is a key principle of feminist therapeutic approaches, and it plays an important role in the feminist multicultural framework (Cattaneo & Chapman, 2010). It is deeply rooted in social justice efforts, as reflected in McWhirter's 1991 definition:

> The process by which people, organizations or groups who are powerless (a) become aware of the power dynamics at work in their life context, (b) develop the skills and capacity for gaining some reasonable control over their lives, (c) exercise this control without infringing upon the rights of others and (d) support the empowerment of others in their community. (p. 224)

As a therapeutic intervention, empowerment involves helping the individual develop a sense of control over his or her own thoughts, behavior, feelings, and development (Worell & Remer, 2003). Empowerment interventions provide a route to resilience and eventual positive outcomes for individuals who do not inherently identify or utilize the resources that are available to them. Specifically, if an individual who encounters adversity does not know how to access resources to respond to that adversity, empowerment therapy provides interventions to help the individual both recognize and obtain the necessary resources to respond, be they internal or external. Ultimately, the use of empowerment interventions are expected to lead to overcoming adversity, developing resilience, and thriving through positive adaptation (O'Leary & Bhaju, 2006).

"Empowerment" is a popular term that has only recently been systematically located in a model and defined as a complex process by Cattaneo and Chapman (2010), who define empowerment as:

> an iterative process in which a person who lacks power sets a personally meaningful goal oriented toward increasing power, takes action toward that goal, and observes and reflects on the impact of this action, drawing on his or her evolving self-efficacy, knowledge and competence related to the goal. Social context influences all sex process components and the links among them. (p. 647)

A full exploration of this complex definition is beyond the scope of this chapter. However, several key components of this definition resonate with the feminist multicultural perspective and will be relevant throughout the exploration of developmental stages. Of particular importance is the emphasis on recognizing the impact of action taken, which implies that there is change in the individual's social influence as well as intrapsychic change (Cattaneo & Chapman). Further, the social context is explicitly acknowledged as influencing the presence of and access to power. Finally, the emphasis on taking action, recognizing the impact of that action, and drawing on self-efficacy to move forward are all relevant to the process of human change and development, and are inherently part of the growth of individuals from infancy to older adulthood.

Childhood and Adolescence

One way to tell the story of a life consists of using a life span development approach and tracing developmental connections from infancy through childhood and adolescence to adulthood (Miller, 2006). Thus, to understand child and adolescent development from a feminist multicultural perspective, Erikson's (1964) stages of psychosocial development provide a helpful starting point. Sorell and Montgomery (2001) explain, "Erikson proposed that people know who they are through participation in particularized sociohistorical contexts, and the ways in which self-definitions are composed vary across the life span as bodies grow and age and social opportunities, expectations, and responsibilities grow and change" (p. 102). In each of Erikson's stages, the individual faces a particular "crisis" or developmental task. These crises or developmental tasks come to the forefront because of not only changing characteristics of the person, such as biological maturation or deterioration and advancing or declining cognitive skills, but also changing attitudes, behaviors, and expectations of others. For school-age children, these developmental tasks include building a sense of industry as a precursor to a sense of competence. For adolescents, Erikson's primary developmental task is developing a sense of identity. Notably, Erikson's lack of focus on the role of relationships in earlier development has been challenged by Carol Gilligan (1982) and other psychologists who emphasize the centrality of the capacity and desire for relationships to women's development and human development in general (Impett, Sorsoli, Schooler, Henson, & Tolman, 2008).

As previously mentioned, a feminist multicultural perspective draws on the foundation provided by Erikson's life span development approach yet also considers sociocultural factors and the interaction between the individual and the environment. For children and adolescents, the transactional nature of multiple systems undoubtedly affects development (Masten, 2003). Ecological models like Bronfenbrenner's (1977) take into account that youth are nested in families, and families are nested in communities and other systems (Wyche, 2006). Dire economic circumstances, political chaos, or a restricted range of beliefs, roles, and activities may adversely impact development and the opportunity to develop a personal sense of identity (Sorell & Montgomery, 2001). In contrast, families, schools, and communities characterized by caring and support, high expectations, and members' active involvement are protective factors for children. Benard (1991) asserts, "It is only at this intersystem level—and only through intersystem collaboration within our communities—that we can build a broad enough, intense enough network of protection for all children and families" (pp. 19–20).

Physical Development

Many noteworthy physical changes occur during childhood and adolescence. From preschool to school years, improvements in gross motor coordination appear. These changes are followed by refinement in fine motor development and eye-hand coordination (Broderick & Blewitt, 2010). With adolescence comes puberty, the process of sexual maturation, as well as a growth spurt, a rapid increase in size. Puberty takes an average of three to four years to complete. The dramatic physical changes in adolescence tend to begin and end about two years earlier for girls than for boys. There is, however, wide variation among individuals. For example, puberty can happen in as little as 18 months for some girls or can take up to five years for other girls (Piran & Ross, 2006).

By adolescence, some areas of the brain, such as those dealing with motor control and eye-hand coordination, are well-developed. However, other areas, including those in the highest regions of the brain, continue to grow during puberty. Consequently, even when much of the adolescent body has matured into an adult form, the adolescent brain functions differently from an adult brain. Skills like organizing ideas, devising strategies, and managing impulses are not fully developed because the frontal lobes, more specifically the prefrontal cortex, are not fully formed (Broderick & Blewitt, 2010).

During adolescence, it is crucial to promote optimal physical development by way of diet, exercise, and social coping skills. It is equally important to prevent risk behaviors, including drug use, unprotected sex, and violence (Abreu & Newcomb, 2002). Given the timing of adolescence of girls relative to boys, girls are more likely than boys to simultaneously face the physical changes and the transition to middle school or junior high (Broderick & Blewitt, 2010). In addition, it can be challenging for girls to go through puberty due to adverse social forces such as sexual harassment, dating violence, objectification of women's bodies, prejudicial treatment, and discrimination (Piran & Ross, 2006). Indeed, while physical appearance is a concern for both adolescent males and females, the standards for women are relatively more strict, so girls may risk more sanctions for violations (Travis, 2006).

It is important to note that the resources necessary for healthy physical development are not equally accessible to all children and families. For example, correlates of poverty in children include inefficient cardiovascular functioning (Evans & Kim, 2007), decreased likelihood of receiving childhood immunization vaccinations (Centers for Disease Control and Prevention, 2007), and increased likelihood of obesity (Chen & Escarce, 2010). Families with limited access to resources are less likely to be able to afford healthy, organic, or even lean foods, and more likely to have diets that include heavily processed foods. Attending to the intersection of social class and the dietary resources available in the community is critical to understanding potential differences in physical development.

Emotional Development

Emotions such as fear, sadness, happiness, anger, and surprise aid human survival, motivate behavior, serve as a mechanism of communication, and facilitate decision making. The ability to identify and express feelings is one component of social competency that aids healthy development, resilience in the face of risk factors, and overall well-being (Bierman, 2004; Broderick & Blewitt, 2010; Werner, 1990). Interventions designed to foster emotional development often focus on self-esteem. Self-esteem is a person's evaluation of her or his attributes. Moreover, it is the positive or negative emotional valence associated with those attributes. Global self-esteem reflects an individual's perception of personal strengths and limitations considered relative to competent performance in areas of personal importance. This is true during childhood, adolescence, and adulthood. In other words, if a child performs poorly in athletics, the negative impact on self-esteem is greater if sports are important to the youth and less adverse if sports are unimportant. Consequently, a child or adolescent could experience high overall self-esteem even if she or he displays low competence in specific areas. It has been hypothesized that marginalized groups have lower global self-esteem than mainstream groups due to internalization of discriminatory appraisals. Current developmental research, however, does not support this unequivocally. Although findings may vary from individual to individual and group to group, in general, strong racial or ethnic identity is correlated positively with global self-esteem (Broderick & Blewitt, 2010).

Self-esteem tends to decline somewhat during middle childhood and early adolescence because children recognize, often for the first time, that they may fall short in comparison to others. A small, but consistently observed gender difference in self-esteem favors males in late childhood and early adolescence (Broderick & Blewitt, 2010). Nonetheless, recent studies have shown that many girls show a steady increase in self-esteem after the age of 13 over the course of adolescence and young adulthood. For example, Impett and colleagues (2008) assessed adolescent girls' tendencies to silence their own thoughts and feelings. They found that congruence between what girls felt, thought, and did in relational contexts (i.e., relationship authenticity) distinguished girls who experienced an increase in self-esteem during adolescence from those who did not. For the girls in the study, self-esteem was tied to the ability to bring themselves fully and authentically into their relationships with others. This is consistent with feminist psychologists' assertion that relationship authenticity is central to self-esteem and well-being. In Impett and colleagues' study, relationship authenticity predicted increases in self-esteem after ethnicity was taken into account.

Social Development

From their earliest moments, people are social. Babies actively create an attachment system through behaviors that keep a caregiver close or elicit caregiving. Examples of such behaviors include clinging, sucking, and smiling. Attachment systems are essential for social development; they provide ongoing protection and nurture emotional bonds (Broderick & Blewitt, 2010). For children, feeling a sense of belongingness is a need and may be established not only at home with primary caregivers, but also in the context of other microsystems such as school and community groups. A youth's sense of belonging reflects a personally felt, active engagement with, and psychological connection to a group (Baskin, Wampold, Quintana, & Enright, 2010).

Relational capacity or social competency serves as a source of strength and resiliency (Brabeck & Brabeck, 2006; Werner, 1990). Specific skills associated with social competency across different social situations include social participation (joining peers and being comfortable in peer contexts), emotional understanding (identifying and expressing feelings), pro-social behavior (being cooperative), self-control, communication skills, fair play (being a good sport), and social problem-solving skills (Bierman, 2004). A child or adolescent who masters social competency is better equipped to contribute to the well-being of self and others. Thus, social competency facilitates accountability, which is, as discussed earlier, one of the core concepts of multicultural feminist therapy (Hurtado, 2010). A related cognitive-developmental milestone is when children can de-center their thinking, understand that the self and each other person has a perspective, and grasp that the perspectives of self and others may differ (Miller, 2006). In other words, the multicultural feminist core concept of self-reflexivity becomes a possibility (Hurtado, 2010). Notably, to be consistent with an ecological model of development, when there are issues in regard to social development, intervention should include not only individual children, but also the peers with whom they are most likely to interact.

In their classic book, *The Psychology of Sex Differences*, Maccoby and Jacklin (1974) concluded that aggression was the only area within social behavior for which sex differences are fairly well-established. Since then, meta-analyses have found that physical aggression with an onset during toddlerhood is more typical of boys, while relational aggression with an onset during middle childhood is more typical of girls (Broderick & Blewitt, 2010). However, counter to common sex stereotypes, girls have not been found to be more dependent, sociable, or pro-social than boys. According to Bem's gender schema theory (1975, 1983) children's self-concepts become sex-typed when they limit their choices and regulate their behavior to conform to cultural definitions of femaleness or maleness. As a result, Bem encouraged moving beyond gender as a way of responding to the world. Werner (1990) found that during the middle childhood years, resilient youngsters possess a broad spectrum of skills, rather than limiting themselves to behavior governed by traditional gender stereotypes. For instance, resilient girls display autonomy and independence, while resilient boys tend to be emotionally expressive, socially perceptive, and nurturing. Gilligan (1996) emphasized the importance of relationship to human development, and suggested that the fluid interaction of resilience and vulnerability to others fosters development for both boys and girls.

As children grow into adolescents, peers have increasing and significant influence. In early adolescence, friends are often chosen due to similarity in behaviors, attitudes, and identities. In later adolescence, individual differences among peers are more common. Meanwhile, adolescents may spend less time at home and may try to negotiate a more egalitarian relationship in the family context (Piran & Ross, 2006). Parents and caregivers, however, remain an important microsystem. For example, parental warmth or responsiveness is associated with adolescents' self-confidence and social competence, while parental control is associated with adolescents' own ability to exert self-control. Through high levels of monitoring and involvement, adults also may positively influence adolescents' choice of peers (Broderick & Blewitt, 2010).

The complicated nature of the relationships between adolescents, peers, and parents is reflected in the risk and mediating factors related to bullying behaviors. Using an ecological model, Barboza and colleagues (2009) elucidated the ways in which gender, race, social support, parental relationships, teacher relationships, school climate, and school-parent interactions can influence whether or not adolescents participate in or are victims of bullying behavior. Specifically, they found that students who perceive the school atmosphere as unwelcoming, unfair, and unpleasant were more likely to bully. The authors also found that Asian American and African American students were significantly less likely to bully than White students. An important follow-up question, consistent with a feminist multicultural perspective, would be to examine the extent to which discrimination might contribute to social climate factors and increase the likelihood of bullying in a school system. A rash of lesbian, gay, and bisexual (LGB) adolescent suicides in the United States in late 2010 drew national attention to this question, as it increased public awareness of the tragic cost of homophobia and bullying based on sexual orientation (Crary, 2010).

Cognitive and Academic/Vocational Development

Piaget's broad framework for describing and explaining cognitive development is one of the grand psychological theories of the twentieth century (Sorell & Montgomery, 2001). Although the specifics of Piaget's cognitive stages of development have been the subject of debate, his general characterizations of children's abilities are useful. Piaget's assertion that the human mind constructs knowledge is an underlying assumption of much of the current research on cognitive development. As they interact with the environment, children try to fit new information into an existing knowledge structure or an organized way of thinking through the process of assimilation. Then, children engage in the process of accommodation, in which they modify the existing knowledge in order to achieve a better match or fit to the environment (Broderick & Blewitt, 2010). Piaget's focus on human agency and learning is compatible with feminist pedagogy because both see students as active learners and teachers as facilitators of self-directed learning (Miller, 2006).

From the perspective of Erikson's psychosocial stages of development, significant events for children and adolescents include things of an academic or vocational nature (Broderick & Blewitt, 2010). Significant events for children aged 6 to 12 years include learning important academic skills and comparing favorably to peers in the school context. In turn, significant events for adolescents moving toward adulthood include making choices about vocational goals as they strive to establish a sense of identity. The future orientation required to make such choices is something that an adolescent is cognitively capable of doing (Gordon, 1996).

Consistent with a feminist multicultural perspective, counselors and psychologists who work in school settings must watch for and remove barriers to student learning and academic/vocational development. Such barriers include low educator expectations and attitudes, biased curriculum, and other inequities that prevent students from experiencing an environment conducive to learning and achieving at high levels. Advocacy in the school setting takes many forms, including empowering students to become leaders and helping families to navigate the bureaucracy of the school system and to access its resources (Chen-Hayes, Miller, Bailey, Getch, & Erford, 2011).

Although key aspects of physical, emotional, social, and cognitive development each have been highlighted in turn, it is crucial to remember that these factors all come into play and interact when individuals of any age navigate daily life and make decisions. As a case in point, Gordon (1996) examined the prevention of early pregnancy at an inner-city high school and found that many of the participants desired pregnancies; that they preferred single parenthood to traditional family structure; and that they experienced low academic skills and poverty prior to pregnancy. For some, getting pregnant was seen as an intentional decision with a desirable outcome. Thus, a prevention program for sexually active teens who want children would need to focus on helping adolescents develop other alternatives to early childbearing. Meanwhile, a prevention program for adolescents who do not want children would focus more on the provision of knowledge about reproduction and contraception. In short, the more carefully and comprehensively we consider cognitive, social/psychological, and cultural social factors, the better positioned we are to understand and assist children and adolescents.

Young Adulthood

Historically, research on the transition to adulthood focused on the timing and transitions of "markers" of an adult status, like completing school, beginning full-time work, getting married, and becoming a parent (Aronson, 2008). In contrast, the work of Arnett (1997) demonstrated that individuals rely less on the attainment of such life markers and more on intangible, psychological indicators of adulthood, including accepting the consequences of one's actions, making decisions independent of parents or other influences, and becoming financially independent. Viewing adulthood as social construction, Aronson's (2008) research on young women's transition from adolescence to young adulthood revealed how objective transitions, such as marriage, which are often used in life course research, are neither subjectively relevant nor universally applicable. After interviewing 42 young women who were part of the Youth Development Study, Aronson commented, "Young women make sense of their lives through perspectives absorbed from the women's movement. They expect to have fulfilling jobs, support themselves economically, develop their own identities, raise children alone if necessary, and pursue their own goals even when they are in relationships with men. Feminism, in this context, is lived through women's everyday experiences" (pp. 77–78). Some of the young women whom Aronson interviewed incorporated feminist attitudes in their lives through a self-reliant and self-sufficient approach; by "living feminism," the young women crafted their life pathways.

Notably, the majority of girls navigate the transition from girlhood to womanhood with success (Currie, Kelly, & Pomerantz, 2006). Piran and Ross (2006) identified factors that contribute to a positive transition from girlhood to womanhood, such as a sense of physical safety, equitable treatment at home and at school, positive peer and adolescent and adult relationships, and participation in empowering experiences.

Physical Development

The period from about age 18 to 25 may be described as a time of emerging adulthood. Sometime between age 18 and 30, all biological systems reach peak potential. Within that time frame, some systems peak early, such as muscle strength, flexibility, speed of movement, and response. Other systems peak later, such as abilities dependent on control (e.g., arm-hand steadiness, precision, and stamina) and performance dependent on cognitive factors like strategy use. Good habits that help maintain peak or near peak functioning include eating a healthy diet, regularly exercising, not smoking, and refraining from excessive drug and alcohol use (Broderick & Blewitt, 2010).

Emotional Development

Erikson identified two developmental tasks as essential for adulthood adjustment: establishing and strengthening bonds with significant others; and becoming a productive worker. For young adults, the development of intimacy may be reflected in a willingness to commit to affiliations and partnerships with the positive outcome of love (Broderick & Blewitt, 2010). Erikson's theory has been criticized for having an androcentric bias because, in line with a tradition male trajectory, it emphasizes independence over connectedness (Sorell & Montgomery, 2001). Sorell and Montgomery asserted that male and female development can be conceptualized as involving different psychosocial trajectories without considering either gender deviant or inferior. In turn, Langdale (1986) asserted that both men and women possess the capacity to develop independence and agency, as well as the capacity to develop relationality and connectedness.

As gendered beings in a gendered society, males and females face different circumstances and expectations and thus tend to balance independence and connectedness differently. Individual people also differ in the degree to which they are relational. Psychologists are encouraged to facilitate the development of both communal and agentic traits in their clients (Brabeck & Brabeck, 2006). Compared to individuals who adopt more traditional gender-role behaviors, individuals who can function in situations requiring agentic, instrumental behaviors as well as situations needing communal, expressive, and emotionally nurturing behaviors are more likely to have relatively high self-esteem, self-confidence, and low depression (Worell, 2006).

The emphasis on gender differences in committed or intimate relationships has contributed to a socially constructed tendency to overlook the experience of same-sex couples forming relationships in young adulthood. While forming attachments that lead to marriage is seen as a fundamental step in young adult development, the same process of attachment for gay and lesbian couples can be viewed as atypical or even psychologically immature (Roisman, Clausell, Holland, Fortuna, & Elieff, 2008). However, empirical evidence suggests that committed gay and lesbian couples do not differ from married heterosexual couples in terms of their relationship quality or their interactions in conflict resolution (Roisman et al., 2008). This is consistent with extensive research on gay families, which suggests that the children of gay parents experience stability and positive outcomes similar to those of the children of heterosexual parents (American Psychological Association [APA], 2005).

Social Development

Closely tied to emotional development is social development. Two ways of conceptualizing adult social development are the nuclear family tradition and the peer/romantic tradition (Broderick & Blewitt, 2010). The nuclear family tradition examines the degree to which a person's earliest attachments to primary caregivers endure throughout life and how these earliest attachments affect the quality of caregiving provided to the next generation. Consistent with this tradition, young adults develop working models of relationships that allow them to process information about people and to respond quickly. Problems arise if people behave in current relationships in ways that were adaptive in past relationships under very different circumstances. Thus, the challenge is to accommodate to the realities of current relationships.

In contrast, the peer/romantic tradition focuses on the peer attachments of young adults and whether partners have a positive sense of themselves and others, expect others to be available and supportive, and are comfortable with both intimacy and autonomy. Research on adult relationships reveals that women and men define romantic relationships similarly, with the most essential features being trust, caring, honesty, and respect (Brabeck & Brabeck, 2006).

Although it is often overlooked in psychological literature, the role of friendship is also important in adult development. For example, in a study of young adult college students, discussing negative events with an ambivalent friend contributed to higher blood pressure and higher heart rates than discussion with a supportive friend (Holt-Lunstad, Uchino, Smith, & Hicks, 2007), suggesting that the quality of friendships may have an effect on physical well-being.

Cognitive and Academic/Vocational Development

There is some debate as to whether additional thinking skills emerge during young adulthood or whether existing abilities are simply sharpened and honed so that thinking becomes more relativistic. What is certain is that in young adulthood, individuals increasingly face circumstances in which the "right answer" is not pre-established and varies with the circumstances and the perspective of the problem solver. Ill-defined or ill-structured problems include choices regarding educational and career paths. Thus, the ability to stand back and use relative judgment is a major achievement in intellectual development (Schaie & Willis, 2000).

Whether or not young adults pursue college, they share similar goals and face some common expectations of work as a microsystem. College and non-college youth see good pay, opportunities for advancement, and the chance to contribute to society as highly desirable characteristics of a job (Broderick & Blewitt, 2010). After studying the requirements for success in the twenty-first century workplace, Achieve, Inc. (2004), concluded that the knowledge and skills needed for success in the workplace are essentially the same as those needed for success in a post-secondary setting. Entry-level jobs require analytic and literary skills. Problem-solving skills and the ability to work in a team are also essential. Despite common goals and expectations of college and non-college youth, the reality is that education is a key predictor of educational success and career advancement. Thus, an education that ends with high school often limits options and opportunities (Broderick & Blewitt, 2010). This reality is of particular importance in the context of an educational macrosystem that continues to be differentially accessed by people of color. For example, the US Department of Education reports that high school dropout rates differ significantly by race: 4.4% of Asian/Pacific Islander, 4.8% of White, 9.9% of African American, 14.6% of American Indian, and 18.3% of Hispanic 16–24-year-olds were not enrolled in or completing a high school credential in 2008 (U.S. Department of Education, 2010a). Among youth who completed high school, 49.2% of White youth, 40% of African American youth, and 36.7% of Hispanic youth were enrolled in a degree-granting institution in 2008 (U.S. Department of Education, 2010b).

Young adulthood contributes to a person's social location, which in turn influences his or her understanding of self. Miller (2006) comments, "Specifically, each phase opens up new possible experiences, denies access to other experiences and constrains how experiences are understood, in part because people enter different social institutions and cultural discourses in each phase" (p. 446). Ideas from Piaget can inform efforts to explain how a young adult might come to understand the new academic or vocational experiences and, in the process, develop an identity. In line with Piagetian theory, a student or worker initially comes to understand a new experience in terms of what he or she already knows. If this current knowledge system cannot successfully make sense of the educational or employment experience, then she or he experiences conflict or disequilibrium. At that point, the individual actively tries to develop a new level of understanding of school or work that resolves any contradictory beliefs. Equilibrium is experienced after a more complex level of understanding of the academic or vocational experience is attained. The cycle will begin again as this new level of understanding proves partial and imperfect. Continued learning and change are inevitable because the person's new cognitive structure makes him or her aware of other novel aspects of life that must be understood. By coming to understand multiple new experiences over time, she or he gradually constructs a new identity that acknowledges the intersection of an academic or vocational identity with race, ethnicity, social class, sexual orientation, and other selves. Reflecting on this identity development, Miller (2006) asserts, "Over time certain aspects of self become stronger and more prevalent, and others diminish. Thus, a self, identity, ability or skill is multiple, fluid and ever changing; the balance simply shifts" (p. 462).

Middle Adulthood

Perhaps because many early developmental theories attached such great importance to the tasks of childhood, adolescence, and relationship formation, limited attention has been paid to midlife and later adult development (Valsiner, 2006). Erikson did address development across the life span, but his proposals about the developmental crises of adulthood have not been widely explored or researched. One recent and notable exception is a study of two midlife adult cohorts, which tested Erikson's assumptions and concluded that personality continues to develop into and throughout midlife (Whitbourne, Sneed, & Sayer, 2009). This study is consistent with the recent interest in midlife development apparent in the emergence of life span development (Baltes, 1987; Baltes, Lindenberger, & Staudinger, 2006) and life course development (Elder & Shanahan, 2006). Certainly the rich literature on the intersection of vocational and family demands (Schultheiss, 2006), examined by counseling psychologists over several decades, has addressed some aspects of midlife development. Finally, a series of research lines have been launched using the National Survey of Midlife Development in the United States (MIDUS), data collected in the mid-1990s by the John D. and Catherine T. MacArthur Foundation (Brim, Ryff, & Kessler, 2004). While these developments suggest that more attention is being paid to midlife, it continues to be overlooked relative to other stages of life span development.

A closer examination suggests that midlife is frequently a period of life filled with transitions in work, family, relational, and health arenas. Lachman (2004) notes, "Middle-aged adults are linked to the welfare of others, including children, parents, coworkers, other family members, and friends.... At the same time, they are addressing their own needs for meaningful work (paid or unpaid), health and well-being" (pp. 306–307). This tension between caring for others, while also undergoing significant transitions, results in midlife being a dynamic and complex phase of the life cycle. Women continue to assume many of these caregiving tasks, in both their roles as mothers and daughters (Tronto, 1993). Among collective cultures, caregiving burdens in midlife are also more likely to be significant, as there is a greater likelihood that aging parents or grandparents will be cared for by family members than in dominant White culture. For example, Latino families in the United States are less likely to use formal caregiving resources and are more likely to assume care of older family members, with that care often being assumed by women in the family (Ibarra, 2003). The interplay of gender and culture therefore has the potential to have a significant impact on midlife development, although this is again the subject of very limited investigation.

Physical Development

Physical changes in midlife are often viewed negatively and as harbingers to old age. In a culture that is generally identified as youth-oriented, even the earliest signs of age can be viewed as cause for anxiety and worry (Etaugh & Bridges, 2006). A single day of television commercials demonstrates the intense fear of wrinkles, age spots, and sagging skin that is being suggested to the average U.S. citizen. In that context, common middle-age changes such as weight gain and decreased physical activity can be ominous.

Concerns about health and physical conditions are likely to be intensified among adults who are uncertain of access to health care, an area in which social identity contributes to meaningful discrepancies. Midlife women are less likely to have access to health care than older women or men of either age group, and are more likely to report delays in receiving health care, even after controlling for access to insurance (Ng & Scholle, 2010). Disparities can also be found in the effectiveness of health care received, with Black and Hispanic midlife adults (ages 45–65) receiving less effective care than Whites of the same age group (Ng & Scholle).

Midlife physical changes related to sexuality are also notable. Normative physical changes, such as menopause and decreased fertility, are also common in midlife, particularly among women. Men's sexual activity and satisfaction may decrease in the presence of health concerns during midlife, as illness can have a disproportionately high impact on male sexual functioning (Carpenter, Nathanson, & Kim, 2009). While menopause may be viewed as a loss, research has also found that some midlife women experience it as an opportunity for increased freedom in sexual activity (Rossi, 1994). Although the experiences of midlife women of color have been generally under-studied (Etaugh & Bridges, 2006), there is some evidence that ethnicity influences the experience of menopause. Specifically, in a qualitative study of 38 women living in Britain, Wray (2007) found that women of color were less likely to think of menopause as an event or condition requiring medical attention than White women. In the words of one participant, "We don't let it stop us doing anything ... we ignore it" (Wray, 2007, p. 39). This attitude is consistent with feminist perspectives on menopause, which suggest that treating it as a medical event contributes to the stigmatization of women's physical selves.

Although some physical changes at midlife are viewed negatively, it is also important to note that many midlife adults remain very physically active and maintain good health (Etaugh & Bridges, 2006). For example, Finn (2000) notes that women "view midlife as a time of positive change" and are "not willing to let peri-menopausal symptoms disrupt their lives" (p. 354).

Emotional Development

Erikson (1964) identified the primary task of midlife as generativity, the need to care for and give back to the next generation. Current research, drawing on a sample of MIDUS participants, demonstrates that generativity does predict psychological well-being (Rothrauff & Cooney, 2008). Interestingly, no differences were detected between parents and non-parents, suggesting that well-being is associated with caring for the next generation, whether or not that generation is one's own offspring.

Psychological well-being has also been examined in the context of discrimination and sense of control (Jang, Chiriboga, & Small, 2008). Based on a sample of approximately 1,500 from the MIDUS database, the authors concluded that perceived discrimination has a negative impact on psychological well-being, but that this effect can be mediated by a sense of control. Participants with a higher sense of control experienced less impact of perceived discrimination, and those with lower sense of control experienced greater negative affect.

Discrimination has also been connected to psychological well-being among lesbian, gay, and bisexual midlife adults. Also drawing from the MIDUS sample, self-identification as LGB was predictive of lower levels of eudaimonic psychological well-being (Riggle, Rostosky, & Danner, 2009), defined as a sense of personal growth, purpose, meaning, and self-actualization. In this same study, women with less education also had lower levels of well-being. Racial/ethnic minority members, however, had higher levels of eudaimonic psychological well-being. The authors posit that the protective factor of community and family support contributes to this higher level of well-being, and suggest that LGB individuals have less overt community support and so may have less protection from perceived discrimination.

These three studies highlight the important impact of social identity and contextual factors on psychological well-being and emotional development. The impact of discrimination, along with the presence or lack of protective factors moderating that discrimination, may determine emotional health in midlife.

Social Development

Changing social relationships are perhaps among the most significant transitions in midlife. Changes in child, parent, grandparent, spousal, and work relationships are all likely to occur during midlife, bringing with them a multitude of emotions, challenges, and opportunities (Kogan & Vacha-Haase, 2002). As midlife adults adjust to their changing roles in these relationships, they may also be juggling the demands of multiple roles, many of which are changing simultaneously. Although a thorough exploration of all of these potential role changes is beyond the scope of this chapter, a few issues of particular salience are highlighted. For example, it is very likely that midlife adults will be caring for family members in multiple generations.

By the mid-1980s, the need to care for aging parents was identified as a "normative family stress" experience (Brody, 1985) for many midlife individuals. As more and more older adults live longer and develop chronic rather than acute illnesses, the ranks of midlife adults in the "sandwich generation" (Raphael & Schlesinger, 1993) has grown significantly in the first decade of the twenty-first century. While this experience may be normative, it is important not to overlook its stressful aspects. Social support can be particularly important in midlife (Lachman, 2004), helping adults manage the multiple responsibilities they have. Further, the lack of social support can increase stress and contribute to illness (Lachman).

Relationships with children also change during midlife. Midlife parents are not a homogenous group, as their family may include young children, adolescents, or young adults leaving or returning to the family home (Lachman). Negotiating the changing expectations in child-parent relationships as children mature can present midlife adults with significant challenges, and these challenges can be intensified for parents who are also preparing their children to deal with life stressors such as discrimination or limited financial resources. Of particular relevance in the current period of economic downturn, many midlife adults are negotiating living arrangements with their adult children who are staying in or returning to the family home into their twenties and beyond. This interaction of the family microsystem and the macrosystem represented by the economy then becomes a source of interpersonal stress that most parents have not anticipated; the financial security that many people hope to achieve during midlife may be delayed as a result.

Intimate and couple relationships can also experience significant change during midlife, at least partly in response to the additional tension placed on couples by the changes in other family relationships. As men and women enter midlife, their expectations regarding gender roles may change. This is particularly likely to occur if work roles are also changing, especially if partners are unequally engaged in or advancing at work. Especially for heterosexual couples, the continuing gender inequity in the workplace and the division of labor at home continue to present very different challenges for men and women (Kossek & Lambert, 2005). Divorce is also fairly common at midlife, and can result in significant change in economic resources and social status (Smock, Manning, & Gupta, 1999). However, divorce can also be viewed as a positive change, particularly if the marriage relationship has been abusive or restrictive in some way (Rice, 2003). In fact, empowerment to leave such relationships is a significant intervention consistent with feminist theory.

Cognitive and Vocational/Academic Development

Midlife adults who have access to work and educational settings are likely to make valuable cognitive contributions, as they hold important positions in the family and work environments (Lachman, 2004). However, it is important not to overlook the contributions of adults who have not had access to experiences that contribute to cognitive development. Research on cognitive development among adults with lower incomes, for example, is quite limited (Hendrie et al., 2006).

This lack of research is inconsistent with the reality that many non-dominant cultures place high values on the wisdom of midlife and older adults (Assmann, 1994). The discrepancy between measuring cognitive development and wisdom is an example of how the dominant culture influences which research questions are pursued and ultimately disseminated. From a feminist multicultural perspective, the wisdom of midlife and older adults is as valuable as memory and processing speed.

Career development is more fully explored elsewhere in this volume (see chapters 14 and 15), so will be only briefly addressed as a developmental issue. In the original life span approach to career development, Super (1990) identified midlife as a period of maintenance, during which time the worker is primarily focused on keeping his or her skills updated to meet job requirements and to obtain advancement. Most of the career development "action" is seen in the earlier stages leading up to having an established career. However, given the significant career changes and flexibility of most workers (Savickas, 2002), at least in the United States, this period of maintenance can no longer be seen as static. Numerous career transitions, both planned and unplanned, can occur during midlife, with both positive and negative outcomes (Juntunen, Wegner, & Matthews, 2002). Beyond transitions from one job or kind of work to another, midlife adults might also experience a re-commitment to their careers. In fact, Bejian and Salomone (1995) proposed career renewal as a stage worthy of further consideration. Little has been done to follow up on this suggestion empirically, but as attention to midlife development increases, this will be a fruitful area of further study.

Older Adulthood

There is general recognition of the need to attend to the unique issues encountered in older adulthood, if for no other reason than the fact that the percentage of older adults is growing in response to the aging of the Baby Boomer generation. Across psychology, there is increased awareness of the unique issues encountered by older adults, as evidenced by documents such as the American Psychological Association Guidelines for Psychological Practice with Older Adults (APA, 2003). However, the research and theoretical literature in counseling psychology does not convey a clear commitment to issues encountered by older adults. The inclusion of chapters in landmark books such as the *Handbook of Counseling Psychology* have called for greater involvement, and have outlined ways in which counseling psychology can contribute to an understanding of aging through the lens of normative development and adaptation (Hill, Thorn, & Packard, 2000). These opportunities are supported by the fact that there are perspectives on aging that are consistent with the strengths-based approach supported in counseling psychology and feminist multicultural theory, such as successful aging (Rowe & Kahn, 1997) and active aging, a policy framework developed by the World Health Organization 2001.

Despite these opportunities for intersection, there is "disturbingly little representation of older adults" (Werth, Kopera-Frye, Blevins, & Bossick, 2003, p. 803) in the two major journals of counseling psychology. This is certainly inconsistent with the life span focus that is central to the counseling psychology identity, and suggests that our understanding of the developmental needs of older adults may be limited. Given that studies of healthy, active, or successful aging are much less common than studies of age-related decline (Hendrie et al., 2006), this lack of attention by counseling psychology and feminist multicultural theorists is particularly unfortunate. It may, in fact, contribute to the perception that aging is primarily a time of decline and support the idea "that 'successful aging' should be distinguished from 'normal aging'" (Hendrie et al., p. 14).

Physical Development

The emphasis on decline has been refuted by feminist scholars, such as Antonucci, Blieszner, and Denmark (2010), who note that most older Americans remain healthy well into old age and also perceive their own health to be good or better. These authors suggest that the negative stereotypes related to aging (ageism) contribute to the perception that age is associated with ill health, as well as related factors such as sexual activity or interest. It is important to acknowledge that such stereotypes could also be at play among researchers, including psychologists, who make the decisions about which areas of behavior or functioning to examine.

In the Report of the National Institutes of Health's (NIH) Cognitive and Emotional Health Project, Hendrie and colleagues (2006) reviewed 96 published studies that were longitudinal in nature, included samples of at least N = 500 who were 65 years and older, and focused on cognitive or emotional health. They found that poor physical health, including chronic illness, disability, and cardiovascular concerns including hypertension, contributed to both poor cognitive health and poor emotional health. The authors also caution that very few large-scale longitudinal studies have examined questions related to healthy or positive physical development in late adulthood, although there is the capacity to do so with the large databases that exist.

In one notable exception to the emphasis on age-related decline, Bowling (2008) interviewed 279 adults age 65 and older about their perceptions of the construct of active aging. The most common response was maintaining physical health and physical function, including physical exercise, endorsed by 43% of the sample. This was followed by leisure and social activities (34%), mental functioning (18%), and social relationships (15%). Importantly, participants rated physical functioning as equally important, whether they were themselves physically fit or not. This may suggest that frail elders are not aging actively, in their own perception, and could also suggest that these perceptions are influenced by stereotypes that place significant salience on physical functioning over other aspects of active aging.

Emotional Development

Emotional well-being among older adults is related to several sociocultural factors, as well as to indicators of physical and cognitive health. Hendrie and colleagues (2006) found that there was a strong relationship between emotional and cognitive well-being, suggesting either a bidirectional relationship or the possibility that both are affected by some common process. Several contextual factors appear to function as protective factors for emotional well-being, including higher levels of education, higher socioeconomic status, and greater social support (Hendrie et al.). Social engagement has also been shown to be related to psychological well-being among older adults living in assisted living facilities (Park, 2009).

Risk factors for emotional well-being include chronic illness, cardiovascular disease, and a history of mood concerns, including depression and anxiety (Hendrie et al.). There is also some evidence that personality traits influence health-related quality of life. Specifically, neuroticism (as measured by the NEO Five Factor Inventory) contributes to lower self-assessment of health-related quality of life among older adults (Chapman, Duberstein, & Lyness, 2007).

Social Development

Understanding social development, and specifically the changes in social relationships, is particularly important for older adults. Social relationships change significantly as partners, family, and friends die, and as grief becomes a part of the lived experience. The lower life expectancy of men means that, as they grow older, heterosexual women are less likely to be married, as they tend to re-partner less than men following widowhood or the end of relationships. Specifically, the U.S. Census Bureau (2009) reports that 41% of women 65 and older are widowed, compared to 13% of men. However, women are also more likely to have close friends and to rely heavily on social networks. For example, evidence suggests that contacts with social networks increases throughout the first three years following widowhood, and then returns to pre-widowhood levels (Guiaux, Tilburg, & Van Groenou, 2007). Such positive social relationships may serve as a protective factor against stigmatization due to marginalized social identities (Antonucci et al., 2010).

Stigma is also related to social well-being among older LGB adults. Specifically, in a study of Dutch LGB adults aged 55 to 85 years, Kuyper and Fokkema (2010) found that minority stress contributes significantly to the experience of loneliness. Not surprisingly, less loneliness was experienced by participants with steady partners, who had good physical health and high levels of self-esteem. Importantly, the presence of an LGB network also served as a protective factor against loneliness. Past experiences with prejudice and expectations of prejudice from others, including caregivers, contributed to greater feelings of loneliness.

It is also critical to note that much of the literature on aging and relationships is also influenced by assumptions that death, dying, and isolation are the primary areas of concern. However, in a review of literature focused on marriage and aging, several studies found that marital satisfaction and sexual relationships are widely experienced among older adults (Melton, Hersen, Van Sickle, & Van Hasselt, 1995). These authors also noted that there is a significant need for more research in the sexual relationships of older adults, but little has been examined in the 15 years since that call.

The use of social media among older adults is also an area that is significantly understudied by counseling psychology. It is estimated that 46% of adults 65 and older use the Internet (Pew Research Center, August, 2010), and the number of older adult users of social media sites, such as Facebook, is growing more quickly than any other age group (Madden, 2010). Older adults reported that they were increasingly likely to use social media for three major reasons: to reconnect with people from their past, to find online support for managing chronic disease, and to stay involved with other generations, particularly grandchildren (Madden, 2010). This increased use of new technology to support social development is another example of older adulthood having the potential to be a time of renewal, rather than decline.

Cognitive and Vocational/Academic Development

Hendrie and colleagues (2006) found consistent support for the protective factor of education in cognitive health among older adults. This may be due to the role of education in developing a "cognitive reserve" (p. 22). It may also be that education is representative of other protective factors, such as socioeconomic resources and healthier contextual environments. Other protective factors include social engagement, social support, self-efficacy, and cultural factors.

Beyond cognitive ability, some researchers have considered the relationship between age and wisdom, defined as consisting of cognitive reflective and affective dimensions. Specifically, wisdom includes the search for a deeper truth, the ability to engage in self-examination, self-awareness, and self-insight, and the ability to feel greater compassionate love for others (Ardelt, 2003, 2010). In a study that compared older adults to college students, Ardelt (2010) found that older adults with a college education scored higher on a three-dimensional wisdom scale than young adults, and concluded that wisdom may increase over time due to learning from life experiences, at least among those with the opportunity and motivation to pursue wisdom. These findings acknowledge both the potential benefit of age in cognitive development, and the importance of contextual factors that support the development of wisdom.

Conclusion

The ecological systems theory (Bronfenbrenner) provides a culturally and contextually informed perspective on the complexities of human development. In the preceding pages, we have attempted to infuse feminist multicultural analysis of key developmental issues, including the role of resilience and empowerment, an emphasis on social support and networks, and a recognition of the stress related to identity and sociocultural status. It is important to note that there is significantly more empirical and theoretical support for this infusion when discussing childhood and adolescence. However, a feminist multicultural understanding of development in adulthood remains relatively limited.

Future Directions

1. There is a significant need for feminist multicultural counseling psychologists to attend more fully to the psychological well-being, relational needs, and optimal functioning of older adults.
2. The cross-cutting impact of socioeconomic status on most domains of development needs to be more fully addressed and integrated into feminist multicultural research.
3. The role of sexual orientation is only sporadically considered in developmental research. This is an area in which culturally competent counseling psychology researchers could make a significant and systematic impact, by considering the interaction of identity development models with other developmental processes.
4. Analyzing development from a strengths-based model of counseling psychology can contribute to increased recognition of positive development over time, which would potentially

mitigate some of the bias toward decline present in current aging literature.

References

Abreu, J. M., & Newcomb, M. D. (2002). Promoting healthy lifestyles among adolescents. In C.L. Juntunen & D. R. Atkinson (Eds.). *Counseling across the lifespan* (pp. 93–111). Thousand Oaks, CA: Sage.

Achieve, Inc. (2004). *American Diploma Project: Ready or not, creating a high school diploma that counts.* Washington, DC: Author.

Allen, L. (2010). The identity salience model: Self-imposed limitations and potential contributions. *Counselling Psychology Review, 25*(4), 56–64.

American Psychological Association (2003). Guidelines for psychological practice with older adults. Author: Washington, DC. Retrieved from http://www.apa.org/practice/guidelines/older-adults.pdf.

American Psychological Association (2005). *Lesbian and gay parenting.* Washington, DC: Author.

Antonucci, T. C., Blieszner, R., & Denmark, F. L. (2010). Psychological perspectives on older women. In H. Landrine, N. Russo, H. Landrine, N. Russo (Eds.), *Handbook of diversity in feminist psychology* (pp. 233–257). New York: Springer Publishing.

Ardelt, M. (2003). Empirical assessment of a three-dimensional wisdom scale. *Research on Aging, 25*(3), 275–324. doi:10.1177/0164027503025003004

Ardelt, M. (2010). Are older adults wiser than college students? A comparison of two age cohorts. *Journal of Adult Development, 17*(4), 193–207. doi:10.1007/s10804-009-9088-5

Arnett, J. J. (1997). Young people's conceptions of the transition to adulthood. *Youth and Society, 29*, 3–23.

Aronson, P. (2008). The markers and meanings of growing up: Contemporary young women's transitions from adolescence to adulthood. *Gender and Society, 22*(1) 56–82. doi: 10.1177/089124307311420

Assmann, A. (1994). Wholesome knowledge: Concepts of wisdom in a historical and cross-cultural perspective. In D. L. Featherman, R. M. Lerner, M. Perlmutter, D. L. Featherman, R. M. Lerner, M. Perlmutter (Eds.), *Life-span development and behavior,* Vol. 12 (pp. 187–224). Hillsdale, NJ: Lawrence Erlbaum Associates.

Baltes, P. B. (1987). Theoretical propositions of life-span developmental psychology: On the dynamics between growth and decline. *Developmental Psychology, 23*(5), 611–626. doi:10.1037/0012-1649.23.5.611

Baltes, P. B., Lindenberger, U., & Staudinger, U. M. (2006). Life Span Theory in Developmental Psychology. In R. M. Lerner, W. Damon, R. M. Lerner, W. Damon (Eds.), *Handbook of child psychology* (6th ed.): Vol. 1, *Theoretical models of human development* (pp. 569–664). Hoboken, NJ: John Wiley & Sons.

Barboza, G. E., Schiamberg, L. B., Oehmke, J., Korzeniewski, S. J., Post, L. A., & Heraux, C. G. (2009). Individual characteristics and the multiple contexts of adolescent bullying: An ecological perspective. *Journal of Youth and Adolescence, 38*(1), 101–121. doi:10.1007/s10964-008-9271-1

Baskin, T. W., Wampold, B. E., Quintana, S. M., & Enright, R. D. (2010). Belongingness as a protective factor against loneliness and potential depression in a multicultural middle school. *The Counseling Psychologist, 38*, 626–651.

Bauman, S. (2002). Fostering resilience in children. In C. L. Juntunen, D. R. Atkinson, C. L. Juntunen, D. R. Atkinson (Eds.), *Counseling across the lifespan: Prevention and treatment* (pp. 42–55). Thousand Oaks, CA: Sage Publications.

Bejian, D. V., & Salomone, P. R. (1995). Understanding midlife career renewal: Implications for counseling. *The Career Development Quarterly, 44*(1), 52–63.

Belgrave, F. Z., Chase-Vaughn, G., Gray, F., Addison, J., & Cherry, V. R. (2000).The effectiveness of a culture- and gender-specific intervention for increasing resiliency among African American preadolescent females. *Journal of Black Psychology, 26*(2), 133–147. doi:10.1177/0095798400026002001

Bem, S. L. (1975). Sex role adaptability: One consequence of sexual androgyny. *Journal of Counseling and Clinical Psychology, 45,* 196–225.

Bem, S. L. (1983). Gender schema theory and its implications for child development: Raising gender-aschematic children in a gender-schematic society. *Signs, 8*, 598–616.

Benard, B. (1991). *Fostering resiliency in kids: Protective factors in the family, school and community.* Portland, OR: Northwest Regional Laboratory.

Betz, N. E. (1989). Implications of the null environment hypothesis for women's career development and for counseling psychology. *The Counseling Psychologist, 17*(1), 136–144. doi:10.1177/0011000089171008

Bierman, K. L. (2004). *Peer rejection: Developmental processes and intervention.* New York: Guilford Press.

Bowling, A. (2008). Enhancing later life: How older people perceive active ageing? *Aging and Mental Health, 12*(3), 293–301. doi:10.1080/13607860802120979

Brabeck, M. M., & Brabeck, K. M. (2006). Women and relationships. In J. Worrell & C. D. Goodheart (Eds.), *Handbook of girls' and womens' psychological health: Gender and well-being across the lifespan* (pp. 208–217). New York: Oxford University Press.

Brim, O., Ryff, C. D., & Kessler, R. C. (2004). The MIDUS National Survey: An overview. In O. Brim, C. D. Ryff, R. C. Kessler, O. Brim, C. D. Ryff, R. C. Kessler (Eds.), *How healthy are we?: A national study of well-being at midlife* (pp. 1–34). Chicago: University of Chicago Press.

Broderick, P. C., & Blewitt, P. (2010). The life span: Human development for helping professionals (3rd ed.). Boston: Pearson.

Brody, E. M. (1985). Parent care as a normative family stress. *The Gerontologist, 25*(1), 19–29.

Bronfenbrenner, U. (1977). Toward an experimental ecology of human development. *American Psychologist, 32*(7), 513–531. doi:10.1037/0003-066X.32.7.513

Bronfenbrenner, U. (1993). The ecology of cognitive development: Research models and fugitive findings. In R. H. Wozniak, K. W. Fischer, R. H. Wozniak, & K. W. Fischer (Eds.), *Development in context: Acting and thinking in specific environments* (pp. 3–44). Hillsdale, NJ England: Lawrence Erlbaum Associates, Inc.

Bronfenbrenner, U., & Morris, P. A. (2006). The bioecological model of human development. In R. M. Lerner, W. Damon, R. M. Lerner, W. Damon (Eds.), *Handbook of child psychology* (6th ed.): Vol. 1, *Theoretical models of human development* (pp. 793–828). Hoboken, NJ: John Wiley & Sons.

Carpenter, L. M., Nathanson, C. A., & Kim, Y. J. (2009). Physical women, emotional men: Gender and sexual satisfaction in midlife. *Archives of Sexual Behavior, 38*(1), 87–107. doi:10.1007/s10508-007-9215-y

Cattaneo, L. B., & Chapman, A. R. (2010). The process of empowerment: A model for use in research and practice. *American Psychologist, 65*(7), 646–659. doi:10.1037/a0018854

Centers for Disease Control and Prevention (August 2007). Nation's childhood immunization rates remain at or above record levels. Retrieved from http://www.cdc.gov/media/pressrel/2007/r070830.htm.

Chapman, B., Duberstein, P., & Lyness, J. M. (2007). Personality traits, education, and health-related quality of life among older adult primary care patients. *The Journals of Gerontology: Series B: Psychological Sciences and Social Sciences, 62B*(6), P343–P352.

Chen A. Y. & Escarce, J. J. (May 2010). Family structure and childhood obesity, Early Childhood Longitudinal Study—Kindergarten Cohort. *Preventing Chronic Disease, 7*(3). Retrieved from http://www.cdc.gov/pcd/issues/2010/may/09_0156.htm.

Chen-Hayes, S. G., Miller, E. M., Bailey, D. F., Getch, Y. Q., & Erford, B. T. (2011). Leadership and achievement advocacy for every student. In B. T. Erford (Ed.), *Transforming the school counseling profession* (pp. 110–128). Upper Saddle River, NJ: Pearson.

Clauss-Ehlers, C. C. (2003). Promoting ecologic health resilience for minority youth: Enhancing health care access through the school health center. *Psychology in the Schools, 40*(3), 265–278. doi:10.1002/pits.10086

Clauss-Ehlers, C. S., & Levi, L. (2002). Violence and community, terms in conflict: An ecological approach to resilience. *Journal of Social Distress and the Homeless, 11*(4), 265–278. doi:10.1023/A:1016804930977

Clauss-Ehlers, C. S. (2004). A framework for school-based mental health promotion with bicultural Latino children: Building on strengths to promote resilience. *The International Journal of Mental Health Promotion, 6*(2), 26–33.

Clauss-Ehlers, C. S., Yang, Y. T., & Chen, W. C. (2006). Resilience from childhood stressors: The role of cultural resilience, ethnic identity, and gender identity. *Journal of Infant, Child, and Adolescent Psychotherapy, 5*, 124–138.

Clauss-Ehlers, C. S. (2008). Sociocultural factors, resilience, and coping: Support for a culturally sensitive measure of resilience. *Journal of Applied Developmental Psychology, 29*(3), 197–212. doi:10.1016/j.appdev.2008.02.004

Coll, C. G., Crnic, K., Lamberty, G., & Wasik, B. (1996). An integrative model for the study of developmental competencies in minority children. *Child Development, 67*(5), 1891–1914. doi:10.2307/1131600

Crary, D. (October 9, 2010). Suicide surge: Schools confront anti-gay bullying. Associated Press. Retrieved from http://www.msnbc.msn.com/id/39593311/ns/us_news-life/.

Currie, D. H., Kelly, D. M., & Pomerantz, S. (2006). 'The geeks shall inherit the earth': Girls' agency, subjectivity, and empowerment. *Journal of Youth Studies, 9*(4), 419–436. Doi:10.1080/13676260600914416

Elder, G. R., & Shanahan, M. J. (2006). The Life Course and Human Development. In R. M. Lerner, W. Damon, R. M. Lerner, W. Damon (Eds.), *Handbook of child psychology* (6th ed.): Vol. 1, *Theoretical models of human development* (pp. 665–715). Hoboken, NJ: John Wiley & Sons.

Enns, C. Z. (2010). Locational feminisms and feminist social identity analysis. *Professional Psychology: Research and Practice, 41*(4), 333–339. doi:10.1037/a0020260

Erikson, E. H. (1964). *Childhood and society* (2nd ed.). Oxford: W. W. Norton.

Etaugh, C. A., & Bridges, J. S. (2006). Midlife transitions. In J. Worell, C. D. Goodheart, J. Worell, C. D. Goodheart (Eds.), *Handbook of girls' and women's psychological health: Gender and well-being across the lifespan* (pp. 359–367). New York: Oxford University Press.

Evans, G. W., & Kim, P. (2007). Childhood poverty and health: Cumulative risk exposure and stress dysregulation. *Psychological Science, 18*(11), 953–957. doi:10.1111/j.1467-9280.2007.02008.x

Finn, S. C. (2000). Women in midlife: A nutritional perspective. *Journal of Women's Health and Gender-Based Medicine, 9*(4), 351–356. doi:10.1089/15246090050020655

Gallo, L. C., & Matthews, K. A. (2003). Understanding the association between socioeconomic status and physical health: Do negative emotions play a role? *Psychological Bulletin, 129*(1), 10–51. doi:10.1037/0033-2909.129.1.10

Gallo, L. C., Penedo, F. J., de los Monteros, K., & Arguelles, W. (2009). Resiliency in the face of disadvantage: Do Hispanic cultural characteristics protect health outcomes? *Journal of Personality, 77*(6), 1707–1746. doi:10.1111/j.1467–6494.2009.00598.x

Garmezy, N., Masten, A. S., & Tellegen, A. (1984). The study of stress and competence in children: A building block for developmental psychopathology. *Child Development, 55*(1), 97–111. doi:10.2307/1129837

Garmezy, N. (1993). Vulnerability and resilience. In D. C. Funder, R. D. Parke, C. Tomlinson-Keasey, K. Widaman, D. C. Funder, R. D. Parke, ... K. Widaman (Eds.), *Studying lives through time: Personality and development* (pp. 377–398). Washington, DC: American Psychological Association. doi:10.1037/10127-032

Gilligan, C. (1982). *In a different voice.* Cambridge, MA: Harvard University Press.

Gilligan, C. (1996). The centrality of relationship in human development: A puzzle, some evidence, and a theory. In G. G. Noam, K. W. Fischer, G. G. Noam, K. W. Fischer (Eds.), *Development and vulnerability in close relationships* (pp. 237–261). Hillsdale, NJ: Lawrence Erlbaum Associates.

Gordon, C. P. (1996). Adolescent decision making: A broadly based theory and its application to the prevention of early pregnancy. *Adolescence, 31*, 561–584.

Guiaux, M., van Tilburg, T., & van Groenou, M. (2007). Changes in contact and support exchange in personal networks after widowhood. *Personal Relationships, 14*(3), 457–473. doi:10.1111/j.1475-6811.2007.00165.x

Hendrie, H. C., Albert, M. S., Butters, M. A., Gao, S., Knopman, D. S., Launer, L. J., Yaffe, K., Cuthbert, B. N., Edwards, E., & Wagster, M. V. (2006). The NIH Cognitive and Emotional Health Project: Report of the Critical Evaluation Study Committee. *Alzheimer's and Dementia, 2*(1), 12–32. doi:10.1016/j.jalz.2005.11.004

Hill, R. D., Thorn, B. L., & Packard, T. (2000).Counseling older adults: Theoretical and empirical issues in prevention and intervention. In S. D. Brown, R. W. Lent, S. D. Brown, R. W. Lent (Eds.), *Handbook of counseling psychology* (3rd ed.) (pp. 499–531). Hoboken, NJ: John Wiley & Sons.

Holt-Lunstad, J., Uchino, B. N., Smith, T. W., & Hicks, A. (2007). On the importance of relationship quality: The impact of ambivalence in friendships on cardiovascular functioning. *Annals of Behavioral Medicine, 33*(3), 278–290. doi:10.1007/BF02879910

Hurtado, A. (2010). Multiple lenses: Multicultural feminist theory. In H. Landrine, N. Russo (Eds.), *Handbook of diversity in feminist psychology* (pp. 29–54). New York: Springer Publishing.

Ibarra, M. L. (2003). The tender trap: Mexican immigrant women and the ethics of elder care work. *Aztlan: A Journal of Chicano Studies, 28*, 87–113.

Impett, E. A., Sorsoli, L., Schooler, D., Henson, J. M., & Tolman, D. L. (2008). Girls' relational authenticity and self-esteem across adolescence. *Developmental Psychology, 44*, 722–733.

Jang, Y., Chiriboga, D. A., & Small, B. J. (2008). Perceived discrimination and psychological well-being: The mediating and moderating role of sense of control. *The International Journal of Aging and Human Development, 66*(3), 213–227. doi:10.2190/AG.66.3.c

Jordan, J. V., Kaplan, A. G., Miller, J., Stiver, I. P., & Surrey, J. L. (1991). *Women's growth in connection: Writings from the Stone Center*. New York: Guilford Press.

Juntunen, C. L., Wegner, K. E., & Matthews, L. G. (2002). Promoting positive career change in midlife. In C. L. Juntunen, D. R. Atkinson, C. L. Juntunen, D. R. Atkinson (Eds.), *Counseling across the lifespan: Prevention and treatment* (pp. 329–347). Thousand Oaks, CA: Sage Publications.

Kogan, L. R., & Vacha-Haase, T. (2002). Supporting adaptation to new family roles in middle age. In C. L. Juntunen, D. R. Atkinson, C. L. Juntunen, D. R. Atkinson (Eds.), *Counseling across the lifespan: Prevention and treatment* (pp. 299–327). Thousand Oaks, CA: Sage Publications.

Kohlberg, L. (1963). The development of children's orientations toward a moral order: I. Sequence in the development of moral thought. *Vita Humana, 6*(1–2), 11–33. Retrieved from http://ezproxy.library.und.edu/login?url=http://search.ebscohost.com.ezproxy.library.und.edu/login.aspx?direct=true&db=psyh&AN=1964-05739-001&site=ehost-live&scope=site.

Kossek, E. (Ed.), & Lambert, S. (Ed.). (2005). *Work and life integration: Organizational, cultural, and individual perspectives*. Mahwah, NJ: Lawrence Erlbaum Associates.

Kuyper, L., & Fokkema, T. (2010). Loneliness among older lesbian, gay, and bisexual adults: The role of minority stress. *Archives of Sexual Behavior, 39*(5), 1171–1180. doi:10.1007/s10508-009-9513-7

Lachman, M. E. (2004). Development in midlife. *Annual Review of Psychology, 55*, 305–331. doi:10.1146/annurev.psych.55.090902.141521

Landrine, H. (Ed.) (1995). *Bringing cultural diversity to feminist psychology: Theory, research, and practice*. Washington, DC: American Psychological Association.

Langdale, C. J. (1986). A revision of structural-developmental theory. In G. L. Sapp (Ed.), *Handbook of moral development: Models, processes, techniques and research* (pp. 15–54). Birmingham, AL: Religious Education.

Lerner, R. (Ed.), & Steinberg, L. (Ed.). (2009a). *Handbook of adolescent psychology*, Vol. 2: *Contextual influences on adolescent development* (3rd ed.). Hoboken, NJ: John Wiley & Sons.

Lerner, R. M. (2002). *Concepts and theories of human development* (3rd ed.). Mahwah, NJ: Lawrence Erlbaum Associates.

Lerner, R. M. (2006). Developmental science, developmental systems, and contemporary theories of human development. In R. M. Lerner, W. Damon, R. M. Lerner, W. Damon (Eds.), *Handbook of child psychology* (6th ed.): Vol. 1, *Theoretical models of human development* (pp. 1–17). Hoboken, NJ: John Wiley & Sons.

Lerner, R. M., & Steinberg, L. (2009b). The scientific study of adolescent development: Historical and contemporary perspectives. In R. M. Lerner, L. Steinberg, R. M. Lerner, L. Steinberg (Eds.), *Handbook of adolescent psychology*, Vol. 1: *Individual bases of adolescent development* (3rd ed.) (pp. 3–14). Hoboken, NJ: John Wiley & Sons.

Luthar, S. S., Cicchetti, D., & Becker, B. (2000). The construct of resilience: A critical evaluation and guidelines for future work. *Child Development, 71*(3), 543–562. doi:10.1111/1467-8624.00164

Maccoby, E. E., & Jacklin, J. A. (1974). *The psychology of sex differences*. Stanford, CA: Stanford University Press.

Madden, M. (August, 2010). *Older adults and social media: Social networking use among those ages 50 and older nearly doubled over the past year.* Pew Internet and American Life Project, A Project of the Pew Research Center. Retrieved from http://www.pewinternet.org/~/media//Files/Reports/2010/Pew%20Internet%20-%20Older%20Adults%20and%20Social%20Media.pdf

Masten, A. (2003). *Commentary: Developmental psychopathology as a unifying context for mental health and education models, research and practice in schools.* Bethesda, MD: National Association of School Psychologists.

Masten, A. S., Best, K. M., & Garmezy, N. (1990). Resilience and development: Contributions from the study of children who overcome adversity. *Development and Psychopathology, 2*(4), 425–444. doi:10.1017/S0954579400005812

McWhirter, E. H. (1991). Empowerment in counseling. *Journal of Counseling and Development, 69*(3), 222–227.

Melton, M. A., Hersen, M., Van Sickle, T. D., & Van Hasselt, V. B. (1995). Parameters of marriage in older adults: A review of the literature. *Clinical Psychology Review, 15*(8), 891–904. doi:10.1016/0272-7358(95)00051-8

Miller, P. H. (2006). Contemporary perspectives from human development: Implications for feminist scholarship. *Signs: Journal of Women in Culture and Society, 31*(2), 445–469.

Neville, H. A., & Mobley, M. (2001). Social identities in contexts: An ecological model of multicultural counseling psychology processes. *The Counseling Psychologist, 29*(4), 471–486. doi:10.1177/0011000001294001

Ng, J., & Scholle, S.H. (May, 2010). Disparities in quality of care for midlife adults (ages 45–64) versus older adults (ages ≥ 65). Report prepared under contract from the Agency for Healthcare Research and Quality and the Office of the Assistant Secretary for Planning and Evaluation. Washington, DC: National Committee for Quality Assurance. Retrieved from http://aspe.hhs.gov/health/reports/2010/qualcare/report.pdf.

O'Leary, V. E., & Bhaju, J. (2006). Resilience and empowerment. In J. Worell, C. D. Goodheart, J. Worell, C. D. Goodheart (Eds.), *Handbook of girls' and women's psychological health: Gender and well-being across the lifespan* (pp. 157–165). New York: Oxford University Press.

Park, N. (2009). The relationship of social engagement to psychological well-being of older adults in assisted living facilities. *Journal of Applied Gerontology, 28*(4), 461–481. doi:10.1177/0733464808328606

Pew Research Center (December 2010). *Trend Data: Demographics of internet users.* Retrieved from http://pewinternet.org/Trend-Data/Whos-Online.aspx

Piaget, J. J. (1926). *The language and thought of the child.* Oxford: Harcourt, Brace.

Piran, N., & Ross, E. (2006). From girlhood to womanhood: Multiple transitions in context. In J. Worrell & C. D.

Goodheart (Eds.), *Handbook of girls' and womens' psychological health: Gender and well-being across the lifespan* (pp. 301–310). New York: Oxford University Press.

Raphael, D., & Schlesinger, B. (1993). Caring for elderly parents and adult children living at home. *Social Work Research and Abstracts, 29*, 3–10.

Rice, J. K. (2003). 'I can't go back': Divorce as adaptive resistance. In L. B. Silverstein, T. Goodrich, L. B. Silverstein, T. Goodrich (Eds.), *Feminist family therapy: Empowerment in social context* (pp. 51–63). Washington, DC: American Psychological Association. doi:10.1037/10615-004

Riggle, E. B., Rostosky, S. S., & Danner, F. (2009). LGB identity and eudaimonic well being in midlife. *Journal of Homosexuality, 56*(6), 786–798. doi:10.1080/00918360903054277

Roisman, G. I., Clausell, E., Holland, A., Fortuna, K., & Elieff, C. (2008). Adult romantic relationships as contexts of human development: A multimethod comparison of same-sex couples with opposite-sex dating, engaged, and married dyads. *Developmental Psychology, 44*(1), 91–101. doi:10.1037/0012-1649.44.1.91

Rossi, A. S. (1994). Eros and caritas: A biopsychosocial approach to human sexuality and reproduction. In A. S. Rossi, A. S. Rossi (Eds.), *Sexuality across the life course* (pp. 3–36). Chicago: University of Chicago Press.

Rothrauff, T., & Cooney, T. M. (2008). The role of generativity in psychological well-being: Does it differ for childless adults and parents? *Journal of Adult Development, 15*(3–4), 148–159. doi:10.1007/s10804-008-9046-7

Rowe, J. W., & Kahn, R. L. (1997).Successful aging. *The Gerontologist, 37*(4), 433–440.

Russo, N., & Landrine, H. (2010). Overview: Diversity in feminist psychology. In H. Landrine, N. Russo (Eds.), *Handbook of diversity in feminist psychology* (pp. 3–27). New York: Springer Publishing.

Rutter, M. (1987). Psychosocial resilience and protective mechanisms. *American Journal of Orthopsychiatry, 57*(3), 316–331. Retrieved from http://ezproxy.library.und.edu/login?url=http://search.ebscohost.com/login.aspx?direct=true&db=psyh&AN=1987-34476-001&site=ehost-live&scope=site.

Savickas, M. L. (2002). Reinvigorating the study of careers. *Journal of Vocational Behavior, 61*(3), 381–385. doi:10.1006/jvbe.2002.1880

Schaie, K. W. & Willis, S. L. (2000). A stage theory model of adult cognitive development revisited. In R. L. Rubinstein, M. Moss, & M. H. Kleban (Eds). *The many dimensions of aging* (pp. 175–193). New York: Springer.

Schultheiss, D. E. P. (2006). The interface of work and family life. *Professional Psychology: Research and Practice, 37*(4), 334–341. doi:10.1037/0735-7028.37.4.334

Silverstein, L. (2006). Integrating feminism and multiculturalism: Scientific fact or science fiction? *Professional Psychology: Research and Practice, 37*(1), 21–28. doi:10.1037/0735-7028.37.1.21

Smith, E. J. (2006). The strength-based counseling model. *The Counseling Psychologist, 34*(1), 13–79. doi:10.1177/0011000005277018

Smock, P. J., Manning, W. D., & Gupta, S. (1999). The effect of marriage and divorce on women's economic well-being. *American Sociological Review, 64*, 794–812.

Sorell, G. T., & Montgomery, M. J. (2001). Feminist perspectives on Erikson's theory: Their relevance for contemporary identity development research. *Identity: An InternationalJournal of Theory and Research, 1*(2), 97–128.

Spencer, M. (2006). Phenomenology and ecological systems theory: Development of diverse groups. In R. M. Lerner, W. Damon, R. M. Lerner, W. Damon (Eds.), *Handbook of child psychology* (6th ed.): Vol. 1, *Theoretical models of human development* (pp. 829–893). Hoboken, NJ: John Wiley & Sons.

Super, D. E. (1990). A life-span, life-space approach to career development. In D. Brown, L. Brooks (Eds.), *Career choice and development: Applying contemporary theories to practice* (2nd ed.) (pp. 197–261). San Francisco, CA: Jossey-Bass.

Travis, C. B. (2006). Risks to healthy development: The somber planes of life. In J. Worrell & C. D. Goodheart (Eds.), *Handbook of girls' and womens' psychological health: Gender and well-being across the lifespan* (pp. 15–23). New York: Oxford University Press.

Tronto, J. (1993). *Moral boundaries: A political argument for an ethic of care*. New York: Routledge.

Ungar, M. (2010). What is resilience across cultures and contexts? Advances to the theory of positive development among individuals and families under stress. *Journal Of Family Psychotherapy, 21*(1), 1–16. doi:10.1080/08975351003618494

U.S. Census Bureau (2009). *America's families and living arrangements: 2009*. Washington, D.C: U.S. Census Bureau. Retrieved from http://www.census.gov/population/www/socdemo/hh-fam/cps2009.html

U.S. Department of Education, National Center for Education Statistics. (2010a). *The Condition of Education 2010* (NCES 2010–028). Retrieved from http://nces.ed.gov/fastfacts/display.asp?id=16.

U.S. Department of Education, National Center for Education Statistics. (2010b). *Digest of Education Statistics*. (Table 204). Retrieved from http://nces.ed.gov/programs/digest/d09/tables/dt09_204.asp.

Valsiner, J. (2006). Developmental epistemology and implications for methodology. In R. M. Lerner, W. Damon, R. M. Lerner, W. Damon (Eds.), *Handbook of child psychology* (6th ed.): Vol. 1, *Theoretical models of human development* (pp. 166–209). Hoboken, NJ: John Wiley & Sons.

Vera, E. M., & Shin, R. Q. (2006). Promoting strengths in a socially toxic world: Supporting resiliency with systemic interventions. *The Counseling Psychologist, 34*(1), 80–89. doi:10.1177/0011000005282365

Werner, E. E. (1990). Protective factors and individual resilience. In S. J. Meisels & J. P. Shonkoff (Eds.), *Handbook of early childhood intervention* (pp. 97–116). New York: Cambridge University Press.

Werth, J. R., Kopera-Frye, K., Blevins, D., & Bossick, B. (2003). Older adult representation in the counseling psychology literature. *The Counseling Psychologist, 31*(6), 789–814. doi:10.1177/0011000003258391

Whalen, M., Fowler-Lese, K., Barber, J. S., Williams, E. N., Judge, A. B., Nilsson, J. E., & Shibazaki, K. (2004). Counseling practice with feminist-multicultural perspectives. *Journal of Multicultural Counseling and Development, 32*, 379–389. Retrieved from http://ezproxy.library.und.edu/login?url=http://search.ebscohost.com/login.aspx?direct=true&db=psyh&AN=2005-00106-012&site=ehost-live&scope=site.

Whitbourne, S., Sneed, J. R., & Sayer, A. (2009). Psychosocial development from college through midlife: A 34-year sequential study. *Developmental Psychology, 45*(5), 1328–1340. doi:10.1037/a0016550

Worell, J., & Remer, P. (2003). *Feminist perspectives in therapy: Empowering diverse women* (2nd ed.). Hoboken, NJ: John Wiley & Sons.

Worell, J. (2006). Pathways to healthy development: Sources of strength and empowerment. In J. Worrell & C. D. Goodheart (Eds.), *Handbook of girls' and womens' psychological health: Gender and well-being across the lifespan* (pp. 25–35). New York: Oxford University Press.

Wray, S. (2007). Women making sense of midlife: Ethnic and cultural diversity. *Journal of Aging Studies, 21*(1), 31–42. doi:10.1016/j.jaging.2006.03.001

Wyche, K. F. (2006). Healthy environments for youth and families. In J. Worrell & C. D. Goodheart (Eds.), *Handbook of girls' and womens' psychological health: Gender and well-being across the lifespan* (pp. 218–227). New York: Oxford University Press.

Yakushko, O., Davidson, M. M., & Williams, E. (2009). Identity salience model: A paradigm for integrating multiple identities in clinical practice. *Psychotherapy: Theory, Research, Practice, Training*, 46(2), 180–192. doi:10.1037/a0016080

CHAPTER

4 Gender and Mental Health in Ecological/Sociocultural Context

Julie R. Ancis *and* M. Meghan Davidson

Abstract

This chapter describes an integrated, ecological perspective on girls' and women's mental health. The interplay of multiple oppressions and their impact on the physical, psychological, and spiritual functioning of girls and women is described. Core values of positive psychology, feminist psychology, and counseling psychology emphasize individual strengths, and are applied to working with girls and women. In addition, the authors review relevant APA (2007) Guidelines for Psychological Practice with Girls and Women and discuss issues in assessment and diagnosis as related to women. Finally, implications for clinical work and future research are discussed. An ecological perspective that attends to the diversity within and between girls and women, as well as their social and environmental contexts, holds great promise for promoting girls' and women's wellness.

Key Words: Ecological theory, positive psychology, benefit finding resilience, bias and discrimination, DSM

A feminist and multicultural approach to counseling psychology has an integrated, ecological perspective on mental health at its core. Such a view acknowledges the multiple social contexts in which individuals are embedded and the interplay between environmental factors and psychological functioning. This chapter describes ecological systems theory and its relevance to understanding women's and girls' issues related to education and the workplace, sexual violence, and legal systems. It then summarizes how social and ecological systems perspectives are embedded in the American Psychological Association's (APA, 2007) Guidelines for Psychological Practice with Girls and Women, and discusses girls' and women's sources of resilience and positive mental health. Final sections of the chapter focus on implications for diagnosis, assessment, and multicultural feminist counseling psychology practice.

Ecological Theory

Over a quarter century ago, Urie Bronfenbrenner (1977) published his ecological theory of human development, asserting that to understand the development of individuals, we must move beyond the observation of behavior in one place with one person. Rather, it is necessary to examine systems of interaction and to account for environmental aspects beyond the immediate individual, situation, and/or context (Bronfenbrenner, 1977). This comprehensive model defined the ecological environment as a nested system, with each structure contained within the next. These five nested structures consist of the *individual*, the *microsystem*, the *mesosystem*, the *exosystem*, and the *macrosystem* (Bronfenbrenner, 1977, 1979, 1992). Additionally, ecological theory emphasizes *bidirectionality*, whereby each ecological context influences the individual, including the individual's ability to create change in each ecological subsytem (Bronfenbrenner, 1977, 1979, 1992; Chronister, McWhirter, & Kerewsky, 2004).

The *individual* is the core of the ecological model and comprises individual characteristics such as sex, ability, and age. The *microsystem* includes the individual's immediate environment at home, school, workplace, and so on, such as close friends, family members, teachers, coworkers, and neighbors. The *microsystem* also includes the individual's roles in the particular setting, as well as an awareness of the importance of relevant characteristics of other individuals in that environment (Bronfenbrenner, 1992).To illustrate roles interacting at the *microsystem* level, consider a woman who was raised in a family with culturally reinforced, traditional gender roles and who subsequently marries a man raised with similar values. The culturally bound gender roles of both the woman and her partner represent important facets of the *microsystem* that in turn affect her at the individual level, as well as through other nested systems. For example, these gender roles may play out in the home, with the woman being responsible for all the household cleaning; in the world of work, she may also face expectations that the man should be the primary breadwinner while the woman remains in the home and focuses on raising the children.

The *mesosystem* is defined as the interrelations of microsystems, that is, the quality of the relationships among the different contexts, such as interactions among family, school, workplace, and peer group (Bronfenbrenner, 1977, 1992). The *exosystem* is an extension of the mesosystem that comprises the environmental contexts and processes that affect the individual, although they may not directly contain the individual (Bronfenbrenner, 1977). Examples of the exosystem include neighborhood/geographic location, available community services, and government agencies.

The last component of the ecological model is the *macrosystem*. The macrosystem differs in some ways from the other nested systems in that it does not refer specifically to an individual's particular contexts that she directly experiences. Rather, it refers to models or ideals that exist in the larger culture, which then set the example or "standard" for activities that occur on a concrete level. Bronfenbrenner (1977, 1992) referred to the *macrosystem* as the culture's institutional patterns and "blueprints" that serve as transmitters of ideology and information that bestow meaning, both implicitly and explicitly, to specific agencies, social networks, roles, activities, and their relations among and between one another. The *macrosystem* is characterized by patterns of belief and behavior, and these patterns are passed on from generation to generation via processes of socialization through various cultural institutions such as school, church, family, workplace, and government.

Applications of the Ecological Model

Many researchers have utilized Bronfenbrenner's (1977, 1979, 1992) model to organize their conceptualizations and research in specific mental health–related areas. Specifically, Bronfenbrenner's subsystems have been used—and in some cases modified—to conceptualize specific social and mental health problems, seemingly individual concerns, and interventions. The ecological model and these applications are particularly relevant to gendered concerns (and other multicultural components, broadly defined), conceptualizations, and interventions. These areas include violence against women (Carlson, 1984; Edleson & Tolman, 1992; Heise, 1998; Smith, White, & Moracco, 2009; White, 2009), the impact of sexual assault and recovery (Campbell, Dworkin, & Cabral, 2009; Neville & Heppner, 1999), behavior problems in youth and adolescents, including alcohol and substance abuse (Robbins, Schwartz, & Szapocznik, 2004; Szapocznik et al., 1997), career development (Cook, Heppner, & O'Brien, 2002), the therapeutic process (Anderson, Holberg, & Carson, 2000; Conyne & Cook, 2004) and psychology practice (Prilleltensky & Nelson, 2002), and counseling immigrant women (Yakushko & Chronister, 2005), and are represented in a model of identity salience (Yakushko, Davidson, & Williams, 2009).

As a specific example, Bronfenbrenner's (1977, 1979) ecological model has been applied to the development of frameworks for understanding domestic violence (Carlson, 1984; Heise, 1998). Ecological approaches to violence against women conceptualize such violence as a "multifaceted phenomenon grounded in an interplay among personal, situational, and sociocultural factors" (Heise, 1998, p. 263). Such frameworks (e.g., Carlson, 1984; Heise, 1998) tend to emphasize the individual, microsystem, exosystem, and macrosystem (omitting the mesosystem). One's personal history, such as being abused as a child, witnessing violence as a child, worldview, and personality are viewed as central to the individual level (Carlson, 1984; Heise, 1998). The microsystem emphasizes roles in the family such as male dominance, male control of wealth, and marital/verbal conflict (Carlson, 1984;

Heise, 1998). Components of the exosystem include socioeconomic and employment factors, economic realities, law enforcement practices, delinquent peer associations, and isolation of women and families (Heise, 1998). Finally, male entitlement, rigid gender roles, acceptance of interpersonal violence, sex-role stereotyping, and masculinity are linked to aggression and dominance as relevant features of the macrosystem (Carlson, 1984; Heise, 1998).

Ecologically influenced conceptualizations of domestic violence (Carlson, 1984) have been applied to the development of interventions for men who physically abuse women (Edleson & Tolman, 1992). Such interventions employ the aforementioned delineations of the individual, microsystem, exosystem, and macrosystem, but also include interventions at the mesosystem level, noting that this system is most often omitted or overlooked (Edleson & Tolman, 1992).

The Gendered Adolescent Interpersonal Aggression (GAIA) model (Smith, White, & Moracco, 2009; White, 2009) is a gendered model of adolescent dating violence that is grounded in a social ecological perspective. Dating violence in adolescent relationships is viewed within the larger context of friendships and romantic relationships, while simultaneously considering peer, family, and broader institutional influence. Specifically, the GAIA is a person-centered social ecological model that incorporates gender, which is seen as socially constructed, at each level of the ecological system, and it includes multiple markers of interacting social identities (e.g., race, class, sex) as a meta-construct.

Sexual assault represents another type of violence against women. Neville and Heppner (1999) developed a Culturally Inclusive Ecological Model of Sexual Assault Recovery (CIEMSAR). Two differences emerged in their model, in comparison to the models of Carlson (1984) and Heise (1998); Neville and Heppner (1999) omitted the exosystem rather than the mesosystem, and the individual and the microsystem are viewed in conjunction with one another. The microsystem/individual level components include (a) rape characteristics such as relationship to perpetrator and severity of injury; (b) person variables such as demographics, previous sexual abuse, and race and ethnicity; (c) coping behaviors and responses such as specific coping strategies; and (d) culture-specific attributions. The mesosystem includes level of social support and institutional interventions. Finally, the rape-prone culture and racial and ethnic-specific sociocultural contexts are emphasized in their conceptualization of the macrosystem (Neville & Heppner, 1999).

Bronfenbrenner's (1977) work has also been the basis of an ecological model of career counseling and development for women and people of color (Cook, Heppner, & O'Brien, 2002, 2005). The model primarily emphasizes the individual, microsystem, and macrosystem, as well as the interactions of the microsystem and macrosystem with the individual. On the microsystem level, exposure to role models and mentors in educational and/or occupational settings for women of color and White women can be helpful. At the macrosystem level, sexual harassment stems from cultural and larger ideological beliefs about women and gender roles (Cook et al., 2002, 2005). Working from an ecologically based career counseling model could assist a women struggling with sexual harassment in the workplace or educational environment to view such oppressive behavior as one of power, rooted in societal/cultural beliefs (macrosystem), rather than operating solely at the individual or microsystem levels (Cook et al., 2005).

Scholars have also more directly employed the ecological model to intervene at the level of the therapeutic process. Interventions focused on group counseling (Bemak & Conyne, 2004), community agency work (O'Connell & Mabry, 2004), organizational consultation (Rapin, 2004), and advocacy and social justice (Watson, Collins, Collins, & Correia, 2004) illustrate the variety of environmental (i.e., microsystem, mesosystem, and macrosystem) contexts that interact with persons, as well as ways to approach counseling with individuals from these nested systems. The construct "contextual therapeutic relationship" (Anderson, Holberg, & Carson, 2000) underscores the notion that the therapeutic relationship is situated within broader environmental contexts, some of which are beyond the client's and/or therapist's control. Managed care, for example, plays a role as an environmental influence on the therapeutic process. "Ecological counseling" (Conyne & Cook, 2004) also highlights person-environment interactions in clinical work. Greater attention to external influences in the process of therapy is advocated within these conceptions, including specific discussion in sessions regarding the influences of family (i.e., gender roles embedded in family roles), neighborhood (i.e., expectations from peers and elders in neighborhood), school/work (i.e., role expectations, race-based discrimination), and culture (i.e., culturally based values).

Several scholars (e.g., Ancis & Jongsma, 2007; Szapocznik et al., 1997; Yakushko & Chronister, 2005) have utilized the ecological model to examine multiple sociocultural contexts and the various levels of the ecology at which to focus interventions. Such interventions have been proposed for a range of populations and concerns, including partner relational issues, balancing multiple roles, single parenting (Ancis & Jongsma, 2007), and working with Hispanic adolescents with disruptive behavior disorders (Robbins, Schwartz, & Szapocznik, 2004). For example, for immigrant women, factors such as acculturation, immigrant stress, relations with family, and the adoption of new gender roles have been identified as specific aspects of the ecology that influence the mental health of immigrant women (Yakushko & Chronister, 2005). Xenophobia, racism, sexism, poverty, and employment discrimination represent dimensions of the exosystem and macrosystem and sources of oppression that impinge upon immigrant women's mental health. Specific intervention strategies across the nested ecological systems to promote more positive mental health for immigrant women have been proposed (Yakushko & Chronister, 2005). These include (a) gaining a thorough history of pre-migration, migration, and post-migration experiences (individual level); (b) assessing changes in family structure (microsystem); (c) strengthening existing support networks and connections to cultural and spiritual communities in their new home (meso- and exosystem); and (d) providing information and teaching skills regarding ways to manage discrimination based on nationality, religion, gender, race, and so forth (macrosystem).

Yakushko, Davidson, and Williams (2009) recently proposed an Identity Salience Model for use in psychotherapy, utilizing perspectives of the ecological model as well as Root's (1997, 1998, 1999, 2000, 2003) racial identity model and Hays's (2001, 2008) ADDRESSING framework. This model highlights the intersectionality of individuals' multiple identities, and provides practitioners with a framework of how these identities may be influenced by oppressive contexts and the myriad realities of people's lived experience. More specifically, the Identity Salience Model provides a scaffold for how (a) the psychotherapy context can consider the multiple identities of an individual; (b) the salience of identities can be distinguished and appreciated; and (c) the ecological factors affecting the person/client, the therapist, and the therapeutic process can be examined and employed (Yakushko et al., 2009). The Identity Salience Model attends to the dynamic nature of multiple and intersecting identities, encompassing gender, sexual orientation, race/ethnicity, social class and ability status, among other social locations. It allows for the exploration of how these identities interact with one another and with the nested systems of the ecology in an effort to positively enhance the therapeutic process and achieve greater mental health for the client.

It is evident that ecological theory has had a profound impact on the way that scholars conceptualize psychological difficulties and provide interventions for individuals, environments, and institutions. It has proved to be a useful framework for integrating feminist and multicultural approaches across the levels of the ecology to enhance the mental health of individuals.

The Relationship Between Social Forces and Mental Health

Consistent with an integrated, ecological perspective, the dynamics of social forces and institutions and their interrelationships with mental and physical health have been empirically explored. Girls and women experience bias, discrimination, and a general lack of opportunities worldwide. The experience of sexist events has been demonstrated to have negative effects on mental health, including anxiety, depression, lowered self-esteem, and decreased well-being (e.g., Briere & Jordan, 2004; Fischer & Holz, 2010; Moradi & Subich; 2003). Bias and discrimination occur in multiple arenas. A description of how sexist events are manifested and their relationships to mental, physical, and behavioral health in the areas of education, the workforce, sexual assault and harassment, and the legal arena are presented below.

Education and the Workforce

Limited educational opportunities prevent many girls and women from personal and professional development and advancement. Approximately one-quarter of girls in developing countries do not attend school (Lloyd, 2005). Out of the world's 130 million out-of-school youth, 70% are girls (Human Rights Watch, 1999). Little to no schooling is associated with early marriage in many parts of the world (International Center for Research on Women, 2007), which has subsequently been found to be associated with abuse within marriage (International Center for Research on Women, 2005).

For those who do attend school, gender bias in education has been documented, including a "null environment," belittling behavior by faculty, and sexual harassment (Fassinger, 2002; Sadker & Sadker, 1994; Sadker, Sadker, & Zittleman, 2009). Educational barriers have multiple effects on occupational choice, implementation, and achievement. Cognitive and affective dimensions often mediate the relationship between educational gender bias and behavior. For example, academic gender bias is associated with lower career self-efficacy (Ancis & Phillips, 1996). Self-efficacy in turn influences such important career-related behaviors as choice of major, career choice, and persistence in the face of obstacles (Betz & Fitzgerald, 1987; Hackett, 1985; Phillips & Imhoff, 1997).

Once in the workforce, women face a number of disadvantages and stressors, including (a) gender inequity in salary; (b) overrepresentation in low paying, low status jobs that underutilize their talent and offer little opportunity for advancement; and (c) discriminatory practices in hiring, evaluation, resource allocation, and promotion (Betz & Fitzgerald, 1987; Fassinger, 2002). Interestingly, in areas such as salary inequity, perceived discrimination actually underreports actual discrimination (Gee, 2002; Stockdale & Vaux, 1993). Research supports the negative impact of perceptions of workplace discrimination on women's health, even after controlling for prior emotional health, physical health limitations, and job characteristics (Pavalko, Mossakowski, & Hamilton, 2003).

Sexual Harassment and Assault

Girls and women are often subject to sexual violence. Females are more likely than males to be victims of childhood sexual rape abuse or sexual assault (Tolin & Foa, 2006; U.S. Department of Justice, 2009). Statistics indicate that one in six women will be sexually assaulted in their lifetime (RAINN, 2009). Both sexual harassment and sexual assault have been shown to have deleterious psychological and behavioral effects (Impett, Schooler, & Tolman, 2006; Lindberg, Grabe, & Shibley Hyde, 2007; Mercurio & Landry, 2008; Rospenda, Richman, & Shannon, 2009). Mental health effects of sexual assault include lowered self-esteem, depression, post-traumatic stress disorder (PTSD), suicidal behavior and attempts, and substance use (Briere & Jordan, 2004; McFarlane et al., 2005a; McFarlane et al., 2005b).

The sexual objectification of women within the larger society is often internalized by women themselves, resulting in self-objectification (Fredrickson & Roberts, 1997). Such self-objectification is associated with low self-esteem and life satisfaction (Mercurio & Landry, 2008), body shame, disordered eating (Noll & Fredrickson, 1998), and decreased sexual functioning (Steer & Tiggemann, 2008). Adolescent girls with higher levels of self-objectification describe their sexual experiences with "regret, concern, or vagueness and rarely described their experiences of sexual pleasure or subjectivity" (Steer & Tiggemann, 2008, p. 11); express greater difficulty in communicating with their partners regarding sexuality; are less likely to communicate with their partners about the use of protection; and are less likely to have conversations with their parents about sex (Hirschman, Impett, & Schooler, 2006).

Relatedly, Campbell, Dworkin, and Cabral (2009) provide an ecologically grounded examination of the impact of sexual assault on women's mental health. More specifically, assault is positioned as an additional nested system that lies between the individual and the microsystem. Campbell et al. assert that the characteristics of the sexual assault itself impact the psychological well-being and mental health of the woman survivor, and thus affect all the interrelated systems. Self-blame is proposed as a meta-level construct that undergirds the entire ecology. This model provides a conceptual map to address mental health outcomes, including PTSD, depression, suicidality, and substance use.

Related to societal messages that are associated with women's sex-role socialization, studies have demonstrated the deleterious effects of internalized conventional ideas about femininity. Inauthenticity in relationships (silencing one's own needs and desires as a strategy to reduce conflict) and body objectification (dissociating from one's own desire and constantly surveilling one's own body from another's perspective), two aspects of internalized conventional ideas about femininity, are associated with poorer sexual self-efficacy. Lower sexual self-efficacy, in turn, predicts less use of protection (Impett, Schooler, & Tolman, 2006). Sexual violence and associated internalized beliefs have deleterious psychological and social effects.

Legal System

The legal system represents another arena in which women experience discrimination. For example, women litigants' particular challenges in divorce and custody disputes have been studied (Ancis, 2009a, 2009b; Ancis, Neelerambam, & Watson, 2009). Court practices regarding custody, child support, alimony, and property division often negatively impact the economic status of women (Ancis, 2008; Bryan, 2006; Gadalla, 2009). Financial limitations may hinder access to legal counsel and the adoption of effective litigation strategies. In addition, the accuracy of financial data and mediation in the courts have been identified as areas that consistently and negatively affect women in all areas of the family law system (Beck & Sales, 2001; Bryan, 2006). Critiques of mediation, as currently practiced, include women's greater likelihood of bargaining away property to obtain their preferred custody or visitation arrangements due to unequal bargaining power and coercion. Inequality between participants is particularly severe when one party has been physically abused by the other.

Women describe the emotional and traumatic effects associated with prolonged litigation and the related violation of voice and dignity, unfair court procedures, harassment and intimidation tactics, and custody loss (Ancis, 2009a,; Ancis2009b; Rettig, 2007; Watson & Ancis, 2010). In addition, women describe a lack of social support, physical health issues, anxiety, and depressive symptoms (Ancis, Neelarambam, & Watson, 2009; Thomas & Ryan, 2008). Inequities within the justice system and larger cultural attitudes regarding women, which represent the exosystem and macrosystem, respectively, negatively impact women's psychosocial functioning. Lack of support on the mesosystem level, which may serve to buffer the deleterious impact of such inequities, leaves them at risk, both physically and psychologically.

Guidelines for Psychological Practice with Girls and Women

The Guidelines for Psychological Practice with Girls and Women, co-chaired by Roberta L. Nutt, Joy K. Rice, and Carol Zerbe Enns and published by the American Psychological Association in 2007, were developed to provide a set of ethical aspirations for psychologists in order to enhance gender- and culture-sensitive practice with diverse girls and women. These 11 guidelines were influenced by an integrated, ecological perspective. Relatedly, the guidelines attend to the nested systems and subsystems of which girls and women are a part, while attending to girls' and women's intra- and inter-diversity.

The first three guidelines focus specifically on issues of diversity and social contexts. Guideline 1 implores psychologists to be aware of the impact of socialization on girls and women. This includes the reinforcement of traditional roles that may be psychologically and behaviorally limiting. Guideline 1 also emphasizes the socialization of girls and women within a set of group memberships, some of which are visible and some of which are invisible. These memberships include race/ethnicity, class, age, sexual orientation, spiritual orientation, and physical or cognitive ability. Group memberships intersect and influence each other and are enacted within larger family and cultural institutions. There is recognition that girls and women have both shared and unique identities and developmental pathways.

Guideline 2 recognizes that girls and women possess multiple personal and social group memberships and that they may simultaneously belong to both socially privileged and disempowered groups. Negotiating multiple identities that are associated with oppression is often stressful and potentially traumatic. This guideline also attends to identity development processes, specifically models that describe movement from internalized prejudice and privilege toward increased awareness, flexibility, and internal standards of self-definition (e.g., Cross & Vandiver, 2001; Downing & Roush, 1985; Moradi, Subich, & Phillips, 2002). As psychologists recognize that girls and women possess multiple group memberships and various identities, they are encouraged to recognize how their own levels of identity awareness influence their clinical assessments.

Guideline 3 emphasizes the impact of bias and discrimination on an individual's physical and mental health. This relationship has been demonstrated in multiple contexts. Bias and inequity occur in multiple arenas, including health systems (Landrine & Klonoff, 2001), educational institutions (AAUW, 1992, 1994, 2004), the workplace (Ortiz & Roscigno, 2009; Yoder, 2007), religious institutions (Para-Mallam, 2010; Starr Sered, 1999), legal systems (Ancis, 2009a, 2009b; Guinier, Fine, & Balin, 1997), family and couple relationships (Sanchez & Kane, 1996; Sanderson & Sanders Thompson, 2002), and in research methods and language (Denmark, Russo, Frieze, & Sechzer, 1988; Gannon, Luchetta, Rhodes, Pardie, & Segrist, 1992; Gill & Floos, 2008; Kimmel & Crawford, 2001).

Acknowledgment of multiple social contexts, the relationships among these contexts, and the interaction of the individual with these contexts is clear throughout the guidelines. The guidelines describe gender, racial, and ethnic socialization; identity development; and discriminatory experiences as they impact girls and women. Individual strengths, resilience, and coping resources are acknowledged as important factors for psychologists to consider (Worell & Remer, 2003; Wyche & Rice, 1997).

The Interplay of Multiple Oppressions

As described in the Guidelines for Psychological Practice with Girls and Women, as women possess multiple memberships and identities, they may also experience multiple oppressions as well as privileges (Ancis & Ladany, 2001, 2010; Comas-Díaz & Greene, 1994a). Oppressive forces such as heterosexism, racism, and sexism negatively impact an individual's psychological (e.g., Krieger, 1990; Thomas & González-Prendes, 2009) and physical well-being (e.g., Clark et al., 1999; Schulz et al., 2006; Williams, 2008). From an ecological perspective, women of color may face challenges at every level, as they experience sexism and oppression within their own racial and ethnic communities and oppression from the dominant group (Comas-Díaz & Greene, 1994a). Similarly, individuals must often struggle with acculturative stressors, cultural adaptation, and identity conflict within the framework of these nested systems. Privileges may accrue for some women as a function of their race (e.g., White), socioeconomic status (e.g., high income), or sexual orientation (e.g., heterosexual). Differences certainly exist among women as a function of particular historical and sociopolitical contexts, the diversity of gender roles within ethnic groups, and individual approaches in coping and functioning (Comas-Díaz & Greene, 1994a, 1994b).

Both gender and race-related stress at the micro-, meso-, exo- and macrosystems levels have been linked to higher levels of emotional and behavioral problems (DuBois, Burk-Braxton, Swenson, Tevendale, & Hardesty, 2002). Subjective experiences of discrimination adversely affect the physical and mental health of minority women (Kessler, Mickelson, & Williams, 1999; Krieger, 1990; Williams, 2008). For example, increases in stress appraisals for individual racism are associated with increases in anxiety and obsessive-compulsive symptoms for African American women (Greer, Laseter, & Asiamah, 2009). Perceived inequity and discrimination as a function of one's personal characteristics such as race, ethnicity, and gender are associated with psychological distress, lower self-esteem, anxiety, cardiovascular effects, low birth weight in infants of mothers experiencing discrimination, and poor self-reported health status (Clark et al. 1999; Gee et al., 2006; Jones, Cross, & DeFour, 2007; Kessler et al., 1999; Krieger 1990; Lewis et al., 2006; Moradi & Subich, 2003; Rospenda et al., 2008; Schulz et al., 2006; Szymanski, & Stewart, 2010; Williams et al., 2003).

In the area of the workforce, gender, racial, or ethnic minorities of color report workplace discrimination more often (Hammond, Gillen, & Yen, 2010; Roberts, Swanson, & Murphy, 2004; Rospenda, Richman, & Shannon, 2009). Institutional discrimination is influential in restricting economic opportunity for racial and ethnic minority women in particular (Williams, 2008; Williams & Collins, 2001). Black women, compared to White women, are disparately concentrated in sex-segregated jobs and in positions of lower occupational prestige (Ortiz & Roscigno, 2009). Harmful mental health effects of workplace discrimination include diminished psychological well-being, increased risk of psychological distress, and pronounced depressive symptoms (Bhui et al., 2005; Roberts et al., 2004; Rospenda et al., 2008; Wadsworth et al., 2007).

As ethnic minority women's bodies have been historically objectified and devalued (Bryant-Davis & Ocampo, 2006; Franklin et al., 2006) by the sexist ideology and attitudes at the macrosystem level, they are particularly vulnerable to sexual assault (Bryant-Davis, Chung, & Tillman, 2009). The impact of multiple oppressions is demonstrated in research on lifetime exposures of perceived racial discrimination and intimate partner violence (IPV). Furthermore, women who reported both exposures show a notably higher prevalence of anxiety and nonspecific physical health symptoms compared with women who report either or neither exposure (Waltermaurer, Watson, & McNutt, 2006). For ethnic minority women, the trauma of sexual abuse overlays the already existing intergenerational trauma of sexism, racism, classism, and heterosexism. The silencing and stereotyping within the judicial, economic, and media systems on the exosystem and macrosystem levels represent further challenges for ethnic minority women in the recovery process and as they seek justice (Bryant-Davis et al., 2009; Neville & Pugh, 1997).

Race, ethnicity, gender, and socioeconomic status are related to the differential distribution of health risks and subsequently variations in the rates of disease (Krieger, Rowley, Herman, Avery, & Phillips, 1993; Williams, 2008). Women face more difficulties with financial resources, racial or ethnic bias, and bias against individuals with specific disability statuses associated with aging (APA 2004; Federal Interagency Forum on Aging-Related Statistics, 2000). Gender inequality is associated with mortality, excess disease, and morbidity around the world (Landrine & Klonoff, 2001). Inequalities in the allocation of food and economic power, as well as male violence on the multiple levels identified by Brofenbrenner, are factors that contribute to morbidity and mortality among women (Landrine & Klonoff, 2001; Ussher, 2000). Whereas gender- and race-related oppression impact women, lesbian women and gay men are subject to heterosexism, and women of color face triple jeopardy in the form of heterosexism, sexism, and racism (Greene, 2004). In fact, studies have demonstrated that racist events, heterosexist events, and internalized heterosexism each correlated positively with psychological distress in African American sexual minority women (Szymanski & Meyer, 2008).

The experience of multiple oppressions is often stressful and traumatizing. These experiences may range from the more subtle to the overt. The ways in which one adapts and copes with the interplay of multiple oppressions have tremendous implications for one's physical, mental, and spiritual well-being, and are the subject of much of the work in the area generally known as positive psychology.

Positive Mental Health

Positive Psychology

Positive psychology emphasizes the scientific study of positive traits, positive emotions, and positive institutions in order to prevent maladies and improve mental health (Seligman & Csikszentmihalyi, 2000). The study of optimal human functioning and the goals of understanding and applying those factors that assist people and communities to thrive and flourish are emphasized (Magyar-Moe, 2009; Snyder & Lopez, 2009; Wood & Tarrier, 2010). Martin Seligman, in his 1998 American Psychological Association presidential address, called attention to *positive psychology* as he urged the psychology profession to focus more on recognizing and cultivating talent, and assisting others to develop more rewarding lives (Seligman & Csikszentmihalyi, 2000). Several authors (e.g., Seligman, 2002b; Seligman & Csikszentmihalyi, 2000) have criticized psychology's focus on pathology, which has resulted in a profession aimed at repairing the worst aspects of people. In a seminal article in the *American Psychologist*, Seligman and Csikszentmihalyi (2000) posited a field of positive psychology that would emphasize well-being, satisfaction, optimism, and hope. Despite not referencing it as such, these authors utilized an ecological framework as they discussed positive psychology at the individual level (e.g., perseverance, capacity for love and vocation) and group level (e.g., institutions that move individuals toward better citizenship). Their overarching message was to remind professionals that "psychology is not just the study of pathology, weakness, and damage; it is also the study of strength and virtue" (2000, p. 7). This is consistent with the foundations of counseling psychology, which have traditionally emphasized preventive, educative and developmental, and remedial approaches, as well as a focus on assets and strengths (Gelso & Fretz, 2001).

Two central theories comprise positive psychology: strengths theory (Clifton & Nelson, 1996; Peterson & Seligman, 2004) and the "broaden and build" theory of positive emotions (Fredrickson, 1998, 2001). Strengths theory emphasizes recognizing and building upon an individual's (or community's) strengths while controlling weaknesses (Clifton & Nelson, 1996), rather than repairing what is wrong and allowing assets and strengths to develop on their own. Clifton and Nelson (1996) described the majority of psychologists and other leaders as endorsing faulty logic in believing that (a) addressing a weakness will result in a stronger individual, community, or organization; and (b) strengths will develop naturally and thus do not need fostering. Additionally, strengths and weaknesses are not opposites and should not be viewed or treated as such (Clifton & Nelson, 1996). For example, studying weaknesses does not inform what we know about strengths.

Relevant research investigations include the study of gifted girls and women. Several scholars (Kerr, 1997; Kerr & Larson, 2008; Yewchuck, Äyst, & Schlosser, 2001) have examined the lives of eminent women and described qualities and characteristics that enabled them to succeed. Particular assets and strengths, including resilience, positive emotionality, and resourcefulness, seem to be critical to the development of gifted girls as they work to become talented women. Interestingly, resistance to stereotyping and discrimination and resistance to the culture of romance—themes often emphasized in women's socialization processes—are other characteristics associated with eminent women. Kerr and Larson (2008) described how these strengths buffer girls from factors that can interrupt and impede their development. These detrimental factors include significant loss (e.g., of a parent); societal pressures to direct interests toward popularity, appearance, and romance; interpersonal threats and attacks (e.g., social scrutiny from peer group); and stereotype threat (e.g., boys are better in math and science). Such investigations of gifted girls and women can potentially guide the development of future interventions for building girls' strengths.

The broaden and build theory suggests that positive emotions play critical roles in people's lives, and are as equally important as negative emotions for their survival and ability to flourish (Fredrickson, 1998, 2001). Five hypotheses comprise Fredrickson's broaden and build theory: broaden hypothesis, build hypothesis, undoing hypothesis, resilience hypothesis, and flourish hypothesis. The broaden hypothesis asserts that when an individual is experiencing positive emotions, she is able to see greater possibilities (Fredrickson, 1998, 2001). In contrast, a person experiencing negative emotions is more likely to see narrowed possibilities and may experience tunnel vision. The build hypothesis maintains that once possibilities have been broadened (by experiencing positive emotions), a number of personal resources are built up and are available. The personal resources that are generated include various physical, social, intellectual, and psychological assets. The undoing hypothesis simply states that positive emotions have the power to undo negative emotions. Because possibilities cannot simultaneously be broadened and narrowed, eliciting positive emotions while struggling with negative emotions may alleviate the negative. The resilience hypothesis affirms that positive emotions trigger the broadening of options, and this broadening in turn fosters resiliency via "upward spirals of well-being" (Fredrickson, 2001). Finally, the flourish hypothesis posits that the critical element in determining whether an individual flourishes is the ratio of positive to negative emotions that the person experiences (Fredrickson & Losada, 2005). More specifically, the ratio of positive to negative emotions must be 3:1 over time for a person to flourish. Related research has demonstrated that the experience of positive emotions is associated with creativity, inventiveness, and a "big picture" perceptual focus (Fredrickson, 2003). In addition, positive emotions are associated with the development of psychological resilience (Fredrickson, 2003).

Resilience, Benefit Finding, and Growth

In line with a focus on strength, resilience, and adaptation, feminist scholars (e.g., Clarke & Griffin, 2008; Connolly, 2006; Harvey & Tummala-Narra, 2007; O'Leary &Bhaju; 2006; Poorman, 2002) and positive psychologists (e.g., Durkin & Joseph, 2009; Fazio, Rashid, & Hayward, 2008; Helgeson, Reynolds, & Tomich, 2006; Keyes & Haidt, 2003; Joseph & Linley, 2006; Linley & Joseph, 2005; Lopez, Snyder, & Rasmussen, 2003; Seligman, 2002b) have examined ways in which resilience buffers traumatic events and how adversity provides opportunities for psychological growth.

Particular personality characteristics, aspects of the individual in the ecosystem, are related to enduring and overcoming stressful circumstances. Hardiness represents a growth-oriented personality buffer that provides the courage and motivation to turn stressful circumstances into growth opportunities (Kobasa, 1979; Maddi, 2006). In addition to normal stressful circumstances, individuals are often confronted with stresses that are not developmentally inevitable. Many studies have demonstrated that hardy attitudes provide the strength and motivation to engage in transformation coping, supportive social interactions, and facilitative self-care under stress (Maddi & Kobasa, 1984). The positive influence of hardiness on performance and mood in diverse samples, including bus drivers (Bartone, 1989), lawyers (Kobasa, 1982), and military personnel (Bartone, Roland, Picano, & Williams, 2008) has been clearly established. Other studies support the mechanisms whereby hardy attitudes lead to hardy actions, thereby positively affecting performance, conduct, and health (Maddi, 2002).

Hardiness is seen as a pathway to resilience under stress (Bonanno, 2004). The construct of resilience, grounded in an emphasis on strengths and resources (Hawley, 2000), has been described as a developmental and dynamic process rather than a stable trait (Hawley & DeHaan, 1996; Patterson, 2002). Poorman (2002), in her qualitative investigation of women who had experienced abuse or status-related oppression (gender, ethnicity, sexual orientation) at the microsystem and/or macrosystem level, determined that for thriving to occur, women needed to experience and then fight against adversity. Research with oppressed and marginalized women (Bradley & Davino, 2007; Clarke & Griffin, 2008; Connolly, 2006; Poorman, 2002) found that thriving and resilience borne from adversity was defined by interdependence and connection with others, a strengthening of the microsystem level. Women describe resilience as a reliance on others' support, being in community, and creating and maintaining a strong network in which they draw from and contribute to others. Greater resiliency seems to be associated with positive feelings about addressing past trauma (Tarakeshwar et al., 2006).

Research has found evidence of psychological growth following trauma or adversity (e.g., Durkin

& Joseph, 2009; Fazio, Rashid, & Hayward, 2008; Helgeson, Reynolds, & Tomich, 2006; Keyes & Haidt, 2003; Lopez, Snyder, & Rasmussen, 2003; Seligman, 2002b). For example, Bradley and Davino (2007) found a high degree of resilience among incarcerated women who had been victims of interpersonal violence as they created significant relationships with others and successfully regulated affect, reflecting positive changes in the women's microsystem and individual levels of their ecology. Similarly, among long-term lesbian couples, successfully navigating adversity, such as homophobia, brought couples a type of relational resiliency and unification, as well as a capacity for mutuality (Connolly, 2006). Traumatic stress may thus serve as a springboard for positive development and growth such that more optimal functioning, and not just resiliency, arises from adverse experiences (see Joseph & Linley, 2006; Linley & Joseph, 2004; Linley & Joseph, 2005). Relatedly, the construct of "benefit finding" (Helgeson, Reynolds, & Tomich, 2006) refers to perceptions of positive changes in one's life after experiencing a stressful or traumatic event. Like resilience, benefit finding may serve to moderate the effects of stress on psychological distress and well-being. Moreover, benefit finding is associated with greater optimism and coping strategies of positive reappraisal, acceptance, and denial (Helgeson et al., 2006).

Meta-analyses of research focused on growth emerging from traumatic or negative events have been conducted (Helgeson et al., 2006), yielding complex results. Greater positive well-being and less depression were found to be related to benefit finding in a range of situations, including in response to HIV-related symptoms (Siegel & Schrimshaw, 2007), although unrelated to anxiety and global distress or global quality of life. Benefit finding was more strongly associated with these positive psychological outcomes when the time since the traumatic event was longer than two years (Helgeson et al., 2006). Interestingly, women, people of color, and younger individuals participate in the most benefit finding (Helgeson et al., 2006). Also, consistent with previous research, women have been found to engage in more positive self-talk and positive reappraisal, compared to men (Tamres, Janicki, & Helgeson, 2002). It seems that members of marginalized and oppressed groups seek to alter their individual experience of the ecological context in an effort to buffer against negative experiences at the microsystem, mesosystem, and macrosystem level.

Applications of Positive Psychology

A wide variety of positive psychology interventions aimed at improving mental health have been investigated. Recent areas and populations in which these interventions have been employed include health psychology (Aspinwall & Tedeschi, 2010), cancer care (Coyne & Tennen, 2010; Coyne, Tennen, & Ranchor, 2010), depression (Sin & Lyubomirsky, 2009), happiness (Seligman, Steen, Park, & Peterson, 2005), goal-striving and coaching (Biswas-Diener, 2009, 2010; Grant & Spence, 2010), children and adolescents (Kirschman, Johnson, Bender, & Roberts, 2009; Miller, Nickerson, & Jimerson, 2009; Norrish & Vella-Brodrick, 2009), and couples (Kauffman & Silberman, 2009). Mental health interventions and other scholarly work with a gendered, positive psychology focus are relatively limited in the published literature. Despite this limitation, relevant gender related work is discussed below.

Approaches to working with adolescent girls have been influenced by positive psychology, feminist psychology, and strengths-based interventions. Previous research has demonstrated the effectiveness of a number of interventions designed to enhance the well-being and health of adolescent girls by emphasizing their strengths and resilience. For example, teaching problem-solving skills to teen girls has been demonstrated to be effective for developing resistance to depression (Chaplin et al., 2006). Teaching positive coping skills at multiple levels, such as the microsystem, mesosystem, and exosystem levels (i.e., individual, family, and community), has demonstrated effectiveness in reducing sexual abuse and substance abuse (Strader, Collins, & Roe, 2000). Johnson (2003) utilized a case example to outline a strengths-based approach in working with an adolescent girl (who exhibited acting-out behaviors, depression, and subclinical attention-deficit/hyperactivity disorder [ADHD]) and her parents that included (a) improving relations between the adolescent and her parents (i.e., microsystem); (b) developing an awareness of possible ethnic, class, and gender stereotypes imposed by parents, peers, teachers, and others (i.e., microsystem, mesosystem, macrosystem); (c) assisting the adolescent in reclaiming her voice rather than expressing herself through risky behaviors (i.e., individual level); (d) teaching problem-solving skills (i.e., individual level); and (e) interacting with both the parents and the school to assist the adolescent (i.e., microsystem, mesosystem). Johnson (2003) reported that such a family-centered, strengths-based approach has been found effective for many adolescent girls and their families who present with a range of concerns including anxiety, dysthymia, ADHD, and adjustment issues.

Positive psychological aspects of assets and strengths are highlighted in feminist therapeutic approaches (Worell & Johnson, 1997), as are ecological parameters of the environment and contexts in which a woman interacts (Comas-Díaz & Greene, 1994a, 1994b; Lerman, 1987). Similarly, empowerment work with adolescent girls involves an assessment of their individual and collective strengths while considering the social construction of gender among other sociocultural influences, including race, ethnicity, class, and ability (Johnson, 2003). Resilience and thriving are often viewed as outcomes of a feminist therapy approach. Feminist empowerment therapy (O'Leary & Bhaju, 2006; Worell, 2001; Wyche & Rice, 1997) involves the validation of women's experiences and the facilitation of personal empowerment. Personal empowerment includes becoming more assertive regarding goal attainment and psychological change and growth.

Reconceptualizing the DSM and Assessment

Steeped in positive psychology and feminist-multicultural perspectives, multiple authors (Association for Women in Psychology Committee on Bias in Psychiatric Diagnosis, 2011; Lopez et al., 2006; Yoder, 2007; Zalaquett, Fuerth, Stein, Ivey, & Ivey, 2008) have discussed the limitations and problems inherent in the *Diagnostic and Statistical Manual of Mental Disorders*-IV-TR (American Psychiatric Association, 2000). Gender bias in psychiatric diagnosis, the *DSM IV-TR*, and previous iterations of the *DSM* have been documented (Broverman, Broverman, Clarkson, Rosenkrantz, & Vogel, 1970; Caplan & Cosgrove, 2004; Caplan & Profit, 2004), such as in the area of personality disorders (Yoder, 2007) and other diagnoses, including premenstrual dysphoric disorder (Offman & Kleinplatz, 2004), female sexual dysfunction (Working Group of a New View of Women's Sexual Problems, 2004), and gender identity disorder (Wilson, Griffin, & Wren, 2002). Women's normal development is often pathologized (Caplan, 1995; Landrine & Klonoff, 2001) and their difficulties are either overdiagnosed or underdiagnosed (Bjorklund, 2006; Jordache & Low, 2010; Riecher-Rössler, 2010), resulting in faulty or no interventions.

A major critique of the *DSM* is that the manual tends to focus on negative parameters of a person's life. Further, Lopez et al. (2006) iterate that a classification system that fails to account for the connections between "the environment, culture, behavior, thoughts, emotions, external supports, and functioning can only hint at implications for treatment" (p. 262). The *DSM* has been criticized for its limited consideration of ecological parameters in defining psychological disorders, and lack of consideration of ways in which racism and sexism could reasonably explain an individual's struggles in coping (Counselors for Social Justice, 2011; Zalaquett, Fuerth, Stein, Ivey, & Ivey, 2008).

Several authors (Ivey & Ivey, 1998) have called for reframing the manual and classification systems to incorporate a positive developmental perspective. More recently, alternative multicultural and social justice conceptualizations of the *DSM* have been proposed (Zalaquett et al., 2008). Attention to ecological factors would allow a woman who has been sexually harassed or discriminated against to understand subsequent anxiety or depression as a valid response to her environment (Ancis & Jongsma, 2007; Zalaquett et al., 2008). Although these authors do not explicitly articulate an ecological model (i.e., Ivey & Ivey, 1998; Lopez et al., 2006; & Zalaquett et al., 2008), their proposal of widening the *DSM's* focus to consider psychological strengths, environmental factors, sociocultural parameters, and developmental influences that shape the expression of people's strengths and weaknesses certainly aligns with an ecological perspective of positive mental health.

In line with these urgings to broaden the perspectives of the *DSM*, the "four-front approach" to psychological assessment has also been suggested. Wright and Lopez (2002, 2009) outlined the four-front approach as focusing attention on (a) deficits and destabilizing characteristics of the individual; (b) assets and strengths of the individual; (c) deficits and destructive influences in the environment; and (d) opportunities and resources in the environment. This approach incorporates both positive and negative factors at the individual and contextual levels. Wright and Lopez (2002, 2009) emphasized the ways that this model increases the possibilities for remediation and supports the discovery and development of strengths and assets. Additionally, they highlighted the dynamic nature of this approach, as the individual's strengths and deficits influence each other, as do the individual's behavior and environment. The four-front approach to assessment clearly aligns with the ecological model, with its interdependent, nested systems, as well as a complete state of mental health model.

Corey Keyes (2002, 2005a, 2007, 2009) has been instrumental, within and outside the field of positive psychology, in promoting the concept of a complete state model of mental health. This model embraces the notion that mental health is not simply the lack of mental illness, nor is mental illness merely the lack of mental health. Rather, building from the World Health Organization's (1948) definition, mental health is described as a *complete state* incorporating the absence of mental illness and the presence of a high level of well-being (Keyes & Lopez, 2002). To investigate this proposed definition, Keyes (2005a) conducted a large-scale, empirical study (N = 3,032) utilizing factor analyses that confirmed mental health and mental illness as comprising distinct, although correlated factors, lending strong support for the complete state model of mental health. Mental health is presented as a complete state delineated by a "flourishing" and "languishing" (Keyes, 2005a, 2007). More specifically, Keyes (2005a) advocated for specific diagnostic criteria for flourishing and languishing. Flourishing requires exhibition of high levels of hedonic well-being (e.g., positive affect in the past 30 days) and high levels of positive functioning (e.g., self-acceptance, personal growth.) Conversely, languishing refers to being devoid of positive functioning and involves a state of being stuck or stagnant.

Despite the consistent findings that women demonstrate higher rates of depression than men (Centers for Disease Control [CDC], 2010; Van de Velde, Bracke, Levecque, & Meuleman, 2010; Weissman et al., 1993), women report equal (e.g., emotional well-being, social integration) or higher levels (e.g., positive relations, social acceptance) of positive functioning on a number of subjective well-being measures (Dwyer & Cummings, 2001; Keyes, 2005b; Lykken, 1999; Myers, 2000; Rueger, Malecki, & Demaray, 2008). Similarly, women indicate levels of autonomy, self-acceptance, personal growth, purpose in life, and environmental mastery similar to those of men (Keyes, 2005b). Also, numerous investigations (Harvard Men's Health Watch, 2010; Hill & Donatelle, 2005; Keyes, 2005b; Marshall, 2010; Yaughn & Nowicki, 1999) have demonstrated that women report significantly higher levels of positive relationships with others, compared to men. These inconsistencies lend credence to the complete state of mental health, in which depression and subjective well-being are viewed as discrete dimensions of a person's overall mental health (Keyes & Ryff, 2003). Utilizing both an ecological framework and a positive psychological approach, the *DSM* and associated clinical assessment could be reconceptualized to better address the lived experiences of individuals, particularly girls and women, and people from marginalized groups.

Implications and Limitations

Ecological approaches have great potential for understanding and promoting human wellness. Women's psychological, physical, and spiritual health is a product of the larger historical, geographic, sociocultural, economic, and political context (Williams, 2008). The importance of counseling psychologists taking an integrated, ecological perspective is clear, and will support the development of sensitive, positive, and effective interventions at the preventive, maintenance, and remedial levels. These include interventions at the microsystem and macrosystem levels that promote girls' and women's health (APA, 2007). On the microlevel, sources of support, extended family ties, and religious involvement may reduce the negative effects of stress (Wallace & Forman, 1998). Learning how to confront an individual about an oppressive practice can increase a sense of empowerment and influence (APA, 2007). Psychological approaches include options for working with clients who are questioning their beliefs based on sexist assumptions that devalue women, and expanding women's perceived range of choice for improving their lives (Ancis & Jongsma, 2007; Atwood, 2001). Similarly, increasing women's awareness of the relationships between sexism, discrimination, and mental health, and developing skills of personal control can alleviate psychological distress (Fischer & Holz, 2010; Major & O'Brien, 2005). At the macrolevel, in order to improve girls' and women's psychological, physical, and spiritual health, changes are needed in policies related to education, employment, housing and transportation, rape, sexual harassment, and child and elder abuse; as well as changes in social mores (APA, 2007; Newman, 2001). Higher levels of political and economic status for women in the United States are associated with lower morbidity and mortality (Williams, 2008).

The field of positive psychology and the focus on strength-based approaches have enormous potential for the well-being of individuals and communities. Development of resilience is shaped by person-environment interactions. Early interventions may foster positive parent-child attachments; interventions for youth may foster wellness and the development of a social milieu that can facilitate a sense of belonging and self-esteem. These interventions set the stage for coping and resilience into adulthood (Harvey & Tummala-Narra, 2007).

Clearly, a significant amount of work has been advanced in the field of positive psychology regarding theory development and mental health. A plethora of investigations have been conducted to examine these theories in the wider population. Counseling psychology has historically focused on individuals' strengths and has advocated for social change (Walsh, 2004). However, more research is needed on the efficacy and effectiveness of strengths-based approaches. It appears that a gap exists in the literature regarding interventions that are specific to girls and women, and gender more broadly. Future research should emphasize gender-specific and culture-specific interventions and investigations that utilize the framework of positive psychology. Doing so would benefit practice and real-world application. Approaches to fostering resilience must take into account cultural context and the identity development of individuals and communities (Harvey & Tummala-Narra, 2007).

Finally, more research is needed that attends to the interaction between biological factors and psychosocial processes and how this interaction creates particular physical and mental health realities (Clark, Anderson, Clark, & Williams, 1999; McEwen, 1998). Understanding the dynamic interplay of environmental, psychological, and biological processes requires more complex methodological approaches. Such work is essential to better understanding the whole person, whose life is embedded in multiple and changing contexts.

Future Directions

We conclude our chapter with a list of questions that can be used to guide the development of future theory and research that considers gender in sociocultural and ecological context.

1.Do counseling psychologists and the mental health profession in general need a diagnostic reference guide? If so, how may this guide take into account diversity among individuals and their social contexts?

2.What types of challenges and concerns should future research address in developing and examining interventions rooted in positive psychology specific to girls and women?

3. What research methodologies should be employed for future research examining ecologically based interventions specific to girls and women and their multiple identities (race, sexual orientation, SES)?

4. How can psychologists foster a reconceptualization of women's issues and challenges as potentially positive and growth producing?

5. How can the profession create new narratives of women's biological processes and foster these narratives among women?

References

American Association of University Women. (1994). Shortchanging girls, shortchanging America. Retrieved from http://www.aauw.org/learn/research/upload/SGSA-2.pdf.

American Association of University Women. (1992). The AAUW Report: How Schools Shortchange Girls. Retrieved from http://www.aauw.org/learn/research/upload/hssg.pdf.

American Association of University Women. (2004). Tenure denied: Cases of sex discrimination in academia. Retrieved from http://www.aauw.org/learn/research/upload/TenureDenied.pdf.

American Psychiatric Association (2000). Diagnostic and statistical manual of mental disorders (4th ed., text rev.). Washington, DC: Author.

American Psychological Association. (2004). Guidelines for psychological practice with older adults. *American Psychologist, 59,* 236–260.

American Psychological Association. (2007). Guidelines for psychological practice with girls and women. *American Psychologists, 62,* 949–979.

Ancis, J. R. (2008, Fall). *Women's legal experiences: Divorce and custody:* Part I. Division F (Division of Women Psychologists, Georgia Psychological Association) Quarterly Newsletter, 7–8.

Ancis, J. R. (April 2009a). *The role of power, control, and dual relationships in divorce and custody disputes.* Paper presented at the Southeastern Regional Counseling Psychology Conference, Athens, Georgia.

Ancis, J. R. (August 2009b). *An empirical investigation of mothers' experiences with guardians ad litem.* Paper presented at the meeting of the American Psychological Association, Toronto, Canada.

Ancis, J. R., & Jongsma, A. E. (2007). *The Complete Women's Psychotherapy Treatment Planner.* Hoboken, NJ: Wiley.

Ancis, J. R., & Ladany, N. (2001). A multicultural framework for counselor supervision. In L. J. Bradley & N. Ladany (Eds.), *Counselor supervision: Principles, process, and practice* (3rd ed.) (pp. 63–90). Philadelphia: Brunner-Routledge.

Ancis, J. R. & Ladany, N. (2010). A multicultural framework for counselor supervision. In L. J. Bradley & N. Ladany (Eds.), *Counselor supervision* (4th ed.) (pp. 53–95). New York: Routledge.

Ancis, J. R., & Phillips, S. D. (1996). Academic gender bias and women's behavioral agency self-efficacy. *Journal of Counseling and Development, 75,* 131–137. doi:10.1002/j.1556-6676.1996.tb02323.x

Ancis, J. R., Neelerambam, K., & Watson, L. (August 2009). *Psychosocial impact of divorce and custody disputes: Clinical implications.* Paper presented at the meeting of the American Psychological Association, Toronto, Canada.

Anderson, T., Holberg, J. L., & Carson, K. L. (2000). The contextual therapeutic relationship: Biological considerations in psychotherapy research and practice. *Psychotherapy: Theory,*

Research, Practice, Training, 37, 107–116. doi:10.1037/h0087727

Aspinwall, L. G., & Tedeschi, R. G. (2010). The value of positive psychology for health psychology: Progress and pitfalls in examining the relation of positive phenomena to health. *Annals of Behavioral Medicine, 39*, 4–15. doi:10.1007/s12160-009-9153-0

Atwood, N. C. (2001). Gender bias in families and its clinical implications for women. *Social Work*, 46(1), 23–36. doi: 10.1093/sw/46.1.23

Association for Women in Psychology Committee on Bias in Psychiatric Diagnosis. Retrieved May 29 2011, from http://www.awpsych.org/index.php?option=com_content&view=article&id=102&Itemi d=126.

Bartone, P. T. (1989). Predictors of stress related illness in city bus drivers. *JournalofOccupationalMedicine, 31*, 657–663. Retrieved from http://journals.lww.com/joem/Abstract/1989/08000/Predictors_of_Stress_Related_Illness_in_City_Bus.8.aspx.

Bartone, P. T., Roland, R. R., Picano, J. J., & Williams, T. J. (2008). Psychological hardiness predicts success in US Army Special Forces candidates. *International Journal of Selection and Assessment, 16*, 78–81. doi: 10.1111/j.1468-2389.2008.00412.x

Beck, C. J. A., & Sales, B. D. (2001). *Family mediation: Facts, myths, and future prospects.* Washington, DC: APA.

Bemak, F., & Conyne, R. K. (2004). Ecological group work. In R. K. Conyne & E. P. Cook (Eds.), *Ecological counseling: An innovative approach to conceptualizing person-environment interaction* (pp. 195–218). Alexandria, VA: ACA Press.

Betz, N. E., & Fitzgerald, L. F. (1987). *The career psychology of women.* New York: Academic Press.

Bhui, K., Stansfeld, S., McKenzie, K., Karlsen, S., Nazroo, J., & Weich, S. (2005). Racial/ethnic discrimination and common mental disorders among workers: Findings from the EMPIRIC study of ethnic minority groups in the United Kingdom. *American Journal of Public Health, 95*(3), 496–501.Retrieved from http://www.ncbi.nlm.nih.gov/pubmed/15727983.

Biswas-Diener, R. (2009). Personal coaching as a positive intervention. *Journal of Clinical Psychology, 65*, 544–553. doi:10.1002/jclp.20589

Biswas-Diener, R. (2010). A positive way of addressing negatives: Using strengths-based interventions in coaching and therapy. In G.W. Burns (Ed.). *Happiness, healing, enhancement: Your casebook collection for applying positive psychology in therapy,* (pp. 291–302). Hoboken, NJ: John Wiley & Sons.

Bjorklund, P. (2006). No man's land: Gender bias and social constructivism in the diagnosis of borderline personality disorder. *Issues in Mental Health Nursing, 27*, 3–23. doi: 10.1080/01612840500312753

Bonanno, G. (2004). Loss, trauma, and human resilience: Have we underestimated the human capacity to thrive after extremely aversive events? *American Psychologist, 51*, 72–82. doi: 10.1037/0003-066X.59.1.20

Bradley, R., & Davino, K. (2007). Interpersonal violence, recovery, and resilience in incarcerated women. *Journal of Aggression, Maltreatment and Trauma, 14*, 123–146. doi:10.1300/J146v14n01_07

Briere, J., & Jordan, C. (2004). Violence against women: Outcome complexity and implications for assessment and treatment. *Journal of Interpersonal Violence, 19*, 1252–1276. doi:10.1177/0886260504269682.

Bronfenbrenner, U. (1977). Toward an experimental ecological of human development. *American Psychologist, 32*, 513–531. doi:10.1037/0003-066X.32.7.513

Bronfenbrenner, U. (1979). *The ecology of human development: Experiments by nature and design.* Cambridge, MA: Harvard University Press.

Bronfenbrenner, U. (1992). Ecological systems theory. In R. Vasta (Ed.), *Six theories of child development* (pp. 187–250). London: Jessica Kingsley Publishers.

Broverman, I. K., Broverman, D. M., Clarkson, F. E., Rosenkrantz, P. S., & Vogel, S. R. (1970). Sex-role stereotypes and clinical judgment on mental health. *Journal of Consulting and Clinical Psychology, 34*, 1–7. doi:10.1037/h0028797

Bryan, P. E. (2006). *Constructive divorce: Procedural justice and sociolegal reform.* Washington, DC: APA.

Bryant-Davis, T., Chung, H., & Tillman, S. (2009). From the margins to the center: Ethnic minority women and the mental health effects of sexual assault. *Trauma, Violence and Abuse, 10*, 330–357. doi: 10.1177/1524838009339755

Bryant-Davis, T., & Ocampo, C. (2006). A therapeutic approach to the treatment of racist-incident-based trauma. *Journal of Emotional Abuse, 6*, 1–22, 450–469. doi: 10.1300/J135v06n04-01.

Campbell, R., Dworkin, E., & Cabral, G. (2009). An ecological model of the impact of sexual assault on women's mental health. *Trauma, Violence, and Abuse, 10*, 225–246. doi:10.1177/1524838009334456

Caplan, P. J. (1995). *They say you're crazy: How the world's most powerful psychiatrists decide who's normal.* Reading, MA: Addison-Wesley.

Caplan, P. J., & Cosgrove, L. (2004). *Bias in psychiatric diagnosis.* Lanham, MD: Rowman and Littlefield.

Caplan, P. J., & Profit, W. E. (2004). Some future contenders. In P. J. Caplan & L. Cosgrove (Eds.), *Bias in psychiatric diagnosis* (pp. 249–254). Lanham, MD: Rowman & Littlefield.

Carlson, B. E. (1984). Causes and maintenance of domestic violence: An ecological analysis. *Social Service Review, 58*, 569–587. doi:10.1086/644239

Centers for Disease Control. (2010). Current depression among adults—United States, 2006 and 2008. *Morbidity and Mortality Weekly Report, 59*, 1229–1235. Retrieved from http://www.cdc.gov/mmwr/preview/mmwrhtml/mm5938a2.htm?s_cid=mm5938a2_x.

Chaplin, T. M., Gillham, J. E., Reivich, K., Elkon, A. G. L., Samuels, B., Freres, D. R., Winder, B., & Seligman, M. E. P. (2006). Depression prevention for early adolescent girls: A pilot study of all girls versus co-ed groups. *The Journal of Early Adolescence, 26*, 110–126. doi:10.1177/0272431605282655

Chronister, K. M., McWhirter, B. T., & Kerewsky, S. D. (2004). Prevention from an ecological framework. In R. K. Conyne & E. P. Cook (Eds.), *Ecological counseling: An innovative approach to conceptualizing person-environment interaction* (pp. 315–338). Alexandria, VA: ACA Press.

Clark, R., Anderson, N. B., Clark, V. R., & Williams, D. R. (1999). Racism as a stressor for African Americans: A biopsychosocial model. *American Psychologist, 54*, 805–816. doi: 10.1037/0003-066X.54.10.805

Clarke, L. H., & Griffin, M. (2008). Body image and aging: Older women and the embodiment of trauma. *Women's Studies International Forum, 31*, 200–208. doi: 10.1016/j.wsif.2008.04.001

Clifton, D. O., & Nelson, P. (1996). Soar with your strengths. New York: Dell Books.

Comas-Díaz, L., & Greene, B. (1994a). Overview: An ethnocultural mosaic. In L. Comas-Díaz & B. Greene (Eds.), *Women of Color: Integrating ethnic and gender identities in Psychotherapy* (pp. 3–9). New York: Guilford.

Comas-Díaz, L., & Greene, B. (1994b) (Eds.). *Women of Color: Integrating ethnic and gender identities in psychotherapy.* New York: Guilford.

Connolly, C. M. (2006). A feminist perspective of resilience in lesbian couples. *Journal of Feminist Family Therapy, 18,* 137–162. doi: 10.1300/J086v18n01_06

Conyne, R., & Cook, E. P. (Eds). (2004). *Ecological counseling: An innovative approach to conceptualizing person-environment interaction.* Alexandria, VA: American Counseling Association.

Cook, E. P., Heppner, M. J., & O'Brien, K. M. (2002). Career development of women of color and white women: Assumptions, conceptualization, and interventions from an ecological perspective. *Career Development Quarterly, 50,* 291–305. doi: 10.1002/j.2161-0045.2002.tb00574.x

Cook, E. P., Heppner, M. J., & O'Brien, K. M. (2005). Multicultural and gender influences in women's career development: An ecological perspective. *Journal of Multicultural Counseling and Development, 33,* 165–179. doi: 10.1002/j.2161-1912.2005.tb00014.x

Counselors for Social Justice. Committee on DSM-5 (2011). *Counselors for Social Justice Position Statement on the Development of the Diagnostic and Statistical Manual of Mental Disorders-5th ed. (DSM-5) and Proposed Draft Revision to DSM Disorders and Criteria.* Retrieved from http://counselorsforsocialjustice.com/advocacy.html.

Coyne, J. C., & Tennen, H. (2010). Positive psychology in cancer care: Bad science, exaggerated claims, and unproven medicine. *Annals of Behavioral Medicine, 39,* 16–26. doi:10.1007/s12160-009-9154-z

Coyne, J. C., Tennen, H., Ranchor, A. V. (2010). Positive psychology in cancer care: A story line resistant to evidence. *Annals of Behavioral Medicine, 39,* 35–42. doi: 10.1007/s12160-010-9157-9

Cross, W. E., Jr., & Vandiver, B. J. (2001). Nigrescence theory and measurement: Introducing the Cross Racial Identity Scale (CRIS). In J. G. Ponterotto, J. M. Casas, L. M. Suzuki, & C. M. Alexander (Eds.), *Handbook of multicultural counseling* (2nd ed.) (pp. 371–393). Thousand Oaks, CA: Sage.

Denmark, F., Russo, N. F., Frieze, I. H., & Sechzer, J. A. (1988). Guidelines for avoiding sexism in psychological research: A report of the Ad Hoc Committee on Nonsexist Research. *American Psychologist, 43,* 582–585. doi: 10.1037/0003-066X.43.7.582

Downing, N. E., & Roush. K. L. (1985). From passive-acceptance to active commitment: A model of feminist identity development for women. *The Counseling Psychologist, 13,* 695–709. doi: 10.1177/0011000085134013

DuBois, D. L., Burk-Braxton, C., Swenson, L. P., Tevendale, H. D., & Hardesty, J. L. (2002). Race and gender influences on adjustment in early adolescence: Investigation of an integrative model. *Child Development, 73,* 1573–1592. doi: 10.1111/1467-8624.00491

Durkin, J., & Joseph, S. (2009). Growth following adversity and its relation with subjective well-being and psychological well-being. *Journal of Loss and Trauma, 14,* 228–234. doi: 10.1080/15325020802540561

Dwyer, A. L. & Cummings, A. L.(2001) Stress, self-efficacy, social support, and coping strategies in university students. *Canadian Journal of Counselling, 35,* 208–220. Retrieved from http://cjc-rcc.ucalgary.ca/cjc/index.php/rcc/article/viewArticle/189.

Edleson, J. L., & Tolman, R. M. (1992). *Intervention for men who batter: An ecological approach.* Newbury Park, CA: Sage Publications.

Fassinger, R. E. (2002). Hitting the ceiling: Gender barriers to occupational entry, advancement and achievement. In L. Diamant & J. Lee (Eds.), *The psychology of sex, gender, and jobs: Issues and solutions* (pp. 21–46). Westport, CT: Greenwood.

Fazio, R.J., Rashid, T., & Hayward, H. (2008). Growth through loss and adversity: A choice worth making. In S. J. Lopez (Ed.), *Positive psychology: Exploring the best in people,* Vol. 3: *Growing in the face of adversity* (pp. 1–27). Westport, CT: Praeger Publishers/Greenwood Publishing Group.

Federal Interagency Forum on Aging-Related Statistics. (2000). *Older Americans 2000: Key indicators of well-being.* Washington, DC: U.S. Government Printing Office.

Fischer, A. R., & Holz, K. B. (2010). Testing a model of women's personal sense of justice, control, well-being, and distress in the context of sexist discrimination. *Psychology of Women Quarterly, 34,* 297–310. doi: 10.1111/j.1471-6402.2010.01576.x

Franklin, A. J., Boyd-Franklin, N., & Kelly, S. (2006). Racism and invisibility: Race-related stress, emotional abuse and psychological trauma for people of color. *Journal of Emotional Abuse, 6,* 9–30. doi: 10.1300/J135v06n02-02

Fredrickson, B. L. (1998). What good are positive emotions? *Review of General Psychology, 2,* 300–319. doi:10.1037/1089-2680.2.3.300

Fredrickson, B. L. (2001). The role of positive emotions in positive psychology: The broaden-and-build theory of positive emotions. *American Psychologist, 56,* 218–226. doi:10.1037/0003-066X.56.3.218

Fredrickson, B. L. (2003). The value of positive emotions. *American Scientist, 91,* 330–335. Retrieved from http://www.bus.umich.edu/positive/pos-research/positivesessions/2003-07fredrickson.pdf.

Fredrickson, B., & Losada, M. (2005). Positive affect and the positive dynamics of human flourishing. *American Psychologist, 60,* 678–686. doi: 10.1037/0003-066X.60.7.678

Fredrickson, B. L., & Roberts, T. A. (1997). Objectification theory: Toward understanding women's lived experiences and mental health risks. *Psychology of Women Quarterly, 21,*173–206. doi: 10.1111/j.1471-6402.1997.tb00108.x

Gadalla, T. M. (2009). Impact of marital dissolution on men's and women's incomes: A longitudinal study. *Journal of Divorce and Remarriage, 50,* 55–65. doi: 10. 1080/10502550802365714

Gannon, L., Luchetta, T., Rhodes, K., Pardie, L., & Segrist, D. (1992). Sex bias in psychological research: Progress or complacency? *American Psychologist, 47,* 389–396. doi: 10.1037/0003-066X.48.10.1093.b

Gee, G. C. (2002). A multilevel analysis of the relationship between institutional and individual racial discrimination and health status. *American Journal of Public Health, 92,* 615–623. Retrieved from http://www.ncbi.nlm.nih.gov/pubmed/11919062.

Gee, G. C., Ryan, A., Laflamme, D. J., & Holt, J. (2006). Self-reported discrimination and mental health status among African descendants, Mexican Americans, and other Latinos in the New Hampshire REACH 2010 initiative: The added dimension of immigration. *American Journal of Public Health, 96,* 1821–1828. Retrieved from http://ajph.aphapublications.org/cgi/content/abstract/96/10/1821.

Gelso, C., & Fretz, B. (2001). *Counseling psychology.* Fort Worth, TX: Harcourt College Publishers.

Gill, R., & Floos, R. R. (2008). Editors' introduction: Secrecy and silence in research: Opening up the debates. *Feminism and Psychology, 18,* 381–383. doi: 10.1177/0959353508092091

Grant, A. M., & Spence, G. B. (2010). Using coaching and positive psychology to promote a flourishing workforce: A model of goal-striving and mental health. In P. A. Linley, S. Harrington, & N. Garcea (Eds.), *Oxford handbook of positive psychology and work* (pp. 175–188). New York, NY: Oxford University Press.

Greene, B. (2004). Lesbian women of color: Triple jeopardy. In L. Comas-Díaz & B. Greene (Eds.). *Women of color: Integrating ethnic and gender identities in psychotherapy* (pp. 389–427). New York: Guilford.

Greer, T. M., Laseter, A., & Asiamah, D. (2009). Gender as a moderator of the relation between race-related stress and mental health symptoms for African Americans. *Psychology of Women Quarterly, 33,* 295–307. doi: 10.1111/j.1471-6402.2009.01502

Guinier, L., Fine, M., & Balin, J. (1997). *Becoming gentlemen: Women, law school, and institutional change.* Boston: Beacon Press.

Hackett, G. (1985). The role of mathematics self-efficacy in the choice of math-related majors of college women and men: A path analysis. *Journal of Counseling Psychology, 32,* 47–56. doi: 10.1037/0022-0167.32.1.47

Hammond, W. J., Gillen, M., & Yen, I. H. (2010). Workplace discrimination and depressive symptoms: A study of multiethnic hospital employees. *Race and Social Problems, 2,* 19–30. doi: 10.1007/s12552-010-9024-0

Harvard Men's Health Watch. (January 2010). Mars vs. Venus: The gender gap in health. Retrieved from http://www.health.harvard.edu/newsletters/Harvard_Mens_Health_Watch/2010/January/mars-vs-venus-the-gender-gap-in-health.

Harvey, M. R., & Tummala-Narra, P. (2007). Sources and expression of resilience in trauma survivors: Ecological theory, multicultural perspectives. *Journal of Aggression, Maltreatment and Trauma, 14,* 1–7. doi: 10.1300/J146v14n01_01

Hawley, D. R. (2000). Clinical implications of family resilience. *The American Journal of Family Therapy, 28,* 101–116. doi: 10.1080/019261800261699

Hawley, D. R., & DeHaan, L. (1996). Toward a definition of family resilience: Integrating life-span and family perspectives. *Family Process, 35,* 283–298. doi: 10.1111/j.1545-5300.1996.00283.x

Hays, P. A. (2001). *Addressing cultural complexities in practice: Assessment, diagnosis, and therapy.* Washington, DC: American Psychological Association.

Hays, P. A. (2008). *Addressing cultural complexities in practice: Assessment, diagnosis, and therapy* (2nd ed.). Washington, DC: American Psychological Association.

Heise, L. L. (1998). Violence against women: An integrated, ecological framework. *Violence Against Women, 4,* 262–290. doi:10.1177/1077801298004003002

Helgeson, V. S., Reynolds, K. A., & Tomich, P. L. (2006). A meta-analytic review of benefit finding and growth. *Journal of Consulting and Clinical Psychology, 74,* 797–816. doi: 10.1037/0022-006X.74.5.797

Hill, W. G., & Donatelle, R. J.(2005). The impact of gender role conflict on multidimensional social support in older men. *International Journal of Men's Health, 4,* 267–276. doi: 10.3149/jmh.0403.267

Hirschman, C., Impett, E. A., & Schooler, D. (2006). Dis/embodied voices: What late-adolescent girls can teach us about objectification and sexuality. *Sexuality Research and Social Policy: Journal of National Sexuality Research Center, 3,* 8–20. Retrieved from http://ezproxy.gsu.edu:2313/10.1525/srsp.2006.3.4.8.

Human Rights Watch. (December, 1999). *Promises broken: An assessment of children's rights on the 10th anniversary of the convention on the rights of the child.* Retrieved from www.hrw.org/campaigns/crp/promises/education.

Impett, E. A., Schooler, D., & Tolman, D. L. (2006). To be seen and not heard: Femininity idealogy and adolescent girls' sexual health. *Archives of Sexual Behavior, 34,* 131–144. doi:10.1007/s10508-005-9016-0

International Center for Research on Women. (2005). Development initiative on supporting healthy adolescents. Retrieved from http://www.icrw.org/publications.

International Center for Research on Women. (2007). Too young to wed: Education & action toward ending child marriage. Retrieved from www.icrw.org/docs/2006_cmtoolkit/cm_all.pdf.

Ivey, A. E., & Ivey, M. B. (1998). Reframing *DSM-IV*: Positive strategies from developmental counseling and therapy. *Journal of Counseling and Development, 76,* 334–350. doi: 10.1002/j.1556-6676.1998.tb02550.x

Johnson, N. G. (2003). On treating adolescent girls: Focus on strengths and resiliency in psychotherapy. *Journal of Clinical Psychology/In Session, 59,* 1193–1203. doi:10.1002/jclp.10210

Jones, H. L., Cross, W. E., DeFour, D. C. (2007). Race-related stress, racial identity attitudes, and mental health among Black women. *Journal of Black Psychology, 33,* 208–231. doi: 10.1177/0095798407299517

Jordache, I., & Low, N. C. (2010). The overdiagnosis of bipolar disorder. *Journal of Psychiatry and Neuroscience, 35,* E3-D4. doi: 10.1503/jpn.100032

Joseph, S. (2009). Growth following adversity: Positive psychological perspectives on posttraumatic stress. *Psychological Topics, 18,* 335–343. Retrieved from http://hrcak.srce.hr/file/74341.

Joseph, S., & Linley, P. A. (2006). Growth following adversity: Theoretical perspectives and implications for clinical practice. *Clinical Psychology Review, 26,* 1041–1053. doi: 10.1016/j.cpr.2005.12.006

Kauffman, C., & Silberman, J. (2009). Finding and fostering the positive in relationships: Positive interventions in couples therapy. *Journal of Clinical Psychology, 65,* 520–531. doi:10.1002/jclp.20594

Kerr, B. A. (1997). *Smart girls.* Scottsdale, AZ: Great Potential Press.

Kerr, B. A., & Larson, A. L. (2008). How smart girls become talented women. In S. J. Lopez (Ed.). *Positive psychology: Exploring the best in people,* Vol. 4: *Pursuing human flourishing* (pp. 131–145). Westport, CT: Praeger Publishers/Greenwood Publishing Group.

Kessler, R. C., Mickelson, K. D., Williams, D. R. (1999). The prevalence, distribution, and mental health correlates of perceived discrimination in the United States. *Health and Social Behavior, 40,* 208–230. doi:10.2307/2676349

Keyes, C. M. (2002). The mental health continuum: From languishing to flourishing in life. *Journal of Health And Social Behavior, 43,* 207–222. doi:10.2307/3090197

Keyes, C. L. M., & Lopez, S. J. (2002). Toward a science of mental health: Positive directions in diagnosis and interventions. In C. R. Snyder & S. J. Lopez (Eds.), *Handbook of positive psychology* (1st ed.) (pp. 45–62). New York: Oxford University Press.

Keyes, C. L. M., & Haidt, J. (2003). *Flourshing: Positive psychology and the life well lived.* Washington, DC: American Psychological Association.

Keyes, C. L. M., & Ryff, C. D. (2003). Somatization and mental health: A comparative study of the idiom of distress hypothesis. *Social Science and Medicine, 57,* 1833–1845. doi:10.1016/S0277-9536(03)00017-0

Keyes, C. L. M. (2005a). Mental illness and/or mental health? Investigating axioms of the complete state model of health. *Journal of Consulting and Clinical Psychology, 73,* 539–548. doi:10.1037/0022-006X.73.3.539

Keyes, C. L. M. (2005b). Gender and subjective well-being in the United States: From subjective well-being to complete mental health. In K.V. Oxington (Ed.), *Psychology of Stress* (pp. 1–15). New York: Nova Biomedical Books.

Keyes, C. L. M. (2007). Promoting and protecting mental health as flourishing: A complimentary strategy for improving national mental health. *American Psychologist, 62,* 95–108. doi:10.1037/0003-066X.62.2.95

Keyes, C. L. M. (2009). Toward a science of mental health. In S. J. Lopez & C. R. Snyder & (Eds.). *Handbook of positive psychology* (2nd ed.) (pp. 45–62). New York: Oxford University Press.

Kimmel, E. B., & Crawford, M. C. (2001). Methods for studying gender. In J. Worell (Ed.), *Encyclopedia of women and gender* (pp. 749–758). San Diego, CA: Academic Press.

Kirschman, K. J. B., Johnson, R. J., Bender, J. A., & Roberts, M. C. (2009). Positive psychology for children and adolescents: Development, prevention, and promotion. In S. J. Lopez & C. R. Snyder (Eds.), *Oxford handbook of positive psychology* (2nd ed.) (pp. 133–148). New York: Oxford University Press.

Kobasa, S. C. (1979). Stressful life events, personality, and health: An inquiry into hardiness. *Journal of Personality and Social Psychology, 37,* 1–11. doi: 10.1037/0022-3514.37.1.1

Kobasa, S. C. (1982). Commitment and coping among stress resistance among lawyers. *Journal of Personality and Social Psychology, 37,* 1–11. doi: 10.1037/0022-3514.42.4.707

Krieger, N. (1990). Racial and gender discrimination: Risk factors for high blood pressure? *Social Science Medicine, 30,* 1273–1281. Retrieved from http://ajph.aphapublications.org/.

Krieger, N., Rowley, D. L., Herman, A. A., Avery, B., & Phillips, M. (1993). Racism, sexism, and social class: Implications for studies of health, disease, and well-being. *American Journal of Preventive Medicine, 9,* 82–122. Retrieved from http://www.ajpm-online.net/.

Landrine, H., & Klonoff, E. A. (2001). Health and health care: How gender makes women sick. In J. Worell (Ed.), *Encyclopedia of women and gender* (pp. 577–594). San Diego, CA: Academic Press.

Lerman H. (1987). *A note in Freud's eye: From psychoanalysis to the psychology of women.* New York: Springer.

Lewis, T. T., Everson-Rose, S. A., Powell, L. H., Matthews, K. A., Brown, C., Karavolos, K., et al. (2006). Chronic exposure to everyday discrimination and coronary artery calcification in African-American women: The SWAN heart study. *Psychosomatic Medicine, 68,* 362–368. doi:10.1097/01.psy.0000221360.94700.16

Lindberg, S. M., Grabe, S., & Shibley Hyde, J. (2007). Gender, pubertal development, and peer sexual harassment predict objectified body consciousness in early adolescence. *Journal or Research on Adolescence, 17,* 723–742. doi: 10.1111/j.1532-7795.2007.00544.x

Linley, P. A., & Joseph, S. (2004). Positive change following trauma and adversity: A review. *Journal of Traumatic Stress, 17,* 11–21. doi: 10.1023/B:JOTS.0000014671.27856.7e

Linley, P. A., & Joseph, S. (2005). The human capacity for growth through adversity. *American Psychologist, 60,* 262–264. doi: 10.1037/0003-066X.60.3.262b

Lloyd, C. B. (Ed). (2005). *Growing up global: The changing transitions to adulthood in developing countries.* Washington, DC: National Academies Press.

Lopez, S. J., Edwards, L. M., Teramoto Pedrotti, J., Prosser, E. C., LaRue, S., Vehige Spalitto, S., & Ulven, J. C. (2006). Beyond the *DSM-IV*: Assumptions, alternatives, and alterations. *Journal of Counseling and Development, 84,* 259–267. doi:10.1002/j.1556-6678.2006.tb00404.x

Lopez, S. J., Snyder, C. R., & Rasmussen, H. (2003). Striking a vital balance: Developing a complementary focus on human weakness and strength through positive psychological assessment. In S. J. Lopez & C. R. Snyder (Eds.), *Positive psychological assessment: A handbook of models and measures* (pp. 3–20). Washington, DC: American Psychological Association.

Lykken, D. (1999). *Happiness: The nature and nurture of joy and contentment.* New York: St. Martin's Griffin.

Maddi, S. R. (2002). The story of hardiness: Twenty years of theorizing, research, and practice. *Consulting Psychology Journal, 54,* 173–185. doi: 10.1037/1061-4087.54.3.173

Maddi, S. R. (2006). Hardiness: The courage to grow from stresses. *The Journal of Positive Psychology, 1,* 160–168. doi: 10.1080/17439760600619609

Maddi, S. R., & Kobasa, S. C. (1984). *The hardy executive: Health under stress.* Homewood, IL: Dow Jones-Irwin.

Magyar-Moe, J. L. (2009). *Therapist's guide to positive psychological interventions.* New York: Academic Press.

Major, B., & O'Brien, L. T. (2005). The social psychology of stigma. *Annual Review of Psychology, 56,* 393–421. doi: 10.1146/annurev.psych.56.091103.070137

Marshall, T. C. (2010). Gender, peer relations, and intimate romantic relationships. In J. C. Chrisler & D. R. McCreary (Eds.), *Handbook of gender research in psychology,* Vol. 2: *Gender research in social and applied psychology* (pp. 281–310). New York: Springer Publishing.

McEwen, B. S. (1998). Seminars in Medicine of the Beth Israel Deaconess Medical Center: Protective and damaging effects of stress mediators. *The New England Journal of Medicine, 338*(3), 171–179. doi:10.1056/NEJM199801153380307

McFarlane, J., Malecha, A., Gist, J., Watson, K., Batten, E., Hall, I., et al. (2005a). Intimate partner sexual assault against women and associated victim substance use, suicidality, and risk factors for femicide. *Issues in Mental Health Nursing, 26,* 953–967. doi: 10.1080/01612840500248262

McFarlane, J., Malecha, A., Watson, K., Gist, J., Betten, E., Hall, I., et al. (2005b). Intimate partner sexual assault against women: Frequency, health consequences and treatment outcomes. *Obstetrics and Gynecology, 105,* 99–108. doi: 10.1097/01.AOG.0000146641.98665.b6

Mercurio, A., & Landry, L. (2008). Self-objectification and well-being: The impact of self-objectification on women's overall sense of self-worth and life satisfaction. *Sex Roles, 58,* 458–466. doi: 10.1007/s11199-007-9357-3

Miller, D. N., Nickerson, A. B., Jimerson, S. R. (2009). Positive psychology and school-based interventions. In R. Gilman, E. S. Huebner, & M. J. Furlong (Eds.), *Handbook of positive psychology in schools* (pp. 293–304). New York: Routledge/Taylor & Francis Group.

Moradi, B., & Subich, L. M. (2003). A concomitant examination of the relations of perceived racist and sexist events to the psychological distress for African American women. *The Counseling Psychologist, 31,* 451–469. doi: 10.1177/0011000003031004007

Moradi, B., Subich, L. M., & Phillips, J. C. (2002). Revisiting feminist identity development theory, research, and practice. *The Counseling Psychologist, 30,* 6–43. doi: 10.1177/0011000002301002

Myers, D. (2000). The funds, friends, and faith of happy people. *American Psychologist, 55,* 56–67. doi:10.1037/0003-066X.55.1.56

Neville, H. A., & Heppner, M. J. (1999). Contextualizing rape: Reviewing sequelae and proposing a culturally inclusive ecological model of sexual assault recovery. *Applied and Preventive Psychology, 8,* 41–62. doi:10.1016/S0962-1849(99)80010-9

Neville, H. A., & Pugh, H. (1997). General and culture-specific factors influencing African-American women's reporting patterns and perceived social support following sexual assault: An exploratory investigation. *Violence Against Women, 3,* 361–381. doi: 10.1177/1077801297003004003

Newman, K. S. (2001). After Acheson: Lessons for American policy on inequality and health. In J. S. Auerbach, & Krim-Gold, B. K. (Eds.). *Income, socioeconomic status, and health: Exploring the relationships* (pp. 107–131). Washington, DC: National.

Noll, S., & Fredrickson, B. L. (1998). A mediational model linking self-objectification, body shame, and disordered eating. *Psychology of Women Quarterly, 22,* 623–636. doi: 10.1111/j.1471-6402.1998.tb00181.x

Norrish, J. M., & Vella-Brodrick, D.A. (2009). Positive psychology and adolescents: Where are we now? Where to from here? *Australian Psychologist, 44,* 270–278. doi:10.1080/00050060902914103

O'Connell, W., & Mabry, A. (2004). The ecology of community and agency counseling: An administrator's perspective. In R. K. Conyne & E. P. Cook (Eds.), *Ecological counseling: An innovative approach to conceptualizing person-environment interaction* (pp. 243–264). Alexandria, VA: ACA Press.

Offman, A., & Kleinplatz, P. (2004). Does PMDD belong in the DSM? Challenging the medicalization of women's sexuality. *Canadian Journal of Human Sexuality, 13,* 17–27. Retrieved from http://www.sieccan.org/cjhs.html.

O'Leary, V. E., & Bhaju, J. (2006). Resilience and empowerment. In J. Worell and C. D. Goodheart (Eds.), *Handbook of girls' and women's psychological health* (pp. 157–165). New York: Oxford University Press.

Ortiz, S. Y., & Roscigno, V. J. (2009). Discrimination, women, and work: Processes and variations by race and class. *The Sociological Quarterly, 50,* 336–359. doi: 10.1111/j.1533-8525.2009.01143.x

Para-Mallam, F. J. (2010). Promoting gender equality in the context of Nigerian cultural and religious expression: Beyond increasing female access to education. *Compare: A Journal of Comparative and International Education, 40,* 459–477. doi: 10.1080/03057925.2010.490370

Patterson, J. M. (2002). Integrating family resilience and family stress theory. *Journal of Marriage and Family, 64,* 349–360. doi: 10.1111/j.1741-3737.2002.00349.x

Pavalko, E. K., Mossakowski, K. N., & Hamilton, V. J. (2003). Does perceived discrimination affect health? Longitudinal relationships between work discrimination and women's physical and emotional health. *Journal of Health and Social Behavior, 44,* 18–33. doi: 10.2307/1519813

Peterson, C., & Seligman, M. (2004). *Character strengths and virtues: A handbook and classification.* New York: Oxford.

Phillips, S. D., & Imhoff, A. R. (1997). Women and career development: A decade of research. *Annual Review of Psychology, 48,* 31–59. doi:10.1146/annurev.psych.48.1.31

Poorman, P. B. (2002). Perceptions of thriving by women who have experienced abuse or status-related oppression. *Psychology of Women Quarterly, 26,* 51–62. doi: 10.1111/1471-6402.00043

Prilleltensky, I., & Nelson, G. B. (2002). *Doing psychology critically: Making a difference in diverse settings.* New York: Palgrave Macmillan.

Rape, Abuse, and Incest National Network [RAINN]. (2009). How often does sexual assault occur? Retrieved from http://www.rainn.org/get-information/statistics/frequency-of-sexual-assault.

Rapin, L. S. (2004). Ecological applications to organizational consultation. In R. K. Conyne & E. P. Cook (Eds.), *Ecological counseling: An innovative approach to conceptualizing person-environment interaction* (pp. 265–288). Alexandria, VA: ACA Press.

Rettig, K. (2007). Divorce injustices: Perceptions of formerly wealth women of the stressors, crises and traumas. *Journal of Loss and Trauma, 12,* 175–198. doi: 10.1080/15434610600854103

Riecher-Rössler, A. (2010). Prospects for the classification of mental disorders in women. *European Psychiatry, 25,* 189–196. doi: 10.1016/j.eurpsy.2009.03.002

Robbins, M. S., Schwartz, S., Szapocznik, J. (2004). Structural ecosystems therapy with Hispanic adolescents exhibiting disruptive behavior disorders. In J. R. Ancis (Ed.), *Culturally responsive interventions: Innovative approaches to working with diverse populations* (pp. 71–99). New York: Brunner-Routledge.

Roberts, R. K., Swanson, N. G., Murphy, L. R. (2004). Discrimination and occupational mental health. *Journal of Mental Health. 13,* 129–142. doi: 10.1080/09638230410001669264

Root, M. P. P. (1997). Multiracial Asians: Models of ethnic identity. *Amerasia Journal, 23,* 29–41. Retrieved from http://www.aasc.ucla.edu/aascpress/ajcollection.asp

Root, M. P. P. (1998). Experiences and process affecting racial identity development: Preliminary results from the biracial sibling project. *Cultural Diversity and Mental Health, 4,* 237–247. doi:10.1037/1099-9809.4.3.237

Root, M. P. P. (1999). The biracial baby boom: Understanding ecological constructions of racial identity in the twenty-first century. In R. H. Sheets, & E. R. Hollins (Eds.), *Aspects of human development: Racial and ethnic identity in school practices* (pp. 67–89). Mahwah, NJ: Lawrence Erlbaum.

Root, M. P. P. (2000). Rethinking racial identity development: An ecological framework. In P. Spickard & J. Burroughs (Eds.), *We are a people: Narrative in the construction and deconstruction of ethnic identity* (pp. 205–220). Philadelphia, PA: Temple University Press.

Root, M. P. P. (2003). Updating models of racial and ethnic identity. In D. K. Freedheim (Ed.), *Handbook of psychology:* Vol. 1, *History of psychology* (pp. 503–508). Hoboken, NJ: John Wiley & Sons.

Rospenda, K. M., Richman, J. A., & Shannon, C. A. (2009). Prevalence and mental health correlates of harassment and discrimination in the workplace: Results from a national study. *Journal of Interpersonal Violence, 24,* 819–843. doi: 10.1177/0886260508317182

Rueger, S. Y., Malecki, C. K., & Demaray, M. K. (2008). Gender differences in the relationship between perceived social support and student adjustment during early adolescence. *School Psychology Quarterly, 23*, 496–514. doi:10.1037/1045-3830.23.4.496

Sadker, D. M., Sadker, M., & Zittelman, K. (2009). *Still failing at fairness: How gender bias cheats girls and boys in school and what we can do about it.* New York, NY: Simon & Schuster.

Sadker, M., & Sadker, D. (1994). *Failing at fairness: How our schools cheat girls.* New York, NY: Simon & Schuster.

Sanchez, L., & Kane, E. W. (1996). Women's and men's constructions of perceptions of housework fairness. *Journal of Family Issues, 17,* 358–387. doi: 10.1177/019251396017003004

Sanderson, S., & Sanders Thompson, V. L. (2002). Factors associated with perceived paternal involvement in childrearing. *Sex Roles, 46,* 99–111. doi: 10.1023/A:1016569526920

Schulz, A. J, Gravlee, C. C, Williams, D. R, Israel, B. A, Mentz, G., & Rowe, Z. (2006). Discrimination, symptoms of depression, and self-rated health among African American women in Detroit: Results from a longitudinal analysis. *American Journal of Public Health, 96,* 1265–1270. doi: 10.2105/AJPH.2005.064543

Seligman, M. E. P., & Csikszentmihalyi, M. (2000). Positive psychology: An introduction. *American Psychologist, 55,* 5–14. doi:10.1037/0003-066X.55.1.5

Seligman, M. E. P. (2002a). *Authentic happiness.* New York: Free Press.

Seligman, M. E. P. (2002b). Positive psychology, positive prevention, and positive therapy. In C. R. Snyder & S. J. Lopez (Eds.), *Handbook of positive psychology* (pp. 3–9). New York: Oxford University Press.

Seligman, M. E. P., Steen, T. A., Park, N., & Peterson, C. (2005). Positive psychology progress: Empirical validation of interventions. *American Psychologist, 60,* 410–421. doi:10.1037/0003-066X.60.5.410

Siegel, K., Schrimshaw, E. W. (2007). The stress moderating role of benefit finding on psychological distress and well-being among women living with HIV/AIDS. *AIDS Behavior, 11,* 421–433. doi: 10.1007/s10461-006-9186-3

Sin, N. L., & Lyubomirsky, S. (2009). Enhancing well-being and alleviating depressive symptoms with positive psychology interventions: A practice-friendly meta-analysis. *Journal of Clinical Psychology, 65,* 467–487. doi:10.1002/jclp.20593

Smith, P. H., White, J. W., & Moracco, B. (2009). Becoming who we are: A theoretical explanation of gendered social structures and social networks that shape adolescent interpersonal aggression. *Psychology of Women Quarterly, 33,* 25–29. doi:10.1111/j.1471-6402.2008.01470.x

Snyder, C. R., & Lopez, S. J. (Eds.). (2009). *Oxford handbook of positive psychology.* New York: Oxford University Press.

Starr Sered, S. (1999). "Woman" as symbol and women as agents: Gendered religious discourses and practices. In M. M. Ferree & J. Lorber, (Eds), *Revisioning gender,* Vol. 5, *The gender lens* (pp. 193–221). Thousand Oaks, CA: Sage.

Steer, A., & Tiggemann, M. (2008). The role of self-objectification in women's sexual functioning. *Journal of Social and Clinical Psychology, 27,* 205–225. doi: 10.1521/jscp.2008.27.3.205

Stockdale, M. S, & Vaux, A. (1993). What sexual harassment experiences lead respondents to acknowledge being sexually harassed? A secondary analysis of a university survey. *Journal of Vocational Behavior, 43,* 221–234. doi: 10.1006/jvbe.1993.1044

Strader, T. N., Collins, D. A., & Roe, T. D. (2000). *Building healthy individuals, families, and communities: Creating lasting connections.* New York, NY: Plenum.

Szapocznik, J., Kurtines, W., Santosteban, D. A., Pantin, H., Scoppetta, M., Mancilla, Y., et al. (1997). The evolution of structural ecosystems theory for working with Latino families. In J. G. Garcia & M. C. Zea (Eds.), *Psychological interventions and research with Latino Populations* (pp. 166–190). Boston: Allyn & Bacon.

Szymanski, D. M., & Meyer, D. (2008). Racism and heterosexism as correlates of psychological distress in African American sexual minority women. *Journal of LGBT Issues in Counseling, 2,* 94–108. doi: 10.1080/15538600802115423

Szymanski, D., & Stewart, D. (2010). Racism and sexism as correlates of African American women's psychological distress. *Sex Roles, 63,* 226–238. doi: 10.1007/s11199-010-9788-0

Tamres, L. K., Janicki, D., & Helgeson, V. S. (2002). Sex differences in coping behavior: A meta-anayltic review and an examination of relative coping. *Personality and Social Psychology Bulletin, 6,* 2–30. doi:10.1207/S15327957PSPR0601_1

Tarakeshwar, N., Hansen, N. B., Kochman, A., Fox, A., & Sikkema, K. J. (2006). Resiliency among individuals with childhood sexual abuse and HIV: Perspectives on addressing sexual trauma. *Journal of Traumatic Stress, 19,* 449–460. doi: 10.1002/jts.20132

Thomas, S. A., & González-Prendes, A. A. (2009). Powerlessness, anger, and stress in African American women: Implications for physical and emotional health. *Health Care for Women, 30,* 93–113. doi: 10.1080/07399330802523709

Thomas, C., & Ryan, M. (2008). Women's perceptions of the divorce experience: A qualitative study. *Journal of Divorce and Remarriage, 49,* 210–224. doi: 10.1080/10502550802222394

Tolin, D. F., & Foa, E. B. (2006). Sex differences in trauma and posttraumatic stress disorder: A quantitative review of 25 years of research. *Psychological Bulletin, 132,* 959–992. doi: 10.1037/1942-9681.S.1.37

U.S. Department of Justice. (2009). *National crime victimization study 2009.* Retrieved from http://bjs.ojp.usdoj.gov/index.cfm?ty=pbdetail&iid=2217.

Ussher, J. M. (2000). *Women's health: Contemporary international perspectives.* London: British Psychological Society.

Van de Velde, S., Bracke, P., Levecque, K., & Meuleman, B. (2010). Gender differences in depression in 25 European countries after eliminating measurement bias in the CES-D 8. *Social Science Research, 39,* 396–404. doi:10.1016/j.ssresearch.2010.01.002

Wadsworth, E., Dhillon, K., Shaw, C., Bhui, K., Stansfeld, S., & Smith, A. (2007). Racial discrimination, ethnicity and work stress. *Occupational Medicine. 57,* 18–24. doi:10.1093/occmed/kql088

Wallace, J. M., & Forman, T. A. (1998). Religion's role in promoting health and reducing risk among American youth. *Health and Education Behavior, 25,* 721–741. doi:10.1177/109019819802500604

Walsh, W. B. (2004). *Counseling psychology and optimal human functioning*. New York: Lawrence Erlbaum.

Waltermaurer, E., Watson, C., & McNutt, L. (2006). Black women's health: The effect of perceived racism and intimate-partner violence. *Violence Against Women, 12*, 1214–1222. doi: 10.1177/1077801206293545

Watson, L., & Ancis, J. R. (August 2010). *The abusive personality: Power tactics during divorce and custody disputes*. Paper presented at the meeting of the American Psychological Association, San Diego, California.

Watson, A. L., Collins, R. L., & Collins Correia, F. (2004). Advocacy and social justice in the context of ecological counseling. In R. K. Conyne & E. P. Cook (Eds.), *Ecological counseling: An innovative approach to conceptualizing person-environment interaction* (pp. 289–314). Alexandria, VA: ACA Press.

Weissman, M. W., Bland, R., Joyce, P. R., Newman, S., Wells, J. E., & Wittchen, H-U. (1993). Sex differences in rates of depression: Cross-national perspectives. *Journal of Affective Disorders, 29*, 77–84. doi:10.1016/0165-0327(93)90025-F

White, J. W. (2009). A gendered approach to adolescent dating violence: Conceptual and methodological issues. *Psychology of Women Quarterly, 33*, 1–15. doi:10.1111/j.1471-6402.2008.01467.x

Williams, D. R. (2008). Racial/ethnic variations in women's health: The social embeddedness of health. *American Journal of Public Health, 98*, 588–597. Retrieved from http://www.ncbi.nlm.nih.gov/pubmed/11919058

Williams, D. R., & Collins C. (2001). Racial residential segregation: A fundamental cause of racial disparities in health. *Public Health Reports, 116*, 404–416. Retrieved from http://www.ncbi.nlm.nih.gov/pmc/articles/PMC1497358/pdf/12042604.pdf.

Williams, D. R, Neighbors, H. W., & Jackson, J. S. (2003). Racial/ethnic discrimination and health: Findings from community studies. *American Journal of Public Health. 93*, 200–208. Retrieved from http://www.ncbi.nlm.nih.gov/pubmed/12554570

Wilson, I., Griffin, C., & Wren, B. (2002). The validity of the diagnosis of gender identity disorder. *Clinical Child Psychology and Psychiatry, 7*, 335–351. doi: 10.1177/135910450200 7003003

Wood, A. M., & Tarrier, N. (2010). Positive clinical psychology: A new vision and strategy for integrated research practice. *Clinical Psychology Review, 30*, 819–829. doi: 10.1016/j.cpr.2010.06.003

Worell, J. (2001). Feminist interventions: Accountability beyond symptom reduction. *Psychology f Women Quarterly, 25*, 335–343. doi:10.1111/1471-6402.00033

Worell, J., & Johnson, N. G. (Eds.). (1997). *Shaping the future of feminist psychology: Research, education, and practice*. Washington, DC: American Psychological Association.

Worell, J., & Remer, P. (2003). *Feminist perspectives in therapy: Empowering diverse women* (2nd ed.). Hoboken, NJ: John Wiley & Sons.

Working Group of a New View of Women's Sexual Problems. (2004). In P. Caplan and L. Cosgrove (Eds.), *Bias in psychiatric diagnosis* (pp. 233–239.) Lanham, MA: Jason Aronson.

World Health Organization. (1948). World Health Organization constitution. In *Basic Documents*. Geneva: Author.

Wright, B. A., & Lopez, S. J. (2002). Widening the diagnostic focus: A case for including human strengths and environmental resources. In C. R. Snyder & S. J. Lopez (Eds.), *The handbook of positive psychology* (pp. 26–44). New York: Oxford University Press.

Wright, B. A., & Lopez, S. J. (2009). Widening the diagnostic focus: A case for including human strengths and environmental resources. In S. J. Lopez & C. R. Snyder (Eds.), *The handbook of positive psychology* (pp. 71–87). New York: Oxford University Press.

Wyche, K. F., & Rice, J. K. (1997). Feminist therapy: From dialogue to tenets. In J. Worell & N. G. Johnson (Eds.), Shaping the future of feminist psychology: Education, research, and practice (pp. 57–71). Washington, DC: American Psychological Association.

Yakushko, O., & Chronister, K.M. (2005). Immigrant women and counseling: The invisible others. *Journal of Counseling and Development, 83*, 292–298. doi: 10.1002/j.1556-6678.2005.tb00346.x

Yakushko, O., Davidson, M. M., & Williams, E. (2009). Identity salience model: A paradigm for integrating multiple identities in clinical practice. *Psychotherapy: Theory, Research, Practice, Training, 46*, 180–192. doi:10.1037/a0016080

Yaughn, E., & Nowicki, S. (1999). Close relationships and complementary interpersonal styles among men and women. *The Journal of Social Psychology, 139*, 473–478. doi: 10.1080/00224549909598406

Yewchuck, C., Äyst, S. O., & Schlosser, G. (2001). Attribution of career facilitators by eminent Women from Canada and Finland. *High Ability Studies, 12*, 89–112. doi: 10.1080/13598130124367

Yoder, J. D. (2007). *Women and gender: Making a difference* (3rd ed.). Cornwall-on-Hudson, NY: Sloan Publishing.

Zalaquett, C. P., Fuerth, K. M., Stein, C., Ivey, A. E., & Ivey, M. B. (2008). Reframing the DSM-IV-TR from a multicultural/social justice perspective. *Journal of Counseling and Development, 86*, 364–371. doi: 10.1002/j.1556-6678.2008.tb00521.x

CHAPTER

5 Critical Questioning of Social and Feminist Identity Development Literature: Themes, Principles, and Tools

Ann R. Fischer *and* Kurt A. DeBord

Abstract

Theory and research in psychology are products of numerous, often unnamed choices made by individuals embedded in systems of power and privilege. Acknowledging and dissecting these effects allow more conscious decision making about the research and theory-making process, ultimately improving work with clients, students, and communities. Building on feminist science studies and the feminist therapy technique of power analysis, the authors take a process-oriented approach, examining the roles of power and privilege in shaping knowledge production and "the literature." In order to model metacognition and systematic questioning of the "unnamed specificity" pervading research, they first identify overarching principles of how societal factors shape the research process. Next, they articulate practical tools for analyzing the roles of power in any body of psychological research. As a case example, they then apply those tools to relevant research and theory, with particular emphasis on critiquing the feminist identity literature to which the first author has contributed.

Key Words: Identity, power, privilege, feminism, feminist identity, social identity, critical thinking, metacognition, research methods, identity development

Imagine the following hypothetical scenario: You are attending a research symposium at a nearby university, sponsored by the Department of Psychology. The title of the talk you are attending is "This Is a What a Feminist Looks Like," and you listen intently as the speaker informs the audience of staff members, students, faculty, and community members about the current state of research on feminist identity development. Among other findings, the presenter summarizes empirical data indicating that women who have progressed into higher stages of feminist identity development have been shown to be more likely to recognize sexism when they see it, to evaluate the work of other women more favorably, and to see themselves as more capable of pursuing and succeeding in various careers. The speaker addresses the research on advancement to higher stages of feminist identity development by noting the positive correlations found between such advancement and strengths in women, such as higher self-esteem and achievement in school. It is clear that many in the audience are engaged and are thinking about implications of such research. You, too, begin thinking about the implications.

What Do You Think?

Now the speaker asks the audience to break into small groups for discussion. Within the small groups, each individual is invited to share reactions to the findings just presented. Group members begin to pose questions, make comments, and talk about how the findings are relevant to their own lives or those of their clients. As a member of this audience, what would you make of these findings, and how would you consider using them to enhance your counseling or other clinical work? Please take a moment right now and jot down a few ideas. (Please do actually write for a moment; you will get more out of the reading this way.) We will come back to your responses to this thought experiment later in the chapter.

Attending to Process and Content

The writing we asked you to complete will, we hope, help to prepare you for engagement in this chapter and for engagement with us in the process of metacognition, or thinking about thinking. We aim to use the tools of critical power analysis and metacognition to reveal flaws in our thinking, holes in our observations, and gaps in our knowledge, rather than to assume that our standard research questions and methods reliably provide us with insights into general principles that govern social identity dynamics because we intend them to do so. Traditionally, many of us in academia have been steeped in a basic research methodology that reflects the values of conventional academic culture. Following from this methodology, students are often presented with a theory, model, or specific research findings and then are asked to apply that material to a client case or more generally to counseling practice. We could have adopted the same method while writing this chapter: presenting theory, describing related research findings, applying the findings generally, identifying caveats, and making recommendations for continuing these lines of research.

However, because this is a book on multicultural and feminist ideas and practices, we thought a different approach might be helpful. Our goal is to apply multicultural, feminist, and social justice–oriented strategies in the moment, during our writing, to focus on the role that social power plays in our research. We invite readers to join us in questioning what assumptions our field's methods contain, what possibilities different research questions might open, and why we should assume that any research can be applied to any client. Although we review literature on feminist and other social identity development, we do not do so in the typical linear way. Instead, we weave this material throughout the chapter, using a more process-oriented and unconventionally structured approach.

Overarching Theme and Goal of This Chapter

As we illustrate below, the dynamics of power and social context matter not only in understanding research participants' social identities but also in understanding our own processes. The production and dissemination of theory and research still reflect structural issues related to power and context. Ironically, much of the research on social identity and societal power is itself embedded in often unnamed structures of power that privilege knowledge production from select kinds of people, in select settings, on select topics, with select methodologies, in select formats. However, within mainstream psychology, these processes are rarely acknowledged explicitly alongside discussion of empirical findings. Instead, they make themselves invisible and thereby increase their acceptance. In sum, our general goal is to shine a light on our embeddedness in power, highlighting ways in which the power structures are not "out there" but "in here," in our work and your work. Power affects not only the literature on feminist and other social identities but all research, theory, and practice (Fine, 2010; Harding, 2004).

Structure of This Chapter

The goal above makes for tricky structuring of this chapter. Therefore, we provide a guide to our organization. First, we describe critical power analysis and our rationale for adopting this approach. Because there are no clear rules for engaging in an analysis of power, we outline the principles that guide our use of it. This chapter is largely intended to equip readers with the metacognitive tools (i.e., questions, challenges) essential for power analysis. Thus, we then identify eight such tools that readers can use when dissecting the literature on social identity theory and feminist identity theory. We set the stage with a brief overview of themes in selected literature on social and feminist identity, followed by a step-by-step analysis of that literature using the aforementioned eight tools. We complete the chapter with reminders of our primary themes and final recommendations for scientific work in this field and in general.

A Caveat about Our Critical Voices

Although many of our comments in this chapter are critical of mainstream research and theory on social identity development, including research that we have conducted ourselves, we would like to emphasize again that we believe a cornerstone of feminism and feminist identity is examining systems and relationships using a lens of power. In this chapter, we hope to model that kind of examination in a research context. Although unearned power and privilege can distort bodies of knowledge, we respectfully acknowledge the importance and utility of scientific methods of inquiry and the results of studies using those methods, despite our pointed critiques.

Critical Power Analysis

Although the feminist tool of critical power analysis is typically used in the context of feminist therapy, we will adopt a broader view of power as it both shapes and is shaped by the research and theory-making process in psychology. While many conceptualizations exist, there appears to be no consensus in defining power (Allen, 2008; see Overbeck, 2010, for an excellent review of theoretical approaches). In a special issue of *Psychology of Women Quarterly* on feminist examination of power, Yoder and Kahn (1992) note that many references to power assume a kind of subjugation or domination. They point out that in addition to this traditional conception, power can also be used to benefit or to help others become empowered. Rather than being exclusively other-focused, power also sometimes refers to an individual's more internal sense of agency, competence, or self-mastery. We found Carolyn Wood Sherif's (1982) classic description of power most helpful:

> control of resources, including human resources, and of core social institutions that enables (a) *effective* initiation of action, decisions, policies, and propaganda, and (b) the use of *effective* sanctions, e.g., opening or closing others' access to power, rewards, or punishments.... (pp. 388–389; italics in original)

Why is it important to conduct a power analysis? We intend to draw attention to the context surrounding research and theory on feminist identity development and to illustrate the implementation of a power analysis on a social level instead of an interpersonal one. Within feminist therapy, power analysis typically involves psycho-education about various kinds of power (e.g., power-over vs. power-to, coercive, legitimate, expert, intrapersonal), as well as about strategies used by individuals and institutions to create, maintain, or break down hierarchies. From this foundation, according to Carolyn Zerbe Enns (2004), "Therapists and clients explore how inequities or institutional and cultural barriers may limit self-definitions, achievements, and wellbeing" (pp. 445–445). Clients are encouraged to think about the roles of power inequalities in their own lives, circumstances, and decision-making and are invited to consider whether their distress may stem, at least in part, from "their experience with power—assuming it, abusing it, and being controlled by it" (Evans, Kincade, & Seem, 2011, p. 139). Paralleling this approach, we uncover ways in which power and resource imbalances shape theory and research in psychology.

Outside the therapy room, Amy Allen has proposed a method for examining the effects and dynamics of power in a variety of fields and situations (1999). Allen draws attention to the distinction between foreground and background analysis, with the latter explicating the influence of "deep structures" such as cultural meanings, social practices, and institutions. To illustrate, when considering a case of domestic violence, a foreground analysis would attempt to investigate what personality, behavioral, and situational factors led to the violence. This level of analysis seems to underlie a great deal of mainstream literature. In contrast, a background analysis would investigate how the violence was affected by cultural meanings (e.g., how internalized gender role norms affect behavior), social practices (e.g., victim blaming as a result of just-world beliefs in an individualistic society), and institutions (e.g., response or lack of response from law enforcement officers). We intend to employ Allen's methods in the examination of academic research and theory on feminist identity development. We would like to examine how the assumption of "objectivity in research" has affected research conclusions; how the dominance of quantitative research methods and the prioritizing of research outlets such as book chapters and journal articles have affected what we say we know about feminist identity development; how researchers are rewarded for publications and how that might affect the body of literature; and how much we truly pay attention to the context of a research study and the many parties involved when we draw conclusions and make generalizations about feminist identity. In the end, we hope to inspire a consistent use of background analysis in the consumers and producers of research in this area.

General Principles for Critical Thinking with Power Analysis

Another field that may inform our understanding and application of critical power analysis is interdisciplinary feminist science studies. Although there are varying perspectives (Wylie, Potter & Bauchspies, 2010), feminist science studies generally investigates "'how social factors may intrude upon science... the products of science... and the process of doing scientific work itself" (Whelan, 2001, p. 544). Importantly, the effects of various aspects of social location and identity must be analyzed, including socioeconomic status, colonization, disability, immigration, sexuality, culture, ethnicity, and others, along with gender. Feminist science studies guide us in investigating the ways that these factors have been constructed and used in all phases of the research process.

We cast this approach to questioning the research process itself as analogous to conducting ongoing analyses of power in counseling and therapy. Below, we attempt to articulate principles for such an approach, and we later narrow in, suggesting specific, practical tools for applying them. We bring together elements that we have distilled over the years in our own teaching and research, grounded broadly in works related to feminist epistemology, philosophy of science, and theories of power.

PRINCIPLE 1: RESEARCH, THEORY, AND KNOWLEDGE GENERATION ALWAYS HAPPEN IN CONTEXTS, WITH OVERT OR COVERT POWER DIFFERENCES

Research is conceived and conducted by individuals and groups who are embedded in social contexts and power structures, as we are so embedded in writing this chapter. Thinking in terms of Allen's (1999) instruction to examine deep structure will be useful in unveiling these effects. Also highlighting the impact of these contexts and structures, Wylie et al. (2010) note the common assumption in feminist science studies that "communities, not individuals, produce knowledge." Recognition that the research process reflects and reinforces systems of privilege is echoed in the field of critical psychology. For example, Fox (2000) implies that cultural values around individualism create a generally unspoken influence on mainstream psychologists' work. He points to an overemphasis on "individualism, the narrow pursuit of personal goals, and either adapting to or bypassing societal norms and expectations." In this way, even clinical and counseling work that is intended to be client-centered and strength-focused may well function to reinforce the status quo and existing power relations.

PRINCIPLE 2: ALL SYSTEMS OF POWER AND PRIVILEGE SHOULD BE EXAMINED, NOT JUST GENDER

As noted, feminist science studies is a broad interrogation of all aspects of privilege—including but moving far beyond gender. This principle will be woven throughout our remaining discussion, as we explore the intersections of gender with disability, sexual orientation, socioeconomic status, culture, colonization, age, nationality, immigration status, gender identity, and ethnicity, for example.

PRINCIPLE 3: RESEARCH, THEORY, AND KNOWLEDGE GENERATION ARE ALWAYS PARTIAL

The kind of critical questioning that we describe in this chapter calls on all of us in psychology to develop and strengthen habits of meta-cognition, or thinking about how we think. An important meta-cognitive skill is to remind ourselves that, even regarding very common assumptions, we could be wrong: tentativeness is a hallmark of science. Rather than proceeding as if we are proving or disproving hypotheses, scientists and scientist-practitioners instead operate under the assumption that it is always possible for the picture to change, with different samples, data, methods, and question framing.

It is basically this habit of mind that we would like to see cultivated more strongly regarding power and inclusiveness in research. When thinking about or conducting research, we should be asking ourselves repeatedly what we are not seeing. What factors are we forgetting to consider? Michele Fine (2010) asks simply, "Who is not in the room?" Whose voices are not being represented in research, theory, and practice? Honest and useful science requires a constant interrogation of the ways that our perspectives are limited by our unique social locations regarding culture, power, and privilege.

PRINCIPLE 4: EVERYTHING MUST BE QUESTIONED, INCLUDING THE FUNCTIONING OF POWER IN ALL ASPECTS OF RESEARCH, THEORY, AND KNOWLEDGE PRODUCTION

Ignoring the influence of systems and power structures as backdrops creates risks at all stages of the research process; it imperils a faithful recounting and understanding of psychological processes and can have serious effects on the individuals and communities involved. Again taking a broad look at the ways in which science is affected by social factors, Wylie et al. (2010) refer to critics' skepticism about the idea that "the institutions of science are a model of gender-neutral meritocracy." Below, we provide examples of how power influences all phases of research, rendering it something short of a meritocracy when considered in almost any light. (For more critical inquiry about the process of making research public, see the special section in the January 2009 issue of *Perspectives on Psychological*

Science, containing a series of articles on "Issues in Publishing, Editing, and Reviewing.")

Tools for Applying the Principles Above: Exploring the Unnamed Specificity of Our Work

In addition to outlining broad principles above, we aim to provide some more specific tools for enacting them. The first two tools we offer are the broadest, and they set the stage for the more specific ones that follow. Elaborated in the application section below, Tools 1 and 2 are guiding questions that we suggest should be kept in mind in any critical power analysis.

Tool 1: Ask, "Who benefits from this situation?"

Tool 2: Ask, "How are privilege and power shaping what we see?"

Although still broad, Tools 3–8 extend and sharpen the underlying questions to focus more narrowly on choices—*often unnamed and unquestioned*—which individuals and groups make during the research process. These choices shape what we ultimately see as "the body of literature."

Tool 3: Question who is and is *not* represented in "the literature," among researchers, theorists, participants, cultures, and communities.

Tool 4: Question the methods.

Tool 5: Question the research questions.

Tool 6: Question the interpretations.

Tool 7: Question the motivations and possible uses of this work, intended or unintended.

Tool 8: Question the ways in which a focus on the individual may obscure contexts and dynamics of power.

Setting the Stage for Examining Feminist and Social Identity Research

Overview, Themes, and Definitions

Karina Korostelina (2007) noted that, despite its popularity in the literature, social identity appears to be "one of the most diffuse and loose concepts in social research" (p. 16). She further pointed out that social identity "is now included in all fields of social science and has become an important part of numerous theoretical conceptions, from psychoanalytical theories to the models of nation building" (p. 18). Although our discipline often fails to recognize ways in which constructs such as social identity have been addressed widely across many disciplines, even within psychology its application and study have been similarly widespread (Brewer, 2001; Thoits & Virshup, 1997).

One of the themes that we observed in the social identity literature is the apparent ambivalence in the field regarding the developmental nature of many of the models. Classic theories of social identity based on psychodynamic principles had clear developmental underpinnings (Erikson, 1968; Marcia, 1966). Building from Cross's (1971) Black identity development model, Atkinson, Morten, and Sue (1989) originally proposed a more general Minority Identity Development Model for generating hypotheses about how members of historically oppressed groups develop a group-level consciousness. Common in such models was the proposition that a person moves progressively through psychological stages, first conforming to majority culture, then (recognizing the peril in this) immersing oneself in one's own minority culture, and eventually transitioning into a newly considered basis for positively valuing aspects of one's own culture and the majority culture.

Inherent in older social identity development models is the notion that one progresses to higher or more sophisticated levels or stages of functioning as one successfully negotiates developmental tasks. Other theories of social identity appear to suggest the same notion but do not commit wholly to developmental principles. Regarding her very popular work on racial identity development, Janet Helms (1995) noted that it has often been misinterpreted and misused, as if her approaches were strong-stage models with clear qualitative differences between stages, rather than, as she intended, permeable stage models. Focusing on "cognitive emotional information-processing strategies" (p. 187) as statuses, not stages, she maintained the assumption of sequential development but clarified that the statuses are expressed according to level of dominance within the individual's personality structure, rather than being mutually exclusive. In a similar vein, Janet Hyde (2002) argued that once a woman achieved *Revelation* in Downing and Roush's (1985) model of feminist identity development (described in a later section), the "subsequent" stages in the model may not be so much true developmental stages as, rather, various ways in which a critical consciousness around gender can be acted out; therefore, she suggests that they be considered dimensions or statuses instead of stages. Given the theoretical and empirical implications of the developmental tenets of a theory, theorists and researchers should be exceedingly clear about the tenets and to what extent research supports them.

We observed many additional patterns and unresolved questions in the literature on social identity (see the July 2007 issue of *Journal of Counseling Psychology* for several very helpful discussions) but, due to space limitations, highlight just one more: whether social identity is better considered as a distinct, stable, individual difference variable or instead as more of a schematic tool, simultaneously shaping and being shaped by one's social environments. Although most psychologists would likely agree that social identity is not static, it is often treated as such within the individual differences research base of counseling and clinical psychology, where results of studies examining personality, behavioral, and mental health correlates of an identity status are regularly published.

In contrast, studies in other areas of psychology tend to pay more attention to contextual factors that strengthen or diminish the salience of a given identity, such as self-esteem (Rubin & Hewstone, 1998) or multiple identity statuses (Purdie-Vaughns & Eibach, 2008). In the latter approach, attention is frequently given to the role of social power in the self-presentation of identity. Experimental manipulations are often used (e.g., Gonzales & Hancock, 2008) to examine the shifting nature of identity, emphasizing the relevance of social factors and noting how individual behavior changes as the context changes. This emphasis reduces the odds of making the fundamental attribution error in research conclusions, which occurs when we fail to carefully dissect the immediate and broader social contexts of individuals' voluntary participation in research. Given our value of analyzing power and considering context, we are fans of this experimental approach when conducted respectfully and sensitively, despite its rather rare appearance in counseling and clinical psychology journals. We also encourage readers to explore sociologists' treatment of the active "identity work" done by individuals to influence other people and social systems (e.g., "deploying" collective identity in order to challenge dominant cultural practices and assumptions, Bernstein, 1997, p. 537)

Given the rich history of work surrounding social identity and the slippery nature of the term itself, we thought it would be useful to address a few common definitions of social identity. In mainstream academic psychology, Tajfel (1974) famously referred to "that part of the individual's self-concept which derives from his [*sic*] knowledge of his [*sic*] membership of a social group (or groups) together with the emotional significance attached to that membership" (p. 69). Although useful and popular, we encourage readers to examine other work, such as the integrative review of Ashmore, Deaux, and McLaughlin-Volpe (2004), who suggest using the term "collective identity" instead of "social identity," in part, because of the conceptual ambiguity related to the latter term. In an attempt to provide more clarity and precision in this area, these authors outline seven core elements of collective identity, some of which were not addressed by Tajfel: "self-categorization, evaluation, importance, attachment and sense of interdependence, social embeddedness, behavioral involvement, and content and meaning" (p. 80).

To illustrate these dimensions, consider Cherita, a lesbian woman who tells others about her sexual orientation (self-categorization), who considers her sexual orientation to be a good (evaluation) and vital part (importance) of who she is, who feels as if she belongs and shares a common fate with other lesbian women (attachment and sense of interdependence), who has a friendship and social support network composed primarily of other lesbian women (social embeddedness), who organizes the weekly "Out on the Town" night for community women (behavioral involvement), and who believes that she has important characteristics and experiences in common with other lesbian women whom she reads about on an international lesbian blog site (content and meaning). We hope that aspects of Ashmore et al.'s (2004) multidimensional framework can be a starting point for addressing collective identity in a way that allows for mutual understandings of the complexity of identity.

Intersectionalities: Human Complexity in Multiple Identities

Although we found the above conceptualizations helpful as starting points, below we address one of the major vulnerabilities of social identity development models within psychology. In their intense focus on specific aspects of identity (e.g., race, ethnicity, gender), these models are unable to explicitly accommodate the immense range of identity issues that group members may experience. In other words, there is probably no "generic" way of experiencing any group-specific social identity, because each identity is embedded within others. No woman is "just" a (generic) woman. She also exists within systems reflecting social meanings around class, religion, disability, culture, and so on. Therefore, any attempt to describe women in general will be an oversimplification. By definition, models are abstractions and oversimplifications, but social identity models have been hotly criticized for their failure to account for within-group variability, especially in recent years.

The insight that each individual is formed by a unique combination of many social identities is not new, of course. Born into enslavement in New York around 1797, Isabella Bomefree (or Baumfree) renamed herself Sojourner Truth in 1843 and went on to become an activist and preacher. At a women's rights convention in Akron, Ohio, in 1851, Truth, as an African American woman, gave her famous "Ain't I a Woman?" speech. In it, she highlighted the intersection of social locations around race, gender, and economic status by directly challenging the common rhetoric around women's rights, which was not truly about *all* women's rights; instead, as she illustrated, it focused on the kinds of rights that would benefit race- and class-privileged women. Some 120 years later, members of the Asian American Women's Movement in late 1960s Los Angeles were expressing similar sentiments and also consciously distancing themselves from the mainstream U.S. women's movement (Ling, 1989) as not reflecting their values and priorities.

Within gender and ethnic studies, although strong critiques echoing these points had been made (e.g., hooks, 1981) and sometimes acknowledged, it was not until the early 1990s that phrases such as "multiple identities" and "intersectionality" began regularly appearing in the psychological literature.[1] Although it would be a rare psychologist who denies that unique combinations of identities within individuals are important, early psychological models of identity were unable to explicitly accommodate intersectionality. Most reflected a "one identity at a time" approach.

In 2008, Stephanie Shields assembled a special issue of the journal *Sex Roles,* bringing together theoretical, empirical, and reflective work on intersectionality. Leah Warner (2008) summarized intersectionality as the idea that combinations of social identities "interact to form qualitatively different meanings and experiences.... [O]ne cannot reduce identity to a summary of the social groups to which a person belongs" (p. 454). This point is easily illustrated through the conundrum created by the phrase "women and minorities," still commonly used in public discussions and U.S. government documents related to diversity. There is much to unpack in this wording, but one aspect is the false assumption that some people fall into the first category while another discrete group falls into the second (extraordinarily and unnecessarily broad as it is). Are Ecuadoran immigrant women "women" or "minorities"? Although they are likely to experience sexism, ethnocentrism, xenophobia, and other prejudices, an intersectional perspective directs us to examine *the gendered* (Ransford & Miller, 1983) experiences. Such a lens conveys the assumption, for example, that racism is gendered and that sexism is racialized, such that these systems are not additive but instead combine to create qualitatively different experiences of oppression.

To give another non-academic example, in the late 1980s and early 1990s, Native American activists called upon each other to actively resist the racist exclusion they experienced within White-dominated lesbian, gay, bisexual, and transgender (LGBT) movements and heterosexist attitudes within some Native communities after colonization (Walters, Evans-Campbell, Simoni, Ronquillo, & Bhuyan, 2006). The concept of "two-spirit" identities claimed by some "encompass[es] all aspects of who we are, including our culture, sexuality, gender, spirituality, community, and relationship to the land" (Wilson, 2008). Unfortunately, the two-spirit identity created from empowered resistance has recently been misappropriated by some non-Native LGBT individuals, in effect erasing the cultural context and replicating the colonizing forces that its use was intended to resist.

Within scholarship in feminist therapy, Brown (2009) notes that the concept of multiple identities is a "normative paradigm" (p. 72). Selected sample works on multiple identities not addressed later in this chapter include Linda James Myers's (1993) Optimal Identity model, Pamela Hays's ADDRESSING model (1996), Beverly Greene's integrative work on intersecting identities (e.g., 2003, 2009), and numerous other authors' contributions (see Benet-Martinez & Haritatos, 2005; McCarn & Fassinger, 1996; Reynolds & Pope, 1991; Worell & Remer, 2003). The proliferation of models may be a good sign, but a great deal of literature, including some "models," do little more toward understanding intersectionality than saying, basically, "We should consider it." Readers are led to understand *that* one kind of identity shapes others, but they often are left wondering *how.* Shields (2008) observes that although *acknowledging* the importance of intersectionality is easy, it is another matter "to [explain] those linkages or the processes through which intersecting identities define and shape one another" (p. 304).

Feminist Identity Development: Caveats and Guiding Theory

In writing the latter half of this chapter, we recognized that its content was devoted largely to consideration of research on one model, Downing and Roush's (1985) Feminist Identity Development model, and its most recent and popular operationalization, the Feminist Identity Composite (FIC), a set of previous instruments' items compiled by Fischer et al. (2000). Why?

Consistent with our commitment to analyze the use of power, we wanted to acknowledge that, in addition to some of the intersectional works cited above and the Downing and Roush (1985) model described below, there are many other ways of conceptualizing what it means to develop a gender-related, sociopolitical identity. For example, although feminism is often cast as a middle- to owning-class[2] White women's club addressing primarily the needs of a small and privileged group, Aaronette White has highlighted ways in which African American men and women have embraced and enacted explicitly feminist identities (2006, 2008). Further, African American women have been creating and shaping feminist visions that have addressed multiple oppressions for many decades. In the nineteenth century, activism and scholarship from Maria W. Stewart, Sojourner Truth, Ida B. Wells-Barnett, and Mary Church Terrell, for example, paved the way for the twentieth-century works of Angela Davis, Audre Lorde, Reverend Dolores Jackson (co-founding what is now the African Ancestral Lesbians United for Societal Change), Barbara Smith (contributor to the Combahee River Collective Statement of 1977), Alice Walker (popularizing the concept of "Womanism" in 1983), bell hooks, and many others. From such thinking emerged the philosophy of Black Feminism, which Patricia Hill Collins notes is "not about what Black women think of White feminist ideas" (2001, p. vii) but instead reflects a radical recentering of African American women's experience and situated knowledge as guides to understanding and promoting social justice agendas. This stands in contrast to unnamed cultural (European-American) specificity of the Downing and Roush (1985) model presented below.

Returning to the concept of Womanism, there is no clear consensus on the meaning of this term, particularly in the context of the experiences of women of color from various backgrounds beyond African American women. Kimberly King (2003) defines "Womanism" as "integration of ethnic and feminist consciousnesses among women of color" (p. 19). Lilian Comas-Díaz (2008) summarizes that Womanism is based in intersectionality and that, in psychology, it both "associates with and departs from feminist, ethnic minority, and multicultural psychologies by challenging these disciplines to become more inclusive" (p. 14). One path of inclusiveness is the strong component of spiritual development contained in some definitions of Womanist identity, which clashes with the historical ambivalence about or avoidance of spirituality in mainstream psychology. Comas-Díaz notes that "... indigenous psychologies acknowledge spirituality as a form of knowledge, method, and development. Indeed, one of the ways that Eurocentric psychology attempts to colonize women of color is through the degradation of their spiritual experiences" (2008, p. 17; see also Estes, 1992).

Comas-Díaz (2008) then presents a five-stage model of Latina Womanist (*mujerista*) spiritual development, potentially relevant for the psychologies of all women, contrasting it with common Eurocentric feminist theologies. In this conceptualization, the Womanist path begins with *rejection of oppression* ("emphasiz[ing] the struggle against external and internal oppression within a decolonization framework," p. 19), and then involves the stages of *reclaiming sacredness* and one's ability to transform oppression into strengths, *endorsement of universal healing* (vs. individual healing only), *international solidarity*, and finally, *r/evolution*, which "sets the stage for transformation and cocreation of a just and safe global society... an active commitment to universal social justice" (p. 19).

An earlier Womanist stage model within psychology, Ossana, Helms, and Leonard's (1992) Womanist Identity Development model, does not explicitly address consciousness around multiple identities (e.g., race, sexual orientation). Instead, the term "Womanist" in this context is used to theorize the possibility that, despite differences in class, race, or other sociopolitical group membership, women move through a common progression of stages. Ossana et al.'s measure has much in common with Downing and Roush's (1985) more widely known feminist identity development model, with language as one of the main distinctions (Womanist vs. feminist labels). Potentially increasing the popularity of this model, these authors offered a pencil-and-paper instrument to assess attitudes consistent with each status via five subscales. However, 20 years later, little research has used this instrument, perhaps in part due to unfavorable performance of the subscales in past research (see Moradi, Yoder, & Berendsen, 2004, for a review).

Even though the models above offer keen insights into complex processes, we focus much of this chapter on Downing and Roush's (1985) model. We made this choice for several reasons, including the facts that we aimed to review empirical literature in this chapter; that it has been the most thoroughly researched model of social identity development around gender consciousness in psychology; and that the first author has been involved in some of this research, providing material with which we could more easily model and practice critical self-reflection. Consideration of whether this model's popularity is deserved or has been good for science in this area are two underlying questions that we consider as we apply the tools of power analysis to this body of work.

Briefly, Nancy Downing and Kristin Roush's model (1985) of Feminist Identity Development was based on ideas paralleling Cross's (1971) model of Black Identity Development but centered from the perspective of two European American women (Hansen, 2002). Both are developmental models positing movement through a series of stages as a person becomes more aware of the impact of oppression and subsequently attempts to cope with and integrate the consciousness of it into one's unique identity. Each stage is described below.

Women in the first stage, *passive acceptance*, do not recognize the sexist, oppressive forces and practices that affect their own lives or those of other women. To some degree, this may involve distorting reality in a way that allows for identification with and appreciation of sexist cultural traditions and the institutions that perpetuate sexism.

In the second stage, *revelation*, a woman's awareness of female oppression is awakened. Her psychological and intellectual readiness for this may stem, in part, from direct confrontation with painful, negative, sexist experiences. Two dominant emotions in this reactionary stage are anger about sexism and guilt over one's past collusion with it. Movement into this stage is marked by the transformative experience of beginning to trust one's own reactions. At the same time, schemas for making sense of these reactions are new and typically reflect either/or thinking.

In *embeddedness-emanation*, women forge bonds of "sisterhood" with like others, which empower and strengthen women by validating their perceptions and emotions. Once grounded in a supportive social collective, a more relativistic perspective allows for and stimulates new, ambivalent, and multifaceted reactions about the people and institutions that perpetuate sexism.

Next, in *synthesis*, women actively fight against sexism after making careful assessments about the nature and sources of sexist offenses. That is, they flexibly consider a range of causal attributions about social interactions and evaluate men on an individual basis, rather than as an ememy class. They aim to rise above expectations of traditional gender roles and make in-the-moment decisions about living in accordance with their own principles and standards.

Finally, Downing and Roush (1985) hypothesized that few women move to the *active commitment* stage, which requires great self-awareness and an ability to fully commit oneself to an ongoing struggle against repressive gender norms. Women at this stage identify how their own strengths and abilities could best be used to fight sociopolitical battles against sexism, providing the promise of future liberation for all genders. "Action" is the key term for this stage.

The Downing and Roush (1985) model clearly provides a useful heuristic for conceptualizing women's awareness of gender oppression and responses to it, but the model is not without its critics. As noted, its singular focus is gender, a weakness that the authors of the model acknowledged. Additionally, as with other models of social identity, the developmental structure of the model has been questioned. Hyde (2002) argued that the final three stages of the model may reflect "just different ways that women turn out after Revelation" (p. 109) and that women probably move among these three ways of being and expressing themselves throughout the rest of their lives.

Walters et al. (2006) take the critique of a linear stage model even further. These authors qualitatively examined Native American two-spirit women's experiences. Based on these women's voices, the authors challenge the basic concept of a stage model as incongruent with many Native American or First Nations cultures' view of time as non-linear: "... [T]he ancestors as well as future generations are viewed as omnipresent... things come in their own time" (p. 140). Thus, the theorized press toward "higher" development meets the importance of waiting as a cultural value.

Principles and Tools in Action: Scrutinizing Research on Feminist Identity Development

A September 2011 cited reference search of the Google Scholar database for Downing and Roush's original (1985) model uncovered 279 scholarly works citing these authors' original introduction to the Feminist Identity Development model. Clearly, their theorizing has influenced a great deal of scholarship in the discipline of psychology, including the three attempts to operationalize their model, the revised Feminist Identity Scale (FIS-R) (Rickard, 1987), the Feminist Identity Development Scale (FIDS) (Bargad & Hyde, 1991), and the derived Feminist Identity Composite (FIC) (Fischer et al., 2000). The latter was created from items from the previous two instruments, primarily in order to address psychometric issues inherent in them (see Moradi & Subich, 2002, for more details). Since its construction, the derived FIC has been used in 46 indexed scholarly works and numerous unpublished conference presentations and undergraduate theses, while 93 have cited the Fischer et al. (2000) study. As detailed below, we are not confident that such an impact has been merited or beneficial for the study of feminism in psychology. However, we also want to acknowledge our privilege in being able to dissect and critically assess this body of research. If the first author of this chapter had not been involved in compiling items for the FIC, we probably would have felt much less comfortable in offering the critique below. But that concerns us, too. If science rests on a foundation of vigorous debate and the free exchange of ideas, shouldn't this kind of questioning be more common?

Applying Tool 1: Ask, "Who Benefits from This Situation?"

Political theorists, feminist and critical scholars, and everyday citizens have noted that any examination of power must focus on how situations serve or hinder the interests of various parties (in legal terms: cui bono?). In other words, we must examine the actual functioning and outcomes of systems, rather than simply the positive intentions of those in positions of power.

The question of who benefits from the status quo runs parallel to recent redefinitions of prejudice focusing on the functions of attitudes in maintaining power and marginalization of subordinate groups, rather than on how superficially positive or negative attitudes are. For example, as Glick and Fiske (2001) posit, the ideas behind benevolent sexist attitudes sound affirming of women on the surface, as they emphasize a kind of valuing of women (e.g., "Women should be cherished and protected by men"). However, such attitudes ultimately serve to maintain women's lower status by defining them as needing protection, as well as men's greater freedom by defining women as more pure. (It is a short step from there to a belief that women are inherently better at childcare, an important but societally lower-status activity). By claiming these positive attitudes, individuals are able to see themselves as unprejudiced supporters of women. However, the simultaneous but unacknowledged function is that this same support serves to justify and maintain the gender hierarchy. In other words, attitudes and behaviors backed with positive intentions often have negative consequences.

Similarly, positive intentions among the community of researchers are not enough. Therefore, we ask ourselves at this moment, "Who benefits from the current state of feminist and other social identity literature?" We hope that the individuals and communities we serve will ultimately benefit from social scientists' and practitioners' evolving knowledge. However, a more direct and practical answer is that we benefit in the academic world: (a) "we" who have been given opportunities to conduct feminist and social identity research for publication, presentation, or thesis/dissertation requirements; (b) "we" institutions and administrators whose faculty, staff, or students are represented as authors; (c) those whose life experiences are reflected in mainstream models of feminist identity development, i.e., European American, middle- or owning class; and, more specifically, (d)"we" as authors of this chapter, being offered the chance to frame the literature in ways that we and the editors select, to spend many months in intellectual dialogue as we conceive and write this piece, and to add to our lists of publications.

Applying Tool 2: Ask, "How Are Privilege and Power Shaping What We See?"

To continue with the previous example, we can approach Tool 2 as a variation of the question above. A foundational example of privilege shaping what we see is the fact that a person reading original, peer-reviewed research on social identity is probably herself or himself a professional or student with resources (money enough, time enough, social support enough) allowing such an educational path. Whoever "we" are, we are not a representative sample of anyone, except possibly of psychology professionals and students, and those specific aspects of our identities necessarily frame the way we read, see, hear, and understand research.

A related way in which privilege shapes what we see and know is reflected in the cliché about what a large proportion of knowledge about "human" behavior comes from studies of college sophomores in the United States. Similarly, a great deal of research on feminist identity development has been conducted with samples who are largely U.S. citizens or residents, White, middle class, and often assumed to be heterosexual, which has been true in the majority of our own work as well. Why?

Power creates paths of least resistance, such that it becomes relatively easy for those with privilege to avoid asking difficult questions about the research process itself (and then to not notice that we are avoiding them). How, where, and when is it easiest to overlook concerns about research methods, such as sampling? Do we engage in equally hardy critiques of problems in all the studies that we read or design? Likely, we do not, in part due to selective attending. A metacognitive goal for all researchers and consumers should be to humbly *assume* that we are selectively attending and to ask how (not whether) that affects our judgments.

As an example, despite the sampling bias noted in the previous paragraph, studies have typically been summarized in literature reviews in ways that ignore this bias, described as involving samples of simply "women" or "female students." When participants reflect multiple non-majority statuses, these are more likely to be marked as special and less prototypical of any social identity group (e.g., "*Latina* women," "*African American lesbians*," "women with *disabilities*"). In this way, dimensions of majority status masquerade as generic or neutral. The implicit norm groups in these examples are men, White women, heterosexual women, and women with no obvious disabilities. Further, Purdie-Vaughns and Eibach (2008) articulate a model of "intersectional invisibility," illustrating ways in which dominant-group ideologies (e.g., heterocentrism, ethnocentrism) together construct individuals with more than one subordinate-group identity as less prototypical of any group and therefore relatively invisible. Caldwell (2010) demonstrates these dynamics in the case of disability and bisexuality.

Should this matter? Why not just consider the marked versus unmarked groups as simply different, rather than better or worse? If we are scientists who simply report observations, then isn't this just a fine point about linguistics—basically irrelevant to our work? Apparently, subtle framing of groups as standard versus "to be explained" does matter, as feminist scholars have argued for decades (de Beauvoir, [1949] 1989; Lorde, 1984). Recent experimental research with female and male German community members demonstrated that members of groups (even arbitrary, fictitious ones) implicitly set up as the referent for further comparisons were perceived as more powerful and more agentic than members of the groups being compared to them (Bruckmuller & Abele, 2010).

Privilege works in part by making itself invisible or at least plausibly deniable, so those with privilege are prone to minimizing awareness of it. While reporting on research, we simultaneously exercise and discount our academic privilege when we discuss bodies of research as if they were baskets full of interchangeable findings to drop into literature reviews as needed. We hope that this is changing, but why, in the past, has it apparently been easier for many researchers and practitioners to think in terms of selectively citing studies in service of specific arguments than to spend time and manuscript space carefully questioning the ways in which they reflect specific social contexts? How do institutionalized "isms" (e.g., classism, ableism, heterosexism, racism) affect the research that is produced? For example, in a qualitative study, if a Native American or First Nations woman participant enters the research lab of a White U.S. faculty researcher, what unspoken expectations may affect (a) the potential participant's subjective comfort in continuing or halting participation; (b) her behavioral willingness to continue; (c) her trust in the researcher's and research community's positive intentions; and (d) if she stays, the answers the participant is willing to give or feels subtly pressed to give? What if the interview questions are about what feminism means in her life? What if the researcher is of Middle Eastern descent? How do the dynamics change if the participant is White and the researcher is Malaysian American?

Probably most researchers would agree that these factors can shape the research process and therefore outcomes, and some authors openly consider and discuss these issues alongside their findings, especially in studies using qualitative paradigms. A bigger question is how frequently consumers of any research weigh these factors in general, in classroom discussions, and when setting up arguments for their own (new) studies. We challenge readers and ourselves to consider how we enact and entrench this research culture through the choices we make along the way.

A final example of the influence of privilege is the unspoken cultural pressure of scientific communities encouraging us to minimize the weight of the personal benefits that we reap as authors. It is an academic privilege to cast the tangible, career-building outcomes of our research (e.g., having work published or completing a dissertation) as incidental or secondary to loftier goals. Many enter psychology with a motivation to help people through research and service; feminist and social justice–oriented researchers additionally focus their careers on work with high potential to benefit communities historically denied access to resources and power. At the same time, though, it is worthwhile to ask how persistently we would pursue the specific research agendas we do if they did not also carry some degree of extrinsic reward (e.g., university degrees, status and tenure with publications, money with grants) associated with power and privilege.

Applying Tool 3: Question Who Is and Is Not Represented in "the Literature," among Researchers, Theorists, Participants, Cultures, and Communities

When we survey theory and research on feminist and other social identity development, in what ways are we looking through the lenses of gender? Culture? Physical ability or disability? Social class? Sexuality? Religion? Intersectionality? Jones (2010) challenges the limited perspectives in mainstream psychology literature, quoting the African proverb, "The true tale of the lion hunt will never be told as long as the hunter tells the story" (p. 705). Whose stories are being told, by whom, and why?

An analysis of power reminds us that "our" understanding of feminist and social identity is limited in part to the theories and models published in academic journals. Although they actually reflect a subset of models conceptualized and used, they may appear to be the only ones available, indicating that they are privileged in academic and professional culture. When we refer to such work collectively with phrases such as "the body of literature," we would do well to remember that a true body of knowledge on identity is much broader. For instance, in the journal *China Media Research*, Jing Yin (2006) challenges the Eurocentric, individualistic focus of academic feminism and instead explicates Confucian principles that may form a foundation for a more collectivistic feminism from a traditional Chinese perspective. Yin highlights "the principle of *ren* (humanness), the notion of rights as *fen* (share), and duty-based ethics in Confucian teaching" as pathways for creating "a communally based critical self-awareness and a common language of justice that foster gender equality" (p. 13) (see also Yin, 2009). As another example, Lisa Grayshield (Washo) and Anita Mihecoby (Comanche) discuss the interconnectedness of self and land in place-based Indigenous Ways of Knowing, noting that humans cannot be separated from the rest of the natural world (2010). (Please also see the Native American Academy, n.d.)

Additional sources of knowledge include less-read and less-promoted works by post-colonial scholars in the global South and indigenous scholars worldwide, as well as knowledge about identity held within traditional cultures, communicated implicitly or explicitly through art, stories, proverbs, music, poetry, and dance, for example. Some of these sources are accessible to some academics, primarily those who are members of these cultures or have sustained personal experience and facility with relevant languages in the case of written and oral sources. Regarding West African griots or griottes (keepers of history and oral traditions), Alex Haley (1976) wrote that "when a griot dies, it is as if a library has burned to the ground" (p. viii). Related, Sandra Harding (2004) advocates questioning of "how different cultures will tend to produce different patterns of knowledge and, equally importantly, of ignorance" (p. 35). What patterns of ignorance are we creating and maintaining in mainstream psychology?

Therefore, "the body of literature" as typically construed in U.S. academic psychology includes a limited subset of understanding, with privileged places for ideas that are (a) written; (b) presented through mainstream academic journals, books, or conferences with high registration fees; (c) in the English language; (d) with discipline-specific jargon; and often (e) from a Western or Northern perspective (and within the U.S., often from perspectives that are White, heterosexual, middle- or owning class, without obvious disabilities, etc.). Our goal is not to diminish such sources but to highlight the unnamed specificity and limited scope of surveying "the literature."

As noted in a previous section, a great deal of recent research on gender consciousness generally and feminist identity specifically is based on Downing and Roush's (1985) model, described above. This model appears to have captured something important about gender and feminism for many readers, some of whom responded with "aha" moments as they heard their familiar yet unarticulated experiences voiced and validated. At the same time, however, many have been critical of the way that this model has been used, such that majority women's experiences remain at the center, along numerous dimensions (e.g., class, culture, disability, nationality, immigration status, sexual orientation, ethnicity, race). In reflecting on development of the model, Nancy Downing Hansen (2002) reiterated the fact that the model was a product of the time and social locations of the authors (both European American).

Again, we encourage readers to consider additional models with explicit attention to intersectionality and multiple identities, such as Myers's (1993) optimal Afrocentric worldview model and others mentioned earlier. In our discussion of applying Tool 4 below, we address at length an additional factor likely contributing to the popularity of the Downing and Roush (1985) model: the ready availability of instruments to measure attitudes consistent with their hypothesized five stages of development. It should also be noted that there are pencil-and-paper measures available for attitudes related to Ossana et al.'s model (see Moradi, Yoder, & Berendsen, 2004), Myers's model (Montgomery, Fine, & Myers, 1990), and Womanism as conceived in the Womanist Consciousness Scale (King & Fujino, 1994).

Although we have touched on this issue at several points above, we would like to explicitly acknowledge again the fact that privilege stemming from our perceived and actual identities has shaped the fact that we two co-authors have the chance to share our ideas in this book. These effects are cumulative, such that our educational and professional careers have been long affected by the constellations of privilege and oppressions that we carry. Our ways have been paved in part by subtle or overt "passes" that we have been given from being perceived as cisgender, middle class, thin, without disability, European- or White American, and, at the moment, as mid-career or seasoned professionals. Despite these commonalities, the meanings of the privilege that we share have changed over time and in varying contexts. For example, as we began our academic careers at roughly the same time, we had many conversations about how different our teaching experiences were. We hypothesize that some of the difference stemmed from mixes of gender privilege (second author) and sexual orientation privilege (first author). At the same time, however, the effects of these privileges have varied with contexts of our institutions and with different makeups of the administrations and student bodies regarding socioeconomic status, ethnicity, and culture.

Applying Tool 4: Question the Methods

Returning to the Downing and Roush (1985) model, what does a careful questioning of the methods used to study it reveal? Several years after the appearance of the model, two paper-and-pencil measures were made public. Kathryn Rickard (1987) developed the Feminist Identity Scale, and Adena Bargad and Janet Shibley Hyde (1991) published the Feminist Identity Development Scale. These tools proved invaluable in helping researchers and practitioners represent and understand women's experiences, leading to a substantial body of empirical studies on feminist identity development, mostly, though not exclusively, with samples of White U.S. university women.

As with any measures, both strengths and weaknesses of the FIDS and FIS had been noted. In response, Fischer et al. (2000) examined FIDS and FIS items as a combined set, in an attempt to bring together the best from each instrument. In the first study, these authors studied primarily White university women's patterns of responding, exploring internal consistency, latent factor structure (via exploratory factor analysis), and outsider reviewers' judgments of content representation. Based on these findings, they tested a shorter composite, best-of-the-best instrument (Feminist Identity Composite; FIC), first in the development sample as an exploratory step and then in a new but similar sample for validation. Results from confirmatory factor analysis, convergent validity coefficients, and discriminant validity coefficients suggested that the "new" subscales (one subscale for each of Downing and Roush's five stages) worked very well. A few years later, Moradi and Subich (2002) examined the structure and performance of the FIDS, FIS, and the derived FIC in another new sample. Although the FIC did not perform as well as it had in Fischer et al. (2000), especially in its poor representation of *embeddedness-emanation* attitudes, Moradi et al. recommended that researchers wishing to operationalize the entire set of Downing and Roush attitudes may fare best with the FIC, although these recommendations were appropriately, in our opinion, unenthusiastic and qualified (see also comments by Hansen [2002] and Hyde [2002]).

Since publication of the composite measure, the first author (Fischer) regularly receives requests from researchers for more information about it. My standard reply (in addition to providing a help sheet on scoring and a referral to Moradi & Subich's 2002 study) has been to suggest asking the original FIDS and FIS authors for permission to use their items, as my co-authors and I did not create the items making up the composite. But my personal reaction is usually quite mixed. First, it is a pleasure to hear of the many creative projects that students and other researchers are doing. Second, though, I often feel discomfort with the process. Specifically, it is common for these e-mail requests to indicate that the researcher would like to somehow "measure feminism" or uncover consequences or correlates of "being more feminist." Often, the researcher does not have a clear measurement goal. Is she or he or ze (transgender pronoun) truly hypothesizing about specific processes of feminist *development*? Or would a clearer articulation of research questions reveal the need for a measure more directly assessing attitudes, beliefs, behaviors, or worldviews about gendered power, rather than identity development per se?

What concerns us about these scenarios is the way that an instrument's popularity may sometimes pave the way for a vague conceptualization of research questions and subsequently chosen methods. Unfortunately, with repeated exposure, measures sometimes begin taking on lives of their own. Researchers may begin "thinking in instruments" (Fischer & Moradi, 2001) instead of clearly articulating well-grounded hypotheses about underlying psychological processes. This proverb comes to mind: "When one is holding a hammer, everything looks like a nail." With an FIC hammer, how many nails have been created with less-than-complete consideration and reflexivity? Particularly in cross-sectional research, we hear people begin to construct research projects around their affection for or familiarity with a specific instrument. ("Hmmm ... what variables might be related to scores on this scale I have?") Creativity is squashed if we *start* by looking at our toolbox, rather than by making careful observations and thinking flexibly to create hypotheses about how the world may work.

This problem is not unique to feminist identity development research, with various scholars commenting for years on the concern in social identity research (e.g., regarding ethnic identity, see Ponterotto & Park-Taylor, 2007). Cokley (2007) refers bluntly to "the continual and loyal usage of scales with demonstrated poor psychometric properties, absent any strong theoretical or even pragmatic rationale for their continued usage" (p. 226). In this way, well-known measures propagate themselves. Regarding feminist identity development specifically, Hyde (2002) comments that progress will not be made "by trying to tweak scales to achieve better internal consistencies, to measure stages [from Downing & Roush, 1985] that, in all likelihood, are not real stages" (p. 209). Instead, she suggests that we should critically question the theoretical model underlying the scales and inform our critiques with longitudinal data. With the current first author (Fischer) as one of the "tweakers" being questioned (as all researchers should be), readers might be surprised to learn that—although we are glad that researchers are studying feminist identity—we do not often recommend use of the FIC. Why? Simply, it does not usually represent the constructs of genuine interest to the researchers involved. Sometimes it seems to be used out of habit, and what effects might that have? The more a researcher's work is cited, by definition, the more opportunities others have to become aware of it. Therefore, a path of least resistance is cleared for the composite measure, based on items that my co-authors and I did not write.

Returning to Hyde's (2002) suggestion for using data to critique and possibly revise models, we would like to highlight the years-long projects of William Cross and his colleagues in revising Cross's original racial identity development model. Cokley (2007) and Ponterotto and Parks-Taylor (2007) showcase this work (along with other teams' work) as illuminating a "best practices" approach to incorporating new information and critiques into revisions of existing theories and measures (Cross Racial Identity Scale; Cross & Vandiver, 2001). As another leading social identity theorist, Helms has consistently raised pointed questions over the years about what we are doing in the field of racial and ethnic identity development when it comes to issues of measurement, psychometrics, and sampling (see Helms, 2007, for more recent commentary).

When models and instruments are revisited and refined in light of new information and perspectives, or simply scrapped to make way for others when their usefulness is past, that is what advances the "technology" of measurement. However, that apparently has not been a priority in the realm of feminist identity development as measured with the FIDS, FIS, or composite FIC. What does continued use of the models and measures mean, who benefits, and who incurs costs? We posit that there are costs to individuals and communities whose experiences are *not* well represented by the model or instruments, particularly those whose unique, intersectional social locations include identities as transwomen, transmen, gender queer individuals, women of color, women with disabilities, very low-income women, multiethnic and multiracial women, and others.

Applying Tool 5: Question the Research Questions

Taking a step back, we can broaden our view of the research process by asking how research questions and hypotheses get posed in the first place. Although some may be led to believe that research questions are selected from a field of equally weighted options, questions are likely to embody the interests of dominant groups (e.g., Gannon, 1998). As Harding (2004) explains,

> [Privilege influences] what situations or conditions get identified as scientific problems, what is supposed to be problematic about them, which hypotheses and concepts are favored, and how the research project is designed. All of these choices and decisions occur *before* sciences' methods kick in to control for scientists' "biases." (pp. 33–34)

Within psychology, critical theorist Dennis Fox (2000) goes so far as to refer to "psychology's historic role as a servant of the state" (see Summers, 2008, for more on ways in which the U.S. military and Department of Defense have overtly or covertly shaped the field of psychology).

As noted above, the popularity of a measure (e.g., the FIC) both reflects and reinforces the influence of the model on which it is based. Let's take a look at the general shape of research questions posed in published research using the FIC to assess feminist identity development attitudes. First, we notice that the majority of projects hypothesize, basically, that "higher" levels of feminist identity development will predict or will be associated with behaviors (e.g., social justice activism), attitudes (e.g., sexual attitudes), or mental or emotional states (e.g., well-being, self-esteem) that are considered positive. The form of the research question, therefore, would be, "Is 'higher' feminist identity development related to Positive Thing X and Positive Thing Y?" A variation of this question is, "Does 'higher' feminist identity development buffer the detrimental effects of Negative Thing Z?" Although the Downing and Roush (1985) model conveys a clear value on *developing* a feminist identity, and therefore these research questions do follow logically, it is also worth noting that one would be hard pressed to find published studies documenting associations of FIC subscale scores reflecting "later" stages (*synthesis* and *active commitment*) with more negative constructs or processes. Could part of the reason be that questions of negative associations are rarely asked? Kaschak (1992) and Baker (1996) remind us that, in some situations, there may be danger associated with seemingly positive "feminist" behaviors. Such risks (e.g., to physical safety in the workplace, public, or home) are too-infrequently discussed.

Questions such as these raise the issue of what is positive or negative, and to whom. Further, possible moderating effects of cultural or other social identity variables are not commonly explored. Although Rederstorff, Buchanan, and Settles (2007) focused on gender role attitudes, rather than feminist identity development per se, their results provide an important reminder to actively explore patterns of findings across and within groups. These authors found gender role attitudes to moderate the link between sexual harassment and symptoms of posttraumatic stress in both African American and White women, but the direction of moderation was opposite for the two groups. The link was stronger for African American women when they endorsed *less* traditional attitudes but stronger for White women when they endorsed *more* traditional attitudes.

In general, we suggest more explicit attention to the varied meanings of gender consciousness and possibly feminist identity that girls and women may construct and how these meanings change over time. As a few examples of research in this vein, we highlight Manago, Spears Brown, and Leaper's (2009) study, analyzing adolescent Latina girls' writing about what feminism meant to them. In another qualitative study, Settles, Pratt-Hyatt, and Buchanan (2008) found both similarities and differences between African American and White women's constructions of gender. Walters et al. (2006) interviewed Native women who identified as two-spirit to learn about ways in which racism, heterosexism, and sexism shaped their understanding and experience of gender and sexuality. We do not believe that qualitative research is a panacea, but these studies are notable in addressing nuances in meaning as voiced by girls and women.

As pointed out by Nancy Downing Hansen (2002; of Downing & Roush, 1985), another potential moderator variable rarely explored in the feminist identity development literature is salience of attitudes. As documented in other research domains (e.g., social support), individuals may "agree strongly" with attitudinal statements as a way of indicating positivity or negativity, but without that positivity or negativity carrying particularly heavy weight in their day-to-day lives.

We wrap up this section with two additional thoughts. First, we are concerned by the scarcity of empirical literature addressing transgender and gender identity issues generally and within the domain of feminist identity specifically. Especially in light of tensions between some feminist and some transgender communities (Namaste, 2009), we encourage researchers to explore meanings of and experiences with inclusion, exclusion, and empowered resistance to unjust systems. What does the relative invisibility of transwomen, transmen, and queer-identifying individuals mean for potential feminist identity development and the maturation or overhaul of political collectives?

Finally, we share this quotation from Leah Warner's (2008) "best practices" guide for intersectional identity research. She admonishes researchers:

> to pay attention to and be critical not only of the questions they ask and the phenomena they test, but also *the questions they do not ask and the phenomena they do not test.* Truly, one of the central issues in the study of intersectionality is that of visibility—who is granted attention, who is not, and the consequences of these actions for the study of social issues. (pp. 462; italics added)

Applying Tool 6: Question the Interpretations

What is the purpose of the discussion section of a journal article? Synthesizing, interpreting, and extracting meaning from the results. The gist of Tool 6 is to remember that specific individuals are doing the interpreting. Who is doing it, for what purposes, from what perspectives, with what limitations, reflecting whose assumptions, and omitting whose ways of understanding?

In the popular press as well as, unfortunately, cultures of research, precise-looking numbers and statistics with many decimals are sometimes treated as if they were always and *only* faithful recordings of "what happened." Sometimes they are, more or less (see Bérubé's [2011] distinction between simple "brute facts" and "social facts"). However, no method (quantitative or qualitative) in social science is perfect, so it is essential that—in addition to questioning the choice points leading to a study's conceptualization—we remain mindful of technical limitations and humble in our interpretations. For excellent examples of context-sensitive interpretations of previously published findings, see Gannon (1998), Yoder and Kahn (2003), and Jones (2010).

Ideally, within psychology, we use metacognitive tools to keep our vulnerability to unintended cognitive errors in the forefront of our thinking. But it is not unusual in research papers, theses, or even research journals to read that the goal of a given project is to "show that X will happen" or "demonstrate the effect of Y on Z." This phrasing appears to condone the cognitive error known as confirmation bias. The goal of quantitative research should not be to show or demonstrate; instead, quantitative methods should be used to *test* hypotheses that are well-grounded in combinations of theory, previous research, and logic, using methods that are solid and as fair as possible. And again, we must attend consciously to the *unasked* research questions.

Our work may be compromised if we drift from scientific goals and the scrutiny of how we interpret the results of our research—in addition to how we pose research questions, formulate hypotheses, choose methods, and collect data. As a collective, we in the research community should be regularly asking ourselves what we may be assuming rather than testing as we interpret results. In principle, peer review of research should minimize problems, as one of the goals of that process is for peers to question each other's work. On the other hand, it is possible that as we become more "socialized"[3] into a discipline or community of researchers in a specific topic, we also may be subtly socialized into a shared set of cognitive errors or assumptions about content.

For example, many years ago, the first author (Fischer) co-authored a manuscript presenting findings from a study testing (among other things) a link between two key variables. The expert reviewers and journal editor recommended rejection, indicating that because the null correlation observed in our data deviated from the widely understood positive correlation seen in other studies, there must be something wrong with our data. Although we rechecked our data many times, that would certainly have been possible. In reality, however, at that time, there had been very *few* published studies examining this association. Perhaps because the hypothesis of a positive correlation was so intuitively compelling and consistent with theory, the research community seems to have shared the belief that the link surely must have been empirically documented many times. But the link had not been documented. In other words, the initial interpretation of our results was colored by a shared, incorrect assumption about "the literature."[4]

Turning specifically to interpretations related to feminist identity development research, we note that within the widely available body of empirical research using established measures, the usual way to interpret subscale scores is to consider them as indicating higher or lower levels of attitudes consistent with a particular stage or status of Downing and Roush's (1985) model. Especially in older research using the FIDS and FIS, some researchers assigned each participant in their studies as "being in" one of the five stages, based on which subscale score was the highest for each participant. In later research, including much that has used the FIC, each subscale's scores have typically been interpreted separately as indicating levels of stage-consistent attitudes or styles within each participant, rather than being used to assign each individual to a stage. This shift echoes patterns in the ethnic identity development literature as well.

Interestingly, when feminist identity development measures have been used in this non-recommended way (assigning stages), the largest proportions of African American (Blue & Berkel, 2010) and European American women (e.g., Fischer & Good, 2004) would have appeared to be "in" the second-to-last *synthesis* stage. Given that *synthesis* was theorized as the second most advanced stage/status/style, this is curious, especially in samples in which participants would not be expected to endorse feminism particularly strongly. For example, Fischer and Good (2004) used the FIC and assigned predominantly White, mostly first-year public university women to stages, not for hypothesis-testing but instead for illustrative purposes, classifying only women who had one subscale score at least 0.5 standard deviations higher than all others. They reported that about one-quarter of the sample could not be classified (with subscores too close together), but a large majority of the remaining sample would have been classified as "being in" *synthesis*.

A related trend observed recently is that, of the five FIC subscales, overall sample scores are often highest for *synthesis*. This pattern has been reported in samples of African American women (Blue & Berkel, 2010; Linnebach, 2004), Iranian women who have immigrated to the United States (Kaighobadi, 2007), predominantly European American lesbian and bisexual women (Szymanski, 2004), ethnically diverse university faculty, staff, and students (Saunders & Kashubeck-West, 2006), and predominantly European American university women (e.g., Linnebach, 2004; Sabik & Tylka, 2006; Yoder, Perry & Saal, 2007; Yoder, Tobias & Snell, 2011).

Synthesis scores also have been high in women specifically rejecting the self-label "feminist," again very curious given that *synthesis* is considered an advanced and committed status, occurring after two transition phases (*revelation* and *embeddedness-emanation*). Mindy Erchull, Miriam Liss, and colleagues (2009) found that among predominantly White young *non*-feminist women and a small sample of older White *non*-feminist women, *synthesis* scores were the highest of all five FIC subscales. Further, the FIC-*synthesis* scores of feminist-identified women were no higher than those of non-feminist women (although feminist vs. non-feminist differences were found on the other FIC subscales). In a similar sample, Liss and Erchull (2010) reported similar results. Less directly comparable but relevant are the findings of White, Strube, and Fisher (1998), who examined African American women's FIDS (not FIC) scores, finding that *synthesis* failed to distinguish anti-rape activists from non-activists.

Why have *synthesis* scores been so high in non-feminist women, both in an absolute sense and relative to scores on other FIC subscales? Erchull et al. (2009) speculated that it may be due to the fact that, basically, the items making up this subscale would be hard for many modern women to disagree with. All five FIC-*synthesis* items are from the original FIS (Rickard, 1987) and collectively emphasize feeling proud, competent, and having blended personal characteristics and "what is female and feminine" in oneself. Given that many women participating in conventional U.S. research probably grew up learning that gender equality is good and perhaps already achieved, it may not require an expansive feminist critical consciousness for young women to endorse these items, although it may have in previous cohorts. The title of Liss and Erchull's (2010) article suggesting this point is apt: "Everyone Feels Empowered." In light of this pattern of findings, Erchull et al. (2009) suggested that the Downing and Roush (1985) model may not be so applicable to the experiences of young women, with *synthesis*-type attitudes possibly illustrating more of a starting point than a struggled-for consciousness. Indeed, Erchull et al. (2009) found that only about one-third of the young women in their sample with high *synthesis* scores (≥4.0 on a 5-point scale) recalled that they had ever thought about the world in ways represented by any theoretically prior status (*passive acceptance, revelation,* or *embeddedness-emanation*). Within the racial identity development literature,

Cross (1995) similarly acknowledged that what would have looked like more advanced statuses among previous cohorts may not work the same way for younger African Americans. These possible changes in applicability reflect changing contexts in terms of historical and cultural shifts in attitudes, societal structures, and power dynamics.

Given the preceding paragraphs, how should we interpret high FIC-*synthesis* scores? Quite cautiously. Before closing this section, we would like to list a few other caveats in interpreting FIC scores: First, beyond just the *synthesis* composite subscale, researchers have identified limitations of the *embeddedness-emanation* composite scale, particularly its incomplete coverage of the attitude domain outlined by Downing and Roush (1986). Second, we should be asking explicitly about the relevance of the FIDS, FIS (and therefore FIC) items to the lives of women from various backgrounds and ages. Whose realities and possibilities do they represent?

Third, we would like to comment on the "end game" of feminist identity implied by the *active commitment* (final phase) items. About half (4 out of 9) of the FIC items representing *active commitment* involve being committed to creating an egalitarian world for "all people." An additional four items are gender-focused, referring to work advancing the women's movement, women's issues, an improved world for women, or a world of equal opportunity for women and men. Although the "all people" referred to in the first set of items logically includes all genders, the gender-focused content of the second set of items does not necessarily reflect issues beyond gender. Thus, it may be possible for a woman to have a moderately high FIC score by virtue of agreeing strongly with all four of the gender-focused items, regardless of reported agreement with statements in the "all people" items. (The ninth item on the AC subscale of the FIC refers to both gender specifically and "all people" generally).

The bigger issue this raises for us, then, is about a troubling representation in some of these items that "advanced" feminism focuses exclusively or primarily on gender. bell hooks (2000) argues that any conception of feminism with a simplistic focus on equal opportunity for women and men ignores classism, racism, and other inequalities, bypassing the critical question, "[W]hich men do women want to be equal to?" (p. 238). Further,

> Women in lower-class and poor groups, particularly those who are non-white, would not have defined women's liberation as women gaining social equality with men since they are continually reminded in their everyday lives that all women do not share a common social status. Knowing that many males in their social groups are exploited and oppressed, they would not deem it liberatory to share their social status. (hooks, 2000, p. 238)

Returning to FIC interpretation, this perspective seems to undermine the possibility that a person can be said to embody an advanced feminist consciousness (high *active commitment*) without endorsing statements about the importance of equality for all people. For example, owning-class White women having equal status with owning-class White men does not seem like a feminist "success story," especially given that the owning comes at the expense of workers and others without class or race privilege. This analysis comes from an intersectional approach to feminism, strongly rooted in opposition to *interlocking systems* of power, dominance, and oppression. Hence, hooks repeatedly uses the phrase "White supremacist capitalist patriarchy," with all elements of the phrase necessary simultaneously. This shift in language is used to convey the reality that racism, capitalism, sexism, and other systems of oppression are inseparable—not parallel, additive, or capable of being reasonably represented without reference to each other.

Taken a step further, Linda Gannon has suggested that another critical level or layer of feminist identity development would reflect not only intersectional thinking but also a consistent, overarching commitment to equality in the structure and functioning of economic and political systems. From this perspective, rather than a focus on "equal rights" and individual group members gaining access to positions of power and wealth, it is the economic and political systems themselves that must be the focus of analysis and change. Ultimately, "gaining access to positions of power and wealth from which to oppress others would no longer be available, possible, or desirable" (personal communication, September 22, 2011).

Applying Tool 7: Question the Motivations and Possible Uses of This Work, Intended or Unintended

Try to remember the last several public service announcements related to a public health problem (e.g., smoking, diabetes) that you have seen, heard, or read. Chances are good that some or all of them included clear statements about how many people are affected: How many thousands or millions of

Americans each year engage in a specific unsafe behavior or are diagnosed with a given disease? Given that prevalence estimates for a group are foundational for efforts to enhance the health of members of that group, collecting prevalence estimates surely must be a good thing.

However, Vivian Namaste (2009) asks, "Good for whom?" We would add, "Good in what *specific* ways?" and "Risky in what ways?" Namaste provides a vivid example of potential negative outcomes of positively intended research on gender identity. She poses the question of why, in Paris, HIV seroprevalence had not been systematically examined in what had been shown in other regions to be a high-risk population of transsexual and transvestite individuals. In her analysis, community leaders had deeply questioned possible negative effects or uses of data from such a study, particularly with the possibility that rates could be high. Connecting issues of gender, identity, sexuality, labor, class, culture, and ethnicity, Namaste summarized questions about whether such results, when publicized, might

> ...conjoin transsexuals and transvestites ("les travelos") with disease in the popular imagination. How could such knowledge impact negatively on the working conditions of transsexual and transvestite prostitutes? Would an association with disease put them at increased risk of violence? Moreover, given the high proportion of transsexual and transvestite populations from migrant communities in Paris... how could such data be used as "evidence" of the need to deport such undesirable, "illegal" migrants? (p. 26)

Namaste does not suggest that there has been consensus about whether potential risks outweigh benefits but instead uses this example to illustrate the fact that possible negative uses of research may not be visible to members of privileged groups who have less at stake than those primarily affected. Without active collaboration, otherwise-unseen risk may accrue to marginalized populations, with potentially brutal consequences. It is our responsibility to critically question what we are doing and to actively forecast unintended negative consequences.

What are some risks of past and future research using the Feminist Identity Composite? At a very basic level, it may perpetuate assumptions that the focus of continued research should be on women's experiences (not those of men [but see Schmidt & Yoder, 2006], queer-identifying, or transgender-identifying individuals); that the Eurocentric focus of the Downing and Roush (1986) model and FIC measure development is adequate to represent "women" generally; implicitly, that attitudes consistent with more "advanced" feminist identity development are good things for everyone, reflecting the best, most desired identity; and that if a subgroup's scores are different from those usually seen in White, middle class, heterosexual women without obvious disabilities, they will be the ones to be explained, with the first group as the referent (see previous section on Applying Tool 2 for why this matters).

Applying Tool 8: Question the Ways in Which a Focus on the Individual May Obscure Contexts and Dynamics of Power

A final broad tool that we invite readers to consider is to habitually ask how research questions, methods, and interpretations in psychology are shaped by assumptions related to individualism. Especially in majority-culture European American theorizing and research, scholars often ground the study of social identity in an individualistic framework, focusing on individual motivations, values, beliefs, attitudes, and behaviors. This work has helped to illuminate important psychological processes in social identity and is certainly consistent with goals of Western psychology, particularly in contrast to the explicit social group emphasis in disciplines such as sociology. However, returning to our theme that much of mainstream psychology rests on *unnamed specificity*, we ask how a specific focus on individuals may obscure other important levels of analysis. This question may sound counterintuitive, given that we are writing about *social* identity, which by definition stems from individuals' experiences related to perceived group membership. Further, social identity development models in psychology very often center around individuals' awareness of, analysis of, and reactions to group dynamics of power and privilege. Despite this, a clear focus on power and privilege sometimes seems to get derailed when researchers turn to quantitative measurement of these cognitive, affective, and behavioral processes.

For example, it is relatively common in the feminist identity development literature, as discussed above, to find that women's higher FIDS/FIS/FIC Passive Acceptance scores are associated with indicators of decreased well-being and increased distress; higher scores on later stages' subscales (especially Active Commitment) generally demonstrate the opposite pattern. A parallel story is often told in the ethnic identity development literature. When this overall pattern of results is found, researchers may be tempted to propose strategies for "advancing" identity (especially if pressed by journal editors to discuss "implications" of results for counseling or other applied work). Our reading is that advancing identity is generally intended to mean "increasing individuals' critical consciousness of societal power structures." On the one hand, this is entirely consistent with mainstream social justice goals of counseling psychology (Goodman et al., 2004). On the other hand, we are uncomfortable with the subtext suggesting that "we" (more advanced) need to fix "their" (less advanced) thinking. This is a perennial struggle within feminist psychology—how to encourage client autonomy (an often unacknowledged *cultural* value) while also encouraging resistance to societal power structures that "we" see as harmful. Smith (2008) illustrates ways in which classist assumptions and dynamics feed this tension. Brown (1994) and other feminist scholars delve deeply into this difficult and often-underplayed paradox.

Another way in which an emphasis on the individual shapes our understanding of social identity is the tendency, in most areas of psychological research, of researchers to interpret results as providing information exclusively or primarily on the processes that the researchers intended to study. In other words, data collected from participants is generally interpreted as indicating something directly related to the researchers' specific questions. In ideal conditions, this assumption makes sense, but conditions are never perfect. We recommend sustained questioning of exactly what individuals experienced and were affected by during the moments they participated in the research, particularly in terms of environmental factors. This is difficult in mainstream psychology, as implied by Victoria Plaut (2010) in her proposal of "diversity science" as a field: "Western thought is more concerned with the actor than with *the subject or context*... help[ing] to explain why the field is so focused on individual bias as opposed to systemic or structural explanations" (p. 91; italics added) for behavior.

Regarding feminist identity, for example, imagine that a participant who uses a wheelchair for mobility spends an extra half-hour or more getting to the researcher's difficult-to-access lab and then is asked questions about feminism. It is entirely possible that her immediate experience has just reminded her of how inattentive to issues of disability much of feminism has been. In that case, the research context itself may have unintentionally primed her to reject feminism as exclusive and insensitive. This creates ambiguity in interpretation, as the unnamed, specific context may partially drive reports of "less feminist" attitudes (or not; this is an empirical question). This hypothetical effect may be exacerbated if the researcher fails to create space for the participant to mention disability as a potential aspect of identity or self-description. More importantly, the context for participation sends a signal to women with mobility limitations that their input is not valued enough to be made accessible, reinforcing the power of those currently without disabilities. As privileged group members in "a brutally unconscious society" (Watermeyer & Swartz, 2008), we have had the power not to notice this mistake in our own research.

Although likely an uncontroversial point within feminist identity research, we rarely see explicit attention to the fact that we are soliciting *very* short-term, in-the-moment state (vs. trait) snapshots of attitudes shaped by layers of social contexts. Again returning to the importance of metacognition in our own work, when we fail to consider micro- and macro-environmental forces we enact the fundamental attribution error, a common cognitive bias. Related, Yoder and Kahn (2003) demonstrate that recurring findings of gender differences or similarities can often be accounted for by social contexts, rather than an essentialist ("that's just how women are") perspective; we strongly recommend this article. What might we find if we were to ask *explicitly* how attitudes about feminist identity are shaped by local, short-term contexts; societal, longer-term contexts; and the layers of context in between? What if we began by assuming that our blind spots will cause us to neglect many contextual forces and we then took responsibility for accounting for as many of them as possible?

A final issue to raise in this short overview of Tool 8 is the fact that focusing on individuals without due attention to context and structural forces distracts us from developing potentially more effective social justice–oriented explanations and interventions. Critical psychologist Dennis Fox (2000) argues that "mainstream psychology's values, assumptions, and practices... reinforce the status quo; they provide ideological support to dominant institutions and channel psychologists' work and resources in system-maintaining rather than system-challenging directions."

Conclusion

At this point, we ask you to return to the first two paragraphs of the chapter. Please take a moment to reread them and write new responses to the questions in the "What Do You Think?" paragraph. Would you consider allowing the speaker's comments to influence your clinical work? If so, how? If not, why? Compare your responses from your second reading to those from your first reading. What similarities and differences do you note? We are aware that the title of the chapter ("Critical Questioning") probably created a mind-set for some readers to have been cautious and critical in their first round of answers. Good. It's also good if your answers did change, as we encourage readers to engage with, extend, and argue with these ideas. We hope that your consideration of the power analysis tools has stimulated and challenged your thinking about the design, methods, and interpretations of research in feminist social identity development.

In terms of application, we further challenge you to consider *your own areas* of research or interest. Do you have four minutes? Please use them to apply two or three of the tools identified in this chapter to that area. If you choose not to do this, how are issues of power affecting your thinking and decision making *in this moment*?

As chapter authors, we were deeply challenged as well. When we first accepted the privilege of addressing feminist and social identity development in this handbook, we were overwhelmed with the prospect of attempting to integrate the enormous complexity and diversity of ways in which such identities manifest. The intense process focus of this chapter only emerged as we talked through our genuine reservations and celebrations about various aspects of "the literature." In order to ground and orient ourselves, we returned to original works related to gender and culture by feminist and non-feminist women, men, and transgender scholars, varying along dimensions such as disability, social class, sexuality, ethnicity, and immigration status, both inside and outside psychology: works by Zitkala-Ša, Uma Narayan, Alma Garcia, Vivian Namaste, Esther Ngan-Ling Chow, Maria Root, bell hooks, Linda Tuhiwai Smith, Paula Gunn Allen, Vine Delorean Jr., Oliva Espín, Rhoda Olkin, and many others. Their words were inspirational, challenging, even daunting. Beyond being freshly (re)humbled by the analyses of our feminist and social justice elders and ancestors, we listened as closely as possible to those resisting feminism or simply not interested in affiliating with it for a variety of reasons. In this process, we were fully confronted with the notion that feminist writing is political and activist-oriented. Although privilege can overshadow this understanding, a main point of our chapter is that *all* psychological theory and research harbors political implications, whether intended or not.

Audre Lorde's words (1984), "The master's tools will never dismantle the master's house," reminded us that an effective approach to reviewing feminist social identity literature would not be to simply list and categorize elements of the status quo. Instead, we challenged ourselves to actively forge tools of feminist inquiry and analysis to question business-as-usual in psychology and then to model the application of those tools. Unresolved in this process is the issue of just how much challenge we can effectively issue from our positions as both beneficiaries and benefactors of the systems that create and maintain injustice. In what ways are you a beneficiary of such systems?

Finally, in drafting the "Principles and Tools in Action" section of this chapter, we found ourselves returning regularly to the conclusion that privilege strives to remain invisible and unquestioned (see Jost, Banaji, & Nosek, 2004, on system justification). Through the repeated unveiling and questioning of such power and privilege, critical feminist research can be freeing. We turn, next, to our final recommendations and questions for future researchers in feminist social identity development.

Future Directions

In many ways, the gist of this chapter has been about the "future directions" of research in feminist social identity. In reviewing the preceding pages, we have clearly posed more questions than we have provided answers in our treatment of the literature. This fact, combined with our value of a process-oriented approach to writing, left us wanting to be part of a public and evolving discussion regarding readers' ideas and reactions to the kinds of questions posed thus far. For now, we end the chapter by highlighting four topic areas whose influence on feminist social identity will likely prove pivotal in the future: the complexity of social identity; the significance of methodology; the relevance of intersectionality; and, of course, the imperceptibility of privilege in scientific work.

The literature on social identity within the clinical and counseling psychology domain has generated useful insights into identity constructs and has produced many applications/interventions related to it. However, professional discussion of social identity suffers, somewhat, from fragmentation and lack of a coherent, unifying framework from which to proceed. Ashmore et al. (2004) have proposed a model of collective identity involving seven major elements, which attempts to map the complexity of social identity, to relate the constructs to lived outcomes, and to reduce redundancy and contradictions commonly published within the area. The model's utility and parsimony are commendable. Ashmore et al.'s final recommendations are similar to ours: they call for advancement of research on social context variables related to collective identity. We agree that a shift from an individual differences focus to an emphasis on situational factors can only promote a better understanding of social identity.

Regarding the methodology frequently used in social identity research, we strongly encourage investigators to begin their research process by considering two important questions: (a) How will power and privilege influence every aspect of the study? and (b) What are my genuine research questions? The first question bears repeating. The second point relates to our dismay at the degree to which research agendas appear to be dictated by popular measures; it is too easy to think in instruments. The future of this area could be wildly unpredictable and wonderfully fruitful if researchers were more often to truly grapple with figuring out what they want to know, not how they might tangentially touch upon a construct related to what they want to know. The latter occurs too often because of the convenience and popularity of extant measures. Will future researchers have the support, courage, and creativity to articulate their own questions and develop new models of feminist identity development? Maybe, maybe not. But the field stands to benefit greatly from attempts to deviate from the standard approaches.

The future of feminist social identity research also requires increased attention to intersectionality. Our immersion into the intersectionality literature left us struggling for months with the issue of how to discuss it in this chapter, and we continue to struggle. Part of our difficulty resides in the recognition that the construct, its operationalization, and its analysis appear to overwhelm many scholars in the field. Thus, intersectional inclusion is frequently referred to but seldom explicated or attempted. Additionally, when serious attempts are made at assessing and including intersectional identities, the research is often implicitly or explicitly criticized (by observers and authors themselves) for not being "intersectional enough." We urge researchers and writers in this area to consider early and articulate explicitly the relevance of including intersectional identities in every empirical and scholarly project. Referring to the recommendations of authors such as Leah Warner (2008), Lisa Bowleg (2008), Stephanie Shields (2008), and Elizabeth Cole (2009) in how to engage with the complexity of intersectionality and how to cultivate the richness it offers will help individuals and communities to expand our knowledge base.

Finally, at the risk of sounding repetitive, our last comment on the future of feminist social identity is a challenge to all. In the spirit of feminist, critical analysis, let us keep enacting the principles of power analysis in all that we do. Do not be cowed by the accusation that your research or professional work is too political. It is *all* political. Too often, we encounter colleagues and well-intentioned students who assert that someone's research is political because it is feminist, while theirs is not because they simply study psychological processes or behaviors (e.g., problem solving, substance abuse), which they assume transcend politics. Nonsense. *Every commitment of time and energy is a statement of value and is therefore political.* All—we mean *all*—researchers need to ask themselves, "How did I get here, studying this topic, with this sample, in this time frame, in this way?" Each of us must own, acknowledge, and wrestle honestly with the ways in which our privilege and power influence our scholarly endeavors. True progress depends on it.

Authors' Note

Many thanks to Eric W. Morris and Linda Gannon for their thoughtful feedback on a draft of this chapter.

Notes

1. PsycInfo searches confirmed this impression: We searched by year for articles or books containing both "intersect*" (* as a wild card, to catch "intersectionality," "intersectional," "intersecting," and "intersection") and "ident*" (* as a wild card again, to catch "identities," "identity," "identify," and "identification"). In the early 1980s, the average was fewer than 3 articles meeting criteria per year; in the early 1990s, it was up to almost 10 per year; by the early 2000s, there were about 70 per year, and in the last few years before this chapter went to press in 2011, the average was 266!

2. We use the term "owning class" in an attempt to minimize the hierarchical implications of "upper" class.

3. According to accreditation guidelines, a key aspect of counseling, clinical, and school psychology doctoral programs and predoctoral internships is "socialization into the discipline and profession of psychology" (APA, 2007, p. 8). Two typical definitions for the term "socialization" refer to "the adoption of behavior patterns of the surrounding culture" (http://www.thefreedictionary.com/socialization) and to "a continuing process whereby an individual acquires a personal identity and learns the norms, values, behavior, and social skills appropriate to his or her social position" (http://dictionary.reference.com/browse/socialization).

However, if a system contains foundational injustices, whose interests are served by socializing students into it? Feminist psychology has always been about resisting the status quo.

4. The editor responded to an immediate rebuttal with understanding and a provisional acceptance of the manuscript, which was published several months later.

References

Allen, A. (2008). Feminist perspectives on power. In E. N. Zalta (Ed.), *Stanford encylopedia of philosophy* (Fall 2008 edition). Retrieved September 8, 2010, from http://plato.stanford.edu/archives/fall2008/entries/feminist-power.

Allen, A. (1999). *The power of feminist theory.* Boulder, CO: Westview Press.

American Psychological Association, Commission on Accreditation. (2007). *Guidelines and principles for accreditation of programs in professional psychology.* Washington, DC: American Psychological Association.

Ashmore, R. D., Deaux, K., & McLaughlin-Volpe, T. (2004). An organizing framework for collective identity: Articulation and significance of multidimensionality. *Psychological Bulletin, 130*(1), 80–114.

Atkinson, D. R., Morten, G., & Sue, D. W. (1989). *Counseling American minorities: A cross cultural perspective.* Dubuque, Iowa: W.C. Brown.

Baker, N. L. (1996). Class as a construct in a 'classless' society. In M. Hill & E. D. Rothblum (Eds.), *Classism and feminist therapy: Counting costs* (pp. 13–23). New York: Harrington Park Press.

Bargad, A., & Hyde, J. S. (1991). A study of feminist identity development in women. *Psychology of Women Quarterly, 15,* 181–201.

Benet-Martinez, V., & Haritatos, J. (2005). Bicultural identity integration (BII): Components and psychosocial antecedents. *Journal of Personality, 73*(4), 1015–1050. doi:10.1111/j.1467-6494.2005.00337.x

Bernstein, M. (1997). Celebration and supression: The strategic uses of identity by the lesbian and gay movement. *American Journal of Sociology, 103*(3), 531–565. doi:10.1086/231250

Bérubé, M. (2011). The science wars redux. *Democracy: A Journal of Ideas, 19,* 64–74.

Blue, E. L., &Berkel, L. A. (2010). Feminist identity attitudes, negative affect, and eating pathology in African American college women. *Journal of Black Psychology, 36*(4), 426–445. doi:10.1177/0095798409353753

Bowleg, L. (2008). When black + lesbian + woman ≠ black lesbian woman: The methodological challenges of qualitative and quantitative intersectionality research. *Sex Roles, 59*(5), 312–325. doi:10.1007/s11199-008-9400-z

Brewer, M. B. (2001). The many faces of social identity: Implications for political psychology. *Political Psychology, 22,* 115–125. doi:10.1111/0162-895X.00229

Brown, L. S. (1994). *Subversive dialogues: Theory in feminist therapy.* New York: Basic Books.

Brown, L. S. (2009). *Feminist therapy.* Washington DC: American Psychological Association.

Bruckmuller, S., & Abele, A. E. (2010). Comparison focus in intergroup comparisons: Who we compare to whom influences who we see as powerful and agentic. *Personality and Social Psychology Bulletin, 36*(10), 1424–1435. doi:10.1177/0146167210383581

Caldwell, K. (2010.). We exist: Intersectional in/visibility in bisexuality and disability. *Disability Studies Quarterly, 30*(3–4). Retrieved January 6, 2011, from http://www.dsq-sds.org/article/view/1273/1303.

Cokley, K. (2007). Critical issues in the measurement of ethnic and racial identity: A referendum on the state of the field. *Journal of Counseling Psychology, 54*(3), 224–234.

Cole, E. R. (2009). Intersectionality and research in psychology. *American Psychologist, 64,* 170–180. doi:10.1037/a0014564

Collins, P. H. (2001). *Black feminist thought: Knowledge, consciousness, and the politics of empowerment* (2nd ed.). New York: Routledge.

Comas-Diaz, L. (2008). 2007 Carolyn Sherif award address: Spirita: Reclaiming womanist sacredness into feminism. *Psychology of Women Quarterly, 32*(1), 13–21.

Combahee River Collective. ([1977] 1983). The Combahee River Collective statement. In B. Smith (Ed.), *Homegirls: A Black feminist anthology* (pp. 264–274). New York: Kitchen Table, Women of Color Press.

Cross, W. E., Jr. (1971). The Negro-to-Black conversion experience: Toward a psychology of Black liberation. *Black World, 20*(9), 13–27.

Cross, W. E., Jr. (1995). The psychology of Nigrescence: Revising the Cross model. In J. G. Ponterotto, J. M. Casas, L. A. Suzuki, & C. M. Alexander (Eds.), *Handbook of multicultural counseling* (pp. 93–122). Thousand Oaks, CA: Sage.

Cross, W. E., Jr., & Vandiver, B. J. (2001). Nigrescence theory and measurement: Introducing the Cross Racial Identity Scale (CRIS). In J. G. Ponterotto, J. M. Casas, L. A. Suzuki, & C. M. Alexander (Eds.), *Handbook of multicultural counseling* (2nd ed.) (pp. 371–393). Thousand Oaks, CA: Sage.

de Beauvoir, S. ([1949] 1989). *The second sex (Le deuxième sexe).* Translated by H. M. Parshley. New York: Vintage.

Downing, N. E., & Roush, K. L. (1985). From passive acceptance to active commitment: A model of feminist identity development for women. *The Counseling Psychologist, 13*(4), 695–709. doi:10.1177/0011000085134013

Enns, C. Z. (2004). *Feminist theories and feminist psychotherapies: Origins, themes, and diversity* (2nd ed.). New York: Haworth Press.

Erchull, M. J., Liss, M., Wilson, K. A., Bateman, L., Peterson, A., & Sanchez, C. E. (2009). The feminist identity development model: Relevant for young women today? *Sex Roles, 60*(11–12), 832–842. doi:10.1007/s11199-009-9588-6

Erikson, E. (1968). *Identity, youth, and crisis.* New York: Norton.

Estes, C. P. (1992). *Women who run with the wolves.* New York: Ballantine.

Evans, K. M., Kincade, E. A., & Seem, S. R. (2011). *Introduction to feminist therapy: Strategies for social and individual change.* London: SAGE.

Fine, M. (2010). Loss and desire in New Jersey. In J. G. Ponterotto, J. M. Casas, L. A. Suzuki, & C. M. Alexander (Eds.), *Handbook of multicultural counseling* (3rd ed.) (pp. 99–105). Thousand Oaks, CA: Sage.

Fischer, A. R., Tokar, D. M., Mergl, M. M., Good, G. E., Hill, M. S., & Blum, S. A. (2000). Assessing women's feminist identity development: Studies of convergent, discriminant, and structural validity. *Psychology of Women Quarterly, 24*(1), 15–29.

Fischer, A. R., & Moradi, B. (2001). Racial and ethnic identity development: Recent developments and future directions. In J. G. Ponterotto, J. M. Casas, L. A. Suzuki, & C. M. Alexander (Eds.), *Handbook of multicultural counseling* (2nd ed.) (pp. 341–370). Thousand Oaks, CA: Sage.

Fischer, A. R., & Good, G. E. (2004). Women's feminist consciousness, anger, and psychological distress. *Journal of Counseling Psychology, 51*(4), 437–446.

Fox, D. (2000). The critical psychology project: Transforming society and transforming psychology. From *Professing: Dennis Fox's Home Page*. Retrieved November 19, 2010, from http://www.dennisfox.net/papers/voices.html.

Gannon, L. (1998). The impact of medical and sexual politics on women's health. *Feminism and Psychology, 8*(3), 285–302. doi:10.1177/0959353598083004

Glick, P., & Fiske, S. T. (2001). An ambivalent alliance: Hostile and benevolent sexism as complementary justifications for gender inequality. *American Psychologist, 56*(2), 109–118.

Gonzales, A. L., & Hancock, J. T. (2008) Identity shift in computer-mediated environments. *Media Psychology, 11,* 167–185.

Goodman, L. A., Liang, B., Helms, J. E., Latta, R. E., Sparks, E., & Weintraub, S. R. (2004). Training counseling psychologists as social justice agents. *The Counseling Psychologist, 32*(6), 793. doi: 10.1177/0011000004268802

Grayshield, L., & Mihecoby, A. (2010). Indigenous ways of knowing as a philosophical base for the promotion of peace and justice in counseling education and psychology. *Journal for Social Action in Counseling and Psychology, 2*(2), 1–16.

Greene, B. (2003). Beyond heterosexism and across the cultural divide—Developing an inclusive lesbian, gay, and bisexual psychology: A look to the future. In L. D. Garnets & D. C. Kimmel (Eds.), *Psychological perspectives on lesbian, gay, and bisexual experiences* (2nd ed.) (pp. 357–400). New York: Columbia University Press.

Greene, B. (2009). The use and abuse of religious beliefs in dividing and conquering between socially marginalized groups: The same-sex marriage debate. *American Psychologist, 64*(8), 698–709.

Haley, A. (1976). *Roots: The saga of an American family.* Garden City, NY: Doubleday.

Hansen, N. D. (2002). Reflections on feminist identity development: Implications for theory, measurement, and research. *The Counseling Psychologist, 30,* 87–95. doi:10.1177/0011000002301005

Harding, S. (2004). A socially relevant philosophy of science? Resources from standpoint theory's controversiality. *Hypatia, 19*(1), 25–47.

Hays, P. A. (1996). Addressing the complexities of culture and gender in counseling. *Journal of Counseling and Development, 74*(4), 332–338.

Helms, J. E. (1995). An update of Helms's White and People of Color racial identity models. In J. G. Ponterotto, J.M. Casas, L.A. Suzuki, & C.M. Alexander (Eds.), *Handbook of multicultural counseling* (pp. 181–198). Thousand Oaks, CA: Sage.

Helms, J. E. (2007). Some better practices for measuring racial and ethnic identity constructs. *Journal of Counseling Psychology, 54,* 235–246.

hooks, b. (1981). *Ain't I a woman? Black women and feminism.* Boston, MA: South End Press.

hooks, b. (2000.) *Feminism is for everybody: Passionate politics.* Cambridge, MA: South End Press.

Hyde, J. S. (2002). Feminist identity development: The current state of theory, research, and practice. *Counseling Psychologist, 30,* 105–110.

Jones, J. M. (2010). I'm white and you're not: The value of unraveling ethnocentric science. *Perspectives on Psychological Science, 5*(6), 700–707. doi:10.1177/1745691610388771

Jost, J. T., Banaji, M. R., & Nosek, B. A. (2004). A decade of system justification theory: Accumulated evidence of conscious and unconscious bolstering of the status quo. *Political Psychology, 25*(6), 881–919. doi:10.1111/j.1467-9221.2004.00402.x

Kaighobadi, F. (2007). Feminist identity development of Iranian immigrant women and its relationship with their psychological well-being. Unpublished master's thesis, California State University, Long Beach.

Kaschak, E. (1992). *Engendered lives: A new psychology of women's experience.* New York: Basic Books.

King, K. R., & Fujino, D. A. (1994). *Measuring integrated identities: Preliminary development of the Womanist Identity Scale.* Presentation at the Annual Convention of the American Psychological Association, Los Angeles, CA.

King, K. R. (2003). Do you see what I see? Effects of group consciousness on African American women's attributions to prejudice. *Psychology of Women Quarterly, 27,* 17–30.

Korostelina, K. V. (2007). *Social identity and conflict: structures, dynamics, and implications.* New York: Palgrave Macmillan.

Ling, S. (1989). The mountain movers: Asian American women's movement in Los Angeles. *Amerasia Journal, 15,* 51–67.

Linnebach, D. (2004). Culture's not so great expectations: Does feminist identity moderate women's experiences with sexism and body image dissatisfaction? Unpublished doctoral dissertation. The Ohio State University.

Liss, M., & Erchull, M. J. (2010). Everyone feels empowered: Understanding feminist self-labeling. *Psychology of Women Quarterly, 34*(1), 85–96. doi:10.1111/j.1471-6402.2009.01544.x

Lorde, A. (1984). *Sister outsider.* Trumansburg, NY: The Crossing Press.

Manago, A. M., Spears Brown, C., & Leaper, C. (2009). Feminist identity among Latina adolescents. *Journal of Adolescent Research, 24*(6), 750–776. doi:10.1177/0743558409341079

Marcia, J. E. (1966). Development and validation of ego-identity status. *Journal of Personality and Social Psychology, 3*(5), 551–558. doi:10.1037/h0023281

McCarn, S. R., & Fassinger, R. E. (1996). Revisioning sexual minority identity formation: A new model of lesbian identity and its implications. *The Counseling Psychologist, 24*(3), 508–534.

Montgomery, D. E., Fine, M. A., & Myers, L. J. (1990). The development and validation of an instrument to assess an optimal Afrocentric world view. *Journal of Black Psychology, 17,* 37–54.

Moradi, B., & Subich, L. M. (2002). Comparing the psychometrics of three instruments. *The Counseling Psychologist, 30*(1), 66–86.

Moradi, B., Yoder, J. D., & Berendsen, L. L. (2004). An evaluation of the psychometric properties of the Womanist Identity Attitudes Scale. *Sex Roles, 50*(3), 253–266.

Myers, L. J. (1993). *Understanding an Afrocentric world view: Introduction to an optimal psychology* (2nd ed.). Dubuque, IA: Kendall/Hunt Publishing.

Namaste, V. (2009). Undoing theory: The "transgender question" and the epistemic violence of Anglo-American feminist theory. *Hypatia, 24*(3), 11–32.

Native American Academy. (n.d.). *Explorations into Native science: A journey into the spirit and nature of science.* Retrieved January 12, 2011, from http://www.silverbuffalo.org/NSA-NativeScience.html.

Ossana, S. M., Helms, J. E., & Leonard, M. M. (1992). Do "womanist" identity attitudes influence college women's self-esteem and perceptions of environmental bias? *Journal of Counseling and Development, 70,* 402–408.

Overbeck, J. R. (2010). Concepts and historical perspectives on power. In A. Guinote & T. K. Vescio (Eds.), *The social psychology of power* (pp. 19–45). New York: Guilford.

Plaut, V. C. (2010). Diversity science: Why and how differences make a difference. *Psychological Inquiry, 21,* 77–99.

Ponterotto, J. G., & Park-Taylor, J. (2007). Racial and ethnic identity theory, measurement, and research in counseling psychology: Present status and future directions. *Journal of Counseling Psychology, 54*(3), 282.

Purdie-Vaughns, V., & Eibach, R. P. (2008). Intersectional invisibility: The distinctive advantages and disadvantages of multiple subordinate-group identities. *Sex Roles, 59*(5), 377–391. doi:10.1007/s11199-008-9424-4

Ransford, H. E., & Miller, J. (1983). Race, sex, and feminist outlooks. *American Sociological Review, 48,* 56–59.

Rederstorff, J. C., Buchanan, N. T., & Settles, I. H. (2007). The moderating roles of race and gender-role attitudes in the relationship between sexual harassment and psychological well-being. *Psychology of Women Quarterly, 31,* 50–61.

Reynolds, A. L., & Pope, R. L. (1991). The complexities of diversity: Exploring multiple oppressions. *Journal of Counseling and Development, 70*(1), 174–180.

Rickard, K. M. (1987). *Feminist identity development: Scale development and initial validation studies.* Paper presented at The Association for Women in Psychology, Denver, CO.

Rubin, M., & Hewstone M. (1998). Social identity theory's self-esteem hypothesis: A review and some suggestions for clarification. *Personality and Social Psychology Review, 2,* 40–62.

Sabik, N., & Tylka, T. (2006). Do feminist identity styles moderate the relation between perceived sexist events and disordered eating? *Psychology of Women Quarterly, 30*(1), 77–84.

Saunders, K. J., & Kashubeck-West, S. (2006). The relations among feminist identity development, gender-role orientation, and psychological well-being in women. *Psychology of Women Quarterly, 30*(2), 199–211.

Schmidt, S., & Yoder, J. D. (August 2006). *Assessing men's profeminist attitudes by extending the Feminist Identity Scale.* Presented at the meeting of the American Psychological Association, New Orleans, LA.

Settles, I. H., Pratt-Hyatt, J. S., & Buchanan, N. T. (2008). Through the lens of race: Black and white women's perceptions of womanhood. *Psychology of Women Quarterly, 32*(4), 454–468. doi:10.1111/j.1471-6402.2008.00458.x

Sherif, C. W. (1982). Needed concepts in the study of gender identity. *Psychology of Women Quarterly, 6*(4), 375–398.

Shields, S. A. (2008). Gender: An intersectionality perspective. *Sex Roles, 59,* 301–311. doi:10.1007/s11199-008-9501-8

Smith, L. (2008). Positioning classism within counseling psychology's social justice agenda. *The Counseling Psychologist, 36*(6), 895.

Summers, F. (2008). Making sense of the APA: A history of the relationship between psychology and the military. *Psychoanalytic Dialogues, 18*(3), 614–637

Szymanski, D. M. (2004). Relations among dimensions of feminism and internalized heterosexism in lesbians and bisexual women. *Sex Roles, 51*(3–4), 145–159. doi:10.1023/B:SERS.0000037759.33014.55

Tajfel, H. (1974). Social identity and intergroup behaviour. *Social Science Information, 13*(2), 65–93. doi:10.1177/053901847401300204

Thoits, P. A., & Virshup, L. K. (1997). Me's and we's: Forms and functions of social identities. In R. D. Ashmore, & L. J. Jussim, (Eds.), *Self and identity: Fundamental issues* (pp. 106–133). New York: Oxford University Press.

Walker, A. (1983). *In search of our mothers' gardens: Womanist prose.* Boston, MA: Houghton-Mifflin.

Walters, K., Evans-Campbell, T., Simoni, J. M., Ronquillo T., & Bhuyan, R. (2006). "My spirit in my heart": Identity experiences and challenges among American Indian two-spirit women. *Journal of Lesbian Studies, 10*(1–2), 125–148.

Warner, L. R. (2008). A best practices guide to intersectional approaches in psychological research. *Sex Roles, 59*(5–6), 454–463. doi:10.1007/s11199-008-9504-5

Watermeyer, B., & Swartz, L. (2008). Conceptualising the psycho-emotional aspects of disability and impairment: The distortion of personal and psychic boundaries. *Disability and Society, 23*(6), 599–610.

Whelan, E. (2001). Politics by other means: Feminism and mainstream science studies. *Canadian Journal of Sociology/ Cahiers Canadiens de Sociologie, 26,* 535–581.

White, A. M., Strube, M. J., & Fisher, S. (1998). A black feminist model of rape myth acceptance. *Psychology of Women Quarterly, 22*(2), 157–175. doi:10.1111/j.1471-6402.1998.tb00148.x

White, A. M. (2006). Racial and gender attitudes as predictors of feminist activism among self-identified African American feminists. *Journal of Black Psychology, 32*(4), 455–478.

White, A. M. (2008). *Ain't I a feminist? African American men speak out on fatherhood, friendship, forgiveness, and freedom.* Albany: State University of New York Press.

Wilson, A. (2008). N'tacimowininna nah': Our coming in stories. *Canadian Woman Studies, 26,* 193–199. Retrieved from Literature Online, http://lion.chadwyck.com.

Worell, J., & Remer, P. (2003). *Feminist perspectives in therapy: Empowering diverse women* (2nd ed.). Hoboken, NJ: John Wiley & Sons.

Wylie, A., Potter, E., & Bauchspies, W. K. (2010). Feminist perspectives on science. *The Stanford encyclopedia of philosophy* (Spring 2010 edition), E. N. Zalta (Ed.). Retrieved January 5, 2011, from http://plato.stanford.edu/archives/spr2010/entries/feminist-science/.

Yin, J. (2006). Toward a Confucian feminism: A critique of Eurocentric feminist discourse. *China Media Research, 2*(3), 9–18.

Yin, J. (2009). Negotiating the centre: Towards an Asiacentric feminist communication theory. *Journal of Multicultural Discourses, 4*(1), 75–88. doi:10.1080/17447140802651660

Yoder, J. D., & Kahn, A. S. (1992). Toward a feminist understanding of women and power. *Psychology of Women Quarterly, 16*(4), 381–388.

Yoder, J. D., & Kahn, A. S. (2003). Making gender comparisons more meaningful: A call for more attention to social context. *Psychology of Women Quarterly, 27*(4), 281–290.

Yoder, J. D., Perry, R. L., & Saal, E. I. (2007). What good is a feminist identity?: Women's feminist identification and role expectations for intimate and sexual relationships. *Sex Roles, 57*(5–6), 365–372.

Yoder, J., Tobias, A., & Snell, A. (2011). When declaring 'I am a feminist' matters: Labeling is linked to activism. *Sex Roles, 64*(1–2), 9–18.

PART 2

Feminist Multicultural Counseling Psychology and Specific Social Identities

CHAPTER

6

From Hottentot to Superwoman: Issues of Identity and Mental Health for African American Women

Suzette L. Speight, Denise A. Isom, *and* Anita J. Thomas

Abstract

We are well aware of the gendered and racialized nature of our social world, from structures and systems to internalized ideologies. The social constructs of race and gender are often viewed comparatively, in parallel, or as additive elements. What is often lost is the particularity of the intersections, the unique social locations, and the myriad ways these two combine. For African American women, the "and" of race and gender marks a troubling and complex sociohistorical context that impacts the identity development and mental health of African American women. This chapter examines the social context from the story of Saartjie Bartmann, the "Hottentot Venus," through the produced images of enslaved African women, to the contemporary projections of "the "strong Black woman." This discussion is held alongside an examination of theories of identity development and the implications for mental health. Ultimately, this work raises a call for further research and continued dialogue on the development of an authentic sense of self in African American women so that they can speak with their own voice and see themselves through their own eyes.

Key Words: African American women, identity development, race, gender

This chapter will explore the complexities of identity for African American women. In a society in which both Black and female are devalued, it can be difficult for African American women to achieve and maintain healthy, self-affirming identities. Of primary consideration in this chapter is the interplay of the social constructions of both race and gender on the identity processes of African American women. Key to any understanding of issues of identity is a critical examination of the larger societal context of contemporary and historical oppression, which provides the meaning of race and gender in our society (Omi & Winant, 1994). Society's production and projection of the meanings of race and gender are embedded in our social structures and systems. Personal identity is the place where social constructions of race and gender are internalized and often projected. A disquieting exemplar of the interweaving of a racialized context, social constructions, and the self for African American women is the tale of the so-called "Hottentot Venus." Her story provides the starting point for this examination of African American women's identity by illustrating the power of others' projections and the longevity of certain societal images about women of African descent. We will examine the historical images of African American women and contemporary projections of what being Black and female means today. Racial identity and gender identity theories will be briefly reviewed and critiqued in light of a more complex intersectional perspective on African American women's identity. Finally, we explore the connection between identity and mental health for African American women.

Socially constructed notions of Black femaleness impact both the self and society. There is a complex interplay of externally created images, their internalization, and subsequent co-creation of a definition of African American women and womanhood. According to Erikson (1968), identity exists at the nexus of the individual and society. It is important to view identity "as relational and grounded in the historically produced social facts which constitute social location" (Alexander & Mohanty, 1997, p. 126). The social location where African American women are forging their identities is characterized by oppression based on both racial and gender markers. Oppression serves as the touchstone for our society's history, as well as economic, political, and social structure, particularly regarding people of color. In a patriarchal, sexist, and racist society, "race is gendered and gender is racialized" (Omi & Winant, 1994, p. 68). Identity is the location where these constructions are projected onto the African American self; internalized, reconfigured, and produced within the lives of African American women; and then projected back out to society, becoming a kind of passport and influencing both the ways in which African Americans are perceived and perceive themselves within society.

Never simply ideas, the concepts and structuring of race and racial systems have worked to justify some of the world's greatest evils and injustices. "Race is not so much a category but a practice" (Myrsiades & Myrsiades, 1998, p. 2). Before the "peculiar institution" of slavery in the United States, early contact between Europeans and Africans began with the social construction of "Blackness." Those initial impressions of Africans as savage, oversexed heathens, have yet to be shaken in the centuries that have followed (Takaki, 1994, 2008). Slavery coupled paradigms of race with deeply imbedded sexist ideologies. Enslaved African females were produced, conceived, and perceived in "the White mind" as the asexual, overweight, dark-skinned mammy and contradistinctively as an animalistic sexual deviant, or the seductive temptress mullato. Not fully a woman, African American women worked the fields in the daylight under the same conditions as a man and tried to avoid their masters' sexual assaults at night. Alongside her stood the African American male, imaged as a brute laborer and sexually charged "buck"; he too experienced the merging of racial and gender constructs in the creation of his constructed identity (Carbado, 1999; Majors & Billson, 1992). However, "sexism ... determined that the lot of the black female would be harsher, more brutal than that of the black male slave," physically, psychologically, socially, and most especially, sexually (hooks, 1981, p. 43). These produced images helped to create a form of social perception that would masquerade as reality.

How easy it would be if slavery remained simply a relic of history, long past and forgotten, but alas, it bleeds into today, carried into our American consciousness through the racial and gender projects that it spawned. Omi and Winant (1994) described race as "a matter of both social structure and cultural representation ... [where] racial projects connect what race *means* ... [with] the ways in which both social structures and everyday experiences are racially *organized*, based upon that meaning" (p. 56). It is these racial and gender projects that display the ways in which both structure and representation work together, manifesting the images and meanings around gender and race that we take for granted.

The experiences of the "Hottentot Venus," an African woman who was "displayed" in Europe in the 1800s, illustrate the power of others' projections and the longevity of certain societal images about women of African descent. In 1810, a young Khoisan woman from the Eastern Cape of South Africa was brought to Europe by Hendrik Cezar, a White South African. She was renamed Saartjie Baartmen by the Dutch, but she soon became known as the Hottentot Venus. She was a domestic worker-slave or servant for a Boer farmer, Peter Cezar. When she was 21 or 22 years of age, it is said that she entered into an agreement with Alexander Dunlop and Hendrick Cezar, which stipulated that, in addition to her domestic duties, she would be exhibited in England and Ireland. She was to be paid a portion of the profits from her exhibitions and was to return to South Africa in five years. Saartjie was four feet six inches tall, with large buttocks and extended genitals, and this is what Europeans were willing to pay to see. Thus, her racial and sexual characteristics were on display due to their "abnormality." Saartjie was a curiosity for the scientific community and the aristocracy alike. She was paraded about at museums, universities, and bars; she was obliged to walk, stand, dance, or sit as her keeper ordered. She was a sensation in England, despite protests by anti-slavery advocates about her maltreatment, and was renamed Sarah Baartmann. After four years in England, she was sold to a showman of wild animals, and in 1814, under the guardianship of Reaux, she was exhibited in Paris. Saartjie was the subject of cartoons, plays, and ballads, as French society was enthralled with her body or, rather, parts of her body. In order to determine her relationship to other animals and human beings, Saartjie was examined for three days in March 1815 by a team of scientists-zoologists, an anatomist, and physiologists (Sharpley-Whiting, 1999). Georges Cuvier, the renowned French naturalist observed:

> When we met her for the first time, she believed herself to be about 26 years old.... Everyone who had been able to see her over the course of eighteen months in our capital could verify the enormous protuberance of her buttocks and the brutal appearance of her face.... Her movements had something of a brusqueness and unexpectedness, reminiscent of those of a monkey. In particular, she had a way of pushing out her lips in the same manner we have observed in the Orangutan. Her personality was happy, her memory good, after several weeks she recognized a person that she had only seen one time... she spoke tolerably good Dutch, which she learned at the Cape... also knew a little English... was beginning to say a few words of French; she danced in the fashion of her country.... Her conformation was initially striking because of the enormous width of her hips, which surpassed forty-two inches, and because of the protrusion of her hips, which surpassed forty-two inches, and because of the protrusion of her buttocks, which were more than half a foot. Of the remaining body parts, she had no other deformities; her shoulders, her back the top of her chest were graceful. The bulging out of her stomach was not at all excessive. Her arms, a bit thin, were very well made, and her hand was charming. Her foot was also very alluring.... Her hair was dark and woolly like that of Negroes, the slits of her eyes were horizontal... like that of Mongols... her eyes were dark and lively; her lips, a bit blackish, and monstrously swelled; her complexion very swarthy.... Her ears were much like those found in many monkey, small and weakly formed. (Cuvier, 1864, as cited in Sharpley-Whiting, 1999, pp. 23–25)

Cuvier's reports of Saartjie are remarkable for what they reveal about his gaze. His fascination is sprinkled with both eroticism and repulsion. She assaults his sensibilities of the standard for female attractiveness because she seems more akin to primates than humans. And at the same time, he finds aspects of her body appealing (Sharpley-Whiting, 1999). To Cuvier she is primitive, inferior, and fascinating, an intriguing specimen.

Upon her death in January 1816, most likely from smallpox or syphilis and alcoholism, Cuvier was permitted to autopsy and dissect Saartjie. He made a plaster mold of her entire body and preserved her genitalia and skeleton. Cuvier was able to verify the existence of the so-called "Hottentot apron," the overdevelopment of the labia minora, which had been the cause of much speculation, myth, and controversy. This (over)sexual body part within the notion of White superiority solidified the idea of the primitive races as less evolved than the civilized Europeans. This supposedly racial trait symbolized the abnormal, over sexualized, bestiality of the Black female. Sarah's pickled body parts, skeleton, and body mold remained on display in the Paris Musée de l'Homme until the mid-1970s. At the request of South African President Nelson Mandela in 1994 and a subsequently lengthy court battle, Saartjie's remains were finally returned to South Africa, where she was buried in 2002.

South African President Thabo Mbeki (2002) asserted on the occasion of the return of Saartjie's remains, "they [the European colonizers] took away her *identity* [emphasis added]. By turning her into a non-person, they defined her as sub-human. As such a subhuman, she became an object to be fully owned, used at will and freely disposed of by those who had robbed her of her identity" (p. 3). The meaning of Saartjie's racialized gender was invented, imagined, reinforced, and propagated by forces external to her. Saartjie stands as a symbol of the distorted ways that Black women exist in the minds of others. The construction of "the Hottentot Venus" represents, still today, the ideas of the savage sexuality and racial inferiority of Black women. Saartjie suffered humiliation, indignity, and disrespect in life and well beyond her death. Her experiences in Europe appear to provide a road map for the degrading, objectifying, and dehumanizing of Black women that would follow. Even today, Black women's identity is often seen from the "outside in" rather than from the "inside out." According to Sharpley-Whiting (1999), "Black females are perpetually ensnared, imprisoned in an essence of themselves created from without" (p. 10).

Racial and Gender Identity Development

The traditional psychological literature focused on the identity development of African American women tends to explore one dimension of identity development, either racial or gender identity. Many theorists and researchers have sought to define racial identity formation, the ways in which African Americans come to know and function as racialized selves. Several models of Black identity development offer descriptions of the process through which African Americans develop positive

Black identity. Though each perspective focuses on African American people as the founding population, each has different assumptions about what healthy Black identity is and what triggers its growth and development. The original Cross (1971, 1995) model of psychological Nigrescence, the Thomas (1971) model of Black identity development, and the Milliones (1980) Stages of Black Consciousness all assume that Black identity develops in response to and as a result of being in an oppressive environment. Cross's theory of psychological Nigrescence, or Black identity development, has been the most influential. Cross maintained that despite the continued conditions of oppression, Black Americans were undergoing a kind of psychological transformation toward a less oppressed state of being. This "Negro-to-Black Conversion" experience was initially described as a five-stage model and was revised by Cross in 1995. Stage one, pre-encounter, has three elements: (a) assimilation, which is characterized by pro-American values and low salience to race; (b) mis-education, which is characterized by negative stereotypes about African Americans; and (c) self-hatred, which involves negative attitudes about the self due to race. The second stage, encounter, begins with an experience, verbal or visual, which causes the person to begin a reinterpretation of her or his world and assumptions. This stage is characterized by confusion, depression, or alarm. In the third stage, immersion, the person immerses him- or herself into a world of Blackness, which is called intense Black involvement. Everything that is Black-oriented is valued; everything that is White-oriented is devalued. The person is energized by rage, guilt, and a developing sense of pride. Stage four, internalization, represents an increased sense of security about one's Blackness. This stage is characterized by an interest in working to empower the Black community (Black nationalist ideology) and/or emphasizing other cultural variables. Cross's racial identity stage theory has been operationalized by Parham and Helms's (1981) Racial Identity Attitudes Scale, and much research has been generated by the scale.

In a noteworthy departure from the stage-wise models, Sellers, Smith, Shelton, Rowley and Chavous (1998) offered the Multidimensional Model of Racial Identity (MMRI). The MMRI focuses on the status of an individual's racial identity rather than its development. Specifically, the MMRI focuses on four dimensions of identity: (a) racial salience, or the relevance of race to one's self-concept; (b) the centrality of the identity to one's self-concept; (c) the extent of positive or negative regard one has toward being Black; and (d) ideology, which is one's beliefs and attitudes about the way that members of the race should behave. The MMRI and Nigrescence each attempt to describe identity by situating the self within a racialized social context. Other approaches broaden the conceptual frame to include philosophical views of reality and sociocultural identity.

The African-centered worldview represents a way of conceptualizing the world that is consistent with an ancient African value system and philosophy. This philosophy contends that all of nature is connected and represents the manifestation of spirit, energy, or God. The Eurocentric worldview is a way of conceptualizing the world that is consistent with the traditionally European value system and philosophy. This philosophy contends that everything is separate; matter is assumed to be different and separate from spirit, energy, or God (Nobles, 1986). Africentric scholars (e.g., Akbar, 1989; Myers, 1988; Nobles, 1986) maintain that viewing the world from an African-centered perspective leads to a radically different experience, as contrasted with a Eurocentric perspective. Baldwin (1984) suggests that "non-Africentric" theories explain the personality of African Americans in terms of oppression experiences. Conversely, Africentric theories conceptualize the personality of African Americans in terms of a natural condition with an African reality base. Mental health is then seen as moving toward an African identity, with integrity and survival tendencies. Being grounded in an African-centered worldview becomes the most natural and self-actualized state for people of African descent. African American identity development is "not simply a reaction to White people or the results of societal oppression and exploitation" (Nobles, 1989, p. 254). The degree to which one's worldview and subsequent self-concept is Eurocentric in nature rather than Afrocentric defines the degree of pathology that one may experience (Akbar, 1979; Baldwin, 1984).

The racial identity models and African-centered philosophy address the development of one's sense of Blackness. What they have not addressed is how other aspects of one's self-concept, such as gender, sexual orientation, or social class, might impact the development of racial identity. With the neglect of gender consideration, these models seem to imply that the process of identity development is the same for African American men and women, with gender playing no significant part. Unfortunately, that assumption would appear to ignore the intricacies of developing African American womanhood.

Like Cross, Gilligan (1982, 1994) works from and moves beyond Erikson (1968) in her efforts to describe female development (personal and moral). Here the female is not simply subject, but is the voice from which her defining is done. Gilligan (1994) and other scholars, including Miller (1976) and Stack (1974), center their discussion of female identity development on themes not found in previous theories (for which the focus was men), but on the lives and philosophies of women, finding a female self formed from and through relationships. Miller (1976) argues that "women . . . develop in a context of attachment and affiliation with others . . ." (p. 86) relationships that vary in power, role expectation, and duration. Miller, Chodorow (1978) and Gilligan (1982) have laid the foundation for the "self-in-relation" theory for women's development. According to Miller (1976), "women's sense of self becomes very much organized around being able to make and then to maintain affiliation and relationships" (p. 83). The writers of the Stone Center at Wellesley College have suggested that the developmental pathway for women may be different from the developmental pathway for men. Contrary to the much taken for granted Freudian and Ericksonian assumptions that the self must individuate and separate for healthy development, the Stone Center writers suggest that women begin with closeness and develop self-in-relation with others. Common models of development stress the importance of separation from mother, from family, and from mentors, with autonomy, self- reliance, and self-actualization being highly prized goals.

The basic assumption of the self-in-relation theory is that "for women, the primary experience of self is relational, that is, the self is organized and developed in the context of important relationships" (Surrey, 1983, p. 3). According to this theory, women's psychology can best be understood through the mother-daughter relationship, since that is where mutual empathy is first experienced. Accurate empathy is a critical concept in women's relational self. Apparently the ability to be in relationship is related to the capacity for empathy. Chodorow (1978) suggested that the female child, through the mother's support and empathy, develops within that relationship. Unlike the male child, the female child can maintain the bond with her primary caretaker into adulthood by identifying with her mother as a woman rather than by separating from her. This uninterrupted bond with the mother gives the female child a sense of connectedness and security. The girl grows up trusting and feeling enhanced by relationships. In contrast, the male child, in order to develop an identity as a man, will find it necessary to break away from his female caregiver. The boy must disassociate himself from "girlishness." The male child learns to distrust connectedness and intimacy as identity threatening and believes that survival as a man depends on being able to function independently.

According to Miller (1976), a "girl's sense of self-esteem is based in feeling that she is a part of relationships and is taking care of these relationships" (p. 16). Being-in-relationship is a goal, thus forming a motivation. Good relationships, characterized by emotional sharing, openness, and a shared sense of understanding and regard, provide validation and opportunities for relational growth. The ability to perceive, respond, and relate to the needs and feelings of others is an important aspect of a woman's self-development (Surrey, 1983).

Similar to other developmental theories, questions remain about how valid the self-in- relation theory is multiculturally. Davenport and Yurich (1991) cautioned:

> This theory, like much of the writing on women in the last 20 years, has been developed primarily by Euro- American women and seems aimed at understanding women who come from that context also. . . . Because the theory is based on development, rather than socialization, it should be generalizable, but it is possible that these theorists have made the same mistake that male theorists are faulted for making—that is, operating from within their own contexts and blind to the errors in generalizing to others. More research needs to be done applying theory to women from other cultures. (p. 66)

Helms developed an identity development model for women of color, namely the "womanist" identity (Ossana, Helms, & Leonard, 1992). The term "womanist" was chosen instead of feminist as it represents the unique experiences of women of color. This model differs from feminist models in that it describes the process of identity development of a self-definition of womanhood. In stage one, pre-encounter, individuals have traditional gender roles, and behave in ways that devalue women. Stage two, encounter, occurs when individuals have experiences that cause them to question previously held beliefs. In stage three, immersion/emersion, idealization of women occurs, as well as rejection of male dominant definitions of women, and later, by an exploration of positive values of womanhood. Finally, in internalization, the new definition of womanhood is incorporated into self-concept.

Generally, these traditional identity development theories have rarely acknowledged or examined the multiple layers of diversity and have instead offered one-dimensional views of individuals (Poston, 1990; Reynolds & Pope, 1991; Yakushko, Davidson, & Williams, 2009). The assumptions underlying these models appear to oversimplify the nature of reality and attempt to categorize individuals within one sphere or another without considering the interrelatedness of identities. As Reynolds and Pope (1991) so aptly describe, "A common example of this frequent dichotomy or segmenting of human identities is found in many job advertisements—'Minorities and women are encouraged to apply'—which implies two separate and unrelated groups and ultimately makes women of color invisible" (p. 174).

The invisibility of African American women is a frequent occurrence. hooks (1981) explains, "No other group in America has so had their identity socialized out of existence as have black women" (p. 7). The Black identity development theories appear to have been written for and about African American men, with gender issues rarely mentioned. The female identity development models appear to have been written for and about White women, with racial issues rarely mentioned. hooks suggests that it is both sexism and racism which mitigate against the acknowledgment of the interests of African American women. The experience of African American women cannot be easily parceled into a Black experience and a female experience, as described by the traditional models. Separately, the racial identity and female identity models may be unable to fully explain the unique experience of being African American and female simultaneously. Within this context of racial and gender oppression and distortion of identity, one is left to wonder, "What about the African American women"?

Images, Intersectionality, and Identity

In order to see the self, women of African descent must contend with the external constructs that form the images, "metaphors and narratives" (Myrsiades & Myrsiades, 1998, p. 2) surrounding their racialized gender. With both race and gender representing positions of powerlessness and exploitation, Black women are subjected to a series of created images designed to colonize and continually re-colonize, which often results in "a psychic, sexual and material usurpation of... self-determination" (Alexander & Mohanty, 1997, p. 66). African American women could be viewed as having at least two strikes against them, being Black and female in a culture that values neither. African American women are "linked to a history of racist and sexist oppression that institutionalizes the devaluation of African American women as it idealizes their White counterparts" (Greene, 1994, p. 10). There is a natural tendency to look toward the larger society to inform one's sense of self. For the African woman, the American context provides little positive reinforcement. Actually, the mainstream society may act to hinder the healthy identity development of African American women. One could argue that mainstream culture negates the identity of African American women by encouraging (in both subtle and obvious ways) the adoption of a new, different, perhaps more palatable identity. This new identity within a White patriarchal society would result in a total rejection of communally situated African American womanhood.

The African American woman is barraged by colonizing images. Due to the legacy of slavery, particularly the requirements for heavy labor and sexual victimization, societal images of African American women differ from those of White women (Bell, 1992; Greene, 1997; West, 1995). Generally, the societal images and expectations of African American women are that they are dominant, aggressive, sexually promiscuous, rebellious, rude, and loud, "the antithesis of the American conception of beauty, femininity and womanhood" (Jewell, 1993, p. 36). Though distorted and uncharacteristic, these stereotypes "have had a profound influence on other people's perceptions and expectations of African American women" (Jewell, 1993, p. 32). There are three particular stereotypes of African American women—Mammy, Sapphire, and Jezebel—that are especially relevant in contemporary times (Abdullah, 1998; Mitchell & Herring, 1998; West, 1995). The most pervasive and enduring image has been the Mammy.

During slavery, Mammy was an obese, dark-skinned woman with broad features who worked in the master's house, often serving as nanny, housekeeper, and cook (Greene, 1994; Mitchell & Herring, 1998; West, 1995). Mammy took care of the needs of others, often to the neglect of her own needs. Mammy was seen by Whites as non-threatening, nurturing, and possessing selfless devotion to others (Abdullah, 1998). She was expected to be uncomplaining, congenial, and a deferential problem solver (Mitchell & Herring, 1998). The role of Mammy was seen as "nonthreatening, nurturing, selfless... [and] who demonstrated love and devotion to their oppressors and the oppressors' families rather than to self or family" (Abdullah, 1998, p. 198). Constructed to obscure any thought of sexual threat and the pervasive sexual abuse of African women, the Mammy was a convenient contrivance. Over time, "Mammy was a role initially played by women of African descent as a survival strategy to preserve their life and the lives of loved ones, the functional use of the role is now extinct" (p. 199), but the image remains alive and well.

Sapphire, a character from the 1940s and 1950s *Amos and Andy* radio and television show, was seen as nagging, emasculating, shrill, loud, argumentative, and a master of verbal assaults (Mitchell & Herring, 1998; West, 1995). The perceptions of African American women that emerged from this character include arrogant, controlling, loud, hostile, obnoxious, and never satisfied (Bell, 1992; Mitchell & Herring, 1998; West, 1995). She is today's "scary" Black woman, a distorted representation of African American female strength. Reflecting the historic co-inflation of constructed Blackness with a savage animalistic nature, the Sapphire has long appeared in movies and television providing comic pathos. More recently, her sharp tongue, quick temper, and unpredictable attitude have made her a staple caricature for reality shows—sure to get into fights and behave outrageously, she is a catch phrase waiting to happen.

Similar to the Mammy, the stereotype of Jezebel was derived from the sexual exploitation and victimization of African American women. Instead of hiding the obvious sexual abuse, this construction was designed to justify sexual relations with enslaved women. Jezebel is perceived as seductive, manipulative, hypersexed, animalistic in desires, and unable to control her sex drives (Mitchell & Herring, 1998; West, 1995). Even today, African American women are viewed as promiscuous, loose, immoral, sexual aggressors, and lacking sexual restraint (Bell, 1992; Greene, 1997, 1994; Jones & Shorter-Gooden, 2003). Constructed and counter-constructed, the African American female has had to work to develop and maintain identity in a context where structures oppress her and concepts obscure her.

To address the multifaceted issues of race and gender in African American women, many authors have sought to interweave the constructions of race and gender. Collins (1991) and hooks (1981, 1990) frame the discussion of African American women on the reference points of colonialization, oppression, sexism, and racism, which both distort and ensnare the identity and threaten the agency of African American females. The colonized mind, the politics of identity, and the ways in which race and gender oppression have affected the minds and selves of African Americans are all important for establishing the context for a discussion of racialized gender constructs and processes.

Though a complex topic, one aspect of identity agreed upon by most is its duality, employing both internal and external processes and domains (Franklin, 1999; Stevens, 1997). Of course, part of that external frame for African American females is the gendered and racial environment in which they are coming to self. Davis and Gandy (1999) describe the role of that context in personal development by defining "racial identity as an organizing mechanism... situationally emergent... shaped by cumulative social experiences and... enacted in reaction to context-specific social interactions" (pp. 367–368). Identity is understood as an internal "ideological position" created by the external racial projects (Davis & Gandy, 1999).

Within a system of oppression, members of the subordinate group can come to accept and believe the dominant group's negative view of them. This internalization of the dominant group's damaging narrative will cause one to think, feel, and act in ways that show one's negative view of not only her group but also of herself as a member of that group (Hardiman & Jackson, 1997). This internalization is very psychologically damaging, as it serves to colonize and re-colonize the victims of oppression (Freire, 1999; Speight, 2007). As a consequence of accepting the dominant group's definition of reality, members of the subordinate group cease to independently define themselves. As Watts-Jones (2002) explained, "when people of African descent internalize racism it is an experience of self-degradation, and self-alienation; one that promotes the assumptive base of our inferiority" (p. 592). Thus, the produced negative images and stereotypes infiltrate the psyches of African American women.

For women in particular, one significant and obvious manifestation of this internalization relates to standards of beauty. Issues of colorism, skin tone, and hair texture have long been of concern for African American women's sense of self (Coard, Breland, & Raskin, 2001; Keith, & Herring, 1991).

Preference for African American women with lighter skin and more Eurocentric features began with the sexual exploitation of enslaved Africans who produced mixed race offspring. Those enslaved men and women with lighter complexions were often given preferential treatment, including not having to work in the fields. Skin color was also used as a social marker after slavery. The "brown paper bag test" was a ritual once practiced by certain African-American fraternities, and sororities, and social clubs that discriminated against people who were "too dark" (Wilder, 2010). Issues of colorism are transmitted within African American communities and families, which may deem lighter complexions and longer, straighter hair as more attractive (Greene, White, & Whitten, 2000). In relation to the dominant society's gender expectations, African American women are judged as less feminine and less physically attractive than White women.

African American women often compare themselves to European standards of beauty, and some may straighten and lighten their hair in order to be closer to European standards of beauty. "In changing her physical appearance to meet the mainstream ideal, her sense of self may start to disintegrate as she rejects and even grows to disdain her natural physical self" (Jones & Shorter-Gooden, 2003, p. 177). This is not to say that every woman who chemically straightens her hair, for instance, believes that she must be White (or approximate White) to be considered beautiful, but for some, "changing their appearance is a subconscious effort to live up to beauty standards set up by others" (p. 179). There can be an erosion of self-esteem resulting from the belief "that one's natural self is not good enough, not attractive enough" (p. 179). The pain of wanting to be accepted by others is real. Cole and Zucker (2007) compared Black and White women's views of femininity and found that African American women were more interested in maintaining a feminine appearance than White women and were also more likely to describe themselves as feminine. These findings certainly raise some interesting questions about the meaning of feminine appearance for African American women. Cole and Zucker wondered if these African American women (drawn from a national study of women ranging in age from 18 to 55 years) believed that they must live up to an external standard of beauty, or alternately, could their concern over appearance really represent a form of resistance?

For African American women, developing internal ideas of beauty not hinged on White standards of attractiveness is an important part of a positive gendered racial identity. African American women who incorporate an African-centered perspective into their sense of self begin to develop more culturally consistent standards of beauty (Makkar & Strube, 1995).

The way in which one sees one's self comes from a larger context that is not only internally and externally derived, but is also frequently self-distorting. Looking at the larger backdrop of society, Davis and Gandy (1999) speak of the existence of a social identity derived from and mixed with the self, and serving to connect one to a group. Within this notion, the internal and external are intricately and reciprocally intertwined. The internal directs how the external or social self appears, and that internal self is influenced by the external, to which it is projecting and from which it is projected.

For instance, popular culture currently serves to produce, maintain, promote, and project several variations of the African American female, as well. Movies, music, icons, TV are:

> filled with images of demonized black women, images created to justify the latest cuts and abdication of government responsibility; [overrun with] reports of yet another woman raped, beaten, or killed, another woman working and living in poverty... [m]usic videos... [have become] inundated with images of black women dismembered by twisted, violent, male sexual fantasies... there is seldom any whole black woman, merely parts... barely dressed... an array of disconnected body parts to be used and abused at the whim of men. (Nelson, 1997, p. 152)

Today's young African American women stand in the shadow of these historical representations, while coming of age in the Hip Hop generation. Their identity development occurs within the crucible of what Tricia Rose (2008) calls the "commercial trinity of the gangsta, pimp, and ho" (p. 7). Efforts to understand sexuality must take place in an "era rife with pornography, the mainstreaming of strip clubs, and the sexualization of everything from blue jeans ads to primetime television" (Sharpley-Whiting, 2007, p. 5). Nearly inescapable in pop culture, the Black female body, in often just its parts, is bounced, pimped, and distorted in order to sell products, provide decoration, or establish another's masculinity. The resultant outcome can appear as stifled voice and truncated identity.

The constructed (and often internalized) African American female image has morphed from nurturing laborer to sexual icon, while her sexual exploitation has moved from masked reality to commercial enterprise. Recently, MEE Productions (2004) conducted 40 focus groups with African American youth in 10 urban cities, finding that Black teenage girls feel pressure from social messages to become sexually active, often viewing sex as a transaction, feeling unvalued and under cared for, and consequently relying on themselves to take care of their own needs. As Sharpley-Whiting (2007) asserts:

> sexual violence, sexism, 'beat-downs', sexual dishonesty, anti-lesbianism, and the legacy of color prejudice all hammer away at self esteem... It is not that these issues never existed before the hip hop global takeover. But the very public celebration and commercial trafficking in such images and behavior has made them appear normal, acceptable, and entertaining. (p. 12)

The African American woman exists largely in society's consciousness as a caricature, exploitable due to her race and gender and what was created at the intersection of those two constructs. Forged into our social behaviors and environments as well as our psychological notions are the images of African American women defining and constraining what slavery had not already distorted (Ani, 1994). Little of the African American female image is her own or is defined by her values. Her blackness and femaleness remain external, constructed, and maintained by society, practically eliminating her from her own picture (Majors & Billson, 1992; Turner, 1994, 2002).

Standing next to the White woman, the African American female is ever aware of the contrasting images. Where the White woman represents beauty, femininity, purity, and grace, "Black" is imaged as ugly. The African American woman is either an asexual servant or a sexualized being; either way she is exploited (hooks, 1981). Animal sexuality and asexuality, masculine yet female, downtrodden while triumphant survivor, strong but victim, pillar of the race and full of attitude, big and loud yet overshadowed, backbone of the family and reason for her man's problems, mystical and down-to-earth, whore and maternal icon, the African American woman is more than complex and multitudinous; her image and construction are built on a house of contradictions. She is simultaneously all and nullified.

Within this cultural context, external and societal-based values or standards will not provide the African American women with many opportunities for healthy identity development and maintenance. Being the target of oppression can create a self-image of worthlessness, leading to internalized feelings of inferiority (Allport, 1954). Furthermore, African American women frequently experience the dilemma of having to choose between their dual identities as African Americans and women (Reid, 1984), wrestling with the dichotomy of sexual exploitation versus female sexual power or having to disassociate themselves into component selves (McCombs, 1986). On occasion, African American women are called upon to be either Black or female, or to fulfill their societal role (e.g., lawyer, teacher), and at times to combine two aspects (e.g., Black lawyer, female teacher) while omitting one. African American women experience a process of "selective affirmation" in the American context (McCombs, 1986).

Selective affirmation is especially true for African American lesbians, who may face difficult issues negotiating the terrain of racial, gender, and sexual constructions. The African American community tends to be homophobic and heterosexist due to the influence of the theologically conservative view of sexuality espoused by "the Black church" (Cone, 1990). Consequently, African American lesbians may not find support within the African American community for their sexual identity, or that support may be conditioned on maintaining the invisibility of their sexual identity. Racism within the gay/lesbian community and heterosexism within the African American community can leave African American lesbians without consistent acceptance and affirmation of all aspects of their identity (Greene, 2000; Loiacano, 1989).

Though the constructed representations of African American women attempted to render them voiceless and powerless, and the racialized and gendered social structures and ideologies worked to constrain them, the African American female has been known for her survival and strength. It is hard to find a word more intimately tied to a group of people than "strength" is to the African American woman. The word was used descriptively by bell hooks (1981) to identify the African American female; Patricia Hills Collins (1991) takes the notion a step further by defining Black womanhood, in part, as "struggle and strength." The African American woman is perceived as the ultimate over-comer; having survived slavery and endured oppression, she continues to be the rock, the anchor for her family. With male help or without it, she will fight poverty, the high crime rate, racism, sexism, and all forms of discrimination wherever she may encounter them. One thing that makes that the pairing of resilience and African American womanhood so interesting is the other word so often attached to her: "victim." From all sides, she is treated as less than, and her contemporary position in society does nothing to refute that. Michelle Wallace (1990) described a part of that dichotomy well by saying, "It made me cringe to hear men referring to me as 'strong,' because I knew they were referring to the historical me... never realizing how imaginary that strength really was" (Wallace, 1991, p. 95).

On the other hand, being strong is an important and effective coping strategy that enables African American women to deal successfully with life's adversities. For instance, Shambley-Ebron and Boyle (2006) conducted a year-long investigation of African American women with HIV/AIDS who were also mothers of a child with HIV. Faced with their own health challenges with HIV, caring for a child with HIV, along with money and employment problems, these women were invested in being strong. The women talked about inheriting a tradition and heritage of being strong from the generations of "strong Black women" before them. The women also garnered significant strength and hope from their faith, which allowed them to get through many difficult times. This strength signifies the resilience and empowerment that many African American women possess.

Alongside the long history of triumphant African American females, at times, African American female strength appears as a "pose" that African American women adopt to conceal other aspects of self—thereby providing the means to cope with a world marked by oppression. That same pose may allow her to venture into and often find success in a White male-dominated world, even though her race and gender may operate to separate, limit, and mis-define her. African American women are perceived by others and themselves as being strong, psychologically invulnerable, and emotionally secure (Romero, 2000). Yet, women often face tremendous challenges to their daily functioning and to their psyches. Although "strong Black women" are often seen as pillars of their communities, this image belies the fact that some may face loneliness and a sense of isolation or disconnection from others. For instance, while praising the career and educational accomplishments of the African American woman, a Newsweek article also lamented the likelihood of her being "stranded, unfulfilled, childless and alone" (Cose, 2003, p. 49).

The "strong Black woman" provides a shield from, but rarely addresses, the real sexual, racial, economic, and structural constraints experienced and the concomitant psychological toll that these hardships may exact. Many women with a developed facade of strength may have difficulty admitting to difficulties or asking for support. According to Shambley-Ebron and Boyle (2006), "when black women internalize stereotypical myths, believing that they possess a greater degree of emotional strength than other women, they are more likely to set high expectations of their own abilities to manage life's difficulties" (p. 204). Mitchell and Herring (1998) discuss the "Superwoman," who believes herself to be capable of accomplishing multiple tasks successfully. African American women often feel weak and like failures if they cannot be successful or need to ask for help. This need to portray an image of survival and strength, being "strong at all costs," often prevents women from expressing their inner desires and needs, psychological distress, depressive or anxiety symptoms, or to seek psychological services (Gainor, 1992; Greene, 1994; Shambley-Ebron & Boyle, 2006; West, 1995). Consequently, the "strong Black woman" pose has important implications for mental health and well-being.

Mental Health and African American Women

The need to appear strong, counteracting negative societal images of African American women, can be taxing and exhausting for women. The mental health and psychological well-being of women are often compromised by the image of strength.

"And herein lies the problem. Because the idea of strength *appears* to honestly reflect Black women's extensive work and family demands, as well as their accomplishments under far from favorable social conditions," it undermines the true purpose of protecting "a stratified social order by obscuring Black women's experiences of suffering, actions of desperation, and anger" (Beauboeuf-Lafontant, 2009, p. 2). African American women feel internal pressure to maintain the facade of strength and are externally reinforced for not displaying distress or negative emotions that would make others feel uncomfortable. African American women's strength must be understood as resilience and armor, having positive, negative, limiting, and elevating functions. The social construction of the identity of African American women, the prevailing stereotypes, and the need to appear strong often limit their ability to engage in healthy self-acceptance and a positive, affirming sense of self.

Research on the mental health and well-being of African American women has been noticeably sparse. Psychology's indifference to women of African descent is not particularly surprising, however, as it is consistent with the social position of African American women within U.S. society. The mental health of women of African descent may, in fact, "look different" from mental health in women from other racial or ethnic groups. Brown (2003) contends "that societal factors are the most salient influences on the mental well-being of African American women" (p. 1). Thus, mental health (and mental illness, for that matter) is context dependent and can only be understood by exploring the reciprocal interaction of the person within her environment.

Two national studies with representative samples offer a glimpse into the mental illness rates of African American women by examining one-year prevalence rates of mental disorders. The Epidemiologic Catchment Area (Robins, Helzer, Croughan, & Ratcliff, 1981) study found that when compared to African American men, White men, and White women, African American women had the highest rates of schizophrenia, generalized anxiety disorder, phobia, somatization, and panic disorder (Brown & Keith, 2003). The National Comorbidity Survey (Kessler et al., 1994) found that African American women had the highest one-year prevalence rates over White men and women and African American men for agoraphobia, dysthymia, mania, simple phobia, and post-traumatic stress disorder. In terms of lifetime prevalence, when compared to White men and women and African American men, African American women are more likely to experience agoraphobia, simple phobia, post-traumatic stress disorder, and non-affective psychosis (Brown & Keith, 2003).

A survey by the National Mental Health Association (NMHA, 1996) found that African Americans were confused about the definition, causes, and symptoms of depression (Mitchell & Herring, 1998). For example, 63% of African Americans believed that depression is a personal weakness. Only 31% of African Americans in the study believed that depression was a health problem. About 40% of the participants indicated that they would not seek treatment because of the difficulty of admitting what is happening, and 38% would not seek treatment because of shame or embarrassment (NMHA, 1996). Thus, the pose of strength belies the real experience of psychic pain. Indeed, the " discourses of strength and depression—the first emphasizing Black women's validation through struggle and imperviousness to harm, the second constructing mental distress as largely a white women's prerogative—reinforce each other to deny both the existence and experience of depression among Black women" (Beauboeuf-Lafontant, 2009, p. 65).

Specifically, depression in African American women may be displayed through irritability or lashing out at others instead of traditional "White female" symptoms of depressed mood and crying spells (Richardson & Wade, 2000). Women are at high risk for being diagnosed with depression, but are also likely to suppress it. Women may demonstrate symptoms through activity, or by taking care of others, often to the neglect of their own needs, or through low self-esteem, shame, and disappointment at not doing enough for others. Depression may also be shown through somatization (Jones & Shorter-Gooden, 2003). African American women also receive the message that it is important to mask or contain signs of depression (Richardson & Wade, 1999).

Schreiber, Stern, and Wilson (2000), as part of a qualitative study of 12 West Indian Canadian women, found that the women attempted to "manage their depression with grace and to live up to the cultural imperative to be strong" (p. 4). The women thought that suffering was a normal part of life and that one endured personal misery privately in isolation. The women attempted to divert themselves, turning to spiritual support, getting involved in activities, and thinking positively; less than half of the women sought professional help. One reason that these Black women did not get treated for depression is that they expected to feel sad and tired, believing that women should continue to function, often past the point of exhaustion (Thomas, 2001).

Additionally, African American women are unlikely to seek help for anxiety-related symptoms but more often seek services for relationship problems or bereavement (Neal-Barnett & Crowther, 2000). African American women often do not seek treatment because they interpret the anxiety as a normal part of their lives as Black women, illustrating the belief that "we have to keep on keeping on." This is the internalized stereotype of the "strong Black woman" who bears all. African American women may also fear that once they disclose the source of the anxiety, they will become flooded by other negative emotions (Neal-Barnett & Crowther, 2000).

The appearance of strength and resulting tension are often visibly represented in African American women's bodies, through obesity or other stress-related illnesses, such as hypertension (Beauboeuf-Lafontant, 2009). African American women may not present with explicit complaints of depressive or anxiety symptoms, but may experience challenges with mental health that are manifested in binge or compulsive eating. Because African American women do not experience body image issues in the same way as White women, being overweight or obese is often overlooked as a possible sign of mental health issues. Overeating often is a form of emotional acting out for women, helping to sublimate the stresses of daily living (Williams, 2008). Compulsive eating also helps women to put on a literal "protective covering" against sexuality, serving as a coping strategy for women who have experiences with sexual assault and abuse (Beauboeuf-Lafontant, 2009; Williams, 2008).

African American women often need to engage in the painful process of confronting and deconstructing negative societal images and expectations, especially if they have been internalized. African American women often fear being vulnerable, as it contradicts the image of strength and togetherness (Adams, 2000). African American women's strength is understood as resilience and armor, having positive, negative, limiting, and elevating functions. Successful treatment needs to be based on encouraging women to be open to examining the fullness of their lives, its peaks and valleys, sadness and joys, insecurities and strengths. Often, African American women will need to deconstruct the message that they need to "keep it together" at all costs. The "perception these women have of themselves is not that they are suffering, but that they are strong, autonomous beings who can survive anything without help, despite any and all difficulties they confront. In fact, many perceive the need to ask for and accept help from anyone as an intolerable expression of weakness" (Thompson, 2000, p. 240). Mental health is compromised by societal reinforcement of the strong image, and women may need to work through their sense of themselves as failures before engaging in therapeutic work.

Matthews and Hughes (2001), in a rare study of African American lesbian and heterosexual women, found some interesting patterns in their utilization of mental health services. Significantly more lesbians (55%) had received therapy for an emotional problem than heterosexual women (33%). The most common reason for seeking therapy was for feeling sad and depressed. Thirty percent of the lesbians and 44% of the heterosexual women said that they had considered but did not seek therapy due to several factors such as "cost and lack of insurance," "lack of perceived need," "kept putting it off," "not liking to talk with a stranger" and, because they "didn't think it would help." The image of the "strong Black woman," coupled with a lack of confidence in the effectiveness of therapy, constitutes a significant barrier to seeking needed mental health services.

Moreover, clinicians must be cognizant of their own acceptance of societal stereotypes of African American women. Constantine (2007), in a focus group study of racial microaggressions experienced by African American former clients, found that some clients described "idealization" from their counselor, who overestimated desirable qualities due to the client's race. An example of this was a counselor who told the client, "I'm sure you can cope with this problem as a strong Black woman." Obviously, this counselor had bought into the image of the "strong Black woman," which would undoubtedly make it difficult for the client to expose her vulnerabilities.

Because the lives of African American women are complex, careful consideration needs to be given in deciding on appropriate intervention strategies to foster psychological well-being. One of the great challenges for women is to find a balance between getting their needs met while taking care of others (Thompson, 2000). In order to get their needs met, African American women must break silences to share their weaknesses and vulnerabilities, thereby trusting and allowing others to take care of them. Relying on others is the antithesis of being a "strong Black woman." Thus, the dilemma involves a decision "to choose appearances and remain unknown to other people, or to choose truth and risk being disregarded by them" (Beauboeuf-Lafontant, 2009, p. 5).

Psychological treatments that are African-centered in nature and focus on restoring the collective are essential (Boyd-Franklin, 1991). African American women need to build support networks and systems of support to reduce isolation. Group therapy is a recommended form of treatment, as it helps to emphasize interdependence, collective survival, and the importance of emotional release (Pack-Brown, Whittington-Clark, & Parker, 1998). Group members benefit from the support and challenge of other group members as they navigate between the ideas and practice of self-care and care for others.

African American women may also need to learn how to become more assertive (Adams, 2000). One by-product of the Sapphire image is that women may restrict feelings of anger in order to avoid being perceived as the "angry Black woman." Assertiveness training may also need to include comfort with competition as African American women are socialized and often rewarded for being self-sacrificial and for giving to others. Or they may experience feeling guilt for being successful or for leaving others in the community behind due to their success (Boyd-Franklin, 1991). Other women, due to internalized oppression, will fail to acknowledge their own success, may feel like an imposter, may feel ambivalent about success, or may engage in self-sabotaging behaviors (Thompson, 2000).

Encouraging spirituality has also been recommended in helping African American women to cope (Boyd-Franklin, 1991; Thomas, 2001), as spirituality and religion have often been reported to be effective coping tools (Eugene, 1995; Mattis, 2002). For example, women can sing spirituals to not only connect with a higher power, but to serve as a cathartic release from the struggles of the day, as spirituals were born from slavery and oppression, and express the collective suffering of African American women (Eugene, 1995). Learning to engage in "spiritual surrender" can help women to effectively reduce stress in other areas of their lives (Mattis, 2002). The church has traditionally provided an outlet for prayer and a source of validation for experiences of oppression. Women need to be encouraged to find healthy churches, however, as women can also be damaged by patriarchal systems, sexism, and sexual harassment within the sanctuary of church.

Conclusion: The Authentic and Whole Self

Clearly, there is much that is unexplored and yet to be understood about the complex lives and identity of African American woman. Though we have raised a number of issues and questions for future research, some key unanswered questions remain. First, where are the locations of resistance that empower African American women, allowing them to combat the deleterious effects of their multiple oppressions? Second, how might the study of African American female identity development processes expand and connect existing race- and gender-based identity models? Third, is socioeconomic class one of several elements of the complex social context for African American women, or does it represent another construction intimately tied to identity? Fourth, given the changing social discourse on sexuality and gender roles, how will young African American challenge, resist, or perpetuate "strong Black womanism? Fifth, what influence will the African American lesbian, gay, bisexual, transgender (LGBT) community have on African American women's view of their own racialized gender identity and broader gender and sexuality constructions?

This chapter has shown that African American women must develop critical consciousness in order to sort and evaluate negative messages and oppressive images. The negative message and oppressive images, "though invisible, wield much power. They can cause the self to diminish, to shrink, or to disappear" (Jones & Shorter-Gooden, 2003, p. 34). The development of an authentic self based on internal standards will allow the negative historical images from slavery to lose their hold on the psyches of individual African American women and the society. Ultimately, it seems clear that African American women must engage in a process of self-definition based on internal standards, values, and beliefs. The process and resulting definition must transcend the limitations of the existing societal standards for African American womanhood in order to fully validate her existence and guide her development. African American women must "reject . . . reconstruct . . . and redefine" cultural images symbolizing African American womanhood for themselves (Jewell, 1993, p. 33).

The development of an authentic sense of self involves seeing, naming, questioning, resisting, and transforming (Isom, 2002). First, African American women must develop an awareness of the pervasiveness of oppression, the reality of racism and sexism, and the history and current manifestation of stereotypes. The second step is the ability to correctly label one's own experiences of oppression when they occur. The next step involves interrogating and scrutinizing individual experience and questioning the system of oppression responsible for it. The fourth step of resistance involves assertively defending the self by expelling the toxic, damaging, effects of oppression. Taken together, these steps will allow African American women to transform themselves and, ultimately, society through this internal revolution (Thomas, Witherspoon, & Speight, 2004). Women who have self-determination are able to develop their identity, make choices, and behave in ways wholly consistent with their own standards, values, and ideals. African American women with positive identity "know who they are... know where they are, and know to deal with their environment" (Speight, Blackmon, Odugu, & Steele, 2008, p. 370).

Saartjie Bartmann did not have the opportunity to develop her own genuine sense of self due to her physical, psychological, social, and cultural colonization. The experiences of Saartjie Bartmann (and countless others) demonstrate that women of African descent can and have survived degradations and humiliations stemming from oppression. But hooks (1981) powerfully reminds us that "endurance is not to be confused with transformation" (p. 6). Simply making it through and finding a way to survive (or appearing as such) is no substitute for the development of the authentic self, for the "perennial process of self-making and self-inventing... propelled by a self-loving and self-trusting made possible by overcoming a colonized mind, body and soul" (West & Gates, 1996, p. 92). The produced societal images that constructed and entrapped Saartjie are still evident and continue to influence the identity processes of African American women. The unique intersections of race and gender constructions necessitate that African American women develop an identity centered on their own voices, seeing themselves through their own eyes. Seeing, acknowledging, naming, questioning, and resisting oppression in the form of damaging societal images will empower African American women to be more fully human—willingly, boldly, and unapologetically able to create their own truths and realities.

References

Abdullah, A. S. (1998). Mammy-ism: A diagnosis of psychological misorientation for women of African descent. *Journal of Black Psychology, 24*(2), 196–210.

Adams, J. (2000). Individual and group psychotherapy with African American women: Understanding the identity and context of the therapist and the patient. In L. C. Jackson & B. Greene (Eds.), *Psychotherapy with African American women: Innovations in psychodynamic perspectives* (pp. 33–61). New York: Guildford.

Akbar, N. (1979). *Mental disorder among African-Americans.* Paper presented at the Thirteenth Annual Convention of the Association of Black Psychologists, Atlanta, GA.

Akbar, N. (1989). Nigrescence and identity: Some limitations. *The Counseling Psychologist, 17,* 258–263.

Allport, G. W. (1954). *The nature of preiudice.* Reading, MA: Addison Wesley.

Alexander, M. J., & Mohanty, C. T. (1997) *Feminist genealogies, colonial legacies, democratic futures.* New York: Routledge.

Ani, M. (1994) *Yurugu.* Trenton: African World Press.

Baldwin, J. A. (1984). African self-consciousness and the mental health of African Americans. *Journal of Black Studies, 15,* 177–194.

Beauboeuf-Lafontant, T. (2009). *Behind the mask of the strong Black woman: Voice and the embodiment of a costly performance.* Philadelphia: Temple University Press.

Bell, E. L. (1992). Myths, stereotypes, and realities of Black women: A personal reflection. *Journal of Applied Behavioral Science, 28,* 363–376.

Boyd-Franklin, N. (1991). Recurrent themes in treatment of African-American women in group psychotherapy. *Women and Therapy, 11,* 25–40.

Brown, D. R. (2003). A conceptual model of mental well-being for African American women. In D. R. Brown and V. M. Keith (Eds.), *In and out of our right minds: The mental health of African American women* (pp. 1–22). New York: Columbia University Press.

Brown, D. R., & Keith, V. M. (2003). The epidemiology of mental disorders and mental health among African American women. In D. R. Brown and V. M. Keith (Eds.), *In and out of our right minds: The mental health of African American women* (pp. 23–58). New York: Columbia University Press.

Carbado, D. W. (1999). *Black men on race, gender, and sexuality.* New York: Routledge.

Chodorow, N. (1978). *The reproduction of mothering.* Berkeley: University of California Press.

Coard, S. I., Breland, A., & Raskin, P. (2001). Perceptions of and preferences for skin color, Black racial identity, and self-esteem among African Americans. *Journal of Applied Social Psychology, 31*(11), 2256–2274.

Cole, E. R., & Zucker, A. N. (2007). Black and White women's perspectives on femininity. *Cultural Diversity and Ethnic Minority Psychology, 13*(1), 1–9.

Collins, P. H. (1991). *Black feminist thought.* New York: Routledge.

Cone, J. (1990). *A Black theology of liberation: Twentieth century edition.* Maryknoll, NY: Orbis Books.

Constantine, M. G. (2007). Racial microaggressions against African American clients in cross-racial counseling relationships. *Journal of Counseling Psychology, 54*(1), 1–16.

Cose, E. (March 3, 2003). From schools to jobs, Black women are rising much faster than Black men: What it means for work, family and race relations. *Newsweek.*

Cross, W. E. (1971). The Negro-to-Black conversion experience. *Black World, 20*(9), 13–27.

Cross, W. E. (1995). Nigrescence theory: Historical and explanatory notes. *Journal of Vocational Behavior, 41,* 119–123.

Davenport, D. S. & Yurich, J. M. (1991). Multicultural gender issues. *Journal of Counseling and Development, 70,* 64–71.

Davis, J. L., & Gandy, O. H., Jr. (1999). Racial identity and media orientation: Exploring the nature of constraint. *Journal of Black Studies, 29*(3), 367–397.

Erikson, E. H. (1968). *Identity: Youth and crisis.* New York: W.W. Norton.

Eugene, T. M. (1995). There is a balm in Gilead: Black women and the Black church as agents of a therapeutic community. *Women and Therapy, 16,* 55–71.

Franklin, A. (1999). Invisibility syndrome and racial identity development in psychotherapy and counseling African American men. *Counseling Psychologist, 2*(6), 761–793.

Freire, P. (1999). *Pedagogy of the oppressed.* New York: Continuum.

Gainor, K. A. (1992). Internalized oppressions as a barrier to effective group work with Black women. *The Journal for Specialists in Group Work, 17,* 235–242.

Gilligan, C. ([1982], 1994). *In a different voice: Psychological theory and women's development.* Cambridge, MA: Harvard University Press.

Greene, B. (1994). African American women. In L. Coas-Diaz & B. Greene (Eds.), *Women of color: Integrating ethnic and gender identities in psychotherapy* (pp.10–29). New York: Guildford Press.

Greene, B. (1997). Psychotherapy with African American women: Integrating feminist and psychodynamic models. *Smith College Studies in Social Work, 67,* 299–322.

Greene, B. (2000). African American lesbian and bisexual women. *Journal of Social Issues, 56*(2), 239–249.

Greene, B., White, J. C., & Whitten, L. (2000). Hair texture, length, and style as a metaphor in the African American mother-daughter relationship: Considerations in psychodynamic psychotherapy. In L. C. Jackson & B. Greene, Beverly (Eds.), *Psychotherapy with African American women: Innovations in psychodynamic perspective and practice* (pp. 166–193). New York: Guilford.

Hardiman, R., & Jackson, B. W. (1997). Conceptual foundations for social justice courses. In M. Adams, L. A. Bell, & P. Griffin (Eds.), *Teaching for diversity and social justice: A sourcebook* (pp. 16–29). New York: Routledge.

hooks, b. (1981). *Ain't I a woman: Black women and feminism.* Boston: South End Press.

hooks, b. (1990). *Yearning: Race, gender, and cultural politics.* Boston: South End Press.

Isom, D. (2002). *"Me, I got a lot of parts." Tainted by, struggling against, striving for: Racialized gender identity constructs in African American children.* Dissertation, Loyola University, Chicago.

Jewell, K. S. (1993). *From Mammy to Miss America and beyond: Cultural images and the shaping of U.S. social policy.* New York: Routledge.

Jones, C., & Shorter-Gooden, K. (2003). *Shifting: The double lives of Black women in America.* New York: HarperCollins.

Keith, V. M., & Herring, C. (1991). Skin tone: A stratification in the Black community. *The American Journal of Sociology, 97,* 760–778.

Kessler, R. C., McGongale, K. A., Zhao, S., Neson, Hughes, M., Eshleman, S., Wittchen, H. U., & Kendler, K. S. (1994). Lifetime and 12-month prevalence of DSM-III-R psychiatric disorders in the United States: Results from the National Comormidity Survey. *Archives of General Psychiatry, 51*(1), 8–19.

Loiacano, D. K. (1989). Gay identity issues among Black Americans: Racism, homophobia, and the need for validation. *Journal of Counseling and Development, 68,* 21–25.

Majors, R., & Billson, J. M. (1992). *Cool pose: The dilemmas of Black manhood in America.* New York: Lexington Books.

Makkar, J. K., & Strube, M. J. (1995). Black women's self-perceptions of attractiveness following exposure to White versus Black beauty standards: The moderating role of racial identity and self-esteem. *Journal of Applied Social Psychology, 25,* 1547–1566.

Matthews, A. K., & Hughes, T. L. (2001). Mental health service use by African American women: Exploration of subpopulation differences. *Cultural Diversity and Ethnic Minority Psychology, 7*(1), 75–87

Mattis, J. S. (2002). Religion and spirituality in the meaning-making and coping experiences of African American women: A qualitative analysis. *Psychology of Women Quarterly, 26,* 309–321.

Mbeki, T. (2002). Letter from the President. *Chicken Bones: A Journal for Literary and Artistic African American Themes.* Retrieved from http://www.nathanielturner.com/saartjie-baartman.htm.

McCombs, H. G. (1986). The application of an individual/collective model to the psychology of Black women. *Women and Therapy, 5,* 67–80. doi: 10.1300/J015V05N02_06

Miller, J. B. (1976). *Toward a new psychology of women.* Boston: Beacon Press.

Milliones, J. (1980). Construction of a Black consciousness measure: Psychotherapeutic implications. *Psychotherapy, 17,* 458–462.

Mitchell, A., & Herring, K. (1998). *What the blues is: Black women overcoming stress and depression.* New York: Perigee.

Motivational Educational Entertainment Productions, Inc. (2004) "This is my reality": The price of sex: An inside look at Black urban youth and sexuality. Philadelphia: MEE.

Myers, L. J. (1988). Understanding an Afrocentric world view: Introduction to an optimal psychology. Dubuque, IA: Kendall-Hunt.

Myrsiades, K., & Myrsiades, L. (1998). *Racing representation: Voice, history, and sexuality,* Landham: Rowman and Littlefield Publishing.

National Mental Health Association (1996). *Clinical depression and African Americans.* Accessed at http://www.nmha.org/ccd/support/africanamericanfact.cfm.

Neal-Barnett, A. & Crowther, J. H. (2000). To be female, middle class, anxious, and Black. *Psychology of Women Quarterly, 24,* 129–136.

Nelson, J. (1997*). Straight, no chaser: How I became a grown-up Black woman.* New York: G. P. Putnam.

Nobles, W. W. (1986). *African psychology: Toward its reclamation, reascension, and revitalization.* Oakland, CA: The Institute for the Advanced Study of Black Family Life and Culture.

Nobles, W. W. (1989). Psychological Nigrescence: An Afrocentric review. *The Counseling Psychologist, 17,* 253–257. doi: 10.1177/0011000089172003

Omi, M., & Winant, H. (1994). *Racial formation in the United States.* New York: Routledge.

Ossana, S. M., Helms, J. E., & Leonard, M. M. (1992). Do "womanist" identity attitudes influence college women's self-esteem and perceptions of environmental bias? *Journal of Counseling and Development, 70,* 402–408.

Pack-Brown, S. P., Whittington-Clark, L. E., & Parker, W. M. (1998). *Images of me: A guide to group work with African-American women.* Boston: Allyn and Bacon.

Parham, T. A., & Helms, J. E. (1981). The influence of Black students' racial identity attitudes on preferences for counselor's race. *Journal of Counseling Psychology, 28,* 250–257.

Poston, W. S. C. (1990). The Biracial Identity Development Model: A needed addition. *Journal of Multicultural Counseling and Development, 69,* 152–156.

Reid, P. T. (1984). Feminism versus minority group identity: Not for Black women only. *Sex Roles, 10,* 247–255.

Reynolds, A. L., & Pope, R. L. (1991). The complexities of diversity: Exploring multiple oppressions. *Journal of Counseling and Development, 70,* 174–180.

Richardson, B., & Wade, B. (2000). *What Mama couldn't tell us about love: Healing the emotional legacy of racism by celebrating our light.* New York: Perennial Currents.

Robins, L. N., Helzer, J. E., Croughan, J., & Ratcliff, K. (1981). National Institute of Mental Health Diagnostic Interview

Schedule: Its history, characteristics, and validity. *Archives of General Psychiatry, 38*(4), 381–389.

Romero, R. E. (2000). The icon of the strong Black woman: The paradox of strength. In L. C. Jackson & B. Greene (Eds.), *Psychotherapy with African American women: Innovations in psychodynamic perspectives* (pp. 225–238). New York: Guilford.

Rose, T. (2008). *The hip hop wars: What we talk about when we talk about hip hop. And why it matters.* Philadelphia: Basic Books.

Schreiber, R., Stern, P. N., & Wilson, C. (2000). Being strong: How Black West-Indian Canadian women manage depression and its stigma. *Journal of Nursing Scholarship, 32,* 39–45.

Sellers, R. M., Smith M. A., Shelton, J. N., Rowley, S. A. J., Chavous, T. M. (1998). Multidimensional model of racial identity: A reconceptualization of African American racial identity. *Personality and Social psychology Review, 2*(1), 18–39.

Shambley-Ebron, D. Z., & Boyle, J. S. (2006). In our grandmother's footsteps: Perceptions of being strong in African American women with HIV/AIDS. *Advances in Nursing Science, 29*(3), 195–206.

Sharpley-Whiting, T. D. (1999). *Black Venus: Sexualized savages, primal fears, and primitive narratives in French.* Durham, NC: Duke University Press.

Sharpley-Whiting, T. D. (2007). *Pimps up, hos down: Hip hop's hold on young Black women.* New York: New York University Press.

Speight, S. L. (2007). Internalized racism: One more piece of the puzzle. *The Counseling Psychologist, 35*(1), 126–134.

Speight, S. L., Blackmon, S. M. Odugu, D., & Steele, J. C. (2008). Conceptualizing mental health for African Americans. In H. Neville, B. M. Tynes, & S. Utsey (Eds.), *The handbook of African American psychology* (pp. 363–374). Thousand Oaks: Sage.

Stack, C. B. (1974). *All our kin.* New York: Harper and Row.

Stevens, J. W. (1997). African American female adolescent identity development: A three-dimensional perspective. *Child Welfare, 76*(1), 145–172.

Surrey, J. L. (1983). Self-in-relation: A theory of women's development. Work in progress (no. 13). Wellesley, MA: Stone Center Working Papers Series.

Takaki, R. ([1994] 2008). *From different shores: Perspectives on race and ethnicity in America.* New York: Oxford University Press.

Thomas, A. J. (2001). African American women's spiritual beliefs: A guide for treatment. *Women and Therapy, 23*(4), 1–12.

Thomas, A. J., Witherspoon, K. M., & Speight, S. L. (2004). Exploring internalized oppression of African American women. In J. L. Chin (Ed.), *The psychology of prejudice and discrimination* (pp. 113–132). Westbrook, CT: Praeger Press.

Thomas, C. (1971). *Boys no more.* Beverly Hills: Glencoe Press.

Thompson, C. L. (2000). African American women and moral masocism: When there is too much of a good thing. In L. C. Jackson & B. Greene (Eds.), *Psychotherapy with African American women: Innovations in psychodynamic perspectives* (pp. 238–250). New York: Guilford.

Turner, P. A. ([1994] 2002). *Ceramic uncles and celluloid mammies: Black images and their influence on culture.* New York: Anchor Books-Doubleday.

Wallace, M. (1990). *Black macho and the myth of the superwoman.* New York: Verso.

Watts-Jones, D. (2002). Healing internalized racism: The role of within-group sanctuary among people of African descent. *Family Process, 4*(4), 591–601.

West, C., & Gates, H. L., Jr. (1996). *The Future of the race.* New York: Alfred A. Knopf.

West, C. M. (1995). Mammy, Sapphire, and Jezebel: Historical images of Black women and their implications for psychotherapy. *Psychotherapy, 32,* 458–466.

Wilder, J. (2010). Revisiting "color names and color notions": A contemporary examination of the language and attitudes of skin color among Black women. *Journal of Black Studies,* 41(1), 184–206.

Williams, T. (2008). *Black pain: It just looks like we're not hurting. Real talk for when there's nowhere to go but up.* New York: Scribner.

Yakushko, O., Davidson, M. M., & Williams, E. N. (2009). Identity salience model: A paradigm for integrating multiple identities in clinical practice. *Psychotherapy: Theory, Research, Practice, Training, 46*(2), 180–192.

CHAPTER

7 Feminist Counseling Psychology and Lesbians, Bisexual Women, and Transgender Persons

Dawn M. Szymanski *and* Angela N. Hilton

Abstract

Feminist counseling psychologists have made important advances to our understanding of lesbian and bisexual women and transgender persons, the challenges that they face as a result of living in a heterosexist context, and the complex interplays of navigating multiple identities and oppressions. The purpose of this chapter is to survey theory, research, and practice in hopes of presenting readers with a snapshot of the current status of scholarship in this area and to foster mental health professionals culturally competent, empirically based services to this population. We critically review nine main areas: (a) sexual identity development, (b) transgender identity development, (c) similarities and differences between lesbian and bisexual women, (d) the links between external and internalized oppression and psychosocial health, (e) coping with and resisting oppression, (f) immigration and acculturation, (g) life span transitions and issues, (h) career development and workplace issues, and (i) counseling and psychotherapy issues.

Key Words: Heterosexism, sexism, lesbians, bisexual women, coping, sexual identity, mental health

During the past decade, research examining psychosocial aspects of lesbian and bisexual women's (LBW) lives has flourished, and a small but growing field on transgender issues has emerged. In this chapter we survey theory, research, and practice related to LBW and transgender persons in hopes of presenting readers with a snapshot of the current status of scholarship in this area and to foster culturally competent, empirically based services by mental health professionals to this population. Before beginning, it is worth noting some challenges related to subpopulations of LBW and transgender persons as discussed in the current literature.

First, there is a debate within the field about whether to include gender identity issues (i.e., one's internal or self-identification as a gender, or one's psychological sense of being male or female) separately or together with sexual orientation issues (i.e., attraction to someone of the same and/or different sex) in theory and research (American Psychological Association, APA, 2004; Moradi, Mohr, Worthington, & Fassinger, 2009). It is important to note that a person's gender identity should not be confused with her or his sexual orientation. For example, most transgender persons have heterosexual identities, but they often work together with sexual orientation minority persons to advocate for those persons who challenge the dominant societal conceptions of sex, gender, attraction, and behavior (Sausa, 2002). In addition, very little systemic, empirically based information exists about transgender persons. Although we try to be inclusive of transgender issues and persons, the main focus of this chapter is on female sexual orientation issues because this reflects the reality of our current state of scholarship. We include a section on transgender identity development, and we integrate transgender issues into our review when we have grounds to make specific points about these issues. As such, we use the acronym LBW when research has specifically focused on sexual minority women, LGB when research has used samples consisting of sexual minority men and women, and add T (LBWT or LGBT) when samples have included a significant number of transgender persons in the study's sample or when gender identity issues have been a particular focus.

Second, research on sexual orientation issues has largely been conducted on samples of highly educated, middle and upper middle class, White LBW or LGB persons, with limited research available on LBWT people of color and LBWT people with other minority sociocultural identities (Moradi et al., 2009; Szymanski, Kashubeck-West, & Meyer, 2008a). In addition, research on LGB persons of color has been narrowly focused on high-risk sexual behavior, condom use, HIV and AIDS, substance abuse, and psychological distress (Huang et al., 2010). Thus, the complexities of sexual identity and its relationship to other sociocultural group identities have not been well explored (Bieschke, Hardy, Fassinger, & Croteau, 2008) and again, our review reflects this reality. Despite these two caveats, feminist counseling psychologists have made significant gains in understanding sexual minority women's lives in the areas of (a) LBW sexual identity development, (b) transgender identity development, (c) similarities and differences between lesbian and bisexual women, (d) the links between external and internalized oppression and psychosocial health, (e) coping with and resisting oppression, (f) immigration and acculturation, (g) life span transitions and issues, (h) career development and workplace issues, and (i) counseling and psychotherapy issues. Thus, we organize this chapter along these nine main categories.

LBW Sexual Identity Development

For feminist counselors working with LBW, it is important to be aware of the process of the development of an individual's sexual identity. First, it is important to clarify the differences between sexual orientation and sexual identity. Sexual orientation is defined as having erotic, or sexual, thoughts, fantasies and feelings for individuals of the opposite sex, same sex, both, or neither; sexual identity is a "socially recognized category that names the perceptions, feelings, and meanings that an individual holds about her or his sexual feelings, attractions, and behaviors" (Savin-Williams, 2001 p. 14). For example, a 15-year-old female may have boyfriends and state that her sexual identity is heterosexual, even though her sexual orientation is toward the same-sex. A young woman could also identify as a lesbian, even though she is more bisexual in orientation, because she feels a stronger bond with the lesbian community (Savin-Williams, 2001).

Numerous sexual identity development models have been proposed in the literature over the past three decades (e.g., Cass, 1979; Lewis, 1984; Sophie, 1982). While models of sexual identity development are useful because they have drawn researchers' attention toward gaining a better understanding of this process, they leave out considerable differences and the diversity that exists in the development of sexual identities (Rust, 2003; Savin-Williams, 2001). Importantly, the models are mostly based on men's experiences, excluding both lesbian and bisexual identity formations (Rust, 2003; Savin-Williams, 2001) and often oversimplify the developmental processes of sexual identity formation for some LBW (Diamond, 2006a; Diamond & Butterworth, 2008). Thus, we draw from Szymanski (2008), who identified four dimensions that seem to be similar across several models of LBW identity development and emphasize the functional aspects of the coming out process. In addition, we integrate emerging research on women's same-sex sexuality and bisexual identity to attend to the complexity of sexual identity development.

The first dimension, *being different*, often involves a general feeling of being different, feelings of confusion, and an initial wondering if one is LBW (Lewis, 1984; Sophie, 1982). The second feature, *coming out to self*, involves acknowledging that one is LBW, working toward self-acceptance of one's same-sex attractions and behavior, and reducing internalized heterosexism and/or internalized bisexism (Cass, 1979; Sophie, 1982; Ochs, 1996; Guidry, 1999). For some LBW, this sexual questioning is not a one-time-only event but is often revisited and revaluated once a woman settles on a sexual minority identity (Diamond, 2006a). Thus, sexuality continues to develop even after this initial phase of coming out to self. In addition, women, especially those with non-exclusive attractions, often change the labels they use to describe their sexual identity over time in response to specific interpersonal and social contexts (Diamond, 2005). Supporting this notion, Diamond (2005) found that 70% of the women in her longitudinal study changed their sexual identity label at least once after their initial coming out. Finally, many sexual minority women openly reject the use of labels such as lesbian, bisexual, or heterosexual, instead opting for the use of questioning or non-labeled identities to denounce the implied restrictions involved in sexual identity labels and to acknowledge their non-exclusive sexual attractions and behaviors (Diamond, 2005, 2006a). Thus, the important focus in this phase should be on acceptance of same-sex sexuality, rather than adoption of a particular sexual identity label.

The third aspect, *coming out to others*, involves making decisions about disclosing one's sexual minority attractions and behaviors and/or identity to others, which often includes both benefits (e.g., more authenticity in personal relationships) as well as risks (e.g., sexual orientation–based rejection, discrimination, and violence; Sophie, 1982; Szymanski, 2008). Disclosure of one's sexual orientation to others may vary according to individual factors (e.g., need for privacy, level of internalized heterosexism and/or bisexism; Szymanski et al., 2008a) as well as relational (e.g., out to family, out to world) and sociocultural/environmental contexts (e.g., affirming versus hostile; Mohr & Fassinger, 2000). For bisexual women, coming out to self and others can be especially confusing because they need to (a) reject two accepted and recognized categories of sexual identity and (b) acknowledge and affirm not only the homosexual components of their identity but also the heterosexual components as well (Fox, 2000). This dual acknowledgment, affirmation, and disclosure process can be ambiguous and challenging, especially given the fluidity of women's sexuality, the essentialist, dichotomous, and often categorical view of sexuality in the larger U.S. culture, the myths that exist concerning bisexuality, and the dual discrimination that they may experience from both the lesbian/gay and heterosexual communities (Diamond, 2005, 2008; Ochs, 1996). The fourth aspect, *identity synthesis*, involves a feeling of pride concerning one's same-sex sexuality, an integration of one's same-sex sexuality into other aspects of the self, and confrontation of heterosexism/bisexism (Cass, 1979; Diamond, 2006a).

Other scholars note the importance of distinguishing between *individual* sexual identity development (i.e., the process of recognizing and accepting one's own same-sex attraction and lifestyle preferences), and *group* membership identity development (i.e., the process involving the acceptance of one's status as a member of an oppressed group and the confrontation of societal oppression as a member of that group; McCarn & Fassinger, 1996). In this model, LBW can form a positive identity around their own individual sexual orientation without developing an identity that involves a strong connection with the larger LGB community. More recently, scholars have begun to develop more comprehensive frameworks for understanding both sexual identity and gender identity within the context of other sociocultural identities (e.g., race/ethnicity, social class, religion). Most notably, Fassinger and Arseneau (2007) posited that psychologists need to consider sexual orientation, gender orientation, and cultural orientation (e.g., a sense of self in relation to other sociocultural identities) when working with LGBT clients. In addition, they need to consider how these three dimensions interact within a context of temporal influences that include taking into account historical and community contexts within four developmental arenas (psychological and physical health, education and work, relationships and families, and legal and political rights). This model recognizes that other sociocultural identities may impact the construction, visibility, and importance of sexual identity to the self and allows for a multitude of ways in which gender and sexual identity are developed and enacted across many life domains.

Transgender Identity Development

Transgender refers to a range of gender–non-conforming behaviors, expressions, and identifications that transcend the typical bipolar gender system paradigms in a given culture (Carroll, Gilroy, & Ryan, 2002). This broad category of people includes cross-dressers (e.g., drag queens, drag kings, transvestites), transsexuals (i.e., individuals whose gender identity is different from their biological sex, who frequently seek sex hormones and/or sex reassignment surgery, and who desire to permanently fulfill their lives as members of the other gender), inter-sex persons or hermaphrodites (i.e., individuals who are born with some mixture of ambiguous genitalia), and gender benders (i.e., individuals who purposefully present an ambiguous gender expression or alternating gender presentations; Carroll et al., 2002; Gainor, 2000).

Due to the diversity of identity categories within this population, self-definition is a complicated process for many transgender persons. This process is often made more difficult due to confusions between sexual orientation and gender identity; the essentialist, dichotomist models of gender identity that invalidate the experiences of gender fluidity and multiplicity for many transgender individuals; and the marginalization, discrimination, and victimization of transgender persons in U.S. society

(Carroll et al., 2002; Diamond & Butterworth, 2008; Gainor, 2000; Grossman & D'Augelli, 2006). These sociocultural pressures can also create or exacerbate mental health issues that transgender persons might present in psychotherapy, such as low self-esteem, anxiety, depression, and substance abuse (Carroll et al., 2002; Denny, 2004; Gainor, 2000). In addition, transgender persons often seek mental health counseling to sort out feelings related to their gender identity, to reduce gender dysphoria associated with incongruence between their psychological sense of gender and their physical appearance and behavior, and to gain assistance in navigating a host of options available to align their psychological sense of gender with their physical appearance and presence (e.g., choosing how to dress, changing one's name, hormone therapy, genital surgery; Denny, 2004, 2007).

Group Comparisons: Lesbians and Bisexual Women

LBW are often lumped together under the same umbrella of sexual minority women; however, there are important differences as well as similarities between these two groups. Using group comparisons, research has begun exploring some of the unique characteristics of these subgroups. For example, research suggests that women's sexual attractions, behavior, and identity are often fluid, variable, and non-exclusive (Diamond, 2005); women may be more likely than men to identify as bisexual (Sheets & Mohr, 2009; Trocki, Drabble, & Midanik, 2005); there are both stable and fluid subtypes of LBW (Diamond, 2005); and the differences among LBW are of degree rather than type (Diamond, 2005, 2008). Particularly notable in this area is Lisa Diamond's (2005, 2008) longitudinal study following lesbian, bisexual, and "unlabeled" women from late adolescence to young adulthood. Diamond (2005) compared patterns of attraction and behavior among three groups of LBW: (a) stable lesbians, or those who consistently maintained a lesbian identification over an eight-year period; (b) fluid lesbians, or those who alternated between lesbian and non-lesbian labels; and (c) stable non-lesbians, or those who never adopted a lesbian label but had same-sex attractions and engaged in same-sex sexual behaviors. She found that fluid lesbians reported more same-sex sexual physical attractions (80%) and sexual behavior (70%) with women than stable non-lesbians (who reported 45% and 32%, respectively) but less than stable lesbians (who reported 93% and 92%, respectively). In addition, she found that fluid and stable non-lesbians reported more absolute fluctuations in their emotional and physical attractions for women from assessment to assessment than stable lesbians over the eight-year period. Finally, Diamond (2008) found that bisexuality can be both a third type of sexual orientation characterized by stable attractions to both women and men, as well as a strong form of all women's capacity for flexibility in sexual response. In contrast, she found no support for the long-standing myth that female bisexuality is a transitional stage to a lesbian identity or just an experimental phase in which heterosexual women try out same-sex same sexual behaviors.

Research comparing lesbians with bisexual women on dimensions of sexual minority experience has found some interesting differences and similarities. For example, self-identified lesbians report less confusion about their sexual identity, higher levels of outness, more identification with and connection to the LGBT community, and greater commitment to LGBT activism then bisexual women (Balsam & Mohr, 2007; Friedman & Leaper, 2010; Herek, Gillis, & Cogan, 2009; Morris & Rothblum, 1999). No differences were found between lesbian and bisexual women on internalized heterosexism, sexual identity superiority, stigma consciousness, social support, sexist discrimination, gendered heterosexism, or feminist activism (Balsam & Mohr, 2007; Friedman & Leaper, 2010). In addition, research suggests that the relationships between dimensions of sexual minority identity and psychosocial health do not differ for lesbians and bisexual women (Balsam & Mohr, 2007). Finally, research suggests that bisexual women are more comparable demographically to lesbians than to heterosexual women (Rothblum, Balsam, & Mickey, 2004), and heterosexual sisters of lesbians are more comparable demographically to the U.S. census data of women in the general population than their lesbian sisters (Rothblum et al., 2004; Rothblum & Factor, 2001).

Oppression and Psychosocial Health

The APA (2007) Guidelines for Psychological Practice with Girls and Women (referred to as the APA Guidelines for the remainder of this chapter) encourage psychologists to attend to external conditions, such as oppressive contexts and experiences that contribute to LBW's psychosocial health, in addition to internal factors. Additionally, feminist theory posits that oppression contributes to LBW's psychosocial distress via both its external (e.g., prejudice, harassment, discrimination, and violence) and internalized (e.g., negative attitudes, beliefs, and feelings about oneself as a minority group member and about one's minority group) forms (Szymanski et al., 2008b). Two methodological approaches have been used to test the feminist principle that oppression is related to poorer mental health among LBW. The first is a between-groups design that typically compares heterosexual women to LBW and/or heterosexual persons to LGB persons. This design is based on the notion that if oppression associated with being a member of a non-dominant or disadvantaged group causes mental health problems, then LGB persons will have higher rates of oppressive experiences and poorer mental health than heterosexual persons (Meyer, 2010). The second methodological approach is a within-groups design that typically examines how external and internalized oppressions are related to psychosocial health outcomes among lesbians, bisexual women, LBW, or LGB persons. Below, we review pertinent literature related to each of these two approaches.

Studies using between-group designs have fairly consistently found that LGB youth and adults report more experiences of oppressive events than their heterosexual counterparts. For example, data from numerous studies have found that LGB youth and adults report experiencing more discrimination, more incidents of victimization, more childhood sexual abuse, and more parental maltreatment (e.g., psychological and physical abuse during childhood) than heterosexual persons (c.f., Balsam, Rothblum, & Beauchaine, 2005; Berlan, Corliss, Field, Goodman, & Austin, 2010; Birkett, Espelage, & Koenig, 2009; Corliss, Cochran, & Mays, 2002; Goodenow, Szalacha, & Westheimer, 2006; Mays & Cochran, 2001; Tjaden, Thoeness, & Allison, 1999). In addition, using heterosexual siblings as the comparison group, Balsam et al. (2005) found that sexual orientation accounts for significant variance in victimization above and beyond family influences. That is, LGB children and adolescents may be specifically targeted for abuse in their families as a function of perceived or known sexual orientation. Several studies have also found that LBW report more experiences of adult sexual assault than heterosexual women (Balsam et al., 2005; Moracco, Runyan, Bowling, & Earp, 2007; Tjaden et al., 1999). For example, Balsam et al. (2005) found that almost twice as many lesbian (15.5%) and bisexual (16.9%) women reported an experience of rape in adulthood than heterosexual women (7.9%), and the majority of perpetrators were men. Furthermore, some of these sexual victimization experiences are directly related to heterosexist bias (e.g., some sexual minority women report being the victim of a sexual orientation–based sexual assault; Szymanski, 2005; Szymanski & Balsam, 2010).

Studies using between-group designs have also found elevated rates of psychosocial distress, including anxiety, depression, post-traumatic stress, suicidal ideation, suicide attempts, and substance use and/or abuse, among youth and adult LGB persons and/or LBW (for reviews, see Cochran, 2001; Meyer, 2003; for more recent studies, see Almeida, Johnson, Corliss, Molnar, & Azrael, 2009; Corliss et al., 2010; Marshal et al., 2008). In addition, some of this research points to the confluence of heterosexism and sexism in LBW's lives. For example, consistent with findings that women are twice as likely than men to develop post-traumatic stress disorder (PTSD) over the life span (for a review, see Norris, Foster, & Weisshaar, 2002), D'Augelli, Grossman, and Starks (2005) found that significantly more sexual minority female youth reported a lifetime PTSD diagnosis than sexual minority male youth. In addition, women with same-sex partners were significantly more likely to report a recent and lifetime history of PTSD diagnosis than women with opposite-sex partners (Gilman et al., 2001). Finally, data from population-based studies indicate that discrimination and victimization experiences explain these sexual orientation differences in psychosocial health (Goodenow et al., 2006; Mays & Cochran, 2001).

Studies using within-group designs have fairly consistently found that many LBW have experienced heterosexist harassment, discrimination, and violence. For example, using a national probability sample, Herek (2009) found that 15.4% of lesbians and 14.6% of bisexual women reported that they had been victims of a sexual orientation–based hate crime or attempted crime, such as physical assault, sexual assault, robbery, or vandalism. In addition, he found that 54.5% of lesbians and 34.3% of bisexual women have experienced heterosexist verbal harassment, 14.6% of lesbians and 6.8% of bisexual women have had objects thrown at them because of their sexual orientation, and 16.3% of lesbians and 6.8% of bisexual women have experienced sexual orientation–based housing or job discrimination. Other studies using primarily convenience samples of LBW have found similar trends (c.f., Descamps, Rothblum, Bradford, & Ryan, 2000; Morris & Balsam, 2003; Szymanski, 2005;

Szymanski & Balsam, 2010). Furthermore, some research indicates that lesbian identification (versus bisexual identification), non-conformity to traditional standards of gender appearance and behavior, and outness are associated with greater risk for heterosexist harassment, rejection, discrimination, and violence (D'Augelli, Pilkington, & Hershberger, 2002; Friedman & Leaper, 2010; Herek, 2009; Waldo, Hesson-McInnis, & D'Augelli, 1998).

Studies using within-group designs have also found that external heterosexism in the forms of (a) sexual orientation based parental maltreatment, (b) heterosexist prejudice, rejection, harassment, and discrimination, (c) sexual orientation–based hate crime or attempted hate crime victimization, (d) workplace specific heterosexism, and (e) anti-LGB legislation, policies, and movements (e.g., Defense of Marriage Amendments initiatives) is related to more psychosocial distress, including low self-esteem, anxiety, depression, PTSD, suicide attempts, and substance abuse in youth and adult LGB persons and/or LBW (for a review, see Szymanski & Moffitt, 2012). Similarly, studies examining internalized heterosexism have also consistently found that more internalized heterosexism is related to a host of psychosocial difficulties, including less sexual identity development, more difficulties with the coming out process, lower self-esteem, more depression, more psychological distress, lower levels of social support, less coping resources, less relationship quality, and less sexual satisfaction (for a review, see Szymanski et al., 2008a). In addition to internalized heterosexism, research also suggests that other sexual minority stressors, including stigma consciousness (i.e., the expectation that one will experience prejudice and discrimination), sexual identity superiority (i.e., feeling better than and devaluing heterosexuals), less "outness" (i.e., disclosing one's sexual identity to others), and gender-atypical behavior are important predictors of LBW's psychosocial health (Balsam, & Mohr, 2007; D'Augelli, Grossman, Salter, Vasey, Starks, & Sinclair, 2005; Jordan & Deluty, 1998; Lewis, Derlega, Clarke, & Kuang, 2006; Morris, Waldo, & Rothblum, 2001).

Recognizing the diversity of LBW, the APA (2007) Guidelines encourage psychologists to attend to LBW's experiences of external and internalized heterosexism within the context of LBW's various minority group memberships. As such, empirical research has recently begun to explore how heterosexism adds to, interacts with, and/or intersects with other forms of oppression to influence psychosocial health. For example, several studies have found that when examined together, both external and internalized heterosexism and sexism emerge as unique, significant, and additive predictors of LBW's psychological distress (Descamps et al. 2000; Szymanski, 2005; Szymanski & Kashubeck-West, 2008; Szymanski & Owens, 2008, 2009). Relatedly, Szymanski (2005) found that the interaction of recent sexual orientation–based hate crime victimization with sexist discrimination was a significant predictor of psychological distress among lesbians. That is, sexist discrimination intensified the relationship between sexual orientation–based hate crime victimization and psychological distress. Finally, Haines et al. (2008) found that more internalized heterosexism is related to more internalized sexism via self-objectification (i.e., the internalization of sexually objectifying experiences that manifests in how frequently a woman watches her appearance and experiences her body according to how it looks; Fredrickson & Roberts, 1997) among lesbians, and self-objectification partially mediated the relations between internalized heterosexism and depression and negative eating attitudes.

Turning to LBW of color, research demonstrates that heterosexism in communities of color, internalized heterosexism, external racism, and race-related dating and relationship problems in the LGB community are unique predictors of psychological distress among LBW and/or LGB persons of color (Szymanski & Gupta, 2009a, 2009b; Szymanski & Meyer, 2008; Szymanski & Sung, 2010). Research using samples of African American women suggests that both external and internalized gendered racism (i.e., the fusion of sexism and racism that occurs from stereotypes or images of specific subgroups of women of color) may also have a significant impact on racial/ethnic minority LBW's low self-esteem and psychological distress (King, 2003; Thomas, Witherspoon, & Speight, 2004, 2008; Woods, Buchanan, & Settles, 2008). Other research suggests that there are more similarities than differences between LGB persons of color and White LGB persons on sexual orientation–based minority stress variables. More specifically, Moradi et al. (2010) found that there were no significant differences between LGB persons of color and White LGB persons in levels of perceived heterosexist stigma, internalized heterosexism, and comfort with disclosing one's sexual orientation to others, and in the relationships between heterosexist stigma and comfort with sexual orientation and actual outness levels. Similarly, Dube and Savin-Williams (1999) found no differences on levels of internalized heterosexism among Asian/Pacific Islander, African American, Latino/a, and White LGB youth. However, Moradi et al. (2010) did find a difference between the racial/ethnic minority and White LGB persons on outness levels, with LGB persons of color reporting lower level of outness than their White counterparts. This finding is consistent with Bowleg, Huang, Brooks, Black, and Burkholder's (2003) qualitative research on African American lesbians who described manifestations of heterosexism in difficulties with sexual identity management, self-silencing, and self-monitoring with family, friends, and co-workers. Moradi et al. (2010) also found that the relationship between perceived heterosexist stigma and internalized heterosexism was weaker for LGB persons of color than for White LGB persons. Finally, some empirical evidence suggests a relationship between ethnic identity attitudes and internalized heterosexism among LGB persons of color, with more positive ethnic identity attitudes associated with lower levels of internalized heterosexism (for a review, see Szymanski et al., 2008a).

Taken together, the existing research suggests that LBW's experiences of heterosexism occur against a backdrop of other forms of oppression, which may influence both their risk and response to heterosexism as well as compounding, interacting, and/or intersecting to negatively affect their psychosocial health. Other forms of oppression, such as gendered heterosexism, bisexism, classism, ableism, and anti-Semitism, are also of likely interest to diverse groups of LBW; however, the relation of these variables to LBW's psychosocial health have not yet been empirically examined.

Coping with and Resisting Heterosexism and Other Forms of Oppression

The APA (2007) Guidelines encourage psychologists to focus on LBW strengths and to assist them in identifying how they have coped with and resisted (currently and in the past) oppressive contexts and to identify and fortify healthy forms of resistance. In their review of the literature on coping with heterosexism and sexism, Szymanski and Moffitt (2012) identified several strategies that LGB persons and women often use to combat and resist oppression: (a) relying on internal resources; (b) building and relying on social support systems; (c) contextualizing behaviors; (d) engaging with the oppressive stressor; (e) disengaging from the oppressive stressor; and (f) engaging in collective action and social activism.

For LBW, relying on internal resources often takes the form of affirmation and self-acceptance of ones' sexual identity and same-sex relationships to counter negative messages and stereotypes about sexual minorities (Levitt et al., 2009; Rostosky, Riggle, Gray, & Hatton, 2007). Other important internal resources found among a sample of African American lesbians included optimism, spirituality, self-esteem, social competencies, and feeling unique (Bowleg et al., 2003). In terms of social support, LBW are more likely to rely on their families for support for major needs than gay and bisexual men, who tend to rely on other LGB individuals for support (Frost & Meyer, 2008). Beals and Peplau (2005) found that having support for one's sexual identity from family and friends was related to greater well-being among lesbians. In addition, they found that devaluation of one's sexual identity from family and friends was related to less well-being. These relations held true even after controlling for other types of social support and stress. Relatedly, Szymanski and Kashubeck-West (2008) found that social support was found to mediate the relationships between both internalized heterosexism and internalized sexism and psychological distress among LBW. That is, LBW who experience low levels of internalized oppression based on sexual orientation and gender have more social support, which in turn results in less psychological distress. Among bisexual college students, Sheets and Mohr (2009) found that general social support from family and general support from friends was most predictive of well-being, whereas support from family and friends for one's sexual identity was most predictive of less internalized bisexism. In addition, they found that the negative relationship between sexuality-specific support from friends and internalized bisexism was driven by support from heterosexual friends and not lesbian/gay friends.

In addition to individual and familial support systems, LBW also build LGBT community social supports. Although actual definitions of the LGBT community vary among LBW, being a part of it is important for many because it often provides a source of support and strength by decreasing isolation through social connection with similar others, providing both social and physical capital and resources, providing a sense of accomplishment regarding LGBT activism and historical achievements, and fostering empowerment through being part of a large group of capable, creative, and independent women (Lehavort, Balsam, & Ibrahim-Wells, 2009; Riggle, Whitman, Olson, Rostosky, & Strong, 2008).

Contextualizing behavior often takes the form of externalizing rather than internalizing heterosexist experiences (Szymanski & Moffitt, 2012). For example, Rostosky et al. (2007) found that many LBW reframed heterosexist experiences in ways that empowered them rather than immobilized or diminished them. Relatedly, Russell and Richards (2003) found that some LBW placed anti-LGB campaigns and political initiatives within a larger sociocultural perspective, which allowed them to focus on their own efforts to engage in social change rather than personalize the events.

Engaging with the oppressive stressor includes resistance strategies such as expressing one's feelings to the perpetrator, directly challenging and confronting the person who offended them, and making a formal complaint, while disengaging from the oppressive stressor includes resistance strategies such as minimizing or ignoring the behavior or perpetrator, avoiding contact with people and situations that place one at risk for oppressive acts, boundary setting, and concealing one's sexual identity in hostile environments (Szymanski & Moffitt, 2012). Finally, engaging in collective action and social advocacy to combat oppression includes activities such as educating others about LGB and/or feminist issues, participating in LGB or feminist demonstrations, boycotts, marches, and/or rallies, writing to politicians and elected officials concerning LGB or feminist issues, and creating empowerment programming, such as National Coming Out Day and Gay Pride Festivals (Levitt et al., 2009; Szymanski, 2004; Szymanski & Chung, 2003).

In addition to coping and resisting, some research indicates that having a sexual minority status can offer LBW opportunities to transform oppressive experiences into behaviors that lead to optional functioning. For example, in a qualitative study on the positive aspects of being lesbian or gay, several characteristics emerged, including having strong connections to others, serving as positive role models and leaders, insight and empathy for self and others who are oppressed, and living authentically and honestly (Riggle et al., 2008). Freedom to explore different expressions of one's sexuality and different constructions of intimate relationships, freedom from societal definitions of roles, particularly traditional gender roles, and freedom from patriarchal power relationships and the creation of egalitarian relationships for lesbians also emerged as positive characteristics (Riggle et al., 2008). In a quantitative study, Konik and Crawford (2004) found that bisexual women scored higher on a measure of cognitive flexibility than lesbians, gay men, or heterosexual persons. Many of these characteristics provide key tools for making meaning out of one's life, creating positive interpersonal relationships, living with integrity, fostering flexible worldviews, cultivating abilities to challenge conventional assumptions and create one's own norms and expectations about ways of being and relating to others, and navigating different cultural worldviews through biculturalism (Riggle et al., 2008).

Immigration and Acculturation

According to the U.S. Census (2000), more than 14,000 bi-national female same-sex couples (i.e., one or both of the partners in the couple are not U.S. citizens) live together in the United States, with more than half of them raising children under the age of 18 years. In addition, children living with same-sex couples are less likely to be citizens than children living with male-female bi-national couples. Despite these growing statistics, LBW couples and families are not recognized under current U.S. immigration law. More specifically, in 1996, Congress passed the Defense of Marriage Act, which states that for purposes of the federal government, marriage means only a legal union between one woman and one man as wife and husband. In addition, it states that no state is obligated to recognize a same-sex marriage that was issued by another state, country, or jurisdiction. Because the U.S. Immigration and Nationality Act states that U.S. citizens and legal permanent residents may sponsor their spouses (and other immediate family members) for immigration purposes, LBW who are U.S. citizens and permanent residents cannot sponsor their same-sex partner or non-biological children because they are not considered "spouses" under federal law. In addition, couples in which one or both partners are transgender may have difficulty obtaining identity documents that match their gender identity and face lack of recognition for their gender identity throughout the immigration process (Tiven & Neilson, 2009). For example, immigration officials may treat the couple as a same-sex couple rather than a heterosexual couple. Thus, lack of legal recognition, coupled with government-sanctioned exclusion, leads to unique challenges and extra stressors associated with the immigration process for LBWT and their families.

Same-sex bi-national couples have limited choices for dealing with these discriminatory immigration policies. These include (a) separating or ending their relationship; (b) trying to obtain a green card for the non-U.S. partner through other methods, such as a student or employment visa, but at the risk of having the existence of a same-sex romantic partner used against them as evidence of unlawful intent to remain in the U.S.; (c) going underground to become an undocumented illegal immigrant, with constant risk of deportation; and (d) leaving the United States to immigrate to a country that allows both partners to live there (e.g., Australia, Belgium, Brazil, Canada, Denmark, England, Finland, France, Germany, Iceland, Israel, the Netherlands, New Zealand, Norway, Portugal, South Africa, Spain, Sweden, Switzerland; Human Rights Watch/Immigration Equality, 2006; Tiven & Neilson, 2009) This discriminatory legislation, along with anti-immigrant sentiments prevalent in the United States, can negatively impact the mental, physical, relational, familial, and financial health of same-sex bi-national couples and their families. However, there is some hope that this federally based discrimination could end sometime in the future. Currently there is a bill being considered by Congress called the Uniting American Families Act (Senate Bill 424, House of Representatives Bill 1024) that, if passed, would amend the Immigration and Nationality Act to eliminate sexual orientation–based discrimination by permitting U.S. citizens and permanent residents to sponsor their same-sex partners (called "permanent partners" in the Act) for family-based immigration.

Another important issue concerning LBW and immigration is refugee and asylum law. A refugee refers to a person who cannot return to their country of origin due to persecution or fear of persecution on the basis of nationality, religion, political opinion, race, or membership in a particular social group. The latter category has been successfully used as a grounds for asylum based on sexual orientation or gender identity in the United States (Tiven & Neilson, 2009). LBW seeking asylum must file a claim within one year of their arrival in the United States and must prove the authenticity of their LBW identity (Heller, 2009). This often requires LBW asylum seekers to highlight characteristics and behaviors based on stereotypes of sexual minorities (e.g., lesbians are masculine), which can be particularly challenging for LBW who have escaped their county of origin, where they may have been encouraged to hide their sexual identity in order to avoid persecution, and for LBW who do not fit these stereotypes (Heller, 2009). Because asylum law is very complex, LBWT should seek legal advice from an LBWT affirmative and knowledgeable immigration lawyer (Heller, 2009; Tiven & Neilson, 2009).

Once in the United States, LBW immigrants are likely to undergo a process of acculturation in which changes occur in practices (e.g., language use, social affiliations), values (e.g., cultural belief systems, such as importance of the family and emphasis on individualism or collectivism), and/or identifications (e.g. attachment to a cultural group) as a result of contact with a culturally dissimilar group (Schwartz, Unger, Zamboanga, & Szapocznik, 2010). In this process, an LBW may combine and synthesize aspects of the two cultures into a unique blend or, if she perceives conflict and incompatibility between her culture of origin and the dominant U.S. culture, may try to keep these two cultures separate (Schwartz et al., 2010). Related to sexual identity, the acculturation process is likely to be influenced by many factors, including attitudes toward homosexuality and bisexuality in the country of origin, and whether these are more or less accepting than attitudes toward homosexuality and bisexuality in the United States; cultural norms in the country of origin; and experiences of racism and/or heterosexism. However, very little empirical research on how the acculturation process impacts sexual identity development and experience exists. Clearly, this is a fruitful area for future inquiry.

Life Span Transitions and Issues

The APA (2007) Guidelines encourage psychologists to attend to developmental issues related to sexual identity that emerge over the life span. In this section, we review relevant research related to youth, developing and maintaining same-sex intimate relationships, parenting, and aging.

Youth

LBW children and adolescents often face the same developmental tasks and issues that heterosexual children and adolescents do. However, one area of difference is dealing with the development of a sexual minority identity in both a heterosexist and sexist context and the process of coming out (Reynolds & Hanjorgiris, 2000). Although there are multiple risks and fears associated with this process, according to recent studies, youths are disclosing to their families of origin more often and at a younger age than their predecessors (Saltzburg, 2004; Savin-Williams, 2001). Among studies that have reviewed the average age of coming out, young women report that they begin to label themselves as lesbian or bisexual between the ages of 14 and 17 years (D'Augelli & Hershberger, 1993; Sears, 1991). Similarly, transgender adolescents and young adults report feeling that they were transgender at puberty (Grossman & D'Augelli, 2006). The earlier coming out experiences of this generation of LBW youth may be due to the increasing tolerance of sexual minorities in U.S. culture. For example, attitudes toward LGB persons, especially among younger cohorts, have become more accepting over the past 20 years, positive portrayals of LGBT persons in various forms of media have increased, and LGBT support groups, such as Gay/Straight Alliance in middle and high schools, have proliferated (Savin-Williams, 2005). Despite positive trends toward increasing acceptance of sexual minorities, some LBW youth do experience difficulties related to heterosexism.

D'Augelli, Grossman, and Starks (2005) examined factors that differentiated youth whose parents knew of their sexual orientation from youth whose parents did not know in a sample of LGB youth who lived with parents who raised them. They found that more LGB self-identification, greater childhood gender non-conformity, less internalized heterosexism, more family support, less fear of parental harassment or rejection, and more past verbal sexual orientation victimization by parents were uniquely related to parental awareness and accounted for over half of the variance. Although youth with aware parents reported more past parental verbal victimization, they also reported more current family support and less fear of future parental sexual orientation–based victimization. In addition, less internalized heterosexism has been found to be related to less negative parental attitudes toward homosexuality, less intergenerational family conflict, more individuation, and less distant, rejecting, and intrusive parental behaviors (for a review, see Szymanski et al., 2008a), suggesting the influence of the family of origin on sexual identity development and minority stress.

For some young persons, disclosure of a lesbian or bisexual sexual identity often results in feelings of alienation and marginalization (Goldman, 2008; Reynolds & Hanjorgiris, 2000). As a result of their sexual orientation, LBW and transgender youth often experience rejection, bullying, and/or victimization from family members and/or peers in school, such as teasing, physical assault, heterosexist name calling, and negative reactions to gender atypical behaviors (GLSEN, 2007; Grossman & D'Augelli, 2006; Rivers, 2001). As reviewed above in the section on oppression and psychosocial health, studies consistently find that LBW youth experience more parental abuse during childhood and more victimization and heterosexist bullying than their heterosexual peers. In addition, other studies indicate that sexual orientation–based prejudice, rejection, harassment, and discrimination are widespread and common in school settings (GLSEN, 2007; Grossman & D'Augelli, 2006). Yet, many LGBT students do not report these victimization experiences to their teachers or other school staff members because they believe that reporting it would either make it worse or that nothing would be done (GLSEN, 2007).

Many young LBW who do not feel safe at school subsequently choose not to attend their classes or skip entire days of school (GLSEN, 2007). In addition, young LBW who are being physically harassed at school because of their sexual orientation have poorer academic performance and are less likely to pursue a college education (GLSEN, 2007). The stress of rejection and prejudice not only contributes to academic issues among LBW, but also to mental health problems, substance use and/or abuse problems, and suicidal ideation and/or attempts, as reviewed above in the section on oppression and psychosocial health.

Studies on heterosexism among youth have also examined both risk and protective factors. In terms of risk, research indicates that LGBT youth in communities with lower adult educational attainment and youth in rural communities encounter more hostile school climates, with increased exposure to heterosexist harassment and victimization (Kosciw, Greytak, & Diaz, 2009). Research also indicates that LGB youth have significantly lower levels of protective factors than heterosexual youth, including lower levels of family connectedness, other adult caring, teacher caring, social support, and school safety (Eisenberg & Resnick, 2006; Saewyc et al., 2009; Williams, Connolly, Debra, & Craig, 2005). In addition, when these factors are present in LGB youths' lives, they often serve to significantly protect them from negative outcomes. For example, Eisenberg and Resnick (2006) found that family connectedness, other adult caring, and school safety protected LGB youth from suicidal ideation and attempts. Relatedly, Birkett et al. (2009) found that a positive school climate (e.g., feeling respected and cared about by adults at their school and feeling that they are getting a good education) and lack of heterosexist teasing buffered the relationships between sexual orientation and both depression/suicidality and alcohol/marijuana use. Finally, having an informal mentor (e.g., a teacher) is related to higher levels of post-secondary participation among LGB youth (Gastic & Johnson, 2009).

Research on heterosexism in the schools has found that the presence of (a) a non-discrimination policy that includes sexual orientation and gender identity, (b) anti-bullying policies, (c) a gay-straight alliance, or similar student groups, (d) a school court or other student judiciary, (e) staff training on sexual diversity and sexual harassment training, (f) six or more supportive staff/educators, (g) peer support groups and/or peer tutoring programs, and (h) LGB related resources in the curriculum are related to less hostile environments, less victimization, more supportive psychosocial climates, and greater safety of LGB students (GLSEN, 2007; Goodenow et al., 2006; Szalacha, 2003). These findings point to the need to target protective factors and organizational policies and practices in efforts to reduce the occurrence and negative effects of heterosexism in the schools.

Female Same-Sex Intimate Relationships

In her review of the research on same-sex couples, Diamond (2006b) concluded that in many ways, same-sex couples are similar to heterosexual couples, and the similarities outnumber the differences. For example, similar factors predict relationship maintenance and satisfaction (e.g., similarities in demographic background, attitudes, and values), sexual satisfaction (e.g., global relationship quality), and relationship dissolution (e.g., lack of barriers). In this section, we highlight some of the distinctive features of LBW's same-sex intimate relationships.

In terms of dating and courtship, Rose and Zand (2002) found that an accelerated path to emotional exclusivity and relationship development, heightened intimacy, freedom from traditional gender roles, and the effects of heterosexism were unique aspects of same-sex relationship development. In addition, they found that LBW tend to develop romantic relationships out of close same-sex friendships. This friendship courtship script was followed by sexually explicit and romance scripts in frequency of occurrence.

In terms of same-sex couples, unique relational dynamics and challenges due to heterosexism have emerged. For example, when lesbians in same-sex couples (both those with civil unions and those without) are compared to their heterosexual married siblings, research indicates that married heterosexual women are more likely to have traditional gendered divisions of household tasks, child care, finances, and relationship maintenance behaviors than their lesbian sisters (Solomon, Rothblum, & Balsam, 2004, 2005). Thus, female same-sex couples tend to be more egalitarian than their heterosexual counterparts. In addition, some research indicates that same-sex couples report lower levels of ineffective arguing, negative problem solving, and withdrawal, lower levels of relationship conflict, and greater relationship quality, compatibility, intimacy, equality, and autonomy than heterosexual married couples (Balsam, Beauchaine, Rothblum & Solomon, 2008; Kurdek, 1998, 2004).

Coupled lesbians report less support from their family of origins than married heterosexual women, but no differences were found on social support from friends (Solomon et al., 2004). LBW also report less frequent contact with their parents, less instances of bringing their same-sex partners along when visiting their parents, less acceptance by their partners' parents, and less instances of receiving holiday gifts or cards addressed to both themselves and their partners than married heterosexual women (Henehan, Rothblum, Solomon & Balsam, 2007). This suggests that heterosexism in some families of origin can lead to a lack of support, the inability to rely on parents' assistance in dealing with relationship difficulties or parenting problems, and/or estrangement for LBW (Henehan et al., 2007).

Lesbians in coupled relationships report attending more social events and engaging in more leisure activity with their partners, having more mutual friends, and having more friends who were ex-lovers than married heterosexual women (Solomon et al., 2004). Similarly, Harkless and Flowers (2005) found that lesbian and gay men were more likely than heterosexual persons to report higher levels of connection to ex-serious relationship partners, and these differences were due to sexual orientation and heterosexism-related system pressure rather than gender. These unique relational approaches for women in same-sex couples suggest that the use of traditional "heterosexual paradigms" when providing counseling services to female same-sex couples may be inappropriate (Harkless & Flowers, 2005).

Research examining external and internalized minority stressors has found that internalized heterosexism and more discrepancy in partner's level of internalized heterosexism is related to poorer relationship quality and satisfaction, as well as sexual satisfaction among LBW (for a review, see

Szymanski et al., 2008a). No support has been found for the relationship between interpersonal experiences of heterosexist harassment, discrimination, and/or violence and relationship quality (c.f., Balsam & Szymanski, 2005; Otis, Rostosky, Riggle, & Harmin, 2006); however, lesbian couples report experiencing more stress related to their family's reaction to their sexual orientation (i.e., rejection, lack of support, lack of understanding) than gay men, and this gay-specific family stressor is related to less relationship satisfaction (Todosijevic, Rothblum, & Solomon, 2005). The lack of legal recognition in most states for same-sex couples and the denial of more than 1,000 federal-level rights, protections, and benefits of marriage (e.g., tax benefits, inheritance rights, social security benefits) can place extra stress and financial burden on female same-sex couples and their families (Szymanski, 2008). Mixed support has been found for the relationship between levels of outness and relationship quality, with some research finding a positive link (c.f., Caron & Ulin, 1997; Murphy, 1989), and others finding no relationship between the two (c.f. Balsam & Szymanski, 2005; Frost & Meyer, 2009).

Examining the influence of legal recognition for same-sex couples, research indicates that same-sex couples not in civil unions were more likely to break up during the three-year duration of the study than same-sex couples in civil unions or heterosexual married couples (Balsam et al., 2008), and participants in committed same-sex couples without legal recognition reported more stress, depression, and internalized heterosexism and less meaning in their lives than participants in same-sex couples with legal recognition (Riggle, Rostosky, & Horne, 2010). Thus, legal recognition of same-sex couple intimate relationship appears to provide not only material benefits but also psychological benefits.

Parenting

The 2000 Census found that one in three lesbian couples are raising children, and that same-sex couples raising children are more likely (41.1%) to be in a long-term relationship than unmarried heterosexual couples with children (19.1%; Bennett & Gates, 2003). In addition, Latina and African American female same-sex couples are more likely to be raising children than their White non-Hispanic female same-sex counterparts (Cianciotto, 2005; Dang & Frazer, 2004). LBW are raising children through foster care or adoption, or birth through donor insemination, and/or from previous heterosexual relationships (Golding, 2006; Patterson, 1995). Again, the lack of legal recognition in most states for same-sex couples and the denial of federal level benefits of marriage can place extra stress on LBW raising children. For example, LBW couples with children (a) are less likely to have access to family health insurance through their employer than heterosexual couples with children; (b) pay more in federal income tax than married heterosexual couples when one parent is a stay-at-home mom; (c) are often denied the rights associated with the Family and Medical Leave Act; (d) are often denied the right to establish legal relationships to their non-biological children through second-parent or joint adoptions; and (e) are denied access to Social Security survivorship benefits in the event of the death of the parent who was not able to establish a legal relationship with the child (Bennett & Gates, 2003). In addition, some states disadvantage or deny LBW parents in visitation, custody, foster care, and adoption proceedings (Patterson, 2009).

For female same-sex parents, internalized heterosexism is not related to the choice to be parents, parental stress, or adjustment issues for children. However, greater internalized heterosexism, more experiences of heterosexist rejection, and perceived negative attitudes of others toward homosexuality are related to feeling that they have to defend their position as a mother more often (for a review, see Szymanski et al., 2008a). Studies also indicate that LBW who had children reached all milestones in the coming-out process several years later than LBW without children. In addition, LBW who had children before coming out reached developmental milestones several yeas later than LBW who had children after coming out (Henehan et al., 2007; Morris, Balsam, & Rothblum, 2002). Finally, LBW with children reported being more out about their sexual orientation and having increased political involvement than LBW who did not have children (Henehan et al., 2007). LBW who had children reported less support from their parents than heterosexual women with children (Henehan et al., 2007), but same-sex couples share child-care duties more evenly than do heterosexual parents (Patterson, 2000).

Researchers who have studied same-sex couples have consistently found that children raised by same-sex parents develop as well as children raised by heterosexual parents, and there are no significant differences between the two on a host of psychosocial variables, including development of gender identity, sexual orientation, self-esteem, school adjustment, moral judgment, intelligence, social relationships, and mental health (for reviews, see Patterson, 2006, 2009; Tasker & Patterson, 2007). Thus, there is no basis for legal discrimination of LBW raising children. In addition, some research indicates that the larger heterosexist climate can negatively impact LBW parents. For example Shapiro, Peterson, and Stewart (2009) compared lesbian and heterosexual mothers living in the United States with those living in Canada, a country that has a more supportive legal climate for same-sex couples and families. They found that lesbian mothers in the United States reported more worries about legal problems and discrimination based on sexual orientation than did lesbian mothers in Canada, but there was no difference between the two groups on general family worries. In addition, there were no differences found between U.S. and Canadian heterosexual mothers, who enjoy legal protection in both countries.

It is important for feminist counselors working with LBW who are parents of school-age children to recognize the difficulties they may face when working with school personnel or other parents, such as exclusion, hostility, or questioning of their ability to parent (GLSEN, 2008). In 2008, GLSEN released a report from a survey of 588 LGBT parents of K–12 children, which revealed that 53% had felt they were excluded from various activities at their child's school, 26% were mistreated by another parent, and 16% believed that as an LGBT parent they would not be accepted if they participated in their child's school community. Fortunately, the majority of the parents in the survey (67%) felt that there were a few staff members or teachers at their child's school who were supportive of LGBT families (GLSEN, 2008). Interestingly, students had higher GPAs (3.4 vs. 2.9) and missed fewer days of school at schools where there were six or more LGBT supportive teachers and staff members (GLSEN, 2008).

Aging

According to estimates by researchers, there are approximately 3% to 7% self-identified LGBT individuals in the United States, or one to 3.5 million, with the largest percentage being made up of lesbian women and gay men (Haber, 2009). It is estimated that with the youngest of the baby boomers approaching older age, by 2030 the number of LGBT adults over the age of 65 will double (Haber, 2009; Jackson, Johnson & Roberts, 2008). As LBW age, they face extra stressors associated with heterosexism, such as economic discrimination from denial of a partner's social security and pension benefits; lack of legal support for coupled and family relationships; the necessity of creating legal documents (e.g. personal will, power of attorney) to protect their wishes regarding medical treatment and disposition of property and to honor their commitment to their same-sex relationship; invisibility within the context of the mainstream aging community; insensitive and biased health care; and discrimination from senior centers, retirement communities, and assisted living facilities (Grossman, D'Augelli & O'Connell, 2001; Haber, 2009; Kimmel, Rose, & David, 2006; Knauer, 2009). In addition, the lower wages of women compared to men (U.S. Department of Labor, 2007), along with lack of domestic partner social security and retirement benefits, can have negative implications for aging LBW.

The experiences of older LBW and the way in which they view their lives in the present is influenced by generational/cohort differences and both the current and past social context concerning LGB issues. Historically, older LBW grew up in a time where it was not as common for LGBT individuals to be open about their sexual identity. They have borne witness to the Stonewall riots in New York City, the removal of homosexuality as a mental illness from the American Psychiatric Association's *Diagnostic and Statistical Manual*, the representation of LGBT characters on television and in film, and the beginnings of same-sex marriage being recognized in the United States (Haber, 2009). Thus, it is important for feminist counselors working with older LBW to acknowledge their life experiences and the ways in which social change and the historical, sociocultural, and political context have played a role, and will continue to, in their lives.

A small but growing number of studies have begun to empirically examine the needs and issues related to aging among LBW. This research has found that social support among elderly LBW is important to their well-being. For example, Masini and Barrett (2007) found that support from friends but not family predicted higher mental health quality of life and lower internalized heterosexism, depression, and anxiety among a sample of 220 LGB adults over 50 years old. Relatedly, in a national sample of 416 LGB adults aged 60 years or older, Grossman and colleagues (2000, 2001) found that the most important factor contributing to LGB older adults' satisfaction with their social support was their social support system members' knowledge of their sexual orientation. Satisfaction with social support and having a live-in partner were associated with less loneliness, while having a live-in partner was associated with better physical and mental health.

Research also indicates that older LBW are heavily involved in family caregiving responsibilities with their family of origin (e.g., parent, child, sibling) and/or family of choice (e.g., partners, close friends), which come with psychological, physical, and financial stresses as well as opportunities to show their commitment and strengths (Grossman, D'Augelli & Dragowski, 2005; Shippy, 2005). Many LBW view caregiving as a way to give back to the LBW community and to build care-giving networks that might assist them in the future (Grossman et al., 2005). In addition, older LBW often create support systems that differ from the traditional ones often established in heterosexual communities. For example, LBW's social support systems most often include female close friends (Grossman et al., 2000, 2001), and LBW are more likely to participate in an LGB social group than in a local senior center (Quam & Whitford, 1992). Finally, both caregiving and care receiving can be complicated when encountering heterosexism and when older LBW have not disclosed their sexual orientation to their children and/or parents (Fredriksen-Goldsen, Kim, Muraco & Mincer, 2009; Grossman et al., 2005).

Career Development and Workplace Issues

LBW face many career and workplace barriers due to their marginalized statuses as both sexual minorities and women. Heterosexism and sexism manifest in the workplace in both indirect and direct ways. Examples of indirect occupational heterosexism include assumptions of heterosexuality and pressures to act straight (Waldo, 1999). Examples of direct forms of occupational heterosexism include anti-LGB jokes and sexual orientation–based harassment and discrimination (Konik & Cortina, 2008; Waldo, 1999). Empirical research on LGB workers indicates that 25% to 60% reported workplace discrimination at some point in their careers, and about 50% anticipated future discrimination (for a review, see Croteau, 1996). In addition, LBWT can be fired in many states on the basis of sexual orientation and/or gender identity (Fassinger, 2008). Indirect occupational sexism is revealed in the lower wages for women; traditionally female occupational options; limited numbers of women in management positions (a.k.a. the "glass ceiling"); lack of support, mentorship, and direction given to women who make it into upper management (a.k.a. the "glass labyrinth"); and backlash (i.e., the perceptions of women's qualifications may increase as a result of behaving in stereotypical masculine ways, but may come at the cost of social acceptance for violating gender norms; Eagly & Carli, 2007; Rudman & Glick, 1999, 2001; U.S. Department of Labor, 2007). Direct occupational sexism manifests in sexual harassment, which has been operationalized to include gender harassment or behaviors that convey hostile and offensive attitudes toward women, unwanted sexual attention, and sexual coercion (Fitzgerald, Gelfand, & Drasgow, 1995).

A recent study by the National Center for Transgender Equality and the National Gay and Lesbian Task Force (2009) found that workplace harassment and discrimination is rampant among transgender persons, with 97% reporting experiencing harassment or mistreatment in the workplace and 47% experiencing adverse job outcomes such as being fired, not hired, or denied promotion. In addition, transgender workplace discrimination is also revealed in their data, showing that transgender persons experience both unemployment and poverty at twice the rate of the population as a whole, and almost one-fifth of transgender persons become homeless due to challenges they face with employment.

Research reveals that LGB workers encounter substantially greater amounts of both sexual and heterosexist harassment than heterosexual workers (Konik & Cortina, 2008). The confluence of heterosexism and sexism in LBW's lives is also revealed in research comparing lesbians with their heterosexual sisters. This research demonstrates that even though lesbians are more educated, have occupations with greater status, are more geographically mobile, are less likely to be homemakers, and are less likely to have children than their heterosexual sisters (Rothblum et al., 2004; Rothblum & Factor, 2001), there is no difference in individual income between lesbians and their heterosexual sisters. This research also reveals that lesbians have a lower household income than their heterosexual sisters. Other research indicates that female same-sex couples have higher poverty rates than male same-sex couples and heterosexual married couples, and children of same-sex couples are twice as likely to live in poverty as children of married heterosexual couples (Albelda, Badgett, Scheebaum, & Gates, 2009). Thus, women's lower salaries and the denial of workplace benefits such as a pension plan, health insurance, and family medical leave to same-sex partners disadvantages LBW couples and their families and results in a considerable deficit in overall earnings (Fassinger, 2008). When race is taken into account, the data are even bleaker for LBW of color and their families. For example, analyses of the 2000 Census data revealed that African American and Latina women in same-sex households reported $18,000 and $24,000 less in median annual household income, respectively, than their White female same-sex counterparts (Cianciotto, 2005; Dang & Frazer, 2004).

In addition to negative effects on financial health, experiences of heterosexism and sexism in the workplace have been linked to negative job, mental health, and physical health outcomes. For example, experiences of heterosexism in the workplace are related to decreased job satisfaction, higher levels of absenteeism, less career commitment, less organizational commitment, stronger intentions to quit one's job, less opportunities for promotion, lower promotion rates, higher levels of depression, greater psychological distress, and more health-related problems among LGB workers (Ragins, & Cornwell, 2001; Smith & Ingram, 2004; Waldo, 1999). Similarly, experiences of sexual harassment in the workplace have also been linked to lower job satisfaction, less organizational commitment, less interpersonal satisfaction with co-workers, more psychological distress, more post-traumatic stress, and poorer physical health among women (for a meta analysis, see Willingness, Steel, & Lee, 2007).

Paralleling research on heterosexism in the schools described earlier, research on heterosexism in the workplace also reveals that organizational policies and practices appear to influence the occurrence of heterosexism in the workplace. For example, Waldo (1999) found that LGB individuals who perceived their organization as tolerant of heterosexism were more likely to experience heterosexist events in their workplaces than those who believed their organization to be intolerant. Furthermore, he found that job gender context was also an important predictor of heterosexist experiences; the presence of more women in the workplace environment was related to less heterosexism. Relatedly, Ragins and Cornwell (2001) found that LGB employees were more likely to experience heterosexist discrimination when employed in organizations that were primarily heterosexual, lacked organizational supportive policies such as offering same-sex domestic partner benefits, and were not covered by regional/local sexual orientation–based protective legislation.

In addition to focusing on workplace climate and discrimination, research on LBW career development has examined categories and correlates of workplace sexual identity management and disclosure (Croteau, 1996). Four categories of workplace sexual identity management strategies that appear to be supported by qualitative data are (a) passing or actively creating a façade that one is heterosexual; (b) covering or concealing information related to one's sexual identity; (c) being implicitly out or being honest about one's personal life, including information that might lead others to believe that one is an LBW but not explicitly stating it; and (d) being explicitly out or making it clear to coworkers that one is an LBW (Croteau, 1996; Griffin, 1992). Examining antecedents of workplace outness, research indicates that an LGB affirmative workplace climate, organizational intolerance of heterosexism, presence of LGB coworkers, presence of LGB supportive heterosexual supervisors and co-workers, and perceptions of past sexual orientation–based workplace discrimination are related to higher levels of workplace outnesss (Ragins, Singh, & Cornwell, 2007; Waldo, 1999). In addition, qualitative research among lesbians indicates that social class may play a role in opportunities to work in more LGB-affirmative workplaces and willingness to be out at work, with working class LBW experiencing more heterosexist contexts than middle class LBW (McDermott, 2006). Examining consequences of disclosure in the workplace, research indicates that more outness is related to more exposure to direct forms of heterosexism but to less indirect forms of heterosexism (Waldo, 1999).

In addition, outness has been found to have positive, negative, and non-significant relations with work attitudes, compensation, and psychological strain (for a review, see Ragins, 2004). These inconsistencies in the research may be explained in part by differentiating fears of workplace outness versus actual level of workplace outness. Ragins et al. (2007) found that for those who had not fully disclosed their sexual orientation at work, the fears associated with disclosure predicted work attitudes (e.g., less job satisfaction, less organizational commitment, less career commitment), work environment (i.e., greater role ambiguity and more role conflict), lower promotion rates, and psychological strain; however, actual disclosure was not significantly related to these variables. These findings highlight the complex processes underlying decisions to come out in the workplace and the fine balance between psychological factors (e.g., need for authenticity) and social support that drive disclosure on the one hand and the fear of negative consequences that inhibit it on the other (Ragins et al., 2007).

A final area of research has focused on predictors of the career development process. Theorists have postulated that coming to terms with a minority sexual identity within a heterosexist context can make career exploration and decision making difficult, especially for LBW who are having a difficult time establishing their sexual identity (Schmidt & Nilsson, 2006). Supporting this notion, research suggests that for a substantial minority of lesbians, the sexual identity development process can negatively influence the career development process, mostly through delays, disruptions, or derailments (Boatwright, Gilbert, Forrest, & Ketzenberger, 1996; Tomlinson & Fassinger, 2003). In addition, research has found that sexual identity conflict, experiencing conflict between developing a sexual minority identity and a career, negative campus climate, and low social support predict less vocational development (e.g., vocational indecision, low career maturity, low career decision-making self-efficacy, more career decision-making barriers) among LGB adolescents and/or young adults (Lyons, Brenner, & Lipman, 2010; Schmidt & Nilsson, 2006; Tomlinson & Fassinger, 2003). Other research has found potential career benefits resulting from connections with other LBW and the LBW community, including networking and business referrals, receiving support, increased self-confidence, a greater acceptance of diversity, and developing career-related skills (e.g. communication in conflict, advocacy, leadership; Boatwright et al., 1996).

Counseling and Psychotherapy Issues

Drawing from the research reviewed above, the APA (2007) Guidelines, and applied articles for working with LBWT clients (c.f., Kashubeck-West, Szymanski, & Meyer, 2008; Szymanski, 2008; Szymanski & Moffitt, 2012), we describe six global treatment strategies: (a) facilitating sexual identity development and the coming out process; (b) facilitating transgender identity development; (c) attending to heterosexism and other forms of oppression in LBW's lives; (d) building on clients' strengths and developing skills for coping with oppression; (e) targeting protective factors and instituting inclusive organizational policies and practices; and (f) engaging in social advocacy and political and legislative action.

Facilitating Sexual Identity Development and the Coming Out Process

Psychologists working with LBW clients who are struggling with issues related to sexual identity development and the coming out process need to provide support, validation, empathy, unconditional positive regard, and complete acceptance of their clients' same-sex feelings (Szymanski, 2008). If internalized heterosexism or bisexism is present, it may be helpful to identify, explore, and challenge the client's negative stereotypes and maladaptive beliefs about lesbians and/or bisexual women by using techniques such as feminist analyses of heterosexual privilege, gender role messages and stereotypes, sexuality, and oppression; cognitive methods to help clients evaluate the validity of these beliefs; and/or providing factual information or affirmative readings about lesbianism/bisexuality (Kashubeck, Szymanski, & Meyer, 2008). In this work it is important to focus on the clients' acceptance of their same-sex sexuality, rather than adoption of a particular sexual identity label (Diamond, 2005, 2006a, 2006b). In addition, it is often important to increase LBW clients' awareness of their other relevant sociocultural identities (e.g., gender, race/ethnicity, ability level, social class, religion), to explore how these other identities influence their sexual identity, and to facilitate identity development within these identities (APA, 2007). For example, a psychologist working with a Latina LBW might help her to explore cultural and family messages concerning sexuality, the impact that being LBW may have on her family relationships and connection with her ethnic community, and experiences of racism within the LGB community and heterosexism within her ethnic community and how these influence her current struggles. Relatedly, a psychologist counseling a working class LBW might help her explore how financial and social capital influence her work environments and ability to be out, as well as her access and connection to the larger, often middle and upper middle class, LGBT culture.

Psychologists might also help clients make decisions about coming out to others. In this work, it is often important to help the client explore (a) her reasons for deciding to come out or not to come out to a particular person; (b) the benefits and risks associated with coming out to each individual of concern; (c) fears, hopes, and expectations about coming out to others; (d) the best and worst case scenarios; and (e) tensions or conflicting loyalties or pressures from family and/or racial, culture, sexual minority, and religious communities (Miville & Ferguson, 2006; Szymanski, 2008). Psychologists might also use techniques such as modeling sexual identity disclosure, empty chair role plays to practice the disclosure and anticipated reactions from others, and educating clients about common initial reactions of family, friends, and colleagues to sexual orientation disclosure (e.g., shock, anger, guilt, hurt, rejection, acceptance; Szymanski, 2008). Finally, after each disclosure occurs, psychologists might facilitate the client's expression of her feelings about both positive and/or negative responses received from others.

Facilitating Transgender Identity Development

When working with transgender clients, it is important for psychologists to understand the issues and needs associated with various subgroups within this population. For example, many transsexuals experience conflict between psychological gender and biological sex and desire permanent identification with the other gender, often through hormone therapy and genital surgery, whereas other subgroups of transgender persons experience more fluidity in their experiences in which an ongoing oscillation between more feminine and masculine aspects of internal gender identity and outward physical appearance and behavior occurs (Denny, 2004; Diamond & Butterworth, 2008). It is also important for psychologists to be aware that feminine and masculine behaviors are often the creation of sociocultural norms and not of biological specification (Carroll, Gilory, & Ryan, 2002; Diamond & Butterworth, 2008).

In working to facilitate gender identity development, psychologists should assess the level of incongruence between clients' gender identity and physical appearance presentation, promote congruence between these two aspects, and facilitate clients' acceptance of their gender identity (Etthner, 1999). Providing factual information about the options to transition, making referrals if necessary, exploring and supporting clients' chosen steps to transition, and promoting comfort with their body may also be helpful (Denny, 2004, Etthner, 1999). Finally, it is important to explore with transgender clients how their psychological symptoms may be connected to societal discrimination and abuse (Denny, 2004).

Attending to Heterosexism and Other Forms of Oppression in LBW's Lives

Given the occurrence of heterosexism and the negative effects that it can have on LBW's lives, it is important for psychologists to routinely assess for both its external and internalized manifestations. As such, psychologists should routinely assess for heterosexist experiences, including negative parental reactions to sexual orientation and/or gender atypical behavior, rejection, exclusion, harassment, discrimination, and violence in their clients' lives. Psychologists are encouraged to ask questions such as "How have your family, friends, coworkers reacted to knowledge of your sexual orientation?" in clinical interviews and use scales designed to measure heterosexist experiences, such as the Heterosexist Harassment, Rejection, and Discrimination Scale (Szymanski, 2006). Furthermore, administering the Lesbian Internalized Heterosexism Scale (Szymanski & Chung, 2001) or the Internalized Homophobia Scale—Women's Version (Martin & Dean, 1987) might be helpful in determining how a client may have internalized cultural messages about homosexuality and/or bisexuality.

Addressing heterosexist experiences can be facilitated by encouraging clients to examine how their current struggles might be related to heterosexist experiences they may have had, as well as in providing corrective emotional experiences for clients who have had such experiences. For example, a psychologist working with an LBW client who has experienced a sexual orientation—based hate crime might assist the client in exploring how her symptoms of anxiety, hypervigilence, and substance use are connected to this event. Similarly, a psychologist working with an LBWT client seeking asylum can help by facilitating the processing of past traumas related to sexual orientation and/or gender identity–based persecution; encouraging the expression of the unique challenges and extra stressors associated with a lack of legal recognition and government-sanctioned exclusion that LBWT immigrants and their families face; and providing support through the very complex, expensive, and emotionally difficult asylum-seeking process (Heller, 2009; Human Rights Watch/Immigration Equality, 2006; Tiven & Neilson, 2009). Relatedly, a psychologist working with a lesbian client with depression might encourage her to examine the ways in which she may have internalized negative messages about homosexuality and translated these experiences into personal endorsements of sociocultural hetero-normative standards of sexuality, relationships, identity, and behavior. Thus, the client begins to see how her depression is connected to cultural and social pressure to be heterosexual rather than to some personal deficiency. Techniques like these may help clients decrease the shame that they experience regarding their struggles and may enable them to work more productively on reducing their psychological distress symptoms. In addition, psychologists might provide clients with information about the research on psychosocial correlates of heterosexism described in this chapter to help clients gain more perspective about their own difficulties and see them in a contextual light (Kashubeck-West et al., 2008). Finally, interventions targeting variables that have been found to mediate or explain the relationships between internalized heterosexism and psychological distress, including self-esteem, avoidant coping, and social support, may be important. Thus, psychologists might lessen the potential negative impact that internalized heterosexism has on LBW's mental health by using therapeutic strategies designed to increase feelings of self-worth, foster development and enhancement of social support, and decrease use of avoidant coping strategies (Szymanski & Gupta, 2009b; Szymanski & Kashubeck-West, 2008; Szymanski & Owens, 2008).

In addition to external and internalized heterosexism, LBW must often deal with sexism as well as other forms of oppression associated with aspects of their identity that are marginalized in U.S. culture (e.g., race/ethnicity, social class, disability.). Thus, it is important for psychologists to promote an awareness of how clients' multiple identities and oppressions influence both external and internalized heterosexism and psychosocial difficulties (Szymanski, 2008). For example, a psychologist might also assess for experiences of sexism in addition to heterosexism and, if appropriate, to link the additive contributions of these oppressions to an LBW client's psychological symptoms (Szymanski & Owens, 2008). Relatedly, a psychologist working with an Asian American LBW might facilitate exploration of how multiple minority stressors associated with heterosexism (particularly within their racial/ethnic community) and racial prejudice and discrimination (particularly in dating and interpersonal relationships within the LGBT community) might be contributing to her psychological distress (Szymanski & Sung, 2010). Creating an oppressive events timeline in which a client develops a poster that marks experiences of heterosexism and racism and psychological struggles across her lifetime may illuminate these links. Similarly, a psychologist might assist an African American LBW client struggling with poor self-esteem to examine how her internalized racism and internalized heterosexism might be contributing to her feelings of low self-worth (Szymanski & Gupta, 2009b).

Building on Clients' Strengths and Developing Skills for Coping with Oppression

As described above, LBW have a number of strengths and use a variety of coping strategies to resist oppression. Psychologists are encouraged to identify and build on their clients' strengths and coping resources, as well as facilitating the growth of positive coping methods to combat experiences of heterosexism and other forms of oppression that they may encounter. For example, a psychologist working with an LBW client who is encountering workplace heterosexism might explore with her the various options she has for coping with it, such as using identity management strategies and coping with discrimination strategies described above. In addition, the psychologist could help her identify the pros and cons of using different strategies; use role-playing, constructive feedback, and modeling on how to use a particular strategy; and process reactions related to the outcome of implementing a particular strategy (Kashubeck-West et al., 2008).

The results of numerous studies reviewed above indicate the importance of social support for LBW identity development and mental health across the life span. Thus, psychologists working with LBW clients are encouraged to attend to issues of social support. For example, a psychologist working with a bisexual female client who is struggling with internalized bisexism and psychological distress symptoms might help her to increase both her general social supports as well as sexuality-specific supports, especially from family and heterosexual allies (Sheets & Mohr, 2009). When increasing family of origin support is not possible, psychologists might encourage their clients' efforts in creating families of choice that provide validation, affirmation, and support (Riggle et al., 2008; Rostosky et al., 2007). Group therapy for LBW who have experienced the effects of heterosexism may also be useful in helping participants feel not so alone by being able to share and compare their experiences with other LBW, to see how their experiences are related to larger sociocultural factors, and to share their own strategies for resisting heterosexism and other forms of oppression (APA, 2007; Kashubeck-West et al., 2008).

Targeting Protective Factors and Instituting Inclusive Organizational Policies and Practices

Our review indicates that it may be helpful for psychologists to implement interventions aimed at fostering variables that appear to protect LBWs from the harmful effects of heterosexism and to institute inclusive and LBW-affirmative organization policies and practices. For example, a psychologist working in the school system might implement interventions designed to increase school safety, teacher caring, informal mentoring, social support, and family connectedness for LBW youth. Psychologists might also help institute anti-bullying non-discrimination policies in schools, workplaces, and other organizational settings that include sexual orientation and gender identity and to develop effective systems for reporting and addressing heterosexist incidents that individuals experience (GLSEN, 2007). In addition, they might advocate for LGB-friendly policies and practices, such as same-sex domestic partner benefits, inclusion of same-sex partners at organizational events, and support groups (Ragins & Cornwell, 2001).

Engaging in Social Advocacy and Political and Legislative Action

There are a variety of ways that psychologists can engage in social advocacy aimed at reducing the incidence and potential negative impact of heterosexism on LBW's lives. For example, in their daily lives they can discourage heterosexist behavior by, for example, confronting others' stereotypes about lesbianism and bisexuality and changing their agency's counseling materials that may be heterosexist (Szymanski, 2008). In addition, they might provide LBW-affirmative outreach programs as part of their work in schools, colleges, or mental health agencies. Relatedly, they might develop written and multimedia materials that provide clear explanations of the detrimental role of heterosexism in LBW's lives and disseminate this information through the media; educate policy makers about the harmful effects that prohibition against marriage for same-sex couples has on LBW couples and families; and publicize the empirical research that demonstrates that children raised in same-sex households are as psychologically healthy as those raised in heterosexual households. Furthermore, they might advocate to defeat and change laws, such as the Defense of Marriage Amendments, that discriminate against LBW and to pass legislation, such as the Uniting American Families Act and federal and state protection from employment discrimination based on sexual orientation and gender identity, that affirms, protects, and gives equal rights to LBW and their families (Fassinger, 2008; Kashubeck-West et al., 2008; Szymanski & Moffitt, 2012).

In conclusion, feminist counseling psychologists have made important advances to our understanding of LBWT, the challenges that they face as a result of living in a heterosexist context, and the complex interplays of navigating multiple identities and oppressions. In addition, feminist counseling psychologists are in a unique position to deliver culturally competent and strengths-based clinical services to clients struggling with issues related to an often oppressive social context.

References

Albelda, R., Badgett, M., Scheebaum, A., & Gates, G. (2009). *Poverty in the lesbian, gay, and bisexual community.* Los Angeles, CA: The Williams Institute, UCLA School of Law. Retrieved July 22, 2010 from http://escholarship.org/uc.item/2509p8r5.

Almeida, J., Johnson, R. M., Corliss, H. L., Molnar, B. E., & Azrael, D. (2009). Emotional distress among LGBT youth: The influence of perceived discrimination based on sexual orientation. *Journal of Youth and Adolescence, 38,* 1001–1014.

American Psychological Association (2004). Answers to your questions about sexual orientation and homosexuality. Retrieved October 24, 2004, from http://www.apa.org/pubinfo/answers.html.

American Psychological Association. (2007). Guidelines for psychological practice with girls and women. *American Psychologist, 62,* 949–979.

Balsam, K. F., Rothblum, E. D., & Beauchaine, T. D. (2005). Victimization over the lifespan: A comparison of lesbian, gay, bisexual, and heterosexual siblings. *Journal of Consulting and Clinical Psychology, 73,* 477–487.

Balsam, K. F., & Szymanski, D. M. (2005). Relationship quality and domestic violence in women's same-sex relationships: The role of minority stress. *Psychology of Women Quarterly, 29,* 258–269.

Balsam, K. F., & Mohr, J. J. (2007). Adaptation to sexual orientation stigma: A comparison of bisexual and lesbian/gay adults. *Journal of Counseling Psychology, 54,* 306–319.

Balsam, K. F., Beauchaine, T. P., Rothblum, E. D., & Solomon, S. E. (2008). Three-year follow-up of same-sex couples who had civil unions in Vermont, same-sex couples not in civil unions, and heterosexual married couples. *Developmental Psychology, 44,* 102–116.

Beals, K. P., & Peplau, L. A. (2005). Identity support, identity devaluation, and well-being among lesbians. *Psychology of Women Quarterly, 29,* 140–148.

Bennett, L., & Gates, G. (2003). *The cost of marriage inequality to children and their same-sex parents: A human rights campaign foundation report.* Retrieved July 29, 2010, from http://www.hrc.org/documents/costkids.pdf.

Berlan, E. D., Corliss, H. L., Field, A. E., Goodman, E., & Austin, S. B. (2010). Sexual orientation and bullying among adolescents in the growing up today study. *Journal of Adolescent Health, 46,* 366–371.

Biesckhe, K. J., Hardy, J. A., Fassinger, R. E., & Croteau, J. M. (2008). Intersecting identities of gender-transgressive sexual minorities: Toward a new paradigm of affirmative psychology. *Biennial Review of Counseling Psychology, 1,* 177–207.

Birkett, M., Espelage, D. L., & Koenig, B. (2009). LGB and questioning students in schools: The moderating effects of

homophobic bullying and school climate on negative outcomes. *Journal of Youth and Adolescence, 38,* 989–1000.
Boatwright, K. J., Gilbert, M. S., Forrest, L., & Ketzenberger, K. (1996). Impact of identity development upon career trajectory: Listening to the voices of lesbian women. *Journal of Vocational Behavior, 48,* 210–228.
Bowleg, L., Huang, J., Brooks, K., Black, A., & Burkholder, G. (2003). Triple jeopardy and beyond: Multiple minority stress and resilience among Black lesbians. *Journal of Lesbian Studies, 7,* 87–108.
Caron, S. L., & Ulin, M. (1997). Closeting and the quality of lesbian relationships. *Families in Society: The Journal of Contemporary Human Services, 78,* 413–419.
Carroll, L., Gilroy, P. J., & Ryan, J. (2002). Counseling transgendered, transsexual, and gender-variant clients. *Journal of Counseling and Development, 80,* 131–139.
Cass, V. C. (1979). Homosexual identity formation: A theoretical model. *Journal of Homosexuality, 4,* 219–235.
Cianciotto, J. (2005). *Hispanic and Latino same-sex couple households in the United States: A report from the 2000 Census.* Retrieved July 29, 2010, from http://www.thetaskforce.org/downloads/reports/reports/HispanicLatinoHouseholdsUS.pdf.
Cochran, S. D. (2001). Emerging issues in research on lesbians' and gay men's mental health: Does sexual orientation really matter? *American Psychologist, 56,* 931–947.
Corliss, H. L., Cochran, S. D., & Mays, V. M. (2002). Reports of parental maltreatment during childhood in a United States population-based survey of homosexual, bisexual, and heterosexual adults. *Child Abuse and Neglect, 26,* 1165–1178.
Corliss, H. L., Rosario, M., Wypij, D., Wylie, S. A., Frazier, A. L., & Austin, S. B. (2010). Sexual orientation and drug use in a longitudinal cohort study of U.S. adolescents. *Addictive Behaviors, 35,* 517–521.
Croteau, J. M. (1996). Research on the work experiences of lesbian, gay, and bisexual people: An integrative review of methodology and findings. *Journal of Vocational Behavior, 48,* 195–209.
Dang, A., & Frazer, S. (2004). *Black same-sex households in the United States: A report from the 2000 Census.* Retrieved July 29, 2010, from http://www.thetaskforce.org/downloads/reports/reports/2000BlackSameSexHouseholds.pdf.
D'Augelli, A. R., & Hershberger, S. L. (1993). Lesbian, gay, and bisexual youth in community settings: Personal challenges and mental health problems. *American Journal of Community Psychology, 21,* 421–448.
D'Augelli, A., Pilkington, N. W., & Hershberger, S. L. (2002). Incidence and mental health impact of sexual orientation victimization of lesbian, gay and bisexual youths in high school. *School Psychology Quarterly, 17,* 148–167.
D'Augelli, A. R., Grossman, A. H., Salter, N. P., Vasey, J. J., Starks, M. T., & Sinclair, K. O. (2005). Predicting the suicide attempts of lesbian, gay, and bisexual youth. *Suicide and Life-Threatening Behavior, 35,* 646–660.
D'Augelli, A. R., Grossman, A. H., & Starks, M. T. (2005). Parents' awareness of lesbian, gay, and bisexual youths' sexual orientation. *Journal of Marriage and Family, 67,* 474–482.
Denny, D. (2004). Changing models of transsexualism. *Journal of Gay and Lesbian Psychotherapy, 8,* 25–40.
Denny, D. (2007). Transgender identities and bisexual expression: Implications for counselors. In B. A. Firestein (Ed.), *Becoming visible: Counseling bisexuals across the lifespan* (pp. 268–284). New York: Columbia University Press.
Descamps, M. J., Rothblum, E., Bradford, J., & Ryan, C. (2000). Mental health impact of child sexual abuse, rape, intimate partner violence, and hate crimes in the National Lesbian Health Care Survey. *Journal of Gay and Lesbian Social Services, 11,* 27–55.
Diamond, L. M. (2005). A new view of lesbian subtypes: Stable versus fluid identity trajectories over an 8-year period. *Psychology of Women Quarterly, 29,* 119–128.
Diamond, L. M. (2006a). What we got wrong about sexual identity development: Unexpected findings from a longitudinal study of young women (pp. 73–94). In A. M. Omoto and H. S. Kurtzman (Eds.), *Sexual orientation and mental health: Examining identity and development in lesbian, gay, and bisexual people.* Washington, DC, US: American Psychological Association.
Diamond, L. M. (2006b). The intimate relationships of same-sex relationships of sexual minorities (pp. 293–312). In A. L. Vangelisti and D. Perlman (Eds.) *The Cambridge Handbook of Personal Relationships.* New York: Cambridge University Press.
Diamond, L. M. (2008). Female bisexuality from adolescence to adulthood: Results from a 10-year longitudinal study. *Developmental Psychology, 44,* 5–14.
Diamond, L. M., & Butterworth, M. (2008). Questioning gender and sexual identity: Dynamic links over time. *Sex Roles, 59,* 365–376.
Dube, E. M., & Savin-Williams, R. C., (1999). Sexual identity development among ethnic sexual minority male youths. *Developmental Psychology, 35,* 1389–1398.
Eagly, A. H. & Carli, L. L. (2007). *Through the labyrinth: The truth about how women become leaders.* Boston, MA: Harvard Business School Press.
Eisenberg, M. E., & Resnick, M. D. (2006). Suicidality among gay, lesbian and bisexual youth: The role of protective factors. *Journal of Adolescent Health, 39,* 662–668.
Etthner, R. (1999). Gender loving care: A guide to counseling gender—variant clients. New York: Norton.
Fassinger, R. E., & Arseneau, J. R. (2007). "I'd rather get wet than be under that umbrella": Differentiating the experiences and identities of lesbian, gay, bisexual, and transgender people. In K. J. Bieschke, R. M. Perez, and K. A. DeBord, *Handbook of counseling and psychotherapy with lesbian, gay, bisexual, and transgender clients* (2nd ed.) (pp. 19–49). Washington, DC: American Psychological Association.
Fassinger, R. E. (2008). Workplace diversity and public policy: Challenges and opportunities for psychology. *American Psychologist, 63,* 252–268.
Fitzgerald, L. F., Gelfand, M. J., & Drasgow, F. (1995). Measuring sexual harassment: Theoretical and psychometric advances. *Basic and Applied Social Psychology, 17,* 425–445.
Fox, R. C. (2000). Bisexuality in perspective: A review of theory & research. In B. Greene and G. L. Croom (Eds.), *Psychological perspectives on lesbian and gay issues:* Vol. 5, *Education, research, and practice in lesbian, gay, bisexual, and transgendered psychology* (pp. 161–206). Thousand Oaks, CA: Sage.
Fredrickson, B. L. & Roberts, T. (1997). Objectification theory: Toward understanding women's lived experiences and mental health risks. *Psychology of Women Quarterly, 21,* 173–206.
Fredriksen-Goldsen, K. I., Kim, H.-J., Muraco, A., & Mincer, S. (2009). Chronically ill midlife and older lesbians, gay men, and bisexuals and their informal caregivers: The impact of the social context. *Sexuality Research and Social Policy, 6,* 52–64.

Friedman, C., & Leaper, C. (2010). Sexual-minority college women's experiences with discrimination: Relations with identity and collective action. *Psychology of Women Quarterly, 34,* 152–164.

Frost, D. M., & Meyer, I. H. (August 2008). *Social support among diverse sexual minority populations.* Paper presented at the annual convention of the American Psychological Association. Boston, MA.

Frost, D. M., & Meyer, I. H. (2009). Internalized homophobia and relationship quality among lesbians, gay men, and bisexuals. *Journal of Counseling Psychology, 56,* 97–109.

Gainor, K. A. (2000). Including transgender issues in lesbian, gay and bisexual psychology: Implications for clinical practice and training. In B. Greene and G. L. Croom (Eds.), *Psychological perspectives on lesbian and gay issues:* Vol. 5, *Education, research, and practice in lesbian, gay, bisexual, and transgendered psychology* (pp. 131–160). Thousand Oaks, CA: Sage.

Gastic, B., & Johnson, D. (2009). Teacher-mentors and the educational resilience of sexual minority youth. *Journal of Gay and Lesbian Social Services, 21,* 219–231.

Gay, Lesbian and Straight Education Network (2007). *The 2007 National School Climate Survey.* New York: GLSEN.

Gay, Lesbian and Straight Education Network (2008). *Involved, invisible, ignored: The experiences of lesbian, gay, bisexual and transgender parents and their children in our nation's K-12 schools.* New York: GLSEN.

Gilman, S. E., Cochran, S. D., Mays, V. M., Hughes, M., Ostrow, D., & Kessler, R. C. (2001). Risk of psychiatric disorders among individuals reporting same-sex sexual partners in the National Comorbidity Survey. *American Journal of Public Health, 91,* 933–939.

Golding, C., (2006). Redefining the nuclear family: An exploration of resiliency in lesbian parents. *Journal of Feminist and Family Therapy, 18*(1–2), 35–65.

Goldman, L. (2008). *Coming out, coming in: Nurturing the well-being and inclusion of gay youth in mainstream society.* New York: Routledge.

Goodenow, C., Szalacha, L., & Westheimer, K. (2006). School support groups, other school factors, and the safety of sexual minority adolescents. *Psychology in the Schools, 43,* 573–589.

Griffin, P. (1992). From hiding to coming out: Empowering lesbian and gay educators. In K. M. Harbeck (Ed.), *Coming out of the classroom closet* (pp. 167–196). Binghamton, NY: Harrington Park Press.

Grossman, A., D'Augelli, A., & O'Connell, T. (2001). Being lesbian, gay, bisexual and 60 or older in North America. *Journal of Gay and Lesbian Social Services, 13,* 23–40.

Grossman, A. H., D'Augelli, A. R., & Hershberger, S. L. (2000). Social support networks of lesbian, gay, and bisexual adults 60 years of age and older. *The Journals of Gerontology: Series B: Psychological Sciences and Social Sciences, 55B,* 171–179.

Grossman, A. H., D'Augelli, A. R., Dragowski, E. A. (2005). Caregiving and care receiving among older lesbian, gay, and bisexual adults. *Journal of Gay and Lesbian Social Services: Issues in Practice, Policy and Research, 18,* 15–38.

Grossman, A. H., & D'Augelli, A. R. (2006). Transgender youth: Invisible and vulnerable. *Journal of Homosexuality, 51,* 111–128.

Guidry, L. L. (1999). Clinical intervention with bisexuals: A contextualized understanding. *Professional Psychology: Research and Practice, 30,* 22–26.

Haber, D. (2009). Gay aging. *Gerontology and Geriatrics Education, 30,* 267–280.

Haines, M. E., Erchull, M. J., Liss, M., Turner, D. L., Nelson, J. A., Ramsey, L. R., & Hurt, M. M. (2008). Predictors and effects of self-objectification in lesbians. *Psychology of Women Quarterly, 32,* 181–187.

Harkless, L. E., & Flowers, B. J. (2005). Similarities and differences in relational boundaries among heterosexuals, gay men, and lesbians. *Psychology of Women Quarterly, 29,* 167–176.

Heller, P. (2009). Challenges facing LGBT asylum-seekers: The role of social work in correcting oppressive immigration process. *Journal of Gay and Lesbian Social Services, 21,* 294–308.

Henehan, D. F., Rothblum, E. D., Solomon, S. E., & Balsam K. F. (2007). Social and demographic characteristics of gay, lesbian, and heterosexual adults with and without children. *Journal of GLBT Family Studies, 3,* 35–79.

Herek, G. M. (2009). Hate crimes and stigma-related experiences among sexual minority adults in the United States: prevalence estimates from a national probability sample. *Journal of Interpersonal Violence, 24,* 54–74.

Herek, G. M., Gillis, J. R., & Cogan, J. C. (2009). Internalized stigma among sexual minority adults: Insights from a social psychological perspective. *Journal of Counseling Psychology, 56,* 32–43.

Huang, Y., Brewster, M. E., Moradi, B., Goodman, M. B., Wiseman, M. C., & Martin, A. (2010). Content analysis of literature about LGB People of Color: 1998–2007. *The Counseling Psychologist, 38,* 363–396.

Human Rights Watch/Immigration Equality (2006). Family, unvalued discrimination, denial, and the fate of binational same-sex couples under U. S. law. Retrieved June 1, 2010, from http://www.immigrationequality.org/uploaded files/FamilyUnvalued.pdf.

Jackson, N., Johnson, M., & Roberts, R. (2008). The potential impact of discrimination fears of older gays, lesbians, bisexuals and transgender individuals living in small- to moderate-sized cities on long-term health care. *Journal of Homosexuality, 54,* 325–339.

Jordan, K. M., & Deluty, R. H. (1998). Coming out for lesbian women: Its relationship to anxiety, positive affectivity, self-esteem, and social support. *Journal of Homosexuality, 35,* 41–63.

Kashubeck-West, S., Szymanski, D. M., & Meyer, J. (2008). Internalized heterosexism: Clinical implications and training considerations. *The Counseling Psychologist, 36,* 615–630.

Kimmel, D., Rose, T., & David, S. (2006). (Eds.). *Lesbian, gay, bisexual and transgeder aging: Research and clinical perspectives.* New York: Columbia University Press.

King, K. R. (2003). Racism or sexism? Attributional ambiguity and simultaneous membership in multiple oppressed groups. *Journal of Applied Social Psychology, 33,* 223–247.

Knauer, N. (2009). LGBT elder law: Toward equity in aging. *Harvard Journal of Law and Gender, 32,* 1–58.

Konik, J., & Crawford, M. (2004). Exploring normative creativity: Testing the relationship between cognitive flexibility and sexual identity. *Sex Roles, 51,* 249–253.

Konik, J., & Cortina, L. M. (2008). Policing gender at work: Intersections of harassment based on sex and sexuality. *Social Justice Research, 21,* 313–337.

Kosciw, J. G., Greytak, E. A., & Diaz, E. M. (2009). Who, what, where, when, and why: Demographic and ecological factors contributing to hostile school climate for lesbian, gay, bisexual, and transgender youth. *Journal of Youth and Adolescence, 38,* 976–988.

Kurdek, L. A. (1998). Relationship outcomes and their predictors: Longitudinal evidence from heterosexual married, gay cohabitating, and lesbian cohabitating couples. *Journal of Marriage and the Family, 60,* 553–568.

Kurdek, L. A. (2004). Are gay and lesbian cohabitating couples really different from heterosexual married couples? *Journal of Marriage and the Family, 66,* 880–900.

Lehavort, K., Balsam, K. F., & Ibrahim-Wells, G. D. (2009). Redefining the American quilt: Definitions and experiences of community among ethnically diverse lesbian and bisexual women. *Journal of Community Psychology, 37,* 439–458.

Levitt, H. M., Ovrebo, E., Anderson-Cleveland, M. B., Leone, C., Jae, Jeong, Y., et al. (2009). Balancing dangers: GLBT experience in a time of anti-GLBT legislation. *Journal of Counseling Psychology, 56,* 67–81.

Lewis, L. A. (1984). The coming out process for lesbians: Integrating a stable identity. *Social Work,* September-October, 464–469.

Lewis, R. J., Derlega, V. J., Clarke, E. G. & Kuang, J. C. (2006). Stigma consciousness, social constraints, and lesbian well-being. *Journal of Counseling Psychology, 53,* 48–56.

Lyons, H. Z., Brenner, B. R., & Lipman, J. P. (2010). Patterns of career and identity interference for lesbian, gay, and bisexual young adults. *Journal of Homosexuality, 57,* 503–514.

Marshal, M., Friedman, M. S., Stall, R., King, K. M., Miles, J., Gold, M.A., Bukstein, O. G., & Morse, J. Q. (2008). Sexual orientation and adolescent substance use: A meta-analysis and methodological review. *Addiction, 103,* 546–556.

Martin, J. L., & Dean, L. L. (1987). Ego-dystonic homosexuality scale. Unpublished manuscript, Columbia University. Retrieved June 1, 2010, from: http://psychology.ucdavis.edu/rainbow/html/ihpitems.html.

Masini, B. E., & Barrett, H. A. (2007). Social support as a predictor of psychological and physical well-being and lifestyle in lesbian, gay, and bisexual adults aged 50 and over. *Journal of Gay and Lesbian Social Services: Issues in Practice, Policy and Research, 20,* 91–110.

Mays, V. M., & Cochran, S. D. (2001). Mental health correlates of perceived discrimination among lesbian, gay, and bisexual adults in the United States. *American Journal of Public Health, 91,* 1869–1876.

McCarn, S. R., & Fassinger, R. E. (1996). Revisioning sexual minority identity formation: A new model of lesbian identity and its implications for counseling and research. *The Counseling Psychologist, 24,* 508–534.

McDermott, E. (2006). Surviving in dangerous places: Lesbian identity performances in the workplace, social class, and psychological health. *Feminism and Psychology, 16,* 193–211.

Meyer, I. H. (2003). Prejudice, social stress, and mental health in lesbian, gay, and bisexual populations: Conceptual issues and research evidence. *Psychological Bulletin, 129,* 674–697.

Meyer, I. H. (2010). Identity, stress, and resilience in lesbians, gay men, and bisexuals of color. *The Counseling Psychologist, 38,* 442–454.

Miville, M. L., & Ferguson, A. D. (2006). Intersections of sexism and heterosexism with racism: Therapeutic implications. In M. Constantine and D. W. Sue (Eds.), *Addressing racism: Facilitating cultural competence in mental health and educational settings* (pp. 87–103). Hoboken, NJ: John Wiley & Sons.

Mohr, J., & Fassinger, R. (2000). Measuring dimensions of lesbian and gay male experiences. *Measurement and Evaluation in Counseling and Development, 33,* 66–90.

Moracco, K. E., Runyan, C. W., Bowling, J. M., & Earp, J. A. L. (2007). Women's experiences with violence: A national study. *Women's Health Issues, 17,* 3–12.

Moradi, B., Mohr, J. J., Worthington, L. R., & Fassinger, E. R. (2009). Counseling psychology research on sexual (orientation) minority issues: Conceptual and methodological challenges and opportunities. *Journal of Counseling Psychology, 56*(1), 5–22.

Moradi, B., Wiseman, M. C., DeBlaere, C., Goodman, M. B., Sarkees, A., Brewster, M. E., & Huang, Y. (2010). LGB of color and white individuals' perceptions of heterosexist stigma, internalized homophobia, and outness: Comparisons of levels and links. *The Counseling Psychologist, 38,* 397–424.

Morris, J. F., & Rothblum, E. D. (1999). Who fills out a "lesbian" questionnaire? The interrelationship of sexual orientation, years "out," disclosure of sexual orientation, sexual experiences with women, and participation in the lesbian community. *Psychology of Women Quarterly, 23,* 537–557.

Morris, J. F., Waldo, C. R., & Rothblum, E. D. (2001). A model of predictors and outcomes of outness among lesbian and bisexual women. *American Journal of Orthopsychiatry, 71,* 61–71.

Morris, J. F., Balsam, K. F., & Rothblum, E. D. (2002). Lesbian and bisexual mothers and nonmothers: Demographics and the coming out process. *Journal of Family Psychology, 16,* 144–156.

Morris, J. F., & Balsam, K. F. (2003). Lesbian and bisexual women's experiences of victimization: Mental health, revictimization, and sexual identity development. *Journal of Lesbian Studies, 7*(4), 67–85.

Murphy, B. C. (1989). Lesbian couples and their parents: The effects of perceived parental attitudes on the couple. *Journal of Counseling and Development, 68,* 46–51.

National Center for Transgender Equality and the National Gay and Lesbian Task Force (2009). National transgender discrimination survey: Preliminary findings. Retrieved July 29, 2010, from http://transequality.org/Resources/NCTE_prelim_survey_Econ.pdf.

Norris, F. H., Foster, J. D., & Weisshaar, D. L. (2002). The epidemiology of sex differences in PTSD across developmental, societal, and research contexts. In R. Kimerling, P. Ouimette, and J. Wolfe (Eds.), *Gender and PTSD* (pp. 3–42). New York: Guilford.

Ochs, R. (1996). Biphobia: It goes more than two ways. In B. A. Firestein (Ed), *Bisexuality: The psychology and politics of an invisible minority* (pp. 3–50). Thousand Oaks, CA: Sage.

Otis, M. D., Rostosky, S. S., Riggle, E. D. B., & Harmin, R. (2006). Stress and relationship quality in same sex couples. *Journal of Social and Personal Relationships, 23,* 81–99.

Patterson, C. (1995). Lesbian mothers, gay fathers and their children. In A.R. D'Augelli & C. Patterson (Eds.), *Lesbian, gay and bisexual identities across the lifespan: Psychological perspectives* (pp. 262–290). New York: Oxford University Press.

Patterson, C. J. (2000). Family relationships of lesbian and gay men. *Journal of Marriage and Family, 62,* 1052–1069.

Patterson, C. J. (2006). Children of lesbian and gay parents. *Current Directions in Psychological Science, 15,* 241–244.

Patterson, C. J. (2009). Children of lesbian and gay parents: Psychology, law, and policy. *American Psychologist, 8,* 727–736.

Quam, J. K., & Whitford, G. S. (1992). Adaptation and age-related expectations among older gay and lesbian adults. *The Gerontologist, 32,* 367–374.

Ragins, B. R., & Cornwell, J. M. (2001). Pink triangles: Antecedents and consequences of perceived workplace discrimination against gay and lesbian employees. *Journal of Applied Psychology, 86,* 1244–1261.

Ragins, B. R. (2004). Sexual orientation in the workplace: The unique work and career experiences of gay, lesbian, and bisexual workers. *Research in Personnel and Human Resources Management, 23,* 35–120.

Ragins, B. R., Singh, R., & Cornwell, J. M. (2007). Making the invisible visible: Fear and disclosure of sexual orientation at work. *Journal of Applied Psychology, 92,* 1103–1118.

Reynolds, A. L. & Hanjorgiris, W. F. (2000). Coming out: Lesbian, gay and bisexual identity development. In R. M. Perez, K. A. DeBord & K. J. Bieschke (Eds.). *Handbook of counseling and psychotherapy with lesbian, gay and bisexual clients* (pp. 35–55). Washington, DC: American Psychological Association.

Riggle, E., Whitman, J., Olson, A., Rostosky, S. & Strong, S. (2008). The positive aspects of being a lesbian or gay man. *Professional Psychology: Research and Practice, 39,* 210–217.

Riggle, E. D. B., Rostosky, S. S., & Horne, S. G. (2010). Psychological distress, well-being, and legal recognition in same-sex couple relationships. *Journal of Family Psychology, 24,* 82–86.

Rivers, I. (2001). The bullying of sexual minorities at school: Its nature and long-term correlates. *Educational and Child Psychology, 18*(1), 33–46.

Rose, S. M., & Zand, D. (2002). Lesbian dating and courtship from young adulthood to midlife. *Journal of Lesbian Studies, 6,* 85–109.

Rostosky, S. S., Riggle, E. D. B., Gray, B. E., & Hatton, R. L. (2007). Minority stress experiences in committed same-sex couple relationships. *Professional Psychology, Research and Practice, 38,* 392–400.

Rothblum, E. D., & Factor, R. (2001). Lesbians and their sisters as a control group: Demographic and mental health factors. *Psychological Science, 12,* 63–69.

Rothblum, E. D., Balsam, K. F., & Mickey, R. M. (2004). Brothers and sisters of lesbians, gay men, and bisexuals as a demographic comparison group. *Journal of Applied Behavioral Science, 40,* 283–230.

Rudman, L. A. & Glick, P. (1999). Feminized management and backlash towards agenic women: The hidden costs to women of a kinder, gentler image of middle managers. *Journal of Personality and Social Psychology, 77,* 1004–1010.

Rudman, L. A., & Glick, P. (2001). Prescriptive gender stereotypes and backlash toward agentic women. *Journal of Social Issues, 57,* 743–762.

Russell, G. M., & Richards, J. A. (2003). Stressor and resilience factors for lesbians, gay men, and bisexuals confronting antigay politics. *American Journal of Community Psychology, 31,* 313–328.

Rust, P.C. (2003). Finding a sexual identity and community: Therapeutic implications and cultural assumptions in scientific models of coming out. In L. D. Garnets & D. C. Kimmel (Eds.). *Psychological perspectives on lesbian, gay, and bisexual experiences.* (pp. 227–269). New York: Columbia University Press.

Saewyc, E. M., Homma, Y., Skay, C. L., Bearinger, L. H., Resnick, M. D., Reis, E. (2009). Protective factors in the lives of bisexual adolescents in North America. *American Journal of Public Health, 99,* 110–117.

Saltzburg, S. (2004). Learning that an adolescent child is gay or lesbian: The parent experience. *Social Work, 49,* 109–118.

Sausa, L. A. (2002). Updating college and university campus policies: Meeting the needs of trans students, staff, and faculty. *Journal of Lesbian Studies, 6,* 43–55.

Savin-Williams, R. C. (2001). *Mom, dad. I'm gay.* Washington, DC: American Psychological Association.

Savin-Williams, R. C. (2005). *The new gay teenager.* Cambridge, MA: Harvard University Press.

Schmidt, C.K., & Nilsson, J. E. (2006). The effects of simultaneous developmental processes: Factors relating to the career development of lesbian, gay, and bisexual youth. *Career Development Quarterly, 55,* 22–37.

Schwartz, S. J., Unger, J. B., Zamboanga, B. L., & Szapocznik, J. (2010). Rethinking the concept of acculturation: Implications for theory and research. *American Psychologist, 65,* 237–251.

Sears, J. T. (1991). *Growing up gay in the South: Race, gender, and journeys of the spirit.* Binghamtom, NY: Haworth.

Shapiro, D. N., Peterson, C., & Stewart, A. J. (2009). Legal and social contexts and mental health among lesbian and heterosexual mothers. *Journal of Family Psychology, 23,* 255–262.

Sheets, R. L., & Mohr, J. J. (2009). Perceived social support from friends and family and psychosocial functioning in bisexual young adult college students. *Journal of Counseling Psychology, 56,* 152–163.

Shippy, R. A. (2005). We cannot go it alone: The impact of informal support and stressors in older gay, lesbian and bisexual caregivers. *Journal of Gay and Lesbian Social Services, 18,* 39–51.

Smith, N. G., & Ingram, K. M. (2004). Workplace heterosexism and adjustment among lesbian, gay, and bisexual individuals: The role of unsupportive social interactions. *Journal of Counseling Psychology, 51,* 57–67.

Solomon, S. E., Rothblum, E. D., & Balsam, K. F. (2004). Pioneers in partnership: Lesbian and gay male couples in civil unions compared with those not in civil unions and married heterosexual siblings. *Journal of Family Psychology, 18,* 275–286.

Solomon, S. E., Rothblum, E. D., & Balsam, K. F. (2005). Money, housework, sex, and conflict: Same-sex couples in civil unions, those not in civil unions, and heterosexual married siblings. *Sex Roles, 52,* 561–575.

Sophie, J. (1982). Counseling lesbians. *Personnel and Guidance Journal, 60,* 341–345.

Szalacha, L. A. (2003). Safer sexual diversity climates: Lessons learned from an evaluation of Massachusetts Safe Schools Program for Gay and Lesbian Students. *American Journal of Education, 110,* 58–88.

Szymanski, D. M., & Chung, Y. B. (2001). The Lesbian Internalized Homophobia Scale: A rational/theoretical approach. *Journal of Homosexuality, 41*(2), 37–52.

Szymanski, D. M., & Chung, Y. B. (2003). Feminist attitudes and coping resources as correlates of lesbian internalized heterosexism. *Feminism and Psychology, 13,* 369–389.

Szymanski, D. M. (2004). Relations among dimensions of feminism and internalized heterosexism in lesbians and bisexual women. *Sex Roles, 51*(3–4), 145–159.

Szymanski, D. M. (2005). Heterosexism and sexism as correlates of psychological distress in lesbians. *Journal of Counseling and Development, 83,* 355–360.

Szymanski, D. M. (2006). Does internalized heterosexism moderate the link between heterosexist events and lesbians' psychological distress? *Sex Roles, 54,* 227–234.

Szymanski, D. M. (2008). Lesbian, gay, bisexual, and transgendered clients. In G. Mcauliffe (Ed.), *Culturally alert counseling: A comprehensive introduction* (pp. 466–505). Thousand Oaks, CA: Sage.

Szymanski, D. M., & Kashubeck-West, S. (2008). Mediators of the relationship between internalized oppressions and lesbian and bisexual women's psychological distress. *The Counseling Psychologist, 36,* 575–594.

Szymanski, D. M., Kashubeck-West, S., & Meyer, J. (2008a). Internalized heterosexism: Measurement, psychosocial correlates, and research directions. *The Counseling Psychologist, 36,* 525–574.

Szymanski, D. M., Kashubeck-West, S., & Meyer, J. (2008b). Internalized heterosexism: A historical and theoretical overview. *The Counseling Psychologist, 36,* 510–524.

Szymanski, D. M., & Meyer, D. (2008). Racism and heterosexism as correlates of psychological distress in African American sexual minority women. *Journal of LGBT Issues in Counseling, 2,* 94–108.

Szymanski, D. M., & Owens, G. P. (2008). Do coping styles moderate or mediate the relationship between internalized heterosexism and sexual minority women's psychological distress? *Psychology of Women Quarterly, 32,* 95–104.

Szymanski, D. M., & Owens, G. P. (2009). Group-level coping as a moderator between heterosexism and sexism and psychological distress in sexual minority women. *Psychology of Women Quarterly, 33,* 197–205.

Szymanski, D. M., & Gupta, A. (2009a). Examining the relationship between multiple oppressions and Asian American sexual minority persons' psychological distress. *Journal of Gay and Lesbian Social Services, 21,* 267–281.

Szymanski, D. M., & Gupta, A. (2009b). Examining the relationship between multiple internalized oppressions and African American lesbian, gay, and bisexual persons' self-esteem and psychological distress. *Journal of Counseling Psychology, 56,* 110–118.

Szymanski, D. M., & Balsam, K. F. (2011). Insidious trauma: Examining the relationship between heterosexist events and lesbians' post-traumatic stress. *Traumatology, 17*(2), 4–13.

Szymanski, D. M., & Sung, M. R. (2010). Minority stress and psychological distress among Asian American sexual minority persons. *The Counseling Psychologist, 38,* 848–872.

Szymanski, D. M., & Moffitt, L. B. (2012). Sexism and heterosexism. In N. Fouad (Ed.), *Handbook of counseling psychology: Volume 2 practice, training, and policy.* Washington, DC: American Psychological Association.

Tasker, F., & Patterson, C. J. (2007). Research on gay and lesbian parenting: Retrospect and prospect. *Journal of Gay, Lesbian, Bisexual and Transgender Family Issues, 3,* 9–34.

Thomas, A. J., Witherspoon, K. M., & Speight, S. L. (2004). Toward the development of the Stereotypic Roles of Black Women Scale. *Journal of Black Psychology, 30,* 426–442.

Thomas, A. J., Witherspoon, K. M., & Speight, S. L., & (2008). Gendered racism, psychological distress, and coping styles of African American women. *Cultural Diversity and Ethnic Minority Psychology, 14,* 307–314.

Tiven, R. B., & Neilson, V. (2009). Working with lesbian, gay, bisexual, and transgender immigrants. In F. Chang-Muy and E. P. Congress (Eds). *Social work with immigrants and refugees: Legal issues, clinical skills and advocacy* (pp. 257–275). New York: Springer.

Tjaden, P., Thoeness, N., & Allison, C. J. (1999). Comparing violence over the life span in samples of same-sex and opposite-sex cohabitants. *Violence and Victims, 14,* 413–425.

Todosijevic, J., Rothblum, E. D., & Solomon, S. E. (2005). Relationship satisfaction, affectivity, and gay-specific stressors in same-sex couples joined in civil unions. *Psychology of Women Quarterly, 29,* 158–166.

Tomlinson, M. J., & Fassinger, R. E. (2003). Career development, lesbian identity development, and campus climate among lesbian college students. *Journal of College Student Development, 44,* 845–860.

Trocki, K. F., Drabble, L., & Midanik, L. (2005). Homosexuals and bisexuals: Results from a national household probability survey. *Journal of Studies on Alcohol, 66,* 105–110.

U.S. Department of Labor, Bureau of Labor Statistics, *Employment and earnings, 2008 annual averages and the monthly labor review*, November 2007.

Waldo, C. R., Hesson-McInnis, M. S., & D'Augelli, A.R. (1998). Antecedents and consequences of victimization of lesbian, gay, and bisexual young people: A structural model comparing rural university and urban samples. *Journal of Community Psychology, 26,* 307–334.

Waldo, C. R. (1999). Working in a majority context: A structural model of heterosexism as minority stress in the workplace. *Journal of Counseling Psychology, 46,* 218–232.

Williams, T., Connolly, J. P., Debra, C., & Craig, W. (2005). Peer victimization, social support, and psychosocial adjustment of sexual minority adolescents. *Journal of Youth and Adolescence, 34,* 471–482.

Willingness, C. R., Steel, P., & Lee, K. (2007). A meta-analysis of the antecedents and consequences of workplace sexual harassment. *Personnel Psychology, 60,* 127–162.

Woods, K. C., Buchanan, N. T., & Settles, I. H. (2008). Sexual harassment across the color line: Experiences and outcomes of cross versus intra-racial sexual harassment among black women. *Cultural Diversity and Ethnic Minority Psychology 34,* 1–11.

CHAPTER

8 Feminist Multicultural Counseling Psychology and Poverty

Laura Smith, Lauren Appio, *and* Jennifer Chang

Abstract

Within social justice theorizing, issues of poverty and social class receive relatively little focused attention, yet the convergence of feminist and multicultural counseling psychology provides a natural context for such considerations. In this chapter, the authors support this idea by outlining trends within feminist and multicultural psychology, and then go on to describe recent innovations by counseling psychologists that point the way toward socially just counseling practice in the context of poverty.

Key Words: Poverty, social class, social justice, counseling, psychotherapy

> Just as feminism has changed the way in which counselors might assess strengths in women clients, multiculturalism has challenged counselors to reexamine strength within clients identified by cultural differences... Feminist and multicultural scholars have challenged traditional ideas about health and provided suggestions about how healthy psychological development might look in people who have had less access to the power that defines health. (Whalen, Fowler-Lese, Barber, Williams, Judge, Nilsson, et al., 2004, p. 381)

Whalen et al.'s 2004 article, quoted above, summarized the efforts of a working group whose goal was to integrate feminist and multicultural psychological theory into counseling psychology practice. Sponsored by the APA Division 17 Section for the Advancement of Women, the working group sought to bring these approaches to bear on the preparation of counselors to work sensitively and effectively with clients and communities across a diverse spectrum of sociocultural identities. The authors pointed out that these two literatures, though often considered in isolation, offer important and converging guidance for the implementation of socially just practice among marginalized groups such as women, people of color, and lesbian, gay. bisexual, transgender, and queer (LGBTQ) individuals. In this chapter, we hope to illuminate that convergence further in its application to the psychological well-being of a marginalized group that is often mentioned in discussions of multiculturalism and social justice only in passing: people living in poverty. We see the convergence of feminist and multicultural frameworks as a natural context for the psychological consideration of social class and poverty, and we will begin our discussion with some observations to illustrate this perspective. Next, we clarify our usage of the terms *social class* and *classism*, and sketch out the statistical parameters of contemporary American poverty. Within this portrait, we bring special attention to women's poverty. We follow this discussion by outlining trends within applied psychology's history of attention (and inattention) to women and to the poor, and finally, we profile the promising work of feminist and multicultural counseling psychologists who are bringing their social justice commitments to life through innovative practice and action in the context of poverty.

Feminist Multicultural Counseling Psychology: The Right Home for an Applied Perspective on Poverty

In 2002, Bernice Lott remarked upon the near-invisibility of the poor within psychology generally, and applied psychology has been no exception to this rule (Smith, 2005). Counseling psychology is, however, historically and philosophically well-situated to lead the exploration of issues of social class and poverty and their impact on the psychotherapeutic process. As Whalen et al. (2004) and other commentators (e.g., Goodman et al., 2004) have noted, counseling psychology has a unique, distinguished history of attention to the impact of sociocultural factors on human development and well-being. One of the notable flowerings of this emphasis occurred with the development of the American Psychological Association's (APA, 2003) Multicultural Guidelines on Education and Training, Research, Practice, and Organizational Development for Psychologists, a profession-wide statement of ethical multicultural practice, which originated in the work of counseling psychologists (Sue, D. W. et al., 1982; Sue, D. W., Arredondo, & McDavis, 1992). Correspondingly, counseling psychologists such as William Liu (2001; Liu et al., 2004), Nadya Fouad (Fouad & Brown, 2000), and David Blustein (Blustein et al., 2002) have been influential in encouraging practitioners to broaden the scope of their theory, research, and practice to encompass issues of social class and the experiences of clients who live in poverty.

During the period when counseling psychologists were formulating conceptions of multicultural competence, feminist psychologists were reexamining their own practice from a similar perspective (e.g., Brown, 1990). As mainstream feminism was being challenged for its predomininantly White, middle class, heterosexual worldview, feminist psychologists responded by examining the relevance of existing models of feminist therapy for women of all races, sexual orientations, and social classes. Feminist psychotherapists who brought attention to the circumstances of poor female clients continued a tradition that traced its roots to the work of early socialist feminists such as Charlotte Perkins Gilman, who explicated the intersections of economic injustice and patriarchy in the oppression of women (Enns, 2004). It also built upon more recent analyses such as Pearce's (1978) articulation of a sociohistorical trend that she called "the feminization of poverty" in an article of the same title. This trend, according to Pearce, referred to the steadily deepening relative poverty of women as the result of such phenomena as the persistent gender earning gap and the exclusionary closure of many professions with regard to the hiring of women. Women have continued to be poorer "because they are women," as Pearce put it (p. 28), through the first decades of the new millennium. Even the educational gains by women in recent years have not turned the tide: though women employees are now better educated than men, they still earn 24% less than men and are 35% more likely to live in poverty (Legal Momentum, 2009).

In applying such considerations to their work with poor women, feminist psychologists substantively addressed considerations of social class earlier than did their colleagues in counseling psychology—or applied psychologists anywhere in the field, for that matter. Underscoring the marginalization of poor women, Patricia Denny (1986) asked provocatively whether "poor women could benefit from, or even survive" mainstream feminist therapy, asserting that "in its present state, feminist therapy has unintentionally perpetrated much the same sort of ignorance on women in poverty that traditional psychotherapy perpetrated on all women" (p. 60). Denny urged feminist therapists to explore their own racism and classism as they sought to improve therapeutic outcomes for poor and working class women. To aid in this effort, she presented a series of issues and questions for exploration, including the proposition that

> poor women have the right to expect the therapist to understand the purpose and function of the socioeconomic class system.... This exploration may be uncomfortable, for it necessitates the reevaluation of White middle-class privileged positions in society, and often, new conclusions about what is possible and what is just. (p. 62)

A decade later, a special edition of the journal *Women and Therapy* was published as the book *Classism and Feminist Therapy: Counting Costs* (Hill & Rothblum, 1996), a volume focused entirely on the impact of economic injustice and classism on both therapists and their clients. This volume contained such work as a study by Chalifoux (1996), who interviewed working class women about their therapeutic experiences. Chalifoux found that these women were very much aware of the class differences between themselves and their middle class therapists, and experienced their therapists as having different worldviews from their own. One participant, for example, commented that her middle class clinician did not seem to understand that "freedom of choice takes money" (p. 30). Women in this study also reported noticing that their therapists avoided issues of class and money, which made *them* feel uncomfortable and too ashamed to bring these issues up themselves. Chalifoux (1996) noted that this disconnection had serious implications for the therapeutic relationship: when participants felt that their therapists could not understand or tolerate their concerns, they edited themselves in session, undermining the establishment of the trust necessary for an effective therapeutic alliance.

Social Class and Poverty

When psychologists do reference social class within their theory or research, it is usually to incorporate one of a number of social class proxies, such as income or socioeconomic status (SES)—each of which is related to, but not the same as, social class itself. In our use of the term *social class*, we follow the work of sociologists who have described the ways that societies are stratified, along with the differing relationships of people within these strata to sources of socioeconomic power. Gilbert (2008) conceptualized theories of social stratification as attempts to account for the operation of 10 key variables: four economic variables (*occupation, wealth, income,* and *poverty*), four social variables (*prestige, association, socialization*, and *social mobility*) and two political variables (*power* and *class consciousness*). The interaction of these variables results in different socioeconomic experiences, obstacles, and opportunities for different groups of people. These experiences, obstacles, and "reward packages" (Grusky & Ku, 2008, p. 5)—or class-related social assets and advantages—tend to clump together in systematic ways that distinguish one social class group from another. Many different social class structures and nomenclatures have been proposed to describe these groups, and there is no one "right" model. Here, we offer a simple class typology that combines the language of Betsy Leondar-Wright (2005), a class activist, and Michael Zweig (2000), a professor of economics. Their approaches echo the class distinctions proposed by many theorists with regard to (a) the sources of socioeconomic power in the ownership of wealth and property, and (b) the operations of socioeconomic power vis-à-vis the process of economic production:

Poverty: Predominantly describes working class people who, because of unemployment, low-wage jobs, health problems, or other crises, are without enough income to support their families' basic needs.

Working class: People who have little power or authority in the workplace, little control over the availability or content of jobs, and little say in the decisions that affect their access to health care, education, and housing. They tend to have lower levels of income, net worth, and formal education than more powerful classes.

Middle class: Professionals, managers, small business owners, often college-educated and salaried. Middle class people have more autonomy and control in the workplace than working class people, and more economic security; however, they rely upon earnings from work to support themselves.

Owning class: People who own enough wealth and property that they do not need to work to support themselves (although they may choose to); people who own and control the resources by which other people earn a living. The owning class includes people who, as a result of their economic power, also have significant social, cultural, and political power relative to other classes.

Consideration of this typology brings poverty into focus as more than a lack of purchasing power (although this is a critical element of life in poverty). Rather, poverty is understood more broadly to be a social location at bottom of the social class spectrum. As such, poverty implies a relative lack of many socially valued opportunities and assets, along with the discriminatory attitudes that accompany social exclusion. We follow social psychologists Bernice Lott and Heather Bullock (2007) in referring to the form of oppression at work in the social class hierarchy as *classism*. According to Lott and Bullock, classism comprises two general forms: *institutional classism*, which refers to the practices, attitudes, assumptions, behaviors, and policies through which social institutions function to perpetuate the deprivation and low status of poor people; and *interpersonal classism*, which is characterized by prejudice, stereotyping, and discrimination.

Just as feminist and multicultural psychologists understand race and gender to represent dimensions of sociocultural identity along which power and oppression can be examined and addressed, we support the conceptualization of social class as another such dimension. Addressing social class stratification directly, rather than through its artifacts (such as income), provides a framework for addressing the dynamics of economic injustice in society—an issue of central relevance for feminist and multicultural psychology (Smith, 2008).

Who Are the Poor? Poverty by the Numbers

Not only do considerations of poverty fit well with the interests and commitments of feminist and multicultural psychologists, a look at the statistics that describe American poverty makes clear the national importance of these issues. According to the 2009 U.S. Census, 43.6 million Americans fell below the poverty line, representing 14.3% of the total population. Between the years 2001 and 2003, a relatively small percentage of the population (2.4%) experienced chronic poverty, meaning that they were poor for at least three years (Stern, 2008). However, nearly a third of Americans have spent at least two months or more living below the poverty line between 2004 and 2007 (DeNavas-Walt, Proctor, & Smith, 2009). Furthermore, the U.S. Department of Labor (2010) estimates that 8.9 million people comprise the "working poor," adults who collect poverty-level incomes despite their participation in the workforce for at least 27 weeks of the year. Working poverty itself is on the increase in the United States, with 1.4 million more Americans identified as "working poor" in 2008 than 2007. Among working poor individuals with histories of full-time employment, 85.8% reported that low wages, periods of unemployment, or forced part-time employment contributed to their financial insecurity. What is clear from this data is that more and more Americans are feeling the direct effects of poverty.

The income gap between the wealthiest and poorest Americans is also growing. Referring to this gap as *economic apartheid*, Collins and Yeskel (2005) found that, while incomes for families in every income bracket had risen proportionately between the years of 1947 and 1979, incomes have not risen at the same rate across the board in the years since. Between 1979 and 2003, income for Americans in the top two quartiles (earning at least $98,200 and $170,000 a year, respectively), rose by 51% and 75%. Comparatively, families in the bottom 20% of earners actually saw their yearly incomes drop by 2% during the same time period. As income and wealth have trickled *up* over the years, a tiny percentage of people at the very top of the economic spectrum have seen their fortunes skyrocket: Johnson (2007) reported that the top 10% of Americans earned nearly 50% of the nation's collective income in 2005, and the top .1% of earners collected nearly as much income as the lower 50% of American earners put together. In other words, 300,000 of the wealthiest Americans earned as much as the 150 million Americans at the bottom of the pyramid. This is a considerable jump from income distribution in the 1970s, when the top 10% of American earned approximately 20% of total income (Johnson, 2007). Collins and Yeskel (2005) contributed another illustration of this trend with an example of the widening gap between the highest-paid worker and the average worker in American firms. In 1975, the ratio was 41 to 1; by 2003, it was 301 to 1.

These statistics paint a startling picture of poverty as an increasingly common part of the American experience, and this is especially true for women. As mentioned, Pearce (1978) noted decades ago that poverty had become increasingly "feminized," in that women comprise a disproportionately higher percentage of the poor than men. Accordingly, U.S. Census data (2008) show that more women and girls are poor than men and boys (21.6 million compared to 16.8 million, respectively). In their study of gender and poverty, Brady and Kall (2008) found that women in affluent, Western countries are at least 10% more likely to be poor than men, with women in the United States being 30% more likely to be poor, supporting the gendered poverty statistics obtained by the U.S. Census. Brady and Kall (2008) additionally reported that poor women tend to experience a deeper, more intense poverty than do poor men. That is, poor women earn lower wages and accrue fewer employment-related benefits than poor men, making their financial circumstances even more precarious.

Women's disproportionate representation among the poor has been linked to a number of factors. First, women are simply paid less than men for their labor. Women earn approximately 78% of men's earnings, and women's median income is less than men's in all 50 states (Semega, 2009). Second, women often work in jobs that pay lower wages and do not provide steady, secure employment. Boraas and Rodgers (2003) confirmed that whenever women predominate within an occupation, such as in service industries, employees earn less than those who work in male-dominated industries. Even then, men seem to be less affected by this trend than are women: men who work in female-dominated industries earn approximately 12% less than men in male-dominated occupations, whereas women in female-dominated occupations earn 25% less than women in male-dominated careers (Boraas & Rodgers, 2003). Women are significantly underrepresented among the highest earners in the U.S. population, comprising only 31% of that quintile (Kline, 2006). Pressman (2003) estimated that if women were proportionately employed and compensated in male-dominated fields, the gender poverty gap would shrink by 33%.

Women's earning potential and vulnerability to impoverishment has also been exacerbated by changes in family structure. The number of single-parent families has increased as divorce, premarital sex, and childbearing outside marriage have become more frequent and socially acceptable, and 92% of children in single-parent families live with their mother (Ellwood & Jencks, 2002). Because women generally earn less than men and households headed by single women must rely on only one income, female-headed households have a higher rate of poverty (29.9%) than single male-headed households (16.9%) and households headed by married couples (5.8%; DeNavas-Walt et al., 2010).

It should be noted that other intersecting oppressions also factor into the demographics of American poverty. The deep historical intertwining of racism with socioeconomic interests (e.g., Marable, 2000) has resulted in the overrepresentation of people of color below the U.S. poverty line. Specifically, the U.S. Census Bureau (2010a) estimated the poverty rate of Whites to be 9.4%, which is less than half the rate for Blacks at 25.8% and Latinos at 25.3%. The percentage of Asians living in poverty is also higher than Whites living in poverty (12.5%). Statistics regarding American Indian poverty are not organized as such by the Census; however, the Census Bureau's American Community Survey (2010b) found that, of the five counties with poverty rates greater than 39%, four contain or are contained within American Indian reservations. Finally, heterosexism's impact can be seen in the fact that 24% of lesbians are estimated to live in poverty as compared to 19% of straight women; gay men, on the other hand, have poverty rates that are approximately equal to those of straight men (Albelda, Badgett, Schneebaum, & Gates, 2009).

The operations of classism, sexism, racism, and heterosexism, therefore, dovetail in the relegation of disproportionate numbers of women and their children to life in poverty, as summarized by Lott and Bullock (2007), who concluded that "the burden of coping with poverty falls most heavily on women" (p. 190). The powerful, persistent intersection of social class with other oppressed identities in American society points compellingly to the need for feminist and multicultural psychologists to capitalize on the promise represented in both literatures to develop an integrated social justice framework for social class and poverty.

Psychotherapists and the Poor

Poverty has long been established as a risk factor for countless varieties of emotional and physical distress and disorder; in fact, the relationship between poverty and mental health has been called "one of the most thoroughly documented relationships in epidemiological research" (Allen & Britt, 1983, p. 149). Nevertheless, psychologists' consideration of the poor has been inconsistent—and frequently negatively biased. Observing that poor clients were more likely to terminate treatment than middle class clients, Auld and Myers (1954) postulated that poor clients did not receive the full rewards of therapy because therapists did not understand their communication style or life experiences. Along these lines, Bernstein (1964) described the form of communication utilized by working class individuals as

> a code which does not facilitate the verbal elaboration of meaning; it is a code which does not help the user put into words his intent, his unique purposes, beliefs and motivations. It also does not help him to receive such communications from others. (p. 56)

Bernstein's (1964) perspective was widely shared by psychotherapists of the day, who often viewed poor and working class clients as "hostile" people (Lorion, 1974a, p. 344) who lacked insight, intelligence, and overall verbal ability (Bernstein, 1964), all of which would seem to render them inappropriate candidates for psychotherapy.

At the same time, when poor people were encountered by clinicians, they were more likely to receive psychiatric diagnoses—and specifically, to be diagnosed as psychotic—than were their middle class and wealthy counterparts, as revealed by Hollingshead and Redlich (1953). In their influential studies of social class patterns in the provision of psychiatric services, Hollingshead and Redlich (1953) found that poor and working class clients were significantly less likely to be receive therapy than middle and upper class clients, with 73.7% of upper class clients and 52.7% of middle class clients receiving therapy referrals, compared to a mere 16.1% of poor clients. Instead, poor clients were more likely to receive organic therapy (that is, medication) or no treatment at all.

Simultaneously regarded, then, as highly pathological and yet undesirable or unsuitable as therapy clients, poor and working class people were routinely denied psychological services (Myers & Schaffer, 1954). This trend was partially and temporarily reversed, however, through the community mental health center (CMHC) movement of the

1970s. The increased contact between poor clients and psychologists in CMHCs promoted the slow emergence of social class issues within the psychological literature, and psychologists began to question the perceived unsuitability of poor clients for psychotherapy. Many did so in a way, however, that revealed the tenacity of existing biases against the poor. Heitler (1976), for example, argued "against premature exclusion of lower-class patients from the more traditional forms of expressive psychotherapy" (p. 339) but went on to repeatedly label poor clients as "unsophisticated," proclaiming the usefulness of pre-therapy preparation programs that "socialize" poor clients and help to manage their unrealistic expectations about therapy (p. 345). By contrast, Lorion (1974a) suggested that researchers had overemphasized the idea that low-income people had misconceptions about psychotherapy, which supposedly acted as barriers to their treatment. To investigate this hypothesis, Lorion (1974b) administered the Mental Health Attitude Survey to psychotherapy clinic applicants from diverse social classes and found no significant effects of social class or gender on mental health attitudes or treatment expectations. Instead, Lorion (1974b) observed that misconceptions about psychotherapy were in fact found among members of all social classes. Siassi and Messer (1976) documented the ways in which negative stereotypes held by therapists could detrimentally impact the treatment of poor clients. In particular, these authors explained that therapists who view poor clients as "primitive" and impulsive were likely to "keep the patient at arm's length" (p. 34). This tendency—what Bernice Lott (2002) would later call "distancing from the poor"—inhibits therapists from establishing rapport with poor clients, who may then experience this therapeutic distance as rejection. Lorion (1974a) noted that, rather than considering the impact of such negative attitudes and biases, therapists often attributed their treatment failures to poor clients themselves, ultimately coming to view them as a "waste" of resources (p. 345).

More recently, Schnitzer (1996) observed similar biases among her colleagues and trainees at a community-based mental health clinic. She summarized the operation of these biases as narratives that mental health practitioners pass on anecdotally regarding their poor clients, narratives that align with common, negative stereotypes about people living in poverty. For example, one such story line maintains that poor clients just "don't come in," (Schnitzer, 1996, p. 574), which translates as attributions of irresponsibility or lack of motivation. Such conclusions by middle class professionals fail to account for the vicissitudes of life in poverty, which are shaped by such necessities as dependence on public transportation and constant, often unpredictable interactions with civic bureaucracies (J. Smith, 2000).

Scholars, therefore, have suggested for decades that unacknowledged classist beliefs can hinder relationships between class-privileged professionals and their poor clients. Lott and Bullock (2007) offered direction as to how such classist distancing can be counteracted, encouraging psychologists to increase their awareness of negative stereotyping of the poor as they examine the value systems that sustain these biases. In particular, class-privileged people can benefit from better understanding the common attributions for poverty and wealth. For example, internal attributions of poverty and endorsement of the Protestant work ethic—a values system that links success to hard work and discipline—have been found to be related to negative stereotypes of poor people (Cozzarelli, Wilkinson, & Tagler, 2001). In contrast, people who recognize the external factors that contribute to poverty—including prejudice and discrimination in hiring and wages, shortage of well-paying jobs, and exploitation by employers—have more positive feelings toward poor people (Cozzarelli et al., 2001). Multicultural and social justice curricula typically comprise opportunities to learn about the sociohistorical foundations of oppressions such as racism and sexism; by extending this learning paradigm to the structural and external factors that contribute to poverty and wealth, we can begin to dislodge the notion that people are individually responsible (or to blame) for their social class positions, thereby undermining false constructions of poor people as inherently inferior (Smith, 2010).

Psychotherapists and Poor Women

Psychology's consideration of poor women has taken place against a historical backdrop according to which not only the poor, but also women themselves, were viewed largely in terms of their deficiencies (Chesler, [1972] 1997). Freud famously helped set this tone with his view of women's problematic psychosexual development, and moreover developed purportedly universal theories of human psychological development based upon the experiences of his educated, class-privileged clients (Rendon, 1996). Furthermore, psychotherapists have traditionally encouraged the acceptance of restrictive sex roles as important to optimal mental health and development, as revealed by Broverman, Broverman, Clarkson, Rosenkrantz, and Vogel (1970). Working from the result of a previous study that found wide consensus as to the qualities that are typically found in men and women (Rosenkrantz, Vogel, Bee, Broverman, & Broverman, 1968), the researchers asked male and female mental health practitioners to identify the traits associated with healthy men, women, and adults in general. In this study, mental health practitioners assigned desirable masculine and feminine traits to healthy men, who were described as both *ambitious* and *warm*. Healthy women, on the other hand, were not assigned desirable masculine qualities. In fact, they were only credited with half of the available desirable feminine qualities, having been typically portrayed as *emotional* and *submissive*. In the eyes of these therapists, therefore, the "healthy woman" was assumed to be largely lacking in positive psychosocial attributes as compared to men; moreover, the qualities attributed to the "healthy woman" were also significantly different from those assigned to the "healthy adult," who more closely matched the "healthy man." Even "healthy" women, therefore, were seen by therapists as somehow inadequate by general adult standards—standards that appeared to be calibrated to the experiences and perspectives of "healthy" men.

Extant research regarding psychotherapy with poor women is limited and narrow in scope, addressing primarily conventional treatments and depressive symptomatology. In a recent review of the literature, Levy and O'Hara (in press) identified 11 clinical trials in the past 30 years that documented therapeutic interventions addressing depression in poor women. Grote, Bledsoe, Swartz, and Frank (2004), for example, discussed the potential usefulness of interpersonal therapy (IPT) as a culturally relevant intervention among poor women. IPT focuses on understanding problems in an interpersonal context, and is a strengths-based approach that encourages women to participate in pleasurable activities and to bolster support systems. Accordingly, Grote et al. (2004) emphasized that depression arises from an interpersonal context—often stemming from social isolation and interpersonal problems—rather than from conflicts among intrapsychic forces. However, the authors also acknowledged that IPT interventions do not change poor women's environments, and thus are not necessarily effective in addressing what Belle and Doucet (2003) called the "depressogenic" and anxiety-creating effects of poverty itself (p. 109). Perhaps because of these considerations, IPT has been alternatively shown to be effective and ineffective in treating psychological distress among poor women. On the one hand, IPT-based interventions have been shown to effectively alleviate post-traumatic stress symptoms (Krupnick, Green, Stockton, Miranda, Krause, & Mete, 2008) and postpartum depression for poor women (Zlotnick, Johnson, Miller, Pearlstein, & Howard, 2001). Conversely, when implementing an IPT-based intervention that focused on stress management, motherhood role transition, anticipating interpersonal problems, and developing conflict-resolution skills, Crockett, Zlotnick, Davis, Payne, and Washington (2008) found that pregnant, low-income African American women from rural areas did not report significantly lower depressive symptoms or parental stress three months postpartum than women who received standard medical, prenatal care.

Cognitive-behavioral therapy (CBT) is another form of treatment whose efficacy for women living in poverty has been studied. Research suggests that CBT can help reduce depressive symptoms among poor women (Foster, 2007; Miranda, Chung, Green, Krupnick, Siddique, Revicki, & Belin, 2003; Peden, Rayens, & Hall, 2005), particularly when it is paired with other social services (Ammerman, Putnam, Stevens, Holleb, Novak, & Van Ginkel, 2005; Miranda, Azocar, Organista, Dwyer, & Areane, 2003). These results are not unequivocal, however: McKee, Zayas, Fletcher, Boyd, and Nam (2006) studied the impact of a three-component intervention combining cognitive-behavioral treatment, psychoeducation, and social-support-building. The intervention did not demonstrate significant effects beyond the other services routinely offered by clinic workers (such as individual counseling and support groups) for poor women of color, although women in both conditions showed reductions in depressive symptoms. Reflecting upon the development of this intervention, Zayas, McKee, and Jankowski (2004) suggested that a true collaboration with community members could have created a program that was more relevant, culturally sensitive, and effective with regard to their clients:

> We encountered differences in what researchers consider relevant patient outcomes and what patients think are relevant outcomes for themselves. Women described themselves as stressed, not depressed; thus, those elements of the intervention aimed toward reducing depressive symptoms may have seemed irrelevant to many women. We learned that getting

> social support or psychoeducational information, having a compassionate listener, or learning about available childcare was more important to them than reducing depression or engaging in pleasurable activities. Participatory research strategies that included patients' and other stakeholders' voices in all stages of the project, even if it involved modifying the goals initially set for the study, would have created a better match in the preferred outcomes of patients and researchers. (p. 506)

Zayas et al.'s (2004) take-away point is an important one. First, their message is not that conventional therapies such as IPT and CBT are necessarily useless among poor women and other clients who live in poverty; rather, counselors should not *assume* that their conventional psychotherapy "toolboxes" contain interventions that are likely to be useful and relevant in the context of poverty. Second, the best way to determine what services might be most useful in a given community is to seek answers to that question in partnership with community members themselves. As the authors noted, participatory strategies represent an approach to such partnerships, as will be described in the following section.

Emerging Approaches to Poverty in Feminist Multicultural Counseling

Feminist and multicultural therapists have begun to move beyond conventional "medical model" treatments to contribute social justice theory, interventions, and actions that can function to subvert the invisibility of the poor generally and of poor women specifically. Many of the characteristics of these approaches can be summed up by the six themes that Goodman and her colleagues (2004) described as foundational to feminist, multicultural, and social justice counseling work: "(a) ongoing self-examination, (b) sharing power, (c) giving voice, (d) facilitating consciousness raising, (e) building on strengths, and (f) leaving clients with tools for social change" (Goodman et al., 2004, p. 798). The ways in which feminist and multicultural therapists have acted on these themes can be expressed as a continuum of alternative approaches ranging from interventions that share much in common with conventional therapeutic dyads to those that function at the community level to incorporate pro-social action and advocacy (Smith, 2010).

Within this continuum, approaches that are closest in format to mainstream psychotherapy can be thought of as socially just, *transformed counseling/psychotherapy* modalities. Feminist therapy can be considered an example of such a modality in and of itself, in that "clients learn to distinguish between internal/psychological and external/social aspects of issues they are dealing with, and to identify both personal change and social change strategies that can be used to deal with these respective areas" (Enns, 2004, p. 12). A specific example of such an approach is Relational Cultural Therapy (RCT; e.g., Miller & Stiver, 1997), developed by feminist theorists and therapists at the Wellesley College Centers for Women. According to RCT theory, individual growth is facilitated by a context of interpersonal connection; the operation of structural forms of oppression such as racism, sexism, and classism are conceptualized as causing profound, chronic disconnections that injure both individuals and society. Already we can see that RCT refutes taken-for-granted patriarchal narratives that fault women who prefer to live in a context of affiliation—instead, affiliation and mutuality are positioned as an optimal medium for personal growth. Moreover, this valuing of mutuality extends to the therapeutic dyad itself, in that therapists and clients are understood to work together collaboratively and to grow in concert: when a therapist has truly joined a client within an RCT intervention, "something happens *in the therapist*: she is changed" (Miller & Stiver, 1997; italics added). RCT therefore can offer special relevance for poor clients and women in that it inherently contradicts the top-down, power-over social interactions that people in marginalized groups frequently encounter. Moreover, as Comstock, Hammer, Strentzsch, Cannon, Parsons, and Salazar (2008) pointed out, it creates a context in which

> marginalized clients can recognize where mutual engagement is possible in multicultural counseling situations, despite what individuals have been taught to expect by the larger culture. It is equally important for counselors who are privileged and/or are members of the dominant group to understand what they have been taught to expect from marginalized members of society. (p. 283)

A transformed approach to vocational theory and practice that incorporates considerations of social class and poverty was developed by David Blustein and his colleagues. Blustein et al. (2002) explored the school-to-work transition of working class young adults. Qualitative data analyses showed that young adults with lower socioeconomic status were more likely than their higher SES peers to report fewer educational resources, less job-related support from parents, less access to career-planning advice, and fewer job leads specific to career interests. The authors noted the many ways in which social class influenced these young adults' transitions from school to work, and encouraged counselors to consider the impact of environmental factors as well as internalized biases upon transition success. Correspondingly, Blustein and Fouad (2008) observed that whereas most career development theories focus on individual values and traits as a way to choose occupations, the reality is that many people do not have the opportunity and freedom to choose. In response to the absence of issues of social class, oppression, and power within career theory and practice, Blustein et al. (2008) proposed an inclusive psychology-of-working that comprised the fostering of empowerment, critical consciousness, skill building, and "scaffolding in support of volition and the role of advocacy" (p. 301). In so doing, the authors hoped to promote a transformed vocational approach that begins with relevant, effective counseling for people in all social class groups and extends to efforts to change an unjust status quo:

> The psychology-of-working perspective, through applied and research contributions, has the potential to pave a road that will inform and promote socially just and meaningful counseling practices and public policies that aim to reduce inequity in the distribution of various resources to schools and communities and to racial, ethnic, lower class, and working-class groups. (p. 306)

As Blustein et al. (2008) indicated, challenging structural barriers to clients' well-being is a key component of socially just, transformed therapeutic practice. In a chapter from *The Handbook for Social Justice in Counseling Psychology*, Toporek and Chope (2006) presented specific issues for counselors to consider with regard to the incorporation of advocacy into counseling practice. A counselor's role, they explained, can be to support a client through *self-advocacy*, to *advocate on behalf of the client*, or to be a *social change agent*, in which case counselors act in support of social issues by participating in efforts to shape legislation and institutional policies. Counselors can help clients feel empowered to advocate for themselves by helping them to plan a course of action, anticipate and prepare for obstacles, and identify important community resources, allies, and sources of information. In so doing, counselors should be knowledgeable about laws and institutional policies and practices that affect clients' everyday lives. Toporek and Chope (2006) encouraged counselors to actively advocate for clients when they themselves have "access to power, beyond that of the client, that is critical to resolving the problem" (p. 283); however, counselors should only assume this role in conjunction with clients' own acts of self-advocacy. Counselors who do not engage clients as partners in this process may actually function to disempower their clients.

Toporek and Chope (2006) furthermore highlighted "informed consent, adherence to client goals, and limits of competence" as key ethical considerations in social justice work (p. 280). In obtaining informed consent prior to advocacy work, counselors should fully disclose any potential interventions; because systemic change may be a goal, counselors must also discuss with the client the potential impact of the intervention on the client and the community. Only after discussions of possible positive and negative outcomes can clients make truly informed decisions about how to proceed—and as the work unfolds, "the psychologist must adhere to the client's wishes" (p. 280), should she decide not to pursue these goals. Toporek and Chope (2006) emphasized that clients' choices should always come before social justice aims if the two are in conflict. Finally, counselors must be open with clients about the extent of their expertise and abilities, and should be willing to make referrals when clients would be better served by specialists from other fields.

Co-created therapeutic interventions are less similar to conventional practice, and are not forms of psychotherapy at all. They are interventions created by practitioners in collaboration with clients or community members, such as the community-based group modalities based on spoken word performance and poetry described by Smith, Chambers, and Bratini (2009). In this example, therapist Debbie-Ann Chambers was faced with the undertaking of developing a counseling intervention in a youth organization in a poor urban community—a community where the young people informed her directly that they wanted nothing to do with conventional mental health services. Rather than conclude that the site and/or its constituents were unsuited to counseling work, Chambers changed the work. She learned from the teens that they did, in fact, deeply value the opportunity to express their feelings. Their preferred modality, however, was through poetry and rhyming, so together, Chambers and the teens collaborated in the creation of a group based on writing and sharing poetry. Do such interventions qualify as counseling practice? Chambers concluded that a social justice context requires us to answer in the affirmative:

> Other practices which met the needs of the students but that broke with traditional methods of doing therapy included counseling students outside of the building while walking down the street, sitting on the sidewalk steps, or playing chess with the students. Some of these practices grew out of the logistical constraints of the building, which, as mentioned, were created by financial limitations.... [D]uring these interactions I observed self-reflection, insight, and eventual behavior change comparable to any that I had facilitated within more traditional therapeutic environments. As a practitioner, I have seen that there are many ways to achieve an end goal, and I believe that participatory modalities are essential to our work in communities that are skeptical of traditional models as a result of their histories of systematic oppression. (Smith, Chambers, & Bratini, 2009, p. 164).

At the end of the continuum farthest from conventional modalities are *community praxis* interventions. These interventions not only partner counselors with community members in collaborative efforts, they also result in programming for well-being that incorporates collective prosocial action. The ROAD (Reaching Out About Depression) project described by Goodman et al. (2007) exemplifies community praxis. ROAD is a multifaceted project that was inspired by a support group comprising poor women. The first component was a supportive workshop series exploring the experience of depression among women living in poverty. The workshops were originally facilitated by counseling graduate students, but the community participants learned to conduct the workshops themselves, subsequently joining the facilitation team. The second component of the program was the resource team, an advocacy group within which community women were matched with law students and counseling students to collectively take on such systemic issues as layoffs and threatened evictions. Programs like ROAD correspond well to the description of successful interventions in the context of poverty offered by the Division 35 (Society for the Psychology of Women) Task Force on Women, Poverty, and Public Assistance (APA, 1998). The characteristics of such programs, according to the Task Force, include being community-focused, collaborative, and addressed to clients as individuals who are part of a larger social context. Such interventions transcend the fragmented, bureaucratic nature of typical human services programming; consequently, "in these programs, no one tells a client that this may be what you need, but helping you get it is 'outside our jurisdiction' or 'not part of my job' (Schorr & Schorr, 1988)" (APA, 1998).

We suggest that participatory action research (PAR) projects also constitute community praxis interventions (Smith & Romero, 2010). PAR is first and foremost an approach to the creation of knowledge through which professional researchers partner with community members to identify important issues and problems, study them together, and then formulate action based on the results. This collaborative, democratic method of seeking knowledge allows for the "expression of meaning that represents (because it comes from) lives and worldview other than those characteristic of university settings and other elite locations" (Smith, 2010, p. 117). One of the elements of PAR, therefore, is the sharing of decision-making power between professional and community co-researchers. When Michelle Fine and her colleagues (2003) studied the impact of college on women in prison, one of her inmate co-researchers reflected, "Most research on prisons is conducted by outside investigators. However, there is an incredible source of skills right inside these walls.... Just because I am in prison does not negate the fact that I am also a competent researcher" (p. 188). Ultimately, such partnerships create an interpersonal context in which members support and challenge each other as they build self-efficacy and critical consciousness. Along these lines, PAR co-researchers have attested to the personal and collective growth-enhancing impact of these participations (Foster-Fishman, Nowell, Deacon, Nievar, & McCann, 2005; Smith, 2010; Smith & Romero, 2010).

Concluding Comments and Future Directions

Feminist and multicultural scholars have highlighted the absence of the voices of poor people from psychological literature (Lott, 2002), particularly the experiences and perspectives of poor women (Reid, 1993; Saris & Johnston-Robledo, 2000). Through their shared social justice values, feminist and multicultural counseling psychologists can address this absence by incorporating considerations of social class and classism into their contextualized analyses of gender, race, and other identities. This work obviously begins with an attitudinal shift: a willingness to learn about social class and a commitment to *see* classism. Subsequently, these new directions will obviously require psychologists to depart from many of the familiar practices in which they were trained, and in some cases, to depart from their offices altogether. In so doing, some of the important issues that they will need to address are identified in the following paragraphs.

Currently, although feminist, multicultural, and social justice theories have gained currency within counseling psychology discourse, many of us still employ techniques that are primarily or entirely based on the conventional 50-minute psychotherapy hour. What innovations of practice will allow us to move beyond conventional roles in our attempts to serve people living in poverty? Theoretical and philosophical elaborations of socially just practice have provided important inspiration and guidance for counseling psychologists, but there is a crucial need now for how-to examples from practitioners who have ventured beyond the traditional parameters of individual and group counseling. As indicated, reports of such interventions are emerging: in addition to the examples cited earlier, Aldarondo (2010) recently presented a network of services and programming meant to support and protect undocumented, unaccompanied immigrant youth; Goodman, Glenn, Bohlig, Banyard and Borges (2009) are building upon the work of the ROAD project by proposing a model called *feminist relational advocacy* that incorporates both emotional and instrumental support. We look forward to many more opportunities to learn from creative, multifaceted interventions like these.

Relatedly, many of us in academic programs continue to train students only or primarily in conventional techniques even when we describe our programs as having multicultural and/or social justice and/or feminist orientations. How can graduate programs expand their focus to *also* train students in the implementation of divergent, "psychopolitically valid" (Prilleltensky, 2003, p. 195) practices and actions in the context of poverty? It seems safe to say that the incorporation of curricula addressing social class and poverty as part of the multicultural/social justice spectrum is a necessary first step in this direction.

As psychologists create and implement new practices and actions in the context of poverty, it will be important to simultaneously develop new ways of assessing their effectiveness. Smyth and Schorr (2009) outlined the futility of applying conventional evaluation methodology to unconventional contextualized interventions. Because such interventions do not lend themselves to circumscribed, easily quantifiable outcomes, they may end up going unevaluated (and therefore unfunded), or having their most effective components trimmed to make way for more countable (yet trivial) results. Smyth and Schorr called for practitioners to envision and implement new, expanded evaluative paradigms, explaining,

> We are among those who value the push toward greater accountability. This is a time when we need more than ever to know whether what we are paying for actually translates into changed lives. Debates about which results matter, which matters can be measured, and whether it counts if you can't count it are important and worth having. But the discussions have largely been dominated by those who advocate a limited definition of evidence in the pursuit of decisive determinants of efficacy. (p. 220)

The foundations, therefore, of socially just practice in the context of poverty are available to counseling psychologists within the work of feminist and multicultural scholars—qualitative researchers like Chalifoux (1996), whose investigation allowed poor women to name their experiences and talk back to psychologists; or social psychologists like Lott and Bullock (2007), who elucidated the importance of understanding social class membership in relation to power; or Lisa Goodman and her colleagues (2007), who reconceptualized counseling practice to directly incorporate social justice action and advocacy. Building upon these foundations will allow counseling psychologists to put their practice to work in the spirit of what Schorr (1999) called the "heroic idea" that underlies the best programs and services in poor communities:

> the idea that we are all interconnected, that we're all in this together; that we must share the burdens and pool some of our rich resources so that all our children will reach adulthood with a realistic stake in the American dream, so that we can achieve our best possibilities as a nation. (p. 423)

References

Albelda, R. Badgett, M. V. L., Schneebaum, A., & Gates, G. J. (2009). Poverty in the lesbian, gay, and bisexual community. Retrieved on September 25, 2009, from the web site of the Williams Institute at http://www.law.ucla.edu/williamsinstitute/pdf/LGBPovertyReport.pdf.

Aldarondo, E. (February 2010). *Promoting the human rights and well-being of unaccompanied immigrant minors.* Workshop conducted at the 27th Annual Teachers College Winter Roundtable on Cultural Psychology and Education, Teachers College, Columbia University, New York.

Allen, L. & Britt, D. (1983). Social class, mental health, and mental illness. In R. Felner, L. Jason, J. Moritsugu, & S. Farber (Eds.), *Preventative psychology: Theory, research, and practice* (pp. 149–161). New York: Pergamon.

American Psychological Association (1998). Making "welfare to work" really work. Report of the Division 35 Task Force on Women, Poverty, and Public Assistance. Retrieved on February 5, 2011, from http://www.apa.org/pi/women/programs/poverty/welfare-to-work.aspx

American Psychological Association (2003). Multicultural guidelines on education and training,research, practice, and organizational development for psychologists. *American Psychologist, 58*, 377–402.

Ammerman, R. T., Putnam, F. W., Stevens, J., Holleb, L. J., Novak, A. L., & Van Ginkel, J. B. (2005). In-home cognitive behavior therapy for depression: An adapted treatment for first-time mothers in home visitation. *Best Practices in Mental Health, 1*, 1–14.

Auld, F., & Myers, J. K. (1954). Contributions to a theory for selecting psychotherapy patients. *Journal of Clinical Psychology, 10*, 56–60.

Belle, D. & Doucet, J. (2003). Poverty, inequality and discrimination as sources of depression among women. *Psychology of Women Quarterly, 27*, 101–113.

Bernstein, B. (1964). Social class, speech systems, and psychotherapy. *The British Journal of Sociology, 15*, 54–64.

Blustein, D. L., Chavez, A. P., Diemer, M. A., Gallagher, L. A., Marshall, K. G., Siring, S., & Bhati, K. S. (2002). Voices of the forgotten half: The role of social class in the school-to-work transition. *Journal of Counseling Psychology, 49*(3), 311–323.

Blustein, D. L. & Fouad, N. A. (2008). Changing face of vocational psychology: The transforming world of work. In W. B. Walsh (Ed.), *Biennial Review of Counseling* (pp. 129–156). New York: Psychology Press, Taylor & Francis Group.

Blustein D. L., Kenna, A. C., Gill, N., & DeVoy, J. E. (2008). The psychology of working: A new framework for counseling practice and public policy. *The Career Development Quarterly, 56*, 294–308.

Boraas, S. & Rodgers, W. M. (2003). How does gender play a role in the earnings gap? An update. *Monthly Labor Review,* 2003, March, 9–15. Retrieved from http://www.bls.gov/opub/mlr/2003/03/art2full.pdf.

Brady, D., & Kall, D. (2008). Nearly universal, but somewhat distinct: The feminization of poverty in affluent Western democracies, 1969–2000. *Social Science Research, 37*, 976–1007.

Broverman, I. K., Broverman, D. M., Clarkson, F. E., Rosenkrantz, P., & Vogel, S. R. (1970). Sex-role stereotypes and clinical judgments of mental health. *Journal of Consulting Psychology, 34*, 1–7.

Brown, L. S. (1990). The meaning of a multicultural perspective for theory-building in feminist therapy. *Women and Therapy, 9*, 1–22.

Chesler, P. ([1972] 1997). *Women and madness*. New York: Four Walls Eight Windows.

Chalifoux, B. (1996). Speaking up: White working class women in therapy. In M. Hill & E. D. Rothblum (Eds.), *Classism and feminist therapy* (pp. 25–34). New York: Harrington Park.

Collins, C., & Yeskel, F. (2005). *Economic apartheid in America: A primer on economic inequality and insecurity.* New York: The New Press.

Comstock, D., Hammer, T., Strentzsch, J., Cannon, K., Parsons, J., & Salazar II, G. (2008). Relational-cultural theory: A framework for bridging relational, multicultural, and social justice competencies. *Journal of Counseling and Development, 86*, 279–287.

Cozzarelli, C., Wilkinson, A. V., & Tagler, M. J. (2001). Attitudes toward the poor and attributions for poverty. *Journal of Social Issues, 57*, 207–228.

Crockett, K., Zlotnick, C., Davis, M., Payne, N., & Washington, R. (2008) A depression prevention intervention for rural low-income African-American pregnant women at risk for postpartum depression. *Archives of Women's Mental Health, 11*, 319–325.

DeNavas-Walt, C., Procter, B. D., & Smith, J. A. (2009). Insurance, poverty, and health insurance coverage in the United States: 2008. Retrieved from http://www.census.gov/prod/2009pubs/p60-236.pdf.

DeNavas-Walt, C., Procter, B. D., & Smith, J. A. (2010). Insurance, poverty, and health insurance coverage in the United States: 2009. Retrieved from http://www.census.gov/prod/2010pubs/p60-238.pdf.

Denny, P. A. (1986). Women and poverty: A challenge to the intellectual and therapeutic integrity of feminist therapy. *Women and Therapy, 5*, 51–64.

Ellwood, D. T., & Jencks, D. T. (2002). The spread of single parent families in the United States since 1960. Cambridge, MA: Harvard University.

Enns, C. Z. (2004). Feminist theories and feminist psychotherapies. New York: Haworth.

Fine, M., Torre, M. E., Boudin, K., Bowen, I., Clark, J., Hylton, D. et al. (2003). Participatory action research from within and beyond prison bars. In P. M. Camic, J. E. Rhodes, & L. Yardley (Eds.), *Qualitative research in psychology: Expanding perspectives in methodology and design* (pp. 173–198). Washington, DC: American Psychological Association.

Foster, R. M. P. (2007). Treating depression in vulnerable urban women: A feasibility study of clinical outcomes in community service settings. *American Journal of Orthopsychiatry, 77*, 443–453.

Foster-Fishman, P., Nowell, B., Deacon, Z., Nievar, M. N., & McCann, P. (2005). Using methods that matter: The impact of reflection, dialogue, and voice. *American Journal of Community Psychology, 36*, 275–291.

Fouad, N. A., & Brown, M. T. (2000). Role of race and social class in development: Implications for counseling psychology. In S. D. Brown & R. W. Lent (Eds.), *Handbook of counseling psychology* (3rd ed.) (pp. 379–408). Hoboken, NJ: Wiley.

Gilbert, D. (2008). *The American class structure in an age of growing inequality.* Los Angeles: Pine Forge Press.

Goodman, L. A., Liang, B., Helms, J. E., Latta, R. E., Sparks, E., & Weintraub, S. (2004). Training counseling psychologists as social justice agents: Feminist and multicultural perspectives. *The Counseling Psychologist, 32*, 793–837.

Goodman, L. A., Litwin, A., Bohlig, A., Weintraub, S. R., Green, A., Walker, J., et al. (2007). Applying feminist theory to community practice: A multilevel empowerment intervention for low-income women with depression. In E. Aldarondo (Ed.), *Advancing social justice through clinical practice* (pp. 265–290). Mahwah, NJ: Erlbaum.

Goodman, L. A., Glenn, A., Bohlig, A., Banyard V., and Borges, A. (2009). Feminist relational advocacy: Processes and outcomes from the perspective of low-income women with depression. *The Counseling Psychologist, 37*, 848–876.

Grote, N. K., Bledsoe, S. E., Swartz, H. A., & Frank, E. (2004) Culturally relevant psychotherapy for perinatal depression in low-income ob/gyn patients. *Clinical Social Work Journal, 32,* 327–347.

Grusky, D. B., & Ku, M. C. (2008). Gloom, doom, and inequality. In D. B. Grusky (Ed.), *Social stratification* (pp. 2–28). Philadelphia: Westview Press.

Heitler, J. B. (1976). Preparatory techniques in initiating expressive psychotherapy with lower class, unsophisticated patients. *Psychological Bulletin, 83,* 339–352.

Hill, M., & Rothblum, E. D. (1996). *Classism and Feminist Therapy: Counting Costs.* Binghamton, NY: Harrington Park Press.

Hollingshead, A. B. & Redlich, F. C. (1953). Social Stratification and psychiatric disorders. *American Sociological Review, 18,* 163–169.

Johnson, D. C. (March 29, 2007). The income gap is widening, data shows. *New York Times.* Retrieved from http://www.nytimes.com/2007/03/29/business/29tax.html.

Kline, S. (March, 2006). Women still underrepresented among highest earners. United States Department of Labor. Retrieved from http://www.bls.gov/opub/ils/pdf/opbils55.pdf.

Krupnick, J. L., Green, B. L., Stockton, P., Miranda, J., Krause, E., & Mete, M. (2008). Group interpersonal psychotherapy for low-income women with posttraumatic stress disorder. *Psychotherapy Research, 18,* 497–507.

Legal Momentum (2009). Women's poverty. Retrieved on October 24, 2010, from http://www.legalmomentum.org/issues/womens-poverty/women-poverty.html

Leondar-Wright, B. (2005). *Class matters.* Gabriola Island, Canada: New Society Publishers.

Levy, L. B., & O'Hara, M. W. (in press). Psychotherapeutic interventions for depressed, low-income women: A review of the literature. *Clinical Psychology Review.*

Liu, W. M. (2001). Expanding our understanding of multiculturalism: Developing a social class worldview model. In D. B. Pope-Davis & H. L. K. Coleman (Eds.), *The intersection of race, class, and gender in counseling psychology* (pp. 127–170). Thousand Oaks, CA: Sage.

Liu, W. M., Ali, S., Soleck, G., Hopps, J., Dunston, K., & Pickett, T. (2004). Using social class in counseling psychology research. *Journal of Counseling Psychology, 51,* 3–18.

Lorion, R. P. (1974a). Patient and therapist variables in the treatment of low-income patients. *Psychological Bulletin,* 6, 344–354.

Lorion, R. P. (1974b). Social class, treatment attitudes, and expectations. *Journal of Consulting and Clinical Psychology, 42,* 920.

Lott, B. (2002). Cognitive and behavioral distancing from the poor. *American Psychologist, 57,* 100–110.

Lott, B., & Bullock, H. E. (2007). *Psychology and economic injustice: Personal, professional, and political intersections.* Washington, DC: American Psychological Association.

Marable, M. (2000). *How capitalism underdeveloped Black America.* Chicago: South End Press

Mckee, D., Zayas, L. H., Fletcher, J., Boyd, R.C., & Nam, S. (2006). Results of an intervention to reduce perinatal depression among low-income minority women in community primary care. *Journal of Social Service Research, 32,* 63–81.

Miller, J. B., & Stiver, I. P. (1997). *The healing connection.* Boston: Beacon Press.

Miranda, J., Azcar, F., Organista, K., Dwyer, E., & Areane, P. (2003). Treatment of depression among impoverished primary care patients from ethnic minority groups. *Psychiatric Services, 54,* 219–225.

Miranda, J., Chung, J. Y., Green, B. L., Krupnick, J., Siddique, J., Revicki, D. A., & Belin, T. (2003). Treating depression in predominately low-income young minority women: A randomized controlled trial. *Journal of American Medical Association, 290,* 57–65.

Myers, J. K., & Schaffer, L. (1954). Social stratification and psychiatric practice: A study of an outpatient clinic. *American Sociological Review, 19,* 307–310.

Pearce, D. (1978). The feminization of poverty. *Urban and Social Change Review,* 11, 28–36.

Peden, A. R., Rayens, M. K., & Hall, L.A. (2005). A community-based depression prevention intervention with low-income single mothers. *Journal of the American Psychiatric Nurses Association, 11,* 18–25.

Pressman, S. (2003). Feminist explanations for the feminization of poverty. *Journal of Economic Issues, 37,* 353–361.

Prilleltensky, I. (2003). Understanding, resisting, and overcoming oppression: Toward psychopolitical validity. *American Journal of Community Psychology, 31,* 195–201.

Reid, P. T. (1995). Poor women in psychological research: Shut up and shut out. In N. R. Goldberger & J. B. Veroff (Eds.), *The culture and psychology reader* (pp. 184–204). New York: New York University Press.

Rendon, M. (1996). Psycho-analysis in an historical-economic perspective. In R. M. Perez-Foster, M. Moskowitz, and R. A. Javier (Eds.), *Reaching Across Boundaries of Culture and Class: Widening the Scope of Psycotherapy* (pp. 47–67). Northvale, NJ: Jason Aronson.

Rosenkrantz, P. S., Vogel, S. R., Bee, H., Broverman, I. K., & Broverman, D. M. (1968). Sex-role stereotypes and self-concepts in college students. *Journal of Consulting and Clinical Psychology, 32,* 287–295.

Saris, R. N., & Johnston-Robledo, I. (2000). Poor women are still shut out of mainstream psychology. *Psychology of Women Quarterly, 24,* 233–235.

Schnitzer, P. K. (1996) "They don't come in!" Stories told, lessons taught about poor families in therapy. *American Journal of Orthopsychiatry, 66,* 572–582.

Schorr, L. B., & Schorr, D. (1988). *Within our reach: Breaking the cycle of disadvantage.* New York: Doubleday.

Schorr, L. B. (1999). Fighting poverty and building community: Learning from programs that work. *American Journal of Orthopsychiatry, 69,* 420–423.

Semega, J. (September 2009). Men's and women's earnings by state: 2008 American community survey. Retrieved from http://www.census.gov/prod/2009pubs/acsbr08-3.pdf.

Siassi, I., & Messer, S. B. (1976). Psychotherapy with patients from lower socioeconomic groups. *American Journal of Psychotherapy, 30,* 29–40.

Smith, J. M. (2000). Psychotherapy with people stressed by poverty. In A. N. Sabo & L. Havens (Eds.), *Real world guide to psychotherapy practice* (pp. 71–92). Cambridge, MA: Harvard University.

Smith, L. (2005). Psychotherapy, classism, and the poor: Conspicuous by their absence. *American Psychologist, 60,* 687–696.

Smith, L. (2008). Positioning classism within psychology's social justice agenda. *The Counseling Psychologist, 36,* 895–924.

Smith, L., Chambers, D. A., and Bratini, L. (2009). When oppression is the pathogen: The participatory development of socially-just mental health practice. *American Journal of Orthopsychiatry, 79,* 159–168.

Smith, L. (2010). *Psychology, poverty, and the end of social exclusion: Putting our practice to work*. New York: Teachers College Press.

Smith, L. & Romero, L. (2010). Psychological interventions in the context of poverty: Participatory action research as practice. *American Journal of Orthopsychiatry, 80,* 12–25.

Smyth, K. F., & Schorr, L. B. (2009). A lot to lose: A call to rethink what constitutes evidence in finding social interventions that work. Malcolm Wiener Center for Social Policy at Harvard Kennedy School of Government, working paper series.

Stern, S. M. (2008). Poverty dynamics: 20012003. Retrieved from http://www.census.gov/hhes/www/poverty/publications/dynamics01/PovertyDynamics.pdf.

Sue, D. W., Bernier, J., Durran, M., Feinberg, L., Pedersen, P., Smith, E.,& Vasquez-Nuttall, E. (1982). Position paper: Cross-cultural counseling competencies. *Counseling Psychologist, 10,* 45–52.

Sue, D. W., Arredondo, P., & McDavis, R. J. (1992). Multicultural counseling competencies and standards: A call to the profession. *Journal of Counseling and Development, 70,* 477–483.

Toporek, R. L., & Chope, R. C. (2006). Individual, programmatic, and entrepreneurial approaches to social justice. In R. L. Toporek, L. H. Gerstein, N. A. Fouad, G. Roysircar, & T. Israel (Eds.), *Handbook for Social Justice in Counseling Psychology* (pp. 276–293). Thousand Oaks, CA: Sage.

U.S. Census Bureau (2008). Poverty status in the past 12 months [Data File]. Retrieved from http://factfinder.census.gov/servlet/STTable?_bm=y&-geo_id=01000US&-qr_name=ACS_2008_3YR_G00_S1701&-ds_name=ACS_2008_3YR_G00_.

U.S. Census Bureau (2010a). Poverty: Overview/highlights. Retrieved from http://www.census.gov/hhes/www/poverty/about/overview/index.html.

U.S. Census Bureau (2010b). U.S. Census Bureau releases first set of 5-year American Community Survey Estimates. Retrieved from http://www.census.gov/newsroom/releases/archives/american_community_survey_acs/cb10-cn90.html.

U.S. Department of Labor (March 2010). A profile of the working poor, 2008. Retrieved from http://www.bls.gov/cps/cpswp2008.pdf.

Whalen, M. W., Fowler-Lese, K., Barber, J., Williams, E., Judge, A., Nilsson, J., et al. (2004). Counseling practice with feminist-multicultural perspectives. *Journal of Multicultural Counseling and Development, 32,* 379–389.

Zayas, L. H., McKee, M. D., & Jankowski, K. R. B. (2004). Adapting psychosocial intervention research to urban primary care environments: A case example. *Annals of Family Medicine, 2,* 504–508.

Zlotnick, C., Johnson, S. L., Miller, I. W., Pearlstein, T., & Howard, M. (2001). Postpartum depression in women receiving public assistance: A pilot study of interpersonal-therapy oriented group intervention. *American Journal of Psychiatry, 158,* 638–640.

Zweig, M. (2000). *The working class majority.* Ithaca, NY: Cornell University Press.

CHAPTER

9 Realidades Culturales y Identidades Dimensionadas: The Complexities of Latinas' Diversities

Alberta M. Gloria *and* Jeanett Castellanos

Abstract

To understand the realities and complexities of Latinas' multidimensionality of identities, this chapter addresses the different sociocontextual considerations and cultural dimensions and roles with which they contend. Implementing a gender-cultural strength lens, the ways by which Latinas infuse their multiplicity of identities as a strength-based and powerful process are examined. Through the bridging of Latinas' cultural and familial *costumbres, valores, y practicas culturales* (customs, values, and cultural practices), the chapter emphasizes the energetically spiritual transmissions of Latinas' internal strength *patron* (blueprint) while (re)defining *una buena mujer* and the process of tranformation to *una* Latina *poderosa* (a powerful Latina).

Key Words: Latinas, identities, cultural values, with-group heterogeneity, gender roles, spirituality, *mestizaj*

Long-standing questions for Latinas are those addressing *¿Quién somos?* (Who are we?), *¿Cómo estamos*? (How are we?), and *¿Qué somos?* (What are we?). From whose voice, from what perception or assumption, or from what role and context are Latinas defined? All too frequently, Latinas are aggregated as a single group, with similar values, beliefs, and behaviors, without consideration of the dimensionalized identities and multiplicity of roles, influencing contexts and circumstances, and complex nuances that create the lived experiences of different Latinas in the United States. In elucidating the intertwining of Latinas' identities and processes, it is necessary to address considerations of context, differences, moderating processes, and cultural considerations in the theory and research of exploring and understanding *¿Quién son Latinas?* (Who are Latinas?).

Estableciendo el Contexto (Setting the Context)

To create a context in describing and lending definition to Latinas' experiences, a brief overview of general descriptors of who Latinas are within the United States is necessary. As this chapter cannot provide the scope, depth, and detail of each characteristic dimension of Latinas, select and consistently identified dimensions from which to understand Latinas are provided. Doing so will call further attention to the range and complexities inherent to Latina identities.

¿Qué es lo que me llaman—Qué es lo que me llamo? (What Am I Called—What Do I Call Myself?)

The term "Latina" in and of itself encompasses multiple identities and the aggregation of identity dimensions. First, the label "Latina" is a gendered term that intertwines gender and race/ethnicity. That is, the term "Latino" is gendered as it refers to both males and females (i.e, Latinos) or males only (i.e., Latinos). The term Latinos places males as the "standard" or norm from which females must call attention to differentiate their gender (e.g., Latino/a). The subjugation of identity through language (and terminology) is a well-known and scholarly debated conversation (Comas-Díaz, 2001; Dernersesian, 1993; Oboler, 1995) in finding voice and identity for Latinas. For example, how does a Latina identify when in a group of Latino males? If she identifies as a Latina, she is inherently placing her gender before her ethnicity and is open to criticism from her male counterparts for not having solidarity to ethnicity. Yet, she is de-emphasizing her womanhood should she identify with her ethnicity first (i.e., Latino). It is an on-going consideration to identify how both gender and ethnicity are identified simultaneously (Latina/o) in order to honor the full range of Latinas' identities. Choosing gender before ethnicity (i.e., a/o) as opposed to ethnicity prior to gender (i.e., o/a) is a seemingly small choice (i.e., spelling), yet the selection of a self-referent and self-identification is an important part of the meaning-making process for Latina identity (Comas-Díaz, 2001). The emphasis of gender before race/ethnicity (i.e., a/o versus o/a) is a political and even ideological struggle, as Latinas have been omitted or marginalized from sociocultural and sociopolitical systems and processes that are male-privileged (Dernersesian, 1993). Nonetheless, choosing a self-referent is one of the first of many layers inherent to the identity of Latinas as a means of resistance (Sandoval, 2008) and a "straddling of borders" that are often imposed by others (Viramontes, 2008, p. x).

Whether a Latina chooses a self-referent that is reflective of ethnicity (e.g., Peruana), ethnicity and geographic region (e.g., Nuyorican), sociopolitical identity (e.g., Xicana), indigenous origins (e.g., Taíno), spiritual connection and indigenous roots (e.g., Mestiza), or generational status and ethnicity (e.g., Boricua), it is the self-ascribed meaning and psychological implications that are ultimately of most relevance (Padilla, 1995; Quintana & Scull, 2009). "Hispanic" was a governmentally imposed term with colonial implications (García & Marotta, 1997), in which ethnicities were not identified as a race (Ennis, Ríos-Vargas, & Albert, 2011; Saenz, 2010), yet a racially-mixed population (Santiago-Rivera, Arredondo, & Gallardo-Cooper, 2002). The ability to name and emphasize salient dimensions of identity through self-referents has become a source of strength and resistance for many Latinas (Comas-Díaz, 2001; Gloria, 2001).

Also inherent to the term "Latina" is the combining and subsuming of vastly different ethnicities and heritages. Specifically, the within-group heterogeneity included within the pan-ethnic term of Latina/o (Comas-Díaz, 2001; Oboler, 1995) includes individuals of Mexican, Puerto Rican, and South and Central American heritage. Similarly, the term commingles and even de-emphasizes the historical and social oppressions, languages, religions, generational and immigration statuses, and processes of being Latina (Gonzalez, 2000; Oboler, 1995). Although no definitive answer has emerged from the long-standing debate as to whether the term "Hispanic" (as per U.S. Census) or "Latino" (i.e., Latina/o, Latino/a, or even Latin@) is the most culturally appropriate or accurate, this chapter will use the term "Latina" to reference a group of women who have culturally similar yet vastly different characteristics and sociocultural realities.

Dimensiones de la identidad (Dimensions of Identity)

Although a discussion of each descriptive dimension influencing Latinas is beyond the scope of this chapter, several of the most salient considerations that engender the multiple differences subsumed within the term are addressed. Despite the assumed homogeneity of Latinas, contradicting realities and processes exist. The way by which Latinas navigate and traverse the contradictions of identities and physical and psychological borders is perhaps best brought to life by the poignant poem of self and identity by Gloria Anzaldúa (1993, p. 97), "To Live in the Borderlands Means You,"

> To survive the Borderlands you must live *sin fronteras*,be a crossroads.

A Large and Growing Population

Counted as individuals of any race, Latina/os are the largest U.S. minority group (Passel, Cohn, & Lopez, 2011), with a projected population of 132.8 million by 2050 (i.e., 30% of the nation's population; Ennis et al., 2011). As of the 2010 U.S. Census, the Latina/o population was estimated at 50.5 million, or 16.3% of the total U.S. population, having increased 15.2 million over the last decade and accounting for more than half of the total U.S. population increase (i.e., 27.3 million; Ennis et al., 2011). Although exceeding four times the national population growth rate since 2000, the overall growth rate for Latina/os was lower than in previous decades (Passel et al., 2011).

Much like the previous 2000 report, Latina/os of Mexican, Puerto Rican, and Cuban origin remain the largest groups as per the 2010 census (Lopez & Dockterman, 2011). Based on country of origin, those of Mexican descent comprise 63% of the U.S. Latina/o population, followed by those of Puerto Rican (9.2%) and Cuban (3.5%) origin (Ennis et al., 2011). Yet, the diversity of Latina/os is changing considerably as the growth rate of the Guatemalan (180%), Salvadorian (152%), Colombian (93%) and Dominican (85%) country-of-origin populations rose substantially over the last decade. By comparison, the Puerto Rican (36%) and Cuban (44%) populations had a lower growth rate (Ennis et al., 2011).

As the diversity of ethnicities has changed, so have the areas in which Latina/os live. Nine states have consistently had the largest established Latina/o communities (i.e., Arizona, California, Colorado, Florida, Illinois, New Mexico, New Jersey, New York, and Texas); however, nine other states had a 100% or more increase in populations in the last ten years. Primarily in the Southeastern portion of the U.S., the Latina/o populations are steadily growing in South Carolina (148%), Alabama (145%), Tennessee (134%), Kentucky (122%), Arkansas (114%), North Carolina (111%), Mississippi (116%), Maryland (106%), and South Dakota (103%) (Passel et al., 2011). Although the numbers of Latina/os who live in the high Latina/o population states have decreased over the decades (i.e., 76% in 2010, 81% in 2000, 86% in 1990), the largest number of Latina/os continue to live in California in Los Angeles county (4.7 million) (Passel et al., 2011). Clearly, the ethnic diversity and subsequent sociopolitical processes of immigration are increasing the diaspora of Latina/os in the United States.

Immigration and Generational Status

As a function of the reason for and the process of immigration to the United States, many Latinas are challenged to define first-time and lifelong identities as "minorities" (Arredondo, 1991; Gloria, 2001; Ginorio, Gutiérrez, Cauce, & Acosta, 1995). The timing (e.g., Puerto Ricans after World War II) and context (e.g., Cubans as political refugees) for different Latina/o racial and ethnic groups coming to the United States create a sociopolitical blueprint that informs the larger conceptualization of what it means to be Latina in the United States (Gloria, 2001; Gloria & Segura-Herrera, 2004). The blueprint is further impacted by Latinas' legal status or citizenship as they adapt and integrate within their communities and access resources and services (Gonzales, 2007; Ortega, Fang, Perez, Rizzo, Carter-Pokras, Wallace, & Gelberg, 2007).

As the time from original immigration increases (i.e., familial generations born in the U.S.), there is the amplified propensity for intergenerational conflict or disagreement regarding the relevance, application, and engagement of cultural values between the generations (e.g., grandparents, parents, children) (Dennis, Basaíez, & Farahmand, 2010). Increasingly, differences in adherence to cultural values and approaches (i.e., acculturative gaps) become part of the lived experiences in claiming and living out different identities (Hurtado & Cervantez, 2009). Given that U.S.-born Latina/os are outpacing immigration as the key source of growth, Suro and Passel (2003) estimated that in the next 20 years, second-generation Latinos (i.e., the U.S.-born children of immigrants) will be the largest subpopulation of Latina/os, which will have immediate consequences for school systems (Suro & Passel, 2003). As a fast-growing and young population, Latina/o children are entering the U.S. educational school system, which is inadequately prepared to provide language resources (e.g., bilingual teachers, translators for parents and families), an integrated curriculum (e.g., Latina/o history and contributions to U.S. history), and professional training considerations (e.g., cultural competence, assessment of student persistence, cultural audits) (Quijada & Alvarez, 2006). Critical to immigration and generation status, however, is the emotional and psychological proximity to those experiences that prompted immigration (e.g., economic need, political unrest, physical violence). It is "the emotional and physical legacy of war and trauma exposure" (Kaltman, Green, Mete, Shara, & Miranda, 2010, p. 32) for Latina/o first-generation immigrants that becomes part of the survival and transmission of different values and practices that shape *Latinidad* (the meaning of being Latina/o) and *la condición de la mujer* (womanhood).

El lenguaje de la identidad (The Language of Identity)

Almost two-thirds (62%) of the 55.4 million who speak a language other than English speak Spanish (34.5 million). From 1980 to 2007, the percentage of individuals who spoke Spanish at home increased 210.8% (23.4 million more individuals) (Shin &

Kominski, 2010). Understandably, Latina/os who were non-U.S. born (73%) were more likely to speak English less than "very well," compared to U.S.-born Spanish speakers (21%). Although language ability differs based on native status for Latina/os of different ethnicities as well as socioeconomic standing, nearly half of Latina/os are bilingual (speaking Spanish at home and speaking English well to very well) (Saenz, 2010).

Although able to speak English, many Latina/os have a strong preference to *hablar Español en casa* (speak Spanish at home) (Santiago-Rivera et al., 2002). The use of Spanish has been linked to comfort and willingness to discuss personal or intimate matters (Gloria, Ruiz, & Castillo, 2004), in particular for conversations that are emotion-oriented (Echeverry, 1997; Santiago-Rivera, Altarriba, Poll, Gonzalez-Miller, & Cragun, 2009). As communication in one's native language (Spanish) is more natural and facilitates free expression, Santiago-Rivera and Altarriba (2002) argued that Spanish-English bilingual Latina/os "represent emotional words differently in their two languages and typically associate these words with a broader range of emotions in their first language..." (p. 33). Despite differences in dialect (based on region and ethnic group) and language ability, the Spanish language is frequently considered a primary process for maintaining cultural tradition and identity (Santiago-Rivera & Altarriba, 2002; Santiago-Rivera et al., 2009).

Yet, being Latina/o and being a heritage-language Spanish speaker are erroneously assumed to be synonymous (Ardila, 2005) and result in the frequent essentialization of Latina/os (e.g., "Real Latina/os speak Spanish," Gloria, 2001). Yet, there exists great variability of Spanish language mastery among Latina/os, from native Spanish speakers who speak no to very little English to those who understand or speak no Spanish at all (Ardila, 2005). This language variability is frequently an artifact of generational status, historical educational and cultural oppression, or processes of survival (Gonzalez, 2000). The blending of English and Spanish (i.e., Spanglish) creates a permanent mixture of both languages and "represents the most important contemporary linguistic phenomenon the United States has faced that has unfortunately been significantly understudied" (Ardila, 2005, p. 65). Although the use of Spanglish is frequently negatively perceived, with an undertone of stigma for Latina/os due to a loss of intergenerational language continuity by other Latina/os, the use of Spanglish can in fact bridge acculturation gaps and solidify evolving identities for Latinas. Indeed, *usando Spanglish puede crear espacios de seguridad y facilita* (using Spanglish creates spaces of security and facilitates) rapport among diverse Latinas. As there are Spanish words that do not translate easily or have the same feeling or meaning when spoken in English, the ability to share the feelings, images, and sensations of certain words in conversation can allow for connection. For example, referring to one's *familia* (family) and telling about the *comida* (food) made *en la cocina* (in the kitchen) of our *abuelitas* (grandmothers) engenders a different conversation than telling about the food made in the kitchen of our grandmothers. Again, it is not the level or sophistication of Spanish spoken; rather, feelings and stories may be rendered incomplete without a combination of Spanish and English.

Education and Socioeconomic Status

As Latinas seek to integrate and acclimate, two key factors influencing their gender and ethnic identities are education and socioeconomic status. Briefly examining but not fully encompassing Latinas' representation in education and the workforce, it is clear that there is a strong relationship between education, occupational attainment, and upward mobility (Chapa & De La Rosa, 2004; Kochhar, 2005; Thomas-Breitfeld, 2003). As a whole, Latina/os are more likely to be of low socioeconomic means and to have lower economic indices (e.g., education, employment, health insurance, and income) (Kochhar, 2005; Saenz, 2010), which influence their adjustment, adaptation, and integration. Underscoring the role of dimensionality, birthplace affects socioeconomic status and education, as foreign-born Latina/os evidence less educational attainment (e.g., lower high school graduation) and lower occupational statuses (Gonzales, 2007; Saenz, 2010). Latinas, however, face high rates of impoverishment (Cawthorne, 2008), regardless of place of birth or generation (Saenz, 2010), reflective of Vasquez's (1994) notion of Latinas being "affected by the triply oppressive experiences associated with being female, ethnic, and...poor" (p. 121).

Although underpaid and underemployed within the work force (Gonzales, 2007), Latinas continue to be viewed as wives and mothers first and foremost, which may create domestic and gender role strains (Niemann, 2004). Linked to economic empowerment and social mobility, Latinas' educational preparation and achievement is abysmal, as only 59% graduated in four years with a high school diploma (National Women's Law Center and Mexican American Legal Defense and Educational Fund, 2009). Although Latinas outpace their male counterparts through the educational pipeline (American Council on Education, 2007; Gloria, Castellanos, Scull, & Villegas, 2009), they encounter unique challenges (Rodriguez, Guido-DiBrito, Torres, & Talbot, 2000) and make familial and cultural "sacrifices" to pursue higher education (González, Jovel, & Stoner, 2004, p. 19). The quality of educational experiences is influenced by stereotyped expectations, cultural incongruity, and unwelcoming academic environments (Castellanos & Gloria, 2007), coupled with familial pressures (González et al., 2004) and guilt for moving beyond the family to pursue an education (Gloria & Castellanos, 2012).

Mediating Processes of Latina Identity: Acculturation, Enculturation, and Ethnic Identity

An accurate understanding of identity for Latinas must include the concepts of acculturation, enculturation, and traditionality to circumvent the process of essentialism and misattributions of behaviors and interactions. The notion of a universal Latina, much less the concept of a universal woman, is perilous, as it renders the understanding, meaning, and application of values and approaches of vastly different realities and lived experiences to oversimplified stereotypes and misassumptions (Gloria, 2001).

The concepts of acculturation and enculturation are two closely related yet different processes in understanding Latina experiences and identities. Considered multidimensional constructs (Alamilla, Kim, & Lam, 2010; Kohatsu, 2005), acculturation and enculturation both address psychological and cultural elements (Berry, 2007; Hurtado & Cervantez, 2009). More specifically, "psychological acculturation describes individual changes resulting from socialization to dominant cultural norms, psychological enculturation describes individual processes or changes resulting from (re)socialization to indigenous cultural norms" (Alamilla et al., 2010, p. 58). That is, acculturation encompasses a cultural exchange between the native and host culture, requiring a psychological adjustment by the recipient. In contrast, enculturation is the learning of one's own culture through socialization into and maintenance of specific practices embedded in native values and beliefs. The individual adaptations of these processes have been described as "assimilation, integration, or biculturality, separation or maintenance of traditionality, and marginalization or peripheral status in both cultures" (Gamst, Dana, Der-Karabetian, Aragón, Arellano, & Kramer, 2002, p. 480), a series of processes that can moderate Latinas' general health and well-being. For example, Latinas who experience minority stress reported higher perceived discrimination, leading to general anxiety symptoms (including tension and nervousness), somatization, and hostility (e.g., resentment, aggression) (Lechuga, 2008).

A simultaneous social-cultural process of identity-making and a person's response to their lived experiences creates ethnic identity—an individual's attitudes, values, knowledge, behaviors, preferences, and affiliation of membership to their own ethnic group (Gonzalez, Fabrett, & Knight, 2009; Ocampo, Bernal, & Knight, 1993; Quintana & Scull, 2009). Concurrent with the process of cultural socialization and maintenance, ethnic identity influences the perception of the experiences and the interpretation of the contrasting expectations for personal encounters. For instance, if a Latina self-identities as Mexican (versus Mexican American or Hispanic), her affiliation to her heritage group or host culture will influence her experiences and perceptions (Lechuga, 2008). Consequently, the straddling of two cultures and the various difficult encounters that accompany the transitional phases and ongoing adjustments of Latinas result in complex psychological functioning (Kim & Omizo, 2006).

As a plethora of research has emphasized the challenges and difficulties of balancing multiple identities, resilience models and frameworks (Hurtado & Cervantez, 2009; Zimmerman, Bingerheimer, & Notaro, 2002) emphasized the protective factors that reduce negative outcomes. Two key factors that influence the process are centrality (i.e., the extent to which an individual places importance on their racial self-concept) and public regard (i.e., one's belief and evaluation of others of one's racial and ethnic group) (French & Chavez, 2010; Sellers, Smith, Shelton, Rowley, & Chavous, 1998). As Latinas negotiate their identities and work toward being culturally-grounded, they are protected by keeping culture at the center of their processes but are simultaneously conflicted as they begin to make other identities more salient during various stages of their lives. Hence, as culture serves as a protective factor, Latinas often use *la familia* (family) as their central resource (Keefe, 1980; Marín, 1993; Padilla, 1980). Simultaneously, the cultural values when shifted by acculturation or traditionality can create cultural incongruence or familial stress (Alamilla et al., 2010; Vasquez, 1994). Moreover, the role of public regard in relation to their family is heightened if Latinas do not maintain and preserve the traditionality of cultural values passed down generationally (Gloria et al., 2004; Ramírez, 1991). Yet, it is the *mujer's* ability to navigate these conflicts and assist in the immersion and continuum of collision of differences (Anzaldúa, 1987; Arredondo, 2002) that allows her to create a seamless integration of successfully living out the multidimensions of her various evolving identities. More simply stated, it is the *mezcla de las diferencias* (intermingling of differences) that manifests a transformed reality of intersecting contrasts in which Latinas are situated.

Complexity of Roles

As Latinas seek to manage the complexity of their roles, the notion of a "wild zone" or the "... contextualization or space that applies to the mental, physical, and spiritual chaos that has enveloped many Latinas" (Arredondo, 2002, p. 308) has emerged. The challenge of identity politics, which are tied to gender, economics, sexual orientation, and spirituality, makes the wild zone and the concept of living within the borderlands of different identities relevant spaces of discussion for Latinas (Arredondo, 2002). As part of the complexity of merging and re-amassing the intersections of identities (Anzaldúa, 1987; Vasquez, 1994), Arredondo (2002) persuasively argued that Latinas must also find grounding or reestablish connection to our *raíces* (roots) of past and present *mestizas* to create opportunities for knowledge and identity. More specifically, *para conocer el presente o el futuro hay que conocer el pasado* (to know the present or future, one must know the past). Knowing the past can assist in the process of claiming and living out different identities, as they often do not come without challenge or question of authenticity. As Latinas broaden the notion of *la condición de mujeres Latinas* (Latina womanhood), or what it means to be *mujeres Latinas* at the individual, group, community, and societal levels, their diversities become evident.

The following section is a discussion of the different roles and identities that are frequently negotiated by Latina women; yet, the conversation must consider moderating constructs of acculturation, enculturation, and traditionality. Considering these processes guards against the essentializing of core values and roles for Latinas and provides a working framework from which to delineate the salience of one's identity and an interpersonal approach.

Madres, comadres, hijas, y pecadoras (Mothers, Co-mothers, Daughters, and Sinners)

Any scholarly investigation or clinical intervention about Latinas inherently involves *la familia* (family), cultural scripts and gendered expectations, and an operationalization in some form of what it means to be *una buena mujer* (a good Latina woman). Central to the discussion is the widely-known and written value of *familismo,* around which many cultural values emanate and are interrelated (Gloria & Castellanos, 2009). *Familismo* is the "preference for maintaining a close connection to family" (Santiago-Rivera et al., 2002, p. 42), which is demonstrated by solidarity, interdependence, and reciprocity (Gloria & Castellanos, 2009). Including both fictive (e.g., *abuelas de crianza* ["adopted" grandmothers]) and nonfictive (e.g., *primas* [cousins]) relationships (Gloria et al., 2004), an allocentric or collectivistic approach often drives the process of emphasizing the well-being of the family first and foremost, despite detriment to individual needs (Marín & Triandis, 1985; Santiago-Rivera et al., 2002).

It is from this context of *familismo* that Latinas negotiate their interactions. Regardless of whether they themselves have children or are married, they are frequently defined by being part of *la familia,* as a woman, daughter, or (co)mother simultaneously. The cultural and gender scripts for Latinas have been described through psychological, sociological, and women's studies literatures, ranging from docile and subservient women who are venerated as saints (Castillo, Perez, Castillo, & Ghosheh, 2010) to *guerreras chingonas* (bad-ass warrioresses) who have fought against male subjugation and traditional conceptualizations of Latina scripts (Gaspar de Alba, 2005). One of the first scholarly discussions of *marianismo,* a Latina gender script, was by Stevens (1973), who described it as a religious manifestation in which Latinas were regarded as semi-divine, morally superior, sexually chaste, and spiritually stronger than their male counterparts. Upholding the roles of mother and caregiver, familial backbone, and cultural transmitter of values was required, or else their womanhood was questioned (Stevens, 1973). Adherence to the role was considered a "maintenance of honor" (p. 94) and responsibility to uphold the cohesion and status of the family (Frevert & Miranda, 1998). In particular, the daughter's chastity and purity were tied to familial dignity (Espín, 1997), such that females who did not conform to the traditional gender script of *marianismo* were considered *una mala mujer* (a bad woman) or even a *malinche* or *malinchistas* (traitors). The original *malinche* was Malintzin Tenepal, an indigenous Mayan woman, who interpreted and assisted Hernán Cortés in the conquest of Mexico and bore his children (Gaspar de Alba, 2005). Inherent to *marianismo* is the assumed heterosexuality of Latinas, as *lesbianas* (Latina lesbians) are charged with the act of favoring the foreign (Gaspar de Alba, 2005). In turn, they seek out alternative spaces away from their families of origin in order to express their sexuality, thereby creating new spaces and families of choice—an act that is considered culturally defiant (Acosta, 2008). By doing so, Latina lesbians are believed to repudiate the concept of family, the most serious of betrayals.

A more recent conceptualization known as the "Maria Paradox" described *marianismo* as an "invisible yoke which binds capable, intelligent, ambitious Latinas...to a no-win lifestyle" (Gil & Vazquez, 1996, p. 7). Their "ten commandments of *marianismo*" (p. 8) identify the strictest of traditional gender scripts and subsequent self-beliefs, interactions, and approaches to self. Each of the beliefs or commandments places the needs of the woman's husband and family first, whereby Latinas are yoked to a role of subservience and without self-expression or power. Drawing out the cultural strengths, there is a reclaiming of positive qualities such as dependability, trustworthiness (Gloria & Segura-Herrera, 2004), loyalty, compassion (Gil & Vazquez, 1996), perseverance, and ability to survive (Comas-Díaz, 1989). Yet, the attempt to fulfill multiple role expectations has been identified as working the *doble jornada* (double duty both at home and work, Comas-Díaz, 1989), giving rise to the *super macha* or *la hembra* (superwoman), who is continuously charged to *hacer algo de lo nada* (to make something from nothing), based on her *espiritu creativo* (creative and innovative spirit of survival) (Nogales & Bellotti, 2003).

Mestizaje y espiritualidad (Practices/Beliefs of Mixed Ancestral Indigenous Heritage and Spirituality): The Sacredness of Open Spaces

Oppression and social injustice have opened the path for Latinas to implement *mestizo* (e.g., a mixture of indigenous and Spanish blood and *cultura* [culture] (Falicov, 1998)) skills, tools, and practices to navigate their current circumstances and spaces. Considering the historical colonization of Latina/o cultures and the ongoing discrimination and marginalization of Latinas' experience (Campesino & Schwartz, 2006), sociopolitical, religious, and gender movements have assisted in the liberation of oppression. At the same time, Latinas' dual minority status has been negated (Aquino, 2002; Campesino & Schwartz, 2006) as they contend with continued and consistent struggles of imposed patriarchy (Arrizón, 2009). It is the synergistic ability to convert difficult realities into manageable experiences that promotes the healing and well-being of women as they forge their pathways. Within the multiple and varied definitions of spirituality (Fukuyama & Sevig, 1999), *mestizaje* ultimately encompasses the experiential encounter of the divine through subjective lenses (Cervantes, 2010). *Mestizo* spirituality recognizes the connection of the psychological adjustment of a people, nurtures the practice of history in context, unifies harmony with all, maintains openness to diversity, and promotes a willingness to learn from differences (Cervantes, 2010).

As a result, Latinas have passed indigenous knowledge (consciously and subconsciously—orally and behaviorally) intergenerationally, having learned the connection of nature, soul, and spirit (Lara, 2008). Latinas understand the holistic role of interpersonal interactions and the centrality of energy, intention, mind-set, and beliefs. Embodied in a culture that offers a range of spiritual beliefs and practices (e.g., folk beliefs, *Espiritismo, Santeria*; Baez & Hernandez, 2001; McNeill & Cervantes, 2008), Latinas are often socialized with a fundamental belief system with dual beliefs rooted in religiosity (e.g., *Dios me ayudara* [God will help me]) and spirituality (*Soy una con el universo—Yo puedo crear mis realidades* [I am one with the universe—I can create my realities]). Given the emphasis of *el espíritu* (spirit), Latinas often gravitate to the teachings of their mothers and grandmothers, who often provide insight into family interactions, how to navigate differences, and shift energies to facilitate *tranquilidad* (tranquility) of differences (Arredondo, 2002; Cervantes, 2008). Cognizant of the psychological impressions that can occur in conflict, Latinas digest old traditions and subsequently create new ones to persist (Gil & Vazquez, 1996). For example, Latinas have converted the energy of *la malinche* (Espín, 1997; Gaspar de Alba, 2005) to *la mujer radical* (a radical woman)—transformed into a survivor through personal stories and intuitive abilities to understand the invisible and parallel spiritual processes (Lara, 2008).

The application and transfer of spiritual knowledge and practice for Latinas to meet their daily demands of *la familia,* work, home, and school (Comas-Díaz, 1989) keeps them conscious of their needs and personal power in the process. One challenge that augments Latinas' dual belief systems includes the separation of sensuality and sexuality as a sacred component of human processes, of which "both are integral aspects of the self" (Lara, 2008, p. 28). As sexuality has been used to promote the subjectification of Latinas with the role of spirituality fragmented from the body, the attraction and energetic pulls that come through personal energy exchanges are minimized and negated (Arrizón, 2009). In the context of larger society, Arrizón (2009) contends that "...Latina sexuality and its representative 'brown' body becomes the product of objectifying stereotypical processes and complex subject formations" (p. 191) from a colonizing perspective. Simultaneously, the practice of identifying Latinas' sexual exchanges as solely corporal necessities and pleasures ignores Latinas' active powers in mutual spiritual exchanges. As Latinas work through the polarizing messages regarding sexuality and sensuality (Arrizón, 2009) by acknowledging, understanding, and working with their personal and spiritual power within multiple dimensions (including sexual identity and sensual being), they create spaces that nurture collective consciousness by awakening a "transformed consciousness" and an empowered *mujer* (Lara, 2008). For example, a sexual encounter becomes more than family honor or cultural script; it can instead be a divine energetic exchange, equally engaging and balancing the sexual powers of reclaiming the self (Acosta, 2008).

Poderosas (The Powerful Ones): A Different Latina Power

Latinas have created a *mujer*-grounded culturally centered skill set in which they translate and transform everyday processes while preserving and nurturing healthy elements of tradition to reinforce their evolving identities and values. For example, Latinas *poderosas* must daily live through negative experiences about who they are and what they represent in today's society. Staying strong to the strengths of their *valores culturales* (cultural values) allows them to maintain a sense of groundedness and meaning of who and what they are as Latinas. With the internal ability to navigate incongruence, Latinas morph and transcend within their multiple identities that harvest changing contexts and cultures, while facilitating the practice of cultural shape-shifting. Understanding the essence of survival and connectivity with their surroundings, Latinas function as transformers, connectors, and key or wisdom keepers to different realities (Cervantes, 2008). They learn to be present in one world, consistently working toward an internal seamless continuity in the midst of change. Their practice of moving and transferring within the changing tapestry of their daily realities, however, is not implemented to meet the needs of others or to lose their person to another, but to grow and persist despite challenges. Given that Latinas' value-centered coping strategies are founded in spirituality and *familia, la condición de la mujer* (the condition of the Latina woman) and their *feminismo* (feminism) are evolving. Consequently, with the goal of remaining culturally grounded, Latinas face the continuous challenge of infusing a combination of their core values of *familismo* and *espiritismo* into their engagement of everyday activities.

Imprinted in their ancestral blueprint and spiritual makeup, Latinas have survival skills that are generationally passed down, both consciously and unconsciously. Through daily encounters, the basic task of sharing time and coexisting (e.g., eating a meal, sitting, and sharing space) transmits ancestors' *costumbres, valores, y practicas culturales* (customs, values, and cultural practices). *Nuestras madres y abuelas* (Our mothers and grandmothers) may take the initiative to share the details of how to *sobrevivir* (survive), but this knowledge is already energetically transmitted via the management of challenges and subsequent strength *patron* (blueprint)—a collective consciousness awaiting to be awakened. A lack of awareness, or self-doubt, or limited confidence to tap into the subconscious will often lead Latinas to borrow from external, oppressive, and non-native systems. Doing so creates a foreign cultural blueprint for *la mujer* that is often inadequate and manifests as incongruence, depression, and other mental health concerns (Ginorio et al., 1995). When Latinas mask their identities with others' words, labels, and practices, they simultaneously dismantle and contaminate their most natural inner support system of self-definition to live out or complete processes in sacred spaces.

Reclaiming ourselves is a strength and powerful process of spirit and energy transformation and creation. As Latinas embrace their range of identities, they move from victims to survivors, fearful fighters to warriors, and ultimately *poderosas,* transforming realities as they engage daily processes and struggles. More specifically, Latinas' active identification, acknowledgment, ownership of their skills, and conscious permission to embrace inner ancestral and spiritual abilities (e.g., intuition, creative practices) reinforce an identity of active healer (Lara, 2008).

As healers of different capacities, Latinas merge and connect dimensionalized realities, which can lead to seamless navigation of identities.

The evolving *poderosa* identity promotes a culturally referenced skill set that instills a preparedness, personal resourcefulness, and intuition regarding the fluidity of life exchanges. In owning these qualities, Latinas slowly and progressively engage the fluidity of their identities (e.g., gender, educational, generational, sexual, spiritual). Although identity fluidity can create discomfort, ambivalence, and ambiguity for *la familia, los hombres*, and other social *conexciones* (connections), it becomes the space of power for the *poderosas* (warrioress) as Latinas engage and express their full scope of being *una buena mujer*.

Implications for Practice, Training, and Research

There are several implications for practice and training, as well as research and advocacy, that emerge from the previous discussion of identities and complexity of roles of Latinas. The following recommendations provide salient considerations and set a baseline for minimal competence for working effectively with Latinas. In particular, we pose questions to generate ideas about and around areas of practice, training, and research in providing best practices.

En terapia (In therapy)

What is the meaning and importance to Latinas' self-referents to their individual and family *patron*? Ask how the client identifies herself racially and ethnically and what it means to her. The self-referents that she uses may mean nothing, or they may mean everything to her (e.g., a source of pride and strength). Either way, a conversation about self-referents can provide a sense of ethnic identity and a way to access the psychological meaning and importance of being of a particular self-referent. Further, ask how others in her family self-identify. Identifying differences may reflect generational and acculturative changes and stresses that can serve to story the client's *patron*.

How is *cultura* integrated into interpersonal and social interactions with Latinas? Engage in the cultural values being emulated in the interaction (e.g., *personalismo, respeto, simpatia*). Knowing cultural values and interacting within the context of cultural values are different processes. That is, knowing the definition of *personalismo* is quite different from interacting in a manner that is steeped in *personalismo*. For example, a client may ask after the therapist's *familia* and expect a response that is genuine in order to engage in harmonious and caring interactions (i.e., *personalismo*). The counselor may recognize that the Latina's question is based in the value of *personalismo*; however, how the counselor responds will influence subsequent counseling interactions. Responding in kind will likely lead to *confianza* (trust) and *respeto* (respect) needed for a strong counselor-client relationship. In addition to implementing culturally-familiar interactions in therapy, counselors can access the resources and systems that represent Latinas' beliefs. For instance, counselors can collaborate with spiritual consultants or include other spiritual healers (e.g., *santero*, priest) as part of the therapeutic process based on the Latinas' beliefs.

What dimensions and contexts need to be considered in the assessment of Latinas' challenges? Include the assessment of psychological (the individual and their struggles), social (external oppressive systems), and cultural (family, gender and cultural scripts) factors in the context of understanding the client (Gloria & Rodriguez, 2000). Ultimately, helping Latinas to traverse and bridge their different realities are of concern within treatment approaches (Flores-Ortiz, 1995) and as a means of empowerment.

What must be considered to create a culturally-seeded treatment plan that integrates the different roles and realities that Latinas may encounter? Develop a treatment plan that incorporates and is parallel to the cultural values (e.g., *familia, espiritualidad*), cultural gender scripts (e.g., *marianismo, madre*), and realities (e.g., educational status, immigration history) of the Latina to understand and address competently her multiple realities and roles. Doing so will require an assessment of the different roles in which Latinas engage to address potential areas of conflict and spaces in which they can be integrated. For example, is the client experiencing a *doble jornada* as she attempts to balance her varied and contrasting roles? How are her cultural and gender scripts influencing her choices and challenges? Importantly, the therapist will need to refrain from defining which behaviors, beliefs, and decisions are grounded in a *poderosas* framework and allow the Latina to define these for herself and within her context.

What are Latinas *podersosas'* strength-based processes? Be aware, sensitive, and reinforcing of those inner strengths that Latinas bring to their challenges and concerns. Empower them to find their own voice and cultural processes that are congruent to their worldview and sociocultural *patron* as they find wellness and balance. Doing so will require that the therapist examine, challenge, and re-work his or her own biases, assumptions, and stereotypes about and for Latinas.

Training Considerations

How do training programs assess their students' readiness, progress, and processes to work with Latinas? Training programs can implement a comprehensive and ongoing cultural audit of students' beliefs, biases, and assumptions as part of their supervision, such that they can understand how their own worldviews and cultural values may interact (e.g., be similar or different) with those of Latina clients.

What venues can be accessed to gain historical, spiritual, and cultural information about Latinas? In that "to know the past is to know the present and future," practice-based training programs should require students to take a course on Chican@/Latin@ histories and psychological processes to understand the diaspora of issues and identities within the different Latina/o communities. In particular, counselors will benefit from learning and understanding the roles that different Latina/o spiritual systems play for Latinas. For example, *espiritualidad,* is often used as a coping response, serving as a moderating factor for everyday decision-making processes (Castellanos & Gloria, 2008). Moreover, understanding how *espiritualidad* influences the counseling interactions and the Latina client's progress warrants conceptualization and assessment.

What specific training components need to be incorporated to most effectively understand Latinas *poderosas*? Expose therapists to the complexity of Latina/o cultures through specific one-on-one interactions that will assist the understanding, implementation, and inclusion of cultural practices familiar to clients. For example, programs can require some portion (if not all) of the practica and externships to work specifically within Latina/o families and communities in outreach and community service. Supervision should intentionally address diversities within the community, its multiple social systems, various means of coping, and venues to work with clients within their worldview, beliefs, and value systems.

Who needs to be included in developing an effective cultural forum within a program curriculum to understand the Latina *poderosas* paradigm? Practicum curricula should consistently include Latina cultural experts as part of the training (including community service providers) to share insight and understanding of Latinas. Latina experts can provide practicum lectures and conceptual consultations using composite vignettes to engage real-life considerations and cultural interactional processes. Addressing cultural nuances, varying levels of diversities, and cultural strengths can provide a working model to facilitate a strong therapist–Latina client relationship for efficacious exchanges and services.

How can *comunidad* be bridged with Latinas' needs to enhance the existing cultural and social networks? Prepare and teach psychologists to access comfortably the resources and health-system networks that include ethnocultural processes and beliefs that support effective services. In particular, there is the need to shift the paradigmatic focus of individual counseling to include those systems and networks of individuals who are the primary constituents working for Latina well-being. For example, counselors can learn to use a collaborative community approach to develop partnerships with local Latina/o communities and community centers, Latina leaders, and gatekeepers to access the wellness services needed to support culturally integrated and comprehensive mental health services.

Conducting Research

What types of research can be implemented to better understand Latinas *poderosas*? Research should be considered (and taught) as the connection between practice and social advocacy for Latinas. By focusing on the value of action research, scholars and students in training can gain the narratives and foundational information (e.g., exchanges with the community) needed to implement a culturally-grounded perspective for the development of strength-based research questions. With students, for example, a required field studies and ethnographic project including participant observation of the social issues within Latina communities will facilitate their identification of salient community concerns and, in turn, the transfer of this knowledge into counseling services.

What are the specific research components necessary to understand Latinas' dimensionalized realities? Research questions need to be dimensionalized so that they include psychological (e.g., self-beliefs), social (e.g., connections), and cultural (e.g., values and behaviors) dimensions within the context or setting of the individual (Castellanos & Gloria, 2007). Engaging in this practice can allow for a holistic and comprehensive approach to explore concerns and processes for Latinas.

Similarly, researchers would do well to formulate questions that are strength-based and to consider the moderating processes of acculturation, enculturation, ethnic identity, and traditionalism.

What is the role of including Latinas' voices and narratives in the context of research? esearchers should consider how addressing narratives or phenomenological processes for Latinas holds prominence equal to that of quantitative investigations. Despite challenges or criticisms of qualitative approaches, it is from individual stories and voices that insight into the deep-structure culture is gained and more nuanced questions can be asked for and about Latinas. Similarly, using mixed-method designs within studies can provide deeper and more comprehensive understanding of Latina issues, concerns, realities, and lives.

What is the added value of creating and implementing an emic versus etic research measure for Latinas *poderosas*? Given the limited culturally emphasized scales developed for Latinas, there exists the need to create, pilot, and validate measures and assessments that are specific to their concerns and cultural constructs. For example, scales that assess how Latinas are *poderosas* or are negotiating the process of intertwining different identities (e.g., sexual, ethnic, gender, education, career, family) could assist in developing new programmatic research agendas.

Direcciones Futuras (Future Directions)

As the process of meaning-making and the struggle to create a strength-based and culture-steeped self-ascribed definition of being Latina continue, there are many directions in which multicultural feminist psychology can address concerns and challenges. The following are offered as areas of continued exploration and reflection.

- As the field of psychology strives to provide socially-just and culturally relevant and competent services for individuals and communities of difference, the development of counseling guidelines and practices for Latinas is warranted. While guidelines exist for the psychological treatment of women and girls (APA, 2007), specific and culturally steeped guidelines are similarly needed to differentiate the community concerns, cultural moderators, and processes unique to Latinas.
- As the immigration processes and histories of different Latina ethnic subgroups are varied, attention to how the immigration process influences the conceptualization and reconfiguration of family is warranted. As a frequent core consideration for many Latinas, an exploration of how the family occurs transnationally and across geographic and psychological borders increasingly warrants examination.
- An examination of the continual balance of identities and competing processes of Latinas' roles that are perceived as strength-based is needed. Identifying how a reclaiming of voice and a redress of the junction and mixing of traditional and contemporary values can be accomplished is pivotal.
- There is a need to acknowledge and facilitate Latinas' efforts to fuse and live out the multidimensionality of their identities, while still encouraging them to perceive themselves as *mujeres buenas* who balance energies and nurture wellness and well-being. In particular, an expansion of what is currently believed to encompass *una buena mujer* to include Latinas with professional identities (e.g., advanced educational degrees), of all sexualities, of different belief systems and practices (e.g., healers, *santeras, curanderas, shamanas, espiritistas*), and with different constellations of family systems (e.g., single *madres*, multigenerational households, *mujers sin hija/os* [women without children]) is warranted.
- As the field has moved to understand the Latina/o cultural values, beliefs, and practices, multiple psychological models have offered culture-based directives for clinical practice. Still, relatively few Latina-specific psychological models integrate multiple dimensions and emphasize the fluidity of identities that are important for addressing the dimensionality of Latinas' varied experiences and processes that support mental health.
- Relative to *Mestizo* and Latina/o psychology, the identities of spirituality, sensuality, and sexuality are fragmented, limiting the understanding of the psychology of *la mujer*. By integrating the identities, Latinas can move beyond the societally-imposed unidimensional stereotypes to a multi-dimensionalized Latina *poderosa* who is connected spiritually and culturally to herself, her contexts, and social networks. In the process of integrating the identities, researchers and practitioners must explore and refine methods to address the dimensions fully and contextually.
- As the transforming identities of *la mujer* have been criticized, it is the acceptance and embracing of Latinas' multidimensional processes by their social and cultural systems that will allow *mujeres* to live out their experiences with increased *tranquilidad* (tranquility), congruence, and continuity of identity. As the cultural and gender-

scripts for Latinas have been formulated from a static rubric, allowing for a fluid, evolving open system invites the voice, needs, and complexity of identities, and the bridging of Latinas' realities.

Authors' Notes

This chapter, Realidades Culturales y Identidades Dimensionadas (Cultural Realities and Dimensioned Identities), is dedicated to our *abuelas maternas* (maternal grandmothers), Refugio Fuentes and Maria Perdigon—the women who transmitted to us the strengths and resources to traverse multiple boundaries and identities via their daughters.

References

Acosta, K. L. (2008). Lesbianas in the borderlands: Shifting identities and imagined communities. *Gender and Society, 22*(5), 639–659. doi: 10.1177/0891243208321169

Alamilla, S. G., Kim, B. S. K., & Lam, N. A. (2010). Acculturation, enculturation, perceived racism, minority status stressors, and psychological symptomatology among Latino/as. *Hispanic Journal of Behavioral Sciences, 32,* 55–76. doi: 10.1177/0739986309352770

American Council on Education (2007). *Minorities in higher education: Twenty-second annual status report: 2007 supplement.* Washington, DC: Author

Anzaldúa, G. (1987). *Borderlands/La frontera.* San Francisco: Spinsters/Aunt Lute Book.

Anzaldúa, G. (1993). To live in the Borderlands means you. In R. D. Rebolledo, & E. S. Rivero (Eds.), *Infinitive divisions: An anthology of Chicana literature* (pp. 96–97). Tucson: University of Arizona Press.

APA (2007). *Guidelines for psychological practice with girls and women.* American Psychological Association. Washington, DC: Author.

Aquino, M. P. (2002). Latina feminist theology: Central features. In M. Aquino, D. Machado, & J. Rodriguez (Eds.), *Reader in Latina feminist theory* (pp. 133–160). Austin: University of Texas.

Ardila, A. (2005). Spanglish: An Anglicized Spanish dialect. *Hispanic Journal of Behavioral Sciences,* 27, 60–81. doi: 10.1177/0739986304272358

Arredondo, P. (1991). Counseling Latinas. In C. C. Lee, & B. L. Richardson (Eds.), *Multicultural issues in counseling: New approaches to diversity* (pp. 143–156). Alexandria, VA: American Association for Counseling and Development.

Arredondo, P. (2002). Mujeres Latinas: Santas y marquesas. *Cultural Diversity and Ethnic Minority Psychology, 8*(4), 308–319. doi: 10.1037/1099-9809.8.4.308

Arrizón, A. (2009). Latina subjectivity, sexuality, and sensuality. *Women and Performance: A Journal of Feminist Theory, 18*(3), 189–198.

Baez, A., & Hernandez, D. (2001). Complementary spiritual beliefs in the Latino community: The interface with Psychotherapy. *American Journal of Orthopsychiatry, 71*(3), 408–415. doi: 10.1037/0002-9432.71.4.408

Berry, J. W. (2007). Acculturation. In J. E. Grusec & P. D. Hastings (Eds.), *Handbook of socialization: Theory and research* (pp. 543–558). New York: Guilford Press.

Campesino, M., & Schwartz, G. E. (2006). Spirituality among Latinas/os: Implications of culture in conceptualization and measurement. *Advances in Nursing Science, 29*(1), 69–81.

Castellanos, J., & Gloria, A. M. (2007). Research considerations and theoretical application for best practices in higher education: Latina/os achieving success. *Journal of Hispanic Higher Education, 6,* 378–396. doi: 10.1177/1538192707305347

Castellanos, J., & Gloria, A. M. (2008). *Rese un Ave Maria y ensendi una velita:* The use of spirituality and religion as a means of coping with educational experiences for Latina/o college students. In B. McNeill & J. Cervantes (Eds.), *Latina/o healing practices: Mestizo and indigenous perspectives* (pp. 195–219). Brunner-Routledge.

Castillo, L. G., Perez, F. V., Castillo, R., & Ghosheh, M. R. (2010). Construction and initial validation of the Marianismo Beliefs Scale. *Counselling Psychology Quarterly, 23*(2), 163–175. doi: 10.1080/09515071003776036

Cawthorne, A. (2008). *The straight facts on women in poverty.* Washington, DC: Center for American Progress.

Cervantes, J. M. (2008). What is indigenous about being indigenous? The Mestiza/o experience. In B. McNeill, & J. M. Cervantes (Eds.), *Latino/a health traditions: Mestizo and indigenous perspectives* (pp. 3–27). New York: Routledge Press.

Cervantes, J. M. (2010). Mestizo spirituality: Toward an integrated approach to psychotherapy for Latina/os. *Psychotherapy Theory: Research, Practice, Training, 47*(4), 527–539. doi: 10.1037/a0022078

Chapa, J., & De La Rosa, B. (2004). Latino population growth, socioeconomic and demographic characteristics, and implications for educational attainment. *Education and Urban Society, 36*(2),130–149. doi: 10.1177/0013124503261320

Comas-Díaz, L. (1989). Culturally relevant issues and treatment implications for Hispanics. In D. R. Koslow, & E. Salett (Eds.), *Crossing cultures in mental health* (pp. 31–48). Washington: Society for International Education Training and Research (SIETAR).

Comas-Díaz, L. (2001). Hispanics, Latinos, or Americanos: The evolution of identity. *Cultural Diversity and Ethnic Minority Psychology, 7,* 115–120. doi: 10.1037/1099-9809.7.2.115

Dennis, J., Basaíez, T., & Farahmand, A. (2010). Intergenerational conflicts among Latinos in early adulthood: Separating values conflicts with parent from acculturation conflicts. *Hispanic Journal of Behavioral Sciences, 32*(1) 118–135. doi: 10.1177/0739986309352986

Dernersesian, A. C. (1993). And, yes...the earth did part: On the splitting of Chicana/o subjectivity. In A. de la Torre & B. M. Pesquera (Eds.), *Building with our hands: New directions in Chicana studies* (pp. 34–56). Los Angeles: University of California Press.

Echeverry, J. J. (1997). Treatment barriers: Accessing and accepting professional help. In J. G. Garcia & M. C. Zea (Eds.), *Psychological intervention and research with Latino populations* (pp. 94–107). Boston: Allyn and Bacon.

Ennis, S. R., Ríos-Vargas, M. & Albert, N. G. (2011). *The Hispanic population 2010.* C2010BR-04. U.S. Census Bureau, Washington, DC.

Espín, O. M. (1997). *Latina realities: Essays on healing, migration, and sexuality.* Boulder, CO: Westview Press.

Falicov, C. J. (1998). *Latino families in therapy: A guide to multicultural practice.* New York: Guilford Press.

Flores-Ortiz, Y. G. (1995). Psychotherapy with Chicanas at midlife: Cultural/clinical considerations. In J. Adeleman & G.

Enguídanos (Eds.), *Racism in the lives of women: Testimony, theory, and guides to antiracist practice* (pp. 251–259). Binghamton, NY: Harrington Park Press.

French, S. E., & Chavez, N. R. (2010). The relationship of ethnic-related stressors and Latino ethnic identity to well-being. *Hispanic Journal of Behavioral Sciences, 32*(3), 410–428. doi: 10.1177/0739986310374716

Frevert, V. S., & Miranda, A. O. (1998). A conceptual formulation of the Latin culture and the treatment of Latinos from an Adlerian psychology perspective. *Journal of Individual Psychology, 54*(3), 291–309.

Fukuyama, M. A., & Sevig, T. D. (1999). *Integrating spirituality in multicultural counseling.* Thousand Oaks: Sage Press.

García, J. G., & Marotta, S. (1997). Characterization of the Latino population. In J. G. García & M. C. Zea (Eds.), *Psychological interventions and research with Latino populations* (pp. 1–14). Boston: Allyn & Bacon.

Garmst, G., Dana, R. H., Der-Karabetian, A., Aragón, M., Arellano, L. M., & Kramer, T. (2002). Effects of Latino acculturation and ethnic identity on mental health outcomes. *Hispanic Journal of Behavioral Sciences, 24,* 479–504. doi: 10.1177/0739986302238216

Gaspar de Alba, A. (2005). Malinche's revenge. In R. Romero & A. N. Harris (Eds.), *Feminism, nation and myth: La Malinche* (pp. 44–57). Houston: Arte Público Press.

Gil, R. M., & Vazquez, C. I. (1996). *The Maria paradox: How Latinas can merge Old World traditions with New World self-esteem.* New York: Berkley Publishing.

Ginorio, A. B., Gutiérrez, L., Cauce, A. M., & Acosta, M. (1995). Psychological issues for Latinas. In H. Landrine (Ed.), *Bringing cultural diversity to feminist psychology: Theory, research, and practice* (pp. 241–263). Washington, DC: American Psychological Association.

Gloria, A. M. (2001). The cultural construction of Latinas: Practice implications of multiple realities and identities. In D. B. Pope-Davis and H. L. K. Coleman (Eds.), *The intersection between race, gender, and class: Implications for multicultural counseling* (pp. 3–24). Thousand Oaks, CA: Sage.

Gloria, A. M., Ruiz, E. L., Castillo, E. M. (2004). Counseling Latinos and Latinas: A psychosociocultural approach. In T. Smith (Ed.), *Practicing multiculturalism: Affirming diversity in counseling and psychology* (pp. 167–184). Boston: Allyn and Bacon.

Gloria, A. M., & Segura-Herrera, T. (2004). ¡*Somos*:! Latinos and Latinas in the U.S. In D. Atkinson, G. Morton, & D. W. Sue (Eds.), *Counseling American minorities: A cross cultural perspective* (6th ed.) (pp. 279–299). McGraw Hill.

Gloria, A. M., & Castellanos, J. (2009). Latinas/os and their communities. In Council of National Psychological Associations for the Advancement of Ethnic Minority Interests, *Psychology education and training from culture-specific and multiracial perspectives: Clinical issues and recommendations* (pp. 12–18). Washington, DC: American Psychological Association.

Gloria, A. M., Castellanos, J., Scull, N. C. & Villegas, F. J. (2009). Psychological coping and well-being of male Latino undergraduates: Sobreviviendo la universidad. *Hispanic Journal of Behavioral Sciences, 31*(3), 317–339. doi: 10.1177/0739986309336845

Gloria, A. M., & Castellanos, J. (2012). *Desafíos y bendiciones*: A multi-perspective examination of the educational experiences and coping responses of first-generation college Latina students. *Journal of Hispanic Higher Education, 11*(1), 81–98. doi: 10.1177/1538192711430382.

Gloria, A. M. & Rodriguez, E. R. (2000). Counseling Latino university students: Psychosociocultural issues for consideration. *Journal of Counseling and Development, 78,* 145–154.

Gonzales, F. (2007). *Hispanic women in the United States 2007.* Washington, DC: Pew Hispanic Center.

Gonzalez, J. (2000). *Harvest of an empire: A history of Latinos in America.* New York: Penguin Press.

González, K. P., Jovel, J. E., & Stoner, C. (2004). Latinas: The new Latino majority in college. In A. M. Ortiz (Ed.), *Addressing the unique needs of Latino America students* (pp. 17–27). San Francisco: Jossey-Bass. DOI: 10.1002/ss.113

Gonzalez, N. A., Fabrett, F. C., & Knight, G. P. (2009). Acculturation, enculturation, and the psychosocial adaptation of Latino youth. In F. A. Villarruel, G. Carlo, J. M., Grau, M. Azmitia, N. J. Cabrera, & T. J. Chahin (Eds.), *Handbook of U.S. Latino psychology: Developmental and community-based perspectives* (pp. 115–134). Thousand Oaks, CA: Sage.

Hurtado, A., & Cervantez, K. (2009). A view from within and from without: The development of Latina feminist psychology. In F. A. Villarruel, G. Carlo, J. M. Contreras, M. Azmitia, N. J. Cabrera, & T. J. Chahin (Eds.), *Handbook of U.S. Latino psychology: Developmental and community-based perspectives* (pp. 171–190). Thousand Oaks, CA: Sage.

Kaltman, S., Green, B. L., Mete, M., Shara, N., & Miranda, J. (2010). Trauma, depression, and comorbid PTSD/depression in a community sample of Latina immigrants. *Psychological Trauma: Theory, Research, Practice, and Policy, 2*(1), 31–39.

Keefe, S. M. (1980). Acculturation and the extended family among urban Mexican Americans. In A. M. Padilla (Ed.), *Acculturation: Theory, models, and some new findings* (pp. 85–110). Boulder, CO: Westview.

Kim, B. S., & Omizo, M. M. (2006). Behavioral acculturation and enculturation and psychological functioning among Asian American college students. *Cultural Diversity and Ethnic Minority Psychology, 12,* 2, 245–258. doi: 10.1037/1099-9809.12.2.245

Kochhar, R. (2005). *The occupational status and mobility of Hispanics.* Washington, DC: Pew Hispanic Center.

Kohatsu, E. L. (2005). *Acculturation: Current and future directions.* In R. T. Carter (Ed.), *Handbook of racial-cultural psychology and counseling: Theory and research* (Vol. 1, pp. 207–231). Hoboken, NJ: Wiley.

Lara, I. (2008). Latina health activists-healers bridging body and spirit. *Women and Therapy, 31*(1), 21–41. doi: 10.1080/02703140802145169

Lechuga, J. (2008). Is acculturation a dynamic construct? The influence of method of priming culture on acculturation. *Hispanic Journal of Behavioral Sciences, 30,*324–339. doi: 10.1177/0739986308319570

Lopez, M. H., & Dockterman, D. (2011). *U.S. Hispanic country-of-origin counts for nation, top 30 metropolitan areas.* Washington, DC: Pew Hispanic Center.

Marín, G., & Triandis, H. C. (1985). Allocentrism as an important characteristic of the behavior of Latin Americans and Hispanics. In R. Diaz-Guerrero (Ed.), *Cross-cultural and national studies in social psychology* (pp. 85–104). Amsterdam: North Holland.

Marín, G. (1993). Influence of acculturation on familism and self-identification among a case study. *Journal of Community Psychology, 21,* 149–161.

McNeill, B. W., & Cervantes, J. M. (Eds.) (2008). *Latina/o healing practices: Mestizo and indigenous perspectives*. New York: Routledge Press.

National Women's Law Center and Mexican American Legal Defense and Educational Fund (2009). *Listening to Latinas: Barriers to high school graduation*. Washington, DC: Author.

Niemann, Y. F. (2004). Stereotypes of Chicanas and Chicanos: Impact on family functioning, individual expectations, goals, and behavior. In R. J. Velásquez, L. M. Arellano, & B. W. McNeill (Eds.), *The handbook of Chicana/o psychology and mental health* (pp. 61–82). Mahwah, NJ: Lawrence Erlbaum Associates Publishers.

Nogales, A., & Bellotti, L. G. (2003). *Latina power! Using 7 strengths you already have to create the success you deserve*. New York: Simon & Schuster.

Oboler, S. (1995). *Ethnic labels, Latino lives: Identity and the politics of (re)presentation in the United States*. Minneapolis: University of Minnesota Press.

Ocampo, K. A., Bernal, M. E., Knight, G. P. (1993). Gender, race and ethnicity: The sequencing of social constancies. In M. E. Bernal & G. P. Knight (Eds.), *Ethnic identity: Formation and transmission among Hispanics and other Minorities* (pp. 11–30). Washington, DC: American Psychological Association.

Ortega, A. N., Fang, H., Perez, V. H., Rizzo, J. A., Carter-Pokras, O., Wallace, S. P., & Gelberg, L. (2007). Health care access, use of services, and experiences among undocumented Mexican and other Latinos. *Archive of Internal Medicine, 167*(21), 2354–2360.

Padilla, A. M. (1980). The role of cultural awareness and ethnic loyalty in acculturation. In A. M. Padilla (Ed.), *Acculturation: Theory, models, and some new findings* (pp. 47–84). Boulder, CO: Westview.

Padilla, A. M. (1995). Introduction to Hispanic psychology. In A. M. Padilla (Ed.), *Hispanic psychology: Critical issues in theory and research* (pp. xi–xxi). Thousand Oaks, CA: Sage.

Passel, J. S., Cohn, D., & Lopez, M. H. (2011). *Census 2010: 50 million Latinos: Hispanics account for more than half of nation's growth in past decade*. Washington, DC: Pew Hispanic Center.

Quijada, P. D. & Alvarez, L. (2006). Cultivando semillas educacionales: Understanding K-8 Latina/o students. In J. Castellanos, A. M. Gloria, & M. Kamimura (Eds.), *The Latina/o pathway to the Ph.D: Abriendo caminos* (pp. 2–17). Sterling, VA: Stylus.

Quintana, S. M., & Scull, N. (2009). Latino ethnic identity. In F. A. Villarruel, G. Carlo, J. M. Grau, M. Azmitia, N. J. Cabrera, & T. J. Chahin (Eds.), *Handbook of U.S. Latino psychology: Development and community-based perspectives* (pp. 81–98). Thousand Oaks, CA: Sage.

Ramírez, M. (1991). *Psychotherapy and counseling with minorities: A cognitive approach to individual and cultural differences*. New York: Pergamon Press.

Rodriguez, A. L., Guido-DiBrito, F., Torres, V., & Talbot, D. (2000). Latina college students: Issues and challenges for the 21st century. *NASPA Journal, 37*, 511–527.

Saenz, R. (2010). Latinos in the United States 2010. *Population Bulletin Update*. Washington, DC: Population Reference Bureau.

Sandoval, A. M. (2008, Ed.). *Toward a Latina feminism of the Americas: Repression and resistance in Chicana and Mexicana literature*. Austin: University of Texas Press.

Santiago-Rivera, A. L., & Altarriba, J. (2002). The role of language in therapy with the Spanish-English bilingual client. *Professional Psychology: Research and Practice, 33*, 30–38. doi: 10.1037//0735-7028.33.1.30

Santiago-Rivera, A. L., Arredondo, P., & Gallardo-Cooper, M. (2002). (Eds.). *Counseling Latinos and la familia: A practical guide*. Thousand Oaks, CA: Sage.

Santiago-Rivera, A. L., Altarriba, J., Poll, N., Gonzalez-Miller, N., & Cragun, C. (2009). Therapists' views on working with bilingual Spanish-English speaking clients: A qualitative investigation. *Professional Psychology: Research and Practice, 40*(5), 436–443. doi: 10.1037/a0015933

Sellers, R. M., Smith, M., Shelton, J. N., Rowley, S. J., & Chavous, T. M. (1998). Multidimensional model of racial identity: A reconceptualization of African American racial identity. *Personality and Social Psychology Review, 2*, 18–39. doi: 10.1207/s15327957pspr0201_2

Shin, H. B., & Kominski, R. A. (2010). *Language use in the United States: 2007*. American Community Survey Reports, ACS-12. U.S. Census Bureau, Washington, DC.

Stevens, E. P. (1973). Marianismo: The other face of machismo in Latin America. In A. Pescatello (Ed.), *Female and male in Latin America essays* (pp. 90–101). Pittsburgh: University of Pittsburgh Press.

Suro, R., & Passel, J. S. (2003). *The rise of the second generation: Changing patterns in the Hispanic population growth*. Washington, DC: Pew Hispanic Center.

Thomas-Breitfeld, S. (2003). *The Latino workforce*. Statistical Brief, ED 481480. Washington, DC: National Council of La Raza.

Vasquez, M. J. T. (1994). Latinas. In L. Comas-Díaz, & B. Greene (Eds.), *Women of Color: Integrating ethnic and gender identities in psychotherapy* (pp. 114–138). New York: Guilford Press.

Viramontes, H. M. (2008). Preface. In A. M. Sandoval, A. M. (Ed.), *Toward a Latina feminism of the Americas: Repression and resistance in Chicana and Mexicana literature* (pp. ix–xvi). Austin, TX: University of Texas Press.

Zimmerman, M. A., Bingerheimer, J. B., & Notaro, P.C. (2002). National mentors and adolescent resilience: A story of urban youth. *American Journal of Community Psychology, 30*, 221–243.

CHAPTER

10 Asian American Women's Feminism: Sociopolitical History and Clinical Considerations

Lisa A. Suzuki, Munínder K. Ahluwalia, *and* Anjali Alimchandani

Abstract

This chapter provides a multicultural counseling psychology perspective highlighting theory and research that conceptualizes the experiences of Asian American women, a group characterized by diverse histories and social locations within the United States. A historical and political context is provided, beginning with the examination of federal legislation that has impacted the immigration patterns of Asian American women for over a century. Controversies surrounding a pan-Asian identity and intersectionality theory are illustrated, along with stereotypical portrayals of Asian women in the media. Asian conceptions of psychology and mental health are outlined, along with clinical considerations from a cultural perspective. Mental health concerns in the Asian American community are identified. The formation of social networks of Asian American women is discussed, as well as their impact on the women's movement within this community. In addition, this chapter cites the unique characterization of feminism within the interdependent and often bicultural community of Asian American women.

Key Words: Asian American women, feminism, history, stereotypes, oppression

Multicultural counseling psychology theory and research pertaining to Asian American women have been influenced by cultural values emphasized within the diverse Asian ethnic subcultures, historical events (e.g., laws governing immigration, war), racism and discrimination, and stereotypes as evidenced in the media. Hall (2002) noted that the passive and subservient gender role of East Asian women has been reinforced by Confucian values emphasizing a patriarchal hierarchy. A similar gender conceptualization has been characterized for South Asian and Southeast Asian women, as they are often treated as property to be obtained and traded as a resource within families. These female gender roles are considered "more rigid and not subject to negotiation and change" within many Asian communities (Hall, 2002, p. 157).

As will be discussed in the historical section of this chapter, immigration laws have supported these patriarchal values within Asian communities and thereby impacted the role assumed by and projected onto Asian women in American society. Stereotypical representations of Asian American women as passive, modest, subservient, and exotic have led to negative portrayals, as these women are viewed as "self-effacing, unworthy, and subservient to men (i.e., as transitional sex objects)" (Chin, 2000, p. 7). Asian American women have been perceived as silent in the face of oppression, which has led to a commonly held, but false, belief that they have been invisible, even absent, in the feminist movement. This invisibility is evidenced in the limited representation of Asian American women in the feminist literature.

> Little is known about the lives and relationships of Asian American women and the characteristics that promote or impede their growth and development... myths continue to perpetuate

the mystique about Asian American women, and stereotypes that objectify and disempower them remain. (Chin, 2000, p. 6)

This chapter focuses on the important contributions that Asian American women have made to society, their lived experiences, and the multiple contexts in which they currently reside. We begin by providing a context of Asians in the United States, as the lives of Asian American women are clearly impacted by the current conditions. Issues pertaining to historical context and a pan-Asian identity are then highlighted, prior to addressing the status of Asian American women in terms of mental health issues and the feminist movement.

Asian Americans in the United States

The term "Asian" refers to "people having origins in any of the original peoples of the Far East, Southeast Asia, or the Indian subcontinent" (U.S. Census Bureau, 2007, n.p.). Sandhu (1997) reports the existence of 40 distinct ethnic subgroups within this category, including: Indian, Bangladeshi, Bhutanese, Burmese, Cambodian, Chinese, Filipino, Hmong, Indochinese, Indonesian, Iwo Jiman, Japanese, Korean, Laotian, Madagascar, Maldovian, Malaysian, Nepalese, Okinawan, Pakistani, Singaporean, Sri Lankan, Taiwanese, Thai, and Vietnamese. Each of these Asian subgroups has a unique history (e.g., migration experience), identification with home country, level of acculturation, language, and culture (Sandhu, 1997). Census estimates indicate that the number of Asians overall residing in the United States is approximately 13.5 million, comprising 4.7% of U.S. households. The largest Asian groups include Chinese, Indians, Filipinos, Vietnamese, and Koreans, and comprise nearly 90% of the total Asian population in the United States.

It is important to note that the census continues to compare racial and ethnic minority groups to Whites as a norm. While we disagree with this practice, for the purposes of this chapter, demographic information is reported as noted in publications on the Asian community in the United States (Reeves & Bennett, 2003; U.S. Census Bureau, 2007). Asians reportedly had larger proportions of college graduates and a higher median income compared to non-Hispanic Whites. Asian and Pacific Islander women were more likely than non-Hispanic White women to have earned a bachelor's degree (44% compared to 22%; Reeves & Bennett, 2003). Asians generally spoke English at home, and 7 of every 10 Asians were United States citizens by birth or naturalization. Fifty-nine percent of Asian and Pacific Islander women participated in the labor force. In addition, Asian communities had reportedly lower rates of divorce, criminal activities, and drug abuse, in comparison to Whites and African Americans (cited in Meyer, Dhindsa, & Sue, 2009).

The origins of the Asian American classification emerged during the civil rights era as college students of Asian descent (i.e., Chinese and Japanese) mobilized to increase awareness of anti-Asian violence and other acts of racism and discrimination. They sought to establish support for pan-ethnic collective action, protesting the wars in Southeast Asia and fighting for the establishment of programs in Asian American Studies (e.g., Leong & Gupta, 2009). The Asian American label has taken on new meanings over time. This plurality is reflected in the increasing number of Asian ethnic subgroups, as well as religious diversity, bicultural experiences, and mixed identification with the "model minority" stereotype. The sociopolitical complexity of Asian American identity is further discussed in a later section of this chapter.

Historical Highlights of Asian American Women: Immigration

The immigration of Asian women to the United States must be understood within the context of political history and oppression for the past 100 years (Root, 1995). Although migration narratives vary greatly across different Asian groups (i.e., many Vietnamese immigrants migrated as refugees and asylees, while many Chinese immigrants migrated to the U.S. as laborers), this section provides a brief overview of some immigration experiences and the U.S. legislation that shaped them. Tien (2000) notes that immigration legislation has systematically impacted this group, given the historical prohibition against entry of Asian women into the United States. Asian men who were laborers were brought over to work during the California Gold Rush and the building of the Transcontinental Railroad. Tien cites three immigration laws as illustrations of oppressive legislation—the Chinese Exclusion Act of 1882, The Immigration Act of 1917, and the National Origins Act of 1924. It is beyond the scope of this chapter to provide information regarding the immigration of all Asian ethnic subgroups; however, readers are referred to asian-nation.org for a more in-depth examination of the arrival of South Asians, Vietnamese, and other Asian groups to the United States.

The Chinese Exclusion Act of 1882 prohibited the immigration of any Chinese person and forbade Chinese immigrants already in the U.S. from attaining citizenship, labeling them "permanent aliens." Prostitution of women was rampant during the 1800s, and Chinese women in the United States were viewed as "sexually subservient" and immoral (Tien, 2000, p. 31).

The Immigration Act of 1917 identified all people from Asia as inadmissible aliens and barred their entry into the United States until the start of World War II. This act was directed primarily at the Japanese, due to conflict between Japan and the United States. In 1885, Japanese workers had arrived in the United States to escape drought conditions in Japan. Japanese women immigrated in larger numbers after 1900 (Gee, 1981). Married men sent for their wives, while other single men returned to Japan to meet women. Most, however, engaged in a long-distance marriage through "picture brides." Many American citizens were prejudiced against "Orientals" and deemed this practice as immoral and un-Christian (Gee, 1981). While some women immigrated with little knowledge of the hardships that awaited them, others came desiring new experiences. These Japanese women knew that they needed to be strong to face the challenges that awaited them in the United States:

> ... my heart had to be as beautiful as Mount Fuji. I resolved that the heart of a Japanese woman had to be sublime, like that soaring majestic figure eternally constant through wind and rain.... (Gee, 1981, p. 55)

The Immigration Act of 1924 expanded the immigration restrictions to other Asian groups, and the National Origins Act of 1924 barred immigration from Asia and the Pacific Islands. Attempts were made to petition for the admission of Asian women into the U.S. in 1935, 1937, and 1939 (i.e., Alien Wife Bill), but they never gained the needed political support due to the "unwillingness of Americans to accept Asian women" (Tien, 2000, p. 32).

Although the United States had adopted anti-Asian immigration policies prior to the outbreak of World War II, the attack by Japan on Pearl Harbor increased anti-Asian sentiments and led to the internment of 100,000 first- and second-generation Japanese Americans. It is estimated by the Federal Reserve Bank that the financial cost of internment to the Asian American community was $400 million (Houston & Houston, 1981). The familial and psychological toll on the community was even greater as "packed sleeping quarters, the communal mess halls, the open toilets—all this was an open insult to that other, private self, a slap in the face you were powerless to challenge" (as cited in Houston & Houston, 1981, p. 154). As one internee wrote: "Whatever dignity or feeling of filial strength we may have known before December 1941 was lost, and we did not recover it until many years after the war" (p. 159).

Anti-Asian, xenophobic sentiments were detrimental to all Asian immigrants; however, Asian American women, as any double minority group, suffered further discrimination. For example, while "Americanization" programs were available to immigrant men, women were often excluded from cultural orientation, English language programs, and vocational training, mediated by Americans who sought to maintain male authority within the family (Kelly, 1981). Without education or work opportunities, in order to support themselves and their families, many women were relegated to paid employment as bar girls, laundresses, farm workers, cooks, domestic servants, seamstresses, and prostitutes (Espiritu, 1996; Kelly, 1981). This exclusion was particularly problematic, given that, as Kelly (1981) notes, "Over 21% of all Vietnamese families that immigrated to the United States were headed by women who claimed to be the sole breadwinner for that household" (p. 236). Kelly (1981) reports about a community of Vietnamese women who participated in English language lessons in a resettlement camp prior to their arrival in the United States in the 1970s. Women were represented in the curriculum through lessons on budgeting, shopping, and conversation. There was a clear differentiation between sex roles, in which women were narrowly depicted as wives and mothers. Despite the lack of opportunity and access to job training and advisement, Kelly notes that a year after the camps were closed, "over 45% of Vietnamese female immigrants were employed in the American labor force, primarily in service occupations requiring a minimum of English language proficiency and work skills" (p. 239).

Throughout the twentieth century, the U.S. government passed various regulations and laws to impose restrictions on Asian Americans' economic, social, educational, and civil rights (Alvarez, 2009). In addition to impacting immigration from various Asian countries, these laws gravely affected the lives of the Asian Americans already in the U.S. Naturalization laws prohibited Asian Americans from obtaining citizenship and the right to land ownership. The laws slowed or banned further immigration, resulting in isolation from families and communities. In addition, because women were not seen as a source of labor and therefore had not been recruited to the United States, and anti-miscegenation laws restricted intermarriage, family life for Asian Americans was further disrupted. Married men were separated from their wives, who were not allowed to immigrate, while single men were often unable to find spouses. Each community managed this challenge differently. One example is seen in the Indian community, as approximately 10 to 20 women entered yearly as immigrants, and the proportion of Indian women to men was the lowest for any group immigrating from Asia (McMahon, 2001, p. 15). With the lack of Indian (Punjabi) women available to marry, many single Indian men in California married Mexican women, resulting in large Punjabi-Mexican communities.

The history of Asian immigration to the United States has had a major impact on members of this community. Legislation controlling the number of women allowed into the United States has clearly affected the formation of family units and the acceptable roles of Asian women in American society.

Pan-Asian Identity and Intersectionality

Although a number of Asian American ethnic groups share some degree of similarity in cultural values (i.e., patriarchal hierarchy) and historical experiences of oppression, characterization of these diverse groups in terms of a pan-Asian American identity has been controversial. According to Espiritu (1993), the term "Asian American" refers to a pan-ethnicity, or a generalized solidarity among particular ethnic groups. "Pan-Asian," however, is largely an imposed group label. The constituents of the term "Asian American" comprise an extremely diverse group of people across culture, race, ethnicity, and religion, among other identity markers. However, in response to a shared American experience of racist subjugation, as well as economic, political, and social discrimination, Asian Americans have forged a communal sociopolitical identity. This shared experience, in addition to the reality of culture as a non-static, dynamic entity, suggests that pan-ethnicity cannot be adequately conceptualized through some notion of a shared common culture, but rather a shared experience of oppressive sociopolitical structures. As Espiritu notes, when the dominant culture "uses the ethnic label as a unit in economic allocations and political representations, ethnic groups find it both convenient and necessary to act collectively" (p. 10).

Maeda (2006) affirms this perception of the sociopolitical context that shaped the formation of Pan-Asian identity, explaining that organizers began advocating against anti-Asian racism and exploitation in the late 1960s. Two of the primary actors in this social movement in the United States were members of the Red Guard Party, who built community programs, organized an Asian American labor movement, and protested the Vietnam War. Artist/critic Frank Chin also engaged in leftist activism through his work as a playwright, artist, and co-editor of AIIIEEEEE! (1991), a foundational anthology of Asian American literature. Chin, however, like many radical leftist activists, was criticized for his privileging of a nationalistic political agenda over feminist consciousness and a refusal to integrate the two. Both the Red Guard Party and writers like Chin relied on performances by the Black radical resistance, including the use of the language and style of the Black Panthers, in modeling their own movements. This reliance speaks to the interconnected nature of racial identity formation among people of color in the United States. Such identities are uniquely American in that their origins are rooted in American experiences of discrimination, rather than any independently perceived notion of a shared cultural identity.

Although Pan-Asian identity provides the political competitive advantage associated with large-scale identity, enabling Asian Americans to build a larger, stronger advocacy movement, this constructed "homogeneity" of identity is not without intense internal conflict. It panders to a racist discourse that views Asian Americans as a homogenous group, asserting a monolithic, stagnant, and sometimes non-inclusive definition of "Asian American." This problematic discourse results in the exclusion of some Asian communities. For example, Shankar and Srikanth (1998) discusses the manner in which South Asian Americans often experience a unique marginalization within Asian American communities, in that they are "a part, yet apart" (p. x). This passive lack of acknowledgment of South Asian Americans within Asian American discourse is rooted in a number of complex intersecting issues, such as the differing migration histories and socio-economic/class experiences of East/Southeast Asians and South Asian Americans. South Asian American immigration includes limited experiences of forced migration and indentured labor, in comparison to other Asian American groups. In addition, U.S. foreign policy with respect to a number of East/Southeast Asian countries has historically seen high levels of political tension, unlike its policy toward South Asian countries. However, following 9/11, South Asian Americans witnessed a dramatic shift in foreign policy enacted within their native countries as well as within their experience as brown people in the United States. Ahluwalia and Zaman (2009) discuss discrimination in the Muslim and Sikh communities following 9/11 and the impact on counseling services.

The homogeneity of the Pan-Asian identity also fails to allow space for the intersectionality of human identity. Intersectionality achieved critical attention in Crenshaw's (1989) work, which recognized the inextricably linked nature of multiple identities of race and gender. The concept was then expanded to include additional identity categorizations, such as sexual orientation, class, and religious affiliation. Those occupying a minority status within more than one of these identities often experience multiple minority stress (Bowleg et al., 2003), the sum of which is greater than the individual parts. In other words, multiple minority stress cannot be holistically understood by isolating experiences associated with single identity categorizations. Individuals forced to choose one identity over another must resort to silencing aspects of the self, which results in a heightened level of insidious trauma, defined as the lifelong trauma associated with social statuses that lack power (Root, 1992). The construction of a Pan-Asian identity, by definition, calls for a concrete, one-dimensional conceptualization of identity. This does not allow Asian Americans to be seen as whole people, shaped by multiple intersecting influences of ethnicity, gender, class, and sexual orientation, among other identity markers.

Intersectionality is particularly relevant for Asian American women as they struggle to negotiate their gender with their racial and cultural identities. Given the historical role that women have played as bearers of authentic cultural identity, many myths about Asian American women are often based in ideas that we have of Asians in their country of origin. This relegates Asian American women to stagnant stereotypical categories. This conceptualization of Asian Americans, however, is also problematic since Asian Americans may be immigrants, refugees, or settled as second or third generation; and therefore they may adopt a bi- or multicultural identity. In addition, Asian Americans sometimes come to the United States as parachute kids (whereby minors from Asian countries immigrate to the U.S. alone), or astronaut parents (whereby one parent immigrates with children, while the other parent stays in the country of origin; e.g., Tsong & Liu, 2009). Some Asian American women are international transracial adoptees. Internationally adopted girls outnumber the boys (Evan B. Donaldson Adoption Institute, n.d.) and have unique cultural identities and reculturation processes that have both similarities and distinct differences from other Asian Americans (Baden, Treweeke, & Ahluwalia, in press). It is important for us to consider the differences in acculturation, as well as sociopolitical histories and identities when working and/or interacting with Asian American women. The factors impacting the formation of identities among Asian American women are discussed further in the sections that follow.

Stereotypes of Asian American Women

Understanding conceptions of mental health for Asian American women requires attention to the stereotypes that have been used to characterize these diverse communities for decades. Stereotypes are insidious as they "limit the behavior to which the observer will attend... depersonalize a person or group, which subsequently allows those in power to disregard them as individuals with rights ..." (Root, 1995, p. 274). Root also notes that if internalized, stereotypes serve to undermine self-esteem. Stereotypical representations of Asian American women include descriptions such as submissive, obedient, and quiet. But stereotypes go far beyond those pertaining solely to women. As Aoki and Mio (2009) suggest, the stereotypic portrayals of Asians and Asian Americans in the media reinforce problematic conceptualizations. "Asians are seen as being: (a) perpetual foreigners; (b) mysterious; (c) exotic; (d) 'arm candy' for White males; and (e) invisible" (p. 422). In this section, we highlight the model minority myth, the perpetual foreigner, the dangerous Asian, and the exoticization of Asian and Asian American women.

Model Minority Myth

Asian Americans are viewed, in contrast to other ethnic minorities, as the model minority, that is, as high achieving, hardworking, self-reliant, and law-abiding— the minority that has overcome hardship, oppression, and discrimination to achieve educational and socioeconomic success (Chao, Chiu, & Lee, 2010; Lee, Wong, & Alvarez, 2009; Takaki, 1998). The idea that all Asian Americans are successful, however, is a socially constructed myth.

The myth of the model minority has had a negative impact in several ways. The myth discounts the diversity within the Asian American experience (and related disparities) to great detriment to individuals and groups, as well as education (Suzuki, 2002) and government policies (Chao, Chiu, & Lee, 2010). Some groups, such as Cambodians, Laotians, and Hmong, are underrepresented in higher education, for example, but because they fall under the umbrella of Asian American, they are excluded from affirmative action policies (Suzuki, 2002). It also masks the reality that while some Asian Americans are indeed successful (e.g., educationally, economically, etc.), other groups, including refugees and immigrants, have not attained the same markers of success.

The Perpetual Foreigner

When we consider images of "all-American" activities, we may envision baseball games and backyard barbeques. And when we consider the people who are engaging in these all-American activities, the image that comes to mind (and that has been perpetuated by the media) is that of White Americans. If being American means being White, Asian Americans are thereby cast as perpetual foreigners, "inherently foreign and therefore truly not 'American'" (Lee, Wong, & Alvarez, 2009, p. 69). Again, this stereotype is deeply problematic; multiple generations of Asian Americans in the United States are still not considered American enough.

The Dangerous Asian

The perpetual foreigner stereotype is exacerbated or taken to the extreme during wartime or times of conflict. Examples of these extreme reactions include the internment of Japanese Americans during World War II (Wu, 2002, as cited in Lee, Wong & Alvarez, 2009) and the discrimination experienced by Muslim and Sikh Americans after the terrorist attacks of September 11, 2001 (Ahluwalia & Zaman, 2009), which suggests that these Americans somehow have sole allegiance to their country of origin (or country of ancestry) and should return to those countries.

Though the stereotype of Asians (i.e., South Asian in particular) as dangerous existed before September 11, 2001, the terrorist attacks of that day solidified the image in the minds of many Americans. Although the media images of terrorists are those of Muslims (and dangerous misconceptions and stereotypes about Muslims have persisted as a result), South Asian men and Arab men of all faiths have been negatively targeted by the media and by individuals. In particular, Sikh men with turbans and beards have been targets (Ahluwalia & Pellettiere, 2010). Women from the community, who may appear more mainstream, are bystanders to the racism and experience it through association with men. This racism by association can result in feelings of paralysis and helplessness (Ahluwalia, 2011). Women who wear clothing that is culturally or religiously different from that of the mainstream, such as Muslim women who wear the *hijab* or head scarf, or Sikh women who wear a *chuni* (or more rarely, a turban), are also targeted and are seen as dangerous.

The Exoticization and Hypersexualization of Asian American Women

Asian American women have been depicted as exotic and hypersexualized in the media, and thus have been permanently labeled as the "other." These stereotypes, specific to women, are layered and juxtaposed against the general stereotypes of Asian Americans. Stereotypes specific to Asian American women include those of the hypersexualized being, the dragon lady, and the perpetually oppressed woman (Espiritu, 1996; Hall, 2009).

In the late nineteenth and early twentieth centuries, Asian women were brought to the United States as prostitutes to service the sexual needs of Asian men who were unable to marry (Espiritu, 1996). The stereotype of the exotic Asian woman in the sexual service of men is one that is clearly linked in origin to this historical context. War brides further reinforced this stereotype, when American servicemen married women from countries with which the United States was in conflict (e.g., Korea).

Associated with the previous stereotype of exotic and hypersexualized women who were prostitutes, the image of the dragon lady who is "...evil, inscrutable, sinister, and dark with long fingernails" (Hall, 2009, p. 198) dates from the time when Asian women's immigration to the United States was prohibited or extremely limited. Further "dehumanization and sinisterization" of Asian women took place during U.S. military involvement throughout the twentieth century with Japan, Korea, and Vietnam (Hall, 2009).

Stereotypes abound of the oppressed Asian woman with no voice and little power. While these stereotypes can be seen across most Asian Americans, stereotypes about oppression of women in the Muslim community are particularly pervasive. "[E]quity is highly prized in Islam, the practice and implementation of it has been significantly affected by patriarchal values of the host cultures. Furthermore, many Muslim women may view men and women's roles as complementary to each other, rather than comparable" (Ahluwalia & Zaman, 2009, p. 469). Although there are "patriarchal barriers" in the Muslim community (Hoodfar, 2001, p. 421), there are also many false assumptions about the community that are fed by Western media. The veil is an excellent example. Hoodfar argues that there is an assumption in the West that the "'veil' equals 'ignorance' and 'oppression'" (p. 421). She explains that while the veil can be used in the service of patriarchy, it can also be perceived by women as a means of freeing themselves from patriarchy.

The stereotypes of exotic and oppressed Asian American women are also projected onto their dating practices, romantic relationships, partnerships, and marriages (Ahluwalia, Suzuki, & Mir, 2009). According to the 2000 U. S. Census, 23% of Asian American women were married to non-Asians (Xie & Goyette, n.d.). These interracial marriages can be perceived to fit the stereotype of the exotic Asian woman, whereas intra-ethnic or intra-religious arranged marriages can be (somewhat incorrectly) perceived as oppressive to women.

Stereotypes about Asian American women are problematic not only because of the inaccurate depiction of these women, but also because of the negative impact they have on the women themselves. As with other oppressive messages, when stereotypes are internalized, they can be harmful to the well-being of Asian American women.

Asian Conceptions of Psychology and Mental Health

Western conceptions of psychology and psychotherapy are relatively new when viewed in the context of healing across the globe. Societies have engaged in diverse rituals and spiritual and/or social practices to promote healing and the mental well-being of their members for centuries before the creation of Western psychology (Moodley & West, 2005). Given the diversity of conceptions of human development and psychology among Asian Americans, a comprehensive description of Asian American psychology is not possible. This section provides a general overview of a common viewpoint within a number of Asian cultures and specific examples of psychological theory emerging from Cambodia, India, and some Buddhist communities.

Indigenous Perspectives

The multiple calls to revise the current understanding of multiculturalism within psychology have catalyzed increased growth of the field of indigenous psychologies. Yeh and Kwong (2009) note that "indigenous healing practices were created from the culture's nature, worldview, history, beliefs, and accessibility of resources in various parts of the world" (p. 559). Yeh and Kwong (2009) cite the importance of collectivistic coping, stressing the importance of relationships and strategies such as family support, respect for authority figures, intracultural coping (e.g., support network within the community), relational universality, forbearance, social activity, and fatalism (i.e., control is derived in context and through external forces). They cite literature supporting the existence of a collectivistic orientation and an interdependent self-construal.

The field outlines the "culture-bound and culture-blind" nature of Western psychology, highlighting the fact that mainstream psychological theories reflect the values of the United States and are not always generalizable to other societies. Culture is embedded in mental health because the ways in which people process, explain, experience, and give meaning to their psychological afflictions are rooted in particular sociocultural contexts. The field calls for the development of a body of psychological knowledge that reflects, explains, and describes mental and physical behaviors within a culturally relevant frame of reference, producing culturally rooted therapeutic methods (Kim & Park, 2005).

Hwang (2009) advocates for the use of indigenous psychology as well. He discusses the ways in which Confucianism, Taoism, and Buddhism shape the daily lives of Chinese individuals. In addition to Hwang, a number of international counseling scholars have published a body of literature focused on counseling practice and conceptualization in varying global contexts. For example, the *Asian Pacific Journal of Counseling and Psychotherapy* (2010) published a special issue focused on the development of indigenous counseling services in different Asian communities. In addition, according to Turner-Essel and Waehler's (2009) research on increased internationalization of the field of counseling psychology, the *Journal of Mental Health Counseling* dedicated an issue to the development of professional counseling in China, Taiwan, Ghana, Japan, Fiji, Turkey, India, Ukraine, and Italy.

Many theories of psychology among Asian communities view human functioning as a fully integrated process of physical, emotional, cognitive, and spiritual elements. One element cannot be treated without attending to others, and in some circumstances, certain elements may only be reached through the others. The relationship between the spiritual realm and the individual can be permeable. And the primary sense of identity, and therefore the root of healing within the context of psychological trauma, is located within the community and social connection.

A study of Cambodian refugees found that nightmare content was frequently related to the experience of trauma and resulted in a decrease in "concentric, ontology, security," or a decrease in the protective layers of the self, making it more vulnerable to physical and spiritual invasions (e.g., attacks by spirits/ghosts) (Hinton, Hinton, Pich, Loeum, & Pollack, 2009). Research findings indicated that many Cambodians engaged in specific cultural rituals to repel attacking forces and to rebuild the protective layers of the self (Hinton et al, 2009).

An analysis of Indian conceptions (primarily Hindu) of psychological healing found that the central difference between Indian and conventional Western treatment methods lies in the conception of the self (Kakar, 1991). Traditional Indian views perceive the person as comprising three intertwined parts: body, self, and social being. The social being includes not only an individual's social network and support, but ancestor spirits as well. The self comprises not only actions in this lifetime, but in the collective karma of actions over multiple lifetimes. Mental health problems may occur as a result of disturbances in any or all of these elements, each of which is integrally tied to the other. Research indicates that Indians, like many other communities, simultaneously approach traditional shamans, mystics, spiritual healers, Ayurvedic and other traditional practitioners, in addition to Western trained doctors for treatment of mental health afflictions (Kakar, 1991).

Buddhist psychology offers theories explicating human experience and the development of psychopathology as well as treatment methods. According to Daya (2000), the theory, rooted in Buddhist religious practices, defines four noble truths. The first states that the human condition is one of disease, or dissatisfaction, which results from the cycle of pursuing personal likes and avoiding personal dislikes. The second is the doctrine of dependent origin, or the idea that the self comprises a series of transient, arising emotional and thought states, rather than a concrete entity that produces such states. Therefore, the self is continually in flux, as it interacts with contextual factors in a bidirectional manner. Human suffering results from attaching oneself to a particular set of feelings/thoughts, defining a persistent unchanging self. The third truth states that humans can release themselves from this conception of self. And the last truth offers mindfulness, or an awareness of arising states without judgment or the need to control them, as the method by which to transcend this psychological suffering. Mindfulness also enables humans to become more comfortable with the constant unstable nature of life. These indigenous perspectives of psychology stand in stark contrast to Western psychology, though a number of attempts have been made to integrate diverse cultural perspectives in multiculturalism.

Current conceptions of multiculturalism within the field of psychology, however, adopt a hierarchical approach in which Western psychological models are deemed the objective norm and culturally competent practitioners and researchers need only integrate multicultural perspectives and/or practices into the existing models. However, recent publications, such as those of the American Psychological Association, report on provision of services for refugee communities, point to the inefficacy of this conception of culturally competent psychological services (APA, 2010). Moodley and West (2005) argue for the current need to travel outside the bounds of Western psychology as a direct result of the failure of current approaches to multicultural counseling to effectively address the psychological needs of non-Western clients. They explain that current multicultural counseling offers cultural competencies as therapeutic techniques, but does not promote human development and conceptualizations of the self and psychopathology across different cultural contexts. From the standpoint of counseling psychology, an emphasis on a holistic and health-oriented life span perspective is critical in working with diverse clients.

This criticism of current conceptions of multiculturalism within psychology has crossed over the border of internal discussions among psychologists and into mainstream discussions regarding globalization. Watters (2010) criticizes the United States' exportation of the *Diagnostic and Statistical Manual of Mental Disorders* (American Psychiatric Association, APA, 2000) as the worldwide standard on categorization of mental diseases—as well as the realities that Western researchers run the top scholarly psychology journals, Western universities train the world's most influential clinicians, and Western drug companies control the vast majority of funding for psychological research. He goes on to comment on the lack of sufficient self-reflection among the dominant psychological canon, as evidenced by the assumption that Western categorizations of mental illness are universal and absolute. He notes that conceptions of mental illness have evolved, with some concepts now relegated as cultural artifacts. For example, the popularity of "hysteria" as a diagnosis for women in the Victorian era, and the rise in numbers diagnosed with multiple personality disorder 15 years ago are now considered historical vestiges. He further notes the minimization of culture-bound syndromes in the latest *Diagnostic and Statistical Manual* (*DSM-IV*). Those noted within particular Asian communities such as *koro* and *amok* could be identified as "Psychiatric Exotica: Two Bits a Gander" (p. 5). While Watters may employ a somewhat sensationalistic style of writing and is admittedly not a psychologist, he poses important ethical questions regarding traditional conceptions of multiculturalism within psychology.

Mental Health Issues in the Asian American Community

In their review, Meyer, Dhindsa, and Sue (2009) note the complexity of factors that impact examination of mental health issues in the Asian communities in the United States. As noted earlier, assumptions of a pan-Asian identity are problematic, and the identities of different Asian subgroups must be considered in examining prevalence rates of mental health concerns. Acculturative stress, intergenerational conflict, migration conditions (e.g., refugee status), experiences in the host country, level of cultural adaptation required to adjust to the new country, and post-migration trauma have been tied to post-traumatic stress disorder (PTSD) and depression and clearly impact the occurrence of mental disorders in the Asian immigrant community (Meyer, Dhindsa, & Sue, 2009). Overall, there are lower rates of self-reported mental health problems among Asians in comparison to Whites. However, these authors cite numerous examples of studies done in specific Asian communities, noting higher rates of PTSD among Southeast Asian refugees; greater occurrences of adjustment disorder, major depression, and paranoia among members of the Hmong community; and more reports of feelings of loneliness and discomfort among Asian college students. The literature also notes consistently low usage of mental health services in Asian communities. Of concern is that those who do access services tend to report severe problems.

As illustrated in earlier sections of this chapter, the diversity among Asian American women's experiences is vast, due to differences in migration narratives, ethnicity, socioeconomic status, sexuality, and gender identity, among other factors. For this reason, a comprehensive analysis of cultural and clinical considerations is impossible to provide within a single chapter. This section provides an overview of common themes that may bring Asian American women into therapy, as well as cultural issues to consider in treatment. Some common concerns include immigration adjustment, domestic violence, shame, living and raising children in a bicultural world, discrimination effects, and eating disorders (Hall, 2009). Hall explains that in dealing with mental health issues, some Asian American women tend to use traditional indigenous healing methods such as their faith or spirituality, while others may use a blend of both Western and traditional methods.

There are many cultural factors to consider when working with Asian American women. To varying degrees, Asian American women may appear mainstream (or not) in their cultural artifacts (e.g., food, clothes), religion, language, gender roles (e.g., carrier of culture), dating and relationship practices, and family systems. Faith life can be very important for some Asian Americans. For example, for Indian Sikhs, the Guru Granth Sahib (the Sikh holy book) acts as a guide and a source of healing, and for Korean Christians, the Bible (the Christian holy book) may serve the same function.

Acculturation levels, as well as other intersecting identities, must be taken into consideration. For example, a Pakistani American immigrant woman may wear a *salwar kameez* (tunic and flowing pants) at family functions but wear dresses to her place of work. If one looks at this woman's family constellation, one may see differences in how other women in her family dress, with a grandmother possibly wearing Punjabi clothes exclusively, a mother who may wear Punjabi and Western clothes interchangeably, and a sibling who engages in some mix of the above. While acculturation does not necessarily mean that things such as dress, language use, gender roles, and so on, will become more mainstream according to how long (or how many generations) one's family has been in the United States, levels of acculturation can be one factor in determining these.

As noted earlier, Asian Americans, as with all other Americans, have multiple intersecting social identities that impact their identity development. "Having multiple social identities means that an individual subjectively experiences being part of more than one social group" (Chen, 2009, p. 173). It is key for clinicians to consider that all identities—race, ethnicity, age, sexual orientation, gender identity, national origin, ability status, socioeconomic status, indigenous heritage—impact the gendered experience of Asian American women. The experience of a lesbian Korean American would be very different from that of a heterosexual Korean American female. If we layer other identities onto this same person (e.g., whether or not they are internationally adopted), we can see the complexity (and identity) of the individual come into focus. Interestingly, theories and research on Asian Americans discuss how Asian Americans may manage their multiple identities (Chen, 2009). Chen discusses three ways in which Asian American women may negotiate their multiple identities: (a) focusing on one of the identities, such as race *or* ethnicity *or* gender; (b) compartmentalizing one's identities into separate categories; and (c) integrating one's identities into one holistic identity.

Identity issues for Asian American women also include those related to body image. Asian Americans are subject to sociocultural messages both from the United States and from their country of origin or ancestry (Kawamura & Rice, 2009). As members of a visibly distinct racial group in the United States (and members of diverse ethnic groups), Asian American women may "become self conscious of physical characteristics that set them apart from people of other racial backgrounds, such as their facial features and skin color" (Kawamura & Rice, 2009, pp. 537–538). Though traditionally many Asian cultures valued obesity as a sign of beauty, prosperity, or good health, current cultural values have shifted toward the Western ideal of thinness (Kawamura & Rice, 2009). There is an idealization among Asian Americans of particular facial features, including a narrower nose and the double eyelid (Kawamura & Rice, 2009; Yokoyama, 2007). In addition, Asian American women value larger breast size and greater height. These facial features and body types are more commonly attributed to mainstream White culture. Though a response to these idealizations may be minor (e.g., dieting or wearing makeup), Asian American women may engage in more serious behaviors (e.g., surgical interventions) and may be at risk for eating disorders (Kawamura & Rice, 2009; Yokoyama, 2007).

Domestic Violence and Human Trafficking

While varying definitions of violence within Asian American communities pose significant challenges in identifying abuse, a brief literature review points to the high prevalence of incidents of domestic violence (DV) and trafficking within this population. The U.S. Department of Justice (2004) reports that Asian Americans comprise the largest group of people trafficked into the United States (5,200–7,800 out of an estimated total of 14,500–17,500 trafficked individuals). According to a review of community studies conducted by the Asian/Pacific Islander Institute on Domestic Violence (APIIDV, 2011), 41–61% of Asian American women survey respondents reported experiencing some form of intimate, physical, and/or sexual violence in their lifetimes. One specific study conducted by Leung and Cheung (2008) found that in a survey of 1,577 Asian Americans, the average partner abuse prevalence was 16.4% (22.4% among Vietnamese participants, 21.8% among Filipino participants, 19.5% among Indian participants, 19.5% among Korean participants, 9.7% among Japanese participants, and 9.7% among Chinese participants). A number of national studies also demonstrate that certain subgroups, such as Asian American women married to military men, have a higher prevalence of DV than the general population. Additionally, research suggests that Asian American victims may face a higher fatality risk than the general population of DV victims (Foo, 2003).

Although many DV victims are silenced by their abusers through such tactics as isolation and threats, Asian American victims of DV with limited English proficiency are doubly silenced by a system that is not equipped to assist them. The U.S. Department of Justice indicates that the deceptively low number of reported cases of DV among immigrant populations is most likely attributed to cultural taboos and a lack of culturally and/or linguistically competent services. Cultural taboos surface in help-seeking attitudes among many Asian American groups. APIIDV's review of community studies (2011) found that Asian American women may refuse to or feel unable to access external social services because of the shameful nature of domestic violence, a need to preserve family dignity, minimization of the serious nature of the violence, a desire to seek support from friends, and unsatisfactory experiences with counseling and/or other social services.

Asian Americans have a low rate of reporting mental health issues, so it is unclear whether Asian American women face particular issues. Mental health problems can vary among specific Asian American communities due to a number of environmental factors, specific cultural issues related to their ethnicity, and other intersecting identities. It is important to note that there are specific issues related to Asian American women, such as a high occurrence of domestic violence and body image issues that are linked to sociocultural messages from both their ethnic groups and the dominant culture in the United States.

Feminism in Asian American Communities

Feminism within Asian American communities must be conceptualized within the context of their respective migration histories. United States immigration policies throughout the twentieth century consistently illustrate xenophobic attitudes and a general fear of difference. Assimilation was repeatedly emphasized and "... the distinctive experiences of immigrant women were usually subsumed under men's history or given perfunctory or patronizing treatment" (Seller, 1981, p. 8). The emphasis on reform of the 1960s brought attention to the political, economic, and educational discrimination facing women in the United States. Louie (2000) cites literature indicating that, "According to the feminist perspective, the experiences of women activists are shaped by the contradiction and inequalities of the larger social world in which they live" (p. 14). She notes that activism is linked to hardship within the larger social context.

The 1960s and 1970s highlighted a "new ethnicity" and the ways in which scholars depicted the plight of immigrant women. As referenced in an earlier section, Asian Americans and other ethnocultural groups "followed the lead of Black Americans by organizing to pursue political and economic justice for their communities and by taking increased pride in their ethnic heritages" (p. 8). Organizing around shared concerns for social justice in the Asian community served as an impetus for bilingual education, ethnic studies programs, the removal of stereotypic images from the media, and an emphasis on resisting oppression.

It should be noted that writers such as Gee (1981) present a cautionary note in judging the role of Asian women prior to this time. "Yet amid the clamor for social change, accompanied at times by loud political rhetoric, we should not disparage the quiet fortitude of these Issei [first generation Japanese] women. In America, quietness and modesty tend to be equated with weakness, but with these Issei women, quietness and modesty are sure signs of strength" (p. 59). Chin (2000) reinforces this point noting, "Adaptation should be considered from the perspective of resiliency and strength, that is the ability of Asian American women to adapt and cope" (p. 226).

According to Chow (1994), Asian American women, like other women of color, were excluded from much of the feminist movement in the 1960s. Following this time period, Asian American women began organizing; however, they faced and continue to struggle with a number of barriers, including, but not limited to, the constraints of culturally prescribed gender roles, language barriers, psychological fears of losing ethnic identity in pursuit of "Americanized" feminism, legal-political and socioeconomic status obstacles, and perceived "invisibility" within mainstream culture. A survey of Asian American social activists (Louie, 2000) highlighted awareness of the injustices (e.g., racism, discrimination) facing this community of women and the importance of collegial relationships formed in the context of social advocacy between Asian Americans and members of the non-Asian community. The lack of organized support and leadership development in the Asian American community is particularly problematic.

This lack of leadership derives in part from the conditions under which the Asian American women's movement was formed. Serafica, Weng, and Kim (2000) note the importance of informal social networks of Asian women that eventually formed the foundation of the women's movement. Studies of informal networking note the importance of chain immigration (e.g., family members or friends immigrating to join others already in the U.S.), the existence of ethnic enclaves (e.g., Chinatowns), community norms emphasizing the need for relationships and support, and community churches (i.e., Protestant denominations) as factors leading to informal networking among Asian American women. Women gathered informally to engage in activities to gain mutual support, self-discovery, and political study around issues of sexism and patriarchy. Louie (2000) explains that "a woman's identity often is defined in the context of relationship" (p. 216). In her study of the Chinatown garment industry, she notes the importance of relationships among women facing oppression and acculturative stress. Eventually these groups evolved from self-study to a focus on addressing the negative plight of Asian American women in society. "Informal networks became the formal national organization seeking to improve the status of Asian American women throughout the country" (Wei, 1992, cited in Serafica, Weng, & Kim, 2000, p. 56).

In her seminal review on the Asian American women's movement, Root (1995) notes that the Asian women's movement was delayed "because their energies were dissipated in the struggle to integrate two cultures, acts that required the violation of proscriptions for female modesty, invisibility, passivity, and support of men" (p. 273). Engaging in the feminist movement was often perceived as conflicting with the cultural norms of the Asian American community. Japanese and Chinese women with longer histories in the United States had access to greater resources and education than other communities of women who focused on economic survival rather than political involvement. In addition, living in ethnic enclaves led to isolation of Asian ethnic groups, and the presence of "a 'culture and racial' hierarchy among Asian groups also may have contributed to the lack of involvement of Filipinos and Koreans, newer immigrants, who had less status in this hierarchical system . . ." (p. 273).

Given the plethora of challenges faced by Asian American women with respect to negotiating gender, race, and class oppression, sexuality remained largely silenced. In recent years, queer Asian American critiques have shed light upon the particular sociopolitical threats posed by non-heteronormativity. Gopinath (1997) suggests that nationalist discourses reify gender hierarchies, perpetually holding women as stagnant bearers of state-promoted cultural identity. Gopinath (1997) advances this gendered critique of nationalism through her commentary upon the construction of non-heteronormative, or queer sexuality during both the colonial and postcolonial periods. Queer sexuality is seen as a significant threat to patriotism, continually challenging the conventional heteronormative female role that defines nation, home, and family. Her examination of queer female subjectivity contributes to essential discussions regarding intersectionality of identity and Asian American feminism.

Feminism and Social Justice

Many Asian and Asian American women do not use the term "feminist" to describe themselves or their work—even work that fits within such a definition. It could be argued that they are not using the term "feminist" for two reasons: because of an alliance with Asian men (race as primary importance); and racism and exclusion from other feminists. Asian American women's voices are absent from mainstream feminism (e.g., White feminism). As Hall (2009) explains, the women's movement (i.e., predominantly White women) began with the fight to have the right to work outside the home, whereas many ethnic minority women were already working outside the home. Asian American women were not included in women of color feminism (e.g., Black women's construction of "womanism") either, which was an alternative to White feminism. Asian American women fought for equal pay, equal rights, and respect as women *and* Asians (Hall, 2009, p. 205).

In addition to feminist movements, Asian Americans have fought for social justice for themselves and for others. The twenty-first century has seen a rise in social justice movements for Asian Americans with sociopolitical and historical markers such as 9/11 (e.g., for South Asian women) and anti-immigration movements and legislation. Women have had a strong voice in these movements and labor rights struggles. For example, the Asian Pacific American Labor Alliance and Asian Immigrant Women Advocates (AIWA) organize against unfair labor practices and are led by Asian American women. AIWA works specifically with low income, limited English–speaking American women. Social activist Bhairavi Desai (http://www.sawnet.org/whoswho/?Desai+Bhairavi) was a founding member of the Taxi Workers Alliance in New York City, an organization created to advocate against the inequities faced by taxi drivers, many of whom are of South Asian descent. Kochiyama (1997) cites a number of Asian American women who have been social advocates, including Janice Mirikitani, who spoke in the 1981–1982 congressional hearings regarding the Japanese internment camps during World War II. In addition, as a lesbian socialist educator at University of California at Berkeley, Merle Woo acted as a trailblazer in her commitment to radical socialist feminism despite significant discrimination, which resulted in the university firing her from her position in the Asian American Studies program. Woo filed a lawsuit against the university, eventually winning a settlement. Woo's decision to share her sexual orientation paved the way for other Asian American lesbian and/or queer women to live freely. In New York City, the Committee Against Anti-Asian Violence (CAAV), in which women play central roles, monitors discrimination faced by Asian Americans, and organizes with other people of color to advocate for social justice. The National Asian Pacific American Women's Forum also advocates for the rights of Asian American women across the nation.

Conclusion

This chapter informs the discourse on feminist multicultural counseling psychology as it pertains to the Asian American community. Asian American women come from diverse ethnic subgroups, each with its own unique history in the United States.

Although the term "Asian American" has benefits in that it allows us to discuss cultural overlaps and to form a political collective, a pan-Asian identity does not do justice to the unique characteristics of women falling within this category. Immigration laws and other historical events, such as Japanese American internment and the backlash after 9/11, provide glimpses of the political landscape of oppression, racism, and discrimination that has governed the arrival and settlement of Asian women in the United States. Legislative acts have shaped the lens through which Asian American women are viewed. Stereotypic characterizations have impacted Asian American women's view of themselves and the world around them, which in turn has created stressors affecting their sense of well-being.

Asian American women are identified in the literature as being relative latecomers to the women's movement in the United States. However, this perception may be, in part, due to a narrow understanding of what activities constitute feminist advocacy. It is critical to understand the context and to recognize their strengths in their adaptation and resilience. There were a number of features of the women's movement that, at first glance, may seem diametrically opposed to Asian cultural norms. Moreover, much of the mainstream movement did not address the concerns of many Asian American women and other women of color, such as labor conditions, immigration laws, and so on. Asian American women, like other women of color, had to find balance, pursue economic survival, and maintain cultural norms and a movement toward social advocacy and social justice. The value of interdependence lent itself to the creation of social networks that built community, provided support, and acted as a political space for Asian American women.

Currently, Asian American women of all generations continue to experience discrimination and oppression due to gender and racial background, among other identity markers. Although many Asian American women would not identify as feminists, their work has clearly promoted a feminist agenda and should be recognized within the larger women's movement.

Future Directions

Based upon our preceding review of theory and research surrounding the development of feminism in the Asian American community, we recognize a number of areas that need to be addressed in future research and practice. First, while group differences within the pan-Asian movement have been touted in the literature, this categorical identification still fails to recognize the importance of existing multiple and intersecting identities present in diverse Asian communities. It is important to note that the creation of a pan-Asian community has enabled this group to gain a stronghold and leverage for change in the American political system; however, the pan-Asian identity becomes particularly problematic in the realm of clinical treatment, given the cultural diversity within and among Asian subgroups. Thus, striking a balance and flexibility in understanding the complex relationship between more general and subgroup-specific identities is critical for Asian Americans as a whole and women in particular.

Related to this balance is the need to recognize the unique histories of each Asian group and the circumstances of their arrival in the United States. While many Asian groups share some degree of similarity in terms of values and beliefs, conflicts between Asian subgroups must also be recognized by Asian American community advocates and psychologists/practitioners. Ultimately, future advocacy should focus on the recognition of this diversity among policy makers, to ensure that race-based social and economic policies do not universally categorize all Asian American subgroups in a single group. Instead, such policies should recognize the diverse economic and social realities of various Asian groups and should be designed in accordance with this reality.

Despite numerous efforts to debunk the model minority myth of Asian Americans, the stereotype continues to prevail and to impact members of the community. The stereotypes pertaining to Asian American women continue to affect their roles within society, as well as the services they receive. For example, Asian American women who may be struggling with mental health or other issues may not receive adequate and timely assistance as a result of the model minority myth. Building on the complexity of these stereotypes, Asian American women must negotiate their own internalization of particular ideals and conceptions of the "ideal" Asian woman, which may, at times, be in conflict with their needs and desires. Asian American women are continuing to work toward a reconciliation of their feminist values with respect for cultural traditions that may run counter to their ideals.

Another area for future research is rooted in the expanding indigenous psychologies movement referenced earlier in the chapter. As Asian American psychologists conceptualize human development within culturally specific frameworks and develop uniquely Asian American psychological theories and associated treatment methods, Asian American women may have a unique opportunity to advance indigenous Asian feminist psychologies. Further research in this realm may result in the integration of indigenous spiritual healing practices, social justice agendas, and/or the community-building methods developed by Asian American women in response to economic injustices, referenced in an earlier section of the chapter.

We offer the following questions to guide future research and practice as it pertains to Asian American women:

1. How can we obtain a greater understanding of Asian American women while acknowledging and attending to the unique experiences of Asian ethnic subgroups?
2. How does our knowledge of intersecting identities inform our understanding of Asian American women?
3. How can we expand the current dialogue regarding Asian indigenous psychologies to integrate feminist perspectives?
4. How can our understanding of the history of social, economic, and political justice in the Asian American community enhance our cultural competence and training for practitioners who seek to work with Asian American women?
5. Given the impact of structural oppression on individual and community mental health, in what ways can practitioners engage in public policy and advocacy efforts to address ongoing discrimination against Asian American women?

Authors' Note

Special thanks to Jennifer Aliosi for her assistance in the outlining of this chapter.

References

Ahluwalia, M. K., Suzuki, L. A., & Mir, M. (2009). Dating, partnerships and arranged marriages. In N. Tewari, and A. N. Alvarez (Eds.), *American psychology: Current perspectives* (pp. 273–294). New York: Lawrence Erlbaum Associates.

Ahluwalia, M. K., & Zaman, N. K. (2009). Counseling Muslims and Sikhs in a post-9/11 world. In J. G. Ponterotto, M. Casas, L. A. Suzuki, and C. Alexander (Eds.), *Handbook of multicultural counseling* (3rd ed.) (pp. 467–478). Thousand Oaks, CA: Sage Publication

Ahluwalia, M. K., & Pellettiere, L. A. (2010). Sikh men post-9/11: Misidentification, discrimination, and coping. *Asian American Journal of Psychology, 1*(4), 303–314.

Ahluwalia, M. K. (2011). Holding my breath: The experience of being Sikh after 9/11. *Traumatology, 17*(3), 39–44.

Alvarez, A. N. (2009). Racism: "It isn't fair." In N. Tewari and A. N. Alvarez (Eds.), *Asian American psychology: Current perspectives* (pp. 399–419). New York: Lawrence Erlbaum Associates.

American Psychiatric Association. (2000). *Diagnostic and statistical manual of mental disorders* (4th ed., text revision). Washington, DC: Author.

American Psychological Association. (2010). *Resilience and recovery after war: Refugee children and families in the United States.* Washington, DC: APA Task Force on the Psychosocial Effects of War on Children and Families Who are Refugees from Armed Conflict Residing in the United States.

Aoki, G. & Mio, J. S. (2009). Stereotypes and media images. In N. Tewari and A. N. Alvarez (Eds.), *Asian American psychology: Current perspectives* (pp. 421–439). New York: Lawrence Erlbaum Associates.

Asian Pacific Islander Institute on Domestic Violence. (2011). Fact Sheet: Violence against Asian and Pacific Islander women. In Asian Pacific Islander Institute on Domestic Violence Fact Sheet. Retrieved May 2011, from http://www.apiidv.org/download/Violence.against.API.Women-FactSheet-APIIDV-2.2011.pdf

Baden, A. L., Treweeke, L. M., & Ahluwalia, M. K. (In press). Reclaiming culture: Reculturation of transracial and international adoptees. *Journal of Counseling and Development.*

Bowleg, L., Huang, J., & Brooks, K. (2003). Triple jeopardy and beyond: Multiple minority stress and resilience among black lesbians. *Journal of Lesbian Studies, 7,* 87–108.

Chao, M. M., Chiu, C., & Lee, J. S. (2010). Asians as the model minority: Implications for U.S. Government's policies. *Asian Journal of Social Psychology, 13,* 44–52.

Chen, G. A. (2009). Managing multiple social identities. In N. Tewari and A. N. Alvarez (Eds.), *Asian American psychology: Current perspectives* (pp. 173–192). New York: Lawrence Erlbaum Associates.

Chin, F., Chan, J. P., Inada, L. F., & Wong, S. (1991). *The big Aiiieeeee! An anthology of Chinese American and Japanese American literature.* New York: Penguin Books.

Chin, J. L. (Ed.) (2000). *Relationships among Asian American women.* Washington, D. C.: American Psychological Association.

Chow, E. N.-L. (1994). The feminist movement: Where are all the Asian American women? In R. Takaki (Ed.), *From different shores: Perspectives on race and ethnicity in America* (pp. 184–191). New York, NY: Oxford University Press.

Crenshaw, K. (1989). Demarginalizing the intersection of race and sex: A black feminist critique of antidiscrimination doctrine, feminist theory and antiracist politics. *University of Chicago Legal Forum,* 139–167.

Daya, R. (2000). Buddhist psychology, a theory of change processes: Implications for counselors. *International Journal for the Advancement of Counseling, 22*(4), 257–271.

Department of Justice. (June 2004). Assessment of U.S. activities to combat trafficking in persons.

Espiritu, Y. L. (1993). *Asian American panethnicity: Bridging institutions and identities.* Philadelphia: Temple University Press.

Espiritu, Y. L. (1996). *Asian American women and men.* Thousand Oaks, CA: Sage Publications.

Evan B. Donaldson Adoption Institute. (n.d.). *International adoption facts.* Retrieved August 22, 2011, from http://www.adoptioninstitute.org/FactOverview/international.html.

Foo, L. J. (2003). *Asian American women: Issues, concerns, and responsive human and civil rights advocacy.* Lincoln, NE: iUniverse, Inc.

Gee, E. (1981). Issei women: "Picture Brides" in America. In M. S. Seller (Ed.) *Immigrant women* (pp. 53–59), Philadelphia: Temple University Press.

Gopinath, G. (1997). Nostalgia, desire, diaspora: South Asian sexualities in motion. *Positions, 5*(2), 467–489.

Hall, C. C. I. (2009). Asian American women: The nail that sticks out is hammered down. In N. Tewari & A. Alvarez (Eds.), *Asian American psychology: Current perspectives* (pp. 193–209). New York: Routledge/Taylor & Francis Group.

Hall, G. C.N. (2002). Culture-specific ecological models of Asian American violence. In G. C. N., and S. Okazaki (Eds.) *Asian American psychology: The science of lives in context* (pp. 153–170). Washington, DC: American Psychological Association.

Hinton, D., Hinton, A., Pich, V., Loeum, J., & Pollack, M. (2009). Nightmares among Cambodian refugees: The breaching of concentric ontological security. *Culture, Medicine and Psychiatry, 33*(2), 219–265.

Hoodfar, H. (2001). The veil in their minds and on our heads: Veiling practices and Muslim women. In E. A. Castelli, *Women, gender, religion: A reader* (pp. 420–446). New York: Palgrave.

Houston, J. W., & Houston, J. D. (1981). A family disrupted. "Shikata Ga Nai—This cannot be helped." In M. S. Seller (Ed.) *Immigrant women* (pp. 152–156), Philadelphia: Temple University Press.

Hwang, K. K. (2009). The development of indigenous counseling in contemporary Confucian communities. *The Counseling Psychologist, 37*(7), 930.

Kakar, S. (1991).*Shamans, mystics, and doctors: A psychological inquiry into India and its healing traditions.* Chicago: University of Chicago Press.

Kawamura, K., & Rice, T. (2009). Body image among Asian Americans. In N. Tewari and A. N. Alvarez (Eds.), *Asian American psychology: Current perspectives* (pp. 537–557). New York: Lawrence Erlbaum Associates.

Kelly, G. P. (1981). "I am a housewife": English lessons for Vietnamese women. In M. S. Seller (Ed.), *Immigrant women* (pp. 235–240). Philadelphia: Temple University Press.

Kim, U., & Park, Y. S. (2005).Integrated analysis of indigenous psychologies: Comments and extensions of ideas presented by Shams, Jackson, Hwang and Kashima. *Asian Journal of Social Psychology, 8*(1), 75–95.

Kochiyama, Y. (1997). Preface: Trailblazing in a white world: A brief history of Asian Pacific American women. In S. Shah (Ed.), *Dragon ladies: Asian American feminists breathe fire* (pp. 5–8). MA: South End Press.

Lee, S. J., Wong, N. A., & Alvarez, A. N. (2009). The model minority myth and the perpetual foreigner: Stereotypes of Asian Americans. In N. Tewari and A. N. Alvarez (Eds.), *Asian American psychology: Current perspectives* (pp. 69–84). New York: Lawrence Erlbaum Associates.

Leong, F. T. L. & Gupta, A. (2009). History and evolution of Asian American psychology. In N. Tewari and A. N. Alvarez (Eds.), *Asian American psychology: Current perspectives* (pp. 31–48). New York: Lawrence Erlbaum Associates.

Louie, K. B. (2000). Asian American women and social advocacy. In J. L. Chin (Ed.) *Relationships among Asian American women* (pp. 13–23). Washington, DC: APA Publications.

Maeda, D. J. (2006). Black panthers, red guards, and Chinamen: Constructing Asian American identity through performing blackness, 1969–1972. *American Quarterly, 57*(4), 1079–1103.

McMahon, S. (2001). *Echoes of freedom: South Asian pioneers in California, 1899–1965.* Berkeley: Center for South Asian Studies, University of California, Berkeley.

Meyer, O., Dhindsa, C. G., & Sue, S. (2009). Psychopathology and clinical issues in Asian American populations. In N. Tewari & A. N. Alvarez (eds.). *Asian American psychology: Current perspectives* (pp. 519–536). New York: Taylor and Francis.

Moodley, R., & West, W. (2005). *Integrating traditional healing practices into counseling and psychotherapy.* Thousand Oaks, CA: Sage Publications.

Reeves, T., & Bennett, C. (2003). *The Asian and Pacific Islander population in the United States: March 2002*, Current Population Reports, P20–540, U.S. Census Bureau, Washington, DC.

Root, M. P. P. (1992). Reconstructing the impact of trauma on personality. In L. S. Brown & M. Ballou (Eds.), *Personality and psychopathology: Feminist reappraisals* (pp. 229–265). New York, NY: Guildford Press.

Root, M. P. P. (1995). The psychology of Asian American women. In H. Landrine (Ed.) *Bringing cultural diversity to feminist psychology: Theory, research, and practice* (pp. 265–501). Washington, DC: American Psychological Association.

Sandhu, D. S. (Ed.) (1997). *Asian Pacific Islander Americans: Issues and concerns for counseling and psychotherapy.* Hauppauge, NY: Nova Science Publications.

Seller, M. S. (Ed.) (1981). *Immigrant women.* Philadelphia: Temple University Press.

Serafica, F. C., Weng, A., & Kim, H. K. (2000). Friendships and social networks among Asian American women. In J. L. Chin (Ed.) *Relationships among Asian American women* (pp. 101–117).Washington, DC: American Psychological Association.

Shankar, L. D., & Srikanth, R. (1998). *A part, yet apart: South Asians in Asian America.* Philadelphia: Temple University Press.

Suzuki, H. B. (2002). Revisiting the model minority stereotype: Implications for student affairs practice and higher education. *New Directions for Student Services, 97*, 21–32.

Takaki, R. (1998). *Strangers from a different shore.* New York: Little, Brown & Company.

Tien, L. (2000). U. S. attitudes toward women of Asian ancestry: Legislative and media perspectives. In J. L. Chin (Ed.) *Relationships among Asian American Women* (pp. 29–470. Washington, DC: American Psychological Association.

Tsong, Y. & Liu, Y. (2009). Parachute kids and astronaut families. In N. Tewari & A. N. Alvarez (eds.). *Asian American psychology: Current perspectives* (pp. 365–380). New York: Taylor and Francis.

Turner-Essel, L., & Waehler, C. (2009). Integrating internationalization in counseling psychology training programs. *The Counseling Psychologist, 37*(6), 877.

U.S. Census Bureau (2007). The American Community—Asians: 2004: American Community Survey Report. Retrieved August 22, 2011, from http://www.census.gov/prod/2007pubs/acs-05.pdf.

Watters, E. (2010).*Crazy like us: The globalization of the American psyche.* New York, NY: Free Press.

Xie, Y., & Goyette, K. A. (n.d.). Asian Americans: A demographic portrait of Asian Americans. Retrieved August 22, 2011, from http://www-personal.umich.edu/~yuxie/Research/brief/Xie-Goyette.pdf.

Yeh, C. J., & Kwong, A. K. (2009). Asian American indigenous healing and coping. In N. Tewari & A. N. Alvarez (eds.). *Asian American psychology: Current perspectives* (pp. 559–573). New York: Taylor and Francis.

Yokoyama, K. (2007). The double binds of our bodies: Multiculturally and informed feminist therapy considerations for body image and eating disorders among Asian American women. *Women and Therapy, 30*(3–4), 177–192.

CHAPTER

11 Women With Disabilities: The Cultural Context of Disability, Feminism, Able-Bodied Privilege, and Microaggressions

Barbara J. Palombi

Abstract

This chapter provides an orientation to the lives and experiences of women with disabilities (WWD); examines the relationship between WWD and feminist psychology, including philosophical differences between feminist theorists and disability feminist theorists; and focuses on therapeutic models that incorporate feminism and multiculturalism. The chapter also (a) addresses the behavioral impact of able-bodied privilege and microaggressions experienced by WWD; (b) describes behaviors within clinical practice associated with microaggressions; (c) provides resources to increase multiculturalism competency when working with WWD; and (d) presents a model of therapy that integrates multiculturalism and feminism when working with WWD.

Key Words: Disabled, women with disabilities, able-bodied privilege, microaggressions, feminism, disability feminist theories, feminism and multiculturalism

The field of counseling psychology has been in the forefront of efforts to advocate for and to be inclusive of marginalized members of society, as evidenced by the number of publications and professional contributions made to feminist psychology and diversity. To date, however, the lives of women with disabilities (WWD) have received limited attention. Feminist counseling psychologists have not yet explored many of the issues of WWD, such as lack of peer contact, isolation and stigmatization, limited media coverage of personal concerns of WWD, social events that are not inclusive of WWD, and the absence of advocacy for shared causes of WWD. These experiences exemplify the discrimination, prejudice, and marginalization experienced by WWD in today's society.

Non-disabled feminists may share society's negative attitudes toward WWD and may distance themselves from WWD in an effort to advance more powerful, competent, and appealing female icons (Asch & Fine, 1988; Lloyd, 1992; Lonsdale, 1990). WWD may also have limited awareness about issues important to WWD (Nosek, 2009). Many WWD are more focused on surviving and may not identify themselves "as having a disability or being part of an oppressed population" (p. 506). Nosek (2009) challenges feminist counseling psychologists as follows: "If the essence of feminism is empowerment, then we must put all theories aside and look specifically at those individual, lifestyles, and social factors that serve to either diminish or enhance the power of women with disabilities to believe they are women of value and to exert control over their lives" (p. 506).

This chapter provides an orientation to the lives and experiences of WWD; examines the relationship between WWD and feminist psychology, including philosophical differences between feminist theorists and disability feminist theorists; and focuses on therapeutic models incorporating feminism and multiculturalism. Feminist psychology focuses on the power difference among members of society and also emphasizes privileges that entitle certain members of society to maintain power and control over others. A privilege that has received little attention in the feminist literature is "able-bodied" privilege. Able-bodied privilege within society contributes to the discrimination and marginalization of WWD. This chapter will examine able-bodied privilege and its relationships to oppression and microaggressions. The concerns addressed by this chapter will provide feminist counseling psychologists with an opportunity to educate the psychological and mental health communities regarding the impact of ableism and how it is embedded in various aspects of feminist counseling psychology (Wolbring, 2008).

Women with Disabilities (WWD)

Persons with disabilities (PWD) represent the largest minority group in the world. If all individuals with a disability were to live in a single country, it would be the third largest country in the world (Freeman, 2002). According to the World Health Organization (WHO), the number of individuals with disabilities continues to expand (2002). The WHO has predicted that by 2020, chronic conditions will contribute to more than 80% of the global burden of disease. These chronic conditions include body impairments and handicaps, as well as diseases that restrict participation in daily activities and require management over years or decades. The WHO and the United Nations estimate that such disability conditions account for about 10% of any national population, and over half of these are women (Coleridge, 1993: Health Canada, 1997; Rioux, 1998). According to the United Nations Development Programme (UNDP), 80% of all persons with disabilities live in developing countries. The World Bank estimates that 20% of the world's poorest people are disabled, viewed in their own communities as the most disadvantaged; WWD are the poorest of the poor (Latin American and Caribbean Women's Health Network, 2006).

As the population within the United States continues to age, the number of individuals with disabilities has also increased. More than 52 million Americans (one in six, or 15% of the population) currently have physical or mental disabilities (Cornish et al., 2008; Longmore, 2009; Mpofu & Conyers, 2004; Olkin, 2002; Rohrer, 2005). Relatively few of these impairments are congenital, and few developed during birth or childhood. Rather, most people have disabilities as the result of an illness or injury sustained during adolescence or adulthood (Asch, 2004), including sensory limitations, mobility impairments, chronic illness, and so-called hidden disabilities, including epilepsy and diabetes (Rohrer, 2005).

WWD constitute one of the largest and most disadvantaged populations in the United States (Nosek & Hughes, 2003). The most prevalent disabling condition in women is back disorder (15.3%), followed by arthritis (13.3%), cardiovascular disease (9.7%), asthma (5.3%), orthopedic impairment of lower extremity (4.2%), mental disorders (3.3%), diabetes (3.3%), and learning disability and developmental disabilities (2.5%). Among the mental disorders, WWD experience anxiety disorders, panic disorders, post-traumatic stress disorder (PTSD), and agoraphobia, as well as mental illnesses such as schizophrenia and bipolar disorder. WWD appear to be at an elevated risk for depression (30%), compared to men with disabilities (26%), women without disabilities (8%), and the population in general (7%). Depression in WWD is associated with lower levels of perceived control, lack of social support, lower income, poverty, and experiences with abuse (Begum, 1992; Curry, Hassouneh-Phillips, & Johnston-Silverberg, 2001; Gilson, Cramer, & DePoy, 2001; Nosek, Howland, Hughes, 2001). The lack of or inability to secure employment also contributes to depression for WWD. Turner and Turner (2004) found that WWD are five times more likely than their non-disabled counterparts to be involuntarily unemployed.

Health is a major consideration for WWD. McDermott, Moran, Platt and Dasari (2007) compared 770 WWD to a group of 1,097 women without disabilities and found that different risks were associated with different disabilities. For example, both groups had similar rates of diabetes, hypertension, and obesity. Yet WWD with sensory, developmental, and trauma disabilities had higher hazard ratios for dementia; women with sensory disabilities had higher risk for minor heart attacks; and those whose disabilities were related to trauma had a higher risk for depression.

Iwasaki and Mactavish (2005) studied stress and identified several areas of stress unique to WWD: (a) added demands associated with daily living and the complications of disability; (b) health concerns; (c) interpersonal relationship and attitudes toward WWD; and (d) issues regarding employment. Landry and Mercurio (2009) identify discrimination as a unique type of stress. Because discriminatory events are demeaning and personal, they have a greater impact on woman's health than generic stressors such as those associated with daily living

(Landrine & Klonoff, 1997; Orbe & Camara, 2010). As a result of being female and having a disability, WWD may be more likely than their male counterparts to experience stress due to higher rates of poverty, social isolation, violence and other forms of victimization, and chronic health problems (Deegan & Brooks, 1985; Fine & Asch, 1988). Contributing to their economic disadvantage are many stress-inducing factors, including earning lower income, having less education, being less likely to be married or employed, and having fewer disability benefits from public programs (Fine & Asch, 1988; Hanna & Rogovsky, 1993; Nosek & Hughes, 2003). These stressors influence their ability to take advantage of legal entitlements to education, employment, or public services and prevent WWD from managing certain impairment-related expenses such as medications, transportation, personal assistance services, particular diet supplements, or items of clothing. Stressors related to major life events and to the demands of daily living are associated with negative mental and physical health outcomes (Krieger, 1999; Landrine & Klonoff, 1997).

Working also creates additional stress for WWD. Environmental barriers (e.g., lack of accommodations in the workplace), interpersonal impediments (e.g., ableist attitudes), and internal obstacles (e.g., low self-esteem) create additional stresses and may exacerbate the disability (Gill, 1997; Shahnasarian, 2001). For example, those with emotional or cognitive impairments may need the assistance of job coaches or other support staff to manage the demands of education or work. WWD who experience chronic pain or limited energy may require special equipment or work schedules adjusted for rest, or medical appointments to successfully maintain employment (Olkin, 1999).

To summarize, feminist counseling psychologists need to be cognizant of the increased stress experiences of WWD due to health concerns, challenges associated with daily living, attitudes and interpersonal relationships, employment, and the impact of discrimination on woman's health. Without accounting for these stressors, it is difficult for feminist counseling psychologists to comprehend or understand the life experiences of WWD.

Diversity, Intersectionality, and WWD

WWD represent multiple categories of social group membership that include women, women with disabilities, and cultural, racial, gender, and social identities, or what Crenshaw has labeled "intersectionality" (Cole, 2009, p. 170). Intersectionality is characterized by the "interplay between person and social location, with particular emphasis on power relations among various social locations" (Mahalingam, 2007, p. 45). WWD's membership in multiple social groups has an impact on their perceptions and experiences, including social inequalities (Cole, 2009), and can contribute to their marginalization and disempowerment (Cronin & King, 2010). In other circumstances, intersectionality can be the source of empowerment and strength. Focusing on intersectionality provides feminist counseling psychologists an opportunity to determine "the interplay of identities in relationship to public and private institutions, families, schools, workplaces, and the law and how they contribution to political, material and social inequality" (Cole, 2009, p. 170).

Research suggests that the struggles of WWD vary; for instance, women who have lived only in an impaired body may experience disability differently from women who acquire a disability later in life (Rohrer, 2005; Sherrill, 1993). Age, time of onset of disability, type of impairment, social class, education, race, ethnicity, and sexuality contribute to intersecting identities and feelings of alienation and marginalization (Clark, 2006; Sherrill, 1993). Also significant is the observation that pre-injury attitudes toward disability influence post-injury attitudes (Hardin, 2007). Because impairments are multiple and various, the same impairment may affect individuals differently, depending upon environment and personal factors in the person's life (Asch, 2004).

Though WWD represent the largest group of diverse women within the United States, their status as being diverse is at times questioned (Weeber, 1999). Many members of society do not believe that WWD experience prejudice, discrimination, and marginalization similar to that experienced by other minorities. According to Davis (1997) "people with disabilities have been isolated, incarcerated, observed, written about, operated on, instructed, implanted, regulated, treated, institutionalized, and controlled to a degree probably unequal to that experienced by any other minority group" (p. 1). When intersecting identities are considered, disability is frequently overlooked and assumes lesser importance within other marginalized groups (Gill, 2001; Tsao, 1998; Vernon, 1998).

Frequently, members of other disadvantaged groups may reflect the prejudices and attitudes of society (Castaneto & Willemsen, 2006; Palombi,

2010). Nowell and Gill (2005) studied the lived experience of Black women with disabilities and found that these women (a) viewed disability as complicating their lives more so than race; (b) described contradictions between wanting their disability needs to be met but not wanting to identify as WWD; (c) did not accept or openly discuss in their societal networks their disability status; and (d) had little affiliation with other WWD or disability groups. The life experiences of these women reflect how disability can be discounted and minimized when considered as part of other intersecting identities. It also highlights the women's personal discomfort in acknowledging their own disabilities. In spite of being WWD, they may isolate themselves from other WWD, which prevents them from receiving mutual support, sharing of information, and developing bonds of "sisterhood" with other WWD (Nosek, 2009). The following section with provide an overview regarding how these factors influence the lives of WWD.

Oppression, Able-Bodied Privilege, and Microaggressions

In examining the lives of WWD, it is apparent that they experience numerous acts of discrimination and prejudice daily, and this section explores the relationship between oppression, able-bodied privilege and microaggressions. Oppression is defined as "an unjust, harsh, or cruel exercise of power over another or others" (Hanna, Talley, & Guindon, 2000, p. 2), is imbedded within the sociocultural fabric of society (Orbe & Camara, 2010), and may contribute to psychological distress or emotional pain and suffering. An important aspect of oppression is an irrational sense of entitlement assumed by the oppressive person or group (Black & Stone, 2005). These irrational beliefs are contrived by the dominant members of society and may remain unsubstantiated (Black & Stone, 2005). For example, WWD are viewed by society as childlike and dependent. These beliefs allow WWD to be easily dismissed and disregarded by members of the dominant culture. Because of these beliefs, WWD receive fewer financial resources and have limited employment opportunities available to them (Nosek, 2009).

Oppression serves as the foundation for the dominant members' beliefs in such concepts as privilege and ableism (Black & Stone, 2005). Black and Stone (2005) define privilege as "any entitlement, sanction, power, immunity, and advantage or right granted or conferred by the dominant group to a person or group solely by birthright membership in prescribed identities" (p. 245). Privileged persons may be unaware of their privilege and therefore can look on "prejudice, bigotry, and conferred dominances with detachment" (p. 248).

A form of privilege rarely discussed in the psychological literature is ableism. "Ableism, just like racism and sexism, is a prejudicial emotion, thought, and/or action against the disabled" (Castaneto & Willemsen, 2006, p. 1218). Ableism values certain abilities, which leads to disableism, the discrimination against the "less able" (Wolbring, 2008, p. 252). Ableism is a set of beliefs, processes, and practices, based on ability, that influences the understanding of the self, the body, relationships with others, and determines how others judge the individual. This preference for certain abilities has been used by various social groups to justify their elevated level of rights and status in relations to other groups. These beliefs provide the foundation and support for able-bodied privilege (Campbell, 2008; Wolbring, 2008).

A chief feature of an ableist viewpoint is a belief that impairment is inherently negative. If an opportunity presents itself, the disability should be ameliorated, cured, or indeed eliminated (Campbell, 2008; Kafer, 2003). The processes of ableism, like those of racism, induce an internalization that devalues disablement (Campbell, 2008). Theorists focused on disability assert "that most non-disabled people feel disabled people symbolize, among other things, imperfection, failure to control the body and everyone's vulnerability to weakness, pain and death. So pervasive are those projected ableist attitudes that many disabled people also internalize them" (Overboe, 1999, p. 19). Because of these beliefs, much of the world is structured as though everyone is physically strong, as though all bodies are "ideally shaped," as though everyone can walk, hear and see well, as though everyone can work and play at a pace that is not compatible with any kind of illness or pain.... Not only the architecture, but the entire physical and social organization of life, assumes that we are either strong and healthy and able to do what the average able-bodied person can do. (Wendell, 1997, p. 266)

The following vignette focuses on the unconscious process of able-bodied privilege. Frequently, oppressors are oblivious that their behavior is a manifestation of able-bodied privilege.

> Flo, who has a hearing impairment and uses hearing aids, is attending a lecture at the local

community center, which has recently been remodeled. Part of the remodeling has included the installation of an electronic "loop" that allows those who use hearing aids to have access to the presentation through the microphone and to adjust their hearing aids to the required frequency. Flo is looking forward to the presentation because of the new "loop." Because of the "loop" Flo does not feel required to sit in the front row to hear and sits with her friends in the middle of the audience. However, the presenter declines to use the microphone, and states that he is uncomfortable using the microphone and that his voice is strong enough to be heard. Flo is angry when she realizes that the presenter is not using the microphone because she will not have access to the "loop" and will be unable to hear the presentation. Again, she feels left out and marginalized. She chastises herself for coming and wonders why she wasted her time coming to the presentation.

This vignette reflects how able-bodied privilege is an unconscious process. Those who currently possess able-privilege see accommodations as an inconvenience that can be easily discounted and ignored. Society defines and operationalizes the belief of what human beings are and what (in that particular society) people think they ought to try to be (Davis, 2005). These beliefs shape or define life in that society, individual choices, and institutions (Hastings & Thomas, 2005). The manner in which disability is perceived affects how society treats able-bodied individuals as normal and grants them the special status as being seen as able-bodied (Davis, 2005, p. 158).

When society uses able-bodied standards, there are three assumptions made regarding disability: (a) it is normal for humans to be able-bodied; (b) a person's disability is a consequence of or results from her not being able-bodied; and (c) not being able-bodied is the reason for being disadvantaged in society (Davis, 2005). These assumptions allow members of society to believe that the pain, suffering, frustration, and disadvantage experienced by WWD result from the fact that they are disabled, and thus, there is no need for further personal connection with WWD. Viewing WWD from the ideology of able-bodied privilege contributes to society's reluctance to endorse policies of accommodation that would make life easier and better for those with disabilities (Davis, 2005; Park, Radford, & Vickers, 1998). Due to these assumptions, WWD may be perceived as having little value (Davis, 2005; Nosek, 2009). The following vignette outlines how perceptions can change when an individual acquires a disability.

Last summer, Tiffany was involved in a car accident and suffered a closed head injury that affected her speech. Now Tiffany's speech is labored and difficult to understand. Prior to her accident, Tiffany and her partner had a large circle of friends and were frequently asked to speak regarding issues affecting the LGBT community. Recently, both Tiffany and her partner have become aware of no longer being asked to participate in many community events and also having less contact with their friends. Finally, Tiffany and her partner contact a leader of the advocacy group. After much reluctance, the leader informs Tiffany and her partner that because of Tiffany's speech impediment, she no longer embodies the image that the LGBT community wants to portray to the outside community.

This vignette reflects how easily individuals may be rejected and devalued when they no longer project the group's image of competence and strength (Asch, 2004; Klein, 1996; Nadal, 2008). Able-bodied persons may find it intolerable to spend time with WWD due to their concern about the possible negative perception by others (Fisher & Galler, 1988; Wertlieb, 1985). Many individuals limit their interaction with WWD because of their fear that a similar situation could happen to them (Hirschberger et al., 2005). Non-disabled individuals may also socially distance themselves from individuals who are close to WWD due to their belief that this distance will prevent them from any possible loss of status (Hirschberger et al., 2005).

Within society there has been an unspoken collaboration to avoid granting access to disabled persons or to acknowledge their presence, even when they are physically present (Davis, 2005). The practices of exclusion become social customs or habits and are passed on from one generation to another. Parents often instruct children to refrain from doing things like staring at "the nice person in the wheelchair" (Davis, 2005, p. 197). This is something that is seen as a matter of courtesy, or good manners, and develops into the familiar "tactful" adult practice of averting one's gaze from those whom one perceives as disabled. What is considered customary or standard practice becomes "willful disregard and discourtesy" (Davis, 2005, p. 197). The traits and abilities people regard as "normal" have been created by previous decisions and determine (a) the construction of the environment, (b) the type of institutions, (c) the specific policies implemented, and (d) cultural norms for how things are done (Davis, 2005).

Therefore, disability is a culturally constructed concept that legitimizes an unequal distribution of resources, status, and power within a biased social and architectural environment (Knoll, 2009). As such, disability encompasses four aspects: (a) a system for interpreting and disciplining body variations; (b) a relationship between bodies and their environments; (c) a set of practices that produce both the able-bodied and the disabled; and (d) a way of describing the inherent stability of the embodied self (Garland-Thomson, 2004). The disability system functions to preserve and validate some privileged designations as beautiful, healthy, normal, fit, competent, and intelligent, all of which provide cultural capital to those who can claim such status, who can reside within these subject positions (Garland-Thomson, 2005).

Those who currently meet able-bodied standards are not guaranteed that the current system of able-bodied privilege will continue to be beneficial in their future (Davis, 2005; Morell, 2003; Overall, 2006; Smith, 2007). In statistical terms, illness, injury, accident, or infirmity will affect most individuals (Morell, 2003; Overall, 2006; Smith, 2007). The longer one lives, the more likely it is that she or he will live some portion of life as a disabled person. If our society continues to marginalize and devalue those who are disabled, then it is likely that most members of society will, at some point, face this marginalization. Those who act from able-bodied privilege will come to see themselves as less worthy, less valued, or less than fully human simply for becoming disabled (Garland-Thomson, 2004; Morell, 2003; Overall, 2006; Smith, 2007; Wendell, 1996).

Feminism and Able-Bodied Privilege

Feminist theorists with disabilities view feminist theorists as neither understanding issues related to WWD nor supporting WWD (Begum, 1992; Ferri& Gregg, 1998; Freeman, 2002; Garland-Thomson, 2004; Kafer, 2003; Sheldon, 1999; Wendell, 1996). Disability is rarely acknowledged as a social identity, or recognized in feminists' litanies of identities that reflect the category of "woman," or explored and/or included in feminist literature (Asch, 2004; Garland-Thomson, 2004; Knoll, 2009; Sheldon, 1999). Feminist issues that are intricately entangled with disability, such as reproductive technology, the place of bodily differences, the particularities of oppression, the ethics of care, and the construction of the subject, are repeatedly discussed without any reference to disability (Garland-Thomson, 2004).

At times, the concerns that feminist theorists may advocate for are in direct conflict with the needs of WWD, reflecting instead aspects of able-bodied privilege. Society's reliance on and use of technology is such an example. Some feminists argue that technology alienates women from natural processes (Freeman, 2002). Yet for WWD, technology is a crucial and necessary part of their lives. Technology provides WWD with (a) increased mobility, (b) energy-saving devices that increase freedom and independence, and (c) numerous possibilities for a more enjoyable life.

According to feminist theorists, "patriarchies are the near-universal hierarchical social systems in which attributes associated with maleness are privileged and those attributed to women are denigrated" (Lerner, as cited in Brown, 2010, p. 5). Due to the oppression of the patriarchal society, both feminists and feminists with disabilities struggle. Certain aspects of women's oppression parallel the experiences of disabled women and non-disabled women, especially regarding gender roles, body image, and sexuality (Begum, 1992). Though the issues may be similar for both groups, the impact of disability means that the implications or effects may differ. The relative privileges of normative femininity are often denied to disabled women (Sheldon, 1999). In regard to laws of patriarchy, WWD are excluded and face a double invisibility—they are neither considered as women nor as objects of sexual desire (Ferri & Gregg, 1998; Kafer, 2003). WWD are perceived as "perennial outsiders" and are seen as powerless. These positions have not been addressed by feminists theorists.

Cultural stereotypes imagine disabled women as asexual, unfit to reproduce, overly dependent, unattractive, or generally removed from the sphere of true womanhood and feminine beauty (Rohrer, 2005). WWD struggle to have their sexuality and their rights to bear children recognized (Begum, 1992). Members of society believe that WWD will give birth to "defective" offspring, or will be unfit mothers (Heyman & Huckle, 1995; Sheldon, 1999) and therefore, WWD have experienced forced sterilization and abortion, and have been denied custody (Breeden, Olkin, & Taube, 2008; Ferri & Gregg, 1998). Because of their inability to fit the prescribed gender roles that have been assigned to women, WWD occupy a position in a "no woman's land" that may either push them (a) to choose very traditional feminine roles to appear normal, or (b) to select non-traditional feminine roles as a process of default rather than personal choice. If WWD choose not to conform to conventional gender roles, they will have difficulty in achieving access to institutions of society, including the family. Although many feminists may consider these institutions oppressive, the struggle against the family or other institutions of society may be different for WWD, who are excluded from the outset. When WWD recognize society's rejection and realize that the socially sanctioned roles are prohibited, they acquire a sense of worthlessness and a negative self-image (Begum, 1992).

Feminist disability theory offers to the feminist literature a comprehensive analysis of the ways that the female body has been medicalized in modernity (Garland-Thomson, 2004). Both women and the disabled have been imagined as "medically abnormal" and have in common the intersections between the politics of appearance and the medicalization of subjugated bodies. Feminist critics have pointed out that society's standard of beauty for the female body has become a goal to be achieved through self-regulation and consumerism (Garland-Thomson, 2004; Haiken, 1997; Neath, 1997; Wold, 1991). Women are also encouraged to modify their bodies through intrusive surgical procedures, including silicone breast implants, face-lifts, liposuction, intestinal bypass, or stomach stapling (Gilman, 1998; Neath, 1997; Wold, 1991). These procedures are viewed as enhancements that correct flaws and improve the health and well-being of women. Those who choose to forego these surgical enhancing procedures are regarded "as unnatural and abnormal," while the surgically altered bodies are portrayed "as normal and natural" (Garland-Thomson, 2004, p. 12).

WWD share similar pressures to modify their bodies. Society's high expectations regarding medical technology have encouraged "the cultural conviction" that disability can be fixed and/or eradicated and therefore reinforces the belief that living with a disability is intolerable. Focusing on changing/curing the "abnormal and dysfunctional" bodies of WWD shifts attention from changing exclusionary attitudinal, environmental, and economic barriers (Garland-Thomson, 2004). Body image has a profound impact on the way in which WWD perceive themselves. "A positive body-image can help to build confidence and promote self-esteem, and a negative image can affirm feelings of inferiority, worthlessness and inadequacies" (Begum, 1992, p. 77).

Another major philosophical difference between feminist theorists and feminist theorists with disabilities involves care and the caring relationship (Sheldon, 1999). For feminist theorists, the emphasis is on the giver of care (usually female), while in disability studies the focus is on the recipient of care (male or female). From the feminist perspective, the caring relationship allows women to express the importance of emotions and their connection to interdependency, which "symbolizes and embodies the genuine intimacy and reciprocity that cannot find expression in society dominated by male imagery" (Hughes et al., 2005, p. 260). Feminists may look upon caring as an ethical responsibility in which "mutuality, reciprocity and tactility" are the foundations for a moral life (p. 264). Through the process of caring, woman's identity begins to emerge (Graham, 1983).

Yet, from the perspective of feminist theorists with disabilities, the concept of the caregiver neglects the citizenship of the recipient of care. Caregivers have the ability to choose how they are willing to help, yet the recipient of care has limited choice regarding care. If she chooses to reject the help offered by the caregiver, the rejection of help may sever the helping relationship (Silvers, 1995). The fact that WWD need care in order to live in today's able-bodied society allows them to be viewed as dependent and to have their competency questioned (Asch, 2004; Hughes et al., 2005; Silvers, 1995). For WWD, it is empowering to transform care into help or assistance, with those needing care as "the employer" and the caretaker as "the employee." Such a transformation breaks the potential domination of the carer and lessens the vulnerability of the recipient of care (Morris, 2001), and reverses the balance of power (Hughes et al., 2005). In the feminist analysis of women's experiences, WWD who needed care were defined as "others," excluded from the category of "women," and regarded as a threat to non-disabled economic opportunities (Morris, 2001). Being regarded as the employer allows WWD to have the same access to the labor market as non-disabled people, as well as the opportunity to participate fully in social and cultural life. Within the feminist literature there is an emphasis on achieving equality. Yet equality may not permit WWD to have their personal needs taken care of, and WWD may consider equality as "a repressive rather than a liberating notion" (Silvers, 1995, p. 32).

Espín (1995) and McIntosh (1988) both assert that feminist theory reflects the privilege of its creators and their inability to acknowledge that privilege. It is also embedded in models that are used to describe specific developmental tasks, including feminist identity development. Most of the research conducted on feminist identity development has used White women who were traditional-age college students, and has not included other groups of women (e.g., ethnic minority women, women of all ages, women with disabilities, lesbian/bisexual women, women of various religions) (Moradi, Mezydlo, Subich, & Phillips, 2002). As previously mentioned, WWD have less access to education, frequently are older, are more likely to live in poverty, and are more likely to represent a higher percentage of women of color; therefore, they would be unlikely to have been included in the sample (Asch & Fine, 1988). Also, activities that serve as benchmarks to determine if a specific developmental stage has been achieved reflect able-bodied privilege. For example, the final stage of the feminist model of identity development is *active commitment* (Downing & Roush, 1985) and is defined as women translating their feminist identities into working toward societal change, with the goal of eliminating oppression. An indicator of achieving this final stage of feminism identity is being engaged in social advocacy.

The developers of this theoretical model have not considered the mental, physical, and environmental demands required to be a social advocate. The documentary film entitled *Rolling* (Berland, 2007) follows the daily life of Vicki Elman, who volunteers at Californians for Disability Rights. To ready herself for volunteering, her day includes (a) falling out of her wheelchair and calling the neighbors for assistance; (b) discovering that her wheelchair does not work and being informed by the insurance company that wheelchair repairs are not considered a medical necessity; (c) experiencing leg spasms, which means that she is unable to put on her slacks, and must leave her home with a towel draped over her legs; and (d) spending four hours outside waiting for an accessible bus that never arrives. In spite of these obstacles and personal challenges, she volunteers when these barriers can be minimized. Architectural, physical, and personal barriers may inhibit WWD from being active in social advocacy and achieving this last stage of development, which means that WWD may need to relinquish social advocacy as feminists due to the additional stress, energy, and time that these activities require. If such models are used to define feminist identity, WWD may never be identified as feminists and may therefore continue to be ignored and/or discounted in the feminist movement.

Microaggressions

The physical environment, institutions, education, policies, and procedures are all designed and created from the point of able-bodied privilege and allow those who are able-bodied to be regarded as "more" (Yuval-Davis, 2006). Able-bodied privilege and microaggression are interrelated. Sue and colleagues (2007) define microaggressions as "the brief and commonplace daily verbal, behavioral, and environmental indignities, whether intentional or unintentional, that communicate hostile, derogatory, or negative, racial, gender sexual-orientation, and religious slights and insults to the target person or group" (p. 273). When one assumes and acts from able-bodied privilege, the results are frequently expressed by microaggressions toward WWD. Much of the daily discrimination that WWD face is not characterized as the overt hostility of demeaning statements or offensive language. Rather, it is the experience of being denied the opportunity to play the social roles expected of one's non-disabled age peers (Gill, 2001). WWD are (a) expected to play no adult social role, (b) assumed to be recipients of help and never providers of assistance, and (c) more disliked by non-disabled others if they are clearly competent than if they are perceived as incompetent at a task (Asch, 2004). Negative attitudes and actions are generally not demonstrated blatantly in personal interactions (Gill, 2001). Society has deemed it unacceptable to act in such a fashion. Consequently, the role of WWD is complicated by the ambiguity inherent in many interactions. It is difficult for WWD to know how to act because it is unclear whether the non-disabled person is being accepting or rejecting (Gill, 2001; Wertlieb, 1985).

Another behavior related to microaggression is disability harassment. Holzbauer and Berven (1996) defined disability harassment as:

> the unwelcome bothering, tormenting, troubling, ridiculing, or coercing of another person related to the disability of the person and is composed of verbal behavior or gestures as distinguished from physical violence or force. The harassing behavior is typically repeated and often takes place in a social context, with the harasser attempting to gain power over the individual being harassed. (p. 478)

Psychological and internally harmful consequences from experiencing harassment include (a) self-doubt—WWD may be bewildered and confused and doubt their perceptions/experiences; (b) denial and self-blame—recipients may deny that harassment behavior has occurred, which then leads to the feeling of self-blame; (c) humiliation—recipients experience the stress of being devalued in a harassing situation as humiliating; and (d) anger and depression—WWD may feel powerless to express these emotions, which may lead recipients to turn the anger inward, which leads to depression.

Microaggressions can be viewed as another form of disability harassment. Those who are perpetrators of microaggressions are frequently unaware that they have engaged in actions that demean the reception of the communication. The vignette that follows provides the reader with an example of how frequently microaggressions are perpetrated against WWD.

> Sally is a doctoral student in counseling psychology, diagnosed with ADD and a previous history of hospitalization due to depression. Because of her inability to concentrate and her tendency to be easily distracted, she receives testing accommodations from Disabled Student Services. She also has received additional accommodations as a result of unintentional absences due to side effects of her medication, which adversely affect her attention, thinking, and/or alertness. She has heard disparaging comments from her peers regarding these accommodations. According to the university's director of disability services, providing extra time for test-taking is akin to giving glasses to someone with vision problems. It creates a more level playing field for taking the test. In spite of this explanation, her peers believe that a competent psychologist should have no need for accommodations.
>
> In preparing for intern selection, Sally did not mention in her application that she had a disability. She also spoke to each of her references regarding the possible bias that might occur and asked that her disability not be mentioned. Recently, the internship match results were announced. Sally was matched with a highly sought-after internship site. When Sally shared that she had received an internship, none of her colleagues offered congratulations. A classmate who did not receive an internship stated that the only reason Sally was matched was due to having a disability. The site was looking for diversity rather than a competent intern. Sally is speechless and does not know how to respond. She finds it difficult to accept that her peers could be that cruel.

Attitudes toward those with psychiatric disabilities have been negative and contribute to inequalities, segregation, and discrimination (Singer, 2001). Research indicates that Women with mental illness (WWMI) often internalize these stigmatizing ideas and see themselves as less valued (Link & Phelan, 2001). They may decide to avoid this stigma by either denying their group status or not seeking treatment that could identify their mental health status. Corrigan and Matthews (2003) label this behavior as "staying in the closet," similar to individuals who are gay but who deny their sexuality.

Those with serious mental health concerns report lower quality of life, worse general health, and greater problems with physical activity (Corrigan, 2004). Challenges facing WWMI include a limited career focus, which contributes to a lack of vocational and educational goals and creates a pattern of educational underachievement or failure, underemployment or unemployment, and lifelong disability (Kiuhara & Huefner, 2008).

Mental illness presents no clear pattern of symptoms, treatment, length or degree of severity of episode, or prognosis (Kiuhara & Huefner, 2008). Treating serious mental illness typically includes implementing a separate or combined pharmacological and psychological intervention with physical and cognitive side effects. Professors and/or employers may perceive WWMI as being manipulative, especially in regard to excessive absenteeism. Missing class and/or employment may be due to side effects of medication, which adversely affect attention, thinking, or alertness (Kiuhara & Huefner, 2008).

Feminist counseling psychologists need to be aware of the stigma attached to mental illness, the reluctance of WWMI to seek services and/or to disclose their mental health status to mental health providers. In regard to lesbian women with disabilities, empirical sources of information have not examined the intersections of lesbians' and disabled women's mental health (O'Toole & Brown, 2003). Psychologists also need to be aware that there remains a lack of relevant mental health information for and about lesbians with disabilities, and for mental health professionals who provide them services (Olkin, 1999; O'Toole & D'aoust, 2000).

Non-disabled peers frequently dislike WWD when they appear competent (Asch, 2004), as in the example of Sally securing an internship. It is considered acceptable to assume that WWD are inferior and to question their competency (Nadal, 2008). Able-bodied individuals may hold these attitudes in order to minimize their loss of personal status

(Davis, 2005). In contrast, experiencing microaggressions (a) affects marginalized individuals' mental health, causing anger, frustration, low self-esteem, and emotional turmoil; (b) creates a hostile and invalidating campus or work environment; (c) perpetuates stereotype threat; (d) creates physical health problems; (e) inundates society with cues that signal devaluation of WWD; and (f) affects work productivity and problem-solving abilities (Sue, 2010). Frequently, the recipient of a microaggression finds it difficult to respond. Sally's inability to respond matches the typical reaction of those who experience microaggressions, which involves (a) struggling with the inability to determine if a microaggression has occurred; (b) not knowing how to respond; (c) finding that the incident was over before a response could be made; (d) pretending that it did not occur; and (e) being concerned about the interpersonal power differentials between perpetrators and recipients. The interaction with her peers may have eroded Sally's self-confidence, leaving her feeling unsupported, leading her to question her competency as a therapist, and leaving her feeling marginalized and discounted as a person (Sue, 2010).

Microaggressions toward WWD are frequently present in the workplace. A study of high-achieving women with physical and sensory disabilities (Noonan et al., 2004) identified numerous examples of anti-disability prejudice and ableism, which also could be labeled as microaggressions toward WWD. Prejudicial experiences that directly affected the career development of these women included: restricted educational opportunities, discriminatory hiring, biased performance evaluations, job tracking, pay inequities, lack of support and mentoring, negative attitudes and chilly workplace climates, lack of accommodations, and general discouragement. These women also identified strategies used to challenge ableism and microaggressions: (a) ignoring it as much as possible; (b) getting support from others; (c) internally reaffirming their goals and worth; (d) using humor to de-escalate hostility and put others at ease; (e) challenging it personally, collectively, and legally; and (f) working actively toward social change. An overall comment expressed by these women was a reference to the resulting exhaustion from continually confronting ableism and microaggressions.

Therapy and Microaggressions

WWD are as likely to seek therapy for similar issues as their able-bodied counterparts (Pelletier, Rogers, & Dellario, 1985). Psychologists (e.g., Ballou & Brown, 1992) have indicated that some of the problems that bring clients to therapy are related to some mishandling or abuse of power. The majority of women who enter therapy or who receive mental health services are in one way or another victims of other persons more powerful than they are (Lerman & Porter, 1990).

Studies have indicated that mental health professionals do not have the education or training to be competent clinicians for working with WWD (Artman & Daniels, 2010; Cornish et al., 2008; Esten & Willmott, 1993; Kemp & Mallinckrodt, 1996; Leigh et al., 2004; Olkin, 1999). A survey of 481 psychologists who were members of APA gathered information regarding their perceptions of access barriers, success factors, and support needs in providing services to client with disabilities. A significant proportion of psychologists without disabilities responded that they needed no additional training or support (in spite of inadequate training, skills, and knowledge) to enhance services (Leigh et al., 2004).

Leigh et al. (2004) believe that therapists mirror society and may perpetuate negative biases and stereotypes. When WWD seek therapy, they may experience microaggressions from well-intentioned therapists. In many cases, the therapists may unconsciously engage in the following behaviors: (a) dispensing the cure—"perhaps you need to respond" forms of advice that are delivered in a proscribed way; (b) identifying with the client—"when I was a graduate student, I had similar experiences"; (c) suggesting that her concerns have psychological origins—"perhaps you should have had a more positive attitude when interacting with your peers"; (d) communicating that a person who is disabled must have lower life expectations—"you should be very proud of yourself, few WWD are accepted into this graduate program"; (e) providing meaningless encouragement—"I am sure that you will do fine on your internship"; (f) engaging in problem solving for the client—"why don't you, have you tried"; (g) participating in the denial of the client's reality—"I am sure that none of these events is related to your disability"; and (h) seeing no difference between the person who is disabled and one who is not—"we are very similar in our reactions to these types of events" (Esten & Willmott, 1993). A recent study of women and psychotherapy found that the experience of microaggressions within therapy (a) were related to lower quality working alliances; (b) affected the ability of clients to engage in collaborative and purposeful therapeutic work; and (c) were negatively related to clients' psychological well-being (Owen, Tao, & Rodolfa, 2010). WWD's reactions to microaggressions in therapy may be to terminate prematurely, to make statements to test the therapist's trustworthiness, to question the therapist's creditability, and to distrust the therapist's reaction due to subtle nonverbal communication (Olkin, 1999; Sue et al., 2007; Sue, 2010).

The following vignette highlights assumptions that therapists may make regarding clients who do not have a visually marked disability, which may result in ignoring therapeutic issues related to disability (Kafer, 2003). Instead of providing helpful therapeutic interventions, the client is exposed to various microaggressions.

> A counseling psychologist is working with Maria, who is a 36-year-old college graduate with a marketable degree. Maria's presenting concern is uncontrollable anxiety, which she attributes to her inability to secure employment. Due to Maria's successful completion of her education, the therapist considers whether there are other factors contributing to her anxiety and her inability to secure employment, including a lack of self-esteem, being overly selective regarding possible employment opportunities, ineffective job-seeking skills, and so on. As the sessions progress, Maria shares that the cold weather has become more difficult for her to tolerate. Her parents live in a warmer climate and have encouraged Maria to join them. After sharing this concern, the therapist changes her clinical conceptualization, and begins to view Maria as unable to take personal risks and to make personal decisions. She regards these issues as possible underlying factors contributing to her anxiety. The focus of therapy shifts to exploring Maria's feelings/thoughts about taking more personal risks, including changing her place of residence, rather than focusing on her anxiety. Yet, Maria continues to report feeling overwhelmed by her anxiety. At this time the therapist refers to several publications she had recently read regarding therapy and WWD, specifically those written by Olkin (2009) and Palombi (2010). Both of these authors stress asking clients about pain and fatigue and possible health complications. These questions may indicate to the client that the therapist is aware of health conditions with these symptoms, even if the client does not appear to have an obvious disability. The therapist took a therapeutic risk and asked Maria if she struggled with symptoms of pain and fatigue or other health complications, thus conveying her awareness and avoiding assumptions that could lead to a microaggression.

Therapists frequently make judgments regarding clients based on appearance. They may assume that if a client appears able-bodied, she must not have a disability. Yet Women with invisible disabilities (WWID) may be hesitant to disclose a disability, since they may be perceived as being inadequate, less than, or simply undesirable when others become aware of a disability (Davis, 2005; Galvin, 2005: Shelton & Matthews, 2001). These types of discriminatory and marginalizing experiences are typically neither addressed nor acknowledged by therapists (Holzbauer & Berven, 1996). Of those with disabilities, at least 40% have disabilities that cannot be seen, or, are "invisible" (Asch, 2004). An invisible disability has been defined as "one that is hidden so as not to be immediately noticed by an observer except under unusual circumstances or by disclosure from the disabled person or other outside source" (Matthews, 1994, p. 7).

People tend to believe that healthy is normal and that illness is a deviance (Hayden, 1993). Therefore, persons with invisible disabilities have great incentive to keep their conditions concealed. WWID face unique stressors including (a) having to make decisions to disclose their hidden status; (b) feeling anxious due to the possibility of being found out; (c) being isolated from similarly stigmatized others; and (d) being detached from one's true self (Pachankis, 2007). Matthews (1994) researched WWID and found that most did not disclose their disability unless practical reasons demanded it. They felt that disclosure would encourage unwanted sympathy, elicit judgment, and damage existing relationships with people who might not understand their disability and might not find them believable. Research has shown that women with invisible disabilities (WWID) experience avoidance, hostile feelings, stereotyping, and similar responses to those experienced by women with visible disabilities when invisible disabilities are made visible (Asch, 2004; Davis, 2005).

At times, able-bodied people do not believe that WWID actually are disabled (Matthews & Harrington, 2000). Often, invisible disabilities are connected to chronic illnesses that may be progressive and their symptoms inconsistent (Milliken & Northcott, 1996). Individuals who are adjusting to chronic illness may show no visible signs of a disability but may often experience being different from others. These individuals spend enormous effort in appearing "normal" in spite of the internal conflict that is created between "the private self and public identity" (Telford et al., 2006).

Concealing disabilities can carry serious negative ramifications in terms of the able-bodied others with whom they interact and, ultimately, the larger community (Shelton & Matthews, 2001). When individuals are not "seen" as disabled, it can be more difficult for them to secure the assistance or accommodation they need to function effectively (Matthews & Harrington, 2000; Rohrer, 2005). WWID may have to convince others that they really are disabled and are not seeking some special—unfair—advantage. They thus face a double bind: either they forgo the assistance of the accommodation they need, or they attempt to do things that they may not be able to do safely (Davis, 2005).

Because Maria's therapist asked a question about possible struggles with pain and fatigue, Maria shared the following information: (a) a history of psychiatric hospitalizations; (b) the fact that the costs of her medication to maintain her current level of mental health were over $100,000 per year; and (c) that she is dependent on Supplemental Security Income for basic living expenses and Medicaid for her extensive medical costs. Often it is an arduous process for an individual to qualify for Social Security disability benefits. Securing full-time employment could place Maria's Social Security benefits in jeopardy (Noblitt & Perskin Noblitt, 2010). There are also discrepancies between states with regard to requirements for maintaining financial and medical benefits. If the therapist encourages Maria to join her parents, Maria could be at risk of losing her state's major medical benefits, including cost for preventive mental health coverage, medication, and psychiatric hospitalizations. Due to the therapist's lack of awareness regarding Maria's financial status, costs regarding disability, and limits regarding personal choices, these were neither identified nor addressed as relevant personal concerns (Kemp & Mallinckrodt,1996). As a result, therapy may prove to be ineffective (Kemp & Mallinckrodt, 1996; Olkin, 1999; Palombi, 2010).

Due to having a disability, WWD are predisposed to lower levels of income (Smart & Smart, 1997). Membership in an ethnic minority compounds the effect of a disability upon economic status. Because of these economic struggles, psychotherapists may engage in therapy with the assumption that being poor makes WWD less interested and less able to benefit from psychotherapy (Smith, 2005). These assumptions may lead to therapist's "negative bias." Therefore, relevant issues such as cultural perspectives, social status, the distinction between mental and physical labor, and the complex interactions among disability, class, race, ethnicity, gender, and/or sexual orientation may be ignored. Classism among psychotherapists also manifests itself in attitudinal barriers that deter advocacy for the funding and development of psychological services for poor people and compromise the delivery of services (Smith, 2005).

An expectation for therapists who are multiculturally competent is being comfortable asking clients about different aspects of their lives including sexuality, gender, and race. Yet few therapists feel comfortable asking about issues regarding disability (Kemp & Mallinckrodt, 1996). Since therapists may reflect society's negative biases and stereotypes, they need to have an awareness of potential counter transference toward WWD (Leigh et al., 2004) that may trigger unresolved feelings and attitudes (Prilleltensky, 1996). Since counseling psychologists who are feminists view themselves as advocates for marginalized groups and individuals, it may be personally difficult to acknowledge that, in spite of extensive clinical training and a personal commitment to diversity and advocacy, these biases remain unresolved and/or acknowledged (Sue et al., 2007). Yet counter-transference strongly influences the formation of therapeutic bonds, assessment of the client's presenting concern, and treatment planning (Constantine, 2007; Nadal, 2008; Olkin, 1999; Sue et al., 2007). If a therapist is to be helpful to clients with disabilities, she must be willing to examine her own perceptions and biases about disability (Esten & Willmott, 1993).

Training Issues Regarding Disability

Most able-bodied therapists are doing cross-cultural counseling with clients without requisite training (Olkin, 2002). The paucity of disability courses in APA accredited programs in clinical, counseling, or school psychology means that few practicing psychologists are trained to work with WWD. Multicultural perspectives on disability remain lacking in theory, research, and practice (Artman & Daniels, 2010). After surveying graduate programs in psychology, Olkin (2002) found that 89% of these programs included neither courses nor information regarding disability. The number of hours of training focused on disability is less than for any other minority group. When WWD were questioned regarding their experience in therapy, they reported that professional experience and training in disability issues were critical strategies for successful service (Leigh et al., 2004). This feedback supports the need for counseling psychology programs to include training in (a) disability issues, (b) awareness of the contextual factors that influence the lives of WWD, (c) legal requirements for providing public accommodations, and (e) information on disability resources and psychological services available to WWD (Artman & Daniels, 2010). Counseling psychologists need to advocate for graduate students with disabilities as representing aspects of diversity similar to those representing racial diversity and LGBT status (Olkin, 2002). Even if graduate students with disabilities are admitted into psychology programs, few role models and/or mentors are represented in these graduate programs. Graduate students with disabilities also have difficulty in finding accessible training sites and receiving accommodations for which they are legally eligible (Vande Kemp, Chen, Erickson, & Friesen, 2003). Olkin (2002) found that 70% of practicum and internship sites surveyed had no employees or students with physical disabilities, 50% of sites had at least one floor not accessible by elevator, 20% lacked handicapped parking, 25% had no ramps, and 81% did not have an automatic door opener. Only 16% of sites had Braille signage, only 38% had emergency alarms with both visible and audible warnings, only 12% had elevators with Braille and audible signals, and 78% had no TTY (telecommunication device for the deaf) available or even less listed TTY numbers on letterhead. The lack of accessibility with practicum/internship sites, plus the lack of disability-related classes in the curriculum, may contribute to students with disabilities feeling invisible in their programs and may discourage them from pursuing their degree. The lack of students with disabilities trained as psychologists continues to contribute to the lack of psychologists competent to work with WWD (Olkin, 2002).

Another limitation that affects psychologists when working with WWD is that psychologists with disabilities are not well represented among psychologists; less than 2% of APA members identify as psychologists with disabilities (Olkin, 2002; Olkin & Pledger, 2003). Significant barriers remain in accepting and accommodating psychologists with disabilities in the psychology profession, as well as including psychologists with disabilities as faculty in pre-service and in-service training programs. Until these issues are addressed, the quality of disability-focused training will be diminished (Artman & Daniels, 2010).

Therapy and WWD: A Feminist and Multicultural Approach

Sue and Sue (1990) believed that "traditional counseling theory and practice have done great harm to the culturally different" and that there is a need to develop "new methods, concepts, and services more appropriate to the life experiences of culturally diverse groups" (p. v). Guidelines focusing on specific populations seem to emphasize the separation of multiple and intersecting identities (Yakushko, Davidson, & Williams, 2009). Therefore, the client may be forced to choose the one identity that is most salient. This practice creates a hierarchy of oppression (Davidson, 2003; Espín, 2005).

Within the feminist and multicultural literature there are many discussions focused on the benefits of feminist and multicultural theoretical approaches in therapy, the conflicts between the two, and the need for integration of these theoretical orientations. Feminist therapy has been criticized for being overly focused on the needs of White, heterosexual, middle class women (Cole, 1986; Greene, 1995) and for being too "slow to extend its own insight to sociocultural factors other than gender" (Espín, 1994, p. 274). Women of color see feminism as (a) downplaying the importance of race and ethnicity in the lives of women; (b) ignoring the fact that gender is not the primary source of oppression for all women; and (c) overlooking the privileged status of being White (Williams & Barber, 2004). Multicultural therapy has received criticism for overlooking the complexity of culture and contributing to strengthening of stereotypes. Also, multiculturalism has been narrowly defined primarily in terms of race/ethnicity, and ignores other aspects of diversity such as class, gender, sexual orientation, and [disability] (Silverstein, 2006).

Brown (1994) stresses the importance of multiculturalism and views it as a requirement of therapy, specifically feminist therapy. Enns (1997) concurs with Brown and sees diversity as a "central and defining characteristic of feminist therapy" (p. 249). Williams and Barber (2004) have identified similarities between feminism and multiculturalism including (a) a focus on the greater context of a person's life; (b) an emphasis on collaboration between the counselor and the client; (c) the acknowledgment of the potential impact of oppression on the therapeutic relationship; (d) a call for a greater level of communication and understanding between therapist and client; and (e) a shared commitment to social change. Yet, there has been little guidance regarding how to integrate these two theoretical approaches.

Both multicultural and feminist approaches are essential in exploring the broad range of social and cultural perspectives that contribute to oppression and marginalization of WWD and in developing comprehensive and effective interventions to address these concerns. Integration of feminist and multicultural approaches to psychotherapy will require that feminist counseling psychologists "continually question what is normative and to constantly promote greater awareness of self and society" (Brown, 1994, p. 5).

The first major concern when working with WWD is the multicultural competency of the therapist. Because of the lack of training regarding disability, feminist counseling psychologists may be hesitant to address issues regarding disability. They may be intimidated when working with clients representing cultural diversity and/or disability, and interact in a timid or apologetic manner due to their fear of being accused of culturocentrism (Ho, 1995). These fears inhibit therapists from addressing disability and issues related to disability in a frank and honest manner. In general, the greater the cultural differences between counselor and counselee, the more critical multicultural awareness becomes (Ho, 1995).

An Integrative Model of Therapy

Palombi and Pace (1996) incorporated a multicultural and feminist perspective in their development of the Community Model of Embeddedness, Interdependence, Intradependence, & Evolution (CMEIIE) (see figure 11.1). The four sections of the model are interrelated and dependent, and reflect the cultural context of the client's environment and relationships. Palombi (2010) expanded CMEIIE to assist mental health practitioners in conducting a more comprehensive and thorough assessment, and identifying possible areas of clinical exploration when working with WWD. She also developed and published Competency Benchmarks for working with WWD. These competencies are presented within a developmental framework and include entry to practicum, internship, professional practice, and advanced practice and specialization.

The use of the CMEIIE model allows feminist counseling psychologists to integrate multiculturalism and feminism within therapy. CMEIIE focuses on the embedded, interconnected, and intradependent aspects of community and relationships, highlights WWD's personal strengths in the process of change, and challenges feminist counseling psychologists to expand their awareness and understanding of life experiences of WWD.To empower WWD who are oppressed is to help them understand that a possible reason for their emotional distress may be connected to social, cultural, or historical facts (Smart, 2009). This model can be easily adopted to explore intersecting identities and their impact on WWD. The model allows each intersecting identity to be discussed, explored, and viewed in the context of the client's culture and relationships. Ho (1995) believes that for individuals with intersecting identities, their different cultural systems are internalized and coexist within the mind. These individuals "are not merely exposed to and knowledgeable of but have in-depth experiences and hence competence

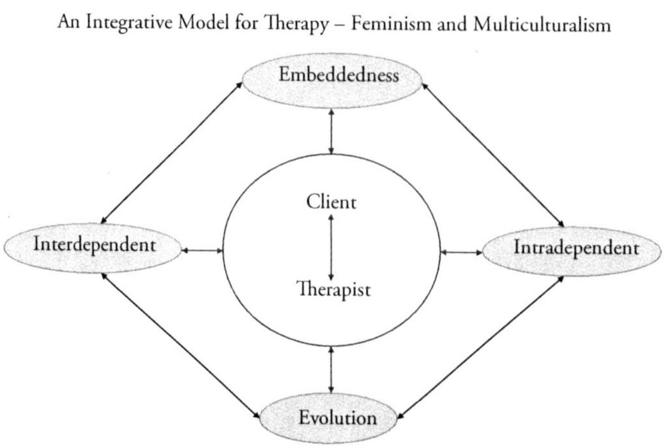

Figure 11.1 Community Model of Embeddedness, Interdependent, Intradependent, and Evolution.

in more than one culture" (pp. 12–13). This model also allows each dimension to be explored as it becomes relevant during the course of therapy. At times, the focus in therapy may change from issues related to embeddedness, then move to intradependence, and then back to embeddedness, and then on to evolution. As WWD explore each dimension, new materials may become more apparent and relevant. In applying the model to WWD and therapy, the dimensions discussed in the following sections need to be explored. Within each of these sections possible topics for exploration are also included.

Embeddedness

Feminist counseling psychologists need to develop an awareness and an understanding of whether and how WWD are embedded into various segments of their communities, including all clinical service interventions provided to other marginalized populations. An aspect of embeddedness is being valued and seen as essential by the community. It is important for WWD to be perceived as making a contribution to their communities, including their families, interpersonal relationships, the workplace, educational settings, and so forth. At times, WWD may perceive themselves as a burden due to being dependent on others for support and needing additional assistance in daily living. Women with acquired disabilities also may perceive themselves as a burden. The newly acquired disability may contribute to increased stress, financial upheaval, and uncertainty within the family. Interpersonal relationships may also change, including loss of shared activities and assumptions of unwanted tasks and responsibilities (Crewe & Krause, 1990). Being embedded in the community is crucial, due to its impact and contribution to positive educational outcomes, life successes, and enhanced physical and mental health (Hayes and Gray, 2008). In neighborhoods where there are high levels of social inclusion, WWD have better access to services.

The principle of embeddedness encourages feminist counseling psychologists to become advocates for clients and assures that WWD receive needed services and become integrated into their communities (Hunt, Matthews, Milsom, & Lammel, 2006). This means that feminist counseling psychologists view the inclusion of WWD as important and ensure the accessibility of the services and program that they sponsor and support (Sue, D. W. & Sue, D, 2003).

Possible topics of exploration include:

Client's role within the community;

Client's contribution to community, family, workplace, educational setting, and so on;

Factors that prevent or inhibit clients from making a contribution;

Support received from community, family, workplace, educational setting, and so on;

Accessibility of the environments and ability to socialize;

Availability of recreational, volunteer, or employment opportunities.

Interdependence

The experience of being oppressed clearly impacts what a person learns about the self and the way the world works and influences her psychological development (Williams & Barber, 2004). WWD's personal experiences in their families and in their culture teach them who they are, as well as how to behave and react in relation to power in society. These forces influence and shape the psychological development of WWD. Interdependence focuses on identifying relationships and the cultural beliefs of these individuals and their impact on WWD.

People without disabilities may not feel comfortable with disability issues, and therefore may make generalizations and categorizations based on the client's medical diagnosis (Smart, 2009). Due to the experiences of being frequently ignored and/or discounted, WWD may be hesitant to develop interpersonal relationships. Failing to do so maintains their sense of isolation and alienation (Nosek, 2009; Palombi & Matteson Mundt, 2006).

Interdependence also focuses on the relationship between the client and therapist. Mental health professionals reflect the prejudices of the culture, including able-bodied privilege and delivering unintentional microagressions. These prejudices and beliefs create therapeutic distance between the client and the therapist and may not allow a strong therapeutic alliance to develop. Feminists counseling psychologists need to (a) understand the power of spread—the process of ascribing greater limitations to the disability and, at the same time, discounting and underrating the strengths and abilities of WWD; (b) recognize that disability as an important aspect of the individual's identity but does not comprise the individual's entire identity; (c) be willing to listen to WWD's experience of prejudice and discrimination; (d) appreciate the way in which the popular media's depiction of disability often results in assaults upon the self-esteem of WWD; and (e) empower their clients—since WWD "lives are saturated with unequal encounters with professionals" (Barnes, Mercer, & Shakespeare, 1999, p. 645) (Smart, 2009). Women who were satisfied with the level of social support within their environments reported less depressive symptoms and a positive impact on psychological well-being (Zea, Belgrave, Townsend, Jarama, & Banks, 1996).

Possible topics of exploration include:

Type and extent of relationships within family, community, health care providers, and so on;

Degree of comfort in asking for additional information from health care providers;

Degree of comfort in interacting or being ignored, discounted, and/or marginalized;

Sense of personal isolation or alienation;

Issues regarding able-bodied privilege;

Personal experiences regarding microaggressions.

Areas for therapist reflection include:

Feelings about working with a client with a disability;

Degree of comfort exploring experiences regarding prejudice, discrimination, or assisting the client in seeing discrimination or marginalization within society and culture;

Focus on client's personal strengths or limitations of her disability;

Ability to share with client how media, institutions, organizations, and members within society perceive WWD and impact psychological well-being and self-efficacy;

Focus on empowering client, awareness of power difference, impact of able-bodied privilege, and unintentional expressions of microaggressions.

Intradependence

The client's personal perception of herself during the therapeutic process and the unique clinical and personal stressors that are currently affecting WWD are the focus of intradependence. WWD are exposed to a wider range of stressors than their able-bodied counterparts (Bramston & Fogerty, 2000). The stress that WWD experience is of a chronic nature, intensified by disability-related factors (Turk & Monarch, 2002), and experienced at multiple levels: personal, social, economic, societal/structural, cultural, and political (anssen, Schuengel, & Stolk, 2002, Noonan et al., 2004). These sources of stress tend to create a cycle that increases personal trauma and contributes to social exclusion and "disability exhaustion," which is the result of dealing with layers and layers of bureaucracy and negotiating a system that is often contradictory (Smart, 2009). These stressors may be unique to the personal experience of WWD, which many clinicians and other members of society do not have to either acknowledge or struggle with (Palombi & Matteson Mundt, 2006).

WWD may also face the impact of institutionalized "enforced idleness"—a combination of public perceptions and laws and policies with built-in financial disincentives that prevent WWD from working. During therapy, WWD continue to struggle, understand, and comprehend the meaning of "chronic" in regard to living with a disability. In the lives of WWD, disabilities are not temporary but "ones we must face again and again for the rest of our lives" (Zola, 1991, p. 16). Also in this dimension of the model, the personal response of WWD to psychological pain can be useful and can provide information regarding their environments and determine aspects and relationships to be changed. Being able to identify these issues within their environments and to develop means to address changes will assist WWD in seeing themselves as empowered, increasing their sense of self-efficacy, and recognizing their ability to impact their world.

Possible topics for exploration include:

Information regarding disability, impact of disability, feelings toward having disability;

Overview of socioeconomic and family background;

Understanding of disability, beliefs, and attitudes of parents/family members;

Beliefs regarding personal care, medically, socially, economically;

Experience with medical community of feeling traumatized, uncomfortable, or discounted;

Information regarding romantic and sexual history, being desired as romantic/sexual partner, role of disability in the relationship;

Ability to choose partner or remaining in relationship due to fear of being unattractive or not desired;

History or current experience of abuse;

"The perfect future," career or means of financial support, and achieving dreams;

Culture meaning and expectations of woman with a disability;

Medical costs, health risks, and financial resources associated with disability.

Evolution

The last phase of the model emphasizes evolution. Evolution focuses on changes that may occur in personal/physical/social dimensions, advances in medical treatment and technology, and new research findings. To be aware of societal, medical, and technological developments and changes, feminist counseling psychologists need to continue to educate themselves through reading and personal contact with WWD (Hunt et al., 2006). Through the process of therapy, WWD begin to see themselves as capable individuals who possess interpersonal strengths, rather than seeing themselves with personality deficits. They will understand that the behaviors and patterns that may appear maladaptive are responses to a harmful and oppressive environment. By focusing on the environmental influences, WWD develop a deeper awareness of how these factors impact their psychological well-being.

A comprehensive process of therapy also includes the goal of social change or liberation from oppression. This is a goal toward which feminist counseling psychology therapists should always strive, both for the benefit of the individual client and for the broader social good (Williams & Barber, 2004). Becoming involved in social change is also a relevant goal for WWD. It is imperative that the therapist does not project onto the client how social change or liberation from oppression would manifest itself or what it would entail. These goals may be as personal as the client learning how to ask others for assistance or being able to share with others when an interaction is perceived as able-bodied privilege or is experienced as a microagression. The model allows feminist counseling psychologists to prepare for the many challenges and modifications created by the changing nature of the community and the field of counseling psychology that may affect WWD (Palombi& Matteson Mundt, 2006).

Possible topics for exploration include:

Personal changes and health changes;

Decisions regarding future including medical care, financial security;

Personal stressors, reactions by others, societal responses;

Personal changes to feel/see self as more empowered;

Activities, organizations, or issues to gain additional information or to become involved;

Recognizing able-bodied privilege and microaggressions and impact.

Conclusions and Future Directions

With new advances in medication and health care, it is likely that the life span of women will increase, and part of their lives will be spent dealing with the ramifications of an acquired disability. According to Callahan (1999), by the age of 85, 50% of women will need assistance with daily living, and by age of 75, most women will have at least, on average, two chronic diseases or disabilities. No matter how diligently individuals focus on their health, weight, diet, level of personal stress, and exercise, they still may acquire a disability (Morell, 2003) and will be faced with their own vulnerability and dependencies (Wendell, 1997). Feminist theorists have worked to idealize women's bodies and emphasize that women can control their bodies, yet continue to exclude disabled and older women (Wendell, 1996). Ableism and ageism are two related constructs; both are systems of oppression; and both are socially constructed conceptually and materially (Overall, 2006). To change the mind-set of feminists counseling psychologists, the mental health community and members of society, a major transformation regarding disability must be manifested. Perhaps using a metaphor that emphasizes the process and journey of life would be applicable.

In her work as a Jungian analyst and through her writings and workshops for over 30 years, Jean Shinoda Bolen addressed the aging/disabling process as the journey of becoming "the crone." The crone could be viewed as a withered old woman living alone, or as the elder who symbolizes and holds the wisdom of the tribe/society. According to Bolen, any person who has made a deep connection to nurturing or sustaining others, who has experienced vulnerability and suffering, and has learned some wisdom from it may embrace her later years with a depth of understanding that is of value to us all. The metaphor of the crone allows women to be more authentic and to make a difference in the world by drawing from personal experiences and therefore acknowledging the wisdom they have gained.

Bolen (n.d., a, b, c, & d) believes that change in society becomes a possibility when small groups of women join together to work on issues regarding social justice that are built on the principle of equality. Through the sharing of their personal stories, women in these small groups or "circles" raise awareness of needed changes within society. The sharing of their stories brings about social justice through ending "outer oppression" and at the same time assists women in dealing with the internalized oppression created by prejudice. Listening to the personal stories of other women is likely to increase self-esteem, allow for the celebration of personal accomplishments, and encourage the development of talent. Providing psychological or practical support allows women to feel empowered and to have the courage to make significant change in their lives. Through women's conviction to the principle of relatedness and interdependency, the third wave of feminism can bring about an evolutionary change in society.

Bolen's views clearly underscores the practice and focus of feminists and counseling psychologists and is inclusive of their values: (a) equality, (b) connection and nurturing, (c) relatedness and interdependency, (d) multicultural orientation, and (e) social justice values. Feminist counseling psychologists must focus on enlarging the circle to be more inclusive of WWD and to ensure that when a member of the circle acquires a disability, that the circle remains unbroken. Such a movement means that able-bodied counseling psychologists and feminists need to acknowledge the power difference that exists between WWD and able-bodied women. Because of this power difference, feminist counseling psychologists need to (a) acknowledge feminism's disregard of issues associated to WWD; (b) recognize the lack of inclusion of WWD in their litany regarding diversity and personal characteristics of women; and (c) actively encourage WWD to become members of the circle.

Another challenging aspect is to approach this mission with vigor, courage, and honesty (Appleby, 1992). Such an approach encourages feminist counseling psychologists to acknowledge their able-bodied privilege and lack of knowledge regarding issues of WWD. Adhering to these practices permits WWD to share their daily experience of lacking able-bodied privilege, the constant experience of microaggressions, and exclusions from the circle of women. Feminist counseling psychologists need to encourage and demand that others within their professions include WWD within publications, research, clinical training, and discussions, and to recognize disability as important and as relevant as race, gender, and sexual orientation. Incorporating aging/disability as a natural process of being women and crones within society may transform the identity of feminist counseling psychologists and allow them to be more inclusive and encompassing of all women who have been marginalized.

WWD also have the responsibility to continue advocating for inclusion and acknowledgment as valued and necessary members of society. Also essential is for WWD to incorporate a new identity that allows them to view themselves from a place of personal value; to have a legitimate place within society, and to admire, respect, and acknowledge the meaningful contributions that they make to their families, friends, professions, and society at large.

Feminist counseling psychologists and WWD need to join together to advocate for change within institutions, cultural practices, physical structures, and environmental constructs, as well as working toward policies and politics are inclusive of all members of society. The image of the crone allows feminist counseling psychologists and WWD to embrace their collective wisdom and personal strength, which will enable them to actively engage in achieving social justice throughout the world. To achieve the mission of social justice, it will be important to recognize the daily occurrence and experiences of able-bodied privilege and the impact of microaggressions directed toward WWD. Acknowledging these issues will lead to personal interactions that respect the integrity and essence of the individual. This process will enable members of society to view disability from a new perspective and to include it as a natural process/occurrence of everyday living. By doing so, the voices of each member of society will be heard, especially those of WWD, thereby assuring that social justice is a normal and expected aspect of society.

References

Appleby, Y. (1992). Disability and 'compulsory heterosexuality.' *Feminism andPsychology*, 2(3), 502–505.

Artman, L. K., & Daniels, J. A. (2010). Disability and psychotherapy practice: Cultural competence and practical tips. *Professional Psychology: Research and Practice*, 1–7. doi:10.1037/a0020864.

Asch, A., & Fine, M. (1988). Introduction: Beyond Pedestals. In M. Fine & A. Asch, *Women with Disabilities: Essays in psychology, culture, and politics* (pp. 1–39). Philadelphia: Temple University Press.

Asch, A. (2004). Critical race theory: Feminism, and disability: Reflections on social justice and personal identity. In B. G. Smith and B. Hutchinson, *Gendering Disability* (pp. 9–44). New Brunswick, NJ: Rutgers University Press.

Ballou, M., & Brown, L. S. (1992). *Rethinking mental health and disorder: Feminist perspectives.* New York: Guilford Press.

Barnes, C., Mercer, G., & Shakespeare, T. (1999). *Exploring disability: A sociological introduction.* Cambridge, UK: Polity.

Begum, N. (1992). Disabled women and the feminist agenda. *Feminist Review, 40,* 70–84.

Berland, G. (2007). *Rolling.* Fourwheeldrive Productions.

Black, L. L., & Stone, D. (2005). Expanding the definition of privilege: The concept of social privilege. *Journal of Multicultural Counseling and Development, 33,* 243–254.

Bolen, J. S. (n.d.) (a). *Circles as Vessels of Healing and Transformation.* Retrieved from http://jeanshinodabolen.com/articles/index.html, June 29, 2011.

Bolen, J. S. (n.d.) (b). *Creative Acts of Expression—Catalyzed in Circles by Jean Shinoda Bolen, M.D.* Retrieved from http://jeanshinodabolen.com/articles/index.html, June 29, 2011.

Bolen, J. S. (n.d.) (c). *Crones Don't Whine—Jean Shinoda Bolen.* Retrieved fromhttp://www.unconventionalwoman.com/meaning-aamp-purpose-resourcemenu-4/midlife-challenges-resourcemenu-24/36-crones-dont-whine.html.

Bolen, J. S. (n.d.) (d). *Mother's Day- Standing for Peace.* Retrieved from http://jeanshinodabolen.com/articles/index.html.

Bramston, P., & Fogarty, G. (2000). The assessment of emotional distress experienced by people with mild intellectual disabilities: A study of different methodologies. *Research in Developmental Disabilities, 21*, 487–500.

Breeden, C., Olkin, R., & Taube, D. J. (2008). Child custody evaluations when one divorcing parents has a physical disability. *Rehabilitation Psychology, 53*(4), 445–455. doi: 10.1037/a0013023.

Brown, L. S. (1994). *Subversive dialogues: Theory in feminist therapy.* New York: Basic Books.

Brown, L. S. (2010). *Feminist therapy.* Washington, DC: American Psychological Association.

Callahan, D. (1999). Age, sex, and resource allocation. In M. Walker (Ed.), *Mother time: Women, aging and ethics.* (pp. 189-199). New York: Rowman & Littlefield Publishers, Inc.

Campbell, F. A. K. (2008). Exploring internalized ableism using critical race theory. *Disability and Society, 23*(2), 151–162.

Castaneto, M. V., & Willemsen, E. W. (2006). Social perception of the personality of the disabled. *Social Behavior and Personality, 34*(10), 1217–1232.

Clark, M. A. (2006). Adult education and disability studies, an interdisciplinary relationship: Research implications for adult education. *Adult Education Quarterly*, 56(4), 308–322. doi: 10.1177/0741713606289661.

Cole, E. R. (2009). Intersectionality and research in psychology. *American Psychologists, 64*(3),170–180. doi: 10.1037/a0014564.

Cole, J. (1986). *All American women: Lines that divide, ties that bind.* New York: Free Press.

Coleridge, P. (1993). *Disability, liberation and development.* Oxford: Oxfam.

Constantine, M. G. (2007). Racial microaggressions against African American clients in cross-racial counseling relationships. *Journal of Counseling Psychology, 54*, 17–31.

Cornish, J. A. E., Gorgens, K. A., Monson, S. P., Olkin, R., Palombi, B. J., & Abels, A. V. (2008). Perspectives on ethical practice with people who have disabilities. *Professional Psychology: Research and Practice, 39*, 488–497. doi:10.1037/a0013092.

Corrigan, P. (2004). How stigma interferes with mental health care. *American Psychologist, 59*(7), 614–625. doi: 10.1037/0003-066X.59.6.614.

Corrigan, P. W., & Matthews, A. K. (2003). Stigma and disclosure: Implications for coming out of the closet. *Journal of Mental Health, 12*, 235–248.

Crewe, N. M., & Krause, J. S. (1990). An eleven-year follow-up of adjustment to spinal cord injury. *Rehabilitation Psychology, 35*(4), 205–210.

Cronin, A., & King, A. (2010). Power, inequality and identification: Exploring diversity and intersectionality amongst older LGB adults. *Sociology, 44*(5), 876–892. doi: 10.1177/00380 38510375738.

Curry, M. A., Hassouneh-Phillips, D., & Johnston-Silverberg, A. (2001). Abuse of women with disabilities. *Violence Against Women, 7*(1), 60–79.

Davidson, M. M. (2003). "A feminist asks: What do we mean by multicultural?" In M. M. Davidson & S. Morrow (Co-Chairs). *Student voices: Feminism in the age of multiculturalism.* Symposium presented at the annual meeting of the American Psychological Association, Toronto, Canada.

Davis, L. (1997). Introduction. In Lennard Davis (Ed.), *The Disability Studies Reader* (pp. 1–6). New York: Routledge.

Davis, N. A. (2005). Invisible disability. *Ethics, 116*, 153–213.

Deegan, M. J., & Brooks, N. A. (Eds.). (1985). *Women and disability: The double handicap.* New Brunswick, NJ: Transaction Books.

Downing, N. E., & Roush, K. L. (1985). From passive acceptance to active commitment: A model of feminist identity development for women. *The Counseling Psychologist, 13*, 695–709.

Enns, C. Z. (1997). *Feminist theories and feminist psychotherapies: Origins, themes, and variations.* New York: Haworth Press.

Espín, O. (1995). On knowing you are the unknown: Women of color constructing psychology. In J. Adleman & G. Enguidanos (Eds.), *Racism in the lives of women: Testimony, theory and guides to practice* (pp. 127–136). New York: Harrington Park Press.

Espín, O. (2005). *The age of the cookie cutter has passed: Contractions in identity at the core of therapeutic intervention.* Paper presented at the bi-annual meeting of the Multicultural Conference and Summit, Los Angeles.

Espín, O. M. (1994). Feminist approaches. In L. Comas-Diaz & B. Greene (Eds.), *Women of color: Integrating ethnic and gender identities in psychotherapy* (pp. 265–286). New York: Guilford Press.

Esten, G., & Willmott, L. (1993). Double bind messages: The effects of attitude towards disability on therapy. *Women and Therapy, 14*, 29–41.

Ferri, B. A., & Gregg, N. (1998). Women with disabilities: Missing voices. *Women's Studies International Forum, 21*(4), 429–439.

Fine, M., & Asch, A. (Eds.). (1988). *Women and Disabilities: Essays in psychology, culture, and politics.* Philadelphia: Temple University Press.

Fisher, B., & Galler, R. (1988). Friendship and fairness: How disability affects friendships between women. In M. Fine & A. Asch, *Women with Disabilities: Essays in psychology, culture, and politics* (pp. 172–194). Philadelphia: Temple University Press.

Freeman, D. (2002). A feminist theology of disability. *The Journal of the Britain and Ireland School of Feminist Theology, 29*, 71–85.

Galvin, R. D. (2005). Researching the disabled identity: Contextualizing the identity transformations which accompany the onset of impairment. *Sociology of Health and Illness, 27*(3), 393–413.

Garland-Thomson, R. (2004). Integrating disability, transforming feminist theory. In B. G. Smith & B. Hutchinson, *Gendering disability* (pp. 73–106). New Brunswick, NJ: Rutgers University Press.

Garland-Thomson, R. (2005). Feminist disability studies. *Signs: Journal of Women in Culture and Society, 30*(2), 1558–1586. Retrieved from EBSCOhost.

Gill, C. (1997). Four types of integration in disability identity development. *Journal of Vocational Rehabilitation, 9*(1), 39–46.

Gill, C. (2001). Divided understanding: The social experience of disability. In G. L. Albrecht, K. D. Seelman, &

M. Bury (Eds.), *Handbook of disability studies* (pp. 351–372). Thousand Oaks, CA: Sage Publication.

Gilman, S. L. (1998). *Creating beauty to cure the soul*. Durham, NC: Duke University Press.

Gilson, S. F., Cramer, E. P., & DePoy, E. (2001). Redefining abuse of women with disabilities: A paradox of limitation and expansion. *Affilia, 16*(2), 220–235.

Graham, H. (1983). 'Caring: Labour of love,' in J. Finch and D. Groves (Eds.), *A labour of love: Women, work and caring*, pp. 13–30. London: Routledge and Kegan Paul.

Greene, B. (1995). An African American perspective on racism and anti-Semitism within feminist organizations. In J. Adleman & G. M. Enguidanos (Eds.), *Racism in the lives of women: Testimony, theory, and guides to antiracist practice* (pp. 303–313). London: Harrington Park Press.

Haiken, E. (1997). *Venus envy: A history of cosmetic surgery*. Baltimore, MD: Johns Hopkins University Press.

Hanna, F. J., Talley, W. B., & Guindon, M. H. (2000). The power of perception: Toward a model of cultural oppression and liberation. *Journal of Counseling and Development, 78*(4), 430–441.

Hanna, W. J., & Rogovsky, B. (1993). Women with disabilities: Two handicaps plus. In M. Nagler (Ed.), *Perspectives on disability* (2nd ed., pp. 109–119). Palo Alto, CA: Health Markets Research.

Hardin, M. (2007). "I consider myself an empowered woman": The interaction of sport, gender, and disability in the lives of wheelchair basketball players. *Women in Sports and Physical Activity Journal, 16*(1), 39–53.

Hastings, J., & Huw, T. (2005). Accessing the nation: Disability, political inclusion and built form. *Urban Studies, 42*(3), 527–544. doi: 10.1080/00420980500035683.

Hayden, S. (1993). Chronically ill and "feeling fine": A study of communication and chronic illness. *Journal of Applied Communication Research, 21*(3), 263–278. doi: 10.1080/00909889309365371.

Hayes, A., & Gray, M. (2008). Social inclusion: A policy platform for those who live particularly challenged lives. *Family Matters, 78*(4), 4–7.

Health Canada. (1997). *The economic burden of illness in Canada, 1993*. Ottawa: Author.

Heyman, B., & Huckle, S. (1995). Sexuality as a perceived hazard in the lives of adults with learning disabilities. *Disability and Society, 11*, 139–155.

Hirschberger, G., Florian, V., & Mikulincer, M. (2005). Fear and Compassion: A terror management analysis of emotional reactions to physical disability. *Rehabilitation Psychology*, 50(3), 246–257. doi: 10.1037/0090-5550.50.3.246.

Ho, D. Y. F. (1995). Internalized culture, culturocentrism, and transcendence. *The Counseling Psychologist, 23*,(1), 4–24.

Holzbauer, J. J., & Berven, N. L. (1996). Disability harassment: A new term for a long-standing problem. *Journal of Counseling and Development, 74*, 478–483.

Hughes, B., McKie, L., Hopkins, D., & Watson, N. (2005). Love's labours lost? Feminism, the disabled people's movement and an ethic of care. *Sociology, 39*(2), 259–275. doi:10.1177/0038038505050538.

Hunt, B., Matthews, C., Milsom, A., & Lammel, J. A. (2006). Lesbians with physical disabilities: A qualitative study of their experiences with counseling. *Journal of Counseling and Development, 84*, 163–173.

Iwasaki, Y., & Mactavish, J. B. (2005). Ubiquitous yet unique: Perspective of people with disabilities on stress. *Rehabilitation Counseling Bulletin, 48*(4), 194–209.

Janssen, C. G.C., Schuengel, C., & Stolk, J. (2002). Understanding challenging behavior in people with severe and profound intellectual disability: A stress-attachment model. *Journal of Intellectual Disability Research, 46*, 445–453.

Kafer, A. (2003). Compulsory bodies: Reflections on heterosexuality and able-bodiedness. *Journal of Women's History, 15*(3), 77–89.

Kemp, N., & Mallinckrodt, B. (1996). Impact of professional training case conceptualization of client with a disability. *Professional Psychology: Research and Practice, 27*, 378–385.

Klein, B. (1996). 'We are who you are.' *Feminism and Disability, 3*, 70–74.

Kiuhara, S. A., & Huefner, D. S. (2008). Students with psychiatric disabilities in higher education settings: The American with Disabilities Act and beyond. *Journal of Disability Policy Studies, 19*(2), 103–114.

Knoll, K. R. (2009). Feminist disability studies pedagogy. *Feminist Teacher, 19*(2), 122–133.

Krieger, N. (1999). Embodying inequality: A review of concept, measures, and methods for studying health consequences of discrimination. *International Journal of Health Services, 29*, 295–352.

Landrine, H., & Klonoff, E. A. (1997). *Discrimination against women: Prevalence, consequences, remedies*. Thousand Oaks, CA: Sage.

Landry, L. J., & Mercurio, A. E. (2009). Discrimination and women's mental health: The mediating role of control. *Sex Roles*, 61,192–203. doi: 10.1007/s11199-009-9624-6

Latin American and Caribbean Women's Health Network. (2006). Women with disabilities speak out: Different bodies, equal rights. *Women's Health Journal, 21*, 3.

Leigh, I. W., Powers, L., Vash, C., & Nettles, R. (2004). Survey of psychological services to clients with disabilities: The need for awareness. *Rehabilitation Psychology, 49*(1), 48–54.

Lerman, H., & Porter, N. (Eds.) (1990). *Feminist ethics in psychotherapy*. New York: Springer.

Link, B. G., & Phelan, J. C. (2001). Conceptualizing stigma. *Annual Reiview of Sociology, 27*, 363–385.

Lloyd, M. (1992). Does she boil eggs? Toward a feminist model of disability. *Disability, Handicap and Society, 7*(3), 207–221.

Longmore, P. K. (July 2009). Making disability an essential part of American history. *OAH Magazine of History*, 11–15.

Lonsdale, S. (1990). *Women and disability: The experience of physical disability among women*. London: Macmillan Education.

Mahalingam, R. (2007). Culture, power and psychology of marginality. In A. Fuligni (Ed.), *Contesting stereotypes and creating identities: Social categories, social identities, and educational participation* (pp. 42–65). New York: Sage.

Matthews, C. K. (1994). *To tell or not to tell: The management of privacy boundaries by the invisibly disabled*. Paper presented at the annual meeting of the Western States Communication Association, San Jose, CA.

Matthews, C. K., & Harrington, N. G. (2000). Invisible Disability. In D. O. Braithwaite and T. L. Thompson (Eds.), *Handbook of communication and people with disabilities: Research and application* (pp. 405–423). Mahway, NJ: Lawrence Erlbaum Associates.

McDermott, S., Moran, R., Platt, T., & Dasari, S. (2007). Health conditions among women with a disability. *Journal of Women's Health, 16*(5), 713–720. DOI: 10.1089/jwh.2007.0363.

McIntosh, P. (1988). *Understanding correspondence between white privilege and male privilege through women's studies work.* (Working Paper No. 189). Wellesley, MA: Center for Research on Women, Wellesley College.

Milliken, F. J., & Northcott, H. C. (1996). Seeking validation: Hypothyroidism and the chronic illness trajectory. *Qualitative Health Research, 6,* 202–223.

Moradi, B., Mezydlo Subich, L., & Phillips, J. C (2002). Revising feminist identity development, therapy research, and practice. *The Counseling Psychologist, 30*(1), 6–43.

Morell, C. (2003). Empowerment theory and long-living women: A feminist and disability perspective. *The Journal of Human Behavior in the Social Environment, 7*(3–4), 225–236. doi: 10.1300/J137v7n03_13.

Morris, J. (2001). Impairment and disability: Constructing an ethics of care that promotes human rights. *Hypatia, 16*(4), 1–16.

Mpofu, E., & Conyers, L. M. (2004). A representational theory perspective of minority status and people with disabilities: Implications for rehabilitation education and practice. *Rehabilitation Counseling Bulletin, 47,* 142–151.

Nadal, K. L. (2008). Preventing racial, ethnic, gender, sexual minority, disability, and religious microaggressions: Recommendations for promoting positive mental health. *Prevention in Counseling Psychology: Theory, Research, Practice and Training, 2,* 22–27.

Neath, J. (1997). Social causes of impairment, disability, and abuse. *Journal of Disability Policy Studies, 8*(1–2), 195–229.

Noblitt, R. & Perskin Noblitt, P. (2010). Psychologists and the economics of social security disability programs. *Professional Psychology: Research and Practice, 41*(3), 274–279. doi: 10.1037/a0019315.

Noonan, B. M., Gallor, S. M., Hensler-McGinnis, N. F., Fassinger, R. E., Wang, S., & Goodman, J. (2004). Challenge and success: A qualitative study of the career development of highly achieving women with physical and sensory disabilities. *Journal of Counseling Psychology, 51*(1), 68–80.

Nosek, M. A. (2009). Feminism and disability: Synchronous agendas in conflict. In H. Landrine and N. Felipe Russo (Eds.), *Handbook of diversity in feminist psychology* (pp. 501–533). New York: Springer Publishing.

Nosek, M. A., Howland, C. A., & Hughes, R. B. (2001). The investigation of abuse and women with disabilities. *Violence Against Women, 7*(4), 477–499.

Nosek, M. A., & Hughes, R. B. (2003). Psychosocial issues of women with physical disabilities: The continuing gender debate. *Rehabilitation Counseling Bulletin, 46*(4), 224–233.

Nowell, N. L., & Gill, C. J. (2005) Illuminating the lives of disabled black women through role and identity narrative. DAI-B 66(04): p. 2327; October 2005 (AN MUI-UWRI0611–001051)

Olkin, R. (1999). *What psychotherapists should know about disability.* New York: Guilford.

Olkin, R. (2002). Could you hold the door for me? Including disability in diversity. *Cultural Diversity and Ethnic Minority Psychology,* 8, 130–137. doi:10.1037/1099-9809.8.2.130.

Olkin, R., & Pledger, C. (2003). Can disability studies and psychology join hands? *American Psychologist, 58,* 296–304.

Olkin, R. (2009). Disability-Affirmative Therapy. In I. Marini & M. A. Stebnicki (Eds.), *The professional counselor's desk reference* (pp. 355–370). New York: Springer.

Orbe, M. P., & Camara, S. K. (2010). Defining discrimination across cultural groups: Exploring the [un-]coordinated management of meaning. *International Journal of Intercultural relations,* 34, 283–293. doi: 10.1016/j.ijintrel. 2010.02.004.

O'Toole, C. J., & D'aoust, V. (2000). Fit for motherhood: Towards a recognition of multiplicity in disabled lesbian mothers. *Disability Studies Quarterly, 20*(2), 145–154.

O'Toole, C. J., & Brown, A. A. (2003). No reflections in the mirror: Challenges for disabled lesbians accessing mental health services. *Journal of Lesbian Studies, 7*(1), 35–39.

Overall, C. (2006). Old age and ageism, impairment and ableism: Exploring the conceptual and material connections. *NWSA Journal, 18*(1), 126–137.

Overboe, J. (1999). 'Difference in itself': Validating disabled people's lived experience. *Body and Society, 5*(4), 17–29.

Owen, J., Tao, K., & Rodolfa, E. (2010).Microaggressions and women in short-term psychotherapy: Initial evidence, *The Counseling Psychologists, 38*(7), 923–946. doi: 10.1177/0011000010376093.

Pachankis, J. E. (2007). The psychological implications of concealing a stigma: A cognitive-affective-behavioral model. *Psychological Bulletin, 133*(2) 328–345. doi: 10.1037/0033-2909.133.2.328.

Palombi, B. J., & Pace, D. (1996). *Site report prepared for the American Psychological Association.* Allendale, MI: Grand Valley State University, Counseling and Career Development Center.

Palombi, B. J., & Matteson Mundt, A. (2006). Achieving social justice for college women with disabilities: A model for inclusion. In T. Israel and R. Toporek (Eds.), *Social justice handbook* (pp. 170–184). Thousands Oaks, CA: Sage.

Palombi, B. J. (2010). Disability: Multiple and intersecting identities-Developing multicultural Competencies. In J. A. Erickson Cornish, B. A. Schreier, L. I. Nadkarni, L. Henderson Metzger, & E. R. Rodolfa (Eds.), *Handbook of multicultural counseling competencies* (pp. 55–92). Hoboken, NJ: John Wiley & Sons.

Park, D. C., Radford, J. P., & Vickers, M. H. (1998). Disability studies in human geography. *Progress in Human Geography, 22*(2), 208–233.

Pelletier, J., Rogers, E., & Dellario, D. (1985). Barriers to the provision of mental health services to individuals with severe physical disability. *Journal of Counseling Psychology, 32,* 422–430.

Prilleltensky, O. (1996). Women with disabilities and feminist therapy. *Women and Therapy 18*(1), 87–97.

Rioux, M. (1998). *Enabling the well-being of persons with disabilities.* Toronto: Roeher Institute.

Rohrer, J. (2005). Toward a full-inclusion feminism: A feminist deployment of disability analysis. *Feminist Studies, 31*(1), 34–63.

Shahnasarian, M. (2001). Career rehabilitation: Integration of vocational rehabilitation and career development in the twenty-first century. *The Career Development Quarterly, 49*(3), 275–283.

Sheldon, A. (1999). Personal and perplexing: Feminist disability politics evaluated. *Disability and Society, 14*(5), 643–657.

Shelton, M. W., & Matthews, C. K. (2001). Extending the diversity agenda in forensics: Invisible disability and beyond. *Argumentation and Advocacy, 28*(2), 121–130.

Sherrill, C. (1993). Women with disabilities, Paralympics and reasoned action contact theory. *Women in Sport and Physically Activity Journal, 2*(2), 51–65.

Silvers, A. (1995). Reconciling equality to difference: Caring (F) or justice for people with disabilities. *Hypatia, 10*(1), 31–55.

Silverstein, L. B. (2006). Integrating feminism and multiculturalism: Scientific fact or science fiction? *Professional Psychology:*

Research and Practice, 37(1), 21–28. doi: 10.10370735-7028.37.1.21.

Singer, O. (2001). Biases toward individuals with psychiatric disabilities as related to community integration. *The International Journal of Psychosocial Rehabilitation, 6,* 21–27.

Smart, D. W., & Smart, J. F. (1997). The racial/ethnic demography of disability. *Journal of Rehabilitation, 63,* 9–15.

Smith, H. M. (2007). Psychological service needs of older women. *Psychological Services, 4*(4), 277–286. doi: 10.1037/1541-1559.4.4.277.

Smart, J. (2009). Counseling individuals with disabilities. In I. Marini & M. A. Stebnicki (Eds.). *The professional counselor's desk reference* (pp. 639–646). New York: Springer.

Smith, L (2005). Psychotherapy, classism, and the poor. *American Psychologist, 60*(7), 687–696. doi: 10.1037/0003-066X.60.7.687.

Sue, D. W., & Sue, D. (1990). *Counseling the culturally different: Theory and practice* (2nd ed.). New York: John Wiley & Sons.

Sue, D. W., & Sue, D. (2003). *Counseling the culturally diverse: Theory and practice* (4th ed.). New York: John Wiley & Sons.

Sue, D. W., Capodilupo, C. M., Torino, G. C., Bucceri, J. M., Holder, A. M., Nadal, K. L., & Esquilin, M. (2007). Racial microaggressions in everyday life: Implications for clinical practice. *American Psychologist, 62,* 271–286. doi: 10.1037/0003-066X.62.4.271.

Sue, D. W. (2010). *Microaggressions in everyday life: Race, gender, and sexual orientation.* Hoboken, NJ: John Wiley & Sons.

Telford, K., Kralik, D., & Koch, T. (2006). Acceptance and denial: Implications for people adapting to chronic illness: Literature review. *Integrative Literature Reviews and Meta-Analyses,* 55(4), 457–464. doi: 10.1111/j.1365-2648.2006.03942.x.

Tsao, G. (1998). *Growing up Asian with a disability.* http://www.colorado.edu/jpournals/standards/V7N1/FIRSTPERSON/tsao.html.

Turk, D. C., & Monarch, E. S. (2002). Biopsychosocial perspective on chronic pain. In D. C. Turk & R. J. Gatchel (Eds.), *Psychological approaches to pain management: A practitioner's handbook* (pp. 3–29). New York: Guilford Press.

Turner, J. B., & Turner, R. J. (2004). Physical disability, unemployment and mental health. *Rehabilitation Psychology,* 49(3), 241–249. doi: 10:1037/0090-5540.49.3.241.

Van de Kemp, H., Chen, J. S., Erickson, G. N., & Friesen, N. L. (2003). ADA accommodation of therapists with disabilities in clinical training. In M. E. Banks & E. Kaschak (Eds.), *Women with visible and invisible disabilities: Multiple intersections, multiple issues, multiple therapies* (pp. 155–168). New York: Haworth.

Vernon, A. (1998). Multiple oppression and the disabled people's movement. In T. Shakespeare (Ed.), *The disability reader* (pp, 201–210). London: Cassell.

Weeber, J. E. (1999). What could I know of racism? *Journal of Counseling and Development, 77,* 20–23.

Wendell, S. (1996). *The rejected body: Feminist philosophical reflections on disability.* New York: Routledge.

Wendell, S. (1997). Toward a feminist theory of disability. In L. J. Davis, *The Disability Studies Reader* (pp. 260–278). New York: Routledge.

Wertlieb, E. C. (1985). Minority group status of the disabled. *Human Relations, 38*(11), 1047–1063.

Williams, E. N., & Barber, J. S. (2004). Power and responsibility in therapy: Integrating feminism and multiculturalism. *Journal of Multicultural Counseling and Development, 32,* 390–401.

Wolbring, G. (2008). The politics of ableism. *Development, 51,* 252–258. doi:10.1057/dev.2008.17.

Wold, N. (1991). *The beauty myth: How images of beauty are used against women.* New York: William Morrow.

World Health Organization (WHO). (2002). *Innovative care for chronic conditions: Building blocks for action.* Global Report. Geneva, Switzerland: Author.

Yakushko, O., Davidson, M. M., & Williams, E. N. (2009). Identity salience model: A paradigm for integrating multiple identities in clinical practice. *Psychotherapy Research, Practice, Training, 46*(2), 180–192. doi: 10.1037/a0016080

Yuval-Davis, N. (2006). Intersectionality and feminist politics. *European Journal of Women's Studies, 13*(3), 193–209. doi: 10.1177/1350506806065752.

Zea, M., Belgrave, F., Townsend, T., Jarama, S., & Banks, S. (1996). The influence of social support and active coping on depression among African Americans and Latinos with disabilities. *Rehabilitation Psychology, 41,* 225–242.

Zola, I. K. (1991). Communication barriers between "the able-bodied" and "the handicapped." In P. M. Ferguson, D. L. Ferguson, & S. J. Taylor (Eds.), *Interpreting disability: A qualitative reader* (pp. 157–164). New York: Columbia Teachers College Press.

CHAPTER

12 Feminist Multicultural Counseling Psychology with American Muslim Women

Amina Mahmood

Abstract

The psychological literature about American Muslim women is sparse, suggesting that little is known about this population. Much of the research conducted on Muslim women originates in the United Kingdom and Canada. The American context experienced in the United States is unique and colors the experiences of, and challenges faced by, American Muslim women. This chapter provides an introduction to the American Muslim population, the Islamic faith that unites and is common to these women, and some common psychosocial concerns experienced by American Muslim women.

Key Words: American Muslim women, Islam, feminism, *hijab*, domestic violence, psychosocial concerns

This chapter introduces the feminist multicultural counseling psychologist to working with American Muslim women. The reader is provided with a brief history of Islam, including basic beliefs and values of Muslims. This is followed by an overview of the presence of Islam in America and the demographics of the American Muslim population, with a specific focus on American Muslim women. Next, representative issues of concern to American Muslim women are discussed. A brief synopsis of therapeutic implications is provided, followed by directions for future research with this population. Although much of the content of this chapter is relevant to Muslim women living throughout the North American region, the demographic information is specific to Muslim women living in the United States.

It should be noted that American Muslim women are bearers of multiple identities, including race, ethnicity, religion, and social class. Some women may only culturally identify themselves as Muslim and may resonate more with their ethnic identity. Thus, the feminist multicultural counseling psychologist is advised to utilize the material presented in this chapter in conjunction with other chapters in this volume that address some of the other identities that their clients consider important.

Introduction to Islam and American Muslims

Contrary to popular belief, most Muslims are not Arabs, and many Arabs are not Muslim. In fact approximately one-fifth of the Muslim population is Arab (Esposito, 1998). Muslims are a heterogeneous group encompassing a diversity of cultural, ethnic, linguistic, professional, and economic backgrounds. The countries with the largest Muslim populations in the world, in order, are: Indonesia, Pakistan, Bangladesh, India, and Nigeria, none of which is located in the Middle East. In order to understand the concerns and issues important to American Muslim women, it becomes imperative to first gain knowledge and understanding of the religious identity that serves as a point of unity for this diverse group. Additionally, it serves the feminist multicultural counseling psychologist well to understand the history of American Muslims in the United States.

Introducing Islam

Islam is the second largest religion in the world, followed by one-fifth of the world's population (Esposito, 1998), at approximately 1.4 billion people. The word "Islam" originates from the Arabic root word *salaam*, which literally translated means "peace" or "surrender." One who follows the religion of Islam is a Muslim, or one who submits or surrenders to the will of Allah (the Arabic term for "God").

Islam was revealed to the Prophet Muhammad (peace and blessings be upon him [this is the usual statement that follows when a reference is made to the Prophet Muhammad, and other prophets of the Judeo-Christian tradition, and from this point it will be assumed rather than stated in the text]) in the early seventh century on the Arabian peninsula, present-day Saudi Arabia. Muslims believe that God communicated His message to Muhammad via the archangel Gabriel, starting in the year 610 of the common era (also referred to as c.e.), until Muhammad's death in 632 c.e. This message is believed to be the continuation of the guidance given to the great Prophets of the Judeo-Christian tradition, such as, Noah, Abraham, Moses, and Jesus. The revelations that Muhammad received are compiled in the Qur'an, which is composed of 114 chapters (in Arabic chapter is referred to as *surah*). The original language of the Qur'an is Arabic, but it has been transliterated into many languages. The Qur'an is the primary source of guidance for Muslims. The bulk of the Qur'an addresses social, legal, and daily life issues, such as inheritance laws, divorce and alimony, conducting business, and so on. Since the Qur'an primarily addresses specific concerns affecting seventh-century Arabian society, contemporary Muslims are encouraged to interpret the message of the Qur'an contextually, and in order to do so are traditionally taught and encouraged to learn about the historical events and social milieu surrounding the revelations to Muhammad (Ali, 2006).

In addition to the Qur'an, Muslims give great importance to the Prophet Muhammad's sayings (*hadith*), and practices (*sunnah*). The Prophet Muhammad is considered to be the role model for humanity and one who best understood the message of the Qur'an. Thus, by emulating Muhammad's example and by seeking a greater understanding of the *hadith* and *sunnah,* Muslims believe that they can attain a clearer understanding of the universal guidance provided by the Qur'an (Ali, 2006). Muslims often turn to numerous examples from Muhammad's life to understand how to conduct business, resolve conflicts, become better leaders, and interact with family members.

Sunni-Shi'ite split

The Muslim population today spans the entire globe; this means that there are cultural differences in the practice of and adherence to Islam. In the context of this cultural diversity it becomes necessary to address the Sunni-Shi'ite split among Muslims. Shiites constitute approximately 20% of the Muslim population globally, and this is also true of the Muslim population in the United States. It should be noted that the commonalities between Shi'ite and Sunni Islam far outweigh the differences.

The death of Muhammad in 632 c.e. created a political division among the Muslim community of the Arabian Peninsula (Mahmood, 2006). Muhammad passed away prior to appointing someone to succeed him in the leadership of the burgeoning Muslim community. However, a group of people believed that Muhammad had intended his son-in-law Ali to succeed him (Armstrong, 2000), and these people came to be known as the Shi'ite Ali (literally translated as "the party of Ali," similar today to identifying oneself with the Democrat or Republican parties), whereas the majority believed that the leadership ought to be decided via consensus among the respected leaders of the community (known as the Sunni). Ali finally did assume the position of leadership in the Muslim community in 656 c.e., as the fourth leader, or *caliph,* of the Muslim community after Muhammad's passing. Ali had to concentrate his governance on resolving residual administrative and governmental problems created during the caliphate of the previous caliph Uthman, during whose term nepotism had flourished. Ali's term saw the first civil war in Islam's history, in 657 c.e., and Ali was assassinated in 661 c.e. by a group within the Muslim community known as the Kharjites.

Ali's son Hasan became the next caliph of the community, but seceded the caliphate in the interest of maintaining the welfare of the Muslim community to Mu'awiya, who had opposed Ali's caliphate. Mu'awiya later poisoned Hasan in 669 c.e., as he was aware that the Shi'ite Ali were planning an uprising against his (that is, Mu'awiya's) caliphate; additionally, Mu'awyia had signed a treaty with Hasan indicating that Hasan would re-assume leadership of the caliphate after Mua'wiya's death (Mahmood, 2006). Thus, in the early history of Islam, the Sunni-Shi'ite split was primarily an issue of political leadership rather than religious practice. However, this political split solidified into a distinct school of thought after the events of Karbala (in modern-day Iraq) in 680 c.e., and led to the development of religious Shi'ism.

It was at Karbala that Muhammad's grandson Husayn and his small army encountered the army of Yazid (Mu'awiya's son and a very corrupt ruler) and were essentially surrounded for nine days with no access to the basic necessities of life, and no provisions of such necessities for even the women and children who were traveling with Husayn (Mahmood, 2006). Husayn was martyred at Karbala, and his surviving family members were taken hostage by Yazid. The events of Karbala further ingrained social justice and standing up against oppression as important values for all Muslims, but moreso for the Shi'ites (Mahmood, 2006), as they had experienced first-hand discrimination and oppression at the hands of those in the majority. The differences in doctrines of faith between Shi'ism and Sunnism emerged in the ninth century, and included who is considered eligible and qualified to be the rightful leader of the Muslim community (Shi'ites believe that leadership belongs to the Prophet's descendants). Over time sub-sects of Shi'ism emerged, including Ismailis and Zaydis, with the primary cause of division concerning the inheritance of leadership of the Muslim community (Mahmood, 2006).

Basic Tenets of Faith

All Muslims, regardless of their cultural practices, adherence to Islam, or affiliation with Sunni Islam, Shi'ism, or Sufism (a mystical practice of Islam), agree on the basic tenets of faith also known as the five pillars of faith. These basic tenets include:

Tawhid: This is the belief that there is only one God and Muhammad is the last messenger of God. The articulation of this belief is known as the *shahada*, and once a person articulates this belief, (s)he is considered Muslim.

Salat (prayer): Muslims are mandated to offer five daily prayers. Each prayer takes a few minutes (typically five to ten), and the prayers are distributed evenly throughout the day: before dawn, midday, late afternoon, at sunset, and at night before going to bed. Muslims are required to perform a ritual cleansing, which is symbolic of a spiritual cleansing, in preparation for prayer. A clean and quiet space is required for prayers, as the prayer has a physical component that can be likened to light yogic poses, such as bending and touching the knees, kneeling, and so on, while meditating and reciting Quranic verses. Thus, many Muslims traditionally prefer to use a prayer rug or mat during the prayer. Muslim women traditionally cover their hair during prayer and have only their hands and face visible.

Zakat (charity): Muslims are required to donate approximately 2.5% of their wealth on an annual basis to those in need. Shi'ites, however, tend to also donate an additional tax to their religious leader, who then is responsible for distributing it to the needy in the community (Mahmood, 2006). Immigrant Muslim communities prefer to donate their annual *zakat* to family members or others in need in their home countries. Historically, American Muslims tended to utilize faith-based charities that distributed aid to primarily Muslim countries; however, with post–9/11 scrutiny, many are hesitant to donate to Muslim-based charitable organizations due to fear of surveillance by the government, and of wrongfully being accused of terrorism.

Sawm (fasting): During the month of Ramadan (the ninth month in the Islamic calendar), healthy and able Muslims are required to refrain from food and drink during the daylight hours. Women are exempt from fasting if they are menstruating or are pregnant and breast-feeding, and these missed fasts can be made up at a later time. Ramadan is also a time of spiritual reflection, and Muslims are encouraged to spend time on self-reflection, meditation, prayers, doing good deeds, and donating to charity. Communal gatherings for *iftar* (the evening meal) are typically held within the Muslim community, and these give the month of Ramadan a festive feel, as well as enhancing feelings of connectedness and community among families and local Muslim communities. Muslims also engage in extra prayers after the night prayer during the month of Ramadan. In American Muslim communities, these prayers usually occur at the local mosque or community center. The end of Ramadan is marked by one of the major religious holidays, known as *Eid-ul-Fitr*. In majority Muslim countries the festivities typically last three or four days, and include feasting and socializing with friends, family, and neighbors. In America, however, with the exception of Eid prayers in the morning, community celebrations are held on the weekend, especially if the holiday falls during a weekday.

Hajj (pilgrimage): Muslims are required to go on a pilgrimage to Makkah Saudi Arabia (the birthplace of Islam), at least once during their lifetime, if their health and finances allow. The pilgrimage commemorates God's command that Abraham sacrifice his son Ishmael in God's name. There are specific rituals involved with the *hajj*, and Muslims who intend to go to the pilgrimage typically have to spend time learning and preparing for the rites and rituals. The *hajj* is a transformative experience for Muslims, as it gives them the experience of being at one with the global Muslim community, regardless of race, ethnic background, culture, or social class. In many ways *hajj* illustrates the social justice and feminist components of Islam. Aside from the spiritual components of *hajj*, it is also a time when all Muslims, regardless of race, ethnicity, social class, and sex/gender, are united in the purpose of completing the pilgrimage. Both men and women have the same rights and responsibilities during the *hajj*, and there is no culturally sanctioned segregation of the sexes. Additionally, being surrounded by Muslims from all walks of life during the *hajj* reminds one that in the eyes of Allah (God), it is not their material power and prestige, but rather their intentions and actions that are valued.

In addition to the five pillars of Islam mentioned above, Muslims follow specific dietary practices known as *halal* (similar to "kosher" in the Jewish tradition). *Halal* means "permissible" in the context of diet. This means that Muslims are not allowed to consume pork or pork products, nor are they allowed to drink alcohol. Additionally, meat for consumption needs to be raised and slaughtered humanely. In the context of daily living, the term *halal* refers to living in accordance with Islamic guidelines. Muslims are also forbidden to engage in gambling. There is also a proscription on engaging in sexual relations outside marriage.

Islam was revealed to Muhammad during a time when Arabian society was plagued with many social injustices and inequities, and thus Muslims believe that Islam was revealed in order to address and resolve these societal concerns and injustices (Ali, 2006).

Beliefs and Values of Muslims

As mentioned previously, Muslims are a heterogeneous group representing all cultures, ethnicities, and social class backgrounds. However, there are certain beliefs and values that all Muslims consider important. These include:

Hijab (modesty): Islam emphasizes modesty in dress and behavior for both genders. Modesty in cross-gender interactions is also emphasized. It should be noted that cross-gender interactions are dictated in part by cultural background. The Qur'an focuses on modesty in the following verses of Surah Nur:

"Tell the believing men to lower their gaze and to be mindful of their chastity: this will be most conducive to their purity—[and,] verily God is aware of all that they do.

And tell the believing women to lower their gaze and to be mindful of their chastity, and not to display their charms [in public] beyond what may [decently] be apparent thereof; hence, let them draw their head-coverings over their bosom"

(The Qur'an,[1] 24:30–31).

However, the term *hijab* is more commonly understood today as the head scarf that many Muslim women choose to wear as an identifier of their faith. Women who wear the head scarf believe that the Quranic injunction for doing so is stated in the verse quoted above. In recent years, there has been an increase in American Muslim women adopting the *hijab*. Reasons postulated for this choice include the reality that many of these women see themselves as asserting their faith identity, experiencing empowerment, and refuting stereotypes of Muslim women that exist in the West as perpetuated by the media. Although the practice of wearing the head scarf or the *hijab* is done of one's own volition in the United States, it is important to note that some Muslim women may practice the *hijab* due to cultural and familial pressures, rather than religious reasons.

Family: Islam emphasizes the importance of the family unit. Great emphasis is placed on heterosexual marriage, and the family unit is viewed as the building block of society. Collectivism is emphasized in that the individual is encouraged to work toward the well-being of one's family, and hence, toward the welfare of the community. Motherhood is highly valued by Muslims, and several religious traditions and sayings emphasize the importance of, and respect for, mothers. One saying of the Prophet Muhammad that emphasizes the honor given to mothers is "Heaven lies beneath the feet of the mother." Although motherhood is important and valued, Muslim women are not required to be stay-at-home moms, but can choose this option if they so desire. It is important to note that cultural gender roles often dictate a woman's role in society, and at times, these cultural roles may be in conflict with religious teachings.

Education: Muslims place great emphasis on education, especially as the first words of the Qur'an to Muhammad were a directive to "read," or to educate oneself. There are many religious sayings and references that emphasize the importance of attaining education. A common religious saying is to "Seek knowledge even if you have to go to China." Another Muslim tradition states that if one has a son and a daughter but only has enough resources to educate one child, then the daughter should be educated as she has the power to educate an entire generation. This was indeed a controversial and feminist idea, especially in patriarchal seventh-century Arabia. It aligns well with the importance given to motherhood in Islam. Individuals are also encouraged to use their education for the betterment of the community. Both women and men are encouraged to share their talents and give back to society.

Ummah (Muslim community): Muslims are encouraged to take care of and help members of the Muslim community. One analogy commonly narrated to Muslims involves likening the global Muslim community to the human body. When one part of the body (that is, a specific Muslim community) is suffering, the rest of the body is also affected. This is a powerful analogy, as it encourages embracing and acting upon the values of social justice and advocacy. This social justice and advocacy should not be solely reserved for the Muslim community, but rather, should expand to the oppressed and disenfranchised of society. Working toward erasing societal injustices is viewed as a religious duty for all Muslims.

American Muslims are embracing these values by opening free medical clinics affiliated with their religious community centers, by joining local and national American Muslim organizations such as the Council of American-Islamic relations (a civil liberties organization), Muslim Public Affairs Council, and Muslim Students' Associations on college campuses. They also show social justice commitments by volunteering at local social service agencies, such as homeless shelters, food banks, and crisis centers; and by creating specific organizations to counter social injustices and oppression. An exemplary organization that emphasizes social justice and advocacy is the Inner-City Muslim Action Network (IMAN) [www.imancentral.org], formed in 1995 in Chicago with a focus on delivering social services in impoverished urban communities. American Muslim women are also involved and are in the frontlines of these efforts of working toward social justice and empowerment. For example, American Muslim women serve as directors and founders of domestic violence organizations such as Turning Point (www.turningpoint-ny.org), and the Peaceful Families Project (www.peacefulfamilies.org). They have also started homeless and battered women's shelters, such as Muslimat Al Nisaa (http://www.mnisaa.org), and have organized Muslim women lawyers for human rights (www.karamah.org). The mission statements of these organizations emphasize serving those in need and working toward eradicating disparities in society.

Muslims in the United States

American Muslims are ethnically diverse, with roots in over 50 different countries in the world (Afridi, 2001). Estimates of the American Muslim population range between 2 to 8 million (U.S. Department of State, 2001), and Islam was estimated to be the second largest religious group in the United States by 2010. In order to work with American Muslim women, it is important to understand the history of Muslims in the United States. In this section, a brief overview of the history of Muslims in America is provided in order to illustrate the socio-cultural-political diversity of American Muslim women.

The presence of Muslims in the United States can be dated back to the early eighteenth and nineteenth centuries, to the times of slavery. Many of the African slaves from West Africa were Muslim. These early Muslim slaves were stripped of their religious identity, but many in the later generations did return to Islam. For many African Americans, this return was through the Nation of Islam, considered by many Muslims to be a heterodox movement and not in accordance with accepted doctrines. However, in recent years the Nation of Islam has moved closer to Sunni Islam in theology and practice. Today, African American Muslims constitute approximately one-third of the American Muslim population.

The first wave of immigrant Muslims to America was in the late nineteenth and early twentieth century, with an influx of Arab Muslim immigrants from Lebanon, Syria, and Jordan (Smith, 2005), who primarily moved to the Midwest to work in the industrial sector (such as in the automobile industry in Michigan, in construction, and on the railroad). Today, the Dearborn, Michigan, area is the most densely Muslim-populated area in the United States. Also, Cedar Rapids, Iowa, is home to the first mosque in the United States, due to the presence of Arab Muslim immigrants who settled in the area.

The next wave of immigrants arrived in the early to mid-twentieth century and consisted of relatives and families of those who immigrated in the first wave (Smith, 2005). This wave of immigration occurred from 1947–1960. Muslims immigrated from Eastern European countries, as well as from the Middle East and South Asia. Finally, the current wave of immigration (1965–present), is primarily composed of South Asian immigrants, making this group the second largest ethnic Muslim group in the United States, and constituting approximately one-third of the Muslim population (Smith, 2005). The 1990s and 2000s have seen an increase in refugee and immigrant groups from Ethiopia, the Sudan, Somalia, and Iraq (countries that are home to a sizable Muslim population). There are sizable refugee resettlement communities in the Midwest (for example, a significant Somali population in the Minneapolis area, recent Iraqi refugees in Nebraska, and a sizable Sudanese, as well as Bosnian, population in Iowa), contributing to the increasing diversity of this region of the United States. The United States government's 1990 immigration law also created a "diversity" visa via a lottery system to people from countries that have had low immigrant rates to the United States, and this has also led to immigration of many individuals from predominantly Muslim countries (Haddad, Smith, & Moore, 2006).

A statistical breakdown of the American Muslim population in the United States indicates that approximately 30% (some estimates would say 40%) of the population is composed of African Americans, and another third is composed of South and Central Asian Muslims. Approximately 25% are Arab American Muslims, 3% are African immigrants, 2% are South East Asians, 2% are European Americans, and the remaining 5% of the population is composed of Latino, Native American, and other ethnic groups (Smith, 2005).

The demographics of the American Muslim community refute the stereotype that Muslims are not indigenous to the United States, as illustrated by the majority of the population being composed of African Americans and European Americans whose families have been in the United States for many generations. It should be noted that the term "indigenous" is commonly used in the research literature on American Muslims to differentiate between American Muslims who have resided in the United States for many generations and other groups, such as South Asians, that have immigrated more recently to the United States.

In addition to cultural, ethnic, and linguistic diversity, American Muslims are diverse in terms of social class, although they do tend to be wealthier and better educated than Muslims in Europe. Data from the Muslims in American Public Squares project (Project MAPS, 2004) indicate that about half of the American Muslim population earns over $50,000 a year. Approximately 58% of American Muslims are college graduates, many of whom go on to achieve graduate education. In terms of political identity, approximately 40% identified as Democrats, 23% as Republicans, and 28% considered themselves to be Independent (Project MAPS, 2004).

In terms of identification with faith, the Masjid Study Project 2000 (Bagby, Perle, & Froehle, 2001) revealed that approximately 7 out of 10 Muslims are active in mosques (*masajid*), and that 35% of men, and 26% of women attend weekly religious services. Another important finding of this project was that approximately one-quarter of the mosque attendees belong to households with incomes below $20,000. These findings suggest that American Muslims are religiously diverse in terms of their practice of, and identification with, their faith. Haddad and Lumis (1987) elaborate on the religious diversity of the American Muslim population in terms of their identification with faith. American Muslims range from individuals who are highly liberal and Westernized, and primarily consider themselves "culturally" rather than practicing Muslims, to those who are highly conservative (evangelical) and believe that public life ought to be governed by Islamic principles. Members belonging to the conservative group tend to isolate themselves from the greater non-Muslim society, and primarily interact with other conservative Muslims. The majority of American Muslims, like Muslims in other parts of the world, are moderate or conservative-moderate (Haddad & Lumis, 1987); they have a strong Muslim identity, but are also well integrated and active in the larger American society. There is also a growing popularity of Sufi Islam in the United States. This is the mystical and spiritual practice of Islam, which emphasizes seeking closeness to God through meditative practice, and love and tolerance of others.

American Muslim Women

The concerns, experiences, and identities of American Muslim women is a burgeoning area of research, and one in need of greater attention in psychological research in the United States. During the past decade there has been an increased focus on American Muslims in general, as well as American Muslim women in particular. Muslim women in general have been an enigma to the West. They have often been stereotyped and portrayed as veiled and oppressed women who are uneducated, unintelligent, at the beck and call of patriarchal men, limited to the domestic domain, or as exotic belly dancing harem girls (Haddad, Smith, & Moore, 2006). The Western media have played a pivotal role in perpetuating these stereotypes. For example, media often focus on the veiled Muslim women in majority Muslim countries, and perpetuate the stereotype of Muslim women as subjugated and oppressed. There have been many *Disney* and Hollywood movies that have portrayed Arabs and Muslims negatively. Dr. Jack Shaheen has done extensive work on the perpetuation of Arab and Muslim stereotypes and addresses these in his documentary *Reel Bad Arabs: How Hollywood Vilifies a People* (for more information, see: http://www.reelbadarabs.com/). The people's revolutions in Egypt and Tunisia in the beginning of 2011 challenged Western stereotypes about Muslims. Media coverage of the revolution reported on men and women, many of them Muslim, veiled and unveiled, as equal participants in overthrowing their country's regimes and strongly voicing their support for democracy in their countries.

American Muslim women reflect the diversity of the American Muslim population at large. Similar to other women, American Muslim women's experiences of discrimination and oppression can be based on sexism, in addition to other variables. Variables including religion, ethnic background, culture, racial background, and sexuality intersect and impact the experience of discrimination and oppression for American Muslim women (Droogsma, 2007; Karim 2009). It cannot be assumed that the Muslim identity is a primary identity for American Muslim women (Haddad, Smith, & Moore, 2006). Culture or social class identities may be salient for many women. However, American Muslim women who identify strongly with their faith identity tend to be active in religious activities in their communities, and are also involved in reinterpreting Islam in the American context, teasing out cultural baggage carried over by immigrant Muslims from religious teachings (Haddad, Smith, & Moore, 2006).

Western stereotypes assume that Islam is oppressive to women, but for many Muslim women, Islam is a positive and empowering force in their lives. There are Muslim women in America and around the world who are unfortunately oppressed. However, it is important to note that such treatment is not in accordance with Islamic teachings or practices, but is usually based on patriarchal culture and traditions. It is important for the feminist multicultural counseling psychologist to understand the religious teachings regarding feminism and the role of women. This can be particularly useful in assisting Muslim clients to differentiate between religious and cultural practices.

Attitudes Toward Feminism and Multiculturalism

"...Behold, We have created you all out of a male and a female, and have made you into nations and tribes, so that you might come to know one another. Verily, the noblest of you in the sight of God is the one who is most deeply conscious of Him. Behold, God is all-knowing, all-aware" (The Qur'an, 49:13).

Islam teaches that each individual is responsible and accountable for her or his actions. At its core, Islam places an emphasis on restoring peace and justice and eradicating oppression (Munir, 2003). There is no hierarchical structure in Islam, and Muslims are encouraged to utilize their intellect, rationality, and logic when interpreting and practicing the faith (Munir, 2003). Gender does not define God. Although the English transliterations and interpretations referred to God using the male pronoun, this does not imply God's maleness; rather, this reference reflects the limitation of the English language. In the eyes of God, everyone is equal. One's race, ethnicity, social class, or sex does not make one better than the other; rather, as indicated by the verse above, it is one's piety and God-consciousness.

In the Qur'anic version of Adam and Eve's fall from grace, both parties are held equally responsible and accountable (see verses 2:30–37), again establishing gender equality. Many would argue that Islam is compatible with feminist principles (Haddad, Smith, & Moore, 2006). Islam also asserts that multiculturalism and diversity are to be embraced. Religious teachings encourage Muslims to interact with and learn from others who are different from them. However, gender inequalities, racism, and classism do exist among American Muslim communities (Karim, 2009).

The teachings of the Qur'an are focused on minimizing power differentials and creating a society free from social hierarchies. In pre-Islamic Arabia, women were treated as property, and female infanticide was widely practiced. With the spread of Islam and the Quranic revelations, female infanticide was immediately abolished, and the equality of women in all spheres of life was established. Many scholars also acknowledge inherent differences between men and women, and use the term "equity" rather than equality. However, it should be noted that these differences do not imply inequality of status. Women in seventh-century Arabia attained the right to inherit, vote, run for and participate in public office, become respected scholars and teachers, operate their own businesses, negotiate their marriage contracts, and choose their marriage partners. It should be noted that many of these rights were not granted to women in the West until the nineteenth or twentieth centuries.

Although Islam established the equality of women in seventh-century Arabia, this does not guarantee that equality is being practiced. Patriarchal cultures have influenced and contorted religious teachings and have subverted the rights granted to Muslim women in many Muslim communities around the globe. A glaring example is that of Afghani women, who have suffered greatly under the rule of the Taliban's warped rulings based on religious pretexts. The media have provided much coverage to the situation in Afghanistan, as well as that of oppressed Muslim women in other countries. The focus on the status of Muslim women around the globe has an impact on how American Muslim women are perceived by fellow Americans, as well as how these women view themselves within a North American context (Haddad, Smith, & Moore, 2006). The media play an important role in the perpetuation of stereotypes regarding Muslim women globally. For instance, much of the global coverage on Muslim women represents the veil as a symbol of oppression. This leads to the belief that American Muslim women who choose to veil are oppressed. It is fairly common for Muslim women who veil to field queries and attempts by concerned others who would like to "save" them from the religion that oppresses them.

American Muslim women range from being conservatively religious to liberal. Some follow traditional gender roles, whereas others are strong in their defiance of these roles. Muslim feminism is becoming increasingly visible in America. Although American Muslim women may resist being labeled as "feminist" due to its association with a White, Western movement incompatible with Islamic values and principles (Haddad, Smith, & Moore, 2006), a recent qualitative investigation suggested that American Muslim women endorse feminist values (Ali, Mahmood, Moel, Hudson, & Leathers, 2008). This rejection of the "feminist" label by American Muslim women is similar to the rejection of the label by many African American women, who choose instead to identify themselves as "womanist," since feminism has, until more recently, by and large ignored the issues of culture and diversity (Enns, 1997; Haddad, Smith, & Moore, 2006).

Contemporary American Muslim women are bringing Islamic feminisms to the forefront by engaging in reinterpreting religious texts and traditions, and thus participating in and informing the evolution of an American Islam. Scholars and activists such as Leila Ahmed, Azizah al-Hibri, Laleh Bakhtiar, Riffat Hassan, Aminah Beverly McCloud, and Amina Wadud are contributing to the American Muslim discourse, as well as the global discourse on Muslim women and Islamic feminisms. American Muslim women's voices are also present in national and local religious and advocacy organizations (for instance, Ingrid Mattson was elected president of the largest North American Muslim organization [Islamic Society of North America] in 2006), groups and forums dedicated to educating American Muslim women of their rights (for example, KARAMAH, an organization of American Muslim women lawyers), and audio-visual and print media (for instance, *AZIZAH* [see www.azizahmagazine.com], a magazine for American Muslim women that addresses religious issues, fashion, and somewhat controversial psychosocial concerns).

The verse quoted at the beginning of this section illustrates the value that Islam places on diversity and multiculturalism. Islamic teachings abhor treating someone unfairly due to her or his racial or ethnic identity. Ideally, in a society based on Islamic values, the color of one's skin should have no bearing on one's access or lack of access to jobs, education, health care, social services, and treatment by others. However, American Muslims are residing in a society where one's social class, ethnic, or racial background has an impact on many aspects of one's life. For example, established immigrants and their first generation children often differentiate themselves as better than newer immigrants from their countries of origin (Karim, 2009). Converts to Islam may find that they are constantly being bombarded by American Muslims of different cultural backgrounds who seek to teach them that only their culture-specific religious practices are correct. Karim's (2009) analysis of African American and South Asian American Muslim women is an intriguing overview of the intersections of race and class within the community due to ethnic- and culture-based divisions among American Muslims. It would be beneficial to further explore the influence of race, ethnicity, and class as they pertain to the interactions of American Muslim women.

It is essential for the feminist multicultural counseling psychologist to gain an understanding of Islamic perspectives on feminism and multiculturalism. It is hoped that this section aids the feminist multicultural counseling psychologist in doing so. Additionally, this information will assist the feminist multicultural psychologist in framing feminist and multicultural clinical interventions when addressing common psychosocial concerns with American Muslim women.

Common Psychosocial Concerns

American Muslim women, like other American women, seek therapy for a variety of concerns, including depression, anxiety, relationship concerns, and grief and loss issues. However, it is important for psychologists/therapists to recognize that the faith identity may not be the primary identity for the client, and if it is, it is one among several identities that determine the manifestation of the client's concerns or issues. Cultural, religious, and social class identities are impacted by the larger sociopolitical context of being Muslim in America today. When working with the American Muslim woman, the feminist multicultural counseling psychologist is encouraged to consider the client's multiple identities, especially as those identities determine how the religious identity is interpreted and practiced. Additionally, it is important for the feminist multicultural counseling psychologist to be aware of the larger sociopolitical context in which the American Muslim woman resides.

Outlined in the following sections are common issues that affect American Muslim women. The first four issues, post–9/11 discrimination and Islamophobia, domestic violence, *hijab* (head scarf), and marriage and dating, are examined in depth. In addition, four emerging issues (areas beginning to receive increasing research attention) are briefly addressed, including body image, conversion to Islam, generational and cultural differences, and acculturation issues. Ali (2006), Ali, Liu, and Humeidan (2004), and Hedayat-Diba (2000) offer a discussion of other clinical and moral issues impacting American Muslims, including dealing with interest, usury, and loans; depression and suicide; and alcohol and substance use.

Living with Islamophobia

The events of September 11, 2001, have resulted in a constant spotlight on the global Muslim population, as well as the marginalization of this population. The American Muslim community, in addition to members of other faith and cultural groups perceived to be Muslim, have been victims of discrimination and hate crimes post–9/11. The events of 9/11 impacted American Muslims twice. First, American Muslims, like their non-Muslim fellow Americans, were emotionally shocked and wounded by this event. Many lost family or friends in the attacks, others were first responders, and some were hurt or killed. Second, while coping with this tragedy, American Muslims simultaneously had to begin coping with being open targets of harassment and discrimination in America (Abu-Ras & Suarez, 2009).

The Council on American-Islamic Relations (CAIR), a not-for-profit civil liberties organization, has produced several reports on discrimination and hate crimes targeting American Muslims since 9/11. "Islamophobia" is a term that has been in use since 1991 and can be defined as the fear or dislike of Muslims. Islamophobia is on the rise in the United States (Sheridan, 2006) and has garnered much media attention, especially through the summer of 2010 up until the United States' mid-term elections in November 2010. Representative Peter King's (Republican, NY) congressional hearings on the radicalization of Muslims in America in March 2011 are another example of Islamophobia in the public realm.

There have been several empirical studies conducted on Islamophobia and its effects on American Muslims since 9/11 (Abu-Raiya, Pargament, & Mahoney, 2010; Abu-Ras, & Suarez, 2009; CAIR, 2006, 2007; Hallak & Quina, 2004; and Zaal, Salah, & Fine, 2007). The Status of Muslim Civil Rights in the United States report published by CAIR (2007) indicates a 25.1% increase in the number of civil rights complaints received from the year 2005 to the year 2006. These complaints include an increase in hate crimes against

Muslims, consisting of defacement and desecration of mosques, sniper attacks on mosques, and physical assaults (especially if one is perceived to be ethnically or religiously Muslim by the perpetrator). Discrimination and hate crimes have also occurred in a variety of other settings, including the workplace, online, at Muslim-owned businesses, in academic settings (schools, colleges, and university settings), in public places (shopping centers, banks), by government agencies (particularly with regard to immigration and citizenship issues), and at airports ("flying while Muslim" is now considered an "enforceable" offense) (CAIR, 2007). A recent article published in the *New York Times* reported that there has been a 20% increase in work discrimination complaints by American Muslims (Greenhouse, 2010). Approximately one-quarter of the 3,386 complaints of religious discrimination in the workplace were filed by Muslims, a population that comprises less than 2% of the American population (Greenhouse, 2010).

This rising Islamophobia is tied to the (mis) information or lack of information available to Americans about Islam and Muslims. Another survey conducted by CAIR (2006) polled the American public's opinion about Islam and Muslims. The results of this survey are sobering, with one in four Americans viewing Islam as "a religion of hatred and violence" (CAIR, 2006); however, with the recent rise in Islamophobia, it is likely that this number is greater today than it was when this particular survey was conducted. Approximately one-fifth of those surveyed were in favor of restricting the civil liberties of American Muslims (CAIR, 2006). Interestingly, the majority of respondents stated that their views of Muslims would probably change if Muslims would condemn terrorism strongly, work to improve the status of Muslim women (implying that women are mistreated by Islam), and seek to improve America's image in the majority Muslim countries (CAIR, 2006). It is important to acknowledge that American Muslim communities and major North American Muslim organizations (including the Islamic Society of North America, Islamic Circle of North America, Muslim Public Affairs Council, and CAIR) have condemned acts of terrorism conducted in the name of their faith; however, these condemnations are not publicized by the mainstream media, which tends to be the source of information for many Americans.

Abu-Ras and Suarez (2009) and Abu-Raiya, Pargament, and Mahoney (2010) conducted empirical research examining the perception of discrimination, post-traumatic stress disorder (PTSD) symptomatology, and coping methods used to deal with these concerns post–9/11. Participants in both studies reported experiencing hate crimes and other acts of discrimination. Approximately 86% of respondents reported being the target of anti-Muslim comments at least once, 68% were subjected to ongoing special security checks, 60% had experienced discriminatory acts against them, 58% reported verbal harassment, and 88% found these events to be stressful (Abu-Raiya, Pargament, & Mahoney, 2010).

Experiencing such events impacts one's sense of self, interpersonal relationships, and psychological well-being. Many American Muslims report experiencing PTSD post–9/11, a by-product of being targeted via hate crimes, acts of discrimination (Abu-Ras & Suarez, 2009), and negative media bias (Hallak & Quina, 2004). Hallak and Quina (2004) and Zaal, Salah, and Fine (2007) researched the effects of and challenges experienced by Muslim women post–9/11. The participants in these studies indicated that they were greatly worried about the status of human rights in America (Zaal, Salah, & Fine, 2007). Additionally, these women found it challenging to navigate the constant prejudice and discrimination directed toward them from their host community (Hallak & Quina, 2004). The participants in Zaal, Salah, and Fine (2007)'s research also identified being constantly vigilant of their surroundings, actions, and speech, as well as feeling the responsibility to speak up and educate others in order to correct misinformation about their faith. However, a very real concern expressed was personal safety and fear of retaliation (Abu-Ras & Suarez, 2009). This concern appears to influence actions undertaken by American Muslim women in society today. American Muslim women, like their male counterparts, feel less safe in the United States post–9/11, and women more than men report being affected negatively by these changes and report lower self-esteem and self-confidence than American Muslim men (Abu-Ras & Suarez, 2009).

American Muslim women, in addition to experiencing gender discrimination, now increasingly have to contend with religious and racial discrimination. Feelings of paranoia and being under constant surveillance (Zaal, Salah, & Fine, 2007) undoubtedly have an impact on this population's help-seeking behaviors. The feminist multicultural counseling psychologist who recognizes the challenges that these women experience post–9/11 should be aware that it will likely take time to establish trust in the therapeutic relationship. Many American Muslim women in need of psychotherapy will be reluctant to pursue therapy due to the aforementioned fear of being under surveillance, feeling that their faith will be blamed for their problems, and distrusting that confidentiality will be maintained.

Challenges for the feminist multicultural counseling psychologist include working to establish trust in the psychotherapeutic relationship. Additionally, in order to establish her credibility, it is also important for the feminist multicultural counseling psychologist to establish relationships with the local American Muslim community, to learn more about the faith and the faith community's perceptions of psychological healthcare providers, and to form alliances within the community. The feminist multicultural counseling psychologist should be aware of the impact that the post–9/11 world has on her or his client and the interaction of this reality with the presenting issue, even if the presenting issue appears to be fairly benign. For instance, a *hijab*-wearing American Muslim college student may seek therapy for academic difficulties at a college counseling center. An exclusive focus on study skills and habits may obscure the effects that being visibly Muslim on a primarily non-Muslim campus may have on this client. For instance, the client may be dealing with discrimination by peers and instructors, leading to social exclusion, stress, and interference with her ability to focus on academics. The feminist multicultural counseling psychologist is encouraged to take into account the potential challenges and impacts of Islamophobia on the American Muslim client and their interplay with the presenting problem.

Domestic Violence

"And among His wonders is this: He creates for you mates out of your own kind, so that you might incline toward them, and He engenders love and tenderness between you ..." (The Qur'an, 30:21).

This verse of the Qur'an underscores not only the important placed on marriage, but also emphasizes the "harmony principle" (al-Hibri, 2000) that guides this relationship. The ideal Muslim marriage is a partnership characterized by affection, mercy, and compassion between husband and wife. The Qur'an further illustrates this partnership with the analogy of clothing, stating that one's spouse is a "garment for you as you are a garment for them" (The Qur'an, 2:187). Clothing serves to protect our bodies from the harshness of weather, and it is a way for us to beautify and present ourselves to others. This verse suggests that in a marital relationship, the spouses serve as clothing for one another; that is, each partner protects and cares for the other, serves as a confidante for the other, and works together to strengthen the marital bond. However, despite the religious emphasis on love and tranquility in the marital relationship, the Muslim community globally, and within America, is affected by domestic violence.

Domestic violence is an issue in all communities, regardless of religion, culture, or social class status. Approximately 1 in 3 American women will be a victim of violence in her lifetime, and for American Muslim women this statistic is 1 in 10 (Alkhateeb, 1999). There is also a great likelihood that domestic violence is underreported. The incidence of domestic violence is increasing in the American Muslim community post–9/11 (Childress, 2003). It is hypothesized that this increase can in part be accounted for by the increased scrutiny, surveillance, discrimination, and general anti-Muslim sentiments in American society (al-Hibri, 2000; Ammar, 2007). In addition to leading to the increase in domestic violence, these aforementioned concerns may also account for a decreased likelihood of reporting such incidents; victims may fear contributing to the existing negativity that exists in society about Islam and American Muslims (Kiely-Froude & Abdul Karim, 2009) as well as their specific ethnic minority group (for example, negative perceptions about Arab Americans, African Americans, and Hispanic Americans).

Similar to other communities, the issue of domestic violence is shrouded in secrecy and shame in American Muslim communities, and there is a tendency to deny that it exists. However, the issue of domestic violence in the American Muslim community entered the limelight in 2009 with a case in New York that garnered media attention. In this case the victim, Aasiya Hassan, a professional American Muslim woman and the founder of the first American Muslim cable television channel, was beheaded by her husband. This case brought attention to the fact that the American Muslim community is not immune from domestic violence, and that there is a need for local and national American Muslim organizations and leadership to address this issue.

There is limited research literature available on domestic violence and its impact on American Muslim women. A qualitative study conducted by Hassouneh-Phillips (2001) revealed that 13 of the 17 participants had experienced emotional abuse, 9 had experienced physical abuse, and 2 had experienced sexual abuse. The Peaceful Families

Project (see www.peacefulfamilies.org), an organization that raises education and awareness, and offers workshops and training to address domestic violence in American Muslim communities, is also actively collecting and analyzing data on the incidence and impact of domestic violence in American Muslim communities. Data from nine domestic violence organizations serving a significant number of Muslim women revealed that approximately 85% of women served were immigrants, and the various forms of abuse and violence experienced included emotional or verbal abuse (82%), financial abuse (65%), spiritual abuse (49%; this can include using a patriarchal and misogynistic interpretation of religion to justify abuse), physical abuse (74%), and sexual abuse (30%) (Alkhateeb, 2010).

Religion and spirituality can offer a powerful framework within which to help a devout American Muslim woman. The importance given to marriage as an integral part of one's faith and the collective, family-oriented nature of Islam leads victims of domestic violence to feel sorrow and confusion at being unable to live up to the ideal of the "perfect" Muslim marriage (Hassouneh-Phillips, 2001). It is common for victims to blame themselves for the abuse, to tolerate the abuse with the hope that faith will help things to improve over time (Hassouneh-Phillips, 2001), and to believe that, as their spouse strengthens his faith, the abuse will end.

It should be emphasized that abuse is not condoned by Islam (see verses 2:187, 4:19, 30:21, & 42:39–42); however, one verse of the Qur'an is often erroneously used to justify abuse (see The Qur'an 4:34). This verse outlines steps for conflict resolution, beginning with engaging in a discussion about the conflict in order to resolve it, and, if this is unsuccessful, to separate in order to diffuse any tension and frustration, prior to returning to resolve the issue (Mubarak, 2004). It is important for therapists to be aware of this verse, as this is erroneously used as a "religious" justification for abuse by the perpetrator and by some religious leaders within the American Muslim communities. There is much discussion of an Arabic word used in this particular verse, since many patriarchal interpretations translate that word as "to beat." However, scholars have determined that this translation is inadequate and contradicts the Qur'an's message of nonviolence and peace, especially in the marital relationship. It is also important to note that in the legal realm, Islamic jurists have argued that men who are abusive should be prohibited from getting married (al-Hibri, 2000).

Issues of ethnicity, culture, immigration status, and social class influence attitudes toward seeking help for domestic violence issues. Women are often fearful to reach for help within the community due to lack of support and disapproval by family or community members (Kiely-Froude & Abdul Karim, 2009). Additionally, there are safety concerns due to the abuse becoming public knowledge (Haddad, Smith, & Moore, 2006). This is a paramount concern since, with the exception of metropolitan areas, American Muslim communities tend to be small and interconnected.

A case example to illustrate this issue involves a Sudanese Muslim woman residing in a small Midwestern community who seeks out assistance from a local domestic violence agency. This is an impressive step to take for someone who is a recent immigrant, has limited knowledge about social services and the justice system in America, and is residing in a small tight-knit community. The advocate assigned to her is not knowledgeable about Islam and begins to blame the woman's "patriarchal" religion and the chauvinism of Muslim men for the abuse. Not realizing that religion is an important source of strength for her client, the advocate succeeds in alienating the victim, increasing the victim's concern of whether this will lead to her husband's deportation, and making the victim feel guilty for shedding negative light on her religion. Additionally, as the victim is meeting with the advocate, a woman from the Sudanese community spots her and is curious about the nature and content of the meeting. This creates several problems, including the undermining of the victim's source of strength (that is, her religion) and threatening confidentiality.

The feminist multicultural counseling psychologist should educate herself/himself about Islam's view on marital relations, and become familiarized with religious sayings or teachings that underscore the importance of love and harmony within the marriage, as religion may serve as an important and positive role in providing strength and helping the victim heal. There are several organizations founded and led by American Muslim women that provide resources and consultation for professionals. For instance, information about a Muslim version of the power and control wheel can be found at http://www.peacefulfamilies.org/dvwheel.html. Clinical services for victims of domestic violence include the Peaceful Families Project (www.peacefulfamilies.org), Islamic Social Services Association (http://www.issaservices.com/), MONSOON United Asian Women of Iowa (www.muawi.org), women's shelters (such as Turning Point NY [http://www.turningpoint-ny.org/], and Muslimat al-Nisaa [http://www.mnisaa.org/]).

Hijab (The Headscarf)

As explained earlier (see the section on beliefs and values of Muslims), *hijab,* or modesty, is an important value for Muslim women. This value is interpreted differently, depending on the woman's interpretation of religious scripture and teachings. Some women believe that the head scarf (or *hijab*) is mandated, and only the face and hands of the woman should be visible when she is out in public; others believe that *hijab* refers to modesty in dress and behavior, and in order to practice modesty, a physical head scarf is not required. In addition, a small group of women practice the *niqab* (face covering in addition to the veil, in which only the eyes are visible).

The *hijab* is often a "hot topic" issue in Western society in discussions about Muslim women. It is often viewed as a patriarchal and oppressive tool meant to suppress a woman's independence and self-determination. Although this is unfortunately true in many cultures globally, it is important to recognize that the use of the *hijab* in order to suppress and seclude women is a pre-Islamic practice, and is rooted in misogynistic and patriarchal cultural traditions that are in direct contradiction with Islamic teachings and practices. The diversity of American Muslim women is reflected in the practice of the *hijab* and the meanings ascribed to it.

The *hijab* is a visible symbol of Muslim identity (Williams, &Vashi, 2007). *Hijab* holds different meanings and serves different purposes for the woman choosing to practice it. It defines one's Muslim identity, serves to keep one's behavior in check within Islamic guidelines, challenges stereotypes, and is a source of liberation (Droogsma, 2007) for many Muslim women. *Hijab* is also seen as a way to "represent Islam," and a way for Muslim women to identify with each other and create a cultural space for themselves (Williams, &Vashi, 2007).

American Muslim women also feel that the *hijab* liberates them from Western patriarchy in which women's sexuality and body image is emphasized rather than their intellect. The liberating effects of the *hijab* include being respected (Droogsma, 2007) and appreciated for their intelligence, and rejecting society's status quo of beauty. Post–9/11 women with the *hijab* have become targets of discrimination and hate. Many Muslim women chose to stop wearing the *hijab* due to safety concerns post–9/11, and others adopted the *hijab* as a way to challenge stereotypes and educate the larger community about Islam. Although there is a scarcity of research literature currently available on *hijab* and discrimination, the existing literature does comment on the impact of 9/11 on women who choose to wear it (Ali, Yamada, Mahmood, & Knupp, Unpublished Manuscript; Droogsma, 2007; Ghumman & Jackson, 2010; Mir, 2009; and Williams & Vashi, 2007). Ghumman & Jackson (2010) conducted an online survey of 219 Muslim women in America; of these women, 117 participants practiced *hijab*. Findings of this survey indicate that women who practice *hijab* have significantly lower expectations of receiving a job offer, and this deters them from pursuing jobs (Ghumman & Jackson, 2010). This is not surprising, considering recent media coverage that reported that Muslim female employees in *hijab* who worked for companies such as Abercrombie and Fitch or Disney were relegated to the stockroom or positions with low public contact; other companies actually have dismissed women from work. One participant in Ali, Yamada, Mahmood, & Knupp's (Unpublished Manuscript) study, which examined the role of *hijab* as related to workplace discrimination and job satisfaction, noted that she only wore the *hijab* outside her work setting, as it would not be accepted by her company.

The feminist multicultural counseling psychologist working with an American Muslim client who practices *hijab* should determine the role that the *hijab* plays in the client's life, as it may relate to the presenting problem. For instance, the *hijab* could represent a cultural rather than a religious practice for the client, and for some clients it may be a restrictive rather than a liberating practice.

In the post–9/11 world, the *hijab* has become a visible symbol of Muslim identity, and a target for hate crimes and discriminatory actions; thus, it is likely that a therapist may encounter women contemplating whether to wear the *hijab* or not. For example, a Muslim woman seeking employment may present with anxiety. This anxiety could be related to her expectations that she will have difficulty finding employment due to her *hijab* (Ghumman & Jackson, 2010). It is important to explore the meaning that the *hijab* holds for the client, and to explore the consequences that its removal would have for her. For instance, is removal of the *hijab* an acceptable personal spiritual and religious option for the client, or will removing it lead to further anxiety and guilt of disobeying God, or will it cause a problem with her family? Alternatively, is the client looking to explore occupations and careers in employment settings where she will not have to compromise her identity and can continue to practice *hijab*?

Marriage and Dating

As previously mentioned, heterosexual marriage and family are emphasized in Islam. A saying of the Prophet states that "marriage is one half of faith," which underscores its importance. American Muslims, like members of other faith communities, emphasize marriage within the faith. From a religious perspective, marriage is considered to be a partnership and the basic building block of a strong community. Muslims are encouraged to marry others with a similar level of faith and piety, and one should give weight to the character of one's partner rather than her or his physical appearance, ethnic or social class background. However, various ethnic groups within the American Muslim community prefer that their children marry someone of the same ethnic group.

American Muslim women across ethnic and cultural groups are socialized from an early age to view marriage as the ideal relationship (Hassouneh-Phillips, 2001). The challenge for American Muslim women, especially those whose parents are immigrants, becomes how to negotiate dating in an American context. Dating in the Muslim context is viewed differently from dating in the mainstream American context. For many Muslims, dating has negative connotations, as it implies sexual intimacy outside the marital relationship. However, within the American Muslim context, dating may consist of "talking" (Mir, 2009) as well as more traditional Western dates, minus the component of physical or sexual intimacy. How "dating" looks for the American Muslim woman depends on the cultural and ethnic background of the woman, her identification with, and interpretation of, the religious norms and mores pertaining to dating.

Being a member of a religious minority means that it is often difficult to find someone of interest in the community in which one is residing. In recent years, there has been an increase in online dating in America, and this is also true of the American Muslim community. Several online relationship sites cater to the American Muslim community, such as www.naseeb.com, www.zawaj.com, and www.shaadi.com. American Muslims organizations also hold social events at major conferences for the purposes of introducing potential partners and their families to one another (for instance, the Islamic Society of North America's matrimonial banquet), and young Muslim professionals have created organizations that host social networking events across the country.

In addition to the challenge of finding a Muslim husband, American Muslim women of some cultural backgrounds may also have to navigate their parents' expectations about finding a marriage partner. For instance, a Pakistani American Muslim woman interested in marrying an Ethiopian American Muslim male may meet resistance from her family for several reasons, such as: she did not involve her parents in the decision-making process of choosing a marriage partner, and he is not Pakistani. The parents may refuse to acknowledge that he is well educated, religious, and of good character; they may also impose cultural and racist restrictions on who their daughter can marry, even when these restrictions are diametrically opposed to religious teachings. Another challenge for American Muslim women is that of immigrant parents' pressure to marry someone from their home country. For instance, an Egyptian Muslim family may pressure their daughter into considering marriage with someone from Egypt. This may be undesirable to their Egyptian American Muslim daughter, who feels she shares nothing in common with someone from her parents' home country, and would prefer to marry an American Muslim.

An additional challenge for American Muslim women, and one that will likely be debated in the American context, is that of marrying outside the faith. Although statistics for the United States are not available, there is an increase in Muslim women marrying non-Muslim men (Haddad, Smith, & Moore, 2006). The Qur'an states that a Muslim man can marry women of good character and morals within the Judeo-Christian tradition (The Qur'an, 5:5) but is silent on whether a Muslim woman can do the same. The feminist multicultural counseling psychologist can expect to see American Muslim clients who are conflicted about making a decision about marrying outside the faith. It is important to process the client's understanding and interpretation of the faith, and to evaluate the implications this would have on the client's relationships with her family.

This section primarily covers heterosexual relationships and marriage. Islam, like the other Judeo-Christian traditions, emphasizes heterosexual marriage. However, it should be acknowledged that homosexuality is present within the American Muslim community, but is not recognized by the mainstream Muslim community. There is an organization for gay and lesbian Muslims (see http://www.al-fatiha.org/), and recently, Irshad Manji's PBS documentary *Faith Without Fear* has given voice to this community in North America. Undoubtedly, American Muslim women who identify as lesbian or bisexual carry the burdens of this identity, and face discrimination and ostracism from within the American Muslim community also.

Emerging Psychosocial Concerns

This section briefly introduces emerging issues, including body image, challenges associated with converting to Islam, generational and cultural differences among American Muslims, and acculturation concerns.

Body Image

Research in the area of body image and eating disorders with American Muslim women is lacking. Tolaymat & Moradi's (2010) survey of 112 Muslim women explored the role that the *hijab* may play in body image issues. The findings indicate that the *hijab* did not protect the participants from being affected by and internalizing societal beauty standards and body image concerns (Tolaymat & Moradi, 2010). A qualitative examination of 22 African American Muslim women in upstate New York revealed the importance of religion and spirituality in perceptions of body image (Odoms-Young, 2008). The participants of this study reported several components that impact their perception of body image: wanting to return to pre-marriage or pre-pregnancy body size; cultural, social, and family norms and expectations about body size and shape; partners' perceptions of participants' bodies; the role of spirituality and religious beliefs; and the importance of the spiritual self versus the physical self (Odoms-Young, 2008). This study is unique as it considers ethnicity, religion, and gender implication on perceptions of body image.

The feminist multicultural counseling psychologist working with an American Muslim client with an eating disorder or body image issue is encouraged to incorporate the client's cultural beliefs and values, as well as religious and spiritual teachings regarding physical health and well-being.

Converting to Islam

Since September 11, the Council of American Islamic Relations cites that approximately 20,000 people in America convert to Islam annually, with the ratio of women to male converts being four to one (Haddad, Smith, & Moore, 2006). This gender discrepancy in conversion rates may be puzzling to the average American who views Islam as a patriarchal religion that oppresses women. American women converts to Islam typically choose the religion after extensive research and study (Haddad, Smith, & Moore, 2006). These women report dissatisfaction with their previous faith or way of life, and a cultural fit between their values and Islam as some of the reasons for conversion (Maslim & Bjorck, 2009). African American, Hispanic, and Native American women in particular find that Islamic values resonate well with their cultural identity (Haddad, Smith, & Moore, 2006).

Converts to Islam have several challenges ahead of them. Conversion at times requires drastic changes to their previous lifestyle, for example, dietary restrictions, cross-gender interactions, changes in dress and attire, rejection by family members for accepting Islam (Rehman & Dziegielewski, 2004), and creating a social support network and space for oneself within the Muslim community (Haddad, Smith, & Moore, 2006). The feminist multicultural counseling psychologist working with a client who is a new convert to Islam or with someone considering conversion needs to be aware of her or his own beliefs and perceptions about Islam. A client who has recently converted to Islam may utilize therapy to adjust to her new lifestyle, to seek ways in which to reconcile with her family members who are not accepting of her decision to become Muslim, to create a social support network within her new religious community, or to differentiate between cultural influences on the practice of Islam and the actual religious teachings (Haddad, Smith, & Moore, 2006).

Generational and Cultural Differences

Recent immigrants constitute an increasing proportion of the American Muslim population. These immigrants have become involved in leadership positions in local religious communities, as well as national organizations. They are also raising American-born children who are defining their Muslim and ethnic identity within the American context. Many American Muslim youth create and identify with hyphenated, bicultural, or multicultural identities (Sirin & Fine, 2008).

Immigrant parents' practice of religion is often influenced by cultural practices and rituals that do not resonate with their American Muslim children, who are engaged in redefining and reevaluating Islam within the American context. Many

American Muslim youth who attend immigrant-run mosques feel alienated by the cultural baggage that is imported into the mosque space. A common complaint by many is the lack of American Muslim imams, or religious leaders. Many mosques (typically those populated by recent immigrant groups) tend to import imams from the Middle East or Asia; these imams are not trained to address concerns facing American Muslims today, and are typically dealing with their own adjustment to life in America. American Muslim women are also negotiating their roles within the mosque, including gaining equal access to mosque space (a cultural import within the immigrant Muslim community involves segregating women, or limiting their access to the mosque space, which is especially prevalent in Mosques influenced by South Asian and Arab cultures [Karim, 2009]).

Other complaints include parents' views on acceptable career paths and academic fields (for instance, South Asians place a premium on the sciences and medicine). Differing views on issues of education, marriage, practice and understanding of religion, and linguistic differences (children preferring to communicate in English, rather than their parents' language) can also be expected sources of intergenerational conflict.

Acculturation Concerns

Women of immigrant backgrounds range from those who immigrated many decades ago, to those who have been in America for only a few years. Years spent in America, education, social class, language fluency, and level of integration with American society all determine where these women are in terms of acculturation. For example, some women may reside in ethnic enclaves; an Arab American immigrant woman residing in Dearborn, Michigan, may interact only with other Arab immigrants in her daily life. Immigrant women are adjusting to a new lifestyle and culture, as well as the challenges of raising children in an environment that is hostile toward Muslims. All of these stressors inevitably affect psychological well-being. One's cultural background and education influence help-seeking behaviors, as does the knowledge and awareness of what psychotherapy encompasses. This population is unique in that the feminist multicultural counseling psychologist would likely have to engage in relationship building and educational efforts in order to develop an understanding of needs, and to provide an awareness of the option of pursuing psychotherapy to alleviate acculturation stresses.

Implications for Therapy

Islam takes a holistic perspective toward psychological health and well-being (Carter & Rashidi, 2004), with many religious scholars from the eighth through twelfth centuries emphasizing a mind-body connection and linking psychology to medicine (Haque, 2004). Psychological distress is often viewed by some devout Muslims to occur as a result of straying away from Islamic teachings and practices (Ali, 2006), and the guilt and shame attached to this may prevent some from seeking help from professionals. American Muslims, like other minority groups in the United States, may not be aware or educated about the nature and extent of psychological services available (Kobeisy, 2004).

There is a scarcity of psychological help-seeking literature for the American Muslim population. Existing literature often does not attend to the complexities of ethnic, culture, age, and social class backgrounds, and the ways in which these identities, in conjunction with religious identity, color one's attitudes and views toward psychological health and help-seeking. Khan (2006) examined help-seeking attitudes and utilization of counseling services among Muslims in Toledo, Ohio. Findings indicated that Muslim women were more likely to hold positive attitudes toward counseling and to identify the need for counseling services than were men (Khan, 2006). The participants in this study also identified religious coping mechanisms, such as prayer and reading the Qur'an, as alleviating their distress; accessing support from family and the community were also preferred means of coping (Khan, 2006).

A qualitative study examining attitudes toward help-seeking among South Asian American Muslim women revealed that the majority of participants (11 of 13) recognized psychologists as necessary and important (Mahmood, 2008). Although participants indicated that their faith recognizes the importance of taking care of their psychological health, cultural beliefs and stigma regarding psychological concerns and issues often contradict religious teachings that affirm the value of seeking help for such concerns (Mahmood, 2008). Participants in this investigation stated that they would prefer a provider from their cultural or religious background, or someone who is knowledgeable about their community, culture, and religion (Mahmood, 2008). This sentiment resonates with research conducted by Kelly, Aridi, and Bakhtiar (1996), who found that only 43.8% of respondents indicated that they would consider working with a non-Muslim counselor who is educated and aware about Islam and Islamic values. Further research on attitudes toward help-seeking among American Muslim women is needed. Such research should also consider culture, education, age, and social class background and the role that they play in facilitating or preventing women from seeking help.

It can be delineated from the research outlined above that, although American Muslim women would prefer Muslim providers, many would consider seeking services from a non-Muslim provider who has an understanding of their religious and cultural backgrounds. This finding has several important implications. First, it would be important to encourage American Muslims to seek careers in behavioral health care. This will certainly require time and focused energy from training programs. Second, providers who are interested in providing services to this population need to educate themselves about the basics of Islam. Next, in these times of anti-Muslim discrimination and Islamophobia, spending time establishing trust with the local American Muslim community by attending open house and other community events held at the mosque will help in building the provider's credibility. Finally, providers are encouraged to use online resources, and to seek consultation via health-focused American Muslim organizations including American Muslim Healthcare Professionals (www.amhp.us) and Muslim Mental Health (www.muslimmentalhealth.com).

It is important for Muslim mental health professionals to establish relationships with and work in collaboration with non-Muslim professionals to raise awareness and education about psychological services, and to counter misconceptions about counseling and psychotherapy. The feminist multicultural counseling psychologist, in addition to collaborating with Muslim colleagues, should build relationships with local religious and community leaders. This can be done by attending open houses at mosques and community centers, and by attending study circles and/or other events at these locations. Establishing these relationships will allow the feminist multicultural counseling psychologist to learn about the needs of the community, and subsequently may lead to psycho-educational workshops and seminars on psychosocial issues identified by the community, even if these are fairly innocuous, such as attaining work-family balance.

Future Directions

Feminism and multiculturalism seek to foster the creation of a society where people operate fairly and without biases (Worell & Remer, 2003). This perspective is well aligned with the teachings of Islam and the beliefs and values of Muslims. Unfortunately, attention to diversity was previously absent from feminist literature (Enns, 1997), as was information on religious and spiritual identities. These newer additions to the theory and research need much more attention.

Religion and spirituality, in particular, are important forces in the lives of many, and it is important for feminist multicultural counseling psychologists to be aware of their clients' religious identities and the importance of these identities to their clients, as this knowledge will undoubtedly help the therapeutic process. This chapter has outlined some psychosocial concerns of American Muslim women, and the challenges that this population is currently undergoing in the United States. In order to better serve this population, more research needs to be done on this population to understand its needs and concerns.

First, there is the need to conduct research on the exploration of attitudes toward help seeking among various ethnic and cultural groups of American Muslim women, including similarities and differences in these attitudes between ethnic and cultural groups, as well as between immigrant and American-born Muslim women. Second, there is a need to conduct research that explores the meaning of feminisms, especially Islamic or Muslim feminisms, in the American Muslim context. Third, given the current marginalization of this population, an examination of the psychosocial impact of Islamophobia is important. For instance, how does the rise in anti-Muslim sentiment affect American Muslim women's self-perceptions, and how are American Muslim mothers coping with parenting and raising children in an environment hostile to their way of life? Do religion, social class, and culture play a role in American Muslim women's conceptualization of gender roles? How are American Muslim women similar to or different from women of other faith groups, and the general populace in their conceptualization of gender roles?

Feminist multicultural counseling psychologists are encouraged to seek continuing education and training opportunities to learn more about this population in order to further their understanding of American Muslim women in the context of their multiple identities.

Note

1. Muslims attribute the Qur'an to be the word of God. Hence, in the text, quotations and verses referred to are cited as such. For the purposes of this chapter, Muhammad Asad's (2003) translation was utilized; the reference can be located under his name in the reference list.

References

Abu-Raiya, H., Pargament, K. I., & Mahoney A. (2010). Examining coping methods with stressful interpersonal events experienced by Muslims living in the United States following the 9/11 attacks. *Psychology of Religion and Sprituality,* Advance online publication. doi: 10.1037/a0020034

Abu-Ras, W., & Suarez, Z. E. (2009). Muslim men and women's perception of discrimination, hate crimes, and PTSD symptoms post 9/11. *Traumatology, 15,* 48–63.

Afridi, S. (2001). *Muslims in America: Identity, diversity and the challenge of understanding.* New York: Carnegie Corp.

Al-Hibri, A. Y. (2000). An Islamic perspective on domestic violence. *Fordham International Law Journal, 27,* 195–224.

Ali, S. R., Liu, W. M., & Humeidan, M. (2004). Islam 101: Understanding the religion and therapy implications. *Professional Psychology: Research and Practice, 35,* 635–642.

Ali, S. R. (2006). Psychology and Sunni Muslims. In E. T. Dowd & S. L. Nielsen (Eds.), *The Psychologies in religion: Working with the religious client* (pp. 221–236). New York: Springer.

Ali, S. R., Mahmood, A., Moel, J., Hudson, C., & Leathers, L. (2008). A qualitative investigation of Muslim and Christian women's views of religion and feminism in their lives. *Cultural Diversity and Ethnic Minority Psychology, 14,* 38–46.

Ali, S. R., Yamada, T., Mahmood, A., & Knupp, T. (Unpublished Manuscript). The practice of *hijab*, workplace discrimination and job satisfaction: An investigation of the relationship of religiosity, *hijab*, discrimination, and job stress to job satisfaction among Muslim American women.

Alkhateeb, M. (2010). *DV organizations serving Muslim women: Preliminary results of a 2009 quantitative survey.* Peaceful Families Project. Retrieved December 8, 2010, from http://www.peacefulfamilies.org/DVOrgsSurvey.pdf.

Alkhateeb, S. (1999). Ending domestic violence in Muslim families. *Journal of Religion and Abuse, 1,* 49–59.

Ammar, N. H. (2007). Wife battery in Islam: A comprehensive understanding of interpretations. *Violence Against Women, 13,* 516–526.

Armstrong, K. (2000). *Islam: A short history.* New York: Random House.

Asad, M. (2003). *The message of the Qur'an.* Bristol, England: The Book Foundation.

Bagby, I., Perle, P. M., & Froehle, B. T. (2001). *The Mosque in America: A national portrait. A report from the Mosque Study.* Council on American-Islamic Relations. Retrieved July 2, 2005, from http://www.cair-net.org.

Carter, D. J., & Rashidi, A. (2004). East meets West: Integrating psychotherapy approaches for Muslim women. *Holistic Nursing Practice, 18,* 152–159.

Council of American-Islamic Relations. (2006). *American public opinion about Islam and Muslims 2006.* Washington, DC: Council of American-Islamic Relations.

Council of American-Islamic Relations (2007). *The status of Muslim civil rights in the United States, 2007: Presumption of guilt.* Washington, DC: Council of American-Islamic Relations.

Childress, S. (2003). Muslim American women are quietly coping with a tragic side effect of the attacks—a surge in domestic violence. *Newsweek, 142,* 2.

Droogsma, R. A. (2007). Redefining hijab: American Muslim women's standpoints on veiling. *Journal of Applied Communication Research, 35,* 294–319.

Enns, C. Z. (1997). *Feminist theories and feminist psychotherapies.* Binghamton, NY: Harrington Park Press.

Esposito, J. L. (1998). *Islam: The straight path.* New York: Oxford University Press.

Greenhouse, S. (2010). Muslims report rising discrimination at work. *New York Times,* September 24, 2010.

Ghumman, S., & Jackson, L. (2010). The downside of religious attire: The Muslim headscarf and expectations of obtaining employment. *Journal of Organizational Behavior, 31,* 4–23.

Haddad, Y. Y., & Lumis, A. T. (1987). *Islamic values in the United States.* New York: Oxford University Press.

Haddad, Y. Y., Smith, J. I., & Moore, K. M. (2006). *Muslim women in America: The challenge of Islamic identity Today.* New York: Oxford University Press.

Hallak, M., & Quina, K. (2004). In the shadows of the twin towers: Muslim immigrant women's voices emerge. *Sex Roles, 51,* 329–338.

Haque, A. (2004). Psychology from Islamic perspective: Contributions of early Muslim scholars and challenges to contemporary Muslim psychologists. *Journal of Religion and Health, 43,* 357–378.

Hassouneh-Phillips, D. (2001). "Marriage is half of faith and the rest is fear Allah": Marriage and spousal abuse among American Muslims. *Violence Against Women, 7,* 927–946.

Hedayat-Diba, Z. (2000). Psychotherapy with Muslims. In P. S. Richards, & A. E. Bergin (Eds.), *Handbook of psychotherapy and religious diversity* (pp. 289–314). Washington, DC: American Psychological Association.

Karim, J. (2009). *American Muslim women: Negotiating race, class, and gender, within the Ummah.* New York: New York University Press.

Kelly Jr., E. W., Aridi, A., Bakhtiar, L. (1996). Muslims in the United States: An exploratory study of universal and mental health values. *Counseling and Values, 40,* 206–218.

Khan, Z. (2006). Attitudes toward counseling and alternative support among Muslims in Toledo, Ohio. *Journal of Muslim Mental Health, 1,* 21–42.

Kiely-Froude, C., & Abdul Karim, S. (2009). Providing culturally conscious mental health treatment for African American Muslim women living with spousal abuse. *Journal of Muslim Mental Health, 4,* 175–186.

Kobeisy, A. N. (2004). *Counseling American Muslims: Understanding the faith and helping the people.* Westport, CT: Praeger

Mahmood, A. (2006). Psychology and Shia Muslims. In E. T. Dowd & S. L. Nielsen (Eds.), *The psychologies in religion: Working with the religious client* (pp. 237–252). New York: Springer.

Mahmood, A. (2008). Attitudes towards help-seeking among South Asian American Muslim Women. Ph.D. dissertation, University of Iowa, Iowa City, IA.

Maslim, A. A., & Bjorck, J. P. (2009). Reasons for conversion to Islam among women in the United States. *Psychology of Religion and Spirituality, 2,* 97–111.

Mir, S. (2009). Not too "college-like," not too normal: American Muslim undergraduate women's gendered discourses. *Anthropology and Education Quarterly, 40,* 237–256.

Mubarak, H. (2004). Breaking the interpretive monopoly: A re-examination of verse 4:34. *Hawwa, 2,* 261–289.

Munir, L. Z. (2003). *Islam, modernity, and justice for women.* Paper presented at the Islam and Human Rights Fellow Lecture, October 14, 2003, organized by the Islam and Human Rights Project, School of Law, Emory University, Atlanta, GA.

Odoms-Young, A. (2008). Factors that influence body image representations of black Muslim women. *Social Science and Medicine, 66,* 2573–2584.

Project MAPS: Muslims in American Public Square, & Zogby International. (2004). *Muslims in the American public square: Shifting political winds and fallout from 9/11, Afghanistan, and Iraq.* Retrieved July 2, 2005, from www.projectmaps.com/AMP2004report.pdf

Rehman, T. F., & Dziegielewski, S. F. (2004). Women who choose Islam: Issues, changes, and challenges in providing ethnic-diverse practice. *International Journal of Mental Health, 32,* 31–49.

Sheridan, L. P. (2006). Islamophobia pre- and post-September 11th, 2001. *Journal of Interpersonal Violence, 21,* 317–336.

Smith, J. I. (2005). Patterns of Muslim immigration. *Muslim Life in America.* Office of International Informational Programs. U.S. Department of State, Retrieved February 13, 2005, from http://usinfo.state.gove/products/pubs/muslimlife/immigrant

Sirin, S. R., & Fine, M. (2008). *Muslim American Youth: Understanding hyphenated identities through multiple methods.* New York University Press: New York.

Tolaymat, L., & Moradi, B. (2010). Muslim women's body image: Links among hijab and objectification theory constructs. Paper presented on August 15, 2010, at the American Psychological Association Annual Convention, San Diego, CA.

U.S. Department of State. (2001). *Fact sheet: Islam in the United States.* Retrieved January 15, 2002, from http://usinfo.state.gov/usa/islam/fact2.htm.

Williams, R. H., & Vashi, G. (2007). *Hijab* and American Muslim women: Creating the space for autonomous selves. *Sociology of Religion, 68,* 269–287.

Worell, J., & Remer, P. (2003). *Feminist perspectives in therapy: Empowering diverse women* (2nd ed.). Hoboken, NJ: John Wiley & Sons.

Zaal, M., Salah, T., & Fine, M. (2007). The weight of the hyphen: Freedom, fusion and responsibility embodied by young Muslim-American women during a time of surveillance. *Applied Development Science, 11,* 164–177.

CHAPTER

13 Feminist Multicultural Counseling Psychology in Transnational Contexts

Sharon G. Horne *and* Kiran S. K. Arora

Abstract

As the field of counseling psychology becomes increasingly global in scope, feminist and multicultural contributions are vital to the development of socially just, transnational counseling psychology. In this chapter we focus on (a) the ways in which both feminist and multicultural theory and practice inform and challenge prevailing approaches to transnational and cross-cultural work, in particular by drawing upon Sharon Horne's experiences with post-communist countries and communities, and Kiran Arora's work within transnational Sikh communities as a second-generation Sikh woman; (b) the foundational work conducted by feminist multicultural counseling psychologists in transnational contexts and with recent immigrants in the United States; (c) the developmental aspects of education and training in feminist-multicultural (F-M) transnational work; and (d) finally, future directions for F-M transnational counseling psychology.

Key Words: International, global, transnational, advocacy, social justice, feminist multicultural, feminism, counseling, counseling psychology

An increasing number of counseling psychologists guided by feminist and multicultural ideals and principles are conducting transnational work in countries other than their own, as well as in local settings serving diverse cultural communities. In this chapter we start with two narratives about our challenges engaging in transnational work, including how feminist-multicultural (F-M) ideas, themes, and principles have aided our development as therapists and researchers, and describing our current engagement in this work. We believe that in sharing our narratives we highlight the developmental aspects of engagement in transnational work, and allow for a richer discussion of the varying degrees of power and privilege associated with citizenship, geopolitical location, as well as educational and professional status in transnational work. An F-M framework prizes self-reflexivity and an ongoing analysis of the roles and relations of power during the creation and development of cross-cultural and international collaboration. We hope that by sharing some of our experience in transnational engagement—admittedly, not our shiniest of moments—that we can encourage further dialogue and exploration of these issues among counseling psychologists engaged in transnational issues. In the next section, we review the current status of F-M transnational counseling psychology, and, finally, we highlight recommendations for future training, research, and practice within F-M transnational counseling psychology.

Personal Narratives: Our Own Engagement in Transnational Work

Sharon Horne

At a Christian camp in the mountains near the Georgia-Tennessee border, 55 women activists from the recently dissolved Soviet empire gather in the main lodge one evening in October 1994. They include Russians, Georgians, Armenians, and Azerbaijanis who are in the United States for a U.S. AID project intended to provide training and support to women leaders from emerging nongovernmental organizations (NGOs) in post-communist countries. This gathering is meant to give a bit of respite after two weeks of intensive training in Atlanta; on site there has been singing and dancing, cross-agency planning and sharing of ideas, and one apology to the camp director for our Siberian activist caught bathing in the buff in the local river. Toward the end of the final evening, even the Georgians and Russians, who refused to be in each other's company earlier in the program, are huddled arm in arm, sitting on the wood floor in sisterhood. The singing stops and I begin my informal presentation. I'm quite certain that it is in no small measure the combination of wine and international collaborative spirit that spurs on their attention as I propose my idea of a woman-owned diaper factory to be built in the heart of Russia. As I go on—describing suggested sites in the middle of the Russian steppe and providing potential profit numbers—the former Soviet women sit there in silence, taking it all in, nodding politely, but not asking questions or engaging in discussion, which is quite unusual for this group. When I finish, there are several women who say it was very interesting (translation: not so much), but there are no follow-up questions and no one says she would like to be involved in the next stage. The group resumes singing Russian folk songs with a "Kumbaya" thrown in to appease the American trainers.

Now I can acknowledge that I may have garnered their undivided attention primarily due to my privileged status as an American (which at the time carried a great deal of valence with this group), combined perhaps with some deference due to my role as chief trainer on the grant. It was early in my feminist edification, and I had yet to complete any multicultural training. I was a White, able-bodied, middle class woman in my mid-twenties whose experience with diapers, I admit, was limited to a brief babysitting job at age 14. I was given the position of chief trainer because I was one of a handful of U.S. women who had experience in the Soviet Union with the feminist NGO movement related to violence against women in the early 1990s. Despite this experience, my proposal was put forward without any regard for Russian cultural ideas about diapers or Soviet beliefs about potty training (i.e., diapers are unhealthy, particularly for boys; potty training should be concluded by age one; diapers are a waste of money), which persist to this day. Nor had I any clue what it would take to establish a business in Russia in the early 1990s and that this arena was largely the domain of men and, in no small part, the emerging Russian mafia. The reason I had proposed this idea was that I had met an Atlanta exporter (male) who thought that Russia was the next great market for diapers, and I thought this might be an ingenious way for women activists to take control of this market and increase NGO profits for their organizations. Even more disturbing was my inability to perceive my proposal as steeped in a colonialist, global capitalist framework.

It's not the first time that my high scores on the enterprising domain of the "Strong Interest Inventory" have gotten me into imprudent situations (e.g., there was the bright idea of selling ice cream and fruit juice at the Olympics during grad school), but this was the one that to this day still causes me to shudder with shame. I can still see the faces of these women, many of whom I'm lucky enough to still consider colleagues and friends, as they sat in this lodge and considered this proposal—women with decades of experience and expertise in fighting the exploitation and oppression of women as they challenged dominant paradigms in their local communities. They were there to relax and enjoy a break from their respective battles, and they didn't need a business proposal developed by a graduate student to consider. A U.S. colleague and friend, who was the same age as me but apparently had a great deal more transnational feminist awareness at the time, sat to the side, propped up against a log with a smirk on her face. I heard someone say *podguzniki* (diapers) and snicker. As I reached my conclusion, having become increasingly quieter until I was now mumbling, I was the embodiment of Western hegemony, complete with good intentions. In less than five minutes, I had managed to bolster every major American stereotype—like other Americans, U.S. feminists were also brash, aggressive, and naïve (Laungani, 2007).

My subsequent education in feminist theory taught me about power-sharing, the exploitations of global capitalism, and about Western hegemony. Reading the works of feminists and global scholars such as Chandra Talpade Mohanty, Ignacio Martin-Baró, Carolyn Enns, Urvashi Vaid, Charlotte Bunch, Lynne Segal, Laura Brown, Lillian Comaz-Diaz, and many, many others allowed me a lens with which to perceive the exchange that occurs as the voices associated with U.S. citizenship and

White privilege, typically located within the global North/West, are given center stage at the same time that the words and experiences of activists, scholars, and human rights activists in global South/East countries often are marginalized and/or disregarded. As I was exposed to U.S. multicultural theory and practice, my awareness of the importance and resilience of cultural beliefs and norms, particularly with respect to transnational contexts, deepened and expanded. I learned that the term "transnational" was being used as an alternative to "global" and "international" because these terms had become associated with the neo-colonizing role that multinational corporations were playing in perpetuating global inequities as they moved into new markets in the South and East. Transnational (as opposed to international) also began to signify the less relevant role in global politics of the nation-state, and was used as a synonym for the diasporic, therefore including migratory and refugee populations (Grewal & Kaplan (2001). Counseling psychologists who are integrating feminist and multicultural approaches into their work in global contexts, often under the rubric of social justice, are exploring and challenging overt and covert power relations (e.g., classist, racist, North/West biased) through reflexivity and collaborative reflection in their global work (Lock Swarr & Nigar, 2010). Therefore, the term "transnational" best captures the diverse work that is being conducted in this realm by F-M counseling psychologists, including collaborative cross-cultural consultation and research; psychological intervention and engagement with refugee, immigrant, migrant, diasporic communities, international students, and other transnational populations that may inhabit multiple positions both physically and psychologically; and peace and reconciliation work that minimizes the role of our contemporary constructions of nation-states (e.g., Tibet, Israeli-Palestinian conflict, etc.).

At this point, I've been engaged in an ongoing learning process within transnational work for more than 24 years, 13 of those as a counseling psychologist, and primarily in Eastern Europe, Russia, and former Soviet countries. As well, I have had the opportunity to mentor counseling psychologists in training who are interested in being engaged on a global level either as students who come to graduate work to pursue international interests, or as international students desiring to bring counseling psychology that is informed by feminist and multicultural theories to their home communities. In my ongoing effort to bring feminist and multicultural principles to my transnational work (and to reduce the occurrence of such cultural impasses and cross-cultural exploitation), I developed, along with my colleague Susan Mathews, a feminist-multicultural collaborative consultation model for working in international contexts (see Horne & Mathews, 2004, 2005), and this model has been used in our approach to cross-cultural research and consultation (e.g., Mathews, Horne, & Levitt, 2005; Horne, Mathews, Brown, & DeGroff, 2009; Horne, Ovrebo, Levitt, & Franeta, 2009).

My work is now primarily in Kyrgyzstan, where I work with the Psychology Department at American University of Central Asia and with an energetic group of women faculty who range in their identification as feminists but rally around women's rights and a commitment to social justice. Together we conduct research, work on curriculum and syllabi, write articles, and work on grants to pursue research and training on mental health issues. For the past four years we have been involved in the development of an ethics code for Kyrgyz psychologists, which is now coming into fruition, thanks to their ongoing efforts to bring psychologists throughout Kyrgyzstan together to draft and agree on a common approach to ethical practice and research within a Central Asian context. My ongoing involvement with this group has been made easier by an academic fellowship with the Open Society Institute that I have held intermittently since 2005.

In many ways, globalization has benefited our relationship and indeed has made it possible to forge a solid and lasting connection. Technology such as Skype has made communication easier, and consequently, our world is shrinking as shared understandings and cross-cultural meanings and symbols increase in scope. For example, on my first visit to work in Kyrgyzstan, standing in front of a Lenin statue with my new colleagues, the chair of the department's cell phone began to ring. I recognized that the ring tone was the title song from the TV show *Sex and the City*, and I gave my colleague a glance. Typically very formal, my colleague shrugged her shoulder and unapologetically said, "I just love that show." What ensued next was a lively discussion of the characters from the popular TV show, and there were many laughs. As a result, our connection deepened—all through a feminist critique of this showcase of Western capitalist values! As enjoyable as this exchange was, there was also no question that this bridge for sharing cultural meanings had been largely forged by the domineering presence of Western media, which principally allows only unidirectional traffic. I can't recall encountering a single Kyrgyz cultural reference while in the United States. Most of the time, any discussion of Kyrgyzstan in which I am engaged involves explaining that Kyrgyzstan is in Central Asia, unlike Kurdistan, which refers to the geocultural region in the Middle East claimed by the Kurdish people. There is a great deal of power in having one's cultural references "known" by a sizable portion of the world's population. As well, my colleagues and I have various degrees of privilege, depending on where we are located sociopolitically; for example, I am able to come and go easily, with easy access to visas, due to my U.S. citizenship, and as a lesbian woman legally married to another woman in my state, I have individual freedoms that would be unthinkable to some of my colleagues who are expected to marry a man—often a man of the family's choosing. These divergent degrees of privilege are also located among the faculty who are a diverse group of women with Russian, Korean, Uzbek, Kyrgyz, and Uighur backgrounds. Somehow these multinational and transnational experiences, privileges, differences, and backgrounds have cohered to create an ever evolving collaborative network and partnership that is supportive, challenging, inspiring, and for which I am very grateful.

However, there is a great deal to question and critique about the nature of our collaboration as we forge our transnational solidarity. The new transnational feminist movement has been critiqued as a "new form of empire" (Mendoza, 2002, p. 316) or neocolonialism (Jameson & Miyoshi, 1998) due to its typical location found within global development, which is only possible if the notion of ingrained inequality between the global North/West and the South/East exists. Mendoza argues that "development becomes the grand equalizer between women in a world divided into developed, developing and less developed nations. In this manner, development becomes the substance of global feminist solidarity" (p. 319). As long as development serves as the backdrop for cross-cultural and transnational feminism, the "developed" world of international development agencies and governments will continue to set the agendas in assisting the developing and less developed worlds. Without a central critique of *development* and the role of culture, nation, and power, the transnational movement will only be, at best, an approximation of globalization. Therefore, F-M transnational solidarity relies not only on a critique of the role of culture and gender but with economic-political debate and analysis. The transnational connection that my colleagues and I have rests upon an understanding of the complex power relations not only within culture and gender, but also of the sociopolitical issues in play. Recently, we had a lively discussion about the different family and societal expectations for Kyrgyz women graduate students as opposed to men in pursuing higher education in the West (e.g., expectations of women to marry and have children young, and expectations that wives take care of extended family on the husband's side often prevents them from being away for extended periods of time). We then took a broader perspective beyond gender socialization and expectations, as it occurred to us that this was also a political-economic issue (i.e., education at a Central Asian university was not deemed as valuable as a U.S. education, and there were limited opportunities and resources available in Kyrgyzstan for both women and men to receive an advanced degree in psychology). Practicing F-M approaches to transnational counseling psychology can open up additional avenues of inquiry.

Kiran Arora

I want to begin by locating myself as a heterosexual woman who belongs to the Sikh diaspora. I am a child of Sikh immigrants from Punjab, India, and I was born in Vancouver, Canada. I feel that it is valuable to be transparent about my intersecting identities, as they inform this section of the chapter, in which I explore feminist multicultural aspects of working with recent transnational communities based on my experience. Inevitably my own perceptions and experiences shape how I make meaning of the experiences of the Sikh diaspora.

As a second-generation Sikh woman, I find myself constantly having to explain my multiple identities. People seem to be intrigued by my Sikh and Punjabi heritage. However, I seem to draw the most attention when I state that I am those things *and* a feminist. My White Irish Roman Catholic female colleague once told me that she found it surprising that I had pursued higher education, given that the men and women in *my Sikh Punjabi culture* would not support a woman who wanted to educate herself. Her statement is problematic on many levels; however, at that time what upset me the most was that she thought my culture was vastly different from her culture when it comes to patriarchy and the systemic support for men's education over women's—that it may be more unlikely for me to pursue my dreams than for her to do so. I remember being taken aback by her comment to me. In an effort to transform this incident and my feelings of frustration into something that could help me grow, I began to consider the possible ways in which I could see myself in her. While I had felt invisible and misunderstood by my colleague, it forced me to think of the time when I had not seen someone, not heard someone. One of those times I felt this disconnection most acutely was when I worked with Suria.

At the time, I had seen Suria in therapy for four sessions. She was my first Sikh Punjabi client. I felt confident in my ability to work with her. Although I was born and raised in Canada and she was born in and had recently immigrated from India, we shared religious, cultural, and gender identities. Suria had been having severe headaches, had several bouts of crying, and was referred by her physician. In my initial session I worked hard to join with her. Nine months prior, she had been married in India to a Sikh man from Canada. After marriage she waited in anticipation for her immigration paperwork to go through so that she could join her husband and they could start their life together. She shared the ways in which she missed her family and felt isolated in her new home country. During the next session, she began telling me that her new life was not what she had expected. She had very little money and spent much of her time on household chores. Suria spoke very little English, which made her an easy target for ridicule by strangers and her husband. Further, what was once subtle pressure to provide a male child was now turning into a demand by her in-laws. Suria called this group of events *kismat*, or fate. She also believed that the unfolding of events was the will of God. Suria presented a contradiction that I had struggled with in my own life. According to general patriarchal norms of Punjabi culture, it is not uncommon for a woman to give up personal agency and resign herself to a life that is handed to her, usually by the men in her life. However, gender equality is a central precept in Sikhism, and a woman is not to acquiesce to *kismat*. Women and men are expected to persevere and work toward living a life of justice and dignity. I had been working to unravel these problematic contradictions, consciously aligning myself with the ideals of Sikhism as they felt the most liberating to me. I may have believed that Suria could also walk this tightrope of contradictions and share my beliefs that the pursuit of gender equality could be the most liberating.

All of my therapist training to that point taught me to ask thoughtful questions, be curious, and to collaborate with the client in developing richer life narratives. Instead, my Western privilege as a Canadian, my own emerging feminist awareness within the Sikh context, and my recent struggles in my marriage and recent divorce from a Sikh man triggered me enough to steer my therapy in a direction that was not necessarily what Suria wanted or found useful. I wanted Suria to feel free and to run her own life, according to my version of feminism. While I believed that I created a space where Suria could explore her conflicting feelings, my questions essentially asked her to take a position against her husband and the life that was waiting for her once she left my office. My shifting feminist ideas were now privileging personal freedom over the desires of others, in particular men. I had responded to my oppression by swinging sharply toward prizing the Western construction of individual agency. Struggling to hold complexity in regard to feminism and my Sikh, Punjabi, and Western cultures, I was unable to understand Suria and what I perceived as her lack of resistance to oppression in her life. Further, I didn't understand the impact of her not having any family or close friends in Canada. I ignored her account of her financial situation while pushing my agenda on her. Nor did I consider that perhaps Suria and her husband could come together and build a strong respectful relationship. At the time, I didn't consider Suria to have feminist consciousness. Her lack of resistance troubled me. Further, I was caught between cultures and was encouraging a Western emphasis on agency, which prioritized autonomy. It limited my understanding of the ways in which our lives as women had been shaped by our traditions. In a phone call after our third session, Suria shared that she was no longer coming to therapy due to travel difficulties. I could not ignore the growing feeling that I had of not being a skilled therapist. Further, I had not weighed our differences as women, and as women from different parts of the world. I had a lot to learn about working with what I considered my culture.

My training in counseling was valuable. I was attuned to examining counseling process and outcomes. I understood that my work with Suria was not effective, and I wanted to examine under what conditions a more favorable result would have occurred. Shortly after working with Suria, an opportunity to participate in a conference that emphasized social justice and working cross-culturally presented itself. At this venue, I was exposed to the idea of using therapy for addressing some of the injustices that occur in people's lives. With their emphasis on challenging mono-cultural therapy, the Just Therapy team from New Zealand, Michael White from Australia, and Kenneth V. Hardy from New York were deeply influential in my development. It is here that I began to embrace my own struggle with my Sikh Punjabi culture. I began to understand and accept that culture was probably the most influential determinant of meaning making in my life, and the life of my clients. Further, I learned that the manner in which I sought information from Suria also conveyed meaning and determined the sort of responses that I received from her.

In an effort to understand my biases and how they inform the therapy process, I enrolled in a marriage and family therapy doctoral program, which emphasized social justice and self of the therapist. Here, I was encouraged to draw connections between my ancestral history, life experiences, and present-day worldview. I learned to acknowledge and be responsible with my power and privilege, and, most importantly, I began to access parts of my voice that had been silenced for too long. Drawing connections between the inequities and cultural messages of my gender, race, and, status as a second-generation Sikh Punjabi, I began to free myself of concrete thinking and embraced complexity. This personal exploration in turn translated into my work, and I began to pay attention to clients' lived realities informed by context, and the implications that context had on their mental health and well-being. Monica McGoldrick, Nancy Boyd-Franklin, Ignacio Martín-Baró, and Laura Brown are a few theorists who continue to influence my work.

Currently I am a faculty member in a counseling department and contribute to a Ph.D. program in counseling psychology that emphasizes social justice informed by feminist and multicultural ideals and values. My current research examines how the tragic events of 9/11 have impacted the lives and relationships of Sikh families in the United States. The backlash and suspicion toward this minority group have been profound (Ahluwalia & Pellettiere, 2010; Arora, 2009). Psychological distress, relational strain, and trauma are often connected to marginalization and discrimination (McGoldrick & Hardy, 2008; Weingarten, 2004). My hope is to contribute to the dearth of literature and research studies on Sikhs in family therapy and the broader mental health field. In order to provide appropriate psychological services to Sikh families in the United States, it is critical to understand the context of Sikhs' experiences against the backdrop of living in a post–9/11 world. This research has been made possible with a fellowship by the Institute for Asian American Studies at UMASS Boston, and will be enhanced by using an F-M lens to explore the complexity of contemporary Sikh experience.

What Makes Transnational Counseling Psychology Feminist and/or Multicultural?

As authors, we have both shared narratives that we believe capture episodes in our lives early in our professional careers and prior to each of us developing a more nuanced, in-depth F-M approach to our transnational work. We like to think we would not make the same choices if these situations presented themselves again. And, although they were glaring examples of times when we were unable to perceive our privilege and its potential impact on others, we recognize that the ability to "see" privilege is always challenging, as it constantly shifts from interaction to interaction. Even more challenging is recognizing privilege or power and ceding it in order to engage in genuine power-sharing.

Increasing cultural and gender awareness is at the heart of F-M transnational work. One of the documents that helps frame our development and learning is Rice and Ballou's (2002) statement on gender and cultural awareness in psychology, which became a foundation for an APA (2004) resolution on the same topic. As Arora shared, her experience with Suria prompted her to receive more training and increase her "respect for pluralism based on differences" (Rice & Ballou, 2002, p. 1). She was able to consider the ways her training and privilege may have obscured her ability to create space for a multiplicity of views about living as a Sikh woman. As Horne related, her humbling experience with her post-communist colleagues brought about recognition of the importance of "awareness and analysis of power" (Rice & Ballou, 2002, p. 1) and engagement in a "critical analysis of Western perspectives" (Rice & Ballou, 2002, p. 1). She felt compelled to question her position of power and her disproportionate access to voice and resources in this context. Other principles of cultural and gender awareness in international psychology, as articulated by Rice and Ballou (2002), were present in each of these scenarios: understanding the experiences of individuals in diverse cultures and contexts, and international and interdisciplinary social-cultural perspective-taking. These principles evolved from feminist and multicultural theories and are increasingly present in counseling psychology transnational research and practice.

Without a doubt, the field of counseling psychology is emerging as a field with a global focus, although there are only a few programs outside the United States and Canada that designate counseling psychology as a sub-field (Leong & Leach, 2007). Still, many universities world-wide are developing counseling psychology specialties, and it is expected that given counseling psychology's emphasis on multiculturalism and social justice, this field will continue to be appealing for inclusion in transnational contexts; therefore, this global trend is expected to continue (Barak & Golan, 2000; Leach, Akhurst, & Basson, 2003; Leung, Guo, & Lam, 2000; Leung, Guo, & Leong, 1997). In addition, there have been many U.S.-based counseling psychologists who have integrated feminist and multicultural principles in their international work.

The guiding values of counseling psychology include a focus on strengths and resiliency; healthy and normative functioning, rather than conceptualizing through a lens toward psychopathology; life span development; career and vocational issues; person-environment and systemic interactions; and prevention and education (Whalen et al., 2004). Within each of these foci, there have been feminist and multicultural contributions (e.g., Comas-Diaz, 1994; Enns, 2004; Sue, Ivey, & Pedersen, 1996; Sue & Sue, 2008). As counseling psychology has become more international in scope, there has been a call for greater attention to multicultural approaches that increase cultural awareness in our training models, collaboration, and research (Leong & Bluestein, 2000; Marsella, 1998; Marsella & Pedersen, 2004). With respect to transnational contexts, this focus on multiculturalism has contributed to (a) the education and training about cross-cultural differences and similarities; (b) the exploration and modification of cultural biases and assumptions; (c) multidisciplinary approaches to global issues (e.g., incorporating cultural and race studies); (d) the privileging of indigenous psychologies; (e) the critiquing of Western approaches to treatment and assessment; and (f) the development of approaches and consultation models that are culturally sensitive and dynamic (e.g., Gerstein & Ægisdóttir, 2005, 2007; Heppner, 2006; Pedersen, 2003; Horne & Mathews 2004, 2005). Without a doubt, multicultural education and training have enhanced the work of counseling psychologists who engage in transnational work by solidifying the importance of cultural awareness and understanding.

Less commonly discussed, but no less important to international counseling psychology, are feminist theory and therapy contributions. Central aspects of feminist psychology include, among others, the value of girls' and women's experiences (Ballou & West, 2000; Lamb, 2010); political empowerment and critical analysis of power relations (McDowell & Hernández, 2010); acknowledgment of the sociocultural impact of environment on psychological distress (Hill & Ballou, 2005); the importance of engagement in reflexivity and exploration of context (Fine, 1985); and the pursuit of egalitarianism as well as social activism (Enns, 2004; Lerman & Porter, 1990). These feminist ideals have informed many counseling psychologists, primarily women, who are engaged in work focused on gender equality and women's empowerment in transnational contexts settings.

Feminism and multicultural theory mainly have been considered as distinct philosophies within psychology (Ali, Mahmood, Moel, Hudson, & Leathers, 2008). Both philosophies have focused on single domains of diversity. While multiculturalism has primarily emphasized race and ethnicity, feminism has primarily focused mainly on white middle class women (Silverstein, 2006). An integration of both philosophies would enable an inclusive understanding of women and their multiple identities.

The current paradigm of feminist theory and practice in Western secular nations is based on a Euro-American model that emphasizes individualism, autonomy, and self-fulfillment (Landrine, 1995). Whereas Western feminism has been a catalyst for feminist consciousness around the globe, it has largely not acknowledged women's voices that do not fit this paradigm. Feminist leaders in the West have been known to call public attention to patriarchy in the lives of women globally; however, their good intentions have mirrored imperialist sexism, racism, and class elitism (hooks, 2000). Although feminism in the West has contributed greatly to informing and challenging patriarchy, these thinkers alone cannot manufacture globally just feminisms. A more ethical practice in working from a feminist multicultural perspective for theorists, practitioners, and researchers would require privileging theories, ideas, and the voices of those who live in the margins both within Western nations and around the world. Women theorists and activists, often from non-Western regions or countries, have critiqued dominant discourses on feminist and multicultural theory (Barret et al., 2005; Mohanty, 2003; Yu, 2009) and, therefore, have pushed feminist ideas beyond the confines of Western feminism. Emerging feminist theory explores decolonizing praxis and emphasizes the importance of intersectionality in transnational work (e.g., McDowell & Hernandez, 2010; Mendoza, 2002); this scholarship is beginning to inform transnational counseling psychology.

Counseling psychologists and colleagues informed by F-M theories and principles are working transnationally in Japan (Carolyn Enns and Sayaka Machizawa); Southeast Asia (Kathryn Norsworthy and Ouyporn Khuankaew); Ukraine (Oksana Yakushko); Mexico and Chile (Benedict and Ellen McWhirter); the United States and Canada with the Sikh diaspora (Kiran Arora); Iceland (Stephanie Ægisdóttir); Asian contexts (Fred Leong and John Romano); with Somalian refugees and international students located in the United States (Johanna Nilsson and Gargi Roysircar Sodowsky); Taiwan and South Africa (Puncky P. Heppner); Tibet (Larry Gerstein); Russia and Kyrgyzstan (Sharon Horne, Elena Molchanova, Elena Kim, and Lena Kosterina); and Central America and India (Scott Moeschberger, Alicia Ordonez, Jui Shankar, and Shonali Raney), and many, many others. In addition, counseling psychologists informed by feminist and multicultural practices were instrumental in creating the Guidelines for Psychological Practice with Girls and Women (2007) and how it applies to international contexts, as well as the Resolution on Cultural and Gender Awareness in International Psychology (2004). In addition, there has been an increase in scholarship on the process of engagement by counseling psychologists in transnational contexts (e.g., Gerstein & Ægisdóttir, 2005, 2007; Norsworthy, 2003; Norsworthy, Leung, Heppner, & Wang, 2005).

The rise of the social justice movement in counseling psychology in the past 15 years has evolved from the focus on multiculturalism and diversity within the field (Leong & Leach, 2007). In terms of counseling psychology, social justice refers to the focus on the equitable distribution of opportunities and resources, and active change designed to challenge institutions and systems that are inequitable through advocacy, multicultural competence, and targeted intervention and prevention for marginalized issues and populations (Fouad, Gerstein, & Toporek, 2005). It may be that because social justice expands the conceptualization of multiculturalism within counseling and includes values often associated with feminist ideas of justice, such as equalizing access to resources, power sharing, and engaging in activism, the contribution of feminism is sometimes overlooked in discussions of international counseling psychology work in the field (e.g., Leong & Leach, 2007; Gerstein & Ægisdóttir, 2007).

However, there may be important reasons for retaining the focus on feminist ideals in addition to multicultural practices when considering transnational work. For example, Lock Swarr and Nigar (2010, p. 7) describe three specific practices that are central to feminism that may be important for transnational work: (a) engagement with positionality and reflexivity, which includes an awareness of one's gender, race, class, and other categories and examining how it produces and influences transnational relationships; (b) representational experiments that aim to intersperse and juxtapose multiple voices along with the researcher or practitioner; and (c) enacting accountability, which includes a process of engagement and follow-up once projects or products are concluded. The ability to combine and negotiate these feminist ideals along with multicultural counseling practices (e.g., the interrogation of cultural assumptions, values, and biases, and the increased valence of indigenous mental health practices and of cultural awareness and competency among counseling psychologists) is vital, we believe, for effective transnational engagement.

Working with Transnational Recent Immigrant and Refugee Populations in the United States and Canada: The Need for Both Multicultural and Feminist Approaches

Our world is becoming increasingly interconnected. The communities in which we live are becoming much more multicultural and diverse. Many of our neighbors have experiences of migration and dislocation, of gender oppression and resiliency. However, many of these people do not seek psychological services. An expansive cultural account of lived experiences, which includes a multiplicity of voices and narratives, is critical in providing competent and ethical psychological services to recent immigrant and refugee populations. Understanding the intersections of gender, race, immigration status, religion, social class, ethnicity, sexual orientation, and abilities is critical to our ability to assist transnational immigrant populations. These dimensions of diversity must be considered as basic structures for understanding psychological wellness and cannot be considered simply independent features. Taking a contextual approach to assessment and healing is critical. Considering a population's "broader ecology" will require us to pay attention to context and to reconsider our definitions of health, pathology, and resiliency (McGoldrick & Hardy, 2008, p. 7). We cannot simply pathologize a particular behavior without considering the impressions that political violence, poverty, or discrimination may leave on an individual. Further, incorporating culturally appropriate rituals would ensure therapy that is reflective of the traditions and healing practices that hold meaning for women and their families (Ali et al., 2008; Enns, 2004).

Whereas having a core understanding of a culture is useful in working with immigrant populations, being mindful of within-group differences is critical. Often, immigrant groups' experiences are lumped together. This clustering only further marginalizes and minimizes the true diversity of people. For example, Asian American communities are commonly referred to as the "model minority." Although some Asian Americans are "successful," as assessed by criteria informed by Western values of material and educational attainment, this perception is problematic and detrimental to many, as it excludes those who are on the margins. For example, Cambodian and Hmong communities have much higher poverty rates and lower rates of education than other Asian communities (Guofang & Wang, 2008). Further, Asian American women's experiences are often vastly different than men's experience and compounded by gender oppression (see also chapter 10 of this handbook).

Engaging F-M transnational approaches in working with immigrant and refugee populations can decrease colonizing experiences and experiences of marginality. For example, Lugones (1987) describes a process of "world traveling" in which awareness exercises allow for increased communication among women around the world and among women who share a similar geopolitical region but not background and culture. Three activities are a part of this process, beginning with (a)seeking awareness about cultural norms that have allowed for the creation of an us/them dichotomy. As part of this awareness, it is important to acknowledge the processes of oppression that have impacted both Western White women and immigrant/refugee women and how these experiences may differ or be similar. The second and third phases involve (b) attempting to see "what it is to be ourselves in their eyes" (p. 18), which explores the role of global hegemony and how it may be propagated during transnational encounters; and (c) endeavoring to see women around the world, including immigrants and refugees in Western contexts, as they see themselves. Such an analysis allows F-M counseling psychologists to engage in reflexivity and to question their own position in society, and how that may come with unearned privileges (Rice & Ballou, 2002).

Engaging in F-M Transnational Counseling Psychology: An Evolving and Ongoing Developmental Process

Learning to perceive privilege and being accountable for it goes beyond exploration exercises commonly encountered in our multicultural courses. Training and educating counseling psychologists to be competent feminist and multicultural theorists and practitioners is challenging work, especially given the short, three- to five-year time frame for graduate studies. Furthermore, when the curriculum is burdened with ever-increasing demands for new knowledge and skills (e.g., health psychology, positive psychology, child and adolescent concerns, as well as prevention efforts), competing demands for time and resources can be challenging to resolve in training programs. Expecting students to also become proficient in transnational issues goes beyond the standard educational objectives of graduate education in counseling psychology. Not every counseling psychology program will make an effort or even desire to be inclusive of transnational issues. However, those counseling psychologists and programs engaged in transnational work could offer suggestions for how transnational F-M issues can be integrated into current social justice and counseling psychology training curricula.

This process could include providing critical readings and works from global East/South psychologists for inclusion in standard multicultural, gender, and foundations courses in counseling psychology. It might also involve opening up opportunities for counseling psychology students in various programs to gain transnational experience through counseling programs that are engaged in transnational training (through transfer credits or cross-listing courses at several universities). To assist with training and development, a web-based course could be developed that features F-M counseling psychologists at work in transnational contexts.

In addition, universities can be encouraged to support international exchange opportunities for graduate students; for example, at some universities, graduate students receive support from student fees toward their travel and engagement with transnational issues. Of course, student exchanges are not inherently informed by feminist or multicultural ideals, and it would be beneficial to have

F-M preparation and training available to students. At the same time, there is no education like on-the-job training; no matter how much introduction to theory and other counseling psychologists' experiences of transnational work students are exposed to, they will primarily learn from their own experience of transnational engagement. Supervisors of these experiences will need to recognize these opportunities for growth, and when the inability to perceive privilege or a lack of cultural awareness is impacting a transnational relationship. Supervisors will need to develop skills to guide students' learning and developmental processes so that our graduates are adept at self-reflection about their social locations and power relations as well as at interrogating their cultural assumptions and biases.

The education in F-M transnational counseling psychology does not end with graduate school, but rather is a lifelong, ongoing learning process. It may be argued that a person can develop a competency in reflective listening or use of open-ended questions; however, it is not possible to ever have a checklist for cultural competence in transnational work—culture is always changing, and our positions within and in relation to culture are always evolving. "To engage in conversations and collaboration across social locations is to essentially occupy space in borderlands" (McDowell & Hernandez, 2011, p. 103).

For example, engaging in transnational work is the ultimate exercise in applied and relational ethics. As Hui Nui Wilcox (Lock Swarr & Nigar, 2010, p. 217) stated, "Border-crossing is an embodied act that demands us to think about ethics." Similar to the process by which beginning counseling psychologists become more comfortable in the therapeutic process as they let go of fears of causing irreparable harm to clients by a mis-statement, those engaged in transnational psychology from the global West/North, who gain an awareness of Western hegemony and the exploitation of processes of globalization, may be concerned that their role in transnational work is reproducing and contributing to global inequities. For example, when counseling psychologists begin to see clients, they are sometimes paralyzed by fear of their power as therapists. This fear often is gradually replaced by a more nuanced understanding of the power relations between client and therapist. The therapist in training learns that she or he does not typically have overwhelming influence and that clients have a great degree of agency and autonomy (Williams & Levitt, 2007). A similar process may occur for Western individuals who begin transnational work. It is imperative that counseling psychologists need to be aware of and accountable for the harmful and debilitating consequences of Western hegemony and global exploitation. They need to make every effort to reduce the centering of Whiteness and North/West subjectivity and domination, and the marginalization and othering of South/East individuals and communities (Chatterjee, 2010). And, without question, we need to infuse social justice principles and actions into all of our work, locally and globally.

Inevitably, the F-M transnational counseling psychologist will find her or his work embedded in enduring ethical dilemmas and challenges. For example, I (Horne) grappled with the role of development in my transnational relationships, and recently struggled with the following internal debate as my group pursued federal funding for a project. In the next sentences, I pose a range of questions and phrase my internal responses in parentheses.

Will the pursuit by a Kyrgyz-U.S. team of psychologists of a U.S. State Department grant aimed at increasing peace and reconciliation efforts in Kyrgyzstan reinforce global inequities and Western hegemony? (Yes—the U.S. government will supply the funds and ultimately determine the direction of the project.) Is the ultimate aim of this grant to maintain U.S. political influence in Central Asia? (Yes—peaceful communities in Central Asia will assist with efforts to continue the U.S. military presence in Central Asia, which helps with the war on terror in Afghanistan.) Will receiving and implementing such a grant create more peaceful communities if conducted within a social justice framework informed by multicultural and feminist principles? (Likely—there could be many benefits in creating communities of peacemakers and dialogues of reconciliation to prevent civil unrest and conflict.) Will my Kyrgyz colleagues benefit personally, materially, and professionally from funded support to do the work they are already doing (pro bono) to create more peaceful communities in their home country and reduce the development of mental health issues or post-traumatic stress disorder as a result of inter-ethnic violence and unrest? (Yes—without a doubt.) Will I as a Western partner and counseling psychologist benefit? (Yes—also without question.)

Numerous questions are important to consider. When do the benefits outweigh the potential harm of reproducing global inequities and power structures that are engaged in exploitation and destruction of indigenous peoples and practices? What is compromised when social action is undertaken by institutions with political motives in the name of development instead of as a grassroots effort? When do we determine that the cost is too great of unilateral (West to East) intervention and determination of needs, aims, and objectives by the more dominant power? There are endless ethical questions that the transnational counseling psychologist must grapple with on a daily basis. We must consider these actions thoroughly, and having a feminist and multicultural framework helps is to make choices in relationship to these questions.

As a family therapist and researcher working with the Sikh community, I (Arora) too am ingrained in ethical challenges. Self-reflection is a process that I engage in consistently in order to keep my work as ethical as possible. To my knowledge, I am one of very few Sikh therapists and researchers who are working with the Sikh diaspora. This puts me in a unique position. While I do not believe that I should know everything there is to know about Sikh families, or that I must have the skills to capture all that could be understood about Sikhs and their psychological and relational experiences, I do have an internal struggle of wanting to do as much as I can for my community, of desiring to give back to a community that has given me so much. I often ask myself whether my work is beneficial, and whether there are more critical areas that I should be focusing on.

I am guided by the idea that the families to whom we belong and the social context in which we live impact our experiences. My belonging in the Sikh community makes it critical that I scrutinize my beliefs and life experiences, as they inevitably shape my interpretations of my clients and the participants in my research. After Suria terminated therapy, I had to interrogate my work to come to some understanding about why therapy ended so abruptly. I had to answer questions such as "Whose voice was I privileging, Suria's or mine?" and "Whose agenda was at the center, Suria's or mine?" In the past, my own struggles with my identity as a Sikh woman in the diaspora often seeped into my perceptions and interpretations of clients and research participants. I have wondered how my own internalized oppression may prohibit or favor particular questions or interpretations and whether I have contributed to perpetuating generalizations about Sikhs. My goal is to make space for stories that speak to the truth of my clients' and participants' experiences.

While I have engaged subsequently in self-of-the-therapist work, which requires that I understand and scrutinize my beliefs, biases, and life experiences, I am never truly free of them. This process has been an integral component of my training and will remain a lifelong pursuit. The degree to which I can appreciate and challenge my subjective experiences while simultaneously embracing, exploring, and nurturing different assumptions held by others is critical. My hope is that my own limitations will not hinder healing or my understanding of those for whom I work.

Future Directions for F-M Transnational Counseling Psychology

Moving away from a purely development lens will allow transnational feminism to be a process that recognizes autonomy and agency as present among all communities of women. There is a Kyrgyz joke about how whenever there is a budget crisis, the government responds by raising the rent the U.S. military pays to land at the airport. As one of my (Horne) feminist Kyrgyz colleagues said once, after a theoretical discussion of feminist and multicultural activism, "Westerners spend a lot of time thinking about how you might affect us, and don't consider how we change you in the process." We must resist the tendency that results from an awareness of the profound impact of Western hegemony and the colonizing processes of globalization that goes to the extreme and equates the East/South as a passive receptor of the vast knowledge produced in the North/West and portrays East/South women and collaborators as submissive victims of the current inequitable world order. There is agency and there is activism found in asymmetrical partnerships, and feminists who are not located in the North/West are known to create their own feminisms by adopting Western concepts that work in their local communities, and including principles arising from their own contexts (Mathews, Horne, & Levitt, 2005). Similar to White guilt, Western guilt may be immobilizing (Neville, Worthington, &Spanierman, 2001).

Rather, an F-M approach to transnational counseling psychology would pose questions such as: What do counseling psychologists and their partners in the East and South have to gain and lose from transnational collaborations with Western/Northern counseling psychologists (and vice versa)? What are the respective needs and desires for collaborative engagement, and how can we increase power sharing, mutuality, and reflexivity to reach social justice aims? Is it possible to utilize world resources and at the same time reduce the harmful impact of globalization? How can we prevent our transnational collaboration from prizing Western models at the expense of the erosion of indigenous cultural values, and is there a way to infuse a multiplicity of approaches to accomplish our work? How do we resist paralysis and change direction when inevitable processes of neo-colonialization and exploitation appear? These are but a few of the questions that should occur to a counseling psychologist engaged in transnational work who is informed by both feminist and multicultural theory. Is it possible to create power-sharing, socially just transnational collaborations within the cushion of *development*? As Mendoza (2002, p. 324) questions, "Can African, Asian, or Latin American women elevate the issues of anorexia and other eating disorders that western women suffer to a human rights issue in the same manner that genital mutilation has been framed by western feminists?" Can women globally commit to a praxis that is just and keeps the welfare of the other in mind?

Finally, F-M U.S. counseling psychologists typically work solo in their transnational collaborations. This individual approach limits the development of a shared knowledge base or the development of best practices for F-M transnational counseling psychology. Although there have been special issues and presidential platforms dedicated to the internationalization of counseling psychology (e.g., Leong, Douce, Chung), very little attention has been given to the practices or ethics of transnational psychology in our field. It is our hope that as our world increasingly becomes more interconnected, F-M counseling psychologists will articulate and expand the field of transnational practice and consultation.

Authors' Note

Correspondence concerning this chapter should be addressed to Sharon G. Horne, Department of Counseling and School Psychology, University of Massachusetts Boston, 100 Morrissey Blvd., Boston, MA 02125. Email: sharon.horne@umb.edu.

References

Ahluwalla, M. K., & Pellettiere, L. (2010). Sikh men post-9/11: Misidentification, discrimination, and coping. *Asian American Journal of Psychology, 1*(4), 303–314.

Ali, S. R., Mahmood, A., Moel, J. M., Hudson, C., Leathers, L. (2008). A qualitative investigation of Muslim and Christian women's views of religion and feminism in their lives. *Cultural Diversity and Ethnic Minority Psychology, 14* (1), 38–46.

American Psychological Association (2004). Resolution on gender and culture awareness in international psychology. Washington, DC: Author.

Arora, K. (2009). *Breaking the silence: The impact of political violence on Sikh diaspora.* Ph.D. dissertation. Retrieved from http://www.umb.edu/library/.

Ballou, M., & West, C. (2000). Feminist therapy approaches. In M. Biaggio & M. Hersen (Eds.), *The psychology of women* (pp. 274–275). New York: Kluwer Academic/Plenum Publishers.m

Barak, A., & Golan, G. (2000). Counseling psychology in Israel: Successful accomplishments of a nonexistent specialty. *The Counseling Psychologist, 28,* 100–116.

Barret, S. E., Chin, J. L., Comas-Diaz., L., Espin, O., Greene, B., & McGoldrick, M. (2005). Multicultural feminist therapy: Theory in context. *Women in Therapy, 28* (3–4), 27–61.

Chatterjee, P. (2010). Continuing coversations: Critical transnational feminsit praxis contributors. In A. Lock Swarr & R. Nigar (Eds.), *Critical feminist transnational praxis* (pp. 206–218). Albany, NY: State University of New York Press.

Comas-Diaz, L. (1994). An integrative approach. In L. Comaz-Diaz & B. Greene (Eds.), *Women of color: Integrating ethnic and gender identities in psychotherapy* (pp. 287–318). New York: Guilford Press.

Enns, C. Z. (2004). *Feminist theories and feminist psychotherapies: Origins, themes, and diversity* (2nd ed.). New York: Harrington Park Press.

Fine, M. (1985). Reflection on a feminist psychology of women: Paradoxes and prospects. *Psychology of Women Quarterly, 9,* 167–183.

Fouad, N., Gerstein, L. H., & Toporek, R. (2005). Social justice and counseling psychology in context. In R. Toporek, L. H. Gerstein, N. Fouad, G. Roysircar-Sodowsky, & T. Israel (Eds.), *The handbook of social justice in counseling psychology: Leadership, vision, and activism* (pp. 1–15). Thousand Oaks, CA: Sage Publications.

Gerstein, L H., & Ægisdóttir, S. (2005). Counseling outside of the United States: Looking in and reaching out. *Journal of Mental Health Counseling, 27,* 95–103.

Gerstein, L. H., & Ægisdóttir, S. (2007). Training international social change agents: Transcending a U.S. counseling paradigm. *Counselor Education and Supervision, 47,* 123–139.

Grewal, I., & Kaplan, C. (2001). *An introduction to women's studies: Gender in a transnational world.* New York: McGraw-Hill.

Guofang, L., & Wang, L. (2008). The old myth in a new time. In L. Guofang & L. Wang, (Eds.), *Model minority myth revisited: An interdisciplinary approach to demystifying Asian American educational experiences* (pp. 1–20). Charlotte, NC: Information Age Publishing.

Heppner, P. P. (2006). The benefits and challenges of becoming cross-culturally competent counseling psychologists. *The Counseling Psychologist, 34,* 147–172.

Hill, M., & Ballou, M. (2005). From the past toward the future. *Women and Therapy, 28,* 161–163.

hooks, b. (2000). *Feminism is for everybody: Passionate politics.* Cambridge. South End Press.

Horne, S., & Mathews, S. (2004). Collaborative consultation: International application of a multicultural-feminist approach. *Journal of Multicultural Counseling and Development, 32,* 366–378.

Horne, S. G., & Mathews, S. (2005). A social justice approach to international collaborative consultation. In R. Toporek, L.H. Gerstein, N. Fouad, G. Roysircar-Sodowsky, & T. Israel (Eds.), *The handbook of social justice in counseling psychology: Leadership, vision, and activism* (pp. 388–405). Thousand Oaks, CA: Sage Publications.

Horne, S. G., Mathews, S. S., Brown, D., DeGroff, S. H. (2009). Not staying home: The experience of Uzbek women

crisis counselors and therapists. *Women and Therapy, 32*, 317–337.
Horne, S. G., Ovrebo, E., Levitt, H. M., & Franeta, S. (2009). Leaving the herd: The lingering threat of difference for same-sex identities in post-communist Russia. *Sexuality Research and Social Policy, 6*, 108–122.
Jameson, F., & Miyoshi, M. (Eds.). (1998). *The cultures of globalization.* Durham, NC: Duke University Press.
Lamb, S. (2010). Feminist ideals of healthy female adolescent sexuality: A critique. *Sex Roles, 62*, 294–306.
Landrine, H. (1995). Introduction: Cultural diversity, contextualism, and feminist psychology. In H. Landrine (Ed.), *Bringing cultural diversity to a feminist psychology: Theory, research and practice* (pp. 1–20). Washington. DC: APA.
Laungani, P. D. (2007). *Understanding cross-cultural psychology: Eastern and Western perspectives.* Thousand Oaks, CA: Sage Publications.
Leach, M. M., Akhurst, J., & Basson, C. (2003). Counseling psychology in South Africa: Current political and professional challenges and future promise. *The Counseling Psychologist, 31*, 619–640.
Leong, F. T. L., & Blustein, D. L. (2000). Toward a global vision of counseling psychology. *The Counseling Psychologist, 28*, 5–9.
Leong, F. T. L., & Leach, M. M. (2007). Internationalising counseling psychology in the United States: A SWOT analysis. *Applied Psychology: An International Review, 56*, 165–181.
Lerman, H., & Porter, N. (1990). *Feminist ethics in psychotherapy.* New York: Springer Publishing.
Leung, S. A., Guo, L., & Lam, M. P. (2000). The development of counseling psychology in higher educational institutions in China: Present conditions and needs, future challenges. *The Counseling Psychologist, 28*, 81–99.
Leung, S. A., Guo, L., & Leong, F. T. L. (1997). Counseling in an international context. *The Counseling Psychologist, 25*, 117–121.
Lock Swarr, A., & Nigar, R. (2010). *Critical feminist transnational praxis.* Albany, NY: State University of New York Press.
Lugones, M. (1987). Playfulness, "World"-Travelling, and loving perception. *Hypatia, 2*, 3–19. doi: 10.1111/j.1527-2001.1987.tb01062.x
Marsella, A. J. (1998). Toward a "Global-Community Psychology": Meeting the needs of a changing world. *American Psychologist, 53*, 1282–1291.
Marsella, A. J., & Pedersen, P. (2004). Internationalizing the counseling psychology curriculum: Toward new values, competencies, and directions. *Counselling Psychology Quarterly, 17*, 413–423.
Mathews, S. S., Horne, S. G., & Levitt, H. M. (2005). Feminism across borders: A Hungarian adaptation of Western feminism. *Sex Roles, 53*(1–2), 89–103.
McDowell, T., & Hernández, P. (2010). Decolonizing academia: Intersectionality, participation, and accountability in family therapy and counseling. *Journal of Feminist Family Therapy, 22*, 93–111.
McGoldrick, M., & Hardy, K. V. (2008). Introduction: Re-visioning family therapy from a multi-cultural perspective. In M. McGoldrick, & K. V. Hardy (Eds.), *Re-Visioning Family Therapy: Race, culture, and gender in clinical practice* (pp. 3–24). New York: Guilford.
Mendoza, B. (2002). Transnational feminisms in question. *Feminist Theory, 3*, 313–332.
Mohanty, C. T. (2003). *Feminism without borders: Decolonizing theory, practicing solidarity.* London: Duke University Press.
Neville, H., Worthington, R., Spanierman, L. (2001). Race, power, and multicultural counseling psychology: Understanding white privilege and color blind racial attitudes. In J. Ponterotto, M. Casas, L. Suzuki, & C. Alexander(Eds). *Handbook of multicultural counseling* (pp. 257–288), Thousand Oaks, CA: Sage.
Norsworthy, K. L. (2003). Understanding violence against women in Southeast Asia: A group approach in social justice work. *International Journal for the Advancement of Counselling, 25*, 145–156.
Norsworthy, K. L., Leung, S. A., Heppner, P. P., & Wang, L. (2005). Crossing borders in collaboration. In R. Toporek, L. H. Gerstein, N. Fouad, G. Roysircar-Sodowsky, & T. Israel (Eds.), *The handbook of social justice in counseling psychology: Leadership, vision, and activism* (pp. 125–139). Thousand Oaks, CA: Sage Publications.
Pedersen, P. B. (2003). Culturally biased assumptions in counseling psychology. *The Counseling Psychologist, 31*, 396–403.
Rice, J., & Ballou, M. (2002). *Cultural and gender awareness in international psychology.* Washington, DC: American Psychological Association, Division 52, International Committee for Women.
Silverstein, L. B. (2006). Integrating feminism and multiculturalism: Science fact or science fiction? *Professional Psychology: Research and Practice, 37*, 21–28.
Sue, D. W., Ivey, A. E., & Pedersen, P. B. (1996). *A theory of multicultural counseling and therapy*. New York: Brooks/Cole.
Sue, D. W., & Sue, D. (2008). *Counseling the culturally diverse: Theory and practice* (5th ed.). New York: John Wiley & Sons.
Weingarten, K. (2004). Witnessing the effects of political violence in families: Mechanisms of intergenerational transmission and clinical interventions. *Journal of Marital and Family Therapy, 30*(1), 45–59.
Whalen, M., Fowler-Lese, K. P., Barber, J. S., Williams, E. N., Judge, A. B., Nilsson, J. E., & Shibazaki, K. (2004). Counseling practice with feminist-multicultural perspectives. *Journal of Multicultural Counseling and Development, 32*, 379–389.
Williams, D. C., & Levitt, H. M. (2007). Principles for facilitating agency in psychotherapy. *Psychotherapy Research, 17*(1), 66–82.
Yu, S. (2009). Third-wave feminism: A transnational perspective. *Asian Journal of Women's Studies, 15*, 7–25.

PART 3

Feminist Multicultural Counseling Psychology Applications: Theory, Research, and Practice

CHAPTER

14 Feminist Vocational/Career Theory and Practice

Gail Hackett *and* Julie D. Kohlhart

Abstract

This chapter reviews the literature on feminist vocational/career theory and practice. In particular, it reviews the theory and research on the major career development theories focused on career choice and critiques their applicability for understanding women's vocational behavior. Major theories reviewed include Holland's person-environment theory, Super's developmental career theory, and social cognitive career theory. Coverage of career development theories that were developed specifically to account for women's vocational behavior and that influence the dominant theories of today are also included, namely, Gottfredson's theory of circumscription and compromise, as well as models proposed by Farmer, Astin, Betz & Fitzgerald, and Fassinger. Research on the applicability of the various theories with respect to diverse groups of women is addressed; issues in the extant empirical literature are explored; and limitations of the theories are discussed. The heuristic value of the various theories for guiding career interventions is discussed.

Key Words: Bandura, career counseling, career development, Gottfredson, Holland, P-E fit, social cognitive, Super, vocational behavior, women's careers

Introduction

Research and scholarship on the theory and practice of career development and counseling has long been a focus of vocational psychology, a subfield within counseling psychology since the earliest days of the discipline (Savickas & Baker, 2005). As Coogan and Chen (2007) so eloquently and rightly put it, "...traditional career development theories were developed with white, able bodied, publicly heterosexual, and ethnically homogeneous, men as a target group" (p. 192). Although the study of women's career development was not a part of the earliest research and theorizing within this research tradition, over the latter part of the past century and the early part of this century, the study of women's vocational behavior has become one of the most robust areas of research within vocational psychology (Fassinger, 2005; Fitzgerald & Harmon, 2001). And when we refer to the study of women's career development, we refer to the theory, research, and practice that have been conducted predominantly from a feminist perspective, regardless of whether it has been so labeled.

The field of vocational psychology has classically been divided into the study of adolescent career choice and adult career adjustment (Crites, 1969). The current literature is quite a bit more sophisticated now than it was during the period when Crites posited that simple dichotomy, but we will nonetheless try to roughly follow his distinction. Thus, this chapter will address the scholarly literature and research touching what has classically been known as the career choice process, leaving the adult career adjustment literature—that is, a focus on women in the workforce—to be covered in the next chapter, although doubtless there will be some degree of overlap. We will begin with a discussion of the current status of vocational theories with regard to women, followed by a discussion of the implications of the theories and research for practice. We will, of necessity, focus this chapter on those theories that are currently receiving the most empirical attention, rather than trying to be comprehensive. We will discuss the implications for practice within our discussion of each theory and will round out the chapter by discussing other issues related to the career counseling of women. Because this review will necessarily be rather general, readers are referred to recent works that have explored some of the issues addressed herein in more depth, particularly the *Handbook of Career Counseling for Women* (Walsh & Heppner, 2006), *Career Development and Counseling* (Brown & Lent, 2005), and the *Handbook of Vocational Psychology* (Walsh & Savickas, 2005).

Vocational Theories and Women's Career Development

The origins of vocational psychology are generally traced back to Frank Parsons's (1909) landmark work, *Choosing a Vocation*, wherein the "matching men and jobs" approach to vocational guidance was presented that gave initial impetus to both the field itself as well as a scientifically based approach to practice (Savickas & Baker, 2005). Within the title of Parsons' approach can be seen the dilemma that proved a challenge for researchers interested in the applicability of theories for female clients for the better part of the last century, namely, an almost exclusive focus on men within this trait-factor tradition. As the formerly pragmatic field of vocational guidance developed into the "scientific" field of vocational psychology, replete with scientific tools (tests and inventories),research methods, and theoretical models, the dominant paradigm until the middle of the last century was the trait and factor (or matching men [*sic*] and jobs) approach.

Several different theories emerged out of this tradition. For example, the theory of work adjustment (Dawis, 2002, 2005; Dawis & Lofquist, 1984) hinges on two primary theoretical constructs, and the correspondence or "fit" between the two, that predict job satisfaction and worker satisfactoriness: reinforcer systems and needs. That is, the theory hypothesizes that work satisfaction is a function of the ability requirements of the work environment corresponding to the individual's work-related needs (Osipow & Fitzgerald, 1996). However, despite the extensive history of research behind the theory of work adjustment and its constructs, this theory is not now the focus of much research in the field (Fassinger, 2005). By far the most widely researched Person-Environment (P-E) fit theory, and, in fact, the most widely researched of any of the vocational theories, is Holland's P-E fit theory (Betz, 2008). But Holland's theory has also garnered a great deal of criticism along the way, particularly as it pertains to its applicability to women, and more recently with respect to its cross-cultural applicability.

P-E Fit Theories: Holland's Theory

STATUS OF THE THEORY

Holland first proposed his theory in the late 1950s and extended and expanded on those ideas in subsequent work (Holland, 1959, 1997). Although it is a variation of the "matching men and jobs" model first introduced by Parsons (1909), Holland's theory went considerably beyond Parsons's simpler notions. Holland (1959) hypothesized not only that a fit between personality and occupation translated into more satisfying occupational choice, but he also presented hypotheses about the relationships among the six personality types in his theory and their relationship to six corresponding occupational environments (Holland, 1959, 1997). Holland's (1959) original six "personality" types, as defined by interest patterns, and corresponding work environments, "motoric, intellectual, supportive, conforming, persuasive and esthetic" (p. 36), reflected labor, scientific, social, office/clerical, sales, and creative work, respectively. He later renamed the six personality/occupational categories as Realistic (R), Investigative (I), Artistic (A), Social (S), Enterprising (E), and Conventional (C), forming the acronym RIASEC, and placed them in a hexagonal structure, in that order, in relation to each other (Spokane, Luchetta, & Richwine, 2002; Weinrach & Srebalus, 1991).

Holland (1959, 1997) described the six interest patterns that correspond to the six work environments, and proposed that any individual could be described by at least one of those six interest or personality patterns. Further, the core of the model is, in essence, the proposition that individuals search for work environments that allow them to "exercise their skills and abilities, express their attitudes and values, and take on agreeable problems and roles" (Spokane et al., 2002, p. 379). Individuals may resemble one, two or three or more of the Holland types, for example, SEC: Social, Enterprising, and Conventional (Spokane & Cruza-Guet, 2005; Weinrach & Srebalus, 1991).

Realistic occupations included those that involve construction and repair, or nature and the outdoors.

Investigative vocations are scientific, or those using analytical and investigative skills. Artistic work is work in which people value aesthetics and creativity. People in Social occupations take interest in caring for others or working collaboratively. Enterprising occupations are described as using sales skills or working toward economic goals and possibilities, and Conventional work is described as positions that use organizational skills and require detailed work (Spokane & Cruza-Guet, 2005; Spokane et al., 2002).

There are also four key constructs within the theory: consistency, differentiation, identity, and congruence (Holland, 1997). Within the hexagonal structure, the closer an individual's types are to each other, the more similar they are and therefore the more consistent the Holland code. The consistency hypothesis yields predictions that the more consistent the Holland code (e.g., Realistic and Investigative) the more predictable the vocational choices for the individual (Spokane et al., 2002); types that are opposite each other on the hexagon are relatively dissimilar from one another (e.g., Conventional and Artistic) and would yield less predictable vocational choices (Kantamneni & Fouad, 2010). The differentiation construct refers to the difference between an individual's highest and lowest theme (Spokane et al., 2002). Some people have a degree of interest across several occupational themes, whereas others are highly differentiated, with interests narrowly focused mainly in one area. The construct of identity refers to how clear, consistent, and stable one's interest are over time (Spokane et al., 2002).

The fourth key construct of Holland's theory, congruence, is one of the most important constructs in the theory, and it is also the construct that has received the most empirical attention over the past 50 years. In fact, most of the research conducted on Holland's theory has examined the congruence hypothesis and the structure of interests across different samples. Congruence refers to the degree of fit between a person's interest pattern and the corresponding work environment in which they find themselves (Holland, 1997). That is, people whose interest code (say, IAS) is congruent with the code of their work environment (e.g., IAS) are likely to be more satisfied and persist longer in that work environment than if they were in a work environment with an incongruent Holland code. In the latter case, the prediction would be that the individual would likely be dissatisfied and/or change fields (Holland, 1997).

In order to study the usefulness of Holland's theory, a number of measures have been developed from Holland's own Self-Directed Search (SDS) to the widely employed Strong Interest Inventory (SII), which, in 1974, adopted Holland's theory as an organizing framework (Fouad & Kantamneni, 2010). Those inventories, however, were grounded in the majority perspectives of their times. For example, Holland (1959) originally described the "Supportive Orientation" (later the "Social" personality or work environment), or people who are attracted to fields such as teaching, therapy, or social work, as "best typified as orally dependent in the sense of being verbal, feminine, and dependent" (p. 37). In fact, early on, Holland's theory was criticized for its lack of gender and cultural relevance (Kantamneni & Fouad, 2010). The original theory was criticized as reinforcing gendered occupational stereotypes, and critics also questioned how the RIASEC hexagon and interest categories fit for women and people of color (Kantamneni & Fouad, 2010).

Dozens of research articles on Holland's theory appeared throughout the 1960s (Holland, 1973). Prediger and Cole (1975) were among the first to openly challenge the use of the interest inventories based on Holland's theory, arguing that they reinforced gender-role stereotypes. Researchers pointed to the possibility that women experienced more complex career choices than men and that interests were not being adequately measured (Blustein & Fouad, 2008). As a consequence of these discussions, some researchers involved in interest inventory development, for example, E. K. Strong of the SII, had suggested as early as the 1940s, that there should be separate interest inventories for women and men (Fouad & Kantamneni, 2010). In the 1970s, the Strong Interest Inventory (SII, then referred to as the Strong Vocational Interest Blank) merged its separate forms so that men and women indicated their interests on the same instrument, but same sex norm groups for each individual were still employed. Many of the other interest inventories also made changes in the 1970s and 1980s to improve reliability and validity for women (Fouad & Kantamneni, 2010). Even into the 1990s, Holland's research and validation on his own instrument, the SDS, were criticized for using raw scores, which produced large discrepancies between the Realistic and Social categories for men and women (Fouad & Kantamneni, 2010). Recent examinations of the SII also reveal large differences on inventoried interests between gender groups on this instrument (Fouad, 2002).

Meta-analyses demonstrate that there are very few differences between men and women on abilities related to occupational choice (Hyde, 2005). Research with regard to occupational interests, however, continues to reveal gender differences (Lonborg & Hackett, 2006). In looking at occupational preferences in almost 5,000 participants with a range of age and sexual orientation, Lippa (2005), for example, found results that suggested distinct masculine and feminine occupational subdomains and gender-related occupational preferences. Arbona (2000) cited several studies showing stereotypical preferences for occupational interests—males indicating interest in Investigative and Realistic occupations, and females expressing interest more toward Social, Conventional, and Artistic occupational areas. Reardon, Vernick, and Reed (2004), using U.S. Census data, compared occupational titles with Holland occupational codes across four decades. They found that 79% to 85% of men worked in occupations categorized in the Realistic or Enterprising categories; women, on the other hand, had more varied occupations over time, but fell mainly into the Conventional and Social occupational areas. In the last half of the twentieth century, the percentage of women in Conventional and Social occupations stayed the same (around 30% and 20%, respectively); the percentage of women in Realistic occupations decreased (33% to 20%); and the percentage of women in Enterprising occupations nearly doubled, from 13% to 24%.

Soon after the period when applications of Holland's theory to women were being challenged, issues of the applicability of the theory to racial/ethnic populations were also raised. Researchers began to explore the relevance of the Holland interest themes to different cultural groups, as well as looking at the applicability of the hexagonal model across cultures (Kantamneni & Fouad, 2010). Early research on Asian, Latino/a, and African American groups demonstrated some differences in interests between these groups and White samples (Fouad & Kantamneni, 2010). A follow-up study by Fouad (2002), with much larger samples, demonstrated few differences across racial groups with regard to interest categories, but also revealed large gender differences. Other studies have generally provided support for the cross-cultural utility of the basic components of Holland's theory, particularly the congruence hypothesis (Betz, 2008), although much less work has been conducted on work environments than on the interest themes (Fassinger, 2005).

The use of the hexagonal model with racial/ethnic groups has also been extensively researched (Fouad & Kantamneni, 2010). This includes Holland's hypothesis that within the hexagonal structure there are equal distances between types, and that types that are closer to each other on the hexagon represent more similar fields of work. In particular, researchers have questioned whether this hexagonal structure is applicable across gender and racial/ethnic groups (Armstrong, Hubert, & Rounds, 2003). The majority of the empirical evidence does show support for the RIASEC order, but there are questions about whether each of the interest categories are equidistant from each other, as in the shape of a hexagon, or if cultural groups associate the interest types differently, creating more of a circumplex mode—one in which there are not equal associations between each interest category (Armstrong, Hubert, & Rounds, 2003; Fouad, Harmon, & Borgen, 1997). For example, African American men and women and Latina women more closely associated Realistic-Investigative to each other on the SII than did other groups (Armstrong, Hubert, & Rounds, 2003; Armstrong & Rounds, 2008). Continued validation is needed to understand the degree of distance or placement between types of interest/career categories to a diversity of groups (Armstrong & Rounds, 2008). Therefore, the picture of Holland's model today shows that, although the structure of interests may vary across race and gender, personality characteristics and interests tend to be moderated by gender.

IMPLICATIONS FOR CAREER COUNSELING

Because there is considerable research support for the multicultural applicability of Holland's theory, it can be helpful in assisting psychologists and counselors with the diverse client populations seen today (Spokane & Cruza-Guet, 2005). There are many interest inventories using Holland's theory that are available, but caution should be exercised when using these instruments with diverse racial and ethnic groups, particularly with individuals from ethnic groups for which collectivistic cultural values, such as the family's influence and expectations, may play an important role (Fouad & Kantamneni, 2010). The use of the Self-Directed Search (SDS), in particular, requires caution, as it should be used with appropriate gender and racial/ethnic group norms. Other instruments created by Holland include the Vocational Preference Inventory (VPI); My Vocational Situation and the Vocational Identity Scale (VI); the Position Classification Inventory (PCI), and the Career

Attitudes and Strategies Inventory (CASI) (Spokane & Cruza-Guet, 2005). The most popular vocational inventory that uses Holland types as an organizing framework is the Strong Interest Inventory (SII), which has recently been revised to reflect contemporary changes in the work world (Kantamneni & Fouad, 2010). The Unisex Edition of the ACT Interest Inventory (UNIACT) was specifically developed to minimize gender differences (Fouad & Kantamneni, 2010). Other assessment instruments also using Holland's theory as a unifying structure for presenting their results include the new Armed Services Vocational Aptitude Battery (ASVAB) workbook; the Vocational Insight and Exploration Kit (VEIK); and different Vocational Card Sorts, as well as the Bolles Party Game (Lonborg & Hackett, 2006).

Despite the continued need to research and revise these instruments according to multicultural findings, application of the theory brings the field of vocational psychology full circle, back to its practical roots (Spokane & Cruza-Guet, 2005). Counselors and psychologists are challenged in clinical settings to integrate a theory that researchers and Holland himself have investigated and improved upon for over half a century in order to help people find work environments that fit interests and personalities.

Developmental Theories

STATUS OF THE THEORY

As with P-E fit theories, there have been numerous developmental theories proposed and researched over the years, and many of these theories have not yielded the scientific or practical returns hoped for by their proponents. In fact, the field of vocational psychology is experiencing something of a convergence, with a few major theories coming to the fore and dominating the research due to their theoretical robustness and supporting empirical evidence, and theoretical cross-fertilization among the dominant theories as well (Betz, 2008). Ironically, among the developmental theories, one of the oldest of these, Super's (1953) developmental theory, as revised by Super himself over the years and as adapted and extended by Savickas (2001, 2002), is the major developmental theory that still predominates in the literature. Super's developmental theory is not actually one theory but rather a series of theoretical propositions that have been revised and updated many times over the decades (Super, 1953, 1954, 1957, 1969, 1980, 1984, 1990; Super, Savickas, & Super, 1996). Super has called his own theory a "segmental model of career development," as it contains a number of discrete propositions only loosely coupled together, rather than being a tightly unified grand theory (Super, 1990).

Super's (1953) original theory went considerably beyond the matching theories of the day, and was based on both developmental theory and self-concept theory. Ginzberg, Ginzberg, Axelrod, and Herma (1951) originally published their seminal work, *Occupational Choice*, wherein they introduced the idea that vocational choice is not a one-time event, as featured in the matching models that prevailed until this time, but rather a process that occurs over a long but limited period of time. Super (1953), responding to this earlier work, extended and elaborated on it by positing that the choice process did not just occur over a circumscribed period of time as proposed by Ginzberg et al., but over a lifetime. Both notions, but particularly Super's, were radical departures from established practice and significantly influenced subsequent theory and practice.

Specifically, Super (1953) posited the existence of a series of developmental stages through which individuals progressed; these were identified as the growth, exploration, establishment, maintenance, and disengagement stages, through which individuals progressed as they tackled the vocationally related developmental tasks in each stage; substages were hypothesized to exist as well. Vocational development was seen as the process of translating the self-concept into a vocational self-concept. Super (1954) also identified the existence and importance of career patterns early in the development of his theory. Career patterns referred to trends in "... typical entry, intermediate, and regular adult occupations of persons from different socio-economic levels" (Super, 1954, p. 17). Another important construct introduced within this theoretical tradition was the idea of vocational or "career maturity" (Super, 1957), or the readiness of the individual for coping adequately with the developmental tasks in her or his stage of life/career development. The theory had important implications for interventions, both individual and group, and important implications as well for assessment.

Super's theory was based on longitudinal research focused primarily but not exclusively on White, middle class boys (Super, 1990). Research over the years has supported some aspects of the theory and has addressed the problems with other aspects of the theory—not only its questionable relevance to women and people of color, but also some core aspects of the theory itself. There has been empirical support for the developmental stages and attendant tasks in general, and also for the importance of the self-concept in career choice (Betz 2008; Swanson & Gore, 2000). One of the areas of the theory to receive serious reconsideration—and one that is therefore now receiving more research support—is Super's updated proposition related to predictable vocational life stages. These theoretical propositions have been reframed to account for individuals recycling back through stages and tasks, as opposed to the earlier proposal of a constant linear, hierarchical progression in vocational development (Super, 1990).

Although rich in theoretical material and clearly advancing the field of vocational psychology—in fact giving the name "career development" to an entire field of research—the limitations of Super's developmental theory with regard to women, people of color, and individuals from lower SES backgrounds were stark until researchers and theorists, including Super himself, began to remedy the omissions in the theory (Warnath, 1975). Super did, very early in his theory building, attempt to make his theory relevant to women, at least White, heterosexual women, first by introducing alternate career patterns based on women's experiences.

In his landmark book *The Psychology of Careers,* Super (1957) pointed out the relevance of homemaking to women's lives, and the importance of that choice to women's vocational development, when he articulated an overlapping but somewhat different set of career patterns for women than for men. Super (1957) identified the stable homemaking pattern for women who married and did not enter the workforce; the conventional career pattern was described for women who entered the workforce but then left after marriage; the stable working pattern was identified for women who did not marry but worked continuously; the double track career pattern was identified for women who balanced both home and work roles; the interrupted career pattern described women who went back into the paid workforce, usually after childrearing; the unstable career pattern characterized unpredictable movement in and out of the workforce; and the multiple-trial career pattern described an unstable vocational history (Super, 1957). Although many of the descriptors used for these patterns are dated, and the numbers of women fitting in each category has shifted markedly with changes in women's workforce participation, the basic notion that women's career choices and behaviors are generally more complex than men's (despite some movement toward increasing acceptance of men's alternate choices as well) is well supported in the literature (Farmer, 2006). The relevance to women of color is not necessarily as well supported in that there is, for example, a different set of roles and expectations for African American women, whose mothers were much more likely to have worked, and therefore more likely to have set an expectation for having a career for their daughters than their White peers (Farmer, 2006). Nor has there been much research on Super's career patterns for men or for women over the years. Overall, the cross-cultural research appears to support Super's hypotheses that individuals progress through predictable developmental stages; however, the research on career maturity points to the need for the development of culturally appropriate measures of that construct (e.g., Fouad & Arbona, 1994).

A seemingly more satisfactory extension of Super's theory concerning its applicability to women occurred in the 1970s with Super's (1980) introduction of his "life space life span approach to career development," wherein he proposed the concept of the life-career rainbow, representing the multiple and changing roles that individuals occupy, sometimes simultaneously, over the course of their life span. This expansion of Super's theory explicitly acknowledged the reality of women's career behavior in that, although both women and men occupy multiple roles in their personal and private lives, women of all backgrounds tend to carry a heavier load with regard to family and domestic duties, even when they are employed full-time (Betz, 2006). Although the life career rainbow per se does not appear to have instigated much research, there is a large and vibrant empirical tradition examining multiple role issues related to women, and the concepts have been applied to developmentally based career counseling (e.g., Niles & Harris-Bowlsbey, 2009).

Over a decade ago, Swanson and Gore (2000) noted the decline in empirical attention to Super's theory that is even more manifest today. Nevertheless, the theory continues in a reformulated version, primarily through Savickas's (2001, 2002, 2005) work. Savickas (2001, 2005) has been both an adherent of Super's theory and a revisionist, proposing reformulations and expansions of Super's work as a result of ongoing critiques and the need to revise and reformulate in response to new empirical and theoretical developments. Savickas (2005), although clearly staying the course set by Super's earlier work, has engaged in theorizing consistent with the trend in vocational psychology toward convergence across major theories (Savickas & Lent, 1994). For example, Savickas (1997, 2001) introduced the notion of "career adaptability" as part of his "career construction theory" to replace the earlier concept of "career maturity" that had been tied to readiness for age-related decision making. Career adaptability, emphasizing as it does a more fluid and constructivist conception of coping with career life stage demands, was an improvement in the theory, not only with respect to characterizing career development in general, but also in enhancing the theory's ability to capture women's vocational experiences more adequately.

Overall, Savickas's constructivist reformulation and extension of Super's theory has much more explanatory power and potential for accounting for women's career development than its earlier incarnations (Betz, 2005). It has been noted, in other reviews of Super's work, that empirical applications to diverse groups are scanty at best (Fassinger, 2005; Swanson & Gore, 2000). A major limitation of the research has been its predominant focus on the early stages of career development, particularly the exploration stage (Fassinger, 2005). Additional research into the applicability of the theory to the career behavior of women of color, in particular, as well as to other groups of women, is needed to test its relevance to diverse populations.

IMPLICATIONS FOR CAREER COUNSELING

The major applications of Super's (1990; Super, Savickas, & Super, 1996) developmental theory and Savickas's (2001, 2005) extension of that theory have been in guiding practice with individuals in the exploratory stage, first by assessing readiness for career decision making—what was formerly called "career maturity" and what has now been reframed as "career adaptability"—and by using the model's life stages and associated developmental tasks to guide individual and group interventions. Savickas's (2005) career construction theory, in particular, extends the earlier constructs associated with career maturity along four dimensions relevant to interventions: concern about one's future work; increased personal control; curiosity about possible selves and the future; and increased confidence about one's ability to pursue vocational aspirations. Although there is not a specific reference to gender in much of the developmental writings on career counseling, the approach, based as it is on constructivist assumptions and a mixture of directive and non-directive interview techniques focused on a concern with the client's experience, does have much in common with feminist approaches to assessment (Lonborg & Hackett, 2006; Super, Savickas, & Super, 1996).

Numerous assessment tools based on the model have also been developed. For example, the Vocational Development Inventory, later relabeled as the Career Maturity Inventory (Crites, 1978), has proven useful in identifying clusters of students in schools who may benefit from focused career interventions. Although a revised version of the scale (CMI-Revised) is still widely used, there are concerns about the instrument, particularly as the revisions of Super's theory have dramatically transformed the concept of career maturity. There are also concerns about how well the scores on the scale predict career maturity for women (Lonborg & Hackett, 2006). The Values scale (Nevill & Super, 1986) is another instrument derived from developmental theory that can assist in exploring both male and female clients' work-related values in career counseling, although counselors may need to be sensitive to the potential for gender differences in work values related to the choice of certain careers (Farmer, 2006). The life career rainbow concept has been used to explore role salience with young girls exploring vocational interests and options (Niles & Harris-Bowlsbey, 2009). And finally, some writers have noted the importance of attending to the experiences of discrimination and bias when working on career development tasks with adolescents of color (Jackson, Leon, & Zaharopolous, 2010).

Social Cognitive Career Theory

STATUS OF THE THEORY

Two closely related and very fruitful research programs have arisen over the past three decades, both of which have their origins in social cognitive theory, namely, career self-efficacy (Hackett & Betz, 1981) and social cognitive career theory (Lent, Brown, & Hackett, 1994); both also arose out of an initial interest in better understanding women's career choices (Hackett & Betz, 1981). These areas of theory and research are also historically related to Krumboltz, Mitchell, and Jones's (1976) social learning theory of career selection, in that all three have their roots in Bandura's empirical and theoretical works that have evolved over the decades (Bandura, 1969, 1977, 1986, 1997). In particular, Bandura's earliest work was entitled "social learning theory" (e.g., Bandura, 1969), wherein the "social" part of the title refers to observational learning and attendant self-regulatory processes. Krumboltz et al. (1976) drew on this version of Bandura's theoretical work to develop their seminal work applying social learning theory, that is, the principles of learning, including classical and operant conditioning as well as observational learning, to career decision making (Hackett & Lent, 2008). Although that work has probably outlived its usefulness as a stand-alone theory, it has influenced other theories in important ways.

Working directly from his ongoing empirical research, Bandura published a landmark theoretical advance in 1977, proposing self-efficacy as a central mediator of behavior and behavioral change. Bandura hypothesized that self-efficacy, or cognitive appraisals about one's ability to successfully perform a given task or behavior, determine whether that task or behavior is initiated and also determine the amount of effort expended in pursuing the task or course of action. More specifically, Bandura (1986) defined self-efficacy as "people's judgments of their capabilities to organize and execute courses of action required to attain designated types of performances" (p. 391). In Bandura's (1977) view, successful interventions, for example, participant modeling, are successful, despite their specific elements, by means of their ability to influence cognitive beliefs in the form of efficacy expectations. The stronger one's self-efficacy, the more likely the behavior will be initiated and the longer the person will persist in his or her efforts at performing that behavior. Bandura (1977) also articulated four sources of learning that influence self-efficacy, including prior behavioral performance (mastery experiences), vicarious learning (modeling), emotional arousal, and verbal persuasion, although he also emphasized the primary role played by self-efficacy in the mediation of the effects of past performance and the other sources of efficacy information on cognitive judgments about future performance. There were other elements of the theory that were important as well, for example, Bandura (1977) discussed outcome expectations, which involved expectations about what would happen if one's performance of a task or behavior was successful. In this theoretical framework, then, self-efficacy refers to one's confidence with respect to performing a task—"Can I do this?"—whereas outcome expectations refer to the response to the question, "If I do this, what will happen?" and get at the possible outcomes of successful performance (Bandura, 1977, 1986).

One of the thorniest problems that has plagued researchers and theorists trying to understand women's career development has been the underutilization of women's talents, abilities, and interests in the vocational domain and the concomitant underrepresentation of women in higher status, higher paying career pursuits (Betz & Fitzgerald, 1987; Farmer, 2006). Hackett and Betz (1981) applied Bandura's (1977) newly minted self-efficacy theory to women's career development, seeing the theory as a valuable tool to both better understand some of the mechanisms whereby socialization limits girls and women's career choices, and also as a heuristic guide for counselors and others to intervene to help girls and women open up realistic options. Although they clearly saw the applicability of self-efficacy theory to the career behavior of men and women, Hackett and Betz (1981) argued that it could be particularly helpful in understanding some of the issues in women's career development. In their first empirical test of their self-efficacy theory of women's career development, Betz and Hackett (1981) found strong support for their initial hypotheses, based on Bandura's (1977) theory, that women's occupational self-efficacy was lower than men's in career areas traditional for men, and significantly higher for occupational areas traditional for women. More specifically, differential access to the sources of efficacy information such as performance accomplishments may limit women's efficacy expectations in areas in which their previous experience is limited, despite their potential for success in those areas. Conversely, exposure to, and particularly successful experiences with, those previously unexplored areas of experience can strengthen efficacy and therefore also strengthen one's interest in and desire to pursue new vocational options.

Betz and Hackett (1983; Hackett, 1985) also did some early research on self-efficacy for mathematics, a potential barrier for women's entrance into science, technology, engineering, and mathematics occupations (STEM), all areas where women were and remain seriously underrepresented. Research in this area was supportive as well of the applicability of self-efficacy theory to understanding both women's career development and vocational behavior in general (Hackett, 1995; Hackett & Betz, 1995). The hypotheses regarding career self-efficacy posited by Hackett and Betz (1981) were not only supported by this earliest research, but subsequent findings extended the earliest hypotheses to demonstrate the relationships of career-related self-efficacy to career decision making, career interests, and job tasks and work activities (Hackett, 1995). The research literature on gender differences in occupational self-efficacy was extended and further supported, and the construct of career self-efficacy more generally was quickly expanded to different populations and cultures (Hackett & Betz, 1995). The literature on career self-efficacy virtually exploded in the 1980s and 1990s, expanding to become one of the most vibrant areas of research in vocational psychology at the time, and career self-efficacy continues to be a focus for researchers to this day (Betz & Hackett, 2006). Generally, the research supports the conclusions that gender differences in career-related self-efficacy predict gender differences in career consideration and gender differences in career interests (Betz & Hackett, 1986; Lent & Hackett, 1987). The research on career self-efficacy has also been supportive of applications to diverse populations (Byars & Hackett, 1998; Hackett, 1995; Hackett, Betz, Casas, & Rocha-Singh, 1992; Hackett & Byars, 1996).

At the same time that the literature on applications of self-efficacy theory to the career area was expanding, Bandura and his colleagues continued to conduct research and to develop his theory (Hackett & Lent, 2008). In yet another seminal contribution, Bandura (1986) presented a fully developed and relabeled "social cognitive theory," emphasizing the role of cognitions and the construction of knowledge in the theory. Yet, despite the relabeling, self-efficacy remained not only an important construct, but the central mediator of human behavior in Bandura's social cognitive theory. Other important elements of the evolving social cognitive theory include all of the aspects of self-efficacy theory, for example, sources of efficacy information and outcome expectations, and some other important constructs, such as goals, emphasizing the importance of cognitive and self-reflective abilities in human functioning (Bandura 1986). In 1997, Bandura summarized additional research and elaborated more extensively on his social cognitive theory in the book *Self-efficacy: The Exercise of Control.*

Just as Bandura's (1969, 1977, 1986, 1997) empirical and theoretical work evolved over time, so too did the applications of his work to the career area. Lent, Brown, and Hackett (1994) proposed a social cognitive career theory (SCCT) to capture the empirical work conducted on career self-efficacy in a fleshed-out theoretical model, and to extend Bandura's full social cognitive to the vocational domain, for example, by explicitly including interests within the causal model; this version of the theory remained largely true to Bandura's work in preserving a central mediational role for self-efficacy. Specifically, Lent et al. (1994) proposed self-efficacy, outcome expectations, and goals as the three central constructs of their theory. In addition, they proposed similar but slightly different predictive models for the development of interests, educational performance/attainment, and occupational choice, with sources of efficacy expectations as the immediate precursors of efficacy beliefs in all models, and person inputs, for example, predispositions, gender, and ethnicity among other influencers, and background contextual affordances as distal influences (Lent et al., 1994). More proximal to choice, Lent et al. (1994) proposed that self-efficacy and outcome expectations influence interests, which in turn influence choice goals, choice actions, and performance. Underlying the entire model is Bandura's conception of the triadic reciprocity over time of behavior, personal factors (cognitive, affective, and biological), and environmental factors in determining human functioning (Bandura, 1997; Hackett & Lent, 2008).

After the initial introduction of SCCT, Lent et al. provided additional clarifications of the theory, for example, by extending the theory to the school to work transition (Lent, Hackett, & Brown, 1996; 1999) and by clarifying the role of contextual influences in the theory (Lent, Brown, & Hackett, 2000). Despite this clarification, a number of reviewers have criticized SCCT because of the paucity of research on the aspects of the theory having to do with contextual influences (e.g., Fassinger, 2005; Swanson & Gore, 2000)—the very parts of the theory that have the most explanatory potential for accounting for the experiences of diverse groups of women in our society. However, there is starting to be more research attention to the related constructs of outcome expectations, barriers, and contextual influences within studies of the SCCT model (e.g., Brenner, Chopra, Davis, Talleyrand, & Suthakaran, 2001; Fouad, Hackett, Smith, Kantamneni, Fitzpatrick, Haag, & Spencer, 2010; Restubog, Florentino, & Garcia, 2010). This emphasis is of particular note for applications to women's career development, as the role of internal and external barriers to women's career choices have long been discussed as important to understanding women's career development (Betz & Fitzgerald, 1987). Researchers have struggled to assess and understand the role of career barriers, defined by Swanson and Woitke (1997) as "events or conditions, either within the person or in his or her environment, that make career progress difficult" (p. 434), in the career development of women and people of color (McWhirter, 1997; Swanson, Daniels, & Tokar, 1996).

Within social cognitive career theory, contextual influences, including environmental supports and career barriers, for example, are both distal and proximal to choice and performance in the model, and serve as mediators as well as direct effects (Lent et al., 2000). Gender, race/ethnicity, and other person variables interact with the environment at two points in the model: first remotely, as early influences on learning experiences and then on the development of self-efficacy, outcome expectations, and interests; and second, more immediately, at the point where interests influence goal setting and actions (Lent et al., 2000). There have been a number of attempts to clarify the relationship between career barriers, a construct of great importance to researchers studying women's career development, and the contextual influences in the SCCT model (Swanson & Gore, 2000). Some of the difficulty lies in the self-efficacy construct, and its effects on other constructs in the model. For example, Lent et al. (2000) hypothesized that coping efficacy may mediate the effects of barriers on choice behavior. That is, strong coping efficacy may result in a strong enough sense of confidence in one's abilities to surmount perceived barriers such that those barriers are not actually perceived as hindrances. Thus, the ongoing interplay and interaction between self-efficacy expectations and other constructs may actually change the constructs themselves, and perceptions of potential career barriers are in fact one of the constructs that are most malleable, given changes in self-percepts (Lent et al., 2000). Conversely, the effects of career self-efficacy on interests and choices may be weakened in the presence of perceived barriers when coping efficacy is also weak (Lent et al., 2000).

Research conducted explicitly on the social cognitive career theory has been extensive and has demonstrated general support for the major hypotheses set forth by Lent et al. (1994, 2000, 2002). Some of the studies in the developing body of research have focused on a small subset of SCCT variables, whereas other studies have attempted to test the causal relationships among a larger set of variables in the SCCT model. In particular, and consistent with earlier research on career self-efficacy theory, the relationships between self-efficacy and interests and performance have consistently received empirical support (Betz, 2008; Swanson & Gore 2000), although the temporal ordering of the self-efficacy/interest relationship continues to receive attention (e.g., Betz, 2007; Bonitz, Larson, & Armstrong, 2010). Tests of the SCCT model also underscore its usefulness, particularly the role of self-efficacy, in understanding women's career development and also the career behavior of diverse groups, for example, Mexican Americans (Flores & O'Brien, 2002; Flores, Ojeda, Huang, Gee, & Lee, 2006; Flores, Robitschek, Celebi, Andersen, & Hoang, 2010; Fouad & Smith, 1996; Navarro, Flores, & Worthington, 2007), African Americans (Gainor & Lent, 1998; Lent, Sheu, Gloster, & Wilkins, 2010), and Asian Americans (Tang, Fouad, & Smith, 1999). Studies conducted with international samples have also yielded generally supportive results (e.g., Lent, Brown, Nota, & Soresi, 2003; Lent, Paixao, da Silva, & Leitao, 2010; Lent & Sheu, 2010). Finally, researchers and theorists have also incorporated important factors such as acculturation and ethnic identity development into SCCT as they endeavor to understand the career-related behavior of people of color (e.g., Flores et al., 2006), and the theory has also proved useful in understanding the vocational behavior of persons from different socioeconomic backgrounds (e.g., Ali, McWhirter, & Chronister, 2005). Conceptual applications to lesbian, gay, and bisexual populations have been proposed, but research attention has been slow to follow (Lindley, 2006; Morrow, Gore, & Campbell, 1996).

IMPLICATIONS FOR CAREER COUNSELING

The SCCT model can be most straightforwardly applied, as originally envisioned by Hackett and Betz (1981) and as elaborated by others (e.g., Lent, 2005), as a guide to expanding the options of girls and women through the four sources of efficacy information. For example, creating opportunities for successful performance experiences can not only create stronger career self-efficacy and therefore influence goals and choice directly, but successful performance in new areas can also create conditions where interests can bloom (Lent, 2005). In fact, one of the most useful features of the SCCT model has long been the inherent implications for intervention contained within Bandura's theory as applied to the career domain. Experimental and correlational research have supported the main propositions of Bandura's (1977, 1986, 1997) social cognitive theory, as well as in the applications to the career area. Specifically, the propositions about the relationship of successive performance accomplishments, vicarious learning, decreasing physiological arousal, and verbal encouragement to self-efficacy and interests with the goal of expanding constricted career options, encouraging realistic and informed decision making, coping with barriers and building supports, and engaging in effective career-related goal setting have been supported (Lent, 2005; Lent et al., 2002). And because, in the SCCT model, interests are a result not only of past learning experiences but also of current levels of efficacy and outcome expectations, the model also suggests that counselors must carefully consider how gender and culturally related patterns of efficacy and outcome expectations may limit goals and choices (Lent et al., 2002; Lonborg & Hackett, 2006).

Conversely, a drawback of this approach has been that most of the assessment conducted within the SCCT framework must be customized, as the self-efficacy construct, in particular, is situation specific (Betz & Hackett, 2006). However, standardized measurement tools have now been developed, guided by self-efficacy theory and SCCT, particularly the Skills Confidence Inventory (SCI) (Betz, Borgen, & Harmon, 1996). The SCI, which can be employed along with the Strong Interest Inventory, can provide women with information about the strength of their confidence in their ability—or self-efficacy—with respect to the occupations clustered according to Holland's six themes. Such information can provide the counselor and the client valuable insight into areas where intervention is warranted.

Writers have also attended specifically to the implications of self-efficacy theory and the SCCT model to diverse client groups. Byars and Hackett (1998; Hackett & Byars, 1996) discussed applications of social cognitive career theory for understanding and intervening with women of color, and included in their discussion attention to the different experiences of groups of women of color in American society with respect to gender role socialization as well as racial and ethnic identity influences, all of which must be taken into account in working with clients. For example, Latino/a ethnic identity may bear an important relationship to self-efficacy and outcome expectations (Gushue, 2006). In addition to applications of SCCT to women of color, applications of the model to lesbian women (Morrow, Gore, & Campbell, 1996), people with disabilities (Szymanski, Enright, Hershenson, & Ettinger, 2003), and psychiatric challenges (Fabian, 2000) have also been explored. It has been suggested by several writers that outcome expectations may play a different and more important role with some populations than others, for example, with African Americans (Brown, 1995), lesbian, and bisexual individuals (Morrow et al., 1996). Coping efficacy is another construct within SCCT theory that may also be more important for people of color than for other groups as they deal with career-related barriers (Byars, 2001; Lindley, 2006). Other writers have addressed the empirical status of SCCT and applications of SCCT with women across cultures more generally (Betz, 2007; Lent, 2005; Lent & Sheu, 2010).

Gendered Theories

In the latter decades of the last century there were not only critiques of mainstream theories of career development and their applicability to women, but there were also attempts at developing theories to specifically account for women's career development (Fitzgerald & Crites, 1980; Osipow, 1975). Most of these early attempts at theory development no longer have much currency due to lack of interest and/or research attention devoted to them and the vigor and empirical support for some of their competitors. However, these pre-theoretical or theoretical attempts warrant coverage herein due to their influence on contemporary theory and research.

Early Models

One of the first theorists to attempt to provide a conceptual model explaining women's occupational behavior was Psathas (1968), who argued that social class, role influences, opportunity for social mobility, and their connection to the desire for a mate all influenced women's occupational choices (Fitzgerald, Fassinger, & Betz, 1995). Although Psathas's (1968) theory is quite dated and has not received empirical support, at the time of its introduction it did influence later writers and researchers, and it did serve to advance the idea that women's career development was more complex than men's (Betz & Fitzgerald, 1987). Zytowski (1969) too, about this time, published a number of propositions regarding women's career development and argued for the need for a separate theory to explain women's career development.

Subsequently, many researchers studying women's vocational behavior in the 1970s focused on the choice between homemaking and having a career, and when studying the career choices of women, examined career orientation/salience or whether the career choice was traditional or non-traditional for women (Betz & Fitzgerald, 1987). In addition, researchers focused on a number of constructs relevant to women's vocational behavior, many of which later became integrated into more formal theoretical statements. For example, gender role socialization and its effects on women's interests and career choices has long been a focus of the research (Betz & Fitzgerald, 1987). Another example can be found in Farmer's (1976) work. She identified internal and external barriers to women's career and achievement behavior. The internal barriers included gender role socialization, self-concept, risk taking, home-career conflict, and low academic self-esteem, whereas the external or environmental barriers included discrimination, family socialization, and availability of resources (Farmer, 1976). As we have already seen, the inclusion of barriers in models of career choice is quite contemporary.

Gottfredson's Theory

One other developmental theory merits mention when discussing career theories of relevance to women; in fact, it could be considered under either the developmental theory section or under this section as a "gendered theory." Gottfredson's (1981, 2002, 2005) theory of circumscription and compromise was originally an explicit attempt to incorporate both gender role socialization and socioeconomic status (SES), along with other individual difference factors, into a theoretical framework predicting how occupational aspirations develop (Gottfredson, 1981). Circumscription, according to Gottfredson, is the process by which children, as they progress through different developmental stages and begin to understand the various factors that play a role in career choices, begin to eliminate certain vocational options as acceptable possibilities for themselves. Compromise, on the other hand, refers to the process of letting go of previously desired but unattainable alternatives in favor of more achievable options. This theory, therefore, underscores that for some in our society, vocational development is sometimes not really a choice, but rather acceptance of the least undesirable among less acceptable options.

Gottfredson's (1981) theory explicitly acknowledged gender as an important influence on career choice and development when it was originally developed, unlike many other career theories. As with other developmental theories, Gottfredson's theory emphasizes developmental stages and self-concept, but also focuses more on the content of choice than other developmental theories, in particular, how sex role socialization and social class constrict aspirations and result in compromises in occupational choice. As we have noted, theorists and researchers interested in understanding why women's career choices underutilize their talents and abilities have long noted that women face barriers to the implementation of their occupational choices (Betz & Fitzgerald, 1987; Betz, 2006). Gottfredson's theory offers one theoretically based explanation as to how that process may occur. Early responses to the theory when it was originally introduced were mixed (Farmer, 2006), and today the empirical support for Gottfredson's theory remains limited; some of the supportive research has been applied post hoc; and the research that has been conducted to explicitly test the theoretical propositions derived from this theory has yielded mixed results (Betz, 2008; Osipow & Fitzgerald, 1996; Swanson & Gore, 2000). Although there is support for the importance of the process of compromise, and there is also some indirect empirical support for the influence over time of interests, gender roles, and SES in determining children's preferred vocational options and aspirations, the priorities in circumscription and compromise posited by Gottfredson (1981) have not yet received strong empirical support (Betz, 2008; Gottfredson, 2005).

Other Gendered Theories

Astin (1984) also presented a theory of women's career development. Her theory was somewhat different from the others covered here in that it was grounded more thoroughly in a sociological framework, although also taking psychological factors into account. Astin's (1984) theory relies on needs and motivations as drivers of career behavior, coupled with expectations of how work will satisfy those needs. But the greatest contribution of her theory, which sought to explain the career-related behavior of both women and men, was the inclusion of the "structure of opportunity" as a major influence on occupational accessibility and career choice (Astin, 1984). There has been very little empirical scrutiny of this theory over the years, possibly due to the difficulty in operationalizing some of the general constructs (Farmer, 2006; Fitzgerald, Fassinger, & Betz, 1995). However, the theory has influenced other research and conceptualizations, particularly with reference to the role of contextual influences on vocational behavior (e.g., Lent, Brown, & Hackett, 2000).

Farmer (1985), too, included the effects of context on women's career choices in her attempt at theorizing. Specifically, Farmer (1985) identified three sets of factors: background factors, personal characteristics, and environmental variables. Background factors include gender, race, SES, age, and ability; personal characteristics, according to Farmer's (1985) model, include gender role socialization, academic self-esteem, independence, and values and attributions; and environmental variables include support for women working and the encouragement of significant adults such as parents and teachers. Farmer (1985) presented research support for the model, including support for the importance of career salience, aspirations, and mastery motivation, as well as its applicability to women of color (Fassinger, 2005), and other researchers have also found support for aspects of Farmer's model and its applicability to ethnically diverse populations (Fitzgerald, Fassinger, & Betz, 1995; McWhirter, Hackett, & Bandalos, 1998). However, this model, as with most of the other gendered theories, is notable mainly for how it has influenced other, mainstream theories.

Betz and Fitzgerald (1987), after comprehensively reviewing the literature on women's career psychology through the mid-1980s, summarized the major factors facilitating women's career development. These included individual variables, for example, high ability, liberated sex role values, and strong academic self-concept; background variables, such as working mother, supportive father, educated parents, and female role models; educational variables, such as going on to higher education, continuation in mathematics, and attendance at girls' schools and women's colleges; and finally, adult lifestyle choices, for example, late marriage or being single and having no or few children (Betz & Fitzgerald, 1987). These variables were then drawn upon to create a proposed model that included previous work experience, academic success, role model influence, and perceived encouragement predicting attitudes toward work, self, and sex role attitudes, which in turn predict lifestyle preferences and plans and, ultimately, realism of career choice (Betz & Fitzgerald, 1987).

Subsequent research by Fassinger (1990; O'Brien & Fassinger, 1993) only partially supported the original model and indicated the need for some refinements (Fitzgerald, Fassinger, & Betz, 1995). Maternal influences, ability, agency (e.g., self-efficacy), liberal gender role attitudes, and career and family orientation all appear to have received some support as important in predicting women's career choices (Fassinger, 2005). Beyond these, it is unclear whether the other variables in the model are not influential or whether measurement difficulties impede our understanding of their importance (Fitzgerald, Fassinger, & Betz, 1995). However, the research on the Betz and Fitzgerald (1987; Fassinger, 1990) model has clearly significantly advanced our understanding of women's career development, of the influences on women's career choices, and has served to inform the major theories of career development.

Finally, there has been an attempt to construct a theoretical framework accounting not only for women's career development, but specifically taking into account the experiences of individuals from divergent racial/ethnic, SES, sexual minority identity, and disability status backgrounds (Fassinger, 2005). Fassinger's (2002) model was based on prior research as well as a series of qualitative studies with notable women in different career fields, for example, Latinas (Gomez, Fassinger, Prosser, Cooke, Mejia, & Luna, 2001), African American, White women (Richie, Fassinger, Linn, Johnson, Prosser, & Robinson, 1997), and women with disabilities (Noonan, Gallor, Hensler-McGinnis, Fassinger, Wang, & Goodman, 2004), as well as lesbian and Asian American women (Fassinger, 2005). Fassinger's (2002) model includes personal, environmental, cognitive, decisional, developmental, and relational variables. More specifically, "in this model career development is seen as the evolving formulation of the self in relation to others, focused on work roles and behaviors in the context of other life roles" (Fassinger, 2005, p. 112). The model includes concentric influences on women's career development, consisting of the innermost influences of self, including various identity constructs. Extending outward, the model posits an interpersonal/relationship context, including the influences of family, educational, occupational, and other experiences, and an outer set of influences of sociopolitical and cultural context, including structural barriers, prejudice and oppression of various sorts, as well as facilitators such as social movements. Fassinger (2002) also proposes developmental vectors, beginning at the core self and extending across the other influences; these generally consist of developmental tasks, such as developing skills and interests or tackling developmental tasks appropriate to other life stages (Fassinger, 2005). Research conducted on this model has underscored some common themes, such as the experience of barriers and oppression and the importance of diverse social movements as positive influences (Fassinger, 2005). The research has also reinforced the importance of the intersection of gender and race in understanding the career development of women of color (Fassinger 2005). For women with disabilities, the experience of disability-based discrimination is most salient, and the intersection of gender, race, and disability is important for women of color with disabilities (Noonan et al., 2004).

Career Counseling with Women

We have already addressed, albeit briefly, the implications of the major theories of career development for interventions. Here we address a few more issues that cut across the major theories and that require additional attention. Some issues have already been touched upon, but all span more than one theoretical framework and are important in their own right. Career counseling, as with any other form of counseling or therapy, should always take place within the context of an intimate familiarity with the most recent guidelines for work with girls and women (APA, 2007); there are also repeated calls in the literature underscoring the importance of career counselors' familiarity with the multicultural guidelines (APA, 2003) and the guidelines for counseling with lesbian, gay, bisexual, and transgender (LGBT) populations (APA, 2000, 2011).

Career Counseling with Women from Diverse Backgrounds

As we have already noted, there are a range of factors that are of importance in the career development of all women; then there are another set of issues with which counselors must be conversant when working with different groups of clients. For example, when conducting career counseling with women of color, culture and racial identity development are often issues that play an important role, not only in the development of interests and the consideration of career options, but also in the counseling process itself (Fouad & Bingham, 1995). This issue of understanding women in their unique cultural context is repeatedly emphasized in the literature (Bingham, Ward, & Butler, 2006). For example, Bingham et al. (2006) and Byars (2001) argued that racial identity development was a very important consideration for African American women. Byars (2001) argued further that career counselors need to not only understand the possible effects of contextual and socialization influences and barriers, but also understand the value to African American women of developing strategies to cope with barriers and potential discriminatory behavior directed at them. Byars also spoke to the importance of coping efficacy, and cautioned that counselors need to understand the multiple sources of oppression experienced by African American women.

Although racial and ethnic identity are also extremely important in working with and understanding the career development of Latinas, the way in which culture influences Latinas' career development and choices may differ from how cultural influences play out for other women of color. Flores, Navarro, and Ojeda (2006), for example, identified acculturation, or "the process of change resulting from contact between two different cultures" [p. 272] as a key variable for Latinas; specifically, the degree of acculturation into the mainstream culture and acculturation into one's culture of origin both have profound influences on Latina's career development and choices (Fouad, 1995). "Understanding the potential influence of these shared cultural values on Latinas' career development is key in the provision of culturally sensitive and effective career counseling to this population" (Flores, Navarro, et al., 2006, p. 277). Family support, financial issues, bicultural stress, the ethnic and gender composition of the academic or work environment, and gender role attitudes as they interact with cultural influences are some of the other issues that may intersect to influence Latinas' career development in unique ways (Flores, Navarro, et al., 2006).

Asian American women face a different set of hurdles and therefore career counselors must understand their unique challenges. Again, the issue of the degree of acculturation is important, but as Asian cultures are largely collectivist, one of the things that career counselors must be sensitive to when working with Asian American women is the extent to which family and community expectations and influences play a part in an Asian American woman's educational and career performance, aspirations, and choices (Ali, Lewis, & Sandil, 2006). As an example, career counselors must be cautious about applying Super's construct of career maturity to Asian American women in that Asian Americans may appear less mature in their career decision making due to the importance of family and community as well as the Eurocentric definitions of the career maturity construct (Leong & Gim-Chung, 1995). Other factors to take into account include, as with other women of color, the issues of coping with discrimination and barriers, other potential family influences such as deference to elders and authority, conformity and obligations to one's family over self, and the possible prioritization of family interests over self-interests. And, finally, because Asian cultures put such a high value on educational and occupational achievement, the career counselor must be sensitive to how this may play out with regard to a given girl's or woman's development, aspirations, and choices (Ali, Lewis, & Sandil, 2006). American Indian/Native American women and girls, too, face their unique set of issues and have corresponding unique factors that influence their career development, including issues related to native ethnic identity and acculturation (McCloskey & Mintz, 2006).

With Native American girls and women, in particular, working with the family, extended family, and tribe/community may be particularly important in career interventions (Johnson, Swartz, & Martin, 1995).

There are many more groups of women that we could discuss in this section: women with disabilities; women from lower SES backgrounds; incarcerated women; women in dual-earner families; immigrant women, and more. Many of these topics will be covered in other chapters in this handbook. However, due to space constraints, we will end with but one more exemplar in our brief discussion of career counseling issues: lesbian and bisexual women. First, in working with lesbian women, as with any of the women we have discussed, there is always the potential for multiple intersecting identities (e.g., an African American lesbian) (Bieschke & Toepfer-Hendey, 2006). Second, the possible effects of a marginalized identity must be understood when working with lesbian and/or bisexual clients; that is, sexual orientation must be understood as a minority status (Atkinson & Hackett, 2003). And third, several researchers have commented on how gender role interacts with sexual orientation to affect career interests and choices; that is, gay men's career development differs from lesbian women's career development, and lesbian women's career development often differs in some important ways from heterosexual women's career development (Bieschke & Toepfer-Hendey, 2006). More specifically, lesbians more often than heterosexual women assume that they need to achieve financial security on their own, which in turn influences career choice (Bieschke & Toepfer-Hendey, 2006). There is also some research to suggest that lesbians have, on average, more liberal gender role attitudes, which also tend to influence career interests, aspirations, and choices (Bieschke & Toepfer-Hendey, 2006). For example, the more liberal gender role attitudes of lesbian women may result in more non-traditional career choices and increased resistance to the pursuit of gender-traditional interests and pursuits (Bieschke & Toepfer-Hendey, 2006). Lesbian women, because of their awareness of the need to provide for themselves, tend to be more aware than heterosexual women of the economic consequences of their career choices (Bieschke & Toepfer-Hendey, 2006).

Barriers to Choice

As noted previously, researchers have long identified the issue of barriers to women's career choices as a central factor in thwarting girls' and women's career choices. Farmer (1976) suggested both internal and external barriers; in their discussion, Betz and Fitzgerald (1987) identified facilitators that helped women to overcome barriers. Astin (1984) incorporated the idea of the "structure of opportunity" into her theory of women's career development, and Lent et al. (1994; 2000) included both outcome expectations as well as contextual affordances into social cognitive career theory. The P-E fit theories have always included the environment (E) as an important part of the career development process. Indeed, it has become increasingly clear that for all individuals, taking into account how the environment, distal and proximal to decision points, supports or thwarts career development, aspirations, and choice is important to understanding vocational choice. But those supports and barriers differ for diverse groups of women: they differ by gender and ethnicity, and also by sexual orientation, disability status, SES, and educational level.

Several studies have examined barriers to high school students' career choices. McWhirter, Hackett, and Bandalos (1998), for example, investigated a causal model of Mexican American high school girls' career expectations. They found that ethnic group membership was a stronger predictor than gender of career expectations, and they also found support for the importance of the role of acculturation in predicting career expectations. Although McWhirter et al. (1998) did not find support for the inclusion of barriers in their predictive model, they found that Mexican American girls did perceive barriers to their occupational pursuits. Flores and O'Brien (2002) reported an inverse association between the perception of barriers and the prestige level of career choice in a sample of Mexican American high school girls. That is, the more barriers that were perceived, the lower the level of prestige of the career that was chosen. Kenny, Blustein, Chaves, Grossman, and Gallagher (2003) also studied the effects of supports and barriers on a younger population, this time conducting research with diverse, urban high school students. They found that lower perceptions of barriers and higher perceived support from family and others were related to commitment to school and career aspirations and expectations for attaining career goals. Clearly, it is important for counselors to incorporate attention to perceived barriers and perceptions of support into their approach to career counseling as they work with girls and women of all backgrounds.

The earliest research on women's career choices looked at so-called "non-traditional" career choices for women, that is, occupations dominated by men. In the professional arena, many of these non-traditional occupations are careers in the STEM fields—science, technology, engineering, and mathematics occupations. Women have made startling inroads into many career areas once heavily or exclusively dominated by men, for example, law and some areas of medicine (i.e., the biological sciences), but the STEM fields have remained remarkably resistant to similar changes (Hill, Corbett, & St. Rose, 2010). A recent study by the American Association of University Women entitled *Why So Few?* (Hill, Corbett, & St. Rose, 2010) sought to examine the current status of the research in the STEM fields. The conclusions of this report are several: first, although progress has been made, men continue to outnumber women in the STEM fields. Girls and boys take mathematics and sciences courses through high school in roughly equal numbers,

> ... and about as many girls as boys leave high school prepared to pursue science and engineering majors in college. Yet fewer women pursue these majors. Among first-year college students, women are much less likely than men to say that they intend to major in science, technology, engineering, or math (STEM). By graduation, men outnumber women in nearly every science and engineering field, and in some, such as physics, engineering, and computer sciences, the difference is dramatic, with women earning only 20% of bachelor's degrees. Women's representation in science and engineering declines further at the graduate level and yet again in the transition to the workplace. (Hill, Corbett, & St. Rose, 2010, p. xiv)

Second, the report explores the reasons for these differences, beginning by debunking some of the commonly held but mistaken beliefs about gender differences in mathematical ability. One of the most common myths about gender differences in mathematical ability and the corresponding occupational gender differences is the assumption that men are biologically superior to women in mathematical ability. Cognitive sex differences in mathematics performance are nonexistent in the general school population (Hyde, Lindberg, Linn, Ellis, & Williams, 2008). Although there are some gender differences on tests of spatial ability, there is also evidence that such skills can be taught (Hill, Corbett, & St. Rose, 2010). The report also reviewed the extant literature on topics relevant to the issue of women and STEM, for example, gender stereotypes, self-assessments of ability, bias, environmental influences, climate, and workplace bias. The report concludes with a set of recommendations for attracting and retaining more girls and women in STEM majors and careers. These recommendations included many relevant to counselors that focused on cultivating girls' and women's achievements in sciences, mathematics, and engineering, for example, spreading the word about women's achievements in mathematics and sciences (e.g., through modeling); encouraging skill development in the STEM areas; encouraging children to develop spatial skills; counteracting bias; helping girls to develop career-relevant skills; and encouraging girls to take science and mathematics classes in high school (Hill, Corbett, & St. Rose, 2010).

Conclusion

Two very general observations may be derived from our overview of theoretical trends in research on theorizing about women's career development: first, although the gendered theories and the research on them have generated a great deal of knowledge about, and have certainly advanced our understanding of, women's vocational behavior, there does not seem to be great promise in any of the models proposed to specifically explain women's career development. There has clearly been a movement away from special theories for women toward the creation of theories applicable to both men and women. Clearly, these integrative theories seeking to encompass career development in general, while also adequately capturing the vocational experience of diverse groups of women, are the models that researchers ought to be investigating. And much more research is needed if the major theories of career choice and development are to adequately capture the experiences of our increasingly diverse population in North America, let alone globally.

Second, despite the fact that there remain many extant theoretical models of career behavior, there is also an increasing trend toward convergence across the three major theories (Betz, 2008), that is, Holland's (1997) P-E fit theory, Super's developmental theory as elaborated by Savickas (2002), and Social Cognitive Career Theory (Lent et al., 1994). This trend toward convergence was first remarked upon by Osipow (1990) on the occasion of the twentieth anniversary of the *Journal of Vocational Behavior*; it was the subject of a conference in the early 1990s (Savickas & Lent, 1994); and it has since only accelerated. Through the 1990s, writers in the field were still talking about Anne Roe's needs-based career theory (Osipow & Fitzgerald, 1996), sociological theories (Brown & Brooks, 1990), Bordin's psychodynamic theory (Brown & Brooks, 1990), Krumboltz et al.'s (1976) Social Learning Theory of Career Decision Making (Brown & Brooks, 1990), and the Theory of Work Adjustment (Dawis, 2002, 2005). Yet today, although one can still find coverage of some these theories in basic texts, very little writing or empirical research can be found in the literature that is focused on these older theories; most of the theory-based investigations in the vocational literature since the turn of the century have focused on the three theories named previously (Betz, 2008). Essentially, aspects of the theories that have exerted an influence on the field have been incorporated into the currently prevailing theoretical models. And this convergence is also occurring with respect to our understanding of women's career behavior. That is, although empirical studies devoid of theoretical underpinnings are found in the literature, the theory-based research on women' career development tends increasingly to be informed by one of the major career theories. Because the career literature in the past has suffered from a lack of theoretically based research (Hackett & Lent, 1992; Swanson & Gore, 2000), this is a very positive trend for the field. We might also add that the convergence observable in the literature is not just a convergence upon the several major theories that dominate the research literature, but rather it is a convergence across these leading theoretical traditions, with much cross-fertilizing between major theories (Betz, 2008). Undoubtedly new models will emerge, as has occurred in the past. We are only describing the literature as it now exists.

Future Directions

One of the biggest changes for women in the workforce that has occurred in the last several decades is the tremendous influx of women into the paid workforce, resulting in dramatic shifts in attitudes toward women and work (Farmer, 2006). And although this has had many positive effects, it has not altogether negated the problems that women face. Formal discrimination against women has not disappeared entirely, although it is no longer the major problem it once was (Fitzgerald & Harmon, 2001). But informal barriers, or what have been termed "thwarting conditions," in various forms from minor to major, remain as challenges for women in the paid workforce (Fitzgerald & Harmon, 2001).

With regard to women's career choice and development, the influences known to be important were summarized almost 25 years ago by Betz and Fitzgerald (1987), and the major facilitators of women's career development that they identified remain, for the most part, current today: background variables such as parental influences and female role models; individual difference variables such as high ability and self-efficacy; educational variables as, for example, continuation in mathematics; and various adult lifestyle and family influences. What research since the late 1980s has revealed, however, is how some of these general influences play out in the lives of diverse groups of women. Researchers and theorists have been trying to understand how these and other influences are important in the lives of women of color and other women whose lives may differ from the groups of White, middle class, college-educated women who have largely served as participants in vocational psychology research in past decades (Betz, 2006).

In terms of future research, one of the most pressing needs is for investigations examining the effects of intersecting identities on career choice and development, that is, examinations of how gender interacts with other identities in the vocational development and career choice process to create truly comprehensive vocational theories (Lindley, 2006). As can be seen from this review, the literature has only just begun to reflect the diversity of our society; there is still a long way to go before the vocational theories adequately capture the experiences of the diverse population in this country, let alone globally. Coupled with that is a need for increased attention to integrating gender and culture into theory-based and theory-building research. For too long the literature has been dominated by atheoretical research (Fassinger, 2005; Hackett & Lent, 1992). Headway has now been made in developing robust theories that are beginning to account for the vocational choices and behavior of diverse populations, but this trend needs to be accelerated. And finally, although there are many research issues demanding attention, the vexing issue of supports and barriers to girls' and women's career choices and development is one of the issues in most need of attention.

We end with a quote that remains relevant today:

> The study of women's career development began both as the study of a 'special' group and as an attempt to integrate knowledge about that group into the more general fabric of vocational psychology. As we have made progress on these goals, it has become increasingly apparent that what we are studying is not

only women per se but also *gender* and its differential influences on the career development of both sexes. As the study of women and gender has become more integrated into the study of vocational psychology more generally, it has also become more apparent that women are not a homogeneous group and that research needs to begin to take this into account.... In learning more about women of color, lesbians, poor women, we will learn more about *all* women, and, if history is any guide, about everyone else (i.e., men) as well. (Fitzgerald, Fassinger, & Betz, 1995, p. 102)

References

Ali, S. R., McWhirter, E., & Chronister, K. (2005). Self-efficacy and vocational outcome expectations for adolescents of lower socioeconomic status: A pilot study. *Journal of Career Assessment, 13*, 40–58.

Ali, S. R., Lewis, S. Z., & Sandil, R. (2006). Career counseling for Asian women. In W. B. Walsh & M. J. Heppner (Eds.), *Handbook of career counseling for women* (2nd ed.) (pp. 241–270). Mahwah, NJ: Lawrence Erlbaum Associates.

American Psychological Association (2000). Guidelines for psychotherapy with lesbian, gay, and bisexual clients. *American Psychologist, 55*, 1440–1451.

American Psychological Association (2003). Guidelines on multicultural education, training, research, practice, and organizational change for psychologists. *American Psychologist, 5*, 377–402.

American Psychological Association (2007). *Guidelines for psychological practice with girls and women.* Washington, DC: American Psychological Association.

American Psychological Association (2011). Guidelines for psychological practice with lesbian, gay, and bisexual clients. *American Psychologist, 67*, 10–42.

Arbona, C. (2000). Practice and research in career counseling and development—1999. *The Career Development Quarterly, 49*, 98–134.

Armstrong, P. I., Hubert, L., & Rounds, J. (2003). Circular unidimensional scaling: A new look at group differences in interest structure. *Journal of Counseling Psychology, 50*, 297–308.

Armstrong, P. I., & Rounds, J. (2008). Vocational psychology and individual differences. In S. D. Brown & R. W. Lent (Eds.), *Handbook of counseling psychology* (4th ed.) (pp. 375–391). New York: John Wiley & Sons.

Astin, H. S. (1984). The meaning of work in women's lives: A sociopsychological model of career choice and work behavior. *The Counseling Psychologist, 12*, 117–126.

Atkinson, D. R., & Hackett, G. (2003). *Counseling diverse populations* (3rd ed.). Boston, MA: McGraw-Hill.

Bandura, A. (1969). *Principles of behavior modification.* New York: Holt, Rinehart, & Winston.

Bandura, A. (1977). Self-efficacy: Toward a unifying theory of behavioral change. *Psychological Review, 84*, 191–215.

Bandura, A. (1986). *Social foundations of thought and action: A social cognitive theory.* Englewood Cliffs, NJ: Prentice-Hall.

Bandura, A. (1997). *Self-efficacy: The exercise of control.* New York: Freeman.

Betz, N. E., & Hackett, G. (1981). The relationship of career-related self-efficacy expectations to perceived career options in college men and women. *Journal of Counseling Psychology, 28*, 399–410.

Betz, N. E., & Hackett, G. (1983). The relationship of mathematics self-efficacy expectations to the selection of science-based college majors. *Journal of Vocational Behavior, 23*, 329–345.

Betz, N. E., & Hackett, G. (1986). Applications of self-efficacy theory to understanding career choice behavior. *Journal of Social and Clinical Psychology, 4*(3), 279–289.

Betz, N. E., & Fitzgerald, L. F. (1987). *The career psychology of women.* New York: Academic Press.

Betz, N. E., Borgen, F., & Harmon, L. (1996). *Skills confidence inventory: Applications and technical guide.* Palo Alto, CA: Consulting Psychologists Press.

Betz, N. E. (2005). Women's career development. In S. D. Brown & R. W. Lent (Eds.). *Career development and counseling* (pp. 253–277). Hoboken, NJ: John Wiley & Sons.

Betz, N. E. (2006). Basic issues and concepts in the career development and counseling of women. In W. B. Walsh & M. J. Heppner (Eds.), *Handbook of career counseling for women* (2nd ed.) (pp. 45–74). Mahwah, NJ: Lawrence Erlbaum Associates.

Betz, N. E., & Hackett, G. (2006). Career self-efficacy theory: Back to the future. *Journal of Career Assessment, 14*, 3–11.

Betz, N. E. (2007). Career self-efficacy: Exemplary recent research and emerging directions. *Journal of Career Assessment, 15*, 403–422.

Betz, N. E. (2008). Advances in vocational theories. In S. D. Brown & R. W. Lent (Eds.), *Handbook of counseling psychology* (4th ed.) (pp. 357–374). New York: Wiley.

Bieschke, K. J., & Toepfer-Hendey, E. (2006). Career counseling with lesbian clients. In W. B. Walsh & M. J. Heppner (Eds.), *Handbook of career counseling for women* (2nd ed.) (pp. 351–385). Mahwah, NJ: Lawrence Erlbaum Associates.

Bingham, R. P., Ward, C. M., & Butler, M. M. (2006). Career counseling with African American women. In W. B. Walsh & M. J. Heppner (Eds.), *Handbook of career counseling for women* (2nd ed.) (pp. 219–239). Mahwah, NJ: Lawrence Erlbaum Associates.

Blustein, D. L., & Fouad, N. A. (2008). Changing face of vocational psychology: The transforming world of work. In W. B. Walsh (Ed.), *Biennial review of counseling psychology* (pp. 129–155). New York: Psychology Press.

Bonitz, V. S., Larson, L. M., & Armstrong, P. I. (2010). Interests, self-efficacy, and choice goals: An experimental manipulation. *Journal of Vocational Behavior, 76*, 223–233.

Brenner, B., Chopra, S. B., Davis, T., Talleyrand, R., & Suthakaran, V. (2001). The role of contextual supports and barriers in the choice of math/sciences educational options: A test of social cognitive hypotheses. *Journal of Counseling Psychology, 48*, 474–483.

Brown, D., Brooks, L., & Associates (1990). *Career choice and development* (2nd ed.). San Francisco, CA: Jossey-Bass.

Brown, M. T. (1995). The career development of African Americans: Theoretical and empirical issues. In F. T. L. Leong (Ed.), *Career development and vocational behavior of racial and ethnic minorities* (pp. 7–36). Mahwah, NJ: Lawrence Erlbaum Associates.

Brown, S. D., & Lent, R. W. (Eds.). (2005). *Career development and counseling: Putting theory and research to work.* Hoboken, NJ: Wiley.

Byars, A. M., & Hackett, G. (1998). Applications of social cognitive theory to the career development of women of color. *Applied and Preventive Psychology, 7*, 255–267.

Byars, A. M. (2001). Rights-of-way: Affirmative career counseling with African American women. In W. B. Walsh, R. P. Bingham, M. T. Brown, & C. M. Ward (Eds.), *Career counseling for African Americans* (pp. 113–137). Mahwah, NJ: Lawrence Erlbaum Associates.

Coogan, P. A., & Chen, C. P, (2007). Career development and counseling for women: Connecting theories to practice. *Counseling Psychology Quarterly, 20*, 191–204.

Crites, J. O. (1969). *Vocational psychology*. New York: McGraw-Hill.

Crites, J. O. (1978). *Theory and research handbook for the Career Maturity Inventory*. Monterey, CA: CTB/McGraw-Hill.

Dawis, R. V., & Lofquist, L. (1984). *A psychological theory of work adjustment*. Minneapolis, MN: University of Minnesota Press.

Dawis, R. V. (2002). Person-environment correspondence theory. In D. Brown & Associates, *Career choice and development*, (4th ed.) (pp. 427–464). San Francisco, CA: Jossey-Bass.

Dawis, R. V. (2005). The Minnesota theory of work adjustment. In S. D. Brown & R. W. Lent (Eds.). *Career development and counseling* (pp. 3–23). Hoboken, NJ: John Wiley & Sons.

Fabian, E. S. (2000). Social cognitive theory of careers and individuals with serious mental health disorders: Implications for psychiatric rehabilitation programs. *Psychiatric Rehabilitation Journal, 23*, 262–269.

Farmer, H. S. (1976). What inhibits career and achievement motivation in women? *The Counseling Psychologist, 6*, 12–14.

Farmer, H. S. (1985). Model of career and achievement motivation for women and men. *Journal of Counseling Psychology, 32*, 363–390.

Farmer, H. S. (2006). History of career counseling for women. In W. B. Walsh & M. J. Heppner (Eds.), *Handbook of career counseling for women* (2nd ed.) (pp. 1–44). Mahwah, NJ: Lawrence Erlbaum Associates.

Fassinger, R. E. (1990). Causal models of career choice in two samples of college women. *Journal of Vocational Behavior, 36*, 225–248.

Fassinger, R. E. (August, 2002). *Honoring women's diversity: A new, inclusive theory of career development*. Presented at the annual meeting of the American Psychological Association, Chicago, IL.

Fassinger, R. E. (2005). Theoretical issues in the study of women's career development: Building bridges in a brave new world. In W. B. Walsh & M. L. Savickas (Eds.), *Handbook of vocational psychology* (3rd ed.) (pp. 85–124). Mahwah, NJ: Lawrence Erlbaum Associates.

Fitzgerald, L. F., & Crites, J. O. (1980). Toward a career psychology of women: What do we know? What do we need to know? *Journal of Counseling Psychology, 27*, 44–62.

Fitzgerald, L. F., Fassinger, R. E., & Betz, N. E. (1995). Theoretical advances in the study of women's career development. In W. B. Walsh & S. H. Osipow (Eds.). *Handbook of vocational psychology* (2nd ed.) (pp. 67–109). Mahwah, NJ: Lawrence Erlbaum Associates.

Fitzgerald, L. F., & Harmon, l. W. (2001). Women's career development: A postmodern update. In F. T. L. Leong & A. Barak (Eds.), *Contemporary models in vocational psychology: A volume in honor of Samuel H. Osipow* (pp. 207–230). Mahwah, NJ: Lawrence Erlbaum Associates.

Flores, L. Y., & O'Brien, K. M. (2002). The career development of Mexican American adolescent women: A test of the social cognitive career theory. *Journal of Counseling Psychology, 49*, 14–27.

Flores, L. Y., Navarro, R. L., & Ojeda, L. (2006). Career counseling with Latinas. In W. B. Walsh & M. J. Heppner (Eds.), *Handbook of career counseling for women* (2nd ed.) (pp. 271–313). Mahwah, NJ: Lawrence Erlbaum Associates.

Flores, L. Y., Ojeda, L., Huang, Y. P., Gee, D., & Lee, S. (2006). The relation of acculturation, problem solving appraisal, and career decision making self-efficacy to Mexican American high school students' educational goals. *Journal of Counseling Psychology, 53*, 260–266.

Flores, L. Y., Robitschek, C., Celebi, E., Andersen, C., & Hoang, U. (2010). Social cognitive influences on Mexican Americans' career choices across Holland themes. *Journal of Vocational Behavior, 76*, 198–210.

Fouad, N. A., & Arbona, C. (1994). Careers in a multicultural context. *Career Development Quarterly, 43*, 96–104.

Fouad, N. A. (1995). Career behavior of Hispanics: Assessment and career intervention. In F. T. L. Leong (Ed.), *Career development and behavior of racial and ethnic minorities* (pp. 165–192). Mahwah, NJ: Lawrence Erlbaum Associates.

Fouad, N. A., & Bingham, R. P. (1995). Career counseling with racial and ethnic minorities. In W. B. Walsh & S. H. Osipow (Eds.), *Handbook of vocational psychology* (2nd ed.) (pp. 131–365). Mahwah, NJ: Lawrence Erlbaum Associates.

Fouad, N. A., & Smith, P. L. (1996). A test of a social cognitive model for middle school students: Math and science. *Journal of Counseling Psychology, 43*, 338–346.

Fouad, N. A., Harmon, L. W., & Borgen, F. H. (1997). Structure of interests in employed male and female members of US racial-ethnic minority and nonminority groups. *Journal of Counseling Psychology, 44*, 339–345.

Fouad, N. A. (2002). Cross-cultural differences in vocational interests: Between-group differences on the Strong Interest Inventory. *Journal of Counseling Psychology, 49*, 283–289.

Fouad, N. A., Hackett, G., Smith, P. L., Kantamneni, N., Fitzpatrick, M., Haag, S., & Spencer, D. (2010). Barriers and supports for continuing in mathematics and sciences: Gender and educational level differences. *Journal of Vocational Behavior, 77*, 361–373.

Fouad, N. A. & Kantamneni, N. (2010). Cultural validity of Holland's theory. In J. G. Ponterotto, J. M. Casas, L. A. Suzuki, & C. M. Alexander (Eds.), *Handbook of multicultural counseling* (3rd ed.) (pp. 703–714). Los Angeles, CA: Sage.

Gainor, K. A., & Lent, R. W. (1998). Social cognitive expectations and racial identity attitudes in predicting the math choice intentions of Black college students. *Journal of Counseling Psychology, 45*, 403–413.

Ginzberg, E., Ginzberg, S. W., Axelrod, S., & Herma, J. L. (1951). *Occupational choice: An approach to a general theory*. New York: Columbia University Press.

Gomez, M. J., Fassinger, R. E., Prosser, J, Cooke, K., Mejia, B., & Luna, J. (2001). Voces abriendo caminos (voices forging paths): A qualitative study of the career development of notable Latinas. *Journal of Counseling Psychology, 48*, 286–300.

Gottfredson, L. S. (1981). Circumscription and compromise: A developmental theory of occupational aspirations. *Journal of Counseling Psychology, 28*, 545–579.

Gottfredson, L. S. (2002). Gottfredson's theory of circumscription, compromise, and self-creation. In D. Brown & Associates, *Career choice and development*, (4th ed.) (pp. 85–148). San Francisco, CA: Jossey-Bass.

Gottfredson, L. S. (2005). Appplying Gottfredson's theory of circumscription and compromise in career guidance and counseling. In S. D. Brown & R. W. Lent (Eds.), *Career development and counseling* (pp. 71–100). Hoboken, NJ: John Wiley & Sons.

Gushue, G. V. (2006). The relationship of ethnic identity career decision making self-efficacy, and outcome expectations among Latino/a high school students. *Journal of Vocational Behavior, 68,* 85–95.

Hackett, G., & Betz, N. E. (1981). A self-efficacy approach to the career development of women. *Journal of Vocational Behavior, 18,* 326–336.

Hackett, G. (1985). Role of mathematics self-efficacy in the choice of mathematics-related majors in college women and men: A path analysis. *Journal of Counseling Psychology, 32,* 47–56.

Hackett, G., Betz, N. E., Casas, J. M., & Rocha-Singh, I. (1992). Gender, ethnicity, and social cognitive factors predicting the academic achievement of engineering majors. *Journal of Counseling Psychology, 39,* 527–538.

Hackett, G., & Lent, R.W. (1992). Theoretical advances and current inquiry in career psychology. In S. D. Brown & R. W. Lent (Eds.). *Handbook of counseling psychology* (2nd ed.) (pp. 419–452). New York: Wiley.

Hackett, G. (1995). Self-efficacy in career choice and development. In A. Bandura (Ed.), *Self-efficacy in changing societies* (pp. 232–258). New York: Cambridge University Press.

Hackett, G., & Betz, N. E. (1995). Self-efficacy in career choice and development. In J. E. Maddux (Ed.), *Self-efficacy, adaptation, and adjustment: Theory, research, and application* (pp. 249–280). New York: Plenum.

Hackett, G., & Byars, A. M. (1996). Social cognitive theory and the career development of African American women. *The Career Development Quarterly, 44,* 322–340.

Hackett, G., & Lent, R. W. (2008). Social cognitive theory. In F. T. L. Leong, H. E. A. Tinsley, & S. H. Lease (Eds.), *Encyclopedia of counseling:* Vol. 2, *Personal and emotional counseling* (pp. 767–769). Thousand Oaks, CA: Sage Publications.

Hill, C., Corbett, C., & St. Rose, A. (2010). *Why so few? Women in science, technology, engineering, and mathematics.* Washington, DC: American Association of University Women.

Holland, J. L. (1959). A theory of vocational choice. *Journal of Counseling Psychology, 6,* 35–45.

Holland, J. L. (1973). *Making vocational choices: A theory of careers.* Upper Saddle River, NJ: Prentice Hall.

Holland, J. L. (1997). *Making vocational choices: A theory of vocational personalities and work environments* (3rd ed.). Odessa, FL: Psychological Assessment Resources.

Hyde, J. S. (2005). The gender similarities hypothesis. *American Psychologist, 60,* 581–592.

Hyde, J. S., Lindberg, S. M., Linn, M. C., Ellis, A. B., & Williams, C. C. (2008). Gender similarities characterize math performance. *Science, 321,* 494–495.

Jackson, M. A., Leon, C. A., & Zaharopolous, M. (2010). Multiculturally competent career counseling interventions with adolescents vulnerable to discrimination. In J. G. Ponterotto, J. M. Casas, L. A. Suzuki, & C. M. Alexander, (Eds.) *Handbook of multicultural counseling* (3rd ed.) (pp. 715–730). Los Angeles, CA: Sage.

Johnson, M., Swartz, J. L., & Martin, W. E. (1995). Applications of psychological theories for career development with Native Americans. In F. T. L. Leong (Ed.), *Career development and behavior of racial and ethnic minorities* (pp. 103–133). Mahwah, NJ: Lawrence Erlbaum Associates.

Kantamneni, N., & Fouad, N. (2010). Structure of vocational interests for diverse groups on the 2005 strong. *Journal of Vocational Behavior.* Advance online publication. doi: 10.1016/j.jvb.2010.06.003

Kenny, M. E., Blustein, D. L., Chaves, A., Grossman, J. M., & Gallagher, L. A. (2003). The role of perceived barriers and relational supports in the educational and vocational lives of urban high school students. *Journal of Counseling Psychology, 50,* 142–155.

Krumboltz, J. D., Mitchell, A. M., & Jones, G. B. (1976). A social learning theory of career selection. *The Counseling Psychologist, 6,* 71–81.

Lent, R. W., & Hackett, G. (1987). Career self-efficacy: Empirical status and future directions [Monograph]. *Journal of Vocational Behavior, 30,* 347–382.

Lent, R. W., Brown, S. D., & Hackett, G. (1994). Toward a unifying social cognitive theory of career and academic interest, choice, and performance [Monograph]. *Journal of Vocational Behavior, 45,* 79–122.

Lent, R. W., Hackett, G., & Brown, S. D. (1996). A social cognitive framework for studying career choice and transition to work. *Journal of Vocational Education Research, 21,* 3–31.

Lent, R. W., Hackett, G., & Brown, S. D. (1999). A social cognitive view of school-to-work transition. *The Career Development Quarterly, 44,* 297–311.

Lent, R. W., Brown, S. D., & Hackett, G. (2000). Contextual supports and barriers to career choice: A social cognitive analysis. *Journal of Counseling Psychology, 47,* 36–49.

Lent, R. W., Brown, S. D., & Hackett, G. (2002). Social cognitive theory. In D. Brown & Associates, *Career choice and development,* (4th ed.) (pp. 255–311). San Francisco, CA: Jossey-Bass.

Lent, R. W., Brown, S. D., Nota, L., & Soresi, S. (2003). Testing social cognitive interest and choice hypotheses across Holland types in Italian high school students. *Journal of Vocational Behavior, 62,* 101–118.

Lent, R. W. (2005). A social cognitive view of career development and counseling. In S. D. Brown & R. W. Lent (Eds.). *Career development and counseling* (pp. 101–127). Hoboken, NJ: John Wiley & Sons.

Lent, R. W., Paixao, M. P., da Silva, J. T., & Leitao, L. M. (2010). Predicting occupational interests and choice aspirations in Portuguese high school students: A test of social cognitive theory. *Journal of Vocational Behavior, 76,* 244–251.

Lent, R. W., & Sheu, H. B. (2010). Applying social cognitive career theory across cultures: Empirical status. In J. G. Ponterotto, J. M. Casas, L. A. Suzuki, & C. M. Alexander (Eds.), *Handbook of multicultural counseling* (3rd ed.) (pp. 691–701). Thousand Oaks, CA: Sage.

Lent, R. W., Sheu, H. B., Gloster, C. S., & Wilkins, G. (2010). Longitudinal test of the social cognitive model of choice in engineering students at historically Black universities. *Journal of Vocational Behavior, 76,* 387–394.

Leong, F. T. L., & Gim-Chung, R. H. (1995). Career assessment and intervention with Asian Americans. In F. T. L. Leong (Ed.), *Career development and behavior of racial and ethnic minorities* (pp. 193–226). Mahwah, NJ: Lawrence Erlbaum Associates.

Lindley, L. D. (2006). The paradox of self-efficacy: Research with diverse populations. *Journal of Career Assessment, 14,* 143–160.

Lippa, R. A. (2005). Subdomains of gender-related occupational interests: Do they form a cohesive bipolar M-F dimension? *Journal of Personality, 73,* 693–729.

Lonborg, S. D., & Hackett, G. (2006). Career assessment and counseling for women. In W. B. Walsh & M. J. Heppner (Eds.), *Handbook of career counseling for women* (2nd ed.) (pp. 103–166). Mahwah, NJ: Lawrence Erlbaum Associates.

McCloskey, C., & Mintz, L. (2006). A culturally oriented approach to career counseling with Native American women. In W. B. Walsh & M. J. Heppner (Eds.), *Handbook of career counseling for women* (2nd ed.) (pp. 315–350). Mahwah, NJ: Lawrence Erlbaum Associates.

McWhirter, E. H. (1997). Perceived barriers to education and career: Ethnic and gender differences. *Journal of Vocational Behavior, 50*, 124–140.

McWhirter, E. H., Hackett, G., & Bandalos, D. L. (1998). A causal model of the educational plans and career expectations of Mexican American high school students. *Journal of Counseling Psychology, 45*, 166–181.

Morrow, S. L., Gore, P. A., & Campbell, B. W. (1996). The application of a sociocognitive framework to the career development of lesbian women and gay men. *Journal of Vocational Behavior, 48*, 136–148.

Navarro, R. L., Flores, L. Y., & Worthington, R. L. (2007). Mexican American middle school students' goal intentions in mathematics and science: A test of social cognitive career theory. *Journal of Counseling Psychology, 54*, 320–335.

Nevill, D. D., & Super, D. E. (1986). *The Values Scale: Theory, application, and research manual.* Palo Alto, CA: Consulting Psychologists Press.

Niles, S. G., & Harris-Bowlsbey, J. (2009). *Career development interventions in the 21st century* (3rd ed). Upper Saddle River, NJ: Pearson.

Noonan, B. M., Gallor, S., Hensler-McGinnis, N., Fassinger, R. E., Wang, S., & Goodman, J. (2004). Challenge and success: A qualitative study of the career development of highly achieving women with physical and sensory disabilities. *Journal of Counseling Psychology, 51*, 68–80.

O'Brien, K. M., & Fassinger, R. E. (1993). A causal model of the career orientation and career choice of adolescent women. *Journal of Counseling Psychology, 40*, 456–469.

Osipow, S. H. (1975). *Emerging woman: Career analysis and outlooks.* Oxford, England: Charles E. Merrill.

Osipow, S. H. (1990). Convergence in theories of career choice and development: Review and prospects. *Journal of Vocational Behavior, 36*, 122–131.

Osipow, S. H., & Fitzgerald, L.F. (1996). *Theories of career development* (4th ed.). Boston: Allyn & Bacon.

Parsons, F. (1909). *Choosing a vocation.* Boston, MA: Houghton-Mifflin.

Prediger, D. J., & Cole, N. S. (1975). Sex-role socialization and employment realities: Implications for vocational interest measures. *Journal of Vocational Behavior, 7*, 239–251.

Psathas, G. (1968). Toward a theory of occupational choice for women. *Sociology and Social Research, 52*, 253–268.

Reardon, R. C., Vernick, S. H., & Reed, C. A. (2004). The distribution of the U.S. workforce from 1960 to 1990: A RIASEC perspective. *Journal of Career Assessment, 12*, 99–112.

Restubog, S. L. D., Florentino, A. R., & Garcia, P. R. J. M. (2010). The mediating roles of career self-efficacy and career decidedness in the relationship between contextual support and persistence. *Journal of Vocational Behavior, 77*, 186–195.

Richie, B. S., Fassinger, R. E., Linn, S., Johnson, J., Prosser, J., & Robinson, S. (1997). Persistence, connection, and passion: A qualitative study of the career development of highly achieving African American/Black and White women. *Journal of Counseling Psychology, 44*, 133–148.

Savickas, M. L., & Lent, R. W. (Eds.). (1994). *Convergence in career development theories: Implications for science and practice.* Palo Alto, CA: Consulting Psychologists Press.

Savickas, M. L. (1997). Career adaptability: An integrative construct for life-span, life-space theory. *Career Development Quarterly, 45*, 247–259.

Savickas, M. L. (2001). Toward a comprehensive theory of career development: Dispositions, concerns and narratives. In F. T. L. Leong & A. Barak (Eds.), *Contemporary models in vocational psychology: A volume in honor of Samuel H. Osipow* (pp. 295–320). Mahwah, NJ: Lawrence Erlbaum Associates.

Savickas, M. L. (2002). Career construction: A developmental theory of vocational behavior. Person-environment correspondence theory. In D. Brown & Associates, *Career choice and development*, (4th ed.) (pp. 149–205). San Francisco, CA: Jossey-Bass.

Savickas, M. L. (2005). The theory and practice of career construction. In S. D. Brown & R. W. Lent (Eds.), *Career development and counseling* (pp. 42–70). Hoboken, NJ: John Wiley & Sons.

Savickas, M. L., & Baker, D. B. (2005). The history of vocational psychology: Antecedents, origin, and early development. In W. B. Walsh & M. L. Savickas (Eds.), *Handbook of vocational psychology* (pp. 15–50). Mahwah, NJ: Lawrence Erlbaum Associates.

Spokane, A. R., Luchetta, E. J., & Richwine, M. H. (2002). Holland's theory of personalities in work environments. In D. Brown & Associates, *Career choice and development* (4th ed.) (pp. 373–426). Mahwah, NJ: Erlbaum.

Spokane, A. R., & Cruza-Guet, M. C. (2005). Holland's theory of vocational personalities in work environments. In S. D. Brown & R. W. Lent (Eds.). *Career development and counseling* (pp. 24–41). Hoboken, NJ: John Wiley & Sons.

Super, D. E. (1953). A theory of career development. *American Psychologist, 8*, 185–190.

Super, D. E. (1954). Career patterns as a basis for vocational counseling. *Journal of Counseling Psychology, 1*, 12–19.

Super, D. E. (1957). *The psychology of careers.* New York, NY: Harper.

Super, D. E. (1969). Vocational development theory: Persons, positions, and processes. *The Counseling Psychologist, 1*, 2–9.

Super, D. E. (1980). A life-span, life-space approach to career development. *Journal of vocational behavior, 16*, 282–298.

Super, D. E. (1984). Career and life development. In D. Brown & L. Brooks (Eds.), *Career choice and development*, (pp. 192–234). San Francisco, CA: Jossey-Bass.

Super, D. E. (1990). A life span, life space approach to career development. In D. Brown, L. Brooks, & Associates, *Career choice and development*, (2nd ed.) (pp. 197–261). San Francisco, CA: Jossey-Bass.

Super, D. E., Savickas, M. L, & Super, C. M. (1996). The life-span, life-space approach to careers. In D. Brown, & L. Brooks (Eds.), *Career choice and development*, (3rd ed.) (pp. 121–178). San Francisco, CA: Jossey-Bass.

Swanson, J. L., Daniels, K. K., & Tokar, D. M. (1996). Assessing perceptions of career-related barriers: The career barriers inventory. *Journal of career assessment, 4*, 219–244.

Swanson, J. L. & Woitke, M. B. (1997). Theory into practice in career assessment for women: Assessment and interventions regarding perceived career barriers. *Journal of Career Assessment, 5*, 431–450.

Swanson, J. L. & Gore, P. A. (2000). Advances in vocational psychology theory and research. In S. D. Brown & R. W. Lent (Eds.), *Handbook of counseling psychology* (3rd ed.) (pp. 233–269). New York: Wiley.

Szymanski, E. M., Enright, M. S., Hershenson, D. B., & Ettinger, J. M. (2003). Career development theories, constructs, and research: Implications for people with disabilities. In E. M. Szymanski & R. M. Parker (Eds.), *Work and disability: Issues and strategies in career development and job placement* (2nd ed.) (pp. 91–153). Austin, TX: ProEd.

Tang, M., Fouad, N. A., & Smith, P. L. (1999). Asian Americans' career choices: A path model to examine factors influencing their career choices. *Journal of Vocational Behavior, 54*, 142–157.

Walsh, W. B. & Savickas, M. L. (Eds.). (2005). *Handbook of vocational behavior: Theory, research and practice* (3rd. ed.). Mahwah, NJ: Lawrence Erlbaum Associates.

Walsh, W. B. & Heppner, M. J. (Eds.) (2006). *Handbook of career counseling for women* (2nd ed.). Mahwah, NJ: Lawrence Erlbaum Associates.

Warnath, C. F. (1975) Vocational theories: Direction to nowhere. *Personnel and Guidance Journal, 53*, 422–428.

Weinrach, S. G., & Srebalus, D. J. (1991). Holland's theory of careers. In D. Brown, L. Brooks & Associates, *Career choice and development* (pp. 37–67). San Francisco, CA: Jossey-Bass.

Zytowski, D. (1969). Toward a theory of career development of women. *Personnel and Guidance Journal, 47*, 660–664.

CHAPTER

15 Career Issues and Challenges Viewed Through a Feminist Multicultural Lens: Work-Life Interface and Sexual Harassment

Alayne J. Ormerod, Dana L. Joseph, Lauren M. Weitzman, *and* Erin Winterrowd

Abstract

This chapter examines research and theoretical perspectives about the work-life interface and sexual harassment in the workplace. Multiple roles and unwanted social and sexual experiences at work are considered from feminist multicultural and organizational perspectives. The chapter focuses on adaptive and contextual factors when considering how women experience and navigate the work-life interface, and how they respond to sexual harassment. In the context of the review, a new meta-analysis of the relationship between sexual harassment and racial/ethnic harassment and a new quantitative review of sexual harassment measurement are presented. The chapter discusses organizational remedies for sexual harassment in the workplace and strategies for addressing work-family conflict and sexual harassment at the individual level, and presents recommendations for future research.

Key Words: Multiple roles, sexual harassment, work-family conflict, workplace harassment, coping, workplace stress, prevention and intervention, outcomes, antecedents, racial/ethnic harassment

Introduction

Betz and Fitzgerald's (1987) foundational text on the career psychology of women identified the interface of home and work, and sexual harassment as major barriers to women's career adjustment, or success and satisfaction. Research on the work-life interface and sexual harassment has expanded greatly in the past 25 years and continues to grow. In reviewing the current literature in these areas, we approached the topics as two teams, with Lauren M. Weitzman and Erin Winterrowd writing about work-life interface and Alayne J. Ormerod and Dana L. Joseph writing about sexual harassment. Working from a feminist multicultural perspective, each team examined theory and definitions, evolution of research in their area, changes in conceptualization over time, and applications of an ecological perspective; and provided recommendations for future research, intervention, and prevention. The section on work-life interface provides a narrative review of the literature, whereas the section on sexual harassment uses both a narrative and quantitative strategy in its review of the literature that includes a quantitative review of sexual harassment measurement and a meta-analysis of the relationship between sexual harassment and racial/ethnic harassment. In the conclusion to the chapter, we examine the similarities and intersections between work-life interface and unwanted social and sexual experiences at work.

Although there are obvious differences between the realities and challenges associated with work-life interface and sexual harassment in the workplace, it was evident from the two reviews that both experiences have similarities. For example, navigating the work-life interface and facing sexual harassment at work can each be sources of stress that are negatively associated with workplace success and satisfaction, and that have a negative impact on psychological and physical health for the individual. Such findings have important implications for counseling psychologists in terms of working with individuals, organizations, and advocacy for policy change. Both areas have generated substantial research and are characterized by complex and multidimensional models for explaining their respective phenomena, and each area continues to be an important and relevant topic for research for counseling psychologists.

Research on the intersection of work-life balance and sexual harassment indicates that they intersect at various levels, including those of the individual, couples, and the organization. At the level of the individual, both topics represent challenges for women because of "spillover" effects of one life area affecting another (e.g., Parker & Griffin, 2002). At the level of a couple, research suggests that not only does the target of workplace aggression and harassment experience stress, but that the target's partner is also vulnerable to that stress (e.g., Haines, Marchand, & Harvey, 2006). Work-life balance and sexual harassment in the workplace can intersect at the level of an organization's culture or climate, with research indicating that when employees perceive that their organization values positive policy about work-life balance, they also perceive less sexual harassment in the workplace (Timmerman & Bajema, 2000). Although little research exists on the intersections of the two areas, the research that is available represents exciting new directions for scholarship and has important implications for intervention and prevention.

Work-Life Interface

This portion of the chapter will examine research and theory specific to the work-life interface as viewed through a feminist multicultural lens. A cross-disciplinary review of relevant theoretical constructs will be provided, followed by a review of the research literature focusing on the social context and cultural factors that influence how women experience and navigate the work-life interface.

Theoretical Conceptualizations of the Work-Life Interface

The trajectory of our theoretical understanding of the interface of work and family roles has followed a path congruent with the evolution of feminist multicultural counseling psychology. Specifically, conceptual frameworks have shifted to incorporate more adaptive viewpoints informed by the sociocultural contexts within which women live and work. For example, constructs such as work-family conflict (Greenhaus & Beutell, 1985) have progressed to include contemporary conceptualizations that affirm empowering, enriching, and facilitative aspects of managing multiple roles (e.g., Barnett & Hyde, 2001; Greenhaus& Powell, 2006). Culturally embedded formulations (Powell et al., 2009) and relational-cultural theory (Walker, 2004) offer further insight that is congruent with this perspective, by conceptualizing the individual within the unique relationships and sociocultural contexts in which she exists. Boundary theory (Zerubavel, 1991, 1996; Voydanoff, 2005) and work/family border theory (Clark, 2000) provide valuable conceptualizations worthy of consideration by feminist multicultural counseling psychologists. Finally, more recent theories have called for expanded definitions of work, more inclusive conceptualizations of family (Badgett, 2008; Fassinger, 2000; Schultheiss, 2006), and implications of intersecting identities (e.g., Ammons & Kelly, 2008; Beauregard et al., 2009; Perrone, 2005). Such focus falls well within a feminist multicultural paradigm.

In his review of the work-family literature, Frone (2003) identifies the major theoretical models of work-family balance and provides a rationale for this conceptual shift toward more contextual and adaptive theoretical formulations. Based on the six basic work-family models identified by Edwards and Rothbard (2000), he differentiates between non-causal and causal models that differ according to whether a reciprocal influence between roles exists (as reviewed by Morf, 1989). Non-causal conceptualizations include the *segmentation model* (e.g., Burke & Greenglass, 1987; Lambert, 1990), which is grounded in the assumption that work and family roles do not interact or influence one another. *Spillover* and *compensation* hypotheses (e.g., Staines, 1980), examples of causal models, outline ways that emotions and behaviors in both arenas mutually affect each other. For example, in the compensation model, an individual may seek satisfaction in leisure or family roles to make up for what is missing in the work role. Frone (2003) further highlights theory and research that takes into consideration the dynamic interplay between life roles. These include *integrative* models of work-family balance (e.g., Edwards & Rothbard, 2000; Frone, et al., 1997) that highlight reciprocal relationships and distinguish the directionality of influence between work and family roles (work-to-family or family-to-work).

Work-family conflict has been a predominant construct in the literature, particularly in initial theoretical formulations and research (e.g., Byron,

2005; Eby, Maher, & Butts, 2010). Greenhaus and Beutell (1985) first articulated the theory of work-family conflict by positing an incompatibility of work and family domains due to a discord in the related obligations and responsibilities. Their definition of *work-family conflict* is "a form of interrole conflict in which the role pressures from the work and family domains are mutually incompatible in some respect. That is, participation in the work (family) role is made more difficult by virtue of participation in the family (work) role" (Greenhaus & Beutell, 1985, p. 71). Similarly, Kreiner, Hollensbe, and Sheep (2009) define *work-home conflict* as "a subset of role conflict and as a generalized state of tension that results from incompatible expectations and challenges associated with work and home" (pp. 704–705). Baltes, Clark, and Chakrabarti (2010) cite work-family scarcity theory (e.g., Marks, 1977) as another form of work-family conflict theory. This work is grounded in the assumption of finite personal resources, with resource demands from one role draining the total pool of existing resources. While it is indeed the case that individuals do not have unlimited time and energy to draw upon, such theories ignore the possibility that experiences in one role can actually augment or enhance experiences in other life roles.

Addressing this criticism, work-family enrichment theory (Greenhaus & Powell, 2006) views work and family as allied with each other, rather than at cross-purposes. These authors highlight three ways in which multiple role participation can result in positive outcomes for individuals: (a) the additive effects on well-being across roles; (b) the buffering of distress from one role when an individual can access other roles; and (c) the transfer of positive experiences from one role to another (e.g., infusing of energy). Greenhaus and Powell's model (2006) emphasizes the bi-directionality of work-family enrichment and resources generated by role accumulation.

Similarly, Barnett and Hyde (2001) present an expansionist theory of gender, work, and family that emphasizes the psychological and health benefits of participating in multiple roles through several processes. These processes include (a) buffering (whereby success and/or satisfaction in one role offsets negative experiences in another role); (b) the pragmatic benefits of added income; (c) an increase in opportunities for social support; (d) additional chances for the experience of success; (e) expanded frames of reference; (f) increased self-complexity; and (g) a shared similarity of experiences between women and men. From these perspectives, the expanded repertoire of life roles is seen to have clear benefits for both women and men.

The work of Ashforth et al. (2000), Kreiner et al. (2009), and Clark (2000) represent work-family balance research that is grounded in role boundaries and role transitions and that captures an increased level of complexity regarding the interface between roles. Ashforth et al. (2000) identified two important characteristics of role boundaries: flexibility and permeability, which emphasize a dynamic integration between roles. Similar to Frone (2003), Ashforth et al. hypothesized a work-family continuum that ranges from segmentation to integration. They identify costs of segmentation that include greater amounts of energy when transitioning between roles. An integrated approach streamlines the transitions between roles, yet risks greater interference between roles and can result in confusion about when to emphasize one role over the other.

Kreiner et al. (2009) emphasize a social construction approach to work-home integration that views the individual as "an active agent in the 'co-construction' of boundaries in negotiated interactions with others" (p. 705). They present a grounded-theory model of work-home boundary work that draws upon Nippert-Eng (1996), who coined the term *boundary work* to define processes of constructing, dismantling, and maintaining work-home borders. This model identifies *boundary work tactics* that fall into behavioral, temporal, physical, and communicative realms and work-home boundary violations that include intrusion (a boundary "puncture" or the inability to prevent unwanted spillover between roles) and distance (when boundary integration is the desired state but the individual experiences forced segmentation).

Work/family border theory (Clark, 2000) defines work and family as two different domains or spheres that influence each other and assumes permeability across borders. This theory was developed using qualitative methodology and is grounded in Lewin's ideas of the "life space" and Anzaldua's (1987) experience of border-crossing as a Mestiza woman. Other central concepts include *flexibility* (the extent to which a border contracts or expands), *blending* (the existence of both permeability and flexibility that can enhance a more integrated, holistic experience of roles), and *border strength* (strong/rigid borders vs. fluid/flexible borders). Finally, Clark differentiates between *border-crossers* and *border-keepers*. Border-crossers vary in terms of being central or peripheral participants in work and/or family domains, which then has an impact on one's influence within domains and the degree of identification with domain responsibilities. Boundary-keepers, such as supervisors or spouses, can work to define what constitutes the expectations for each domain.

Early theories of the work-life interface focused on conflict and role segregation (e.g., Greenhaus & Beutell, 1995). Later theories (e.g., Barnett & Hyde, 2001; Greenhaus & Powell, 2006) broadened the constructs to include enrichment and facilitation across roles. Perhaps best representing the complex lives of working women, boundary and border theories (e.g., Ashforth et al., 2000; Clark, 2000; Kreiner et al., 2009) make room for more dynamic interactions among life and work roles. Finally, Clark (2000) reminds us that there is no one superior approach to work-family balance and individual personal satisfaction across the segmentation-integration continuum, as each individual navigates these boundaries dependent on personal preferences and unique work-family configurations. This theoretical assumption has significant applications for counseling, where thoughtful exploration of the intersection of personal values, unique family contexts, and current role demands can occur when making choices about managing and navigating work and other life roles.

Research on the Work-Life Interface

ANTECEDENTS AND OUTCOMES OF WORK-FAMILY CONFLICT AND FACILITATION

The majority of research on the work-life interface has focused on the work-family conflict construct, particularly the antecedents and consequences of work-family conflict. In a meta-analysis of 61 studies examining the antecedents of work-family conflict, Byron (2005) found work interference with family (WIF) and family interference with work (FIW) to be unique constructs with unique antecedents. WIF was associated with increased job involvement, higher levels of job stress, more hours at work, less supportive coworkers and supervisors, and less flexible work schedules. In contrast, FIW was associated with a greater number of hours spent with family-related tasks (e.g., housework, child care), increased family stress, more children, and being a single parent. Despite the differing antecedents, Byron (2005) noted that job stress, family stress, and family conflict were the strongest correlates of both work-family interference and family-work interference.

In their comprehensive review of work-family studies published in organizational journals between 1980 and 2002, Eby, Casper, Lockwood, Bordeaux, and Brinley (2005) identified similar antecedents to work-family conflict. These included factors such as conflict, pressure, and stress at work; unpredictable work routine and non-standard work hours; increased involvement and investment in work (e.g., demands, time commitment, hours); and having an abusive supervisor. Family-related predictors of work-family conflict consisted of having children at home, child care difficulties, family stress and tension, increased family involvement and time demands, and reduced family support (Eby et al., 2005). In their review of the literature on affect and the work-family interface, Eby, Maher, and Butts (2010) also described increased workload, dissatisfaction with work schedule, inadequate feedback and training at work, and work-role ambiguity as important correlates of work-family conflict.

Work-family conflict results in a number of affective, psychological, and physiological consequences. For example, as work and family demands increase, negative affective states increase (e.g., anxiety, tension, worry, frustration, guilt, distress, irritation) and positive affect decreases (Eby et al., 2010). Work-family conflict is associated with hypertension and other physical health complaints, as well as stress, depression, substance abuse, and a reduction in overall psychological well-being (Eby et al., 2005; Eby et al., 2010). Furthermore, workers experiencing work-family conflict report decreases in life, family, home, and non-work satisfaction (Eby et al., 2005; Eby et al., 2010). In regard to organizational consequences, work-family conflict is associated with reduced engagement at work, increased intention to leave one's job (risking greater personnel turnover), diminished job satisfaction, and lower perceived career success (Eby et al., 2005; Eby et al., 2010).

Consistent with theoretical advancements, more recent research on the work-life interface has focused on work-family facilitation and positive spillover. For example, studies have found momentary work satisfaction to be associated with momentary marital satisfaction, and greater job satisfaction has been found to be associated with greater daily marital satisfaction and improved affect at home (Eby et al., 2010). Both findings point to positive spillover of mood from one domain to the other. Work-family facilitation is also associated with a number of positive outcomes, including greater work, non-work, and partner satisfaction, improved psychological health, richer interpersonal engagement with partner, and lower rates of burnout (Eby et al., 2010).

SOCIAL CONTEXT AND CULTURAL FACTORS IN THE WORK-LIFE INTERFACE

Many critics have pointed out that past research has ignored contextual and cultural influences on the work-family interface. For example, the experience of work and family likely varies by culture, above and beyond individual differences. Cultures that are more collectivistic (i.e., value close relationships between people) and are high on humane orientation (i.e., encourage humane interactions) may provide more financial and social support for balancing work and family thus leading to lower work-family conflict (Powell, Francesco, & Ling, 2009). Furthermore, people in collectivistic cultures may be more likely to benefit from work-family facilitation because of increased integration across roles and stronger relationships with employers (Powell et al., 2009). Other cultural dimensions theoretically relevant to experiences of work and family include specificity/diffusion (degree of wholeness or integration versus compartmentalization) and gender egalitarianism (extent to which societal norms endorse gender equality and minimize gender-role differences). Workers who live in cultures high on specificity may be more likely to segment their work and family lives, leading to reduced work-family conflict and facilitation because factors in one domain will have less impact on the other domain (Powell et al., 2009).

A number of studies have demonstrated the role of culture in the work-life interface. For example, U.S. women in upper middle management are more likely to have children, to identify benefits of work-family balance, to use strategies to cope with work-family balance (e.g., make lateral career moves, seek jobs with flexibility, utilize support from a spouse or paid help), and to receive support from family and organizations than are German women in upper middle management (Peus & Traut-Mattausch, 2008). Furthermore, given differences in cultural beliefs around work and parenting, German women are more likely to perceive work-life balance as a barrier to a woman's career development and, compared to U.S. women, to see work and children as mutually exclusive. This perception is present despite Germany's additional laws designed to support work-family balance (Peus & Traut-Mattausch, 2008). In another study, family demands (vs. work demands) were more strongly associated with U.S. employees' reports of work-family conflict, whereas work demands (vs. family demands) were more strongly associated with work-family conflict for Chinese employees (Yang, Chen, Choi, & Zou, 2000). In China, sacrificing family time is seen as necessary for long-term benefits to the family, community, and nation, whereas sacrificing family time is seen as selfish and therefore more stressful in the U.S. (Yang et al., 2000). Studies such as these reflect differing cultural meanings of family and work. Additionally, they suggest that dominant societal values may be more influential than governmental laws in one's ability to balance work and family and to combine a career with motherhood.

In addition to culture, contextual influences on the work-family interface also include different meanings and experiences by gender. For example, antecedents of work-family conflict seem to vary by gender. In her meta-analysis, Byron (2005) reported that job involvement was more strongly related to work-family conflict (both WIF and FIW) for men than for women. In contrast, family involvement was more strongly related to work-family conflict (both WIF and FIW) for women than men. Similarly, job involvement was a stronger predictor of work-family conflict for men, whereas family involvement was a stronger predictor for women (Byron, 2005). Although findings on gender differences in physical and psychological health consequences of work-family conflict are mixed, women seem to experience more stress related to work when measured by blood pressure, adrenaline, and other physiological measures (Eby et al., 2005). The experiences of work and family may also vary by gender-role orientation. For example, the relationship between work-family conflict and negative mood states (e.g., guilt) is stronger among women with egalitarian gender-role ideology, whereas it is stronger among men with traditional gender-role orientations (Eby et al., 2010).

Despite reported gender differences in the antecedents and consequences of work-family conflict, findings on gender differences in the overall level of work-family conflict are mixed. Some studies report no gender differences, whereas other studies report women as experiencing more work-family conflict than men (Eby et al., 2005; Frone, 2003). For example, in her meta-analysis of mostly Canadian and U.S. studies, Byron (2005) reported that gender was only weakly related to work-family conflict, suggesting that women and men experience similar levels of interference overall. In contrast, using a large sample (N = 11,800) of dual-earning couples from the International Social Survey

Program, Edlund (2007) reported that women consistently struggle with work-family conflict more than men, though the sources of their stress differed by the wealth of the country. In poorer countries, women reported higher risk of both work and family overload, whereas in wealthier countries, women reported higher risk of work overload only (Edlund, 2007).

The literature appears to be clearer in regard to the influence of children and marriage on women's and men's experiences with the work-family interface. Women are significantly more likely to report work interfering with childbearing decisions and experiences of parenthood (e.g., relationship with child) compared to men (Ammons & Kelly, 2008). Similarly, mothers report more career interruptions than women who do not have children, and the negative effects of child care and having children on the work-family interface are greater for women than men (Eby et al., 2005). In regard to marriage, married female managers report more career interruptions than men (married or not) and are less likely to have a stay-at-home spouse compared to married male colleagues, leading to more work-family conflict (Eby et al., 2005). Furthermore, having a stay-at-home spouse is associated with increased pay and organizational level for men. The same is not true for women with a stay-at-home spouse (Eby et al., 2005). Taken together, the research suggests that being married and having children is generally beneficial to men at work but less so for women at work.

A related line of research examines the influence of occupational and industry gender composition on individual's experiences with work and family. The percent of women in an industry or occupation interacts with gender to predict perceived coworker support, supportive work-family culture, and work-family conflict. Specifically, as the number of women in an occupation or industry increases, women perceive more supportive work-family culture, greater coworker support, and less family-to-work conflict (Cook & Minnotte, 2008). In contrast, men perceived less coworker support, and slightly more family-to-work conflict as the number of women increases (Cook & Minnotte, 2008). The seeming disadvantage of men in female-dominated occupations and industries is somewhat surprising. It is possible that men in these fields are already engaging in less traditionally masculine roles, such as child care and domestic labor, thereby increasing their experiences of work-to-family conflict. Men in female-dominated workplaces may also be more aware of work-family conflict because of their female coworkers (Cook & Minnotte, 2008).

In addition to nationality and gender, contextual influences on the work-family interface include different experiences by socioeconomic status. Lower levels of education (i.e., less than a bachelor's degree) are associated with greater family-to-work conflict, whereas higher levels of education are associated with greater work-to-family conflict, particularly for women (Ammons & Kelly, 2008). This is consistent with findings from other studies suggesting that work-to-family conflict is greater for those with higher income (e.g., Byron, 2005). Ammons and Kelly (2008) also noted that low-wage workers in their sample of young adults reported fewer resources overall, including less access to unpaid and paid family leave, pre-tax dependent care expense accounts, information and referrals for dependent care, and telecommuting options, all of which contributed to their difficulties with balancing work and life. Reduced resources for low income workers are particularly relevant for women, who, on average, are more likely to work at or below the minimum wage, earn less money overall, and live below the poverty level compared to men (U.S. Department of Labor, 2009).

Broader Definitions of Family in Work-Life Interface Research: Challenges and Strengths

Understanding contextual influences on the work-life interface also requires expanding the concept of family to include single parents, same-sex couples, extended and multigenerational families, caretaking of parents, and other "non-traditional" familial structures (Beauregard, Ozbilgin, & Belle, 2009; Fassinger, 2000; Gilbert & Kearney, 2006; Powell et al., 2009; Schultheiss, 2006). Governmental limits on the definition of family provide significant barriers to these non-traditional family structures. The U.S. Department of Labor defines family as those who "reside together and are related by birth, marriage, or adoption" (U.S. Department of Labor, 2009, p. 97). This definition excludes same-sex couples and other-sex couples who are not married. Similarly, the Family and Medical Leave Act (FMLA, 1993) originally restricted the definition of family to spouses, parents, foster children, biological children, and adopted children. Although the definition of child was recently clarified as any child (or adult incapable of self-care due to mental or physical disability), independent of the worker's legal or biological relationship to the child (FMLA, 2010), FMLA continues to exclude adult siblings, parents-in-law, grandparents, and other unrelated adults. Institutionalized definitions of family privilege the minority of workers who fit those definitions while marginalizing all others. Such marginalization can lead to a lack of structural and emotional support as well as greater work-family conflict (Beauregard et al., 2009). Using more inclusive definitions of family is particularly important when considering the differential impact of the "family" domain on women's experiences since female workers, particularly women of color, are significantly more likely to be single mothers, to be providing care for a child, grandchild, or older adult, and to be living in an extended family (Beauregard et al., 2009).

Many U.S. workers (20%) care for both children and an older adult (Beauregard et al., 2009). Workers with elder care responsibilities report increased family-to-work interference, higher levels of stress, more symptoms of depression and other emotional difficulties, reduced overall well-being, and poorer job performance, compared to employees without elder care responsibilities and retired workers caretaking older adults (Beauregard et al., 2009). Furthermore, as the number of hours involved in caretaking an older adult increases, reports of depression and reduced emotional health also increase, particularly for women (Eby et al., 2005). Compared to child care responsibilities, workers caretaking older adults face added stress from awareness of the older person's degeneration and reversal of roles (especially when caretaking a parent), as well as difficulty finding alternative care providers such as sitters (Beauregard et al., 2009). Women are more likely than men to be caring for an older adult, and women report elder care to be more stressful than caring for a child (Beauregard et al., 2009). In the United States, experiences with elder care also vary by ethnicity, with Asian American and Latina/o workers reporting more elder care responsibilities than African American and European American workers (Beauregard et al., 2009), contributing to potentially greater work- and home-related stress.

In addition to caring for older adults, many older workers have caretaking responsibilities themselves. For example, 11% of grandparents provide at least six months of childcare for their grandchildren each year, and most grandparent caregivers are of working age (Beauregard et al., 2009). Rates of caretaking grandchildren are highest for African American and Native American adults (Beauregard et al., 2009). Adults who are caretaking grandchildren face a number of difficulties. Compared to middle-age parents, grandparents experience lower levels of energy, health difficulties due to age, frequently changing family roles, and less family support and cohesion. Such difficulties often result in physical health problems, depression, stress, and anxiety (Beauregard et al., 2009).

Another non-traditional family structure is that of same-sex couples (with and without children). According to the American Community Survey, 0.6% of U.S. households from 2005 to 2009 were made up of same-sex couples (U.S. Census Bureau, 2009). Many work-family struggles are the same for same-sex and other-sex couples, including negotiating time spent at work and home as well as the effects of job and family stress on work and family. However, same-sex couples also face unique struggles with work and family. As described above, such families are typically not covered under FMLA, and most states do not have a mandate to provide pensions, health care, or health-related leave to same-sex partners. Therefore, compared to other-sex couples, same-sex couples typically experience an increased financial burden as a result of job loss because partners are less likely to be covered by insurance (Perrone, 2005).

Same-sex couples are more likely to be dual earners than other-sex couples (Beauregard et al., 2009), which increases the risk of work-family conflict despite the potential financial benefits. Lesbian women are also more likely to have children than gay male couples (Perrone, 2005), resulting in greater amounts of work-family conflict. Facing potential workplace discrimination, many same-sex couples choose not to disclose their sexual orientation to coworkers. This can place additional stress on both the worker and her or his partner, leading to difficulty accessing essential social networks at work and feelings of isolation and psychological distress (Beauregard et al., 2009; Perrone, 2005). Finally, same-sex couples report lower levels of parental and familial support, both of which are important buffers in work-family conflict (Perrone, 2005).

Women continue to earn significantly less than men (U.S. Department of Labor, 2009), putting lesbian couples at a double disadvantage in terms of income; however, lesbian women also earn more money on average than straight women (Beauregard et al., 2009). Lesbian women are also perceived as less likely to quit their jobs for children and as more competent and committed to work than straight women (Beauregard et al., 2009), which may lead to decreased work-family conflict and fewer experiences of sex discrimination in the workplace. Defining family more inclusively allows us to see these complexities, as well as the strengths of diverse family structures. For example, lesbian and gay couples often report more support from friends, perceptions of increased egalitarianism in their relationship, and more egalitarian distribution of actual paid and unpaid work (Beauregard et al., 2009; Perrone, 2005). All of these factors contribute to reduced work-family conflict. Lesbian couples, specifically, report more positive problem-solving experiences, increased relationship cohesion and equality, and fewer costs from the relationship compared to heterosexual couples (Beauregard et al., 2009). In summary, navigating the interface of work and family is an everyday experience for most adults, with having a same-sex partner, raising children, and/or caretaking an older adult adding to the complexity.

Other Non-Work Variables

Consistent with the recent movement to expand work-life research to include more cultural and contextual influences and broader definitions of family, many researchers (e.g., Byron, 2005; Frone, 2003; Powell et al., 2009) have called for additional attention to non-work, non-family roles in investigations of the work-life interface. These include community, leisure, religious, and student roles. Byron (2005) even suggests that researchers should focus more on the diverse factors that contribute to role distress and role fulfillment, rather than the "intersection of work and family" specifically.

In response to the need to view non-work factors more broadly, Fisher, Bulger, and Smith (2009) developed and validated a measure of work/non-work interference and enhancement with two U.S. samples of workers diverse in occupation, gender, age, and family composition. They found evidence for four factors: work interference with personal life (e.g., "I often neglect my personal needs because of the demands of my work"); personal life interference with work (e.g., "When I am at work, I worry about things I need to do outside of work"); work enhancement of personal life (e.g., "Because of my job, I am in a better mood at home"); and personal life enhancement of work (e.g., "My personal life gives me the energy to do my job"). According to Fisher and colleagues, the work/non-work measure predicted interference and facilitation equally well as work/family measures, while being more inclusive to all types of personal life issues, including family.

To investigate the application of "family-friendly" work policies to singles, Casper, Weltman, and Kwesiga (2007) surveyed 208 ethnically diverse, single college students who were working 20 to 40 hours a week. They found evidence for a "singles-friendly" culture that included five factors: social inclusion, equal work opportunities, equal access to benefits, equal respect for non-work life, and equal work expectations. The researchers reported that workers' experiences of singles-friendly culture impacted various organizational factors, including turnover intention, affective commitment, and perceived organizational support. Perhaps most importantly, Casper and colleagues (2007) found that factors typically intended to reduce work-family conflict also reduced work–non-work conflict for singles. These included flexibility and perceived managerial, coworker, and organizational support for non-work life (Casper et al., 2007).

Using the National Survey of Midlife Development, Voydanoff (2005) was one of the first researchers to investigate community context and the work-life interface. Voydanoff examined the role of community participation and resources in job and marital quality among working adults who were partnered and living in the United States. This study found that community participation (i.e., volunteering, having contact with neighbors and friends) was generally unrelated to job and marital quality, whereas affective community resources (i.e., sense of belonging, neighborhood attachment, support from friends) were positively related to job and marital quality. It was also reported that work-to-family conflict and facilitation as well as family-to-work conflict and facilitation mediated the relationship between community, job quality, and marital quality. Studies by Fisher et al. (2009), Casper et al. (2007), and Voydanoff (2005) all contribute to our understanding of the broader context of people's individual lives as they play out in the work and non-work domains.

Future Directions in the Research and Theory of Work-Life Interface

As described above, social context plays an important role in the work-life interface. The culture of the workplace and coworkers directly impact experiences of work-family conflict and facilitation. Additionally, the social context of the worker, including gender, nationality, and socioeconomic status, impact experiences of work and life, as well as cultural meanings and practices of family and work. Academic theories, organizational/governmental policies, and other interventions must therefore be implemented with culture and context in mind. For example, we have much more to learn about the impact of diverse family structures on navigating the work-life interface. Having extended family members in the home might facilitate child care but may also be a stressor, depending on acculturation or cultural differences between family members. In regard to organizational policies and interventions, "family-friendly" policies will not work if they do not match national culture, which is particularly important for multinational corporations. Additionally, organizational culture must support such policies. A family-friendly policy is worth little if the employee is afraid of the repercussions of utilizing that policy.

With this in mind, research suggests that organizations should work to decrease job-related stress (e.g., role conflict, job ambiguity, overload), increase flexibility and control in work scheduling (e.g., flextime), develop a sense of work community and climate that is supportive of work-life issues, offer on-site childcare, and create opportunities for work load reduction for all workers (e.g., Ammons & Kelly, 2008; Byron, 2005; Eby et al., 2005). Improving organizational support for work-life issues is associated with increased job satisfaction, more organizational commitment, fewer turnover intentions, improved work and family functioning, and more trust in management (Eby et al., 2005).

Organizations and governments outside the U.S. may provide examples of inclusive work-life policies. For example, child care is generally more available in Chinese communities and workplaces than in the United States, potentially decreasing some family-related demands (Yang et al., 2000). Additionally, the United Kingdom includes same-sex couples in their governmental family policies. Workers in the United Kingdom can also request flexible work hours and can take time off for any dependent (i.e., person reliant upon the worker for assistance; Beauregard et al., 2009). De-marginalizing families through broader governmental definitions of family may also lead to increased structural and emotional support for these workers and subsequently less work-life conflict and greater life and work satisfaction.

Clark (2000) defines balance as "a consequence of artful border and domain management" and states that balance is "nearly unattainable without identification with roles and activities associated with membership in both work and home domains" (p. 761). Several authors have proposed a shift away from the metaphor of "work-family balance" (MacDermid et al., 2001; Schultheiss, 2006; Weitzman, 2004). MacDermid et al. (2001) draw upon the work of Galinsky (1999) and suggest the dynamic metaphor of *navigation*. Along with Weitzman's (2004) suggestion to focus on the process of creating balance (a verb) rather than the outcome of balance (a noun), the navigation metaphor is consistent with a feminist multicultural approach and focuses on "staying the course" in both calm and rough waters, rather than on the "destination" of work-life balance. Related research questions may more deeply explore the nuances of how individuals navigate the work-life interface. For example, investigations of how an individual perceives the fluidity versus rigidity of work-life boundaries and how this perception shifts over time might be explored from a qualitative, life span perspective. Similarly, "critical incidents" (e.g., becoming partnered or having a child, starting a new job, or encountering resistance from an employer regarding a flexible working schedule) that impact how one chooses to negotiate these boundaries can be identified, keeping the sociocultural context in mind. Finally, traditional vocational constructs, such as person-environment fit, can be applied to better understanding the process of aligning personal values and aspirations with a particular organization or job environment to maximize the achievement of individual life goals.

Sexual Harassment in the Workplace

In this portion of the chapter, we focus on major findings about sexual harassment, particularly those originating from large-scale, systematic, or longitudinal research, and meta-analytic studies. Topics include definitions, measurement, frequency, antecedents and causal explanations, harassment's relationship with other forms of workplace deviance, outcomes of sexual harassment, responses to sexual harassment, and intervention and prevention.[1] We examine the existing literature from a feminist multicultural standpoint and make new contributions to the empirical literature by presenting a quantitative review of sexual harassment measurement and conducting a meta-analysis of the relationship between sexual harassment and racial/ethnic harassment. Although much of the research on workplace sexual harassment originates from an organizational perspective, the findings have direct relevance to the practice and scholarship of counseling psychologists.

Construct Definitions of Sexual Harassment

Scientific and legal definitions of sexual harassment have changed over time, often informed by new knowledge and decisions arising from legal proceedings. Recent scholarship has classified the various definitions of sexual harassment as falling into one of two categories: subjective or objective (O'Leary-Kelly, Bowes-Sperry, Bates, & Lean, 2009). Subjective definitions conceptualize sexual harassment from the perspective of the victim, and include the *psychological* definition and the *sex-based* definition. The psychological definition describes sexual harassment as "unwanted sex-related behavior at work that is appraised by the recipient as offensive, exceeding her resources, or threatening her well-being" (Fitzgerald, Swan & Magley, 1997, p. 15), suggesting that it is the recipient's appraisal of the harassing behavior that mediates its impact. The sex-based definition depicts sexual harassment as "behavior that derogates, demeans, or humiliates an individual based on that individual's sex" (Berdahl, 2007a, p. 644). This definition clarifies that sexual harassment may not necessarily be *sexual* (e.g., based on sexual desires), but rather any derogatory behavior that is directed toward an individual's *sex.* Both of the above definitions (i.e., psychological and sex-based) require a subjective evaluation of a behavior as harassing or derogatory in order for the behavior to be classified as sexually harassing.

In contrast, objective definitions of sexual harassment depict the construct as consisting of a given set of behaviors that need not cause psychological distress to be considered sexual harassment (O'Leary-Kelly et al., 2009). For example, *behavioral definitions* of sexual harassment specify three categories of sexually harassing behaviors: *gender harassment, unwanted sexual attention,* and *sexual coercion* (Fitzgerald, Gelfand, & Drasgow, 1995; Gelfand, Fitzgerald, & Drasgow, 1995). Gender harassment involves "a broad range of verbal and nonverbal behaviors not aimed at sexual cooperation but that convey insulting, hostile, and degrading attitudes about women" (Fitzgerald, Gelfand, et al., 1995, p. 430), while unwanted sexual attention refers to "a wide range of verbal and nonverbal behavior that is offensive, unwanted, and unreciprocated" (Fitzgerald, Gelfand, et al., 1995, p. 431). Finally, sexual coercion is described as "the extortion of sexual cooperation in return for job-related considerations" (Fitzgerald, Gelfand, et al., 1995, p. 431). In studies of the U.S. military, gender harassment has been further delineated into two subcategories, *sexist hostility* (also referred to as *sexist behavior*), which is discriminatory behavior based on one's sex, and *sexual hostility* (also referred to as *crude/offensive behavior*), or sexual behavior that is insulting or demeaning (Fitzgerald, Magley, Drasgow, & Waldo, 1999).

Legal definitions of sexual harassment are based on the Equal Employment Opportunity Commission's guidelines (EEOC, 1980, 1993, 1997) and involve both objective and subjective elements. For a sexually harassing behavior to be considered illegal, it must involve *quid pro quo* behavior or a *hostile work environment.* Quid pro quo behavior is similar to sexual coercion in that it requires an attempt to coerce an individual by threatening his or her employment status. Because quid pro quo harassment does not involve a subjective evaluation of a behavior, it can be classified as an objective definition of sexual harassment. A hostile work environment, in comparison, exists when the environment is intimidating, hostile, or offensive enough such that a "reasonable person" would be negatively affected by the environment. As such, this definition involves both objective (i.e., the "reasonable person" standard) and subjective (i.e., the victim must be negatively affected) elements (Bowes-Sperry & Tata, 1999; Gutek & Done, 2001; O'Leary-Kelly et al., 2009).

Recently, literature on sexual harassment has gone beyond broad definitions of sexual harassment to recognize specific types of sexual harassing behavior. For example, *client sexual harassment,* or sexual harassment committed by clients or customers (Gettman & Gelfand, 2007), differs from traditional definitions of sexual harassment in that it focuses on sexually harassing behaviors emanating from individuals *outside* the organization. *Ambient sexual harassment* is a type of indirect sexual harassment that refers to the general level of sexual harassment in a work group (Glomb, Richman, Hulin, Drasgow, Schneider, & Fitzgerald, 1997). Another recently defined specific type of sexual harassment, *racialized sexual harassment,* focuses on behaviors that are harassing toward one's race and gender simultaneously (Buchanan & Ormerod, 2002). Meanwhile, *not-man-enough harassment* involves harassing behaviors directed at one's courage, strength, and toughness (Berdahl, Magley, & Waldo, 1996; Berdahl & Moore, 2006; Waldo, Berdahl, & Fitzgerald, 1998). Examining specific types of harassment can contribute further understanding to women's experiences of harassment in the workplace that might otherwise be overlooked. For example, earlier definitions of sexual harassment at work focused on harassment from coworkers and/or supervisors but did not allow for the possibility of examining harassment from customers or experiences of indirect (ambient) harassment.

The Measurement of Sexual Harassment

Two primary approaches to the measurement of sexual harassment have predominated the literature: direct queries and behavioral assessments (Ilies, Hauserman, Schwochau, & Sibal, 2003; Magley, Hulin, Fitzgerald, & DeNardo, 1999). Assessment via direct query typically involves a single-item question, such as "Have you ever been sexually harassed?" Conversely, the behavioral approach presents a series of harassing behaviors to which a respondent indicates the frequency of experiencing each behavior (e.g., "made unwanted attempts to stroke or fondle you"; Fitzgerald, Gelfand, et al., 1995). The most obvious difference between these approaches is whether the respondent is required to label the experience as sexual harassment. In the direct query approach, the respondent is required to define the experience as sexual harassment, which may introduce perceptual bias into the measurement of the construct. Meanwhile, the behavioral approach asks about specific behaviors, and thus reduces the potential for a perceptual bias and, if similar methodology is used, allows for comparison of rates across time and samples (Ilies et al., 2003). These different measurement approaches have resulted in disparate incidence rates for sexual harassment (e.g., in a meta-analytic study, the direct query method resulted in 24% of women indicating sexual harassment, and the behavioral experiences method resulted in 58% of women indicating sexual harassment; Ilies et al., 2003). Despite differential effects on incidence rates, research has demonstrated that negative outcomes result, regardless of whether the experience is labeled as sexual harassment (Magley et al., 1999; Munson, Miner, & Hulin, 2001). The behavioral approach is the more common of the two measurement practices because the direct query approach results in reports of sexual harassment that are dependent on each respondent's definition of sexual harassment. However, the behavioral approach has been criticized for neglecting the extent to which a respondent is bothered by each of the behaviors included in the measure (e.g., Gutek, Murphy, & Douma, 2004), which may lead to overestimation of incidence rates because it includes experiences that may be considered trivial by the respondent (Fitzgerald, Magley, et al., 1999). Contemporary advances are attempting to address this criticism by expanding the behavioral approach to include both frequency and the extent to which each behavior bothers the respondent (e.g., Berdahl, 2007b; Berdahl & Moore, 2006).

The behavioral approach to measurement of sexual harassment has largely been dominated by the Sexual Experiences Questionnaire (SEQ; Fitzgerald, Shullman, et al., 1988). Introduced in 1988 (Fitzgerald, Shullman, et al.), the SEQ has undergone two major revisions, one in 1995 (Fitzgerald, Gelfand, et al., 1995; Gelfand et al., 1995), the other in 2002 (Stark, Chernyshenko, Lancaster, Drasgow, & Fitzgerald, 2002), which resulted in the 16-item, four-factor[2] SEQ. The SEQ has been translated into various languages (e.g., Spanish, Portuguese, Turkish, Japanese), used with diverse samples (e.g., men and women, various racial/ethnic groups, occupational types, and socioeconomic status levels), and has been adapted for use within various contexts (e.g., the number of items, response scale, dimensions measured, time frame of responses, and wording changes for use in U.S. military, public and private organizations, educational settings from middle through graduate school, and the assessment of harassment by landlords and customers). The SEQ has been criticized because of the adaptations described above, which are thought to lessen comparability across studies that use different versions (Gutek et al., 2004). However, the authors of the SEQ have provided a body of research supporting its structure and measurement capabilities (e.g., Fitzgerald, Gelfand, et al., 1995; Gelfand et al., 1995; Fitzgerald, Drasgow, Hulin, Gelfand, & Magley, 1997), and it is generally considered to be the most psychometrically sound measure of sexual harassment (e.g., Willness et al., 2007). In a study by Lee and Ormerod (2003), the four-factor structure of the SEQ remained invariant across gender and diverse samples and despite differences in item wording or, in some cases, unique items, providing strong support for its construct validity.

The SEQ is also considered to be the most widely used measure of sexual harassment (e.g., Berdahl & Raver, 2010; Chan, Lam, Chow, & Cheung, 2008; Gutek & Done, 2001; Willness et al., 2007). However, the actual proportion of studies operationalizing sexual harassment with the SEQ is relatively unknown. A recent meta-analysis demonstrates that sexual harassment has been measured with a version of the SEQ in approximately 60% of the studies included in the meta-analysis (Willness et al.), although this work does not represent the proportion of all sexual harassment literature published in peer-review journals that have used the SEQ. To better understand the extent to which sexual harassment literature in peer-reviewed journals is utilizing the SEQ and what alternative measures are being used most often, we conducted a quantitative review of sexual harassment measurement. The review involved a keyword search for *sexual harassment* in American Psychological Association's PsycINFO (1887–2010) and subsequent coding of all available peer-reviewed studies that measured sexual harassment. Attitudes toward sexual harassment and beliefs about definitions of sexual harassment were excluded. Only studies that explicitly measured sexual harassment were included. Results of the review are presented in figures 15.1 and 15.2.

Figure 15.1 presents a general time line of sexual harassment research, indicating the number of studies that explicitly measured sexual harassment in each year from 1980 to 2010 (i.e., our search did not identify any studies prior to 1980 that had explicitly measured sexual harassment). As figure 15.1 illustrates, the number of studies measuring sexual harassment appears to have steadily increased over the life course of the construct, suggesting that interest in the construct of sexual harassment may still be growing. Our literature search located 372 studies in peer-reviewed journals that explicitly measured sexual harassment. The resulting database of studies appeared to be fairly well distributed across journals, with only four journals containing 10 or more of the studies located through the literature search: *Sex Roles* (45 studies), *Psychology of Women Quarterly* (18 studies), *Journal of Interpersonal Violence* (11 studies), and *Journal of Applied Psychology* (11 studies).

As illustrated by figure 15.2, the SEQ is the single most commonly used measure in the sexual harassment literature (i.e., the SEQ was used in 31% of the studies identified in the literature search). However, "homemade" measures, or measures that were unpublished and were developed for the current study, were slightly more common than the SEQ (i.e., 34% of the studies identified in the literature search used a homemade measure). These findings point to a problematic proportion of studies that have measured sexual harassment with homemade (34%) or one-item measures (16%). That is, our results show that *half* of the studies assessing sexual harassment in peer-reviewed journals used an unvalidated or one-item measure of sexual harassment. Of the 19% of studies using a measure designated as "other measure" in figure 15.2 (i.e., a measure other than the SEQ, a homemade measure, or a one-item direct query measure), no single measure was identified as a commonly used alternative to the SEQ. For example, other than the SEQ or versions of the SEQ, the second most commonly cited measure was the AAUW Sexual Harassment Questionnaire (American Association of University Women Educational Foundation, 2001), and only 15 of the 372 studies (4%) reported having used this measure. Thus, the results of our quantitative review appear to confirm previous assertions that the SEQ is the most widely used measure of sexual harassment (e.g., Berdahl & Raver, 2010; Chan et al., 2008; Gutek & Done, 2001; Willness et al., 2007). However, it should be noted that studies measuring sexual harassment that do not appear in PsycINFO or peer-review journals, those that do not include the keyword "sexual harassment," or those that were not available electronically were not included in the current review. In summary, the amount of research on sexual harassment has steadily increased over the last three decades, and results of this quantitative review suggest that the dominant measure in sexual harassment research is the SEQ.

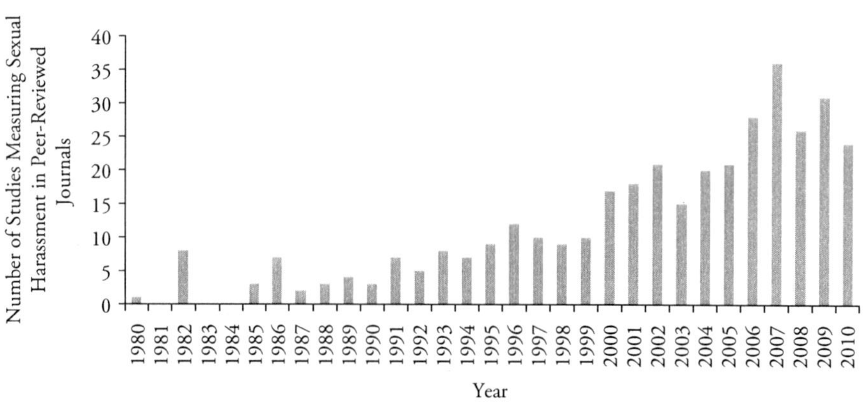

Figure 15.1 A Time Line of Sexual Harassment Measurement.

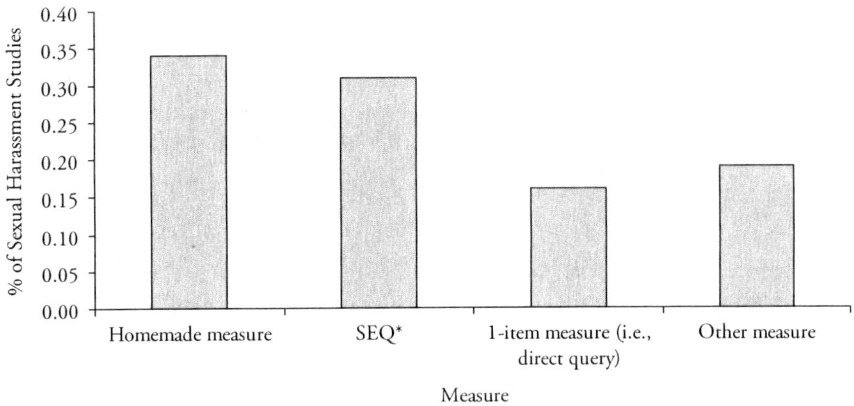

Figure 15.2 Sexual Harassment Measures.
N = 372 studies that measured sexual harassment. "Homemade measure" refers to an unpublished measure that was developed for the purposes of the current study. SEQ = Sexual Experiences Questionnaire (Fitzgerald et al., 1988). *Studies that used any version of the SEQ (e.g., SEQ-DoD, SEQ-L) were included in the "SEQ" category. "Other measure" refers to published multi-item measures other than the SEQ.

Incidence: How Frequent Is Sexual Harassment?

There is a high degree of variability among published incidence rates for sexual harassment in the workplace (Ilies et al., 2003). Some of the factors that affect incidence rates include *who is asked* about the harassment (i.e., the sampling procedures), *how harassment is defined* (i.e., the construct definition), *what is asked* (i.e., the content validity and reliability of the measure), and the *time frame* for the harassing behavior (i.e., the length of time the respondents are to refer to when recalling past harassment; Ilies et al., 2003; Koss et al., 1994). Such factors affect not only whether an estimate of sexual harassment is considered accurate and representative of a target population, but also whether it is comparable to other estimates of sexual harassment. Thus, direct comparisons across studies are not meaningful when different methodologies are used. In the discussion of incidence rates below, we will consider rates that come from large-scale studies using nationally representative samples and valid, reliable, and behaviorally worded measures.

In a meta-analytic study of sexual harassment incidence rates in the workplace, Ilies et al. (2003) found that incidence rates are moderated by sampling methodology (probability, non-probability), survey questions (behavioral vs. direct query), and type of workplace (academic, private sector, government, military). Convenience (non-probability) samples demonstrated a sample selection bias, resulting in overestimates of sexual harassment, and the direct query method resulted in lower estimates of harassment (likely due to a perceptual bias in reporting sexual harassment). These findings underscore the importance of using psychometrically sound instruments and rigorous methods when assessing sexual harassment in the workplace.

When considering only those studies that used probability samples and behavioral measures, Ilies et al. (2003) found that incidence rates of sexual harassment varied by work setting, with military samples experiencing the highest incidence (69%), followed by academic samples (58%), private sector samples (46%), and government samples (43%), with an average incidence rate of 58% for female workers. No comparable meta-analytic study exists for men. Considering only large-scale studies, estimates for the sexual harassment of men have ranged from 14% to 43% (Das, 2009; Gutek, 1985; Rospenda, Richman, & Shannon, 2009; U.S. Merit Systems Protection Board, USMSPB, 1981, 1988, 1995); however, such figures represent studies using widely differing methodologies.

Although overall incidence rates of sexual harassment provide general information about how many people experience one or more harassing behaviors within a specified time frame, examining the type of sexual harassment experienced (i.e., gender harassment, unwanted sexual attention, sexual coercion) and demographic correlates (e.g., work setting) of those who are targeted can contribute more detailed information about the frequency of harassment. For example, when considering type of harassment, sexist hostility (63%, 15%) and sexual hostility (69%, 35%) are far more common than unwanted sexual attention (42%, 8%) or sexual coercion (13%, 2%) for women and men, respectively (Fitzgerald, Magley, et al., 1999).[3] In addition to being more common, gender harassment may occur in isolation from other forms of sexual harassment, whereas unwanted sexual attention and sexual coercion rarely occur without the existence of gender harassment (Fitzgerald, Magley, et al., 1999).

Although women tend to experience higher rates of overall harassment (Rospenda et al., 2009) and higher rates of each individual form of sexual harassment, there is some recent research suggesting that among younger workers, overall rates of harassment across genders may be approaching parity (Das, 2009; Rospenda et al., 2009). However, as noted above, reporting frequency alone is not necessarily informative to our understanding of its effect and meaning. It is also important to consider the degree to which the respondent is bothered by harassing behavior (i.e., subjective appraisals), and research demonstrates that women are more likely to evaluate such behavior as bothersome or threatening (Berdahl, 2007b).

In contrast to research on the incidence rates of sexual harassment across genders, the literature is mixed about whether racial/ethnic status affects incidence rates for sexual harassment (e.g., Bergman & Drasgow, 2003; USMBSP, 1988). Simply counting who is harassed by race/ethnicity is likely to ignore other more complex factors, such as the influence of cultural affiliation (e.g., Shupe, Cortina, Ramos, Fitzgerald, & Salisbury, 2002) or the interplay of multiple status identities with sexual and other forms of harassment (e.g., Berdahl & Moore, 2006). For example, Shupe and colleagues examined the rates of sexual harassment and degree of cultural affiliation to mainstream U.S. culture for three groups of women (Hispanic low cultural affiliation, Hispanic moderate cultural affiliation, non-Hispanic White) working in the same organization, and found that Hispanic women with low cultural affiliation reported far fewer incidents of sexual harassment than did moderately acculturated Hispanic women or non-Hispanic White women, with the latter reporting the most harassment. These findings suggest that the frequency of sexual harassment may be moderated by more complex factors than ethnicity alone, and point to the need to consider culture and identity when examining women's experiences.

Antecedents and Causal Explanations for Harassment

In 1987, Betz and Fitzgerald noted that our theoretical understanding of sexual harassment was underdeveloped and that the literature on sexual harassment included "more data than theory" (p. 245). Twenty-five years later, this characterization still holds true, despite a wider array of theoretical offerings. Tests of existing theories have been few, and the reasons for this are many, including the difficulty of gaining access to organizations that allow research on harassment, the fact that some of the broader-based theories (e.g., biological or evolutionary explanations) do not lend themselves to testing, and the ethical considerations of studying harassment in a lab setting (Berdahl & Raver, 2010).

Theories about sexual harassment have been broadly characterized in various ways, including those with biological, organizational, sociocultural, and social psychological assumptions (e.g., Berdahl & Raver, 2010; Betz & Fitzgerald, 1987). In actuality, many of the theories contain elements of more than one characterization. Biological or natural theories of sexual harassment arise from the belief that sexual harassment is a "natural" behavior based on libido and attraction, typically targeted toward women by men (e.g., Tangri, Burt, & Johnson, 1982). However, this perspective has not received support in the research literature (Berdahl, 2007b). For example, when considering harassment by type, hostile behaviors (gender harassment) are far more common than harassment based on sexual attention or sexual coercion (e.g., see Berdahl, 2007a, for a recent critique of the biological theory). Other explanations that contain underlying biological assumptions include mechanisms such as sex-role spillover (e.g., expectations for women workers, or their work, based on socially ascribed gender roles; Gutek & Morasch, 1982), the power of the harasser (e.g., harassment arises in situations of unequal power; Bargh, Raymond, Pryor, & Strack, 1995; Farley, 1978; MacKinnon, 1979), and the contact hypothesis (e.g., harassment as a function of the amount of contact with individuals of another gender; Gutek, Cohen, & Konrad, 1990).

Of those explanations that are considered organizational, Fitzgerald and colleagues' integrated model of sexual harassment (Fitzgerald, Hulin, & Drasgow, 1994; Fitzgerald, Drasgow, et al., 1997; Hesson-McInnis & Fitzgerald, 1997) has been influential in explaining the antecedents of sexual harassment. In this model, sexual harassment is considered to be a function of organizational and group processes, in that it is theorized to arise from employee perceptions that management tolerates the harassment of employees (i.e., organizational climate; Hulin, Fitzgerald, & Drasgow, 1996), and the job-gender context of one's workgroup, which refers to the degree to which one's job context is considered gender-traditional (e.g., the sex ratio of one's immediate workgroup, the sex of one's supervisor, or the degree to which one's job or occupation has traditionally been held by men or women; Fitzgerald, Drasgow, & Magley, 1999). Individual studies (e.g., Glomb, Munson, Hulin, Bergman, & Drasgow, 1999) and meta-analytic research (Willness et al., 2007) provide strong support for the relationship between perceptions of organizational climate and incident rates of sexual harassment, and moderate support for job-gender context as an antecedent of sexual harassment. Related research on organizational practices finds that perceptions of organizational leaders who do *not* take action in response to sexual harassment (e.g., do not investigate complaints, enforce existing policy, or provide penalties to harassers) are associated with increased incidence of harassment (Williams, Fitzgerald, & Drasgow, 1999). Interestingly, this same study demonstrated that training about harassment and organizational resources for targets of harassment did not add much explanatory power in predicting the incidence of harassment beyond leadership actions.

Sociocultural/sociological explanations suggest that sexual harassment arises from sexual hostility, which results from a gendered hierarchy. Fiske and Glick (1995) utilize theory about ambivalent sexism and gender stereotypes to explain different types of sexual harassment (e.g., gender harassment, unwanted sexual attention) and suggest that harassment arises from different motivations (e.g., paternalism, gender differentiation, heterosexual attraction) on the part of the harasser. For example, hostile harassment (similar to gender harassment) is thought to arise from hostile sexists beliefs, whereas earnest harassment (similar to unwanted sexual attention) is considered to originate from benevolent sexist beliefs about intimacy seeking (Fiske & Glick, 1995).

Finally, theories that can be considered as arising from the social psychology literature include Berdahl's (2007a) recent explanation for sexual harassment, which conceptualizes sexual harassment as sex-based behavior that is motivated to protect or enhance the social status of the harasser (male or female) when that status is threatened. Such behavior is located within the context of a socially gendered hierarchy, with men having higher social status than women. Thus, Berdahl's theory emphasizes the social environment in which the harassment takes place. Research on Berdahl's propositions supports that women within socially gendered organizations who do not conform to the gender hierarchy (e.g., assertive women) are more often harassed (Berdahl, 2007b).

Sexual Harassment and Other Forms of Workplace Deviance

Although research on sexual harassment has flourished for several decades, only recently has the literature begun to examine the construct of sexual harassment within the larger nomological net of workplace deviance (O'Leary-Kelly et al., 2009). Specifically, recent work has investigated the relationship of sexual harassment with *broader* constructs such as workplace aggression (Hershcovis & Barling, 2010), incivility (Lim & Cortina, 2005), bullying (Crawford, 1997; Martin, 2008), and generalized workplace harassment (Rospenda & Richman, 2004; Rospenda, Richman, Ehmke, & Zlatoper, 2005; Rospenda, Richman, & Shannon, 2006; Shannon, Rospenda, & Richman, 2007). Similarly, recent literature has also examined the relationship of sexual harassment with other *specific* types of harassment/deviance, including racial/ethnic harassment (Berdahl & Moore, 2006; Buchanan & Fitzgerald, 2008; Raver & Nishii, 2010), heterosexist harassment (Konik & Cortina, 2008), racialized sexual harassment (Woods, Buchanan, & Settles, 2009), sexual assault (Harned, Ormerod, Palmieri, Collinsworth, & Reed, 2002), and stalking (Martin, 2008; Schell, 2003). Across studies, there tend to be positive relationships between sexual harassment and other broad and specific workplace deviance behaviors, suggesting that sexual harassment may co-occur with other forms of workplace deviance.

Several scholars have elaborated on the theoretical backdrop for the co-occurrence of sexual harassment with other forms of deviant behaviors. Berdahl's (2007a) theory of sex-based harassment, for example, suggests that the desire to protect one's social status when it is threatened is a common motive that underlies *all* types of harassment. Based on this theory, one might expect that when an individual's social status is threatened, he or she may respond with any form of deviant behavior that does not necessarily correspond to the type of social status that has been threatened. For example, if a man has been denied a promotion and discovers that an equally qualified woman received the promotion, he may feel his sex-based status has been threatened; however, he may retaliate by making jokes about the promoted woman's sex (i.e., sexual harassment), or about the woman's weight, religion, sexual orientation, and so on. That is, a threat to one's social status does not necessitate a response with in-kind deviance behaviors. This may result in perpetrators responding to status threats with multiple acts of deviance, thereby increasing the co-occurrence of the deviant acts.

Others have pointed to organizational climate as the antecedent to the co-occurrence of deviant behaviors (e.g., Raver & Nishii, 2010). Hulin et al. (1996) theorized that harassment is "a manifestation of an organizational culture that permits dominance of certain groups of employees over other groups" (p. 133). Therefore, if one group is dominant over another, any form or combination of deviant behaviors is likely to occur to support the exertion of dominance (i.e., the dominant group may exercise its dominance through a combination of sexual harassment, racial harassment, generalized workplace harassment, and so on, rather than promoting one deviant behavior in particular). Again, this type of organizational climate would promote the co-occurrence of workplace deviance behaviors.

Finally, the co-occurrence of sexual harassment with other types of deviant behavior in the workplace may be due to a characteristic or set of characteristics of the victim that predisposes him or her toward the experience of multiple deviant behaviors. Negative affect of the victim has been proposed as a type of personal characteristic that may explain why some individuals experience multiple types of deviant behaviors (Raver & Nishii, 2010). It is also possible that the routine characteristics of an individual's workplace may predispose him or her toward the experience of multiple deviant behaviors, such as a workplace where one interacts with the public often, or very large workplaces (De Coster, Estes, & Mueller, 1999).

Thus, recent theoretical and empirical work has begun to incorporate sexual harassment into the literature on other types of workplace deviance. To illustrate the relationship between sexual harassment and another form of workplace deviance, we have quantitatively summarized the current state of this literature by conducting a small-scale meta-analysis on the relationship between sexual harassment and racial harassment. We focused on this specific relationship because of the recent increase in research examining this relationship and because a quantitative summary of this literature may serve to inform future investigations of sexual harassment with other specific types harassment or broader forms of workplace deviance. Moreover, recent theory on this relationship has emphasized the need to integrate the literatures on sexual and racial harassment because the dissociation of race and gender experiences of workers is not true to the actual experience of the worker (Buchanan & Ormerod, 2002; Woods et al., 2009; Yoder & Aniakudo, 1996).

To calculate the meta-analytic relationship between sexual harassment and racial harassment, we began by searching the American Psychological Association's PsycINFO (1887–2010), Google Scholar, and Dissertation Abstracts International (1861–2010) for the following keywords (and variations thereof): *sexual harassment, sexual discrimination, sexism, gender harassment, gender discrimination, racial harassment, racial discrimination, racism, ethnic harassment,* and *ethnic discrimination.* References of the available studies were searched, and several authors were contacted for unpublished work. The search identified 57 studies that were then examined for their correspondence with several inclusion criteria. First, the study had to provide an effect size for the relationship between sexual harassment or discrimination and racial/ethnic harassment or discrimination.[4] Second, the sample had to consist of employed individuals. Third, the sample had to consist of adult participants (over age 16) and report the sample size. The inclusion criteria resulted in a final database of 20 samples with a total sample size of 9,135. This final database included one unpublished data set (Ormerod, 2004) of 1,259 participants (1,125 women, 134 men) who worked in diverse occupations and organizations. In this sample, sexual harassment was measured with the Sexual Experiences Questionnaire (Fitzgerald, Gelfand, et al., 1995; Fitzgerald, Shullman, et al., 1988) and racial/ethnic harassment with the Racial Experiences Questionnaire (Ormerod, 1999).

Results of the meta-analysis are displayed in table 15.1. Results show a moderately strong correlation between sexual harassment and racial harassment (ρ = .37, CI [.29, .45]), indicating individuals who experience sexual harassment also tend to experience racial harassment. We examined sex and race as moderators, although neither appeared to moderate the relationship between sexual and racial harassment (as evidenced by overlapping confidence intervals).

These results indicate that sexual and racial harassment tend to co-occur, and that the co-occurrence is not necessarily greater in women or racial/ethnic minorities. These findings suggest that sexual and

Table 15.1. Meta-Analytic Results of the Relationship between Sexual Harassment and Racial Harassment

						95% Conf. Int.		95% Cred. Int.	
	k	*N*	*r*	ρ	*SD*ρ	*LL*	*UL*	*LL*	*UL*
Overall Relationship	20	9135	.34	.37	.15	.29	.45	.08	.67
Women	10	4055	.32	.36	.16	.25	.48	.05	.68
Men	6	936	.33	.36	.25	.14	.58	–.13	.85
Non-Hispanic Whites	7	2888	.28	.31	.09	.21	.40	.12	.49
Racial/Ethnic Minorities	12	1984	.40	.43	.20	.31	.55	.03	.83

Note: k = number of effect sizes in the meta-analysis; *N* = total sample size in the meta-analysis; *r* = sample-size weighted mean correlation; ρ = correlation corrected for attenuation in the predictor and criterion; SD%= standard deviation of corrected correlation; 95% Conf Int. = 95% confidence interval; 95% Cred. Int. = 95% credibility interval; *LL* = lower limit; *UL* = upper limit.

racial experiences cannot be disentangled without losing information that is critical to the experience of mistreatment in the workplace (e.g., Moradi & Subich, 2003), and that future examinations of sexual harassment would benefit from measuring additional types of harassment to better understand the full spectrum of deviant behavior directed toward a target. Finally, future research in this area would benefit from meta-analytically summarizing the relationship among all types of harassment and deviant behavior to investigate whether *all* types of deviant behaviors tend to co-occur (i.e., whether a broad harassment/deviance factor exists that represents the shared variance among all specific types of harassment).

Outcomes of Sexual Harassment

The organizational or integrated model of sexual harassment (Fitzgerald, Drasgow, et al., 1997; Fitzgerald, Hulin, et al., 1994) summarizes those organizational factors thought to contribute to the frequency of sexual harassment and outcomes for targets of harassment. Described in part earlier, the frequency of sexual harassment is considered to be a function of one's organizational climate and the gendered nature of one's workgroup and job duties. Organizational climate is also posited to have a direct influence on outcomes, such that perceptions that one's organization is more tolerant or accepting of sexual harassment is considered to be associated with less satisfaction with one's job, coworkers, and supervisor, and ultimately organizational withdrawal (e.g., lateness, turnover) and reduced organizational commitment. The frequency of sexual harassment is conceptualized to be associated directly and indirectly with harm to one's job, psychological well-being, and health. Psychological well-being is also conceived of as mediating the relationship between harassment and health. In addition, the integrated model proposes that the effects of harassment are moderated by an individual's personal vulnerability and coping response (Fitzgerald, Drasgow, et al., 1997). Meta-analytic research provides support for the integrated model of sexual harassment (Chan et al., 2008; Willness et al., 2007) and tests of moderation suggest that younger workers may be more vulnerable than older workers and that the direct query approach has a weaker association between harassment and job satisfaction (Chan et al., 2008). Furthermore, the integrated model has been found to apply equally well across racial/ethnic groups (Bergman & Drasgow, 2003), culture (Wasti, Bergman, Glomb, & Drasgow, 2000), and gender (Chan et al., 2008).[5]

There is a large body of research that links sexual harassment to job-related, psychological, and physical health-related harm for the target of harassment. Although much of this research is cross-sectional (e.g., Fitzgerald, Drasgow, et al., 1997), meta-analytic studies (e.g., Willness et al., 2007) provide support for those relationships found across studies, and longitudinal research suggests that there is a causal relationship between harassment and outcomes (e.g., Sims, Drasgow, & Fitzgerald, 2005). Harassment is associated with job attitudes such as decreased overall job satisfaction (Chan et al., 2008; Lapierre, Spector, & Leck, 2005; Willness et al., 2007), decreased satisfaction with coworkers, supervisors, and one's work (Willness et al., 2007), and decreased psychological attachment to one's organization or organizational commitment (Chan et al., 2008; Willness et al., 2007). Job-related behaviors such as withdrawal from work (e.g., avoiding work tasks or work) or one's job (e.g., turnover) are associated with harassment (Chan et al., 2008), as is decreased work productivity (Fitzgerald, Drasgow, et al., 1999; Schneider, Swan, & Fitzgerald, 1997). Providing particularly strong support for the harmful effect of sexual harassment on women's jobs and careers, a longitudinal study found that harassment had direct and indirect (as mediated by job attitudes and satisfaction) influences on actual job turnover in a sample of military women (Sims et al., 2005).

Harassment is also related to poorer physical and psychological health. It has been associated with increases in physical health symptoms and conditions (Chan et al., 2008; Willness et al., 2007), such as headaches and nausea (e.g., Magley et al., 1999), changes in cardiovascular reactivity (Schneider, Tomaka, & Palacios, 2001), and decreased satisfaction with one's health (Chan et al., 2008). Harassment is also linked to problem drinking in both cross-sectional and longitudinal studies (e.g., Freels, Richman, & Rospenda, 2005; Richman et al., 1999). The psychological correlates of sexual harassment include increased symptoms of psychological distress (Chan et al., 2008; Willness et al., 2007) such as post-traumatic stress, depression, and anxiety (e.g., Dansky & Kilpatrick, 1997; Fitzgerald, Drasgow, et al., 1997; Glomb et al., 1999; Vogt, Pless, King, & King, 2005), and decreased psychological well-being (Chan et al., 2008; Willness et al., 2007) such as lowered self-esteem (e.g., Harned & Fitzgerald, 2002) and satisfaction with life (e.g., Lim & Cortina, 2005). Longitudinal research suggests that the effects of harassment (psychological, health, work) persist over time (Glomb et al., 1999; Rospenda et al., 2005), and that harassment at an earlier time point predicts self-reported use of services (mental health, health) at a later time point (Rospenda, 2002; Rospenda et al., 2006).

Organizational outcomes of sexual harassment have been less researched, with several studies attempting to determine the monetary costs of harassment to a particular organization (e.g., USMSPB, 1981, 1988). Faley, Knapp, Kustis, and Dubois (1999) provided a costing model of harassment that summarized costs as productivity (e.g., increased job and work withdrawal due to the harassment), administrative (e.g., costs associated with loss of workers such as hiring and training new workers), and other costs associated with handling a harassment complaint or those related to providing services (e.g., medical, counseling) for the victim. Taking a conservative approach, they estimated that for one year (using 1994 dollars) sexual harassment would cost the U.S. Army in excess of $250 million (Faley et al., 1999). The USMSPB extrapolated the annual cost of sexual harassment, based on surveys of the federal workforce in 1981 and 1988, to be $188.7 million and $267.3 million, respectively (USMSPB, 1981, 1988).

Individual Responses to Sexual Harassment

Research on responses to sexual harassment has focused on individual responses particularly studies categorizing the type and frequency of coping responses (e.g., Gruber & Bjorn, 1986) and the determinants of coping (e.g., Knapp, Faley, Ekeberg, & DuBois, 1997). Various theoretical frameworks to describe the structure and determinants of coping with sexual harassment have been proposed, with current findings supporting that the structure of coping is multidimensional and the process of employing a coping response is complex and multidetermined (e.g., Knapp et al; Magley, 2002; Wasti & Cortina, 2002).[6] Older conceptualizations of coping that categorized each type of coping response by its degree of assertiveness or effectiveness (e.g., Gruber & Bjorn, 1986) have been critiqued as inherently biased toward certain types of coping (e.g., reporting or asserting) as most appropriate in harassing situations (Fitzgerald, Swan, & Fischer, 1995; Magley, 2002).

At the broadest level, the structure of coping can be classified as emotion-focused (internal) or problem-focused (external; Fitzgerald, 1990; Schneider et al., 1997). *Emotion-focused* responses are strategies that attempt to manage the thoughts and feelings that arise in response to harassing behavior and include minimizing or enduring the harassment, denial, detachment, reattribution (e.g., assuming the harasser meant well), and self-blame (also called illusory control). *Problem-focused* responses are strategies that attempt to deal with the harassing behavior and include seeking institutional or organizational relief (e.g., reporting), assertive or confrontational responses (e.g., asking the initiator of the harassment to stop), seeking social support (e.g., talking with supportive others), avoiding the harasser, and attempting to appease the harasser (e.g., making up an excuse to be left alone). The internal-external conceptualization draws on Lazarus and Folkman's (1984) stress and coping framework and suggests that responses to sexual harassment are attempts to manage a stressor that include primary appraisals (e.g., the target's emotional assessment about the harmfulness or threat to personal well-being) of the harassing situation and secondary appraisals about how to respond. Casting coping with harassment into a stress and coping framework allows coping response to be conceptualized as an ongoing process that is multidetermined by the circumstances (e.g., individual resources, primary appraisal, personal and organizational limitations) of the situation (Fitzgerald, Swan, et al., 1995).

Beyond classifying coping responses, Fitzgerald and colleagues (Fitzgerald, Swan, et al., 1997) described the determinants of coping in a framework called the Model of Harm. The Model of Harm conceptualizes coping as an interactive process between person and environment for the purpose of managing a stressor and, as described above, is grounded in the stress and coping literature. According to the Model of Harm, coping response is considered to be multidetermined by *stimulus* factors (objective aspects of the harassing behavior, such as the frequency, duration, and intensity or severity of the harassment), *context* factors (the organizational context within which the harassing behavior occurs such as climate, management norms, whether other types of harassment are present, gender context of the job), and *individual* factors or characteristics of the target (e.g., victimization history, resources, attributions). These three factors are thought to influence primary appraisals about the harassment and the coping response. Coping (along with the objective and context factors) is in turn believed to influence outcomes.

Another major framework for classifying coping responses is that of Knapp and colleagues (1997) who incorporated Gruber's (1989) categories of coping with a 2 x 2 typology (focus of coping response—the self or harasser, and mode of coping response—self-response or use of outside resources) suggested by Gutek and Koss (1993). This typology attempts to account for coping with harassment by classifying responses and describing their effectiveness based on the quadrant in which they fall. The quadrants are described as *avoidance/denial* (self-focus, self-response; for example, ignore, go along with, treat it like a joke, quit or transfer, do nothing), *social coping* (self-focus, supported response; for example, seeking support from peers, friends, family, or health care professionals), *confrontation/negotiation* (harasser focus, self-response; for example, asking or telling the harasser to stop or threatening the harasser), and *advocacy seeking* (harasser focus, supported response; for example, reporting the harassment, taking legal action, asking someone else to tell the harasser to stop). Empirical research suggests support for Fitzgerald et al.'s internal-external framework as a higher order conceptualization of coping behavior (Magley, 2002) and Knapp et al.'s typology (Malamut & Offermann, 2001; Wasti & Cortina, 2002).[7]

Knapp et al. (1997) also advanced a model to explain the determinants of coping, based on findings from the whistle-blowing, stress and coping, and sexual harassment literatures. Four elements were proposed to influence coping response to sexual harassment: the characteristics of the *reporting process* (e.g., perceptions about one's organizational policies and procedures related to sexual harassment); the target's *expectations about the outcome* of the response; the *severity* of the harassment; and the target's level of psychological or somatic *distress,* given the harassment. This model also described the antecedents of outcome expectancies (individual, workgroup, and organizational characteristics; organizational power of the target; macro-level legal and economic context) and the severity of the harassment. Coping response is conceptualized as leading to outcome, and there is a reciprocal loop between outcomes (positive or negative) and future expectations and distress.

Empirical research on coping (including those studies stemming from the Model of Harm and Knapp et al.'s model) has revealed a complex set of relationships among coping responses, determinants, and outcomes (e.g., Bergman, Langhout, Palmieri, Cortina, & Fitzgerald, 2002; Collinsworth, Fitzgerald, & Drasgow, 2009; Cochran, Frazier, & Olson, 1997; Cortina & Wasti, 2005; Malamut & Offermann, 2001; Wasti & Cortina, 2002; Wright & Fitzgerald, 2009).[8] Targets of harassment typically utilize multiple forms of coping (e.g., Cortina & Wasti, 2005; Magley, 2002; Malamut & Offermann, 2001), but the most common forms are those that involve avoidance, minimization, and putting up with the harassment, whereas least common are self-blame, confrontation, and seeking organizational relief (Fitzgerald, Swan, et al., 1995; Magley, 2002; Schneider et al., 1997; USMSPB, 1981, 1995).

Coping response may be differentially influenced by a number of personal and environmental determinants (Malamut & Offermann, 2001). Although there have been theoretical and empirical advancements, and some consistent findings across studies, no systematic program of research for studying coping has yet emerged. One finding that is fairly consistent across studies is that primary or subjective appraisals appear to fully or partially mediate many of the proposed determinants of coping (e.g., occupational status, climate, gender, power differences between the target and harasser, frequency and duration of harassment) and many, but not all, coping strategies (e.g., appraisals did not mediate determinants and avoidance-denial responses; Malamut & Offermann).

It is also important to consider the outcomes of coping response. Reporting, one of the least common coping strategies in response to harassment (USMSPB, 1981), has received far more attention than other forms of coping (e.g., Fitzgerald, Swan et al., 1995). Despite being the focus of organizational policy recommendations, reporting is not necessarily associated with a cessation of harassment or positive outcomes. Research links reporting sexual harassment with retaliation, decreased job satisfaction, and increased distress (Bergman et al., 2002; Hesson-McInnis & Fitzgerald, 1997). Not surprisingly, fear of retaliation from the harasser or the organization is a commonly cited reason for why individuals do not formally or informally report harassment or confront the harasser (Fitzgerald, Swan, et al., 1995; Gutek & Koss, 1993). Similarly, assertion or confronting the harasser has been linked to negative psychological and work-related outcomes for sexually harassed women (Hesson-McInnis & Fitzgerald, 1997; Stockdale, 1998).

In sum, understanding the process and correlates of coping with sexual harassment is important for those who work with targets of harassment. It is critical for psychologists, courts, and organizational leaders to keep in mind that filing a formal report is not the normative response to harassment, that emotion-focused responses are the most common type of response, and that one individual might employ a variety of responses over the course of a harassing situation. Further, such responses are multi-determined by a complex set of person and situational factors, and the outcome to the target from asserting or reporting may include actions that are not necessarily positive. Put another way, current research supports that there is no correct choice for coping strategy in response to every sexual harassment situation.

Sexual Harassment Prevention, Intervention, and Future Directions

The empirical literature on remedies for sexual harassment in the workplace is somewhat sparse. However, it should be clear from our review of antecedents and causes that leadership behavior is a key component in preventing harassment (e.g., Williams et al., 1999). Organizational leaders are in positions to create organizational climates where harassing behaviors are considered unacceptable in the workplace, to address such behaviors when they occur, and to offer resources for the targets of harassment. Policy and training related to sexual harassment are necessary for establishing an ethical organizational climate, but are insufficient on their own to prevent harassing behavior (Williams et al., 1999). It is critical that policy be supported by the behavior of organizational leaders to prevent harassment (Offermann & Malamut, 2002). Research suggests that when leaders are perceived as willing to prevent harassment and to sanction harassers, incidences are lower, targets feel safer to report harassing behavior, and work-related outcomes are more positive (Offermann & Malamut, 2002; Williams et al., 1999).

Leaders are also in positions to create gender balance in the workplace and to reduce stereotyping based on gender, race/ethnicity, and other social identities. Consistent with empirical findings and a feminist multicultural perspective, creating work environments that have gender balance (e.g., relative number of women and men in workgroups and positions of power and leadership) should be associated with reductions in sexually harassing behavior (e.g., Fiske & Glick, 1995; Willness et al., 2007). Fiske and Glick (1995) offer concrete suggestions for reducing masculine culture and power asymmetries, such as the use of language that does not evoke gender-associated characteristics, minimizing sexual joking, and emphasizing interdependence and accountability. Following from her theory of sex-based harassment, Berdahl supports similar recommendations for reducing harassment, along with creating work environments that value interpersonal cooperation rather than competition and that reduce social hierarchy, particularly hierarchy based on gender (Berdahl & Raver, 2010).

The literature on sexual harassment is also lacking in research on interventions for the targets of harassment. Several authors have suggested the utility of applying an ecological model to counseling targets of harassment (e.g., Perrone, 2002). Cook, Heppner, and O'Brien (2002) present an ecological model of career counseling focused on women of color and White women that takes into account the context of an individual's experiences and behavior by considering the dynamic interplay among the various systems within which a person interacts (e.g., microsystems, macrosystems). Cortina and Wasti (2005) apply an ecological model to better understand the determinants of coping with sexual harassment from a person-centered perspective. Their findings support that the determinants of coping come from various system levels, but that cultural affiliation (macrocontext) and the severity of the harassment (microcontext) are among the strongest predictors of coping (Cortina &Wasti). The ecological model offers a promising direction to pursue for developing feminist multicultural interventions for targets of harassment.

As demonstrated in our time line of sexual harassment measurement, the literature on sexual harassment has grown since its beginnings and will likely continue to expand. There is still much to understand about sexual harassment, and the literature is in need of systematic research that addresses underrepresented areas (e.g., theory, prevention and intervention, multiple forms of workplace deviance, culture and harassment) and that integrates findings within some of the more established areas, such as the literature on individual coping. Methodologically, cross-sectional designs and convenience samples are overrepresented in the sexual harassment literature, as are analog designs. Studies that incorporate more sophisticated methods and designs are needed to advance the literature. For example, research that utilizes prospective designs can answer causal questions about the effects of sexual harassment and would allow a longitudinal examination of the effects of harassment on women's career development. Multilevel designs can be useful for understanding how harassment occurs at various levels within the workplace (e.g., individual, workgroup, organizational; Raver & Gelfand, 2005). Research that includes diverse nationally representative samples of working women and men can inform incidence and prevalence of sexual harassment.

It would also be valuable to examine sexual harassment within the context of research on interpersonal violence, trauma, and recovery. For example, research suggests that sexual harassment co-occurs with other forms of interpersonal violence, such as sexual assault (e.g., Harned et al., 2002; Sadler, Booth, Cook, & Doebbeling, 2003) and has begun to examine the effects of multiple forms of victimization (e.g., Campbell, Greeson, Bybee, & Raja, 2008). Given that sexual harassment is so ubiquitous in the workplace, and that a harassing event is likely to take place over time, understanding those factors that both exacerbate and reduce harm, particularly within the context of multiple forms of interpersonal violence, is a critically important topic for research. As our meta-analysis earlier in this chapter highlighted, it is important to consider the "intersectionality" of multiple experiences such as gender and racial/ethnic discrimination, particularly for racial/ethnic minority individuals (e.g., Moradi & Subich, 2003, p. 463). Counseling psychologists may be particularly well positioned to examine sexual harassment from career development and intervention perspectives, and to contribute to our understanding of this phenomenon from feminist multicultural standpoints.

Moving Toward Healthy and Affirmative Organizational Environments: Conclusion and Future Directions

Navigating the work-life interface and the experiences of sexual harassment at work are sources of workplace stress that can act as barriers to women's career advancement and satisfaction. Although these barriers likely differ in impact and scope, there are striking similarities between the affective, psychological, physical, and organizational outcomes when work-life conflict and sexual harassment are encountered. Both can result in psychological symptoms and problematic health concerns and can have a negative effect on job and life satisfaction (Bergman, 2003). The process by which this can occur was examined in a study of women in a male-dominated workplace. Findings indicated that both gender harassment and family-to-work conflict were related to overperformance demands or "an individual's perception that they need to overperform to gain acceptance and recognition within the workplace" (Parker & Griffin, 2002, p. 1996). Overperformance demands were then directly related to psychological distress (as was family-to-work conflict), and gender harassment had a mediated relationship with distress through overperformance demands (Parker & Griffin, 2002). It is not only discrimination based on gender that affects overperformance demands at work. Research with African American nurses suggests that overperformance demands can be a response to racial discrimination in the workplace (Gipson-Jones, 2009). These findings have important implications for psychologists and other practitioners in understanding the ways in which individuals respond to discrimination and family-to-work conflict. The findings also have implications about the process and effects of gender and racial/ethnic discrimination in the workplace and can be useful for psychologists who engage in consultation with organizations (Parker & Griffin, 2002).

Negative effects can also extend beyond the individual. For example, research on ambient sexual harassment demonstrates that others in the immediate work environment (e.g., coworkers) experience decrements in job satisfaction and increased psychological distress from indirect exposure to sexual harassment (Glomb et al., 1997). As seen in the section on work-life interface, one's personal relationships outside work can be affected by experiences encountered at work. Although it is reasonable to assume that harassment at work would affect relationships outside of work, research connecting sexual harassment to work-life issues is quite sparse. However, one study addressed the cross-over effects of workplace aggression (including sexual harassment) on one's partner and found that job stress as a result of workplace aggression crosses over from the target to the target's partner (Haines et al., 2006). These findings imply that interventions aimed at victims of workplace aggression and harassment should also consider the effects on the victim's partner and immediate family.

Research findings also suggest that the work-life interface and sexual harassment may intersect at the level of organizational culture or climate. For example, employees who perceive that management supports work-life balance policy report less observed harassment of others at work, perhaps because a workplace culture that values work-life balance is also intolerant of sexual harassment (Timmerman & Bajema, 2000). This finding is intriguing because it suggests that studying various work environments for those factors that both inhibit harassment and create perceptions of positive management support would be a productive direction for researchers (Timmerman & Bajema, 2000).

We take the perspective that although individuals are directly affected by sexual harassment and work-life issues, response to these challenges at the level of the individual is not sufficient for prevention, particularly in the context of an unsupportive organization. Organizations must take an active role in creating cultures where employees have safe and supportive workplaces in which to be productive. Thus, we suggest that workplace issues and challenges (e.g., work-life demands, sexual harassment) are best conceptualized and studied from a multilevel perspective that includes not only individual level variables but those that are able to account for environmental influences and processes. We also suggest that it would be useful to study healthy, affirmative workplaces to better understand those factors that create such environments. For example, distal or overarching factors such as a culture of cooperation or a strong positive sense of work community may contribute to creating workplaces both low in harassment and high in facilitating an effective work-life interface.

It is clear that organizations have much to gain by facilitating an effective interface between work and life roles and taking active steps to create a workplace free of harassing behavior. As this chapter suggests, such a stance is congruent with a feminist multicultural perspective in its assertion of the importance of sociocultural contextual factors and its emphasis on an adaptive, empowering approach that fosters the ability of all individuals to achieve their highest potential in the workplace.

Notes

1. We do not review the literature on perceptions of sexual harassment; see Rotundo, Nguyen, and Sackett (2001) for a meta-analytic study that reviews gender differences in perceptions of behaviors that constitute harassment.

2. The four factors correspond to the dimensions described earlier: sexist hostility, sexual hostility, unwanted sexual attention, and sexual coercion.

3. Percentages are from a study of military personnel, which are likely to be higher than those found in the civilian workforce.

4. In the case of one study (Wright & Fitzgerald, 2009) the effect size for the measure of sexual harassment and racial/ethnic harassment (as measured by the Racial Experiences Questionnaire, Ormerod, 1999) was provided with permission from the second author.

5. When examining whether sex moderates the impact of harassment, there were no differences for women and men; however, fewer male samples were available for inclusion in the analyses, and the authors urged caution in interpreting the results (Chan et al., 2008).

6. Space precludes a comprehensive review of coping frameworks. Readers are referred to Magley (2002) and O'Leary-Kelly et al. (2009) for reviews.

7. For an exception, see Magley (2002), which did not find support for Knapp et al.'s (1997) coping typology, and presents an alternate multidimensional conceptualization of coping response.

8. Although we highlight some of the findings from studies of determinants, readers are referred to the original studies for further information.

References

*Indicates that the study was included in the meta-analysis

American Association of University Women Educational Foundation (2001). *Hostile hallways: Sexual harassment and bullying in schools.* Washington, DC: Harris/Scholastic Research.

Ammons, S. K., & Kelly, E. L. (2008). Social class and the experience of work-family conflict during the transition to adulthood.

New Directions for Child and Adolescent Development, 119, 71–84. doi:10.1002/cd.210

Anzaldua, G. (1987). *Borderlands: The new Mestiza.* San Francisco, CA: Aunt Lute Book Co.

Ashforth, B. E., Kreiner, G. E., & Fugate, M. (2000). All in a day's work: Boundaries and micro role transitions. *Academy of Management Review, 25,* 472–491. doi:10.5465/AMR.2000.3363315

*Avery, D. R., McKay, P. F., & Wilson, D. C. (2008). What are the odds: How demographic similarity affects the prevalence of perceived employment discrimination. *Journal of Applied Psychology, 93,* 235–249.

Badgett, M. L. (2008). Bringing all families to work today: Equality for gay and lesbian workers and families. In A. Marcus-Newhall, D. F. Halpern, & S. J. Tan (Eds.), *The changing realities of work and family* (pp. 140–154). Malden, MA: Blackwell Publishing Ltd.

Baltes, B. B., Clark, M. A., & Chakrabarti, M. (2010). Work-life balance: The roles of work-family conflict and work-family facilitation. In P. A. Linley & S. Harrington (Eds.), *Oxford handbook of positive psychology and work* (pp. 201–212). New York: Oxford University Press.

Bargh, J. A., Raymond, P., Pryor, J. B., &Strack, F. (1995). Attractiveness of the underling: An automatic power → sex association and its consequences for sexual harassment and aggression. *Journal of Personality and Social Psychology, 68,* 768–781. doi:10.1037/0022-3514.68.5.768

Barnett, R. C., & Hyde, J. S. (2001). Women, men, work, and family: An expansionist theory. *American Psychologist, 56,* 781–796. doi:10.1037/0003-066X.56.10.781

Beauregard, T. A., Ozbilgin, M., & Belle, M. P. (2009). Revisiting the social construction of family in the context of work. *Journal of Managerial Psychology, 24,* 46–65. doi:10.1108/02683940910922537

Berdahl, J. L., Magley, V. J., & Waldo, C. R. (1996). The sexual harassment of men: Exploring the concept with theory and data. *Psychology of Women Quarterly, 20,* 527–547.

*Berdahl, J. L., & Moore, C. (2006). Workplace harassment: Double jeopardy for minority women. *Journal of Applied Psychology, 91,* 426–436.

Berdahl, J. L. (2007a). Harassment based on sex: Protecting social status in the context of gender hierarchy. *Academy of Management Review, 32,* 641–658.

Berdahl, J. L. (2007b). The sexual harassment of uppity women. *Journal of Applied Psychology, 92,* 425–437.

Berdahl, J. L., & Raver, J. L. (2010). Sexual harassment. In S. Zedeck (Ed.), *APA handbook of industrial and organizational psychology* (Vol. 3, pp. 641–669). Washington, DC: APA.

Bergman, B. (2003). The validation of the Women Workplace Culture Questionnaire: Gender-related stress and health for Swedish working women. *Sex Roles, 49,* 287–297.

Bergman, M. E., Langhout, R. D., Palmieri, P. A., Cortina, L. M., & Fitzgerald, L. F. (2002). The (un)reasonableness of reporting: Antecedents and consequences of reporting sexual harassment. *The Journal of Applied Psychology, 87,* 230–242. doi:10.1037/0021-9010.87.2.230

Bergman, M. E., & Drasgow, F. (2003). Race as a moderator in a model of sexual harassment: An empirical test. *Journal of Occupational Health Psychology, 8,* 131–145.

Betz, N. E., & Fitzgerald, L. F. (1987). *The career psychology of women.* Orlando, FL: Academic Press.

Bowes-Sperry, L., & Tata, J. (1999). A multiperspective framework of sexual harassment: Reviewing two decades of research. In G. N. Powell (Ed.), *Handbook of gender and work* (pp. 263–280). Thousand Oaks, CA: Sage.

Buchanan, N.T., & Ormerod, A. J. (2002). Racialized sexual harassment in the lives of African American women. *Women and Therapy, 25,* 107–124.

Buchanan, N. T., & Fitzgerald, L. F. (2008). Effects of racial and sexual harassment on work and the psychological well-being of African American women. *Journal of Occupational Health Psychology, 13,* 137–151.

Burke, R. J., & Greenglass, E. (1987). Work and family. In C. L. Cooper & I. T. Robertson (Eds.), *International review of industrial and organizational psychology* (pp. 273–320). New York: Wiley.

Byron, K. (2005). A meta-analytic review of work-family conflict and its antecedents. *Journal of Vocational Behavior, 67,* 169–198. doi:10.1016/j.jvb.2004.08.009

Campbell, R., Greeson, M. R., Bybee, D., & Raja, S. (2008). The co-occurrence of childhood sexual abuse, adult sexual assault, intimate partner violence, and sexual harassment: A meditational model of posttraumatic stress disorder and physical health outcomes. *Journal of Consulting and Clinical Psychology, 76,* 194–207.

Casper, W. J., Weltman, D., & Kwesiga, E. (2007). Beyond family-friendly: The construct and measurement of singles-friendly work culture. *Journal of Vocational Behavior, 70,* 478–501. doi:10.1016/j.jvb.2007.01.001

Chan, D. K. S., Lam, C. B., Chow, S. Y., & Cheung, S. F. (2008). Examining the job-related, psychological, and physical outcomes of workplace sexual harassment: A meta-analytic review. *Psychology of Women Quarterly, 32,* 362–376.

Clark, S. C. (2000). Work/family border theory: A new theory of work/family balance. *Human Relations, 53,* 747–770. doi:10.1177/0018726700536001

Cochran, C., Frazier, P., & Olson, A. (1997). Predictors of responses to unwanted sexual attention. *Psychology of Women Quarterly, 21,* 207–226.

Collinsworth, L. L., Fitzgerald, L. F., & Drasgow, F. (2009). In harm's way: Factors related to psychological distress following sexual harassment. *Psychology of Women Quarterly, 33,* 475–490.

Cook, A., & Minnotte, K. L. (2008). Occupational and industry sex segregation and the work-family interface. *Sex Roles, 59,* 800–813. doi:10.1007/s11199-008-9484-5

Cook, E. P., Heppner, M. J., & O'Brien, K. M. (2002). Career development of women of color and White women: Assumptions, conceptualization and interventions from an ecological perspective. *Career Development Quarterly, 50,* 291–305.

Cortina, L. M., & Wasti, S. A. (2005). Profiles in coping: Responses to sexual harassment across persons, organizations, and cultures. *Journal of Applied Psychology, 90,* 182–192. doi:10.1037/0021-9010.90.1.182

Crawford, N. (1997). Bullying at work: A psychoanalytic perspective. *Journal of Community and Applied Psychology, 7,* 219–225.

Dansky, B. S., & Kilpatrick, D. G. (1997). Effects of sexual harassment. In W. O'Donohue (Ed.), *Sexual harassment: Theory, research, and treatment* (pp. 152–174). Needham Heights, MA: Allyn & Bacon.

Das, A. (2009). Sexual harassment at work in the United States. *Archives of Sexual Behavior, 38,* 909–921. doi:10.1007/s10508-008-9354-9

De Coster, S., Estes, S. B., & Mueller C. W. (1999). Routine activities and sexual harassment in the workplace. *Work and Occupations, 26,* 21–49.

Eby, L. T., Casper, W. J., Lockwood, A., Bordeaux, C., & Brinley, A. (2005). Work and family research in IO/OB: Content analysis and review of the literature (1980–2002). *Journal of Vocational Behavior, 66,* 124–197. doi:10.1016/j.jvb.2003.11.003

Eby, L. T., Maher, C. P., & Butts, M. M. (2010). The intersection of work and family life: The role of affect. *Annual Review of Psychology, 61,* 599–622. doi:10.1146/annurev.psych.093008.100422

Edlund, J. (2007). The work-family time squeeze: Conflicting demands of paid and unpaid work among working couples in 29 countries. *International Journal of Comparative Sociology, 48,* 451–480. doi:10.1177/0020715207083338

Edwards, J. R., & Rothbard, N. P. (2000). Mechanisms linking work and family: Clarifying the relationship between work and family constructs. *Academy of Management Review, 25,* 178–199. doi:10.5465/AMR.2000.2791609

Equal Employment Opportunity Commission. (1980). Guidelines on discrimination because of sex. (Sect 1604.11). *Federal Register, 45,* 74676–74677.

Equal Employment Opportunity Commission. (1993). Policy guidelines. 29 C.F.R. 1609.1, Washington DC: US Government Printing Office.

Equal Employment Opportunity Commission. (1997). Guidelines on discrimination because of sex 29 (Sect 1604.11) (b). *Federal Register, 62,* 12033–12051.

Faley, R. H., Knapp, D. E., Kustis, G. A., & Dubois, C. L. Z. (1999) Estimating the organizational costs of sexual harassment: The case of the U.S. Army. *Journal of Business and Psychology, 13,* 461–484. doi:10.10231/A:1022987119277

Family and Medical Leave Act of 1993. (1993). Pub. L. No. 103–3, 29 U.S.C. § 2601.

Family and Medical Leave Act of 1993 (2011). *Administrator's Interpretation* (No. 2010–2013). Retrieved January 7, 2011, from http://www.dol.gov/WHD/opinion/adminIntrprtn/FMLA/2011/FMLAAI2010_3.htm.

Farley, L. (1978). *Sexual shakedown: The sexual harassment of women on the job.* New York: Warner Books.

Fassinger, R. E. (2000). Gender and sexuality in human development: Implications for prevention and advocacy in counseling psychology. In S. D. Brown & R. W. Lent (Eds.), *Handbook of counseling psychology* (3rd ed.) (pp. 346–378). New York: Wiley.

Fisher, G. G., Bulger, C. A., & Smith, C. S. (2009). Beyond work and family: A measure of work/nonwork interference and enhancement. *Journal of Occupational Health Psychology, 14,* 441–456. doi:10.1037/a0016737

Fiske, S. T., & Glick, P. (1995). Ambivalence and stereotypes cause sexual harassment: A theory with implications for organizational change. *Journal of Social Issues, 51,* 97–115.

Fitzgerald, L. F., Shullman, S. L., Bailey, N., Richards, M., Swecker, J., Gold, Y., Ormerod, A. J., & Weitzman, L. (1988). The incidence and dimensions of sexual harassment in academia and the workplace. *Journal of Vocational Behavior, 32,* 152–175. doi:10.1016/0001-8791(88)90012-7

Fitzgerald, L. F. (March, 1990). *Assessing strategies for coping with sexual harassment: A theoretical/empirical approach.* Paper presented at the annual meeting of the Association for Women in Psychology, Tempe, AZ.

Fitzgerald, L. F., Hulin, C. L., & Drasgow, F. (1994). The antecedents and consequences of sexual harassment in organizations: An integrated model. In G. P. Keita & J. J. Hurrell, Jr. (Eds.), *Job stress in a changing workforce: Investigating gender, diversity and family issues* (pp. 55–73). Washington, DC: American Psychological Association.

Fitzgerald, L. F., Gelfand, M. J., &Drasgow, F. (1995). Measuring sexual harassment: Theoretical and psychometric advances. *Basic and Applied Social Psychology, 17,* 425–445. doi:10.1207/sl5324834baspl704_2

Fitzgerald, L. F., Swan, S., & Fischer, K. (1995). Why didn't she just report him?: The psychological and legal implications of women's strategies for responding to sexual harassment. *Journal of Social Issues, 51,* 117–138.

Fitzgerald, L. F., Drasgow, F., Hulin, C. L., Gelfand, M. J., & Magley, V. J. (1997). The antecedents and consequences of sexual harassment in organizations: A test of an integrated model. *Journal of Applied Psychology, 82,* 578–589. doi:10.1037/0021-9010.82.4.578

Fitzgerald, L. F., Swan, S., & Magley, V. J. (1997). But was it really sexual harassment? Legal, behavioral, and psychological definitions of the workplace victimization of women. In W. O'Donohue (Ed.), *Sexual harassment: Theory, research, treatment* (pp. 5–28). Boston, MA: Allyn & Bacon.

Fitzgerald, L. F., Drasgow, F., & Magley, V. J. (1999). Sexual harassment in the armed forces: A test of an integrated model. *Military Psychology, 11,* 329–343.

Fitzgerald, L. F., Magley, V. J., Drasgow, F., & Waldo, C. R., (1999). Measuring sexual harassment in the military: The Sexual Experiences Questionnaire (SEQ-DoD). *Military Psychology, 11,* 243–263.

Freels, S. A., Richman, J. A., Rospenda, K. M. (2005). Gender differences in the causal direction between workplace harassment and drinking. *Addictive Behaviors, 30,* 1454–1458. doi:10.1016/j.addbeh.2005.01.014

Frone, M. R., Yardley, J. K., & Markel, K. (1997). Developing and testing an integrative model of the work-family interface. *Journal of Vocational Behavior, 50,* 145–167.

Frone, M. R. (2003). Work–family balance. In J. C. Quick & L. E. Tetrick (Eds.), *Handbook of occupational health psychology* (pp. 143–162). Washington, DC: American Psychological Association.

Galinsky, E. (1999). *Ask the children.* New York: William Morrow.

Gelfand, M. J., Fitzgerald, L. F., & Drasgow, F. (1995). The structure of sexual harassment: A confirmatory factor analysis across cultures and settings. *Journal of Vocational Behavior, 47,* 164–177.

Gettman, H. J., & Gelfand, M. J. (2007). When the customer shouldn't be king: Antecedents and consequences of sexual harassment by clients and customers. *Journal of Applied Psychology, 92,* 757–770.

Gilbert, L. A., & Kearney, L. K. (2006). Sex, gender, and dual-earner families: Implications and applications for career counseling for women. In W. B. Walsh & M. Heppner (Eds.), *Handbook of career counseling for women* (2nd ed.) (pp. 193–217). Mahwah, NJ: Lawrence Erlbaum.

Gipson-Jones, T. (2009). Perceived work and family conflict among African American nurses in college. *Journal of Transcultural Nursing, 20,* 304–312.

Glomb, T. M., Richman, W. L., Hulin, C. L., Drasgow, F., Schneider, K. T., & Fitzgerald, L. F. (1997). Ambient sexual harassment: An integrated model of antecedents and consequences. *Organizational Behavior and Human Decision Processes, 71,* 309–328.

Glomb, T. M., Munson, L. J., Hulin, C. L., Bergman, M. E., & Drasgow, F. (1999). Structural equation models of sexual harassment: Longitudinal explorations and cross-sectional generalizations. *Journal of Applied Psychology, 84,* 14–28.

Greenhaus, J. H., & Beutell, N. J. (1985).Sources of conflict between work and family roles. *Academy of Management Review, 10,* 76–88.

Greenhaus, J. H., & Powell, G. N. (2006). When work and family are allies: A theory of work-family enrichment. *Academy of Management Review, 31,* 72–92.doi:10.5465/AMR.2006.19379625

Gruber, J. E., & Bjorn, L. (1986). Women's responses to sexual harassment: An analysis of sociocultural, organizational, and personal resource models. *Social Science Quarterly, 67,* 814–826.

Gruber, J. E. (1989). How women handle sexual harassment: A literature review. *Sociology and Social Research, 74,* 3–9.

Gutek, B. A., & Morasch, B. (1982). Sex-ratios, sex-role spillover, and sexual harassment of women at work. *Journal of Social Issues, 38,* 55–74.

Gutek, B. A. (1985). *Sex and the workplace: Impact of sexual behavior and harassment on women, men and organizations.* San Francisco: Jossey-Bass.

Gutek, B. A., Cohen, A. G., & Konrad, A. M. (1990). Predicting social-sexual behavior at work: A contact hypothesis. *Academy of Management Journal, 33,* 560–577.

Gutek, B. A., & Koss, M. P. (1993). Changed women and changed organizations: Consequences of and coping with sexual harassment. *Journal of Vocational Behavior, 42,* 28–48.

Gutek, B. A., & Done, R. (2001). Sexual harassment. In R. K. Unger (Ed.), *Handbook of the psychology of women and gender* (pp. 367–387). New York: Wiley.

Gutek, B. A., Murphy, R. O., & Douma, B. 2004. A review and critique of the Sexual Experiences Questionnaire (SEQ). *Law and Human Behavior, 28,* 457–482.

Haines, V. Y., Marchand, A., & Harvey, S. (2006). Crossover of workplace aggression experiences in dual-earner couples. *Journal of Occupational Health Psychology, 11,* 305–314.

Harned, M. S., & Fitzgerald, L. F. (2002). Understanding a link between sexual harassment and eating disorder symptoms: A meditational analysis. *Journal of Clinical and Consulting Psychology, 70,* 1170–1181.

Harned, M. S., Ormerod, A. J., Palmieri, P. A., Collinsworth, L. L., & Reed, M. (2002). Sexual assault and other types of sexual harassment by workplace personnel: A comparison of antecedents and consequences. *Journal of Occupational Health Psychology, 7,* 174–188.

Hershcovis, M. S., & Barling, J. (2010). Comparing victim attributions and outcomes for workplace aggression and sexual harassment. *Journal of Applied Psychology, 95,* 874–888.

Hesson-McInnis, M. S., & Fitzgerald, L. F. (1997). Sexual harassment: A preliminary test of an integrative model. *Journal of Applied Social Psychology, 27,* 877–901.

*Huerta, M. (2007). *Intersections of race and gender in women's experiences of harassment.* Unpublished doctoral dissertation, The University of Michigan.

Hulin, C. L., Fitzgerald, L. F., &Drasgow, F. (1996). Organizational influences on sexual harassment. In M. Stockdale (Ed.), *Sexual harassment in the workplace* (Vol. 5, pp. 127–150). Thousand Oaks, CA: Sage.

Ilies, R., Hauserman, N., Schwochau, S., & Sibal, J. (2003). Reported incidence rates of work-related sexual harassment in the United States: Using meta-analysis to explain reported rate disparities. *Personnel Psychology, 56,* 607–631.

Knapp, D. E., Faley, R. H., Ekeberg, S. E., & DuBois, C. L. Z. (1997). Determinants of target responses to sexual harassment: A conceptual framework. *Academy of Management Review, 22,* 687–729.

Konik, J., & Cortina, L. M. (2008). Policing gender at work: Intersections of harassment based on sex and sexuality. *Social Justice Research, 21,* 313–337.

Koss, M. P., Goodman, L. A., Brown, A., Fitzgerald, L. F., Keita, G. P., & Russo, N. F. (1994). *No safe haven: Male violence against women at home, at work, and in the community.* Washington, DC: American Psychological Association.

Kreiner, G. E., Hollensbe, E. C., & Sheep, M. L. (2009). Balancing borders and bridges: Negotiating the work-home interface via boundary work tactics. *Academy of Management Journal, 52,* 704–730. doi:10.5465/AMJ.2009.43669916

*Krieger, N., Chen, J. T., Waterman, P. D., Hartman, C., Stoddard, A. M., Quinn, M. M., Sorensen, G., & Barbeau, E. M. (2008). The inverse hazard law: Blood pressure, sexual harassment, racial discrimination, workplace abuse and occupational exposures in US low-income black, white, and Latino workers. *Social Science and Medicine, 67,* 1970–1981.

Lambert, S. J. (1990). Processes linking work and family: A critical review and research agenda. *Human Relations, 43,* 239–257.

*Landrum, T. L. (2000). *Major concerns of workers at three stages of life.* Unpublished doctoral dissertation, Arizona State University.

Lapierre, L. M., Spector, P. E., & Leck, J. D. (2005). Sexual versus nonsexual workplace aggression and victims' overall job satisfaction: A meta-analysis. *Journal of Occupational Health Psychology, 10,* 155–169.

Lazarus, R. S., & Folkman, S. (1984). *Stress, appraisal, and coping.* New York: Springer.

*Lee, A. E. (2005). *Towards a model of coping for Black women public school teachers experiencing racism, sexism, and work-related stressors.* Unpublished doctoral dissertation, Howard University.

Lee, W. C., & Ormerod, A. J. (August, 2003). "Constructing" the SEQ: A multiple-group analysis across samples and versions of the SEQ. In A. J. Ormerod (Chair), *Sexual Experiences Questionnaire—What it can and can't do (yet).* Symposium presented at the annual meeting of the American Psychological Association, Toronto, Canada.

Lim, S., & Cortina, L. M. (2005). Interpersonal mistreatment in the workplace: The interface and impact of general incivility and sexual harassment. *Journal of Applied Psychology, 90,* 483–496.

MacDermid, S. M., Leslie, L. A., & Bissonnette, L. (2001). Walking the walk: Insights from research on helping clients navigate work and family. *Journal of Feminist Family Therapy, 13,* 21–40.

MacKinnon, C. A. (1979). *Sexual harassment of working women.* New Haven, CT: Yale University Press.

Magley, V. J., Hulin, C. L., Fitzgerald, L. F., & DeNardo, M. (1999). Outcomes of self-labeling sexual harassment. *Journal of Applied Psychology, 84,* 390–402.

Magley, V. J. (2002). Coping with sexual harassment: Reconceptualizing women's resistance. *Journal of Personality and Social Psychology, 83,* 930–946.

Malamut, A. B., & Offermann, L. R. (2001). Coping with sexual harassment: Personal, environmental, and cognitive determinants. *Journal of Applied Psychology, 86,* 1152–1166.

Marks, R. S. (1977). Multiple roles and role strain: Some notes on human energy, time, and commitment. *American Sociological Review, 42,* 921–936.

Martin, J. L. (2008). Gendered violence on campus: Unpacking bullying, harassment, and stalking. In M. A. Paludi (Ed.), *Understanding and preventing campus violence* (pp. 3–26). Westport, CT: Praeger/Greenwood.

Moradi, B., & Subich, L. M. (2003). A concomitant examination of the relations of perceived racist and sexist events to psychological distress for African American women. *The Counseling Psychologist, 31,* 451–469. doi:10.1177/0011000003031004007

Morf, M. (1989). *The work/life dichotomy: Prospects for reintegrating people and jobs.* New York: Quorum.

Munson, L. J., Miner, A. G., & Hulin, C. L. (2001). Labeling sexual harassment in the military: An extension and replication. *Journal of Applied Psychology, 86,* 293–303.

Nippert-Eng, E. C. (1996). *Home and work: Negotiating boundaries through everyday life.* Chicago: University of Chicago Press.

Offermann, L. R., & Malamut, A. B. (2002). When leaders harass: The impact of target perceptions of organizational leadership and climate on harassment reporting and outcomes. *Journal of Applied Psychology, 87,* 885–893. doi:10.1037//0021-9010.87.5.885

O'Leary-Kelly, A. M., Bowes-Sperry, L., Bates, C. A., & Lean, E. R. (2009). Sexual harassment at work: A decade (plus) of progress. *Journal of Management, 35,* 503–536.

Ormerod, A. J. (August 1999). *Development of the racial/ethnic experiences questionnaire.* Poster session presented at the annual meeting of the American Psychological Association, Boston, MA.

*Ormerod, A. J. (2004). [Occupationally diverse community sample assessed for sexual harassment and other stressors]. Unpublished raw data.

Parker, S. K., & Griffin, M. A. (2002). What is so bad about a little name-calling? Negative consequences of gender harassment for overperformance demands and distress. *Journal of Occupational Health Psychology, 7,* 195–210.

Perrone, K. M. (2002). Sexual harassment and dual-career issues: The case of Megan. *Career Development Quarterly, 50,* 317–320.

Perrone, K. M. (2005). Work-family interface for same-sex, dual-earner couples: Implications for counselors. *Career Development Quarterly, 53,* 317–324.

Peus, C., & Traut-Mattausch, E. (2008). Manager and mommy? A cross-cultural comparison. *Journal of Managerial Psychology, 23,* 558–575. doi:10.1108/02683940810884531

Powell, G. N., Francesco, A. M., & Ling, Y. (2009). Toward culture-sensitive theories of the work-family interface. *Journal of Organizational Behavior, 30,* 597–616. doi:10.1002/job.568

Raver, J. L., & Gelfand, M. J. (2005). Beyond the individual victim: Linking sexual harassment, team processes, and team performance. *Academy of Management Journal, 48,* 388–400.

*Raver, J. L., & Nishii, L. H. (2010). Once, twice, or three times as harmful? Ethnic harassment, gender harassment, and generalized workplace harassment. *Journal of Applied Psychology, 95,* 236–254.

Richman, J. A., Rospenda, K. M., Nawyn, S. J., Flaherty, J. A., Fendrich, M., Drum, M. L., & Johnson, T. P. (1999). Sexual harassment and generalized workplace abuse among university employees: Prevalence and mental health correlates. *American Journal of Public Health, 89,* 358–363.

Rospenda, K. M. (2002). Workplace harassment, services utilization, and drinking outcomes. *Journal of Occupational Health Psychology, 7,* 141–155.

Rospenda, K. M., & Richman, J. A. (2004). The factor structure of generalized workplace harassment. *Violence and Victims, 19,* 221–238.

Rospenda, K. M., Richman, J. A., Ehmke, J. L. Z., & Zlatoper, K. W. (2005). Is workplace harassment hazardous to your health? *Journal of Business Psychology, 20,* 95–110.

Rospenda, K. M., Richman, J. A., & Shannon, C. A. (2006). Patterns of workplace harassment, gender, and use of services: An update. *Journal of Occupational Health Psychology, 11,* 379–393.

*Rospenda, K. M., Richman, J. A., & Shannon, C. A. (2009). Prevalence and mental health correlates of harassment and discrimination in the workplace: Results from a national study. *Journal of Interpersonal Violence, 24,* 819–843.

Rotundo, M., Nguyen, D. H., & Sackett, P. R. (2001).A meta-analytic review of gender differences in perceptions of sexual harassment. *Journal of Applied Psychology, 86,* 914–922.

Sadler, A. G., Booth, B. M., Cook, B. L., & Doebbeling, B. N. (2003). Factors associated with women's risk of rape in the military environment. *American Journal of Industrial Medicine, 43,* 262–273.

Schell, B. H. (2003). The prevalence of sexual harassment, stalking, and false victimization syndrome (FVS) cases and related human resource management policies in a cross-section of Canadian companies from January 1995 through January 2000. *Journal of Family Violence, 18,* 351–360.

Schneider, K. T., Swan, S., & Fitzgerald, L. F. (1997). Job-related and psychological effects of sexual harassment in the workplace: Empirical evidence from two organizations. *Journal of Applied Psychology, 82,* 401–415.

Schneider, K. T., Tomaka, J., & Palacios, R. (2001). Women's cognitive, affective, and psychological reactions to a male coworker's sexist behavior. *Journal of Applied Social Psychology, 31,* 1995–2018.

Schultheiss, D. E. P. (2006). The interface of work and family life. *Research and Practice, 37,*334–341. doi:10.1037/0735-7028.37.4.334

Shannon, C. A., Rospenda, K. M., & Richman, J. A. (2007). Workplace harassment patterning, gender, and utilization of professional services: Findings from a US national study. *Social Science and Medicine, 64,* 1178–1191.

Shupe, E. I., Cortina, L. M., Ramos, A., Fitzgerald, L. F., & Salisbury, J. (2002). *Psychology of Women Quarterly, 26,* 298–308.

Sims, C. S., Drasgow, F., & Fitzgerald, L. F. (2005). The effects of sexual harassment on turnover in the military: Time-dependent modeling. *Journal of Applied Psychology, 90,* 1141–1152.

Staines, G. L. (1980). Spillover versus compensation: A review of the literature on the relationship between work and nonwork. *Human Relations, 33,* 111–129.

Stark, S., Chernyshenko, O. S., Lancaster, A. R., Drasgow, F., & Fitzgerald, L. F. (2002).Toward standardized measurement of sexual harassment: Shortening the SEQ-DoD using item response theory. *Military Psychology, 14,* 49–72.

Stockdale, M. S. (1998). The direct and moderating influences of sexual-harassment pervasiveness, coping strategies, and gender on work-related outcomes. *Psychology of Women Quarterly, 22,* 521–535.

Tangri, S. S., Burt, M. R., & Johnson, L. B. (1982). Sexual harassment at work: Three explanatory models. *Journal of Social Issues, 38,* 33–54.

Timmerman, G., & Bajema, C.(2000). The impact of organizational culture on perceptions and experiences of sexual harassment. *Journal of Vocational Behavior, 57,* 188–205.

*Wade-Golden, K. (2006). *Work and family conflict: Understanding the role of race, gender, racial discrimination, and sexual discrimination.* Unpublished doctoral dissertation, Wayne State University.

United States Merit Systems Protection Board (1981). *Sexual harassment of federal workers: Is it a problem?* Washington, DC: United States Government Printing Office.

United States Merit Systems Protection Board (1988). *Sexual harassment of federal workers: An update.* Washington, DC: United States Government Printing Office.

United States Merit Systems Protection Board (1995). *Sexual harassment in the federal workplace: Trends, progress, continuing challenges.* Washington, DC: United States Government Printing Office.

U.S. Census Bureau (2011). *2005–2009 American community survey: Households and families* (Table S1101). Retrieved January 7, 2011, from http://factfinder.census.gov.

U.S. Department of Labor (2011). *Women in the labor force: A databook* (Report 1018). Retrieved January 7, 2011, from http://stats.bls.gov/cps/wlf-databook-2011.pdf.

U.S. Merit Systems Protection Board. (1995). *Sexual harassment in the federal workplace: Trends, progress, and continuing challenges.* Washington, DC: U.S. Government Printing Office.

Vogt, D., Pless, A. P., King, L. A., & King, D. W. (2005). Deployment stressors, gender, and mental health outcomes among Gulf War I veterans. *Journal of Traumatic Stress, 18,* 115–127.

Voydanoff, P. (2005). Social integration, work-family conflict and facilitation, and job and marital quality. *Journal of Marriage and Family, 67,* 666–679.

Waldo, C. R., Berdahl, J. L., & Fitzgerald, L. F. (1998). Are men sexually harassed? If so, by whom? *Law and Human Behavior, 22,* 59–79.

Walker, M. (2004). How relationships heal. In M. Walker & W. B. Rosen (Eds.) *How connections heal: Stories from relational-cultural therapy* (pp. 3–21). New York: Guilford Press.

Wasti, S. A., Bergman, M. E., Glomb, T. M., & Drasgow, F. (2000). Test of the cross-cultural generalizability of a model of sexual harassment. *Journal of Applied Psychology, 85,* 766–778.

Wasti, S. A., & Cortina, L. M. (2002). Coping in context: Sociocultural determinants of responses to sexual harassment. *Journal of Personality and Social Psychology, 83,* 394–405.

Weitzman, L. M. (July, 2004). *Multiple role realism revisited: A personal and professional journey seeking balance.* Paper presented at the meeting of the American Psychological Association, Honolulu, HI.

Williams, J. H., Fitzgerald, L. F., & Drasgow, F. (1999). The effects of organizational practices on sexual harassment and individual outcomes in the military. *Military Psychology, 11,* 303–328.

Willness, C. R., Steel, P., & Lee, K. (2007). A meta-analysis of the antecedents and consequences of workplace sexual harassment. *Personnel Psychology, 60,* 127–162.

Woods, K. C., Buchanan, N. T., & Settles, I. H. (2009). Sexual harassment across the color line: Experiences and outcomes of cross-versus intraracial sexual harassment among Black women. *Cultural Diversity and Ethnic Minority Psychology, 15,* 67–76.

*Wright, C. V., & Fitzgerald, L. F. (2009). Correlates of joining a sexual harassment class action. *Law and Human Behavior, 33,* 265–282.

Yang, N., Chen, C., Choi, J., & Zou, Y. (2000). Sources of work-family conflict: A Sino-U.S. comparison of the effects of work and family demands. *Academy of Management Journal, 43,* 113–123.

Yoder, J. D., & Aniakudo, P. (1996). When prank become harassment: The case of African American women firefighters. *Sex Roles, 35,* 253–270.

Zerubavel, E. (1991). *The fine line: Making distinctions in everyday life.* New York: Free Press.

Zerubavel, E. (1996). Lumping and splitting: Notes on social classification. *Sociological Forum, 11,* 421–433.

CHAPTER

16 Feminist Therapy in Counseling Psychology

Pam A. Remer *and* Katharine Hahn Oh

Abstract

In this chapter, the authors discuss the development of feminist psychological practice and identify similarities between feminist approaches and counseling psychology, including multicultural and social justice perspectives. Empowerment Feminist Therapy (Worell & Remer, 1992, 2003) is highlighted as a model of feminist practice that applies the Guidelines for Psychological Practice with Girls and Women (APA, 2007) and incorporates social justice principles. The authors explain methods for using feminist assessment and conceptualization as collaborative and empowering interventions. They describe specific techniques for cultural analysis, exploration of privilege and oppression, analysis of identity development, and exploration of intersecting identities. The authors explore feminist perspectives on several ethical issues and stress the importance of using the Guidelines as a model of effective practice. Future directions for feminist theory and practice are provided.

Key Words: Collaborative, cultural analysis, empowering, Empowerment Feminist Therapy, Guidelines for Psychological Practice with Girls and Women, identity development, intersecting identities, oppression, privilege, social justice

Introduction

Feminist psychological practitioners view individuals in their cultural contexts and assert that clients' problems in living are often caused by unhealthy societal and cultural environments. Further, feminist therapists assert that unequal power relationships in the forms of privilege and oppression contribute to the toxicity of social contexts. Feminist psychological approaches are in sharp contrast to the intrapsychic perspectives of traditional therapeutic approaches that locate problems in the internal feelings, thoughts, and behaviors of clients and ignore the influences of socialization and systemic discrimination. Feminist psychological practitioners appreciate the skills used by women and girls and members of other diverse disadvantaged groups to cope with these toxic cultural contexts as strengths and as signs of resiliency. While much has been written about feminist therapy, feminist psychological perspectives are applied to a variety of psychological practices, including therapy, assessment and diagnosis, prevention, consultation, advocacy, pedagogy, training, social activism, and research (APA, 2007; Worell & Johnson, 1997).

The Development of Feminist Psychological Practice in Counseling Psychology

Feminist psychological practice was created as the broader feminist movement collided with and became incorporated into the established discipline of psychology. Feminist psychology has been challenged to incorporate the diverse experiences of women and to engage with emerging feminist epistemologies. In the following section, we provide a brief and admittedly simplified narrative of the theories, therapies, and historical events relevant to the development of feminist psychological practice in counseling psychology, and we briefly describe some feminist therapies in current use.

The Herstory of Feminist Therapy

Since the 1970s, the dominant scientific and social paradigms have shifted considerably. Ballou (2005) describes this shift as moving from a positivist paradigm to "systems thinking with relational consciousness and a social and environmental justice ethic" (p. 207). The threads of different feminist theories remain in feminist counseling psychology but have been transformed by challenges and new modes of thought. For instance, the original goal of consciousness-raising (CR) groups to change society is still a goal of feminist counseling psychology, but multicultural and social justice perspectives have broadened the aims of feminist activism to include other social problems, in addition to sexism. In this section, we describe the development of feminist therapy through the lens of prominent feminist theories, and we describe important events in the development of feminist therapies.

CONSCIOUSNESS-RAISING GROUPS: RADICAL AND SOCIALIST FEMINISMS

CR groups were perhaps the earliest form of feminist therapy, arising as part of the second wave of feminism in the 1970s. The purpose of CR groups was not originally to empower or support individual women but, in the tradition of radical philosophy, to change society (Sarachild, 1975). The women who participated in these groups viewed each other as being essentially healthy within a pathological society. Through sharing stories of their lives, women began to hear the similarities in their experiences and to form an analysis of how society needed to be changed (Hanisch, 1971; Sarachild, 1970). These analyses and new understandings often led to activism, a cornerstone of radical feminism. Radical and socialist feminisms called for revolutionary change in society, placing the blame for problems on the patriarchal and, in the case of socialist feminist, capitalist structures of society (Jagger & Rothenberg, 1984; Students for a Democractic Society, 1969). Within CR groups, women gained understanding of how gender socialization and patriarchal oppression affected their own lives—in other words, how the personal is political (the ways in which their personal experiences were reflective of societal discrimination). For White women in CR groups, the analyses were focused primarily on raising consciousness about sexism and the impact of patriarchy. For African American women in CR groups, sharing their stories led to a discussion of multiple forms of oppression, especially oppression based on race, sex, and class (Combahee River Collective, 1982).

The CR groups themselves functioned as a different space for women, separate from patriarchal spaces. Relationships within CR groups were egalitarian rather than hierarchical, and women's experience and understanding were considered extremely valuable as tools for changing what was wrong in the world. Although CR groups were not designed primarily to improve individuals' well-being, White (mostly middle-class) women in CR groups reported gaining greater self-esteem, more autonomy, the ability to express anger, and improved relationships with women (Kravetz, 1978, Kravetz, 1987).

African American women described a sense of common struggle and support tempered by the realities of racism and classism that acted simultaneously with sexism in their lives. For one African American woman (Wallace, 1982), the process of creating a CR group was discouraging, and the group eventually dissolved. Wallace wrote, "We exist as women who are Black who are feminists, each stranded for the moment, working independently because there is not yet an environment in this society remotely congenial to our struggle—because, being on the bottom, we would have to do what no one else has done: we would have to fight the world" (p. 12). Due to the lack of privilege and its attendant resources, African American women experienced more barriers to organizing than did middle-class White women. We may presume that other groups of women experienced similar constraints (e.g., Asian American women, lesbian women).

EMPOWERING INDIVIDUALS: LIBERAL AND CULTURAL FEMINISMS

Women therapists began to use the CR group model to lead feminist therapy groups and to inform individual therapy with women. Some of the emphasis then shifted from revolutionizing society to empowering women. Several articles in *The Journal of Counseling Psychology* during the 1970s describe how feminist therapy was practiced among counseling psychologists. Holroyd (1976) described feminist therapy as "a combination of radical therapy philosophy with humanist therapy techniques and behaviorism, but it focuses on one particular type of oppression which has retarded the growth of women—sexism" (p. 25). Interventions focused on allowing women to feel and express anger, encouraging women to embrace both masculine and feminine traits within themselves (androgyny therapy), enhancing women's sense of choice, increasing sexual agency, supporting career options for women, and training women to be more assertive (APA, 1975; Holroyd, 1976; Nutt, 1979). These early feminist therapy approaches were developed and written about primarily by White women, with little attention to issues of race and class.

In the 1970s, women psychologists raised concern about the sexist treatment of women in therapy. The American Psychological Association (APA) appointed a Task Force on Sex Bias and Sex Role Stereotyping in Psychotherapeutic Practice, which found that (a) therapists tended to emphasize women's contentment with traditional roles, pathologizing other desires (e.g., for a career); (b) therapists encouraged women to be passive and used demeaning labels; (c) therapists employed sexist psychoanalytic concepts; and (d) therapists related to women as sex objects (APA, 1975). The report of the task force also mentioned that poor, African American, and lesbian women encountered specific bias with therapists who stereotyped or pathologized them. The task force recommended that consciousness-raising about sexism be done at both organizational and individual levels, that guidelines be developed for "nonsexist psychotherapeutic practice" (p. 1174), that therapist training include education about the psychology of women, and that ethical standards for psychologists address sexism.

In 1979, the Society for Counseling Psychology's ad hoc committee on women developed 13 "Principles Concerning the Counseling and Psychotherapy of Women," which were then updated in 1986. These principles emphasized that therapists must be aware of theories that limit women and must have knowledge of those that are useful to women; Fitzgerald and Nutt (1986) held up feminist therapy as "the example *par excellence* of a psychological mode that has particular usefulness for women clients" (p. 186).

At the same time, cultural feminism, which played a significant role in the nineteenth century, again became prominent and influenced feminist psychological theory and therapy (Belenky, Clinchy, Goldberger, & Tarule, 1986; Chodorow, 1978; Gilligan, 1982; Miller, 1976). Cultural feminism focuses on the strengths and perspectives of women, honoring both biological and social aspects of womanhood (e.g., mothering, connection, and cooperation) and revaluing traditionally feminine attributes. Although this approach has been criticized for essentializing particular traits as inherent to women or men, cultural feminist psychology contributes to feminist theory by challenging the assumption that true psychological health involves utter independence and competence, insisting that both men and women depend on others for support and connection (Miller, 1976).

EMBRACING COMPLEXITY: WOMEN OF COLOR, INTERNATIONAL, AND POSTMODERN FEMINISMS

Women psychologists of color in the late 1980s and early 1990s mounted an effective challenge to feminist therapy's emphasis on sexism as the *prime* oppression for women and critiqued feminist psychology as written by and for White women. Comas-Díaz (1991) pointed out that White feminists could be just as unaware of their cultural assumptions as other White women, and she challenged White feminist psychologists to continue listening to the voices of women of color in order to make feminist psychology applicable to diverse women's realities. Brown (1995) urged feminist psychologists to reconstruct feminist therapy as anti-racist. At the 1993 National Conference on Education and Training in Feminist Practice at Boston College, White and women of color feminist psychologists began to grapple with the challenge of integrating diverse experiences and perspectives (Chin, 1994; Worell & Johnson, 1997). Describing the discussion in the working group on diversity, Greene and Sanchez-Hucles (1997) wrote that "gender and gender oppression are not the primary locus of identity or oppression for all women. We agreed that all women share gender oppression but that they experience this oppression through their individual historical, social, political, economic, ecological, and psychophysical realities" (p. 183). Although the working group met resistance from others at the conference, meaningful collaborations between White and women of color feminists emerged, and feminist psychology began to embrace the mandate for a multicultural feminism. In 1997, the first National Multicultural Conference and Summit was held, cosponsored by APA Divisions 17, 35, 44, and 45, and in 2001 the National Counseling Psychology Conference, held in Houston, focused on social justice as a necessary part of cultural competency (Fouad et al., 2004). In 1998, the Division 17 Section for the Advancement of Women met in Michigan with the express purpose of integrating feminism and multiculturalism (Fassinger, 2004).

The results of these efforts to speak and listen, to break down and rebuild theory, and to rewrite the herstories of feminist psychology have resulted in rich theories and therapies. Multicultural perspectives have been integrated into feminist therapy texts (Worell & Remer, 2003) and are evident in the delineation of feminist therapy principles and in the Guidelines for Psychological Practice with Girls and Women (APA, 2007). As the Society of Counseling Psychology (Division 17) and the Society for the Psychology of Women (Division 35) collaborated on the Guidelines, these understandings of multiple women's experiences were powerfully utilized to inform the broader practice of psychology. As a consequence, analysis of gender as a feminist therapy intervention has been supplemented by an analysis of the client's intersecting identities (Worell & Remer, 2003). Feminist psychologists now attend to issues of race, class, ability, age, immigration, religion, and sexual orientation, as well as additional salient aspects of identity presented by clients.

The multicultural challenge to White feminist psychology also created interest among American feminists in the international perspectives of women. Understanding the limitations of the White American feminist lens, current feminist psychologists attempt to comprehend the particular experiences of women in other countries. International feminist psychologists consider the cultural, legal, religious, and economic situations of women and promote understanding of how women in particular countries imagine liberation or social justice for themselves. Enns (2004) suggests that by listening to men and women outside the United States, American feminist psychologists can understand the limitations of Western psychology and the impact of developed countries' actions on people in less developed nations. Feminist psychologists are also working to create alliances across borders in order to advance global women's rights in areas such as domestic violence and reproductive rights.

At the same time that feminism was responding to the challenge of multicultural awareness, poststructural and constructionist understandings of identity and knowledge began to emerge in feminist psychology. The third wave of feminism experienced by younger feminists resulted in an understanding of feminism as flexible and personal. Many younger feminists view themselves as having many intersecting identities and various interests, which may result in internal or apparent contradictions that may not be resolvable. Thus, just as feminist therapy became more cohesive, understandings about the unique cultural and personal perspectives of women have created a push toward understanding the many experiences of different women and attending to the unique client. In spite of embracing the complexity of women's experiences, however, most contemporary feminist psychology theorists do not wholeheartedly endorse the moral relativism often associated with postmodern theory. Instead, many feminist psychologists acknowledge that all theories are partial maps of the complex territory of personal and cultural reality, while also holding to the set of principles developed by diverse feminists (Enns, 2004). Porter (2005) sums up this distinction in her heading "Contexualism, Yes. Moral Relativism, No" (p. 157). Feminist psychologists thus manage the tension between holding clear principles and allowing space for individual and cultural phenomenologies.

Contemporary Feminist Therapies

Feminist therapists today use multiple feminist approaches and methods in their work with individuals and groups. For example, a therapist working with an African American woman client may help the client become aware of how systemic racism has influenced her life (using a multicultural feminist approach) and may also work to increase the client's awareness of her choices (using a liberal feminist approach). Thus, in contemporary usage, the categories of feminist theory and therapy are not often separated. Because theories are based in different philosophies and epistemologies, several feminist psychologists have suggested that feminist therapists take a thoughtful and systematic approach when developing their own feminist theories/therapies and when integrating feminism with other psychological theories (Enns, 2004; Worell & Remer, 2003). Brief descriptions of several feminist therapies currently in use may help psychologists identify the specific feminist theories and therapies from which they draw.

LIBERAL FEMINIST APPROACHES TO THERAPY

When therapists use liberal feminist approaches, they assist clients to understand their gender socialization and to access opportunities and experiences that might normally be denied based on their gender identity. For example, a therapist might work with a male client to experience a broader range of emotion, with a female client to assert her needs in a relationship, or with a transgender client to transition into a new gender. Humanistic therapies such as person-centered therapy and Gestalt therapy are integrated with feminist therapy to broaden clients' awareness of their choices and to support clients' goals. Cognitive behavioral therapy is used by feminists to teach skills that empower clients to reach their goals. Some critiques of liberal feminist therapy approaches are that this approach focuses on helping individuals change rather than working directly to radically change society, and that the goal of gender equality is not radical or transformative enough.

CULTURAL FEMINIST APPROACHES TO THERAPY

When therapists use cultural feminist approaches, they do not seek simple gender equality but work to revalue traditionally feminine qualities and values, such as nurturing, mothering, relational connection, cooperation, and peace. Therapists using cultural feminist approaches may value the client-therapist relationship as the primary tool of therapy and may seek to enhance the clients' quality of connection with self and others. Relational cultural therapy is based on Miller's (1976) retelling of human development based on women's development rather than men's. Using relational cultural theory, therapists identify ways in which clients do not bring themselves fully into connection and then help them heal their ability to connect through use of the therapeutic relationship. Cultural feminist approaches have been criticized for the essentialism (i.e., the belief that gender traits are inherent and unchanging) expressed by some theorists and for the way in which White women's perspectives were privileged in the original framing of the theory.

MULTICULTURAL FEMINIST APPROACHES TO THERAPY

When therapists use multicultural feminist approaches, they help clients become aware of the effects of oppression/colonization and privilege in their lives, and they honor clients' cultural ways of thinking, talking, and interacting in the world (e.g., talking in non-linear ways, holding a relational rather than individualistic sense of self). An important aspect of multicultural feminist therapy is therapists' own identity development and self-reflective awareness of privilege and oppression. When employing a multicultural feminist approach, therapists use frameworks and interventions that are consistent with clients' worldviews and may use culturally specific interventions (e.g., a therapist working with a Native American client may collaborate with a Native American healer to incorporate appropriate healing rituals). They attend not only to race/ethnicity, but also to disability, age, religion, and other aspects of identity that hold cultural meaning or differential status, applying feminist principles to empower clients in all aspects of life and identity.

POSTMODERN FEMINIST APPROACHES TO THERAPY

When therapists use postmodern feminist approaches, they attend to clients' unique language and meaning-making, and they view identity as fluid and context-dependent. Therapists challenge dualistic thinking, working with meanings and identities independent from either/or categories (e.g., bicultural identity, gender queer identity). Narrative therapy is integrated with feminist therapy to help clients make new meanings of their experiences, with awareness of multiple aspects of identity. Postmodernism has been critiqued as too morally relativistic; however, a "weak" postmodern approach may be useful in valuing different perspectives and appears to fit current conceptions of knowledge as constructed, partial, and context-bound (Waugh, 1998).

ONGOING TRANSFORMATIONS OF FEMINIST THERAPY

Feminist therapies continue to evolve as practitioners integrate feminist therapy with other therapies and find forms of feminist thought and practice that fit for them. Worell and Remer (2003) provide a model for systematic feminist integration or transformation of other theories. They recommended transforming other approaches with a feminist perspective at the levels of both theory and intervention. Lee (1997) integrated feminist and narrative therapies: she highlighted the similarities and differences in theories and provided an example of a feminist narrative approach with body image concerns. Lee emphasized how narrative theory can contribute to a feminist approach by conceptualizing women's stories as constructive of reality or "that through which women become who they are" (p. 10). Other feminist psychologists have integrated feminist therapy with Gestalt approaches (Enns, 1987), psychodrama, and cognitive behavioral therapies (Worell & Remer). Because most therapy approaches primarily aim to change the individual rather than society, one consistent aspect of feminist transformations is to shift the focus of interventions to raising awareness of societal context and the need for social change.

Enns (2004) encouraged feminists to explore different feminist therapy theories and thoughtfully develop their own personal feminist therapy approach. Brown (1994), for instance, combined a radical feminist philosophy with multicultural awareness in her writings about feminist therapy. As a radical feminist, she asserted that the primary goal of feminist therapy is to subvert patriarchy, either by creating awareness of patriarchy for clients or by supporting clients to change the patriarchal contexts in which they live. Embracing multicultural perspectives, Brown insisted that feminist therapy must provide analyses that include clients' multiple sources of oppression and/or privilege, and she highlighted the benefits of seeing through different lenses and committing to continued multicultural understanding.

Consensus Values

As discussed in the previous section, a variety of feminist psychological approaches have been developed, and these approaches reflect a range of philosophical foundations (Enns, 2004). However, at the APA Division 35 First National Conference on Education and Training in Feminist Practice in 1993, over 75 feminist psychologists, many of them counseling psychologists, unanimously agreed to 17 Common Themes of Feminist Psychological Practice. These themes included (a) defining feminist psychological practice as including therapy, teaching, political action, research, supervision, pedagogy, consultation, administration, and community service; (b) promoting social change; (c) assuming that the personal is political; (d) embracing diversity; (e) examining power and privilege and oppression; (f) empowering women; (g) emphasizing collaboration; (h) embracing the value of diverse methodologies (i) asserting the importance of feminist consciousness (j) promoting the importance of self-reflection (k) encouraging the lifelong examination of values; (l) asserting that inequalities among people have negative consequences; (m) encouraging demystification of theories and practice; (n) believing theory and practice should always be evolving and emerging, (o) embracing the importance of the process of feminist practice; (p) emphasizing the importance of the sociocultural context; and (q) defining learning as the integration of cognitions, knowledge, emotions, and experience (Worell & Johnson, 1997). Thus, despite the diverse range of feminist approaches that are currently used, feminist psychological approaches have some important and unifying similarities.

Feminist Psychological Practice, Multicultural Psychology, and Social Justice

These feminist psychological common themes or values fit very well with diversity and social justice lenses. All three perspectives focus on privilege and oppression as significant contexts in individuals' lives and as a significant source of problems in living. All three emphasize the importance of working to change society to reduce privilege and oppression. All three perspectives include embracing diversity and understanding multiple cultural perspectives. Further, practitioners of the three approaches assert that because value-free practice is not possible, psychological practitioners must be aware of their personal and professional values and biases and must engage in lifelong reflection about the impact of these values and biases on their work. Finally, practitioners using feminist and/or social justice lenses declare that challenging cultural contexts and the institutionalization of oppression and privilege is often a crucial aspect of accomplishing social change.

Feminist Psychological Practice and Counseling Psychology

Although feminist psychological practice did not develop exclusively within the field of counseling psychology, its principles and practices are consonant with the identity and core values of counseling psychologists. First, social justice, with its emphasis on reducing privilege and oppression, historically has been a focus for both counseling psychology and many feminist psychological approaches (Goodman et al., 2004). Currently, both counseling psychologists and feminist psychologists have increasingly centralized the importance of accomplishing social change and social justice (Council of Counseling Psychology Training Programs, Association of Counseling Center Training Agencies, & Society of Counseling Psychology, 2009; Remer, 2008b; Worell & Remer, 2003). Second, both counseling psychologists and feminist psychologists assert that individuals are strongly affected by their environments and that individuals must be understood within their cultural contexts (Goodman et al., 2004; Packard, 2009). Third, both feminist and counseling psychology approaches embrace a respect for and inclusion of diverse groups. Thus, both approaches focus on identifying and understanding the multiple, intersecting identities of those with whom they work. Fourth, with an understanding of the negative impact of societal oppression, feminist and counseling psychologists recognize the strengths inherent in the acts of those who survive the realities of disadvantaged lives. Fifth, both feminist and counseling psychologists believe that all practitioners hold values and biases that impact their professional work. Thus, both stress the importance of practitioner critical self-awareness and the value of reflective practice (Council of Counseling Psychology Training Programs, Association of Counseling Center Training Agencies, & Society of Counseling Psychology, 2009; Worell & Remer, 2003).

Empowerment Feminist Therapy

An in-depth exploration of multiple feminist approaches to therapy is impossible in a single chapter. Instead, we have chosen to highlight one feminist therapy approach, Empowerment Feminist Therapy (EFT; Worell & Remer, 2003), because it integrates feminist, multicultural, and social justice perspectives. Further, EFT theory and techniques match counseling psychology's foci on respect for diversity, promotion of social justice, reflective practice, strength-based interventions, collaboration, and healthy development (Council of Counseling Psychology Training Programs, Association of Counseling Center Training Agencies, & Society of Counseling Psychology, 2009; Packard, 2009). EFT was also chosen because of its compatibility with and operationalization of the Guidelines for Psychological Practice with Girls and Women (APA, 2007). EFT is based on a set of value assumptions that are reflected in the four principles that guide psychological practice.

Value Assumptions of Empowerment Feminist Therapy

Most feminist therapists believe that all psychological theories and practices are built on personal and cultural values that often remain unnamed and invisible. Thus, value-free counseling does not exist and is not possible. Further, feminist therapists believe that all counselors' professional work is influenced by personal and cultural values. Feminist therapists seek to make their values visible and to engage in lifelong critical self-evaluation of their values and their social identities. Therefore, feminist therapists disclose their values to clients so that clients can make informed choices about who will be their therapists and what methods will be used.

Empowerment Feminist Therapy has a set of values and assumptions that form its foundations.

1. "Women have individual problems because of living in societies that devalue them, limit their access to resources, and discriminate against them economically, legally, and socially. Thus, sexism is institutionalized in all areas of society—families, religion, education, recreation, the workplace, and laws—and is a major source of problems" (Worell & Remer, 2003, p. 65).
2. Racism, ethnocentrism, ageism, ableism, classism, sexism, heterosexism, and other forms of societal oppression are external societal realities that negatively impact individuals' lives.
3. "Because societal oppression negatively affects the mental health of all individuals, all forms of oppression need to be eliminated. Thus, social change is crucial to mental health. Individual change is not sufficient. Social change includes altering how people are socialized (e.g., gender-role socialization) and how social institutions are structured" (Remer, 2008b, p. 409).
4. "Psychopathology, which is defined by the dominant culture, is primarily environmentally induced. Likewise, what is considered 'normal' is defined and maintained by the dominant culture" (Worell & Remer, p. 65).
5. " A culturally diverse range of values and perspectives need to be understood and respected. Individuals cannot be understood outside of their cultural contexts" (Remer, 2008b, p. 409).

The Four Principles of Empowerment Feminist Therapy

Based on the values assumptions described in the previous section, a central goal of EFT is to empower clients. "Empowerment is a broad goal of feminist interventions that enables individuals, families, and communities to exert influence over the personal, interpersonal, and institutional factors that impact their health and well-being" (Worell & Remer, 2003, p. 24). The four principles of EFT represent how feminist and social justice perspectives are used to guide therapeutic practice. The four principles of EFT are (a) personal and social identities are interdependent; (b) the personal is political; (c) relationships are egalitarian; and (d) women's perspectives are valued (Worell & Remer).

EFT PRINCIPLE I: PERSONAL AND SOCIAL IDENTITIES ARE INTERDEPENDENT

The first section of the Guidelines for Psychological Practice with Girls and Women (APA, 2007) (Guidelines 1, 2, and 3) stresses that psychologists need to be aware of and understand how diversity, social context, and power impact the lives of individuals (see table 16.1.). Diverse experiences with socialization, discrimination, privilege, and oppression and their impact on the lives of girls and women must be understood by psychologists. This first section of the Guidelines (Guidelines 1, 2, and 3) sets a daunting challenge for all psychologists because very few therapeutic models have theoretical constructs for understanding the impact of societal context, nor do they include interventions for exploring the cultural contexts of clients' lives. EFT Principle I (personal and social identities are interdependent) provides a framework and techniques for understanding clients in their diverse and complex cultural contexts and for assessing how experiences with privilege and oppression have impacted their clients' identities and counseling issues (Worell & Remer, 2003).

According to EFT Principle I, all societies construct categories of social locations, that is, discrete social groups (e.g., racial and ethnic groups, gender-based groups, groups based on sexual orientation) (Worell & Remer, 2003). Individuals are viewed and treated differently based on the social locations to which they are perceived by others to belong. Individuals' views of themselves are also impacted by these social locations. In all societies, social locations exist on a continuum from privileged to oppressed (Remer, Worell, & Remer, 2005). Privileged groups benefit from having greater access to societal resources, being judged to fit the norms of the culture, and being stereotypically seen as having desirable characteristics. On the other hand, oppressed groups are viewed as inferior and defective and

Table 16.1. Guidelines for Psychological Practice with Girls and Women

Guideline Number	Guideline Text
Guideline 1:	Psychologists strive to be aware of the effects of socialization, stereotyping, and unique life events on the development of girls and women across diverse cultural groups.
Guideline 2:	Psychologists are encouraged to recognize and utilize information about oppression, privilege, and identity development as they may affect girls and women.
Guideline 3:	Psychologists strive to understand the impact of bias and discrimination on the physical and mental health of those with whom they work.
Guideline 4:	Psychologists strive to use gender sensitive and culturally sensitive, affirming practices in providing services to girls and women.
Guideline 5:	Psychologists are encouraged to recognize how their socialization, attitudes, and knowledge about gender may affect their practice with girls and women.
Guideline 6:	Psychologists are encouraged to use interventions and approaches that have been found to be effective in the treatment of issues of concern to girls and women.
Guideline 7:	Psychologists strive to foster therapeutic relationships and practices that promote initiative, empowerment, and expanded alternatives and choices for girls and women.
Guideline 8:	Psychologists strive to provide appropriate, unbiased assessments and diagnoses in their work with girls and women.
Guideline 9:	Psychologists strive to consider the problems of girls and women in their sociopolitical context.
Guideline 10:	Psychologists strive to acquaint themselves with and utilize relevant mental health, education, and community resources for girls and women.
Guideline 11:	Psychologists are encouraged to understand and work to change institutional and systemic bias that may impact girls and women.

Adapted from Guidelines for Psychological Practice with Girls and Women, American Psychological Association, 2007, *American Psychologist, 62*, 960–970. Copyright 2007 by the American Psychological Association.

are denied access to societal resources. Oppressed group members are negatively stereotyped and are discriminated against. These negative views of oppressed groups are institutionalized into societal systems (e.g., government, educational institutions, religious organizations, legal structures, and families). The negative views are also transmitted to the members of a society through socialization. Societal oppression has many manifestations in the United States, including sexism, ethnocentrism, ableism, ageism, racism, classism, and heterosexism (Worell & Remer).

While societies socially construct and maintain these social locations, individuals differ in the ways that they perceive and identify with their social locations and in their perceptions of whether each of their social locations is oppressed or privileged. Individuals' perceptions of their social locations comprise their social identities. Additionally, all individuals comprise multiple, intersecting social identities. Most individuals simultaneously have privileged and oppressed social identities. For example, an individual may be White and heterosexual (privileged locations) and be a woman of low socioeconomic status (oppressed locations). Further, she may perceive that she does not have an ethnic, racial identification and sees herself as a poor (SES identity), divorced woman (gender identity).

Social identities are in part influenced by one's social identity development level. "Identity development models describe the processes by which individuals' social identities are impacted by the advantaged or disadvantaged social positions of their social locations" (Remer, 2008b, p. 412). Understanding the complexity of clients' multiple, social identities is a major goal of EFT Principle I. In order to have an identity development model that would simultaneously include individuals' multiple, intersecting social identities, Worell and Remer (2003) created a multiple social identities development model that synthesized existing and more specific identity development models (e.g., Cass, 1979; Cross, 1980; Downing & Roush, 1985; Helms, 1995; Sue & Sue, 1999). According to this Personal/Social Identities Model, individuals progress through four levels that range from non-awareness of privilege and oppression (Level One) to full awareness and involvement in working for social change (Level Four). In Level One (Pre-Awareness), individuals are not aware of the privileged or oppressed status of their social identities. At Level Two (Encounter), individuals become aware of the privileged or oppressed status of the social identity. At Level Three (Immersion), individuals understand the impact of discrimination and negative stereotypes of oppressed groups. At Level Four (Integration and Activism), individuals challenge societal discrimination and work to create a more socially just society.

According to Worell and Remer's (2003) social identity development model, individuals may be at differing levels of development for each of their social identities, and a major goal of EFT's Principle I is to facilitate clients' progression through the relevant social identity development concerns. According to Principle I, therapists use techniques to open up discussion of the clients' social locations and social identities in order to understand the cultural context of their clients' lives. That is, therapists use social identity exploration to increase both their own and their clients' understanding of the unique impact of clients' social realities on the issues that are the foci of therapy. Any two clients with the same presenting general problem (e.g., depression following a rape) will have varying specific struggles related to their unique, intersecting societal contexts. For example, a White male rape survivor will often struggle with what it means for a man to have been victimized and with how the rape threatens both his gender and sexual identities (Remer & Rostosky, 2003). An Asian American rape survivor may fear that if her rape becomes known to others she will bring shame to her family. EFT practitioners also use interventions to explore the similarities and differences in social identities between themselves and their clients and the impact these identities may have on their therapeutic relationships and on therapy outcomes.

EFT PRINCIPLE II: THE PERSONAL IS POLITICAL

Helping clients understand their issues in the context of their societal experiences is a key element in empowering them (Worell & Remer, 2003). Consistent with EFT Principle I, early explorations of clients' social identities and their social identity development levels begin the process of both clients and therapists being aware of how sociocultural environments impact clients' lives. Principle II (the personal is political) extends and expands Principle I. In EFT and in most feminist therapies, the external, social environment is viewed as the main source of clients' issues (Wyche & Rice, 1997). "Thus, a primary source of clients' 'pathology' is not intrapsychic or personal, but rather, social and political" (Worell & Remer, p. 68). This view of societal factors as the main sources of clients' problems in living requires therapists to shift their interventions from changing clients' feelings, behaviors, and thoughts to changing societal structures and socialization processes that oppress and negatively impact people. Thus, EFT practitioners use social justice lenses through which to view their clients' lives and actively work for social change. The idea that the personal is political is not only a unifying theme among feminist therapies; it is also central to Guidelines 1, 2, and 3 in the *APA* (2007) Guidelines for Psychological Practice with Girls and Women. EFT Principles I and II qualify EFT as a social justice approach.

Whereas traditional therapeutic approaches focus on identifying client symptoms and finding the correct APA *Diagnostic and Statistical Manual* (*DSM*) diagnostic category, EFT practitioners view "symptoms" as ways of coping with toxic environments (Wyche & Rice, 1997), as socialization messages that have been internalized (Greenspan, 1993), and as the effects of being oppressed (Brown, 2000). Thus, when "symptoms" or problems in living are examined within their societal contexts of socialization messages, structured inequalities, and experiences with oppression, these reactions are reframed as coping skills, trauma reactions, and strengths. The source of the problem is no longer primarily individual and *personal*, but is social and *political*. By embracing Principle II that the personal is political, feminist therapists challenge the symptom-driven, individual pathology models that currently dominate psychological practice. "Subordinated individuals are not blamed or pathologized for thinking, feeling, and behaving in ways that are congruent with living in an oppressive society" (Worell & Remer, 2003, p. 68).

A crucial goal of Principle II is to raise clients' awareness about how institutionalized oppressions and cultural socialization processes have impacted their lives and the issues they have brought to counseling. Consistent with Guidelines 1, 2, 3, and 9, EFT therapists are generally knowledgeable about the cultural contexts of their clients' lives and employ counseling techniques that help clients explore the unique specific aspects of the cultural contexts associated with each of the intersecting social identities of their clients. Understanding how the *personal is political* requires techniques for assessing cultural contexts. Cultural analysis techniques, such as gender-role analysis and power analysis, have been developed for helping both therapists and clients identify how socialization messages have been internalized by clients and how institutionalized hierarchical societal structures limit clients' access to societal resources. The shift from "internal to external causes of problems is a major source of empowerment for clients because the burden of their self-blame and self-insufficiency is lifted" (Remer, 2008b, p. 415).

EFT PRINCIPLE III: RELATIONSHIPS ARE EGALITARIAN

The 1975 APA Task Force on Sex Bias and Sex Role Stereotyping in Psychotherapeutic Practice found that women were treated in sexist and patronizing ways by therapists and at times were also sexually exploited. Ethnic minority, poor, immigrant, sexual minority, and disabled women have been exposed to even more ill treatment by the mental health profession. Because of the history of abuses and misuses of power in therapy relationships, Guideline 7 of the Guidelines for Psychological Practice with Girls and Women (APA, 2007) emphasizes that therapeutic relationships should "promote initiative, empowerment, and expanded alternatives and choices" (p. 55). In order to create a space of empowerment for clients, EFT Principle III asserts that relationships are egalitarian (Worell & Remer, 2003). EFT therapists strive to equalize power with clients in order to avoid re-creating the harmful discriminatory contexts in which many clients' problems emerged. According to Principle III, EFT therapists recognize the inherent power difference in their position as therapists but use strategies to involve clients in an egalitarian relationship. Although therapists have expertise about psychology and therapy techniques, clients hold the expertise about themselves, their worlds, and their experiences.

Strategies to create egalitarian therapy relationships include demystification of therapy, assessment of strengths, collaborative goal-setting, appropriate self-disclosure and self-involving responses, acceptance of clients' reactions, and explicit discussion of differences. EFT therapists explain their approach to therapy in order to educate clients to be informed consumers of therapy. They assess clients' problems but also assess strengths and acknowledge clients' resilience and coping. When setting goals for therapy and choosing which strategies or approaches to use, therapists work together with clients to make decisions that fit for them.

Self-disclosure and self-involving responses are used carefully by EFT therapists when these interventions will move clients toward their goals. For example, a woman therapist working with a client who was sexually harassed may self-disclose about her own experience of harassment, helping the client reframe her experience as an example of societal sexism. EFT therapists use self-involving responses when they share their own thoughts or feelings in the moment in response to the client. Self-involving responses serve several functions: making the therapist vulnerable and thus reducing distance/power, illustrating the interpersonal impact or power of the client, and modeling direct expression of feeling.

When clients have a reaction (positive or negative) to the therapist, EFT therapists do not automatically interpret the reaction as transference. Instead, they consider clients' responses as valid reactions to their therapists and work with their reactions in the context of the mutual relationship. Finally, EFT therapists can directly discuss their points of difference with clients. For example, a young White woman therapist working with a middle-aged African American woman client may share that she wonders how being young and White affects the clients' ability to trust her, acknowledging that these differences may affect the relationship and opening a discussion of how they can develop trust in spite of these differences.

PRINCIPLE IV: WOMEN'S PERSPECTIVES ARE VALUED

Because women have multiple roles and social locations, no single "woman's perspective" is privileged in EFT. Throughout the Guidelines for Psychological Practice with Girls and Women (APA, 2007), the authors emphasize that the conceptualization of women and girls must include their multiple aspects of identity and their particular socialization. Most women are socialized to take responsibility for relationships and to provide nurturing and support for others. However, these traits are devalued in Western societies, while stereotypically White masculine traits are valued. Aspects of multiple social locations are similarly devalued; for instance, a Chinese American woman who favors traditional Chinese medicine may experience her belief as devalued in the United States. Guideline 4 states that "psychologists strive to use gender and culturally sensitive, affirming practices in providing services to girls and women" (p. 46). Principle IV of EFT states that women's perspectives are valued. Thus, the perspectives of women clients, in all the complexity of their social locations, are valued and affirmed.

The effects of revaluing the devalued aspects of women's experiences are many: clients learn to nurture themselves, to gain more self-trust, to expand their behavioral repertoire, and to appreciate the experiences of other women. Although many women are adept at nurturing others, EFT encourages women to turn their compassion on themselves and to begin to develop a habit of self-nurturing. Male clients may also benefit from enhanced self-care and from recognizing the ways in which others nurture them. Second, when women's perspectives are valued by therapists, women begin to trust their own wisdom and intuition more, becoming more self-confident and certain about their needs and decisions. Third, both men and women clients can benefit from valuing traditionally feminine qualities (including qualities taught to African American women, Latinas, etc.). When clients begin to revalue these aspects of themselves, prizing their relational and nurturing qualities, for instance, they are free to expand their roles and to choose behaviors that are most adaptive in the moment. Finally, valuing women's perspectives allows women to appreciate the ways in which they have solidarity with other women. A sense of solidarity can facilitate women's organizing for social change.

Assessment and Conceptualization as Feminist Interventions

The feminist processes of assessment and case conceptualization are collaborative. In other words, although the therapist has frameworks, such as the *DSM* or another theoretical orientation, which may shape the therapeutic conceptualizations, the clients' phenomenology is given equal importance. Together, therapist and client discover and name what is happening for the client. A feminist approach to assessment can empower clients. Thus, feminist assessment and conceptualization are considered to be direct interventions.

ENVIRONMENTAL ASSESSMENT

In contrast to the intra-psychic focus of the medical model, feminist therapy recognizes that pathology is not located within the individual but is located in society (Brown, 2000). Thus, in addition to asking clients about signs of distress and levels of functioning, feminist therapists assess clients' contexts. Santos de Barona and Dutton (1997) wrote, "placement of the client's assessment within the multifaceted social, political, and economic context within which she or he lives is a hallmark" of feminist psychology (p. 39). Using a feminist ecological model, therapists ask about family, community, and larger systems (Ballou, Matsumoto, & Wagner, 2002). Feminist therapists ask about gender socialization, salient social locations and identity development, and about relevant events in relationships to determine how they are affecting clients (e.g., trauma history, current conflict with partner). Specific interventions, such as gender analysis or a social locations exercise (Worell & Remer, 2003), can be used as collaborative assessment methods. The feminist process of assessment can lead not only to a holistic conceptualization, but to clients' empowerment.

Signs of distress are not automatically considered symptoms of disorder; rather, symptoms may be (a) coping strategies to deal with the environment; (b) the clients' natural responses to the environment (Greenspan, 1993); or (c) the effects of resisting an oppressive system. For example, dissociating can be a very effective way of modulating the effects of trauma by blocking sensation, thus preventing the client from becoming emotionally overwhelmed. Mild forms of dissociating may help clients succeed in their daily tasks. Framing "symptoms" as coping can help clients understand what they already do to help themselves, empowering them to act further. Some symptoms may not be coping strategies but may be natural responses to events in clients' lives. For instance, if a client is in a new situation with little support and is not succeeding, feelings of hopelessness would be natural, not pathological. Similarly, if a client resists oppressive societal norms, the social backlash or policing behaviors of others may result in distress.

Environmental assessment with the client may bring into awareness discrimination, victim-blaming, or other pathological aspects of society. Expressing dismay at continued societal wrongs can help clients recognize that society should be changed. Therapists can connect clients to organizations working for social change related to clients' experience (for instance; a client who is struggling with discrimination against a family member who is mentally ill may benefit from reading about what the National Alliance on Mental Illness is doing to help). Clients who are survivors of abuse or sexual assault can discuss what should have been different in the response they received from others when they sought help. By helping clients identify what should be changed in the environment, therapists help reduce self-blame and guilt, allowing more room for acceptance and healing.

At times, the environment can be changed. Sometimes clients will choose to become involved in social action as a final act of healing for themselves or to help others in similar situations. Therapists can also work with clients to make changes in unsupportive relationships, to spend more time in positive environments, or to choose a workplace or career path that is a better fit. Therapists can often advocate for clients or help them connect to resources that will materially change their situation. Taking the time to focus on what can be changed in the environment continues to communicate the message that the pathology is not located in the individual.

STRENGTHS ASSESSMENT

A feminist assessment process also involves understanding clients' strengths and current ways of coping. Therapists might ask, "How have you coped with these difficult situations?" or "What strengths have helped you get through this?" Clients may identify sources of support (e.g., family or faith), name internal resources (e.g., perseverance), or describe specific strategies (e.g., focusing on others). Simply by asking these questions, therapists communicate belief in clients' ability to cope. Assessing strengths is one way of applying EFT Principle IV (women's perspectives are valued*)*. Therapists can model valuing clients' strengths and thus help clients recognize their own power to cope with and transform their lives.

FEMINIST CONCEPTUALIZATION

Feminist conceptualization follows from an assessment of environment, signs of distress, and strengths. Conceptualization may incorporate other theoretical perspectives when these have been transformed to fit with feminist principles. Most importantly, conceptualization is done collaboratively with clients. Rather than impose a label or use standard formulae for what constitutes "abnormal," in a feminist conceptualization, clients help decide what is abnormal for them (Brown, 2000). Feminists acknowledge that biological factors are important in clients' distress; however, even biological conditions bear meanings that are constructed in cultural contexts. Rather than simply "downloading" a medical model for diagnoses, feminist therapists explore the meanings of symptoms and disorders and help clients to untangle personal experience from imposed cultural meaning.

Although a *DSM* diagnosis may be one aspect of a total conceptualization, it is not the primary aspect for feminist therapists. For instance, a client with schizophrenia may be well served to have a diagnosis and receive medical treatment; however, a feminist conceptualization would involve a more holistic understanding, including the person's aspects of identity, support systems, meaningful ways of engaging the world, financial situation, resources, skills, and strengths. In order to receive payment for services, many therapists are required to use *DSM* diagnoses; however, feminist therapists use diagnoses in therapy with critical awareness of their limitations, and many feminist therapists actively reject diagnostic categorization.

When clients ask for a diagnosis, feminist therapists can explore with them what a diagnosis would mean for them, what the purpose of diagnosis would be, whether being diagnosed would be helpful or disempowering, and they can explain the broader conceptualization process. For instance, therapists can explain that they develop their understanding of clients by interacting with them and by learning about their background, current situation, strengths, and resources, as well as their forms of distress. Feminist therapists might explain that *DSM* diagnoses are based in the medical model, which does not fit the therapist's more contextual approach to understanding people's problems. Diagnosis and conceptualization can also be presented as a "snapshot" of clients that will change over time (Santos de Barona & Dutton, 1997). These explanations are important because of the influence of the medical model and because of misunderstandings about mental health. Feminist conceptualization empowers clients to understand their experience as intertwined with their socio-cultural contexts.

Other Feminist Interventions

This section describes several interventions that are either unique to feminist and diversity theoretical practice perspectives or borrowed from traditional theoretical approaches and then used in unique ways. All of the described interventions are ways of raising conscious awareness about the impacts of privilege, oppression, and social identities. Many also provide ways of assessing cultural, political, economic, social, legal, educational, and historical contexts and structures.

CULTURAL ANALYSES

Cultural analyses include a variety of techniques designed to assess and make visible the often invisible sociocultural contexts of individuals' lives. The general goals of these interventions are to examine and assess how privilege and oppression are structured into the fabrics of societal institutions and are transmitted via socialization practices. These critical cultural analyses are also designed to identify and increase individuals' awareness about how these cultural forms of privilege and oppression impact their lives. That is, cultural analyses are designed to help individuals see how external, social processes impact their internal experiences (Remer, 2008b).

Cultural analyses can be generally structured around collaboratively exploring with clients answers to the following questions posed by Worell and Remer (2003). For each question, the answers should reflect clients' intersecting social identities.

> How are clients' problems and issues (e.g., eating disorders, depression, rape) defined by the dominant privileged culture? How are they defined by all of the clients' communities and how do these definitions reflect intersecting social identities? How are the values of the dominant privileged culture reflected in all of these definitions? How do these societal contexts contribute to or create this problem?
>
> What societal myths or misinformation exist about the client's issue? What stereotypes associated with social locations are connected to these myths? For example, what gender-role stereotypes are connected to these myths?
>
> How do the labels, language used, and diagnoses relevant to the client issue locate the problem in the individual and obscure the role of societal contexts? How do they blame the victims?
>
> Are the incidence or prevalence rates for the client issue higher for marginalized groups? Higher rates often represent the negative impacts of oppression.
>
> How are all of clients' social identities related to their problems or issues and to their strengths?

More specific therapeutic interventions aimed at consciousness-raising about cultural contexts include bibliotherapy, information giving, therapist self-referent responses, and client self-reflections. Three more cultural analysis interventions that have been created by feminist practitioners are social identities, gender-role, and power analyses.

SOCIAL IDENTITIES ANALYSIS

An analysis of clients' intersecting social identities begins by asking clients to discuss how they identify with each of their social locations (e.g., gender, race, ethnicity, sexual orientation, class, age, cognitive and physical ability groups). For example, Worell and Remer (2003) suggest that individuals choose a label for each of their social locations. This label should characterize how they identify with the social location. For example, a female client might label her gender social location as "wise woman," "girlie woman," or "non-traditional woman." Secondly, the client is asked to describe what that label means to her. A third step in the analysis of social identities is to ask clients to describe their levels of social identity development for each identity and to name which of their social identities are most salient, or important, for them in relation to their counseling issues.

GENDER-ROLE ANALYSIS

Gender-role analysis interventions have been created to identify how individuals have been differentially socialized to be girls and women or boys and men. Gender-role socialization messages are conveyed by a variety of societal sources, including family members, peers, teachers, churches, schools, and the media. Some of these messages are stated explicitly (e.g., "women should not go out at night alone") or implicitly (e.g., women do most of the cooking). These socialization messages also vary across cultural/ethnic groups and social locations. These messages are internalized and impact the thoughts, feelings, behaviors, and relationships of all individuals in that society. Thus, societal gender-role messages and expectations may be conflicting, may be sent directly or indirectly, and may be internalized to varying degrees. These messages so permeate everyday life that they become as invisible as the air we breathe. The main purpose of gender-role analysis therapeutic interventions is to make these invisible messages visible to both clients and their counselors. Once these messages are visible, they can be analyzed for their influences on clients' lives. Clients can then make more informed choices about the internalized messages by which they want to live.

Worell and Remer (2003) created a gender-role analysis that has six steps. The first step is to have clients name the gender-role societal messages that they have received and learned throughout their lives about how they should and should not behave as women. The second step is to discover the external societal sources (e.g., family, teachers, peers, media) of these messages. Next, clients evaluate the positive and negative impacts of each message on their lives, especially the messages that are relevant to their current struggles. Additionally, clients often benefit from assessing the positive and negative impacts of their messages on society in general because doing so helps them to see how the "personal is political." The fourth step involves clients' decisions regarding which of these internalized messages they want to change—a feminist version of cognitive restructuring. For those who they wish to change, they create new self-messages that are more self-enhancing. Finally, they develop an implementation plan for replacing their old messages with their newly created ones.

POWER ANALYSIS

Power analysis interventions are aimed at identifying and analyzing societal power differentials and their influences on clients' lives. Power analyses are crucial for understanding the contexts of clients' lives. Power analysis allows clients to recognize how the privileged or oppressed status of each of their social identities has impacted their lives. Power analyses also can help clients identify how they can have more influence on external situations in their lives (Worell & Remer, 2003).

Basic power analysis begins with clients and counselors collaboratively defining power in a way that fits with feminist principles and perspectives. Worell and Remer's (2003) definition of power as the "ability to access personal and environmental resources to effect personal and/or external change" (p. 78) is one such definition. Second, therapists give clients information about the different kinds of power (e.g., role, legal, reward, physical, resource, economic, institutional, referent, normative). Third, they identify how clients' social locations and social identities have impacted their access to and use of different kinds of power and how these structured inequalities are related to their counseling issues. Fourth, clients explore how both external and internalized barriers created by societal sexism, racism, heterosexism, classism, and so on, impact their use of power. Fifth, clients and their therapists explore the potential benefits and costs of using different power strategies. In expanding their power strategy repertoire, clients often need to change the internalized messages that limit their use of various kinds of power and challenge the societal oppression barriers to their use of power.

REFRAMING AND RELABELING

Reframing and relabeling—techniques originally developed for family therapy (Grunebaum & Chasin, 1978)—are strategies for viewing clients' issues from a different perspective. In family therapy, a reframed perspective shifts the focus from an individual family member having a problem (the identified patient) to the family having a problem that causes distress for one or more family members. Feminist therapists reframe clients' personal and individual problems as societal problems rooted in oppressive structures. Thus, viewing the personal as political is a reframing technique.

EFT therapists use relabeling interventions to change the evaluation of clients' behaviors or feelings from a negative one to a positive one. For example, women who freely express sadness or happiness are often judged by society and themselves as "too emotional." In feminist approaches, this emotional expressiveness can be relabeled as having emotional intelligence.

CONSCIOUSNESS-RAISING GROUPS

Consciousness-raising (CR) groups were a part of the women's movement from the 1970s. They comprised groups of women who met to share about their lives as women. These groups were usually leaderless and were run collaboratively. Currently, CR groups are often led by mental health practitioners to provide women with an opportunity to share and reflect on their lived experiences. Despite having a leader, these CR groups are conducted collaboratively with group members. These groups may be general in nature or may be more specifically focused on a particular women's issue (e.g., body image) or diverse intersecting identity (e.g., Latina women). By sharing their experiences and identifying the commonalities in these experiences, women in a CR group become more aware of how their issues emanate from societal sources (i.e, how the personal is political). They also increase group members' awareness of the strengths that they have used to cope with sexism and other forms of oppression. These groups often result in women working together for some kind of social change or in supporting individual women's engagement in social change.

Research on Feminist Psychological Practice

Over the past 30 years, feminist-based research has been plentiful, providing psychologists with important knowledge about women's lives and women's issues. This research has informed feminist psychological practice in innumerable ways. (See the Guidelines for Psychological Practice with Girls and Women [APA, 2007] as an example.) Some feminist researchers have examined the effectiveness of feminist therapy and other feminist psychological practices (e.g., prevention programs). Researchers have found feminist-based treatments to be effective with depressed and anxious adolescent girls (Cook, 1999; D'Haene, 1995) and with adult survivors of childhood sexual abuse (Westbury & Tutty, 1998). Similarly, feminist-based rape prevention programs have demonstrated effectiveness with college students (Medley, 2000; Remer et al., 2004), and feminist relational advocacy interventions have positively impacted low-income women (Goodman, Glenn, Bohlig, Banyard, & Borges, 2009). Feminist researchers have used quantitative and qualitative methodologies and outcome measures ranging from symptom reduction to increased empowerment (Chandler, Worell, Johnson, Blount, & Lusk, 1999).

Given psychology's current emphasis on empirically supported or evidence-based practice, more research is needed on the effectiveness of feminist-based treatments. One of the reasons for the low number of outcome research studies on feminist therapy outcomes is that the culture surrounding evidence-based practice is not a compatible fit with feminist perspectives. For example, currently quantitative research on the effectiveness of psychological treatments is based on the medical model and on reducing the presence or severity of symptoms. Feminist and diversity researchers also emphasize more strength-based, positive therapy outcomes (e.g., increasing empowerment, resiliency in oppressive environments, psychological well-being), and feminist research on therapy outcomes would need to include this non-medical focus.

Current evidence-based therapy research is also driven by diagnoses. That is, specific treatments are created for individuals with specific psychological disorders. As we have indicated earlier in this chapter, feminist practitioners are very cautious about (or reject) assigning diagnoses to their clients. Furthermore, the client-participants in the research studies on evidence-based treatments have overwhelmingly been Caucasians, and the treatments generally have been created using European cultural lenses. Thus, very little evidence exists about whether these treatments are effective or appropriate with ethnically diverse individuals. Finally, the psychological treatments that have been researched and supported all focus on changing individuals' thoughts, feelings, and behaviors (an intrapsychic focus). Feminist practitioners believe that society is a major source of individual problems in living. Thus, from a social-change perspective, the outcomes for feminist treatment, prevention programs, and advocacy interventions would be reduction in oppressive life events (e.g., fewer incidents of sexual harassment) and reduction in societal privilege and oppression.

Thus, the current culture of evidence-based psychology treatment conflicts with many feminist perspectives (Worell, 2001). Feminist practitioners not only need to create, label as feminist, and research the effectiveness of feminist interventions and models, they need to challenge the culture governing the establishment of efficacious treatments. We need to advocate for the use of strength-based outcomes, more qualitative methodology as well as innovative approaches to evaluating the impact of feminist therapies, and measurement of the impact of interventions on societal contexts. In essence, we need to change the existing culture to include feminist methods for researching feminist psychological practice.

Feminist Perspectives on Ethical Practice

As for all psychologists, feminist approaches are grounded in the American Psychological Association's Ethical Principles of Psychologists and Code of Conduct (2010). First, feminist practice is philosophically grounded in the aspirational Ethical Principles. Principle A (Beneficence and Non-Maleficence), Principle D (Justice), and E (Respect for Human Rights and Dignity) are especially important philosophical underpinnings for addressing societal privilege and oppression. These principles remind psychologists to provide benefit and not do harm to those whom we serve, to make psychology and its contributions accessible to all groups of people, to make sure that psychologists' biases do not lead to unjust practices, and to be aware of and honor cultural and individual differences in their work. The Codes of Conduct most relevant to work with diverse groups are 2.01 (Boundaries of Competence), 3.01 (Unfair Discrimination), 3.02 (Sexual Harassment), and 3.03 (Other Harassment). According to these codes, when providing services to diverse groups, psychologists are to have knowledge of these diverse groups and are not to engage in unfair discrimination or harassment (sexual or other). The codes do not specify the nature or depth of the required knowledge or the discriminatory acts.

While the Guidelines for Psychological Practice with Girls and Women (APA, 2007) are considered aspirational for psychologists, feminist psychological approaches, especially EFT, are also fundamentally grounded in these guidelines, which were written by psychologists using contextual and social justice lenses to view women's lives. The Guidelines for Psychological Practice with Girls and Women offer feminist practitioners a more specific map for working with diverse groups of women and girls than do the APA's Ethical Principles of Psychologists and Code of Conduct (2010). Included in each of the 11 guidelines is an explicatory narrative that is grounded in psychological research findings. The Guidelines for Psychological Practice with Girls and Women provide a series of challenges for all psychological practitioners (Remer, 2008a).

Remer (2008a) identified six challenges associated with the Guidelines for Psychological Practice with Girls and Women. The first challenge for psychologists is to be knowledgeable about the issues that impact the lives of women and girls and to understand how sociocultural contexts create or contribute to the existence of these issues and impede healing from them. The second challenge for psychologists is to be aware of and have tools for exploring the intersecting social identities of their clients and of their experiences with privilege and oppression. Psychologists must also understand how these gendered and oppressive experiences impact the lives of girls and women. They must develop tools for measuring occurrences of privilege and oppression in individuals' environments. The third challenge presented by the Guidelines is to develop theories and interventions to identify, use, and celebrate women's and girls' strengths. The fourth challenge for psychologists is to be involved in creating social change of societal structures, cultural beliefs, and hierarchical relationships that create and maintain oppression and distress in the lives of girls and women. Challenge five is for psychologists to be aware of their own social identities, cultural values, experiences with privilege and oppression, and the impacts of these on their professional interactions with others. The final challenge is for all psychologists to understand and embrace feminist, diversity, multicultural, and/or social justice approaches to psychological practice.

Feminist psychological practice meets most of the challenges reflected in the Guidelines. Feminist psychological practitioners have increased our understanding of diverse perspectives, have created interventions for changing societal structures, have provided tools for understanding the lives of women and girls in their societal contexts, and have researched the impact of societal oppression on the lives of women and girls. However, despite these important feminist practitioner contributions, the challenges reflected in the Guidelines are ongoing ones for feminist practitioners. These challenges provide both current and future directions for the work of feminist practitioners.

Future Directions

How do feminist practitioners manage the tension between using *DSM* diagnoses and resisting intrapsychic explanations of distress?

How does the transgender activist movement, which calls for acknowledgment of fluid gender identities, challenge or enrich feminist therapy theory?

How should feminist researchers respond to the trend for empirically validated treatments: by developing empirically validated feminist treatments, by challenging the assumptions behind the EVT movement, or with other responses?

How can feminist practitioners navigate the territory between our differences and our common, shared struggles?

How does feminist psychological practice apply to clients' privileged social identities?

How do we help psychologists who hold feminist philosophical beliefs to learn the skills to implement feminist and social justice theories?

How do we facilitate practitioners' integration of the Guidelines for Psychological Practice with Girls and Women into their professional services?

References

American Psychological Association. (1975). Report of the task force on sex bias and sex-role stereotyping in psychotherapeutic practice. *American Psychologist, 30,* 1169–1175.

American Psychological Association. (2007). Guidelines for psychological practice with girls and women. Washington, DC: American Psychological Association. doi:10.1037/0003-066X.62.9.949

American Psychological Association. (2010). Ethical principles of psychologists and code of conduct. Retrieved from http://www.apa.org/ethics/code/index.aspx.

Ballou, M. (2005). Threats and challenges to feminist therapy. In M. Hill & M. Ballou (Eds.), *The foundation and future of feminist therapy* (pp. 267–284). New York: Hayworth Press.

Ballou, M., Matsumoto, A., & Wagner, M. (2002). Toward a feminist ecological theory of human nature: Theory building in response to real-world dynamics. In M. Ballou & L. S. Brown (Eds.), *Rethinking mental health and disorder: Feminist perspectives* (pp. 99–144). New York: The Guilford Press.

Belenky, M. J., Clinchy, B. M., Goldberger, N. R., & Tarule, J. M. (1986). *Women's ways of knowing.* New York: Basic Books.

Brown, L. S. (1994). *Subversive dialogues: Theory in feminist therapy.* New York: Basic Books.

Brown, L. S. (1995). Cultural diversity in feminist therapy: Theory and practice. In H. Landrine (Ed.), *Bringing cultural diversity to feminist psychology: Theory, research, and practice* (pp. 143–162). Washington, DC: American Psychological Association.

Brown, L. S. (2000). Discomforts of the powerless: Feminist constructions of distress. In R. A. Neimeyer & J. D. Raskin (Eds.), *Constructions of disorder: Meaning-making frameworks for psychotherapy* (pp. 287–308). Washington, DC: American Psychological Association.

Cass, V. (1979). Homosexual identity formation: A theoretical model. *Journal of Homosexuality, 4,* 219–235.

Chandler, R., Worell, J., Johnson, D., Blount, A., & Lusk, M. (August 1999). Measuring long-term outcomes of feminist counseling and psychotherapy. In J. Worell (Chair), *Measuring process and outcomes of feminist counseling and therapy.* Presented at the annual meeting of the American Psychological Association, Boston, MA.

Chin, J. L. (Ed.). (1994). *Proceedings of the national conference on education and training in feminist practice.* Washington, DC: Office of Women's Affairs, American Psychological Association.

Chodorow, N. J. (1978). *The reproduction of mothering.* Berkeley: University of California Press.

Comas-Díaz, L. (1991). Feminism and diversity in psychology: The case of women of color. *Psychology of Women Quarterly, 15,* 594–610. doi:0361-6842/91.

Combahee River Collective (1982). A Black feminist statement. In G. T. Hull, P. B. Scott, & B. Smith (Eds.), *All the women are White, all the Blacks are men, but some of us are brave: Black women's studies* (pp. 13–22). Old Westbury, NY: Feminist Press.

Cook, D. A. (1999). Gestalt treatment of adolescent females with depressive symptoms: A treatment outcome study. *Dissertation Abstracts International, 60,* (8b), 4210.

Council of Counseling Psychology Training Programs, Association of Counseling Center Training Agencies, and Society of Counseling Psychology. (2009). Counseling psychology model training values statement addressing diversity. *The Counseling Psychologist, 37,* 641–643. DOI:10.1177/0011000009331930.

Cross, W. E. (1980). Models of psychological nigressence. In R. L. Jones (Ed.), *Black psychology* (pp 81–98). New York: Harper & Row.

D'Haene, M. T. (1995). Evaluation of feminist-based adolescent group therapy. *Smith College Studies in Social Work, 65*(2), 153–165.

Downing, D. E., & Roush, K. L. (1985). From passive acceptance to active commitment: A model of feminist identity development. *The Counseling Psychologist, 13,* 695–709.

Enns, C. Z. (1987). Gestalt therapy and feminist therapy: A proposed integration. *Journal of Counseling and Development, 66,* 93–95.

Enns, C. Z. (2004). *Feminist theories and feminist psychotherapies: Origins, themes, and diversity* (2nd ed.). New York: Hawthorne Press.

Fassinger, R. E. (2004). Centralizing feminism and multiculturalism in counseling. *Journal of Multicultural Counseling and Development, 32,* 344–345. Retrieved from http://vnweb.hwwilsonweb.com.ezproxy.uky.edu/hww/results/results_single_fulltext.jhtml;hwwilsonid=1IKQ1GTGN2KSTQA3DIOSFGOADUNGIIV0.

Fitzgerald, L. F., & Nutt, R. (1986). The Division 17 principles concerning the counseling/psychotherapy of women: Rationale and implementation. *The Counseling Psychologist, 14,* 180–216. doi: 10.1177/0011000086141019.

Fouad, N. A., McPherson, R. H., Gerstein, L., Blustein, D. L., Elman, N. S., Ihle Helledy, K., et al. (2004). Houston 2001: Context and legacy. *The Counseling Psychologist, 32,* 15–77. doi:10.1177/0011000003259943.

Gilligan, C. (1982). *In a different voice.* Cambridge, MA: Harvard University Press.

Goodman, L. A., Glenn, C., Bohlig, A., Banyard, V., & Borges, A. (2009). Feminist relational advocacy: Processes and outcomes from the perspective of low-income women with depression. *The Counseling Psychologist, 37,* 848–876. doi: 10:1177/0011000008326325

Goodman, L. A., Liang, B., Helms, J. E., Latta, R. E., Sparks, E., & Weintraub, S. R. (2004). Training counseling psychologists as social justice agents: Feminist and multicultural principles in action. *The Counseling Psychologist, 32,* 793–837.

Greene, B., & Sanchez-Hucles, J. (1997). Diversity: Advancing an inclusive feminist psychology. In J. Worell & N. G. Johnson (Eds.), *Shaping the future of feminist psychology: Education, research, and practice* (pp. 173–202). Washington, DC: American Psychological Association.

Greenspan, M. (1993). *A new approach to women and therapy.* New York: Wiley.

Grunebaum, H., & Chasin, R. (1978). Relabeling and reframing reconsidered: The beneficial effects of a pathological label. *Family Process, 17,* 449–456.

Hanisch, C. (1971). The personal is political. In J. Agel (Ed.), *The radical therapist* (pp. 152–157). New York: Ballantine.

Helms, J. (1995). An update of Helm's White and people of color racial identity models. In J. G. Pomeratto, J. M. Casas, I. A. Suzuki, & C. M. Alexander (Eds.), *Handbook of multicultural counseling* (pp. 181–198).Thousand Oaks, CA: Sage.

Holroyd, J. (1976). Psychotherapy and women's liberation. *Journal of Counseling Psychology, 6,* 22–28. doi:10.1177/001100007600600207

Jagger, A. M., & Rothenberg, P. S. (Eds.) (1984). *Feminist frameworks.* New York: McGraw-Hill.

Kravetz, D. (1978). Consciousness-raising groups in the 1970s. *Psychology of Women Quarterly, 3,* 168–186. doi:0361–6843/78/1600-0168$00 95

Kravetz, D. (1987). Benefits of consciousness-raising groups for women. In C. Broday (Ed.), *Women's therapy groups: Paradigms of feminist treatment* (pp. 55–66). New York: Springer.

Lee, J. (1997). Women re-authoring their lives through feminist narrative therapy. *Women and Therapy, 20*(3), 1–22. doi: 10.1300/J015v20n03_01.

Medley, S. (2000). Effect of self-persuasion on date rape prevention. Lexington: University of Kentucky.

Miller, J. B. (1976). *Toward a new psychology of women.* Boston: Beacon Press.

Nutt, R. (1979). Review and preview of attitudes and values of counselors of women. *Journal of Counseling Psychology, 8,* 18–20. doi:10.1177/001100007900800112.

Packard, T. (2009). The 2008 Leona Tyler Award Address: Core values that distinguish Counseling psychology: Personal and professional perspectives. *The Counseling Psychologist, 37,* 610–624. DOI: 10.1177/0011000009333986.

Porter, N. (2005). Location, location, location: Contributions of contemporary feminist theorists to therapy theory and practice. In M. Hill & M. Ballou (Eds.), *The foundation and future of feminist therapy* (pp. 143–160). New York: Hayworth Press.

Remer, P. (August 2008a). Challenges of implementing the Guidelines for clinical practice. In P. Remer (Chair), *The Guidelines for Psychological Practice with Girls and Women: Inspirations and challenges.* Symposium presented at the American Psychological Association annual conference, Boston, MA.

Remer, P. (2008b) Feminist counseling and psychotherapy. In J. Frew & M. Spiegler (Eds.) *Counseling and psychotherapy for a world of diversity: Theory and practice* (pp. 397–441). Boston, MA: Lahaska Press/Houghton Mifflin.

Remer, P., & Rostosky, S. (Spring, 2003). Practice talk: Feminist empowerment for rape survivors—Part 1. *The Feminist Psychologist, 30*(2), 22–23.

Remer, P., & University of Kentucky Counseling Psychology Date Rape Prevention Team (April 2004). *Preventing date rape: Research and treatment challenges.* Symposium presented at University of Kentucky, Lexington.

Remer, P., Worell, J., & Remer, R. (January, 2005). *Feminist psychological practice strategies for exploring the intersection of multicultural identities.* Workshop presented at the National Multicultural Conference and Summit, Hollywood, CA.

Santos de Barona, M., & Dutton, M. A. (1997). Feminist perspectives on assessment. In J. Worell & N. G. Johnson (Eds.), *Shaping the future of feminist psychology: Education, research, and practice* (pp. 37–56). Washington, DC: American Psychological Association.

Sarachild, K. (1970). A program for feminist "consciousness raising." In S. Firestone & A. Koedt (Eds.), *Notes from the second year* (pp. 78–80). New York: Redstockings, Inc.

Sarachild, K. (1975). Consciousness-raising: A radical weapon. In Redstockings (Eds.), *Feminist revolution* (pp. 144–150). New York: Redstockings, Inc.

Students for a Democratic Society (1969). National resolution on women. In B. Roszak & T. Roszak (Eds.), *Masculine/Feminine: Readings in sexual mythology and the liberation of women* (pp. 254–258). New York: Harper and Row.

Sue, D. W., & Sue, D. (1999). *Counseling the culturally different: Theory and practice.* New York: Wiley.

Wallace, M. (1982). A Black feminists search for sisterhood. In G. T. Hull, P. B. Scott, & B. Smith (Eds.), *All the women are white, all the Blacks are men, but some of us are brave: Black women's studies* (pp. 5–12). Old Westbury, NY: Feminist Press.

Waugh, P. (1998). Postmodernism and feminism. In S. Jackson and J. Jones (Eds.), *Contemporary feminist theories* (pp. 177–193). New York: New York University Press.

Westbury, E., & Tutty, L. M. (1998). *Child Abuse and Neglect, 23,* 31–44.

Worell, J. (2001). Feminist interventions: Accountability beyond symptom reduction. *Psychology of Women Quarterly, 25,* 335–343.

Worell, J., & Johnson, N. G. (Eds.). (1997). *Shaping the future of feminist psychology: Education, research, and practice.* Washington, DC: American Psychological Association.

Worell, J., & Remer, P., (1992). *Feminist perspectives in therapy: An empowerment model for women.* Chichester, UK: Wiley.

Worell, J., & Remer, P. (2003). *Feminist perspectives in therapy: Empowering diverse women* (2nd ed.). Hoboken, NJ: John Wiley & Sons.

Wyche, K. F., & Rice, J. K. (1997). Feminist therapy: From dialogue to tenets. In J. Worell & N. G. Johnson (Eds.), *Shaping the future of feminist psychology. Education, research, and practice* (pp. 55–72). Washington, DC: American Psychological Association.

CHAPTER

17 Feminist Therapy with Male Clients: Empowering Men to Be Their Whole Selves

Laurie B. Mintz *and* David Tager

Abstract

Empowerment is the overarching goal of feminist therapy. This is accomplished through an analysis of power, gender, and social location, with key strategies including the creation of an egalitarian therapy relationship and the framing of distress as attempts at gaining power in an oppressive and patriarchal society. The field of men and masculinity, emanating from feminist scholarship and created by the pioneering work of counseling psychologists, also strives to empower men. Like feminist therapy, the field of men and masculinity focuses heavily on analyzing gender roles and also, more recently, albeit less thoroughly, attends to issues of social location. This chapter attempts to do what surprisingly has not been done before: systematically integrate scholarship from the field of men and masculinity with the tenets and processes of feminist therapy. Through this integration, it is demonstrated that feminist therapy is an excellent therapeutic modality for doing psychotherapy with men.

Key Words: Feminist therapy, psychology of men and masculinity

Introduction

Toward the end of the 1960s, when therapists first began to use the term "feminist" to describe their work (Brown, 2010), few would have envisioned—or even endorsed—a chapter being written on feminist therapy with men. Then, in the 1980s, some clinicians and theorists began to champion feminist therapy for use with men (e.g., Collins, 2002; Ganley, 1988). Nevertheless, had this chapter been written in that era, many would have still questioned whether feminist therapy was applicable to male clients. An even more contentious issue would have been the question of whether men could be feminist therapists. Indeed, it has only been over the course of the first decade of the twenty-first century, as feminist therapy has increasingly recognized the importance of intersecting identities, that feminist therapists have generally come to advocate the value of feminist therapy for both male and female clients, as well as embrace the idea that feminist therapists can be of any gender (Ballou, Hill, & West, 2008; Brown, 2010; Enns, 2004; Levant & Silverstein, 2005; Walker, 2001; Worell and Remer, 2003). In the last decade, a body of work has begun to emerge that outlines specific utilizations of feminist therapy involving men, with much of this work in the area of couples and family therapy (e.g., Hill & Rothblum, 1996; Nutt, 2005; Rampage 2000; Silverstein, 2005; Silverstein & Goodrich, 2003; Zimmerman & Besel, 2008). Some scholarship has also focused on treating presenting concerns such as men's trauma (Mejia, 2005) and anorexia nervosa among men (Soban, 2006). Clearly, feminist therapy has moved past questions regarding the place of men as clients and therapists. Feminist therapy has "evolved significantly from its roots as a psychotherapy for women . . . into a sophisticated postmodern, technically integrative model of practice that utilizes the analysis of gender, social location, and power as primary strategies for comprehending human difficulties. It has become a practice that encompasses work with women and men..." (Brown, 2010, p. 2).

During the same era that feminist therapy was undergoing this significant transformation to include men as therapists and clients, a new field of study concerning men was emerging. In 1995, Division 51 of the American Psychological Association, the Society for the Psychological Study of Men and Masculinity, was founded. In 1997, the APA Council recognized this Division with permanent status. In 2000, the associated journal, the *Psychology of Men and Masculinity*, made its debut. Of note, counseling psychologists have been at the forefront of this field of study. According to the American Psychological Association (APA, 2009), 21% of Division 51 members are also members of Division 17, the highest percentage of overlap with any APA Division. Even more striking, the vast majority of Division 51 presidents (e.g., Gary Brooks, Glenn Good, Mark Kiselica, Sam Cochran, John Robertson, Fred Rabinowitz, Chris Kilmartin, Jay Wade, Aaron Rochlen) were trained as counseling psychologists. Likewise, many of the scholars in the field of men and masculinity have been counseling psychologists. Just a few examples of the many important works by counseling psychologists on providing more effective therapy with men are Good and Brooks's (2001) two-volume *Handbook of Psychotherapy and Counseling with Men*, and Rabinowitz and Cochran's (2002) *Deepening Psychotherapy with Men*. Other important works by counseling psychologists have included contributions regarding theoretical models of masculinity (e.g., O'Neil, Helms, Gable, David, & Wrightsman, 1986) and on marketing mental health services to men and barriers to help-seeking (e.g., Aaron Rochlen's "Real Men. Real Depression." campaign sponsored by the National Institute of Mental Health; Rochlen, McKelly, & Pituch, 2006). The work of these counseling psychologists, and many others, will be highlighted in this chapter.

Given counseling psychologists' central role in the field of the psychology of men and masculinity, it seems fitting that a chapter in *The Oxford Handbook of Feminist Multicultural Counseling Psychology* would focus on this work. Indeed, this chapter will attempt to do what has surprisingly not been systematically done before: to draw upon knowledge from the study of the psychology of men and masculinity to explain why and how feminist therapy is an excellent therapeutic modality for doing psychotherapy with men.

Integrating Feminist Therapy and the Psychology of Men

In an attempt to integrate feminist therapy with scholarship and knowledge from the field of men and masculinity, the historical debt that the latter owes to the former will first be articulated. This section will also highlight the overlapping missions between the two fields. Following this, the three key elements of feminist therapy as defined by Brown (2010), specifically the analysis of power, gender, and social location, will each be examined for their applicability to therapy with men. These three sections will first integrate feminist therapy with the theory and research in the field of the psychology of men and masculinity. Then, within each of these sections, specific therapy suggestions stemming from the analyses of power, gender, and social location will be detailed and case examples provided. A final, detailed case example will illustrate the interplay among all three realms of analysis and associated strategies. This will be followed by a section on the importance of therapist self-awareness, recommendations for bringing such awareness into the therapy room, and two case examples of when a failure to do so impeded the therapy process. Finally, conclusions will be drawn and future directions suggested.

Historical Debt and Overlapping Mission

Feminist thinking, and in particular the analysis of gender roles, has had a strong influence on the development of the field of the psychology of men and masculinity. The Division 51 mission statement (American Psychological Association, n.d.) explicitly documents this notable influence when it states that the Society for the Psychological Study of Men and Masculinity (SPSMM), "acknowledges its historical debt to feminist-inspired scholarship on gender..." While feminist scholarship is explicitly recognized in the SPSMM mission statement, the tenets of feminist therapy are implicitly reflected throughout.

Key elements of feminist therapy are analyzing gender, power, and social location with the goal of understanding and alleviating distress (Brown, 2010). All three are reflected in the SPSMM mission statement. Specifically, analyzing power and social location are briefly alluded to when it is noted that this professional society "commits itself to the support of groups such as women, gays, lesbians and people of color that have been uniquely oppressed by the gender/class/race system." Likewise, the feminist therapy notion that "...patriarchal realities serve as a source of distress and as a brake on growth and personal power for all humans" (Brown, 2010, p. 4) is reflected in the SPSMM mission statement that "constraining definitions of masculinity . . . have . . . contributed to the oppression of other people." In short, the feminist therapy concepts of analyzing both social location and power are reflected within the mission of SPSMM.

Central to the SPSMM mission statement is the analysis of gender. Specifically, feminist therapy's foundation " . . . in a close and careful analysis of the meanings and contributions of gender . . . to the etiologies . . . [and alleviation] of distress and dysfunction" (Brown, 2010, p. 3) is essential to the SPSMM mission statement. Specifically, SPSMM (a) "Promotes the critical study of how gender . . . constricts men's lives"; (b) "Endeavors to erode constraining definitions of masculinity which historically have inhibited men's development [and] their capacity to form meaningful relationships"; and (c) "Contends vigorously that the empowerment of all persons beyond narrow and restrictive gender role definitions leads to the highest level of functioning in individual women and men. . . . " Most certainly, such statements make it clear that the feminist therapy concept of analyzing gender is front and center in the field of men and masculinity. Such statements also lead to the conclusion that the field of the psychology of men and masculinity holds the same mission as that of feminist therapy: social change. Feminist therapy "accomplishes the overarching goal of psychotherapy as a key for social change at the individual level by analyzing gender, power and social location/multiple identities as strategies for comprehending how and why a person feels distress or behaves in dysfunctional ways" (Brown, 2010, p.5).

These three levels of analysis—power, gender, and social location/multiple identities—as well as their implications for doing feminist therapy with men, will each be considered in turn. Dividing the chapter into these three distinct arenas is a bit artificial, in that there is much overlap between them. Even more importantly, while the analysis of power, gender, and social location are identified by Brown (2010) as three key elements of feminist therapy, they are not three equally situated elements. Feminist therapy's main goal is empowerment, with one specific strategy for accomplishing this being the nurturance of a client's multiple identities resulting from an analysis of gender and social location (Brown, 2010). In short, the analysis of power is the primary level of analysis and intervention within feminist therapy.

The Analysis of Power and Powerlessness

The analysis of power dynamics and their impact within personal, familial and societal contexts lies at the heart of feminist therapy. Feminist therapists view distress as primarily the result of disempowerment in the lives of individuals (Ballou, Hill, & West, 2008; Brown, 2010; Worell & Remer, 2003). As stated by Brown (2010), " . . . the theory behind feminist therapy argues that much powerlessness can be transformed . . . and that one disempowerment strategy of patriarchies has been the creation of a trance of powerlessness that is both cultural and personal, in which various messages are conveyed that a client cannot empower themselves" (p. 35). Continuing further, Brown states that "feminist therapy subverts and interrupts the trance of powerlessness by inviting its participants to notice where and how greater power is actually available to them" (Brown, 2010, p. 35). Importantly, client empowerment is "the superordinate goal" of feminist therapy (Brown, 2010, p. 29).

At first glance, it may seem strange to speak of empowering male clients, since men, especially men of European descent, belong to a group that is historically privileged. The second author remembers well the response from pre-doctoral psychology interns at a workshop on men's issues and psychotherapy with Glenn Good, a counseling psychologist who has contributed enormously to the field of the psychology of men and masculinity. During this training, one of the interns who had been trained in the impact of gender, race and ethnicity on women and minority clients, said: "I never thought of men as having difficulties related to power." This intern was acknowledging that adherence to cultural norms of masculinity brings benefits to men, including feelings of competence, rewards of status and power, and respect by peers (e.g., Connell, 1995; Mahalik, Good, & Englar-Carlson, 2003; Mahalik, Locke, et al., 2003). Nevertheless, what the intern was not fully cognizant of is that power in one area of life does not preclude disempowerment in another. This intern was just beginning to recognize that "patriarchal systems . . . intentionally and unintentionally disempower almost all people . . . " (Brown, 2010, p. 34), including men.

Even men, whose lives seem emblematic of male power and privilege, are disempowered by patriarchy. The first author recalls vividly a wealthy White executive with whom she worked; his wealth and Whiteness bestowed him with much power and privilege in our culture, yet his morbidly obese weight disempowered him though shame, discrimination, and his wife's repulsion of him sexually. She recalls another male client, a handsome African American businessman who had also been a star athlete in college. In the boardroom and on the basketball court, his power was obvious. However, when he wore his jeans and t-shirt and walked down the city streets at night, he reported being aware of his imposing muscularity and his Blackness—and he felt disempowered by the palpable fear that others exhibited toward him.

Clearly, men who are powerful in one arena may be disempowered in any number of other ways, including within the other realms of analysis (i.e., gender and social location) to be discussed subsequently. Men may experience disempowerment based on socioeconomic status or physical ability. Men experience racism and discrimination. Men struggle to negotiate cultural differences. Men can feel conflicted about, and hated for, their sexual orientation. Men are often even disempowered by internalizing and embracing the masculine expectations of power.

Many men who embrace traditional masculine mandates of power become disempowered through disconnection with others. Men who experience privilege and power in most social realms can find themselves isolated from their partners and children, able to command but unable to share their vulnerabilities or to let anyone matter in their lives. A man's consuming pursuit of status and power may deprive him of his ability to experience his emotional world and to establish fulfilling personal connections based on mutual care and support (Levant, 1996; Pollack, 2005; Real, 1998). One way that feminist therapy can empower men is through assisting them in connecting more deeply with others.

A first step to helping men become empowered in therapy is through fostering an egalitarian therapy relationship. For some men, the act of connecting on a deep level with the therapist represents an achievement in itself (Good & Mintz, 2005). The therapeutic relationship is also one that they can use as a springboard for growth in other relationships. Feminist therapy stresses an egalitarian relationship as central to feminist practice, not only because it helps foster trust between therapist and client, but also because it begins the process of empowering the client to make choices about her or his life (e.g., Ballou, Hill, & West, 2008; Brown, 2010; Worell & Remer, 2003). Fostering an egalitarian relationship can thus be viewed as a critical therapy strategy that stems from a feminist therapist's analysis of power and his or her attempt to empower the client. Framing symptoms as resistance to powerlessness is another key strategy related to a power analysis in feminist therapy. Both of these therapy strategies related to power analysis are discussed subsequently.

THERAPY STRATEGIES RELATED TO POWER ANALYSIS

Feminist therapy does not use the term "psychopathology"; instead, the terms "distress" and "behavioral dysfunction" are used (Brown, 2010). A key aspect of feminist therapy is conceptualizing the source of a client's distress and behavioral dysfunctions as external rather than internal. Writings in the field of men and masculinity also emphasize this concept; Johnson (2005) recommends that (female) therapists view male clients' responses not as individual pathology, but rather as a product of male socialization. Indeed, a goal of feminist therapy is to help clients to understand the "...patriarchal context and its role as the ultimate distal source of the client's problems" (Brown, 2010, p. 59). In feminist therapy, symptoms are seen as a resistance to powerlessness.

The notion of distress and problematic behaviors being a form of resistance to a sense of disempowerment is quite useful in conducting feminist therapy with men. Attempting to live up to masculine expectations of power can result in myriad problems for men. It can result in the denial of psychological pain, and the transformation of fear and hurt into risk-taking, anger, and violence (e.g., Jakupcak, Tull, & Roemer, 2005; Tager, Good, & Brammer, 2010). Men are four times more likely to commit suicide and much more likely than women to develop problems related to substance abuse (Cochran & Rabinowitz, 2000; NIMH, 2009), as well as more likely to struggle with workaholism and aggressive behaviors (Cochran & Rabinowitz, 2000). If we begin to talk about men of color, and African American men in particular, we can cite a bevy of statistics about unemployment, poverty, murder rates, and discrimination. Additionally, writings about African American men underscore the hyper-tough masculine norms of gangsta rap and "cool pose" (Majors & Billsun, 1993), which can be interpreted as acts of resistance to the disempowerment of an imposed invisibility (Franklin, 2002). In short, in feminist therapy with men, coping strategies such as guardedness and aggression are viewed as attempts to solve an experience of powerlessness. Once therapists feel genuine empathy for the client and recognize his behavior as coping, they are in a better position to build the necessary therapeutic relationship through which to assist him to develop alternative strategies of resistance.

There is a great deal of literature stressing the importance of the therapeutic relationship for therapy outcomes (e.g., Norcross & Lambert, 2005; Wampold, 2001). In feminist therapy, fostering an egalitarian relationship between the therapist and the client is the first step toward empowering clients. Empowering the client begins with an effort to reduce the power differential between therapist and client, so that the client becomes invested in shaping the direction of therapy. Common factors research reports that when clients experience ownership of the direction of therapy, positive outcomes are enhanced (Bohart, 2005). Feminist therapy makes this common factor core (Brown, 2010). Likewise, those writing about effective therapy with men (e.g., Good & Brooks, 2005; Englar-Carlson & Stevens, 2006) highlight the importance of the therapist engaging with the client in a collaborative process of identifying the focus of therapy and setting mutually agreed-upon goals. Good and Mintz (2005) emphasize that establishing collaborative working alliances and setting mutually agreed-upon goals are central to working with male clients. However, they also note that male norms of self-reliance, strength, and independence can make bonding with a therapist quite difficult. If men are in distress, but not accustomed to displaying vulnerability, they may attempt to keep the therapist at a distance.

The therapist can set the stage for a more egalitarian and trusting relationship by setting up a collaborative framework that establishes the expertise of both the therapist and the client. The therapist can recognize the client's autonomy by pointing out that he is the expert on himself, while the therapist has training and experience working with other people. It can also be useful to give voice to any doubts that the client may display. Men coming to therapy for the first time are often skeptical of its value. If, for example, a client implies that he's not sure the therapist has what it takes to help, a useful response might be something along the lines of: "Well, I don't know if I can either. I've helped a good many, but I'm not a good match for everyone. I'm willing to try, though, if you are." From the very beginning of therapy, the feminist therapist attempts to model non-defensiveness, to invite collaboration, and to respect the client's limits, while also establishing the trust and safety necessary for difficult feedback to flow in either direction.

Establishing such a relationship with a male client can be challenging. Some male clients may defer to a therapist's supposed expertise and may seek the answer on how "to fix" the problems they identify. Here, the therapist may have to point out the limits of his or her power. This can be done by assisting the client in revising the therapist's feedback to make it more valid for him, and by helping the client to develop trust in his ability to understand and negotiate his situation. An opposite challenge occurs when male clients contest the power in the room in an effort to dominate the relationship. This may occur with either male or female therapists, though the risks tend to be different due to gender socialization. In male-male pairings, the therapist, aware of his own socialization, has to be careful not to react by exerting his power or engaging in a competitive process (Sher, 2005). With the same type of client, female therapists may have to fight against feeling dismissed (Johnson, 2005). A feminist therapist working with such men must continually keep in mind that an egalitarian relationship in which the client can feel safe, heard, and empowered is the goal. The feminist approach of attending to power dynamics in the room and working to create a more egalitarian relationship is a crucial tool in establishing collaboration, setting mutual goals, and ultimately, empowering the client to make the changes that he desires for himself.

Establishing an egalitarian relationship in therapy is not a one-time event that occurs at the start of therapy. Continually monitoring the balance of power and the degree of collaboration is an ongoing part of the therapy process (e.g., Brown, 2010; Johnson, 2005). Asking permission to make observations, framing these observations in tentative language, and inviting clients to clarify and revise are all techniques that build collaboration. Brown (2010, p. 87) emphasizes "the no-coercion rule" of feminist therapy, which means that the client needs to set the agenda, pace, and goals of therapy, regardless of what the therapist thinks would be useful. The therapist's task is not to direct the client, but to offer her or his knowledge, insight, and experience in the form of invitations that the client is free to accept or reject. Negotiation and re-negotiation of the direction and goals of therapy empower the client to tackle his difficulties as he defines them and to strive for changes that make him feel more competent to handle challenges as they occur.

One specific tool for maintaining an egalitarian relationship in feminist therapy is self-disclosure (e.g., Ballou, Hill, & West, 2008; Brown, 2010; Worell & Remer, 2003). A therapist might mention his or her own struggles when doing so seems clinically relevant to the client's issues. The authors of this chapter frequently use limited self-disclosure as a means of increasing trust in the relationship and creating a balance of power. The idea is not to make the therapist the focus of discussion, or to claim knowledge about the client's situation, but to acknowledge the therapist's humanity and to thereby equalize the power dynamics in the room. Similarly, when clients ask questions of therapists, their queries are conceptualized as clients legitimately wanting to know something about the person with whom they are working in order to have a better context for understanding the therapist's feedback. Answering such questions, and processing the meaning of the answer to the client, is another means of fostering an egalitarian therapy relationship. Essentially, self-disclosure is one tool in a feminist therapist's effort to be transparent about the process of therapy and to attend to issues of power both in the room and in the world, thereby fostering a respectful and equalitarian therapy relationship.

THE CASE OF BOB

Bob, a 65-year-old European American male, came to therapy at the suggestion of his wife to deal with issues of compulsive gambling. He initially indicated that he did not want to be in therapy and that he most certainly did not want the therapist to talk to him about feelings. He explained that his wife, a survivor of sexual abuse at the hands of a therapist, had been exploring these issues in therapy for years and had not been making progress. He did not trust therapists and he did not trust the process of therapy for helping him to change. Still, he was here because he wanted to save his marriage, and his wife indicated that going to therapy could assist with this goal. The therapist reflected Bob's ambivalence regarding therapy and invited him to collaboratively set goals and a method for approaching therapy that would be useful. It was agreed that therapy would focus strictly on the behavior (compulsive gambling) that Bob was attempting to eliminate. The therapist continually checked in with Bob on both his progress and, importantly, his comfort with the process of therapy. On one occasion, when the therapist did ask a feeling question, Bob told her in no uncertain terms that this was not what he was there for. The therapist apologized and explained that while she wanted very much to meet him where he was, she was oriented to asking such questions because of her theoretical viewpoint regarding the relationship between buried feelings and compulsive behaviors. Nevertheless, she also ceased asking feeling questions, explaining to the client that she wanted to honor his view of what he needed in therapy. When the client asked questions about the therapist's training, experience, and orientation to therapy, she answered them non-defensively and inquired as to the effect of her answers on the client.

The client eventually decreased his behaviors, thus creating trust in the therapist and in therapy. He then began to explore some of the root causes of his compulsive behaviors, including physical abuse suffered at the hands of his alcoholic father, and his resultant feelings of self-loathing. He also began to explore how his choice of behaviors—gambling—was related to his views of himself as a man and of expectations for masculine risk-taking and success. In short, fostering a feminist egalitarian relationship with Bob both assisted him in meeting his initial therapy goals and also allowed him to feel safe enough to explore the second realm of feminist therapeutic analysis: the analysis of gender.

The Analysis of Gender

Both feminist therapists and psychologists who specialize in the study of masculinity (e.g., scholars in Division 51) have long noted that gender roles create a powerful set of norms that encourage certain types of gendered self-construal (self-perception and self-presentation) by labeling them as "feminine" or "masculine" (e.g., Cross & Madson, 1997; Eagly, Wood, & Diekman, 2000; Guimond et al., 2007). We learn as children, long before we are conscious of gender roles, that conforming to these norms tends to garner positive attention and to raise our self-esteem, while non-conformity can bring disapproval and cause us to feel bad about ourselves.

According to the most prominent psychological models of masculine socialization, men often experience conflict related to the attempt to live up to masculine norms in specific contexts. This conflict has been variously labeled the *gender role strain paradigm* (Pleck, 1981, 1995), *gender role conflict* (O'Neil, et al., 1986), *gender role stress* (Eisler & Skidmore, 1987) and *masculine role conflict* (Good, Borst, & Wallace, 1994). Pleck (1981, 1995) theorized that men can experience strain when they fail to live up to male role expectations (e.g., hurting when they shouldn't), when they are traumatized by the process of fulfilling expectations (e.g., attempting to save a fellow soldier in battle), and when they experience the negative side effects of fulfilling a particular set of expectations (e.g., self-reliance and devotion to work leading to isolation). O'Neil and colleagues (e.g., O'Neil, 2008; O'Neil et al., 1986) lay out a similar model that emphasizes the restriction of human experience when men adhere rigidly to masculine norms and therefore cannot allow themselves or others to deviate in least from the stereotypic expectations of masculine ideology for fear of appearing unmanly. One illustrative example of this pertains to norms for career and financial success.

Men have long measured their worth by their ability to provide for their families and by career success. The most common psychological models of American masculinity all include the idea of the breadwinner, the sturdy oak, the man in pursuit of status as a key element of socialized masculine expectations (e.g., Brannon, 1976; O'Neil, 1981; Pleck, 1981; Mahalik, Good, et al., 2003; Mahalik, Locke, et al., 2003). Even in contemporary dual-earner families that embrace an egalitarian ideology, men, gay or straight, tend to invest more of their sense of self-worth in their status as workers and economic providers than in their ability to nurture and emotionally provide for their partners and children. Dual-earner heterosexual couples may now represent the majority of couples with children, but men are still expected to be the chief providers, and women are still expected to be the chief custodians of emotional expressiveness and child-rearing (Pleck, 1997; Vogel, Wester, Heesacker, & Madon, 2003). Gay male couples, while free of typical heterosexual gender role expectations with regard to division of labor, still report struggling with their self-concepts as men when faced with the reality of sacrificing some measure of career success to raise children (Silverstein, Auerbach, & Levant, 2003).

Masculine expectations related to work and earning can wind up disempowering men in several ways. Men who devote a tremendous amount of energy to fulfilling career expectations may find themselves disempowered in terms of their ability to establish lasting, satisfying relationships with partners, children, and friends. At the same time, men who are not as successful at their jobs as they feel they should be may struggle with low self-esteem and a sense of having failed to live up to expectations of being a man. Even men who willingly give up jobs or career advancement for the sake of raising children often experience some conflict with expectations about their masculine identity. From a feminist therapy perspective, gender role expectations become disempowering when they conflict with an individual's experience, restrict an individual's ability to fulfill needs, or generally serve to oppress the client's sense of self and ability to function.

One of feminist therapy's great contributions to psychotherapy has been to insist on an exploration of how gendered expectations can disempower clients when they do not conform or when they sacrifice their well-being in an effort to conform (e.g., Ballou, Hill, & West, 2008; Brown, 2010; Worell & Remer, 2003). Stated simply, feminist therapy usefully requires an exploration of a client's gender role schemata and its impact on the individual. This element of feminist practice fits well with recommendations from the psychology of men.

Good, Gilbert, and Sher (1990) integrated feminist therapy and knowledge of gender into Gender Aware Therapy in an early influential description of how principles of feminist therapy could be beneficially applied to both men and women. More recent recommendations for clinical practice with men (e.g., Good & Brooks, 2005; Englar-Carlson & Stevens, 2006) also include an exploration of clients' gender roles and their implications. Exploring gender-role expectations in therapy with men and underlining the ways in which masculine expectations may contribute to presenting concerns can empower male clients to see themselves in a more positive light and can liberate them to make changes that align with their needs and current goals. The goal is not to transform men into a particular way of being, but to assist them in reevaluating what it means to be themselves as men and as human beings.

THERAPY STRATEGIES RELATED TO GENDER ANALYSIS

Three related therapeutic strategies associated with the analysis of gender are those of normalizing distress, re-framing help-seeking as strength, and specifically examining the gendered context of men's distress. First, men often view help-seeking as a sign of weakness, and as a threat to their masculine identity (e.g., Addis & Mahalik, 2003; Mahalik, Good, et al., 2003). Men who think this way tend to perceive their desire for help as confirmation that they have failed to live up to expectations of self-reliance, independence, and leadership. If this is a client's perspective, then he is likely to be guarded and defensive, and feel ashamed or defeated when he does ask for help. It can thus be helpful for the therapist to explicitly recognize how difficult it is to seek help, to note how the process can feel shameful or embarrassing to many men, and to emphasize the courage that it takes to confront one's difficulties. Additionally, we also suggest normalizing distress as something that happens to everyone in the course of a lifetime and of framing therapy as a useful strategy for overcoming the difficult periods that every human being, no matter how capable and strong, must somehow struggle through. We also advocate praising clients for the courage that it takes to acknowledge their struggles.

Framing the process of change as one that requires courage and strength can create a bridge between masculine norms and the expression of vulnerability. It can assist male clients in becoming more flexible in their idea of what strength is and can begin the process of assisting them to a more nuanced and better-fitting gender identity. Certainly, developing a better fitting gender identity requires an explicit examination of gender role messages and expectations, another key feminist therapy technique.

THE CASE OF SIMON

Simon was a thirty-something European American who presented with career concerns and symptoms of depression that he had difficulty acknowledging. Simon reported that the main problem was indecision about what to do next in his career. He said he liked teaching high school, but could not see doing it for the rest of his life. He described having looked at various options, including joining a research team or going back to school for a Ph.D., possibly in political science or economics. He also considered trying to becoming a stand-up comic, since he had had success in small venues throughout his college and graduate school years. However, Simon said that the more he investigated various career options, or imagined a career as a comic, the worse he felt about himself and the more uncertain and apathetic he became. Simon noted that an additional uncertainty for him was that he and his wife were trying to have a child. He reported that his wife was a physician who worked long hours and made three times the money he did. Simon considered himself a "modern" young man. From his perspective, if anyone was going to stop working to take care of a child, it should be him. In fact, he said he liked the idea of being a stay-at-home father, though he also reported being scared by the idea.

As the therapist and Simon began to explore gender roles and expectations related to work and family, Simon described being proud that he had supported his wife's move from medical school in a big Western city to a job in the rural Midwest where she would be given loan forgiveness. He acknowledged that he had given up his social support networks and his access to familiar comedy clubs to a live in a small town that he did not particularly like. He reported feeling isolated and different from the other teachers at his school, who had mostly grown up in or near the small city where he and his wife had located. But mostly, Simon spoke about how he had always thought he would do something "great" that stood out and showed him to be among the best in his career. He reported feeling that it was not enough for him to be a teacher, even a very good one, and acknowledged that while he was excited by the idea of being a stay-at-home father, he was also terrified that by doing so he would give up his chance to make his professional mark on the world.

By exploring gendered expectations, Simon was able to recognize that he was caught between the desire to take on the non-traditional role of stay-at-home father (which was a natural extension of his choices to teach and move out of his preferred environment in support of his wife) and the fear of not being successful in the more conventional sense of passionately rising to the top of an esteemed profession in a competitive big city or at a research university. In the course of therapy, Simon realized that his conflict was not about finding a career. He was torn between wanting to meet gender role expectations of achievement and status and wanting to prioritize the effort to have a direct positive impact on relationships with his and other families.

By underlining the impact of gender socialization and the societal devaluation of parenting and teaching, Simon was empowered to make a choice. In his case, Simon decided that he did want to become a stay-at-home father, and that he did like teaching, which he could return to when his child was in school. He and his therapist discussed the hard work of parenting, the difficulties of being a male primary caregiver, and the challenges that Simon might face. He was living in a community where men were expected to be at work during the day, not feeding a baby while pushing a cart in the supermarket or leading a toddler into the bathroom of the public library. Also discussed in therapy were ways of connecting with other stay-at-home fathers and the need to create a social network and to remain engaged with his adult interests. Simon left therapy excited about the future and with a sense of purpose for the first time since moving to the Midwest.

The purpose of gender-role analysis with Simon was to collaborate in discovering the type of gender-role conflict that he was experiencing. In the simplest terms, he found that he was caught between the more dominant societal expectations of masculine achievement and the kind of relational expectations that are associated with stay-at-home fathers, egalitarianism, and "sensitive" men. The goal was not to advocate for a certain choice, but to give Simon the ability to see that he had a choice and to empower him to reshape his masculine identity to better fit his needs and desires, rather than simply reacting to masculine norms.

The same exploration could have taken place with a man who conformed much more to ideals of masculine achievement, but felt disempowered by economics, or perhaps by egalitarian ideals that might suggest that he should be the one to become a full-time parent. In that case, a feminist approach to gender-role analysis might have helped the hypothetical client to decide, for example, that it was time for him to pursue his dreams of success and achievement while negotiating parenting in the model of dual-earning couples, rather than following the original plan of becoming a stay-at-home father.

Regardless of the client's attitudes toward gender, gender-role analysis cannot take place in isolation. Gender is just one of many critical social locations and multiple identities that must be examined in feminist therapy with men.

The Analysis of Social Location

Feminist therapy stresses the need for a multicultural and ecological approach to gender that takes into account intersecting identities and overlapping social contexts (e.g., Brown, 2010; Hays, 2008; Root, 2000). The multicultural emphasis of contemporary feminist therapy (e.g., Ballou, Hill, & West, 2008; Brown, 2010; Worell & Remer, 2003) provides for an essential analysis of social contexts that intersect with gender and, at times, may feel even more salient to individuals experiencing distress in some dimension of their lives. In its broadest sense, this multicultural framework highlights not only race, ethnicity, and sexual orientation, but every diverse context in the lives of clients, from belief systems and socioeconomic status to geography, physical appearance, and the various environments through which an individual moves in the course of daily existence. This sort of multicultural framework is also emphasized in the literature on the psychology of men and on the practice of psychotherapy with men (e.g., Good et al., 1994; Good & Brooks, 2005; Smiler, 2004; Englar-Carlson & Stevens, 2006).

As many scholars have pointed out, scripts of male identity vary depending on socio-cultural location, are affected by other aspects of identity, and may, at times come in conflict with each other (e.g., Caldwell & White, 2005; Cervantes, 2006; Connell, 1995; Majors & Billsun, 1993; Smiler, 2004; Wade, 2008). To illustrate, gay and bisexual African American male students at predominantly White institutions experience both racial and sexual prejudice from peers that can affect their ability to build relationships within both LGBT and African American communities (Goode-Cross & Good, 2009; Harris, 2003; Washington & Wall, 2006). These young men often choose to very selectively disclose their sexual orientation; they often work to conform to masculine expectations in order to gain the social support from African American peers and mentors needed to thrive in a predominantly White environment (Goode-Cross & Tager, 2011). In essence, these young men are forced to navigate multiple oppressions, and may find themselves struggling to conform to different expectations in different contexts, sometimes restricting vital aspects of their identity.

The former example illustrates how male identity can be scripted by a variety of social locations, including race, ethnicity, and sexual orientation. Religious views and socioeconomic status are additional aspects of social location that intersect with both male and ethnic/racial identity. Hondagneu-Sotelo and Messner (1994) identify a "New Man" version of masculinity defined by ideals of greater gender-egalitarianism and sensitivity, a stance that the authors identify with economic privilege and which, they note, often comes in conflict with the more "traditional" masculinity that is fairly typical of ethnic minorities and of communities of lower socioeconomic status. Abreu, Goodyear, Campos, and Newcomb (2000) concur, identifying both SES and ethnic identity differences in male role attitudes, with men from lower SES groups tending to display more "traditional" masculine attitudes. Ojeda, Rosales, and Good (2008) found that Mexican American college men endorse "traditional" masculine norms at higher levels than a predominantly White sample of college men.

Certainly, however, even "traditional" masculinity can vary by social location. We can imagine a farm worker, an L.A. lawyer, a gang member, and a gay teacher all sharing a Mexican heritage and the values associated with machismo (Cervantes, 2006), but varying in education, acculturation, and economic resources. These four diverse men, although all having Mexican heritage, would differ in their views of what constitutes strength, honor, male family roles, respect, the legitimate use of force, male spirituality, and the acceptability of emotional displays (Cervantes, 2006). There is no doubt that various aspects of social location (e.g., cultural background, SES, sexual orientation) intersect with gender identity, and that an analysis of social location must therefore be front and center in feminist therapy with men.

Also critical to an analysis of men's concerns in feminist therapy with men is context. Specifically, an individual man's values and behavior tend to vary according to his milieu. Indeed, individuals often move between contexts in which masculine behavioral expectations vary and a sort of multicultural fluency becomes necessary to comfortably negotiate diverse cultural codes. Addis, Mansfield, and Syzdek, in their recent critique of the empirical project of measuring the impact of masculine socialization (2010), note how men learn a repertoire of different responses for different situational contexts. For example, there is a discernible difference between how men tend to behave in a fraternity dining hall and in a majority female psychology class. The expectations that an African American male faces on the streets of an urban Black neighborhood may vary considerably from expectations in a White neighborhood or in the boardroom of a majority White company, with racism and microaggressions more palpable in the latter environments (e.g., Sue, 2010). Our clients' social location and multiple identities affect their masculine sense of self, presenting concerns, and what feels empowering and disempowering in their lives.

THERAPY STRATEGIES RELATED TO SOCIAL LOCATION ANALYSIS

In order to understand the identity of our male clients, empathize with their struggles, and assist in alleviating their distress and empowering them, we need to work with them to explore the impact of their sociocultural location as men. Discussing with clients how their various aspects of identity and environment contribute to their distress and sense of empowerment or disempowerment is a crucial strategy for feminist therapy with men. Some critical topics of discussion include how our male clients identify and what conflicts they experience between such identities. What sorts of bias do they encounter? What do our clients experience when they move between environments, and how do these experiences influence their sense of themselves as individuals, men, community members, and human beings? In order to collaborate with our clients, we need to understand as best we can their sense of their own identity in its complex and potentially conflicted richness.

A key element of feminist therapy that is essential when working with men, then, is an exploration of intersecting identities and social location. Certainly, such an analysis cannot be separated from the other key elements of feminist therapy: the analysis of gender and the analysis of power, including the overarching goal of client empowerment. Given this, all three elements of feminist therapy are woven together into an integrated case example.

Putting It All Together: The Case of Derrick

Derrick was a 26-year-old African American law student attending a land-grant university in the Midwest. During his first session, he stated that he had come solely on the suggestion of his fiancé, and expressed ambivalence about counseling. The therapist, a European American male, responded with, "I understand that you're skeptical, and I'm sure you have good reason to be. Whether or not coming in here might help is up to you to decide. I'd be interested in hearing more about your views on therapy, and also why you came in."

Derrick reported that, lately, he had found himself in situations in which he could not control his anger. He also stated that he couldn't see how talking about this would help, describing himself as a "man of action, not of talking." Derrick referred to his experiences as a soldier and as a former football player; he described watching videotapes with coaches who were able to help him see what he was doing wrong and how to fix it. He noted that there were rules to playing football and also to being a good soldier, just as there were rules to being a good lawyer. He said that he felt he was good at following the rules. The problem, he said, was that he had found himself becoming so angry lately that he wasn't always following the rules.

"So you're looking for a coach, someone to help you follow the rules?"

Derrick laughed. "Maybe" he said.

The therapist noted that they might be able to work together as a pair of coaches, using the expertise that each had and collaborating on a plan to address whatever changes Derrick wanted to make. The therapist emphasized that it was ultimately up to Derrick to evaluate whether their work was beneficial. In this way, the therapist set the tone of collaboration from the start and empowered Derrick to decide what he wanted to work on and how. The therapist, who was middle-aged, recognized the complex power dynamic in the room (e.g., male-male, therapist-client, father-son, coach-player, White man–Black man) and tried to set up as egalitarian a relationship as possible.

During the initial session, Derrick reported that he felt the need to do something, though he wasn't sure what. He said that he was stressed by law school, by his classmates, by what he saw as his fiancé's neediness, and by a run-in with security at a local shopping mall, all of which were things "that shouldn't bother me." He reported feeling like he was losing control of his temper, something that he said hadn't happened for years. He explained that he felt like he was on the edge of fighting way too often, and fighting was dangerous—not because he was afraid of getting hurt, but because he might hurt someone and get in trouble with the law, which could ruin his career aspirations. "You can't be a professional and solve problems with your fists."

Looking down, he added that hitting a woman was against his personal rules. Derrick then described trying to disengage from a long-running argument in order to study and finally, "losing it," grabbing his fiancé by the arms and pushing her up against the wall. "She was scared. I swore I would never do that. I saw enough of that growing up." Derrick again emphasized that he had learned how to deal with anger long ago, but that suddenly he was having trouble again.

The therapist found himself wondering if race was as palpable for Derrick at that moment as the masculine norms of toughness and self-reliance, which Derrick had alluded to with his earlier statement about how he should not be bothered by stressors. The therapist asked permission to check out a hunch with Derrick. When permission was granted, the therapist noted the existence of the stereotype of the "angry Black man" and asked the client if he ever found himself fighting this stereotype. Derrick nodded. He stated that he had been fighting that image all his life. "But sometimes, it's impossible not to be angry." He described being followed through a store in the shopping mall in such a blatant way that he finally pulled a shirt off a rack and flung it in the direction of the security guard who was watching him. When the security guard looked right past him and began speaking into a two-way radio, Derrick reported that he clenched with rage. He said that it took every ounce of restraint not to tackle the security guard. Instead, he described yelling at the top of his lungs about how he didn't need to shop there. He reported throwing his intended purchases on the ground and stomping out of the store with disgust. He noted feeling ashamed that he could not control himself because "that shit happens all the time." He looked hard at the therapist. The therapist acknowledged that this was not an experience he had had, and also stated that he could see right now how angry the memory made Derrick. The therapist stated, "Seems like you had good reason to be angry, even if you didn't want to be."

When asked how this issue of race might affect their relationship, Derrick responded that he was used to dealing with White people, which the therapist interpreted and honored as an indication that this was not an area that Derrick currently wanted to explore. The remainder of the session was spent collaboratively developing a set of goals that included the usual anger management strategies of identifying stressors, triggers, and coping skills for anger, exploring Derrick's means of handling conflict, and working on communication with his partner. The therapist noted that in his experience, anger was often a reaction—an attempt to gain control over the experience of pain or injustice—and invited Derrick to think about if this interpretation fit for him.

Over the course of therapy, gender, race, and power came up repeatedly as major intersecting themes. At times, the therapist was able to join with Derrick by expressing empathy for his experience, and Derrick seemed to accept this empathy; at other times, Derrick would maintain his distance. In several instances in therapy, Derrick appropriately, though often implicitly, reminded the therapist that he could not possibly understand what it was like to be a Black man in America. The therapist worked with Derrick to articulate his experience of his identity in various contexts.

The therapist and client explored how Derrick's experience of being stereotyped as a Black man not only sparked anger from a sense of invisibility (Franklin, 2002), but also created a bind between different male gender role expectations. As a man, a football player, and a soldier, Derrick had been encouraged to stand up for himself and his comrades. One of his rules was that he did not initiate "dirty tactics" such as throwing a punch, although he did believe in the necessity of responding forcefully, and ever since he was a boy, he had earned respect by fighting back on the rare occasions that he was provoked. At the same time, Derrick endorsed norms of self-control and emotional control that he acknowledged caused him to ignore his feelings until they sometimes overwhelmed him. He reported feeling ashamed by his reaction in the store. It was unprofessional. Not manly. And though he knew his anger was justified, he also knew that there were potential negative consequences to a reactive response. When he was stereotyped, not only did he become invisible as the worthy, intelligent individual he was, but he became a representative of African American male invisibility in general, that is, visible only as a perceived threat. If he did not respond to oppression, his identity as a man and as an African American was demeaned. But reacting with anger reinforced the stereotypes that demeaned him in the first place. Derrick came to understand that, during the encounter with the mall security guard, he had resorted to the one emotional display that was most acceptable for men, but least acceptable to him because of the stereotype of the "angry Black man" and because of his own father, whose anger had destroyed his family.

Over the course of therapy, Derrick and his therapist explored the connections between Derrick's sense of disempowerment and the reactive assertions of power that made him feel ashamed, especially in the case of his partner. They also focused, as Derrick had initially requested, on developing strategies to deal with anger, including identifying anger more quickly, and utilizing such skills as progressive relaxation. They worked to increase self-care and to build Derrick's social support.

They also analyzed Derrick's interaction patterns with his partner, and he began to notice how he did not make his needs clear to his fiancé, but tended to try to solve every conflict with a rule or set of rules. He noticed his tendency to be inflexible and to become upset when his fiancé expressed her difficulties, but didn't follow his advice, or just didn't follow the rules that he thought should be obvious. An exploration of Derrick's ideas about male and female gender roles revealed that he feared becoming like his father and wanted instead an equal partnership, but did know how to establish this. Therapy included reframing Derrick's relationship as teamwork, as in doubles tennis, with two captains who had to mutually set the rules because there was no top-down organization.

Over the course of therapy, Derrick became more aware of the stressful contexts that precipitated his anger. He began developing better coping skills, including acknowledging his feelings and communicating them to his partner at well-chosen moments. He began to feel empowered. He noticed that small successes led him to have increased tolerance and flexibility, and he reported proudly that his anger was "under control." At this point, the therapist discussed with Derrick the notion that being under control didn't mean not feeling anger, but instead finding ways to express anger that felt constructive rather than destructive. Therapist and client discussed such options as using his verbal skills calmly to make a point and then either walking away from conflict with people who didn't matter in his life, or going the extra mile to understand his partner. Derrick reported these discussions to be freeing.

As is usually the case with clients, we don't know how Derrick fared in the future. But at the end of therapy, he reported benefiting from a collaborative and contextual approach that examined the impact of gender and race on his presenting concerns. Compared to when he entered therapy, Derrick left therapy feeling more empowered to experience and appropriately express the full range of human emotions. He also reported enjoying and appreciating the deeper connection with his fiancé that has emanated from these changes. The therapist told Derrick that he was deeply moved by the honor of collaborating with such a hard-working, deeply committed person. In a feminist framework, the therapists' awareness of self is crucial to therapy, and we turn to this next.

Therapist Self-Awareness

In order to effectively attend to the therapeutic relationship and to gauge the quality of collaboration, feminist therapy stresses the need for therapist self-awareness (e.g., Ballou, Hill, & West, 2008; Worell & Remer, 2003). This is particularly true when it comes to the therapist's own gender identity and sociocultural location. To serve a wide range of clientele, therapists must educate themselves not only about the diversity of human experience, but must also work to foster their own self-awareness. Similarities and differences with clients need to be monitored for their potential impact, and the influence of a therapist's own issues and biases needs to be continually checked.

Therapists must be continually cognizant of their own biases, and must work to eliminate them, lest they enter the therapy room. Particularly important is that therapists monitor themselves to avoid what recent research has uncovered: that is, microagressions against minority clients that harm the working alliance (e.g., Sue, 2010). To do this, therapists must continually ask themselves what kinds of reactions they are having (positive or negative) to aspects of the client's social location and multiple identities, and how these reactions are related to the therapist's own multiple identities and locations.

At times, a male therapist may react to clients based on his own experiences as a man. In this case, the male therapist may rush to conclusions about the client's situation. In a word, similarities can shift a therapist's stance from more egalitarian and collaborative to more coercive. For example, if the client appears to be struggling with the sort of gender role conflict that the therapist believes that he has already resolved, then he may push the client to adapt his preferred strategy rather than offering potentially useful paths that the client is free to accept or reject. Empathy, and indeed the relationship, can be easily lost when therapists attempt to teach the client how to resolve distress with their given solutions, rather than securing mutual agreement on goals for therapy and working collaboratively toward those goals.

The therapy relationship can also be severely harmed when therapists react to male clients based on views of men, or a subgroup of men. Therapists, whether male or female, must ask themselves how they feel about men in general, based on their experience. It is easy to imagine how a therapist might carry biases against men into the therapy room, perhaps diminishing trust of a male client or of his ability to grow or change. Johnson (2005) specifically advises women therapists to not rely on their stereotypes of men when conducting therapy with them. Yet, a preliminary analysis of qualitative data from over 450 therapists which inquired into harmful and beneficial practices with men found that many therapists, both male and female, do just this (Mahalik et al., 2012). Adherence to stereotypes about men's inability to engage in the therapy and to access emotions was frequently noted as a harmful practice when working with men (Mahalik et al., 2012).

There is no doubt that empowering clients in a feminist therapy framework requires continual therapist self-monitoring. Quality supervision during graduate training, as well as continual peer consultation as a professional, can facilitate this self-monitoring. Failures in self-awareness, as in the case examples below, can impede the therapy process.

THE CASE OF A TRAINEE'S NEGATIVE TRANSFERENCE

Heather was an African American counselor-in-training. She was good at forging relationships with clients, both female and male, and with her European American supervisor, a male counseling psychology doctoral student. He was surprised one day to watch a video of Heather's work with James, a new client who was an African American male. Instead of listening and reflecting the client's concerns, Heather seemed to be waiting, tight-lipped, for him to finish what he was saying. Her style with him was curt and dismissive, and her interventions were mostly suggestions about what James might do to improve his situation. Heather did not seem to be responding to James in the session, and when her supervisor noted how uncharacteristic her work with him was, she became somewhat defensive. Heather acknowledged, however, that she did not feel much empathy for James. She reported that she thought he wasn't trying to solve his difficulties.

The supervisor had a hunch that Heather was reacting from her own experience with African American males, but was also aware that processing this with a White male supervisor might be difficult. Deciding that it was important to try to explore Heather's uncharacteristic response to James, the supervisor acknowledged his concerns about race and gender affecting their supervision, as well as her session with James. After some exploration of power, race, and gender and the discomfort of talking about them, Heather was able to acknowledge that she had trust issues with African American men. She reported that she was having difficulty with a partner and with her father, and she was able to see how these issues were negatively affecting her work with James.

Once she had become conscious of her reaction, Heather's demeanor in sessions changed, and she worked hard to ensure that she found the empathy needed to assist James in exploring his concerns and identifying appropriate goals.

THE CASE OF A THERAPIST'S OVER-IDENTIFICATION

Mark, a college student involved in social justice and women's issues, sought therapy, in part because he felt he wasn't living up to his pro-feminist principles. Not living up to these expectations hurt his self-esteem. Mark was embarrassed by his struggle to keep from looking at women and thinking of them sexually, and by his attraction to women who were more conventionally "hot," even though he believed that sex appeal was socially constructed and destructive to women in general. He was ashamed of his privilege as a male. For example, he noted that when he spoke in a group, he commanded attention even if he was saying the same thing a woman had just said. In general, Mark, who was White, saw himself as a member of a dominant and oppressive class and felt unable to reconcile his privilege, thoughts, and behavior with his feminist, multicultural critique.

His therapist saw in Mark a younger version of himself. The therapist felt he knew Mark's struggle intimately. He believed from his own experience that Mark's struggle arose from a kind of perfectionism that sought moral clarity and compensation for low self-esteem by attempting to adhere to a rigid, simplistic version of feminist ideology. As in his own case, the therapist suspected that family-of-origin issues, particularly difficulties in the client's relationship with his father, played a significant role in the client's feelings of shame about his masculinity.

The therapist might have been right in his assessment of the client's intra-psychic dynamic and of the contextual pressure from his activist circle to be an exemplar pro-feminist male within a patriarchal society. However, his identification with the client caused him to assume too much and to diminish his efforts at collaboration in favor of veiled attempts to teach the client what the therapist had learned on his own journey. While at first glance client and therapist might seem to be a good match, the relationship never became strong, the client did not feel understood, and when therapy ended, neither Mark nor the therapist felt he had made much progress. In retrospect, the therapist felt he had tried to impose his experience on the client, engendering resistance rather than trust and collaboration. Certainly, there might have been other factors that contributed to an insufficient working alliance, but the therapist's over-identification with the client undermined the egalitarian relationship and contributed to the client's disempowerment within the very context in which he should have been empowered: feminist therapy.

Conclusions

Empowerment is the overarching goal of feminist therapy. This is accomplished through an analysis of power, gender, and social location, and with key strategies such as creating an egalitarian therapy relationship and framing distress and problematic behaviors as attempts at gaining power in an oppressive and patriarchal society. The field of men and masculinity, emanating from a feminist framework and created by the pioneering work of counseling psychologists, also strives to empower men. This chapter has attempted to do what surprisingly has not been done before: to systematically integrate scholarship from the field of men and masculinity with the tenets and processes of feminist therapy.

We hope that what has been made clear is that feminist therapy and the psychology of men and masculinity are ideally suited to such integration. Both fields seem to have a shared goal of social change through individual empowerment, although this goal is explicitly stated in feminist therapy writings and implicitly implied in writings in the field of men and masculinity. In fact, while the mission statement of the Society for the Psychological Study of Men and Masculinity was quoted at the start of this chapter, perhaps the most important mission was omitted: the "...enhancement of men's capacity to experience their full human potential" (APA, n.d.). Integrating feminist therapy with scholarship from the field of men and masculinity is the most powerful route to achieving this lofty and important goal. While it is hoped that this chapter took one very small step toward this objective, there are many topics that require further examination.

Future Directions

Some of the needed directions for feminist therapy with men are those that are also needed within feminist therapy in general, including (a) more outcome research; (b) examining the implications of sex as a construct on feminist therapy; and (c) a fuller integration of the analysis of all aspects of social location into feminist therapy. Particularly needed are continued examinations of intersections of gender and other social identities (e.g., race/ethnicity, age, sexual orientation, ability status).

First, as is true for all of feminist therapy, more outcome studies are needed. While there are a few studies on feminist therapy (Chandler, et al., 1999; Rader & Gilbert, 2005), more are sorely needed. Particularly relevant to this chapter is the need for outcome studies on feminist therapy conducted by male therapists and/or with male clients.

Second, as eloquently articulated by Brown (2010), while early feminism deconstructed the concept of gender, the concept of sex is currently being deconstructed. To illustrate, while the phenomenon of transgender was at one point attacked by feminist thinkers, "...for growing numbers of the younger generations of feminists...arguments about essential femaleness or maleness are greeted with skepticism" (Brown, 2010, p. 118). As eloquently stated by Brown (2010), "If sex is no longer seen as any more essential than gender, but rather as phenomenology related to a somatic state that is subject to modification both biologically and legally, theory in feminist therapy will be required to change in order to encompass this new way of understanding one of its most basic precepts" (Brown, 2010, p. 118). Such a shift in thinking certainly includes vast implications for feminist therapy, particularly with transmen (born biologically female), and transwomen (born biologically male).

Third, and most important, as is true for all feminist therapy, continued attention to issues of social location and multiple identities must be kept at the forefront of feminist therapy with men. While feminist therapy has made great strides in becoming a more global and multicultural therapy, much is left to be done. Likewise, mirroring psychology in general and feminist therapy in particular, the field of men and masculinity has only recently begun to examine and embrace the full diversity of human experience. What is sorely needed is a complete integration of feminist therapy, the psychology of men and masculinity, and scholarship and practice recommendations from those in the field of multicultural therapy. Future work should carefully and thoroughly consider how gender intersects with other social identities, including but not limited to racial and ethnic identities. Additionally, multiple identities need to be considered in specific social contexts, within the diverse and fluid environments of clients' lives. For example, feminist therapists working with men will need to consider how the salience of particular aspects of identity fluctuate in response to the norms of a particular environment, and how these fluctuations impact the well-being of their clients. Also worthy of scholarly consideration and therapeutic attention is the question of under what circumstances social identities come in conflict and what (successful and unsuccessful) strategies people use to resolve these conflicts. Counseling psychologists have led the field of both the psychology of men and masculinity and that of multicultural counseling; we are thus ideally suited to lead the field to articulate a model of therapy that equally honors the analysis of gender and social location, with the goal of empowering all individuals to reach their full and joyous human potential, for and with one another.

References

Abreu, J. M., Goodyear, R. K., Campos A., & Newcomb, M. D. (2000). Ethnic belonging and traditional masculine ideology among African Americans, European Americans and Latinos. *Psychology of Men and Masculinity, 1,* 75–86. doi:10.1037/1524-9220.1.2.75

Addis, M. E., & Mahalik, J. R. (2003). Men, masculinity, and the contexts of help-seeking. *American Psychologist, 58,* 5–14. doi:10.1037/0003-066X.58.1.5

Addis, M. E., Mansfield, A. K., & Syzdek, M. R. (2010). Is masculinity a problem?: Framing the effects of gendered social learning in men. *Psychology of Men and Masculinity, 11,* 77–90. doi:10.1037/a0018602

American Psychological Association (2009). Demographic characteristics of Division 51 members by membership status, 2009. Retrieved September 20, 2010, from hhtp://www.apa.org/about/division/div51-2009.aspx.

American Psychological Association (n.d.) About Us: Mission Statement. Retrieved September 20, 2010, from, http://www.apa.org/divisions/div51/aboutus/mission.htm.

Ballou, M., Hill, M., & West, C. (Eds.). (2008). *Feminist therapy theory and practice.* New York: Springer.

Bohart, A. C. (2005). The active client. In J. Norcross, L. Buetler, & R. Levant (Eds), *Evidence-based practices in mental health: Debate and dialogue on fundamental questions* (pp. 218–226). Washington, DC: American Psychological Association.

Brannon, R. (1976). The male sex role: Our culture's blueprint for manhood, what it's done for us lately. In D. David and R. Brannon (Eds.), *The forty-nine percent majority: The male sex role* (pp. 1–48). Reading: Addison-Wesley.

Brown, L. S. (2010). *Feminist therapy.* Washington, DC: American Psychological Association.

Caldwell, L. D., & White, J. L. (2005). African-centered therapeutic and counseling interventions for African American males. In G. Good & G. Brooks (Eds.), *The new handbook of psychotherapy and counseling with men* (pp. 323–336). San Francisco: Jossey-Bass.

Cervantes, J. M. (2006). A new understanding of the macho male image: Exploration of the Mexican American man. In M. Englar-Carlson and M. Stevens (Eds.), *In the room with men: A casebook of therapeutic change* (pp. 197–224). Washington, DC: American Psychological Association.

Chandler, R., Worrell, J., Johnson, D., Blount, A., & Lusk, M. (August 1999). Measuring long-term outcomes in feminist counseling and psychotherapy. In J. Worrrell (Chair), *Measuring process and outcomes in short- and long- term feminist therapy.* Symposium presented at the annual meeting of the American Psychological Association, Boston.

Cochran, S. V., & Rabinowitz, F. E. (2000). *Men and depression: Clinical and empirical perspectives.* San Diego: Academic.

Collins, K. A. (2002). An examination of feminist psychotherapy in North America during the 1980's. *Guidance and Counseling, 17,* 105–112.

Connell, R. W. (1995). *Masculinities.* Berkeley: University of California Press.

Cross, S. E., and Madson, L. (1997). Models of the self: Self-construals and gender. *Psychological Bulletin, 122,* 5–37. doi:10.1037/0033-2909.122.1.5

Eagly, A. H., Wood, W., & Diekman, A. B. (2000). Social role theory of sex differences and similarities: A current appraisal. In T. Eckes & H. M. Trautner (Eds.), *The developmental social psychology of gender* (pp. 123–174). Mahwah, NJ: Erlbaum.

Eisler, R. M., & Skidmore, J. R. (1987). Masculine gender role stress: Scale development and component factors in the appraisal of stressful situations. *Behavior Modification, 1,* 123–136. doi:10.1177/01454455870112001

Englar-Carlson, M., & Stevens, M. A. (2006). *In the room with men: A casebook of therapeutic change.* Washington, DC: American Psychological Association.

Enns, C. Z. (2004). *Feminist theories and feminist psychotherapies: Origins, themes and variations.* Binghamton, NY: Haworth Press.

Franklin, A. J. (2002). *From brotherhood to manhood: How black men rescue their relationships and dreams from the invisibility syndrome.* New York: Wiley.

Ganley, A. L. (1988). Feminist therapy with male clients. In M. Dutton-Douglas & L. E. Walker (Eds.), *Feminist psychotherapies: Integration of therapeutic and feminist systems* (pp. 186–205). Norwood, NJ: Ablex Publishing Corporation.

Good, G. E., Gilbert, L. A., & Sher, M. (1990). Gender aware therapy: A synthesis of feminist therapy and knowledge about gender. *Journal of Counseling and Development, 68,* 376–380.

Good, G. E., Borst, T. S., & Wallace, D. L. (1994). Masculinity research: A review and critique. *Applied and Preventive Psychology, 3,* 3–14. doi:10.1016/S0962-1849(05)80104-0

Good, G. E., & Brooks, G. R. (Eds.). (2001). *The new handbook of psychotherapy and counseling with men: A comprehensive guide to settings, problems and treatment approaches.* San Francisco: Jossey-Bass.

Good, G. E., & Brooks, G. R. (Eds.). (2005). *The new handbook of psychotherapy and counseling with men: A comprehensive guide to settings, problems and treatment approaches* (Rev. ed.). San Francisco: Jossey-Bass.

Good, G. E., & Mintz, L. B. (2005). Integrative therapy for men. In G. Good & G. Brooks (Eds.), *The new handbook of psychotherapy and counseling with men* (pp. 248–263). San Francisco: Jossey-Bass.

Goode-Cross, D. T., & Good, G. E. (2009). Managing multiple minority identities: African American men who have sex with men at predominately white universities. *Journal of Diversity in Higher Education, 2,* 103–112. doi:10.1037/a0015780

Goode-Cross, D. T., & Tager, D. (2011). Negotiating multiple identities: How African American gay and bisexual men persist at a predominantly white institution. *Journal of Homosexuality, 58,* 1235–1254. doi: 10.1080/00918369.2011.605736

Guimond, S., Branscombe, N. R., Brunot, S., Buunk, A. P., Chatard, A., Désert, M., et al., (2007). Culture, gender, and the self: Variations and impact of social comparison processes. *Journal of Personality and Social Psychology, 92,* 1118–1134. doi:10.1037/0022-3514.92.6.1118

Harris, W. G. (2003). African American homosexual males on predominately white college and university campuses. *Journal of African American Studies, 7,* 47–56. doi:10.1007/s12111-003-1002-9

Hays, P. A. (2008). *Addressing cultural complexities in practice: Assessment, diagnosis, and therapy.* Washington, DC: American Psychological Association.

Hill, M., & Rothblum, E. D. (1996). *Couples therapy: Feminist perspectives.* New York: Harrington Park Press.

Hondagneu-Sotelo, P., & Messner, M. (1994). Gender displays and men's power: The "new man" and the Mexican immigrant man. In H. Brod & M. Kaufman (Eds.), *Theorizing masculinities* (pp. 200–218). Thousand Oaks, CA: Sage Publications.

Jakupcak, M., Tull, M. T., & Roemer, L. (2005). Masculinity, shame, and fear of emotions as predictors of men's expressions of anger and hostility. *Psychology of Men and Masculinity, 6, 275–284.* doi:10.1037/1524-9220.6.4.275

Johnson, N. G. (2005). Women helping men: Strengths of and barriers to women therapists working with men clients. In G. Good & G. Brooks (Eds.), *The new handbook of psychotherapy and counseling with men* (pp. 291–307). San Francisco: Jossey-Bass.

Levant, R. F. (1996). The new psychology of men. *Professional Psychology, 27, 259–265.* doi:10.1037/0735-7028.27.3.259

Levant, R. F., & Silverstein, L. B. (2005). Gender is neglected by both evidence-based practice and treatment as usual. In J. Norcross, L. Beutler, & R. Levant (Eds.), *Evidence-based practices in mental health: Debate and dialogue on fundamental questions* (pp. 338–345). Washington DC: American Psychological Association

Mahalik, J. R., Good, G. E., & Englar-Carlson, M. (2003). Masculinity scripts, presenting concerns, and help seeking: Implications for practice and training. *Professional Psychology: Research and Practice, 34,* 123–131. doi:10.1037/0735-7028.34.2.123

Mahalik, J. R., Good, G. E., Tager, D., Levant, R. F., & Mackowiak, C. (2012). *Developing a taxonomy of helpful and harmful practices for clinical work with boys and men.* Manuscript submitted for publication.

Mahalik, J. R., Locke, B., Ludlow, L., Diemer, M., Scott, R. P. J., Gottfried, M., & Freitas, G. (2003). Development of the Conformity to Masculine Norms Inventory. *Psychology of Men and Masculinity, 4,* 3–25. doi:10.1037/1524-9220.4.1.3

Majors, R., & Billsun, J. M. (1993). *Coolpose: The dilemmas of black manhood in America.* New York: Touchstone.

Mejia, X. E. (2005). Gender matters: Working with adult male survivors of trauma. *Journal of Counseling and Development, 83,* 29–40.

National Institute of Mental Health (2009). Men and depression. Retrieved October 27, 2010, from http://www.nimh.nih.gov/health/publications/men-and-depression/md-men-and-depression-research.shtml.

Norcross, J. C., & Lambert, M. J. (2005). The therapy relationship. In J. Norcross, L. Beutler, & R. Levant (Eds.), *Evidence-based practices in mental health: Debate and dialogue on fundamental questions* (pp. 208–218). Washington DC: American Psychological Association.

Nutt, R. L. (2005). Feminist and contextual work. In M. Harway (Ed.), *Handbook of couples therapy* (pp. 228–249). Hoboken, NJ: Wiley & Sons.

Ojeda, L., Rosales, R., & Good, G. E. (2008). Socioeconomic status and cultural predictors of male role attitudes among Mexican American Men: ¿Son más machos? *Psychology of Men and Masculinity, 9,* 133–138. doi:10.1037/1524-9220.9.3.133

O'Neil, J. M. (1981). Patterns of gender-role conflict and strain: Sexism and fear of femininity in men's lives. *Personnel and Guidance Journal, 60,* 203–210.

O'Neil, J. M., Helms, B. J., Gable, R. K., David, L., & Wrightsman, L. S. (1986). Gender-Role Conflict Scale: College men's fear of femininity. *Sex Roles, 14,* 335–350.

O'Neil, J. M. (2008). Summarizing 25 years of research on men's gender role conflict using the Gender Role Conflict Scale. *The Counseling Psychologist, 36,* 358–445. doi:10.1177/0011000008317057

Pleck, J. (1981). *The myth of masculinity*. Cambridge, MA: MIT Press.

Pleck, J. (1995). The gender role strain paradigm: An update. In R. F. Levant & W. S. Pollack (Eds.), *A new psychology of men* (pp. 11–32). New York: Basic Books.

Pleck, J. H. (1997) Paternal involvement, sources and consequences. In: M.E. Lamb (Ed.), *The role of the father in child development* (3rd ed.) (pp. 43–55). New York: Lexington Books.

Pollack, W. S. (2005). "Masked men": New psychoanalytically oriented treatment models for adult and young adult men. In G. Good & G. Brooks (Eds.), *The new handbook of psychotherapy and counseling with men* (pp. 203–216). San Francisco: Jossey-Bass.

Rabinowitz, F. E., & Cochran, S. V. (2002). *Deepening psychotherapy with men*. Washington, DC: American Psychological Association.

Rader, J., & Gilbert, L. A. (2005). The egalitarian relationship in feminist therapy. *Psychology of Women Quarterly, 29*, 427–435. doi:10.1111/j.1471-6402.2005.00243.x

Rampage, C. (2000). Feminist couples therapy. In F. M. Dattilio & Bevilacqua L. J. (Eds.), *Comparative treatments for relationship dysfunction* (pp. 325–341). New York: Springer Publishing.

Real, T. (1998). *I don't want to talk about it: Overcoming the secret legacy of male depression*. New York: Simon & Schuster.

Rochlen, A. B., McKelly, R. A., & Pituch, K. A. (2006). A preliminary investigation of the "Real Men. Real Depression" Campaign. *Psychology of Men and Masculinity, 7*, 1–13. doi:10.1037/1524-9220.7.1.1

Root, M. P. P. (2000). Rethinking racial identity development: An ecological framework. In P. Spickard & J. Burroughs (Eds.), *We are a people: Narrative in the construction and deconstruction of ethnic identity* (pp. 113–122). Philadelphia: Temple University Press.

Sher, M. (2005). Male therapist, male client: Reflections on critical dynamics. In G. Good & G. Brooks (Eds.), *The new handbook of psychotherapy and counseling with men* (pp. 308–319). San Francisco: Jossey-Bass.

Silverstein, L. B., Auerbach, C. F., & Levant, R. F. (2003). Contemporary fathers reconstructing masculinity: Clinical implications of gender role strain. *Professional Psychology: Research and Practice, 33*, 361–369. doi:10.1037/0735-7028.33.4.361

Silverstein, L. B., & Goodrich, T. J. (2003). *Feminist family therapy: Empowerment in social context*. Washington, DC: American Psychological Association.

Silverstein, L. B. (2005). Bowen family systems theory as feminist therapy. In M. Harway (Ed.), *Handbook of couples therapy* (pp. 103–118). Hoboken: Wiley & Sons.

Smiler, A. P. (2004) Thirty years after the discovery of gender: Psychological concepts and measures of masculinity. *Sex Roles, 50*, 15–26. doi:10.1023/B:SERS.0000011069.02279.4c

Soban, C. (2006). What about the boys?: Addressing issues of masculinity within male Anorexia Nervosa in feminist therapeutic environment. *International Journal of Men's Health, 5*, 251–267. doi:10.3149/jmh.0503.251

Sue, D. W. (2010) *Microaggressions in everyday life: Race, gender, and sexual orientation*. Hoboken: Wiley & Sons.

Tager, D., Good, G. E., & Brammer, S. (2010). Walking over 'em: An exploration of relations between emotion dysregulation, masculine norms and intimate partner abuse in a clinical sample of men. *Psychology of Men and Masculinity, 11*, 233–239. doi:10.1037/a0017636

Vogel, D., Wester, S. R., Heesacker, M. & Madon, S. (2003). Confirming gender stereotypes: A social role perspective. *Sex Roles, 48*, 519–528. doi:10.1023/A:1023575212526

Wade, J. C. (2008). Masculinity ideology, male reference group identity dependence, and African American men's health-related behaviors. *Psychology of Men and Masculinity, 9*, 5–16. doi:10.1037/1524-9220.9.1.5

Walker, L. E. A. (2001). A feminist perspective on men in emotional pain. In Good, G. E., & Brooks, G. R. (Eds.), *The new handbook of psychotherapy and counseling with men* (pp. 683–695). San Francisco: Josey-Bass.

Wampold, B. E. (2001) *The great psychotherapy debate: Models, methods, and findings*. Mahwah, NJ: Lawrence Erlbaum.

Washington, J., & Wall, V. A. (2006). African American gay men: Another challenge for the academy. In M. J. Cuyjet (Ed.), *African American men in college* (pp. 174–188). San Francisco, CA: Jossey-Bass.

Worell, J., & Remer, P. (2003). *Feminist perspectives in therapy: Empowering diverse women*. Hoboken: Wiley and Sons.

Zimmerman, T. S., & Besel, A. (2008). Feminist family theory and therapy. In K. Jordin (Ed.), *The quick theory reference guide: A resource for expert and novice mental health professionals* (pp. 501–510). Hauppauge, NY: Nova Science Publishers.

CHAPTER

18 Political Analysis: Cornerstone of Feminist Multicultural Counseling and Psychotherapy

Susan L. Morrow *and* Donna Hawxhurst

Abstract

During its first decade of practice and scholarship, feminist therapy was rich with political analysis. As feminist therapy has become more professionalized, political analysis has been de-emphasized (Morrow & Hawxhurst, 1998). Multicultural counseling has focused on the importance of building cross-cultural relationships and examining issues related to counselor and client identity development, as well as engaging clients in understanding the context and cultural variables surrounding their lives and the problems they bring to counseling. However, engaging clients in analyzing the sociopolitical forces impacting their lives has been a nebulous activity, left to the counselor or therapist to figure out on her or his own. This chapter addresses points of convergence and paradoxes surrounding the integration of feminist and multicultural perspectives, including issues of inclusion. We also define feminist multicultural counseling (FMC) as an integrative approach to counseling and therapy. Next, we address the implementation of FMC, including the underlying components. Finally, we offer a process-oriented empowerment model for use in FMC.

Key Words: Feminist multicultural counseling, feminist multicultural therapy, empowerment, colonization, social justice counseling

During its first decade of practice and scholarship, feminist therapy was rich with political analysis. As feminist therapy has become more professionalized, political analysis has been de-emphasized (Morrow & Hawxhurst, 1998). Multicultural counseling has focused on the importance of building the cross-cultural relationship and examining issues related to counselor and client identity development, as well as engaging clients in understanding the context and cultural variables surrounding their lives and the problems they bring to counseling. However, engaging clients in analyzing the sociopolitical forces impacting their lives has been a nebulous activity, left to the counselor or therapist to figure out on her or his own.

Feminist and multicultural perspectives on gender- and culturally competent practice have many parallels; however, the approaches have not always found common ground (Morrow, Hawxhurst, Montes de Vegas, Abousleman, & Castañeda, 2006). This disconnection may have its roots in the early development of feminist therapy and multicultural counseling, in which early feminists in the women's liberation movement were predominantly white and middle class and, for the most part, unaware of the ways in which their theory and practice excluded women of color. In addition, multicultural counseling failed to integrate gender into its analysis and practice, leaving the particular concerns of women of color in the sidelines. As theorists and activists in both movements have become more concerned with the intersections of race, gender, and other statuses, greater focus on intersectionality has become possible. As a result, it is now possible to integrate the strengths from feminist and multicultural counseling theory and practice to better address the needs of clients. As we will see, however, this integration is not without challenges, which we will address below. In this chapter, we will address the points of convergence and paradoxes surrounding the integration of feminist and multicultural perspectives, including issues of inclusion. We will define feminist multicultural counseling (FMC) as an integrative approach to counseling and therapy and will discuss the relevance of liberation psychology to the integrated approach. Next, we will address the implementation of FMC, including the underlying components. Finally, we will offer a process-oriented empowerment model for use in FMC.

Feminist and Multicultural Perspectives in Counseling and Psychotherapy: Paradoxes and Convergence

It might appear that feminist and multicultural perspectives would be natural partners in the process of liberating and empowering clients. Our earliest connections stem back to the anti-slavery and women's suffrage movements, and throughout history efforts toward equality for women have followed closely upon and become integrated with civil rights efforts. Weitzman (Bowman, Rasheed, Ferris, Thompson, McRae, & Weitzman, 2001) identified common elements of both multiculturalism and feminism, including "(a) reducing power imbalances between dominant and oppressed cultures, (b) respecting diversity,...(c) overcoming oppression through empowerment, [and (d)] an examination of the socio-cultural-political context" (p. 794). However, by the very nature of White privilege and its associated lenses, it has been difficult for White feminists to fully understand how their privilege has caused women of color to be invisible. It is to the credit of feminist/womanist women of color that they have persisted in raising their voices and facilitating an increasingly integrative approach to counseling and psychotherapy that addresses the intersections of gender, race, and class.

Espín (1994) argued that White feminists' "nearsightedness" led to feminism being defined narrowly and in a way that marginalized and excluded women of color. She wrote, citing Anzaldúa (1990), hooks (1984), Lorde (1984), and the Combahee River Collective (1979), that "White middle-class women do not 'own' feminism, nor is feminism irrelevant to the experiences of women of color" (p. 265). Espín continued by describing the inseparability of gender and race (and often poverty) for both women and men of color. Thus, not only do women of color bear their own burdens of racism and sexism, they also bear the consequences of the oppression of the men of color in their lives, including violence; pressure to emulate White, middle class women; and the expectation that gender concerns be laid aside in the interests of race struggle (Espín, 1994). Subsequently, when White feminists fail to understand the pressures that feminists of color experience, they may be invalidating the unique challenges facing women of color.

Speaking of contradictions in feminist therapy with women of color, Espín (1994) found it

> rather ironic that a theory that evolved from the awareness that sociocultural factors are essential determinants in the psychology of women has been so slow to extend its own major insight to sociocultural factors other than gender, thus excluding the experiences of the vast majority of women who are not White, and in that process excluding the impact of sociocultural factors other than gender (e.g., race, class, and ethnicity) on the lives of all women, including White women. (p. 274)

Reflecting on the experiences of women of color at a conference hosted in the fall of 1998 by the Division 17 (Counseling Psychology) Section for the Advancement of Women on feminist multicultural perspectives on research, theory, practice, and activism, Thompson wrote that "feminists tended to be European American, and multiculturalists tended to be women of color" (Bowman et al., 2001, p. 789). She noted the paradox for White feminists of engaging in a movement (feminism) that appears "to be the struggle of White women to share in the power of White men" and argued that "fundamental to sharing [that] power is having the power to oppress" (p. 790). Thompson further argued that, in order to create a working alliance among White women and women of color, gender cannot be prioritized over "race, ethnicity, class, age, religion, and sexual identity" (p. 790). Instead, "multiculturalism challenges us to look at biases, prejudices, privileges, and quests for power" (p. 790) that arise from diversities of all types.

McRae (Bowman et al., 2001) further articulated some of the challenges to a real multicultural feminism as she asked, "How do I talk to you, my White sister?" (p. 791). She noted that differences between White women and women of color in opportunities and in gendered expectations limit understanding and collaboration and create barriers to meaningful dialogue. In particular, she noted the inseparability of race and gender for women of color and wondered how White women "manage the duality of race and feminism, of White privilege and feminism" (pp. 791–792). She added, "It is hard for Black women and White women to talk about these issues if there is no understanding of where we stand on issues that affect at least one side so deeply" (p. 792).

Feminist Multicultural Counseling and Therapy: An Integrated Approach

Early calls for an integrated approach came from women of color. Both Espín (1994) and Comas-Díaz (1994) wrote, in *Women of Color* (Comas-Díaz & Greene, 1994), of the integration of feminist and multicultural approaches. Espín advocated feminist therapy as an approach that is appropriate to women of color, particularly in light of the emphasis of feminist therapy on the analysis of sociopolitical forces affecting women. Espín argued that the guidelines for feminist therapy outlined by Butler (1985) coincided with what women of color need from therapy and included:

> Recognition of women's oppression based on gender, race, and class;
> Relevance of the sociocultural context;
> Focus on women's empowerment;
> Diverse therapeutic modalities;
> Demystification of power in the therapeutic relationship;
> The therapist and other women as role models;
> The therapist's ongoing self-examination and reflection on her values;
> Encouragement of growing experiences in addition to therapy (Espín, 1994, pp. 271–272).

Espín noted, "In particular, it is relevant that [feminist therapists working with women of color] emphasize the importance of empowerment, choice, and active social action as healing factors that would foster mental health for all women" (1994, p. 272). She recommended that the most appropriate therapeutic approach for women of color is a "feminist ethno-specific approach" (p. 275) in which the counselor and client come from the same racial/ethnic background. Acknowledging that such a pairing is rare, she argued that White feminist therapists must be aware of and deal with their own privilege, must be committed to self-reflection, and must have an analysis of the social world that includes not only gender but "race, ethnicity, class, sexual orientation, disability, and age" (p. 283).

Comas-Díaz (1994), citing the importance of integration and pluralism in psychotherapy, focused particularly on the needs of women of color for an integrative approach. She described integration as "combining traditional psychotherapeutic models with sociocultural,... ethnoracial, and gender contexts" (p. 288). The underpinnings of an integrative approach, according to Comas-Díaz, include understanding concepts of "colonization, decolonization, and *conscientizaçáo*" (p. 289). She focused on colonization, rather than oppression, because of the necessity for people of color in the United States to adopt the norms of White U.S. culture.

Kanuha (2002) defined colonization as "the domination of a particular nation, community, society or peoples by a foreign or outside nation, society, force or country" (p. 1). Colonizers depend on particular strategies to maintain dominance, including (a) claiming ethnocultural superiority, placing themselves at the center of the defined universe and "othering" the colonized; (b) using physical, psychological, emotional, and spiritual violence; (c) seizing and controlling economic resources; (d) exerting control over the culture; and (e) excluding the colonized from access to power. Kanuha pointed out that patriarchal colonization uses the same strategies to maintain dominance over women. An understanding of the interplay between cultural and gender colonization is important to the process of "psychotherapeutic decolonization" (Comas-Díaz, 1994, p. 287). Comas-Díaz wrote:

> The dynamics of liberation and decolonization involve a three stage process: (1) recovery of the self; (2) achievement of autonomous dignity; and (3) action toward fundamental change of self and/or the colonial condition.... The integrative approach mirrors this process by helping women of color recover and reclaim the self through increasing positive self-attribution and self-esteem; achieve autonomous dignity through self-efficacy, self-mastery, and self-determination; and transform themselves and their situation by developing a critical consciousness (*conscientizaçáo*). (p. 290)

Conscientizaçáo, according to Freiere (1970), is "the process whereby people achieve an illuminating awareness both of the socioeconomic and cultural circumstances that shape their lives and their capacity to transform that reality" (p. 799). *Conscientizaçáo* has its counterpart in feminist consciousness-raising, designed to assist women in understanding, through a collective process, the political nature of their personal experiences (thus the slogan, "the personal is political"). Psychological colonization is so successful specifically because it convinces its victims that their distress is due to personality characteristics, individual flaws, and personal pathology. *Conscientizaçáo,* or consciousness-raising, is effective because it frames personal distress in terms of oppression rather than individual psychopathology.

Applying the concept of *conscientizaçáo* to psychotherapeutic decolonization for women of color, Comas-Díaz (1994) outlined the following therapeutic processes:

> Recognizing the systemic and societal context of colonialism and oppression, thus, becoming aware of the colonized mentality;
>
> Correcting cognitive errors that reinforce the colonized mentality, for example, working through dichotomous thinking (superior-inferior, the colonized is good, the colonizer is bad, etc.) and acknowledging ambivalence (toward self and others);
>
> Self-asserting and reaffirming racial and gender identity, as well as developing a more integrated identity;
>
> Increasing self-mastery and achieving autonomous dignity;
>
> Working toward transformation of self and/or the colonized condition (e.g., improving the condition of women, men, and children of color) (p. 291).

Feminist therapy had its roots in feminist consciousness-raising (Mander & Rush, 1974), although Brown (1994) problematized this evolution in that therapy has traditionally been apolitical, whereas the purpose of consciousness-raising was to move "from anger to action" (p. 32). Weitz (1982) found that feminist consciousness-raising groups increased self-esteem and decreased depression in women. An important aspect of consciousness-raising has always been its absence of hierarchy; the group facilitator, if there is one, is a full participant in the work of self-exploration and sharing her experiences and thoughts with the rest of the group. Thus, feminist multicultural counselors find themselves needing to be diligent to remain true to the spirit of *conscientizaçáo,* or consciousness-raising.

Referring to the limitations of a monocultural perspective, Brown (1994) described a journey that is familiar to many White feminist-now-multicultural therapists from a narrow focus on gender to an increasingly integrative perspective. A feminist multicultural integrative perspective is not just anti-sexist or anti-racist, but has an anti-domination emphasis (hooks, 1989). We engage in a process of self-reflection to understand and uncover the ways in which we have internalized domination on multiple levels. Sinacore-Guinn (1995) recommended that students and practitioners engage in a self-reflective process about their own gender, cultural, and trauma backgrounds. In addition, hooks (1994) described a process of "teaching to transgress" in which teachers engage in the experiential processes that they demand of their students; she invited us to "be actively committed to a process of self-actualization that promotes [our] own well-being" (p. 14), emphasizing that healers and helpers must focus first on themselves if they are to help others. Thus, feminist multicultural therapy addresses not only gender and race/ethnicity, but the multiple forms of dominance that affect the well-being of the people with whom we engage in a healing relationship.

Toward an Inclusive Feminist Multicultural Therapy

In addition to a herstorical neglect of women of color by White feminists, feminism and multiculturalism have often neglected the experiences of other groups, including the poor, disabled people, lesbian/gay/bisexual/transgender/intersex/queer people, people with disabilities (physical and mental), the young, the old, immigrants and refugees, people whose appearance falls outside an acceptable norm (e.g., size, skin tone or color, disfigurement) and many others. Smith (2005) noted that the poor are largely absent from psychotherapeutic research, literature, and practice and suggested that unexamined class privilege and personal and institutional classism contribute to this phenomenon. She referred to "the poor" as those who live at or below the poverty level for the duration of their lives, whose families were poor, and whose chances of moving out of poverty are highly unlikely. Although both multicultural psychology and feminist therapy have addressed class, there is not much evidence of a substantial focus on cultural competency directed to impoverished individuals in our society. Smith makes a strong case for advocacy for focused training and scholarship to facilitate awareness of classism, as well as advocacy for funding and the development of adequate psychological/social services for the poor.

Feminists and multiculturalists have been criticized for neglecting various statuses and identities beside race/ethnicity and class. Brown (1994) noted that lesbian women have been the least neglected by feminist therapists, as many feminist therapists are, in fact, lesbians. Likewise, multiculturalists have recognized the importance of religion and spirituality to people of color. In this handbook, feminist counseling psychologists have addressed many of these issues in Part II, "Feminist Multicultural Counseling Psychology and Specific Social Identities," including African American Women (Speight, Isom, & Thomas, chapter 6); lesbian and bisexual women and transgender persons (Szymanski & Hilton, chapter 7); poverty (Smith, Appio, & Chang, chapter 8); Latinas (Gloria & Castellanos, chapter 9); Asian American women (Suzuki, Ahluwalia, & Alimchandani, chapter 10); women with disabilities (Palombi, chapter 11); American Muslim women (Mahmood, chapter 12); and transnational contexts (Horne & Arora, chapter 13). These and other statuses and identities, as well as intersections of statuses and identities, are critical areas for attention by feminist multicultural counseling psychologists.

Components of Feminist Multicultural Counseling

Morrow et al. (2006) identified the following components in the implementation of feminist multicultural counseling: feminist multicultural perspectives on assessment and diagnosis; the personal as political, including consciousness-raising, *conscientization* (or *conscientização*); analysis of power in psychotherapy; the importance of group work to empower clients, and political action and activism. We have added the therapeutic relationship as the initial step in implementing feminist multicultural counseling.

The Therapeutic Relationship: Issues for Feminist Multicultural Counseling

The therapeutic relationship is central to almost every theoretical orientation to psychotherapy and has been identified as one of the "common factors" in successful counseling (Norcross & Wampold, 2011), particularly with people of color and with women (Comas-Díaz, 1994). Comas-Díaz addressed the therapeutic relationship as the crux of an integrative approach to psychotherapy. She wrote, "In the decolonization process, the therapeutic relationship functions as a dialog that facilitates the process of critical consciousness" (p. 292). Feminist therapists have long addressed power dynamics in the client-counselor relationship as central to the development of the therapeutic relationship (Brown, 1994; Enns, 1997; McWhirter, 1994; Morrow & Hawxhurst, 1998; Morrow, Hawxhurst, Montes de Vegas, Abousleman, & Castañeda, 2006). Feminist multicultural counseling requires the counselor to engage in a self-reflective process regarding her or his own experiences and biases, as well as understanding how race, culture, gender, and other variables impact the client, the counselor, and their relationship (Comas-Díaz, 1994). The inherent power differential between counselors and clients can mimic other inequities experienced by clients, thus reinforcing the client's powerlessness. Comas-Díaz emphasized the impact of unconscious processes in which the therapist unwittingly repeats the colonizer-colonized relationship in the therapy situation. Majority-culture therapists may have internalized domination and superiority and may perpetuate those dynamics in the counselor-client relationship.

The language of counseling and psychotherapy can serve to reinforce this dominance. In this chapter, we have used the terminology common to our field in such words as "therapy," "psychotherapy," "therapist," and "client." Even feminist multicultural counseling psychologists use the medical concepts and language of "patients," "psychopathology," "cases," and "treatment." Brown (1984) pointed out that feminist therapists are vulnerable to the need for legitimacy in the "eyes of their patriarchal colleagues" (p. 75) and demonstrate this need by using traditional psychoanalytic terminology. Clients of color, working class clients, rural clients, older clients, and others may experience psychotherapy as stigmatizing and may avoid placing themselves in a situation where they may perceive themselves or may be perceived by others as "sick" or "crazy." Thus, feminist multicultural counselors might think of new, more egalitarian ways in which to describe our work. Brown (1984, 1994) originated the term "symbolic relationship" instead of "transference" and "counter-transference" to describe the ways that all of us (including therapists) relive prior relationships in the present. The concept of "symbolic relationship" honors the here-and-now relationship between counselor and client while recognizing the impact of past relationships on the present. Likewise, feminist multicultural counselors will be sensitive to the messages communicated by our choices of words such as "therapist" or "psychotherapist" to describe ourselves, implying that someone is ill or injured and needs to be fixed. The word "counselor" may be more acceptable to some clients and may communicate a more egalitarian stance on the part of the therapist.

Walter and Peller (2000) called for a new language beyond therapy and the discourses of pathology and deficits. They moved to a language that replaced "therapy" with "personal consultation," away from the language of "pathology and assessment" toward an orientation to and vocabulary of "conversation, personal consultation, possibilities, and optimism" (p. xii). The authors maintained that this shift in vocabulary better enables them to see their clients as "well intentioned people who want to create something positive in their future" (p. xii). As personal consultants, they saw themselves standing alongside their clients as "they seek out and create these preferred futures" (p. xii). In our age of plurality and diversity, an orientation and language of preferences and possibilities replaces the more traditional language of problems and solutions. They argued that the language of personal consultation enables them to be more respectful of their clients and the diversity of their lives. They were clear about stepping out of the position of "expert" and "evaluator" into a position of "interest, curiosity, and encouraging in the joint exploration of client desires" (p. 178).

Boundaries have been particularly complex issues in the evolution of feminist therapy and remain so for multicultural and feminist multicultural counseling. Citing well-known multicultural authors (e.g., Sue, Boyd-Franklin, Lazarus, and Carrera), Kiselica and Robinson (2001) noted that ethical standards in counseling, psychology, and social work discourage, if not prohibit, dual relationships between counselor and client. These strict standards of boundary enforcement, characteristic of counseling and psychology ethical codes and training practices, have been questioned by multicultural and feminist theory and practice. In the early development of feminist therapy, its practitioners held a relatively naïve view of the possibility of full equality between themselves and their clients. Thus, many feminist therapists were less careful than they should have been regarding overlapping and dual relationships. In addition, feminist and lesbian therapists and their clients in community found themselves subject to a "small town" phenomenon in which dual relationships were often unavoidable. At the same time, feminist psychologists and therapists, responding to the rampant violation of women clients' sexual boundaries by male therapists, led the way for the development of explicit ethical guidelines regarding dual relationships.

Dominant culture ethical guidelines frequently are absolutist and fail to take cultural context into consideration (Ridley, Liddle, Hill, & Li, 2001). In addition, they are intended to be implemented without regard to the relational, familial, religious/spiritual, or political contexts in which clients and counselors engage together. Vasquez (2010) reminded us of the distinction between boundary crossings and boundary violations. Although boundary violations are harmful, boundary crossings may lie on a continuum from harmful, through neutral, to beneficial. Rather than thinking of boundary maintenance as dichotomous, Brown (1994) encouraged practitioners to think of it as continuous. Vasquez (2010) argued:

> Practitioners are encouraged to recognize the importance of multicultural sensitivity/responsiveness, knowledge, and understanding about ethnically and racially different individuals to the area of professional boundaries, such as receiving/giving gifts, attending clients' transitional life events, answering clients' questions and self-disclosure, and nonsexual touch. Sometimes maintaining strict boundaries does more harm than engaging in a humane, genuine, authentic manner that is culturally congruent. (p. 141)

Further, feminist multicultural counselors and the individuals they counsel are frequently partners in social action (Brown, 1994). Political action is a core principle of feminist multicultural counseling, sometimes providing even greater healing for clients who have been sexually traumatized or are the victims of racist microaggressions than "talk therapy." In addition, we believe that it is unethical for practitioners—who earn their living providing services to people who have been injured by a racist, misogynist, homonegative society—not to be engaged in changing that society. When counselors work hand in hand with their clients to create change, not only do they model empowered behavior for clients, but the therapeutic relationship can be deeply impacted. These boundary crossings must be managed thoughtfully to insure that clients do not become confused or come to harm, much like in other therapeutic overlaps.

Feminist Multicultural Perspectives on Assessment and Diagnosis

The second component of implementing feminist multicultural counseling includes assessment and diagnosis. Diagnosis, from a feminist multicultural perspective, may appear to be contradictory. Within a framework that regards context as an essential part of understanding human distress, traditional diagnosis, with its focus on the individual and her or his intrapsychic reality, would seem to be the epitome of "blaming the victim" of injustice, colonization, and societally induced trauma. In fact, traditional psychiatric diagnosis can serve to further injure and oppress clients (Caplan & Cosgrove, 2004).

A feminist multicultural approach to assessment and diagnosis does not ignore or reject the intrapsychic aspect of people's distress. Rather, it recognizes that what is thought of as intrapsychic is a combination of biological and individual characteristics that have been impacted by the environment in a number of ways. Brown (2010) described the biopsychosocial/spiritual-existential axes of personal power that included somatic power, intrapersonal/intrapsychic power, interpersonal/social-contextual power, and spiritual/existential power. Distress, in a patriarchal context, results from interference with one or more of these systems. Morrow and Hawxhurst (1998) developed a model for integrating political analysis in counseling that identified personal, interpersonal, and sociopolitical areas of power; in the model that will be presented later in this chapter, we will expand on these areas.

Traditional mental health theory and practice attributes emotional distress to "brain disease" (Poland & Caplan, 2004). Traditional psychodiagnostics are based on an etic approach, which assumes that we can generalize across cultures in our assessment and diagnosis of human distress and can treat "mental illness" symptomatically based on assumed scientific evidence. In this system, the authors of the *Diagnostic and Statistical Manual of Mental Disorders* (*DSM-IV, TR*; American Psychiatric Association, 2000), insurance companies, and drug companies have the power and authority to identify most, if not all, serious emotional distress as brain disease. Human anguish is "medicalized" and is handled in the mental health system. Poland and Caplan identified sources of bias that may misguide practitioners in their diagnostic efforts, including those based on the psychology of the clinician, professional identity, and contextual factors. Of these, contextual factors have great relevance to feminist multicultural counselors. Exploring the deeper cultural and ideological roots of bias, they examined the interlocking structures and institutions that contribute to viewing human distress as mental illness: pharmaceutical companies, the authors of the *DSM*, insurance companies, and textbook companies all profit from the view that the brain, not society, is responsible for mental illness. This creates a climate in which a feminist multicultural analysis of power can be ignored. Poland and Caplan reminded us that "health issues are, after all, issues of social justice, and, in matters of social justice, it is important to be relentlessly vigilant about identifying and rooting out biases that can harm those members of our society who have little or no power" (p. 20).

Proposing a culturally relevant client-centered psychiatry, Castillo (1997) distinguished between disease-centered psychiatry and client-centered psychiatry. He suggested that, although mental disorders are conceptualized as being caused by brain diseases (primarily chemical imbalances in neurotransmitters), there is no empirical evidence to support the existence of brain disease in mental health problems. He proposed a holistic, client-centered approach to assessment and diagnosis that integrated the following factors:

> Culture-based socio-environmental stress and emotional trauma affecting groups, and differential individual experience of stress and emotional trauma affecting the microstructures of neural networks in the brain;
>
> Individual genetic sensitivity to socio-environmental stress and emotional trauma;
>
> Individual culture-based thinking-feeling responses to the environment structured in and altering neural networks in the brain;
>
> Fluid boundary between mental health and mental illness;
>
> Factors affecting the duration of illness: that is, self-limiting, adaptive, maladaptive and progressive influences (biological and sociocultural);
>
> Culture-based clinical realities: that is, culture-bound syndromes, idioms of distress, professional diagnoses, and forms of deviant behavior structured in neural networks;
>
> Culture-based treatments affecting the psychology and neurology of the client;
>
> Culture-based psychological and neurological outcomes (p. 263).

From this perspective, diagnosis and treatment are concerned with "an individual who has thoughts, emotions, a social context, and a set of cultural schemas" rather than a disease (p. 262).

"Abnormalities" in personality and psychological functioning, according to Castillo, do have some psychobiological basis, but he views these problems as modifiable conditions resulting from patterns of thinking, behavior, or experience (including socio-environmental stress). He emphasized that "the culture-based structure of dominance hierarchies" (p. 263) can have dramatic effects on individuals, and these effects can vary according to the specific types of social and economic stressors.

Castillo described mental illness as "tuning of the mind-brain" (p. 271), that is, the organizing systems of the mind and the associated structures of the brain become "tuned" to certain patterns based on life experiences, including language, culture, and individual experiences. Based on recent investigations of the neurobiology of mental illness, he hypothesized that the sociocultural environment becomes physically structured in the brains of individuals, based on cultural patterns as well as individual experiences such as trauma; "thus people walk around with their culture and their personal history literally inside their heads" (p. 268). Castillo described culture-specific ways of being "abnormal" and emphasized that an accurate diagnosis of mental illness or distress cannot be made without consideration of the cultural context and that treatments must be culturally specific. He wrote, "Culture-based clinical realities, including professional diagnosis, cultural biases, culture-bound syndromes, idioms of distress, and forms of deviance should be recognized as preexisting, culture specific patterns of abnormality and included in any client-centered model of mental illness" (p. 277).

Using a feminist multicultural approach, if we were working with a person from a specific culture who was characterized as having a mental illness, what are some of the things we might want to know? What might we use as sources of information? It would be important to understand broadly the systems and structures of the person's culture(s), recognizing that she or he could be situated in more than one culture. In addition, it would be important to look at community structure and other elements that would impact the client's life and well-being (Sinacore-Guinn, 1995). Sinacore-Guinn emphasized the importance of examining cultural systems and structures, cultural values, gender socialization, and trauma.

Sinacore-Guinn argued that cultural systems and structures must be considered broadly, looking at "community structure, family, schools, interaction styles, concepts of illness, life stage development, coping patterns, and immigration history" (p. 21). She emphasized the importance of understanding the cultural meanings for the client of each of these systems and structures.

Sinacore-Guinn also addressed cultural values, including the client's cultural orientation to:

> Time, focusing on the past, present, or future;
> Activity, emphasizing doing, being, or developing and growing;
> Relational orientation, focusing on the individual, the communal group, or the hierarchical structure;
> Person-nature orientation, focusing on how individuals relate to nature in terms of being in harmony with nature, having control over or being subjugated to it;
> Basic nature of people, involving attitudes about the innate goodness or evil in human behavior (p. 22).

Gender socialization plays an important role in Sinacore-Guinn's model. Noting the gender bias inherent in many diagnostic categories, Enns (1993) explored the ways in which women are pathologized based on gender role stereotypes. Sinacore-Guinn argued that "gender becomes even more complex when one looks beyond the White Western culture" (p. 23). Feminist multicultural therapists need to understand the beliefs, attitudes, and rules about gender in the client's culture, as well as what the cultural consequences are for deviation or variation.

Sinacore-Guinn identified trauma as another critical source of information in working to assess a person from any given culture. Understanding the cultural context is a critical component of understanding trauma and its impact on an individual. Castillo (1997) noted that social stressors that lead to trauma differ across cultures and that these social stressors tend to be greater in societies that are hierarchical rather than egalitarian. Sinacore-Guinn's attention to cultural systems and structures, cultural values, and gender socialization provides a critical context for understanding the nature and impact of trauma.

Many of our clients, particularly those who are marginalized, are located in more than one culture and experience conflict between aspects of those cultures. For example, a first-generation daughter of immigrant Vietnamese parents is likely to feel torn between the traditional culture and language of her family and the dominant U.S. culture into which she is attempting to function and fit. The bicultural struggle that this conflict imposes is present both within and across the systems and structures of both cultures. The complexity of this struggle is likely to necessitate coping strategies that may be pathologized by a counselor who is not considering the complex cultural contexts or the intersections of statuses and identities of the client.

Sinacore-Guinn's model of culture and gender-sensitive assessment and diagnosis offer a powerful feminist multicultural training framework that incorporates a synthesis of theory and personal experience. Sinacore-Guinn suggested a process involving five progressive steps for training students. We recommend these activities to seasoned feminist multicultural counselors as well as our students.

"Critique general theories as well as specifics of the DSM system" (p. 27). It is important to be knowledgeable and critical of the biases that exist in systems and theory of psychopathology and development.

"Examine the cultural systems and structures, values, gender roles, and trauma that exist in their own lives" (p. 27), sharing their insights and awareness with their peers. "The goals of this step are for the students to (a) recognize that they, as all of their clients, are culturally and socially conditioned; (b) learn how that conditioning affects their own lives and their understanding of the world; and (c) discover how that conditioning creates biases that may lead to misunderstanding and misdiagnosing clients" (p. 27).

"Identify a personal bicultural struggle" or dilemma, identifying "personal strengths, weaknesses, coping mechanisms, and ways in which they may be misunderstood and perhaps viewed as pathological" (p. 28).

Look at a variety of "case" studies and analyze cultural systems and structures, values, gender roles, and trauma that exist in the clients' lives, identifying bicultural dilemmas that may exist.

Integrate the theoretical and cultural components of their training, analyzing cases from both particular theoretical orientations and cultural/gender/trauma perspectives. This will help students understand the connection between theoretical orientation and diagnosis and become critical thinkers as they develop their own theoretical orientations. In this way, they may better "avoid inherent cultural and gender biases that may influence diagnosis" (p. 28).

From a feminist multicultural perspective, assessment and diagnosis include a critique of dominant diagnostic practices and tools. Assessment is always conducted through a lens that includes the client's culture, gender, and experiences of oppression and trauma.

The Personal as Political: Consciousness-raising, Conscientization, Conscientização

Although we have addressed these concepts earlier in the chapter, we acknowledge that consciousness-raising is a complex process that can easily drift into a subtle form of colonization. The moment the counselor views the client as having "false consciousness" about her or his condition, that counselor has adopted the role of expert on the client's life, running afoul of one of the basic tenets of feminist therapy: that the client is the expert on her or his own life and experience. However, working as a partner with the client in her or his process of self-liberation, we can, with the client's permission, share our observations and raise questions about ways in which we hear the client internalizing oppression. As we continually reframe the client's self-perceptions in the larger sociopolitical context, the client is given the opportunity to externalize self-blame, which can lead to anger and ultimately to activism.

Analysis of Power in Psychotherapy

It is typical of traditional, individualistic Western psychotherapeutic perspectives to encourage clients to take responsibility for themselves. Although this is an important component of counseling, utilizing a power analysis in counseling engages the client and counselor in a paradigm shift in which, often, the client is encouraged to externalize "blame" for her or his experience. An analysis of power in the client's life includes helping the client understand the actual limits of her or his power in a situation or in society, distinguish between perceived and real limitations, and identify what part of a problem belongs to self as opposed to others, including the larger culture.

Of equal importance to assisting clients in analyzing power in their lives is the analysis of power in the client-counselor relationship. This analysis includes (a) an understanding of the basic structure of therapy, as well as its underlying assumptions and how they influence counselor-client power dynamics; (b) an understanding of the dynamics of colonization; (c) an understanding of cultural and other variables that manifest within the specific client-counselor relationship; and (d) exploration (and self-exploration) of individual client and counselor experiences, assumptions, and biases that may affect power in the therapy relationship.

The therapy relationship is basically unequal. Despite the best intentions of the feminist multicultural counselor and the personal empowerment of the client, the underlying assumptions of psychotherapy are that the client is in need of help and the therapist is able to be the helper (Brown, 1994). Extreme forms of this frame include a traditional psychodynamic therapy relationship of psychoanalyst and patient, in which the patient is assumed to be pathological and the psychoanalyst capable of unearthing and curing the pathology. However, even the most benign counselor-client relationship carries at least unaware assumptions of the different statuses of the two partners. The egalitarian nature of many feminist multicultural relationships can be misleading; thus, the therapist is in the position of needing to be explicit about power and boundaries in the relationship.

It is important to be cognizant of the client's cultural views of the therapy relationship, expertness, and authority. Flexibility in terms of the degree of directiveness will enable the feminist multicultural counselor to meet the client where she or he is. Exploring with the client what she or he believes counseling is supposed to be and do can give valuable information as the counselor attempts to enter the client's worldview and to be culturally sensitive. Regardless of the degree of egalitarianism or hierarchy in the relationship, collaboration is a central goal.

Group Work as Empowerment

A feminist multicultural focus on the importance of group counseling and psychotherapy was a natural outgrowth of feminist consciousness-raising (Morrow et al., 2006). As a tool for balancing power in the therapeutic relationship, "groups help to reduce the power discrepancy between client and counselor, and group dynamics serve to better facilitate clients challenging the power and mystique of the group facilitator" (p. 241). Using feminist consciousness-raising as a model, facilitators of counseling and therapy groups may work to facilitate this process by being transparent about group dynamics, collaboratively establishing the more political goals of the group (e.g., suggesting that one purpose of the group would be to look at how our personal experiences are part of a larger context), and rotating leadership among group members. Transparency in group dynamics and processes may be facilitated by questions such as these provided in a handout to group members at the University of Utah's Women's Resource Center:

How does my presence and participation contribute to safety within the group, the empowerment of myself, others, mutuality, and power sharing?

How many times do I speak and for how long?

How well do I invite others to share their perspectives?

Do others in the group know me well enough to feel safe in my presence?

Do I demonstrate respect for differences, validating the experiences of others without diminishing my own presence, participation, and unique perspectives?

Am I clear about my own and others' boundaries related to disclosure, and do I respect the limits established by others in the group?

Am I assuming some responsibility as a co-facilitator as well as a participant and learner?

Groups create the opportunity for members to address issues of diversity (Brown, 1994), thereby increasing multicultural awareness and skills among the members. Groups serve a unique purpose for members of oppressed groups in that members learn that they are not alone in their experiences, thoughts, feelings, or fears. Such groups combat the isolation that is so common in people who experience oppression (Morrow et al., 2006) and normalize participants' experiences. Conventional group therapy often discourages members from meeting outside the group setting; however, feminist multicultural groups encourage such connections as a tool to end isolation, encouraging transparency of group members about these outside relationships. Morrow et al. framed groups themselves as

> . . . microcosms of societal dynamics; thus, issues of privilege, power, and oppression can be dealt with in an open environment in the group, with facilitators modeling intercultural communication and respect. When people are able to successfully address their experiences of isolation, alienation, and oppression within the group setting, they are empowered to take steps on their own behalf and that of others in the world outside. (p. 241)

Advocacy Counseling, Social Action, and Social Justice

Conventional counseling and psychotherapeutic approaches have emphasized therapist neutrality and thus have failed to see the relevance of social action to the therapy endeavor. However, Bradley and Lewis (2000) countered this tradition by saying:

> Regardless of the particular setting in which he or she works, each counselor is confronted again and again with issues that cannot be resolved simply through change within the individual. All too often, negative

aspects of the environment impinge on a client's wellbeing, intensifying personal problems or creating obstacles to growth. When such situations arise, effective counselors speak up! We think of advocacy as the act of speaking up or taking action to make environmental changes on behalf of our clients. (p. 3)

Morrow et al. (2006) further argued that "counselors and psychotherapists earn their living trying to heal the wounds of an unjust society" (p. 241) and that it is "unethical to do so without taking steps to change social systems that oppress our clients" (p. 241). Thus, social justice work on the part of counselors and therapists is an essential component of being a feminist multicultural counseling psychologist. Engagement in social action can serve to empower the counselor her- or himself, thus becoming a form of self-care; it also serves as an adjunct to the personal work that we do with clients by helping to change the systems and structures that contribute to our clients' distress; finally, our work on behalf of social change models empowered behavior for our clients and may serve as an inspiration to them.

In addition to counselors taking action for social change, Kiselica and Robinson (2001) viewed advocacy counseling, social action, and social justice as tools to increase clients' personal power and to foster sociopolitical change that better addresses the circumstances and needs of clients. Morrow et al. (2006) described client activism and social action as multifaceted, including clients whose first steps as activists are on behalf of themselves or those closest to them. Not all clients will have the resources, physical, economic, or psychological, to engage in larger social justice efforts. However, it is impossible to fully describe the empowerment and transformation that can result from a client's engagement in political action or social change. Lee (1998) wrote that "helping clients challenge institutional and social barriers that impede academic, career, or personal-social development" (pp. 8–9) was a key component of advocacy counseling, social action, and social justice work. Thus, in addition to counselors being aware of resources in the community to meet the personal and social needs of clients, feminist multicultural counselors will be aware of social change and political action initiatives in their community as well as nationally and globally. The counselor's own engagement in these activities will provide the grounding to assess which clients will benefit from these actions and will facilitate communication with clients about activism.

Implementation of Feminist Multicultural Counseling: Strategies for Empowerment

Although numerous feminist, multicultural, and feminist multicultural theorists have emphasized the importance of conducting political analysis in counseling and psychotherapy, few have offered specific guidelines for this process. Morrow and Hawxhurst (1998) expanded on the conceptual work of Dorothy Riddle (unpublished) to develop an empowerment framework for analyzing power and facilitating the empowerment of clients. This framework includes a model illustrating the dimensions and conditions of empowerment as well as feminist process guidelines.

Empowerment Process Guidelines: Dimensions and Conditions of Empowerment

Using their empowerment model for political analysis in psychotherapy, Morrow and Hawxhurst (1998) suggested that client concerns and distress could be analyzed with the client, using an empowerment grid (p. 43) that places dimensions and conditions of empowerment on different axes, then entering information in each of the resulting cells. The purposes of this exercise are many, including identifying specific areas of client powerlessness for further work, understanding the exact nature of the problem, developing counselor interventions to address the various aspects of powerlessness, and giving the client complete information about the problem so that she or he is able to take action.

DIMENSIONS OF EMPOWERMENT: PERSONAL, INTERPERSONAL, AND SOCIOPOLITICAL

Kitzinger and Perkins (1993) criticized feminist models of empowerment for focusing solely on the personal dimension. The intrapersonal or intrapsychic perspective that dominates psychology and psychotherapy often focuses exclusively on personal power and responsibility. Alternatively, Morrow and Hawxhurst (1998) identified three dimensions of empowerment: the personal, the interpersonal, and the sociopolitical. Each is defined and illustrated below.

The Personal Dimension

The personal, or intrapersonal, dimension of empowerment emphasizes *power within.* Empowerment at the personal level involves gaining, maintaining, and/or restoring power and control over an aspect of ourselves and our lives. It is important to recognize that we do have power, as well as the right and potential to exercise it. Even though options for choices may in fact be limited, we are still left with choices. According to Hill Collins (1990), "The existence of Afrocentric feminist thought suggests that there is always choice, and power to act, no matter how bleak the situation may appear to be" (p. 238). However, she was not referring to the personal-responsibility, make-your-own-reality view characteristic of some contemporary perspectives. Instead, she went on to say, "Viewing the world as one in the making raises the issue of individual responsibility for bringing about change. It also shows that, while individual empowerment is key, only collective action can effectively generate lasting social transformation of political and economic institutions" (p. 238). Thus, personal empowerment is always considered in the context of the other dimensions.

The personal dimension of empowerment includes past experiences that are no longer overtly disempowering (e.g., parental messages, traumatic events). Others did have the power to control or victimize us but are no longer overtly present as forces of power in our lives. These disempowering events, experiences, and messages become internalized at the personal level after the external controls are gone. It is at the personal level that we internalize institutionalized oppression and colonization, which are enforced and maintained both interpersonally (i.e., microagressions) and through social enforcement (i.e., institutionalized racism). The voices of oppression and colonization are reflected in an individual's self concept, attitudes, and behaviors. "The true focus of revolutionary change is never merely the oppressive situations which we seek to escape, but that piece of the oppressor which is planted deep within each of us, and which knows only the oppressors' tactics, the oppressors' relationships" (Lorde, 1984, p. 123).

At a personal level, the therapy goal might be to move from self-hatred and self-denial to self-love and nurturing, recognizing the strengths of inner resources, the brilliance of coping strategies (which may have been pathologized), and the often improbable reality of one's survival in the face of seemingly impossible circumstances. From a feminist multicultural perspective, we would replace the language of "pathology" or "dysfunction" with a language of "positive coping strategies." Metaphors often used in therapy might include the internal self-helper, the wise woman within, the Amazon warrior, or the inner child.

As part of the personal dimension of empowerment, we would also include Brown's (2010) concepts of *somatic power* and *intrapersonal/intrapsychic power*. According to Brown, somatic power includes being "in contact with body." The body is "accepted as it is" and experienced as a safe place to be. The client is connected to her or his "bodily desires for food, sexual pleasure, and rest." Brown noted that power at this level "does not require the ability to see, hear, walk, or talk, nor is a powerful body necessarily free of pain or illness, nor strong or physically fit" (p. 32). The individual experiences compassion regarding her or his body.

Brown defined intrapersonal/intrapsychic power as knowing what one thinks, being able to think critically, and being flexible. Such a person trusts her or his intuition and "knows feelings as they are felt. Feelings [are] a useful source of information about the here and now." The person has the "ability to experience powerful emotions, to contain affect, . . . [and] to self-soothe in ways that are not harmful to self or others physically, psychosocially, or spiritually" (p. 32).

Brown also identified the spiritual/existential dimension of power, which we view as overarching or as experienced very personally but encompassing the interpersonal and sociopolitical or collective dimensions as well. Brown noted that people who are empowered at this level "have systems of meaning making that assist with responding to the existential challenges of life and that have the potential to give a sense of comfort and well-being." They have a "sense of [their] own heritage and culture integrated into [their] identity in ways that allow for better understanding of self." They "have a raison d'etre and can integrate that into important aspects of daily life." They have "access to capacities for creativity and fantasy, yet have [a] sense of reality" (p. 32).

The Interpersonal Dimension

The interpersonal dimension of empowerment includes overt experiences of power and powerlessness occurring at the interpersonal level or that have an interpersonal overlay. Often, personal power issues stem from or become interpersonal power struggles or power failures (e.g., when a friend, partner, or therapist is invested and takes responsibility for the individual's process or outcomes). Also, at the interpersonal level we find what Daly (1978) referred to as "token torturers" (p. 132) or cases of mistaken identity: the ones who enforce the rules and support the institutions of a racist patriarchy (e.g., teachers, parents, and even therapists—those who carry out the socializing activities that enforce societal oppression). Daly writes about token torturers, often women/mothers, who enforce such practices as clitoridectomy and foot binding; however, in the United States there is also a history of extreme practices, such as sterilization of young, poor women of color (sometimes with nurses as token torturers), the gifting of a breast implant by a mother to her daughter for her 18th birthday, and the many more subtle socialization practices that limit freedom and lead to internalized "isms" in their victims.

At the interpersonal level of empowerment, egalitarian relationships are valued. Egalitarian relationships involve addressing issues of power in relationships, including therapy; striving for mutuality; consensual decision making; and collaboration. When hierarchy is unavoidable (e.g., in traditional work settings and educational systems, between parents and children), it is important to recognize and name the limits of equality and to develop strategies for remaining empowered in these situations.

Brown (2010) combined interpersonal and social-contextual power. Focusing on her definition of interpersonal power, people who are interpersonally empowered are "interpersonally effective" and "have desired impacts on others" (p. 32). They have "no illusions of control; [they] forgive [themselves] and others" (p. 32). They are appropriately self-protective. They are capable of forming relationships with others and are "able to create and sustain intimacy, to be close without loss of self or engulfment of other, and to be differentiated without being distant or detached" (p. 32). They can end relationships when it is time but also persevere in relationships and work out conflict. They can "enter roles in life—parent, partner, worker—most often from a place of choice, intention, and desire, not accidentally, although serendipity and the opportunity to encounter the new are welcomed" (p. 32).

The Sociopolitical Dimension

The sociopolitical dimension of empowerment involves access and avenues to choice within the social system. Limits and barriers are imposed by cultural norms, values, rules, sanctions, taboos and violence within systems of privilege, dominance, and power in the larger social system. It is important to understand power relations in regard to, for example, gender, race, and ethnicity, as well as the politics of domination, colonization, domestication, and resulting institutionalized systems of oppression that are presented to us as "reality." Hagan (1993) noted:

> Efficient domination and effective internalization occurs when subordinates are convinced that their subordination is inevitable, even natural. Such internalized oppression creates the illusion of agreement.... As a form of social control, internalization is definitely a long-range strategy. This method requires that over many generations, the values of domination must be passed down through family and other societal forms. Our conditioning from birth trains us to conform and to assume those values as our own. Given no alternatives, domination and subordination becomes our reality, our universe. It's just the way things are. (p. 85)

Social empowerment requires group support and social justice action and change in order to ultimately move beyond or through the barriers imposed by the existing sociocultural-political structures. We argue that any form of counseling or psychotherapy that does not in some way include a political analysis of the broader social context falls short as a form and process of feminist multicultural counseling.

Incorporating Brown's (2010) notion of spirituality at the sociopolitical dimension, we note the importance of the transmission of spiritual values through communities and cultures. Brown argued that spiritually/existentially powerful people are "aware of the social context and can engage with it rather than being controlled by it or unaware of its impact" (p. 32).

CONDITIONS OF EMPOWERMENT: PERMISSION, ENABLEMENT, AND INFORMATION

In addition to identifying the dimensions of empowerment, Morrow and Hawxhurst (1998) described three conditions: permission, enablement, and information. Each of these conditions can be assessed to identify power or powerlessness in clients' lives, to provide a map to effective counseling interventions, and to guide clients in their own self-empowerment.

Permission

Permission involves addressing the questions, "May I?," "Do I have the right?," and "Am I deserving?" At the *personal dimension,* permission involves recognizing, knowing, naming, and believing that we have individual rights, without disregard for the other individuals in our lives. Permission at the personal level results in self- affirmation, validation, and self-esteem.

At the *interpersonal dimension,* permission is the real or perceived requirement of permission-giving by another. What are the consequences, in relationship, of acting on one's own behalf? Traditional patriarchal models for heterosexual relationships frequently assume that the man "owns" the woman's time and even her body and that his permission is required for her to act autonomously. Even some lesbian and gay relationships perpetuate the permission-giving model. Partners in empowered couples will exercise autonomy while considering the impact of their actions on the other partner.

Family relationship dynamics manage to extend well beyond childhood, for better or worse. Empowered and empowering parenting and families will produce a next generation who can achieve a balance between autonomy and responsibility to family that is individually and culturally appropriate.

It is important to consider the power of approval and disapproval by others as well as more overt risks that could lead to violence and abuse. We can look at many examples of overt risks within the context of domestic violence. Understanding permission at the interpersonal level might include an analysis of power and control as well as an understanding of entitlement. For example, an abuser likely believes that he is entitled to his partner's time, her undivided attention, and her sexual compliance. Her refusal on any level could result in emotional and/or physical abuse. Empowerment at the interpersonal level, in this case, may include such practical steps as a safety plan in addition to integrating personal and sociopolitical empowerment.

Permission at the *sociopolitical dimension* includes laws, rules, norms, values, taboos, and prohibitions that either support or undermine one's freedoms or curb one's personal power. At this level it is important to understand the consequences of breaking the spoken and unspoken rules in the interest of personal empowerment, obeying or disregarding the law, or even participating in civil disobedience. Exploring permission at the social level asks about the costs and benefits of compliance as well as of non-compliance with societal expectations, norms, and rules.

Enablement

Enablement addresses the questions, "Can I?" and "How can I?" At the *personal dimension,* enablement involves knowledge, skills, abilities, efficacy, and other personal resources that may be developed or enhanced through self-help and personal exploration, including reading, journaling, practicing, and training.

At the *interpersonal dimension,* enablement involves mentoring, support, assistance, or facilitation within the context of individual or group relationships. Enablement activities might include networking, classes, support or consciousness-raising groups, as well as individual advocacy. Counseling could be an example of enablement at the interpersonal level.

At the *sociopolitical dimension,* enablement involves the implementation and enforcement of affirmative action policies, civil rights laws, and provision for and access to resources, opportunity, and freedoms.

Information

In addition to permission and enablement as conditions of empowerment, information addresses the questions: "What do I need to know?" and "Where do I find it?" At all levels, information is power that can be used to limit or expand one's possibilities. At the *personal dimension,* information involves self-awareness (e.g., interests, needs, priorities, identities). Empowerment at this level involves "knowing oneself" in as many aspects as possible.

At the *interpersonal dimension,* information involves interpersonal relationships and exchanges exemplified by acts of telling our stories, giving voice to our experience, and sharing our truths. The personal becomes political through these acts of sharing: "The most notable fact that culture imprints on women is the sense of our limits. The most important thing one woman can do for another is to illuminate and expand her sense of actual possibilities" (Rich, 1976, p. 246).

At the *sociopolitical dimension,* information involves discovering and understanding the lenses through which information is presented via educational institutions and the media in all its varied forms. This includes information about the information (e.g., institutionalized censorship designed to maintain the status quo; the power of the media through selective information, distortion, and withholding of information; and biases presented as reality and incorporated into the presentation of history, science, and religion). Who has the power to share, withhold, or distort information? Identifying and illuminating alternative sources of information that are typically not available through mainstream educational and media sources can be a powerful component of empowerment.

Empowerment Process Guidelines

In our training of feminist multicultural counselors and therapists, we have developed training materials to assist ourselves and our trainees in conducting an analysis of power in counseling and psychotherapy. Empowerment includes three components: (a) both an analysis of power (understanding the dynamics of power relationships) and an action component; (b) gaining power or control on three levels: personal, interpersonal, and social; and (c) making informed choices from all the available alternatives. The following Empowerment Process Guidelines are not intended as a cookbook approach. Although they may be used in order, it is frequently more useful to skip to a guideline that seems especially relevant to your client's situation. The guidelines may be used either as a self-help tool or as an aid to facilitate the empowerment of another person. We frequently give them to our clients as a handout. A condensed version of these guidelines, created by our students, appears in Appendix A of this chapter.

To use the guidelines, first choose a *specific* problem or issue of concern. Then:

1. *Assess the situation.* Be as clear as you can about:

a. Describing the situation in detail, including examples and interactions.

b. Your own experience of powerlessness, including your feelings and how the experience affects your functioning.

c. Where do you believe the power lies? Is it in your own hands? Does someone else have real or imagined control? Is the source of power specific, or is it a nebulous "they?" Work to identify where the power lies, both specifically (the people and institutions who have power) and accurately (one's immediate supervisor may only *appear* to have the power). Explore all the options. The power may lie in many places.

2. *Affirm yourself.*

a. What do you value about yourself? What are your strengths?

b. What are your limitations? How do you work against yourself?

c. What are your vulnerabilities? Are you seeing them as weakness or strengths? Sharing our vulnerabilities can be either empowering (such as when the sharing is mutual in a friendship) or disempowering (for example, when we reveal them to people who have power over us—a "belly-up" approach).

3. *Acknowledge your power.*

a. At the personal level: What can you do for yourself?

b. At the interpersonal level: Who are your advocates or allies? How can they be supportive of you?

c. At the social level: What larger realities are in your favor (groups, laws, other support)?

4. *Identify areas of powerlessness.*

a. At the personal, interpersonal, social levels.

b. Are you lacking permission, enablement, information? On which level(s): personal, interpersonal, and/or social?

c. You may need to stop here in order to increase your power in one of the above areas.

5. *Analyze your possibilities.*

a. Decide what would fit best. What is your fantasy of the perfect situation? What do you want?

b. What is preventing the best fit?

i. At the personal, interpersonal, social levels?

ii. In the areas of permission (May I? Do I have the right?), enablement (Can I? How can I?), information (What do I need to know? How do I find out? How reliable are my sources of information? Are there alternative sources or networks?).

iii. In the area of vulnerabilities?

iv. In the area of responsibility? Am I taking responsibility for others? Am I deciding for someone else their capability to be responsible ? (Taking responsibility for another person takes power from her or him. There are few areas in which this is productive.) Am I allowing or encouraging others to take responsibility for me?

v. In the area of limits? Do I set clear limits about my own rights and space without imposing on others' rights and space? Are there clear consequences to violating my limits? Have I communicated them clearly?

vi. In the area of protection? Am I protecting another person? Is someone protecting me? Protection usually weakens, except in extreme circumstances in which we are unable to protect ourselves. This is a "gray area," but the effects of protecting another person can serve to demoralize her or him and convey that she or he is incompetent.

vii. In the area of fears? It is helpful to clearly identify any fears and then to do some careful reality checking in terms of possible risks and consequences.

viii. In the area of labeling? Although labels are commonly thought of as descriptive of behavior patterns, they can in fact create unhelpful behavior patterns. How do the labels you use to describe yourself or others help to determine your/their behavior and feelings about self (e.g., disorganized, lazy, intelligent, sensitive, aggressive)?

c. What have you tried? What worked? What didn't? Why? Why not? Is it worth trying again?

d. What have you thought of and not tried? Why not? Is it worth trying?

e. What are your instincts/intuitions? What feels right?

6. *Weigh the risks.*

a. What are the possible consequences of trusting and following your intuition?

b. What are the possible consequences of other courses of action?

c. What are the possible consequences of "staying put" or not acting to change?

7. *Make a choice.* Empowerment lies in making a clear choice (staying put, leaving, changing). Once you have chosen, know that you have made the best possible choice for you at that time. Know also that you have the right to change your mind. Empowerment is a process. What fits now may not fit in the future. Guilt-tripping never fits!

Questions Facilitating Political Analysis

Numerous feminist therapists have developed their own approaches to conducting political analysis in therapy. However, in our training we have also heard feminist therapists ask, "Political analysis? What is that?" Collaboratively with our students, we have developed a brief set of questions to guide beginning feminist multicultural counselors in asking relevant questions of clients that will facilitate political analysis. We encourage feminist multicultural counselors to add to this list when they find questions that help to move into political analysis with clients.

Where did you learn that?

What lessons did you learn about gender as you were growing up? Race? Class? Culture? Other?

Who were your role models? How have they served you?

What are the costs? Benefits?

Who has the power?

Who benefits?

What are the rules? Who made the rules?

What happens when you break the rules?

What and from whom did you learn about relationships?

What would a healthy relationship look like?

What does "love" mean for you? Where did you learn this?

What cultures do you navigate?

What stresses or dilemmas do you experience in navigating more than one culture?

Is that a problem for you? If not, whose problem is it?

Who decides what it means to "get better?" To "be healthy?" To "be normal?"

What roles do you play in your life? Who wrote the scripts?

In conclusion, it is sometimes helpful to use the empowerment grid and guidelines specifically and directly with clients. At other times, they will be more appropriate to use conceptually. We recommend tailoring these tools to the needs of the client as well as the personal style of the counselor.

Feminist Multicultural Counseling and Psychotherapy: Conclusion and Future Directions

This chapter has just scratched the surface of what it means to conduct feminist multicultural counseling and psychotherapy. Our goal was to provide practical guidance to practitioners who hope to practice an integrative approach that encompasses both feminist and multicultural perspectives. As White feminists, it has been our challenge to write a chapter that does not continue to relegate multicultural issues to the background. It is in the spirit of humility and self-reflection that we welcome feedback on how well we have achieved this goal. We are very cognizant that our White privilege and internalized colonization allow us the luxury to choose when we focus on issues that go beyond gender to a more inclusive, integrative feminist multicultural perspective.

We have identified future directions as we consider areas that we lacked the space to include in this chapter, areas for further research, and problems yet to be addressed (or addressed more completely).

First, we want to give credit to those feminist multiculturalists in counseling psychology whom we mentioned in this chapter as well as those who did not appear but have made important contributions to an integrative approach. A complete chapter on feminist multicultural counseling and psychotherapy would include a herstory of their contributions. We hope to remedy this in the future.

Our focus in this chapter was on theory and implementation of feminist multicultural counseling and psychotherapy. The research in this area is extremely sparse, likely because most of the writing about feminist multicultural counseling comes from practitioners rather than researchers; but it should be reviewed more fully. The field is in great need of both qualitative and quantitative research on therapy process and outcome.

In terms of assessment, there are a few instruments (e.g., Johnson, Worrell, & Chandler, 2005) that measure feminist therapy outcome, but only one of which we are aware (Feminist Multicultural Therapy Outcome Measure, or FMTOM, Abousleman, 2006) that fully integrates feminist and multicultural aspects of therapy. Research is in process on this instrument. As further psychometric data are available, feminist multicultural therapists should have a tool that will measure the effectiveness of their work.

We neglected issues related to feminist multicultural counseling and therapy with international, indigenous, and immigrant/refugee populations. This was not an indication of the value we place on these issues. In particular, much of the theorizing on colonization mentioned above comes from indigenous and international feminists. It is crucial that feminist multicultural therapists and researchers expand their focus in these areas.

Self-reflection and "doing our own work" are a central part of our research, teaching, and practice. Although this was mentioned in this chapter, an entire chapter could be dedicated to reflection, self-critique, and self-exploration for feminist multicultural counselors and the students we teach and supervise.

Authors' Note

Correspondence concerning this chapter should be addressed to Susan Morrow, Department of Educational Psychology, University of Utah, Salt Lake City, UT 84112–9255. E-mail: sue.morrow@utah.edu.

References

Abousleman, T. M. (2006). Feminist Multicultural Therapy Outcomes Measure: Instrument development and psychometric validity evidence. Unpublished master's thesis, University of Utah.

American Psychiatric Association. (2000). *Diagnostic and statistical manual of mental disorders* (4th ed., text revision). Washington, DC: Author.

Anzaldúa, G. (Ed.). (1990). *Making face, making soul—Haciendocaras: Creative and critical perspectives by feminists of color.* San Francisco: Aunt Lute.

Bowman, S. L., Rasheed, S., Ferris, J., Thompson, D. E., McRae, M., & Weitzman, L. (2001). Interface of feminism and multiculturalism: Where are the women of color? In J. G. Ponterotto, J. M. Casas, L. A. Suzuki, & C. M. Alexander (Eds.), *Handbook of multicultural counseling* (2nd ed.) (pp. 779–800). Thousand Oaks, CA: Sage.

Bradley, L., & Lewis, J. (2000). Introduction. In J. Lewis & L. Bradley (Eds.), *Advocacy in counseling: Counselors, clients, and community* (pp. 3–4). Greensboro, NC: ERIC Clearinghouse on Counseling and Student Services.

Brown, L. S. (1984). Finding new language: Getting beyond analytic verbal shorthand in feminist therapy. *Women and Therapy, 3*(1), 73–80.

Brown, L. S. (1994). *Subversive dialogues: Theory in feminist therapy.* New York: Basic Books.

Brown, L. S. (2010). *Feminist therapy.* Washington, DC: American Psychological Association.

Butler, M. (1985). Guidelines for feminist therapy. In L. B. Rosewater & L. Walker (Eds.), *Handbook of feminist therapy* (pp. 32–38). New York: Springer.

Caplan, P. J., & Cosgrove, L. (2004). *Bias in psychiatric diagnosis.* Lanham, MD: Jason Aronson.

Castillo, R. J. (1997). *Culture and mental illness: A client-centered approach.* Pacific Grove, CA: Brooks/Cole.

Comas-Díaz, L. (1994). An integrative approach. In L. Comas-Díaz & B. Greene (Eds.), *Women of color* (pp. 287–318). New York: Guilford.

Comas-Díaz, L., & Greene, B. (Eds.) (1994). *Women of color: Integrating ethnic and gender identities in psychotherapy.* New York: Guilford.

Combahee River Collective. (1979). A Black feminist statement. In Z. Eisenstein (Ed.), *Capitalist patriarchy and the case for socialist feminism* (pp. 135–139). New York: Monthly Review Press.

Daly, M. (1978). *Gyn/Ecology: The metaethics of radical feminism.* Boston: Beacon.

Enns, C. (1993). Twenty years of feminist counseling and therapy: From naming biases to implementing multifaceted practice. *The Counseling Psychologist, 21,* 3–87.

Enns, C. Z. (1997). *Feminist theories and feminist psychotherapies: Origins, themes, and variations.* Binghamton, NY: Harrington Park.

Espín, O. M. (1994). Feminist approaches. In L. Comas-Díaz & B. Greene (Eds.), *Women of color: Integrating ethnic and gender identities in psychotherapy* (pp. 265–286). New York: Guilford.

Freire, P. (1970). *Cultural action for freedom.* Cambridge, MA: Harvard Educational Review.

Hagan, K. L. (1993). The invisible obvious. In K. L. Hagan, *Fugitive information: Essays from a feminist hothead* (pp. 81–92). New York: HarperCollins.

Hill Collins, P. (1990). *Black feminist thought: Knowledge, consciousness and the politics of empowerment.* Boston: Uniwin Hyman.

hooks, b. (1984). *Feminist theory: From margin to center.* Boston: South End Press.

hooks, b. (1989). *Talking back: Thinking feminist, talking black.* Boston: South End Press.

hooks, b. (1994). *Teaching to transgress.* New York: Routledge.

Johnson, D. M., Worrell, J. & Chandler, R. K. (2005). Assessing psychological health and empowerment in women: The Personal Progress Scale Revised. *Women and Health, 41,* 109–128.

Kanuha, V. K. (June, 2002). *Colonization and violence against women.* National Summit on Domestic Violence in Asian and Pacific Islander Communities, San Francisco, CA.

Kiselica, M. S., & Robinson, M. (2001). Bringing advocacy to life: The history, issues, and human dramas of social justice work in counseling. *Journal of Counseling and Development, 79,* 387–397.

Kitzinger, C., & Perkins, R. (1993). *Changing our minds: Lesbian feminism and psychology.* New York: New York University Press.

Lee, C. C. (1998). Counselors as agents for social change. In C. C. Lee & G. R. Walz (Eds.), *Social action: A mandate for counselors* (pp. 3–16). Alexandria, VA: American Counseling Association.

Lorde, A. (1984). *Age, race, class, and sex: Women redefining difference.* In A. Lorde, Sister outsider (pp. 114–123). Freedom, CA: Crossing Press.

Mander, A. V., & Rush, A. K. (1974). Feminism as therapy. San Francisco: Random House/Bookworks.

McWhirter, E. H. (1994). *Counseling for empowerment.* Alexandria, VA: American Counseling Association.

Morrow, S. L., & Hawxhurst, D. M. (1998). Feminist therapy: Integrating political analysis in counseling and psychotherapy. *Women and Therapy, 21*(2), 37–50.

Morrow, S. L., Hawxhurst, D. M., Montes de Vegas, A. Y., Abousleman, T. M., & Castañeda, C. L. (2006). Toward a radical feminist multicultural therapy: Renewing a commitment to activism. In R. L. Toporek, L. H. Gerstein, N. A. Fouad, G. Roysircar, & T. Israel (Eds.), *Handbook for social justice in counseling psychology: Leadership, vision, and action* (pp. 231–247). Thousand Oaks, CA: Sage.

Norcross, J. C., & Wampold, B. E. (2011). Evidence-based therapy relationships: Research conclusions and clinical practices. *Psychotherapy, 48,* 98–102.

Poland, J. & Caplan, P. J. (2004).The deep structure of bias in psychiatric diagnosis. In P. J. Caplan & L. Cosgrove (Eds.) *Bias in psychiatric diagnosis* (pp. 9–23). Lanham, MD: Jason Aronson.

Rich, A. (1976). *Of woman born: Motherhood as experience and institution.* New York: Norton.

Ridley, C. R., Liddle, M. C., Hill, C. L., & Li, L. C. (2001). Ethical decision making in multicultural counseling. In J. G. Ponterotto, J. M Casas, L. A Suzuki, & C. M. Alexander (Eds.), *Handbook of multicultural counseling* (2nd ed.) (pp. 165–188). Thousand Oaks, CA: Sage.

Sinacore-Guinn, A. L. (1995). The diagnostic window: Culture- and gender-sensitive diagnosis and training. *Counselor Education and Supervision, 35,* 20–31.

Smith, L. (2005).Psychotherapy, classism, and the Poor: Conspicuous by their absence. *American Psychologist, 60,* 687–696.

Vasquez, M. J. T. (2010). Ethics in multicultural counseling practice. In J. G. Ponterotto, J. M. Casas, L. A. Suzuki, & C. M. Alexander (Eds.), *Handbook of multicultural counseling* (3rd ed.) (pp. 127–145). Thousand Oaks, CA: Sage.

Walter, J. L., & Peller, J. E. (2000). *Recreating brief therapy: Preferences and possibilities.* New York: Norton.

Weitz, R. (1982). Feminist consciousness raising, self-concept, and depression. *Sex Roles, 8,* 231–241.

Appendix A: Empowerment Process Guidelines

Assess the Situation	In what ways are you experiencing a lack of power? Who has the power?
Affirm Yourself	What are your strengths? Limitations? Vulnerabilities?
Acknowledge Your Power	At the personal level: What can you do for yourself? At the interpersonal level: Who are your advocates? How can they be supportive to you? At the social level: What larger realities are in your favor: groups, laws, other support?
Identify Areas of Powerlessness	At the personal, interpersonal, social levels: Are you lacking permission, enablement, information? On which level(s)? You may need to stop here in order to increase your power in one of these areas.
Analyze Your Possibilities	What would best fit? What is your fantasy of the perfect situation? What do you want? What is preventing the best fit (at each level of power)? What have you tried? What worked? What didn't? Why? Why not? What have you thought of & not tried? Why not? What are your instincts/intuitions? What feels right?
Weigh the Risks	What are the possible consequences of trusting and following your intuition? What are the possible consequences of other courses of action? What are the possible consequences of "staying put" or not acting to change?
Make a Choice	Empowerment lies in making a clear choice (staying put, leaving, changing). Once you have chosen, know that you have made the best possible choice for you at that time. Know also that you have the right to change your mind. Empowerment is a process. What fits now may not fit in the future. Guilt-tripping never fits!

CHAPTER

19 Couples and Family Counseling In Multiple Contexts

Roberta L. Nutt

Abstract

Working with couples and families fits the historic emphasis in counseling psychology of considering the individual in context. As many trains of feminist thought also emphasize the importance of relationships, a chapter tying together feminist couples and family counseling within counseling psychology is an important area of integration. This chapter provides an overview of the feminist critique of traditional couples and family counseling, followed by a description of couples and family counseling from a feminist perspective that is informed by multicultural contexts. Feminist couples and family counseling is more a philosophical and political viewpoint than a specific set of techniques, so a variety of strategies may be employed. Descriptions of intervention possibilities are grouped by their intent, including to demystify the therapy process and empower, aid communication, build empathy and connection through mutual understanding of gender roles in cultural context, analyze and negotiate power issues, and negotiate the redistribution of work within the family. Applications to diverse families and research findings are also discussed.

Key Words: Feminist multicultural couples counseling, feminist multicultural family counseling, feminist couples therapy, feminist family therapy, gender issues in couples counseling/therapy, gender issues in family counseling/therapy

Introduction

Both counseling and family psychology share a common emphasis on the importance of context to understanding the life circumstances of clients (Gelso & Fretz, 2001; Nutt, 2007; Sexton, Alexander, & Mease, 2004), while feminist and cross-cultural or multicultural psychology emphasize the role that political, social, cultural, and economic circumstances play in clients' lives, problems, and their solutions (Arredondo, 2002; Brown, 2006; Sue & Sue, 2003; Worell & Remer, 2003). A long history of cultural and gender bias in psychology and therapy has been covered in earlier chapters in this handbook and will also be summarized in this chapter. Efforts to enhance practice based on the recognition of this history have resulted in a number of American Psychological Association publications and guidelines aimed to help trainers, researchers, and practitioners avoid future bias (APA, 2003, 2004, 2007, 2012a,b).

It is important to include a chapter devoted to feminist couples and family counseling in this *Handbook of Feminist Multicultural Counseling Psychology* because of the many similarities between counseling and couples/family psychology. Both emphasize normal growth and development and consider the person in context. They also have increasingly considered the importance and impact of issues of diversity, including ethnicity, socioeconomic status, gender, sexual orientation, religion, immigration status, and other factors. They recognize the importance of individual and system strengths and work with them in treatment, and both integrate science and practice (Nutt, 2007). In fact, a series of articles in 1980 in *The Counseling Psychologist* predicted a growing emphasis on systems thinking and working with families. The systemic perspective that has grown from the family orientation also fits well with multicultural studies that emphasize community and collectivism (Nutt, 2007). As feminism has also suggested, through the products of Stone Center scholars (Jordan, 2003; Jordan, Kaplan, Miller, Stiver, & Surrey, 1991) and other writers, the most adaptive and healthy development occurs in relationship to others and not through the rugged individualism so prevalent in U.S. culture and psychology.

The Feminist Critique of Couples and Family Counseling

Theory as well as the practice of couples and family counseling have suffered from gender bias in the same way as other aspects of psychology and mental health professions. The feminist critique of couples and family counseling was a major emphasis in the 1980s and examined both the structure of theory and practice and a number of specific, damaging concepts. In general, feminist critics suggested that many approaches were based upon patriarchal models that disadvantaged women, with particularly strong criticism leveled at strategic approaches such as those of Jackson and Bateson, the problem-solving approach of Haley and the Milan approach, the structural model of Minuchin, and the multigenerational approaches such as the psychodynamic view of Paul and Framo and the Bowen model (Ault-Riche, 1986; MacKinnon & Miller, 1987; Walsh & Scheinkman, 1989).

Interventions in some approaches, particularly systemic ones that emphasize structure and hierarchy, blatantly put husbands/fathers in charge of the relationship/family (an executive function), fostering traditional roles and thereby reinforcing the devaluation and oppression of women (Goodrich, Rampage, Ellman, & Halstead, 1988; Hare-Mustin, 1978; Pittman, 1985). They did not honor the importance of women's roles in family life, nor did they leave much room for alternative styles of decision-making based upon consensual agreement and collective participation, such as those often used by women (Gilligan, 1982; Miller, 1986).

In work with families, mothers were often blamed for family pathology because they were seen as overinvolved or enmeshed with their children due to theorists' failure to recognize the importance of connectedness and relatedness in women's lives (Gilligan, 1982; Hare-Mustin, 1978; Miller, 1986; Silverstein, 2003; Walters, Carter, Papp, & Silverstein, 1988), or mothers were viewed as responsible for family problems since it was seen as their job to maintain family relationships and emotional well-being (Haddock & Lyness, 2002). Given the matriarchal stereotype given to African American women at the time, they were blamed even more heavily for family problems, including the absence of men from families because they were too "overbearing" (Pinderhughes, 1986). Similarly, lesbian couples have often been criticized as being too bonded, fused, or merged, when in reality, their closeness can sometimes represent a deep level of empathic understanding and connection, as well as boundary flexibility (Morton, 1998). Interventions of the time were aimed at unbalancing the family by moving the mother away from the role of disciplinarian and getting the disengaged father more involved with his children. The mother was blamed for being unwilling to allow the father to be involved with the family, thereby devaluing the mother as inadequate and idealizing the father as he was brought into the picture to save the family from its problems (Minuchin & Fishman, 1981; Silverstein, 2003). Overemphasis on the maintenance of strict boundaries often damaged or violated connectedness as well as disempowering the woman in the only arena in the family in which she had strength (Walsh & Scheinkman, 1989). Many practitioners of the time also failed to see how the picture of the enmeshed mother and the peripheral father, or the mother who was overfunctioning at home and the father who was overfunctioning at work, were actually the products of gender role socialization created by the larger culture for women and men, merely acted out within the family system (Silverstein, 2003).

Also during this time, feminists strongly objected to the concept of counselor neutrality as not only impossible but actually dangerous in that it could overlook some outcomes of power differentials, such as family or couple violence (Avis, 1985; Carmen, Russo, & Miller, 1981; Dankoski & Deacon, 2000; Enns, 1988; Hare-Mustin, 1987). Ignoring the differences in gender role socialization and the resulting power differential in many heterosexual relationships reinforces the status quo and therefore the oppression and even victimization of women (Hare-Mustin, 1987; Philpot & Brooks, 1995).

Also specifically targeted by critics were constructs that mistakenly assumed the presence of gender equity, such as circularity, complementarity, and reciprocity. Circularity assumes that people are involved in recursive behavior patterns that are mutually reinforcing, which results in viewing both partners in a couple or all members of a family as equally responsible for events that happen, with no one accountable for anything. Circularity only works as theorized when all players are equal in power. However, if a wife does not have equal power in a marital relationship because she makes less money or perhaps is not even employed, she should not be held equally responsible as her husband for the outcome of all their interactions. Circularity can also be misused to blame the victims—in this case, wives, girlfriends, children, and so on—for their own abuse. Similarly, the complementarity principle posits that the behavior of one person induces behavior in the other and suggests that they complement each other. Again, it assumes that, at a deep level, the partners are equal and denies the real-life oppression and power differential that makes domination a reality in many relationships. Reciprocity suggests that persons in a relationship reinforce each other, and it has also been misused to blame victims for their abuse. It assumes that the persons in the interaction have equal roles and therefore equal power in influencing the outcome of their interaction. All three of these concepts ignore the realities of power differentials in couple and family interactions/relationships (Goldner, 1985; Goodrich et al., 1988; MacKinnon & Miller, 1987; Walters et al., 1988).

What Is Feminist Couples and Family Counseling?

Feminist couples and family counseling is more a philosophical and political viewpoint than a specific set of techniques (Goodrich et al., 1988; Nutt, 2005). It may draw from a variety of couples and family strategies that are informed by feminist principles. Like all feminist therapy/counseling, it first requires that the therapist/counselor become aware of his or her own values regarding gender (Brosi & Rolling, 2007) and examine the extent to which she or he has been influenced by sexist stereotypes. Similarly, McGeorge and Carlson (2011) have suggested a three-step process for a therapist's self-examination of heterosexism that could be expanded to fit other types of self-examination. The steps include examining heteronormative assumptions, such as heterosexuality being healthy and normative, heterosexual privilege and its benefits, and heterosexual identity development. To be able to assist clients in understanding their gender role socialization, the therapist/counselor must have traveled her or his own gender role journey (O'Neil & Egan, 1992), both to understand one's personal process of gender socialization and to examine personal biases. There is a long history of evidence of therapist gender bias in individual, couples, and family counseling and therapy (Fischer, 1989; Harris, Moret, Gale, & Kampmeyer, 2001; Stabb, Cox, & Harber, 1997). After personal understanding, the therapist/counselor must then be able to analyze and critique theoretical orientations and strategies for sexist bias before choosing useful and appropriate interventions (Worell & Remer, 2003). This principle is equally true for examining one's own cultural history and biases, as cultural competence also requires a personal journey of self-examination of life experiences, cultural values, and personal identity (APA, 2003; Sue & Sue, 2003).

Worell and Remer (2003) have designed a system for assessing how well a theory meets feminist principles. Their assessment model contains eight steps of analysis. The first is to analyze the history of the theory to ascertain how the data to support the theory were gathered. The second is to list the key constructs or concepts of the theory. The third and fourth are to consider how the theory conceptualizes normal personality development and psychopathology or maladjustment. The fifth is to examine the role of assessment and diagnosis in the theory, while the sixth is to examine the role of the therapist and the client. The seventh step is to list the major techniques for the theoretical orientation, and the last step describes the theory's fit with the counselor's own personal views. After these eight steps are completed, each is evaluated for androcentrism (i.e., the use of male-oriented constructs); whether it is intrapsychic or interactionist; whether it is deterministic or life span oriented; and whether it is ethnocentric or flexible (i.e., does not assume that all cultures are similar, particularly that all are like Anglo-European populations). The goal is to assess whether theories are or can be adapted to be gender-free, flexible, interactionist, and life span developmental and also compatible with feminist principles such as valuing women's perspectives and egalitarian relationships.

Using Worell and Remer's system, one can see how its analysis would concur with other feminists' (Ault-Riche, 1986; Luepnitz, 1988) critique of Minuchin and other structural family therapists whose approach included encouraging fathers to take on stereotyped executive roles in the family while wives were to be expressive caregivers. That stance and the assumptions behind it would certainly be considered sexist and androcentric. On the other hand, the approaches of Satir and other experiential family therapists that emphasize growth, dealing with feelings, living in the present, and active engagement of the therapist in the therapy process (Gladding, 2011) fit well with the model for assessing feminist principles.

Whipple (1996, 2000) conducted a qualitative study of what it meant to be a feminist family therapist. To obtain her data, she interviewed self-identified feminist family therapists to find out how they had integrated feminist theory into family therapy theory. Many participants described struggles with sexism in their family therapy training and their awareness of sexism in the profession. Some had encountered chauvinistic bosses and colleagues. Each had a personal journey of integrating her personal and professional identity as a feminist family therapist. Whipple concluded from interviewing her participants that the main characteristics of feminist family therapy included encouraging a non-hierarchical therapeutic relationship, including gender as a therapy topic, valuing and encouraging egalitarian relationships, affirming women and their experiences, supporting empowerment and social change in general and for clients (including making non-traditional choices), and conveying a belief that feminism includes concern for stereotypes about men as well as women. Her study provided assurance that men need not be excluded from feminism and feminist family therapy work.

Core Tenets of Feminist Couples and Family Counseling

While, as stated earlier, feminist couples and family counseling is primarily a philosophical and political viewpoint rather than a specific set of techniques, there are a variety of strategies and principles that are often used by feminist counselors and feminist multicultural counselors. A sample of these interventions will be described and illustrated in this section.

Demystify and Empower

Feminist couples and family counseling, like all feminist counseling, aims to demystify counseling and to empower the couple or the family members so that their sense of options and reciprocity increases. In particular, feminist family counselors validate the experiences, strengths, and skills of clients and develop collaborative, egalitarian relationships with them to work toward clients' goals (Bryan, 2001). In this egalitarian relationship, the counselor does not pretend to be neutral but shares her or his biases and recognizes how they may influence the therapeutic process while remaining respectful of the clients' values, beliefs, and expertise about self. The counselor also recognizes that many traditional therapeutic approaches maintain and legitimize the societal oppression of women (Simola, 1992). One typical technique is the use of gender role analysis to aid in understanding roles and impasses in relationships. In some early examples, Goodrich et al. (1988) described the family-oriented approach by stating that "feminist family therapy examines how gender roles and stereotyping affect (1) each individual in the family, (2) relationships between individuals in the family, (3) relationships between the family and society, and (4) relationships between the family and the therapist" (p. 12). Pittman (1985) coined the term "gender broker" (p. 29) to describe the counselor who helps individuals and families identify traditional gender roles and values that they have adopted and decide which ones they wish to retain or discard. He wrote that it is the counselor's job "to help people of both sexes see that they have each been misinformed about the meaning, the responsibilities, and the limitations of their gender" (p. 30).

One particular intervention that has grown out of family systems theory and practice has been the genogram (McGoldrick, Gerson, & Petry, 2008), which was originally used to illustrate and understand family history and relationships, but has now been used for broadened applications. The standard genogram records information about family members for three generations in graphic form, with specific symbols representing individual family members and their relationships. Family structures and patterns become evident as the genogram is drawn. Used with couples, it can help partners understand the family history/baggage that they bring into their relationship and about which they may not be aware, including gender role messages and expectations. Because the genogram structure is graphic and factual, there is no inherent gender or cultural bias, so it fits well into a feminist and multicultural framework. The genogram has also been used specifically to deepen the understanding of cultural and other social forces on individuals and families (Hardy & Laszloffy, 1995; Hodge, 2005; Kosutic et al., 2009; Limb & Hodge, 2011; Marchetti-Mercer & Cleaver, 2000; Sanchez & Davis, 2010).

Communication

Another important aspect of feminist couples and family counseling is the examination of family communication patterns and how these may be following gender patterns that are creating miscommunications and misunderstandings (Hare-Mustin, 1978; Philpot & Brooks, 1995; Tannen, 1990). Learning to use language in a way that does not put down the other but creates feelings of equal partnership is critical to working together in the home (Haddock & Lyness, 2002).

A classic misunderstanding, for example, as described by Tannen (1990), occurs when a woman approaches her husband with a problem, just wanting him to listen, and he responds with a solution. The wife feels frustrated because she just wanted to be heard and understood. The husband feels frustrated because he feels that his well-meaning solution was rejected. With the assistance of a counselor, if both can understand that the issue involves two different styles of communicating and can learn to validate each other's style, then hurt feelings can be avoided in the future and intimacy and closeness can be increased.

Another example might be a lesbian couple in which the partners are from different cultures. If both partners hold minority group status, they share the experience of oppression as women of color and as lesbians, whereas if one is a member of the dominant culture, she will not share the same level of oppression (Long, 2003). In either case, however, the couples will likely suffer prejudice from coworkers, friends, family, and society. Their ability to explain their feelings about this prejudice to each other and to understand each other's point of view may not come easily because of their differences.

It is important for the counselor to be aware of the cultural differences in communication styles that may be also be present and how these may interact with gender patterns. These differences may be in actual word usage, style of communicating, or choice of persons with whom one shares information.

Building Empathy and Connection Through the Mutual Understanding of Gender Roles

In feminist couples counseling, in particular, it is assumed that a significant part of a couple's problems, especially for heterosexual couples, arises from differences in and misunderstandings about gender-role socialization and expectations (Goldenberg & Goldenberg, 2004; Nutt, 2005; Philpot, Brooks, Lusterman, & Nutt, 1997). Both partners carry with them nearly archetypal expectations of relationships, different styles of problem solving, and different beliefs about how families should function that are often not in their awareness, so these expectations are not shared and often create conflicts. Assuming that the goal is to create a closer connection between the couple by means of empathic understanding (Bergman & Surrey, 1999; Johnson, 2004; Laennec & Syrotinski, 2003; Lyness & Lyness, 2007; Vatcher & Bogo, 2001), then one important role for the couples counselor is to bring these expectations into awareness and to help the couple understand each other's gender worldview, socialization process and expectations, and language usage. Therefore, it is essential for the counselor to be well-trained in understanding the gender role development of both genders (Gilbert & Scher, 1999; Nutt, 2005) and to have worked through his or her own gender role journey (O'Neil & Egan, 1992), that is, his or her own attitudes toward gender and power and their influence on the counselor's own life and outlook toward others, also termed "gender discourse" (Keeling, Butler, Green, Kraus, & Palit, 2010).

The first step may be to help the couple understand that both have been negatively affected by gender role socialization; hence, neither is the enemy. Both partners need to learn to be empathic toward the socialization process of the other. Both must appreciate "affiliation and autonomy, cooperation and competition, control and nurturance, and reason and emotion" (Philpot et al., 1997, p. 166), the traditional attributes of both genders. The goal is empathic knowing, which will lead to trust and growing commitment in the relationship. Understanding the struggles of each other allows for greater acceptance. The counseling relationship must create an environment of safety so that the couple can discard their feelings of defensiveness and entitlement and can truly develop empathy for each other. To feel safe, each partner must feel heard, understood, and valued.

One method for reaching this understanding is the use of gender inquiry (Philpot et al., 1997). Gender inquiry uses questions to identify gender messages that clients have received from their families, peers, teachers, and other sources to help them identify the gender identities that they have developed. For example, the counselor might ask a client the following: What were the things you were expected to do or forbidden to do because you were a boy (or a girl) by your parents? Father? Mother? In school, did teachers encourage you in science, art, sports, academics, appearance, social activities, competitiveness, mathematics, business? What career choices were you encouraged to pursue by your family, teachers, peers, others? Whom did you consider to be your mentors/role models? How are you like and not like your mother? Father? There are no correct or incorrect answers, and all answers lead to useful information. In working with couples, it can be particularly helpful to their communication to teach them to use gender inquiry to interview each other as a way to deepen their understanding of each other. They are encouraged to listen carefully to each other, and are often asked first to paraphrase each other's statements to test their understanding and to be sure they get both the content and affect of the message. Eye contact is also emphasized. This process gives them a tool to take away with them from counseling.

Keeling et al. (2010) have developed a Gender Discourse in Therapy Questionnaire to aid trainees in examining their attention to gender and power issues with clients during counseling sessions. It has been used to help the counselors observe their own therapy process and notice gender discourse opportunities that they may have overlooked. It has the potential to aid counselors to increase their gender analysis skills in assisting couples and families to build gender equity during the counseling process.

Another strategy based upon the assumption that gender is a primary construct affecting clients' identities, relationships, and families is the Power Equity Guide (Haddock & Zimmerman, 2001; Haddock, Zimmerman, & MacPhee, 2000). The Guide is a series of Likert items focusing on the relationship and the gender role of the individuals in the relationship to help them evaluate the extent to which gender messages are influencing their relationship. The Power Equity Guide can be used to analyze societal messages about gender and to make new decisions about gender messages, thus developing a more equitable relationship. The authors consider it useful for both heterosexual and homosexual couples. They have suggested several uses for the Guide, including introducing a discussion of gender and power, discussing the benefits of egalitarian relationships, assessing the strengths and growth needs of the couple, setting therapeutic goals, and tracking therapeutic progress. As it is helpful for therapists to normalize the need for couples to work continuously to maintain relationship equality, a recommendation for them to review the Guide periodically, such as every month, six months, or yearly, can help cement therapeutic gains.

Power Issues

Related to the analysis of gender roles is the issue of distribution of power between the couple or within the family, leading Parker (2009) to conclude that power disparities are the main issue underlying most of the problems that couples bring to counseling. One of the earlier criticisms of some family therapy approaches was the assumption that fathers should be the executives of the family, with mothers and children in subordinate positions. Women were to reign in home territories in which men had no interest, such as deciding which brands of detergent or cooking oil the family might use (Goodrich, 2003). However, many therapists and theorists have steered or strayed away from dealing directly with the issue that, in heterosexual marriage, power is generally distributed unevenly in the husband's favor, with problematic consequences (Rampage, 2002). In the United States, only since the second wave women's movement have women questioned taking their husband's names at marriage, although there are other cultures in which this is not the standard practice. Some families may be so gendered that mothers are subordinate not only to their husbands, but also to their sons (Goodrich, 2003). In feminist counseling it is critical to look at power as a shared phenomenon rather than a property that one person has and others do not (the "one puck" theory). When the couple, family, or group assumes that one person has all the power, then it becomes natural to fight for that power.

When there is an understanding that power can be shared, then negotiation is possible and fighting over power is avoided. Parker (2009) suggested asking questions that go beyond what is typical, for example, inquiring about financial decision making, how child care is negotiated, and how household labor is divided or negotiated, because the answers to these questions will reveal issues of power and privilege. One might ask a wife how the fact that her husband makes many times more money than she does affects their decision-making, or when a child is sick, who leaves work to provide child care. These types of questions communicate to the couple the idea that their domestic arrangements are related to the power structure in their relationship.

Other writers have suggested using narrative therapy to validate women, in particular, for their relational and caregiving skills and also to redirect them to better self-care. The wife in heterosexual relationships is empowered by the recognition of her worth as a nurturer. By encouraging narrative accounts of the woman's nurturance of self and others, the husband may feel empowered to try some new nurturing skills himself (Blanton & Vandergriff-Avery, 2001).

Parker (2009) also described multi-couple groups in which several couples work together on issues. These groups are preceded by six to eight weeks of same-gender consciousness-raising orientation groups. The model assumes that couple issues, particularly those of power and privilege, are best addressed in "community healing circles where witnesses are available to both support and hold partners accountable for change" (p. 252).

It is also important to consider how these power issues vary by one's cultural background, sexual orientation, religion, socioeconomic status, and other life experiences (Rabin, 1998). Some particular stressors may include immigration status among Latina/os and Asian refugees/immigrants (including both legal residents and those who are undocumented), the impact of racism and colonialism on Native Americans, and the history of slavery for Black Americans and its disruptive influence on the family (Sue & Sue, 2003). In terms of therapeutic strategies, Sue and Sue (2003) have pointed out that most traditional Western thinking, with its adherence to mastery and control, leads therapists to active problem-solving interventions with clients that stress controlling or changing the environment. In contrast, they describe Asian Americans, Native Americans, Black Americans, and Latino/a Americans as typically viewing people in harmony with nature, family, and environment, therefore valuing different strategies for solving problems. For example, Asians may often accommodate or use deflection. Also, definitions of the family may vary by culture and may include grandparents, aunts and uncles, even non-blood relatives. Gay/lesbian couples whose biological families have rejected them may have developed "families of choice," whose members play important roles in their lives. In addition, the negotiations around decision making within the couple or family can be altered over time as family members age, roles shift, finances change, and so on (Qualls, 1995).

The Cultural Context Model has been used in family counseling to develop critical consciousness, accountability, and empowerment (Hernandez, Almeida, & Dolan-Del Vecchio, 2005). This model assumes that family difficulties and their solutions are interconnected to their social identities of gender, race, class, and sexual orientation. Working with a family includes consideration of the family's intergenerational history of oppression and privilege and its place within the large societal community. For example, a counselor working with a Native American family regarding issues of domestic violence or substance abuse must acknowledge the intergenerational impact of Native American genocide, exile onto reservations, kidnapping of children into boarding schools, the stealing of native lands, and other abuses as a historical background and context to the individual family's struggles. Putting the family's issues in context provides understanding of problems resulting from "longstanding institutionalized terrorism suffered by a colonized people" (p. 106), rather than family or individual psychopathology.

In the Cultural Context Model, first a genogram of the family is drawn, then all family members join small, ongoing same-gender culture circles. Each family member also is assigned a same-gender mentor in the circle. In the circles, family members are assisted in developing critical consciousness of the ways in which gender, ethnicity, class, and sexual orientation have influenced their relationships via psycho-educational materials, paying particular attention to the intersections of power, privilege, and oppression. The point of the same-gender circles is to create a coalition of women to help women increase their power in their relationships and a coalition of men to challenge male privilege and to support male partners as they struggle with power redistribution in their families (Almeida, 2003). The goal is to help family members become better listeners; to question their own sexism, racism, classism, and homophobia; and to develop equity in their family relationships. The authors consider this an empowerment model, as family members are liberated from prior patterns of domination.

Redistribution of Work in the Family

Early in the feminist critique of family therapy and counseling, Avis (1986) and Goodrich et al. (1988) noted the power issues related to household tasks assigned to both parents and children. They suggested removing the gendered task assignment of household chores to children and challenged the traditional arrangement of housekeeping and child-rearing tasks present in most households of the time. Bordeau, Briggs, Staton, and Wasik (2008) suggested rotating chores in the household so that boys had equal responsibility for doing dishes and laundry and girls took out the garbage and washed vehicles. Reis (2001) later expanded this research by looking at the gender-typing of household chores for children, and also by exploring their involvement in family decision making, the toys they were given, and the activities in which they were encouraged to participate. Avis (1986) went on to define parenting and homemaking as important concerns for both men and women, therefore challenging the traditional arrangements of housekeeping and child-rearing tasks and suggesting a more balanced distribution.

In 1989, Hochschild coined the term "second shift" to describe the world of the typical working wife and mother whose household chores constituted her second work shift when she returned home from her paid employment. At that time, statistics showed few husbands engaging in household chores. In the following decades, these statistics have improved, with husbands taking on a greater proportion of these chores, but women continue to assume a disproportionate responsibility for household management, child care, and elder care (Kulik, 2002; Sanderson & Thompson, 2002; Sayer, Cohen, & Casper, 2004; Steil, 2001). In today's world, in intact families in which both parents are employed outside the home, it is important for both adults in the dual-earner couple to balance career and family and to enjoy the satisfactions of both (Haddock & Bowling, 2001; MacDermid, Leslie, & Bissonnette, 2001; Zimmerman, Haddock, Ziemba, & Rust, 2001). It is also important that girls and boys learn a wide range of skills in the home to equip them to live in the world. Girls need to learn to take out garbage, do yard work, fix lawn mowers, change oil in cars, and make sound financial investments; and boys need to learn to wash dishes, cook meals, do laundry, and care for children and others in need.

Applications to Diverse Couples/Families

In the APA Guidelines for the Psychological Practice With Girls and Women (2007), under Guideline 2, the Rationale states: "Because girls and women have multiple personal and social group memberships, they may simultaneously belong to both socially privileged and disempowered groups (e.g., White, heterosexual, lower SES, and female) or to multiple socially oppressed groups (African American, female, lesbian, disabled)" (p. 961). The same issues of multiple identities may be true for couples and families that come for counseling, requiring sensitivity and understanding on the part of the counselor.

Bryan (2001) cautioned that feminism and multiculturalism may at times be in conflict within a couple or family when gender versus ethnic issues vary in salience. The five ethical principles that guide the integration of feminist and multicultural family practice—autonomy, beneficence, justice, nonmaleficence, and fidelity—may come into conflict on certain issues. For example, supporting a wife's voice in a couple's argument may violate her role in marriage in a patriarchal culture. Sometimes feminist family counselors have attempted to address these conflicts by making clients aware of them and then letting clients decide on their course of action, but these decisions have sometimes left clients separated from their cultures in unfortunate and unforeseen ways.

Lesbian/Gay/Bisexual Couples/Families

Many authors have applied feminist therapy/counseling principles to working with lesbian/gay/bisexual couples and families, based on the knowledge that this is another group which has experienced historical and ongoing oppression, stigma, and even recent increases in violence (APA, 2000; Gordon & Meyer, 2008; Herek, 2009; National Coalition of Anti-violence Programs [NCAVP], 2008; Negy & McKinney, 2006). These negative experiences have been shown to impact the mental health of LGBT individuals, and that impact may vary according to interaction of LGBT status with other social identities (D'Augelli, Grossman, & Starks, 2006; Meyer, Dietrich, & Schwartz, 2008). For example, in the Meyer et al. study, Blacks in New York City were found to exhibit a lower rate of mental health concerns than Whites or Latina/os, and Latina/os had made more suicide attempts than Whites.

Therefore, similar perspectives of respecting the client's point of view, attending to the client's language, understanding the impact of the sociocultural variables causing distress in the couple or family, understanding what part of symptoms may be cultural and not internal to the client, and collaborating with the client(s) in setting the goals of therapy would apply. Particular sensitivity to family-of-origin issues and family expectations may be important, as families may have accepted clients and their partners, rejected them, or chosen many variations between these options (Connolly, 2006; Green, 2000; Green & Mitchell, 2002). Specific external issues that may affect the relationship and with which the counselor should be familiar include legal issues related to adoption, child custody, parental rights, domestic partnership rights, and so on, as these may impact counseling issues (Wilton, 2010). Issues that are culture-specific to other social identities also bear examination, such as issues related to biological family, extended family, or family of choice.

Counselors need to be mindful of particular economic stressors that may bear upon lesbian relationships given the likelihood that a dual-career lesbian couple may be earning less than either a comparable heterosexual couple or gay male couple (Carroll, 2010). Whitcomb, Wettersten, and Stolz (2006) have suggested a list of important career issues to consider when counseling same-sex couples, including discrepant incomes, varying degrees of outness between partners, possible job relocation of one partner, lack of role models, employee benefits, and level of acceptance at employee social functions. Some other recommendations to consider in working with lesbian/gay couples include validating their same-sex relationship, understanding the impact of their coming-out process on the larger network of their families of origin and friends, and helping them examine their own internalized homophobia (Halstead, 2003).

Lesbian relationships have often been shown to be characterized by emotional resilience built upon mutuality, interdependence, and flexibility of gender roles (Connolly, 2005; Harkless & Fowers, 2005). Lesbians generally enter relationships without roles clearly defined, which allows them to evolve over time to fit family and individual needs and circumstances (Tasker & Golombok, 1997). Their relationships can be strengthened through building their connections, examining power issues, and sharing power (Hernandez, Rickard, & Giambruno, 2008).

Families of Color

There are a number of paradoxes in families of color that are different from the historical context of White families. For example, in both Latino/a and African American families, it has historically been easier for women to obtain employment (Boyd-Franklin & Garcia-Preto, 1994). However, both cultures have still elevated the man to a superior role within the household, including the dictates of *machismo* that wives should submit to their husbands. Therefore, these women have gained power from their roles in the workforce but suffer conflicting messages from the culture about their home roles.

The declining marriage rate has had a negative impact on African American families, with more families being headed by single women (Pinderhughes, 2002). Some reasons suggested for this change have included the decline in blue-collar jobs for African American men, the unbalanced gender ratio, and the number of African American men in prison. There is also evidence that African American men are more likely to favor a traditional division of household labor. Power may become a particularly complex issue, as African American men are denied power in the larger culture and may therefore be especially sensitive about power issues in the home. In addition, counselors working with African American families need to be attuned to the importance of multigenerational family systems (Hines, Garcia-Preto, McGoldrick, Almeida, & Weltman, 1992), the importance of and respect due to elderly family members, and the need to involve possible other social institutions, such as churches (Gladding, 2011).

Comas-Diaz (2003) has suggested the use of genograms with Latina clients to address "multigenerational ethnic and gender dynamics" (p. 148). The genogram can address the structure of the family and also the importance of spiritual issues in family life and can aid the negotiation of power struggles within the family due to gender, race, and class.

Acculturation may be particularly important in working with Asian American families, and gender role issues may vary widely by level of acculturation. There may be acculturation gaps between generations, resulting in miscommunication and even conflict (Lee, Choe, Kim, & Ngo, 2000). Sensitivity to issues of living in a collectivistic-oriented culture is also important, as these values may outweigh or conflict with emerging issues related to the new culture and new gender and cultural identities.

There is considerable complexity in understanding the mental health needs and issues of Native Americans and Alaska natives given the number of tribal identities within each group and their histories of being underserved by the mental health community (Dixon & Portman, 2010; Dixon Rayle, Chee, & Sand, 2006). One commonly reported feeling is that of being culturally dislocated, such as not fitting into mainstream culture. Many Native American tribes were historically physically dislocated from their homelands. Multiple tribes were oppressed, and their cultures, identities, and traditions were disrespected. In many tribal cultures, family relationships are of particular importance, and elders are widely respected, so it may be especially important when working with such clients to assess the importance of their connections to their extended family (Dixon & Portman, 2010; Garrett & Pichette, 2000).

In working with Muslim couples or families, one must realize that while gender equity has been highly valued in Islam, its implementation and practice have varied widely within the culture of host countries (Ahluwalia & Zaman, 2010). Roles for women and men may be viewed as complementary rather than comparable, with both professional and family roles being highly valued for women (Ali, Mahmood, Moel, Hudson, & Leathers, 2008). Beitan and Allen (2005) have suggested that counselors help couples create new meaning in their identities and roles as both Arabs and Americans and find ways to support each other. Genograms that assess both the strength of each partner and the successes of their ancestors can be used to help them develop new coping skills as a couple. Communication about stress, particularly stress that may be created by relatively strict gender roles that might isolate the wife at home, away from social support systems, may be necessary. The authors, however, cautioned therapists to address power imbalances with cultural sensitivity. In addition, building ties to religious and social communities that support the couple was seen as helpful.

Issues of social class, classism, and possible poverty may add complexity to family issues in any category. Liu and Ali (2008) have suggested a framework of interview questions to aid clients in understanding the impact of classism on their lives, relationships, and worldview. Given the amount of stress that economic issues often cause in families and relationships, the benefits of this understanding can be widespread.

Immigration issues may be relevant for any cultural group that has entered this country from another. If the gender roles in the country of origin are more traditional than those in the United States, then a couple may feel challenged to change, which results in marital stress. Women may wish to enter the workforce or challenge their husbands' patriarchal authority or request more help at home, thereby creating a power struggle in the marriage (Maciel, Van Putten, & Knudson-Martin, 2009). Within a family context, parents may struggle with a teenager who wants to engage in behaviors that may violate cultural norms in their culture of origin, such as wearing makeup or dating, but represent mainstream behavior in the adopted country (Inman & Tummala-Narra, 2010).

Of course, Gushue, Sciarra, and Mejia (2010), among many others, have cautioned that one must never assume that all couples or families from a particular culture are alike, or we risk further stereotyping our clients. Understanding their cultural background is foundational to gaining additional knowledge of what makes them and their issues unique.

Partners from Different Backgrounds

Daneshpour (2003) reported typical strengths and struggles for couples in which the husband was Muslim and of Middle Eastern descent and the wife was either European American or Asian American. In general, the relationships were strong and flourishing, but many had struggled with understanding from their families of origin and misunderstandings about religious practices and customs. Some of the wives had converted to Islam and some had not. The biggest stressors were around issues of parenting and child rearing and deciphering which practices were truly Islamic and which were cultural or familial. The author emphasized the importance of multicultural training for counselors of such couples, particularly concerning interracial/interfaith relationships, and also cautioned counselors not to assume an understanding of a member of the couple with whom counselors may share a similar background.

Hill and Thomas (2002) described Black-White interracial heterosexual couples as those who often face the most hostility of all mixed couples. One result of this partnering is that the White partner loses part of her or his White status. Black women who marry White men are often considered sellouts or traitors. White women who marry Black men are often described are rule-breakers and suffer rejection. Killian (2001) described a number of Black-White interracial couples who faced a variety of problems, including criticism from family and friends, loss of family ties, imbalances of power in the relationship, concerns about their children, and difficulty in talking about the issues. Working with such couples or families requires sensitivity to a complexity of gender and ethnic issues.

Families with Issues of Disabilities

Awareness of the special problems of families in which disabilities are present is critical. The person with the disability will face discrimination in the world outside the family and may bring those issues and feelings into the couple/family relationship. There may also be employment problems that will add stress to the system. Depending upon the type of disability, there may be medical issues, access to care problems, or chronic pain issues that complicate relationships. There are types of disabilities that alter a person's gender identity and may lead her or him to question whether she is an attractive woman or whether he really is a man (Marini, 2005; Olkin, 1999).

Artman and Daniels (2010) have detailed a number of practical competencies for practitioners working with clients and families with disability issues including ensuring building accessibility, making recruitment materials accessible, scheduling appointments to fit transportation needs, and implementing possible testing accommodations. As persons with disabilities are the largest minority group in the United States, the authors have heavily stressed the need for counselor sensitivity and competency in dealing with disability issues, as the likelihood of seeing such persons in practice is great. Palombi (2010) has stressed the need for counselors to be well-versed in both the intersecting identities of persons with disabilities and the external forces that affect their lives and mental health.

Research

Unfortunately, research on feminist couples and family counseling is in its infancy. In 2006, Murray reported a 20-year review of the feminist family and couples counseling literature and found no research that explored the client's experience of feminist-informed couples and family counseling, for one example. Others issues have been addressed to some extent. There have been studies that addressed the gender awareness of the counselor and how that may impact the outcome of therapy (Ivey & Conoley, 1994; Newberry, Alexander, & Turner, 1991; Werner-Wilson, Price, Zimmerman, & Murphy, 1997). Of these, two studies were done with counselors-in-training and one with practicing counselors.

There is a clear literature showing that marital satisfaction increases when relationship equality increases with regard to issues as decision-making, sharing of household tasks and child rearing, and shared power in general (DeMaris, 2007; Glass & Fujimoto, 1994; Gottman, 1999; Gottman & Notarius, 2002; Gray-Little & Burks, 1983; Moller, Hwang, & Wickberg, 2008; Steil, 1997; Whisman & Jacobson, 1989). These studies did not focus on feminist counseling/therapy, but they did assess outcomes relevant to counseling. One study, in particular, found that an inequitable division of labor in the household led to lower marital satisfaction for both partners (Klumb, Hoppmann, & Staats, 2006). Whisman and Jacobson (1989) found increased levels of depression in women who reported inequality in their marital relationships; and perceptions of unequal decision making have been linked to relationship stress and dissatisfaction (Zak, Collins, Harper, & Masher, 1998). In addition, women were found to be more likely to seek divorce when they bore the greater proportion of household tasks (Frisco & Williams, 2003).

Therefore, while these studies did not research feminist couples or family counseling directly, they did study an important outcome of such feminist work. These results can be considered to offer some support for the utility of feminist couples and family counseling while more specific research is conducted.

Conclusions

In conclusion, feminist couples and family counseling is a philosophical and political approach to counseling that may borrow its actual techniques from a variety of compatible sources. It is an integration of feminist principles with the systems perspective of family therapy. Because it is open to the understanding that individuals and groups have multiple identities of varying salience, its application is flexible and broadly appropriate to many populations. Feminist couples and family counseling may be characterized by a number of basic tenets:

The counseling relationship is as egalitarian as possible for all family members in terms of setting counseling goals, outcomes, and procedures.

The counselor aims to demystify the counseling process, asks all family members about their expectations of counseling, and explains the counseling process as fully as possible.

The counselor respects the voices of all clients and aims to empower all members of the couple or family.

Couple or family communication patterns are analyzed for miscommunications and misunderstandings, and new ways of communicating more directly/effectively may be taught.

Gender role socialization of members of the couple/family may be analyzed in order to see ways in which old patterns may be creating problems to establish the goal of creating mutual empathic understanding.

Power issues in the couple/family are analyzed and power redistribution may be negotiated.

Household chores may be analyzed for gender stereotyping, and assignments among family members may be renegotiated.The counselor may use couples/family counseling–specific interventions, such as genograms with gender and cultural emphases or the Power Equity Guide, and may teach gender inquiry strategies to a couple to further gender and power equity goals within the couple/family.

As stated earlier, while there are some encouraging study results, there is not enough definitive research. There is a significant body of research on some of the desired similar outcomes from other research that are promising, but that research is not directly on topic.

Future Directions

As noted earlier, research on feminist couples and family counseling is still in its infancy, and much more research is needed on feminist multicultural couples and family counseling. Some particular questions to be answered include:

Which theories of couples and family interventions best fit a feminist and multicultural framework?

Which research methodologies best answer feminist and multicultural research questions for systemic frameworks?

How do researchers deal with the intersection issues of multiple social identities of clients within the complexity of family relationships?What approaches to couples and family counseling work best with particular ethnic groups and under what circumstances? What approaches are most effective for working with couples/families in which there are multiple social identity issues?

References

Ahluwalia, M. K., & Zaman, N. K. (2010). Counseling Muslims and Sikhs in a post–9/11 world. In J. G. Ponterotto, J. M. Casas, L. A. Suzuki, & C. M. Alexander (Eds.), *Handbook of multicultural counseling* (3rd ed., pp. 467–478). Los Angeles: Sage.

Ali, S. R., Mahmood, A., Moel, J., Hudson, C., & Leathers, L. (2008). A qualitative investigation of Muslim and Christian women's views of religion and feminism in their lives. *Cultural Diversity and Ethnic Minority Psychology, 14,* 38–46.

Almeida, R. V. (2003). Creating collectives of liberation. In L. B. Silverstein & T. J. Goodrich (Eds.), *Feminist family therapy: Empowerment in social context* (pp. 293–305). Washington, DC: American Psychological Association.

American Psychological Association (2003). Guidelines on multicultural education, training, research, practice, and organizational change for psychologists. *American Psychologist, 58,* 377–402.

American Psychological Association (2004). Guidelines for psychological practice with older adults. *American Psychologist, 59,* 236–260.

American Psychological Association (2007). Guidelines for psychological practice with girls and women. *American Psychologist, 62,* 949–979.

American Psychological Association. (2012a). Guidelines for psychological practice with lesbian, gay, and bisexual clients. *American Psychologist, 67,* 10–42.

American Psychological Association. (2012b). Guidelines for assessment of and intervention with persons with disabilities. *American Psychologist, 67,* 43–62.

Arredondo, P. (2002). Counseling individuals from specialized, marginalized and underserved groups. In P. Pederson, J. G. Draguns, W. J. Louver, & J. E. Trimble (Eds.), *Counseling across cultures* (5th ed.,pp. 241–250). Thousand Oaks, CA: Sage.

Artman, L. K., & Daniels, J. A. (2010). Disability and psychotherapy practice: Cultural competence and practical tips. *Professional Psychology: Research and Practice, 41,* 442–448.

Ault-Riche, M. (Ed.). (1986). *Women and family therapy.* Gaithersburg, MD: Aspen.

Avis, J. (1985). The politics of functional family therapy: A feminist critique. *Journal of Marital and Family Therapy, 11,* 145–148.

Avis, J. M. (1986). Feminist issues in family therapy. In F. Piercy & D. Sprenkle (Eds.), *Family therapy sourcebook* (pp. 214–232). New York: Guilford.

Beitan, B. K., & Allen, K. R. (2005). Resilience in Arab American couples after September 11, 2001: A systems perspective. *Journal of Marital and Family Therapy, 31,* 251–267.

Bergman, S. J., & Surrey, J. L. (1999). Couple therapy: A relational approach. *Journal of Feminist Family Therapy, 11,* 21–48.

Blanton, P. W., & Vandergriff-Avery, M. (2001). Marital therapy and marital power: Constructing narratives of sharing relational and positional power. *Contemporary Family Therapy, 23,* 295–308.

Bordeau, W. C., Briggs, M. K., Staton, A. R., & Wasik, S. Z. (2008). Feminism lives on: Incorporating feminism into counseling practice with families and youth. *Journal of Humanistic Counseling, Education and Development, 47,* 42–55.

Boyd-Franklin, N., & Garcia-Preto, N. (1994). Family therapy: A closer look at African American and Hispanic women. In B. Greene and L. Comas Diaz (Eds.), *Women of color: Integrating ethnic and gender identities in psychotherapy* (pp. 239–264). New York: Guilford Press.

Brosi, M. W., & Rolling, E. S. (2007). The effect of value conflicts on therapists' work with abusive clients: Implications for the integration of feminist tenets. *Journal of Feminist Family Therapy, 19,* 63–89.

Brown, L. S. (2006). Still subversive after all these years: The relevance of feminist therapy in the age of evidence-based practice. *Psychology of Women Quarterly, 30,* 15–24.

Bryan, L. A. (2001). Neither mask nor mirror: One therapist's journey to ethically integrate feminist family therapy and multiculturalism. *Journal of Feminist Family Therapy, 12,* 105–121.

Carmen, E. H., Russo, N. F., & Miller, J. B. (1981). Inequality and women's mental health: An overview. *American Journal of Psychiatry, 138,* 1319–1330.

Carroll, L. (2010). *Counseling sexual and gender minorities.* Upper Saddle River, NJ: Merrill.

Comas-Diaz, L. (2003). The Black Madonna: The psychospiritual feminism of Guadalupe, Kali, and Monserrat. In L. B. Silverstein & T. J. Goodrich (Eds.), *Feminist family therapy: Empowerment in social context* (pp. 147–160). Washington, DC: American Psychological Association.

Connolly, C. M. (2005). A qualitative exploration of resilience in long-term lesbian couples. *Family Journal, 13,* 266–280.

Connolly, C. M. (2006). A feminist perspective of resilience in lesbian couples. *Journal of Feminist Family Therapy, 18,* 137–162.

Daneshpour, M. (2003). Lives together, worlds apart? The lives of multicultural Muslim couples. *Journal of Couple and Relationship Therapy, 2,* 57–71.

Dankoski, M. E., & Deacon, S. A. (2000). Using a feminist lens in contextual therapy. *Feminist Process, 39,* 51–67.

D'Augelli, A. R., Grossman, A. H., & Starks, M. T. (2006). Childhood gender a typicality, victimization, and PTSD among lesbian, gay, and bisexual youth. *Journal of Interpersonal Violence, 21,* 1462–1482.

DeMaris, A. (2007). The role of relationship inequality in marital disruption. *Journal of Social and Personal Relationships, 24,* 177–195.

Dixon, A. L., & Portman, T. A. A. (2010). The beauty of being native: The nature of Native American and Alaska native identity development. In J. G. Ponterotto, J. M. Casas, L. A. Suzuki, & C. M. Alexander (Eds.), *Handbook of multicultural counseling* (3rd ed., pp. 215–225.

Dixon Rayle, A. L., Chee, C., & Sand, J. K. (2006). Honoring their way: Counseling American Indian women. *Journal for Multicultural Counseling and Development, 34,* 66–79.

Enns, C. Z. (1988). Dilemmas of power and equality in marital and family counseling: Proposals for a feminist perspective. *Journal of Counseling and Development, 67,* 242–248.

Fischer, E. H. (1989). Gender bias in therapy? An analysis of patient and therapist causal explanations. *Psychotherapy, 26,* 389–401.

Frisco, M. L., & Williams, K. (2003). Perceived housework equity, marital happiness, and divorce in dual earner families. *Journal of Family Issues, 24,* 51–73.

Garrett, M. T., & Pichette, E. F. (2000). Red as an apple: Native American acculturation and counseling with or without reservation. *Journal of Counseling and Development, 78,* 3–13.

Gelso, C. J., & Fretz, B. R. (2001). *Counseling psychology* (2nd ed.). Orlando, FL: Holt, Rinehart and Winston.

Gladding, S. T. (2011). *Family therapy: History, theory, and practice* (5th ed.). Boston: Pearson.

Glass, J., & Fujimoto, T. (1994). Housework, paid work, and depression among husbands and wives. *Journal of Health and Social Behavior, 35,* 179–191.

Gilbert, L. A., & Scher, M. (1999). *Gender and sex in counseling and therapy.* Boston: Allyn and Bacon.

Gilligan, C. (1982). *In a different voice.* Cambridge, MA: Harvard University Press.

Goldenberg, I., & Goldenberg, H. (2004). *Family therapy: An overview* (6th ed.). Pacific Grove, CA: Brooks/Cole.

Goldner, V. (1985). Warning: Family therapy may be hazardous to your health. *Family Therapy Networker, 9,* 19–23.

Goodrich, T. J., Rampage, C., Ellman, B., & Halstead, K. (1988). *Feminist family therapy: A casebook.* New York: Norton.

Goodrich, T. J. (2003). A feminist family therapist's work is never done. In L. B. Silverstein & T. J. Goodrich (Eds.), *Feminist family therapy: Empowerment in social context* (pp. 3–15). Washington, DC: American Psychological Association.

Gordon, A. R., & Meyer, I. H. (2008). Gender nonconformity as a target of prejudice, discrimination, and violence against LGB individuals. *Journal of LGBT Research, 3,* 55–71.

Gottman, J. M. (1999). *The seven principles for making marriage work.* New York: Crown Publishers.

Gottman, J. M., & Notarius, C. I. (2002). Marital research in the 20th century and a research agenda for the 21st century. *Family Process, 41,* 159–197.

Gray-Little, B., & Burks, N. (1983). Power and satisfaction in marriage: A review and critique. *Psychological Bulletin, 93,* 513–538.

Green, R. J. (2000). "Lesbians, gay men, and their parents": A critique of LaSala and the prevailing clinical "wisdom." *Family Process, 39,* 257–266.

Green, R. J., & Mitchell, V. (2002). Gay and lesbian couple in therapy: Homophobia, relational ambiguity, and social support. In A. S. Gurman & N. S. Jacobson (Eds.), *Clinical handbook of couple therapy* (pp. 536–568). New York: Guilford Press.

Gushue, G. V., Sciarra, D. T., & Mejia, B. X. (2010). Family counseling: Systems, postmodern, and multicultural perspectives. In J. G. Ponterotto, J. M. Casas, L. A. Suzuki, & C. M. Alexander (Eds.), *Handbook of multicultural counseling* (3rd ed., pp. 677–688). Los Angeles: Sage.

Haddock, S., & Bowling, S. W. (2001). Therapists' approaches to the normative challenges of dual career couples: Negotiating outdated societal ideologies. *Journal of Feminist Family Therapy, 14,* 91–120.

Haddock, S., & Lyness, K. P. (2002). Three aspects of the therapeutic conversation in couples therapy: Does gender make a difference? *Journal of Couple and Relationship Therapy, 1,* 5–24.

Haddock, S. A., & Zimmerman, T. S. (2001). The Power Equity Guide: An activity to assist couples in negotiating a fair and equitable relationship. *Journal of Clinical Activities, Assignments and Handouts in Psychotherapy Practice, 1,* 1–15.

Haddock, S. A., Zimmerman, T. S., & MacPhee, D. (2000). The Power Equity Guide: Attending to gender in family therapy. *Journal of Marital and Family Therapy, 26,* 153–170.

Halstead, K. (2003). Over the rainbow: The lesbian family. In L. B. Silverstein & T. J. Goodrich (Eds.), *Feminist family therapy: Empowerment in social context* (pp. 39–50). Washington, DC: American Psychological Association.

Hardy, K. V., & Laszloffy, T. A. (1995). The cultural genogram: Key to training culturally competent family therapists. *Journal of Marital and Family Therapy, 21,* 227–237.

Hare-Mustin, R. T. (1978). A feminist approach to family therapy. *Family Process, 17,* 181–194.

Hare-Mustin, R. T. (1987). The problem of gender in family therapy theory. *Family Process, 26,* 15–27.

Harkless, L., & Fowers, B. (2005). Similarities and differences in relational boundaries among heterosexuals, gay men, and lesbians. *Psychology of Women Quarterly, 29,* 167–176.

Harris, T., Moret, L. B., Gale, J., & Kampmeyer, K. L. (2001). Therapists' gender assumptions and how these assumptions influence therapy. *Journal of Feminist Family Therapy, 12,* 33–59.

Herek, G. M. (2009). Hate crimes and stigma-related experiences among sexual minority adults in the United States: Prevalence estimates from a national probability sample. *Journal of Interpersonal Violence, 24,* 55–64.

Hernandez, P., Almeida, R., & Dolan-Del Vecchio, K. (2005). Critical consciousness, accountability, and empowerment: Key processes for helping families heal. *Family Process, 44,* 105–119.

Hernandez, P., Rickard, J., & Giambruno, P. (2008). Transformative family therapy with a lesbian couple: A case study. *Journal of Feminist Family Therapy, 20,* 281–298.

Hill, M. R., & Thomas, V. (2002). Racial and gender identity development for Black and White women in interracial partner relationships. *Journal of Couple and Relationship Therapy, 1,* 1–35.

Hines, P. M., Garcia-Preto, N., McGoldrick, M., Almeida, R., & Weltman, S. (1992). Intergenerational relationships across cultures. *Families in Society: The Journal of Contemporary Human Services, 73,* 323–338.

Hochschild, A. R. (1989). *The second shift: Working parents and the revolution at home.* New York: Viking Press.

Hodge, D. R. (2005). Spiritual ecograms: A new assessment instrument for identifying clients' strengths in space across time. *Families in Society: The Journal of Contemporary Social Services, 86,* 287–296.

Inman, A. G., & Tummala-Narra. P. (2010). Clinical competencies in working with immigrant communities. In J. A. E. Cornish, B. A. Schreier, L. I. Nadkarni, L. H. Metzger, & E. R. Rodolfa (Eds.), *Handbook of multicultural counseling competencies* (pp. 117–152). Hoboken, NJ: Wiley.

Ivey, D. C., & Conoley, C. W. (1994). Influence of gender in family evaluations: A comparison of trained and untrained observer perceptions of matriarchal and patriarchal family interviews. *Journal of Family Psychology, 8,* 336–346.

Johnson, S. M. (2004). *The practice of emotionally focused couple therapy: Creating connection* (2nd ed.). New York: Brunner-Routledge.

Jordan, J. V., Kaplan, A. G., Miller, J. B., Stiver, I. P., & Surrey, J. L. (1991). *Women's growth in connection.* New York: Guilford.

Jordan, J. V. (2003). Relational-cultural therapy. In M. Kopala & M. A. Keitel (Eds.), *Handbook of counseling women* (pp. 22–30). Thousand Oaks, CA: Sage.

Keeling, M. L., Butler, J., Green, N., Kraus, V., & Palit, M. (2010). The Gender Discourse in Therapy Questionnaire: A tool for training in feminist-informed therapy. *Journal of Feminist Family Therapy, 22,* 153–169.

Killian, K. D. (2001). Crossing borders: Race, gender, and their intersections in interracial couples. *Journal of Feminist Family Therapy, 13,* 1–31.

Klumb, P., Hoppmann, C., & Staats, M. (2006). Division of labor in German dual-earner families: Testing equity theoretical hypotheses. *Journal of Marriage and Family, 68,* 870–882.

Kosutic, I., Garcia, M., Graves, T., Barnett, F., Hall, J., Haley, E., Rock, J., Bathon, A., & Kaiser, B. (2009). The critical genogram: A tool for promoting critical consciousness. *Journal of Feminist Family Therapy, 21,* 151–176.

Kulik, L. (2002). The impact of social background on gender-role ideology. *Journal of Family Issues, 23,* 53–73.

Laennec, C., & Syrotinski, M. (2003). Insiders' perspectives on a feminist marriage. *Feminism and Psychology, 13,* 454–458.

Lee, R. M., Choe, J., Kim, G., & Ngo, V. (2000). Construction of the Asian American family conflicts scale. *Journal of Counseling Psychology, 47,* 211–222.

Limb, G. E., & Hodge, D. R. (2011). Utilizing spiritual ecograms with Native American families and children to promote cultural competence in family therapy. *Journal of Marital and Family Therapy, 37,* 81–94.

Liu, W. M., & Ali, S. R. (2008). Social class and classism: Understanding the psychological impact of poverty and inequality. In S. D. Brown & R. W. Lent (Eds.), *The handbook of counseling psychology* (4th ed., pp. 159–175). Hoboken, NJ: Wiley.

Long, J. (2003). Interracial and intercultural lesbian couples: The incredibly true adventures of two women in love. *Journal of Couple and Relationship Therapy, 2,* 85–101.

Luepnitz, D. A. (1988). *The family interpreted: Feminist theory in clinical practice.* New York: Basic Books.

Lyness, A. M. P., & Lyness, K. P. (2007). Feminist issues in couple therapy. *Journal of Couple and Relationship Therapy, 6,* 181–195.

MacDermid, S., Leslie, L. A., & Bissonnette, L. (2001). Walking the walk: Insights from research on helping clients navigate work and family. *Journal of Feminist Family Therapy, 14,* 21–40.

Maciel, J. A., Van Putten, Z., & Knudson-Martin, C. (2009). Gendered power in cultural contexts: Part I. Immigrant couples. *Family Process, 48,* 9–23.

MacKinnon, L. K., & Miller, D. (1987). The new epistemology and the Milan approach: Feminist and sociopolitical considerations. *Journal of Marital and Family Therapy, 13,* 139–155.

Marchetti-Mercer, M. C., & Cleaver, G. (2000). Genograms and family sculpting: An aid to cross-cultural understanding in the training of psychology students in South Africa. *The Counseling Psychologist, 28,* 61–80.

Marini, I. D. (2005). Issues of males with physical disabilities in rehabilitation settings. In G. R. Brooks & G. E. Good (Eds.), *The new handbook of counseling and psychotherapy with men* (pp. 88–103). San Francisco: Jossey Bass.

McGeorge, C., & Carlson, T. S. (2011). Deconstructing heterosexism: Becoming an LGB affirmative heterosexual couple and family therapist. *Journal of Marital and Family Therapy, 37,* 14–26.

McGoldrick, M., Gerson, R., & Petry, S. (2008). *Genograms: Assessment and intervention* (3rd ed.). New York: Norton.

Meyer, I. H., Dietrich, J., & Schwartz, S. (2008). Lifetime prevalence of mental disorders and suicide attempts in diverse lesbian, gay, and bisexual populations. *American Journal of Public Health, 98,* 1004–1006.

Miller, J. B. (1986). *Toward a new psychology of women* (2nd ed.). Boston: Beacon.

Minuchin, S., & Fishman, H. C. (1981). *Family therapy techniques.* Cambridge, MA: Harvard University Press.

Moller, K., Hwang, C., & Wickberg, B. (2008). Couple relationship and transition to parenthood: Does workload at home matter? *Journal of Reproductive and Infant Psychology, 26,* 57–68.

Morton, S. B. (1998). Lesbian divorce. *American Journal of Orthopsychiatry, 68,* 410–419.

Murray, K. (2006). A call for feminist research: A limited client perspective. *The Family Journal: Counseling and Therapy for Couples and Families, 14,* 169–173.

National Coalition of Anti-Violence Programs (2008). *Anti-lesbian, gay, bi-sexual, and transgender violence in 2007.* New York: Author.

Negy, C., & McKinney, C. (2006). Application of feminist therapy: Promoting resiliency among lesbian and gay families. *Journal of Feminist Family Therapy, 18,* 67–83.

Newberry, A. M., Alexander, J. F., & Turner, C. W. (1991). Gender as a process variable in family therapy. *Journal of Family Psychology, 5,* 158–175.

Nutt, R. L. (2005). Feminist and contextual work. In M. Harway (Ed.), *Handbook of couples therapy* (pp. 228–249). Hoboken, NJ: Wiley.

Nutt, R. L. (2007). Implications of globalization for training in counseling psychology: Presidential address. *The Counseling Psychologist, 35,* 157–171.

Olkin, R. (1999). *What psychotherapists should know about disability.* New York: Guilford.

O'Neil, J. M., & Egan, J. (1992). Men's and women's gender role journeys: A metaphor for healing, transition, and transformation. In B. R. Wainrib (Ed.), *Gender issues across the life cycle* (pp. 107–123). New York: Springer.

Palombi, B. J. (2010). Disability: Multiple and intersecting identities—Developing multicultural competencies. In J. A. E. Cornish, B. A. Schreier, L. I. Nadkarni, L. H. Metzger, & E. R. Rodolfa (Eds.), *Handbook of multicultural counseling competencies* (pp. 55–92). Hoboken, NJ: Wiley.

Parker, L. (2009). Disrupting power and privilege in couples therapy. *Clinical Social Work Journal, 37,* 248–255.

Philpot, C. L., & Brooks, G. R. (1995). Intergender communication and gender-sensitive family therapy. In R. H. Mikesell, D.-D. Lusterman, & S. H. McDaniel (Eds.), *Integrating family therapy: Handbook of family psychology and systems theory* (pp. 303–325). Washington, DC: American Psychological Association.

Philpot, C. L., Brooks, G. R., Lusterman, D.-D., & Nutt, R. L. (1997). *Bridging separate gender worlds: Why men and women clash and how therapists can bring them together.* Washington, DC: American Psychological Association.

Pinderhughes, E. (1986). Minority women: A nodal position in the functioning of the social system. In M. Ault-Riche (Ed.), *Women and family therapy* (pp. 51–63). Rockville, MD: Aspen Systems.

Pinderhughes, E. B. (2002). African American marriage in the 20th century. *Family Process, 41,* 269–282.

Pittman, F. (1985). Gender myths: When does gender become pathology? *Family Therapy Networker, 9,* 25–33.

Qualls, S. H. (1995). Marital therapy with later life couples. *Journal of Geriatric Psychiatry, 28,* 139–163.

Rabin, C. (1998). Gender and intimacy in the treatment of couples in the 1990s. *Sexual and Marital Therapy, 13,* 179–190.

Rampage, C. (2002). Marriage in the 20th century: A feminist perspective. *Family Process, 41,* 261–268.

Reis, S. M. (2001). External barriers experienced by gifted and talented girls and women. *Gifted Child Today, 24,* 26–35.

Sanchez, D., & Davis, C. (2010). Becoming a racially competent therapist. In J. A. E. Cornish, B. A. Schreier, L. I. Nadkarni, L. H. Metzger, & E. R. Rodolfa (Eds.), *Handbook of multicultural counseling competencies* (pp. 267–290). Hoboken, NJ: Wiley.

Sanderson, S., & Thompson, V. L. S. (2002). Factors associated with perceived paternal involvement in childrearing. *Sex Roles, 46,* 99–111.

Sayer, L. C., Cohen, P. N., & Casper, L. M. (2004). *Women, men, and work.* New York: Russell Sage Publications.

Sexton, T. L., Alexander, J. F., & Mease, A. L. (2004). Levels of evidence for the models of mechanisms of therapeutic change in family and couples therapy. In M. J. Lambert (Ed.), *Bergin and Garfield's handbook of psychotherapy and behavior change* (5th ed.) (pp. 590–646). Hoboken, NJ: Wiley.

Silverstein, L. B. (2003). Classic texts and early critiques. In L. B. Silverstein & T. J. Goodrich (Eds.), *Feminist family therapy: Empowerment in social context* (pp. 17–35). Washington, DC: American Psychological Association.

Simola, S. K. (1992). Differences among sexist, nonsexist, and feminist family therapies. *Professional Psychology: Research and Practice, 23,* 397–403.

Stabb, S. D., Cox, D. L., & Harber, J. L. (1997). Gender-related therapist attributions in couple's therapy: A preliminary multiple case study investigation. *Journal of Marital and Family Therapy, 23,* 335–346.

Steil, J. (2001). Marriage: Still "his" and "hers?" In J. Worell (Ed.), *Encyclopedia of women and gender* (pp. 677–686). San Diego: Academic Press.

Steil, J. M. (1997). *Marital equality: Its relationship to the well-being of husbands and wives.* Thousand Oaks, CA: Sage.

Sue, D. W., & Sue, D. W. (2003). *Counseling the culturally diverse: Theory and practice* (4th ed.). Hoboken, NJ: Wiley.

Tannen, D. (1990). *You just don't understand: Women and men in conversation.* New York: Ballantine.

Tasker, F. L., & Golombok, S. (1997). *Growing up in a lesbian family: Effects on child Development.* New York: Guilford.

Vatcher, C., & Bogo, M. (2001). The feminist/emotionally focused therapy practice model: An integrated approach for couple therapy. *Journal of Marital and Family Therapy, 27,* 69–83.

Walsh, F., & Scheinkman, M. (1989). (Fe)male: The hidden gender dimension in models of family therapy. In M. McGoldrick, C. M. Anderson, & F. Walsh (Eds.), *Women in families: A framework for family therapy* (pp. 16–41). New York: Norton.

Walters, M., Carter, B., Papp, P., & Silverstein, O. (1988). *The invisible web: Gender patterns in family relations.* New York: Guilford.

Werner-Wilson, R. J., Price, S. J., Zimmerman, T. S., & Murphy, M. J. (1997). Client gender as a process variable in marriage and family therapy: Are women clients interrupted more than men clients? *Journal of Family Psychology, 11,* 373–377.

Whipple, V. (1996). Developing and identity as a feminist family therapist: Implications for training. *Journal of Marital and Family Therapy, 22,* 381–396.

Whipple, V. (March, 2000). *What does it mean to be a feminist family therapist?* Poster presented at the annual conference of the American Counseling Association: Washington, DC.

Whisman, M. A., & Jacobson, N. S. (1989). Depression, marital satisfaction, and marital and personality measures of sex roles. *Journal of Marital and Family Therapy, 15,* 177–186.

Whitcomb, D. H., Wettersten, K. B., & Stolz, C. L. (2006). Career counseling with gay, lesbian, bisexual, and transgender clients. In D. Capuzzi & M. D. Stauffer (Eds.), *Career counseling: Foundations, perspectives, and applications* (pp. 386–411). Boston: Allyn & Bacon.

Wilton, L. (2010). Where do we go from here? Raising the bar of what constitutes multicultural competence in working with lesbian, gay, bisexual, and transgender communities. In J. G. Ponterotto, J. M. Casas, L. A. Suzuki, & C. M. Alexander (Eds.), *Handbook of multi- cultural counseling* (3rd ed., pp. 313–327). Los Angeles: Sage.

Worell, J., & Remer, P. (2003). *Feminist perspectives in therapy: Empowering diverse women* (2nd ed.). Hoboken, NJ: Wiley.

Zak, A., Collins, C., Harper, L., & Masher, M. (1998). Self-reported control over decision-making and its relationship to intimate relationships. *Psychological Reports, 82,* 560–562.

Zimmerman, T. S., Haddock, S. A., Ziemba, S., & Rust, A. (2001). Family organizational labor: Who's calling the plays? *Journal of Feminist Family Therapy, 13,* 65–90.

CHAPTER

20 Feminist Multicultural Counseling with Traumatized Individuals

Christine A. Courtois

Abstract

Feminism has greatly contributed to the treatment of trauma, especially of the sort that involves interpersonal victimization. Additionally, contemporary feminism has been crucial in identifying the scope of interpersonal violence against females, identifying these events and experiences as traumatic, and providing philosophical foundations and strategies for psychotherapy. It has also encouraged the understanding of the victimization in terms of cultural and other contextual considerations that contributed to its occurrence. Trauma victims and survivors benefit from a treatment that is oriented toward re-empowerment, encouragement of their personal strength and resilience, an understanding of adaptations to trauma as survivor skills rather than pathology, an understanding of their unique individual and social characteristics and the influence they have on both the occurrence of their victimization and their recovery. Therapists who treat traumatized clients from a feminist/multicultural model must attend to the potential points of accord, as well as to the points of disagreement between the two, and to the multiple identities and individual needs of each client.

Key Words: Psychological trauma, interpersonal violence, trauma treatment, feminist treatment

This chapter provides an overview of feminist contributions to the understanding of interpersonal traumatization of girls and women and further demonstrates how these contributions are consistent with a multicultural approach that attends to the personal and social identities of traumatized individuals. Both feminism and multiculturalism offer highly complementary ways of understanding and treating clients of all types. Both address the individual in his or her personal and family context and in terms of diverse and multiple social identities. These intersecting feminist and multicultural perspectives are especially salient in working with traumatized individuals. It is now well understood that the occurrence and the impact of trauma are highly influenced by the individual's particular personal, family, and social identities, and some (such as age, gender and gender identity, sexual orientation, ableness including physical and emotional limitations, poverty, or political affiliation in a repressive regime) may actually set the individual up to be victimized by virtue of being a member of that group and might contribute to ongoing victimization. These identities or contexts also determine whether the traumatized receive support and assistance from their community or whether they are shunned and stigmatized—critical factors to recovery. At present, some sociocultural and religious traditions are at odds with the empowerment or the emancipation of women. These also must be considered as part of the multicultural perspective.

This chapter is devoted to the application of feminist thought and analysis to the understanding of gender-based interpersonal victimization and trauma (applicable to other forms of traumatization as well), to the conceptualization of aftereffects of such trauma, and to the choice and application of treatment approaches and strategies. Feminist psychology and multicultural counseling psychology are shown to be highly compatible with what has been identified as necessary to healing from traumatic experiences.

These psychologies and their respective ethics contribute to a treatment that places the individual's experience in context in terms of culture, ethnicity, family, religion, economic and social status, ability, age, and politics, while also emphasizing the uniqueness of the victim's experience, response, and recovery. Many of these overlap, and a client rarely presents with only one relevant social identity or context; rather, these interact in unique ways for each individual. The therapist's attention to and respect toward these multiple identities and contexts are often of direct benefit to the client, making him or her feel as though the therapist wants to know about his or her personal background and identity. This approach serves to support the feeling of being individually acknowledged and respected. In contrast, the therapist's lack of awareness and inquiry can convey disregard or disrespect—even ignorance, discrimination, or antipathy—and can cause the client to feel misunderstood, disliked, and judged. Both types of responses assist or impede the individual in recovering from the victimization and in being able to lead a life that is less impeded and less in decline as a result of the trauma. These psychologies also have in common an emphasis on communal connections and healing and the construction of a narrative of the client's life and traumatic experience in order to assist in the processing and integration of the trauma. An overview model of feminist-based multicultural treatment is presented, with the understanding that it provides an umbrella under which individualized goals and strategies are developed. In a similar vein, it is understood that healing itself is idiosyncratic; different individuals heal in their own way and at their own pace, often consistent with the idioms of distress, teachings, and values of their various personal and social identities.

Therapists who work with traumatized women must come to understand their own upbringing and their loyalty to the teachings of their own contexts and belief systems in order to understand them and their possible impacts (both positive and negative) on their work. They should also understand and take a stance that supports clients in making their own informed decisions about whether, how, and to what extent they engage in treatment and how they approach healing and resolution, taking into account the teachings, idioms of distress, and healing resources and practices (if any) of their particular background and their need for ongoing communal attachment. Some clients will choose to distance or separate from backgrounds that support victimization, while others will attempt to change their dominant ideologies and practices, and still others will stay within their imposed limitations. Recovery from trauma is highly individualized; different outcomes might suit victim/survivors influenced by their own life circumstances and contexts. The therapist is oriented toward helping clients to explore their options and to make informed choices, taking into consideration their personal beliefs and the influence of their backgrounds. Espín (2005) described how such as stance recognizes that "the age of the cookie cutter has passed."

Feminist Influence on Identifying Gender-Based Interpersonal Victimization

Historically, in many cultures and societies, girls and women have been treated as less valued and important than boys and men, a fact that has resulted in the withholding of basic rights and that has involved a massive amount of discrimination, mistreatment, danger, and death—in other words, in victimization and traumatization of girls and women (United Nations, 2010). According to feminist theory, females have been discriminated against, disempowered, attacked, harassed, disfigured, or even killed on the sole basis of their gender or gender identity by those who have more power and influence (mostly males) who hold specific beliefs about roles, positions, and prerogatives based on gender (Reilly, 2009; WHO, 2005).

Over the course of the past 50 years, contemporary feminism has expanded beyond a sole focus on gender to include attention to other contexts or social identities and how these provide the basis for discrimination, attacks against, and disempowerment/disenfranchisement of the lower status (usually female) individual. These include (a) ethnic, cultural, religious, political/historical traditions, values, and teaching regarding gender and ascribed roles of lesser power/authority; (b) issues of power and status between the genders with the resultant general disempowerment of women, and its underprivileging of the experience and wisdom of females as compared to the experience and wisdom of males. This power differential additionally results in the economic impoverishment of women as compared to men and their not being paid at rates that are comparable to or equitable with the work done by men; and (c) myths regarding women (i.e., women are the "weaker sex;" women do not have rights, nor should they have them; women are inherently evil and unclean, and so on) that are associated with particular groups or factions.

Along with identification of these dimensions, feminist theorists have countered them with those that (a) show respect for the individual and her personal narrative and social context; (b) show respect for personal resilience and the adaptations that she made when faced with adverse circumstances, especially when they were chronic and debilitating in conditions of entrapment; (c) identify adaptations as survivor skills versus personal pathology (destigmatization); (d) support personal and social empowerment; and, (e) endorse "women's ways of knowing" (Belenky, Clinchy, Goldberger, & Tarule, 1986) as valid and as distinct from those of men and as having unique value to the nurturance and well-being of offspring and to the society at large.

As a major part of bringing attention to discrimination based on gender, contemporary Western feminism, supplemented more recently by transnational feminism, has played a significant role in bringing family and societal/cultural interpersonal violence against women to public awareness. Were it not for the contemporary feminist movement that began in the 1960s, these forms of abuse would continue to be hidden, their victims enshrouded in the pain of stigmatization-based shame and isolation. Unfortunately, this is still the case in many developing countries where traditional values and traditions are enforced and where women and girls may have few, if any, rights (Kristof & WuDunn, 2009; United Nations Women, 2007).

Rape was the first form of violence against women to be identified and addressed by feminists. In contrast to predominant myths about its occurrence (i.e., that it was deserved or wanted, that the woman was to blame or was responsible for saying no and stopping it), rape was clearly labeled as sexual victimization and exploitation, perpetrated through the use of coercion or force on a woman (or man), for which the victim was not to blame. It was labeled as an assault on the very selfhood of the individual victim. The legal definition of rape specifies that it involves lack of consent and physical penetration of the vagina or anus. Gender-based power dynamics involving objectification and degradation of the victim for the gratification of the perpetrator were identified as the predominant motivations of rape, as well as its *modus operandi*. Rape was also identified as a form of humiliation that is brought upon enemies in conflict and upon those who are defeated (mass rapes as social degradation or mass terrorization of a social group, or as spoils of war that soldiers have "earned" or are rewarded with or to which they are entitled) (Brownmiller, 1975).

As rape issues were increasingly publicized in the 1970s and 1980s, large numbers of women who had been raped sought help in the aftermath of its occurrence. Many women also divulged other forms of sexual violence against them, some of it outside the family (i.e., sexual harassment and assaults, hostile atmospheres, sexual microaggressions), but the majority perpetrated within the family by male relatives or intimates or by others known to the victim (i.e., incest, domestic violence, date and acquaintance rape). Feminist scholars began to describe the family (backed up by its ethnic/cultural and religious values and beliefs) as the breeding ground for women's sexual exploitation in the larger society, a radical formulation when it was first made, but one that has held up, as more is learned about incest and other forms of intimate partner and domestic violence, and about cultural contributions concerning the role and status of women that are conveyed through families (Courtois, 2010; Kristof & WuDunn, 2009; Rush, 1977).

Although the early formulations were solely about girls and women, they were expanded to include males when it became apparent that boys and men can be and are victims of sexual assault inside or outside the family (especially as children) and that many of the same power and control dynamics are at play. Males and females also are enculturated into roles ascribed by their gender, males usually as dominant victimizers, and females as acquiescent victims. Research consistently shows that males are the most likely to perpetrate sexual abuse and assault, while females make up the highest percentage of those who are victimized. Males are sometimes victims, particularly when they are young (due to their smaller size, accessibility, physical and emotional immaturity, and lower status), although male victims assaulted as adults (especially in military and paramilitary settings) are now coming forward in greater numbers. Females sometimes perpetrate but in far lesser numbers than males. Infrequently, they are solo offenders; more frequently, if and when they offend, they co-offend with men or on their behalf. In some cases and some sociocultural contexts, women subscribe to the same belief system that undergirds female victimization, and they help to impose it on their male and female children. Tragically, this sometimes results in their assisting in the victimization, punishment, mutilation, or killing of their own children or other female kin (i.e., genital mutilation, honor maiming and killings) (see Kristof & WuDunn, 2009, for descriptions, examples and documentation).

As research findings about sexual violence within and outside the family accrued, researchers such as Courtois (1979, 1988), Herman (1981), Herman and Hirschman (1977), Holmstrom and Burgess (1974), and Walker (1984) identified the consequences in terms of post-traumatic syndromes (i.e., rape trauma syndrome, seduction and incest trauma, battered woman syndrome). The diagnosis of post-traumatic stress disorder (PTSD) was first included in the *Diagnostic and Statistical Manual-III (DSM-III,* American Psychiatric Association, 1980), and feminist scholars and clinicians immediately adopted it as also applicable to women's trauma and as contrary to what had then come to be identified as the "victim-to-patient process" (Carmen, Rieker, & Mills, 1984) in which victims were shamed, blamed, and labeled for their post-traumatic responses, both at the time of the trauma and later. What started as an experience of victimization for many often resulted in their becoming so debilitated by aftereffects that they sought mental health treatment and became patients, often with a lack of attention to the origin of symptoms by the treating professional. The use of the PTSD diagnosis was heralded as one that was less stigmatizing for the victim/survivor, since it derived from real events that the individual experienced (and were therefore not based solely on the individual's psyche or on internal factors) that were emotionally overwhelming and to which she responded with an understandable and typical set of responses (normal responses to abnormal circumstances versus abnormal responses and an impaired, hysteric, or "borderline" personality or gross psychopathology). *Causation of distress* was therefore *outside the individual,* and responses did not imply personal pathology, although these responses could cause a wide range of disturbances in the individual's life, many of which met criteria for a variety of diagnoses (e.g., depression, anxiety, eating disorders, substance abuse, avoidant personality, borderline personality, and so on).

The Scope of Gender-Based Victimization of Women

The scope of the gender-based victimization and traumatization of women around the globe is truly sobering and as horrifying as it is tragic. The recently published book by Kristof and WuDunn (2009) provides an update on the extent of such victimization and describes it in its historical as well as present-day manifestations. In addition to the sheer magnitude of the problem around the globe, these authors reinforce the position taken by feminist authors over the last half of the twentieth century and into the twentiy-first: namely, that the victimization of women is at epidemic proportions but, perhaps more important, is endemic but hidden in many cultures and societies. They also document how some types have changed and even expanded in certain cultures in recent years, citing the increase in acid attacks and "honor killings" that occur when a woman has been accused of having sex outside marriage or of not sexually satisfying her husband in their marriage. Furthermore, mass rapes and mass "disappearances" become a means of terrorizing whole communities and ethnic groups in sectarian, political, and drug-related conflicts. They suggest that gender-based victimization is so common and embedded within some cultural, religious, ethnic, and political traditions that it has become accepted as the norm and has been paradoxically rendered largely invisible as a result.

In some ways, it has been the "affliction that had no name" and little or no social recognition as to its personal, familial, societal, and cultural toll. Kristof and WuDunn (2009) aptly (but perhaps shockingly for many) labeled it "gendercide." These researchers put it on par with other forms of genocide and compared it to slavery conditions of the past in which human beings were treated like chattel, more like animals than humans, and thus as expendable and subject to being murdered. They highlight what they call the "the missing millions," girls and women who are missing due to their eradication through a number of common practices in different ethnic groups and cultures across the globe, including gender-selective abortion, infanticide, lack of adequate medical attention especially in childbirth, lack of contraception, and increased susceptibility to HIV/AIDS and other STDs. "Erasure killings" and other "disappearances," poverty and malnutrition, and extensive physical and sexual assault, abuse, sexual trafficking, and slavery occur across the entire life span.

In Western countries, where the rights of women are incorporated into law, the situation may not seem as dire; however, gender-based discrimination, abuse, physical and sexual assault of girls and women, sexual slavery, and other forms of interpersonal victimization continue at unacceptably high rates (United Nations, 2010; UN Women, 2007; World Health Organization, 2005). Research has determined that children are the most vulnerable members of society (in Western countries as well as around the world) and are highly likely to suffer one or more forms of victimization due to their physical and emotional immaturity, dependence on adults, accessibility, and lack of power and status, in addition to their gender (Finkelhor, 2008). When boys are victimized, they are more likely to be physically abused within the family and sexually abused outside it, while for girls, the opposite is true. Boys are more likely to be physically assaulted, while girls are more likely to be sexually victimized (although there is certainly considerable overlap between these two forms of abuse).

Another two dimensions of interpersonal victimization have been identified repeatedly in research findings: *poly-victimization* and *re-victimization*. In poly-victimization, more than one form of victimization takes place within its original context (i.e., the family, the school, the community) and victims may be routinely victimized by more than one person and in more than one context, thus adding to the potential for their traumatization. Research findings have also accumulated to demonstrate that when abuse occurs during childhood (especially repetitive and chronic sexual abuse that was entrapping—whether it occurs within or outside the family—and where there is no effective intervention), re-victimization of some sort, especially sexual, is highly likely (Courtois, 2011; Duckworth & Follette, 2011). That is, the victim is at high risk to be sexually re-victimized at different points in adolescence and adulthood, often in serial relationships with abusive/exploitive partners, and is further at high risk for abuse/assault by strangers. Other types of trauma (relational, identity, and layered/cumulative) have also come to light in recent years. *Relational trauma* refers to trauma in the context of primary relationships between infants/toddlers and their parents/primary caregivers, set in their individualized family, religious, and sociocultural context. Patterns of insecure attachment occur when the primary caregiver or attachment figure is not attuned to, protective of, nurturing toward, or responsive to his or her immature, developing, and dependent offspring/child. Failure to provide the child with such a "secure base" or "safe haven" has been implicated in the development of insecure or highly disorganized styles of attachment that render children and later adults vulnerable to problems with self-regulation, self-worth, and relationships with others (Bowlby, 1969). Those with the most insecure patterns (identified as disorganized/unresolved) have a higher likelihood of lifetime difficulties, including ongoing dissociation/dissociative disorders and other forms of psychopathology (Hesse & Main, 2000) and difficulties in effectively parenting their own children.

Identity trauma has been discussed recently by Kira (2010). Core aspects of the individual's very identity (i.e., gender/gender identity, sexual orientation, and racial, ethnic, and cultural membership and related characteristics such as skin color or language) result in victimization due to discrimination against the group. Thus, victimization and trauma become *imbedded in the individual's very being*, and shame, personal negativity, and self-blame are incorporated as part of the individual's core identity. *Cumulative trauma*, as the name suggests, is just that: repetitive, chronic, and layered, in ways that aggregate and exacerbate its aftereffects. Repetitive victimization/re-victimization results in re-traumatization, which, in turn, leaves the victim more injured and more susceptible to additional victimization in a quite vicious cycle that can last a lifetime and that contributes to the intergenerational cycle of violence identified by Widom and her research associates (Widom, 1989). Individuals who are repeatedly victimized or threatened have little or no chance to heal and must use their energy to anticipate and fend off re-occurrence.

Interpersonal victimization has other characteristics that deserve mention, especially as they relate to gender. As opposed to more impersonal forms of victimization (i.e., weather-related or resulting from other forms of natural disasters or "acts of God"), human-perpetrated forms are more likely to be repeated and to become chronic, especially when they occur in the context of a family or other closed setting and when the abuser is related to or otherwise known to the victim. In such a situation, the role and relationship between them are violated and result in what Freyd (1996) termed *betrayal-trauma*, a factor that has been found to be highly correlated with higher degrees of distress and more serious reactions in the victim. Additionally, traumatization can occur when expected help or protection from those individuals or agencies charged with responding is not forthcoming and/or reactions to disclosure are negative and shaming, rather than receptive and caring. *Secondary traumatization* may be due to non-response by a particular individual, such as a parent who is indifferent or judgmental in response to her or his daughter's disclosure of sexual abuse by a family member, or a mother who responds to disclosure of incest by her husband by blaming and castigating her daughter while exonerating him. Alternatively, secondary traumatization may be caused by an organization, especially one that has responsibility to provide assistance, such as a critical response on the part of police or medical personnel when their aid is sought after an assault; and/or non-response within a workplace, a religious hierarchy, or a chain of command that essentially covers up the crime while punishing the victim for speaking out. Non-response, judgment, or actions on the part of societal/cultural/religious groups can also trigger secondary traumatization, such as when a raped woman is labeled as defiled/unclean and therefore is ineligible for marriage or is sentenced to be stoned to death; when a family punishes a woman who has been sexually assaulted by further assaulting or killing her for bringing shame on her family by not living up to social traditions, or alternatively when she is forced to marry her rapist to maintain her family's honor; when the disappearance of a woman is not treated as a crime or is not sufficiently investigated.

To summarize, there are a number of types and aspects of interpersonal victimization to which women and children (and some men and boys) are routinely subjected. Responses from others run the gamut from those that are compassionate and caring to those that are castigating and inconsiderate at best, and judgmental, cruel, punishing, and life-ending at worst. Responses vary according to the values, beliefs, and traditions—especially to those that are ascribed to gender—of the woman's membership groups. Thus, *identity trauma* can be seen as extending to the individual's gender and the type of response that she is likely to receive that is based on the group's determination of how female members ought to behave, be treated, and how they should be responded to (or not). As can further be seen, multiple social identities and contexts can also contribute to interpersonal victimization. They therefore have a major role in the understanding of the individual and his or her unique experience (Brown, 2008), including opportunities for post-traumatic growth (Tedechi & Calhoun, 1995), as opposed to the usual course of post-traumatic decline.

The Impact of Interpersonal Victimization on Psychological and Physical Health

As would be expected, the impact of interpersonal violence can be severe and long-lasting, although individual response varies in terms of two primary dimensions related to the trauma: objective and subjective aspects. Examples of objective characteristics include the age and life stage of the victim at onset and over the course of the victimization; the relationship to the perpetrator and the degree of betrayal involved; the use of force or violence; the duration, frequency, and degree of physical intrusion or injury, severity, and so on. Examples of the subjective characteristics of the victim may include gender or sexual orientation; psychological temperament and physiological hardiness; previous experiences of trauma; resilience and personal strength; values and beliefs (individual and religious/sociocultural); and the degree of recognition and support received post-victimization. At the present time, PTSD is a much more common response in traumatized children than in traumatized adults (where it is documented as the atypical response to being traumatized; see McFarlane & Yehuda, 1996) since it takes much less to traumatize a child than it does an adult and is more common in those who have been repeatedly, multiply, and/or progressively traumatized, or those who are re-victimized and re-traumatized. Moreover, PTSD has been found in an almost a 2:1 female/male ratio (Tolin & Foa, 2006), a finding that might be due to a biological determinant of vulnerability/response or to the fact that females are more routinely and seriously victimized and traumatized, starting in childhood and lifelong.

As research data have accumulated concerning all forms of child abuse and other forms of interpersonal violence, it has become evident that the major criteria for the diagnosis of PTSD, as codified in the *DSM* (American Psychiatric Association, 1980, 1994, 2000), are not always a good fit with some of the common aftereffects that have been identified. The three primary categories of symptoms for the diagnosis of PTSD (re-experiencing, numbing, and hyper-arousal) were originally derived from the study of response to combat, or what Herman (1992) identified as "men's trauma." In contrast, the aftereffects associated with childhood and domestic trauma (identified by Herman as "women's trauma"), are more far-reaching and developmental in impact. Research findings regarding aftereffects grouped them into seven primary categories. An expanded diagnostic conceptualization, complex PTSD/disorders of extreme stress not otherwise specified (CPTSD/DESNOS), which included these seven categories to account for major psychological and physical/health aftereffects that were *in addition to or apart from* those necessary for the diagnosis of PTSD, was first introduced by Herman (1992). These were *primarily developmental* and included *personality and interpersonal* impact. The criteria for the CPTSD diagnosis are the following:

1. *Alterations in the regulation of affective impulses,* including difficulty with modulation of anger, including risk-taking, self-injury, and self-destructiveness. This category includes all methods used for emotional regulation and self-soothing, even those that are paradoxically self-harming but are used in the interest of emotional soothing or self-management.

2. *Alterations in attention and consciousness* leading to amnesias and dissociative episodes and depersonalization. This category includes all forms of dissociative response and disorders.

3. *Alterations in self-perception,* predominantly negative and involving a chronic sense of guilt and responsibility, and ongoing feelings of intense shame. Chronically abused individuals (especially children) incorporate abuse messages and post-traumatic responses into their developing sense of self and self-worth.

4. *Alterations in perception of the perpetrator,* including incorporation of his or her belief system in some cases. This criterion addresses the complex relational attachments that develop in response to repetitive and premeditated abuse by related or known individuals and the lack of appropriate and protective response by others. Traumatic bonding refers to the inconsistent attachment resulting from abuse in which a relationship is first formed with the victim, who is then exploited and betrayed.

5. *Alterations in relationship to others,* such as not being able to trust the motives of others and not being able to feel intimate with them. Another "lesson of abuse" internalized by victim/survivors is that other people are dangerous, out to get what they can by whatever means, including using/abusing others. Abuse survivors may be unaware that other people can be empathic, benign, and caring.

6. *Somatization and/or medical problems.* These somatic reactions and medical conditions may relate directly to the type of abuse suffered and any physical damage that was caused, or they may be more diffuse. They have been found to involve all major body systems and to include many pain syndromes, medical illnesses, sexual dysfunctions and disorders, and somatic conditions.

7. *Alterations in systems of meaning.* Chronically abused and traumatized individuals often feel hopeless about anyone being able to understand them or their suffering. They despair of being able to recover from their psychic anguish.

Despite the fact that a field trial established the validity of these seven categories of aftereffects, complex PTSD was included in the *DSM-IV* (American Psychiatric Association, 1994) only as an associated feature of PTSD, rather than as a freestanding diagnosis, At the time of this writing, the diagnosis has again been introduced in hopes of its inclusion in the *DSM5*, scheduled to be published in 2013, but this is not guaranteed. It appears that the PTSD diagnosis will be expanded somewhat to accommodate some of the criteria associated with its complex variant but again will not be included as a freestanding diagnosis. A diagnosis of developmental trauma disorder (DTD; van der Kolk, 2005) is being considered, possibly as an alternative. In contrast to this position, the *International Classification of Disorders-10* (*ICD-10*), published by the World Health Organization (WHO, 1992), includes a diagnosis characterized by "enduring personality change after catastrophic experiences" that refers to the developmental/personality impact that can occur at any point in the life span in response to severe traumatization.

Feminist theorists have been very vocal about the misuses of psychiatric diagnoses with women, especially those who have been traumatized. Although PTSD and especially complex PTSD are more descriptive and less pejorative, the traumatized are often not understood in terms of *what happened to them* and instead are treated for *what is wrong with them* (Bloom, 1997). Such a perspective is often based on a lack of recognition or identification of trauma (especially in childhood and especially relational trauma) and its widespread impact and how it interferes with and interrupts normal development. Traumatized adults seeking mental health services are often misidentified as suffering from personality disorders and as not being able to relate to others, rather than being understood as having personalities affected by trauma, which impedes their ability to trust and to get close to others.

And yet, abuse and trauma survivors make up a large percentage of individuals who seek medical care and mental health treatment. In fact, when they seek help, those who experience post-traumatic reactions and symptoms of physical distress most often approach primary care physicians and other medical personnel. The extent and severity of their needs can vary dramatically and can shift over the course of their lives by their age and stage of development, by the occurrence of other life events, and during their course of medical treatment or psychotherapy. For example, a victimized infant or toddler will react in ways that are consistent with his or her age or stage of development, as will the victimized adolescent or elderly individual. Many aspects of the personal subjectivity will interact to determine response at these various life stages, as will the availability (or lack thereof) of response and support of intimates and the more broad-based "social surround." In addition, PTSD has been found to be dynamic and fluid rather than static in its presentation; therefore, it might be highly evident at some points and hidden and dormant at others.

The complex group of symptoms that make up CPTSD/DESNOS is often at root of the difficulties that are routinely presented to therapists and medical professionals, usually in forms that are disguised and disconnected from their traumatic origin. If the therapist or medical practitioner fails to ask about past or current abuse, victimization, and trauma, these symptoms are likely to not be understood as related to each other, nor are they likely to be identified as part of an array of symptoms, or even as post-traumatic. As a result, they are frequently misdiagnosed (for which clients might be ineffectively and inappropriately treated and medicated) and their symptoms treated in piecemeal fashion that is disconnected from their trauma etiology.

Another reason that symptoms become disconnected from their origin rests with the ability of trauma survivors to identify and disclose their trauma history, a process that also has been found to be highly variable. Research findings suggest that the ability to disclose is related to whether past disclosures were effective or not (i.e., whether they were responded to and whether they made the situation better or worse); whether the individual remembers the traumatic circumstances or not (and how and when it is remembered); and whether he or she chooses to disclose or not based on fears of judgment, shaming, abandonment, or other negative response, and the degree to which authority figures are mistrusted. Not infrequently, disclosures are followed by recantations, especially in those cases when the victim is blamed and his or her disclosure is challenged and disbelieved. Disclosure may be virtually impossible in some sociocultural contexts, especially those in which the victimized are routinely faulted for what befell them or those who would be shunned or severely punished (up to and including incarceration or killing) due to proscriptions of the group. In treatment contexts, disclosure may only occur after a modicum of trust has developed with the therapist or the medical practitioner and, even then, may only be made in bits and pieces and with great testing and reluctance on the part of the victim/survivor. Therapists should be aware that in some circumstances victims are violating the codes of their family's cultural, religious, or ethnic traditions by divulging abuse and other forms of victimization (especially when it occurred in the context of family and was perpetrated by family members, or in religious or other community contexts, perpetrated by revered authority figures), so disclosures should be handled with utmost discretion and attention to confidentiality.

Feminist Multicultural Perspectives on Interpersonal Victimization

The feminist multicultural perspective extends beyond the individual and the family unit to examine the relevant political/societal/cultural/ethnic/religious/economic contexts that influence the occurrence of interpersonal victimization and reactions to it. It also includes attention to issues of diversity such as gender identity, sexual orientation, and various age, physical, developmental, and emotional challenges (Brown, 2008). To be multiculturally competent, therapists must have specific awareness, knowledge, and skills. This includes an awareness of their own assumptions, values, and biases, that is, their beliefs and attitudes. They must also seek to understand the worldview and cultural outlook of the client—how his or her particular identity impacts interactions in the world. They should also know that one client may have various different identities to learn about and to seek to understand. Lastly, they should develop specific skills through education and clinical skill-building with diverse populations.

From the feminist perspective (and often in keeping with the values and traditions of particular sociocultural groups), men are conditioned into roles of power and domination with regard to females, who are conditioned to be passive and dependent. Gender-based victimization is seen as the tragic manifestation of these beliefs and values and the power imbalance between the sexes and a within-the-family conditioning of women to their subservient and sexual roles in society. Instead of receiving nurturance geared toward their full development as individuals, girls and women are subjugated and abused based on their gender and their lack of power (boy children are also abused due to their small size as children and relative lack of power). Girls and women can therefore learn from an early age that to be female means to be less valued and less important, and to be sexually used and abused or otherwise treated with contempt and disregard.

As twentieth-century Western feminists more systematically studied rape and incest, they challenged the Freudian shift in the foundation of his psychoanalytic theory from the seduction theory, which posited incest as etiological to many psychological disturbances found primarily in women and falling under the rubric of hysteria, to the Oedipal theory, which posited instead that it was based on fantasy and desire on the part of the child. They argued that Freud's original theory (relabeled the *trauma theory*) was accurate and that its replacement was nothing short of a cover-up that denied the reality of the sexual abuse of female children and adults while excusing those who abused (Rush, 1977). They argued against the sexism of psychoanalysis of the day, best exemplified by the position of blaming the child and the "colluding" mother for their own victimization while exonerating the abusing father or other abuser. And they held that the Oedipal theory, by reinforcing the dynamics of denial, disbelief, and blame of the victim, had the effect of perpetuating incest/child sexual abuse and its negative effects rather than ameliorating them.

Incest/child sexual abuse was re-conceptualized by feminists as *interpersonal victimization by intimates with high traumatic potential for the exploited child and serious consequences that could span a lifetime.* As a form of rape—but one repeatedly perpetrated by intimates and those on whom the child depends—it was and is viewed as the ultimate violation of the self, short of homicide. Anna Freud (1981, p. 34) wrote, "Where the chances of harming a child's normal developmental growth are concerned, it ranks higher than abandonment, neglect, physical maltreatment or other forms of abuse." In fact, it often involves all of these forms along with the sexual violation. Shengold (1989), another psychoanalyst, called incest "soul murder." Its occurrence within the family by kin, who, by definition, are supposed to be trustworthy and protective, was seen as *compounding its traumatic impact and its potential to seriously injure the developing child.* Freyd's (1996) conceptualization of *betrayal-trauma* has increased understanding of the additional burden that abuse of this type puts on victims, especially children who remain dependent on and accessible to primary attachment figures and other family members who prey on them in alternation with caring for them. Moreover, attachment dynamics are highly skewed in such a circumstance, resulting in the victim having ambivalent attachment to the perpetrator and others (for which she is often blamed) and simultaneous generalized mistrust of others.

Feminism has as its focus *women's reality.* It stresses the subjective knowledge of the individual in the context of differing sociocultural identities and validates women's experience in a world where the experience of men has been the standard. Feminism also offers a conceptualization of symptom formation not as pathology but rather as adaptation to highly negative circumstances. Symptoms are viewed as survival skills or methods of self-soothing that allowed (and may continue to allow) the individual to cope with the victimization and its aftermath. Subsequently, these same coping mechanisms may (and often do) become maladaptive, spawning secondary elaborations and associated major life difficulties. The work of therapy is, in part, to validate the original injury, to identify survival skills/adaptations, and to replace those that are maladaptive in order for the injury to be healed and the arrested process of development resumed. Thus, treatment involves the development of new and healthier skills in emotional self-regulation, stopping post-traumatic decline, and opening the potential for a future that is less fraught with post-traumatic "baggage." The survivor is assisted in facing rather than avoiding the trauma and its associated emotions in order to process them to the point of some resolution and the diminishment of post-traumatic symptoms. The survivor is seen as the authority on her or his own experience, and therapy as a means of self-exploration, with the process geared toward resolving the impact of the trauma. Because control and a positive sense of self are usually so definitively negated (especially in chronic and cumulative interpersonal victimization), treatment is oriented to helping with the reestablishment of a positive identity, a sense of personal power and efficacy, and improved capacity to relate to and trust others. This is modulated by what is allowed or disallowed in the client's larger sociocultural "surround" and whether he or she continues to be bound by those traditions and beliefs.

A Feminist Multicultural Treatment Model for Interpersonal Trauma

Feminist multicultural treatment encompasses all of the dimensions described above. It also includes the following additional foundations of treatment:

It is overtly based on *professionalism, professional behavior, and a scientific attitude* on the part of the therapist, including the standards of practice and codes of ethical conduct that have been developed over the years by the mental health/medical professions to guide the responsible practice of treatment. This is supplemented with information about the client's background and context and is adapted and explained to the client as needed. Additional philosophical foundations include the following.

Treatment is organized around recognition of the primacy and uniqueness of the individual in his or her sociocultural and personal contexts and the maintenance of her or his welfare. Treatment is not one-size-fits all (Courtois, 1999; Espín, 2005); rather, each individual is assessed and treatment is planned differentially and in a way that attends to the multiple contexts of the client's identity but within the overarching sequenced treatment framework presented below. A "whole person" and a "person with survivor resources" philosophy is used: although symptoms, deficits, and distress are reasons for seeking treatment and generally become the targets for intervention, the client's strengths, resources, and resilience, as well as specific personalized needs, values, and contexts, are identified, reinforced, and worked with. The client's welfare is paramount—major efforts must be directed toward safety to the degree that it is possible in the victim's world. The therapist must guard against further harming the client and should attempt to "do no more harm." Moreover, the therapist must strive to understand the makeup of the victim's world and how it has and continues to influence him or her (in positive as well as negative ways). L. S. Brown (2008, 2009) strongly suggested that the therapist be open to learning from the client about the traditions and beliefs associated with sociocultural/religious background as a means of understanding the uniqueness of each client and as a means of tailoring treatment to the client's needs and context.

A philosophy of *personal empowerment and self-determination* encourages the understanding of the individual's phenomenological experience and context and their specific meaning and relationship to symptoms, distress, and treatment goals. The individual has authority over the meaning and interpretation of her personal life history, current needs and preferences, and goals for the future (Harvey, 1996) and idioms of distress and healing practices are understood within their broader context. These might be drawn on during the course of the treatment (e.g., an iman might bless and "forgive" a Muslim woman raped during wartime who is believed to be unclean; a shaman might be asked to conduct a healing ritual for the victim that is associated with a particular tribal or cultural tradition; a clergy member might be called on to discuss human suffering and religious faith, in general and as associated with the client's victimization).

The therapist must be an *active, empathic, and responsive listener/helper* who enables the client to openly voice, examine, and therapeutically work through feelings that have been suppressed or forbidden, especially shame, self-hatred, self-blame, alienation, and anger. The therapist works to *create relational conditions where the client is emotionally validated and "seen" in order to counter the invalidation of old.* The client's attachment history will have bearing on how he or she relates to the therapist, as will the trauma history and its consequences. The therapy relationship is both the context and the catalyst for self- and relational development in the client. The therapist's ability to self-regulate and to respond to the client in an attuned way that provides "good enough" containment and support sets the stage for self- and relational development.

The therapist strives to *create conditions that are as egalitarian as possible,* with the understanding that some clients will always view the therapist as the authority figure or teacher and/or one who should be treated with deference and respect. Whatever the client's viewpoint, the responsibilities and inherent power differences in the treatment relationship should be explicitly acknowledged. The therapist seeks to use power on the individual's behalf while simultaneously encouraging individualization and differentiation, while keeping in mind the client's personal and social contexts and her or his ability to tolerate or support such change. This includes an openness to the client's questioning of authority (including that of the therapist) in order to support the client's ultimate authority over his/her life, memories, therapeutic engagement and progress; however, it is also understood that some clients may never be able to do this due to the ongoing influence of their sociocultural values and traditions. In fact, these may need to take precedence for particular clients, and the therapist must understand that healing often takes place within a particular context and in a particular way. It is helpful for the therapist to further understand that the healing trajectories of different clients with different backgrounds and resources will also differ. In other words, not all clients heal in the same way and to the same degree, something of which the therapist should be cognizant.

Furthermore, the therapist must uphold appropriate boundaries and limits and is responsible for avoiding dual relationships and situations in which the client might be subject to pressure, coercion, or exploitation within the therapy. Whenever possible, treatment should be based on a shared and collaboratively developed plan, be systematic, and closely follow the evolving evidence base concerning use of the most effective treatment practices, all the while taking into account the client's individualized contexts with its needs, resources, idioms of distress and recovery, and/or constraints. Close attention to ethics, especially pertaining to boundaries, dual relationships, and competence to treat, is required on the part of the therapist.

Treatment relies on a *foundation of professional training, suitable qualifications, and competence (emotional as well as interventional)*. Unfortunately, at the present time, issues of interpersonal victimization have not been included in the curricula of most mental health or other human service/medical professions, nor is specific training or supervision readily available in the treatment of post-traumatic conditions, in general and especially concerning complex post-traumatic disorders (Courtois & Gold, 2009). Nor has professional training particularly emphasized a feminist viewpoint or multicultural perspective from which to understand the client. As a result, the therapist may need to seek out specialized training for working with issues of interpersonal victimization and attending to feminist and multicultural concerns. APA has thus far published two sets of treatment guidelines that address dimension of these topics, one on multicultural education, practice, and policy development, and one on the treatment of lesbian, gay, and bisexual clients (American Psychological Association, 2003; Division 44, 2000). A more general guideline for the treatment of PTSD is scheduled to be developed in the next few years. The International Society for Traumatic Stress Studies (ISTSS) has published a pertinent treatment guideline on international training in mental health and psychosocial interventions for trauma-exposed populations in clinical and community settings (Weine et al., 2000). Other treatment guidelines are now available for PTSD and acute stress disorder (ASD) and the dissociative disorders (American Psychiatric Association, 2004; Australian Centre for Posttraumatic Mental Health, 2007; Clinical Efficiency Support Team, 2003; Foa, Keane, Friedman, & Cohen, 2009; Institute of Medicine, 2006; International Society for the Study of Dissociation, 2011; National Institute for Clinical Excellence, 2005; U.S. Department of Veteran Affairs, 2004. Despite the fact that most are from Western countries and may not attend to or be applicable to the more specialized needs of non-Western cultures, and that most are most pertinent to PTSD and not its more complex and developmental variants, they are essential resources for therapists treating the traumatized.

It has become increasingly evident that, in addition to a specialized base of knowledge, skills, and interventions, therapists must have sufficient emotional maturity to deal with disclosures of horrific experiences that are difficult and painful both to verbalize and to hear, in addition to the relational challenges presented by clients with long-standing and complex trauma histories and symptoms (Pearlman & Courtois, 2005; Pope & Brown, 1996). As discussed above, these may be compounded by histories of other chronic trauma and related problems and by past treatment that was marginally effective or ineffective. Clients who come from backgrounds that are different or distinct from those of the therapist might be especially challenging making it important for the therapist to learn about the client's background directly from the client, and additional research and training might be warranted (Brown, 2008). As therapists learn about beliefs, values, and practices that support victimization, they must be mindful to not scapegoat or attack the context of this behavior while, at the same time, not endorsing victimizing behaviors and practices. This can be an extremely delicate balance to maintain, and the therapist should take the lead from the client, who is likely to express ambivalent attachment and even trauma–bonding, that is, attachment to the perpetrator or justification of his or her behavior, given the larger culture and the practices that support it. Where these need to be challenged and dismantled, the therapist approaches them gradually, according to the client's capacity and willingness to do so.

Therapists who have not had training and supervised experience to anticipate these issues may have great difficulty managing transference, countertransference, and vicarious trauma reactions, in turn, leading to their making therapeutic errors that they might not make otherwise (Pearlman & Caringhi, 2009). Without specific preparation, therapists may become frustrated and angry with the client, the values and traditions of the client's particular sociocultural context, the client's significant others, or themselves in ways that may add to the client's sense of stigma, thus re-activating or intensifying the client's distress rather than ameliorating it. Numerous resources are now available on therapist self-care and resilience in their work as generalist psychotherapists (Norcross & Guy, 2007; Wicks, 2008) and more specifically as trauma therapists (Perlman, 1999; Saakvitne & Pearlman, 1996). Virtually all writers on therapist well-being suggest the importance of ongoing consultation with other professionals, supervision as needed, and ongoing reading and continuing education.

I now turn to a discussion of the consensus-based treatment of complex trauma. It is presented in summary form but has received more extended discussion elsewhere (Courtois, 1999; Courtois & Ford, 2009, 2012; Courtois, Ford, & Cloitre, 2009; Herman, 1992).

Treatment: Pre-treatment Assessment and Three Main Phases

The treatment model for complex traumatic stress disorders involves a preliminary assessment phase and three sequential phases that progressively attend to specific issues and skills, following recommendations first made by feminist psychiatrist Herman (1992) in her influential book *Trauma and Recovery*. This treatment approach gives focal attention to the individual's safety, her or his ability to regulate emotions, and ability to develop trusting relationships with others, the major consequences of interpersonal trauma. Because post-traumatic decline and developmental deficits are often difficult to reverse and because the development of trust and new skills (post-traumatic growth) requires time and effort in particular—and these may counter learning or beliefs associated with the client's cultural, ethnic, and religious context and so may need to be introduced slowly—progress is made in starts and stops. Although the treatment sequence is generally linear, it can be conceptualized as a recursive spiral that involves a back-and-forth process within and between each of three phases. It is also specifically a relapse model in which the client progresses and then regresses. It is modified according to issues that emerge during the initial assessment and over the course of treatment and according to the client's personal and interpersonal means and resources.

Pre-treatment Assessment: Suggested Strategies

Clinical strategies and instruments for the assessment of traumatized individuals are relatively recent developments. A variety of specialized measures are now available; however, they may not cover the full range of the complex traumatic stress disorder symptoms, including such issues as developmental and relational/attachment aspects of the trauma history, functional and self-regulatory impairment, personal resources and resilience, and patterns of re-victimization (Briere & Spinazzola, 2005, 2009). Additionally, they may not take into account the client's particular sociocultural context, which can certainly influence what symptoms develop and how they are manifest and are interpreted within a particular culture. At the present time, a number of trauma assessments have been developed within specific cultural contexts or ethnic traditions. Others developed by Western professionals have been translated into different languages and modified to meet the needs of the sociocultural group under consideration. Therapists should seek out these specialized formats and utilize them when available.

EMBED ASSESSMENT OF TRAUMA WITHIN A STANDARD PSYCHOSOCIAL ASSESSMENT

As part of a standard intake, the therapist should include questions about attachment issues and experiences in the family, various types of trauma and victimization in the individual's past and/or current life, and post-traumatic and dissociative symptomatology. Such inquiry does not automatically result in disclosure, as discussed earlier, because some individuals are unwilling or unable to disclose much about themselves and their victimization, especially early in the assessment or treatment process, or because doing so violates family or sociocultural norms and bans; however, asking conveys that these issues are important and the therapist is open to them. Whether the therapist is asking questions about traumatic experiences and stress symptoms in an initial assessment or later in the treatment process, a sensitive and cautious approach is warranted since disclosure may feel dangerous or disloyal, or may only occur as the individual comes to know and trust the therapist. If a client recants a disclosure or destabilizes after having made one, therapists need to recognize these as rebound reactions to having divulged forbidden material resulting in feelings of vulnerability as a result. Efforts need to be made to assist them in regaining a sense of safety, often with reassurances of confidentiality and slowing the pace of any additional disclosures.

SUPPORTIVE AND CAUTIOUS INQUIRY

Each client must be approached with an understanding that being asked about or disclosing traumatic victimization, traumatic stress symptoms, and personal, family, religious, cultural, or community problems can be difficult and can run counter to the prohibitions of her particular sociocultural context or the ways that she has maintained safety (i.e., by keeping quiet, by maintaining the secret). The therapist must convey an attitude of openness and support. When a trauma history is disclosed, the therapist then must pay careful attention to the individual's condition in-session and afterward (mindful of the possibility of delayed reactions), with reduction or even cessation of inquiry if the client becomes emotionally dysregulated and destabilized.

ASSESS PROGRESS

Specialized assessment may need to be repeated several times over the course of treatment. Post-traumatic and dissociative symptoms may emerge gradually, only after safety and stabilization increase, some precursor issues have been addressed, or when the individual is triggered in some way. These defenses and symptoms might themselves be culture or context-specific, as has been found with dissociation in particular (Speigel, 1994). Although some of these symptoms are blatant and highly evident, others are very subtle, and their function is to maintain secrecy and safety. Unfortunately, most clinicians are not trained to recognize post-traumatic numbing/dissociative, flashback, or hyper-arousal phenomena and so might miss, misunderstand, or misdiagnose them. The therapist who has training in post-traumatic symptoms is obviously in a much better position to recognize and then to address them.

ASSESSMENT BEGINS IN A GENERAL WAY AND BECOMES MORE SPECIALIZED ACCORDING TO THE SYMPTOMS AND NEEDS OF THE INDIVIDUAL

Since this population has such an array of comorbid medical and psychological conditions and symptoms, specialized instruments (e.g., for attachment style, dissociation, quality of relationship, substance abuse, eating disorders, sexual addictions, sexual functioning) are incorporated as needed. As noted above, some of these are now available in different languages and are adapted to cultural conventions. In some cases, outside consultations or specialized corollary assessments (e.g., neuropsychological testing, sleep monitoring, hormonal functioning, pharmacological, to name but a few) might be in order. The findings of all form the basis for initial therapeutic formulation and updating of the treatment plan and the monitoring of treatment progress and outcome.

In addition to assessment, this pre-treatment phase is devoted to education about interpersonal victimization and trauma, including the range of post-traumatic reactions and symptoms, provided in a way that is sensitive to diversity issues. Expectations of psychotherapy and how to interact with the therapist might be highly influenced by ethno/cultural issues, and these should be explored and the psychotherapy process and goals adapted to the needs of the client. Additionally, motivation enhancement may be needed, and these should also be context- and culture-sensitive. Initial treatment goals are established during this pre-treatment phase, in consultation and collaboration with the client and according to the client's needs and resources. Treatment of complex trauma is generally of longer duration than for other forms of trauma; however, it might be done in segments and episodically for some clients, and new approaches and shorter-term models are under development, as described in Courtois and Ford (2009, 2012).

Treatment Phase I: Safety, Stabilization, and Skill Building

This phase involves enhancing safety by stabilizing the client and her life. This involves, among other things, supporting personal safety—to the degree possible in terms of the client's personal situation, context, and community; developing self-regulatory skills; developing communication and other needed life skills; developing positive coping methods where these are lacking; reversing self-defeating or self-harming behaviors and attitudes; building self-esteem; identifying and expanding the client's beliefs and cognitions about abuse and trauma and, more generally, in accordance with those of her social identity and context; and developing a safe therapeutic relationship/working alliance, among others.

Phase I is usually the longest stage of the treatment and the most important to its success. Some clients never move beyond or complete this stage. It is now recognized that good work at this stage is likely to stabilize and substantially improve the client's life. With successful accomplishment of the goals of this stage, some clients may have no need to complete the other two stages, or may choose not to. On the other hand, some clients stay in this stage because they need the support that it provides them in their struggles with daily living (including pressures and expectations regarding their role in the family and in the larger community), with ongoing and unremitting symptoms, or both.

As discussed above, a fairly high number of survivors of chronic interpersonal trauma live in conditions of socioeconomic deficit and relational chaos. Many traumatized women lack basic forms of safety in relation with others (e.g., domestic or community violence, reprisals from others) and themselves (e.g., self-harm, suicidality, addictions, risk taking). A first order of treatment is therefore to establish conditions of safety to the extent possible. This includes safety in the therapeutic relationship, by establishing an interpersonal "secure base" from which to develop and experience sufficient stability necessary for outside safety and therapeutic change. While relational safety in the treatment relationship is essential in all psychotherapies, it is particularly crucial for clients who have suffered extensive interpersonal victimization and whose primary relationships were or continue to be fraught with insecurity/lack of protection or continue to be outright dangerous or life-threatening. Where clients are living in ongoing danger, much therapeutic effort should go toward the development of safety and escape plans and connection with domestic violence shelters and professionals. A reality in domestic violence is that the abused may be at greatest risk of harm at the point of separation or leave-taking. Therapists must be mindful of these types of risks and must educate the client about them, in an effort to safeguard her from ongoing and imminent danger. In some cases, clients may be unable to do much work on their past trauma because present-day trauma is ongoing. It is not advisable to work against or decrease the client's ongoing defenses when they are still needed, nor is it advisable to open a full treatment of past trauma while current crises are ongoing and unresolved. Setting out specified goals and resources for the client's safety may be all that is possible initially.

Education is an integral component of Phase I. Among other things, it can demystify the treatment, a process that might be quite foreign to the client. Being in a small room and being asked about one's most private and taboo experiences with a perceived and real authority figure may feel terrifying. Teaching the client about therapy and how it typically works can therefore be an essential first step. Since many traumatized individuals (quite ironically) know nothing about trauma, they may not label accurately what happened to them and have little or no understanding that their symptoms are associated with their past experiences. Education about trauma and its impact is of considerable importance and may effectively help a client to understand reactions and to develop increased self-understanding and compassion. Education is also the foundation for teaching specific skills that cover a number of domains, many of which may have been missed during childhood: the identification and regulation of emotional states and the development of such skills as personal mindfulness, self-care, coping, problem solving, decision making, assertiveness, and social functioning.

Emotion identification, regulation, and modulation are perhaps the most important self-regulatory skills needed by these clients. At whatever level the treatment is undertaken, it is oriented toward assisting the client in labeling emotions, self-monitoring states of arousal, and learning to manage and modulate the extremes of hyper-arousal (i.e., panic, impulsive risk-taking, rage, dissociation) or hypo-arousal (i.e., emotional numbing, relational detachment, exhaustion, paralysis, hopelessness) associated with traumatic stress disorders, clarifying individual perceptions and thoughts, developing other life skills, and carrying through on other therapeutic tasks. As clients learn to self-regulate, their need for problematic ways in which they have self-soothed (self-injury, suicidality, risk taking, eating disorders, addictions, and so on) will lessen.

Avoidance is a hallmark of traumatic stress disorders, so challenging avoidance is a necessary component of successful treatment. Developing ways to actively engage in both positive and negative experiences and memories requires a shift from reactivity and passivity, the hallmarks of gender-based behaviors taught to and reinforced in women and girls. A fundamental challenge in all phases of treatment, therefore, is to help the client become progressively more able to recognize ways in which she copes with actual or anticipated danger by avoidance and then to identify how to modulate anxiety and to use more effective and active coping tactics. These strategies of course differ according to the needs and the contextual challenges of each client.

Developmentally adverse interpersonal trauma interferes with the acquisition of a sense of positive identity, personal control, and self-efficacy (Ford, 2005), as well as the ability to have satisfying and secure relationships with others. Particular attention needs to be paid to assisting clients to recognize ways that they are (or can be) personally and interpersonally effective and able to safely feel a sense of pride and confidence without being overwhelmed by distress (i.e., fear, shame). This involves analysis of the client's self-perceptions, current and past relationship capacities and interpersonal problems, and personal resources. Again, these need to be addressed with attention to any constraints imposed by the client's particular social identity.

Since mistrust is a major hallmark of interpersonally victimized clients, social/relational deficits and problems are often in evidence. Building support networks and relations with trustworthy others is addressed at this stage. The insecure attachment style is most associated with severe and multiple forms of childhood trauma and results in attachment styles reflective of what was learned in primary relationships: some children become excessively self-sufficient or are controlling or caretaking of others, while others are constantly anxious and insecure. Those who were exposed to the most abusive and disorganized of family backgrounds often develop disorganized/dissociative styles (i.e., involving shifting states of identity, emotional lability, shifting relationships with others, self-injury as a means of self-soothing, and so on). Therapists must work directly with these various styles while providing a secure relational base from which to acquire more interpersonal skills, including the ability to negotiate relationships and to develop intimacy with others. With these interpersonal goals as a focus (as well as goals for self-regulation and safety), therapy can move to the next phase by helping clients commit to enhancing her or his skills for emotional and interpersonal self-regulation and using those skills to recall and reconstruct memories that cause posttraumatic reactions and other distress.

Although Phase II does not specifically focus on trauma processing and resolution, much of the work described above does, either directly or indirectly, relate to traumatic antecedents. The major difference is that in Phase I the treatment alliance is developed and is the context for beginning to explore emotions and cognitions, and the traumatic material is addressed primarily using a dyadic/cognitive perspective. The client is educated about trauma and short- and long-term post-traumatic and developmental adaptations. Ongoing symptoms become the basis for determining whether more directed work with the trauma is required. If the client continues to suffer from PTSD as well as other symptoms and is willing to work more directly on the trauma, treatment proceeds to the second phase. At times, the shift into Phase II will be explicitly initiated by the therapist, based on the assessment of client readiness. And, at still others, it will proceed from some of the cognitive work that then moves naturally to include discussion of associated feelings. Clients often move back and forth between phases, especially in times of crisis and/or when they need to refresh skills or apply or reformulate their safety plan if they become overwhelmed while addressing the trauma. If they become more symptomatic (heightened or lessened reactivity) during trauma-processing, that is taken as a sign to slow the pace and to reinforce safety and other stabilizing skills.

Treatment Phase II: Integrating Traumatic Memories with Emotions

The processing of traumatic memories and associated emotions to some point of resolution and the organization of autobiographical memories into a coherent story line are the primary tasks of this phase. Memory processing and narrative reconstruction must be timed and structured to support the client's ability to not only tolerate trauma memories or symptoms but also to gain a coherent life story. Whether the processing utilizes a specialized approach or technique or occurs more spontaneously as the client comes to understand and feel more about past events and their impact, other issues usually emerge. For example, grief and mourning for all that was lost are common, as are strong feelings of sadness, shame, and rage. Phase II work focuses on processing whatever emotions emerge to the point of some resolution, in order for symptoms to diminish. Additionally, the client might undertake specific actions to resolve relationships with abusers or others, such as disclosures and discussions, boundary development, separation from or reconnection with others, all from a position of increased strength, awareness, understanding, and improved interpersonal as well as self-regulatory skills. Actions such as these are also likely to be impacted by the client's social-cultural context. For example, in some cultures, it is virtually impossible to leave the community without losing one's social context and identity. This may inhibit some clients from taking actions that they might take in other circumstances or to decide to take certain actions and to be faced with dire social consequences.

Memory recollection and reconstruction can be done using different therapeutic modalities, some more structured than others. Generally, traumatic memory work is done in individual psychotherapy, although innovative approaches are now available specifically for group therapy or can be adapted to group. A recently published book by Courtois and Ford (2009) provides an overview and evidence base that is currently available for a variety of approaches. Throughout the treatment process but especially during memory integration work, the client is assisted in maintaining a level of functioning consistent with her past and current lifestyle and circumstances; however, the ability to function may be reduced temporarily at critical junctures in therapy (e.g., at the start; when accessing and working through distressing emotions or memories; when approaching completion). In addition to facing and processing memories, clients are faced with what was lost as the result of their traumatic experiences, and this phase might well be prolonged as clients react with rage, sadness, grief, and other emotions related to past and present losses. Losses are highly idiosyncratic; some are quite obvious, while others are more subtle and thus less easily identified more subtle and less easily identified.

Phase III: Reintegration and Life Reconsolidation

Phase III is the culmination of the work of the previous two phases and is a time of growth; time of growth; however, it may also be fraught with difficulty for those who have never had the opportunity for a "normal" life, or one without personal or social constraints or chaos and danger. This phase is often when the client develops increased understanding of the dysfunction, pathology, and restrictions of the trauma and its surround as she or he continues to attempt to escape their influence. It involves work on remaining unresolved developmental issues, on fine-tuning self-regulation skills, and on relational skill building. Some of the most common issues involve the development of trustworthy relationships and intimacy, sexual functioning, parenting, career and other life decisions, ongoing discussions with or confrontations with abusive or neglectful others, determining courses of action for ongoing self-protection, and so on. All of these are determined according to the client's degree of healing, and personal, economic, and social resources and limitations. This is another treatment phase in which the duration is determined by the number of outstanding issues and their complexity. In this phase, as in the others, clients need to determine their individual courses of action with attention to sociocultural contextual demands and traditions. Some clients will be severely limited in their actions based on restrictions imposed upon them if they stay within a traditional context, while others will choose to make changes that are contradictory to their upbringing and backgrounds and that might cause them to break with their group or to seek a community within their group that is more liberal and less restrictive.

When Feminism and Multiculturalism Collide

Although feminism and multicultural approaches have much overlap in terms of philosophical orientation to traumatized clients and treatment, these approaches can sometimes be incompatible. This is especially likely to be the case when the empowerment of the client puts him or her at odds with the dominant traditions of her background, especially those that espouse gender-based roles, discrimination, and related mistreatment. Therapists should be mindful in assisting their clients in understanding the effect of their backgrounds on both their victimization and their recovery efforts and how individual recovery may not be encouraged or supported by the family or the larger community/culture due to traditions and beliefs. Clients must have the freedom to make their own determinations about the courses of action they will pursue, with the therapist's support. For example, a Central American woman who was raped by an acquaintance from her same cultural background made the choice to never disclose the rape to her family. She had come to terms with the fact that they would never be able to reconcile to the fact that she was raped and that she would therefore be seen as permanently defiled and an embarrassment to her husband and both sides of the family. After carefully examining her options with her therapist, she chose to keep the relationship she had with her parents, not wanting to cause them pain or anguish and not wanting to suffer their disapproval. She also decided never to disclose the fact that she had sought and received mental health treatment—something her family would also have frowned upon and not supported. A male rape or incest survivor might be even more stigmatized in a culture and may decide not to disclose due to shame and the fear of additional attack.

Other examples encompass additional aspects of the client's personal and social context. For example, some male or female victims of clergy abuse might decide not to go public within his or her parish/congregation/temple/ashram, knowing that disclosures of similar abuses by others have resulted in blame, ridicule, and disbelief that caused them to be shunned by or to leave the community. Others decide that they must go public despite the cost to them, in order to publicize the occurrence of clergy abuse and its prevalence. In another example, a gay man, beaten by his father for being an effeminate boy and "to make a man out of him" and bullied throughout his school years, might choose to confront his father and discuss with him how devastating his attacks were on his self-esteem and how the negative effects have shadowed him throughout his life.

Thus, an already complicated therapy can be further compounded by these issues and by any actions taken to resolve them. Many healing trajectories and options are possible, and it is part of the therapist's job to help clients to assess the pros and cons of particular actions, with attention to helping them decide on strategies that are least likely to cause them more harm. Multicultural/transnational feminists have made important contributions that highlight these difficulties and that suggest ways to approach and manage them.

Conclusion

This sequenced model of treatment for interpersonal trauma and complex traumatic stress disorders presented here is based upon and consistent with the tenets of feminist multicultural philosophy and values. It involves individual assessment of the client, including both symptoms and strengths, while allowing for and inquiring about the influence of the client's social identities and context. This is followed by education of the client regarding victimization/trauma and post-traumatic reactions that are also discussed in terms of the client's particular context—this is something that the therapist might need to specifically elicit from the client (Brown, 2008). Symptoms are viewed as having developed as survival skills and as adaptations needed to contend with repeated victimization in the absence of effective intervention and assistance, or in an atmosphere or context where the victimization is viewed as normative.

Phase I stresses safety from further victimization (to whatever degree possible) as a starting point of treatment, after which education and skill building are provided to the client on topics such as self-regulation, communication and life skills, and relationship skills, according to her specific needs and symptoms. These are defined in the treatment plan, which is first based on the preliminary assessment but is modified as needed over the course of the treatment. Some clients do not progress beyond the tasks of Phase I; however, comprehensive work in that phase can result in a less encumbered life and considerable re-empowerment. Emotional processing of the trauma occurs throughout the treatment but especially in Phase II, where a number of specialized techniques can be employed. This phase typically involves the direct acknowledgment of the victimization and its consequences. It can be especially painful and poignant regarding the losses that have resulted and accumulated over time and resultant grief. Phase III involves consolidation of gains that the client has made, including continued emphasis on separating past from present and making life choices that are more personalized to the individual. Throughout the process, the client is encouraged in understanding the victimization in his or her life context as a means of greater self-understanding and compassion and in terms of challenging the status quo and in support of increased social justice and equality. This is also necessary in terms of the client's determination of personal courses of action and how they build upon or conflict with his or her dominant social context. Treatment often takes a considerable period of time to accomplish these complex goals, but new shorter models of treatment are under development and research investigation at the present time.

Future Directions

How can we continue the identification and typology of complex forms of trauma?

How can we get the complex PTSD diagnostic formulation (or the associated "Developmental Trauma Disorder") into the *DSM-V* and the *ICD-11*?

How can we incorporate training about psychological trauma and its treatment into the curriculum of psychology and other related human service professions?

How can we best train clinicians to treat traumatized individuals from feminist and multicultural perspectives?

How can we disseminate the ethics of trauma treatment?

References

American Psychiatric Association. (1980). *Diagnostic and statistical manual of mental disorders* (3rd ed.). Washington, DC: Author.

American Psychiatric Association. (1994). *Diagnostic and statistical manual of mental disorders* (4th ed.).Washington, DC: Author.

American Psychiatric Association. (2000). *Diagnostic and statistical manual of mental disorders* (4th ed., text revision). Washington, DC: Author.

American Psychiatric Association. (2004). *Practice guideline for the treatment of patients with acute stress disorder and posttraumatic stress disorder*. Washington, DC: Author.

American Psychological Association. (2003). *Guidelines on multicultural education, training, research, practice and organizational change*. Retrieved from www.apa.org/pi/multiculturalguidelines/homepage.html.

Australian Centre for Posttraumatic Mental Health. (2007). *Australian guidelines for the treatment of adults with acute stress disorder and posttraumatic stress disorder*. Melbourne: Author.

Belenky, M. F., Clinchy, B. M., Goldberger, N. R., & Tarule, J. M. (1986). *Women's ways of knowing: The development of self, voice, and mind*. New York: Basic Books.

Bloom, S. (1997). *Creating sanctuary: Toward the evolution of sane societies*. New York: Routledge.

Bowlby, J. (1969). *Attachment and loss. Vol.1: Attachment*. New York: Basic Books.

Briere, J., & Spinazzola, J. (2005). Phenomenological and psychological assessment of complex posttraumatic states. *Journal of Traumatic Stress, 18*(5), 401–412.

Briere, J., & Spinazzola, J. (2009). Assessment of the sequelae of complex trauma: Evidence-based measures. In C. A. Courtois & J. D. Ford (Eds), *Treating complex traumatic stress disorders: An evidence-based guide* (pp. 104–123). New York: Guilford Press.

Brown, D. (2009). Assessment of attachment and abuse history, and adult attachment style. In C. A. Courtois & J. D. Ford (Eds), *Treating complex traumatic stress disorders: An evidence-based guide* (pp. 124–144). New York: Guilford Press.

Brown, L. S. (2008). *Cultural competence in trauma practice: Beyond the flashback.* Washington, DC: American Psychological Association.

Brown, L. S. (2009). Cultural competence. In C. A. Courtois & J. D. Ford (Eds), *Treating complex traumatic stress disorders: An evidence-based guide* (pp. 166–182). New York: Guilford Press.

Brownmiller, S. (1975). *Against our will: Men, women and rape.* New York: Simon and Schuster.

Carmen, E. H., Rieker, P. R., & Mills, T. (1984). Victims of violence and psychiatric illness. *American Journal of Psychiatry, 143*, 378–383.

Clinical Efficiency Support Team. (2003). *The management of post traumatic stress disorder in adults.* Belfast: Author.

Courtois, C. A. (1979). Characteristics of a volunteer sample of adult women who experienced incest in childhood and adolescence. *Dissertation Abstracts International, 40*A, November–December 1979, 3194-A.

Courtois, C. A. (1988). *Healing the incest wound: Adult survivors in therapy.* New York: W. W. Norton.

Courtois, C. A. (1999). *Recollections of sexual abuse: Treatment principles and guidelines.* New York: W. W. Norton.

Courtois, C. A. (2010). *Healing the incest wound: Adult survivors in therapy* (Rev. ed.). New York: W. W. Norton.

Courtois, C. A. (2011).Retraumatization and complex traumatic stress: A treatment overview. In M. P. Duckworth & V. M. Follette (Eds.), *Retraumatization: Assessment, treatment, and prevention.* (pp. 163–190) New York: Routledge.

Courtois, C. A., & Ford, J. D. (Eds.). (2009). *Treating complex traumatic stress disorders: An evidence-based guide.* New York: Guilford Press.

Courtois, C. A., Ford, J. D., & Cloitre, M. (2009). Best practices in psychotherapy for adults. In C. A. Courtois & J. D. Ford (Eds.), *Treating complex traumatic stress disorders: An evidence-based guide* (pp. 82–103). New York: Guilford Press.

Courtois, C. A., & Ford, J. D. (2012). *Treatment of complex trauma: A sequenced, relationship-based approach.* New York: Guilford Press.

Courtois, C. A., & Gold, S. N. (2009). The need for inclusion of psychological trauma in the professional curriculum: A call to action. *Psychological Trauma: Theory, Research, Practice, and Policy, 1*, 1, 3–23.

Division 44/Committee on Lesbian, Gay, and Bisexual Concerns Joint Task Force on Guidelines for Psychotherapy with Lesbian, Gay, and Bisexual Clients (2000). Guidelines for psychotherapy with lesbian, gay, and bisexual clients. *American Psychologist, 55*, 12, 1440–1451.

Duckworth, M. P., & Follette, V. M. (2011). *Retraumatization: Assessment, treatment, and prevention.* New York: Routledge.

Espín, O. (January, 2005). *The age of the cookie cutter has passed: Contradictions in identity at the core of therapeutic intervention.* Keynote presentation at the National Multicultural Conference and Summit, Los Angeles, CA.

Finkelhor, D. (2008). *Childhood victimization: Violence, crime, and abuse in the lives of young people.* New York: Oxford University Press.

Ford, J. D. (2005). Treatment implications of altered neurobiology, affect regulation and information processing following child maltreatment. *Psychiatric Annals, 35*, 410–419.

Freud, A. (1981). A psychoanalyst's view of sexual abuse by parents. In P. B. Mrazek & C. H. Kempe (Eds.), *Sexually abused children and their families.* New York: Pergamon Press.

Freyd, J. J. (1996). *Betrayal-trauma: The logic of forgetting childhood abuse.* Boston: Harvard University Press.

Harvey, M. R. (1996). An ecological view of psychological trauma and trauma recovery. *Journal of Traumatic Stress, 9*, 3–23.

Herman, J. L., & Hirschman, L. (1977). Father-daughter incest. *Signs: Journal of Women in Culture and Society, 2*, 735–756.

Herman, J. L. (1981). *Father-daughter incest.* Cambridge, MA: Harvard University Press.

Herman, J. L. (1992). *Trauma and recovery: The aftermath of violence—from domestic to political terror.* New York: Basic Books.

Hesse, E., & Main, M. (2000). Disorganized infant, child, and adult attachment: Collapse in behavioral and attentional strategies. *Journal of the American Psychoanalytic Association, 48*, 1097–1127.

Holmstrom, L. L., & Burgess, A. N (September 1974). Rape trauma syndrome. *American Journal of Psychiatry, 131*, 981–986.

Institute of Medicine of the National Academies. (2006). *Posttraumatic stress disorder: Diagnosis and assessment.* Washington, DC: Author.

International Society for the Study of Dissociation. (2011). Guidelines for treating dissociative identity disorder in adults. *Journal of Trauma and Dissociation, 6*(4), 69–149.

Kira, I. (May 2010). Etiology and treatment of post-cumulative traumatic stress disorders of different cultures. *Traumatology, 4*, 1–14.

Kristof, N., & WuDunn, S. (2009). *Half the sky: Turning oppression into opportunity for women worldwide.* New York: Vantage Press.

Linehan, M. (1993). *Cognitive-behavioral treatment of borderline personality disorder.* New York: Guilford Press.

McFarlane, A. C., & Yehuda, R. (1996). Resilience, vulnerability, and the course of posttraumaticreactions. In B. A. van der Kolk, A. C. McFarlane, and L. Weisaeth (Eds.), *Traumatic stress: The effects of overwhelming experience on mind, body, and society.* (pp. 417–440). New York: Guilford Press.

National Institute for Clinical Excellence (2005). *Posttraumatic stress disorder (PTSD): The management of PTSD in adults and children in primary and secondary care.* London: Author.

Norcross, J. C., & Guy, J. D. (2007). *Leaving it at the office: A guide to psychotherapist self-care.* New York: Guilford Press.

Pearlman, L. A., & Caringhi, J. (2009). Living and working self-reflectively to address vicarious trauma. In C. A. Courtois & J. D. Ford (Eds), *Treating complex traumatic stress disorders: An evidence-based guide* (pp. 202–224). New York: Guilford Press.

Pearlman, L. A., & Courtois, C. A. (2005). Clinical applications of the attachment framework: Relational treatment of complex trauma. *Journal of Traumatic Stress, 18*, 449–460.

Perlman, S. D. (1999). *The therapist's emotional survival: Dealing with the pain of exploring trauma.* Northvale, NJ: Aronson.

Pope, K. S., & Brown, L. S. (1996). *Recovered memories of abuse: Assessment, therapy, forensics.* Washington, DC: American Psychological Association Press.

Reilly, N. (2009). *Women's human rights: Seeking gender justice in a globalizing age.* Malden, MA: Polity Press.

Rush, F. (1977). The Freudian cover-up. *Chrysalis, 6,* 31–45.

Saakvitne, K. W., Pearlman, L. A., & The Staff of the Traumatic Stress Institute (1996). *Transforming the pain: A workbook on vicarious traumatization.* New York: W. W. Norton.

Shengold, R. (1989). *Soul murder: The effects of child abuse and deprivation.* New York, NY: Forcett Columbine.

Speigel, D. (Ed.). (1994). *Dissociation: Culture, mind, and body.* Washington, DC: American Psychiatric Press, Inc.

Tedeschi, R. G., & Calhoun, L. G. (1995). *Trauma and transformation: Growing in the aftermath of suffering.* Thousand Oaks, CA: Sage.

Tolin, D. F., & Foa, E. B. (2006). Sex differences in trauma and posttraumatic stress disorder: A quantitative review of 25 years of research. *Psychological Bulletin, 132*(6), 959–992.

United Nations, Department of Economic and Social Affairs. (2010). *The world's women 2010: Trends and statistics.* United Nations publication No. E.10.XVII.11. Retrieved from unstats.un.org/unsd/demographic/products/Worldswomen/WW2010pub.htm.

UN Women. (2007). *Facts and figures on VAW.* Retrieved from www.unifem.org.

U.S. Department of Veterans' Affairs (2004). *Management of posttraumatic stress.* Washington, DC: Author.

van der Kolk, B. A. (2005). Developmental trauma disorder: Toward a rational diagnosis for children with complex trauma histories.*Psychiatric Annals, 35,* 401–408.

Walker, L. E. (1984). *The battered woman syndrome.* New York: Springer.

Weine, S., Danieli, Y., Silove, Y., Van Ommeren, M., Fairbanks, J., & Saul, J. (2000). Guidelines for international training in mental health and psychosocial interventions for trauma exposed populations in clinical and community settings. *Psychiatry, 65*(2), 279–298.

Wicks, R. J. (2008). *The resilient clinician.* Oxford: Oxford University Press.

Widom, C. S. (April, 1989). The cycle of violence. *Science 244,* 160–166.

World Health Organization. (1992). *ICD-10 Classification of Mental and Behavioural Disorders.* Geneva: Author.

World Health Organization. (2005). *WHO multi-country study on women's health and domestic violence against women.* Geneva, Switzerland: WHO.

CHAPTER

21 Feminist Multicultural Perspectives on Body Image and Eating Disorders in Women

Susan Kashubeck-West *and* Lori Tagger

Abstract

This chapter discusses feminist multicultural approaches to the understanding and treatment of eating disorders and body image dissatisfaction. Historical and contemporary feminist conceptualizations are presented, including a multicultural critique of feminist perspectives. Current approaches to treatment are detailed, including the lack of attention to feminist approaches in the research literature on therapeutic effectiveness. Integration of feminist therapy tenets with other therapeutic approaches is encouraged.

Key Words: Body image, eating disorders, women, feminist multicultural perspectives

Many counseling psychologists work with clients who struggle with issues related to body dissatisfaction and eating disordered behavior. Although full-syndrome disorders of anorexia nervosa and bulimia nervosa that meet *Diagnostic and Statistical Manual for Mental Disorders* (*DSM-IV*) criteria are rare (1–2% of the population or less), the high morbidity, high mortality, and serious psychological pain associated with eating disorders illustrates how serious they are (Kashubeck-West & Mintz, 2001). Importantly, many women (perhaps a third of women in the U.S.) suffer from some eating disorders symptoms (Mulholland & Mintz, 2001). In addition, body dissatisfaction is so common among women in the United States that 25 years ago it was referred to as a normative discontent (Rodin, Silberstein, & Striegel-Moore, 1985). Depending on the population studied, research indicates that up to 80% of women (including those who are deemed to be normal weight or even underweight) report body dissatisfaction; for many females, this negative attitude toward their body starts in elementary school (Kashubeck-West, Saunders, & Coker, 2012). Recent research suggests that women may feel pressure from their social groups to feel dissatisfied with their bodies (Britton, Martz, Bazzini, Curtin, & Lea Shomb, 2006). Thus, women may not only feel dissatisfied with their bodies, they may feel that they *should* be dissatisfied with their bodies (Salk & Engeln-Maddox, 2011).

According to the *Diagnostic and Statistical Manual for Mental Disorders* (DSM-IV-TR; American Psychiatric Association [APA], 2000), the primary characteristics of anorexia nervosa (AN) are (a) a refusal to maintain a minimally normal body weight; (b) an intense fear of gaining weight; and (c) a disturbance in how one's body shape or size is perceived. In addition, women with anorexia are amenorrheic. The primary features of bulimia nervosa (BN) are binge eating, the use of inappropriate compensatory methods to prevent weight gain, and evaluation of the self that is unduly influenced by weight and body shape. For eating disorder symptoms that do not meet the *DSM-IV-TR* criteria for anorexia or bulimia, the Eating Disorders Not Otherwise Specified (EDNOS) category is used. Within the category is a diagnosis that was proposed for further study, binge eating disorder (BED). This disorder is characterized by recurrent episodes of binge eating, extreme distress over the binge eating, and no inappropriate compensatory behaviors. Research on the prevalence of BED suggests that it is more common than AN or BN, with lifetime prevalence estimates from a national comorbidity survey of 3.5% for women and 2.0% for men (Hudson, Hiripi, Pope, & Kessler, 2007).

Feminist Theoretical Perspectives on Body Dissatisfaction and Eating Disorders

Because so many women report body dissatisfaction and because women are about 10 times more likely than men to develop eating disorders (APA, 2000), researchers and theorists have tried to understand why women are at such risk for these problems. Initial sociocultural conceptualizations focused on how women with eating disorders seemed to overvalue size and weight and linked this overvaluation to sociocultural pressures for thinness as a standard of beauty for women in the United States. Thus, a sociocultural understanding of eating disorders and body dissatisfaction has focused upon the pressure to be thin, placed on girls and women, which comes from parents, siblings, peers, dating partners, and, perhaps most importantly, from the mass media (Stice & Shaw, 2002).

A great deal of research has focused upon the relationship between body dissatisfaction and exposure to media (e.g., television, movies, music videos, magazines, and the Internet) that depict women who are thin and attractive. Studies have shown clearly that media exposure and body dissatisfaction are correlated (Smolak 2009); even stronger evidence has been provided by experimental studies. These studies demonstrate that exposure to a barrage of thin, idealized women has the effect of promoting standards for thinness that are unattainable for most women, leaving them with greater levels of body dissatisfaction (Nemeroff et al. 1994). A recent meta-analysis by Grabe, Ward, and Hyde (2008) demonstrated that exposure to mass media images that show the thin-ideal body is related to body image concerns in women. More specifically, greater media exposure was related to stronger internalization of the thin-ideal, greater body dissatisfaction, and a higher frequency of anorexic and bulimic behaviors and attitudes.

Thus, girls and women in our society are confronted regularly with media images that emphasize attractiveness and thinness as necessary attributes of femininity. In addition, girls and women get strong messages from family and friends about the importance of being thin and attractive. In fact, perceived pressure from parents to be thin is believed to be one of the primary factors related to body discontent among adolescents (Ata et al., 2007; Phares et al., 2004). Peers and family members who tease or criticize young women about their weight may also contribute to the development of negative views of their bodies. J. K. Thompson (1992) and Coovert et al. (1988) reported that teasing directly influenced body image disturbance and overall psychological distress in adolescent females. Similarly, Thompson and colleagues (Thompson, 1991; Thompson et al., 1991; Thompson & Psaltis, 1988) and Cash and colleagues (Cash, 1995; Rieves & Cash, 1996) reported that a history of teasing about appearance during adolescence was strongly related to body dissatisfaction in adults. In fact, weight teasing in adolescence was shown to influence a person's self-esteem and body dissatisfaction at a five-year follow-up (Eisenberg et al. 2006). Overall, it is clear that girls are taught at young ages that being thin and attractive is an important part of being female.

Feminist Understandings

For decades, feminist theorists have discussed how women in our society face more pressure than men to be thin and attractive (e.g., Fallon, Katzman, &Wooley, 1994). Rodin et al. (1985) indicated that the female gender role has two central features: the pursuit of beauty and preoccupation with beauty. Thus, to be a real woman, a woman has to be attractive (which includes thinness) *and* focused on her appearance. Fallon (1990) noted that women in many cultures across time have spent their lives attempting to modify their bodies to fit society's notions of what is attractive and acceptable. Importantly, feminist theory *goes beyond* the sociocultural perspective and states that the purpose of these unrealistic body ideals and the gendered emphasis on appearance is to perpetuate gender inequality (Bordo, 1993; Jung, Forbes, & Lee, 2009). Pressuring women to focus on their appearance diverts their attention from developing their competencies and achieving accomplishments. In addition, this focus on appearance leads to exhausting and expensive attempts to fit society's unrealistic standards of appearance, attempts that typically fail (Jung et al.). Thus, women's resources (financial and emotional) are reduced, and their self-confidence is undermined. Wolf (1991) noted that the more success women have had in overcoming barriers to equality in society, the more unrealistic and cruel society's standards of beauty have become. In sum, this feminist perspective has viewed social and cultural influences that promote body dissatisfaction and eating disorders as a method by which society intentionally oppresses women and strengthens patriarchal social structures (Forbes & Jung, 2008).

Objectification theory describes how (via gender role socialization, media exposure, parents and peers) girls and women are taught that their bodies are objects to be looked at, especially with a sexual gaze (Fredrickson & Roberts, 1997; Moradi et al., 2005). When women are viewed primarily as objects of male physical desire (Bartky, 1990), this sexual objectification is posited to have deleterious consequences for the mental health of girls and women (Szymanski, Moffitt, & Carr, 2011). Indeed, sexual objectification of women permeates U.S. society and can be seen in depictions of women in the media, in the high rates of sexual assault, sexual harassment, and rape, and in women's ongoing daily interactions with both women and men (Szymanski et al., 2011). An important consequence is that girls and women internalize this sexual objectification, resulting in self-objectification, the judging and continual monitoring of their bodies to ensure that they are meeting societal standards of attractiveness (Smolak, 2009). Numerous studies have supported the existence of self-objectification and its relation to (a) body image and eating disorders in women (e.g., Augustus-Horvath & Tylka, 2009; Calogero, Davis, & Thompson, 2005; Moradi et al., 2005; Smolak & Murnen, 2008; Tiggemann & Kuring, 2004; Tylka & Hill, 2004); (b) subjective well-being (Breines, Crocker, & Garcia, 2008); (c) self-esteem and life satisfaction (Mercurio & Landry, 2008); (d) cognitive performance (Fredrickson, Roberts, Noll, Quinn, & Twenge, 1998); (e) increased risk for self-harm (Muehlenkamp, Swanson, & Brausch, 2005); (f) greater endorsement of cosmetic surgery (Calogero, Pina, Park, & Rahemtulla, 2010); and (g) a higher rate of psychological distress, such as depression (Calogero & Jost, 2011).

McKinley and Hyde (1996) theorized that women who engage in self-objectification experience three components that make up what they called *objectified body consciousness*. These three components are (a) body shame (belief that one's body does not meet cultural standards); (b) body surveillance (experiencing one's body as an outside observer would experience it); and (c) control beliefs (the ideas that women should be able to achieve cultural standards for beauty by controlling one's appearance, weight, and shape). Lindberg, Hyde, and McKinley (2006) posited that objectified body consciousness develops in girls during puberty. Indeed, data from their study of 10- and 11-year-old children indicated that girls reported greater levels of body surveillance than boys.

Through gender socialization (from parents, peers, and the media), girls are taught to see themselves as sexual objects and are taught that thinness is a critical part of attractiveness and thus an important aspect of the female gender role. Self-objectification and internalization of the thin ideal lead to ongoing body surveillance, body shame, and control beliefs in women, which, in turn, are associated with disordered eating (Smolak, 2009). It is clear that sociocultural forces play a large role in determining how women feel about their bodies. Unfortunately, our culture emphasizes a thin ideal that is not attainable for the vast majority of women. Consequently, the majority of women are dissatisfied with their bodies. This dissatisfaction has consequences for many women; one of the most drastic consequences of a negative body image is the development of eating disorders in some women. Research on body dissatisfaction and eating disorders has established clearly that they are linked (Cash & Deagle, 1997; Nelson & Gidycz, 1993; Williamson et al., 1993; Veron-Guidry et al., 1997), although not everyone with a negative body image develops an eating disorder (Smolak, 2009).

Burns (2004) presented a fascinating exploration of how the language used to describe anorexia and bulimia presents them in hierarchical opposition to each other. Anorexia is glamorized and described in positive terms such as *total control* and *total denial*, terms that can lead to a sense of perfectionism, achievement, success, and pride. Anorexic symptoms, such as dieting and the pursuit of slimness, reflect normal concerns for women; these are considered desirable qualities for women in the dominant culture, especially when paired with low sexual desire (Burns, 2004). On the other hand, bulimia represents a lack of control, someone who is abnormal, disgusting, and shameful. Women with bulimia are often seen as lacking in discipline, immoral, and greedy. More specifically, a link is drawn between bulimia and sexuality, in that women with this eating problem are often characterized as sexually active and promiscuous. Thus, women with bulimia fail at a femininity that values slimness, sexuality structured around male desire, and putting other's needs before one's own. Bulimia is a rejection of ideal femininity (as defined by the dominant culture), whereas anorexia can reflect a valued, traditional femininity (Burns, 2004). Unfortunately, women with eating problems and the therapists who treat them are likely to adhere to such notions. Burns pointed out that these conceptualizations of eating disorders tend to focus on the physical bodies of women, without attention to the meanings of these behaviors in women's lives.

Multicultural Critique

Early feminist approaches focused on the gendered nature of eating disorders (e.g. Fallon et al., 1994), mirroring the almost exclusive focus of feminism on the gender oppression experienced by White women. Over time, numerous calls arose for feminist theory to value *all* women's experiences, not just those of women who were White and middle class. For example, Brown (1991) stated that feminist therapy theory was not complex or diverse. Several writers noted that many feminist theorists and therapists conducted research with and developed theories based on the experiences of White women and then used such research and theories with all women, without regard for their social class, race and ethnicity, sexual orientation, ability status, and other important cultural identities (e.g., Brown, 1994; Enns & Byars-Winston, 2010; Yoder & Kahn, 1993). More recently, the field of feminist theory and therapy has moved to incorporate a more multicultural focus that emphasizes a contextual understanding (Enns & Byars-Winston, 2010). Although feminist therapy still has many challenges related to being truly multicultural, more and more progress is being made.

This movement within feminist theory and therapy, from an exclusive focus on White women's experience to one that decentralizes White women and incorporates a contextual focus on the experience of all women, has been reflected in the literature on body image and eating disorders. Body image disturbance and eating disorders typically were conceptualized (by feminist and non-feminist theorists alike) as the province of White, heterosexual, middle and upper class women. Theoretical models that focused on the beauty ideals of Western culture and the emphasis on thinness contributed to the myth that women of color are immune to eating disorders and body dissatisfaction (Dohm, Brown, Cachelin, & Striegel-Moore, 2010). Not surprisingly, most research in the field of eating disorders and body image has focused primarily on White women, usually college students. If research has included women of color, the focus has often been a comparison of women of color to White women, with an underlying assumption that the experience of White women is the norm or standard to which all other women are to be compared. Alternatively, some work has sought to identify what protects women of color from body dissatisfaction and eating disorders (e.g., Harris, 1994; Kelly et al., 2005; Nishina et al., 2006; Paxton et al., 2006). Unfortunately, women of color, lesbian and bisexual women, and women from impoverished or working class backgrounds are often not perceived by therapists to be at risk for problems with body image and disordered eating (e.g., Dohm et al., 2010). Recently, more attention has been focused on how such groups of women do experience body dissatisfaction and eating disorder problems, contrary to popular belief.

Indeed, research indicates that although White women experience more eating disorders (as defined by the *DSM*) than women of color, levels of disordered eating do not seem to differ across women from different ethnic groups in the United States (Dohm et al., 2010). More specifically, Crago and Shisslak (2003) reported that across empirical studies over a period of 20 years, binge eating was equally common among African American, European American, Hispanic, Asian American, and Native American girls and women. Dieting was reported more frequently by European American women, compared to all other ethnic groups, whereas the use of vomiting, diuretics, and laxatives was either equally as common among girls and women from all ethnic groups or less common for White females than for girls and women in the other ethnic groups. Thus, their findings indicated that women from all ethnic backgrounds show disordered eating and that there are some ethnic differences in the specific types of disordered eating behavior. An important conclusion reached by Crago and Shisslak (2003) was that the meanings women associate with their bodies were dependent on their cultural and social group contexts. Much more research is needed on how women from different cultural groups make meaning of their bodies.

Research on body dissatisfaction among women from different ethnic backgrounds has indicated that no group of women is immune to feelings of body dissatisfaction (Grabe & Hyde, 2006). At the same time, culture clearly plays a role in the definition of standards of beauty (Gilbert, 2003). For example, Striegel-Moore, Schreiber, Pike, Wilfley, and Rodin (1995) proposed that African American standards for beauty incorporate a larger range of sizes than that found in the European American beauty standard, resulting in less pressure about weight and more acceptance of overweight body sizes. Collins

(1990) stated that African American beauty ideals incorporate creativity and uniqueness, freeing women and girls from conforming to a rigid standard of beauty. In a similar fashion, Gil-Kashiwabara (2002) showed that Latin American women who are large and full-bodied are often considered to be healthy and of higher status, suggesting a less narrow definition of beauty than that presented by the European American dominated media (Grabe & Hyde, 2006). However, it is important to remember that all women in the United States are exposed to the dominant culture's beauty standards, and many women from all ethnic backgrounds have internalized these standards of beauty. Indeed, a recent meta-analysis of ethnic differences in body dissatisfaction in samples of women from the United States indicated that White women had higher levels of body dissatisfaction than women of color, but these differences were not large, and all of the women appeared to have some level of body dissatisfaction (Grabe & Hyde, 2006). Such findings reflect the importance of examining within-ethnicity differences in body image and eating disordered behavior, rather than assuming homogeneity within ethnic groups (Gilbert, 2003).

For example, Poran (2006) used focus groups to explore the experiences of Black women college students with regard to whether or not they felt protected by "Black culture" from the negative effects of dominant cultural portrayals of thin, White bodies as the ideal. Rather than feeling protected, these African American women reported feeling vulnerable to social pressures to be slim and felt misrepresented by the media. The participants described a plethora of African American body images in the media that did not reflect the range of body types of African American women living within their communities (i.e., the images were of women who were thin, predominantly light-skinned, had long hair, and displayed European facial features). Thus, these African American women did not feel empowered, but rather felt significant pressure to be thin and to conform to the dominant culture's definitions of beauty.

Patton (2006) stated that it was important to understand African American women's body image challenges within the intersections of race, gender, and class, as all three of these social constructs influence a woman's experience in the world. This perspective is important to take with regard to all women of color. Further, it is important to consider the complexities of women's concerns beyond weight, which can include other body features such as skin tone, hair texture, and facial features (e.g., Falconer & Neville, 2000; Hall, 1995; Patton, 2006). More sophisticated research on body image among subgroups of women is needed (Grabe & Hyde, 2006). Acculturation is another factor that may be important in understanding body image in racial and ethnic minority women (Gordon et al., 2010). Examinations of the relationship of acculturation to body image have resulted in mixed findings, both within and across ethnic groups, and much more research in this area is needed. As Gilbert (2003) stated, research on eating disorders in women of color is in its infancy; we would argue that this is true also with regard to the topic of body dissatisfaction.

Investigations with women in developed and developing countries have revealed that both body dissatisfaction and disordered eating are now worldwide issues (e.g., Nasser, Katzman, & Gordon, 2001). Often, exposure to Western media (with its emphasis on thinness and attractiveness) has been seen as the reason for the emergence of these problems. However, Lee (2004) pointed out that such conceptualizations are simplistic, fail to go beyond paying "lip service to culture" (p. 617), and result in stereotypical conclusions. Lee argued for the examination of eating disorders and body image using research methods that conceptualize culture in deeper ways, such as ethnographic methods. Indeed, the limited work in this area, using qualitative methodology, has shown the importance of research that prioritizes the voices of women within varying cultural contexts (Lee, 2004).

One interesting line of research has investigated the utility of sociocultural and feminist theories in predicting body image and eating disordered behaviors in college women from Korea, China, and the United States. Jung and Forbes (2007) stated that sociocultural theory would predict that college women from the United States would show the highest body dissatisfaction and disordered eating, due to lifelong exposure to Western media, and that college women from China would show the lowest, due to lesser exposure to Western media. In contrast, Jung and Forbes proposed that feminist theory (e.g., Bordo, 1993; Jeffreys, 2005) would argue that in cultures where a marked shift toward gender equality has occurred, there also has been a concomitant increase in sociocultural pressures for thinness (to counter the increased opportunities for women). Feminist theory would support the hypothesis that body dissatisfaction and disordered eating would be higher in the Korean sample of college women, given that Korea has seen the most change in social roles and opportunities for women in the past 20 years, compared to the United States and China. Using measures of body dissatisfaction, dieting behavior, and attitudes, Jung and Forbes found that the Korean women reported greater body dissatisfaction and disordered eating than the U.S. sample, supporting the predictions made by feminist theory. In a follow-up study with middle school students (ages 12–15) in Korea and the United States, Jung et al. (2009) predicted that Korean girls would have the greatest body dissatisfaction and eating disordered behavior. Interestingly, Jung et al. predicted Korean boys would have higher levels of body dissatisfaction than their U.S. counterparts, also because of the dramatic social changes occurring in Korea in the past 20 years. Their results indicated that Korean girls showed the strongest body dissatisfaction and the most disordered eating, followed, in order, by Korean boys, U.S. girls, and U.S. boys. Jung and Forbes noted the importance of including ethnic-specific concerns and more study of appearance standards across cultures in order to more fully understand body dissatisfaction in women from different cultures.

Intersections of Identity

As noted above, the feminist approach to eating disorders began with a primary focus on gender, ignoring other systems of oppression, examining how women's roles in society could result in problematic eating and distorted body images (Katzman & Lee, 1997). This focus emphasized the experience of White, middle class women and ignored issues related to poverty, immigration, racism, and heterosexism. A separate body of work that focused on cross-cultural explorations of eating disorders and body image tended to ignore gender and instead examined factors related to "Westernization" (Katzman & Lee, 1997). Neither approach addressed the ways in which the intersections of systems of oppression might be a factor in how women feel about their bodies and in what kinds of eating behaviors they exhibit. There is a clear need for theory development at the intersections of identity that explores how these multiple identities are related to eating disorders and body image. Importantly, this work has begun, but much more remains to be done.

B. W. Thompson (1992) was an early author who critiqued the research on eating disorders for not including an analysis of how class, race, and sexual oppression relate to the development of eating problems. She described eating problems as coping strategies for women who had experienced trauma related to (a) various forms of oppression, such as sexism, racism, and heterosexism; (b) sexual, physical, and emotional abuse; and (c) poverty and class injuries. Thus, rather than viewing eating problems as issues of appearance, Thompson characterized them as survival strategies. In a related vein, Katzman and Lee (1997) argued that conceptualizing eating disorders, especially the self-starvation of AN, as due solely to the pursuit of thinness and attractiveness masks women's real concerns related to a lack of access to power and ongoing experiences of trauma and oppression. As Thompson noted, conceptualizing eating disorders as appearance-based promotes a notion of femininity as frivolous, vain, and obsessive; such a conceptualization certainly contributed to the notion that working class White women and women of color were not susceptible to eating problems.

Harrington, Crowther, and Shipherd (2010) examined the cultural ideology of the "strong Black woman" (SBW), wherein African American women are seen as inherently resilient and strong, capable of handling all challenges, and as nurturing caretakers of family and community. Harrington et al. (2010) suggested that this cultural imperative may foster shame, low self-esteem, guilt, and depression in African American women who perceive themselves to be falling short of the ideal, and it may foster maladaptive coping strategies in response to trauma. A large body of research has documented significant relationships between the experience of trauma and disordered eating (e.g., Carter, Bewell, Blackmore, & Woodside, 2006; Rayworth, Wise, & Harlow, 2004; Smyth, Heron, Wonderlich, Crosby, & Thompson, 2008). In a sample of African American women, Harrington et al. found that a history of trauma predicted stronger internalization of the SBW, which, in turn, predicted binge eating. In other words, African American women trauma survivors seemed to use binge eating as a means of coping with negative affect related to their traumatic experiences. Thus, the function of binge eating (to regulate or manage negative affect) may be similar for African American and European American women, but the internalization of the SBW may promote binge eating as an acceptable coping strategy that maintains the SBW ideology. Importantly, this culturally specific model of binge eating developed by Harrington et al. (2010) is an example of the type of research needed in the multicultural feminist paradigm. Indeed, it reflects the position of Oyewumi (1999), who called for research that views racism and sexism as forming interlocking oppressions, rather than providing a simple, additive analysis of racism and sexism.

Cummins and Lehman (2007) discussed how eating disorders are often not recognized in ethnic minority individuals, even though the frequency of such problems is steadily increasing in women and men from all cultural backgrounds. Part of the reason for the lack of recognition is that eating disorders have been defined from a White middle class perspective, and individuals from other cultural backgrounds may have different symptoms that are not part of the DSM clinical criteria. Given that different cultures may have different standards of attractiveness and beauty, these different expectations will affect symptom presentation (Cummins & Lehman, 2007). Thus, we need to broaden our understanding of what constitutes an eating disorder, just as we need to broaden our conceptualization of body dissatisfaction.

Katzman and Lee (1997) argued that the eating disorders field should move away from a focus on thinness and fear of fatness (fat phobia) as the defining feature of anorexia to an emphasis on understanding the meaning (both individual and cultural) of food refusal. Some women in the United States and many women in other countries engage in anorexic behavior (food refusal) without experiencing any fear of fatness. Katzman and Lee pointed out that food refusal may be a means for women to gain some control and power in their lives. Limiting the conceptualization of AN to a body image disorder (fear of fatness) or to a Western culture-bound syndrome (a result of sociocultural pressures to be thin and attractive), means that cases in which a person does not experience fat phobia are not considered "real cases" of anorexia. In addition, such a limited conceptualization misses the power dynamics in which women's lives are situated.

A complicating issue is the high-profile war on obesity currently being waged in the United States (e.g., Michelle Obama's fight against childhood obesity) and around the world. As Malson, Clarke, and Finn (2007) noted, the recent construction of obesity as an epidemic and the emphasis on weight-loss strategies as global health care priorities represent a shift in how body weight has been constructed and regulated. Indeed, Malson et al. (2007) noted that the key diagnostic criteria for AN (intense fear of fatness, overvaluing of thinness, insistence on avoidance of fattening foods) have now become health care policy in many nations. Thus, behaviors and values that have been pathologized as anorexic are now indistinguishable from current health care policies for healthy weight management. Such a state of affairs makes it more urgent that we move away from considering eating problems and body dissatisfaction as solely issues related to thinness and appearance. If we conceptualize eating problems and body dissatisfaction as reflective of women's lack of power and control in their lives (Katzman & Lee, 1997; B. W. Thompson, 1992), we broaden the possibilities for how we might effectively prevent and intervene with such problems.

Therapeutic Approaches for Treating Eating Disorders and Body Dissatisfaction

Evidence-Based Approaches

Over the past 25 years, significant progress has been made in the treatment of eating disorders (Wilson, Grilo, & Vitousek, 2007). A range of treatment approaches have been developed, and many others have been suggested as appropriate. Currently, several evidence-based approaches (EBTs) are widely used. These approaches focus on treatment of the individual with the primary goal of therapy directed at cognitive restructuring and behavioral change (Carolan, Bak, Hoppe-Rooney, & Burns-Jager, 2010). Three main types of eating disorders have been the focus of research on treatment: bulimia nervosa, anorexia nervosa, and binge eating disorder.

Manual-based cognitive-behavioral treatment (CBT) continues to be regarded as the treatment of choice for BN (Wilson, 2005). CBT interventions focus on identifying and changing beliefs about food and eating as well as changing unrealistic cognitions that overvalue body shape and weight, as these cognitions are believed to maintain the disordered eating behavior and are at the core of an eating disorder (Carolan et al., 2010; Mitchell, Agras, & Wonderlich, 2007; Wilson et al., 2007). CBT also includes a focus on the development of coping skills for high-risk situations and relapse prevention (Wilson, 2005). CBT is widely recommended in evidence-based treatment guidelines and has received an "A" for the treatment of bulimia from the National Institute for Clinical Excellence (NICE, 2004). NICE is part of the National Health Service for England and Wales and is responsible for developing evidence-based guidelines of best practices for health professionals. Recommendations are granted a grade from A (reflecting strong empirical data) to C (reflecting expert opinion in the absence of strong data). Additionally, CBT has demonstrated efficacy in improving body image distortions in women and for altering negative affect and negative cognitions in the treatment of body dissatisfaction (Hrabosky et al, 2009). Unfortunately, not all individuals with BN get better with CBT. It typically eliminates binging and purging in roughly 30–50% of all BN cases (Wilson et al., 2007). While CBT demonstrates better outcomes than the use of medication and CBT is superior to other psychotherapies in the short term, it still fails to help a large number of individuals (Vanderlinden, 2008; Wilson et al., 2007).

Interpersonal psychotherapy (IPT) has also demonstrated evidence of success in the treatment of BN. IPT was originally developed as a short-term therapy for depression and was adapted for the treatment of BN by Fairburn in 1997. IPT for the treatment of BN is based on the belief that difficulties in interpersonal relationships are thought to contribute to the development and maintenance of the eating disorder. The eating disorder symptoms are not the specific focus, and treatment is longer than CBT (e.g., 8–12 months for IPT vs. 4–5 months for CBT). While IPT has been researched less than CBT in the treatment of BN, there have been comparable outcomes at one-year follow-up after treatment (Fairburn, 1997; Mitchell et al., 2007). The NICE granted IPT the grade of B in the treatment of BN and suggests it as an alternative to CBT (NICE, 2004; Wilson et al., 2007).

In the past 20 years, a very limited number of comparative studies have been completed and published regarding the treatment for anorexia nervosa (Wilson et al., 2007). At this time, AN has remained "impressively resistant to a wide variety of interventions" (Walsh, 2004, p. 6), such that no specific approach can be recommended (Hay et al., 2003). Family systems therapy and psychodynamic therapy both have long histories of application and research in the treatment of AN; however, outcomes have varied. Treatment for AN can involve various settings, such as inpatient, intensive day programs and/or outpatient therapy, and clients may cycle through some or all of these. Treatment requires not only a multidisciplinary team, but also an approach that considers and utilizes multiple therapeutic modalities (Hay et al., 2009). It is possible that the complexity of this disorder, characterized by low frequency rates, a high rate of comorbidity with other psychological distress, the length of treatment, variance in the level of treatment needed, and the common necessity for medical interventions, is a likely contributor to this paucity of research. In a review of the research evidence in the treatment of AN, Fairburn (2005) addressed the difficulty in developing evidence-based treatments with this population and advocated for increased effort directed toward developing and testing different approaches. We think it is also possible that limitations in how AN has been conceptualized might contribute to the lack of effective therapeutic approaches. For example, if AN is viewed primarily as a fear of fatness (Katzman & Lee, 1997), then problems that women face such as oppression, trauma, and powerlessness will not be addressed in treatment, leading to ineffective outcomes.

Binge-eating disorder (BED) has received a fair amount of attention since its definition and inclusion in the appendix of the *DSM-IV* (American Psychiatric Association, 1994). BED has been conceptualized as (a) an inability to regulate or tolerate negative affect; (b) motivated by a desire to avoid negative internal states or to escape awareness of these states; and (c) often triggered by an unwanted stressor (Telch, Agras, & Linehan, 2001; Wilson, 2005). Treatment typically targets the elimination of binging, improvement in mood, and weight reduction for obese individuals (Walsh, 2004). Several treatments for BED have received empirical support, including CBT, IPT, and dialectical behavior therapy (Baer, Fischer, & Huss, 2005). The NICE (2004) granted a grade of A to the strength of evidence supporting CBT for BED. Other therapies, such as feminist, stress reduction, nutritional management, and Gestalt therapies, have been suggested but are seen as lacking an adequate research base (Stein et al, 2001).

The treatments for eating disorders described above have historically been imbedded in the medical or quasi-medical model of psychopathology that, essentially, conceptualizes mental health issues as a flaw or dysfunction within the individual, rather than as a reflection of the individual's experience within the environment. Such a view fails to capture the broad picture of an individual or the complex nature of eating disorders. Thus, much of the work on EBTs for eating disorders has failed to incorporate a contextual focus. No EBTs that we know of incorporate a feminist, multicultural perspective. A wider range of effective treatment choices would provide therapists the ability to individualize their approach to clients, thus increasing the likelihood of successful outcomes.

Promising New Approaches

Many approaches show promise and are in the early stages of demonstrating their effectiveness in the treatment of eating disorders. Several acceptance-based models (considered the third generation of CBT approaches), such as acceptance and commitment therapy (Heffner, Sperry, Eifert, & Detweiler, 2002), dialectical behavioral therapy (Telch et al. 2001; Wisnewkni, Safer, & Chen, 2007), and mindfulness (Baer, 2003), have been suggested in the treatment of eating disorders. Such approaches essentially aim for clients to gain acceptance of their thoughts and emotions rather than asking clients to make changes in them. Vanderlinden (2008) suggested that current CBT approaches may focus too much on the content of thoughts and that some individuals may benefit from this shift. As noted above with regard to EBTs, these newer approaches still operate from an individualistic, medical model focus and do not incorporate a feminist, multicultural view.

Acceptance and commitment therapy (ACT) is a cognitive-behavioral treatment that targets the difficulty many clients have with being present with unpleasant or uncomfortable thoughts, emotions, and feelings and the strategies used to avoid them (Hayes, Strosahl, & Wilson, 1999). ACT does not attempt to change these thoughts, feelings, and emotions, but instead encourages an acceptance of them as separate from the individual having them (i.e., I am not my thoughts) and as simply a part of the process of working toward one's goals (Hayes et al., 1999; Heffner et al., 2002). In working with an anorexic client, Heffner et al. (2002) demonstrated positive results through adaptation of ACT techniques, which typically involve metaphors or imagery, and combined them with family support, rapport, and standard cognitive-behavioral techniques. The authors encouraged further exploration of these techniques and their adaptation for use with the eating disorder population (Heffner et al., 2002).

Dialectical behavior therapy (DBT) is an approach developed to treat borderline personality disorder that specifically targets problems with emotional regulation and teaches skills to better regulate one's emotional experience (Linehan, 1993). Some efficacy has been demonstrated in the treatment of BED with DBT that has been specifically adapted for this population (Telch et al., 2001; Wisniewski et al., 2007). Based on the conceptualization that binge eating involves difficulty with emotional regulation, the binge is viewed as a means to regulate and cope with emotional distress. Telch et al. (2001) hypothesized that the DBT approach may have worked by reducing the urge to eat when upset, rather than directly targeting the negative affect. They suggested also that the identification of differential predictors of binge eating, such as the inability to regulate affect, the intolerance of negative emotions, or the reaction to dietary restraint, would inform the treatment course for individual clients, allowing for a more precise and personalized course of treatment.

Mindfulness is a way of paying attention, in a nonjudgmental way, to one's emotions, cognitions, bodily sensations, and perceptions (Kabat-Zinn, 1990). The most common method of mindfulness training is the mindfulness-based stress reduction program (MBSR; Kabat-Zinn). This treatment approach suggests that as individuals increase their ability to correctly identify physical and emotional sensations, to tolerate negative emotional states, and to decrease involvement with negative thoughts, they will make different decisions when upset. It has been used successfully in the treatment of depression, anxiety, panic, and chronic pain (Baer, 2003). Mindfulness-based cognitive therapy (MBCT) is a manualized program, based on MBSR, that emphasizes mindfulness and acceptance of emotions, and incorporates elements of CBT that help one gain distance from one's thoughts. MBCT has demonstrated efficacy with people with depression and has been applied to a number of other clinical populations, and would appear to be theoretically consistent and useful in treating BED. Kristeller and Hallett (1999) explored the effects of MBCT with binge eating and found significant improvements in participants in both eating and mood. Baer et al. (2005) applied MCBT in a case study of an individual with BED. Results were positive, demonstrating significant reductions in symptoms and an increase in mindfulness and the thoughtful connection of eating with emotions, thoughts, and sensations. While still in the beginning stages of developing evidence of efficacy, MBCT appears to have relevance and promise in the treatment of eating disorders.

Feminist Therapy

Conceptualization and treatment are shaped by how eating disorders, body image, body dissatisfaction, and weight management practices are understood (Malson et al., 2004). Factors such as the overvaluation and focus on shape and weight are at the core of eating disorders for many women (but not all). Given the fact that 90% of people with eating disorders are women (APA, 2000), the application of a feminist frame of understanding to these disorders is particularly relevant. However, there is a paucity of eating disorder treatment studies and manuals for treatment that incorporate feminist tenets (Fairburn, 2008; Garner & Garfinkel, 1997; Hay et al., 2003; Maine, 2009; Stein et al., 2001; Wilson, 2005; Wilson et al., 2007). Additionally, ethnic minorities rarely have been included in the research on the treatment of eating disorders, even though disordered attitudes, thoughts, and behaviors related to eating, shape, and size exist across most ethnic and socioeconomic groups (Stein et al., 2001). Maine pointed out that even though the feminist perspective has long informed clinicians in their practice, research evaluating feminist therapy seems to be ignored and marginalized.

PRINCIPLES OF FEMINIST THERAPY

A major tenet, goal, and technique of feminist therapy is increasing awareness. Through conscious raising and education, women are encouraged to recognize the impact of various forces and expectations on their lives, such as the pressure to be thin or the norm of being dissatisfied with one's body (Salk & Engeln-Maddox, 2011). Women learn to make sense of their experience, to understand how social processes have influenced them, to view their struggles with body image, eating, or self-esteem as an attempt to cope with what they are experiencing, to externalize blame from self onto society when appropriate, and most important, to recognize that they are not alone in their struggles (Brown, Weber, & Ali, 2008; Israeli & Santor, 2000).

Women's psychological health is often linked to the social context of their lives (Israeli & Santor, 2000; Orbach, 1978); therefore, to understand any woman, one must consider her within her context of family, community, and social identities (Barrett, 1998). A basic premise of feminist therapy is that the *personal is political,* meaning that clients and their issues are tied to a larger picture and truly can only be understood within their sociopolitical and cultural context (Enns et al., 1993). Understanding women's relationship with their bodies and with food requires placing these concerns within this larger sociocultural context (Cummins & Lehman, 2007; Gilbert & Kearney, 2006). Therapists need to recognize that for many women, the omnipresent focus on weight, appearance, and food, and the need to control these factors, is directly and strongly connected to their sense of identity and self-worth. Gender is a sociocultural and political construct and is closely tied to power. In our culture, if a woman is attractive (i.e., thin) she is perceived as having more power, as she has demonstrated "control" of her eating and her body. However, this focus and overvaluing of weight and appearance are more oppressive than empowering, and are directly related to lower self-esteem and disordered eating (Smolak, 2009).

Historically, therapists have paid little attention to these issues of gender or power within society, relationships, in families, and within the therapeutic relationship (Evans et al., 2005). "If any one factor is central to women's and girl's development, it would be gender" (Gilbert & Kearney, 2006, p. 232). Therefore, it is essential that gender and power be considered in the conceptualization and treatment of the issues women bring to therapy, such as body image disturbance and eating disorders. Through techniques such as gender and power analyses and psycho-education, feminist therapists are able to help clients identify gender role messages from the past as well as the present, and the oppressive nature of these traditional gender roles is openly addressed. For example, clients are shown how society's pressure on women to focus on their appearance diverts their attention from their competencies and achievements. Beliefs are not labeled as irrational; rather, they are seen as a reflection of how society views or minimizes women (Israeli & Santor, 2000).

Empowerment is another central tenet in feminist therapy. An empowered person can be identified as someone who has a sense of self-worth, self-efficacy, and power or control over her life and body, someone who has experienced righteous anger and is able to use that anger as a motivating force for social change, and someone who values both autonomy and the importance of community (Rogers, Chamberlain, Ellison, & Crean, 1997). Empowerment involves the development of a new belief system, a broader definition of self beyond one's body shape or appearance, and a set of skills to better manage one's life. There can be no true healing of an eating disorder without attending to the relationship between one's self and one's body image (Hutchinson, 1994). This relationship underlies not only a woman's relationship with food, but it is often the foundation of her identity (Hutchinson, 1994). A lack of empowerment is related significantly to body dissatisfaction and eating disorders. Specifically, as one's sense of powerlessness increases, so does the likelihood of disturbances in body image and eating (Peterson, Grippo, & Tantleff-Dunn, 2008). Feeling empowered in one's life is likely to reduce a woman's tendency both to objectify herself and to tie her self-worth to her appearance, which, in turn, may decrease negative body image and eating issues (Peterson et al., 2008). Therefore, therapeutic interventions must go beyond simple symptom reduction. Treatment must deal with negative body image as a shared experience by most women and as a destructive attempt to cope with a culture that is sick (Hutchinson, 1994) and should aim to help clients to see themselves as whole, rather than parts or objects of societal constructs (Carolan et al., 2010).

The therapeutic relationship is a central component in feminist therapy. Minimization of an unequal hierarchy between the therapist and client and the creation of a therapeutic process that is genuinely valuing of women are hallmarks of feminist therapy (Cummins & Lehman, 2007; Israeli & Santor, 2000; Worell & Remer, 2003). The APA's (2006) practice guidelines for treating eating disorders stressed the importance of clinicians developing a relationship with clients that is based on trust and mutual respect. A strong therapeutic alliance can be thought of as the "heart" of therapy (Maine, 2009) and, regardless of strategy or theoretical approach, most therapists readily acknowledge the power of this relationship. However, feminist therapists focus explicitly on fostering an egalitarian relationship with clients and fostering the empowerment of clients (Worell & Remer, 2003).

Developing a therapeutic relationship with clients with eating disorders is particularly important and is a core component of feminist therapy. The circumstances under which these clients enter treatment may differ from the more typical client who readily admits to a problem and seeks help. Eating disorder clients often present at the insistence of others—parents, family members, or medical personnel. The course of therapy is often quite lengthy in treating someone with an eating disorder, and it is important for clients to feel that the therapist is someone with whom they could work over time. The process of change may be frightening for clients if they perceive it to have negative consequences and/or to be inconsistent with core beliefs about the self. For example, treating body image dissatisfaction and eating concerns means educating clients about the insidious nature of the messages they have received regarding their appearance and their worth. Letting go of these long-held beliefs is scary and often very difficult. The therapeutic relationship is a factor in the continuation of therapy and provides insulation against premature termination. In all of these circumstances, the formulation of a strong and safe connection is pivotal (Tagger, 2008).

Integrating Feminist Therapy and Other Approaches

As shown earlier, there is a dire need for the exploration and development of innovative approaches to treat eating disorders. The demonstrated eating behavior is often just the tip of the iceberg in the conceptualization of these complex disorders. Underlying factors of an eating disorder, such as cognitions, emotions, family, race and ethnicity, social class, trauma history, sociopolitical factors, gender, and other cultural variables, are important aspects of the disorder that often go unrecognized Additionally, the limited success of current treatments highlights the complex nature of eating disorders. The need to consider all options available for treatment (Carolan et al., 2010), as well as the development and/or integration of different theories and approaches of treatment, seems reasonable and has been suggested by many (e.g., Mitchell et al., 2007). However, Wilson (2005), in evaluating treatments for BN, cautions against pursuing a "psychotherapy integration" strategy (p. 205) and expresses concern about combining treatments that may not be conceptually and clinically compatible or that may lack an adequate research base. This is a valid and worthy consideration. Rather than attempting to blend CBT with another approach, Tobin (as cited in Wilson, 2005) suggests treating those who do not respond to CBT with some other form of psychotherapy as an alternative, while Fairburn (2008) suggests more intensive CBT treatment rather than an alternate approach.

Importantly, past research has shown that most psychotherapists ascribe to multiple orientations and integrate various relevant aspects of many theories into their practice (Gilbert & Kearney, 2006). In an interesting study, Haas and Clopton (2003) explored the gap between research and practice in treating eating disorders, specifically in the use of CBT. They found that psychotherapy in practice was substantially different from that conducted in research settings. Less than a third of the psychologists in clinical practice reported formal training in EBTs, although most were actually willing to learn about such treatments. Reasons for the gap between research and practice included issues with increased comorbidity in clinical settings, longer treatment, and the need to be more flexible with clients with more severe symptoms. Overall, Haas and Clopton (2003) called for more treatment studies to address the needs of those individuals who do not respond to CBT.

Thus, there is a split in views on how to approach the treatment of eating disorders, with some authors advocating for use of CBT only and others pushing for more integration of therapeutic approaches. The lack of attention to feminist therapeutic approaches is apparent. Given the widespread nature of body dissatisfaction in women and the fact that women are the primary sufferers of eating disorders, inclusion of a feminist framework seems critical. This framework needs to be a broad, multicultural perspective that examines how issues of power, privilege, and oppression are factors involved in women's body dissatisfaction and disordered eating, and that uses this understanding to develop treatment approaches. Feminist therapy has values and principles that can be integrated easily with other theoretical approaches, and feminist therapy allows the clinician to utilize a variety of techniques that are appropriate for a client's needs. Feminist therapy also has particular relevance in the treatment of eating disorders. Researchers have suggested that a collaboration and integration that utilizes key aspects of individual and family systems, the best aspects of CBT, psycho-education, and feminist therapy would provide a holistic, efficient, and empowering experience for the client with an eating disorder (Carolan et al., 2010; Dorian, 2001).

An example of such integration was proposed by Brown et al. (2008). They hypothesized that traditional treatments of eating disorders may actually perpetuate women's overvaluing of weight and size by their focus on these self-management factors in treatment and suggested the combination of feminist and narrative therapy as an alternative approach. Narrative therapy posits that people organize and give meaning to their experiences through stories (White & Epston, 1990). These stories can be changed or modified, thus producing an alternate, more helpful story of one's identity or "truth." In this integration, discussion of conformity and resistance to gender scripts of self-regulation is combined with narrative therapy. A woman with an eating disorder is encouraged to see the context for the development and maintenance of her eating disorder, and to reconceptualize or externalize her eating disorder, leading to the development of a more preferred view of herself. Additionally, the therapist's power is minimized, fostering the empowerment of the client through developing her ability to write her own "story." This integration is an example of how feminist principles could be used in developing a wider range of treatment options.

In order to address the concern for maintaining the integrity of a particular treatment, Worell and Remer (2003) suggested five steps to synthesize feminist ideals into an existing theory. These steps include (a) identifying any sources of bias; (b) restructuring or eliminating components of the theory that were found to be biased; (c) determining the viability of the theory with these changes; (d) assessing the compatibility of the revised theory with feminist criteria; and (e) highlighting feminist components of the theory. Worell and Remer (2003) noted that some theories are more conducive to integration with feminist principles than others. McKay, Hill, Freedman and Enright (2007) used this model to combine forgiveness theory and therapy with feminist ideals. The integration of these two theories is particularly interesting and a good example of how different theories thought to be incompatible can be effectively combined. Historically, feminists have criticized forgiveness theory on the belief that it may reinforce unhealthy gender expectations, such as pressure on women to resolve conflict in relationships, and overpathologize or prevent the processing of a woman's anger (Lamb, 2002). However, through the use of Worell and Remer's (2003) integration process, the two models were found to be quite compatible. In working with eating disorder clients, the integrated theory of feminism and forgiveness allows therapists and clients to not only identify the negative messages received about their appearance from society or specific individuals, but to process and release their anger, to understand how they have been harmed by these expectations, to find meaning in the process and, ultimately, to realize a new purpose in life.

Using Worell and Remer's (2003) integration model could be very beneficial with some of the newer approaches, such as ACT and mindfulness, that are being used with eating disorders in an attempt to incorporate this important feminist lens with strategies that show promise. Additionally and importantly, researchers and practitioners alike must develop and maintain cultural competency in working with women of color who struggle with eating disorders. If using EBTs, they should be balanced with clinical flexibility and individualism, as well as with cultural adaptations and accommodations (Cummins & Lehman, 2007; Smart, 2010). As the need for effective treatments for eating disorders is dire and a culturally informed feminist framework is clearly relevant, an integration of EBTs with feminist multicultural therapy is worthy of exploration and research on its effectiveness.

Prevention

Given that eating disorders are associated with significant medical complications and psychological effects, preventive measures are warranted. Currently, less than a third of women with eating disorders receive treatment (Fairburn, Cooper, Doll, Norman, & O'Connor, 2000), so strategies to insulate young women against negative cultural influences, and to interrupt the progression of disordered eating behavior as early as possible, are vital (Mussell, Binford, & Fulkerson, 2000).

In a meta-analytic review, Stice and Shaw (2004) reported that prevention programs have come in three waves. The first wave was an attempt to provide education about eating disorders to all available adolescents, in the hope that by learning of the negative effects, teens would be deterred from starting the behaviors. These initial efforts were not successful (Perez, Becker, & Ramirez, 2010; Stice & Shaw, 2004). The second wave targeted all adolescents as well and highlighted the strong sociocultural pressures for thinness in the United States, thus offering support for young women to resist this pressure while also promoting healthy weight management behaviors. These efforts showed somewhat more success, as they went beyond simply providing information and offered strategies to combat negative social forces. However, there was still room for improvement and a need for more specific and effective preventive measures. The third wave of prevention programs has targeted individuals considered to be high risk, such as those with warning signs of eating disorders or mild symptoms. These interventions have gone beyond psycho-education, are interactive in nature, and have focused on risk factors shown to be predictive of eating disorders (e.g., body dissatisfaction).

Teaching adolescents who are at risk for the development of eating disorders about exercise, nutrition, and how to resist sociocultural pressures with regard to thinness and attractiveness has been shown to decrease thin-ideal internalization and negative body image (Stice, Shaw, & Marti, 2007). For younger children (typically ages 4–7), universal prevention programs that teach about healthy eating, respect for differences (e.g., in size, interests, talents), and the importance of being active have been shown to be helpful (Levine & Smolak, 2009). Overall, the data suggest that universal prevention programs for younger children and targeted prevention programs for high-risk individuals (especially female adolescents) are very promising avenues in the prevention of body dissatisfaction and disordered eating.

Effective prevention requires a comprehensive conceptualization of eating disorders. However, Stice and Shaw (2004) pointed out that the design of many prevention efforts have not been based on etiologic models of eating disorders. For example, the first wave of interventions focused initially on providing information about eating disorders; however, lack of information is not a risk factor for the development of an eating disorder (Stice & Shaw, 2004). Mussell, Binford, and Fulkerson (2000) reviewed risk factors and prevention for eating disorders and stressed the importance of considering the sociocultural context in which body image dissatisfaction and eating disorders develop. In a similar vein, Stice and Shaw (2004) suggested that interventions should focus on reducing specific risk factors (e.g., glorification of thinness) and, at the same time, should strengthen preventive factors.

Currently, there is growing support for a dissonance-based prevention program, in which young women are taught to critique the messages espoused for women in our society, such as the drive for thinness (Perez et al., 2010; Stice, Marti, Rohde, & Shaw, 2011). This process theoretically creates cognitive dissonance, thus causing a domino effect—reducing the internalization of the thin-ideal, in turn, reduces body dissatisfaction, weight control efforts, and negative affect, thereby reducing symptoms of eating disorders (Stice et al., 2011). Research on dissonance-based programs shows reductions in body dissatisfaction, internalization of the thin-ideal, dietary restraint, bulimic behaviors, and the use of media as a viable source of information regarding beauty (Perez et al., 2010). Such programs reflect the dominant cultural pressures regarding thinness and attractiveness and may need to be modified to be effective with women of color, lesbian and bisexual women, working class women, and so on.

Although prevention methods have not specifically taken a feminist approach, the current approaches are consistent with the principles of feminist multicultural theory, and we urge more direct inclusion of this perspective. Initial efforts in prevention focused on increasing awareness about eating disorders; however, with time, programs have refined their focus by incorporating and confronting the sociocultural pressures placed on women. By attacking media messages, challenging the internalization of the thin-ideal, pointing out gender inequality, educating about power dynamics and differentials, and combating women's shame for their bodies (Stice & Shaw, 2004), prevention programs are encouraging women to have their own thoughts about what is attractive and important, rather than accepting the dictates of society, thus building a sense of empowerment. When sociocultural messages for all women are challenged on a larger, societal level, real systemic change in how women view their bodies and their relationships with food may occur.

Feminist Attitudes, Body Dissatisfaction, and Eating Disordered Behavior

A question of interest to feminist researchers over the decades (e.g., Guille & Chrisler, 1999; Sabik & Tylka, 2006) has been whether feminist attitudes serve to protect women from body dissatisfaction and eating disorders. If feminist attitudes are protective, then prevention programs could be developed that encouraged feminist beliefs in girls and women, thus preventing future body dissatisfaction and eating disorders. Research in this area has been somewhat supportive of this notion. For example, Sabik and Tylka (2006) examined whether feminist identity styles acted as a moderator of the relationship between experiencing sexist events and disordered eating in a sample of college women that was primarily European American. Their results indicated that feminist identity styles reflective of greater feminist attitudes moderated the relations between perceived sexist events and problems with eating. More specifically, for women who did not endorse feminist identity attitudes, both recent sexist events and lifetime sexist events predicted higher disordered eating scores. For women who scored high on feminist identity, there was no relation between perceived sexist events and disordered eating.

Using meta-analytic techniques, Murnen and Smolak (2009) examined the association between feminist identity and body image in 26 studies (most samples were from North America and comprised European American women). The results indicated that there was a significant, positive relationship between feminist identity and body attitudes, and that this relationship was strongest for older women, when more purposeful samples (such as women's studies students) were examined, and when the word "feminist" was used in assessing feminist identity. In addition, the effect size was larger when using dissatisfaction with weight and body shame as the body image variables and smaller when using body parts satisfaction as the body image variable. It is important to note that many of the effect sizes were small, suggesting that feminists are not necessarily immune to sociocultural pressures related to body size. However, feminist identity appeared to be related negatively to internalization of the thin ideal, so perhaps feminism helps women to be more critically evaluative of cultural messages related to the importance of thinness.

Given that the majority of participants in the studies used in the Murnen and Smolak (2009) meta-analysis were European American, an important study in this area examined the relations between feminist attitudes and eating problems in African American women. Blue and Berkel (2010) investigated whether feminist identity attitudes and negative affect (a combination of depression and anxiety) predicted eating pathology in a sample of African American college women. The results indicated that negative affect predicted disordered eating, but feminist identity was unrelated to eating disturbance. Clearly, understanding the meaning of feminism to African American women (Collins, 2000) has ramifications for understanding the relations between feminism and body image and disordered eating in African American women. In addition, the findings highlight the critical importance of examining whether measures of feminist identity have validity when used with samples of African American women (Blue & Berkel, 2010). Much more research is needed to examine how feminist identity might operate to protect women from higher levels of body image problems.

Future Directions

This chapter has traced the development of feminist perspectives on the widespread problem of body dissatisfaction in women and the accompanying symptoms of eating disorders. Although the feminist view of eating disorders and body dissatisfaction began from the perspective that gender was the primary source of oppression, the field has moved to a recognition of the importance of understanding intersections of identity and how these may factor into a woman's body image and her risk for an eating disorder. One clear need is for feminist research that focuses on intersections of identity, such as ethnicity, class, and sexual orientation, and that places women at different levels of risk for body dissatisfaction and eating disorders. Research that places women of color, lesbian and bisexual women, women from lower social classes, women who have disabilities, and other marginalized women at the center of focus is critical.

This chapter reflects the lack of research on feminist approaches to therapy with individuals who struggle with body dissatisfaction and eating disordered behavior. In this era in which evidence-based approaches are prioritized by practitioners and insurance companies alike, research that builds a base of empirical support for feminist therapy is critical. Key to this work will be an examination of how feminist therapy approaches can be integrated with other empirically supported approaches (such as CBT and IPT) to achieve change in body dissatisfaction and disordered eating. A necessary part of this research should be a focus on developing treatment approaches that are suited for working with women from particular cultural backgrounds, rather than assuming that all approaches will work with all women.

Finally, a stronger focus on prevention from a feminist perspective is needed. Much of the work on preventing body dissatisfaction and eating disorders has not included an explicit feminist viewpoint. Inclusion of a feminist, multicultural understanding of women's relationships with their bodies and food may lead to more effective means of preventing problems in the first place. At a broader level, changing the social context such that a woman's value is not based on her physical appearance might lead to the development of a society in which women are able to develop their full potential.

Author's Note

Correspondence about this manuscript should be sent to Susan Kashubeck-West, Department of Counseling & Family Therapy, University of Missouri-St. Louis, One University Blvd., St. Louis, MO, 63121–4400 or to SusanKW@umsl.edu.

References

American Psychiatric Association. (1994). *Diagnostic and statistical manual of mental disorders* (4th ed.). Washington, DC: Author.

American Psychiatric Association. (2000). *Diagnostic and statistical manual of mental disorders* (4th ed., Text Revision). Washington, DC: Author.

American Psychiatric Association. (2006). *Practice guidelines for the treatment of patients with eating disorders* (2nd ed.). Washington, DC: Author.

Ata, R. N., Ludden, A. B., & Lally, M. M. (2007). The effects of gender, and family, friend, and media influences on eating behaviors and body image during adolescence. *Journal of Youth and Adolescence, 36*, 1024–1037. doi:10.1007/s10964-006-9159-x

Augustus-Horvath, C. L., & Tylka, T. L. (2009). A test and extension of objectification theory as it predicts disordered eating: Does women's age matter? *Journal of Counseling Psychology, 56*, 253–265. doi:10.1037/a0014637

Baer, R. A. (2003). Mindfulness training as a clinical intervention: A conceptual and empirical review. *Clinical Psychology: Science and Practice, 10,* 125–143. doi:10.1093/clipsy/bpg015

Baer, R. A., Fischer, S., & Huss, D.B. (2005). Mindfulness-based cognitive therapy applied to binge eating: A case study. *Cognitive and Behavioral Practice, 12*, 351–358. doi:10.1093/clipsy/bpg015

Barrett, S. E. (1998). Contextual identity: A model for therapy and social change. *Women and Therapy, 21*(2), 51–64. doi: 10.1300/J015v21n02_04

Bartky, S. L. (1990). *Femininity and domination: Studies in the phenomenology of oppression*. New York: Routledge.

Blue, E. L., & Berkel, L. A. (2010). Feminist identity attitudes, negative affect, and eating pathology in African American college women. *Journal of Black Psychology, 36,* 426–445. doi:10.1177/0095798409353753

Bordo, S. (1993).*Unbearable weight: Feminism, Western culture, and the body.* Berkeley: University of California Press.

Breines, J. G., Crocker, J., & Garcia, J. A. (2008).Self-objectification and well-being in women's daily lives. *Personality and Social Psychology Bulletin, 34*, 583–598. doi: 10.1177/0146167207313727

Britton, L. E., Martz, D. M., Bazzini, D. G., Curtin, L. A., & LeaShomb, A. (2006). Fat talk and self-presentation of body image: Is there a social norm for women to self-degrade? *Body Image, 3*, 247–254. doi: 10.1016/j.bodyim.2006.05.006

Brown, C. G., Weber, S., & Ali, S. (2008). Women's body talk: A feminist narrative approach. *Journal of Systemic Therapies, 27*, 92–104. doi:10.1521/jsyt.2008.27.2.92

Brown, L. S. (1991). Anti-racism as an ethical imperative: An example from feminist therapy. *Ethics and Behavior, 1*, 113–127. doi:10.1207/s15327019eb0102_4

Brown, L. S. (1994). *Subversive dialogues: Theory in feminist therapy*. New York: Basic Books.

Burns, M. (2004). Eating like an ox: Femininity and dualistic constructions of bulimia and anorexia. *Feminism and Psychology, 14*, 269–295. doi:10.1177/0959-353504042182

Calogero, R. M., Davis, W. N., & Thompson, J. K. (2005). The role of self-objectification in the experience of women with eating disorders. *Sex Roles, 52*, 43–50. doi: 10.1007/s11199-005-1192-9

Calogero, R. M., Pina, A., Park, L. E., & Rahemtulla, Z. (2010). Objectification theory predicts college women's attitudes toward cosmetic surgery. *Sex Roles, 63*, 32–41. doi: 10.1007/s11199-010-9759-5

Calogero, R. M., & Jost, J. T. (2011). Self-subjugation among women: Exposure to sexist ideology, self-objectification, and the protective function of the need to avoid closure. *Journal of Personality and Social Psychology, 100*, 211–228. doi: 10.1037/a0021864

Carolan, M., Bak, J., Hoppe-Rooney, T., & Burns-Jager, K. (2010). An integrated feminist approach to disordered eating intervention in a university campus outpatient setting. *Journal of Feminist Family Therapy, 22*, 43–56. doi:10.1080/08952830903453612

Carter, J. C., Bewell, C., Blackmore, E., & Woodside, D. B. (2006). The impact of childhood sexual abuse in anorexia nervosa. *Child Abuse and Neglect, 30*, 257–269. doi:10.1016/j.chiabu.2005.09.004

Cash, T. (1995). Developmental teasing about physical appearence: Retrospective descriptions and relationships with body image. *Social Behavior and Personality, 23*(2), 123–130. doi: 10.2224/sbp.1995.23.2.123

Cash, T. F., & Deagle, E. A. III. (1997). The nature and extent of body-image disturbances in anorexia nervosa and bulimia nervosa: A meta-analysis. *International Journal of Eating Disorders, 22*, 107–125. doi: 10.1002/(SICI)1098-108X(199709)22:2<107::AID-EAT1>3.0.CO;2-J

Collins, P. H. (1990). *Black feminist thought: Knowledge, consciousness, and the politics of empowerment.* New York: Routledge.

Collins, P. H. (2000). *Black feminist thought: Knowledge, consciousness, and the politics of empowerment.* New York: Routledge.

Coovert, D. L., Thompson, J. K., & Kinder, B. N. (1988). Interrelationships among multiple aspects of body image and eating disturbance. *International Journal of Eating Disorders, 7,* 495–502. doi:10.1002/1098-108X(198807)7:4<495::AID-EAT2260070407>3.0.CO;2-A

Crago, M., & Shisslak, C. M. (2003). Ethnic differences in dieting, binge eating, and purging behaviors among American females: A review. *Eating Disorders: The Journal of Treatment and Prevention, 11*(4), 289–304. doi: 10.1080/10640260390242515

Cummins, L. H., & Lehman, J. (2007). Eating disorders and body image concerns in Asian American women: Assessment and treatment from a multicultural and feminist perspective. *Eating Disorders, 15,* 217–230. doi:10.1080/10640260701323474

Dohm, F. A., Brown, M., Cachelin, F. M., & Striegel-Moore, R. H. (2010). Ethnicity, disordered eating, and body image. In H. Landrine & N. F. Russo (Eds.), *Handbook of diversity in feminist psychology* (pp. 285–309). New York: Springer Publishing.

Dorian, B. J. (2001). An integration of feminist and self-psychological approaches to bulimia nervosa. *Eating and Weight Disorders, 6,* 107–114.

Eisenberg, M. E., Neumark-Sztainer, D., Haines, J., & Wall, M. (2006). Weight-teasing and emotional well-being in adolescents: Longitudinal findings from Project EAT. *Journal of Adolescent Health, 38,* 675–683. doi: 10.1016/j.jadohealth.2005.07.002

Enns, C. Z., & Byars-Winston, A. M. (2010). Multicultural feminist therapy. In H. Landrine & N. F. Russo (Eds.), *Handbook of diversity in feminist psychology* (pp. 367–388). New York: Springer Publishing.

Enns, C. Z., Rawlings, E. I., Worell, J., Robinson, D., Gilbert, L. A., Rossman, K. M., & Espin, O. (1993). Twenty years of feminist therapy: From naming biases to implementing multifaceted practice. *The Counseling Psychologist, 21,* 3–87. doi:10.1177/0011000093211001

Evans, K. M., Kincade, E. A., Marbley, A. F., & Seem, S. R. (2005). Feminism and feminist therapy: Lessons from the past and hopes for the future. *Journal of Counseling and Development, 83*(3), 269–277. doi: 10.1002/j.1556-6678.2005.tb00342.x

Fairburn, C. (1997). Interpersonal psychotherapy for bulimia nervosa. In D. Garner and P. Garfinkel (Eds.), *Handbook of treatment for eating disorders* (2nd ed.) (pp. 278–294). New York: The Guilford Press.

Fairburn, C. (2005). Evidence-based treatment of anorexia nervosa. *International Journal of Eating Disorders, 37,* 526–530. doi:10.1002/eat.20112

Fairburn, C. (2008). *Cognitive behavior therapy and eating disorders.* New York: The Guilford Press.

Fairburn, C. G., Cooper, Z., Doll, H. A., Norman, P., & O'Connor, M. (2000). The natural course of bulimia nervosa and binge eating disorder in young women. *Archives of General Psychiatry, 57*(7), 659–665. doi: 10.1001/archpsyc.57.7.659

Falconer, J. W., & Neville, H. A. (2000). African American college women's body image: An examination of body mass, African self-consciousness, and skin color satisfaction. *Psychology of Women Quarterly, 24*(3), 236–243. doi: 10.1111/j.1471-6402.2000.tb00205.x

Fallon, A. (1990). Culture in the mirror: Sociocultural determinants of body image. In T. F. Cash & T. Pruzinsky (Eds.), *Body images: Development, deviance, and change* (pp. 80–109). New York: Guilford Press.

Fallon, P., Katzman, M. A., & Wooley, S. C. (1994). *Feminist perspectives on eating disorders.* New York: Guilford Press.

Forbes, G. B., & Jung, J. (2008). Measures based on sociocultural theory and feminist theory as predictors of multidimensional measures of body dissatisfaction among Korean and U.S. college women. *Journal of Social and Clinical Psychology, 27*(1), 70–103. doi: 10.1521/jscp.2008.27.1.70

Fredrickson, B. L., & Roberts, T. A. (1997). Objectification theory: Toward understanding women's lived experiences and mental health risks. *Psychology of Women Quarterly, 21,* 173–206. doi: 10.1111/j.1471-6402.1997.tb00108.x

Fredrickson, B. L., Roberts, T.-A., Noll, S. M., Quinn, D. M., & Twenge, J. M. (1998). That swimsuit becomes you: Sex differences in self-objectification, restrained eating, and math performance. *Journal of Personality and Social Psychology, 75*(1), 269–284. doi: 10.1037/0022-3514.75.1.269

Garner, D., & Garfinkel, P. (1997). *Handbook of treatment for eating disorders* (2nd ed.). New York: The Guilford Press.

Gilbert, L. A., & Kearney, L. (2006). The psychotherapeutic relationship as a positive and powerful resource for girls and women. In J. Worrell & C. Goodheart (Eds.), *Handbook of girls' and women's psychological health* (pp. 229–241). New York: Oxford University Press.

Gilbert, S. C. (2003). Eating disorders in women of color. *Clinical Psychology: Science and Practice, 10,* 444–455. doi: 10.1093/clipsy/bpg045

Gil-Kashiwabara, E. F. (2002). Body image disturbance and disordered eating in African-American and Latina women. In L. H. Collins, M. R. Dunlap & J. C. Chrisler (Eds.), *Charting a new course for feminist psychology* (pp. 282–306). Westport, CT: Praeger Publishers/Greenwood Publishing Group.

Gordon, K. H., Castro, Y., Sitnikov, L., & Holm-Denoma. J. M. (2010). Cultural body shape ideals and eating disorder symptoms among White, Latina, and Black college women. *Cultural Diversity and Ethnic Minority Psychology, 16,* 135–143. doi:10.1037/a0018671

Grabe, S., & Hyde, J. S. (2006). Ethnicity and body dissatisfaction among women in the United States: A meta-analysis. *Psychological Bulletin, 132*(4), 622–640. doi: 10.1037/0033-2909.132.4.622

Grabe, S., Ward, L. M., & Shibley, H. J. (2008). The role of the media in body image concerns among women: A meta-analysis of experimental and correlational studies. *Psychological Bulletin, 134,* 460–476. doi: 10.1037/0033-2909.134.3.460

Guille, C., & Chrisler, J. C. (1999). Does feminism serve a protective function against eating disorders? *Journal of Lesbian Studies, 3,* 141–148. doi:10.1300/J155v03n04_18

Haas, H. L., &Clopton, J. R. (2003). Comparing clinical and research treatments in eating disorders. *International Journal of Eating Disorders, 33,* 412–420. doi:10.1002/eat.10156

Hall, C. C. I. (1995). Asian eyes: Body image and eating disorders of Asian and Asian American women. *Eating Disorders: The Journal of Treatment and Prevention, 3,* 8–19. doi:10.1080/10640269508249141

Harrington, E. F., Crowther, J. H., & Shipherd, J. C. (2010). Trauma, binge eating, and the "Strong Black Woman."

Journal of Consulting and Clinical Psychology, 78, 469–479. doi:10.1037/a0019174
Harris, S. M. (1994). Racial differences in predictors of women's body image attitudes. *Women and Health, 2*, 89–104. doi: 10.1300/J013v21n04_06
Hay, P., Bacaltchuk, J., Byrnes, R.T., Claudino, A.M., Ekmejian, A.A. & Yong, P.Y. (2003). Individual psychotherapy in the outpatient treatment of adults with anorexia nervosa. *The Cochran Database of Systemic Reviews. Issue 4*. Art. No.: CD003909. doi:10.1002/14651858.CD003909
Hayes, S. C., Strosahl, K. D., & Wilson, K. G. (1999). *Acceptance and commitment therapy: An experiential approach to behavior change*. New York: The Guilford Press.
Heffner, M., Sperry, J., Eifert, G.H., & Detweiler, M. (2002). Acceptance and commitment therapy in the treatment of an adolescent female with anorexia nervosa: A case example. *Cognitive and Behavioral Practice, 9*, 232–236. doi:10.1016/S1077-7229(02)80053-0
Hrabosky, J. I., Cash, T. F., Veale, D., Neziroglu, F., Soll, E. A., Garner, D., Strachen-Kinser, M., Bakke, B., Clauss, L. J., & Phillips, K. A. (2009). Multidimensional body image comparisons among patients with eating disorders, body dysmorphic disorder, and clinical controls: A multisite study. *Body Image, 6*, 155–163. doi:10.1016/j.bodyim.2009.03.001
Hudson, J. I., Hiripi, E., Pope, H. G., & Kessler, R. C. (2007).The prevalence and correlates of eating disorders in the National Comorbidity Survey Replication. *Biological Psychiatry, 61*, 348–358. doi:10.1016/j.biopsych.2006.03.040
Hutchinson, M. (1994).Imagining ourselves whole: A feminist approach to treating body image disorders. In P. Fallon, M. Katzman & S. Wooley (Eds.), *Feminist perspectives on eating disorders* (pp. 152–170). New York: The Guilford Press.
Israeli, A.L., & Santor, D. A. (2000). Reviewing effective components of feminist therapy. *Counseling Quarterly, 13*, 233–247.
Jeffreys, S. (2005). *Beauty and misogyny: Harmful cultural practices of the West.* New York: Routledge.
Jung, J., & Forbes, G. B. (2007). Body dissatisfaction and disordered eating among college women in China, South Korea, and the United States: Contrasting predictions from sociocultural and feminist theories. *Psychology of Women Quarterly, 31*(4), 381–393. doi: 10.1111/j.1471-6402.2007.00387.x
Jung, J., Forbes, G. B., & Lee, Y.-J. (2009). Body dissatisfaction and disordered eating among early adolescents from Korea and the US. *Sex Roles, 61*(1–2), 42–54. doi: 10.1007/s11199-009-9609-5
Kabat-Zinn, J. (1990). *Full catastrophe living: Using the wisdom of your body and mind to face stress, pain and illness.* New York: Delta.
Kashubeck-West, S., & Mintz, L. B. (2001). Eating disorders in women: Etiology, assessment, and treatment. *The Counseling Psychologist, 29*, 627–634. doi:10.1177/0011000001295001
Kashubeck-West, S., Saunders, K. J., & Coker, A. (2012). Body image. In K. L. Goodheart, J. Clopton, & J. J. Robert-Mccomb (Eds.), *Eating disorders in women and children: Prevention, stress management, and treatment* (2nd ed., pp. 163–180). Boca Raton, FL: CRC Press.
Katzman, M. A., & Lee, S. (1997). Beyond body image: The integration of feminist and transcultural theories in the understanding of self starvation. *International Journal of Eating Disorders, 22*, 385–394.doi:10.1002/(SICI)1098-108X(199712)22:4‹385::AID-EAT3›3.0.CO;2-I
Kelly, A. M., Wall, M., Eisenberg, M. E., Story, M., & Neumark-Sztainer, D. (2005). Adolescent girls with high body satisfaction: Who are they and what can they teach us? *Journal of Adolescent Health, 37*(5), 391–396. doi: 10.1016/j.jadohealth.2004.08.008
Kristeller, J. L. & Hallett, C. B. (1999). An exploratory study of a meditation-based intervention for binge eating disorder. *Journal of Health Psychology, 4*, 357–363. doi:10.1177/135910539900400305
Lamb, S. (2002). Women, abuse and forgiveness: A special case. In S. Lamb & J. G. Murphy (Eds.), *Before forgiveness: Cautionary views of forgiveness in psychotherapy* (pp. 155–171). New York: Oxford University Press.
Lee, S. (2004). Engaging culture: An overdue task for eating disorders research. *Culture, Medicine and Psychiatry, 28*, 617–621. doi:10.1007/s11013-004-1072-8
Levine, M. P., & Smolak, L. (2009). Recent developments and promising directions in the prevention of negative body image and disordered eating in children and adolescents. In L. E. Smolak & J. K. Thompson (Eds.), *Body image, eating disorders, and obesity in youth: Assessment, prevention, and treatment* (2nd ed.) (pp. 215–238). Washington, DC: American Psychological Association.
Lindberg, S. M., Hyde, J. S., & McKinley, N. M. (2006). A measure of objectified body consciousness for preadolescent and adolescent youth. *Psychology of Women Quarterly, 30*(1), 65–76. doi: 10.1111/j.1471-6402.2006.00263.x
Linehan, M.M. (1993). *Cognitive behavioral therapy of borderline personality disorder.* New York, NY: The Guilford Press.
Maine, M. (2009). Beyond the medical model: A feminist frame for eating disorders. In M. Maine, W. Davis, & J. Shure (Eds.), *Effective clinical practice in the treatment of eating disorders: The heart of the matter* (pp. 3–18). New York: Routledge.
Malson, H., Finn, D.M., Treasure, J., Clarke, S. & Anderson, G. (2004). Constructing the eating disordered patient: A discourse analysis of accounts of treatment experiences. *Journal of Community and Applied Social Psychology, 14*, 473–489. doi:10.1002/casp.804
Malson, H., Clarke, S., & Finn, M. (2007). "I don't think that's normal": A reflection on accounts of experiences of treatment for eating disorders. *Feminism and Psychology, 17*, 417–424. doi:10.1177/0959353507083097
McKay, K. M., Hill, M.S., Freedman, S. R., & Enright, R.D. (2007). Towards a feminist empowerment model of forgiveness psychotherapy. *Psychotherapy: Research, Practice and Training, 44*, 14–29.doi:10.1037/0033-3204.44.1.14
McKinley, N. M., & Hyde, J. S. (1996). The Objectified Body Consciousness Scale. *Psychology of Women Quarterly, 20*, 181–215. doi:10.1111/j.1471-6402.1996.tb00467.x
Mercurio, A. E., & Landry, L. J. (2008). Self-objectification and well-being: The impact of self-objectification on women's overall sense of self-worth and life satisfaction. *Sex Roles, 58*(7–8), 458–466. doi: 10.1007/s11199-007-9357-3
Mitchell, J., Agras, S., &Wonderlich, S. (2007). Treatment of bulimia nervosa: Where are we and where are we going? *International Journal of Eating Disorders, 40*, 95–101. doi:10.1002/eat.20343
Moradi, B., Dirks, D., & Matteson, A. V. (2005). Roles of sexual objectification experiences and internalization of standards of beauty in eating disorder symptomatology: A test and extension of objectification theory. *Journal of Counseling Psychology, 52*(3), 420–428. doi: 10.1037/0022-0167.52.3.420
Muehlenkamp, J. J., Swanson, J. D., & Brausch, A. M. (2005). Self-objectification, risk taking, and self-harm in college

women. *Psychology of Women Quarterly, 29*, 24–32. doi: 10.1111/j.1471-6402.2005.00164.x

Mulholland, A. M., & Mintz, L. B. (2001). Prevalence of eating disorders among African American Women. *Journal of Counseling Psychology, 48*, 111–116. doi: 10.1037/0022-0167.48.1.111

Murnen, S. K., & Smolak, L. (2009). Are feminist women protected from body image problems? A meta-analytic review of relevant research. *Sex Roles, 60*, 186–197. doi:10.1007/s11199-008-9523-2

Mussell, M. P., Binford, R. B., & Fulkerson, J. A. (2000). Eating disorders: Summary of risk factors, prevention programming, and prevention research. *The Counseling Psychologist, 28*, 764–796. doi: 10.1177/0011000000286002

Nasser, M., Katzman, M. A., & Gordon, R. A. (2001). *Eating disorders and cultures in transition.* New York: Taylor & Francis.

Nelson, C. L., & Gidycz, C. A. (1993). A comparison of body image perception in bulimics, restrainers, and normal women: An extension of previous findings. *Addictive Behaviors, 18*, 503–509. doi: 10.1016/0306-4603(93)90067-J

Nemeroff, C. J., Stein, R. I., Diehl, N. S., & Smilack, K. M. (1994). From the Cleavers to the Clintons: Role, choices and body orientation as reflected in magazine article content. *International Journal of Eating Disorders, 16*, 167–176. doi:10.1002/1098-108X(199409)16:2<167::AID-EAT2260160208>3.0.CO;2-D

NICE Guidelines. (2004). *Eating disorder guidelines: Core interventions in the treatment and management of anorexia nervosa, bulimia nervosa and related eating disorders.* London: National Institute of Clinical Excellence.

Nishina, A., Ammon, N. Y., Bellmore, A. D., & Graham, S. (2006). Body dissatisfaction and physical development among ethnic minority adolescents. *Journal of Youth and Adolescence, 35*(2), 189–201. doi: 10.1007/s10964-005-9012-7

Orbach, S. (1978). *Fat is a feminist issue.* London: Paddington Press.

Oyewumi, O. (1999). Multiculturalism or multibodism: On the impossible intersections of race and gender in American white feminist and black nationalist discourses. *The Western Journal of Black Studies, 23*, 182–189.

Patton, T. O. (2006). Hey girl, am I more than my hair? African American women and their struggles with beauty, body image, and hair. *National Women's Studies Association Journal, 18*, 24–51.doi:10.1353/nwsa.2006.0037

Paxton, S. J., Eisenberg, M. E., & Neumark-Sztainer, D. (2006). Prospective predictors of body dissatisfaction in adolescent girls and boys: A five-year longitudinal study. *Developmental Psychology, 42*(5), 888–899. doi: 10.1037/0012-1649.42.5.888

Perez, M., Becker, C. B., & Ramirez, A. (2010). Transportability of an empirically supported dissonance-based prevention program for eating disorders. *Body Image, 7*(3), 179–186. doi: 10.1016/j.bodyim.2010.02.006

Peterson, R., Grippo, K. & Tantleff-Dunn, S. (2008). Empowerment and powerlessness: A closer look at the relationship between feminism, body image and eating disturbances. *Sex Roles, 5*, 639–648.doi:10.1007/s11199-007-9377-z

Phares, V., Steinberg, A. R., & Thompson, J. K. (2004). Gender differences in peer and parental influences: Body image disturbance, self-worth, and psychological functioning in preadolescent children. *Journal of Youth and Adolescence, 33*(5), 421–429. doi: 10.1023/b:joyo.0000037634.18749.20

Poran, M. A. (2006). The politics of protection: Body image, social pressures, and the misrepresentation of young Black women. *Sex Roles, 55*, 739–755. doi:10.1007/s11199-006-9129-5

Rayworth, B. B., Wise, L. A., & Harlow, B. L. (2004). Childhood abuse and risk of eating disorders in women.*Epidemiology, 15*, 271–278. doi:10.1097/01.ede.0000120047.07140.9d

Rieves, L., & Cash, T. F. (1996). Social developmental factors and women's body-image attitudes. *Journal of Social Behavior and Personality, 11*, 63–78.

Rodin, J., Silberstein, L. R., & Striegel-Moore, R. H. (1985). Women and weight: A normative discontent. In T. B. Sonderegger (Ed.), *Nebraska symposium on motivation: Psychology and gender* (pp. 267–307). Lincoln: University of Nebraska Press.

Rogers, E., Chamberlain, J., Ellison, M., & Crean, T. (1997). A consumer-constructed scale to measure empowerment among users of mental health services. *Psychiatric Services, 48*, 1042–1047.

Sabik, N. J., & Tylka, T. L. (2006). Do feminist identity styles moderate the relation between perceived sexist events and disordered eating? *Psychology of Women Quarterly, 30*, 77–84. doi:10.1111/j.1471-6402.2006.00264.x

Salk, R. H., & Engeln-Maddox, R. (2011). "If you're fat, then I'm humongous!": Frequency, content, and impact of fat talk among college women. *Psychology of Women Quarterly, 35*, 18–28. doi:10.1177/0361684310384107

Smart, R. (2010). Treating Asian American women with eating disorders: Multicultural competency and empirically supported treatment. *Eating Disorders: The Journal of Treatment and Prevention, 18*, 58–73. doi:10.1080/10640260903439540

Smolak, L., & Murnen, S. K. (2008). Drive for leanness: Assessment and relationship to gender, gender role and objectification. *Body Image, 5*, 251–260. doi: 10.1016/j.bodyim.2008.03.004

Smolak, L. (2009). Risk factors in the development of body image, eating problems, and obesity. In L. E. Smolak & J. K. Thompson (Eds.), *Body image, eating disorders, and obesity in youth: Assessment, prevention, and treatment* (2nd ed.) (pp. 135–155). Washington, DC: American Psychological Association.

Smyth, J. M., Heron, K. E., Wonderlich, S. A., Crosby, R. D., & Thompson, K. M. (2008). The influence of reported trauma and adverse events on eating disturbance in young adults. *International Journal of Eating Disorders, 41*, 195–202. doi:10.1002/eat.20490

Stein, R., Saelens, B., Dounchis, J., Lewczyk, C., Swenson, A., & Wilfely, D. (2001).Treatment of eating disorders in women. The *Counseling Psychologist, 29*, 695–732. doi:10.1177/0011000001295004

Stice, E., Marti, C. N., Rohde, P., & Shaw, H. (2011). Testing mediators hypothesized to account for the effects of a dissonance-based eating disorder prevention program over longer term follow-up. *Journal of Consulting and Clinical Psychology, 79*(3), 398–405. doi: 10.1037/a0023321

Stice, E., & Shaw, H. E. (2002). Role of body dissatisfaction in the onset and maintenance of eating pathology: A synthesis of research findings. *Journal of Psychosomatic Research, 53*, 985–993. doi:10.1016/S0022-3999(02)00488-9

Stice, E., & Shaw, H. (2004). Eating disorder prevention programs: A meta-analytic review. *Psychological Bulletin, 130*, 206–227. doi: 10.1037/0033-2909.130.2.206

Stice, E., Shaw, H., & Marti, C. N. (2007). A meta-analytic review of eating disorder prevention programs: Encouraging findings. *Annual Review of Clinical Psychology, 3*, 207–231. doi:10.1146/annurev.clinpsy.3.022806.091447

Striegel-Moore, R. H., Schreiber, G. B., Pike, K. M., Wilfley, D. E., & Rodin, J. (1995). Drive for thinness in black and white preadolescent girls. *International Journal of Eating Disorders, 18*, 59–69. doi: 10.1002/1098-108X(199507)18:1‹59::AID-EAT2260180107>3.0.CO;2-6

Szymanski, D. M., Moffitt, L. B., & Carr, E. R. (2011). Sexual objectification of women: Advances to theory and research. *The Counseling Psychologist, 39*(1), 6–38. doi: 10.1177/0011000010378402

Tagger, L. (2008). We can do it together. *Perspectives: A Professional Journal of the Renfrew Center Foundation.* Philadelphia, PA: Renfrew Organization.

Telch, C. F., Agras, W. S., & Linehan, M. M. (2001). Dialectical behavior therapy for binge eating disorder. *Journal of Consulting and Clinical Psychology, 69,* 1061–1065. doi:10.1037//0022-006X.69.6.1061

Thompson, B. W. (1992). "A way outa no way": Eating problems among African-American, Latina, and white women. *Gender and Society, 6*, 546–561. doi:10.1177/089124392006004002

Thompson, J. K., & Psaltis, K. (1988). Multiple aspects and correlates of body figure ratings: A replication and extension of Fallon and Rozin (1985). *International Journal of Eating Disorders, 7*, 813–817. doi: 10.1002/1098-108X(198811)7:6‹813::AID-EAT2260070612>3.0.CO;2-4

Thompson, J. K. (1991). Body shape preferences: Effects of instructional protocol and level of eating disturbance. *International Journal of Eating Disorders, 10*, 193–198. doi: 10.1002/1098-108X(199103)10:2‹193::AID-EAT2260100208>3.0.CO;2-M

Thompson, J. K., Fabian, L. J., Moulton, D. O., Dunn, M. F., & Altabe, M. N. (1991). Development and validation of the physical appearance related testing scale. *Journal of Personality Assessment, 56*, 513–521. doi: 10.1207/s15327752jpa5603_12

Thompson, J. K. (1992). Body image: Extent of disturbance, associated features, theoretical models, assessment methodologies, intervention strategies, and a proposal for a new DSM IV diagnostic category—Body Image Disorder. In M. Hersen, R. M. Eisler, & P. M. Miller (Eds.), *Progress in behavior modification* (Vol. 29, pp. 3–54). New York: Sage.

Tiggemann, M., & Kuring, J. K. (2004). The role of body objectification in disordered eating and depressed mood. *British Journal of Clinical Psychology, 43*(3), 299–311. doi: 10.1348/0144665031752925

Tylka, T. L., & Hill, M. S. (2004). Objectification theory as it relates to disordered eating among college women. *Sex Roles, 51*, 719–730. doi: 10.1007/s11199-004-0721-2

Vanderlinden, J. (2008). Many roads lead to Rome: Why does cognitive behavioral therapy remain unsuccessful for many eating disorder patients? *European Eating Disorders Review, 16*, 329–333. doi:10.1002/erv.889

Veron-Guidry, S., Williamson, D. A., & Netemeyer, R. G. (1997). Structural modeling analysis of body dysphoria and eating disorder symptoms in preadolescent girls. *Eating Disorders: The Journal of Treatment and Prevention, 5*(1), 15–27. doi: 10.1080/10640269708249200

Walsh, B. T. (2004). Thefuture of research in eating disorders. *Appetite, 42*, 5–10. doi:10.1016/j.appet.2003.01.001

White, M., & Epston, D. (1990). *Narrative means to therapeutic ends.* New York: Norton.

Williamson, D. A., Cubic, B. A., & Gleaves, D. H. (1993). Equivalence of body image disturbances in anorexia and bulimia nervosa. *Journal of Abnormal Psychology, 102*, 177–180. doi: 10.1037/0021-843X.102.1.177

Wilson, G. T. (2005). Psychological treatment of eating disorders. *Annual Review of Clinical Psychology, 1*, 439–465. doi:10.1146/annurev.clinpsy.1.102803.144250

Wilson, G. T., Grilo, C., & Vitousek, K. (2007). Psychological treatment of eating disorders. *American Psychologist, 62*, 199–216. doi:10.1037/0003-066X.62.3.199

Wisniewski, L., Safer, D., & Chen, E. (2007). Dialectical behavior therapy and eating disorders. In L. Dimeff & K. Koerner (Eds.), *Dialectical behavior therapy in clinical practice: An application across disorders and settings* (pp. 174–221). New York: Guilford Press.

Wolf, N. (1991). *The beauty myth: How images of beauty are used against women.* New York: Morrow.

Worell, J., & Remer, P. (2003). *Feminist perspectives in therapy: Empowering diverse women* (2nd ed.). Hoboken, NJ: John Wiley & Sons.

Yoder, J. D., & Kahn, A. S. (1993). Working toward an inclusive psychology of women. *American Psychologist, 48*(7), 846–850. doi: 10.1037/0003-066x.48.7.846

PART 4

Education, Advocacy, and Social Justice

CHAPTER

22 Feminist, Multicultural, and Social Justice Pedagogies in Counseling Psychology

Ada L. Sinacore, Freda Ginsberg, *and* Anusha Kassan

Abstract

This chapter provides a review of the extant literature on multicultural education and related competencies and pedagogy, feminist theories and pedagogy, and queer pedagogy. In this light, we analyze the literature on the feminist classroom and the challenges that educators experience when employing feminist pedagogy. This discussion is followed by a review of the relationship between multicultural and feminist pedagogies in light of the social justice agenda proposed at the 2001 Houston Counseling Psychology Conference and the challenges of implementing its goals. Lastly, the authors identify future directions and encourage counseling psychologists to build upon the intersections of feminism and multiculturalism to develop a social justice pedagogy for the discipline.

Key Words: Feminist theory, feminist pedagogy, multicultural education, multicultural competencies, social justice

Introduction

In the past 30 years, a number of approaches to multicultural and feminist pedagogy in education and psychology have been proposed. Unfortunately, many of these models have been developed in parallel, with little integration or overlap among them. Central to a number of these pedagogical approaches are the concepts of human rights, equal opportunities, and social justice. These theories seek to inform curricula and assist students in developing a positive orientation toward multiculturalism and building cultural competence. Likewise, educators in counseling and psychology have become concerned with developing appropriate multicultural, feminist, and social justice pedagogies to adequately train students (Crethar, Torres Rivera, & Nash, 2008). Therefore, this chapter provides a brief review of the literature on multicultural education, and competencies, followed by a more in-depth analysis of feminist theories, pedagogies, and the feminist classroom. Next, a review of the relationship between multicultural and feminist pedagogies in light of social justice theory and pedagogy is provided. Finally, recommendations on ways in which one can build upon the intersections of feminism and multiculturalism to develop a social justice pedagogy for the discipline are presented.

Multicultural Education and Counseling: Evolution and Basic Concepts

In order to understand the evolution of feminist and social justice pedagogies, it is necessary to situate this discussion in the literature on multicultural education. As such, in this section the authors provide a brief review of early approaches to multicultural education, followed by a discussion of multicultural counselling competencies.

Early multicultural approaches to education are rooted in liberation pedagogy and were originally developed to educate elementary, secondary, and college students about issues of diversity (Rasheed & Ancis, 2005). These educational approaches were exemplified by Freire's (1973) philosophy, wherein the primary goal of teaching is to help students build a critical consciousness necessary for praxis, or "reflection and action upon the world meant to transform it" (Freire, 1993, p. 51). According to this tradition, the method used to develop praxis is called "problem-posing education," whereby course content is designed in collaboration between teachers and students. Harris Nixon et al. (2010) explained that Freire's critique of traditional education requires the implementation of a transformative pedagogy, critical and creative teaching, and ultimately, societal change. The goal of liberation pedagogy, then, is "second-order change," whereby students not only celebrate difference, but also critique the theoretical assumptions and practices of potentially oppressive and marginalizing professional cultures in which they are embedded (McDowell, Fang, Brownlee, Gomez Young, & Khanna, 2002).

This philosophical shift from traditional pedagogy to one that strives for social change, however, is only realized in protective and supportive teaching communities. Consequently, education aiming at social change and multicultural discussion requires intentionality, honesty, and safety. Therefore, instructors acting as educational catalysts for change must foster a safe and open atmosphere in their classrooms (Harris Nixon et al., 2010; Steele, 2008).

More recent multicultural teaching approaches include the idea that educators must aim to end oppression and achieve social justice in teaching institutions (e.g., Fouad & Arredondo, 2003). For example, the multicultural/social reconstructionist approach to multicultural education is based on this goal and integrates the strengths of a variety of other approaches to multicultural education (Rasheed & Ancis, 2005). Multicultural/social reconstructionist education calls for educational reform and transformation, and the eradication of ethnocentric teaching (Elicker, Thompson, Snell, & O'Malley, 2009). To this end, this approach advocates for a radically changed curriculum and supports education about injustice, inequality, oppression, privilege, and social justice to empower students to become agents for social change (Sue & Sue, 2008).

Though not the primary focus of this chapter, it is also essential to acknowledge the importance of multicultural counseling competencies when discussing the application of multicultural education in the discipline of counseling psychology. Multicultural counseling competencies have been emphasized in the majority of psychology graduate training programs in North America (Mollen, Ridley, & Hill, 2003). To improve multicultural training in psychology, a number of competency models have been proposed, although none emanates entirely from one particular theory. Instead, these frameworks emphasize cultural competence as equated with counselor awareness, knowledge, and skills (Ridley & Kleiner, 2003), and, at times, include the client counselor working relationship (Vinson & Neimeyer, 2000).

Sue and colleagues (1982) were the first to put forth a comprehensive tripartite model of multicultural counseling competencies. In a landmark article published in *The Counseling Psychologist,* these authors proposed that becoming culturally competent entails the development of particular awareness, knowledge, and skills. In this framework, awareness is described as professionals' personal attitudes and beliefs about racial and ethnic minority individuals. Knowledge is defined as understanding individuals' worldviews, having specific information regarding diverse cultural groups, and recognizing sociopolitical influences on human experience. Likewise, skills refer to the ability to deliver culturally appropriate therapeutic interventions.

Ultimately, six divisions of the American Counseling Association (ACES, AADA, AGLBIC, ASCA, ASGW, IAMFC) and three divisions of the American Psychological Association (17, 35, 45) adopted competencies based on Sue et al.'s (1982) original model and later revisions (Sue, Arredondo, & McDavis, 1992; Sue, 2001) as guidelines for counselor training, service delivery, and research activity (Sue & Sue, 2008). Many other models of multicultural counseling competence have, for the most part, been extensions of this tripartite model. Each contributes to the understanding of the complex construct of cultural competency (Mollen et al., 2003; Parham 2002) and aims to train individuals to deliver culturally sensitive services to clients of diverse backgrounds.

A pedagogy of multiculturalism is based on the main theories of multicultural education and multicultural counseling competencies. The concepts shared by these two bodies of theory are power, discrimination, worldview, racial/ethnic identity, and acculturation. Power has been described as the ability to control, influence, and have authority over others. The attainment of power by the dominant groups within a society often leads to the oppression and unfair treatment of various minority groups (Buckley & Gabrielle Foldy, 2010). Additionally, discrimination has been described as the act of perceiving differences, similarities, and distinctions among individuals or groups. This action typically leads to favoritism and one-sided perspectives used to define the realities of minority groups within a particular culture (Swim, Cohen, & Hyers, 1998). Hence, educators must attend to power and discrimination in the classroom so as not to reproduce the discriminatory power dynamics that exist in the broader society.

Worldview, another important concept, pertains to the manner in which individuals perceive, experience, and interpret the world, including the beliefs, values, and assumptions that they hold about the world (Dana, 1993). The worldview that is privileged in the traditional classroom typically reflects that of the majority culture and thereby sets a standard of comparison whereby minority group worldviews are often pathologized, rather than understood and accepted (Vázquez & García-Vázquez, 2003). As such, to counter the broader academic and social reality, the multicultural classroom needs to incorporate and value a diversity of worldviews.

Starting in the early 1970s, models of racial/ethnic identity development (e.g., Atkinson, Morten, & Sue, 1983; Cross, 1971; Helms, 1990) were put forth to describe the cultural identity development of minority groups growing up in a predominantly Caucasian society (Reynolds & Pope, 1991). Within all of these models, the point of reference in describing "the process of growth" is based on minorities' interactions with the majority culture (Vázquez & García-Vázquez, 2003). Since the inception of these models, there has been a move away from conceptualizations exploring the development of single identities and a move toward a consideration of the role of multiple identities (e.g., Fukuyama & Ferguson, 2000). Within the multicultural classroom, these models serve to sensitize students to the complex and challenging process of racial/ethnic or multiple identity development.

Finally, acculturation has historically been used to describe the process by which immigrants adapt to the majority culture of a new country (Berry, Trimble, & Olmedo, 1986). In the early 1990s, the concept of acculturation was extended to include the experiences of minority populations in educational, occupational, and cultural systems in a society (LaFromboise, Coleman, & Gerton, 1993). In recent years, research has examined the central role that educational institutions play in the cultural transitioning experiences of immigrants and ethnic minority populations. (e.g., Sinacore, Mikhail, Kassan, & Lerner, 2009). Therefore, the experiences of acculturation (Vázquez & García-Vázquez, 2003) and cultural transitioning (Sinacore et al., 2009) need to be integrated into the multicultural classroom.

In sum, the literature on multicultural education and counseling competencies highlight the importance of attending to students' experiences of diversity, both inside and outside the classroom. These literatures highlight the importance of understanding cultural context and identities and the social political implications of culture within the classroom. Moreover, these approaches emphasize the importance of being cognizant of both how and what we teach about diversity, power and privilege. Similarly, the following section will explore the feminist pedagogy literature and how it attends to these issues in the classroom.

Feminist Pedagogy

Feminist scholars have played an important role in the development of pedagogy (Enns & Forrest, 2005; Forrest & Rosenberg, 1997), offering a critique of traditional educational practices and exploring the role of patriarchy within the psychology curriculum (e.g. Lewis, 1993; Luke & Gore, 1992). The core tenet of feminist education calls for a transformation of the traditional curriculum and the creation of teaching and learning experiences that challenge the status quo (Forrest & Rosenberg, 1997). These curricular changes include balancing and integrating educational dichotomies, rethinking the role of authority and power in the classroom, creating communal classrooms, respecting diversity within the classroom, exploring different forms of knowledge including personal experiences, as well as incorporating social action into teaching (Valle, 2002; Forrest & Rosenberg, 1997). As such, feminist educators ask alternative questions regarding the human experience and seek differential conceptualizations to guide teaching and learning (Forrest & Rosenberg, 1997). A variety of schools of feminism have emerged over the years, each putting forth unique ideas about the concepts of power, oppression, privilege, and social action. Accordingly, each school of feminism offers different pedagogical models and related tools. In the following sections, the authors provide a brief review of second wave, diversity, postmodern, third wave, global and lesbian feminisms, and queer theory, as well as their respective pedagogical approaches.

Second Wave Feminisms

Second wave feminism, which informed many of the early statements about feminist pedagogy that were written during the 1970s and 1980s, included liberal, cultural, socialist, and radical feminisms (Enns & Sinacore, 2005). Liberal feminist theory postulates that oppression is the result of gender role socialization and sexism within society and emphasizes that women should be entitled to the same civil rights and economic opportunities as men. As such, liberal feminists have promoted the ideas of human dignity, equality, self-fulfillment, and autonomy, while reforming legal and political systems that limit individual freedom (e.g., Jaggar, 1983).

Pedagogy based on liberal feminist theory aims to help women access educational resources and institutional structures, contend with prejudiced attitudes, and overcome socialization experiences that limit aspirations (Acker, 1994). Liberal feminist pedagogy calls for educational reform and advocates for gender-neutral policies, affirmative action, and gender role flexibility. In addition, liberal feminist pedagogy employs cooperative learning, skill and self-esteem development, gender-fair teaching, and support for student success in non-traditional areas of study (Enns & Sinacore, 2005).

Likewise, socialist feminist theories, which suggest that oppression is embedded in hierarchical institutional structures, focus on multiple oppressions related to the cultural variables of class, race, and gender, among others. Additionally, socialist feminists see social action as an essential feminist activity and that the realization of human potential can only be achieved through the restructuring of the personal and public experiences of men and women (Donovan, 2000). Consequently, to create change and achieve learning, socialist feminist pedagogy purports that it is imperative to challenge institutional structures that reinforce classism, racism, and sexism. Thus, socialist feminist pedagogy involves consciousness-raising, examination of hidden assumptions, and challenging educational and social structures that reproduce inequalities.

Alternatively, cultural feminist theory highlights the unique qualities of women as well as the importance of intuitive and non-rational aspects of human experience (Freedman, 2002). Cultural feminists state that oppression is caused by the devaluation of "women's ways of knowing" (Belenky, Clinchy, Goldberger, & Tarule, 1986) and relatedness, while overvaluing masculine values. Thus, a pedagogy based on this theory claims that change requires that women's unique types of knowledge be highlighted and their relational strengths valued (Belenky et al., 1986).

In contrast, radical feminist theorists believe that oppression is the direct result of a patriarchal system wherein men have control over women's bodies. Radical feminists believe that women were the first oppressed group, and that women's oppression occurs in all cultures, and is therefore the most widespread of all oppressions. Further, these feminists argue that gender oppression is the most potent and difficult to eradicate (Jaggar & Rothenberg, 1984). A central tenet of radical feminism is that "the personal is political" (Hanisch, 1969), wherein a high value is placed on social action and social change. Additionally, radical feminists value consciousness-raising as the means to bring about women's empowerment, and view group processes as central to increasing awareness and transforming society (Schniedewind, 1987). As such, a pedagogy emerging out of radical feminism would attend to the politics of the classroom, women's empowerment, and social action, and would view the classroom as a vehicle wherein social change can occur by integrating both affective and cognitive learning.

In summary, second wave feminisms have provided the foundation for educational policy reform and affirmative action programs that confront discriminatory institutional practices and increase the educational opportunities for disadvantaged groups. Yet, these theories are not without their limitations, as historically they have largely promoted a White, heterosexual hegemony, while ignoring the challenges of women of color and lesbians. Though these theories have evolved and have attended to many of these critiques, diversity feminist theories emerged to address the problems inherent in second wave feminist conceptualizations.

Diversity Feminisms

Similar to liberation feminist educators, feminists of color and anti-racist feminists argue that education can either contribute to the oppression of others or can serve a "liberatory function" (hooks, 1989). In this light, many people of color have experienced the suppression or eradication of their cultures and have been required to accommodate themselves to dominant colonizing cultures in order to survive. As a result, people of color have experienced victimization, alienation, self-denial, assimilation within the dominant culture, and/or ambivalence about their role in a dominant culture (Comas-Diaz, 1994; Ng, 1995). In response, feminists of color and anti-racist feminists argue that pedagogy and teaching need to be transformative in order to bring about lasting change in oppressed peoples' lives.

Feminists of color and anti-racist feminists call for a pedagogy that is inclusive of multiple voices and encourages women of color and other marginalized groups to hold a central role in the learning environment. The classroom becomes a place where "students engage in political struggle to learn enough and know enough to transform our mutual futures within and without the academy" (Omolade, 1987, p. 39). That is, women of color and anti-racist feminists propose that the feminist classroom includes (a) analysis of multiple oppressions, (b) assessment of access to privilege and power, (c) inclusion of the personal experiences and worldviews of women of color, and (d) activism (Ng, 1995; Sinacore & Enns, 2005a).

Conscientizaçao, or the development of a critical consciousness (Freire, 1973) is a central component of feminist pedagogy for people of color. Through an educational decolonization process, students become aware of how they have internalized the racist and sexist beliefs held by the dominant culture and develop skills to counter these stances. In essence, to address the effects of colonization, teachers and students examine the ways in which people of color, and women in particular, have been marginalized. These educators then use this awareness to propose feminisms and visions of equality that place women of diversity at the center of inquiry (Omolade, 1987).

Feminists of color and anti-racist feminists also argue that an important aspect of deconstructing traditional pedagogies involves examining the learning environment and related power dynamics of the teacher-student relationship, both in and outside the classroom. Educators act as consultants to this learning process rather than as controllers of it, and thereby avoid taking the position of "the all knowing one." Additionally, they explain their pedagogical strategies and are open to criticism. Likewise, the educator opens herself up to being seen as "not knowing," and this deconstructs the power in the classroom (hooks, 1989, 1994; Omolade, 1987). As such, the classroom becomes a democratic community wherein information is shared and students learn to "generalize their life experiences within a community of fellow intellectuals" (Hess, 1995, p. 39). Accordingly, "teachers need to break the dependence that students have on them for the right answers" (Hess, 1995, p.111), and students must contribute to the dialogue.

In this vein, numerous feminist pedagogy scholars state that the classroom comprises a community of knowers (e.g., Clinchy et al., 1985), suggesting that safety in the classroom, wherein all voices can be heard, is important. However, bell hooks (1989, 1994) asserted that this feminist educational premise supports the "politics of domination" by those who are most vocal and argued that students from exploited groups may be afraid to speak. Thus, in this educational tradition, "the goal is to enable all students, not just an assertive few, to feel empowered in a rigorous critical discussion" (hooks, 1989, p. 53). Collins (2000) proposed that individuals who remain quiet in the classroom but have something to say are "cheating" because they are withholding from others. In contrast, Hess (1995) suggested that educators must create a democratic classroom so that the voices of more confident students do not overshadow others.

Moreover, educators employing a women of color and anti-racist pedagogy must attend to the presence of racism, sexism, and other "isms" that exist in their classroom. For example, in certain educational settings, some students believe that people of color and lesbians are no longer marginalized, and that centralizing the voices of these women represents a form of reverse discrimination. A major challenge for educators is helping these students understand that "naming one's position in the world is not the same as erasing others' existence" (Elenes, 2001, p. 697; Ng, 1995). As such, educators applying a women of color and anti-racist pedagogy may have students explore their own cultural identities and social locations that contribute to their own lives, and in so doing, students may begin to understand the value in exploring the lives of people of color (TuSmith, 1989).

Many of these feminist strategies are also consistent with postmodern and positional pedagogies (discussion to follow) that call for constant self-reflective attention to issues of power, position, and difference in the classroom. For example, Elenes' (2001) proposal for a transformative Chicana feminist pedagogy focuses on undoing dualistic and oversimplified thinking and facilitates the exploration of complex analyses of race, class, gender, and sexual orientation, which she calls "intersections at the borderlands." This author believes that one should work with students to forge a "common language through which multiple and even contradictory discourses can be discussed, respected, and understood" (Elenes, 2001, p. 693).

In addition to classroom practices, women of color and anti-racist feminist educators argue that course content needs to be inclusive and pluralistic. When integrating literature about women of color into course content, academicians need to be cognizant of the writer's perspective and resist relying on content about women of color emanating from White women's scholarship (Green & Sanchez-Hucles, 1997). Instead, to ensure that content reflects women of color on their own terms, texts and readings (both academic and autobiographical) should be written by women of color themselves, should be based on culturally sensitive definitions, and should focus on the strengths of women of color (Ginorio & Martinez, 1998).

Postmodern Feminism

In contrast to feminist pedagogies centered on social activism, postmodern feminist pedagogy arose in academic circles as a method for understanding the limitations and changing nature of knowledge. Postmodernism makes clear the fallibility of the inquirer and asserts that all knowledge is subjective and open to interpretation. As such, postmodernism points to the changing nature of reality, while emphasizing differences rather than commonalities and uniformity (Fraser & Nicholoson, 2008).

Additionally, postmodern feminists employ a technique called discourse analysis with the goal of identifying and analyzing dualities (e.g., femininity and masculinity). These binaries are often considered fixed truths yet may cloud one's understanding of a particular object of study (Mills, 1997). The goal of discourse analysis, therefore, is to deconstruct reality and to illustrate how fixed truths are, in fact, socially constructed and situated within hierarchal structures.

Many publications on feminist pedagogy were built upon postmodern positions (e.g., Dipalma & Ferguson, 2006, Luke & Gore, 1992; Maher & Tetreault, 2001; Tisdell, 1998), perhaps because they explore the complex nature of teaching and learning. A postmodern pedagogical perspective reminds us to explore the privileged position of academic feminist scholarship, as well as the influence of power on knowledge production and acquisition. Additionally, the postmodern classroom calls students to analyze their varying and intersecting identities (e.g. race, gender) and how these relate to classroom power dynamics and student-teacher relationships.

Seven interrelated themes are typically linked to postmodern feminist pedagogies, namely: knowledge, voice, safety, empowerment, authority, positionality, and reflexivity (Maher & Tetreault, 2001; Tisdell, 1998). Each of these themes will be discussed below.

The first theme is based on the contention that "knowledge" is situated within systems of power and privilege, requiring consumers of knowledge to identify the context from which information is conveyed and understood. For example, when a professor selects a textbook, it is important for students to understand the theoretical and philosophical frame that guided the professor's selection in order to fully identify the context of their course reading material. Second, the concept of "voice" in postmodern pedagogy challenges educators and students to speak about their experiences of power and privilege, as well as discrimination and oppression. Third, similar to hooks' (1989) critique of classroom safety, postmodern feminist educators state that students from privileged groups are more likely to feel safe than students from marginalized groups. Rather than attempting to guarantee safety, these educators attend to the conditions that are likely to lead to safe or unsafe classrooms. Likewise, the fourth notion of "empowerment" requires educators to review power dynamics in the classroom such that students are able to present alternative and even unpopular points of views. Next, the theme of "authority" suggests that educators need to scrutinize their pedagogical practices and be aware of ways in which they may inadvertently replicate oppressive power dynamics in the classroom (Luke & Gore, 1992; Tisdell, 1998).

A sixth characteristic of postmodern feminist pedagogy is "positionality," whereby people are situated in a variety of continuously changing social networks. The goal of positional pedagogy is for educators and students to develop an awareness of the various contexts in which they experience empowerment or oppression. That is, students and educators must observe the intersections of power, privilege, and identity (e.g., gender, race), and identify how these intersections influence the learning process (Maher & Tetreault, 2001).

Lastly, "reflexivity" is considered an important aspect of the postmodern classroom (Sinacore-Guinn, Blaisure, Justin, Healy, & Brawer, 1998). Initially, feminist scholars used the practice of reflexivity to critically examine and locate themselves in the research process, and later adapted the concept for teaching (Allen & Farnsworth, 1993; Cook & Fonow, 1986; Harding, 1987). Reflexivity, as applied in the postmodern classroom, promotes self-awareness and scholarly accountability by imploring teachers and students to observe and locate themselves as knowers within certain cultural and socio-historical contexts (see Allen & Farnsworth, 1993). In this way, reflexivity helps to prevent the privileging of any one individual's or group's experiences, and requires students to use their personal experience to critique the accepted knowledge in a field and the ways in which this accepted knowledge has influenced them. In other words, by "refusing to let others do your thinking, talking, and naming for you" (Rich, 1979, p. 231), students become involved with class material on cognitive, affective, and experiential levels, thereby linking their personal lives and the social world (Sinacore-Guinn et al., 1998).

Another form of postmodern thought is represented by the social constructionist model (see Bohan, 2002), which has become a dominant perspective within feminist psychology (Gergen, 2001). Within this approach, gender is considered a verb and not a noun. Social constructionist feminist thought suggests that the act of gender is shaped and changed through one's interaction with the environment, and therefore, is neither a permanent nor static set of characteristics. As such, gender "is a pattern of social organization that structures the relations, especially the power relations, between women and men" (Riger, 1992, p. 737). Likewise, social constructivism suggests that other social identities (e.g., class, race, ethnicity, sexual orientation) are continually evolving and are shaped by context and perceptions.

Critics of postmodernism purport that the ontological assumptions embedded in this theory promote a "slide into relativism"; if all truth is socially constructed, it is therefore relative. As a result, no one can ever legitimately claim to create new knowledge (Alcoff, 1988). In contrast, Gergen (2001) explained that postmodernism is not only associated with reconstructive aspects of knowledge, but deconstructive ones as well. Deconstruction is the dissolving of meanings, while construction offers opportunities to create meanings that emphasize how social influences are integral to interactions among persons and communities. Although meanings associated with experiences vary from person to person, phenomena such as racism and sexism actually occur, and are not merely made up or constructed (Bohan, 2002). As such, in the postmodern and social constructionist classroom, the meaning that students ascribe to experience is analyzed, while acknowledging that there is a complex reality that is the basis of activism and social change.

Third Wave and Global Feminisms

Third wave feminisms, which encompass the belief systems of women who defined themselves as feminist in the early 1990s to the present, were built upon the contributions of second wave feminists. Yet, third wave feminists reclaim feminism on their own terms and correct what they perceive as the inflexibilities, mistakes, and distortions of the previous generation. For example, some third wave feminists have critiqued second wave feminists for being inflexible, dogmatic, or too concerned with being politically correct (e.g., Walker, 1995). Additionally, while second wave feminists raised awareness of sexism and other oppressions through consciousness raising, third wave feminists have had to come to terms with backlash and negative descriptions of feminisms. As such, these generational dynamics and differences between second and third wave feminists are an important consideration in the feminist classroom. Consequently, it is important for these feminist educators to identify ways of discussing generational themes and differences in a manner that demonstrates appreciation and respect (Sinacore & Enns, 2005a).

Because younger feminist women may feel intimidated by the erudite writings of academic feminists, it is important to have a variety of spaces where they can formulate their own feminisms. Specifically, a wide variety of new contexts provides avenues for younger feminists to explore their views on activism, including informal discussion groups, focus groups, Internet chat options, and local "zines" (Rubin & Nemeroff, 2001). In contrast to the consciousness-raising groups of second wave feminists that focused on shared oppression (e.g., civil rights, the women's movement, gay rights, and peace movements), these modern vehicles of discussion emphasize the subjective diversity of feminist views. Chapters on third wave feminist pedagogy, thus, focus on facilitating "cybergrrrl education and virtual feminism" (McCaughey & Burger, 1998), meeting in cyberspace (Rose, 1998), and becoming "webbed women" (Pramaggiore & Hardin, 1998).

As a result, third wave feminisms contribute important knowledge about the complex intersection of historical events and feminisms. In a time of "political correctness," third wave feminists live in a society where opportunities for activism are not readily apparent. That is, the day-to-day experiences of racism, sexism, and heterosexism, as well as the benefits of privilege, are covertly interwoven into the fabric of society. Although equally harmful as the "isms" addressed by second wave feminists, these oppressions are often more difficult to identify and challenge. Hence, third wave feminists catalyze academic feminists, historically the most prolific of theorists, to rethink their work and methods and implore them to be more flexible when defining feminism and activism. Resultantly, third wave feminist pedagogy requires older feminist educators to imagine the world as their students now see it.

While third wave feminists focus predominantly on a North American context, global and transnational feminisms emerged from an effort to examine women's experiences across national boundaries. Specifically, transnational feminists analyze global interdependencies and build feminist coalitions around the world and interconnections among religion, colonialism, nationalism, multinational systems, and gender (see Tong, 1998). Global feminists thus operate from the assumption that the circumstances and experiences of women in one part of the world impact those in other regions (Burn, 2000).

Accordingly, international feminist approaches focus not only on North American ethnic minority group issues, but also on the concerns of people worldwide (Sinha, Guy, & Woollacott, 1999). Educational efforts challenge North American ethnocentrism, Western psychology's version of multicultural concepts, and impart multinational and transnational views. Moreover, transnational feminist education emphasizes the interdependency of the global village, how privileged countries disadvantage less privileged ones, and how Western practices may perpetuate the colonial practices of the past. By being informed about global feminisms, Western feminists can gain insight into the limitations of their own feminism and borrow international strategies to address challenges faced in North America. Coalition building is clearly essential, as global changes in telecommunication, transportation, and economics increasingly link citizens around the world (Kirk & Okazawa-Rey, 2001).

Lesbian Feminism and Queer Pedagogy

Lesbian feminists argue that feminist teaching must be committed to making the invisible visible and, as such, must educate students about social change (Crumpacker & Vander Haegen, 1993). To do so, feminist pedagogy must include the experiences of sexual minorities and be attentive to diversity within this group. Moreover, feminist education must decentralize heterosexuality and examine homophobic oppression.

Lesbian feminists state that the inclusion of lesbian experience in the classroom, ranging from a single lecture to full integration of the topic throughout the course, is the first step to transforming the classroom environment (Rose, 1997). Through the systematic integration of literature and discourse on lesbianism, heterosexuality becomes decentralized in the classroom, and students are required to analyze the differences and similarities among women. For classroom discussion to be truly inclusive, feminist educators address the diversity of heterosexuals and lesbians with regard to age, social class, race, ethnicity, gender identity, and other social positions. This process can become difficult, however, and educators must be willing to address the complexity of multiple identities (Esterberg, 1997; Greene, 1997).

Homophobia, the most extreme form of oppression experienced by sexual minorities, represents "a deadly form of prejudice and discrimination, not merely a phobic reaction" (Crumpacker & Vander Haegen, 1993, p. 65). Thus, an analysis of homophobia is essential to lesbian feminist pedagogy, and educators must address their own homophobia and resistance to addressing lesbian and bisexual women's concerns (Chesler & Zuniga, 1991; Rose, 1997). The first step in addressing homophobia and heterosexism involves defining these constructs to broaden students' perceptions of the role that these phenomena play in the oppression of lesbians and bisexual women (Crumpacker & Vander Haegen, 1993).

Lesbian feminist pedagogy requires educators to address the process of "coming out"; however, they disagree about who should be "out" and when. Many lesbian academics are conflicted about being "out" in academe due to tenure concerns and potential backlash (see Wright, 1998). Nonetheless, radical lesbian feminist theory proposes that coming out is an essential act required to decentralize heterosexuality, and therefore an essential feminist pedagogical undertaking. However, many lesbian academics feel at risk by coming out, and may include lesbian course content but remove personal disclosure from the equation.

As well, feminist heterosexual academics share the belief that self-disclosure and sharing personal narratives are useful tools for deconstructing classroom hierarchies and providing alternative standpoints (Enns, 2004). As a result, heterosexual feminist educators who cover lesbian course content risk being seen as lesbian or bisexual, thereby requiring them to clarify these misperceptions. In addition to their own personal decisions about coming out, feminist educators must be sensitive to students' concerns in this regard and avoid placing pressure on them to come out (Sinacore & Enns, 2005a). Feminist educators should create an atmosphere wherein coming out is possible but not mandatory.

Even though lesbian feminists have articulated an inclusive vision of lesbian identity for the classroom, some argue that this does not go far enough. In other words, pedagogical approaches that merely provide adequate representations of lesbian, gay, and bisexual individuals assume that "with representation comes knowledge, with learning about lesbians and gays comes the realization of the latter's normalcy and finally a happy end to discrimination" (Luhmann, 1998, p. 143). In sum, although educators seek to expand the definition of "normal" in these frameworks, heterosexuality is not necessarily deconstructed and often remains the implicit standard of normal (Britzman, 1995).

Influenced by the social reform movement, queer theory deconstructs the very concept of "normalcy" (Luhmann, 1998, p. 148) by focusing on difference rather than similarity and thereby initiating a dialogue to explore the "infinite proliferation of new identifications" (p. 151). Thus, queer theory requires the rethinking of traditional concepts and definitions, such as identity, psychopathology, gender, and sexuality. Proponents of this theory challenge the status quo, as they believe it is responsible for perpetuating the homophobia and heterosexism found in social systems (Gloria & Pope-Davis, 1997; Tierney, 1997). Thus, while counseling and psychology educators generally acknowledge that the needs of diverse students should be recognized within the curriculum, specific issues pertaining to lesbian, gay, bisexual, and transgender (LGBT) individuals are frequently omitted or ignored (Cannon, 2008). Consequently, the experiences of women, racial/ethnic minorities, people with disabilities, and LGBT individuals have been discounted in counseling and psychology curricula and classrooms (Bieschke & Matthews, 1996). This exclusion is particularly evident for "trans" individuals (Lev, 2004).

Some authors have proposed that queer theory can serve as a unifying framework for diversity training within the fields of counseling and psychology (Frank & Cannon, 2010). Given that most practitioners are insufficiently prepared to work with LGBT clients (Sherry, Whilde, & Patton, 2005) and receive minimal training in this area (Israel & Hackett, 2004), queer theorists argue that queer competencies should be part of the multicultural curricula. With respect to "trans" concerns, there is an even greater lack of understanding in counseling, psychology, educational institutions, and society at large, causing discrimination toward this population to be extremely pervasive (Silvestre & Arrowood, 2006). It is difficult to establish how many trans individuals are actually affected by this level of prejudice, as mixed statistics have been presented with respect to this population. Some sources report percentages as low as 0.3% to 1% of the population at large (Gates, 2011); while others employ a more inclusive definition of the term "trans" and indicate a greater prevalence of 2% to 5% of the population (Gates, 2011; National Council of la Raza, 2002; Rosser, Oakes, Bockting, & Miner, 2007; Van Kesteren et al., 1996). Regardless of the actual percentages, the reality of this prejudice is very disheartening. Hence, it is unacceptable for the educational needs and contributions of this population to be ignored.

According to Gainor (2000), the inclusion of trans issues in counseling psychology cannot be fully realized until broader societal competencies are adopted by the discipline. This situation requires that ingrained systemic ways of viewing sexuality and gender must no longer remain unchallenged. To this end, queer theory can assist educators to confront ethnocentrism and monoculturalism (Sue & Sue, 2008), binary gender systems (Gainor, 2000), as well as trans-phobia and violence (Kirk & Kulkarni, 2006).

Yet, in order to increase the use of queer theory in counseling and psychology, scholars must attend to their own assumptions about LGBT individuals and homophobia (Logan, 1996). If this self-exploration does not occur, educators run the risk of passing along their misconceptions to their students (Logan & Barret, 2005). Moreover, the underrepresentation of LGBT individuals in academia results in these individuals rarely being in positions to influence training programs' curricula and course content (Frank & Cannon, 2010).

In sum, lesbian feminism and queer theory call for a pedagogy that values the diversity of LGBT individuals' voices and the decentralizing of heterosexuality. Accordingly, the classroom can be a place that analyzes both individual and societal heterosexism, homophobia, and transphobia, and that engenders tolerance in the learning environment. Further, queer theorists have argued that the current manifestations of multicultural education perpetuate the historical productions of heterosexuality and homosexuality that regulate power relationships of inequality (Sumara & Davis, 1999). Instead, counseling psychology programs must be revamped to include accurate and realistic multicultural content, including that of LGBT individuals. More specifically, policy makers and scholars in positions of power must advocate for the needs of LGBT individuals and integrate queer theory into counseling psychology training programs.

The Multicultural Feminist Classroom

Feminist pedagogy is recognized as a unique and distinct pedagogy (Forrest & Rosenberg, 1997) with a set of unifying principles linked to a specific set of techniques (Kahn & Ferguson, 2009; Sinacore, Healy, & Justin; 2002). Specifically, techniques associated with feminist teaching include; reflexivity (Sinacore-Guinn, et al., 1998), self-disclosure (hooks, 1994), discourse analysis (Mills, 1997), and journaling (Forrest & Rosenberg, 1997). The common principles of feminist pedagogy include valuing multiple sources of knowledge, attending to diversity, and acknowledging the intersection of multiple identities, while attending to power differentials and reducing hierarchies. Finally, feminist pedagogy is associated with a political standpoint and is transformational.

The first principle, valuing multiple sources of knowing, necessitates that both personal and intellectual sources of knowledge are considered valid and are utilized in classroom settings (Smith-Adcock, Ropers-Huilman, & Choate, 2004). As such, experiential knowledge as well as that derived from research and scholarly reflection are deemed important. Hence, feminist teachers use affective, experiential (Cummings, 1998), and cognitive methods (Sinacore & Boatwright, 2005) to elicit and support students' ways of knowing. In feminist classrooms, students are encouraged to engage in open discourse and share personal stories to compare and contrast the personal with the theoretical. Feminist educators, therefore, encourage their students to critically examine how their lives inform their knowledge and how this knowing is related to broader societal phenomena. To this end, Cummings (1998) suggests alternating discussion groups that focus on scholarship with dialogues that are more experiential in each class session.

Student responses to the inclusion of personal experience in the classroom are mixed, with some indicating that by telling personal stories they give voice to their experience and are heard by their professors. Likewise, some educators have noted that when students are in a classroom where the voicing of personal experiences is encouraged, students may resist shifting gears to the more abstract study of theory. Nonetheless, classrooms that promote students' opportunities to experience the intersection of affective learning with critical scholarly analysis result in students becoming well equipped to understand the social construction of knowledge (Wetzel, 1999; Sinacore & Boatwright, 2005). The second and third unifying principles that adherents of feminist pedagogy incorporate in their educational activities is attention to diversity and multiple intersecting identities. Feminist educators pay particular attention to the ways in which individuals' multiple identities influence educational processes and outcomes (Sinacore et al., 2002). Moreover, feminist educators believe that people experience their social and educational lives differently, depending on their various social locations. In this light, personal identities such as gender, race, social class, disability, and sexual orientation shape social realities and interactions. Specifically, feminist teaching attends to the intersection of various social identities that place students and educators in positions of power and oppression in the classroom (Maher & Tetreault, 2001). As such, feminist teachers pay attention to the implicit (e.g., underlying assumptions) and explicit points of view in their classrooms.

Moreover, educators need to address their own identity and the ways in which it affects their interactions with students' multiple identities in the classroom. Specific attention is paid to the intersection of teacher identity characteristics with those of students. One way that feminist teachers can recognize the contribution of students with diverse identities is by insuring that they have multiple ways to express their knowledge (Smith-Adcock et al., 2004). As well, dialogues that address the intersections of multiple identities between students and teacher are important. To generate productive conversation, Locke and Kiselica (1999) recommended that students be well read on a diversity of topics (e.g. racism, sexism, sexual orientation, disabilities, social class) prior to group discussions. Concomitantly, journaling about the course material allows students to reflect both on reading material as well as classroom experiences, and to process their thoughts and feelings that go unexpressed in group discussions.

According to Sinacore and Boatwright (2005), students' responses to discussions of diversity in the classroom are complex, and are typically presented in terms of their single identity versus the intersection of multiple identities. The predominant areas that have been researched with regard to students' responses to these discussions are gender, commitment to tradition, race and socioeconomic status. With regard to gender, male students often respond with resistance and anger, while females tend to respond through the lens of "male bashing." That is, female students often express concern about how male students are experiencing the feminist classroom (Lewis, 1993). Male responses are further complicated by socioeconomic status (SES) in that White male students from low SES have been reported to become angry at members of minority groups who have benefited from programs like affirmative action (Bell, Morrow, & Tastsoglou, 1999). In contrast, men and women of color typically respond more favorably to the feminist classroom and its interactive nature (Ferguson, 1992). Additionally, students' responses are often filtered through a traditional or non-traditional world view. That is, students who hold more traditional worldviews are less likely to hold a positive view of feminism, and as a result may respond more negatively to the feminist classroom (Sinacore & Boatwright, 2005).

Fourth, feminist pedagogy calls upon educators to pay specific attention to the hierarchies and power differentials between students and teachers. In so doing, feminist educators attend to the ways in which teachers' and students' multiple identities influence power dynamics and interactions in the classroom (Smith-Adcock et al., 2004). Though feminist educators must acknowledge the traditional role expectations of student and teacher, they attempt to influence the complex power structures in the classroom in order to empower students (Cummings, 1998; Hashizume, Greggs, & Cairns, 1994). Thus, feminist pedagogy requires educators to critically examine teacher-student relationships, while simultaneously encouraging students to take an active role in their learning. As such, teachers take on an active role in the cognitive, interpersonal, and affective processes in the classroom.

A technique designed to equalize power and authority in the classroom is self-disclosure (hooks, 1994). Self-disclosure may result in teachers openly acknowledging their own cultural awareness, biases, and prejudices. Shrewsbury (1993) describes a process wherein "both teacher and students engage in the process of thinking, and they talk out what they are thinking in a public dialog" (p. 219). Therefore, applying a feminist pedagogy requires educators to carefully examine their influence on students' processes and thinking while simultaneously attempting to empower them. Although for the most part students have responded favorably to these non-traditional egalitarian approaches to teaching, some perceive feminist instructors as "overly nurturing" (Sinacore & Boatwright, 2005, p. 113) and have demanded that the instructor take back authority (Gardner, Dean, & McKaig, 1989). That is, some students prefer the traditional classroom structure wherein the professor indicates to students what they must learn and how they are to learn it. These students often accuse feminist professors of "not teaching them anything" or that they were not sure what they were "supposed" to learn. Similarly, others find self-disclosure on the part of professors uncomfortable (Sinacore et al., 2002). Finally, multicultural feminist pedagogy is associated with a political standpoint and is transformational (Sinacore & Boatwright, 2005). That is, multicultural feminist pedagogy acknowledges the role of education in social change (e.g., Smith-Adcock et al., 2004). As such, feminist teachers view education as a form of social action and consciousness-raising, with the goal of making a difference in broader society. Consistent with this worldview, feminist pedagogy places value on diversity, respectful conflict, uniqueness, and choice, as well as empowerment through educational activities. Hashizume et al. (1994) suggested that students may be discouraged as a result of addressing racism, sexism, poverty, and discrimination. They proposed that focusing on solutions, however out of reach they might be, can be reassuring to students. The extant empirical and anecdotal literature indicates that student responses to the social action components of feminist pedagogy are predominantly positive in that they have inspired them to get involved in social action (Sinacore & Boatwright, 2005).

Challenges and Barriers to Feminist Pedagogy

Though the feminist classroom is meant to be a place where individuals articulate and explore a diversity of issues, resulting in empowerment and social action, it is not without its challenges. In a study of feminist psychology educators, Sinacore et al. (2002) identified four barriers faced by this group, including managing time demands, managing classroom dynamics, negotiating power differentials between students and professors, and backlash. The participants in this study indicated that feminist teaching required more time than did traditional pedagogical approaches to the classroom, which created a conflict between teaching the content required by the program in a manner that was consistent with a collaborative and exploratory learning environment. Further, managing classroom dynamics in a manner that allowed students to question the validity of feminism as a pedagogical strategy resulted in some students refusing to participate in classroom activities. With regard to negotiating these power differentials, feminist educators reported experiencing conflict between creating a collaborative learning environment where students have a sense of personal power, and their responsibility as educators to manage classroom dynamics and facilitate discussion. Additionally, backlash from both students and colleagues took the forms of lack of collegiality, lack of support, devaluation of feminist course content, and devaluation of the professor.

Despite these challenges, feminist educators have identified a number of benefits to feminist teaching, indicating that congruence between their teaching and their value system and political position is a primary benefit. The second benefit encompasses students' positive responses, such as feelings of empowerment and validation. Other benefits include (a) developing long-term collaborations with former students, (b) challenging and changing the university environment by affecting policies, and (c) receiving teaching awards and positive evaluations from students (Sinacore et al., 2002).

A Call for Social Justice Pedagogy

Presently, there is an emerging interest by many professionals in counseling psychology to articulate a social justice paradigm for the field. In fact, a decade ago, the reality of this phenomenon was revealed by the 88% of the 2001 Houston Counseling Psychology Conference attendees "who voted at a town hall meeting for reclaiming a social advocacy agenda" (Goodman et al., 2004, p. 793). Similarly, the topic of social justice has been given substantial coverage in prominent works such as *The Handbook for Social Justice in Counseling Psychology* (Toporek, Gerstein, Fouad, Roysircar, & Israel, 2006), along with a host of other publications addressing the topic (e.g., Baluch, Pieterse, & Bolden, 2004; Burnes & Manese, 2008; Lewis, 2010; Constantine, Hage, Kindaichi, & Bryant, 2007; Singh, Hofsess, Boyer, Kwong, Lau, & McLain, 2010)

For the most part, however, a reliance on feminist and multicultural analyses has served as the main source of inquiry and practice in the field relating to diversity education. While some authors have argued that feminism and multiculturalism are at the roots of social justice theory (Goodman et al., 2004), the topic of social justice pedagogy has largely remained an ideal in the philosophical margins. As well, most counseling psychology training programs encourage trainers and trainees to consider a rudimentary analysis of gender issues and diversity (Lewis, 2010; Watts, 2004). Moreover, the vast majority of counseling psychology programs employ a stand-alone course on multiculturalism to accomplish the American Psychological Association's (APA) accreditation requirement that states, "The program has and implements a thoughtful and coherent plan to provide students with relevant knowledge and experiences about the role of cultural and individual diversity in psychological phenomena as they relate to the science and practice of professional psychology" (Commission on Accreditation, 2009, p. 10). Thus, despite the growing interest in the topic of social justice in the discipline, counseling psychology has continued to comfortably rely on the status quo.

Although some observers are documenting an increased interest in social justice in the field, the reality of a social justice agenda remains theoretical, rather than one that has been actualized (Ratts, 2006). As a result, it is clear that the actuality of a social justice agenda and its manifestation in counseling psychology are merely in the beginning stages of development. In other words, despite the documented interest in social justice and the growing body of work on the topic, "little discussion has taken place to describe what this actually looks like" (Goodman et al., 2004, p. 793).

For a social justice agenda to take form in counseling psychology, it must move beyond good intentions (Baluch, Pieterse, & Bolden, 2004) and be fully articulated in all realms of the field. In this light, counseling psychologists must conceptualize and embrace a social justice paradigm in the teaching, practice, and research of the discipline. Moreover, despite the emerging interest in social justice by some, it is certainly not a focus and paradigm that all members of the discipline support. For a social justice paradigm to fully take form in counseling psychology, there is a need for widespread discussion on the topic, a process that should aim at ensuring a broader buy-in by those who can bring this goal to fruition. In other words, "The challenge therefore is moving from commitment to an idea to action" (Goodman et al, 2004, p. 793).

There are, however, some noteworthy exceptions to a status quo stance that are evidenced in a few unique counseling training programs for which social justice is one of the main tenets upon which these educational programs are built (see Caldwell & Vera, 2010; Lewis, 2010). It is important to note that, in part, the key to the success of these counseling psychology training programs is that they are housed in very progressive educational settings (e.g., the University of Oregon, Boston College,

Focus of Empowerment

Individual empowerment «---» Social change as well as individual empowerment

Knowledge and the Knower

Reformation of teaching/knowing «----------------------» Transformation of teaching/knowing

Oppression, Privilege, and Social Identity

Single, salient oppression «---» Multiple intersecting identities

Reflexivity and Self-awareness

Awareness of personal attitudes «-----------------------------------» Awareness of systemic power, privilege, & personal values

Figure 22.1 Dimensions/Goals of Multicultural Feminist Pedagogies.

George Mason University) (Talleyrand, Chi-Ying Chung, & Bemak, 2006). Thus, for those educators located in more traditional settings, the goal of fully embracing a social justice agenda and employing a social justice pedagogy is certainly more complex.

Additionally, there are some noteworthy pieces of scholarship that have directly taken on the challenge of moving from the idealized support of social justice in counseling psychology to concrete practice (e.g., Burnes & Singh, 2010; O'Brien, Patel, Hensler-McGinnis & Kaplan, 2006; Toporek & Vaughn, 2010). To support a move toward concrete practice, Sinacore and Enns (2005b) provided an analysis of the commonalities and differences in multicultural and feminist approaches that are relevant to social justice pedagogy. They identified dimensions which focus on features such as pedagogical priorities, or the degree to which an approach emphasizes gender or culture and ethnicity, and the degree to which the approach highlights personal identity or social locations embedded in systems (see figure 22.1).

More specifically, these authors identified four dimensions relevant to social justice pedagogy, including the degree to which an approach emphasizes (a) individual empowerment and/or social change; (b) knowledge as revised frameworks or transformed frameworks; (c) single or multiple oppressions and privileges; and (d) reflexivity and self-awareness that emphasizes self-awareness alone or self-awareness embedded in knowledge of systemic aspects of power and privilege (see figure 22.1). Sinacore and Enns (2005b) believe that approaches that accent the second option relevant to each dimension (depicted on the right side of the figure) tend to hold the greatest promise for supporting social justice goals. In other words, optimal frameworks emphasize combined social and individual change, transformed knowledge and knowers, multiple oppressions and privileges, and self-awareness lodged in awareness of power systems.

With regard to the first dimension of individual empowerment and social change, Sinacore and Enns (2005b) recommend working to facilitate change within individuals, dyads, or small groups while also seeking to transform traditional social and institutional structures. Regarding the second dimension, transformed knowledge (rather than revised knowledge) is acquired by learning from individuals who have been ignored or marginalized in traditional approaches to education. By centralizing previously ignored voices, the psychology curriculum has the potential to both reflect the voices and worldviews of diverse groups and gain new tools for analyzing the role of privilege and oppression. Optimal approaches to the third dimension call educators to deal simultaneously with multiple and intersecting identities, privileges, and oppressions. From this perspective, concepts of power, privilege, and oppression are explored and considered in relation to how their salience can change across time and situations. Finally, the self-reflection and self-awareness dimension involves the exploration of personal biases, assumptions, and attitudes in light of systems of power in which one is embedded and with respect to the subject matter being studied (Sinacore & Enns, 2005b). In conclusion, a social justice pedagogy should draw upon the strengths and pedagogical priorities emanating from the feminist and multicultural theoretical traditions in order to transform the counseling psychology classroom and train future professionals to be agents of social change.

Future Directions

Given the substantial literature that has emerged on the topic, the existence of training programs based on social justice principles, and significant social justice pedagogical resources available to counseling psychology educators, the field has the assets to move forward to adopt a social justice agenda. To do so, however, a number of challenges and barriers must be addressed.

First, according to Speight and Vera (2008), counseling psychology must once and for all centralize the well-being of others, as required by the APA Code of Ethics (American Psychological Association, 2002). That is, the core tenet of a field that aims to improve the lives of others must be re-conceptualized to include a broader definition of well-being, one that includes the societies in which counseling psychology students, clients, and research participants live. To this end, the field of counseling psychology must reconsider its widespread adherence to the scientist-practitioner model and consider one that is founded upon social action, namely a scientist-advocate model (Baker & Benjamin, 2000). Sadly, in a field designed to improve the lives of others, the very model, upon which, the discipline rests serves as a fundamental constraint to the field's ability to fully adopt a social justice agenda and thereby fully help those it serves. That is, the very nature of a scientist-practitioner model, which largely looks at academic theoretical analysis and controlled data collection to inform service delivery does not necessarily require the producers and consumers of psychological knowledge to employ an analytic framework that examines societal injustice. Alternatively, by employing a scientist-advocate approach, counseling psychologists would be required to fully contextualize all matters in their social complexity and seek solutions to problems that extend well beyond the literature, classroom, and counseling center.

In addition to the limitations of the operating zeitgeist of the field, several structural issues also make it challenging for counseling psychologist educators to fully embrace a social justice agenda and pedagogy. In particular, the restraints of tenure and other related academic advancements require teachers of psychology to stay squarely focused on academic activities that will lead to their promotion. That is, the academy itself does not readily reward social action activities when assessing counseling psychologists' contributions to the university. Specifically, tenure reviews rarely take into consideration social action–based projects when calculating a scholar's petition for scholarly advancement. Instead, the number of publications, number of courses taught, number of students graduated, and university service are valued above all. Given this reality, Toporek and McNally (2006) believe that working as a social activist in most counseling psychology environments might ultimately lead to one's "economic self-destruction" (p. 41), whereas employing a more traditional route is more highly rewarded.

Likewise, licensing requirements for counseling psychologists focus heavily on the products of a more traditional educational framework, namely standard coursework, practice hours, and assessment proficiency. These elements require a substantial amount of clinical work, leaving little time for social action activities outside the therapy room, let alone coursework that is not based on the traditional checklist. Therefore, meeting the milestones necessary for counseling psychologists to have fulfilling careers requires students and teachers to stick to the educational and pedagogical "straight and narrow"; otherwise they may compromise their ability to achieve professionally. So, for a social justice pedagogy and the related goals of such endeavors to be more widely adhered to, counseling psychologists need to challenge the field to reconsider what constitutes the criteria for advancement and licensure.

Another related structural issue in the field of counseling psychology is accreditation and related curricular requirements of training programs. Currently, the content of most counseling psychology training programs, both in the classroom and therapy room, takes place in traditional settings and focus on historically agreed upon topics (Watts, 2004). The insularity of counseling psychology training and practice neither promotes scholars and practitioners to focus on topics outside the discipline nor encourages them to employ interventions that do not take place in traditional formats or settings. As such, accreditation requirements and curricula need to be reviewed in light of social justice such that programs would be required to integrate social justice pedagogical and training models throughout the curricula. In this light, educators need to develop course content that trains students in the areas of advocacy and social justice systems consultation. Additionally, curriculum could be expanded such that social justice issues are integrated throughout course content versus being located in a single multicultural class. This expansion necessitates that counseling psychologists articulate and apply a social justice pedagogy in the classroom and clinical training such that the students' learning environments are reflective of the values put forth in the discipline.

Social justice scholars have pointed out that the most daunting obstacle that counseling psychologists may have to contend with is the emotional toll that social justice work takes on educators and practitioners alike (Goodman et al., 2004). For social activism to take hold in the discipline, supports must be staunchly in place for social justice pedagogical work and new ways of thinking to develop. Watts (2004) recommends that curricula be informed by social activists themselves, rather than academic researchers, traditional service providers, and administrators.

Finally, recent interest in the integration of social justice work into the educating of future psychologists has increased; however, there is still a dearth of literature that explains how to train psychologists to do social justice work (Speight & Vera, 2008). The call for social justice within the profession of counseling psychology demands that psychologists move beyond multicultural competence to become agents of social change for clients (Ivey & Collins, 2003; Vera & Speight, 2003). As such, the development of social justice theories and pedagogies that emanate from within the discipline of counseling psychology are essential in moving the social justice agenda forward. Only then can the counseling psychology classroom and curricula be re-evaluated in light of a social justice agenda, with particular attention being given to training students in the areas of advocacy and social action. Additionally, counseling psychology social justice principles and related competencies should be articulated, as other helping professions have done, such as the American Counseling Association (see Toporek, Lewis, & Crethar, 2009). The creation of a sanctioned and widely supported social justice pedagogy and related educational practices can then be embedded in course syllabi and in practica with clearly defined goals, objectives, and pedagogical approaches that lead to students successfully achieving social justice competence.

Author's Note

Corresponding Author: Ada Sinacore, Department of Educational and Counselling Psychology, Education Building, 3700 McTavish Street, Montreal, Quebec, H3A 1Y2, Tel: 514–398–3446 Fax: 514–398–6968; ada.sinacore@mcgill.ca.

References

Acker, S. (1994). Feminist theory and the study of gender and education. In S. Acker (Ed.), *Gendered education: Sociological reflections on women, teaching and feminism* (pp. 43–54). Buckingham, UK: Open University Press.

Alcoff, L. (1988). Cultural feminism versus post-structuralism: The identity crisis in feminist theory. *Signs: Journal of Women in Culture and Society, 13,* 405–436.

Allen, K. R., & Farnsworth, E. B. (1993). Reflexivity in teaching about families. *Family Relations, 42*(3), 351–356.

American Psychological Association. (2002). Ethical principles of psychologists and code of conduct. *American Psychologist, 57*(12), 1060–1073. doi: 10.1037//0003-066X.57.12.1060

Atkinson, D., Morten, G., & Sue, D. (1983). *Counseling American minorities.* Dubuque, IA: Wm. C. Brown.

Baker, D. B., & Benjamin, L. T. (2000). The affirmation of the scientist-practitioner: A look back at Boulder. *American Psychologist, 55*(2), 241–247. doi:10.1037/0003-066X.55.2.241

Baluch, S. P., Pieterse, A. L., & Bolden, M. A. (2004). Counseling psychology and social justice: Houston ... We have a problem. *The Counseling Psychologist, 32*(1), 89–98. doi: 10.1177/0011000003260065

Belenky, M. J., Clinchy, B. M., Goldberger, N. R., & Tarule, J. M. (1986). *Women's ways of knowing.* New York: Basic Books.

Bell, S., Morrow, M., & Tastsoglou, E. (1999). Teaching in environments of resistance: Toward a critical, feminist, and antiracist pedagogy. In M. Mayberry & E. C. Rose (Eds.), *Meeting the challenge: Innovative feminist pedagogies in action* (pp. 23–46). New York: Routledge.

Berry, J., Trimble, J., & Olmedo, E. (1986). Assessment of acculturation. In W. Lonner & J. Berry (Eds.), *Field methods in cross-cultural research* (pp. 291–324). Newbury Park, CA: Sage.

Bieschke, K. J., & Matthews, C. (1996). Career counselor attitudes and behaviors toward gay, lesbian, and bisexual clients. *Journal of Vocational Behavior, 48*(2), 243–255. doi: 10.1006/jvbe.1996.0021

Bohan, J. S. (2002). Sex differences and/in the self: Classic themes, feminist variations, postmodern challenges. *Psychology of Women Quarterly, 26,* 74–88. doi: 10.1111/1471-6402.00045

Britzman, D. (1995). Is there a queer pedagogy? Or, stop reading straight! *Educational Theory, 45,* 151–165. doi: 10.1111/j.1741-5446.1995.00151.x

Buckley, T. R., & Gabrielle Foldy, E. (2010). A pedagogical model for increasing race-related multicultural counseling competency. *The Counseling Psychologist, 38*(5), 691–713. doi: 10.1177/0011000009360917 2010

Burn, S. M. (2000). *Women across cultures: A global perspective.* Mountain View, CA: Mayfield.

Burnes, T. R. & Manese, J. E. (2008). Social justice in an accredited internship in professional psychology: Answering the call. *Journal of Training and Education in Professional Psychology, 2,* 176–181. doi: 10.1037/1931-3918.2.3.176

Burnes, T. R., & Singh, A. A. (2010). Integrating social justice training into the practicum experience of psychology trainees: Staring earlier. *Training and Education in Professional Psychology, 4*(3), 153–162. doi: 10.1037/a0019385

Caldwell, J. C., & Vera, E. M. (2010). Critical incidents in counseling psychology professionals' and trainees' social justice orientation development. *Training and Education in Professional Psychology, 4*(3), 163–176. doi: 10.1037/a0019093

Cannon, E. (2008). Promoting moral development and multicultural competence during internship. *Journal of Moral Education, 37*(4), 503–518.

Chesler, M. A., & Zuniga, X. (1991). Dealing with prejudice and conflict in the classroom: The pink triangle exercise. *Teaching Sociology, 19,* 173–181.

Clinchy, B. M., Belenky, M. H., Goldberger, N., & Tarule, J. M. (1985). Connected education for women. *Journal of Education, 167*(3), 28–45.

Collins, P. H. (2000). *Black feminist thought: Knowledge, consciousness, and the politics of empowerment* (2nd ed.). New York: Routledge.

Comas-Diaz, L. (1994). An integrative approach. In L. Comas-Diaz & B. Greene (Eds.), *Women of color: Integrating ethnic and gender identities in psychotherapy* (pp. 287–318). New York: Guilford Press.

Commission on Accreditation. (2009). *Guidelines and principals for the accreditation of programs in professional psychology*. Washington, DC: American Psychological Association. Retrieved September 14, 2010, from http://www.apa.org/ed/accreditation/about/policies/guiding-principles.pdf.

Constantine, M. G., Hage, S. M., Kindaichi, M. M., & Bryant, R. M. (2007). Social justice and multicultural issues: Implications for the practice and training of counselors and counseling psychologists. *Journal of Counseling and Development, 85*(1), 24–29.

Cook, J. A., & Fonow, M. M. (1986). Knowledge and women's interests: Issues of epistemology and methodology in feminist sociological research. *Sociological Inquiry, 56*, 2–29. doi: 10.1111/j.1475-682X.1986.tb00073.x

Crethar, H. C., Rivera, E. T., & Nash, S. (2008). In search of common threads: Linking multicultural, feminist, and social justice counseling paradigms. *Journal of Counseling and Development, 86*(3), 269–278.

Cross, W. E. (1971). The Negro-to-Black conversion experience. *Black World, 7*, 13–27.

Crumpacker, L., & Vander Haegen, E. M. (1993). Pedagogy and prejudice: Strategies for confronting homophobia in the classroom. *Women's Studies Quarterly, 21*(3–4), 94–106.

Cummings, A. L. (1998). A feminist approach to teaching women's issues in counselor education. *Canadian Journal of Counselling, 32*(1), 64–74.

Dana, R. H. (1993). *Multicultural assessment perspectives for professional psychology.* Needham Heights, MA: Allyn & Bacon.

Dipalma, C., & Ferguson, K. E. (2006). Clearing ground and making connections: Modernism, postmodernism, feminism. In K. Davis, M. Evans, & J. Lorber (Eds.), *Handbook of gender and women's studies* (pp. 127–145). Thousand Oaks, CA: Sage Publications.

Donovan, J. (2000). *Feminist theory: The intellectual traditions of American feminism* (3rd ed.). New York: F. Ungar.

Elenes, C. A. (2001). Transformando fronteras: Chicana feminist transformative pedagogies. *International Journal of Qualitative Studies in Education, 14*(5), 689–702. doi: 10.1080/09518390110059865

Elicker, J. D., Thompson, M. N., Snell, A. F., & O'Malley, A. F. (2009). A training framework and follow-up observations for multiculturally inclusive teaching: Is believing that we are emphasizing diversity enough? *Journal of Diversity in Higher Education, 2*(2), 63–77. doi: 10.1037/a0015374

Enns, C. Z. (2004). *Feminist theories and feminist psychotherapies: Origins, themes, and diversity* (2nd ed.). Binghamton, NY: Haworth Press.

Enns, C. Z., & Forrest, L. M. (2005). Toward defining and integrating multicultural and feminist pedagogies. In C. Z Enns & A. L. Sinacore (Eds.), *Teaching and social justice: Integrating multicultural and feminist theories in the classroom* (pp. 3–23). Washington, DC: American Psychological Association.

Enns, C. Z., & Sinacore, A. L. (Eds.). (2005). *Teaching and social justice: Integrating multicultural and feminist theories in the classroom.* Washington, DC: American Psychological Association.

Esterberg, K. G. (1997). *Lesbian and bisexual identities: Constructing communities, constructing selves.* Philadelphia, PA: Temple University Press.

Ferguson, M. (1992). Is the classroom still a chilly climate for women? *College Student Journal, 26*, 507–511.

Forrest, L., & Rosenberg, F. (1997). A review of the feminist pedagogy literature: The neglected child of feminist psychology. *Applied and Preventive Psychology, 6*(4), 179–192. doi: 10.1016/S0962-1849(97)80007-8

Fouad, N. A., & Arredondo, P. (2003). *Becoming culturally oriented: Practical advice for psychologists and educators.* Washington, DC: American Psychological Association.

Frank, D. A., & Cannon, E. P. (2010). Queer Theory as pedagogy in counselor education: A framework for diversity training. *Journal of LGBT Issues in Counseling, 4*, 18–31. doi: 10.1080/15538600903552731

Fraser, N. & Nicholoson, L. J. (2008). Social criticism without philosophy: An encounter between feminism and postmodernism. In A. M. Jaggar (Ed.), *Just methods: An interdisciplinary feminist reader* (pp. 352–362). Boulder, CO: Paradigm Publishers.

Freedman, E. B. (2002). *No turning back: The history of feminism and the future of women.* New York: Ballantine Books.

Freire, P. (1973). *Education for critical consciousness.* New York: Seabury Press.

Freire, P. (1993). *Pedagogy of the oppressed.* New York: The Continuum International Publishing Group.

Fukuyama, M. A., & Ferguson, A. D. (2000). Lesbian, gay, and bisexual people of color: Understanding cultural complexity and managing multiple oppressions. In M. P. Ruperto et al. (Eds.), *Handbook of counseling and psychotherapy with lesbian, gay, and bisexual clients* (pp. 81–105). Washington, DC: American Psychological Association.

Gainor, K. A. (2000). Including transgender issues in lesbian, gay, and bisexual psychology: Implications for clinical practice and training. In B. Greene & G. L. Croom (Eds.), *Education, research, and practice in lesbian, gay, bisexual and transgendered psychology: A resource manual,* Vol. 5 (pp. 131–160). Thousand Oaks, CA: Sage Publications.

Gardner, S., Dean, C., & McKaig, D. (1989). Responding to differences in the classroom: The politics of knowledge, class and sexuality. *Sociology of Education, 62*(1), 64–74.

Gates, G. J. (April 2011). How many people are lesbian, gay, bisexual, and transgender? *UCLA School of Law: The Williams Institute Newsletter*, 1–8.

Gergen, M. (2001). *Feminist reconstructions in psychology.* Thousand Oaks, CA: Sage.

Ginorio, A. B., & Martinez, L. J. (1998). Where are the Latinas? Ethno-race and gender in psychology courses. *Psychology of Women Quarterly, 22*(1), 53–68.

Gloria, A. M., & Pope-Davis, D. B. (1997). Cultural ambience: The importance of a culturally aware learning environment in the training and education of counselors (pp. 242–262). In D. B. Pope-Davis & H. L. K. Coleman (Eds.), *Multicultural counseling competencies: Assessment, education and training, and supervision.* Thousand Oaks, CA: Sage.

Goodman, L. A., Liang, B., Helms, J. E., Latta, R. E., Sparks, E., & Weintraub, S. R. (2004). Training counseling psychologists as social justice agents: Feminist and multicultural principles in action. *The Counseling Psychologist, 32*(6), 793–837. doi: 10.1177/0011000004268802

Greene, B. (1997). Lesbian women of color: Triple jeopardy. *Journal of Lesbian Studies, 1*(1), 109–147.

Greene, B., & Sanchez-Hucles, J. (1997). Diversity: Advancing an inclusive feminist psychology. In J. Worell & N. G. Johnson (Eds.), *Shaping the future of feminist psychology: Education, research, and practice* (pp. 173–202). Washington, DC: American Psychological Association.

Hanisch, C. (1969). *The Personal Is Political.* Retrieved from http://www.carolhanisch.org/CHwritings/PersonalisPol.pdf\.

Harding, S. (1987). Introduction: Is there a feminist method? In S. Harding (Ed.), *Feminism and methodology* (pp. 1–14). Bloomington: Indiana University Press.

Harris Nixon, D., Marcelle-Coney, D., Torres-Greggory, M., Huntley, E., Jacques, C., Pasquet, M., & Ravachi, R. (2010). Creating community: Offering a liberation pedagogical model to facilitate diversity conversations in MFT graduate classrooms. *Journal of Marital and Family Therapy, 36*(2), 197–211. doi: 10.1111/j.1752-0606.2009.00180.x

Hashizume, L., Greggs, R., & Cairns, K. (1994). Feminist practice in counselor education: Student and faculty experience. In J. Gallivan, S. D. Crozier, & V. M. Lalande (Eds.), *Women, girls, and achievement* (pp. 170–184). North York, ON: Captus University Publications.

Helms, J. E. (1990). *Black and White racial identity: Theory, research, and practice.* Westport, CT: Greenwood.

Hess, G. (1995). *Restructuring urban schools: A Chicago perspective.* New York: Teachers College Press.

hooks, b. (1989). *Talking back: Thinking feminist, thinking black.* Boston, MA: South End Press.

hooks, b. (1994). *Teaching to transgress: Education as the practice of freedom.* New York: Routledge.

Israel, T., & Hackett, G. (2004). Counselor education on lesbian, gay, and bisexual issues: Comparing information and attitude exploration. *Counselor Education and Supervision, 43*(3), 179–191.

Ivey, A. E., & Collins, N. (2003). Social justice: A long-term challenge for counseling psychology. *The Counseling Psychologist, 31*(3), 290–298. doi: 10.1177/0011000003031003004

Jaggar, A. M. (1983). *Feminist politics and human nature.* Totowa, NJ: Rowman and Allenheld.

Jaggar, A. M., & Rothenberg, P. S. (1984). *Feminist frameworks.* New York: McGraw-Hill.

Kahn, J. S., & Ferguson, K. (2009). Men as allies in feminist pedagogy in the undergraduate psychology curriculum. *Women and Therapy, 33*(1), 121–139. doi: 10.1080/02703140903404853

Kirk, G., & Okazawa-Rey, M. (Eds.). (2001). *Women's lives: Multicultural perspectives* (2nd ed.). New York: McGraw Hill.

Kirk, S. C., & Kulkarni, C. (2006). The whole person: A paradigm for integrating the mental and physical health of trans clients. In M. D. Shankle (Ed.), *The handbook of lesbian, gay, bisexual, and transgender public health: A practitioner's guide to service* (pp. 145–172). Binghamton, NY: Harrington.

LaFromboise, T., Coleman, H. L. K., & Gerton, J. (1993). Psychological impact of biculturalism: Evidence and theory. *Psychological Bulletin, 114*(3), 395–412.

Lev, A. I. (2004). *Transgender emergence: Therapeutic guidelines for working with gender- variant people and their families.* New York: The Haworth Press.

Lewis, B. L. (2010). Social justice in practicum training: Competencies and developmental implications. *Training and Education in Professional Psychology, 4*(3), 145–152. doi: 10.1037/a0017383

Lewis, M. G. (1993). *Without a word: Teaching beyond women's silence.* New York: Routledge.

Locke, D. C., & Kiselica, M. S. (1999). Pedagogy of possibilities: Teaching about racism in multicultural counseling courses. *Journal of Counseling and Development, 77,* 80–86.

Logan, C. (1996). Homophobia? No homoprejudice. *Journal of Homosexuality, 31*(3), 31–53.

Logan, C., & Barret, R. (2005). Counseling competencies for sexual minority clients. *Journal of LGBT Issues in Counseling, 1*(1), 3–22.

Luhmann, S. (1998). Queering/querying pedagogy? Or, pedagogy is a pretty queer thing. In W. F. Pinar (Ed.), *Queer theory in education* (pp. 141–156). Mahwah, NJ: Erlbaum.

Luke, C., & Gore, J. (1992). *Feminism and critical pedagogy.* New York: Routledge.

Maher, F. A., & Tetreault, M. K. T. (2001). *The feminist classroom: Dynamics of gender, race, and privilege* (Expanded ed.). Lanham, MD: Rowman & Littlefield.

McCaughey, M., & Burger, C. J. (1998). Cybergrrrl education and virtual feminism: Using the Internet to teach introductory women's studies. In B. S. Winkler & C. DiPalma (Eds.), *Teaching introduction to women's studies: Expectations and strategies* (pp. 151–162). Westport, CT: Bergin & Garvey.

McDowell, T., Fang, S., Brownlee, K., Gomez Young, C., & Khanna, A. (2002). Transforming an MFT program: A model for enhancing diversity. *Journal of Marital and Family Therapy, 28,* 179–191. doi:10.1111/j.1752-0606.2002.tb00355.x

Mills, S. (1997). *Discourse.* London: Routledge Press.

Mollen, D., Ridley, C. R., & Hill, C. L. (2003). Models of multicultural counseling competence: A critical evaluation. In D. B. Pope-Davis et al. (Eds.), *Handbook of multicultural competencies in counseling and psychology* (pp. 21–37). Thousand Oaks, CA: Sage.

National Council of la Raza. (2002). *NCLR agenda for Hispanic families: A public policy briefing book.* Washington, DC: NCLK.

Ng, R. (1995). Teaching against the grain: Contradictions and possibilities. In R. Ng, P. Staton, & J. Scane (Eds.), *Anti-racism, feminism, and crucial approaches to education* (pp. 129–152). Westport, CT: Greenwood Press.

O'Brien, K. M., Patel, S., Hensler-McGinnis, N., & Kaplan, J. (2006). Empowering undergraduate students to be agents of social change: An innovative service learning course in counseling psychology. In R. Toporek, L. Gerstein, N. Fouad, G. Roysircar, & T. Israel (Eds.), *Handbook for social justice in counseling psychology: Leadership, vision, and action.* (pp. 59–74). Thousand Oaks, CA: Sage.

Omolade, B. (1987). A black feminist pedagogy. *Women's Studies Quarterly, 15*(3–4), 32–39.

Parham, T. A. (2002). Counseling models for African Americans: The what and how of counseling. In T. A. Parham (Ed.), *Counseling persons of African descent: Raising the bar of practitioner competence* (pp. 100–118). Thousand Oaks, CA: Sage.

Pramaggiore, M., & Hardin, B. (1998). Webbed women: Information technology in the introduction to women's studies classroom. In B. S. Winkler & C. DiPalma (Eds.), *Teaching introduction to women's studies: Expectations and strategies* (pp. 163–174). Westport, CT: Bergin & Garvey.

Rasheed, J. R., & Ancis, S. R. (2005). Multicultural education and critical pedagogy. In C. Z Enns & A. L. Sinacore (Eds.), *Teaching and social justice: Integrating multicultural and feminist theories in the classroom* (pp. 69–84). Washington, DC: American Psychological Association.

Ratts, M. J. (2006). Social Justice Counseling: A Study of Social Justice Counselor Training in CACREP-accredited Counselor Preparation Programs (Doctoral dissertation, Oregon State University). Retrieved October 8, 2010, from http://ir.library.oregonstate.edu/xmlui/bitstream/handle/1957/1929/Manivong%20Ratts%20-%20Dissertation.pdf?sequence=1.

Reynolds, A. L., & Pope, R. L. (1991). The complexity of diversity: Exploring multiple oppressions. *Journal of Counseling and Development, 70*(1), 174–180.

Rich, A. (1979). *On lies, secrets, and silence: Selected prose—1966–1978.* New York: Norton.

Ridley, C. R., & Kleiner, A. J. (2003). Multicultural counseling competence: History, themes, and issues. In D. B. Pope-Davis et al. (Eds.), *Handbook of multicultural competencies in counseling and psychology* (pp. 3–19). Thousand Oaks, CA: Sage.

Riger, S. (1992). Epistemological debates, feminist voices: Science, social values, and the study of women. *American Psychologist, 47,* 730–740.

Rose, E. C. (1998). The class meets in cyberspace: Women's studies via distance education. In G. E. Cohee, E. Däumer, T. D. Kemp, P. M. Krebs, S. Lafky, & S. Runzo (Eds.), *The feminist teacher anthology: Pedagogies and classroom strategies* (pp. 114–134). New York: Teachers College Press.

Rose, G. (1997). Situating knowledges: Positionality, reflexivities and other tactics. *Progress in Human Geography, 21*(3), 305–320. doi: 10.1191/030913297673302122

Rosser, S. B. R., Oakes, M. J., Bockting, W. O., & Miner, M. (2007). Capturing the social demographics of hidden sexual minorities: An Internet study of the transgender population in the United States. *Sexuality Research And Social Policy, 4*(2), 50–64. DOI: 10.1525/srsp.2007.4.2.50

Rubin, L., & Nemeroff, C. (2001). Feminism's third wave: Surfing to oblivion? *Women and Therapy, 23*(2), 91–104. doi: 10.1300/J015v23n02_07

Schniedewind, N. (1987). Teaching feminist process. *Women's Studies Quarterly, 15*(3–4), 17–29.

Sherry, A., Whilde, N., & Patton, J. (2005). Gay, lesbian, and bisexual training competencies in American Psychological Association accredited programs. *Psychotherapy: Theory, Research, Practice, and Training, 42*(1), 116–120. doi: 10.1037/0033-3204.42.1.116

Shrewsbury, C. M. (1993). What is feminist pedagogy? *Women's Studies Quarterly, 21*(3–4), 8–15.

Silvestre, A. J., & Arrowood, S. H. (2006). Strategies for improving state, county, and city government health and welfare services for LGBT people. In M. D. Shankle (Ed.), *The handbook of lesbian, gay, bisexual, and transgender public health: A practitioner's guide to service* (pp. 263–288). Binghamton, NY: Harrington.

Sinacore, A. L., Healy, P. A., Justin, M. (2002). A qualitative analysis of the experiences of feminist psychology educators: The classroom. *Feminism and Psychology, 12*(3), 339–362. doi: 10.1177/0959353502012003007

Sinacore, A. L., & Boatwright, K. (2005). The feminist classroom: Feminist strategies and student responses. In C. Z. Enns & A. L. Sincaore (Eds.), *Teaching social justice: Integrating multicultural and feminist theories in the classroom* (pp. 109–124). Washington, DC: American Psychological Association Press.

Sinacore, A.L. & Enns, C.Z. (2005a). Diversity feminisms: Postmodern, women-of-color, antiracist, lesbian, third-wave and global perspectives. In C. Z. Enns & A. L Sinacore (Eds.), *Teaching and social justice: Integrating multicultural and feminist theories in the classroom* (pp. 41–67). Washington, DC: American Psychological Association.

Sinacore, A. L., & Enns, C. Z. (2005b). Multicultural and feminist literatures: Themes, dimensions, and variations. In C. Z. Enns & A. L. Sinacore (Eds.), *Teaching and social justice: Integrating multicultural and feminist theories in the classroom* (pp. 99–107). Washington, DC: American Psychological Association.

Sinacore, A. L., Mikhail, A. M., Kassan, A., & Lerner, S. (2009). Cultural transition of Jewish immigrants: Education, employment, and integration. *International Journal for Educational and Vocational Guidance, 9*(3), 157–176. doi: 10.1007/s10775-009-9166-z

Sinacore-Guinn, A. L., Blaisure, K. R., Justin, M., Healy, P., & Brawer, S. (1998). Promoting reflexivity in the classroom. *Teaching of Psychology, 26*(4), 267–270.

Singh, A. A., Hofsess, C. D., Boyer, E. M, Kwong, A., Lau, A. S. M., McLain, M., et al. (2010). Social justice and counseling psychology: Listening to the voices of doctoral trainees. *The Counseling Psychologist, 38*(6), 766–795. doi: 10.1177/0011000010362559

Sinha, M., Guy, D. J., & Woollacott, A. (1999). Why feminism and internationalism? In M. Sinha, D. Guy, & A. Woollacott (Eds.), *Feminisms and Internationalism* (pp. 1–13). Oxford, UK: Blackwell Publishers.

Smith-Adcock, S., Ropers-Huilman, B., & Choate, L. H. (2004). Feminist teaching in counselor education: Promoting multicultural understanding. *Journal of Multicultural Counseling and Development, 32,* 402–413.

Speight, S. L., & Vera, E. M. (2008). Social justice and counseling psychology: A challenge to the profession. In S. D. Brown, & R. W. Lent (Eds.) *Handbook of counseling psychology* (4th ed.) (pp. 54–67). Hoboken, NJ: Wiley.

Steele, J. M. (2008). Preparing counselors to advocate for social justice: A liberation model. *Counselor Education and Supervision, 48*(2), 74–85.

Sue, D. W. (2001). Multidimensional facets of cultural competence. *The Counseling Psychologist, 29*(6), 790–821. doi:10.1177/0011000001296002

Sue, D. W., Arredondo, P., & McDavis, R. J. (1992). Multicultural counseling competencies and standards: A call to the profession. *Journal of Counseling and Development, 70*(4), 477–483.

Sue, D. W., Bernier, J. B., Durran, M., Feinberg, L., Pedersen, P., Smith, E., et al. (1982). Position paper: Cross-cultural counseling competencies. *The Counseling Psychologist, 10*(2), 45–52. doi: 10.1177/0011000082102008

Sue, D. W., & Sue, D. (2008). *Counseling the culturally different: Theory and practice* (5th ed.). New York: Wiley.

Sumara, D., & Davis, B. (1999). Interrupting heteronormativity: Toward a queer curriculum theory. *Curriculum Inquiry, 29*(2), 191–208. doi: 10.1111/0362-6784.00121

Swim, J. K., Cohen, L. L., & Hyers, L. L. (1998). Experiencing everyday prejudice and discrimination. In J. K. Swim & C. Stangor (Eds.), *Prejudice: The target's perspective* (pp. 37–60). New York: Academic.

Talleyrand, R. M., Chi-Ying Chung, R. & Bemak, F. (2006). Incorporating social justice in counselor training programs: A case study example. In R. Toporek, L. Gerstein, N. Fouad, G. Roysircar, & T. Israel (Eds.), *Handbook for social justice in counseling psychology: Leadership, vision, and action.* (pp 44–58). Thousand Oaks, CA: Sage.

Tierney, W. G. (1997). *Academic outlaws: Queer theory and cultural studies in the Academy.* Thousand Oaks, CA: Sage.

Tisdell, E. J. (1998). Poststructural feminist pedagogies: The possibilities and limitations of feminist emancipator adult learning and practice. *Adult Education Quarterly, 48*(3), 139–156. doi: 10.1177/074171369804800302

Tong, R. P. (1998). *Feminist thought* (2nd ed.). Boulder, CO: Westview Press.

Toporek, R.L., Gerstein, L. H., Fouad, N.A., Roysircar, G. & Israel, T. (2006). *Handbook for social justice in counseling psychology: Leadership, vision and action.* Thousand Oaks, CA: Sage Publications.

Toporek, R. L., Lewis, J. A., & Crethar, H. C. (2009). Promoting systemic change through the ACA Advocacy Competencies. *Journal of Counseling and Development, 87*(3), 260–268.

Toporek, R. L., & McNally, C. J. (2006). Social justice training in counseling psychology: Needs and innovations. In R. Toporek, L. Gerstein, N. Fouad, G. Roysircar, & T. Israel (Eds.), *Handbook for social justice in counseling psychology: Leadership, vision, and action.* (pp. 37–43). Thousand Oaks, CA: Sage.

Toporek, R. L., & Vaughn, S. R. (2010). Social justice in the training of professional psychologists: Moving forward. *Training and Education in Professional Psychology, 4*(3), 177–182. doi: 10.1037/a0019874

TuSmith, B. (1989). The cultural translator: Toward an ethnic womanist pedagogy. *Melus, 16*(2), 17–29. Retrieved December 10, 2010, from http://www.jstor.org/stable/467208/

Valle, M. E. (2002). Antiracist pedagogy and conscientización: A Latina professor's struggle. In A. A. Macdonald & S. Sánchez-Casal (Eds.), *Twenty-first-century feminist classrooms* (pp. 155–173). New York: Palgrave Macmillan.

Van Kesteren et al. (1996). An epidemiological and demographic study of transsexuals in the Netherlands. *Archives of Sexual Behavior, 25*(6), 589–600. doi:10.1007/BF02437841

Vázquez, L. A., & García-Vázquez, E. (2003). Teaching multicultural competence in counseling curriculum. In D. B. Pope-Davis, H. L. K. Coleman, W. M. Liu, & R. L. Toporek (Eds.), *Handbook of multicultural competencies in counseling and psychology* (pp. 546–561). Thousand Oaks, CA: Sage.

Vera, E. M., & Speight, S. L. (2003). Multicultural competence, social justice, and counseling psychology: Expanding our roles. *The Counseling Psychologist, 31*(3), 253–272. doi: 10.1177/0011000003031003001

Vinson, T. S., & Neimeyer, G. J. (2000). The relationship between racial identity development and multicultural counseling competence. *Journal of Multicultural Counseling and Development, 28*, 177–192.

Walker, R. (Ed.) (1995). *To be real.* New York: Doubleday.

Watts, R. J. (2004). Integrating Social Justice and Psychology. *The Counseling Psychologist, 32*(6), 855–865. doi: 10.1177/0011000004269274

Wetzel, J. (1999). Assessment and feminist psychology. In M. Mayberrry & E. C. Rose (Eds.), *Meeting the challenge: Innovative feminist pedagogies in action* (pp. 99–119). New York: Routledge.

Wright, J. (1998). Lesbian instructor comes out: The personal is pedagogy. In G. E. Cohee, E. Däumer, T. D. Kemp, P. M. Krebs, S. Lafky, & S. Runzo (Eds.), *The feminist teacher anthology: Pedagogies and classroom strategies* (pp. 191–207). New York: Teachers College Press.

CHAPTER

23 Multicultural Feminist Training, Supervision, and Continuing Education: Concepts, Competencies, and Challenges

Marie L. Miville

Abstract

This book chapter summarizes key concepts of multicultural feminist training and education, including an intersectional conceptualization of multiple identity dimensions; the development of a consciousness or awareness regarding the impact of oppression of individuals, particularly interlocking oppressions; self-reflection; themes of power and empowerment; collaborative and systemic working relationships; and the promotion of advocacy and social change. Pedagogical and curriculum considerations are presented, and individual program and professional organizational initiatives are discussed. Best practices at the individual program level typically infuse multicultural feminist concepts throughout the entirety of training. Organizational efforts include the Counseling Psychology Model Training Values Statement Addressing Diversity, the Integrated Training Model, and the Advocacy Competencies. Challenges involved in adopting a multicultural feminist training program are discussed, and recommendations are made for resolving these dilemmas. Sections on supervision and continuing education highlight concepts and strategies that have been proposed for these types of training activities. Future directions and relevant discussion questions are described.

Key Words: Multiculturalism, feminism, social justice, training and education, supervision, continuing education

> If I have to summarize my development as a psychotherapist, I would say that it is similar to an *arpillera*. The Latin American way of expressing stories of oppression, pain, and resistance, *arpillera* is an artistic weaving that is both liberating and transformative. I have not separated my personal identity from that of a multicultural psychotherapist. Culture, ethnicity, gender, race, among many other diversity variables, have infused plurality into my development... instead of a central ethos, I was given the blessings and the terrors of multiplicity. (Comas-Diaz, 2005, p. 979)

The above personal narrative by Latina psychologist Lillian Comas-Diaz highlights the intense personal and professional journeys that individuals may travel in their efforts to become competent multicultural feminist professionals. What roles can and do training programs play in the development of such professionals? How are training programs today meeting the challenges of organizing a curriculum that encourages attitudes, knowledge, and skills that promote a multicultural feminist stance that, at the same time, reflects accreditation and licensing standards, including the requirements of evidence-based interventions and competence-oriented approaches?

A recent survey of training directors of counseling psychology doctoral programs (Miville et al., 2009) reported that the vast majority of these programs incorporate the multicultural practice guidelines (American Psychological Association [APA], 2003) as well as guidelines for working with lesbian, gay, and bisexual individuals (LGB; APA Division 44 Committee on Lesbian, Gay, & Bisexual Concerns Task Force, 2000) into their training programs (93% and 88%, respectively). The same survey revealed, however, that very few programs, only 17%, incorporated APA practice guidelines relevant to girls and women (APA, 2007). Given the disproportionate numbers of women who both seek counseling psychology services and those who provide them, it is important to explore what these differences reveal regarding the field's current training philosophy as this applies to a complex and nuanced approach to diversity, as well as the professional competence of newly trained counseling psychologists for working with a diverse clientele. Moreover, how might these stark contrasts be effectively mitigated in future program development, particularly in light of many multicultural feminist scholars' call to incorporate multiple aspects of individual and cultural diversity (e.g., Enns & Sinacore, 2005)?

The current chapter reviews literature relevant to multicultural feminist issues for training, supervision, and continuing education in counseling psychology today. First, critical multicultural feminist themes will be reviewed, highlighting key concepts from this approach relevant to training. Next, pedagogical and curriculum considerations within a multicultural feminist framework will be described, followed by a discussion of supervision and continuing education within this framework. The chapter concludes with a consideration of future directions for training and education in counseling psychology.

What's in a Name? Convergence and Divergence Between Multicultural and Feminist Approaches in Training and Education

The 1970s and early 1980s saw an emergence of dual movements within counseling psychology and other fields of professional psychology calling for the inclusion of multicultural (e.g., racial-ethnic) and gender issues into all aspects of research, training, and practice. However, as has been noted by numerous authors (e.g., Hays, 1996; Silverstein, 2006; Reid, 2002; Russo &Vaz, 2001), these movements evolved separately from each other to the extent that race-ethnicity variables often were not incorporated into discussions of gender-oriented issues, and vice versa. This separation was rooted in the sociohistorical context going at least as far back as the nineteenth-century civil rights movements. For example, the critical Seneca Falls Declaration, "the articulated consciousness of women's rights" in the mid-1800s, completely ignored the predicaments of poor women and women of color (Davis, 1983, p. 53). Moreover, although some women's rights activists wisely called for unity between Black Liberation and Women's Liberation movements in the nineteenth century, others disagreed, suggesting "it is more important that women should vote than that the black man should vote ..." (H. W. Beecher, 1887, in Davis, 1983, p. 72). Similarly, Cole (2009) notes that Black male leaders were exhorted "to include sexist discrimination faced by Black women in their race-based agenda" (p. 170). Unfortunately, it would be many decades before the concerns of individuals affected by multiple types of oppressions were acknowledged and included both in sociopolitical movements as well as in more professional and scientific theories and interventions, including psychology.

During the 1980s, a number of women of color scholars in the social sciences began to critique "the single-axis framework...dominant in...feminist theory and anti-racist politics...for its focus on the experiences of the most privileged members of subordinate groups" (Cole, 2009, p. 171). That is, these scholars argued that many, if not most, women of color "often experience double discrimination—the combined effects on practices which discriminate on the basis of race, and on the basis of sex ..." (Crenshaw, 1989/1993, in Cole, p. 171). As Bowman and King (2003) poignantly wrote regarding the dilemmas that women of color face: "Choosing to emphasize sexism in their communities could lead to alienating men and other women who are not interested in confronting their brothers, but choosing to emphasize racism results in a negation of oneself as a woman" (p. 60). The combined effects of discriminatory practices also presumably apply to other individuals from multiple oppressed social groups (e.g., lesbian/gay/bisexual people of color; Hays, 2001).

In professional psychology, Silverstein (2006) wrote that multiculturalism "has generally been narrowly defined in terms of race/ethnicity, overlooking the intersections of other aspects of diversity, such as class, gender, and sexual orientation" (p. 22). She further decried the "virtual invisibility of gender and feminism" in the Multicultural Guidelines (APA, 2003) in which the "emphasis on race and ethnicity in multiculturalism...eclipsed feminism" (p. 21). In an earlier article, Arredondo, Psalti, and Cella (1993, in Silverstein) similarly critiqued multicultural counseling textbooks as having "only a cursory mention of gender if any" (p. 22). And when women of color were mentioned, "they were often portrayed in terms of negative ethnic stereotypes, such as the submissive Asian woman" (p. 22).

Feminist therapy and training modules similarly have been critiqued for ignoring critical issues of race, ethnicity, and class (Enns, 2004; Espin, 1994). Feminist therapists in the 1970s, many of whom were White and middle class, "proposed that gender oppression is the fundamental form of oppression ..., thus implying that the most important form of oppression is discrimination on the basis of sex" (Enns, 2004, p. 202). This singular emphasis on sexism invalidated the experiences of women of color for whom race and racism were often a more salient, hostile, and daily experience. Espin (1994) further argued that "the nearsightedness of White feminists as to the possibilities of the movement and the far-reaching consequences of its ideas [was] very much to blame for the narrowness of definitions of feminism and for the movement's goals being perceived as limited and exclusionary" (p. 265). Bowman and King (2003) also asserted that "the connection to a White feminist description of men as oppressors [served] to separate women of color from their ethnic community" and that as a result, "it appears that women of color may indeed consider race more salient than gender and choose to remain connected to their ethnic community" (p. 61).

Unfortunately, the limits of the singular focus of both the multicultural and feminist movements in psychology have made it "difficult... to understand both the uniqueness and complexity of... clients" (Silverstein, 2006, p. 22). Moreover, as the survey findings of training directors indicated above, many, if not most, doctoral programs have been slow to adopt an inclusive (i.e., multi-axial) framework for achieving professional competence regarding individual and cultural diversity.

To facilitate a more complex understanding of individuals in psychology, the concept of *intersectionality* has been proposed "to describe analytic approaches that consider the meaning and consequences of multiple categories of social group membership" (Cole, p. 170). Intersectionality in understanding self and others is the hallmark of most multicultural feminist approaches: "such attention is critical because failure to attend to how social categories depend on one another for meaning renders knowledge of any one category both incomplete and biased" (Cole, p. 173). Black feminist leaders have been at the forefront of developing frameworks that incorporate more complex understandings of the intersections of multiple identities and social group memberships. For example, the Combahee River Collective of the early 1970s (1982, in Enns, 2004, and Cole, 2009) promoted "the interconnections between race, class, and sex oppression... [and called for] expanding the definition of 'the personal is political' to include issues of race" (Enns, p. 205). They also highlighted the importance of building "solidarity with progressive Black men and a rejection of separatism" (Enns, p. 205). Collins (2000) and others (Smith, 1983, in Enns) further expanded Black feminist themes by emphasizing (a) the critical importance of self-definition, given the history of racist stereotypes, and self-valuations; (b) interlocking factors and the "simultaneity of oppression" (Smith, 1983, in Enns, p. 207); and (c) a legacy of activism and "a commitment to resisting oppression and bettering the lives of oppressed persons" (Enns, p. 207).

Hurtado (2010) also notes the importance of intersectionality from a Chicana feminist perspective, using a borderlands metaphor:

> Living in many liminal spaces... results in the development of a *mestiza* (hybrid) consciousness that simultaneously embraces and rejects contradictory realities so as not to exclude what is critically assessed... women who are exposed to multiple social worlds, as defined by cultures, languages, social classes, sexualities, nation states, and colonization, develop the agility to navigate and the ability to challenge linear conceptions of social reality. *As such, oppressions are not ranked nor are they conceptualized as static; rather they are recognized as fluid systems that take on different forms and nuances depending on the context...* (p. 33, emphasis added)

Israel (2004), writing from the perspective of a biracial (White-Jewish/Asian) bisexual woman, poignantly described the impact of "intersecting identities" on her personal and professional life as a counseling psychologist: "Although parallels may exist, my experience is that these identities intersect and inform each other rather than exist as parallel experiences. The intersections of my bi-identities highlight the importance of *complexity, context, and self-definition* in identity development" (p. 180, emphasis added).

Applying Multicultural Feminist Principles to Training and Practice

Within the past decade, a number of scholars have identified important themes or principles that undergird both multicultural and feminist approaches and a more complex, contextualized, and holistic approach to multiple social group memberships and interlocking oppressions. These themes are critical to articulate in helping shape training programs and activities that promote greater competency for all counseling psychologists regarding individual and cultural diversity.

For example, Funderburk and Fukuyama (2001) noted that both feminist and multicultural approaches place emphasis on "consciousness, context, and connection in order to heighten awareness regarding suffering, liberation, and enlightenment" (p. 6). These approaches also "emphasize group membership and group social identities, many of which carry social stigmatization based upon socially constructed dimensions" (p. 6). Moreover, both perspectives require that professionals "are responsible to become culturally literate and sensitive to both their own and clients' cultural backgrounds... [and they] must acquire cultural knowledge, awareness, and skills, including dynamics of privilege and oppression" (p. 6).

Nishimura (2004) explored how feminist and multicultural approaches necessarily intersect in the effective treatment of biracial clients. She highlighted the multicultural counseling competencies (Sue, Arredondo, & McDavis, 1992, in Nishimura, 2004) involving beliefs and attitudes, knowledge, and skills. She also emphasized multicultural counseling and therapy (MCT; Sue, Ivey, & Pedersen, 1996, in Nishimura, 2004) Principles 2, 3, and 6, which together emphasize that (a) the counselor is as much a factor of the counseling relationship as the client, (b) cultural identity is an important feature in counseling, and (c) the liberation of consciousness is a basic therapy goal. Nishimura then drew on the feminist principles of (a) the "personal is the political" (i.e., counseling issues are driven by social problems and norms), (b) an egalitarian approach to professional relationships, and (c) valuing the diverse, complex, and unique experiences of female perspectives. Finally, she noted that a multicultural feminist counseling perspective can be summarized as incorporating the following: "(1) consideration of who the counselor is as a person who impacts the counseling relationship; (2) acknowledging and valuing multiple aspects of the client's identity; and (3) creating a therapeutic alliance that allows the client to work with the counselor in choosing an appropriate intervention" (p. 142).

Williams and Barber (2004) also discussed how multicultural and feminist approaches might be integrated for more competent practice. They first noted how both approaches help "counselors become more aware of the external factors impacting their clients' lives" and focus on "the greater context" including "social, cultural, economic, familial, [and] political contexts" (p. 391), rather than only individual or intrapsychic concerns. Both frameworks also emphasize a collaborative relationship between therapists and clients. Williams and Barber suggested several principles that can guide a more integrative multicultural feminist approach. These include emphases on (a) power (impact of oppression and privilege as well as learning healthy and responsible approaches to power) and social responsibility; (b) culture and context; (c) the reality that psychological pain can be adaptive; (d) the capabilities and strengths of the client; and (e) the need for social change.

With respect to education and training, Enns and Forrest (2005) described several principles from multicultural perspectives that they also linked with liberation and critical pedagogies, as well as feminist pedagogy. Paulo Freire (1970, 1994, in Enns & Forrest, 2005) has long been credited as a major leader in the development of liberation pedagogies, a key process of which includes *conscientização*, "learning to perceive social, political, and economic contradictions, and to take action against the oppressive elements of reality" (Freire, 1970, in Enns & Forrest, 2005, p. 6). Empowerment is the central activity for multicultural/critical pedagogies.

Principle 1 refers to *problem-posing*, "a group process that draws on personal experience to create social connectedness and mutual responsibility" (Wallerstein, 1987, in Enns & Forrest, 2005, p. 7) and *participatory dialogue*, involving the adaption of the dominant perspective in order to challenge it. In short, "Education becomes the practice of freedom rather than domination. Liberatory education is associated with demythologizing and reinventing reality" (Enns & Forrest, 2005, p. 7). Teaching and learning occurs for both students and teachers who are considered "coparticipants in a shared learning process" (p. 8) such that the traditional role of the teacher is "withered away," although it is recognized that educators can play a dynamic set of roles that may include "convener, facilitator, advocate, adversary, lecturer, recorder, mediator, and librarian" (p. 8) with their initial roles reflecting that of a "provocateur of conceptual inquiry" (Shor, 1987, in Enns & Forrest, 2005, p. 8).

Principle 2 involves *self-reflection*, a four-stage process moving from being unable to perceive one's capacity to influence the environment to being able to critically examine issues and test/adapt new perspectives. Principle 2 also involves *praxis,* which refers to translating reflection into action, such that an "action-reflection-action" cycle is facilitated (Enns & Forrest, 2005). Training activities that encourage self-reflection and praxis involve journaling, reflective essays, and autobiographies, as well as engaging in creative arts, such as photojournaling, poetry, and drama.

With respect to feminist pedagogy, Enns and Forrest drew several principles and strategies from the 1993 Conference on Education and Training in Feminist Practice, which were summarized by Kimmel and Worrell (1997) and Chin and Russo (1997), among others: "These principles reflect a web of assumptions and underlying values, which underlie the development of knowledge (i.e., what we know) and aid the acquisition of skills (i.e., how we practice)... They elicit a feminist process of thoughtful examination rather than a blueprint of what people should teach" (Chin & Russo, 1997, p. 96). Enns and Forrest (2005) begin with Principle 1, *power,* "the importance of rethinking power and authority in the classroom as well as creating communal and democratic learning environments" (Enns & Forrest, 2005, p. 11). Power is redefined as "a source of energy, potential, and capacity" (p. 11). Power is to be shared, for example in the classroom, by teachers and students, and communication skills are facilitated to build cohesion, cooperation, collaboration, and consensus. Educators' self-disclosure is viewed as "an important method for decreasing power differentials, humanizing the classroom, establishing one's authenticity,... validating diversity and difference, and empowering students" (p. 12). Evaluation methods (e.g., group grading) also emphasize decreasing power differences.

Principle 2 involves *holistic learning and integrating dichotomies* such that traditional binary ways of thinking (thinking vs. feeling) are deemphasized, and replaced with a more systemic, contextual approach that balances "personal experience with a broader understanding of oppression (p. 13)." Principle 3, *diversity,* involves recognizing multiple intersections of privilege and oppression, "developing knowledge of and sensitivity to a wide arrange of cultural realities... [as well as fostering] healthy and productive forms of disagreement and conflict resolution (p. 14)." Principle 4 emphasizes *social change,* which entails not only changing oneself but helping to change the larger society.

Enns and Forrest (2005) acknowledge several similarities between multicultural/critical and feminist pedagogies that revolve around "the content, the process, and the goals of education" (p. 16). These pedagogies draw from a wide range of disciplines and challenge traditional definitions of knowledge. They emphasize articulating the impact of privilege and oppression and centralizing nondominant approaches. There also is an emphasis on building awareness and lifting the silence among oppressed individuals and groups. Language is considered critical, both in understanding it as a tool of oppression by colonizing and masculine forces, as well as its potential to "give voice" to marginalized people. The relationship between teachers and students are more equalized, with training activities helping to promote group dialogue and reflection. Finally, a call to action is the goal of education, with "group empowerment and structural change, rather than individual change alone" (p. 17) being its primary purpose.

Goodman et al. (2004) delineated six recurring themes that overlap multicultural and feminist perspectives specifically for counseling psychology training, including ongoing self-examination, sharing power, giving voice, facilitating consciousness-raising, building on strengths, and leaving clients with the tools for social change. Goodman et al. (2004) further noted that these themes overlap within the even larger framework of social justice involving social change and advocacy within communities and through public policy. Goodman et al. (2004) asserted that the history and values of counseling psychology in particular are consistent with such an approach. Moreover, "promoting complete health means promoting social justice for there cannot be health in the absence of justice" (Prilleltensky, 1999, in Goodman et al., 2004, p. 797).

Ongoing examination involves reflecting on and making explicit the values and biases that counseling psychologists bring into their clinical practices or the assumptions on which their research questions are based. Examination involves recognizing the role that power plays in interpersonal interactions with clients and participants as well as one's *positionality* or relative power with respect to race, ethnicity, and culture as well as gender. In short, ongoing examination requires becoming attentive "to hierarchies of power and dominance... We notice the ways in which we are both oppressed and oppressor, dominant and marginal, as well as the interactive relationships that emerge from these different positions of power" (Brabeck and Brown, 1997, in Goodman et al., 2004, p. 799). Counseling psychologists need to ask, "What kinds of strengths and vulnerabilities do members of the collaboration bring to the table, and how do these shape the relative power of each member?" (p. 800). The notion of multiple or intersecting selves is relevant here, since roles shift and change and must be recognized in the course of professional work.

Sharing power or mutuality means that the helper's expertise is simply another source of information, not the best or most "objective." This theme also emphasizes that counseling psychologists do not abuse power and must be vigilant against placing themselves in the position of "the-ones-who-know-how-to-emancipate-the-oppressed" (Lather, 1991, in Goodman et al., 2004, p. 801). Both in therapy and training, it is important to establish oneself as resources or "co-learners":

> because "sharing power" involves collaboration, it privileges the empowerment of groups and the development of the community as a whole over the empowerment of the individuals.... Sharing power not only allows the voices of marginalized and oppressed groups to emerge, but it also requires that those who traditionally hold power reexamine their perceptions and opinions about the strengths of the more marginalized group.... If undertaken authentically, sharing power thereby enhances the growth of each collaborator (p. 802)

Giving voice refers to a "kind of a megametaphor representing presence, power, participation, protest, and identity" (Reinharz, 1994, p. 183, in Goodman et al., 2004, p. 802) as well as "desilencing the oppressed" (Brabeck and Brown, 1997), which involves helping clients to learn their "mother tongue" or "native language" to give life to devalued narratives. Counseling psychologists can help communities "develop shared narratives about their lives, questions, and goals" (Goodman et al., 2004, p. 803). Two strategies can guide this work: (1) "counseling psychologists should approach communities with the belief that communities themselves know what questions or problems they want addressed, and (2) find ways to amplify the voices of community members so that others can learn about their needs, wishes, strengths, and vision" (p. 803).

Consciousness raising involves "helping clients understand the extent to which individual and private difficulties are rooted in larger historical, social, and political forces... [in short,] the personal is rendered political" (Goodman et al, 2004, p. 804). For example, immigrants need to be oriented to the racist hierarchy in the United States as well as other forms of discrimination and domination, and women (and men) need to be made aware of sexism and male privilege. Consciousness raising allows "clients to locate the source of their distress in the social context... that very awareness is treated not through medication and psychotherapy but through social action" (pp. 804–805). However, Goodman et al. (2004) caution that it is important not to denigrate or silence but instead to "*engage people with humility and pluralism,* acknowledging that our views arise from our own sociocultural experiences and may not be true for the people with whom we are working" (p. 805, emphasis added).

Focus on strengths is a chief goal of a multicultural feminist and social justice framework by identifying "clients' strengths, skills, and talents and to help them recognize themselves as competent, powerful individual with the capacity to enact solutions to problems" (Goodman et al., 2004, p. 806). For example, the use of cognitive reframing can help reinterpret problem behaviors as adaptive responses to oppressive circumstances. It also is important to help systems "shift to accommodate the strengths already in the community ..." (p. 806). For instance, bilingualism can be viewed as a strength of children and their families, not a deficit that negatively affects test-taking skills.

Leaving clients with tools arises from feminist perspectives emphasizing the shift in relationships from dependent to mutual, as well as multicultural counseling approaches involving self-help and indigenous support systems. It also is critical to consult with community members about "what tools they feel are necessary for sustainability ..." such that the community "will continue to thrive beyond our explicit involvement" (p. 807).

Other counseling psychologists have written on the importance of incorporating key social justice concepts (which incorporate multicultural and feminist approaches) into training paradigms. Toporek and Vaughn (2010) recently highlighted several themes: developmental perspectives of trainees (e.g., knowledge and attitudes/enthusiasm); multiculturalism (defined broadly to include both racism and sexism, as well as many other forms of discrimination and marginalization); and learning through action (e.g., service-learning projects in the community). They also emphasized the importance of training programs and the departments that house them being more directly and actively involved in emphasizing these themes, such as through a mission statement and the overall curriculum.

In sum, a number of important multicultural feminist principles have been identified as being important to incorporate in training counseling psychologists. These include (a) a more complex and nuanced understanding of diversity, also known as intersectionality; (b) the development of a consciousness or awareness regarding the impact of oppression of individuals, particularly interlocking oppressions; (c) the value of self-reflection; (d) attentiveness to themes of power and empowerment, with power being defined as positive change, rather than domination; (e) the importance of working with others collaboratively and systemically; and (f) the promotion of advocacy and social change. The following section will review best practices for incorporating multicultural feminist approaches at the curriculum/program level.

Pedagogical and Curriculum Considerations and Challenges

Over the past several decades, a number of training models that promote multicultural or feminist approaches, or both, in education and psychology have been proposed. Ali and Ancis (2005) and Ancis and Ali (2005) recently reviewed these different approaches. They identified four major frameworks in multicultural counseling training: existential or universal, emphasizing the similarities among people; ubiquitous/existential, involving a broad definition of culture as including multiple variables, such as age and gender; culture-specific focus, with a major emphasis on race and ethnicity; and race-based, focusing primarily on visible racial factors. Because of these different emphases, each framework promotes different pedagogies. For example, the ubiquitous/existential approach focuses on developing "counselor qualities such as acceptance of one's own and client's worldview," whereas a race-based approach might emphasize developing "counselor racial self-awareness and understanding of racism" (p. 87). These different frameworks also lead trainees to develop different counseling goals, for example, emphasizing identity development as a means of promoting individual well-being (e.g., race-based) or highlighting shared features with culturally similar others (e.g., culture-specific). Suffice to say, no framework is best or always effective for all clients. However, it is important for program faculty to be aware that the choice of framework for multicultural feminist training in counseling psychology will result in consequences regarding their students' overall cultural competence, as well as the clients and systems they serve.

Ancis and Ali (2005) also identified four additional dimensions of multicultural feminist pedagogies that may be reflected in these training models. These parallel several themes identified in the previous section: individual empowerment and social change, knowledge and the knower, oppression and privilege, and reflexivity and self-awareness. Ancis and Ali (2005) suggest that each dimension can range in focus from individual to collective or socially based outcomes. For example, one training program might choose a model that emphasizes the dimension of knowledge and the knower in terms of increasing client access to education as well as the social constructions of "the truth" (p. 103). At the same time, another program can incorporate this dimension to emphasize transforming knowledge:

> to combat the hegemony of dominant perspectives, one must have curricula that reflect the voices and worldviews of diverse groups as well as analyze privilege and multiple oppressions. Common to all these points of view is the notion that pedagogy must address, value, and incorporate multiple forms of knowing and diversity... [These approaches] provide a critical analysis of oppression that has contributed to the disregard of specific ways of knowing and experiencing (e.g., classist, sexist, heterosexist ...). Forms of knowing that have been marginalized are centralized and revalued (e.g., Afrocentric, collectivist, or connected knowing), incorporated within educational systems, and used to empower those who have previously had limited or no voice. (p. 104)

Similarly, programs that incorporate the dimension of individual empowerment and social change might focus on promoting the individual liberties and opportunities of individuals, even promoting success in mainstream society, without any call for change in social structures. Other programs, such as the one described by Goodman et al. (2004), can seek to transform social structures by revealing hidden norms about power and privilege, identifying the political nature of education, critiquing stereotypes and social inequities that are often perpetuated by educational institutions, providing counter-discourses and pedagogies as an alternative to dominant methods, and advocating for social and structural change (Ancis & Ali, 2005, p. 103).

As noted earlier, there are no right or wrong approaches in program decisions regarding the focus on individual or collective outcomes. However, as Ancis and Ali (2005) suggest, the more promising and comprehensive approaches "are those that are attentive to borders and intersections and are... associated with (a) social change perspectives;

(b) transformation; (c) multiple identities and oppressions; and (d) the integrated analysis of privilege, oppression, and personal attitudes" (p. 107).

Program and Organizational Initiatives

Goodman et al. (2004) presented an excellent example of a comprehensive multicultural feminist approach in their description of the doctoral training program in counseling psychology at Boston College (BC). Students in this program are trained to become social justice agents and are informed of this goal from the beginning, through the mission statements of the university, the school of education, and the program. A First Year Experience (FYE) also is structured into the curriculum, in which first year doctoral students spend about six hours a week at "urban, community sites including public schools, courts, detention centers, community-organizing agencies, and public health departments" (Goodman et al, 2004, p. 808). Moreover, during the FYE, instead of a focus on traditional one-on-one counseling skills, "students develop skills in prevention, interprofessional collaboration, and advocacy" (p. 808). Training goals of the FYE "are to help students (a) gain an awareness of systemic factors impacting mental health, psychological growth, and career development; (b) experience collaboration across professions; (c) do collaborative work, advocacy, or indirect service with underserved populations; and (d) engage in the design, delivery, and/or evaluation of preventive interventions" (BC, 2003, in Goodman et al., 2004, p. 808). Students learn to negotiate among members of marginalized communities, as well as those in positions of power who can provide important resources. Students also take part in a bimonthly FYE seminar that meets at the university to engage in important self-reflection as well as dialogue with each other and faculty members about their experiences.

Goodman et al. (2004) also described how many other courses, such as ethics, assessment, and consultation, are geared toward social justice and ecological issues. During the FYE, students are asked to engage in self-disclosure regarding, for example, their attitudes and biases, and, along with this process, struggle with some of the risks associated with doing so. Faculty similarly engage in self-disclosure and expressing their vulnerabilities in the process, such as the risk of appearing incompetent or offensive, negotiating dual relationships, and feeling unsafe in academia for engaging in these efforts.

Regarding the multicultural feminist principles summarized earlier, such as sharing power, Goodman et al. (2004) note the challenges of "practice sometimes [needing] to catch up with rhetoric" (p. 814). For example, feedback in response to evaluation questions posed to clients as part of one FYE project indicated that these questions were too negative and that clients felt they were being "checked-up on." As a result, a new evaluation process—which clients helped to create—emerged, proving to be "a pivotal moment in moving beyond an ideological commitment to sharing power to actually shifting processes and methods to ensure that power was shared in a practical way" (p. 814). The responses of students participating in this project also point to the power of this training approach: "Part of my socialization into psychology has been to think of myself as a skilled and competent expert. But with ROAD [an FYE project], I am being told that the women participating are the experts of their own lives. They are teaching me more than I am teaching them" (p. 815). The student further pointed out that this kind of learning "is sometimes confusing as it goes counter to the message I get in many other professional contexts" (p. 815).

Talleyrand, Chung, and Bemak (2006) presented another example of a counseling psychology program comprehensively incorporating multicultural feminist principles, under the framework of social justice, at George Mason University (GMU). Like BC, the counseling program at GMU conveys the centrality of social justice work in their program mission statement, including an "emphasis on social justice, multiculturalism/internationalism, leadership, and advocacy" (p. 48). Moreover, the program emphasizes interdisciplinary training that includes "public policy, public health, political science, sociology, anthropology, and education as important components toward social justice work" (p. 47). Talleyrand et al. (2006) describe how the evolution of the program took place over time and with great effort. That is, the program did not simply emerge out of thin air or by accident. Instead, diverse faculty members specifically committed to issues of diversity and social justice were recruited by the university to administer and coordinate the counseling program. They then engaged in a deliberative process involving many meetings in which they developed their social justice training framework and curriculum. Part of these efforts also involved active efforts to recruit a diverse student body.

With respect to the curriculum, Talleyrand et al. (2006) note that they developed a specific course, Foundations in Counseling, which introduced the program's social justice mission, as well as having students engage in self-reflection about their worldviews and biases. Like BC, the faculty also created numerous practicum and externship placements that allowed students to go off-campus to work with a variety of organizations. In addition to community sites described by Goodman et al. (2004), GMU also places students in government bodies engaged in public policy and legislative work. Other program courses also support the social justice framework. For example, their career counseling course involves experiences outside the typical testing-in-an-office paradigm. The faculty additionally developed three unique courses in advanced internship for social justice, leadership, and multiculturalism, respectively: "There is no counseling emphasis in these courses; rather students are prepared to be leaders in the counseling field by taking on positions such as client, policy, research, or community and school advocates" (Talleyrand et al., 2006, p. 52).

In addition to individual program initiatives, a number of efforts to incorporate multicultural, feminist, and social justice principles into training have taken place at the organizational level of counseling psychology. For example, the Council of Counseling Psychology Training Programs (CCPTP) took the initiative to develop *the Counseling Psychology Model Training Values Statement Addressing Diversity* (hereafter, the Values Statement, which may be viewed in its entirety at http://www.ccptp.org/trainingdirector page6.html). Impetus for the Values Statement arose in response to a training director's query of the CCPTP listserv of how programs were handling situations in which students' personal values (e.g., religious beliefs) seemed to conflict with counseling psychology professional values (e.g., working with diverse clients, including gay/lesbian/bisexual clients). The Values Statement acknowledges that "respect for diversity and for values different from one's own is a central value of counseling psychology training programs" and that both trainers and trainees "agree to work together to create training environments that are characterized by respect, safety, and trust." Moreover, "both trainers and trainees are expected to demonstrate a willingness to examine their personal values, and to acquire and utilize professionally relevant knowledge and skills regardless of their beliefs, attitudes, and values." The Values Statement was fully endorsed by CCPTP, APA Division 17 Society of Counseling Psychology, and the Association of Counseling Center Training Agencies (ACCTA).

A series of articles was published in *The Counseling Psychologist* addressing the need for the Values Statement (Mintz et al., 2009) as well as ways of operationalizing the Values Statement in academic programs (Winterowd, Adams, Miville, & Mintz, 2009), the admissions process (Loewy, Juntunen, & Duan, 2009), and pre-doctoral internship sites (Illfelder-Kaye, Lese-Fowler, Bursley, Reyes, & Bieschke, 2009). As Mintz et al. (2009) noted,

> our stance is that values in therapy should not be avoided, nor can they... we instead need to come to social consensus about what we value and acknowledge these values (e.g., social justice, the imperative to working with diverse others, and understanding how refusal may serve to further oppress marginalized groups) as a significant aspect of all we do, including research, counseling, training, and supervision. (p. 656)

Winterowd et al. (2009) operationalized the statement through a series of virtues and dispositions, including being respectful, inclusive, collaborative, open, inquisitive, self-aware and introspective, culturally aware, socially just, and committed to professional growth and improvement. They also provided suggestions for specific structural changes that programs can make to create "an environmental context that facilitates exploration regarding the assumptions and previous life experiences of trainees and trainers" (p. 686). These include (a) recruiting and retaining diverse faculty and students; (b) infusing the Values Statement into program mission statements, goals, and materials; (c) introducing the Values Statement during new student orientation; (d) incorporating the Values Statement virtues and dispositions as part of student evaluations in practicum settings as well as annually; (d) incorporating the Values Statement virtues and dispositions throughout courses, practicum experiences, research experiences, faculty-student discussions, and colloquia; and, finally, (e) ensuring that program faculty are familiar with and emulate the Values Statement as role models.

Another organizational effort to promote multicultural and feminist training approaches was through a Special Task Group (STG) established through APA Division 17 by President Roberta Nutt "to develop a model that could facilitate the development of competence in multiple aspects of diversity, so that various aspects of diversity (e.g., race, ethnicity, gender, sexual orientation, age, etc.) become present in all aspects of trainees' and current professionals' work ..." (Miville et al., 2009, p. 521). A major source of information regarding diversity was the series of practice guidelines published by APA regarding multicultural concerns (APA, 2003), girls and women (APA, 2007), gay/lesbian/bisexual individuals (APA Division 44 Committee on Lesbian, Gay, & Bisexual Concerns Task Force, 2000), and aging (APA, 2004). The STG, co-chaired by Marie Miville and Changming Duan, developed and conducted the survey of counseling psychology training directors described at the beginning of the chapter. Miville et al. (2009) concluded from the overall findings of a review of literature, as well as the survey, that although many programs were incorporating training approaches emphasizing some aspects of diversity, including race-ethnicity and sexual orientation, "less clear was the consistent incorporation of other guidelines, such as those related to gender and aging, into the same curricula, pointing to potential deficits in training in these important areas of diversity" (p. 532). Miville et al. (2009) then presented a comprehensive framework, the Integrated Training Model (ITM) "to facilitate competence in multiple diversity dimensions" (p. 533), which they felt would be a more effective strategy.

The ITM consists of four stages or levels of learning: (a) understanding the multicultural self; (b) understanding others based on common themes across diversity, particularly those focusing on oppression, developing a critical consciousness, and social justice; (c) understanding others based on specific factors, involving cultural sensitivity and accurate empathy; and (d) developing specific strategies for interventions at individual, cultural, and systemic levels. Miville et al. (2009) also discussed specific components of evaluation of trainees at each level. For example, understanding the multicultural self can involve self-reflection about the "privileges associated with their respective identities, their role in the oppression of others, and the implications of their social oppression" (pp. 545–546).

Another important organizational training initiative was achieved by the American Counseling Association (ACA), a related professional body, whose Governing Council approved the Advocacy Competencies in 2003 (Toporek, Lewis, & Crethar, 2009). This set of competencies was developed to promote advocacy competence, "the ability, understanding, and knowledge to carry out advocacy ethically and effectively" (Toporek et al., 2009, p. 262). The competencies are organized along two dimensions: extent of client involvement (including "acting with" or "acting on behalf" of clients), and level of intervention ("client/student [i.e., individual], school/community, and public arena [i.e., public or societal]"; p. 262). The model consists of six domains: "client/student empowerment, client/student advocacy, community collaboration, systems advocacy, public information, and social/political advocacy" (p. 262). The development and approval of these competencies by ACA was a clear acknowledgment that oppression and systemic barriers interfere with clients' health and well-being and may even be the cause of their distress. Advocacy extends the impact that counseling may have by increasing the likelihood that environmental stressors and barriers will play a less significant role in the lives of clients (p. 265).

As further evidence of organizational support for multicultural feminist training, the primary APA training journal, *Training and Education in Professional Psychology,* recently published a special section on this topic under the rubric of social justice. Of particular note was the development of specific practicum competencies aimed at preparing doctoral students in professional psychology, including counseling psychology, to have a strong social justice focus in their clinical skills (Lewis, 2010). The competencies were based on an expanded definition of social justice originally put forth by Goodman et al. (2004):

> the fair and equitable distribution of rights, opportunities, and resources between individuals and between groups of individuals within a given society, and the establishment of relationships within this society such that all individuals are treated with an equal degree of respect and dignity. (Lewis, 2010, p. 146)

Lewis (2010) contends that the latter half of the definition highlights treatment of individuals because "the manner in which people are treated in interpersonal exchanges has a profound effect on one's experience of fairness" (p. 146), separate and beyond the simple distribution of goods and resources. Lewis defines this as *interactional justice,* that is, "what is taking place between people" (p. 148). He distinguishes between training at earlier stages of practicum training, which can focus on establishing interactional justice in relationship-building or initial assessment procedures, and training at later stages. For example, during the initial clinical interview, while obtaining a personal history of their client, students can be taught to ask directly about clients' experiences of injustice in their lives. More advanced training, likely in external sites, can focus on coming to "appreciate procedural justice as it is practiced in a real-world community setting" (p. 149). For example, students can learn how funding is obtained, by whom, and for whom. Like Winterowd et al. (2009), Lewis provides a number of recommendations for training programs regarding structural changes to emphasize social justice work throughout the entirety of doctoral training.

In another article in the same issue, Burnes and Singh (2010) describe specific learning activities that may be used to socialize students into a social justice framework. These activities include examining the current literature, journaling to encourage self-reflection, and examining larger systems, for example, through field observation. Burnes and Singh (2010) also provide specific suggestions for practicum training, such as reevaluation of clinical hours, typically counted as direct service hours within an agency. They suggest that programs instead add "specific social justice language and activities" (p. 156), including outreach programming outside a counseling center that focuses on marginalized students in academia. They also urge skills training in psycho-educational workshops on outreach and prevention, such as meeting with stakeholders to co-construct the actual programming event. Both Lewis (2010) and Burnes and Singh (2010) encourage programs to partner with sites in order to set up practicum placements that will provide social justice training.

Challenges in Adopting a Multicultural Feminist Approach

Providing multicultural feminist and social justice training comes with a number of challenges. One issue addressed previously is structuring the curriculum to enhance this focus from the first day of training to the last. Thus, a major challenge is ensuring that program faculty are on board to develop and maintain this curriculum. Clearly, the recruitment of a diverse faculty and student body is essential to this goal. However, once these individuals are gathered, much time and discussion needs to occur to develop the program, while at the same time ensuring that it meets important accreditation standards.

Another major challenge is in building coursework that provides didactic and experiential activities that promote multicultural feminist principles. A number of excellent resources currently exist that present and summarize specific courses and activities (e.g., Adams, Bell, & Griffin, 2007; Alvarez & Miville, 2003; Sinacore & Boatwright, 2005; Vazquez & Garcia-Vazquez, 2003). In particular, Adams et al. (2007) provided a wealth of specific activities for training across a number of diversity dimensions, including race, gender, and sexual orientation, nested within a social justice framework.

Moreover, as noted earlier, multicultural feminist training also will lead to different organization of traditional courses, such as ethics, assessment, consultation, even research design. For example, ethics training might need to be reconceptualized from its traditional underpinnings to adequately prepare students for their work with social change and advocacy (Sparks & Park, 2000). Sparks and Park recommend viewing the intersections of multicultural and feminist principles as a "borderlands" to help conceptualize ethical dilemmas. They recommended several ways to navigate this challenging terrain: (a) understanding the cultural context (e.g., cultural norms and immigration concerns in dealing with domestic violence); (b) awareness of oppressive forces (e.g., lack of trust of mental health professionals); (c) enhancing self-awareness (e.g., potential cultural conflicts with egalitarian views); and (d) flexibility in determining solutions (e.g., indigenous or culturally sanctioned forms of "fighting back"). Sparks and Park (2000) urge practitioners to "undergo an ethical reasoning process" (p. 221) in negotiating mutual resolutions to ethical concerns.

Goodman et al. (2004) described two broad ethical mandates: "First, the idea that values should and do shape our endeavors... [and second] that the processes and outcomes of our work should entail empowerment and collaboration rather than exploitation and objectification" (p. 819). The actual practice of multicultural feminist training can lead to a number of ethical dilemmas. For example, in line with the tenet of ongoing self-evaluation, what happens when "strongly held values (political, religious, or other) [arise that are] different from those of the community members" (p. 820)? Goodman et al. (2004) describe how an "empowerment" project with Asian American middle school girls left them feeling distant and marginalized. These girls wanted to maintain their cultural values of "modesty, respect, honor, and collectivism" (p. 820) which they felt were not being incorporated into the project. Providing students with the tools to respond to these situations is critical. For example, the recent work regarding the Values Statement (Mintz et al., 2009; Winterowd et al., 2009) and their virtues and dispositions can guide initial training on attitudes and decision-making skills to students in their ethics courses.

Another potential ethical dilemma relates to the multicultural feminist principle of "'giving voice,' and [asking] which communities' voices should be amplified? On what basis should choices be made to direct limited resources toward one community over another?" (Goodman et al., 2004, p. 822). Further, "should a social justice agent support community members' voices even when they seem self-destructive?" (p. 823). Although there are no easy or immediate answers to such ethical questions, programs can take the initiative by presenting potential social justice dilemmas in their ethics and practicum courses for class discussion. A case example I have used in my doctoral ethics course for first year students centers on a psychologist working in an agency where state law forbids providing services to undocumented immigrants. On the one hand, the professional may behave unethically by not providing services to people clearly in need, yet on the other hand, may not only break the law by doing so, but also endanger the funding status of the entire agency and its ability to serve the population at large. What should be done? The class discussion usually is quite intense and thoughtful, with a variety of strategies suggested by students. The key point is for faculty to develop courses that predict potential dilemmas and problems that will arise from conducting research and engaging in health services within a multicultural feminist framework, particularly as these training activities promote social change and advocacy.

Other challenges that can arise from teaching within this framework involve the holistic or intersectional framework regarding diversity. As Miville et al. (2009) pointed out, "Of greatest concern is how to incorporate an integrative approach in a way that does not minimize the unique experiences of individual trainees, namely, ensuring that important unique experiences do not lose their emotional valence ..." (pp. 548–549). Miville et al. (2009) cite an example in which, during the process of self-reflection and dialoguing with peers, a student inappropriately responds to another's experience of racism by comparing it to her experience of sexism. Although there may be some important parallels, it is important for the student to understand what the comparison truly meant to her, and how it may have led to the other student feeling minimized, perhaps degraded. Miville et al. (2009) strongly urge that "any effective integrative approach must incorporate space and time to allow for the expression of thoughts and feelings about critical experiences of oppression and unique struggles associated with each dimension of diversity" (p. 549).

Miville et al. (2009) also caution that teaching within this framework must "allow for the expression of differing meanings or the impact of similar issues across individuals without leaving some feeling minimized or even revictimized" (p. 549). For example, violence against women is experienced differently by women and men: "Fear of victimization, differential power and status ..., and gendered privilege" are just a few ways that women and men will differ in their reactions to these topics (p. 549). It is therefore important that emphasis be given to "empower oppressed groups and prevent any potential revictimization in training" (p. 549).

The notion of "safety" in the classroom has been addressed by a number of scholars. Byars-Winston et al. (2005) suggest that these concerns may arise to mask the anxiety and fear of more socially privileged individuals. Tatum (2002) advises the establishment of ground rules from the first class onward (e.g., speaking from one's own experiences) as a means of opening up dialogue in this area. Also, within a multicultural feminist framework, students can be invited to co-construct these ground rules, perhaps suggesting specific readings and class discussions. Byars-Winston et al. (2005) suggest clarifying important terms, such as "race," "ethnicity," and "gender," from the outset, and then building to more complex terms and models, such as "deconstruction, positionality, privilege, and social location" (p. 131). Faculty also can serve as role models in self-disclosing about their experiences and understanding of the complexities of their identities. Finally, the overall experiences of resistance can be addressed directly, either in class dialogue or individual conversation and journaling (Alvarez & Miville, 2003).

Goodman et al. (2004) acknowledge that the greatest challenge in conducting training within a multicultural feminist and social justice framework "is simply its emotional costs" (p. 827). Student effort and work may go unrewarded and unrecognized, leaving some to feel overwhelmed. However, they assert that "the rewards are greater than the costs...We have had the privilege of participating in interesting, complex, challenging, meaningful, and valuable work that embodies values about which we care deeply" (p. 827). Certainly these words convey that although social justice work is difficult, persistence can lead to important changes, albeit small and distal. Program faculty can play a tremendous role in helping students develop realistic expectations about change and the inevitability of failure, as well as to deal with the hopelessness and anger that can arise; faculty can help students to understand that "their work represents just one small brick in an edifice that must be built by many, many people" (p. 829).

In sum, providing multicultural feminist training creates exciting opportunities for learning for trainees and trainers that can lead to genuine changes in the communities and clients they serve. However, a focus on client empowerment and community collaboration also comes with a number of challenges. If these challenges are resolved thoughtfully, they can lead to further positive changes for those involved. Moreover, planning for and developing training activities based on these challenges, as well as other concerns that arise, will better prepare trainees for working effectively as multicultural feminist psychologists.

Supervision

Given the importance of faculty role modeling and support in multicultural feminist training, relationship building between faculty and students must be given a prime focus within a program. Moreover, as with curriculum and specific courses, supervision and mentoring need to be congruent with the principles and goals of multicultural feminist training. As Nelson et al. (2006) described, "By virtue of its evaluative function, supervision is a power-disproportionate relationship. Yet because it involves assisting a supervisee to develop along both personal and clinical dimensions, it is also a highly personal relationship" (p. 105). And because this is such a difficult mixture of goals, Nelson et al. (2006) suggest that there can be great potential for conflict. Moreover, as Miville, Rosa, and Constantine (2005) noted, a primary finding available about supervision in this area is "the critical importance of supervisor competence.... Unfortunately, lack of multicultural training coupled with a position of power on the part of supervisors is often a recipe for neglect and potential harm to supervisees and their clients" (p. 196). Porter and Vasquez (1997) reported that the most negative supervisory experiences generally were overly directive or not directive enough; inappropriately pathologized supervisees; were not encouraging of supervisees' alternative views; and promoted oppressive views regarding race, gender, and class.

Alternatively, several scholars have described multicultural feminist supervision as it might be positively experienced. In an early attempt to discuss supervision from this vantage point, several scholars participating in the aforementioned *1993 National Conference on Education and Training in Feminist Practice*, sponsored by APA Division of the Psychology of Women (Division 35), formed a group to focus on this topic. Porter and Vasquez (1997) summarized these findings, noting that a hallmark characteristic of feminist supervision was the exploration of sociocultural and historical factors, that is, multiculturalism. They provide a definition of feminist supervision that also incorporates multicultural concerns:

> Feminist supervision encompasses a collaborative relationship that is mutual and reflexive in nature. It is not egalitarian; rather it is predicated on the principle of mutual respect characterized by clear, direct, and honest dialogic communication and responsible action. It encompasses awareness of and attention to the social, contextual nature of both the supervisory and the therapeutic processes. A feminist supervisory context embodies the feminist principles of therapy, including the analyses of power, boundaries, and hierarchy; an emphasis on social context and diversity; an examination of the relationship of language to the social construction of gender; and the promotion of social activism, ethics, and lifelong self-examination and professional development. (p. 161)

Porter and Vasquez (1997) also described important qualities of supervisors who practice in this context: they know and model feminist (and multicultural) concepts; initiate discussion on intimate aspects of therapy while maintaining good boundaries; and engage in lifelong self-examination. Finally, Porter and Vasquez provided several principles that may guide multicultural feminist supervision:

1. Proactive analysis of power dynamics and differentials;
2. Mutually respectful and collaborative relationship that encourages supervisees' autonomy and diverse views;
3. Promotion of self-reflection through "openness, authenticity, reflexivity, and the value of lifelong learning" (p. 164);
4. Emphasis on social context;
5. Emphasis on the social constructions of gender;
6. Promotion of advocacy and activism;
7. Maintenance of standards for competent and ethical practice;
8. Use of a developmental perspective; and
9. Advocacy by supervisors for their supervisees and clients within the training setting.

Another group of diverse scholars similarly discussed multicultural feminist supervision during a 1998 conference sponsored by Division 17 Section for the *Advancement of Women, Advancing Together: Centralizing Feminism and Multiculturalism in Counseling Psychology Conference*, the findings of which were published by Nelson et al. (2006). Unlike Porter and Vasquez (1997), this group did not feel ready to describe guidelines for multicultural feminist supervision. Instead they presented key discussion points that they believed might encourage others to further the dialogue. In short, they found that dialogue itself, rather than formalizing a model, seemed to be important to the process, as were their individual and group reflections. Similar to Porter and Vasquez (1997), the central focus of their dialogue was power and power differences in the supervision relationship, and they felt that this topic should be the responsibility of the supervisor to initiate. Nelson et al. (2006) acknowledged that there were risks for supervisors in taking this approach, particularly novice professionals, such as alienation from supervisees who might not be ready to engage in authentic self-reflection, and from supervisees' mentors who might not value this approach to supervision. Similar risks also apply to supervisees, and may be magnified by the evaluative power that supervisors have.

Nelson et al. (2006) provided several suggestions for supervisors. First, supervisors were invited to deconstruct current models of supervision for their potential Eurocentric bias and to embrace a more complex or intersectional approach to diversity in their own theoretical stance as well as their supervisees' development. Supervisors also were encouraged to take risks, and to share their vulnerabilities with students. As one participant stated, "My students respond so positively when I share my mistakes" (p. 112). The authors also promoted the importance of helping supervisees develop cognitive complexity regarding themselves, others, and their clinical work. Moreover, supervisors need to create a context in which anxiety can be tolerated: "Naming race and gender issues in supervision may be seen as a process of coming out. As with any process of coming out, the input of supportive others is essential" (p. 113).

Indeed, the difficulty of genuinely supporting each other was evident in another article by Steward and Phelps (2004), who shared their perspectives as African American women participating in the Nelson et al. (2006) group. They noted stark differences between themselves and their White colleagues, noting their ease in discussing racial issues, a practice that was not evident in their White colleagues, and Steward and Phelps's (2004) own hesitation in sharing what they referred to as "personal" issues, likely dealing with gender, also not evident in their colleagues. Moreover, Steward and Phelps did not share others' discomfort with hierarchical relations, as these were seen as a norm within many African American communities (as they are in many other diverse cultures). They also questioned the presumed universal power differential between supervisee and supervisor, asserting that there were situations in which the supervisee may have the upper hand, given their potential privileged backgrounds. Steward and Phelps concluded by noting the importance of continuing these dialogues: "we believe that to further advance the understanding and compatibility of feminism and multiculturalism in supervision content, process, and outcome, as well as to ensure the success of future work groups, these points of difference must be honestly and openly examined and resolved.... The future of the profession can and should begin with us" (p. 364).

Miville et al. (2005) provided a number of suggestions for supervisors seeking to become culturally competent. First, supervisors need to explore identity dimensions of themselves and their supervisees for areas of convergence and divergence. Supervisors should prepare to negotiate with each supervisee the unique resolutions for tensions and biases that may exist between them. Miville et al. (2005) cautioned that similarities between supervisors and supervisees do not necessarily mean that multicultural or feminist topics should not be discussed, nor that tensions and biases may not exist. Second, supervisors need to initiate dialogue that helps assess the knowledge base and identify strengths and weaknesses of both themselves and their supervisees. Finally, "supervisors greatly affect the quality of multicultural supervision both by what they do and by what they do not do" (p. 198). Activities beyond the supervisory dyad (e.g., engaging in social justice advocacy work in the community or serving in leadership roles of advocacy organizations) can communicate overt support for complex multicultural feminist issues within the dyad.

A number of supervision models have been proposed that emphasize multicultural or feminist or both themes (e.g., Ancis & Ladany, 2001; Norton & Coleman, 2003; Barnes & Bernard, 2003). One particularly useful model is the heuristic model of non-oppressive interpersonal development (Ancis & Ladany, 2001) because of its intersectional approach toward inclusion of diverse identity dimensions, including race and gender, within a supervisory context. The model focuses on both supervisees' and supervisors' multiple identities as well as their social interactions. Ancis and Ladany (2001) note that for any demographic variable, individuals can be part of either a socially privileged group (SOP) or a socially oppressed group (SOG). People have thoughts, feelings, and behaviors that are associated with each of their identities, and their level of awareness about oppression and privilege for each identity can progress across four stages, ranging from apathy and distance to acceptance and awareness. Level of awareness also may vary across different identity dimensions. Ancis and Ladany (2001) note that clinically relevant behaviors are associated with each stage, referred to as adaptation, incongruence, exploration, and integration.

Worrell and Remer (2003) noted that any multicultural feminist supervision model should include (1) attention to process; (2) application of diversity analyses to supervisee-client relationships; (3) exploration of supervisee theoretical orientation; (4) examination of therapy goals; (5) a redefinition of health and pathology, particularly damaging labels; (6) a focus on both internal and external sources of client problems; (7) provision of continuous constructive feedback to client emphasizing strengths; (8) a focus on prevention as well as remediation, including outreach and programming; and (9) the provision of respect and validation of the supervisee, "assisting trainee to trust [his/her] own experience" (p. 326). They also suggest that supervision may be more effective in a group setting; as it maximizes faculty resources, more students can be exposed to this approach, and peers can learn from each other.

In sum, supervision within a multicultural feminist framework occurs within a collaborative, mutually respectful relationship that incorporates intersectional identity dimensions. Open dialogue is key to effectively socializing supervisees to promote social justice in their clients' lives, both through individual and systemic interventions, as is the supervisor's competence. Future work in this area might focus on developing a supervision model that directly incorporates multicultural feminist principles.

Continuing Education

As Miville et al. (2009) noted, "for practitioners and educators who graduated several years ago, developing, updating, or maintaining diversity competencies may be a challenge involving intentional and self-directed behavior" (p. 554). Unfortunately, little information is available about how to conduct continuing education within a multicultural feminist or social justice framework (Toporek et al., 2009). Moreover, Miville et al. (2009) and Toporek et al. (2009), among others, have called for the inclusion of multicultural feminist and social justice issues to be a part of licensure renewal standards in all states, given the great likelihood of current practitioners in need of upgrading their cultural competence with clients and students alike. Although no specific model currently exists that incorporates multicultural feminist concepts, a number of authors have provided suggestions for creating continuing education programs within this format.

As Parham and Whitten (2003) noted, in many continuing education sessions, "participants sit and listen passively for most of the program and are allotted 2 or 3 minutes at the end of the program to 'ask questions'" (p. 566). Unfortunately, this kind of format does not promote a multicultural feminist perspective in either training or practice. Rather than sitting and listening passively, a more effective approach "occurs when professionals are most likely to be aware of a need for better ways to think about what they do" (Cervero, 2000, in Miville et al., 2009, p. 553), particularly if professionals already have a lifelong learning orientation. This approach engages professionals in accord with their level of clinical expertise and life experience, and helps prepare them for the psychological work that must ensue to establish cultural competence.

Mott (2000, in Miville et al., 2009) also suggested using a performance-based approach with current professionals. This focus goes beyond novice questions of what the psychologist must know or do, instead centering on "What is the professional all about?" This focus is well-suited for the more reflexive aspects critical to multicultural feminist pedagogies. Miville et al. (2009) recommended small-group formats "to create the space and time needed for current professionals to process their professional and life experiences and their potentially intense reactions to content material," particularly since the groups are likely to be heterogeneous (p. 554). The approach also presumes and incorporates the level of knowledge and experience that professionals already have, minimizing power differentials and struggles that might occur.

With respect to dealing with resistance to learning, using a variety of teaching modes is ideal, for example, "reading assignment, journaling activities, lectures, discussion, role plays, group encounters, [and] case reviews" (Miville et al., 2009, p. 555). Media outlets, such as movies, books, and biographies, also can be helpful ways to stimulate self-reflection and small group discussion. One important perspective is to view professionals more like a consultation group in which "resistance may be explored, and learning could be linked to (a) increased practice effectiveness being associated with flexibility, self-assessment, and adaptability... and (b) increased career satisfaction, which might promote professional activity in one's senior years" (Miville et al., 2009, p. 555).

Parham and Whitten (2003) also offered several helpful suggestions for envisioning continuing education leading to cultural competence, first, viewing learning as "a process rather than a plateau," that is, lifelong (p. 572). Second, continuing education should be viewed not as simply something to be done to keep one's license, but rather as "the cultivation of the human spirit," a means of enlightenment and path toward competence (p. 572). Third, for long-lasting impact, continuing educators also need to assume that learning does not only occur in a classroom, but "must come from real experiences in living, sharing, and bonding outside of the classroom setting" (p. 572). Finally, rather than a focus on accrual of hours, continuing education programs must emphasize "mastery of the skills and knowledge necessary to be effective service providers" (p. 572).

For more formalized postgraduate training, Johnson and Remer (1997) summarized principles identified by a working group at the 1993 feminist training conference previously described. These included (a) incorporating feminist pedagogical principles, such as collegial environment, local and national support groups, and mentors; (b) centralizing attitude and values change to developing knowledge and skills; (c) focusing on diversity, both cultural norms and oppression issues; (d) incorporating systems analyses; and (e) infusing principles throughout the entire program. Johnson and Remer (1997) also provided year-by-year program suggestions for both novice and experienced clinicians.

As can be seen, although some excellent information is currently available about continuing education, a great deal more work needs to be conducted in terms to developing and providing continuing education programs from a multicultural feminist stance. Given the large numbers of practitioners who are still active and who likely have not received this kind of training, engaging in this work will be of great service to the profession, as well as to many communities.

Concluding Remarks and Future Directions

In this chapter, I have reviewed concepts and strategies reflecting multicultural feminist training, supervision, and continuing education. Given the comprehensive nature of this approach, one major recommendation is for training programs to take a structural perspective and infuse multicultural feminist concepts and strategies throughout all aspects of training. Thus, it is critical for programs as a whole to be on board with this approach. Otherwise, the impact is likely to be piecemeal or disjointed, based on the interests of a particular instructor or supervisor. Recent conferences and publications in the field reflect a level of unprecedented organizational support for multicultural feminist approaches to training in the fields of psychology and counseling. This level of public discourse is necessary, though not sufficient, for moving the field forward in taking a more complex and proactive approach to individual and cultural diversity. What remains is for this work to be applied at the individual program level, where inconsistency exists regarding the breadth and depth of training in multiple diversity dimensions, including race-ethnicity and gender.

In reviewing the current literature, a number of questions for future directions in multicultural feminist training and education arise. These include:

What types of support do programs need today that will help them move forward in taking a more proactive multicultural feminist and social justice stance in training the next generation? This question is particularly salient in light of accreditation procedures and the need to maintain professional standards in all aspects of professional work, including practice, assessment, ethical decision making, research, and so on. Clearly, maintaining a diverse faculty, particularly at the senior level, has long been identified as central in helping move programs forward. Moreover, this question becomes ever more important in light of continuing financial pressures and fewer faculty resources devoted to maintaining sites, courses, and supervisory experiences that are timely and intensive.

What other organizational efforts can be carried out to further support individual programs? In other words, when will the next conference occur on multicultural feminism in psychology? Given the critical impact that previous conferences have had on the field, it seems timely to organize the next generation of educators to take on this important task and discuss what are the next (and recurring) set of challenges for multicultural feminist training, practice, and research.

Given the dearth of existing research exploring the effectiveness of multicultural feminist training approaches, what would studies in this area need to explore? Our field emphasizes empirically based approaches that also are multiculturally sensitive. What qualitative and quantitative approaches can be undertaken to explore what educational activities are effective, as well as how these activities could be further improved? Student responses to training would be an excellent starting point, as well as their efficacy with their clients as they advance through the program.

I began this chapter with a quote from Lillian Comas-Diaz highlighting both the "blessings and terrors" (2005, p. 979) of being a multicultural feminist professional. By all accounts, the path is lifelong, unpredictable, and arduous, and involves the joy and pain of self-discovery and making connections with others in many diverse ways:

> Culture, ethnicity, gender, and social class unfolded the "enigma of my arrival." Julia de Burgos' (1967) poem "*Yo misma fui mi ruta*" (I was my own path) taught me to chart my voyage, and Antonio Machado's (1983) composition, "*Caminante no hay camino, se hace camino al andar*" (There is no way; the way is made by walking) was my compass. I have journeyed with masters, teachers, and peers who value global connectedness. My clients, fellow travelers from diverse areas of the world, taught me that we all are part of the same circle. In psychotherapy, as in life, the philosopher's stone is to recognize yourself in the other. (Comas-Diaz, 2005, p. 979)

¡Buen viaje! Have a good journey!

References

Adams, M., Bell, L. A., & Griffin, P. (2007). *Teaching for diversity and social justice* (2nd ed.). New York: Routledge.

Ali, S. R., & Ancis, J. R. (2005). Multicultural education and critical pedagogy approaches. In C. Z. Enns & A. L. Sinacore (Eds.), *Teaching and social justice: Integrating multicultural and feminist theories in the classroom* (pp. 69–84). Washington, DC: American Psychological Association.

American Psychological Association. (2003). Guidelines on multicultural education, training, research, practice, and organizational change for psychologists. *American Psychologist, 58,* 377–402.

American Psychological Association. (2004). Guidelines for psychological practice with older adults. *American Psychologist, 59,* 236–260.

American Psychological Association. (2007). Guidelines for psychological practice with girls and women. *American Psychologist, 62,* 949–979.

American Psychological Association Division 44 Committee on Lesbian, Gay, & Bisexual Concerns Task Force. (2000). Guidelines for psychotherapy with lesbian, gay, and bisexual clients. *American Psychologist, 55,* 1440–1451.

Alvarez, A. N., & Miville, M. L. (2003).Walking a tightrope: Strategies for teaching undergraduate multicultural counseling courses. In D. Pope-Davis, W. Liu, & R. Toporek (Eds.),, *Handbook of multicultural competencies in counseling and psychology* (pp. 528–547). Thousand Oaks, CA: Sage.

Ancis, J. R., & Ladany, N. (2001). A multicultural framework for counseling superivision. In L. J. Bradley & N. Ladany (Eds.), *Counselor supervision: Principles, process, and practice* (pp. 63–90). Philadelphia, PA: Brunner-Roudtledge.

Ancis, J. R., & Ali, S. R. (2005). Multicultural counseling training approaches: Implications for pedagogy. In C. Z. Enns & A. L. Sinacore (Eds.), *Teaching and social justice: Integrating multicultural and feminist theories in the classroom* (pp. 85–97). Washington, DC: American Psychological Association.

Barnes, K. L., & Bernard, J. M. (2003). Women in counseling and psychotherapy supervision. In M. Kopala & M. A. Keitel (Eds.), *Handbook of counseling women* (pp. 535–545). Thousand Oaks, CA: Sage.

Bowman, S. L., & King, K. D. (2003). Gender, feminism, and multicultural competencies. In D. Pope-Davis, W. Liu, & R. Toporek, *Handbook of multicultural competencies in counseling and psychology* (pp. 59–71). Thousand Oaks, CA: Sage.

Brabeck, M., & Brown, L. (1997). Feminist theory and psychological practice. In J. Worrell & N. G. Johnson (Eds.), *Shaping the future of feminist psychology: Education, research, and practice* (pp. 15–35). Washington, DC: American Psychological Association.

Burnes, T. R., & Singh, A. A. (2010). Integrating social justice training into the practicum experience for psychology trainees: Starting earlier. *Training and Education in Professional Psychology, 4,* 153–162.

Byars-Winston, A. M., Akcali, O., Tao, K. W., Nepomuceno, C. A., Anctil, T. M., Acevedo, V., Benally, N., & Wilton, G. (2005). The challenges, impact, and implementation of critical multicultural pedagogies. In C. Z. Enns & A. L. Sinacore (Eds.), *Teaching and social justice: Integrating multicultural and feminist theories in the classroom* (pp. 125–141). Washington, DC: American Psychological Association.

Chin, J. L., & Russo, N. F. (1997). Feminist curriculum development: Principles and resources. In J. Worrell & N. G. Johnson (Eds.), *Shaping the future of feminist psychology: Education, research, and practice* (pp. 93–120). Washington, DC: American Psychological Association.

Cole, E. R. (2009). Intersectionality and research in psychology. *American Psychologist, 64,* 170–180.

Comas-Diaz, L. (2005). Becoming a multicultural psychotherapist: The confluence of culture, ethnicity, and gender. *Journal of Clinical Psychology, 61,* 973–981.

Davis, A. Y. (1983). *Women, race, and class.* New York: Vintage.

Enns, C. Z. (2004). *Feminist theories and feminist psychotherapies: Origins, themes, and diversity* (2nd ed.). Binghamton, NY: Haworth Press.

Enns, C. Z., & Forrest, L. M. (2005). Toward defining and integrating multicultural and feminist pedagogies. In C. Z. Enns & A. L. Sinacore (Eds.), *Teaching and social justice: Integrating multicultural and feminist theories in the classroom* (pp. 3–23). Washington, DC: American Psychological Association.

Enns, C. Z., & Sinacore, A. L. (2005). Second-wave feminisms and their relationships to pedagogy. In C. Z. Enns & A. L. Sinacore (Eds.), *Teaching and social justice: Integrating multicultural and feminist theories in the classroom* (pp. 25–39). Washington, DC: American Psychological Association.

Espín, O. (1994). Feminist approaches. In L. Comas-Diaz & B. Greene (Eds.), *Women of color: Integrating ethnic and gender identities in psychotherapy* (pp. 265–286). New York: Guildford Press.

Funderburk, J. R., & Fukuyama, M. A. (2001). Feminism, multiculturalism, and spirituality: Convergent and divergent forces in psychotherapy. *Women and Therapy, 24*, 3, 1–18.

Goodman, L. A., Liang, B., Helms, J. E., Latta, R. E., Sparks, E., and Weintraub, S. R. (2004). Training counseling psychologists as social justice agents: Feminist and multicultural principles in action. *The Counseling Psychologist, 32*, 793–837.

Hays, P. A. (1996). Addressing the complexities of culture and gender in counseling. *Journal of Counseling and Development, 74*, 332–338.

Hurtado, A. (2010). Multiple lenses: Multicultural feminist theory. In H. Landrine & N. F. Russo (Eds.), *Handbook of diversity in feminist psychology* (pp. 29–54). New York: Springer.

Ifelder-Kaye, J., Lese-Fowler, K., Bursley, K., Reyes, E., & Bieschke, K. J. (2009). Implementing the Training Values Statement Addressing Diversity in university counseling center internship. *The Counseling Psychologist, 37*, 721–743.

Israel, T. (2004). Conversations, not categories: The intersection of biracial and bisexual identities. *Women and Therapy, 27*, 1, 173–184.

Johnson, N. G., & Remer, P. (1997). Postdoctoral training in feminist psychological practice. In J. Worrell & N. G. Johnson (Eds.), *Shaping the future of feminist psychology: Education, research, and practice* (pp. 203–225). Washington, DC: American Psychological Association.

Kimmel, E., & Worrell, J. (1997). Preaching what we practice: Principles and strategies of feminist pedagogy. In J. Worrell & N. G. Johnson (Eds.), *Shaping the future of feminist psychology: Education, research, and practice* (pp. 121–154). Washington, DC: American Psychological Association.

Lewis, B. L. (2010). Social justice in practicum training: Competencies and developmental implications. *Training and Education in Professional Psychology*, 4, 145–152.

Loewy, M. I., Juntunen, C. L., Duan, C. (2009). Application of the Counseling Psychology Model Training Values Statement Addressing Diversity to the admission process. *The Counseling Psychologist, 37*, 705–720.

Mintz, L. B., Jackson, A. P., Neville, H. A., Illfelder-Kaye, J., Winterowd, C. L., & Loewy, M. I. (2009). The need for a counseling psychology model training values statement addressing diversity. *The Counseling Psychologist, 37*, 644–675.

Miville, M. L., Rosa, D., & Constantine, M. G. (2005). Building multicultural competence in clinical supervision contexts. In M. G. Constantine & D. W. Sue (Eds.), *Building multicultural competence in mental health and educational settings* (pp. 192–211). New York: Wiley.

Miville, M. L., Duan, C., Nutt, R., Waehler, C., Suzuki, L., Pistole, M. C., Arredondo, P., Duffy, M., Mejia, B., & Corpus, M. (2009). Integrating practice guidelines into professional training: Implications for diversity competence. *The Counseling Psychologist, 37*, 519–563.

Nelson, M. L., Gizara, S., Hope, A. C., Phelps, R., Steward, R., & Weitzman, L. (2006). A feminist multicultural perspective on supervision. *Journal of Multicultural Counseling and Development, 34*, 105–115.

Nishimura, N. (2004). Counseling biracial women: An intersection of multiculturalism and feminism. *Women and Therapy, 27*, 1, 133–145.

Norton, R. A., & Coleman, H. L. K. (2003). Multicultural supervision: The influence of race-related issues in supervision process and outcome. In D. Pope-Davis, W. Liu, & R. Toporek, *Handbook of multicultural competencies in counseling and psychology* (pp.114–134). Thousand Oaks, CA: Sage.

Parham, T. A., & Whitten, L. (2003). Teaching multicultural competencies in continuing education for psychologists. In D. Pope-Davis, W. Liu, & R. Toporek, *Handbook of multicultural competencies in counseling and psychology* (pp. 562–574). Thousand Oaks, CA: Sage.

Porter, N., & Vasquez, M. (1997). Covision: Feminist supervision, process, and collaboration. In J. Worrell & N. G. Johnson (Eds.), *Shaping the future of feminist psychology: Education, research, and practice* (pp. 155–172). Washington, DC: American Psychological Association.

Reid, P. T. (2002). Multicultural psychology: Brining together gender and ethnicity. *Cultural Diversity and Ethnic Minority Psychology, 8*, 103–114.

Russo, N. F., & Vaz, K. (2001). Addressing diversity in the decade of behavior: Focus on women of color. *Psychology of Women Quarterly, 25*, 280–294.

Silverstein, L. B. (2006). Integrating feminism and multiculturalism: Scientific fact or science fiction. *Professional Psychology: Research and Practice*, 37, 21–28.

Sinacore, A. L, & Boatwright, K. J. (2005). The feminist classroom: Feminist strategies and student responses. In C. Z. Enns & A. L. Sinacore (Eds.), *Teaching and social justice: Integrating multicultural and feminist theories in the classroom* (pp. 109–124). Washington, DC: American Psychological Association.

Sparks, E. E., & Park, A. H. (2000). The integration of feminism and multiculturalism: Ethical dilemmas at the border. In M. M. Brabeck (Ed.), *Practicing feminist ethics in psychology* (pp. 203–224). Washington, DC: American Psychological Association.

Steward, R. J, & Phelps, R. E. (2004). Feminist and multicultural collaboration in counseling supervision: Voices from two African American women. *Journal of Multicultural Counseling and Development, 32 (Extra)*, 358–365.

Talleyrand, R. M., Chung, R. C.-Y., & Bemak, F. (2006). Incorporating social justice in counselor training programs: A case example. In R. L. Toporek, L. H. Gerstein, N. A. Fouad, G. Roysircar, & T. Israel (Eds.), *Handbook of social justice in counseling psychology: Leadership, vision, and action* (pp. 44–58). Thousand Oaks, CA: Sage.

Tatum, B. D. (2002). *Why are all the Black kids sitting together in the cafeteria? And other conversations about race* (Rev. ed.). New York: Basic Books.

Toporek, R. L., Lewis, J. A., & Crethar, H. C. (2009). Promoting systemic change through the ACA advocacy competencies. *Journal of Counseling and Development, 87*, 260–268.

Toporek, R. L., & Vaughn, S. R. (2010). Social justice in the training of professional psychologists: Moving forward. *Training and Education in Professional Psychology*, 4, 177–182.

Vazquez, L. A., & Garcia-Vazquez, E. (2003). Teaching multicultural competence in the counseling curriculum. In D. Pope-Davis, W. Liu, & R. Toporek, *Handbook of multicultural competencies in counseling and psychology* (pp. 546–561). Thousand Oaks, CA: Sage.

Williams, E. N., & Barber, J. S. (2004). Power and responsibility in therapy: Integrating feminism and multiculturalism. *Journal of Multicultural Counseling and Development, 32 (Extra),* 390–401.

Winterowd, C. L., Adams, E. M., Miville, M. L., & Mintz, L. (2009) Operationalizing, instilling, and assessing counseling psychology training values in academic programs. *The Counseling Psychologist, 37*, 676–704.

Worrell, J., & Remer, P. (2003). *Feminist perspectives in therapy: Empowering diverse women* (2nd ed.). New York: Wiley.

CHAPTER

24 Feminist Multicultural Mentoring in Counseling Psychology

Barbara Gormley

Abstract

This theoretical chapter presents a feminist perspective of mentoring relationships. A recent history of efforts related to feminist mentoring within the field of counseling psychology is described, including efforts to integrate multiculturalism into feminist mentoring. The contributions of a leader in the field of feminist mentoring, Ruth Fassinger, are highlighted. The Multicultural Feminist Mentoring Model (Benishek, Bieschke, Park, & Slattery, 2004) is presented, and its limitations are discussed. A brief review of literature regarding effective mentoring relationships is provided and critiqued from a multicultural and feminist perspective. This chapter argues for a systemic perspective that concurrently considers cultural, organizational, interpersonal, and individual contributors to successful mentoring relationships. Dysfunctional mentoring relationship dynamics are addressed, including misuses of power and cultural differences in approaches to managing conflict. A global perspective of the use of feminist versus traditional mentoring approaches is included. Future directions for practice and research are suggested.

Key Words: Mentoring, graduate training, counseling psychology, feminism, gender differences, culture, multiculturalism, cultural competence, social justice.

Introduction

One of the attractions of counseling psychology to students is the availability of high-quality mentors who are sensitive to dynamics related to cultural differences (i.e., gender, race, ethnicity, nation of origin, age, sexual orientation, socioeconomic status, religion). Over the past several decades, increased representation of feminist and culturally competent psychologists in this academic discipline has led to the cultivation of colleagues and students with related knowledge and skills. As a result, feminism and multiculturalism have become more centralized in counseling psychology. Mentoring is central to counseling psychology and to feminist psychology, as evidenced by the awards given by related divisions of the American Psychological Association (APA). Division 17, the Society of Counseling Psychology, gives a Lifetime Achievement in Mentoring Award, and Division 35, the Society for the Psychology of Women, gives the Strickland-Daniel Mentoring Award.

As increasing numbers of students from marginalized groups, such as female students of color, have sought graduate degrees in applied psychology, counseling psychologists have nurtured their careers, bringing a greater diversity of voices into the field. To accomplish this, many mentoring dyads have engaged in a journey to discover the nuances and needs of cross-gender and cross-cultural mentoring relationships. Although it is traditional for students to seek mentors with similar research interests, students who are culturally different from the dominant group (i.e., those who are not White, middle class, heterosexual, Christian, American, and male) may be more drawn to a professor's commitment to mentoring. A mentor's ability to create a healthy and productive relationship across gender and cultural differences may be what these students believe will sustain them throughout their professional development. This relational and contextual emphasis is stressed by both feminism and multiculturalism and has become an important consideration in the mentoring literature.

A Leader in Feminist Mentoring: Ruth E. Fassinger, Counseling Psychologist

Ruth Fassinger is one of the most influential practitioners and researchers in the field of feminist mentoring and one of the most effective leaders in the movement to integrate multiculturalism and feminism and centralize them in counseling psychology. Dr. Fassinger worked as a professor of counseling psychology at the University of Maryland from 1988 to 2008, where she was recognized as a Distinguished Scholar-Teacher. She has produced hundreds of peer-reviewed theoretical and empirical journal articles, book chapters, and national presentations on topics related to gender, sexual orientation, race, mentoring, career development, and vocational issues. She has won many awards for her work, and her students also have tended to win awards for their work, which is a strong indication of her effectiveness as a mentor. Currently, Ruth Fassinger is the Dean of the College of Professional Studies at John F. Kennedy University in the San Francisco Bay area.

Dr. Fassinger gave a talk in 1997 that sparked momentum in the feminist mentoring movement in counseling psychology. Because she received the Woman of the Year award the previous year in the Counseling Psychology Division's Section for the Advancement Women (SAW), she was invited to speak at the next annual convention of APA. Her paper presentation was entitled, "Dangerous Liaisons: Reflections on Feminist Mentoring" (Fassinger, 1997). The first feminist mentoring model was presented in this unforgettable, inspiring, and unpublished address. In her speech, Ruth Fassinger movingly described the obstacles faced by women, people of color, and other marginalized groups when they seek satisfying and effective mentoring relationships. She called for mentors to more carefully attend to issues related to power, a central theme in those obstacles. She described feminist mentoring as founded on the premise that the empowerment of others affords them the ability to recognize their own authority and potential.

Dr. Fassinger, along with Dr. Linda Forrest and some of their colleagues and students, went on to organize SAW's 1998 working conference, Advancing Together: Centralizing Feminism and Multiculturalism in Counseling Psychology. A primary objective of this meeting was to provide a network of mentors to female counseling psychologists of all racial and ethnic backgrounds at all career levels. During that conference, Dr. Fassinger coordinated the work group that focused on the topic of mentoring and that later published the Multicultural Feminist Mentoring Model (Benishek, Bieschke, Park, & Slattery, 2004). In addition, Fassinger edited the 2004 double special issue on the Integration of Feminism and Multiculturalism in Counseling for the *Journal of Multicultural Counseling and Development*, which published many of the work group products from that conference (Fassinger, 2004). Her actions created mentoring and publication opportunities for hundreds of women, facilitating many careers. From the conception of the project to its culmination, women at all career stages worked together in small groups to accomplish what is usually done individually or through strict hierarchies, demonstrating that a feminist model can meet the demands of a traditional academic system.

Although Fassinger's academic and feminist credentials are irrefutable, what may be more important to those of us who consider her a role model or a mentor is her interpersonal style. An informal conversation with her and a small group of colleagues about shared experiences as mentees and mentors could easily turn into a proposal for a conference panel presentation—often a proposal that would be accepted and would be very well received. During one of our planning meetings to organize the SAW working conference, she looked directly at me and told me definitively that I could do something that I was quite sure I couldn't do, and the next thing I knew, I was doing it. Her interest in helping everyone feel that they can be as successful as she is has a contagious quality—she makes others want to bring out the best in themselves, and she does this continuously, unselfishly, and out of friendship. What Ruth gives to everyone whom she helps with their professional development is not only academic, it is also personal. And although it is work, it's also irresistible fun.

I chose to highlight Ruth Fassinger in this chapter because she is the example I think about when I am struggling to figure out how to be helpful to mentees from diverse cultural backgrounds. My own questions about how a minority sexual orientation might hinder my academic aspirations led me to value her as a role model in the first place. Many other individuals offer mentoring that is feminist and multicultural in nature, and most of them are never publicly acknowledged. I would encourage readers to stop for a moment and think of those people who have influenced their careers in this way. What personal attributes do they have? What skills have they helped you acquire? What is it about how they work with you that matters most, especially from a gendered or cultural perspective? How do your needs or hopes influence the attributes you seek in a mentor? If you have not yet found a mentor, what qualities are you looking for? What might they do that would be helpful to you?

How Multicultural is Feminist Mentoring?

In the aftermath of the SAW Conference and the publication of the work groups' writing products, a flurry of panel discussions at professional conferences tackled a topic that was raised at the conference—how multicultural is feminist mentoring? What evolved was a conversation and a more integrated understanding of two social movements. So many different voices needed to be heard that this conversation could not easily develop within one institution or through an e-mail exchange. Some of those involved in maintaining the momentum of this ongoing dialogue were members of the SAW Mentoring Task Force, which was created in 2005, including Ruth Fassinger, Michele Boyer, Carol Enns, Sue Morrow, Lauren Weitzman, Jill Barber, Libby Nutt Williams, Corinne Datchi-Phillips, the author of this chapter, and many others who became involved in the various projects developed by the task force.

Two panels at annual conventions of APA presented topics related to "Understudied Aspects of Mentoring: Feminist and Multicultural Perspectives" (Williams, 2006) and "The Mentoring Kaleidoscope: Addressing Human Differences in Mentoring Relationships" (Datchi-Phillips, 2010). In 2011, Meghan Davidson organized a mentoring roundtable event at APA. At the International Counseling Psychology Conference, a pre-conference workshop devoted a full day to mentoring research and practice. A panel discussion was featured in the morning ["Powerful and Personal: Mentoring from Multiple Perspectives" (Morrow & Barber, 2008)], and in the afternoon, small groups engaged in the discussion of various mentoring topics. Again, the goal was to stimulate research on the topic as well as offer people opportunities to form connections that could develop into mentoring relationships. One interesting presentation in this panel involved Annaliese Singh and Jill Barber's description of Becky Packard's (2000) work on composite mentoring, which suggests that multiple mentors may be needed to address the topical and cultural needs of mentees. For instance, a student might have one mentor who knows her research area and another mentor who helps her understand how her cultural background will interact with her future job environment. Other topics included self-care for mentors (Lauren Weitzman) and boundaries (Barbara Gormley). At the annual conference of the Association for Women in Psychology (AWP), a panel presentation focused on "Multicultural Feminist Mentoring: Mentor and Mentee Perspectives of the Impact of Cultural Differences and Similarities" (Gormley, 2006). Presenters and attendees were urged by the panel discussant, Michele Boyer, to consider sharing negative as well as positive cross-cultural mentoring experiences. This led to a panel at AWP the next year on "Multicultural Feminist Mentoring Relationships: Influences of Cultural Differences and Similarities on Negative Experiences" (Gormley, 2007). Panelists who spoke on the topic of "Second Wave New York Meets Third Wave Miami: Navigating Cultural Differences in Feminist Mentoring" (Fassinger, Gallor, & Risco, 2007) shared some of the conflicts in assumptions between feminist and Latina cultural values as they intersected with conflicts among feminists of different eras.

Many insights emerged from these activities, and most of them expanded our vision of what we could do and how we might work together to do it. The panels offered opportunities for students to be presenters, for previous presenters to chair a panel, for previous chairs to be discussants, and so on, as power was shared among us. We made new friends with similar interests by offering panel slots through professional listservs. We reexamined our feminist assumptions as they were challenged from various cultural perspectives, but this happened in the company of others who were having similar exchanges, so we could hear how they were working things through. We also learned that we need more training, because very few psychologists begin their careers well prepared to become effective cross-cultural and gender-sensitive mentors. We learned that we don't have to face obstacles alone, that there are national and international networks of people who care about the same things and are trying to make the same kind of difference. And we learned that having these difficult discussions made our mentoring relationships better, shifted our perspectives in interesting ways, and enlivened our professional work.

A Multicultural Feminist Mentoring Model

It is useful to have a theoretical model from which to work when trying to consider the mentoring needs of widely diverse mentees. This section introduces a feminist approach to mentoring, provides specific tenets that foster the application of social justice principles to mentoring relationships, and reviews literature that illuminates some of the known limitations to applying this model.

Providing the kind of mentoring that benefits cultural groups that are underrepresented in academic or other top-level positions reflects a commitment to diversity and a willingness to take a social justice stance. Over three-quarters of counseling psychology faculty members in the United States are White, while one-third of graduate students in this field are from diverse racial and ethnic backgrounds (CCPTP, 2005). As a result, marginalized students who seek to create positive mentoring matches by finding mentors who are similar to themselves in terms of gender, race, and ethnicity (a strategy that has some preliminary empirical support; Santos & Reigadas, 2002; Scandura & Williams, 2001), might not be able to find such matches. Numerous experts (Fassinger & Hensler-McGinnis, 2005; Johnson & Nelson, 1999; Ragins, 1999) have suggested that mentoring relationships are not only more important for the professional advancement of women, ethnic minorities, and members of other marginalized groups, especially in order for them to be as successful as members of mainstream cultural groups, but also that high-quality mentoring relationships are harder for members of marginalized groups to find. In order to be equitable, it is important for those working in academic positions to learn how to be of benefit to those who may be culturally different from the dominant group. A feminist approach, which helps mentees navigate the differences between their cultural backgrounds and traditional systems, is different from traditional mentoring approaches, which often expect those from other groups to conform to the status quo.

According to Fassinger and Hensler-McGinnis (2005), another important difference in a feminist approach is that mentoring relationships are developed to be mutually satisfying, real relationships that are reciprocal and that benefit both parties. These authors suggest that the nature of the relationship itself determines how effective the mentoring process is for the mentee, rather than whether mentors effectively wield their power within the institution to aid the careers of their mentees. This emphasis on relational learning serves to expand the groups that can benefit from mentoring beyond those that easily fit into individualistic and hierarchical traditions to those that work better in collectivistic and collaborative environments.

Furthermore, the way that power is managed is an important consideration in feminist mentoring. Traditional mentoring might maximize the power differential between the mentor and mentee and the hierarchical nature of the mentoring relationship, resolving conflicts by demonstrating who is in charge. In feminist mentoring, the power differential between the mentor and the mentee is acknowledged, but how and when power might be used is carefully considered and might even be openly analyzed within the relationship (Fassinger & Hensler-McGinnis, 2005). For instance, from a feminist perspective, conflicts can be resolved using any number of interpersonally healthy relationship strategies, such as negotiation, sharing perspectives, collaborating, and discovering win-win solutions. Reducing the autocratic aspect of mentoring reduces the chances that power over the other person might be abused.

The feminist mentoring model (Fassinger, 1997; Fassinger & Hensler-McGinnis, 2005) offers mentors six tenets: (a) *rethinking power*, which includes sharing power with mentees and openly talking about the power differentials in the mentoring relationship; (b) *emphasizing the relational*, which includes sharing personal feelings congruently, encouraging mutual feedback, offering to connect mentees with additional mentors, and valuing the personal lives of mentees; (c) *collaborating*, which includes working together on projects and inviting mentees into professional networks; (d) *committing to diversity*, which includes valuing marginalized voices and challenging prejudice in oneself, others, and systems; (e) *integrating dichotomies*, which includes linking abstract knowledge to personal experience; and (f) *incorporating political analysis*, which includes teaching that the personal is political and challenging patriarchal values.

The revision of this model incorporated issues related to cultural diversity into all of the tenets, rather than delineating *commitment to diversity* as a separate tenet. Generally, the multicultural feminist mentoring model (Benishek et al., 2004) described mentoring as an interactive process in which cultural differences are identified and explored as they arise and impact mentoring activities or the professional development of either the mentor or the mentee. These authors advocate a willingness to address tensions between feminism and multiculturalism so that mentoring relationships can be satisfying and effective. Specifically, this revised model recommends that mentors (a) examine their cultural privilege within their mentoring relationships (e.g., White mentors have White privilege when mentoring students of color, in addition to higher professional status); (b) demonstrate valuing of non-majority cultural experiences (e.g., by providing social advocacy); and (c) initiate discussions of gender, race, and other cultural differences with all mentees to facilitate mutual understanding and growth.

Limitations of the Model

The current multicultural feminist mentoring model emerged as a result of many people pooling their experience and wisdom; however, the model may continue to evolve as the dialogue between multiculturalism and feminism continues to evolve. In addition, it is necessary to empirically test whether these tenets are the critical issues to consider in mentoring relationships and to discover whether there are other issues that need to be addressed. Finally, interpersonal relationships are highly variable, and mentoring relationships are no exception, so the application of these tenets should be integrated with other knowledge bases, such as the supervision literature, what is known about working with individual differences, and what works to manage conflicts in general. The current model serves as a guideline for mentoring practice, and it raises questions worth thinking about.

One of the issues raised by this model is whether it is wise for mentors to explicitly address cultural differences with every mentee. Early empirical evidence suggests that the effectiveness of discussions about cultural differences in mentoring relationships may depend on other factors. Members of cross-race mentoring dyads have been found to either avoid discussion of differences or to actively engage in such dialogue; in contrast to the expectations of the researchers, the most functional relationships were not those in which dialogue occurred but those in which the mentor and mentee shared the same preference for dialoguing or avoiding (Thomas, 1993). Therefore, if a professor prefers to have those discussions with students, but some of that professor's students prefer to avoid those conversations, there is a conflict. Should this conflict be resolved based on the professor's preference (which could constitute a use of power), the student's preference (which could be the result of cultural values regarding respect for authority), or some other method of conflict resolution? A thoughtful consideration of this issue might result in different decisions within different relationships, or different decisions at different stages of a mentoring relationship.

Another important consideration is that cross-cultural or cross-gender mentoring relationships are rarely just that simple. Multiple cultural identities occur within each person, which is consistent with *intersectionality*. For example, Latina students will have diverse nations of origin, diverse language variances, diverse socioeconomic statuses, diverse degrees of adherence to Hispanic cultural norms and/or to American cultural values, diverse degrees of adherence to feminine gender role socialization, diverse sexual orientations, and diverse relational styles. Because of this level of complexity, mentors are advised (a) to consult mentees about their most important cultural identities; (b) to recognize that mentee identity development is likely to differ along different demographic lines; and (c) to recognize the impact that mentor demographics have on mentee perceptions of how safe it is to discuss their opinions (Prieto, 2006). For instance, the effectiveness of empowering female mentees (Hammer, 2006) may depend on racial and ethnic values regarding femininity. Women of color who perceive their racial and ethnic identities to be more salient than their gender identities may experience conflicts between achieving greater independence (a feminist value) and their commitment to their families and communities (a cultural value). Furthermore, it is possible for mentees to have more cultural privilege in certain aspects of their identity than their mentors, such as when a heterosexual, wealthy African American woman has a mentor who is a lesbian African American woman from a working class background.

Another issue involves addressing perceptions or experiences of bias or unfairness, whether they occur within the mentoring relationship or outside it. Recommendations for mentees in cross-cultural mentoring relationships who encounter such barriers were not found in the professional literature. Rather, such students are likely to be referred to mentors, who are then advised to help students with these problems. Specifically, it is recommended that mentors understand the effects of racism and sexism so that they can provide relevant psychosocial support (Alvarez, Blume, Cervantes, & Thomas,

2009) and can help students overcome systemic barriers to become productive in their research areas (Evans & Cokley, 2008). Cultural barriers that may be extremely difficult for mentees and mentors to surmount include sexist and racist stereotypes that influence their perceptions of each other (Johnson & Huwe, 2002). Such situations can be painful, and many organizations provide little assistance to mentoring dyads who encounter these kinds of problems. Often, it is only when these issues have escalated into legal concerns that institutions become involved. Other barriers faced by marginalized mentors and mentees may include biased systems of promotion and downsizing efforts (Johnson, 2002). Mentors' efforts to bring marginalized voices into the field can be undermined when mentees witness unfair treatment of their mentors and learn directly what they might expect in their future careers.

When mentees experience bias or discrimination, the multicultural feminist mentoring model (Benishek et al., 2004) suggests that mentors use social advocacy to challenge unfair systems; however, what are the consequences to mentors who do challenge systems? What are the consequences to their mentoring relationships and mentees? Mentors who engage in social advocacy may become less effective due to resulting conflicts with the organization (Fassinger & Hensler-McGinnis, 2005). Recommendations for institutions include (a) developing mentoring strategies designed for racial and ethnic minorities, women, and other diverse groups; (b) providing training on how to mentor marginalized mentees; and (c) rewarding effective mentoring (McGregor, 2006). Whether organizations understand the complexity of cross-cultural mentoring and provide needed support has not been studied.

Further suggestions for how psychologists might effectively work with women mentees of diverse cultural backgrounds are provided in the Guidelines for Psychological Practice with Girls and Women (APA, 2007). Psychologists are advised (a) to be aware of the effects of socialization, oppression, bias, and discrimination on women's development; (b) to recognize their own attitudes about gender and the resulting impact on their practice; (c) to use gender- and culturally sensitive and affirming practices, including interventions found effective with women and those that foster empowerment and expanded alternatives and choices for women; (d) to consider the problems that women encounter in their sociopolitical context and to work to change institutional and systemic biases; and (e) to acquaint themselves with educational and community resources available to women. These suggestions are proactive and pragmatic, but they do not address interactive process problems, such as when there are differences in perceptions or other conflicts between mentors and mentees.

Effective Mentoring Relationships

Since mentees from marginalized cultural groups want effective mentoring relationships, a brief review of the effectiveness literature is provided and considered from a multicultural and feminist perspective. The stereotype of a mentoring relationship is that it is a positive experience for both mentor and mentee. Many people consider the only exception to this scenario to be those rare instances in which either the mentor or mentee sets out to destroy the career of the other person, as characterized in popular movie or television dramas. A more realistic view of mentoring is that all mentoring relationships are different from one other, just like other interpersonal relationships. Mentoring relationships have been described as occurring along a spectrum from dysfunctional to neutral to helpful, with most of them falling somewhere in the middle of this spectrum (Gormley, 2008). As in other types of relationships, the quality of mentoring relationships depends, at least in part, on the relationship skills, abilities, and styles of those involved (for discussion, see Gormley, 2008). Looking for a good mentoring match can be compared to a romantic courtship, because shared individual, relational, professional, and cultural values all may contribute to compatibility.

Beyond basic relationship requirements, other factors to consider are (a) the likelihood that the two parties are operating from different cultural perspectives and so may misinterpret each other's intentions without realizing it; (b) the variation in organizational culture, including whether mentoring is rewarded, tolerated, or devalued; and (c) the pressure that both parties may be under to be productive, such as mentors who are working to achieve tenure while a small group of mentees work to complete their dissertations. Mentors need mentees to help them with their research, and mentees need to have their professional development nurtured by their mentors. In such high-achieving climates, misperceptions and conflicts may interfere with productivity, but time spent on relationship building or conflict resolution may be considered to be off task. Different cultures address relational issues in different ways, including ways that may be in direct opposition to each other. For example, Northern regions of the United States demonstrate a cultural preference for a direct approach to resolving conflict, which is considered rude in Southern regions of the United States, which demonstrate a cultural preference for indirect approaches. Very little is known about what is required to create a culturally competent and academically productive mentoring relationship.

Past research has focused primarily on the ways that mentoring relationships are influenced by mentor personality characteristics, although some preliminary examination of mentee personality characteristics has begun. Very few studies have investigated the negative effects of mentoring relationships, and those studies are limited to surveys of mentees about their perceptions of problematic mentors (for a review, see Noe, Greenberger, & Wang, 2002). This leaves out (a) problematic mentees, (b) mentor and observer perspectives of problematic situations, and (c) the influences of misperceptions or mismatches between mentors and mentees on mentoring relationship problems. Other neglected areas include the influences of organizational climates and interactions between mentors and mentees, such as the influences of similarities and differences in (a) gender, race, age, and nationality; (b) personality traits; and (c) relationship skills (for a review, see Scandura, 1998).

To summarize, the cultural contexts and organizational climates in which they occur have the potential to influence the effectiveness of mentoring relationships, but these systemic influences are seldom studied. Most research focuses on individual differences among mentors and mentees but not the interactions between the two or the processes that two people use to manage their relationship. Especially neglected are negative interactions between mentors and mentees and their impact on the relationship. Therefore, very little is known about how mentors and mentees successfully work together within various types of organizations and cultures within the field of psychology (see figure 24.1).

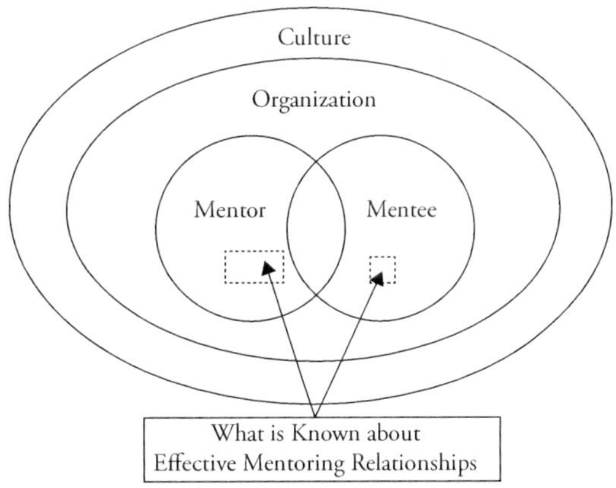

Figure 24.1 Limited Knowledge of Effective Mentoring Relationships.

Cultural, Organizational, Relational, and Individual Contributors to Effectiveness

Cultural differences are likely to influence the effectiveness of mentoring relationships. For example, gender differences in processes and outcomes of mentoring relationships continue to be found, which suggests that cultural bias related to gender still exists among individuals and institutions. In one study, professional women who had male mentors went on to earn more money, while professional women with female mentors experienced more career satisfaction, and their professional expectations were met to a greater degree (Wallace, 2001). Perhaps this outcome can be explained by the finding that male mentors provided more vocational advice in mentoring relationships, whereas female mentors provided more psychosocial support (Allen & Eby, 2004). However, female mentees found mentoring relationships with male mentors more challenging than with female mentors, which decreased their satisfaction with those cross-gender relationships (Ensher & Murphy, 2011). One example of challenges faced by women was reported in a Canadian study. Female graduate students were more often the targets of sexual harassment than male graduate students, and male faculty were more often than female faculty the ones exhibiting the harassing behavior (Schneider, Baker, & Stermac, 2002). There is evidence that mentor perceptions can be biased in traditionally stereotypical ways, but mentee bias has not been studied. For instance, mentors of both genders have reported perceiving greater benefits from working with married men and single women (for a review, see Ragins, 1999), which seems to indicate that only women are expected not to allow family demands to interfere with their work commitments. Additionally, male mentors have reported gaining esteem for female mentees who complied with their wishes, but not for male mentees exhibiting the same behavior (for a review, see Ragins, 1999); this finding seems to indicate that women are rewarded for adhering to feminine gender role expectations. Women are more often in cross-gender mentoring relationships than men, which are the kind of relationships that (primarily White male) mentors perceived as most likely to cause difficulties; specifically, mentors reported that their spouses were jealous of these relationships and that sexual tension within such relationships was an issue (for a review, see Ragins, 1999). Whether the influence of gender stereotypes has changed in recent years and whether stereotypes similarly affect cross-race or cross-ethnicity mentoring relationships merit further investigation, but the need to consider the cultural contexts in which mentoring relationships occur is clear.

Organizational differences can have an impact on the perceived effectiveness of mentoring relationships. Most of what we know about mentoring relationships comes from mentor and mentee self-reports (Noe et al., 2002), but perceptions of relationships are not always accurate. Multiple perspectives of the same experience can be equally valid, and systemic influences can shape individual perceptions. An example of the need to consider organizational influences is found in a study in which perceptions within the mentoring dyad were influenced by factors outside the dyad. When both mentors and mentees reported that their mentoring relationships met their expectations, they only evaluated the relationship as effective when the organizational climate also supported mentoring (Eby, Lockwood, & Butts, 2006; Young & Perrewé, 2000). Institution-level influences can be quite powerful. Whether institutional values related to maintaining the mainstream cultural status quo affect the ability of mentoring relationships to effectively manage diversity issues deserves investigation.

The interactions between mentor and mentee characteristics, including the processes they use to manage relationships, are quite likely to influence the effectiveness of these relationships. Effective mentoring has been linked with relationship quality, which has been found to be enhanced by mutual attraction and interest (for reviews, see Fassinger & Hensler-McGinnis, 2005; Johnson, 2002), a sense of closeness (for a review, see Johnson, 2002), and trust. Mentors trusted mentees more when they performed well, but mentees trusted mentors more after receiving psychosocial support from them (Young & Perrewé, 2000). Low quality relationships were described by mentees as mismatches involving (a) different work styles; (b) personality clashes; or (c) value differences, including occasions when mentors preferred to maintain the status quo while mentees valued diversity (Eby et al., 2000). Further study of cultural issues has been recommended, including the influences of the cultural identity development statuses of mentors and mentees on the quality of their relationships (Davidson & Foster-Johnson, 2001) and the mentor's competence to work with women or racial and ethnic minorities (Johnson, 2002). It is necessary to consider the interactions between the two people involved and the quality of their relationship in order to understand whether mentoring is effective.

Individual differences also influence the effectiveness of mentoring relationships. Mentor and mentee perceptions of each other have been studied, but what they believe about their own contributions to creating effective mentoring relationships has not. Mentees reported preferring mentors with interpersonal skills, intellectual success, and psychological health (for reviews, see Johnson, 2002; Noe et al., 2002) but not mentors whom they perceived as exclusionary, tyrannical, self-absorbed, neglectful, or sabotaging (Eby, McManus, Simon, & Russell, 2000). Mentors reported preferring mentees with high levels of ability, potential, independence, self-direction, self-monitoring, and emotional stability (for a review, see Noe et al., 2002). However, what is considered interpersonally skillful by mentees may vary by gender and cultural background, and the self-direction and independence valued by mentors may not be valued as much by members of some marginalized cultural groups. Rather, some mentees, including those from collectivistic backgrounds, may expect protective relational behavior from mentors. Individual differences contribute to a mentoring match, but further study of how individuals manage their relational and cultural identities and expectations is needed.

To summarize, cultural, institutional, interactional, and individual aspects of mentoring relationships are related to their effectiveness. Female mentees typically work under different sets of mentor expectations from those applied to male mentees, and women's career experiences tend to depend on the gender of their mentors. The degree to which institutions support mentoring and the quality of mentoring relationships is an important variable. In addition, mentors and mentees tend to bring different sets of strengths to their relationships. Each of the four areas described deserves further investigation, especially with regard to the influences of race, ethnicity, nation of origin, and other cultural differences. Furthermore, the manner in which cultural, institutional, interactional, and individual differences contribute to dysfunctional mentoring relationships has seldom been studied.

Dysfunctional Mentoring Relationships

Very little is known about how gender and cultural differences contribute to dysfunctional mentoring relationships. Dysfunction has been linked to negative consequences for mentees, mentors, and organizations, including stress, anxiety, depression, feeling inadequate or incompetent, job dissatisfaction, job performance problems, and a reduced interest in mentoring relationships (for a review, see Scandura, 1998). Two types of dysfunctional mentoring relationships were described in the literature. In the first type of dysfunction, mentors or mentees misuse their power in ways that cause harm to the other party, including through overt abuses of power (e.g., sexual harassment, discrimination) or more subtle power plays (e.g., psychological abuse, prejudice, behaving destructively toward each other's work; for reviews, see Feldman, 1999; Scandura, 1998). In the second type of dysfunction, ongoing interactions may be characterized by chronic conflict or by one or both parties experiencing a high level of distress as a result of being in the relationship (Johnson & Huwe, 2002). Each type of dysfunctional mentoring relationship is elaborated below.

One example of a misuse of power is turning mentoring relationships into romantic relationships. Many mentees later perceived this as having interfered with their career development, especially female mentees who became involved with male mentors (Glaser & Thorpe, 1986). No studies were found to examine whether sexual harassment or discrimination occurs in the context of mentoring relationships. What has been suggested is that misuses of power by mentors may result from the need for elevated levels of power (Eby et al., 2000). Areas that have not been studied include whether mentees misuse their power in mentoring relationships, whether certain types of interactions or relationships provoke this kind of behavior, or whether some organizational climates foster this kind of behavior. Mentees who are members of historically oppressed groups may perceive the power differential between themselves and mentors from dominant cultural groups as an indicator of the potential for oppression rather than as an opportunity to develop a helpful relationship (Farber, Lippert, & Nevas, 1995). Given the significant changes in the field in recent years, mentors may be less multiculturally aware than their mentees. Embracing and discussing multiple perspectives are useful tactics, but practicing these behaviors can be difficult when one or both parties feel violated by misuses of power. Intervention at the organizational or collegial level may be most effective in such cases.

Conflict resolution skills have been found to increase the effectiveness of mentoring relationships (Eby & McManus, 2004), but little is known about the circumstances under which conflict escalates into dysfunction. When the perceptions of the mentor and mentee are in conflict, especially when one person is focused on cultural differences and the other person is focused on work productivity, it can be difficult to find a resolution. For example, mentees in cross-cultural mentoring relationships may attribute interactional problems to mentor prejudice, while their mentors may attribute problems to inadequate mentee work performance. Such disagreements may never be discussed or clarified, given how difficult such dialogues can be. In these circumstances, it is recommended that both parties expand their perspective to include all of the possible contributors to the situation, including factors that have not yet been considered in the literature. Simultaneously considering individual, interactional, organizational, and cultural contributions to highly conflictual interactions (see figure 24.1) reduces the risk of making common errors, such as pathologizing individuals for adhering to various cultural norms or misattributing one person's difficulties to "personality conflicts" that implicate both parties.

Some mentors prefer conflicts to be resolved by mentee compliance with their wishes. Cultural values related to power and authority may predict differences in how mentors and mentees evaluate and respond to conflicts, although this idea has not been tested. Those with *autocratic* cultural values are more likely to (a) perceive authorities as distant, (b) care more about outcomes than relationships, and (c) dislike subordinate disagreement, whereas those with *consultative* cultural values (a) perceive authorities as close and similar to themselves, (b) care more about being treated with respect and having a personal connection than the outcome, and (c) believe that discussion involving subordinate disagreement and criticism of authorities is desirable (Tyler, Lind, & Huo, 2000). Whether mentoring dyads in which one autocratic person and one consultative person try to resolve conflict suffer difficulties that interfere with productivity needs to be investigated. Furthermore, this question should be considered in the context of whether same-gender or cross-gender dyads are involved.

Global Cultural Implications for Mentors

In an increasingly global society, with international students seeking graduate training in the United States and professors interacting with international colleagues, the need to consider cultural context when evaluating mentoring and other work-related relationships expands to global proportions. For example, relationships that begin by North American psychologists mentoring international students may evolve into collaborative and co-mentoring relationships in which both parties gain from cross-cultural exchanges. North Americans have much to learn about other cultures, as well as their own, through interfacing in a more intimate way with colleagues from other countries. For example, they can provide editing assistance for complex grammatical questions when collaborative partners for whom English is a second language submit their work to Western academic journals. In addition, collaborative research projects across nations can add to knowledge about cultural differences and similarities (Enns, Kasai, & Machizawa, 2006).

Perhaps most relevant to this discussion are the international differences in ways that people view authority and power and determine how to interact with those in supervisory positions, which could be extended to mentors in academic and clinical settings. This orientation toward authority figures has been described as the power-distance index (PDI; Hofstede, 1980). According to Hofstede, people from high PDI countries tend to prefer autocratic decision making, hierarchical relationships, conformity, and close supervision. They typically treat supervisors with great respect and distance and act as if supervisors and supervisees are very different kinds of people. In these nations, use of coercive power is more likely, the underdog often is blamed when things go wrong, and there may be a general fear of disagreeing with the boss. It is also relevant to note that supervisors and persons in authority are expected to show beneficence toward subordinates and to protect the best interests of those with less power (Sun, 2008). People from low PDI countries tend to prefer participatory decision making, cooperation, and egalitarian relationships that are close, friendly, and mutual. They typically have a strong independent work ethic and view supervisors and supervisees as similar kinds of people. In these nations, disagreements often are encouraged, the use of legitimate or expert power is more likely, and the system may be blamed when things go wrong.

In a mentoring relationship, if one person has a high PDI cultural background and the other person has a low PDI cultural background, their expectations may be in conflict. If the mentors have high PDI cultural backgrounds, they are likely to expect conformity to their style even if this interactional style is not a good cultural fit for some of their mentees. These mentees may not understand the cultural context of the mentor and are likely to interpret mentor behavior and respond based on their own cultural context. If the mentors have low PDI backgrounds, they may not understand that some of their mentees with high PDI cultural backgrounds are trying to conform to the mentor's style, when what these mentors really want is to collaborate with their mentees in developing a relationship that meets both parties' needs. Either way, this sort of mismatch can look like two people trying to dance together without realizing that one person dances salsa while the other does the foxtrot. Both people may take the steps to develop an effective relationship that they believe to be correct, but these sets of steps may not work well together. Although it may be obvious that something feels awkward about the relationship, such deeply imbedded cultural expectations can be difficult to identify, articulate, and share while remaining open to other views.

One of the implications of Hofstede's (1980) model is that traditional mentoring approaches in the United States may be considered high PDI, whereas feminist mentoring approaches may be considered low PDI. This difference reveals one way in which integrating feminist and multicultural approaches becomes complicated: What if reducing the power differential in a mentoring relationship does not reflect sensitivity to cultural differences among mentees? Both traditional and feminist mentors have opportunities to work with international students, but being able to articulate a mentoring stance and relate it to the mentee's cultural values might be helpful in conversations about whether there is a good match. In addition, an awareness of the other culture's implicit expectations and the mentee's degree of adherence to those national values is likely to be useful. Furthermore, it may be necessary to maintain a certain level of complexity in assessments of whether or not individual students ascribe to both social justice values and the expectations of their high or low PDI countries.

It is worth noting that Hofstede's (1980) theory contains four dimensions of cultural difference (power-distance, uncertainty-avoidance, masculinity-femininity, and individualism-collectivism), all of which are relevant to future multicultural and feminist mentoring research. For instance, international students may have different expectations for male and female mentors based on the cultural norms related to masculinity and femininity found in their nation of origin. When we consider the conflicts that arise in mentoring relationships and how difficult it is to determine whether the differences in perspectives are status-related or culturally derived, it seems critically important to further our understanding of the many cultural dynamics that might impact mentoring relationships.

Conclusion

If one counts all of the female graduate students in counseling psychology as well as all of the racial and ethnic minority students, lesbian, gay, bisexual, and transgender students; students from working class and low income backgrounds; and international students; mentees described as coming from marginalized groups actually constitute the majority (CCPTP, 2005). Because many of these students may hold cultural values that are relational, collectivistic, and process-oriented and may prefer collaborative learning styles, they also may want similar mentoring relationships. However, for graduate students in traditional academic settings, the systemic values, and therefore the values of many of the mentors, are more likely to be hierarchical, individualistic, and product-oriented. By applying feminist and multicultural lenses, both of which emphasize relational and contextual elements of society and embrace cultural differences as enrichments of our work and learning environments, we can expand our perspective to become more inclusive of these differences. The traditional perspective of teacher and student involves two separate individuals trying to create work product. Multicultural and feminist approaches allow us to additionally consider an interconnected view of contextual, organizational, and relational influences on the two individuals in mentoring relationships.

The review of effective mentoring relationship literature contained in this chapter reveals how traditional approaches to studying psychology tend to overemphasize individual differences and to neglect cultural contexts, systemic influences, and relationship processes (see figure 24.1). Because past literature has not addressed many important aspects of what mentees from marginalized groups may consider most salient, it cannot answer some of the most crucial questions facing mentors and mentees in cross-cultural and cross-gender mentoring relationships today. This chapter argues for a need to broaden our view of effective mentoring relationships to consider the contributions of (a) additional individual characteristics of mentors and mentees that have not been studied, such as the kinds of values and value conflicts that are likely to impact their relationships; (b) relational processes, such as how mentors and mentees actually work together, including to resolve conflicts that may be cultural in nature; (c) organizational climates that support or work against healthy approaches to addressing diversity issues; and (d) cultural contexts within which the mentoring relationships occur, which includes not only the interaction between the cultural backgrounds of the mentor and mentee but also the regional cultural influences where they work and study (see figure 24.1). We need to expand our view of effective mentoring relationships so that we can begin to accommodate a more culturally diverse group of mentees.

It is also important to consider how variable diversity is within each of the four systemic levels (i.e., cultural, organizational, relational, and individual). It is not only mentors and mentees who may be similar or different in their demographic characteristics (gender, race, ethnicity, nation of origin, age, sexual orientation, socioeconomic status, religion); institutions and regions also can be dominated by or show preferences toward certain cultural attitudes. For example, the mentor and mentee may work and study in a setting that serves an urban, working class population of predominantly Christian students of color, which influences both institutional policy and the kinds of conversations that may be difficult to initiate. The manner in which such regional influences might impact mentoring efforts, such as interactions between a Buddhist mentor and a Muslim mentee in a predominantly Christian region, needs to be explored. Furthermore, issues of power are not as dualistic as they might first appear, (i.e., that the mentor holds all of the power and the mentee has none). In a feminist power analysis of mentoring relationships, mentors need to examine their own areas of privilege (e.g., teacher, White, middle class) and areas in which they might face obstacles in society (e.g., female, bisexual, non-tenured), and then compare their statuses with those of their mentees to discover the ways in which they do and do not have power in the relationship. For example, an Asian gay male mentor with tenure may hold more or less power over his mentees, depending on their gender, nation of origin, sexual orientation, and professional status. Consider a mentee who is also tenured and who is American, White, heterosexual, and female. There are many privileges that this mentee enjoys in the United States that the Asian gay male mentor does not hold, with the exception of those related to gender. Although mentees initially may seek shared characteristics in mentors, recognizing important cultural differences helps mentors and mentees avoid misuses of power so that mentoring relationships can keep working.

The requirements described above might seem overwhelming, especially because working with cultural differences can stir up deeply held views that we may not realize we hold. As a result, it is fortunate that we have a theoretical model that provides focus. The multicultural feminist mentoring model (Benishek et al., 2004) reminds us (a) to consider when and how to use our power so that we do not inadvertently reinforce the power structures that maintain the status quo; (b) to think about how to cultivate and maintain real relationships where power differentials exist, without violating boundaries; and (c) to take action to promote social justice where we can. Whether launching an investigation into mentoring processes that are useful to resolve conflicts in cross-gender dyads or trying to increase the research productivity of one's African American female mentees, mentors may gain guidance by simply looking at their work's perspective on power, relatedness, and social justice. Remembering that this work also can be fun and invigorating is also beneficial.

Future Directions

The following questions are provided to stimulate conversations, thoughts, papers, research projects, and explorations in practice that are likely to increase understanding of how to create effective cross-cultural and cross-gender mentoring relationships:

Does the multicultural feminist mentoring model contribute to positive outcomes? Does employing the multicultural feminist mentoring model contribute to the upward mobility of members of marginalized groups? Does adhering to the multicultural feminist mentoring model reduce the chances that misuses of power will occur, especially in comparison to traditional mentoring approaches? Does social advocacy lead to positive change in the institutions in which multicultural feminist mentors work?

How can efforts to further integrate multiculturalism and feminism be facilitated? What kinds of conversations, practices, work products, and processes are needed? What are the obstacles to these two social movements learning from each other and growing accordingly? How can these obstacles be addressed in respectful, open, and productive ways by large groups, as we have learned to do in dyads and small groups?

How can we help people find effective, culturally sensitive, and gender-sensitive mentors? Can we institute standard training components that help graduate students to understand what constitutes effective and dysfunctional mentorship and menteeship and informs them about what to do if they find themselves in dysfunctional situations?

What do mentoring dyads do when they experience an ongoing conflict that involves gender or cultural differences? When biases arise within the mentoring relationship or when they perceive their situation in very different ways (e.g., the mentor is focused on work productivity and the mentee is focused on social equity), what kinds of strategies for resolving these conflicts are effective or dysfunctional? What happens when there are cultural differences in approaching conflict, and one person has local regional support for her or his cultural approach? What do effective mentees do (e.g., do they initiate difficult conversations)? What do effective mentors do (e.g., do they consider it part of their job to have difficult dialogues about gender and culture)? Does consultation or mediation help? What do organizations offer that helps with this process?

Are there organizations that provide training to mentors regarding (a) how to manage individual and cultural differences, (b) how to implement mutual conflict resolution strategies, and (c) how to identify and intervene in dysfunctional mentoring relationships? Have any such programs been tested for effectiveness? How might we learn what works and for whom?

Can we "go global" with the multicultural feminist mentoring model and what we know about effective mentoring relationships to create an internationally relevant approach to mentoring? Can North American multicultural feminist mentors work effectively with international students who hold the values of their high PDI countries? Or is it better to match feminist mentors with students from low PDI countries and traditional mentors with students from high PDI countries? How can social justice and hierarchical perspectives be integrated to address the needs of mentees who value both?

Author's Note

A portion of this chapter was presented in August 2006 in E. N. Williams (Chair), Understudied Aspects of Mentorship: Feminist and Multicultural Perspectives, a symposium conducted at the annual convention of the American Psychological Association, New Orleans, LA. Correspondence should be sent electronically to Barbara Gormley, Ph.D., at bgormley@govst.edu. Although the author worked for ten years as a practitioner before becoming an academic, all of her experiences providing cross-cultural and cross-gender mentoring have occurred in academic settings, and she acknowledges the chapter's bias in the direction of academia.

References

Allen, T. D., & Eby, L. T. (2004). Factors related to mentor reports of mentoring functions provided: Gender and relational characteristics. *Sex Roles, 50,* 129–139.

Alvarez, A. N., Blume, A. W., Cervantes, J. M., & Thomas, L. R. (2009).Tapping the wisdom tradition: Essential elements to mentoring students of color. *Professional Psychology: Research and Practice, 40,* 181–188.

American Psychological Association, A Joint Task Force of Divisions 17 & 35. (February 2007). Guidelines for psychological practice with girls and women. Retrieved July 30, 2011 from http://www.apa.org/practice/guidelines/girls-and-women.pdf.

Benishek, L. A., Bieschke, K. J., Park, J., & Slattery, S. M. (2004). A multiculturalfeminist model of mentoring. *Journal of Multicultural Counseling and Development, 32,* 428–442.

Council of Counseling Psychology Training Programs. (2005). CCPTP Survey Data 2005. Retrieved July 30, 2011 from http://www.ccptp.org/resources/surveydata.html

Datchi-Phillips, C. C. (Chair; August 2010), *Mentoring kaleidoscope: Addressing human differences in mentoring relationships.* Symposium conducted at the annual convention of the American Psychological Association, San Diego, CA.

Davidson, M. N., & Foster-Johnson, L. (2001). Mentoring in the preparation of graduate researchers of color. *Review of Educational Research, 71,* 549–574.

Eby, L. T., McManus, S. E., Simon, S. A., & Russell, J. E. A. (2000). The protégé's perspective regarding negative mentoring experiences: The development of a taxonomy. *Journal of Vocational Behavior, 57,* 1–21.

Eby, L. T., & McManus, S. E. (2004). The protégé's role in negative mentoring experiences. *Journal of Vocational Behavior, 65,* 255–275.

Eby, L. T., Lockwood, A. L., & Butts, M. (2006). Perceived support for mentoring: A multiple perspectives approach. *Journal of Vocational Behavior, 68,* 267–291.

Enns, C. Z., Kasai, M., & Machizawa, S. (August, 2006). Co-mentoring: Applying APA's resolution on culture and gender awareness. In C. Z. Enns (Chair), *Personal perspectives on collaborating and co-mentoring across cultures.* Symposium conducted at the annual convention of the American Psychological Association, New Orleans, LA.

Ensher, E. A., & Murphy, S. E. (2011). The Mentoring Relationship Challenges Scale: The impact of mentoring stage, type, and gender. *Journal of Vocational Behavior, 79,* 253–266.

Evans, G. L., & Cokley, K. O. (2008). African American women and the academy: Using career mentoring to increase research productivity. *Training and Education in Professional Psychology, 2,* 50–57.

Farber, B. A., Lippert, R. A., & Nevas, D. B. (1995). The therapist as attachment figure. *Psychotherapy, 32,* 204–212.

Fassinger, R. E. (August, 1997). *Dangerous liaisons: Reflections on feminist mentoring.* Paper presented at the annual convention of the American Psychological Association, Chicago, IL.

Fassinger, R. E. (2004). Centralizing feminism and multiculturalism in counseling: An introduction to the special section. *Journal of Multicultural Counseling and Development, 32,* 344–345.

Fassinger, R. E., & Hensler-McGinnis, N. F. (2005). Multicultural feminist mentoring as individual and small-group pedagogy. In C. Z. Enns & A. L. Sinacore (Eds.), *Teaching and social justice: Integrating multicultural and feminist theories in the classroom* (pp. 143–161). Washington, DC: American Psychological Association.

Fassinger, R. E., Gallor, S., &Risco, C. (March 2007). Second wave New York meets third wave Miami: Navigating cultural differences in feminist mentoring. In B. Gormley (Chair), *Multicultural feminist mentoring relationships: Influences of cultural differences and similarities on negative experiences.* Symposium presented at the annual conference of the Association for Women in Psychology, San Francisco, CA.

Feldman, D. C. (1999). Toxic mentors or toxic protégés? A critical re-examination of dysfunctional mentoring. *Human Resource Management Review, 9,* 247–278.

Glaser, R. D., & Thorpe, J. S. (1986). Unethical intimacy: A survey of sexual contact and advances between psychology educators and female graduate students. *American Psychologist, 41,* 43–51.

Gormley, B. (Chair; April, 2006). *Multicultural feminist mentoring: Mentor and mentee perspectives of the impact of cultural differences and similarities.* Symposium presented at the annual conference of the Association for Women in Psychology, Ypsilanti, MI.

Gormley, B. (Chair; March, 2007). *Multicultural feminist mentoring relationships: Influences of cultural differences and similarities on negative experiences.* Symposium presented at the annual conference of the Association for Women in Psychology, San Francisco, CA.

Gormley, B. (2008). An application of attachment theory: Mentoring relationship dynamics and ethical concerns. *Mentoring and Tutoring: Partnership in Learning, 16,* 45–62.

Hammer, E. Y. (2006). Mentoring female students. In W. Buskist and S. F. Davis (Eds.), *Handbook of the teaching of psychology* (pp. 159–163). Malden, MA: Blackwell.

Hofstede, G. (1980). Motivation, leadership, and organization: Do American theories apply abroad? *Organizational Dynamics, 9*(1), 42–63.

Johnson, W. B., & Nelson, N. (1999). Mentor-protégé relationships in graduate training: Some ethical concerns. *Ethics and Behavior, 9,* 189–210.

Johnson, W. B. (2002). The intentional mentor: Strategies and guidelines for the practice of mentoring. *Professional Psychology: Research and Practice, 33,* 88–96.

Johnson, W. B., & Huwe, J. M. (2002). Toward a typology of mentor dysfunction in graduate school. *Psychotherapy, 39,* 44–55.

McGregor, L. N. (2006). Teaching and mentoring racially and ethnically diverse students. In W. Buskist and S. F. Davis (Eds.), *Handbook of the teaching of psychology* (pp. 164–174). Malden, MA: Blackwell.

Morrow, S. L., & Barber, J. (March, 2008). *Powerful and personal: Mentoring from multiple perspectives.* Pre-conference workshop conducted at the International Counseling Psychology Conference, Chicago, IL.

Noe, R. A., Greenberger, D. B., & Wang, S. (2002). Mentoring: What we know and where we might go. In G. R. Ferris & J. J. Martocchio (Eds.), *Research in personnel and human resources management* (pp. 129–173). Oxford, England: Elsevier Science/JAI Press.

Packard, B. W. (2000). To construct a "composite mentor": College women's conceptions of mentoring, future images, and motivation in science. *Dissertation Abstracts International, 60* (7-A), 2373.

Prieto, L. R. (2006). Multiple cultural identities: Will the real student please stand up? In W. Buskist and S. F. Davis (Eds.), *Handbook of the teaching of psychology* (pp. 175–178). Malden, MA: Blackwell.

Ragins, B. R. (1999). Gender and mentoring relationships: A review and research agenda for the next decade. In G. N. Powell (Ed.), *Handbook of gender and work* (pp. 347–370). Thousand Oaks, CA: Sage.

Santos, S. J., & Reigadas, E. (2002). Latinos in higher education: An evaluation of a university faculty mentoring program. *Journal of Hispanic Higher Education, 1,* 40–50.

Scandura, T. A. (1998). Dysfunctional mentoring relationships and outcomes. *Journal of Management*, 24, 449–467.

Scandura, T. A., & Williams, E. A. (2001). An investigation of the moderating effects of gender on the relationships between mentorship initiation and protégé perceptions of mentoring functions. *Journal of Vocational Behavior, 59,* 342–363.

Schneider, M., Baker, S., & Stermac, L. (2002). Sexual harassment experiences of psychologists and psychological associates during their graduate school training. *The Canadian Journal of Human Sexuality, 11,* 159–170.

Sun, C. T. (2008). *Themes in Chinese psychology.* Singapore: Cengage Learning Asia.

Thomas, D. A. (1993).Racial dynamics in cross-race developmental relationships. *Administrative Science Quarterly, 38,* 169–194.

Tyler, T. R., Lind, E. A., & Huo, Y. J. (2000). Cultural values and authority relations: The psychology of conflict resolution across cultures. *Psychology, Public Policy, and Law, 6,* 1138–1163.

Wallace, J. E. (2001). The benefits of mentoring for female lawyers. *Journal of Vocational Behavior, 58,* 366–391.

Williams, E. N. (Chair, August, 2006), *Understudied aspects of mentorship: Feminist and multicultural perspectives.* Symposium presented at the annual convention of the American Psychological Association, New Orleans, LA.

Young, A. M., & Perrewé, P. L. (2000). The exchange relationship between mentors and protégés: The development of a framework. *Human Resource Management Review, 10,* 177–209.

CHAPTER

25 Activism, Advocacy, and Social Justice in Feminist Multicultural Counseling Psychology

Kathryn L. Norsworthy, Elizabeth M. Abrams, *and* Stefanie Lindlau

Abstract

The fields of feminist, multicultural, and counseling psychology have historical roots in activism, advocacy, and social justice. Most of the existing literature exploring the intersections of these three fields of psychology has focused at the micro-level. In this chapter we (a) define and elaborate on the concepts of social justice, activism, and advocacy, particularly focusing on the meso and macro levels within feminist multicultural counseling psychology; (b) discuss the various contexts in which social justice work is taking place; (c) weave together the existing literature with interview data to illustrate the multifaceted work of feminist multicultural counseling psychologists involved in activism, advocacy, and social justice activities at these larger systemic levels; and (d) make recommendations for future directions in feminist-social justice counseling psychology.

Key Words: Activism, advocacy, social justice, feminist multicultural, feminism, counseling, counseling psychology

Social justice, advocacy, and activism have long been at the heart of feminist multicultural psychologies arising from a diversity of locations around the world, including countries of the Global South/East as well as the Global North/West. Citing Unger (1998) and Wilkinson (1986), Brinton Lykes and Geraldine Moane pointed out that emerging feminist multicultural psychologies have converged around "a political focus that included acknowledgment of oppression and domination, the links between the personal and the political, and the aim of contributing to greater equality and social justice" (Lykes & Moane, 2009, pp. 284). Early U.S. feminist multicultural psychologies, for example, challenged the legitimacy of the discipline of psychology, a field originally predicated on knowledge about White, heterosexual, middle and upper class men and masculinity (Unger, 1998; Weisstein, 1968, 1993).

From its inception, counseling psychology hailed strong roots in social justice, as evidenced by the work of pioneers in career and vocational psychology such as Frank Parsons and Donald Paterson (Fouad, Gerstein, & Toporek, 2006). Early counseling psychologists also took up social activism, focusing on equity in employment and access to work for diverse and often marginalized groups, illustrating the focus on systemic and structural change. While the profession's expressed commitment to social justice waned to some extent in the 1980s and early 1990s, the late 1990s brought in a resurgence of interest that has endured and continues to grow. Goodman, Liang, Helms, Latta, Sparks, and Weintraub (2004) pointed out that as counseling psychology entered the twenty-first century, professionals in the field such as Allen Ivey, Derald Wing Sue, Elizabeth Vera, Suzette Speight, and others have increasingly "echoed calls from critical, community, and liberation psychologies that we engage more systematically in social justice" (p. 793). Further, social justice was a prominent and clearly articulated theme of the last two Division 17 counseling psychology conferences in Houston (2001) and Chicago (2008), although there is debate about the commitment of the profession to centralizing and operationalizing social justice values, principles, and practices explicitly and systematically (Fouad, McPherson, Gerstein, Blustein, Elman, Helledy, & Metz, 2004; Speight & Vera, 2004). Several authors suggest that one of our current challenges is how to infuse social justice into our identities and our practices of counseling psychology at the social and systemic levels (Baluch, Pieterse, & Bolden, 2004; Goodman et al., 2004; Palmer & Parish, 2008; Vera & Speight, 2003).

During the early years of the profession, the voices and activism of feminist multicultural counseling psychologists emerged around social justice issues such as sex bias in assessment, counseling, and career theory and development; the representation of women in the structure and policy making in Division 17 and the field at large; and in training and research (Fitzgerald, 1973; Gilbert & Osipow, 1991; Meara & Harmon, 1989). Out of these concerns, the Division 17 Committee on Women was formed in 1970 as an Ad Hoc committee, transforming into a standing committee in 1982, and finally into the Section for the Advancement of Women (SAW) in 1996. The committee has been an example of grassroots organizing devoted to carrying out feminist multicultural goals connected to disrupting institutionalized gender inequality. Much has been accomplished since the first formal discussions took place in 1970. Twenty years later, reflecting on the contributions of the committee, Gilbert and Osipow (1991) pointed out that, as of 1990, significantly more women held leadership positions in Division 17 and APA and occupied faculty positions in counseling psychology training programs. Further, a body of feminist multicultural scholarship had been generated and was being integrated into counseling psychology training and textbooks. More gender-sensitive, feminist multicultural approaches to counseling women were emerging.

Challenging the hegemony of this predominantly White, heterosexual middle class feminist movement, in the late 1980s and early 1990s, women of color and lesbians within the field brought forward their long-standing justice agenda—inclusion and visibility of their lives, experiences, and professional contributions to feminist multicultural counseling psychology scholarship. For example, Espin (1993) pointed out that the contributions of feminist multicultural psychologists of color, though often unacknowledged, have been central in the development of feminist multicultural therapy and should be treated as such in the developing feminist multicultural counseling psychology literature. Further, they also called attention to the lack of representation of women holding diverse backgrounds, identities, and social locations in positions of organizational leadership and influence (Enns, 1993; Espin, 1990, 1993; Espin & Gawalek, 1992; Rawlings, 1993).

Despite the fact that counseling psychologists have been committed to and actively involved in feminist multicultural activism, advocacy, and social justice work at the systemic level almost since the specialty was formed a half century ago, until recently little has actually been written on this topic. Yet, in preparing to write this chapter, we knew that many feminist multicultural counseling psychologists were engaging in activism and social justice activities focusing on systemic, structural, political, organizational, and community change. The scarcity of representation of this work in the literature revealed that our colleagues' and our own contributions to social change were one of counseling psychology's "best kept secrets"—illustrating the struggles of multicultural feminists in counseling psychology and elsewhere with invisibility, representation, and valuing of diverse, out-of-the box scholarships and practices that interrogate and challenge mainstream theory and praxis and illuminate the powerful interconnections of the personal, the professional, and the political. Further, counseling psychologists typically have not been equipped with skills in systemic level social justice intervention or in defining the "client" as a larger system, rather than an individual, family, or small group (Helms, 2003). Further, as Helms (2003) also pointed out, the organizations and institutions in which counseling psychologists are employed are often resistant to social justice ideas and practices, discouraging professionals from engaging in applying these skills in their work. Thus, we, as coauthors, became even more committed to the idea that this chapter should go beyond a discussion of the commitment of feminist multicultural counseling psychology to social justice; it needs to explore the hyphenated and intersecting spaces of feminist multicultural, social justice–oriented counseling psychology, to articulate the principles underlying the praxis, and to offer a picture of what activism, advocacy, and social justice in feminist multicultural counseling psychology actually looks like in all of its complexity, particularly research, scholarship, and practice focusing on the structural and systemic levels.

Thus, in this chapter we (a) define and elaborate on the concepts of social justice, activism, and advocacy within the context of feminist multicultural counseling psychology praxis; (b) discuss the various contexts in which social justice work is taking place; (c) describe our process of generating primary data presented in this chapter; (d) detail the complicated, multifaceted work of feminist multicultural counseling psychologists involved in systemic activism, advocacy, and social justice activities; and (e) make recommendations for future directions in a socially just feminist multicultural counseling psychology. The ideas and information we share in the following sections stem from our own work in feminist–social justice counseling and counseling psychology, the sparse reports in the literature, as well as from discussions and interviews with several other self-identified feminist multicultural counseling psychologists who have been engaging in system-focused activism and social change in a variety of venues and contexts.

Social Justice in Feminist Multicultural Counseling Psychology

Defining social justice necessitates envisioning a socially just world. Goodman, Liang, Helms, Latta, Sparks, and Weintraub (2004) visualize a socially just world as one in which resources are equitably distributed in support of loving relationships so that people can participate in the world under conditions of safety, security, freedom from exploitation or violence, and with adequate access to health care, food, education, sleep, and other basic needs. They go on to describe the social justice work of counseling psychologists as "scholarship and professional action designed to change societal values, structures, policies, and practices, such that disadvantaged or marginalized groups gain increased access to these tools of self-determination" (Goodman et al., 2004, p. 795). Vera and Speight (2003) note Bell's (1997) comment that the goal of social justice is "full and equal participation of all groups in a society that is mutually shaped to meet their needs" (p. 3, as cited by Vera & Speight, 2003).

Bell's emphasis on the importance of mutuality is consistent with a feminist multicultural perspective on social justice. Further, weaving a feminist multicultural perspective into this picture involves analyzing how gender intersects with multiple identities and social locations in understanding the effects of oppression, domination, and other social forces in people's lives with a "relentless insistence on the importance of incorporating the influence of the social context to our understanding of intrapsychic phenomena" (Espin, 1993, p. 103). To do so requires understanding how power is distributed at the individual, relational, institutional, and structural levels; linking the personal with the social and the political; and actively working to oppose, eliminate, and transform unjust social systems and structures and to create a socially just world (Enns, 1993; Espin, 1993; Goodman et al., 2004). Liberatory in nature, the practice of a socially just feminist multicultural counseling psychology involves the cultivation of a critical consciousness, a praxis of reflecting on and analyzing oppressive and unjust conditions, and taking action to transform them (Freire, 1972; Goodman et al., 2004; Martin-Baro, 1994).

Janet Helms (2003) observed, "Whereas most multicultural counseling literature focuses on integrating principles of social justice at the micro level, very little addresses strategies for intervening at a systemic level" (p. 309). We find this to also be the case within the literature documenting social justice research and practice in feminist multicultural counseling psychology. For example, significant scholarship has focused on documenting and understanding the effects of intersecting oppressions on the lived experiences of women, people of color, people with disabilities, and people living in poverty or economically challenging circumstances. This scholarship is embedded in career and vocational psychology, psychotherapy, counseling psychology training, and pedagogy. Many graduate students in counseling psychology learn to consider social, political, and cultural contexts in locating client problems, in diagnosis, treatment planning, and psychotherapy, and in the development and lived experiences of consultees and research participants. Yet, feminist multicultural counseling psychologists have emphasized that focusing on individual and micro-level change alone does not address the inequitable systems that create or contribute to human suffering—the social, political, and cultural systems of inequality that permeate most of the world's societies. Eliminating human suffering involves expanding our social justice focus to the transformation of communities, organizations, social institutions (i.e. media, schools, religious institutions, law enforcement systems), political systems, and other sociocultural structures. We need to regularly analyze the root causes of human suffering that arise from discriminatory, oppressive, and unjust policies, social conditions, cultural practices, and other societal institutions and structures. Thus, a social justice focus necessitates taking action to change these systems and structures or to create new ones based in social justice values such as equity (distribution of resources, opportunities, and rights in a just way), access (being able to access the resources, opportunities, and power needed to maintain a basic standard of living), participation (involvement or direct influence in decision making), and harmony (periodically sacrificing individual interests in the service of the needs of the larger social system) (Crethar, Torres Rivera, & Nash, 2008).

Social Justice Feminist Counseling Psychologists: Agents of Social and Systemic Change

The authors of previous chapters in this volume have primarily situated social justice values, principles, and practices within their discussions of important micro-level practices in feminist multicultural counseling psychology. Thus, in this chapter, we are emphasizing activism, advocacy, and social justice work in feminist multicultural counseling psychology as actions and activities that go beyond individual, family, and small group change to focus on social, political and cultural change at the meso (communities, organizations, smaller social institutions such as universities, churches, schools, and so forth) and macro (ideologies, policies, and social structures such as mass media, the institution of religion, the legal system etc.) levels. We want to highlight the activism of colleagues who are engaged in systemically focused efforts aimed at the creation of socially just communities, institutions, organizations, policies, cultures, and so on; the dismantling or transformation of systems of oppression and inequality; and the removal of cultural, social, and political barriers that block human access to resources, self-determination, and self-definition. Additionally, we will present examples of our own social justice work in relevant sections.

In order to more completely document and portray the current picture of activism, advocacy, and social justice scholarship and practice in feminist multicultural counseling psychology, we decided to interview several feminist multicultural counseling psychologists about their work in this realm, particularly work that has not appeared in the literature. In preparation for writing this chapter, we interviewed approximately 14 colleagues from around the United States, ranging from early career to very experienced members of the profession (most located in an academic institution as faculty or counseling center staff), as well as feminist multicultural counseling psychology graduate students nominated by their faculty mentors. We, the co-authors, also responded to the interview questions. Interviewees hold diverse racial, ethnic, and cultural identities, sexual orientations, ages, genders, social class backgrounds, and physical abilities, to name a few attributes. We e-mailed the group of potential interviewees, described the project, and requested their participation and permission to include portions of their narratives in the chapter in the form of personal communications. We included the following five questions, requesting a response to each if the colleague agreed to participate.

1. As a feminist counseling psychologist, are you engaged in activism and social justice work at the community, institutional, professional organizational, and/or international levels (that focuses on change beyond the individual or small group levels)? If so, can you please describe your work?
2. How do you see your work (above) emerging from and/or interconnected with your preparation/training, knowledge, and skills as a feminist counseling psychologist?
3. Please describe two examples of positive outcomes in your work that you feel have had an important impact in terms of systemic and/or social change.
4. What are some challenges and conundrums that emerge in your work (particularly in relation to enacting feminist and social justice values, principles, and practices)?
5. Is there any information you would like to add here to help us really "see" your work and you as an activist feminist counseling psychologist?

If necessary, we e-mailed some of our interviewees for further elaboration on particular information they shared. We recognize that our interview sample does not represent the whole of feminist multicultural counseling psychologists engaging in meso- and macro-level social and systemic change. Hopefully, these initial steps will inspire others to more extensively document this underrepresented and deeply influential array of contributions by feminist multicultural counseling psychologists.

By analyzing the existing literature and the narrative content from our interviews, we organized current meso- and macro-level feminist multicultural counseling psychology activism, advocacy, and social justice activities and practices based on the system(s) identified as the target of change. These categories include activities focused (a) at the grassroots community level; (b) at the community organization level; (c) at the professional organization level (e.g., the Association for Women in Psychology or the American Psychological Association, one of its divisions or subsystems); (d) within the academy and other educational institutions, including counseling psychology training programs; (e) within political and legal systems; (f) in employment settings; and (g) at the international level in an array of settings. We also included a category for (h) social justice feminist psychologist researchers and scholars who are intentionally and systematically engaged in activist research and scholarship aimed at changing social policy or sociocultural ideologies.

Feminist Multicultural Counseling Psychologists Engaging in Social Justice Activism

In this section we will weave a narrative that integrates existing literature with the perspectives and experiences of our respondents (including our own), beginning with their training and development in feminist multicultural psychology and praxis as well as counseling psychology. Then we will explore the multiple levels of feminist multicultural and social justice activism in which our respondents are participating (and all of the respondents are participating at multiple levels). In the last section, respondents describe the challenges and conundrums they, as feminist multicultural counseling psychologists, face as they engage in activism. Finally we offer an exchange of ideas among respondents and ourselves for overcoming these challenges.

Feminist Connections and Disconnections with Formal Counseling Psychology Training

As a doctoral student in counseling psychology who also identifies as a feminist and social justice activist, co-author Liz Abrams is aware that her education in feminist multicultural activism began long before she entered graduate school. She reflects:

> Having graduated with a minor in Women's Studies in college, I specifically looked for graduate training programs in counseling and counseling psychology that had a solid commitment to feminist, multicultural, and social justice process and issues. As we began our interviews I was curious to know where and how our respondents received training and experience with activism. Would our respondents view their training in multicultural feminism and counseling psychology as separate ventures or would we see overlap? Do counseling psychologists learn about multicultural feminism and activism while studying in a graduate program in counseling psychology? Would various answers to these questions show differences in identity, perspective, and engagement with activism?

Sharon Horne, a feminist multicultural counseling psychologist and faculty member at the University of Massachusetts, Boston, clearly delineates her development of these identities as separate yet intersecting, and emphasizes the centrality of social justice:

> I believe being a feminist counseling psychologist requires a delicate "holding" of both perspectives. Because of my counseling psychology training, I'm able to empathize with and respect cultural institutions and how they assist individuals to be resilient, connected, and form identities and communities, and my feminist training allows me a lens to see ways cultural institutions and systems can oppress and silence individuals. I think together they provide many means and methodologies for exploring questions. (personal communication, July 25, 2010)

Donna Hawxhurst, feminist multicultural counseling psychologist and director of training at the University of Utah Women's Resource Center, completed her Ph.D. in counseling psychology in 1972. At that time, there was no training regarding feminist multicultural therapy in her department, so she actively sought it out elsewhere:

> Most of my training, knowledge, and skills as a feminist counseling psychologist were developed and enhanced by grassroots feminist therapy consultation groups, local "on the ground" involvement and leadership in the feminist and feminist lesbian communities, a lot of "learning by doing," my active, ongoing participation and involvement in AWP [Association for Women in Psychology], ongoing immersion in the literature of feminist and feminist therapy theory and practice, ongoing participation in several radical feminist affinity groups, and the opportunity to direct a community college mental health paraprofessional training program in which I could institute and implement feminist pedagogy and practice under the radar. (personal communication, July 14, 2010)

Britney Brinkman, feminist multicultural counseling psychologist and faculty member at Chatham University, reports, "I was a feminist before I was a psychologist" (personal communication, July 6, 2010). Britney pursued a certificate in women's studies in addition to her doctorate in counseling psychology, remains active in the National Women's Studies Association, and teaches classes in Chatham's Gender Studies department. Britney's background in feminism and activism drew her to the field of counseling psychology: "My commitment to social justice influences all that I do. It informs my teaching, research, clinical work, supervision, mentoring, and volunteer work. While I wear many hats as a psychologist, my feminist-colored lens never change" (personal communication, July 6, 2010).

Pilar Hernandez, feminist multicultural counseling psychologist and faculty member at Johns Hopkins University, revealed that her feminist multicultural journey began in her home country, Colombia. As an undergraduate student, she had a psychology professor who identified as a feminist and postmodern thinker. The identities of psychologist and feminist began to form together under the tutelage of this mentor. She continued her training as a feminist multicultural therapist in the United States with other feminist mentors who also specialized in family therapy, intersectionality, and "Third World feminism." Pilar explains that she had to seek out these experiences of mentoring, though, because her traditional training in counseling psychology did not offer feminist multicultural and social justice training models (personal communication, July 5, 2010).

Although many of the women we interviewed reported that they acquired feminist multicultural and counseling psychology knowledge in distinctly different training experiences, Carolyn Enns has a different story to tell. She writes, "I was fortunate to be in my [counseling psychology] Ph.D. program at a time when feminist perspectives were beginning to appear. In 1984 (during my first quarter of work), my advisor (Gail Hackett) offered a course entitled Counseling Women, which introduced emerging feminist approaches to counseling." From this experience, Carolyn was encouraged to seek out more knowledge regarding the psychology of women and women's studies. Although there were few formal courses in her program at the time, her feminist mentors (Gail Hackett and Louise Fitzgerald) reinforced her interest in feminist multicultural counseling psychology, providing a space for both identities to emerge simultaneously (personal communication, July 5, 2010).

Clearly, the "herstories" of feminist multicultural counseling psychologists who have embraced social justice activism and advocacy are interesting and varied. Whatever the points of convergence of feminist multicultural and counseling psychology in their professional development process, the literature and our interviewees reveal that feminist multicultural counseling psychologists around the country are applying feminist multicultural counseling psychology in their activism and social justice activities at multiple levels. The feminist, multicultural, and social justice values about which our respondents write appear to be central to their identities and permeate all that they do. Rather than compartmentalizing activism into one part of their lives, their voices are unified around the observation that social justice and social change is important in every space they occupy. Although the broader field of psychology has ties to imperialism, colonization, and social control, we (the co-authors) wonder if feminist multicultural and social justice activists feel more at home in the subfield of counseling psychology due to our history of activism, prevention, and focus on diversity and multiculturalism.

Levels of Feminist Multicultural Counseling Psychologist Social Justice Activism

Vera and Speight (2003) remind us that while counseling psychology's multicultural competencies emphasize skills and abilities to work with diverse populations within the counseling setting, multicultural competence needs to be intertwined with social justice. This necessitates that professionals serve as agents of change within the community through actions such as advocacy, public awareness and consciousness-raising, community outreach, policy-making, and facilitating indigenous support systems. When only fulfilling the minimum requirement of our multicultural competence standards, we are practicing mandatory ethics. Raising the bar within the profession and assuming a social justice role within our communities constitutes practicing aspirational ethics.

Counseling psychology training programs typically do not prepare students to engage in social justice advocacy and activism at the systemic level (Helms, 2003). Most often, the focus is intervention at the individual, family, and group levels, which are, of course, crucial elements of our work. However, feminist multicultural psychology and, more recently, counseling psychology, have recognized the necessity of engaging in systemically focused social change if we are truly going to address the root causes of the suffering experienced by members of marginalized and target groups. For example, feminist multicultural counseling psychologist Rebecca Toporek was a driving force behind the development of the American Counseling Association's (ACA) Advocacy Competencies, enacted in 2003. The ACA Advocacy Competencies (Toporek, Lewis, & Crethar, 2009) call for intervention at the community level and argue for the need to train counselors (and counseling psychologists) to engage in advocacy and activism within communities. Yet, even with increased awareness of the importance of developing knowledge and skills in social justice activism and advocacy, this focus remains largely absent from most counseling psychology programs (Helms, 2003).

Since our training programs have not historically emphasized training in social justice and activism, taking on this work can be uncomfortable even when we are devoted to it (Pitts, Margolies, & Leeder, 2008). In addition, activism is not considered therapeutic work and therefore is not subject to reimbursement, leaving professionals to pursue it pro bono. They cannot bill for services or seek reimbursement for personal resources used, potentially losing out on income due to lost time in the office seeing clients for billable services (Vera & Speight, 2003; Helms, 2003, Pitts, Margolies, & Leeder, 2008). Another major variable may be the climate of the profession, which places greater value on traditional forms of research over activist research or social action in the tenure and promotion of academic counseling psychologists (Kiselica, 2004).

Nonetheless, feminist multicultural counseling psychologists have engaged in activism and social justice activities despite the challenges and discomforts commonly associated with the work. These systemically focused efforts have taken place at multiple levels, from the community grassroots level all the way to the larger social, political, cultural, and international levels. In the following section, we discuss the ways in which feminist multicultural counseling psychologists engage in social justice and social action at the meso and macro levels.

Community Level

Working at the grassroots level in our own communities can be powerful and transformative, with far-reaching effects on individual and collective lives. For some, grassroots social justice activism has been an ongoing, lifelong process. Susan Morrow (2009) details her journey, including an extensive history of grassroots level activism in the civil rights, peace, women's liberation, environmental, and lesbian/gay/bisexual movements. She has participated in consciousness-raising groups, including Black-White and feminist groups. In 1968, she participated in the Poor People's March in Washington, D.C., and during the Vietnam War she went door to door for the peace movement as a part of Another Mother for Peace. Along with Donna Hawxhurst, she became active in feminist and lesbian consciousness-raising, community building, and civil rights as active members in the Feminist Lesbian Activist Coalition (previously the Lesbian Rights Task Force of the Phoenix National Organization of Women). Morrow and Hawxhurst are not alone in their commitments to grassroots activism. Laura Palmer (2004) is actively involved in the Child Abuse Network (CAN), a grassroots multidisciplinary organization focusing on professional networking, advocacy, and public education with the goal of preventing child abuse.

Professional Organization Level

Feminist multicultural counseling psychologists have long been actively engaged in social justice and social change work and bringing multicultural and social justice values to the profession and within our professional organizations. This activism has included, for example, increasing the representation of women in membership and leadership, infusing social justice into professional standards, training, and psychotherapy guidelines (Sue, Bingham, Porche-Burke, & Vasquez, 1999), and special organizational projects aimed at changing systems of inequality in the organization and society at large.

Within our own APA division, the Society of Counseling Psychology (Division 17), feminist multicultural counseling psychologists established the Ad Hoc Committee on Women, first chaired by Jean Parsons and Louise Vetter, in 1970 to address the "neglect and discrimination women were experiencing within the counseling field" (Farmer, 2002, p. 417), the academy, the division, within the APA, and in society at large. The ad hoc committee was transformed into a standing committee in 1982 due to its reputation and effectiveness, and morphed yet again in 1996 to become the Division 17 Section for the Advancement of Women (SAW). Helen Farmer (2002) documents, "By 1990, the Committee on Women had grown in influence and accomplishments.... The formation and approval of the Section on Women within Division 17 was accomplished by a group of dedicated women in 1996. The groundwork for this organizational shift was begun several years earlier (1993–1995) during the period when Linda Forrest, Judy Ellickson, and Ruth Fassinger chaired the committee. Debra Noumair was the first chair of the new section"

(p. 419). Throughout its "herstory" SAW has been a powerful force in transforming the division as well as the "institution" of the APA by ongoing advocacy and social justice efforts aimed at, for example, increasing representation of women in leadership and advocating for the production and dissemination of awareness, knowledge, and skills in feminist multicultural psychology within the profession and in society at large.

The process of development and passage of the APA Guidelines for the Psychological Practice for Girls and Women (APA, 2007) is a powerful example of an institutionally focused social change endeavor deeply anchored in the activism of Division 17 feminist multicultural psychologists, particularly members of SAW and its earlier iterations. Following within-division work by the Ad Hoc Committee, the Committee on Women, and then SAW, to develop and institutionalize Division 17 Principles Concerning the Counseling/Psychotherapy of Women: Rationale and Implementation (Fitzgerald & Nutt, 1986), feminist multicultural psychologists from Divisions 17 and 35 formed a task force aimed at developing guidelines for psychological practice with girls and women, particularly due to ongoing concerns about the institutionalized sexism and other forms of oppression and bias inherent in mainstream psychology. In 2002, two feminist multicultural counseling psychologists, Roberta Nutt and Carolyn Enns, joined Joy Rice, co-chaired joint task force (APA Divisions 17 and 35) comprised of many feminist multicultural counseling psychologists who ultimately created and spearheaded the ratification of the APA Guidelines for Psychological Practice with Girls and Women (APA, 2007). Carol Enns writes that the project took seven years to complete and involved "substantial efforts and struggle to integrate multicultural and feminist frameworks within the guidelines" (personal communication, July 5, 2010). Although they met with some resistance, she and her feminist collaborators continued to push for feminist multicultural process and felt satisfied that the end result had been informed substantially by feminist multicultural values. The guidelines serve as a source of accountability and a set of standards of practice for the profession of psychology, as well as other related professions, such as counselor education and social work, including a guideline encouraging psychologists to engage in social justice activism aimed at understanding and working to "change institutional and systemic bias that may impact girls and women" (APA 2007, p. 64).

A measure of the success of SAW efforts is evidenced not only by the many feminists who have, in recent years, held governance positions within the APA and its various divisions, but also by the ways that they have used their power and influence to carry out social justice projects and agendas aimed at institutional change. Feminist multicultural counseling psychologist Melba Vasquez, current president of the APA, relayed, "Part of the responsibility of a counseling psychologist is to interject social justice in every aspect of one's work. As a feminist multicultural leader, it means promoting related ethics and principles, including modeling ethical leadership, prioritizing fairness and justice and reaching back to support others" (personal communication, January 17, 2011). When we asked Melba about her institutional-level social justice work, she reminded us, "I have focused much of my professional career engaged in promoting social justice. As president of the APA, three of my initiatives focus on social justice issues: immigration; preventing prejudice and enhancing diversity; and educational disparities, particularly for poor and racial/ethnic minority students" (personal communication, January 17, 2011). Melba's explicit goal for these initiatives, involving the appointment of a presidential task force to address each, is to bring about change in the discipline of psychology and in society at large (Azar, 2011). Prior to her election, Melba has had a long "herstory" of feminist multicultural activism within various parts of the APA and other organizations. For example, "As a member of APA's Board of Social and Ethical Responsibility for Psychologists (later renamed the Board for the Advancement of Psychology in the Public Interest), she helped to spur APA to cancel its investments in South Africa during apartheid and raised awareness within the association about HIV/AIDS" (Novotney, 2010, p. 60).

Within the context of another organization, feminist multicultural counseling psychologist Donna Hawxhurst chronicles her long-standing work within the feminist activist organization, the Association for Women in Psychology (AWP), at both the local and national levels. She organized and coordinated local chapters of the AWP in both Utah and Arizona, which have been two of the most active chapters across the country, particularly in the areas of state and community-based anti-oppression work. Over the last three years, Donna has served as collective-coordinator for the national organization, making it her mission to provide leadership in directly addressing White privilege and racism at multiple levels within the organization. Donna reflects:

> The Collective has embraced this mission and sees the work as ongoing, sponsoring sessions for White women to address privilege and racism during the last three annual conferences, with plans to continue this work at future conferences and beyond. More recently the Implementation Collective has been exploring ways to incorporate a clearer focus for inclusion of international and immigrant women's issues and concerns in AWP. (personal communication, July 14, 2010)

The Academy and Other Educational Institutions

Although the academy has long been considered a bastion of progressive and radical values, as the United States continues to embrace a pro-capitalist and pro-corporate ethic, the world of academia moves forward in that direction as well. Though it may have once been considered a given, social justice activism within the academy and other educational institutions now seems required for the survival of progressive values. Feminist multicultural counseling psychologists can be found advocating for diversity and social justice at the larger college and university level and within its subsystems, particularly within counseling and counseling psychology training programs and internship settings.

COLLEGE AND UNIVERSITY LEVEL

Although feminists in the academy are often situated on the margins, there are times when we have opportunities to assert our influence toward institutional and systemic change. As a feminist multicultural counseling psychologist and supervisor at the Women's Resource Center at the University of Utah, Donna Hawxhurst sees the effects of her activism in "politicizing others" and disrupting "business as usual," both within the Women's Resource Center as well as the greater campus. She sits on several committees across campus and speaks out, even when a social justice perspective is being diminished or trivialized by administrators, staff, and others (personal communication, July 14, 2010). Like Donna, Dawn Szymanski, University of Tennessee–based feminist multicultural counseling psychologist and professor, shares that within her institution, she is involved in organizational efforts focusing on systemic change. Dawn reports, "at the university level I have been involved in getting a university Safe Zone program [training allies for LGBT members of the university community] up and running and in developing a department strategic plan to enhance equal opportunity and cultural diversity" (personal communication, July 21, 2010). Carolyn Enns has been a member of many tenure and promotion committees at her college and writes that she uses this opportunity "to raise questions about how we evaluate, think about gender and culture during the faculty evaluation process, etc." Carolyn also reminds us that feminist mentorship within the academy is another way to use feminist multicultural principles to engage others in capacity building and empowerment—another method of changing the culture of an academic institution or unit. She is particularly aware of the importance of staying connected to younger feminists and bridging the generation gap by acknowledging that today's up-and-coming feminists may bring different approaches to activism from which older feminists can learn (personal communication, July 5, 2010).

COUNSELING AND COUNSELING PSYCHOLOGY TRAINING PROGRAMS

Some counseling and counseling psychology graduate programs and internship training sites have organized their programs based on social justice values, principles, and practices. For example, at Boston College, several feminist multicultural counseling psychologists helped spearhead the transformation of the counseling psychology graduate program to more explicitly incorporate social justice as a central theme in the training process. In their 2004 feature article in *The Counseling Psychologist*, Lisa Goodman, Belle Liang, Janet Helms, Rachel Latta, Elizabeth Sparks, and Sarah Weintraub (2004) describe how feminist multicultural counseling psychology faculty and their colleagues have integrated systems-focused social justice training into the core curriculum, emphasizing in particular their first year experience (FYE). "The FYE is designed to expose students to work at the meso (community, organizations) and macro (government, policy, social norms) levels instead of, or in addition to, the more traditional micro (individual) level (Moane, 2003)" (p. 808). They emphasize that students also learn that social justice work can "involve collaborating with those marginalized communities whose situations counseling psychologists are interested in improving or with those groups with the power to make changes happen—those who hold the purse strings, develop policies, or run programs" (Goodman et al, 2004, p. 808).

Within the Rollins College Graduate Program in Counseling, co-author Kathryn Norsworthy and her feminist counseling psychologist colleague, Alicia Homrich, provided key leadership in an organized faculty effort to infuse diversity, multicultural and social justice values, principles, and practices throughout the counseling training program. For example, in addition to providing consultation to faculty as they redesign courses, Norsworthy reports her satisfaction about a new requirement recently implemented—the social justice pre-practicum—during which each student is required to apprentice with a community-based activist organization engaged in systemic-level social change (personal communication, July 7, 2010).

Donna Hawxhurst and colleagues have developed a feminist multicultural therapy practicum site in Salt Lake City, Utah, that utilizes a train-the-trainer model and focuses on feminist multicultural process, advocacy, and social justice activism. She writes, "The students who spend a year in practicum or internship with us report transformative changes in their own work toward and commitments to social justice. Perhaps we contribute to systemic and social change by contributing to individual change of that nature" (personal communication, July 14, 2010). Each student whom she supervises, trains, and collaborates with will go on to affect hundreds or thousands of other lives.

Political and Legal Systems

Political activism and social change are perhaps one of the least documented levels of action in which feminist multicultural counseling psychologists engage. Both the APA Guidelines for Psychological Practice with Women and Girls (APA, 2007) and the APA Multicultural Guidelines (APA, 2003) emphasize the importance of social justice advocacy and activism in creating or changing public policy, laws, and practices within the legal system, including, for example, court procedures. Arredondo and Perez (2003) call for counseling psychologists to take public positions on political issues.

Sharon Horne describes her local and state activist efforts toward the goal of achieving full civil rights for the gay/lesbian/bisexual/transgender communities. In Memphis, Tennessee, Sharon was actively involved in successful efforts to add county non-discrimination policies for LGBT individuals, specifically through her testimony during public hearings and by providing Tennessee-specific statistics and research that strengthened the arguments for equal rights for LGBT individuals and families (personal communication, July 25, 2010). As we discuss later in this chapter, activists fighting against these amendments in states around the country have also cited Sharon's research focusing on the detrimental effects of anti–gay marriage amendments.

Similarly, for almost a decade, co-author Kathryn Norsworthy has been a leader in the central Florida LGBT activist community, where, as a member of the Orlando Anti-discrimination Ordinance Committee (OADO), she has been part of several successful efforts to create human rights ordinances that include sexual orientation and gender identity and to add domestic partner benefits for city and county employees. Norsworthy's current political activism is focused on establishing a city and county domestic partner registry. At the state level, she actively worked to defeat the 2008 anti–gay marriage amendment and to repeal the state law banning gays and lesbians from adopting children. Drawing on her knowledge and skills as a feminist multicultural counseling psychologist and, interestingly, Sharon Horne's research on the negative psychological effects of anti–gay marriage amendments, Norsworthy has testified at public hearings, consulted with public officials, and trained other activists. She writes, "Feminist multicultural counseling psychologists have a role to play in bringing our knowledge about privilege, oppression, trauma, well-being, social justice, and activism to the process of social change within the governmental, policy, and legal systems" (personal communication, July 7, 2010).

International Social Justice Activism

The last few years have seen a surge of interest in international issues within the field of counseling psychology. Sharon Horne is one of a handful of counseling psychologists who works and publishes her international work from an explicitly feminist multicultural and social justice–oriented perspective (Horne & Mathews, 2006; Yakushko, Razzhavaikina, & Horne, 2009; Molchanova, Kim, Horne, Aitpaeva, Ashiraliev, Ten, & Pohilko, 2009). Sharon Horne and feminist multicultural counseling psychologist Susan Mathews (Horne & Mathews, 2004) have been traveling to Russia, Macedonia, Hungary, Uzbekistan, and Romania to train community crisis center counselors working with women on social issues of violence against women and other significant projects. They combine multicultural and feminist orientations in their collaborative consultation model. In their work, they emphasize supporting those with whom they consult in engaging in a sociopolitical analysis of their concerns—Freirian "conscientization" (Freire, 1972). Sharon writes, "Our projects have included ambivalent sexism in cross-cultural contexts, understanding local healing methods as they relate to postmodern psychology, and locating the role of gender in development networks." As an academic fellow with the Soros Foundation Open Society Institute, Sharon collaborates with the American University of Central Asia in Kyrgyzstan, reporting, "I work with local feminist scholars who are creating a socially just academic department that values academic freedom, feminist research, and student empowerment despite existing within a traditional post-communist context that favors hierarchy and authoritarian styles of leadership" (personal communication, July 25, 2010).

Co-author Kathryn Norsworthy's international projects in South and Southeast Asia are well documented (Norworthy & Khuankaew, 2004; Norsworthy & Khuankaew, 2005; Norsworthy, 2008; Norsworthy & Khuankaew, 2008; Norsworthy & Buranajaroenkij, 2011). Along with her primary Thai collaborator, Ouyporn Khuankaew, Kathryn incorporates principles of liberation theory, feminist multicultural psychology, participant action research methodology, and critical theory while taking a decolonizing, power sharing, and empowerment stance (Norsworthy & Khuankaew, 2005). Through a decade of work together, Norsworthy and Khuankaew have developed a strong global North/South partnership, requiring that Norsworthy confront her own biases and appreciate the indigenous wisdom of those with whom she works (for a detailed description of her journey and the evolution of this relationship, see Norsworthy & Khuankaew, 2005).

Since 1997, Norsworthy's international work has involved a wide range of projects and social issues in Thailand, with the refugee communities of Burma, and with regional and international groups. Examples of projects include feminist liberation–based workshops in which groups engage in sociopolitical analysis of violence against women in their cultural contexts, identify impact, develop contextually based action plans for prevention, social change, and community-based response systems for survivors. Many of these projects also involve training participants (at their request) to take the workshop methodology back to their communities (Norsworthy & Khuankaew, 2004, 2005). Ouyporn and Kathryn have also conducted similar workshops focused on community-based prevention, social change, and feminist counseling in response to the needs and concerns of Thai women with HIV/AIDS (Norsworthy & Khuankaew, 2008). More recently, Kathryn has been collaborating with several second-generation activists trained in Norsworthy and Khuankaew's methodology on trauma and peace-building projects in collaboration with mixed ethnic Malay Muslim and ethnic Thai Buddhist groups in southern Thailand, a site of serious intractable ethno-political conflict (Norsworthy, 2008; Norsworthy & Buranajaroenkij, 2011). All of these projects focus on meso- and macro-level social change, whether at the community, organizational, institutional, or structural levels, and center indigenous, feminist multicultural, and social justice counseling psychological knowledge and skills.

Activist Research and Scholarship

The field of counseling psychology has embraced and pursued multicultural and social justice values in various research topics such as training, clinical practice, teaching, and vocational interests. Recently we have begun to see feminist multicultural counseling psychology literature representing socially just, liberatory, and participatory research processes. Our field has been slow to adopt participatory action research, and there still appears to be a firm hierarchy in place that privileges traditional psychology and highly values post-positivist research. Vera and Speight (2003) remind us that research informed by social justice is collaborative, action oriented, and socially relevant, and might concentrate on the needs of specific communities, the evaluation of programs designed to meet community needs, or surveys of research with the potential to influence policies. Feminist social psychologist Michelle Fine (2007) has issued a call to expand our "methodological imaginations" to be in greater solidarity with our social justice values and principles.

Oksana Yakushko has taken this call seriously in her position as faculty in a counseling psychology program. She was expected to teach a counseling psychology research seminar; instead of focusing solely on traditional forms of research, she developed a radical feminist research seminar in which students read texts from bell hooks and Angela Davis and reflected on the intersections of their own identities and experiences as graduate students and feminists. She writes:

> We talked about the continued realities of predominately White male leadership on campus and our field. We discussed the continued dismissal

of research methods that focus on empowerment of participants (such as many qualitative methods) versus those who view participants as mere subjects of data collection. We talked about what it meant for students to have a voice as well as to face their privilege as holders of graduate degrees. I believe the results of this seminar were profound in not only helping students to have a place to give voice to their experiences, but also to encourage them to do amazing scholarly work that intended to address issues of oppression. (personal communication, July 5, 2010)

Putting this kind of training into action, Dawn Szymanski and her students conduct research focusing on identifying factors that help non-dominant groups resist and overcome oppressive social messages and experiences, and articulating how members of dominant groups can become agents for change in the fight to confront and transform sexism, racism, and other forms of oppression (personal communication, July 21, 2010).

Laura Smith, a professor at Teacher's College at Columbia University, has also created a research program that is based on participatory and liberatory perspectives with a social action component. The students on her research team are each engaged in a participatory action research (PAR) project. By modeling a PAR paradigm with her students, she is helping each of them break out of the ivory tower, connect with their local communities, and value research participants as more than "subjects." Instead research participants are co-investigators who bring wisdom, knowledge, competence, and the capacity to carry out interesting, effective, and creative social change. She writes, "PAR can provide psychologists and community members with another paradigm for working with people, an alternative to the top-down, expert-helper model that our conventional [counseling psychology] training prepares us for" (personal communication, July 6, 2010). And the research process and outcomes serve as vehicles for social change at the larger systems levels—particularly the community meso level.

Britney Brinkman's research is founded on principles of feminist action research and much of it involves designing, implementing, and evaluating programs related to social justice at the institutional level. For example, her dissertation research involved evaluating a school-based program called Fairness for All Individuals Through Respect (FAIR). The program's aim is to teach elementary school students about inequality and to promote social justice. Although she wondered initially if this program changed student awareness and behavior, she found that the participants significantly decreased their engagement in gender prejudice behaviors, such as exclusion and name-calling (Brinkman, Jedinak, Rosén, & Zimmerman, 2010). Based on her analysis of focus group interviews, she writes, "I also found that the children were very aware of the potential backlash they might experience if they questioned traditional gender roles and the struggles that come with challenging people who are engaging in discrimination." Using feminist principles and applied research that directly impact school-age children and their formation of gender schemas leaves Brinkman with a hopeful feeling that combats some of the challenges and conundrums that emerge for feminist counseling psychologists. Now, as a relatively new faculty member at Chatham University, Britney immediately began connecting with her community and building a foundation for the extension of her dissertation research in the form of action research with girls. She has recently implemented the FAIR + program (a revised version of the original program) to third, fourth, and fifth graders in an inner-city school in Pittsburgh (personal communication, July 6, 2010). Often, faculty and staff working within academic institutions are discouraged from engaging in community work and action research because, from a traditional social science research perspective, it is deemed "service" rather than research. By pursuing relationships with organizations working toward social justice in her community, Britney is actively rejecting this traditional paradigm while making a statement that feminist-based action research and capacity building is valued, is real research, and has direct application to building socially just communities.

Sharon Horne, who also engages in activist research and scholarship, writes, "I work with students and mentor them to engage with research with social inquiry at the core. We begin by exploring positions of injustice in social arrangements and explore how we can raise awareness of these inequities, and how our work may benefit or alter inequitable social networks." Recently, she initiated a PAR project with young African American men in her local community who are most at risk for HIV infection. She explains that "youth act as architects of the research exploration alongside graduate students and faculty investigators to locate the ways stigmatized sexual and racial identities interplay with sexual risk-taking." She also comments that she "makes concerted efforts to translate her research into practical information for community use to help prevent minority stress" (personal communication, July 25, 2010).

Oksana Yakushko's experiences with activist research and scholarship have led her to take a different path for her own work. She reports that she has been very passionate and engaged with extending justice to immigrants, especially immigrants without legal documents, in the United States. She has offered a social justice analysis of the root causes and negative effects of U.S. xenophobia on our immigrant population (Yakushko, 2009), along with specific recommendations for the role of counseling psychologists as agents of social change at the levels of practice, training, research and policy. Yet, she reported that she has continued to experience the feeling that her work was trapped in the "ivory tower" of academia. Instead of proceeding down the same path and feeling ineffective, Oksana is breaking outside the box by writing a book of fiction about undocumented immigrants. She writes, "In this book I bring all of my counseling psychology and feminist training and sensibilities to the project of bringing to life the voices of people who are marginalized in this country. In addition to issues of immigration, my book will weave together themes of sexism, gendered violence, social class, heterosexism, and unconscious privilege" (personal communication, July 5, 2010).

From the graduate student perspective, co-author Liz Abrams recalls that when applying to graduate school, she searched for mentors who would support feminist activist-based research. This careful search paid off and, under the supervision of her mentor, Susan Morrow, she is now beginning work on a participatory action research dissertation project in collaboration with older lesbians living in Salt Lake City, Utah. This project, called "Living Our Visions," aims to increase the well being and thriving of this community and to support the creation of a more vibrant older lesbian community through social action and self-advocacy (personal communication, September 8, 2010).

Student Activism

Anneliese Singh and six pre-doctoral interns (2010a) have documented counseling psychology students' strong desire for education and experience in social justice during their doctoral programs. They find that some graduate students are currently engaging in systems-level social justice activism on their university campuses and in their communities. For example, one of their research participants reported, "I analyze and oppose the systems that cause and perpetuate oppression and injustice through advocacy, outreach, legislative action, protesting, and education efforts" (Singh et al., 2010a, p. 782). But many of them lament the lack of mentoring and opportunities to increase their knowledge and skills in social justice action.

Among our interviewees, we heard several accounts of feminist multicultural counseling psychology students engaging in meso- and macro-level social justice work. Teresa Reeves, a feminist counseling psychology graduate student at the University of Memphis, incorporates activism into her research, clinical, and teaching activities. She has published research that makes a case for equity for LGBT individuals and families. She also shares her research with her local LGBT community center so that the information is available to people working on the ground with LGBT policy initiatives. As a form of political activism, Teresa notes that she has "attended local rallies to support including LGBT employees in a workplace non-discrimination policy" (personal communication, July 20, 2010).

Manijeh Badiee, a graduate student at the University of Lincoln-Nebraska, was recently awarded the Hammed Shahidian Critical Feminist Award for her qualitative feminist multicultural research with Iranian women and empowerment. She observes:

> On the international level, I am committed to doing qualitative research on Iranian women and men fighting for women's rights. Although I plan to publish in scholarly journals, I also want my research to reach an audience outside of the academic world. There is a lot of misinformation and mystery about Iranian people, and one of my goals with my advocacy work is to raise the voices of strong Iranian women fighting for change. When women are empowered, societies change. (personal communication, February 21, 2011)

Upon moving to Utah in 2009, student co-author Liz Abrams wanted to become connected with anti-racist social justice work in her own community.

> Initially I was disheartened due to the racial and ethnic landscape of my Salt Lake community, which is predominantly White. I soon realized that there were other women wanting to connect around this work so I approached some of the radical feminists with whom I had built relationships about starting a group based on a paper I recently co-authored on the dialectics of White identities and how to

work with White folks around White privilege (Todd & Abrams, 2011). Together, we began a community-based group called WWIRE—White Women Working on Issues of Race & Equity. During bi-weekly meetings, members rotate in co-leading discussions, experiential activities, post-film dialogues, and debriefing our experiences with community-based anti-racist work. The members now do work as a group in the community while continuing our individual activities. (personal communication, September 8, 2010)

Co-author Stefanie Lindlau is involved in a grassroots student organization in her master's program at Rollins College. The community-based activist and social change–focused Legacy Group was started in 2007 by a group of counseling student interns, without request or direction from the faculty, with a goal of implementing the social justice skills they learned in their graduate training. Stefanie writes:

> I am currently coordinating a community-based event focusing on the systemic oppression and needs of homeless veterans in our community. The ultimate goal is to raise awareness about the needs of this population and how to best meet those needs, raise awareness about the social and political issues, take a supportive stance in our interactions, and ensure that each veteran is remembered and celebrated on Veteran's Day. Being a veteran myself, this experience aided me in realizing the ways the personal can be transformed into a tool for sociopolitical change. (personal communication, October 3, 2010)

Challenges and Conundrums for Feminist Multicultural Counseling Psychologists

Just as important as engaging in activism is how to navigate the rough waters and challenges that lie ahead without extinguishing that bright flame in our hearts. Do feminist multicultural counseling psychologist activists fare better in terms of burnout due to our counseling psychology training, or do the multiple roles put us in an even more precarious and vulnerable place, positioning us for burnout? Donna Hawxhurst writes that some of the biggest challenges that emerge for her involve "individuals, offices, departments, organizations, and institutions that are invested in maintaining existing matrixes of practice, privilege, and power." She describes feeling overwhelmed at times, especially when she can see no evidence of a positive outcome. At the same time, Donna feels that the work itself is energizing and can lead to opportunities for each of us to transform our processes which can lead to more effective outcomes (personal communication, July 14, 2010).

Britney Brinkman writes that challenges facing feminist and social justice activist counseling psychologists include "the limited nature of resources," and "resistance." She encourages us to involve a network of people in our work so that it does not fall on a few individuals, communities, or systems. Regarding resistance, Brinkman talks about her challenges in encountering people with an investment in privileged positions and the status quo. She observes, "It can be difficult to sustain energy and hope for activism when one is constantly coming up against these kinds of resistances from individuals, communities, organizations, and institutions" (personal communication, July 6, 2010).

Carolyn Enns notes that there are "too many possibilities and too little time." As an academic, she often runs out of time for herself and for becoming involved with political activism. One of her solutions is to weave social justice knowledge and skills into her classroom by assigning students to write letters to political leaders based on the information about the social issues they have covered in class. As a trained counseling psychologist, Carolyn finds that she has many tools for individual or small group work with others, but feels less equipped with knowledge and experience of large group process. She posits that additional training in community psychology would be useful for counseling psychologists. Further, Carolyn also observes, "My experience in other countries (e.g., Japan and Korea) tells me that social change does not always follow a 'Western' model." She recommends that feminist multicultural counseling psychologists collaborate with and learn from feminist colleagues around the globe (personal communication, July 5, 2010).

Even when we are surrounded by and collaborating with other feminist multicultural colleagues and students around activism, the reality is that we are also surrounded by values of competition and conventional forms of training, practice, and research. Laura Smith writes, "My work looks different from the work of my colleagues who are involved in more conventional forms of psychological research. How will these efforts be valued when I come up for tenure?" (personal communication, July 6, 2010).

Another challenge for many who engage in feminist multicultural and social justice activism is our struggle to spend time taking care of ourselves. For many of us, as women, we have been socialized to take care of others and to make the care of ourselves secondary. As therapists, we enact our enculturated inclination toward helping and caring for others. As social justice activists, we may also struggle with the feelings of "survivor guilt," where we feel we have to keep working, working, working for social justice because we have survived, while others have perished for the cause. When we push ourselves to these outer limits we board a fast track to burnout, yet many of us have not learned, or perhaps have not taken the time, to practice self-care tools that will keep us safe, full of joy, and working for a very long time.

Britney Brinkman observed that her training and experience in counseling psychology offers tools for the prevention of activist burnout through a set of knowledge and skills that have helped her find ways to engage effectively with individuals in difficult dialogues about social justice matters and to stay dedicated to the slow and often arduous process of systemic change (personal communication, July 6, 2010). Oksana Yakushko is deeply self-reflexive on this issue:

> I want to reflect on the challenge of self-care and boundaries. I am still learning to recognize that attending to my inner life and my development (i.e., spiritual, emotional, and physical) is also feminist and is psychologically healthy. Moreover, my partner and my children also require and deserve my full-hearted participation in their lives. For example, I chose a home birth and natural attachment-based parenting, which I believe to be feminist choices but ones that involve more of my active participation in the care for myself and my family. I am growing in a reaction to a challenge to see all these commitments as something that feminist counseling psychologists strive to be—full human beings seeking that their lives contribute meaningfully to their immediate and extended communities. (personal communication, July 5, 2010)

Conclusion

The discipline of counseling psychology has a demonstrated history and commitment to social justice, activism, and advocacy. Feminist multicultural counseling psychologists have been central in this movement and in providing the impetus for enacting our commitment to these values and guiding principles (Gilbert & Osipow, 1991). We see more evidence in the counseling psychology literature in recent years of feminist driven micro-level social justice and advocacy efforts, particularly the incorporation of social justice principles and practices in counseling psychology training and research devoted to articulating the dimensions of privilege and oppression and their effects. Earlier chapters in this book reveal how feminist multicultural counseling psychologists are infusing social justice in pedagogy, training, mentoring, and research. This chapter details the "herstory" of meso- and macro-level social justice and activism in feminist multicultural counseling psychology, weaving together the historical development of counseling psychology and the participation of feminists in this evolution. We emphasize and offer examples of how feminist multicultural counseling psychologists and graduate students with diverse identities and backgrounds have been applying principles and practices from feminist multicultural and counseling psychology in social and systemic change. To do so, we draw from existing literature as well as primary interview data with a number of feminist multicultural counseling psychologists engaged in social justice–based research and praxis, from the local community level to the international arena. We also note the challenges for feminist multicultural counseling psychologists in getting our social justice work published and caring for ourselves to prevent role strain and burnout.

Future Directions

As we have discussed earlier, based on our interview data and those of Anneliese Singh and colleagues, clearly more feminist multicultural counseling psychologists and graduate students are engaging in social justice activism, particularly at the meso and macro levels, than have been included in the literature. We hope to see more research documenting and detailing not only these activities, but also articulating the knowledge and skills necessary to be effective social justice activists, following the examples and advice of such feminist multicultural counseling psychologists as Anneliese Singh (Singh et al., 2010a, b) and Lisa Goodman and her colleagues (2004). This research would serve to further legitimize and value social action by feminist multicultural counseling psychologists and to establish the key role that we play in enacting counseling psychology's social justice agenda. As noted by feminist multicultural counseling psychologists Libby Nutt Williams and Sue Morrow (Williams & Morrow, 2009), qualitative studies, in particular, would be very useful in addressing these questions; in fact, Williams and Morrow (2009) emphasize that one of the purposes of qualitative research should be social justice. We call upon counseling psychology faculty to support feminist multicultural doctoral students who wish to investigate these questions through their dissertation research.

At the same time, we pose the following question: Given that social and political activism is such a long-standing focus of feminism, why are there so few feminist multicultural counseling psychologists represented in the literature? Is it the case that there are many more feminist multicultural counseling psychologists who are engaging in social and political activism, or are there, in fact, very few, and if so, why is that? Several feminist multicultural counseling psychologists have briefly commented on these questions in this chapter; however, further elaboration is needed, both in terms of the work being done and on the social justice issue of the barriers and challenges that feminist multicultural counseling psychologists face in carrying out and publishing their social justice work. These data would be helpful in raising awareness about this particular social justice issue in the field of counseling psychology and would assist in making the case for the importance of this knowledge if we are to prepare the next generation of counseling psychologists to effectively carry out the profession's social justice charge.

Further, as Elizabeth Vera and Suzette Speight (2003) point out, "One way of integrating a commitment to social justice into counseling psychology is through the training of the next generation of counseling professionals" (p. 267), specifically in the enactment of social justice work. They remind us of feminist bell hooks's (1994) observation that we must change our methods of education and training, "transforming students from being passive learners to active participants" (p. 267) and viewing education as a process of liberation. Of course, counseling psychology programs would need to make and enact a commitment to infuse social justice values, principles, and practices into the training process. Counseling psychology faculty would need to acquire the awareness, knowledge, and skills necessary to both engage in social justice activism and to guide students in the practice of systems-level social change. Activism would also be required at the organizational level, particularly within the APA accreditation and counseling psychology training guidelines, to strengthen this commitment to action.

The students involved in this project also posed the question: How can we make the social justice work of feminist multicultural counseling psychologists more accessible beyond direct mentorship and training in the academy, which can be a challenge for students in programs without feminist multicultural counseling psychologists or other faculty with a social justice and/or multicultural sensibility? They call for the institutionalization of the training of feminist multicultural counseling psychologists, particularly in understanding feminist and social justice principles and practices and how to operationalize them in activism, political analysis, and social justice. We envision feminist multicultural counseling psychology social justice institutes that transcend academic programs as a more immediate step, given the slow process of change in organizations and in the academy. How might such a vision become a reality, particularly given the already heavy workloads of feminist multicultural counseling psychologists?

Finally, as our interviewees reminded us, self-care and effective negotiation of role strain and multiple stressors connected to feminist work is ever in the forefront for those of us who answer the feminist call. Extending the preliminary information offered in this chapter, for example, by Oksana Yakushko, we believe it would be extremely useful to hear from feminist multicultural counseling psychologists engaging in systemic social change about effective strategies for preventing burnout and for proactive self care and self regulation. General information on these topics is of course helpful; however, hearing from our colleagues who share our deep commitment to engage in practices of *tikkun olam* (a Hebrew phrase which translates into "repairing the world") would offer meaningful revelations about how to sustain ourselves while traveling this fulfilling, yet often difficult and challenging path.

We close this chapter with the observations of Lisa Goodman, Belle Liang, Janet Helms, Rachel Latta, Elizabeth Sparks, and Sarah Weintraub (2004), Boston College Counseling Psychology program:

> Shifting our standards to reflect a commitment to understanding and intervening in the systems and structures that shape individual lives will require numerous personal and structural transformations. However, we must consider the costs of not making these changes. As feminist and multicultural theorists have underscored for decades, individual mental health cannot be fully achieved until we eradicate the multiple forms of oppression faced by so many. (p. 830)

Feminist multicultural counseling psychologists are clearly in the forefront in responding to this call to action, bringing our feminist knowledge, skills, experiences, as well as the strengths of our identities and commitments as feminists and activists.

Author's Note

Correspondence concerning this chapter should be addressed to Kathryn L. Norsworthy, Graduate Studies in Counseling, Rollins College, 1000 Holt Ave, Box 2726, Winter Park, FL 32789. E-mail: knorsworthy@rollins.edu.

References

American Psychological Association. (2003). APA multicultural guidelines. Washington DC: Author.

American Psychological Association. (2007). Guidelines for psychological practice with girls and women. Washington DC: Author.

Arredondo, P., & Perez, P. (2003). Expanding multicultural competence through social justice leadership. *The Counseling Psychologist, 31*(3), 282–289.

Azar, B. (January, 2011). Meet your 2011 president. *Monitor on Psychology,* 42(1), 64.

Baluch, S. P., Pieterse, A. L., & Bolden, M. A. (2004). Counseling psychology and social Justice: Houston... We have a problem. *The Counseling Psychologist, 32*(1), 89–98.

Bell, L. A. (1997). Theoretical foundations for social justice education. In M. Adams, L. A. Bell, & P. Griffin (Eds.). *Teachings for diversity and social justice* (pp. 3–15). New York: Routledge.

Brinkman, B. G., Jedinak, A., Rosén, L. A., & Zimmerman, T. S. (2010). Teaching children fairness, decreasing gender prejudice amongst 5th graders. *Analyses of Social Issues and Public Policy, 10,* 171–191.

Crethar, H.C., Torres Rivera, E., & Nash, S. (2008). In search of common threads: Linking multicultural, feminist, and social justice counseling paradigms. *Journal of Counseling and Development, 86,* 269–278.

Enns, C. Z. (1993). Twenty years of feminist counseling and therapy: From naming biases to implementing multifaceted practice. *The Counseling Psychologist, 21*(1), 3–87.

Espin, O. M. (1990, Fall). How inclusive is feminist psychology? *Association for Women in Psychology Newsletter,* 1–2.

Espin, O. M. & Gawalek, M. A. (1992). Women's diversity: Ethnicity, race, class, and gender in theories of feminist psychology. In L. S. Brown & M. Ballou (Eds.). *Personality and psychopathology: Feminist reappraisals* (pp. 88–107). New York: Norton.

Espin, O. M. (1993). Feminist therapy: Not for or by white women only. *The Counseling Psychologist, 21*(1), 103–108.

Farmer, H.S. (2002). Focus on Division 17's Committee on Women/Section for the Advancement of Women (SAW) 1970–2030: Achievements and challenges. *The Counseling Psychologist, 30*(3), 417–440.

Fine, M. (2007). Expanding the methodological imagination. *The Counseling Psychologist, 35*(3), 459–473.

Fitzgerald, L. F. (1973). Women's changing expectations: New insights, new demands. *The Counseling Psychologist, 4,* 90–95.

Fitzgerald, L. F., & Nutt, R. (1986). The division 17 principles concerning the counseling/psychotherapy of women: Rationale and implementation. *The Counseling Psychologist, 14*(1), 180–216.

Fouad, N. A., McPherson, R. H., Gerstein, L., Blustein, D. L., Elman, N. S., Helledy, K. I., & Metz, A. J. (2004). Houston, 2001: Context and legacy. *The Counseling Psychologist, 32*(1), 15–77.

Fouad, N. A., Gerstein, L., & Toporek, R. L. (2006). Social justice and counseling psychology in context. In R. L. Toporek, L. Gerstein, N. Fouad, G. Roysircar, & T. Israel, *Handbook for social justice in counseling psychology: Leadership, vision, and action* (pp. 1–16). Thousand Oaks, CA: Sage.

Freire, P. (1972). *Pedagogy of the oppressed.* New York: Herder and Herder.

Gilbert, L.A., & Osipow, S. H. (1991). Feminist contributions to counseling psychology. *Psychology of Women Quarterly, 15,* 537–547.

Goodman, L. A., Liang, B., Helms, J. E., Latta, R. E., Sparks, E., & Weintraub, S. R. (2004). Training counseling psychologists as social justice agents: Feminist and multicultural principles in action. *The Counseling Psychologist, 32*(6), 793–837.

Helms, J. E. (2003). A pragmatic view of social justice. *The Counseling Psychologist, 31*(3), 305–313.

Horne, S. G., & Mathews, S. S. (2004). Collaborative consultation: International applications of a multicultural feminist approach. *The Counseling Psychologist, 32,* 366–378.

Horne, S. G., & Mathews, S. S. (2006). Social justice through international collaborative consultation. In R. L. Toporek, L. Gerstein, N. Fouad, G. Roysircar, & T. Israel, *Handbook for social justice in counseling psychology: Leadership, vision, and action* (pp. 388–405). Thousand Oaks, CA: Sage.

hooks, b. (1994). *Teaching to transgress: Education as the practice of freedom.* New York: Routledge.

Kiselica, M. S. (2004). When duty calls: The implications of social justice work for policy, education, and practice in the mental health professions. *The Counseling Psychologist, 32*(6), 838–854.

Lykes, M. B., & Moane, G. (2009). Editors' introduction: Whither feminist liberation psychology: Critical explorations of feminist and liberation psychologies for a globalizing world. *Feminism and Psychology, 19*(3), 283–297.

Martin-Baro, I. (1994). *Writings for a liberation psychology.* Cambridge, MA: Harvard University Press.

Meara, N. M., & Harmon, L. W. (1989). Accomplishments and disappointments of the Division 17 Committee on Women, 1970–1987. *The Counseling Psychologist, 17*(2), 314–331.

Moane, G. (2003). Bridging the personal and the political: Practices for a liberation psychology. *American Journal of Community Psychology, 31*(1–2), 91–101.

Molchanova, E., Kim, E., Horne, S., Aitpaeva, G., Ashiraliev, N. Ten, V. & Pokhilko, D. (2009). Status of counseling and psychotherapy in Kyrgyzstan. In L. Gerstein, P. P. Heppner, S. Ægisdóttir, A. Leung, & K. L Norsworthy, *International handbook of cross-cultural counseling: Cultural assumptions and practices worldwide* (pp. 265–280). Thousand Oaks, CA: Sage.

Morrow, S. L. (2009). Roots of activism and my evolution as a social justice advocate in academe. In Ponterotto, J. G., Casas, J. M., Suzuki, L., & Alexander, C. M. *Handbook of multicultural counseling* (pp. 71–77). Thousand Oaks, CA: Sage.

Norsworthy, K. L., & Khuankaew, O. (2004). Women of Burma speak out: Workshops to deconstruct gender-based violence and build systems of peace and justice. *The Journal for Specialists in Group Work, 29*(3), 259–283.

Norsworthy, K. L., & Khuankaew, O. (2005). Bringing social justice to international practices of counseling psychology. In R. L. Toporek, L. Gerstein, N. Fouad, G. Roysircar, & T. Israel, *Handbook for social justice in counseling psychology: Leadership, vision, and action.* (pp. 421–441). Thousand Oaks, CA: Sage.

Norsworthy, K. L. (2008). Peacework with Thai Muslim and Buddhist communities in conflict. In T. Ilter, N. Kara, M. Atabey, Y. Arslan, & M. Orun, *Communication in peace/conflict in communication* (pp. 153–158). Famagusta, Northern Cyprus: Eastern Mediterranean University Press.

Norsworthy, K. L. & Buranajaroenkij, D. (2011). Crossing borders, building bridges, and swimming upstream: Feminist liberatory work within South Thailand communities in conflict. *Women and Therapy, 34*(3), 242–260.

Norsworthy, K. L., & Khuankaew, O. (2008). A new view from women of Thailand about gender, sexuality, and HIV/AIDS. *Feminism and Psychology, 18*(4), 527–536.

Novotney, A. (2010). Members elect Vasquez as APA's next president. *Monitor on Psychology, 41*(2), 60.

Palmer, A., & Parish, J. (2008). Social justice and counseling psychology: Situating the role of graduate student research, education, and training. *Canadian Journal of Counseling, 42*(4), 278–289.

Palmer, L. K. (2004). The call to social justice: A multidisciplinary agenda. *The Counseling Psychologist, 32*(6), 879–885.

Pitts, C., Margolies, L., & Leeder, E. (2008). Ethics and activism: Application. In M. Ballou, M. Hill, & C. West, *Feminist therapy theory and process* (pp 127–134). New York: Springer.

Rawlings, E. I. (1993). Reflections on "Twenty years of feminist counseling and therapy." *The Counseling Psychologist, 21*(1), 88–91.

Singh, A., Urbano, A., Haston, M., & McMahon, E. (2010b). School counselors' strategies for social justice change: A grounded theory of what works in the real world. *Professional School Counseling, 13*(3), 135–145.

Singh, A. A., Hofsess, C. D., Boyer, E. M., Kwong, A., Lau, A. S. M., McLain, M., & Haggins, K. L. (2010a). Social justice and counseling psychology: Listening to the voices of doctoral trainees. *The Counseling Psychologist, 38*(6), 766–795.

Speight, S., & Vera, E. (2004). A social justice agenda: Ready or not. *The Counseling Psychologist, 32*(1), 109–118.

Sue, D. W., Bingham, R. P., Porche-Burke, L., & Vasquez, M. (1999). The diversification of psychology: A multicultural revolution. *American Psychologist, 54*(12), 1061–1069.

Todd, N., & Abrams, E. M. (2011). White dialectics: A new framework for theory, research, and practice with white students. *The Counseling Psychologist* (Major contribution), *39*(3), 353–395.

Toporek, R. L., Lewis, J. A., & Crethar, H. C. (2009). Promoting systemic change through the ACA advocacy competencies. *Journal of Counseling and Development, 87,* 260–268.

Unger, R. (1998). *Resisting gender: Twenty-five years of feminist psychology.* London: Sage.

Vera, E. M., & Speight, S. L. (2003). Multicultural competence, social justice, and counseling psychology: Expanding our roles. *The Counseling Psychologist, 31*(3), 253–272.

Weisstein, N. (1968). *Kinder, kuche, kirche as scientific laws: Psychology constructs the female.* Boston, MA: New England Free Press.

Weisstein, N. (1993). Power, resistance, and science: A call for a revitalized feminist psychology. *Feminism and Psychology, 3,* 239–245.

Wilkinson, S. (1986). Introduction. In S. Wilkinson (Ed.), *Feminist social psychology: Developing theory and practice* (pp. 1–7). Milton Keynes, UK: Open University Press.

Williams, E. N., & Morrow, S. L. (2009). Achieving trustworthiness in qualitative research: A pan-paradigmatic perspective. *Psychotherapy Research, 19,* 576–582.

Yakushko, O. (2009). Xenophobia: Understanding the roots and consequences of negative attitudes toward immigrants. *The Counseling Psychologist, 37*(1), 36–66.

Yakushko, O., Razzhavaikina, T. & Horne, S. (2009). Counseling in countries experiencing political, cultural, and economic transition: The case of the former USSR. In L. Gerstein, P. P. Heppner, S. Ægisdóttir, A. Leung, & K. L. Norsworthy, *International handbook of cross-cultural counseling: Cultural assumptions and practices worldwide* (pp. 337–344). Thousand Oaks, CA: Sage.

PART 5

Afterword

CHAPTER

26 Making the Political Personal

Elizabeth Nutt Williams *and* Carolyn Zerbe Enns

Abstract

This chapter highlights the themes that have emerged across the various chapters in this work, the *Oxford Handbook of Feminist Multicultural Counseling Psychology*. Specifically, three primary themes arose. First, the authors spoke to the need for a new paradigm for understanding power and privilege in everyday decisions. They detailed the importance of questioning what is considered normative and of confronting oppression and discrimination at all levels. Second, the authors emphasized the need for the true integration of feminist and multicultural approaches, a recurring and yet unrealized call for change in the literature. Third, the authors raised the importance of refocusing on the roots of counseling psychology (e.g., hygiology, individual differences, prevention, and social justice). Finally, the perceived roadblocks to positive change as well as specific advice to the next generation of feminist multicultural counseling psychologists are overviewed, as feminist multicultural counseling psychologists are called to examine the ways in which the political is personal.

Key Words: Advice, challenges, feminism, multiculturalism, counseling psychology

As editors of the *Oxford Handbook of Feminist Multicultural Counseling Psychology*, we began with high hopes for the diversity and complexity of the chapters that we would include in this volume. Those hopes have been realized in the smart, sophisticated, and cutting-edge work of the authors of the chapters included herein.

Specifically, we wanted to ensure coverage of enduring themes, including our herstorical roots (chapter 1, Enns, Williams, and Fassinger); the ethical foundations of our profession (chapter 2, Brabeck and Brabeck); the life span perspective inherent to counseling psychology (chapter 3, Juntunen and Bauman); and the importance of ecological context (chapter 4, Ancis and Davidson). As our field changes and matures, the willingness to engage in critical questioning (chapter 5, Fischer and DeBord) is also crucial to expanding our understanding of our field.

Intersectionality and diversity are becoming increasingly central to feminist multicultural perspectives, and we wanted to include attention to specific social identities that are consistent with a "complexity paradigm" (Reid, 2002). In Part II, chapters explore the concerns and experiences of African American women (chapter 6, Speight, Isom, and Thomas); lesbian, bisexual, and transgender women (chapter 7, Szymanski and Hilton); women in poverty (chapter 8, Smith, Appio, and Chang), Latinas (chapter 9, Gloria and Castellanos); Asian American women (chapter 10, Suzuki, Ahluwalia, and Alimchandani); women with disabilities (chapter 11, Palombi); American Muslim women (chapter 12, Mahmood); and women in transnational contexts (chapter 13, Horne and Arora). Although our goal was to be inclusive, we realize that we have not been exhaustive in featuring the complexity and diversity of women's social and collective identities. We are hopeful that the diverse perspectives and approaches that the authors have used to discuss women's experiences will offer useful tools for expanding attention to women with multiple identities that are not discussed in this handbook.

As a third goal, we wanted to highlight feminist multicultural issues in theory, research, and practice. Part III investigates unique issues in vocational (see chapter 14, Hackett and Kohlart; and chapter 15, Ormerod, Joseph, Weitzman, and Winterrowd) and psychotherapy contexts (see chapter 16, Remer and Hahn; chapter 17, Mintz and Tager; chapter 18, Morrow and Hawxhurst; chapter 19, Nutt; chapter 20, Curtois; and chapter 21, Kashubeck-West and Tagger). The chapters in this section bring particular attention to male clients, political analysis, family counseling, trauma, and eating disorders.

Finally, in Part IV, we wanted to emphasize counseling psychology's roles in education, advocacy, and social justice (see chapter 22, Sinacore, Ginsberg, and Kassan; chapter 23, Miville; chapter 24, Gormley; chapter 25, Norsworthy, Abrams, and Lindlau) by exploring issues around pedagogy, training, mentoring, and activism.

To draw meaningful conclusions at the end of such an enormous project seemed daunting. As a result, we did what any good feminist multicultural counseling psychologists would do—we invited our chapter authors to collaborate with us by providing their responses to several questions. We frame our conclusions by elucidating themes that we found emerging from the author responses, their chapters, and from our own visions of feminist multicultural counseling psychology.

What Comes Next: Necessary Changes

Three primary themes arose regarding what the authors deemed as necessary changes for the future.

A New Paradigm

First, feminist multicultural counseling psychologists will need to participate in creating and advancing a new paradigm for the profession. This new paradigm will shift what is considered normative, what is encouraged, what is rewarded. The paradigm will be one in which issues of power and privilege are considered first and always, and where genuine critical questioning is valued. It will be, as Ann Fischer and Kurt DeBord suggested, a paradigm where "power is treated not as an afterthought but as shaping all aspects of our work" (personal communication, 2011). The idea that power, privilege, oppression, and discrimination are often unseen, ignored, or unexamined was emphasized by a number of chapter authors. For example, Speight et al. called for us to develop a "critical consciousness" (chapter 6) such that power and oppression do not "remain invisible and unquestioned" (Fischer and DeBord, chapter 5).

Along with this call to open our eyes, remain vigilant, and question everything, the chapter authors remind us of the core importance of social justice work in counseling psychology. Beyond understanding, we are called to action, activism, and advocacy. Nearly every chapter makes mention of these principles and calls us to confront all forms of oppression, from the formal to the informal, from the structural to the relational, from the obvious discrimination to the more subtle microaggressions. As Horne and Arora noted (chapter 13), we must "resist paralysis," and Morrow and Hawxhurst (chapter 18) reminded us to return to political analysis as a basic and foundational method to help facilitate empowerment.

Integration and Complexity

A second theme that arose was dedicated to the true integration of feminist and multicultural approaches in which all forms of bias, all forms of privilege, and all social and collective identities are relevant to the frameworks that we employ (Ormerod et al., chapter 15). Counseling psychologists have long denounced the lack of integration between multicultural and feminist perspectives (Brown, 1994; Comas-Diaz & Greene, 1994; Enns, Sinacore, Ancis, & Phillips, 2004; Yakushko, Davidson, & Williams, 2009) and have yet noted their many points of connection (Raja, 1998; Williams & Barber, 2004). As one of the first voices in applied psychology to focus on issues of diversity (Baker & Subich, 2008), counseling psychology should also lead the charge in fully and finally creating a true focus on intersectionality of identities (Cole, 2009; Worell & Remer, 2003). This concurrent focus on different social identities must also include transnational and global perspectives (Enns, 2010; Tong, 2009).

Nearly all of the authors emphasized the importance of recognizing the complexities of our unique identities and intersectionalities at all levels (from micro to macro). Without an understanding of and embracing of these complexities, we will have a difficult time developing an authentic sense of self or helping others do the same. Multiple authors in this volume also spoke of the value of integrating counseling tools with community and social approaches (e.g., Brabeck and Brabeck, chapter 2) as well as ecological and systems-based frameworks (e.g., Ancis and Davidson, chapter 4). The use of integrated ecological frameworks offers options for implementing an intersectional and integrated multicultural and feminist perspective. Such models help us move toward understanding how some personal issues and identities vary in salience as they become part of the foreground or background in interaction with the complex systems and niches in which individuals are embedded.

Core Values of Counseling Psychologists

While it is important to advance our thinking in new directions, it is also important to reexamine our core values as counseling psychologists. Thus, the third theme that arose comprised a variety of ways in which counseling psychologists should attend to their roots (see Gelso & Fretz, 2001, for an overview of counseling psychology's unifying themes). Several fundamental aspects of counseling psychology were noted: hygiology, individual differences, prevention, and social justice. As counseling psychologists, we have a long history using strengths-based approaches (or what Donald Super, 1955, called hygiology). As noted by contributors to this handbook, a move away from more pathology-based models will be critical from a feminist multicultural perspective, allowing for a greater focus on issues of empowerment, resiliency, and well-being (e.g., Juntunen and Bauman, chapter 3; Ancis and Davidson, chapter 4; Mintz and Tager, chapter 17). Although the strengths and resilience of those with whom we work are central to feminist multicultural counseling psychology (e.g., Szymanski and Hilton, chapter 7), we also need to be cautious about inadvertently perpetuating stereotypes about strength (e.g., the "strong Black woman") that can lead to distorted perceptions about the challenges and oppressions that women face (Speight et al., chapter 6). A major implication of a strengths-based perspective entails valuing the life experience and expertise of those with whom we work and believing that they, in collaboration with trained psychologists, can develop positive tools for coping with oppression as well as contributing to advocacy and social change (Szymanski and Hilton, chapter 7).

Counseling psychologists have also focused on issues of individual difference, one theme that represents "the bedrock, as well as the cutting edge, of counseling psychology" (Hansen, 2011, p. 917). Yet several authors (e.g., Brabeck and Brabeck, chapter 2; Gormley, chapter 24) caution us that we must retain a focus on both the individual *and* the broader cultural context. Counseling psychologists often push past broad and sweeping categorizations to a more complex, textured, and sophisticated approach to understanding and honoring the individual. One recent example of this nuanced work was presented by Worthington and Reynolds (2009) in their work on redefining categories of sexual identity.

As counseling psychologists, multiple authors in the volume indicate that we need to refocus on our historical emphasis on prevention (Kashubeck-West and Tagger, chapter 21), early interventions (Juntunen and Bauman, chapter 3), and systems thinking (e.g., Norsworthy et al., chapter 25). Finally, we will need to publicize our social justice projects, our action orientation, and our focus on advocacy. These important emphases define counseling psychology, and feminist multicultural counseling psychologists are often the most vocal proponents of these issues. Perhaps it begs the question: Aren't all counseling psychologists feminist multicultural counseling psychologists? Or, if the answer to that question is no, perhaps we need to ask: Shouldn't they be?

Significant Roadblocks to Change

In addition to asking the chapter authors about their visions for the future, we also asked what they thought were the most significant roadblocks to change. Many referred to the academic structure and the creation, ownership, and dissemination of "knowledge." For example, who creates the professional literature we read... the articles we use for training purposes, the research we build dissertations on, and the knowledge base we rely on for learning about sound and successful strategies for helping people? Academics, as well as some practitioners who retain strong ties to the academy. All academics are trained within a traditional system, and, if they go on to achieve tenure and promotion within the academy, they are beholden to the system's reward (and punishment) structure. The traditional, mainstream values in the academy (individualistic focus, competition, winner-takes-all mentality) discourage risk-taking and innovation. To publish too far outside what one's institution values means to risk tenure, among other rewards. Yet, that research, theory, and calls to apply our findings to practice govern what new generations learn about the profession. While naming a problem is an important step (Brown, 2000; Friedan, 1963; Morris, 1997), more is necessary. It is a worthy ambition to hope that the naming of this roadblock will garner growing attention over time, allowing us to reject its premise.

In a similar vein, chapter authors worried about the business mentality in research—where it is difficult to obtain funding for smaller, "progressive" projects. It appears that it is becoming harder and harder to reject the power of the pharmaceutical industry in defining both mental health issues and their treatment. A recent example of a grassroots approach to pushing back against more medicalized visions of mental health concerns can be seen in the open letter to the American Psychiatric Association (led by Division 32, Humanistic Psychology) in 2011 regarding updates to the in-process *DSM-V*. The strength-based approaches that define counseling psychology are a good antidote to the illness model of mental health; however, the challenges are significant.

A more personal challenge noted by the chapter authors is the difficulty that we all have owning our own privilege (Ancis & Szymanski, 2001; Liu, Pickett, & Ivey, 2007; Neville, Worthington, & Spanierman, 2001; Pleasants, 2011). Many chapters in this handbook provide a number of suggestions for confronting privilege and oppression and for becoming more self-aware and knowledgeable about these important issues. We were pleased, for example, to have chapters that reflect some of the least studied or newest trends in feminist multicultural research, such as on transgender issues (Szymanski and Hilton, chapter 7), women with disabilities (Palombi, chapter 11), and American Muslim women (Mahmood, chapter 12), and hope that readers will find ways to stretch their knowledge base and ask new questions.

A final roadblock to change noted by the chapter authors is our ability to communicate effectively—with those who oppose our views, with new generations—in order to explain and encourage a more nuanced understanding of oppression and privilege. We need to develop sophisticated communication styles such that we can use (and not be used by) the media to explain our findings and musing to the public at large.

Advice for the Next Generation

When asked to give advice to the next generation of feminist multicultural counseling psychologists, our chapter authors had five primary pieces of advice:

Question everything—keep an open mind in your pursuit of knowledge and expertise.

Be an activist, unapologetically committed to social change.

Fight the *good* fight but focus on the *good* (what we are fighting for) and know that it is really *fun* to do this kind of work and collaborate with others.

Value differences of all kinds.Make the political personal—understand your own history and roots and work to own your own privilege. Perhaps most important, you should choose to do social justice work *for you*. Laura Smith noted poignantly that it is important to ensure that advocacy work "isn't just about wanting to be a savior for other people—the pitfall in that is that you risk becoming just another privileged 'charitable' person who ultimately acts in such a way as to maintain distance and power differentials between yourself and others. Rather, know that you are saving your own humanity by working for justice. Or perhaps you are helping to bring into being the kind of world that you want to live in. Get clear on how justice for everyone would enhance your *own* well-being" (personal communication, 2011).

We chose to sum up that last piece of advice with a twist on the well-known feminist phrase "the personal is political." We hope that in reading the many, varied, and challenging chapters in this handbook, you will consider ways to "make the political personal" and will find ways to push the boundaries of feminist multicultural counseling psychology.

References

Ancis, J., & Szymanski, D. (2001). Awareness of white privilege among white counseling trainees. *The Counseling Psychologist, 29*(4), 548–569.

Baker, D. B., & Subich, L. M. (2008). Counseling psychology historical perspectives. In W. B. Walsh (Ed.), *Biennial review of counseling psychology* (pp. 1–26). New York: Routledge.

Brown, L. S. (1994). *Subversive dialogues: Theory in feminist therapy.* New York: Basic Books.

Brown, L. S. (2000). Feminist therapy. In C. R. Snyder & R. E. Ingram (Eds.), *Handbook of psychological change: Psychotherapy processes and practices for the 21st century* (pp. 358–380). Hoboken, NJ: Wiley.

Cole, E. R. (2009). Intersectionality and research in psychology. *American Psychologist, 64,* 170–180.

Comas-Diaz, L., & Greene, B. (Eds.). (1994). *Women of color: Integrating ethnic and gender identities in psychotherapy.* New York: Guilford Press.

Enns, C. Z., Sinacore, A. L., Ancis, J. R., & Phillips, J. (2004). Toward integrating feminist and multicultural pedagogies. *Journal of Multicultural Counseling and Development, 32,* 414–427.

Enns, C. Z. (2010). Locational feminisms and feminist social identity analysis. *Professional Psychology: Research and Practice, 41,* 333–339.

Friedan, B. (1963). *The feminine mystique.* Oxford, UK: Norton.

Gelso, C., & Fretz, B. (2001). *Counseling psychology* (2nd ed.). New York: Harcourt.

Hansen, J. C. (2012). Contemporary counseling psychology. In E. M. Altmaier & J. C. Hansen (Eds.), *The Oxford handbook of counseling psychology* (pp. 917–922). New York: Oxford University Press.

Liu, W. M., Pickett, T., & Ivey, A. E. (2007). White middle-class privilege: Social class bias and implications for training and practice. *Journal of Multicultural Counseling and Development, 35,* 194–206.

Morris, C. (1997). Mental health matters: Toward a non-medicalized approach to psychotherapy with women. *Women and Therapy, 20,* 63–77.

Neville, H. A., Worthington, R. L., & Spanierman, L. B. (2001). Race, power, and multicultural counseling psychology: Understanding White privilege and color-blind racial attitudes. In J. Ponterotto, J. M. Casas, L. A. Suzuki, & C. M. Alexander (Eds.), *Handbook of multicultural counseling* (pp. 257–288). Thousand Oaks, CA: Sage.

Pleasants, R. K. (2011). Men learning feminism: Protecting privileges through discourses of resistance. *Men and Masculinities, 14,* 230–250.

Raja, S. (1998). Culturally sensitive therapy for women of color. *Women and Therapy, 21,* 67–84.

Reid, P. T. (2002). Multicultural psychology: Bringing together gender and ethnicity. *Cultural Diversity and Ethnic Minority Psychology, 8,* 103–114.

Super, D. E. (1955). Transition from vocational guidance to counseling psychology. *Journal of Counseling Psychology, 2,* 3–9.

Tong, R. (2009). *Feminist thought* (3rd ed.). Boulder, CO: Westview Press.

Williams, E. N., & Barber, J. (2004). Power and responsibility in therapy: Integrating feminism and multiculturalism. *Journal of Multicultural Counseling and Development, 32,* 390–401.

Worell, J., & Remer, P. (2003). *Feminist perspectives in therapy: Empowering diverse women* (2nd ed.). New York: Wiley.

Worthington, R. L., & Reynolds, A. L. (2009). Within-group differences in sexual orientation and identity. *Journal of Counseling Psychology, 56,* 44–55.

Yakushko, O., Davidson, M. M., & Williams, E. N. (2009). Identity salience model: A paradigm for integrating multiple identities in clinical practice. *Psychotherapy, 46,* 180–192.

INDEX

G

H

P

Q

R

T

U

V

W

Y

Z